P9-DFN-158

CRYPTOGRAPHY AND NETWORK SECURITY, FIFTH EDITION

A tutorial and survey on network security technology. Each of the basic building blocks of network security, including conventional and public-key cryptography, authentication, and digital signatures, are covered. Thorough mathematical background for such algorithms as AES and RSA. The book covers important network security tools and applications, including S/MIME, IP Security, Kerberos, SSL/TLS, SET, and X509v3. In addition, methods for countering hackers and viruses are explored. **Second edition received the TAA award for the best Computer Science and Engineering Textbook of 1999.** ISBN 0-13-6097049

COMPUTER SECURITY (WITH LAWRIE BROWN)

A comprehensive treatment of computer security technology, including algorithms, protocols, and applications. Covers cryptography, authentication, access control, database security, intrusion detection and prevention, malicious software, denial of service, firewalls, software security, physical security, human factors, auditing, legal and ethical aspects, and trusted systems. **Received the 2008 Text and Academic Authors Association (TAA) award for the best Computer Science and Engineering Textbook of the year.** ISBN 0-13-600424-5

WIRELESS COMMUNICATIONS AND NETWORKS, SECOND EDITION

A comprehensive, state-of-the-art survey. Covers fundamental wireless communications topics, including antennas and propagation, signal encoding techniques, spread spectrum, and error correction techniques. Examines satellite, cellular, wireless local loop networks, and wireless LANs, including Bluetooth and 802.11. Covers Mobile IP and WAP. ISBN 0-13-191835-4

HIGH-SPEED NETWORKS AND INTERNETS, SECOND EDITION

A state-of-the-art survey of high-speed networks. Topics covered include TCP congestion control, ATM traffic management, Internet traffic management, differentiated and integrated services, Internet routing protocols and multicast routing protocols, resource reservation and RSVP, and lossless and lossy compression. Examines important topic of self-similar data traffic. ISBN 0-13-03221-0

Need help with your homework?

Networking harder than you thought?

Help is here. Now.

With the purchase of a new copy of this textbook, you immediately have access to **Premium Content** and **Web Chapters.**

Use a coin to scratch off the coating and reveal your student access code. Do not use a knife or other sharp object as it may damage the code.

HSDCC-FLANK-BRAYS-BURAN-HELOT-LINES

To redeem your access code:
1. Go to **www.pearsonhighered.com/stallings**.
2. Select your textbook.
3. Click on the **Premium Content** and **Web Chapters** link.

Note to Instructors: **Instructors: Premium instructional material and Web Chapters** *for this title are available in the Instructor Resource Center. Contact your Pearson representative if you do not have IRC access.*

IMPORTANT: The access code on this page can only be used once to establish a subscription to the premium content for Stallings, ***Data and Computer Communications, Ninth Edition.*** If the access code has already been scratched off, it may no longer be valid. If this is the case, follow steps 1-3 and select **"Get Access"** to purchase a new subscription.

Technical Support is available at **www.247pearsoned.com.**

Pearson Education | One Lake Street, Upper Saddle River, NJ 07458

DATA AND COMPUTER COMMUNICATIONS

DATA AND COMPUTER COMMUNICATIONS

Ninth Edition

William Stallings

Prentice Hall

Boston   Columbus   Indianapolis   New York   San Francisco   Upper Saddle River
Amsterdam   Cape Town   Dubai   London   Madrid   Milan   Munich   Paris   Montreal   Toronto
Delhi   Mexico City   Sao Paulo   Sydney   Hong Kong   Seoul   Singapore   Taipei   Tokyo

Editor in Chief: Michael Hirsch
Acquisitions Editor: Tracy Dunkelberger
Assistant Editor: Melinda Haggerty
Editorial Assistant: Allison Michael
Director of Marketing: Margaret Waples
Marketing Coordinator: Kathryn Ferranti
Managing Editor: Jeffrey Holcomb
Project Manager: Wanda Rockwell

Production Supervisor: Heather McNally
Creative and Art Director: Jayne Conte
Cover Designer: Suzanne Behnke
Cover Art: Shutterstock
Media Editor: Daniel Sandin
Media Project Manager: Katelyn Boller
Full-Service Project Management: Integra

Access the latest information about Prentice Hall titles from our World Wide Web site:

http://www.pearsonhighered.com/cs

Credits and acknowledgments borrowed from other sources and reproduced, with permission, in this textbook appear on appropriate page within text.

Microsoft® and Windows® are registered trademarks of the Microsoft Corporation in the U.S.A. and other countries. Screen shots and icons reprinted with permission from the Microsoft Corporation. This book is not sponsored or endorsed by or affiliated with the Microsoft Corporation.

The programs and applications presented in this book have been included for their instructional value. They have been tested with care, but are not guaranteed for any particular purpose. The publisher does not offer any warranties or representations, nor does it accept any liabilities with respect to the programs or applications.

Copyright © 2011, 2007, 2004, 2000, 1997 Pearson Education, Inc., publishing as Prentice Hall, 1 Lake Street, Upper Saddle River, New Jersey, 07458. All rights reserved. Manufactured in the United States of America. This publication is protected by Copyright, and permission should be obtained from the publisher prior to any prohibited reproduction, storage in a retrieval system, or transmission in any form or by any means, electronic, mechanical, photocopying, recording, or likewise. To obtain permission(s) to use material from this work, please submit a written request to Pearson Education, Inc., Permissions Department, Prentice Hall, 1 Lake Street, Upper Saddle River, New Jersey, 07458.

Many of the designations by manufacturers and sellers to distinguish their products are claimed as trademarks. Where those designations appear in this book, and the publisher was aware of a trademark claim, the designations have been printed in initial caps or all caps.

Library of Congress Cataloging-in-Publication Data

Stallings, William.
   Data and computer communications / William Stallings.—9th ed.
     p. cm.
   Includes bibliographical references and index.
   ISBN-13: 978-0-13-139205-2 (alk. paper)
   ISBN-10: 0-13-139205-0 (alk. paper)
   1. Data transmission systems.   2. Computer networks.   I. Title.
TK5105.S73 2011
004.6--dc22

                         2010025052

10 9 8 7 6 5 4 3—EBM—15 14 13

Prentice Hall
is an imprint of

www.pearsonhighered.com

ISBN 10:   0-13-139205-0
ISBN 13: 978-0-13-139205-2

For my brave, extraordinary and fascinating wife ATS

CONTENTS

PREFACE

Begin at the beginning and go on till you come to the end; then stop

—*Alice in Wonderland*, Lewis Carroll

OBJECTIVES

This book attempts to provide a unified overview of the broad field of data and computer communications. The organization of the book reflects an attempt to break this massive subject into comprehensible parts and to build, piece by piece, a survey of the state of the art. The book emphasizes basic principles and topics of fundamental importance concerning the technology and architecture of this field and provides a detailed discussion of leading-edge topics.

The following basic themes serve to unify the discussion:

- **Principles:** Although the scope of this book is broad, there are a number of basic principles that appear repeatedly as themes and that unify this field. Examples are multiplexing, flow control, and error control. The book highlights these principles and contrasts their application in specific areas of technology.

- **Design approaches:** The book examines alternative approaches to meeting specific communication requirements.

- **Standards:** Standards have come to assume an increasingly important, indeed dominant, role in this field. An understanding of the current status and future direction of technology requires a comprehensive discussion of the related standards.

INTENDED AUDIENCE

The book is intended for both an academic and a professional audience. For the professional interested in this field, the book serves as a basic reference volume and is suitable for self-study. As a textbook, it can be used for a one-semester or two-semester course. It covers the material in Networking (NET), a core area in the Information Technology body of knowledge, which is part of the Draft ACM/IEEE/AIS Computing Curricula 2005. The book also covers the material in Computer Networks (CE-NWK), a core area in Computer Engineering 2004 Curriculum Guidelines from the ACM/IEEE Joint Task Force on Computing Curricula.

PLAN OF THE TEXT

The book is divided into seven parts, which are described in Chapter 0:

- Overview
- Data Communications
- Wide Area Networks

- Local Area Networks
- Internet and Transport Protocols
- Network Security
- Internet Applications

The book includes a number of pedagogic features, including the use of animations and numerous figures and tables to clarify the discussions. Each chapter includes a list of key words, review questions, homework problems, suggestions for further reading, and recommended Web sites. The book also includes an extensive online glossary, a list of frequently used acronyms, and a reference list. In addition, a test bank is available to instructors.

The chapters and parts of the book are sufficiently modular to provide a great deal of flexibility in the design of courses. See Chapter 0 for a number of detailed suggestions for both top–down and bottom–up course strategies.

WHAT'S NEW IN THIS EDITION

This ninth edition is seeing the light of day less than four years after the publication of the eighth edition. During that time, the pace of change in this field continues unabated. In this new edition, I try to capture these changes while maintaining a broad and comprehensive coverage of the entire field. To begin the process of revision, the eighth edition of this book was extensively reviewed by a number of professors who teach the subject. The result is that, in many places, the narrative has been clarified and tightened, and illustrations have been improved.

Beyond these refinements to improve pedagogy and user-friendliness, there have been major substantive changes throughout the book. Highlights include:

- **Animations:** Animation provides a powerful tool for understanding the complex mechanisms of network protocols. The ninth edition incorporates a number of separate animations covering such protocols as Hypertext Transfer Protocol (HTTP), Simple Mail Transfer Protocol (SMTP), and Transmission Control Protocol (TCP). A directory of the animations is provided after the Preface.

- **Examples:** The number of examples incorporated in the book has been significantly expanded.

- **Twisted-pair transmission standards:** This new edition covers the 2009 ANSI/TIA 568-C standards and the recent ISO/IEC 11801 twisted-pair transmissions, which are important for gigabit-range Ethernet and other high-speed twisted-pair applications.

- **Expanded coverage of broadband Internet access:** The sections on cable modem and DSL broadband access have been expanded.

- **New coverage of fourth-generation (4G) mobile wireless networks:** Includes the key 4G technology of orthogonal frequency division multiple access (OFDMA).

- **New coverage of virtual LANs:** VLAN technology is covered, as well is the IEEE 802.1Q standard.
- **Updated coverage of high-speed Ethernet:** The new 100-Gbps standard is covered, including the multilane distribution (MLD) transmission technique, plus expanded coverage of 64B/66B encoding.
- **Updated coverage of Wi-Fi/IEEE 802.11 wireless LANs:** IEEE 802.11 and the related Wi-Fi specifications have continued to evolve. New coverage includes 802.11n.
- **Mobile IP:** New to this edition is coverage of Mobile IP, which standardizes techniques for IP addressing and routing for mobile end systems.
- **MPLS:** New to this edition is full chapter devoted to Multiprotocol Label Switching, which is becoming increasingly important on the Internet and other IP-based networks, as well as in telecommunications networks.
- **Expanded coverage of security:** The coverage of security, in Part Six, has been completely rewritten and expanded to two chapters. It is more detailed, covering a number of new topics.

In addition, throughout the book, virtually every topic has been updated to reflect the developments in standards and technology that have occurred since the publication of the eighth edition.

ONLINE DOCUMENTS FOR STUDENTS

For this new edition, a tremendous amount of original supporting material has been made available online, in the following categories:

- **Online chapters:** To limit the size and cost of the book, two chapters of the book are provided in PDF format. The chapters are listed in this book's table of contents.
- **Online appendices:** There are numerous interesting topics that support material found in the text but whose inclusion is not warranted in the printed text. A total of 23 appendices cover these topics for the interested student. The appendices are listed in this book's table of contents.
- **Homework problems and solutions:** To aid the student in understanding the material, a separate set of homework problems with solutions are available. These enable the students to test their understanding of the text.
- **Key papers:** Several dozen papers from the professional literature, many hard to find, are provided for further reading.
- **Supporting documents:** A variety of other useful documents are referenced in the text and provided online.

Purchasing this textbook new grants the reader six months of access to this online material. See the access card in the front of this book for details.

INSTRUCTIONAL SUPPORT MATERIALS

To support instructors, the following materials are provided:

- **Solutions Manual:** Solutions to all end-of-chapter Review Questions and Problems.
- **Projects Manual:** Suggested project assignments for all of the project categories listed below.
- **PowerPoint Slides:** A set of slides covering all chapters, suitable for use in lecturing.
- **PDF files:** Reproductions of all figures and tables from the book.
- **Test Bank:** A chapter-by-chapter set of questions.

All of these support materials are available at the Instructor Resource Center (IRC) for this textbook, which can be reached through the Publisher's Web site www.pearsonhighered.com/stallings or by clicking on the button labeled "Book Info and More Instructor Resources" at this book's Web site WilliamStallings.com/DCC/DCC9e.html. To gain access to the IRC, please contact your local Prentice Hall sales representative via pearsonhighered.com/educator/replocator/requestSalesRep.page or call Prentice Hall Faculty Services at 1-800-526-0485.

In addition, the book's Web site supports instructors with:

- Links to Web sites for other courses being taught using this book
- Sign-up information for an Internet mailing list for instructors

INTERNET SERVICES FOR INSTRUCTORS AND STUDENTS

There is a Web site for this book that provides support for students and instructors. The site includes links to other relevant sites, transparency masters of figures in the book, and sign-up information for the book's Internet mailing list. The Web page is at WilliamStallings.com/DCC/DCC9e.html. For more information, see Chapter 0. The Publisher's Web site www.pearsonhighered.com/stallings provides instructors and students with direct links to the Companion Web site, Instructor Resources, Premium Content, and Web chapters.

New to this edition is a set of homework problems with solutions. Students can enhance their understanding of the material by working out the solutions to these problems and then checking their answers.

An Internet mailing list has been set up so that instructors using this book can exchange information, suggestions, and questions with each other and with the author. As soon as typos or other errors are discovered, an errata list for this book will be available at WilliamStallings.com. In addition, the Computer Science Student Resource site at WilliamStallings.com/StudentSupport.html provides documents, information, and useful links for computer science students and professionals.

PROJECTS AND OTHER STUDENT EXERCISES

For many instructors, an important component of a data communications or networking course is a project or set of projects by which the student gets hands-on experience to reinforce concepts from the text. This book provides an unparalleled degree of support for including a projects component in the course. The IRC not only includes guidance on how to assign and structure the projects but also includes a set of User's Manuals for various project types plus specific assignments, all written especially for this book. Instructors can assign work in the following areas:

- **Animation assignments:** Described in the following section.
- **Practical exercises:** Using network commands, the student gains experience in network connectivity.
- **Sockets programming projects:** The book is supported by a detailed description of Sockets (Appendix T). The IRC includes a set of programming projects. Sockets programming is an "easy" topic and one that can result in very satisfying hands-on projects for students.
- **Wireshark projects:** Wireshark is a protocol analyzer that enables students to study the behavior of protocols. A video tutorial is provided to get students started.
- **Simulation projects:** The student can use the simulation package *cnet* to analyze network behavior.
- **Performance modeling projects:** Two performance modeling techniques are provided: a *tools* package and OPNET.
- **Research projects:** The IRC includes a list of suggested research projects that would involve Web and literature searches.
- **Reading/report assignments:** The IRC includes a list of papers that can be assigned for reading and writing a report, plus suggested assignment wording.
- **Writing assignments:** The IRC includes a list of writing assignments to facilitate learning the material.
- **Discussion topics:** These topics can be used in a classroom, chat room, or message board environment to explore certain areas in greater depth and to foster student collaboration.

This diverse set of projects and other student exercises enables the instructor to use the book as one component in a rich and varied learning experience and to tailor a course plan to meet the specific needs of the instructor and students. See Appendix B for details.

ANIMATIONS

New to this edition is the incorporation of animations. Animations provide a powerful tool for understanding the complex mechanisms of network protocols. A number of Web-based animations are used to illustrate protocol behavior. Each animation allows the user to step through the operation of the protocol by selecting the next step at each point in the protocol exchange. The entire protocol exchange is illustrated by an animated diagram as the exchange proceeds. The animations can be used in two ways. In a **passive mode**, the student can click more or less randomly on the next step at each point in the animation and watch as the given concept or principle is illustrated. In an **active mode**, the user can be given a specific set of steps to invoke and watch the animation, or be given a specific end point and devise a sequence of steps that achieve the desired result. Thus, the animations can serve as the basis for student assignments. The IRC includes a set of assignments for each of the animations, plus suggested solutions so that instructors can assess the student's work.

ACKNOWLEDGMENTS

This new edition has benefited from review by a number of people, who gave generously of their time and expertise. The following people reviewed all or a large part of the manuscript: Mike Kain (Drexel University), Linda Xie (University of North Carolina), Jean-Claude Franchitti (New York University), Xiaobo Zhou (University of Colorado), James Jerkins (University of Northern Alabama), Ahmed Kamal (Iowa State), Mohammed Chouchane (Columbus State), Dr. Eslam Al Maghayreh (Yarmouk University), S. Jay Yang (Rochester Institute of Technology), John Doyle (Indiana University), Maria Villapol (University of Central Florida), Murat Yukse (University of Nevada), Anura Jayasumana (Colorado State University), and Szhi-Li Zhang (University of Minnesota).

Thanks also to the many people who provided detailed technical reviews of a single chapter: Robert H Greenfield, Abhilash V R (VVDN Technologies), Glen Herrmannsfeldt, Fernando Lichtschein, John South (University of Dallas), Edmond Pitt, John Traenkenschuh (CISSP-ISSAP, CCSA/CCSE, Microsoft MVP), and Rick Jones (Hewlett-Packard Company). Loa Andersson and Elisa Bellagamba, both of Ericsson, provided reviews of the MPLS chapter. And Valerie Maguire of The Seimon Company reviewed the material on ANSI/TIA-568.

In addition, Larry Owens of California State University and Katia Obraczka of the University of Southern California provided some homework problems. Nikhil Bhargava (IIT Delhi) contributed to the set of online homework problems and solutions.

Thanks also to the following contributors. Zornitza Prodanoff of the University of North Florida prepared the appendix on Sockets programming. Larry Tan of the University of Stirling in Scotland developed the animation assignments. Michael Harris of Indiana University initially developed the Wireshark exercises and user's guide. Dave Bremer, a principal lecturer at Otago Polytechnic in New Zealand, updated the material for the most recent Wireshark release; he also developed an online video tutorial for using Wireshark. Kim McLaughlin produced the PowerPoint lecture slides.

Finally, I would like to thank the many people responsible for the publication of the book, all of whom did their usual excellent job. This includes the staff at Prentice Hall, particularly my editor Tracy Dunkelberger, her assistants Melinda Haggerty and Allison Michael. Also, Jake Warde of Warde Publishers managed the reviews.

With all this assistance, little remains for which I can take full credit. However, I am proud to say that, with no help whatsoever, I selected all of the quotations.

ABOUT THE AUTHOR

William Stallings has made a unique contribution to understanding the broad sweep of technical developments in computer security, computer networking, and computer architecture. He has authored 17 titles, and counting revised editions, a total of 42 books on various aspects of these subjects. His writings have appeared in numerous ACM and IEEE publications, including the *Proceedings of the IEEE* and *ACM Computing Review*.

He has 11 times received the award for best Computer Science textbook of the year from the Text and Academic Authors Association.

In over 30 years in the field, he has been a technical contributor, technical manager, and an executive with several high-technology firms. He has designed and implemented both TCP/IP-based and OSI-based protocol suites on a variety of computers and operating systems, ranging from microcomputers to mainframes. As a consultant, he has advised government agencies, computer and software vendors, and major users on the design, selection, and use of networking software and products.

He created and maintains the **Computer Science Student Resource Site** at WilliamStallings.com/StudentSupport.html. The site provides documents and links on a variety of subjects of general interest to computer science students and professionals. He is a member of the editorial board of *Cryptologia*, a scholarly journal devoted to all aspects of cryptology.

Dr. Stallings holds a Ph.D. from Massachusetts Institute of Technology in Computer Science and a B.S. from Notre Dame in Electrical Engineering.

ANIMATIONS DIRECTORY

This table lists the animations that are available online at www.pearsonhighered. com/stallings.

DATA AND COMPUTER COMMUNICATIONS

READER'S AND INSTRUCTOR'S GUIDE

"In the meanwhile, then," demanded Li-loe, *"relate to me the story to which reference has been made, thereby proving the truth of your assertion, and at the same time affording an entertainment of a somewhat exceptional kind."*

"The shadows lengthen," replied Kai Lung, *"but as the narrative in question is of an inconspicuous span I will raise no barrier against your flattering request, especially as it indicates an awakening taste hitherto unexpected."*

—*Kai Lung's Golden Hours,* Earnest Bramah

This book, with its accompanying Web site, covers a lot of material. Here we give the reader some basic background information.

0.1 OUTLINE OF THE BOOK

The book is organized into seven parts:

Part One. Overview: Provides an introduction to the range of topics covered in the book. This part includes a general overview of data communications and networking and a discussion of protocols and the TCP/IP protocol suite.

Part Two. Data Communications: Concerned primarily with the exchange of data between two directly connected devices. Within this restricted scope, the key aspects of transmission, interfacing, link control, and multiplexing are examined.

Part Three. Wide Area Networks: Examines the internal mechanisms and user-network interfaces that have been developed to support voice, data, and multimedia communications over long-distance networks. The traditional technologies of packet switching and circuit switching are examined, as well as the more contemporary ATM and wireless WANs. Separate chapters are devoted to routing and congestion control issues that are relevant both to switched data networks and to the Internet.

Part Four. Local Area Networks: Explores the technologies and architectures that have been developed for networking over shorter distances. The transmission media, topologies, and medium access control protocols that are the key ingredients of a LAN design are explored and specific standardized LAN systems examined.

Part Five. Network and Transport Protocols: Explores both the architectural principles and the mechanisms required for the exchange of data among computers, workstations, servers, and other data processing devices. Much of the material in this part relates to the TCP/IP protocol suite.

Part Six. Security: Covers security threats and techniques for countering these threats.

Part Seven. Internet Applications: Looks at a range of applications that operate over the Internet.

A number of online appendices cover additional topics relevant to the book.

0.2 A ROADMAP FOR READERS AND INSTRUCTORS

Course Emphasis

The material in this book is organized into four broad categories: data transmission and communication, communications networks, network protocols, and applications and security. The chapters and parts of the book are sufficiently modular to provide a great deal of flexibility in the design of courses. The following are suggestions for three different course designs:

- **Fundamentals of Data Communications:** Parts One (overview) and Two (data communications) and Chapters 10 and 11 (circuit switching, packet switching, and ATM).
- **Communications Networks:** If the student has a basic background in data communications, then this course could cover Parts One (overview), Three (WAN), and Four (LAN).
- **Computer Networks:** If the student has a basic background in data communications, then this course could cover Part One (overview), Chapters 6 and 7 (data communication techniques and data link control), Part Five (protocols), and part or all of Part Seven (applications).

In addition, a more streamlined course that covers the entire book is possible by eliminating certain chapters that are not essential on a first reading. Chapters that could be optional are Chapters 3 (data transmission) and 4 (transmission media), if the student has a basic understanding of these topics; Chapter 8 (multiplexing); Chapter 9 (spread spectrum); Chapters 12 through 14 (routing, congestion control, cellular networks); Chapter 18 (internetworking); and Part Six (network security).

Bottom–Up versus Top–Down

The book is organized in a modular fashion. After reading Part One, the other parts can be read in a number of possible sequences. Figure 0.1a shows the bottom–up approach provided by reading the book from front to back. With this approach, each part builds on the material in the previous part, so that it is always clear how a given layer of functionality is supported from below. There is more material than can be comfortably covered in a single semester, but the book's organization makes it easy to eliminate some chapters and maintain the bottom–up sequence. Figure 0.1b suggests one approach to a survey course.

Some readers, and some instructors, are more comfortable with a top–down approach. After the background material (Part One), the reader continues at the application level and works down through the protocol layers. This has the advantage of immediately focusing on the most visible part of the material, the applications, and then seeing, progressively, how each layer is supported by the next layer down. Figure 0.1c is an example of a comprehensive treatment and Figure 0.1d is an example of a survey treatment.

Finally, it is possible to select chapters to reflect specific teaching objectives by not sticking to a strict chapter ordering. We give two examples used in courses

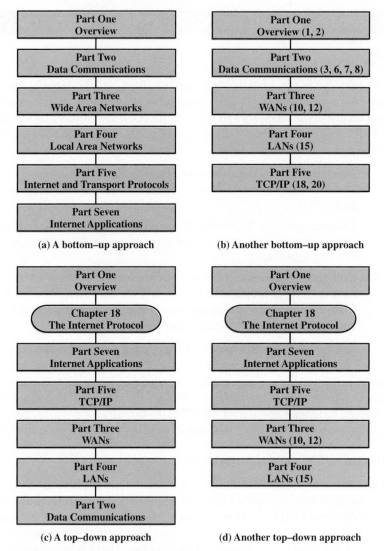

(a) A bottom–up approach   (b) Another bottom–up approach

(c) A top–down approach   (d) Another top–down approach

Figure 0.1 Suggested Reading Orders

taught with the eighth edition. One course used the sequence Part One (Overview); Chapter 3 (Data Transmission); Chapter 6 (Digital Data Communications Techniques); Chapter 7 (Data Link Control); Chapter 15 (LAN Overview); Chapter 16 (High-Speed LANs); Chapter 10 (Circuit and Packet Switching); Chapter 12 (Routing); Chapter 18 (Internet Protocols); and Chapter 19 (Internet Operation). The other course used the sequence Part One (Overview); Chapter 3 (Data Transmission); Chapter 4 (Guided and Wireless Transmission); Chapter 5 (Signal Encoding Techniques); Chapter 8 (Multiplexing); Chapter 15 (LAN Overview); Chapter 16 (High-Speed LANs); Chapter 10 (Circuit and Packet Switching); Chapter 20 (Transport Protocols); Chapter 18 (Internet Protocols); and Chapter 19 (Internetwork Operation).

0.3 INTERNET AND WEB RESOURCES

There are a number of resources available on the Internet and the Web to support this book and to help one keep up with developments in this field.

Web Sites for This Book

Three Web sites provide additional resources for students and instructors. I maintain a special Web page for this book at WilliamStallings.com/DCC/DCC9e.html. For students, this Web site includes a list of relevant links, organized by chapter, an errata sheet for the book, and links to most of the animations used throughout the book. For access to the animations, click on the rotating globe. For instructors, this Web site links to course pages by professors teaching from this book, PowerPoint slides, and pdf copies of all figures and tables in the book.

There is also an access-controlled Web site that provides a wealth of supporting material, including additional online chapters, additional online appendices, a set of homework problems with solutions, copies of a number of key papers in this field, and a number of other supporting documents. See the card at the front of this book for access information.

Finally, additional material for instructors including the complete set of animations is available at the Instructor Resource Center (IRC) for this book. See Preface for details and access information.

Computer Science Student Resource Site

I also maintain the Computer Science Student Resource Site at WilliamStallings. com/StudentSupport.html. The purpose of this site is to provide documents, information, and links for computer science students and professionals. Links and documents are organized into five categories:

- **Math:** Includes a basic math refresher, a queuing analysis primer, a number system primer, and links to numerous math sites
- **How-to:** Advice and guidance for solving homework problems, writing technical reports, and preparing technical presentations
- **Research resources:** Links to important collections of papers, technical reports, and bibliographies
- **Miscellaneous:** A variety of other useful documents and links
- **Computer science careers:** Useful links and documents for those considering a career in computer science.

Other Web Sites

There are numerous Web sites that provide information related to the topics of this book. In subsequent chapters, references to specific Web sites can be found in the *Recommended Reading and Web Sites* section. Because the addresses for Web sites tend to change frequently, the book does not provide URLs. For all of the Web sites listed in the book, the appropriate link can be found at this book's Web site. Other links not mentioned in this book will be added to the Web site over time.

The following are Web sites of general interest related to data and computer communications:

- **Network World:** Information and links to resources about data communications and networking.
- **IETF:** Maintains archives that relate to the Internet and Internet Engineering Task Force (IETF) activities. Includes keyword-indexed library of RFCs and draft documents as well as many other documents related to the Internet and related protocols.
- **IEEE Communications Society:** Good way to keep up on conferences, publications, and so on.
- **ACM Special Interest Group on Communications (SIGCOMM):** Good way to keep up on conferences, publications, and so on.
- **International Telecommunications Union:** Contains a listing of ITU-T recommendations, plus information on obtaining ITU-T documents in hard copy or on DVD.
- **International Organization for Standardization:** Contains a listing of ISO standards, plus information on obtaining ISO documents in hard copy or on CD-ROM.
- **CommsDesign:** Contains lot of useful articles, tutorials, and product information. A bit hard to navigate, but worthwhile.

USENET Newsgroups

A number of USENET newsgroups are devoted to some aspect of data communications, networks, and protocols. As with virtually all USENET groups, there is a high noise-to-signal ratio, but it is worth experimenting to see if any meet your needs. The most relevant are as follows:

- **comp.dcom.lans, comp.dcom.lans.misc:** General discussions of LANs
- **comp.dcom.lans.ethernet:** Covers Ethernet, Ethernet-like systems, and the IEEE 802.3 CSMA/CD standards
- **comp.std.wireless:** General discussion of wireless networks including wireless LANs
- **comp.security.misc:** Computer security and encryption
- **comp.dcom.cell-relay:** Covers ATM and ATM LANs
- **comp.dcom.frame-relay:** Covers frame relay networks
- **comp.dcom.net-management:** Discussion of network management applications, protocols, and standards
- **comp.protocols.tcp-ip:** The TCP/IP protocol suite.

0.4 STANDARDS

Standards have come to play a dominant role in the information communications marketplace. Virtually all vendors of products and services are committed to supporting international standards. Throughout this book, we describe the most important standards in use or being developed for various aspects of data communications and networking. Various organizations have been involved in the development or promotion of these standards. The most important (in the current context) of these organizations are as follows:

- **Internet Society:** The Internet SOCiety (ISOC) is a professional membership society with worldwide organizational and individual membership. It provides leadership in addressing issues that confront the future of the Internet and is the organization home for the groups responsible for Internet infrastructure standards, including the Internet Engineering Task Force (IETF) and the Internet Architecture Board (IAB). These organizations develop Internet standards and related specifications, all of which are published as Requests for Comments (RFCs).

- **IEEE 802:** The IEEE (Institute of Electrical and Electronics Engineers) 802 LAN/MAN Standards Committee develops local area network standards and metropolitan area network standards. The most widely used standards are for the Ethernet family, wireless LAN, bridging, and virtual bridged LANs. An individual working group provides the focus for each area.

- **ITU-T:** The International Telecommunication Union (ITU) is a United Nations agency in which governments and the private sector coordinate global telecom networks and services. The ITU Telecommunication Standardization Sector (ITU-T) is one of the three sectors of the ITU. ITU-T's mission is the production of standards covering all fields of telecommunications. ITU-T standards are referred to as Recommendations.

- **Broadband Forum:** The Broadband Forum is a global consortium of approximately 200 leading industry players covering telecom equipment, computing, networking and service provider companies. This organization develops specifics in a wide variety of areas, including digital subscriber line (DSL), frame relay, asynchronous transfer mode (ATM), and IP-based protocols.

- **ISO:** The International Organization for Standardization (ISO)[1] is a worldwide federation of national standards bodies from more than 140 countries, one from each country. ISO is a nongovernmental organization that promotes the development of standardization and related activities with a view to facilitating the international exchange of goods and services, and to developing cooperation in the spheres of intellectual, scientific, technological, and economic activity. ISO's work results in international agreements that are published as International Standards.

A more detailed discussion of these organizations is contained in Appendix C.

---

[1]ISO is not an acronym (in which case it would be IOS), but a word, derived from the Greek, meaning *equal*.

CHAPTER 1

DATA COMMUNICATIONS, DATA NETWORKS, AND THE INTERNET

The fundamental problem of communication is that of reproducing at one point either exactly or approximately a message selected at another point.

— *The Mathematical Theory of Communication,* Claude Shannon

KEY POINTS

◆ The scope of this book is broad, covering three general areas: data communications, networking, and protocols; the first two are introduced in this chapter.

◆ Data communications deals with the transmission of signals in a reliable and efficient manner. Topics covered include signal transmission, transmission media, signal encoding, interfacing, data link control, and multiplexing.

◆ Networking deals with the technology and architecture of the communications networks used to interconnect communicating devices. This field is generally divided into the topics of local area networks (LANs) and wide area networks (WANs).

This book aims to provide a unified view of the broad field of data and computer communications. The organization of the book reflects an attempt to break this massive subject into comprehensible parts and to build, piece by piece, a survey of the state of the art. This introductory chapter begins with a general model of communications. Then a brief discussion introduces each of the Parts Two through Four of this book.

1.1 DATA COMMUNICATIONS AND NETWORKING FOR TODAY'S ENTERPRISE

Effective and efficient data communication and networking facilities are vital to any enterprise. In this section, we first look at trends that are increasing the challenge for the business manager in planning and managing such facilities. Then we look specifically at the requirement for ever-greater transmission speeds and network capacity.

Trends

Three different forces have consistently driven the architecture and evolution of data communications and networking facilities: traffic growth, development of new services, and advances in technology.

Communication **traffic**, both local (within a building or building complex) and long distance, both voice and data, has been growing at a high and steady rate for decades. The increasing emphasis on office automation, remote access, online transactions, and other productivity measures means that this trend is likely to continue. Thus, managers are constantly struggling to maximize capacity and minimize transmission costs.

As businesses rely more and more on information technology, the range of **services** expands. This increases the demand for high-capacity networking and transmission facilities. In turn, the continuing growth in high-speed network offerings with a simultaneous drop in prices encourages the expansion of services. Thus, growth in services and growth in traffic capacity go hand in hand. Figure 1.1 gives some examples of information-based services and the data rates needed to support them [ELSA02].

Finally, trends in **technology** enable the provision of increasing traffic capacity and the support of a wide range of services. Four technology trends are particularly notable:

1. The trend toward faster and cheaper, both in computing and communications, continues. In terms of computing, this means more powerful computers and clusters of computers capable of supporting more demanding applications, such as multimedia applications. In terms of communications, the increasing use of optical fiber and high-speed wireless has brought transmission prices down and greatly increased capacity. For example, for long-distance telecommunication

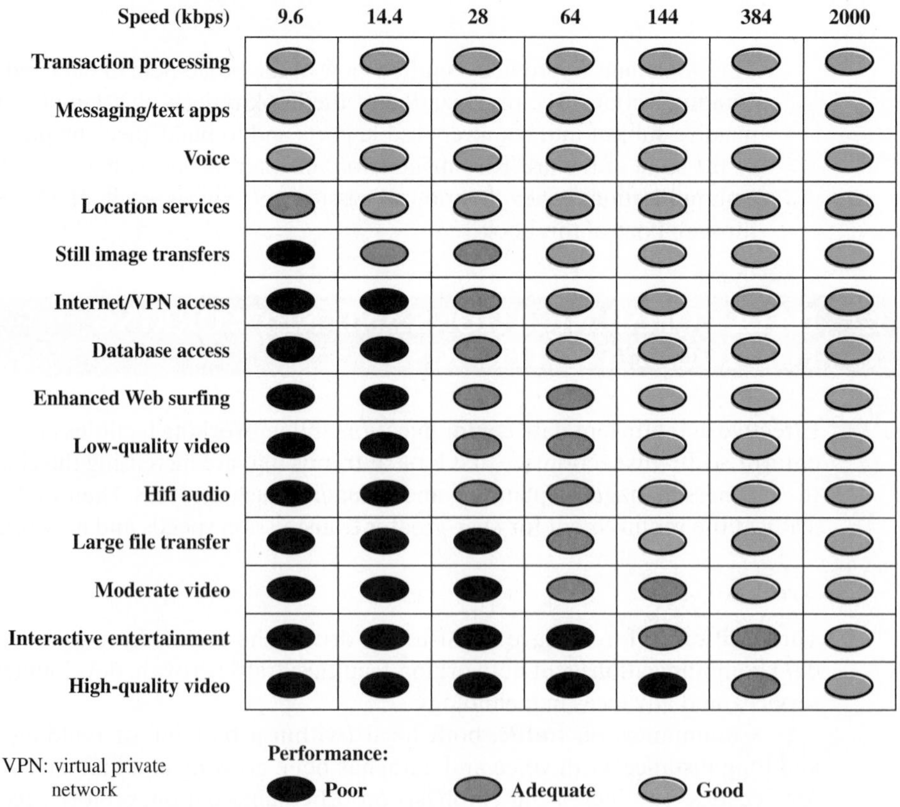

Speed (kbps)	9.6	14.4	28	64	144	384	2000
Transaction processing	Good	Good	Good	Good	Good	Good	Good
Messaging/text apps	Adequate	Adequate	Good	Good	Good	Good	Good
Voice	Good	Good	Good	Good	Good	Good	Good
Location services	Adequate	Good	Good	Good	Good	Good	Good
Still image transfers	Poor	Adequate	Good	Good	Good	Good	Good
Internet/VPN access	Poor	Poor	Good	Good	Good	Good	Good
Database access	Poor	Adequate	Adequate	Adequate	Good	Good	Good
Enhanced Web surfing	Poor	Poor	Adequate	Adequate	Good	Good	Good
Low-quality video	Poor	Poor	Adequate	Adequate	Adequate	Adequate	Good
Hifi audio	Poor	Poor	Adequate	Good	Good	Good	Good
Large file transfer	Poor	Poor	Poor	Good	Good	Adequate	Good
Moderate video	Poor	Poor	Poor	Adequate	Good	Good	Adequate
Interactive entertainment	Poor	Poor	Poor	Poor	Good	Good	Good
High-quality video	Poor	Poor	Poor	Poor	Poor	Adequate	Good

VPN: virtual private network

Performance:
● Poor   ◐ Adequate   ○ Good

Figure 1.1   Services versus Throughput Rates

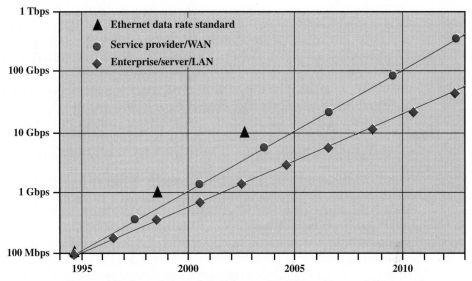

Figure 1.2 Past and Projected Growth in Ethernet Data Rate Demand Compared to Existing Ethernet Data Rates

and data network links, recent offerings of dense wavelength division multiplexing (DWDM) enable capacities of many terabits per second. For local area networks (LANs), many enterprises now have Gigabit Ethernet or 10-Gbps Ethernet backbone networks.[1] Further, the need for the next-generation 100-Gpbs is pressing, and products at this data rate should appear in the near future. Figure 1.2, based on [MELL07], indicates the Ethernet demand trend. As shown, usage statistics indicate that Internet backbone data rate demand in the network core doubles every 12 to 18 months, while demand in enterprise/LAN applications doubles approximately every 24 months.

2. Both voice-oriented telecommunications networks, such as the public switched telephone network (PSTN), and data networks, including the Internet, are more "intelligent" than ever. Two areas of intelligence are noteworthy. First, today's networks can offer differing levels of quality of service (QoS), which include specifications for maximum delay, minimum throughput, and so on. Second, today's networks provide a variety of customizable services in the areas of network management and security.

3. The Internet, the Web, and associated applications have emerged as dominant features of both the business and personal world, opening up many opportunities and challenges for managers. In addition to exploiting the Internet and the Web to reach customers, suppliers, and partners, enterprises have formed intranets and extranets[2] to isolate their proprietary information free from unwanted access.

---

[1]An explanation of numerical prefixes, such as *tera* and *giga*, is provided in the document *Prefix.pdf*, available at the access-controlled Web site for this book.

[2]Briefly, an intranet uses Internet and Web technology in an isolated facility internal to an enterprise; an extranet extends a company's intranet out onto the Internet to allow selected customers, suppliers, and mobile workers to access the company's private data and applications.

4. There has been a trend toward ever-increasing mobility for decades, liberating workers from the confines of the physical enterprise. Innovations include voice mail, remote data access, pagers, fax, e-mail, cordless phones, cell phones and cellular networks, and Internet portals. The result is the ability of employees to take their business context with them as they move about. We are now seeing the growth of high-speed wireless access, which further enhances the ability to use enterprise information resources and services anywhere.

Data Transmission and Network Capacity Requirements

Momentous changes in the way organizations do business and process information have been driven by changes in networking technology and at the same time have driven those changes. It is hard to separate chicken and egg in this field. Similarly, the use of the Internet by both businesses and individuals reflects this cyclic dependency: The availability of new image-based services on the Internet (i.e., the Web) has resulted in an increase in the total number of users and the traffic volume generated by each user. This, in turn, has resulted in a need to increase the speed and efficiency of the Internet. On the other hand, it is only such increased speed that makes the use of Web-based applications palatable to the end user.

In this section, we survey some of the end-user factors that fit into this equation. We begin with the need for high-speed LANs in the business environment, because this need has appeared first and has forced the pace of networking development. Then we look at business WAN requirements. Finally, we offer a few words about the effect of changes in commercial electronics on network requirements.

THE EMERGENCE OF HIGH-SPEED LANS Personal computers and microcomputer workstations began to achieve widespread acceptance in business computing in the early 1980s and have now achieved virtually the status of the telephone: an essential tool for office workers. Until relatively recently, office LANs provided basic connectivity services—connecting personal computers and terminals to mainframes and midrange systems that ran corporate applications, and providing workgroup connectivity at the departmental or divisional level. In both cases, traffic patterns were relatively light, with an emphasis on file transfer and electronic mail. The LANs that were available for this type of workload, primarily Ethernet and token ring, are well suited to this environment.

In the last 20 years, two significant trends altered the role of the personal computer and therefore the requirements on the LAN:

1. The speed and computing power of personal computers continued to enjoy explosive growth. These more powerful platforms support graphics-intensive applications and ever more elaborate graphical user interfaces to the operating system.

2. MIS (management information systems) organizations have recognized the LAN as a viable and essential computing platform, resulting in the focus on network computing. This trend began with client/server computing, which has become a dominant architecture in the business environment and the more

recent Web-focused intranet trend. Both of these approaches involve the frequent transfer of potentially large volumes of data in a transaction-oriented environment.

The effect of these trends has been to increase the volume of data to be handled over LANs and, because applications are more interactive, to reduce the acceptable delay on data transfers. The earlier generation of 10-Mbps Ethernets and 16-Mbps token rings was simply not up to the job of supporting these requirements.

The following are examples of requirements that call for higher-speed LANs:

- **Centralized server farms:** In many applications, there is a need for user, or client, systems to be able to draw huge amounts of data from multiple centralized servers, called server farms. An example is a color publishing operation, in which servers typically contain tens of gigabytes of image data that must be downloaded to imaging workstations. As the performance of the servers themselves has increased, the bottleneck has shifted to the network.

- **Power workgroups:** These groups typically consist of a small number of cooperating users who need to draw massive data files across the network. Examples are a software development group that runs tests on a new software version, or a computer-aided design (CAD) company that regularly runs simulations of new designs. In such cases, large amounts of data are distributed to several workstations, processed, and updated at very high speed for multiple iterations.

- **High-speed local backbone:** As processing demand grows, LANs proliferate at a site, and high-speed interconnection is necessary.

CORPORATE WIDE AREA NETWORKING NEEDS As recently as the early 1990s, there was an emphasis in many organizations on a centralized data processing model. In a typical environment, there might be significant computing facilities at a few regional offices, consisting of mainframes or well-equipped midrange systems. These centralized facilities could handle most corporate applications, including basic finance, accounting, and personnel programs, as well as many of the business-specific applications. Smaller, outlying offices (e.g., a bank branch) could be equipped with terminals or basic personal computers linked to one of the regional centers in a transaction-oriented environment.

This model began to change in the early 1990s, and the change accelerated since then. Many organizations have dispersed their employees into multiple smaller offices. There is a growing use of telecommuting. Most significant, the nature of the application structure has changed. First client/server computing and, more recently, intranet computing have fundamentally restructured the organizational data processing environment. There is now much more reliance on personal computers, workstations, and servers and much less use of centralized mainframe and midrange systems. Furthermore, the virtually universal deployment of graphical user interfaces to the desktop enables the end user to exploit graphic applications, multimedia, and other data-intensive applications. In addition, most organizations require access to the Internet. When a few clicks of the mouse can trigger huge volumes of data, traffic patterns have become more unpredictable while the average load has risen.

All of these trends mean that more data must be transported off premises and into the wide area. It has long been accepted that in the typical business environment, about 80% of the traffic remains local and about 20% traverses wide area links. But this rule no longer applies to most companies, with a greater percentage of the traffic going into the WAN environment. This traffic flow shift places a greater burden on LAN backbones and, of course, on the WAN facilities used by a corporation. Thus, just as in the local area, changes in corporate data traffic patterns are driving the creation of high-speed WANs.

DIGITAL ELECTRONICS   The rapid conversion of consumer electronics to digital technology is having an impact on both the Internet and corporate intranets. As these new gadgets come into view and proliferate, they dramatically increase the amount of image and video traffic carried by networks.

Two noteworthy examples of this trend are digital versatile disks (DVDs) and digital still cameras. With the capacious DVD, the electronics industry has at last found an acceptable replacement for the analog video home system (VHS) videotape. The DVD has replaced the videotape used in videocassette recorders (VCRs) and replaced the CD-ROM in personal computers and servers. The DVD takes video into the digital age. It delivers movies with picture quality that outshines laser disks, and it can be randomly accessed like audio CDs, which DVD machines can also play. Vast volumes of data can be crammed onto the disk. With DVD's huge storage capacity and vivid quality, PC games have become more realistic and educational software incorporates more video. Following in the wake of these developments is a new crest of traffic over the Internet and corporate intranets, as this material is incorporated into Web sites.

A related product development is the digital camcorder. This product has made it easier for individuals and companies to make digital video files to be placed on corporate and Internet Web sites, again adding to the traffic burden.

Convergence

Convergence refers to the merger of previously distinct telephony and information technologies and markets. We can think of this convergence in terms of a three-layer model of enterprise communications:

- **Applications:** These are seen by the end users of a business. Convergence integrates communications applications, such as voice calling (telephone), voice mail, e-mail, and instant messaging, with business applications, such as workgroup collaboration, customer relationship management, and other back-office functions. With convergence, applications provide features that incorporate voice, data, and video in a seamless, organized, and value-added manner. One example is multimedia messaging, which enables a user to employ a single interface to access messages from a variety of sources (e.g., office voice mail, office e-mail, beeper, and fax).

- **Enterprise services:** At this level, the manager deals with the information network in terms of the services it supplies to support applications. The network manager needs design, maintenance, and support services related to the deployment of convergence-based facilities. Also at this level, network managers deal with the enterprise network as a function-providing system. Such management services may include setting up authentication schemes; capacity management for various users, groups, and applications; and QoS provision.

- **Infrastructure:** The infrastructure consists of the communication links, LANs, WANs, and Internet connections available to the enterprise. The key aspect of convergence at this level is the ability to carry voice and video over data networks, such as the Internet.

Figure 1.3, based on [MILL05], illustrates the three layers and their associated convergence attributes. In simple terms, convergence involves moving voice into a data infrastructure, integrating all the voice and data networks inside a user organization into a single data network infrastructure, and then extending that into the wireless arena. The foundation of this convergence is packet-based transmission using the Internet Protocol (IP). Convergence increases the function and scope of both the infrastructure and the application base.

Convergence brings many benefits, including simplified network management, increased efficiency, and greater flexibility at the application level. For example, a converged network infrastructure makes it easier to add applications that combine video, data, and voice. [POL07] lists the following three key benefits of convergence:

- **Efficiency:** Provides a double-digit percent reduction in operating costs through the convergence of legacy networks onto a single global IP network; better use of and reduction in existing resources; and implementation of centralized capacity planning, asset management, and policy management.
- **Effectiveness:** The converged environment has the potential to provide users with great flexibility, irrespective of where they are. Such a company-wide

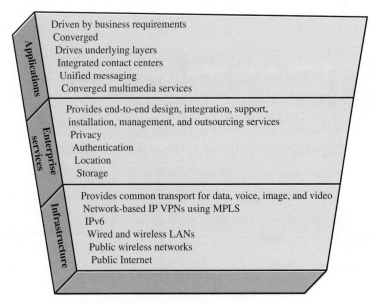

Figure 1.3 Business-Driven Convergence

environment provides for rapid standardized service deployment and enhanced remote connectivity and mobility.

- **Transformation:** Convergence also enables the enterprise-wide adoption of global standards and associated service levels, thus providing better data, enhanced real-time global decision-making processes, and improved execution in business planning and operations. This leads to greater agility for the enterprise in providing new services to its customers and employees.

1.2 A COMMUNICATIONS MODEL

This section introduces a simple model of communications, illustrated by the block diagram in Figure 1.4a.

The fundamental purpose of a communications system is the exchange of data between two parties. Figure 1.4b presents one particular example, which is communication between a workstation and a server over a public telephone network. Another example is the exchange of voice signals between two telephones over the same network. The key elements of the model:

- **Source:** This device generates the data to be transmitted; examples are telephones and personal computers.

- **Transmitter:** Usually, the data generated by a source system are not transmitted directly in the form in which they were generated. Rather, a transmitter transforms and encodes the information in such a way as to produce electromagnetic signals that can be transmitted across some sort of transmission system. For example, a modem takes a digital bit stream from an attached

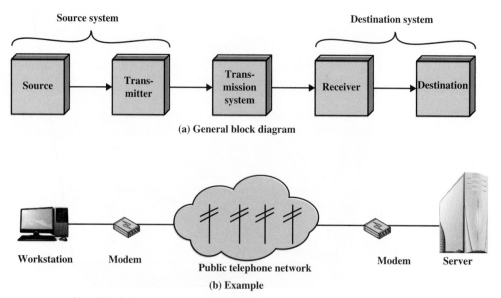

(a) General block diagram

(b) Example

Figure 1.4   Simplified Communications Model

device such as a personal computer and transforms that bit stream into an analog signal that can be handled by the telephone network.

- **Transmission system:** This can be a single transmission line or a complex network connecting source and destination.

- **Receiver:** The receiver accepts the signal from the transmission system and converts it into a form that can be handled by the destination device. For example, a modem will accept an analog signal coming from a network or transmission line and convert it into a digital bit stream.

- **Destination:** Takes the incoming data from the receiver.

This simple narrative conceals a wealth of technical complexity. To get some idea of the scope of this complexity, Table 1.1 lists some of the key tasks that must be performed in a data communications system. The list is somewhat arbitrary: Elements could be added; items on the list could be merged; and some items represent several tasks that are performed at different "levels" of the system. However, the list as it stands is suggestive of the scope of this book.

The first item, **transmission system utilization**, refers to the need to make efficient use of transmission facilities that are typically shared among a number of communicating devices. Various techniques (referred to as multiplexing) are used to allocate the total capacity of a transmission medium among a number of users. Congestion control techniques may be required to assure that the system is not overwhelmed by excessive demand for transmission services.

To communicate, a device must **interface** with the transmission system. All the forms of communication discussed in this book depend on the use of electro-magnetic signals propagated over a transmission medium. Thus, once an interface is established, **signal generation** is required for communication. The properties of the signal, such as form and intensity, must be such that the signal is (1) capable of being propagated through the transmission system, and (2) interpretable as data at the receiver.

Not only must the signals be generated to conform to the requirements of the transmission system and receiver, but also there must be some form of **synchronization** between transmitter and receiver. The receiver must be able to determine when a signal begins to arrive and when it ends. It must also know the duration of each signal element.

Beyond the basic matter of deciding on the nature and timing of signals, there is a variety of requirements for communication between two parties that might be

Table 1.1   Communications Tasks

Transmission system utilization	Addressing
Interfacing	Routing
Signal generation	Recovery
Synchronization	Message formatting
Exchange management	Security
Error detection and correction	Network management
Flow control	

collected under the term **exchange management**. If data are to be exchanged in both directions over a period of time, the two parties must cooperate. For example, for two parties to engage in a telephone conversation, one party must dial the number of the other, causing signals to be generated that result in the ringing of the called phone. The called party completes a connection by lifting the receiver. For data processing devices, more will be needed than simply establishing a connection; certain conventions must be decided on. These conventions may include whether both devices may transmit simultaneously or must take turns, the amount of data to be sent at one time, the format of the data, and what to do if certain contingencies such as an error arise.

The next two items might have been included under exchange management, but they seem important enough to list separately. In all communications systems, there is a potential for error; transmitted signals are distorted to some extent before reaching their destination. **Error detection and correction** are required in circumstances where errors cannot be tolerated. This is usually the case with data processing systems. For example, in transferring a file from one computer to another, it is simply not acceptable for the contents of the file to be accidentally altered. **Flow control** is required to assure that the source does not overwhelm the destination by sending data faster than they can be processed and absorbed.

Next are the related but distinct concepts of **addressing** and **routing**. When more than two devices share a transmission facility, a source system must indicate the identity of the intended destination. The transmission system must assure that the destination system, and only that system, receives the data. Further, the transmission system may itself be a network through which various paths may be taken. A specific route through this network must be chosen.

Recovery is a concept distinct from that of error correction. Recovery techniques are needed in situations in which an information exchange, such as a database transaction or file transfer, is interrupted due to a fault somewhere in the system. The objective is either to be able to resume activity at the point of interruption or at least to restore the state of the systems involved to the condition prior to the beginning of the exchange.

Message formatting has to do with an agreement between two parties as to the form of the data to be exchanged or transmitted, such as the binary code for characters.

Frequently, it is important to provide some measure of **security** in a data communications system. The sender of data may wish to be assured that only the intended receiver actually receives the data. And the receiver of data may wish to be assured that the received data have not been altered in transit and that the data actually come from the purported sender.

Finally, a data communications facility is a complex system that cannot create or run itself. **Network management** capabilities are needed to configure the system, monitor its status, react to failures and overloads, and plan intelligently for future growth.

Thus, we have gone from the simple idea of data communication between source and destination to a rather formidable list of data communications tasks. In this book, we elaborate this list of tasks to describe and encompass the entire set of activities that can be classified under data and computer communications.

1.3 DATA COMMUNICATIONS

Following Part One, this book is organized into seven parts. Part Two deals with the most fundamental aspects of the communications function, focusing on the transmission of signals in a reliable and efficient manner. For want of a better name, we have given Part Two the title "Data Communications," although that term arguably encompasses some or even all of the topics of Parts Three through Seven.

A Data Communications Model

To get some flavor for the focus of Part Two, Figure 1.5 provides a new perspective on the communications model of Figure 1.4a. We trace the details of this figure using electronic mail as an example.

Suppose that the input device and transmitter are components of a personal computer. The user of the PC wishes to send a message m to another user. The user activates the electronic mail package on the PC and enters the message via the keyboard (input device). The character string is briefly buffered in main memory. We can view it as a sequence of bits (g) in memory. The personal computer is connected to some transmission medium, such as a local area network, a digital subscriber line (DSL), or a wireless connection, by an I/O device (transmitter), such as a local network transceiver or a DSL modem. The input data are transferred to the transmitter as a sequence of voltage shifts $[g(t)]$ representing bits on some communications bus or cable. The transmitter is connected directly to the medium and converts the incoming stream $[g(t)]$ into a signal $[s(t)]$ suitable for transmission; specific alternatives will be described in Chapter 5.

The transmitted signal $s(t)$ presented to the medium is subject to a number of impairments, discussed in Chapter 3, before it reaches the receiver. Thus, the received signal $r(t)$ may differ from $s(t)$. The receiver will attempt to estimate the original $s(t)$, based on $r(t)$ and its knowledge of the medium, producing a sequence of bits $g'(t)$. These bits are sent to the output personal computer, where they are briefly buffered in memory as a block of bits (g'). In many cases, the destination system will attempt to determine if an error has occurred and, if so, cooperate with the source system to eventually obtain a complete, error-free block of data.

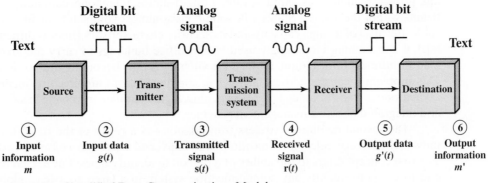

Figure 1.5   Simplified Data Communications Model

These data are then presented to the user via an output device, such as a printer or screen. The message (m') as viewed by the user will usually be an exact copy of the original message (m).

Now consider a telephone conversation. In this case the input to the telephone is a message (m) in the form of sound waves. The sound waves are converted by the telephone into electrical signals of the same frequency. These signals are transmitted without modification over the telephone line. Hence the input signal $g(t)$ and the transmitted signal $s(t)$ are identical. The signal $s(t)$ will suffer some distortion over the medium, so that $r(t)$ will not be identical to $s(t)$. Nevertheless, the signal $r(t)$ is converted back into a sound wave with no attempt at correction or improvement of signal quality. Thus, m' is not an exact replica of m. However, the received sound message is generally comprehensible to the listener.

The discussion so far does not touch on other key aspects of data communications, including data link control techniques for controlling the flow of data and detecting and correcting errors, and multiplexing techniques for transmission efficiency.

The Transmission of Information

The basic building block of any communications facility is the transmission line. Much of the technical detail of how information is encoded and transmitted across a line is of no real interest to the business manager. The manager is concerned with whether the particular facility provides the required capacity, with acceptable reliability, at minimum cost. However, there are certain aspects of transmission technology that a manager must understand to ask the right questions and make informed decisions.

One of the basic choices facing a business user is the transmission medium. For use within the business premises, this choice is generally completely up to the business. For long-distance communications, the choice is generally but not always made by the long-distance carrier. In either case, changes in technology are rapidly changing the mix of media used. Of particular note are *fiber optic* transmission and *wireless* transmission (e.g., satellite and cellular communications). These two media are now driving the evolution of data communications transmission.

The ever-increasing capacity of fiber optic channels is making channel capacity a virtually free resource. During the past 20 years, the cost of fiber optic transmission has dropped by several orders of magnitude, and the capacity of such systems has grown at almost as rapid a rate. Long-distance telephone communications trunks within the United States will soon consist almost completely of fiber optic cable. Because of its high capacity and its security characteristics (fiber is difficult to tap), it is becoming increasingly used within office buildings to carry the growing load of business information. However, switching is now becoming the bottleneck. This problem is causing radical changes in communications architecture, including asynchronous transfer mode (ATM) switching, highly parallel processing in switches, and integrated network management schemes.

The second medium—wireless transmission—is a result of the trend toward universal personal telecommunications and universal access to communications. The first concept refers to the ability of a person to identify himself or herself easily and to use conveniently any communication system in a large area (e.g., globally, over a continent, or in an entire country) in terms of a single account. The second refers to the capability of using one's terminal in a wide variety of environments to connect to information services (e.g., to have a portable terminal that will work equally well in the office, on the street, and on airplanes). This revolution in personal computing obviously involves wireless communication in a fundamental way.

Despite the growth in the capacity and the drop in cost of transmission facilities, transmission services remain the most costly component of a communications budget for most businesses. Thus, the manager needs to be aware of techniques that increase the efficiency of the use of these facilities. The two major approaches to greater efficiency are multiplexing and compression. *Multiplexing* refers to the ability of a number of devices to share a transmission facility. If each device needs the facility only a fraction of the time, then a sharing arrangement allows the cost of the facility to be spread over many users. *Compression*, as the name indicates, involves squeezing the data down so that a lower-capacity, cheaper transmission facility can be used to meet a given demand. These two techniques show up separately and in combination in a number of types of communications equipment. The manager needs to understand these technologies to assess the appropriateness and cost-effectiveness of the various products on the market.

TRANSMISSION AND TRANSMISSION MEDIA Information can be communicated by converting it into an electromagnetic signal and transmitting that signal over some medium, such as a twisted-pair telephone line. The most commonly used transmission media are twisted-pair lines, coaxial cable, optical fiber cable, and terrestrial and satellite microwave. The data rates that can be achieved and the rate at which errors can occur depend on the nature of the signal and the type of medium. Chapters 3 and 4 examine the significant properties of electromagnetic signals and compare the various transmission media in terms of cost, performance, and applications.

COMMUNICATION TECHNIQUES The transmission of information across a transmission medium involves more than simply inserting a signal on the medium. The technique used to encode the information into an electromagnetic signal must be determined. There are various ways in which the encoding can be done, and the choice affects performance and reliability. Furthermore, the successful transmission of information involves a high degree of cooperation between the various components. The interface between a device and the transmission medium must be agreed on. Some means of controlling the flow of information and recovering from its loss or corruption must be used. These latter functions are performed by a data link control protocol. All these issues are examined in Chapters 5 through 7.

TRANSMISSION EFFICIENCY A major cost in any computer/communications facility is transmission cost. Because of this, it is important to maximize the amount of information that can be carried over a given resource or, alternatively, to minimize the transmission capacity needed to satisfy a given information communications requirement. Two ways of achieving this objective are multiplexing and compression. The two techniques can be used separately or in combination. Chapter 8 examines the three most common multiplexing techniques: frequency division, synchronous time division, and statistical time division, as well as the important compression techniques.

1.4   NETWORKS

The number of computers in use worldwide is in the billions. Moreover, the expanding memory and processing power of these computers means that users can put the machines to work on new kinds of applications and functions. Accordingly, the pressure from the users of these systems for ways to communicate among all these machines is irresistible. It is changing the way vendors think and the way all automation products and services are sold. This demand for connectivity is manifested in two specific requirements: the need for communications software, which is previewed in the next section, and the need for networks.

One type of network that has become ubiquitous is the local area network. Indeed, the LAN is to be found in virtually all medium- and large-size office buildings. As the number and power of computing devices have grown, so have the number and capacity of LANs to be found in an office. Although standards have been developed that reduce somewhat the number of types of LANs, there are still half a dozen general types of local area networks to choose from. Furthermore, many offices need more than one such network, with the attendant problems of interconnecting and managing a diverse collection of networks, computers, and terminals.

Beyond the confines of a single office building, networks for voice, data, image, and video are equally important to business. Here, too, there are rapid changes. Advances in technology have led to greatly increased capacity and the concept of integration. *Integration* means that the customer equipment and networks can deal simultaneously with voice, data, image, and even video. Thus, a memo or report can be accompanied by voice commentary, presentation graphics, and perhaps even a short video introduction or summary. Image and video services impose large demands on wide area network transmission. Moreover, as LANs become ubiquitous and as their transmission rates increase, the demands on the wide area networks to support LAN interconnection have increased the demands on WAN capacity and switching. On the other hand, fortunately, the enormous and ever-increasing capacity of fiber optic and wireless transmission provides ample resources to meet these demands. However, developing switching systems with the capacity and rapid response to support these increased requirements is a challenge not yet conquered.

The opportunities for using networks as an aggressive competitive tool and as a means of enhancing productivity and slashing costs are great. The manager who understands the technology and can deal effectively with vendors of service and equipment is able to enhance a company's competitive position.

In the remainder of this section, we provide a brief overview of various networks. Parts Three and Four cover these topics in depth.

Wide Area Networks

Wide area networks generally cover a large geographical area, require the crossing of public right-of-ways, and rely at least in part on circuits provided by a common carrier. Typically, a WAN consists of a number of interconnected switching nodes. A transmission from any one device is routed through these internal nodes to the specified destination device. These nodes (including the boundary nodes) are not concerned with the content of the data; rather, their purpose is to provide a switching facility that will move the data from node to node until they reach their destination.

Traditionally, WANs have been implemented using one of two technologies: circuit switching and packet switching. Subsequently, frame relay and ATM networks assumed major roles. While ATM and, to some extent frame relay, are still widely used, their use is gradually being supplanted by services based on gigabit Ethernet and Internet Protocol technologies.

CIRCUIT SWITCHING In a circuit-switching network, a dedicated communications path is established between two stations through the nodes of the network. That path is a connected sequence of physical links between nodes. On each link, a logical channel is dedicated to the connection. Data generated by the source station are transmitted along the dedicated path as rapidly as possible. At each node, incoming data are routed or switched to the appropriate outgoing channel without delay. The most common example of circuit switching is the telephone network.

PACKET SWITCHING A different approach is used in a packet-switching network. In this case, it is not necessary to dedicate transmission capacity along a path through the network. Rather, data are sent out in a sequence of small chunks, called packets. Each packet is passed through the network from node to node along some path leading from source to destination. At each node, the entire packet is received, stored briefly, and then transmitted to the next node. Packet-switching networks are commonly used for terminal-to-computer and computer-to-computer communications.

FRAME RELAY Packet switching was developed at a time when digital long-distance transmission facilities exhibited a relatively high error rate compared to today's facilities. As a result, there is a considerable amount of overhead built into packet-switching schemes to compensate for errors. The overhead includes additional bits added to each packet to introduce redundancy and additional processing at the end stations and the intermediate switching nodes to detect and recover from errors.

With modern high-speed telecommunications systems, this overhead is unnecessary and counterproductive. It is unnecessary because the rate of errors has been dramatically lowered and any remaining errors can easily be caught in the end systems by logic that operates above the level of the packet-switching logic. It is counterproductive because the overhead involved soaks up a significant fraction of the high capacity provided by the network.

Frame relay was developed to take advantage of these high data rates and low error rates. Whereas the original packet-switching networks were designed with a data rate to the end user of about 64 kbps, frame relay networks are designed to operate efficiently at user data rates of up to 2 Mbps. The key to achieving these high data rates is to strip out most of the overhead involved with error control.

ATM Asynchronous transfer mode, sometimes referred to as cell relay, is a culmination of developments in circuit switching and packet switching. ATM can be viewed as an evolution from frame relay. The most obvious difference between frame relay and ATM is that frame relay uses variable-length packets, called frames, and ATM uses fixed-length packets, called cells. As with frame relay, ATM provides little overhead for error control, depending on the inherent reliability of the transmission system and on higher layers of logic in the end systems to catch and correct errors. By using a fixed packet length, the processing overhead is reduced even further for ATM compared to frame relay. The result is that ATM is designed to work in the range of 10s and 100s of Mbps, and in the Gbps range.

ATM can also be viewed as an evolution from circuit switching. With circuit switching, only fixed-data-rate circuits are available to the end system. ATM allows the definition of multiple virtual channels with data rates that are dynamically defined at the time the virtual channel is created. By using small, fixed-size cells, ATM is so efficient that it can offer a constant-data-rate channel even though it is using a packet-switching technique. Thus, ATM extends circuit switching to allow multiple channels with the data rate on each channel dynamically set on demand.

Local Area Networks

As with WANs, a LAN is a communications network that interconnects a variety of devices and provides a means for information exchange among those devices. There are several key distinctions between LANs and WANs:

1. The scope of the LAN is small, typically a single building or a cluster of buildings. This difference in geographic scope leads to different technical solutions, as we shall see.

2. It is usually the case that the LAN is owned by the same organization that owns the attached devices. For WANs, this is less often the case, or at least a significant fraction of the network assets is not owned. This has two implications. First, care must be taken in the choice of LAN, because there may be a substantial capital investment (compared to dial-up or leased charges for WANs) for both purchase and maintenance. Second, the network management responsibility for a LAN falls solely on the user.

3. The internal data rates of LANs are typically much greater than those of WANs.

LANs come in a number of different configurations. The most common are switched LANs and wireless LANs. The most common switched LAN is a switched Ethernet LAN, which may consist of a single switch with a number of attached devices, or a number of interconnected switches. Two other prominent examples are ATM LANs, which simply use an ATM network in a local area, and Fibre Channel. Wireless LANs use a variety of wireless transmission technologies and organizations. LANs are examined in depth in Part Four.

Wireless Networks

As was just mentioned, wireless LANs are widely used in business environments. Wireless technology is also common for both wide area voice and data networks. Wireless networks provide advantages in the areas of mobility and ease of installation and configuration. Chapters 14 and 17 deal with wireless WANs and LANs, respectively.

1.5 THE INTERNET

Origins of the Internet

The Internet evolved from the ARPANET, which was developed in 1969 by the Advanced Research Projects Agency (ARPA) of the U.S. Department of Defense. It was the first operational packet-switching network. ARPANET began operations in four locations. Today the number of hosts is in the hundreds of millions, the number of users in the billions, and the number of countries participating nearing 200. The number of connections to the Internet continues to grow exponentially.

The network was so successful that ARPA applied the same packet-switching technology to tactical radio communication (packet radio) and to satellite communication (SATNET). Because the three networks operated in very different communication environments, the appropriate values for certain parameters, such as maximum packet size, were different in each case. Faced with the dilemma of integrating these networks, Vint Cerf and Bob Kahn of ARPA started to develop methods and protocols for *internetworking*—that is, communicating across arbitrary, multiple, packet-switched networks. They published a very influential paper in May of 1974 [CERF74] outlining their approach to a Transmission Control Protocol. The proposal was refined and details filled in by the ARPANET community, with major contributions from participants from European networks eventually leading to the TCP (Transmission Control Protocol) and IP (Internet Protocol) protocols, which, in turn, formed the basis for what eventually became the TCP/IP protocol suite. This provided the foundation for the Internet.

Key Elements

Figure 1.6 illustrates the key elements that comprise the Internet. The purpose of the Internet, of course, is to interconnect end systems, called **hosts**; these include PCs, workstations, servers, mainframes, and so on. Most hosts that use the Internet are connected to a **network**, such as a local area network or a wide area network (WAN). These networks are in turn connected by **routers**. Each router attaches to two or more networks. Some hosts, such as mainframes or servers, connect directly to a router rather than through a network.

In essence, the Internet operates as follows. A host may send data to another host anywhere on the Internet. The source host breaks the data to be sent into a sequence of packets, called **IP datagrams** or **IP packets**. Each packet includes a unique numeric address of the destination host. This address is referred to as an **IP address**, because the address is carried in an IP packet. Based on this destination address, each packet travels through a series of routers and networks from source to destination. Each router, as it receives a packet, makes a routing decision and forwards the packet along its way to the destination.

Internet Architecture

The Internet today is made up of thousands of overlapping hierarchical networks. Because of this, it is not practical to attempt a detailed description of the exact architecture or topology of the Internet. However, an overview of the common,

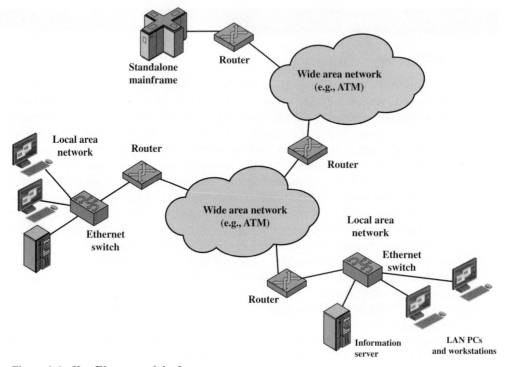

Figure 1.6 Key Elements of the Internet

general characteristics can be made. Figure 1.7 illustrates the discussion and Table 1.2 summarizes the terminology.

A key element of the Internet is the set of hosts attached to it. Simply put, a host is a computer. Today, computers come in many forms, including mobile phones and even cars. All of these forms can be hosts on the Internet. Hosts are sometimes grouped together in a LAN. This is the typical configuration in a corporate environment. Individual hosts and LANs are connected to an **Internet service provider (ISP)** through a **point of presence (POP)**. The connection is made in a series of steps starting with the **customer premises equipment (CPE)**. The CPE is the communications equipment located onsite with the host.

For a number of home users, the CPE was traditionally a 56-kbps modem. This was adequate for e-mail and related services but marginal for graphics-intensive Web surfing. Today's CPE offerings provide greater capacity and guaranteed service in some cases. A sample of these access technologies includes DSL, cable modem, terrestrial wireless, and satellite. Users who connect to the Internet through their work often use workstations or PCs connected to their employer-owned LANs, which in turn connect through shared organizational trunks to an ISP. In these cases the shared circuit is often a T-1 connection (1.544 Mbps), while for very large organizations T-3 connections (44.736 Mbps) are sometimes found. Alternatively, an organization's LAN may be hooked to a WAN, such as a frame relay network, which in turn connects to an ISP.

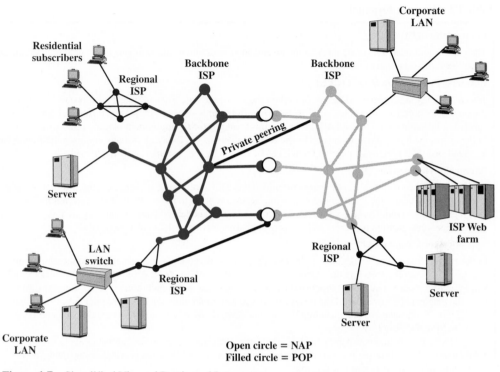

Figure 1.7 Simplified View of Portion of Internet

The CPE is physically attached to the "local loop" or "last mile." This is the infrastructure between a provider's installation and the site where the host is located. For example, a home user with a 56K modem attaches the modem to the telephone line. The telephone line is typically a pair of copper wires that runs from the house to a **central office (CO)** owned and operated by the telephone company. In this instance the local loop is the pair of copper wires running between the home and the CO. If the home user has a cable modem, the local loop is the coaxial cable that runs from the home to the cable company facilities. The preceding examples are a bit of an oversimplification, but they suffice for this discussion. In many cases the wires that leave a home are aggregated with wires from other homes and then converted to a different media such as fiber. In these cases the term *local loop* still refers to the path from the home to the CO or cable facility. The local loop provider is not necessarily the ISP. In many cases the local loop provider is the telephone company and the ISP is a large, national service organization. Often, however, the local loop provider is also the ISP.

Other forms of CPE-ISP connection do not go through a telephone company CO. For example, a cable link would connect the local user to the cable company site, which would include or link to an ISP. Mobile users can take advantage of a wireless link to a WiFi that provides access to the Internet. And corporate access to

Table 1.2 Internet Terminology

Central Office (CO)

The place where telephone companies terminate customer lines and locate switching equipment to interconnect those lines with other networks.

Customer Premises Equipment (CPE)

Telecommunications equipment that is located on the customer's premises (physical location) rather than on the provider's premises or in between. Telephone handsets, modems, cable TV set-top boxes, and digital subscriber line routers are examples. Historically, this term referred to equipment placed at the customer's end of the telephone line and usually owned by the telephone company. Today, almost any end-user equipment can be called customer premises equipment and it can be owned by the customer or by the provider.

Internet Service Provider (ISP)

A company that provides other companies or individuals with access to, or presence on, the Internet. An ISP has the equipment and the telecommunication line access required to have a POP on the Internet for the geographic area served. The larger ISPs have their own high-speed leased lines so that they are less dependent on the telecommunication providers and can provide better service to their customers.

Network Access Point (NAP)

In the United States, a network access point (NAP) is one of several major Internet interconnection points that serve to tie all the ISPs together. Originally, four NAPs—in New York, Washington, D.C., Chicago, and San Francisco—were created and supported by the National Science Foundation as part of the transition from the original U.S. government–financed Internet to a commercially operated Internet. Since that time, several new NAPs have arrived, including WorldCom's "MAE West" site in San Jose, California and ICS Network Systems' "Big East."

The NAPs provide major switching facilities that serve the public in general. Companies apply to use the NAP facilities. Much Internet traffic is handled without involving NAPs, using peering arrangements and interconnections within geographic regions.

Network Service Provider (NSP)

A company that provides backbone services to an Internet service provider (ISP). Typically, an ISP connects at a point called an Internet exchange (IX) to a regional ISP that in turn connects to an NSP backbone.

Point of Presence (POP)

A site that has a collection of telecommunications equipment, usually refers to ISP or telephone company sites. An ISP POP is the edge of the ISP's network; connections from users are accepted and authenticated here. An Internet access provider may operate several POPs distributed throughout its area of operation to increase the chance that their subscribers will be able to reach one with a local telephone call. The largest national ISPs have POPs all over the country.

an ISP may be by dedicated high-speed links or through a wide area network, such as an asynchronous transfer mode or frame relay network.

The ISP provides access to its larger network through a POP. A POP is simply a facility where customers can connect to the ISP network. The facility is sometimes owned by the ISP, but often the ISP leases space from the local loop carrier. A POP can be as simple as a bank of modems and an access server installed in a rack at the CO. The POPs are usually spread out over the geographic area where the provider offers service. The ISP acts as a gateway to the Internet, providing many important services. For most home users, the ISP provides the unique numeric IP address needed to communicate with other Internet hosts. Most ISPs also provide name resolution and other essential network services. The most important service an ISP provides, though, is access to other ISP networks. Access is facilitated by formal peering agreements between providers. Physical access can be implemented by connecting POPs from different ISPs. This can be done directly with a local connection if the POPs are collocated or with leased lines when the POPs are not collocated. A more commonly used mechanism is the **network access point (NAP)**.

A NAP is a physical facility that provides the infrastructure to move data between connected networks. In the United States, the National Science Foundation (NSF) privatization plan called for the creation of four NAPs. The NAPs were built and are operated by the private sector. The number of NAPs has grown significantly over the years, and the technology employed has shifted from Fiber Distributed Data Interface (FDDI) and Ethernet to ATM and Gigabit Ethernet. Most NAPs today have an ATM core. The networks connected at a NAP are owned and operated by **network service providers (NSPs)**. A NSP can also be an ISP but this is not always the case. Peering agreements are between NSPs and do not include the NAP operator. The NSPs install routers at the NAP and connect them to the NAP infrastructure. The NSP equipment is responsible for routing, and the NAP infrastructure provides the physical access paths between routers.

A small hypothetical example can help make the picture clearer. In this example there are two companies, one named A, Inc. and the other B, Inc. and they are both NSPs. A, Inc. and B, Inc. have a peering agreement and they both install routers in two NAPs, one located on the east coast of the United States and the other on the west coast. There are also two other companies known as Y, Inc. and Z, Inc. and they are both ISPs. Finally, there is a home user named Bob and a small company named Small, Inc.

Small, Inc. has four hosts connected together into a LAN. Each of the four hosts can communicate and share resources with the other three. Small, Inc. would like access to a broader set of services so they contract with ISP Y, Inc. for a connection. Small, Inc. installs a CPE to drive a leased T-1 line into a Y, Inc. POP. Once the CPE is connected, software automatically assigns a numeric address to each Small, Inc. host. The Small, Inc. hosts can now communicate and share resources with any other host connected to the larger ISP network. On the other side of the country, Bob decides to contract with ISP Z, Inc. He installs a modem on his phone line to dial into a Z, Inc. POP. Once the modem connects, a numeric address is automatically assigned to his home computer. His computer can now communicate and share resources with any other computer connected to the larger ISP network.

Bob's home machine and the hosts owned by Small, Inc. cannot yet communicate. This becomes possible when their respective ISPs contract with NSPs that have a peering agreement. In this example, the ISP Y, Inc. decides to expand its service coverage to the opposite coast and contracts with the NSP A, Inc. A, Inc. sells bandwidth on its high-speed coast-to-coast network. The ISP Z, Inc. also wishes to expand its service coverage and contracts with the NSP B, Inc. Like A, Inc., B, Inc. also sells bandwidth on a high-speed coast-to-coast network. Because A, Inc. and B, Inc. have a peering agreement and have implemented the agreement at two NAPs, Bob's home machine and the hosts of Small, Inc. can now communicate and share resources. Although this example is contrived, in principle this is what the Internet is. The differences are that the Internet has millions of hosts and many thousands of networks using dozens of access technologies, including satellite, radio, leased T-1, and DSL.

1.6 AN EXAMPLE CONFIGURATION

To give some feel for the scope of concerns of Parts Two through Four, Figure 1.8 illustrates some of the typical communications and network elements in use today. In the upper-left-hand portion of the figure, we see an individual residential user connected to an Internet service provider through some sort of subscriber connection. Common examples of such a connection are the public telephone network, for which the user requires a dial-up modem (e.g., a 56-kbps modem); a digital subscriber line, which provides a high-speed link over telephone lines and requires a special DSL modem; and a cable TV facility, which requires a cable modem. In each case, there are separate issues concerning signal encoding, error control, and the internal structure of the subscribe network.

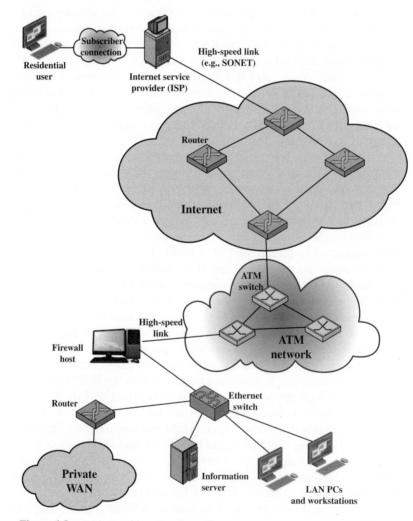

Figure 1.8 A Networking Configuration

Typically, an ISP will consist of a number of interconnected servers (only a single server is shown) connected to the Internet through a high-speed link. One example of such a link is a SONET (synchronous optical network) line, described in Chapter 8. The Internet consists of a number of interconnected routers that span the globe. The routers forward packets of data from source to destination through the Internet.

The lower portion of Figure 1.8 shows a LAN implemented using a single Ethernet switch. This is a common configuration at a small business or other small organizations. The LAN is connected to the Internet through a firewall host that provides security services. In this example the firewall connects to the Internet through an ATM network. There is also a router off of the LAN hooked into a private WAN, which might be a private ATM or frame relay network.

A variety of design issues, such as signal encoding and error control, relate to the links between adjacent elements, such as between routers on the Internet or between switches in the ATM network, or between a subscriber and an ISP. The internal structure of the various networks (telephone, ATM, Ethernet) raises additional issues. We will be occupied in Parts Two through Four with the design features suggested by Figure 1.8.

CHAPTER 2

PROTOCOL ARCHITECTURE, TCP/IP, AND INTERNET-BASED APPLICATIONS

*To destroy communication completely, there must be no rules in common between
transmitter and receiver—neither of alphabet nor of syntax.*

— *On Human Communication,* Colin Cherry

KEY POINTS

◆ A protocol architecture is the layered structure of hardware and software
that supports the exchange of data between systems and supports
distributed applications, such as electronic mail and file transfer.

◆ At each layer of a protocol architecture, one or more common protocols
are implemented in communicating systems. Each protocol provides a
set of rules for the exchange of data between systems.

◆ The most widely used protocol architecture is the TCP/IP protocol
suite, which consists of the following layers: physical, network access,
internet, transport, and application.

◆ Another important protocol architecture is the seven-layer OSI model.

This chapter provides a context for the detailed material that follows. It shows
how the concepts of Parts Two through Five fit into the broader area of
computer networks and computer communications. This chapter may be read
in its proper sequence or it may be deferred until the beginning of Part Three,
Four, or Five.[1]

We begin this chapter by introducing the concept of a layered protocol
architecture. We then examine the most important such architecture, the
TCP/IP protocol suite. TCP/IP is an Internet-based protocol suite and is the
framework for developing a complete range of computer communications
standards. Another well-known architecture is the Open Systems Interconnection (OSI) reference model. OSI is a standardized architecture that is often
used to describe communications functions but that is now rarely implemented.
OSI is examined in Appendix D.

2.1 THE NEED FOR A PROTOCOL ARCHITECTURE

When computers, terminals, and/or other data processing devices exchange data, the
procedures involved can be quite complex. Consider, for example, the transfer of a
file between two computers. There must be a data path between the two computers,

---

[1]The reader may find it helpful just to skim this chapter on a first reading and then reread it more
carefully just before embarking on Part Five.

either directly or via a communication network. But more is needed. Typical tasks to be performed:

1. The source system must either activate the direct data communication path or inform the communication network of the identity of the desired destination system.

2. The source system must ascertain that the destination system is prepared to receive data.

3. The file transfer application on the source system must ascertain that the file management program on the destination system is prepared to accept and store the file for this particular user.

4. If the file formats used on the two systems are different, one or the other system must perform a format translation function.

It is clear that there must be a high degree of cooperation between the two computer systems. Instead of implementing the logic for this as a single module, the task is broken up into subtasks, each of which is implemented separately. In a protocol architecture, the modules are arranged in a vertical stack. Each layer in the stack performs a related subset of the functions required to communicate with another system. It relies on the next lower layer to perform more primitive functions and to conceal the details of those functions. It provides services to the next higher layer. Ideally, layers should be defined so that changes in one layer do not require changes in other layers.

Of course, it takes two to communicate, so the same set of layered functions must exist in two systems. Communication is achieved by having the corresponding, or **peer**, layers in two systems communicate. The peer layers communicate by means of formatted blocks of data that obey a set of rules or conventions known as a **protocol**. The key features of a protocol are as follows:

- **Syntax:** Concerns the format of the data blocks
- **Semantics:** Includes control information for coordination and error handling
- **Timing:** Includes speed matching and sequencing

Appendix 2A provides a specific example of a protocol, the Internet standard Trivial File Transfer Protocol (TFTP).

2.2 A SIMPLE PROTOCOL ARCHITECTURE

In very general terms, distributed data communications can be said to involve three agents: applications, computers, and networks. Examples of applications include file transfer and electronic mail. These applications execute on computers that typically support multiple simultaneous applications. Computers are connected to networks, and the data to be exchanged are transferred by the network from one computer to another. Thus, the transfer of data from one application to another involves first getting the data to the computer in which the application resides and then getting it to the intended application within the computer.

With these concepts in mind, it appears natural to organize the communication task into three relatively independent layers: network access layer, transport layer, and application layer.

The **network access layer** is concerned with the exchange of data between a computer and the network to which it is attached. The sending computer must provide the network with the address of the destination computer, so that the network may route the data to the appropriate destination. The sending computer may wish to invoke certain services, such as priority, that might be provided by the network. The specific software used at this layer depends on the type of network to be used; different standards have been developed for circuit switching, packet switching, local area networks (LANs), and others. For example, IEEE 802 is a standard that specifies the access to a LAN; this standard is described in Part Three. It makes sense to put those functions having to do with network access into a separate layer. By doing this, the remainder of the communications software, above the network access layer, need not be concerned about the specifics of the network to be used. The same higher-layer software should function properly regardless of the particular network to which the computer is attached.

Regardless of the nature of the applications that are exchanging data, there is usually a requirement that data be exchanged reliably. That is, we would like to be assured that all of the data arrive at the destination application and that the data arrive in the same order in which they were sent. As we shall see, the mechanisms for providing reliability are essentially independent of the nature of the applications. Thus, it makes sense to collect those mechanisms in a common layer shared by all applications; this is referred to as the **transport layer**.

Finally, the **application layer** contains the logic needed to support the various user applications. For each different type of application, such as file transfer, a separate module is needed that is peculiar to that application.

Figures 2.1 and 2.2 illustrate this simple architecture. Figure 2.1 shows three computers connected to a network. Each computer contains software at the network access and transport layers and software at the application layer for one or more applications. For successful communication, every entity in the overall system must have a unique address. In our three-layer model, two levels of addressing are needed. Each computer on the network has a unique network address; this allows the network to deliver data to the proper computer. Each application on a computer has an address that is unique within that computer; this allows the transport layer to support multiple applications at each computer. These latter addresses are known as **service access points** (SAPs), or **ports**, connoting the fact that each application is individually accessing the services of the transport layer.

Figure 2.1 indicates that modules at the same level (peers) on different computers communicate with each other by means of a protocol. An application entity (e.g., a file transfer application) in one computer communicates with an application in another computer via an application-level protocol (e.g., the File Transfer Protocol). The interchange is not direct (indicated by the dashed line) but is mediated by a transport protocol that handles many of the details of transferring data between two computers. The transport protocol is also not direct, but relies on a network-level protocol to achieve network access and to route data through the network to

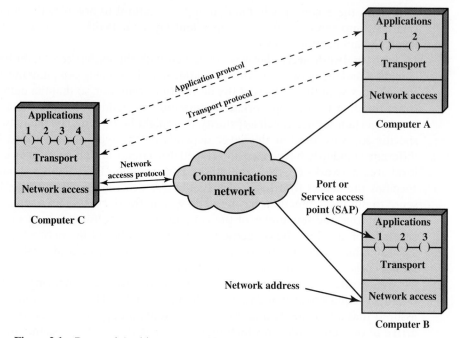

Figure 2.1   Protocol Architectures and Networks

the destination system. At each level, the cooperating peer entities focus on what they need to communicate to each other.

Let us trace a simple operation. Suppose that an application, associated with port 1 at computer A, wishes to send a message to another application, associated with port 2 at computer B. The application at A hands the message over to its transport layer with instructions to send it to port 2 on computer B. The transport layer hands the message over to the network access layer, which instructs the network to send the message to computer B. Note that the network need not be told the identity of the destination port. All that it needs to know is that the data are intended for computer B.

To control this operation, control information, as well as user data, must be transmitted, as suggested in Figure 2.2. Let us say that the sending application generates a block of data and passes this to the transport layer. The transport layer may break this block into two smaller pieces for convenience, as discussed subsequently. To each of these pieces the transport layer appends a transport **header**, containing protocol control information. The addition of control information to data is referred to as **encapsulation**. The combination of data from the next higher layer and control information is known as a **protocol data unit (PDU)**; in this case, it is referred to as a transport PDU. Transport PDUs are typically called **segments**. The header in each segment contains control information to be used by the peer transport protocol at computer B. Examples of items that may be stored in this header include the following:

- **Source port:** This indicates the application that sent the data.
- **Destination port:** When the destination transport layer receives the segment, it must know to which application the data are to be delivered.

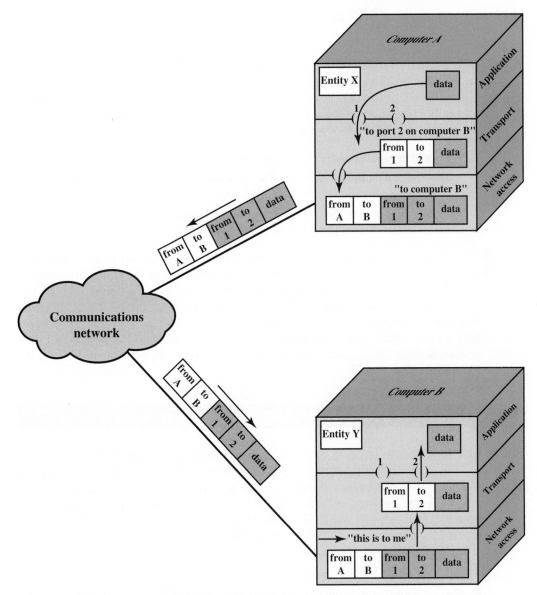

Figure 2.2 Protocols in a Simplified Architecture

- **Sequence number:** Because the transport protocol is sending a sequence of segments, it numbers them sequentially so that if they arrive out of order, the destination transport entity may reorder them.

- **Error-detection code:** The sending transport entity may include a code that is a function of the contents of the segment. The receiving transport protocol performs the same calculation and compares the result with the incoming code. A discrepancy results if there has been some error in transmission. In that case, the receiver can discard the segment and take corrective action. This code is also referred to as a **checksum** or **frame check sequence**.

The next step is for the transport layer to hand each segment over to the network layer, with instructions to transmit it to the destination computer. To satisfy this request, the network access protocol must present the data to the network with a request for transmission. As before, this operation requires the use of control information. In this case, the **network access protocol (NAP)** appends a network access header to the data it receives from the transport layer, creating a network access PDU, typically called a **packet**. Examples of the items that may be stored in the header include the following:

- **Source computer address:** Indicates the source of this packet.
- **Destination computer address:** The network must know to which computer on the network the data are to be delivered.
- **Facilities requests:** The network access protocol might want the network to make use of certain facilities, such as priority.

Note that the transport header is not "visible" at the network access layer; the network access layer is not concerned with the contents of the transport segment.

The network accepts the network packet from A and delivers it to B. The network access module in B receives the packet, strips off the packet header, and transfers the enclosed transport segment to B's transport layer module. The transport layer examines the segment header and, on the basis of the port field in the header, delivers the enclosed record to the appropriate application, in this case the file transfer module in B.

2.3 THE TCP/IP PROTOCOL ARCHITECTURE

TCP/IP is a result of protocol research and development conducted on the experimental packet-switched network, ARPANET, funded by the Defense Advanced Research Projects Agency (DARPA), and is generally referred to as the TCP/IP protocol suite. This protocol suite consists of a large collection of protocols that have been issued as Internet standards by the Internet Activities Board (IAB). Appendix C provides a discussion of Internet standards.

The TCP/IP Layers

In general terms, computer communications can be said to involve three agents: applications, computers, and networks. Examples of applications include file transfer and electronic mail. The applications that we are concerned with here are distributed applications that involve the exchange of data between two computer systems. These applications, and others, execute on computers that can often support multiple simultaneous applications. Computers are connected to networks, and the data to be exchanged are transferred by the network from one computer to another. Thus, the transfer of data from one application to another involves first getting the data to the computer in which the application resides and then getting the data to the intended application within the computer. With these concepts in mind, we can organize the communication task into five relatively independent layers (Figure 2.3):

- Physical layer
- Network access layer
- Internet layer
- Host-to-host, or transport layer
- Application layer

The **physical layer** covers the physical interface between a data transmission device (e.g., workstation, computer) and a transmission medium or network. This layer is concerned with specifying the characteristics of the transmission medium, the nature of the signals, the data rate, and related matters.

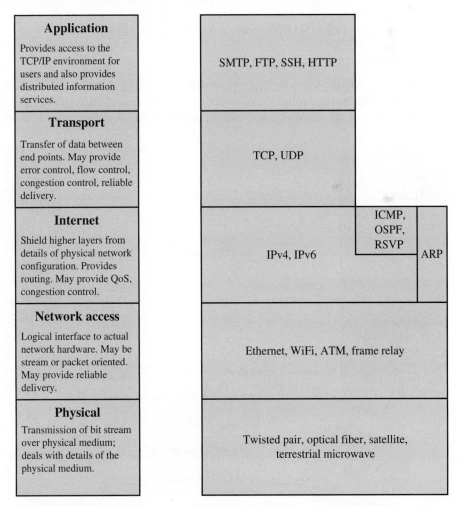

Figure 2.3   The TCP/IP Layers and Example Protocols

The **network access layer** is discussed in Section 2.2. The network access layer is concerned with access to and routing data across a network for two end systems attached to the same network. In those cases where two devices are attached to different networks, procedures are needed to allow data to traverse multiple interconnected networks. This is the function of the **internet layer**. The Internet Protocol (IP) is used at this layer to provide the routing function across multiple networks. This protocol is implemented not only in the end systems but also in routers. A router is a processor that connects two networks and whose primary function is to relay data from one network to the other on its route from the source to the destination end system.

The **host-to-host layer**, or **transport layer** may provide reliable end-to-end service, as discussed in Section 2.2, or merely an end-to-end delivery service without reliability mechanisms. The Transmission Control Protocol (TCP) is the most commonly used protocol to provide this functionality.

Finally, the *application layer* contains the logic needed to support the various user applications. For each different type of application, such as file transfer, a separate module is needed that is peculiar to that application.

Operation of TCP and IP

Figure 2.4 indicates how these protocols are configured for communications. To make clear that the total communications facility may consist of multiple networks, the constituent networks are usually referred to as **subnetworks**. Some sort of

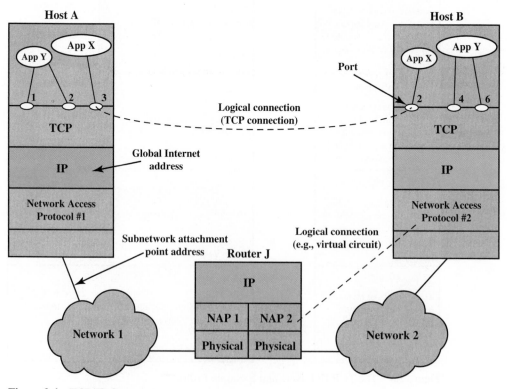

Figure 2.4   TCP/IP Concepts

network access protocol, such as the Ethernet or WiFi logic, is used to connect a computer to a subnetwork. This protocol enables the host to send data across the subnetwork to another host or, if the target host is on another subnetwork, to a router that will forward the data. IP is implemented in all of the end systems and the routers. It acts as a relay to move a block of data from one host, through one or more routers, to another host. TCP is implemented only in the end systems; it keeps track of the blocks of data to assure that all are delivered reliably to the appropriate application.

As is mentioned in Section 2.2, every entity in the overall system must have a unique address. Each host on a subnetwork must have a unique global internet address; this allows the data to be delivered to the proper host. Each process with a host must have an address that is unique within the host; this allows the host-to-host protocol (TCP) to deliver data to the proper process. These latter addresses are known as *ports*.

Let us trace a simple operation. Suppose that a process, associated with port 3 at host A, wishes to send a message to another process, associated with port 2 at host B. The process at A hands the message down to TCP with instructions to send it to host B, port 2. TCP hands the message down to IP with instructions to send it to host B. Note that IP need not be told the identity of the destination port. All it needs to know is that the data are intended for host B. Next, IP hands the message down to the network access layer (e.g., Ethernet logic) with instructions to send it to router J (the first hop on the way to B).

To control this operation, control information, as well as user data, must be transmitted, as suggested in Figure 2.5. Let us say that the sending process generates a block of data and passes this to TCP. TCP may break this block into smaller pieces to make it more manageable. To each of these pieces, TCP appends control information known as the TCP header, forming a **TCP segment**. The control

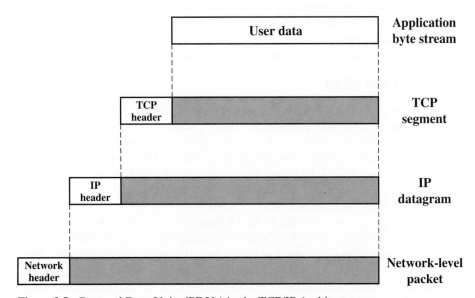

Figure 2.5   Protocol Data Units (PDUs) in the TCP/IP Architecture

information is to be used by the peer TCP entity at host B. Examples of items in this header include:

- **Destination port:** When the TCP entity at B receives the segment, it must know to whom the data are to be delivered.
- **Sequence number:** TCP numbers the segments that it sends to a particular destination port sequentially, so that if they arrive out of order, the TCP entity at B can reorder them.
- **Checksum:** The sending TCP includes a code that is a function of the contents of the remainder of the segment. The receiving TCP performs the same calculation and compares the result with the incoming code. A discrepancy results if there has been some error in transmission.

Next, TCP hands each segment over to IP, with instructions to transmit it to B. These segments must be transmitted across one or more subnetworks and relayed through one or more intermediate routers. This operation, too, requires the use of control information. Thus IP appends a header of control information to each segment to form an **IP datagram**. An example of an item stored in the IP header is the destination host address (in this example, B).

Finally, each IP datagram is presented to the network access layer for transmission across the first subnetwork in its journey to the destination. The network access layer appends its own header, creating a packet, or frame. The packet is transmitted across the subnetwork to router J. The packet header contains the information that the subnetwork needs to transfer the data across the subnetwork.

At router J, the packet header is stripped off and the IP header examined. On the basis of the destination address information in the IP header, the IP module in the router directs the datagram out across subnetwork 2 to B. To do this, the datagram is again augmented with a network access header.

When the data are received at B, the reverse process occurs. At each layer, the corresponding header is removed, and the remainder is passed on to the next higher layer, until the original user data are delivered to the destination process.

TCP and UDP

For most applications running as part of the TCP/IP architecture, the transport layer protocol is TCP. TCP provides a reliable connection for the transfer of data between applications. A connection is simply a temporary logical association between two entities in different systems. A logical connection refers to a given pair of port values. For the duration of the connection each entity keeps track of TCP segments coming and going to the other entity, in order to regulate the flow of segments and to recover from lost or damaged segments.

Figure 2.6a shows the header format for TCP, which is a minimum of 20 octets, or 160 bits. The Source Port and Destination Port fields identify the applications at the source and destination systems that are using this connection. The Sequence Number, Acknowledgment Number, and Window fields provide flow control and error control. The checksum is a 16-bit frame check sequence used to detect errors in the TCP segment. Chapter 20 provides more details.

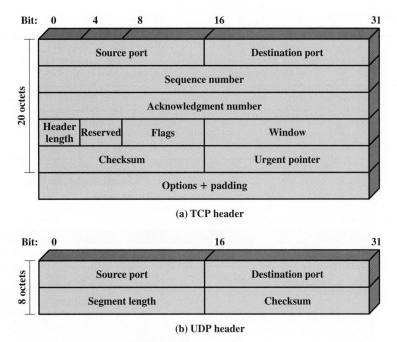

(a) TCP header

(b) UDP header

Figure 2.6 TCP and UDP Headers

In addition to TCP, there is one other transport-level protocol that is in common use as part of the TCP/IP protocol suite: the User Datagram Protocol (UDP). UDP does not guarantee delivery, preservation of sequence, or protection against duplication. UDP enables a procedure to send messages to other procedures with a minimum of protocol mechanism. Some transaction-oriented applications make use of UDP; one example is SNMP (Simple Network Management Protocol), the standard network management protocol for TCP/IP networks. Because it is connectionless, UDP has very little to do. Essentially, it adds a port addressing capability to IP. This is best seen by examining the UDP header, shown in Figure 2.6b. UDP also includes a checksum to verify that no error occurs in the data; the use of the checksum is optional.

IP and IPv6

For decades, the keystone of the TCP/IP architecture has been IPv4, generally referred to simply as IP. Figure 2.7a shows the IP header format, which is a minimum of 20 octets, or 160 bits. The header, together with the segment from the transport layer, forms an IP-level PDU referred to as an IP datagram or an IP packet. The header includes 32-bit source and destination addresses. The Header Checksum field is used to detect errors in the header to avoid misdelivery. The Protocol field indicates which higher-layer protocol is using IP. The ID, Flags, and Fragment Offset fields are used in the fragmentation and reassembly process. Chapter 18 provides more detail.

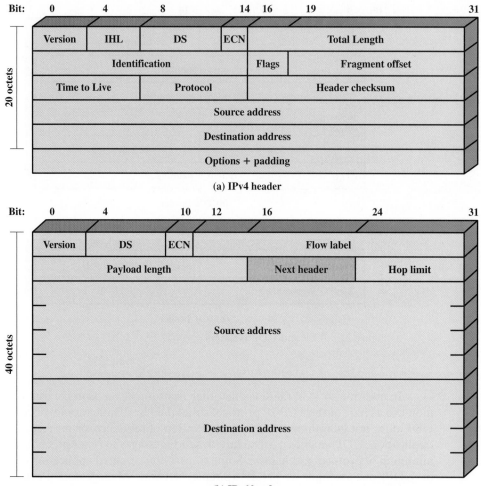

(a) IPv4 header

(b) IPv6 header

DS = Differentiated services field
ECN = Explicit congestion notification field

Note: The 8-bit DS/ECN fields were formerly known as the Type of Service field in the IPv4 header and the Traffic Class field in the IPv6 header.

Figure 2.7 IP Headers

In 1995, the Internet Engineering Task Force (IETF), which develops protocol standards for the Internet, issued a specification for a next-generation IP, known then as IPng. This specification was turned into a standard in 1996 known as IPv6. IPv6 provides a number of functional enhancements over the existing IP, designed to accommodate the higher speeds of today's networks and the mix of data streams, including graphic and video, that are becoming more prevalent. But the driving force behind the development of the new protocol was the need for more addresses. IPv4 uses a 32-bit address to specify a source or destination. With the explosive growth of the Internet and of private networks attached to the Internet, this address length became insufficient to accommodate all systems needing addresses. As Figure 2.7b shows, IPv6 includes 128-bit source and destination address fields.

Ultimately, all installations using TCP/IP are expected to migrate from the current IP to IPv6, but this process will take many years, if not decades.

Protocol Interfaces

Each layer in the TCP/IP suite interacts with its immediate adjacent layers. At the source, the application layer makes use of the services of the end-to-end layer and provides data down to that layer. A similar relationship exists at the interface between the transport and internet layers and at the interface of the internet and network access layers. At the destination, each layer delivers data up to the next higher layer.

This use of each individual layer is not required by the architecture. As Figure 2.8 suggests, it is possible to develop applications that directly invoke the services of any one of the layers. Most applications require a reliable end-to-end protocol and thus make use of TCP. Some special-purpose applications do not need the services of TCP. Some of these applications, such as the Simple Network Management Protocol (SNMP), use an alternative end-to-end protocol known as the User Datagram Protocol (UDP); others may make use of IP directly. Applications that do not involve internetworking and that do not need TCP have been developed to invoke the network access layer directly.

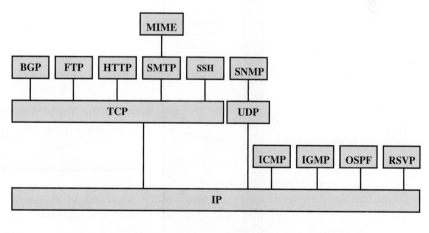

BGP	=	Border Gateway Protocol	OSPF	=	Open Shortest Path First
FTP	=	File Transfer Protocol	RSVP	=	Resource ReSerVation Protocol
HTTP	=	Hypertext Transfer Protocol	SMTP	=	Simple Mail Transfer Protocol
ICMP	=	Internet Control Message Protocol	SNMP	=	Simple Network Management Protocol
IGMP	=	Internet Group Management Protocol	SSH	=	Secure Shell
IP	=	Internet Protocol	TCP	=	Transmission Control Protocol
MIME	=	Multipurpose Internet Mail Extension	UDP	=	User Datagram Protocol

Figure 2.8   Some Protocols in the TCP/IP Protocol Suite

2.4 STANDARDIZATION WITHIN A PROTOCOL ARCHITECTURE

Standards and Protocol Layers

A protocol architecture, such as the TCP/IP architecture or OSI, provides a framework for standardization. Within the model, one or more protocol standards can be developed at each layer. The model defines in general terms the functions to be performed at that layer and facilitates the standards-making process in two ways:

- Because the functions of each layer are well defined, standards can be developed independently and simultaneously for each layer. This speeds up the standards-making process.
- Because the boundaries between layers are well defined, changes in standards in one layer need not affect already existing software in another layer. This makes it easier to introduce new standards.

Figure 2.9 illustrates the use of a protocol architecture as such a framework. The overall communications function is decomposed into a number of distinct layers. That is, the overall function is broken up into a number of modules, making the interfaces between modules as simple as possible. In addition, the design principle of information hiding is used: Lower layers are concerned with greater levels of detail; upper layers are independent of these details. Each layer provides services to the next higher layer and implements a protocol to the peer layer in other systems.

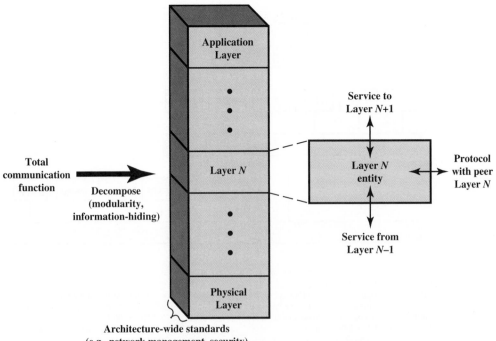

Figure 2.9   A Protocol Architecture as a Framework for Standardization

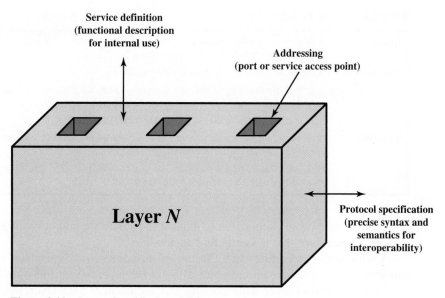

Figure 2.10 Layer-Specific Standards

Figure 2.10 shows more specifically the nature of the standardization required at each layer. Three elements are key:

- **Protocol specification:** Two entities at the same layer in different systems cooperate and interact by means of a protocol. Because two different open systems are involved, the protocol must be specified precisely. This includes the format of the protocol data units exchanged, the semantics of all fields, and the allowable sequence of PDUs.

- **Service definition:** In addition to the protocol or protocols that operate at a given layer, standards are needed for the services that each layer provides to the next higher layer. Typically, the definition of services is equivalent to a functional description that defines what services are provided, but not how the services are to be provided.

- **Addressing:** Each layer provides services to entities at the next higher layer. These entities are referenced by means of a port, or service access point (SAP). Thus, a network service access point (NSAP) indicates a transport entity that is a user of the network service.

The need to provide a precise protocol specification for open systems is self-evident. The other two items listed warrant further comment. With respect to service definitions, the motivation for providing only a functional definition is as follows. First, the interaction between two adjacent layers takes place within the confines of a single open system and is not the concern of any other open system. Thus, as long as peer layers in different systems provide the same services to their next higher layers, the details of how the services are provided may differ from one system to another without loss of interoperability. Second, it will usually be the case that adjacent layers are implemented on the same processor. In that case, we would like to

Table 2.1 Service Primitive Types

Request	A primitive issued by a service user to invoke some service and to pass the parameters needed to specify fully the requested service.

Indication	A primitive issued by a service provider either to
	
	    1. indicate that a procedure has been invoked by the peer service user on the connection and to provide the associated parameters, or
	    2. notify the service user of a provider-initiated action.

Response	A primitive issued by a service user to acknowledge or complete some procedure previously invoked by an indication to that user.
Confirm	A primitive issued by a service provider to acknowledge or complete some procedure previously invoked by a request by the service user.

leave the system programmer free to exploit the hardware and operating system to provide an interface that is as efficient as possible.

With respect to addressing, the use of an address mechanism at each layer, implemented as a service access point, allows each layer to multiplex multiple users from the next higher layer. Multiplexing may not occur at each layer, but the model allows for that possibility.

Service Primitives and Parameters

The services between adjacent layers in a protocol architecture are expressed in terms of primitives and parameters. A primitive specifies the function to be performed, and the parameters are used to pass data and control information. The actual form of a primitive is implementation dependent. An example is a procedure call.

Four types of primitives are used in standards to define the interaction between adjacent layers in the architecture. These are defined in Table 2.1. The layout of Figure 2.11a suggests the time ordering of these events. For example,

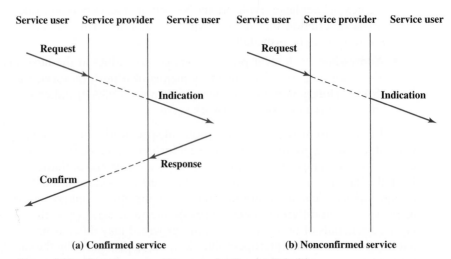

Figure 2.11 Time Sequence Diagrams for Service Primitives

consider the transfer of data from an (N) entity to a peer (N) entity in another system. The following steps occur:

1. The source (N) entity invokes its $(N - 1)$ entity with a *request* primitive. Associated with the primitive are the parameters needed, such as the data to be transmitted and the destination address.

2. The source $(N - 1)$ entity prepares an $(N - 1)$ PDU to be sent to its peer $(N - 1)$ entity.

3. The destination $(N - 1)$ entity delivers the data to the appropriate destination (N) entity via an *indication* primitive, which includes the data and source address as parameters.

4. If an acknowledgment is called for, the destination (N) entity issues a *response* primitive to its $(N - 1)$ entity.

5. The $(N - 1)$ entity conveys the acknowledgment in an $(N - 1)$ PDU.

6. The acknowledgment is delivered to the (N) entity as a *confirm* primitive.

This sequence of events is referred to as a *confirmed service*, as the initiator receives confirmation that the requested service has had the desired effect at the other end. If only request and indication primitives are involved (corresponding to steps 1 through 3), then the service dialog is a *nonconfirmed service*; the initiator receives no confirmation that the requested action has taken place (Figure 2.11b).

2.5 TRADITIONAL INTERNET-BASED APPLICATIONS

A number of applications have been standardized to operate on top of TCP. We mention three of the most common here.

The **Simple Mail Transfer Protocol (SMTP)** provides a basic electronic mail transport facility. It provides a mechanism for transferring messages among separate hosts. Features of SMTP include mailing lists, return receipts, and forwarding. SMTP does not specify the way in which messages are to be created; some local editing or native electronic mail facility is required. Once a message is created, SMTP accepts the message and makes use of TCP to send it to an SMTP module on another host. The target SMTP module will make use of a local electronic mail package to store the incoming message in a user's mailbox.

The **File Transfer Protocol (FTP)** is used to send files from one system to another under user command. Both text and binary files are accommodated, and the protocol provides features for controlling user access. When a user wishes to engage in file transfer, FTP sets up a TCP connection to the target system for the exchange of control messages. This connection allows user ID and password to be transmitted and allows the user to specify the file and file actions desired. Once a file transfer is approved, a second TCP connection is set up for the data transfer. The file is transferred over the data connection, without the overhead of any headers or control information at the application level. When the transfer is complete, the control connection is used to signal the completion and to accept new file transfer commands.

SSH (Secure Shell) provides a secure remote logon capability, which enables a user at a terminal or personal computer to logon to a remote computer and function as if directly connected to that computer. SSH also supports file transfer between the local host and a remote server. SSH enables the user and the remote server to authenticate each other; it also encrypts all traffic in both directions. SSH traffic is carried on a TCP connection.

With the increasing availability of broadband access to the Internet has come an increased interest in Web-based and Internet-based multimedia applications. The terms *multimedia* and *multimedia applications* are used rather loosely in the literature and in commercial publications, and no single definition of the term *multimedia* has been agreed (e.g., [JAIN94], [GRIM91], [PURC98], [PACK99]). For our purposes, the definitions in Table 2.2 provide a starting point.

One way to organize the concepts associated with multimedia is to look at a taxonomy that captures a number of dimensions of this field. Figure 2.12 looks at multimedia from the perspective of three different dimensions: type of media, applications, and the technology required to support the applications.

Media Types

Typically, the term *multimedia* refers to four distinct types of media: text, audio, graphics, and video.

From a communications perspective, the term **text** is self-explanatory, referring to information that can be entered via a keyboard and is directly readable and printable. Text messaging, instant messaging, and text (non-html) e-mail are common examples, as are chat rooms and message boards. However, the term often is used in the broader sense of data that can be stored in files and databases and that does not fit into the other three categories. For example, an organization's database may contain files of numerical data, in which the data are stored in a more compact form than printable characters.

The term **audio** generally encompasses two different ranges of sound. Voice, or speech, refers to sounds that are produced by the human speech mechanism. Generally, a modest bandwidth (under 4 kHz) is required to transmit voice. Telephony and related applications (e.g., voice mail, audio teleconferencing, and telemarketing) are the most common traditional applications of voice communications technology.

Table 2.2 Multimedia Terminology

Media
Refers to the form of information and includes text, still images, audio, and video.
Multimedia
Human–computer interaction involving text, graphics, voice and video. Multimedia also refers to storage devices that are used to store multimedia content.
Streaming media
Refers to multimedia files, such as video clips and audio, that begin playing immediately or within seconds after it is received by a computer from the Internet or Web. Thus, the media content is consumed as it is delivered from the server rather than waiting until an entire file is downloaded.

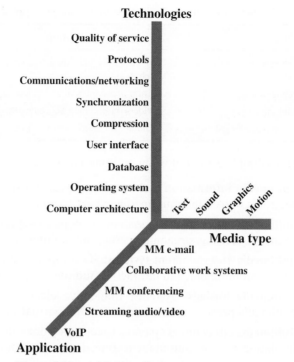

Figure 2.12   A Multimedia Taxonomy

A broader frequency spectrum is needed to support music applications, including the download of music files.

The **image** service supports the communication of individual pictures, charts, or drawings. Image-based applications include facsimile, computer-aided design (CAD), publishing, and medical imaging. Images can be represented in a vector graphics format, such as is used in drawing programs and PDF files. In a raster graphics format, an image is represented as a two-dimensional array of spots, called pixels.[2] The compressed JPG format is derived from a raster graphics format.

The **video** service carries sequences of pictures in time. In essence, video makes use of a sequence of raster-scan images.

Multimedia Applications

The Internet, until recently, has been dominated by information retrieval applications, e-mail, and file transfer, plus Web interfaces that emphasized text and images. Increasingly, the Internet is being used for multimedia applications that involve massive amounts of data for visualization and support of real-time interactivity. Streaming audio and video are perhaps the best known of such applications. An example of an interactive application is a virtual training environment involving distributed simulations and real-time user interaction [VIN98]. Some other examples are shown in Table 2.3.

---

[2]A pixel, or picture element, is the smallest element of a digital image that can be assigned a gray level. Equivalently, a pixel is an individual dot in a dot-matrix representation of a picture.

Table 2.3 Domains of Multimedia Systems and Example Applications

Domain	Example Application
Information management	Hypermedia, multimedia-capable databases, content-based retrieval
Entertainment	Computer games, digital video, audio (MP3)
Telecommunication	Videoconferencing, shared workspaces, virtual communities
Information publishing/delivery	Online training, electronic books, streaming media

[GONZ00] lists the following multimedia application domains:

- **Multimedia information systems:** Databases, information kiosks, hypertexts, electronic books, and multimedia expert systems.
- **Multimedia communication systems:** Computer-supported collaborative work, videoconferencing, streaming media, and multimedia teleservices.
- **Multimedia entertainment systems:** 3D computer games, multiplayer network games, infotainment, and interactive audiovisual productions.
- **Multimedia business systems:** Immersive electronic commerce, marketing, multimedia presentations, video brochures, virtual shopping, and so on.
- **Multimedia educational systems:** Electronic books, flexible teaching materials, simulation systems, automatic testing, distance learning, and so on.

One point worth noting is highlighted in Figure 2.12. Although traditionally the term *multimedia* has connoted the simultaneous use of multiple media types (e.g., video annotation of a text document), the term has also come to refer to applications that require real-time processing or communication of video or audio alone. Thus, voice over IP (VoIP), streaming audio, and streaming video are considered multimedia applications even though each involves a single media type.

Multimedia Technologies

Figure 2.12 lists some of the technologies that are relevant to the support of multimedia applications. As can be seen, a wide range of technologies is involved. The lowest four items on the list are beyond the scope of this book. The other items represent only a partial list of communications and networking technologies for multimedia. These technologies and others are explored throughout the book. Here, we give a brief comment on each area.

- **Compression:** Digitized video, and to a much lesser extent audio, can generate an enormous amount of traffic on a network. A streaming application, which is delivered to many users, magnifies the traffic. Accordingly, standards have been developed for producing significant savings through compression. The most notable standards are JPG for still images and MPG for video.
- **Communications/networking:** This broad category refers to the transmission and networking technologies (e.g., SONET, ATM) that can support high-volume multimedia traffic.

- **Protocols:** A number of protocols are instrumental in supporting multimedia traffic. One example is the Real-time Transport Protocol (RTP), which is designed to support inelastic traffic. RTP uses buffering and discarding strategies to assure that real-time traffic is received by the end user in a smooth continuous stream. Another example is the Session Initiation Protocol (SIP), an application-level control protocol for setting up, modifying, and terminating real-time sessions between participants over an IP data network.

- **Quality of service (QoS):** The Internet and its underlying local area and wide area networks must include a QoS capability to provide differing levels of service to different types of application traffic. A QoS capability can deal with priority, delay constraints, delay variability constraints, and other similar requirements.

All of these matters are explored subsequently in this text.

2.7 RECOMMENDED READING AND WEB SITES

For the reader interested in greater detail on TCP/IP, there are two three-volume works that are more than adequate. The works by Comer and Stevens have become classics and are considered definitive [COME06, COME99, COME01]. The works by Stevens and Wright are equally worthwhile and more detailed with respect to protocol operation [STEV94, STEV96, WRIG95]. A more compact and very useful reference work is [PARZ06], which covers the spectrum of TCP/IP-related protocols in a technically concise but thorough fashion, including coverage of some protocols not found in the other two works.

[GREE80] is a good tutorial overview of the concept of a layered protocol architecture. Two early papers that provide good discussions of the design philosophy of the TCP/IP protocol suite are [LEIN85] and [CLAR88].

Although somewhat dated, [FURH94] remains a good overview of multimedia topics. [VOGE95] is a good introduction to QoS considerations for multimedia. [HELL01] is a lengthy and worthwhile theoretical treatment of multimedia.

CLAR88 Clark, D. "The Design Philosophy of the DARPA Internet Protocols." *ACM SIGCOMM Computer Communications Review*, August 1988.

COME99 Comer, D., and Stevens, D. *Internetworking with TCP/IP, Volume II: Design Implementation, and Internals.* Upper Saddle River, NJ: Prentice Hall, 1999.

COME01 Comer, D., and Stevens, D. *Internetworking with TCP/IP, Volume III: Client-Server Programming and Applications.* Upper Saddle River, NJ: Prentice Hall, 2001.

COME06 Comer, D. *Internetworking with TCP/IP, Volume I: Principles, Protocols, and Architecture.* Upper Saddle River, NJ: Prentice Hall, 2006.

FURH94 Furht, B. "Multimedia Systems: An Overview." *IEEE Multimedia*, Spring 1994.

GREE80 Green, P. "An Introduction to Network Architecture and Protocols." *IEEE Transactions on Communications*, April 1980.

HELL01 Heller, R., et al. "Using a Theoretical Multimedia Taxonomy Framework." *ACM Journal of Educational Resources in Computing*, Spring 2001.

LEIN85 Leiner, B.; Cole, R.; Postel, J.; and Mills, D. "The DARPA Internet Protocol Suite." *IEEE Communications Magazine*, March 1985.

PARZ06   Parziale, L., et al. *TCP/IP Tutorial and Technical Overview.* IBM Redbook GG24-3376-07, 2006, http://www.redbooks.ibm.com/abstracts/gg243376.html

STEV94   Stevens, W. *TCP/IP Illustrated, Volume 1: The Protocols.* Reading, MA: Addison-Wesley, 1994.

STEV96   Stevens, W. *TCP/IP Illustrated, Volume 3: TCP for Transactions, HTTP, NNTP, and the UNIX(R) Domain Protocol.* Reading, MA: Addison-Wesley, 1996.

VOGE95   Vogel, A., et al. "Distributed Multimedia and QoS: A Survey." *IEEE Multimedia,* Summer 1995.

WRIG95   Wright, G., and Stevens, W. *TCP/IP Illustrated, Volume 2: The Implementation.* Reading, MA: Addison-Wesley, 1995.

Recommended Web sites:

- **TCP/IP resources list:** A useful collection of FAQs, tutorials, guides, Web sites, and books about TCP/IP.
- **Networking links:** Excellent collection of links related to TCP/IP.
- **Bongo project:** Running IP over bongo drums. An excellent demonstration of the flexibility of a layered protocol architecture and a source of ideas for projects.

2.8   KEY TERMS, REVIEW QUESTIONS, AND PROBLEMS

Key Terms

application layer	multimedia	router
checksum	network layer	service access point (SAP)
elastic traffic	Open Systems Interconnection	Simple Mail Transfer Protocol
encapsulation	(OSI)	(SMTP)
File Transfer Protocol (FTP)	packet	SSH (Secure Shell)
frame check sequence	peer layer	subnetwork
header	physical layer	TCP segment
inelastic traffic	port	Transmission Control Protocol
Internet	protocol	(TCP)
Internet Protocol (IP)	protocol architecture	transport layer
Internetworking	protocol data unit (PDU)	User Datagram Protocol
IP datagram	quality of service (QoS)	(UDP)

Review Questions

2.1   What is the major function of the network access layer?

2.2   What tasks are performed by the transport layer?

2.3   What is a protocol?

2.4 What is a protocol data unit (PDU)?

2.5 What is a protocol architecture?

2.6 What is TCP/IP?

2.7 What are some advantages to layering as seen in the TCP/IP architecture?

2.8 What is a router?

2.9 Which version of IP is the most prevalent today?

2.10 Does all traffic running on the Internet use TCP?

2.11 Compare the address space between IPv4 and IPv6. How many bits are used in each?

Problems

2.1 Using the layer models in Figure 2.13, describe the ordering and delivery of a pizza, indicating the interactions at each level.

2.2 **a.** The French and Chinese prime ministers need to come to an agreement by telephone, but neither speaks the other's language. Further, neither has on hand a translator that can translate to the language of the other. However, both prime ministers have English translators on their staffs. Draw a diagram similar to Figure 2.13 to depict the situation, and describe the interaction at each level.

  b. Now suppose that the Chinese prime minister's translator can translate only into Japanese and that the French prime minister has a German translator available. A translator between German and Japanese is available in Germany. Draw a new diagram that reflects this arrangement and describe the hypothetical phone conversation.

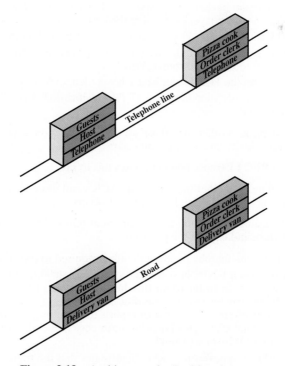

Figure 2.13 Architecture for Problem 2.1

2.3   List the major disadvantages with the layered approach to protocols.

2.4   Two blue armies are each poised on opposite hills preparing to attack a single red army in the valley. The red army can defeat either of the blue armies separately but will fail to defeat both blue armies if they attack simultaneously. The blue armies communicate via an unreliable communications system (a foot soldier). The commander with one of the blue armies would like to attack at noon. His problem is this: If he sends a message to the other blue army, ordering the attack, he cannot be sure it will get through. He could ask for acknowledgment, but that might not get through. Is there a protocol that the two blue armies can use to avoid defeat?

2.5   A broadcast network is one in which a transmission from any one attached station is received by all other attached stations over a shared medium. Examples are a bus-topology local area network, such as Ethernet, and a wireless radio network. Discuss the need or lack of need for a network layer (OSI layer 3) in a broadcast network.

2.6   In Figure 2.5, exactly one protocol data unit (PDU) in layer N is encapsulated in a PDU at layer $(N - 1)$. It is also possible to break one N-level PDU into multiple $(N - 1)$-level PDUs (segmentation) or to group multiple N-level PDUs into one $(N - 1)$-level PDU (blocking).

   a.   In the case of segmentation, is it necessary that each $(N - 1)$-level segment contain a copy of the N-level header?

   b.   In the case of blocking, is it necessary that each N-level PDU retain its own header, or can the data be consolidated into a single N-level PDU with a single N-level header?

2.7   A TCP segment consisting of 1500 bits of data and 160 bits of header is sent to the IP layer, which appends another 160 bits of header. This is then transmitted through two networks, each of which uses a 24-bit packet header. The destination network has a maximum packet size of 800 bits. How many bits, including headers, are delivered to the network layer protocol at the destination?

2.8   Why is UDP needed? Why can't a user program directly access IP?

2.9   IP, TCP, and UDP all discard a packet that arrives with a checksum error and do not attempt to notify the source. Why?

2.10   Why does the TCP header have a header length field while the UDP header does not?

2.11   The previous version of the TFTP specification, RFC 783, included the following statement:

> All packets other than those used for termination are acknowledged individually unless a timeout occurs.

The RFC 1350 specification revises this to say:

> All packets other than duplicate ACK's and those used for termination are acknowledged unless a timeout occurs.

The change was made to fix a problem referred to as the "Sorcerer's Apprentice." Deduce and explain the problem.

2.12   What is the limiting factor in the time required to transfer a file using TFTP?

2.13   A user on a UNIX host wants to transfer a 4000-byte text file to a Microsoft Windows host. In order to do this, he transfers the file by means of TFTP, using the netascii transfer mode. Even though the transfer was reported as being performed successfully, the Windows host reports the resulting file size is 4050 bytes, rather than the original 4000 bytes. Does this difference in the file sizes imply an error in the data transfer? Why or why not?

2.14   The TFTP specification (RFC 1350) states that the transfer identifiers (TIDs) chosen for a connection should be randomly chosen, so that the probability that the same

APPENDIX 2A THE TRIVIAL FILE TRANSFER PROTOCOL **57**

number is chosen twice in immediate succession is very low. What would be the problem of using the same TIDs twice in immediate succession?

2.15 In order to be able to retransmit lost packets, TFTP must keep a copy of the data it sends. How many packets of data must TFTP keep at a time to implement this retransmission mechanism?

2.16 TFTP, like most protocols, will never send an error packet in response to an error packet it receives. Why?

2.17 We have seen that in order to deal with lost packets, TFTP implements a timeout-and-retransmit scheme, by setting a retransmission timer when it transmits a packet to the remote host. Most TFTP implementations set this timer to a fixed value of about 5 seconds. Discuss the advantages and the disadvantages of using a fixed value for the retransmission timer.

2.18 TFTP's timeout-and-retransmission scheme implies that all data packets will eventually be received by the destination host. Will these data also be received uncorrupted? Why or why not?

2.19 This problem concerns material in Appendix D. Based on the principles enunciated in Table D.1.

 a. Design an architecture with eight layers and make a case for it.
 b. Design one with six layers and make a case for that.

APPENDIX 2A   THE TRIVIAL FILE TRANSFER PROTOCOL

This appendix provides an overview of the Internet standard Trivial File Transfer Protocol (TFTP), defined in RFC 1350. Our purpose is to give the reader some flavor for the elements of a protocol. TFTP is simple enough to provide a concise example, but includes most of the significant elements found in other, more complex, protocols.

Introduction to TFTP

TFTP is far simpler than the Internet standard FTP (RFC 959). There are no provisions for access control or user identification, so TFTP is only suitable for public access file directories. Because of its simplicity, TFTP is easily and compactly implemented. For example, some diskless devices use TFTP to download their firmware at boot time.

TFTP runs on top of UDP. The TFTP entity that initiates the transfer does so by sending a read or write request in a UDP segment with a destination port of 69 to the target system. This port is recognized by the target UDP module as the identifier of the TFTP module. For the duration of the transfer, each side uses a transfer identifier (TID) as its port number.

TFTP Packets

TFTP entities exchange commands, responses, and file data in the form of packets, each of which is carried in the body of a UDP segment. TFTP supports five types of packets (Figure 2.14); the first two bytes contain an opcode that identifies the packet type:

 • **RRQ:** The read request packet requests permission to transfer a file from the other system. The packet includes a file name, which is a sequence of ASCII[3] bytes

---

[3] ASCII is the American Standard Code for Information Interchange, a standard of the American National Standards Institute. It designates a unique 7-bit pattern for each letter, with an eighth bit used for parity. ASCII is equivalent to the International Reference Alphabet (IRA), defined in ITU-T Recommendation T.50. See Appendix E for a discussion.

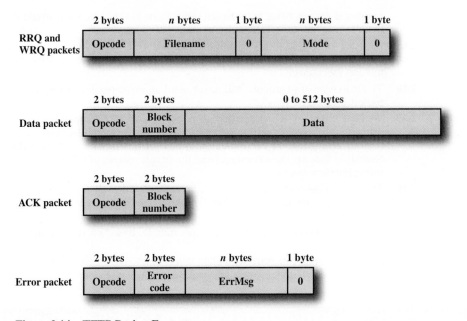

Figure 2.14 TFTP Packet Formats

terminated by a zero byte. The zero byte is the means by which the receiving TFTP entity knows when the file name is terminated. The packet also includes a mode field, which indicates whether the data file is to be interpreted as a string of ASCII bytes (netascii mode) or as raw 8-bit bytes (octet mode) of data. In netascii mode, the file is transferred as lines of characters, each terminated by a carriage return, line feed. Each system must translate between its own format for character files and the TFTP format.

- **WRQ:** The write request packet requests permission to transfer a file to the other system.

- **Data:** The block numbers on data packets begin with one and increase by one for each new block of data. This convention enables the program to use a single number to discriminate between new packets and duplicates. The data field is from zero to 512 bytes long. If it is 512 bytes long, the block is not the last block of data; if it is from zero to 511 bytes long, it signals the end of the transfer.

- **ACK:** This packet is used to acknowledge receipt of a data packet or a WRQ packet. An ACK of a data packet contains the block number of the data packet being acknowledged. An ACK of a WRQ contains a block number of zero.

- **Error:** An error packet can be the acknowledgment of any other type of packet. The error code is an integer indicating the nature of the error (Table 2.4). The error message is intended for human consumption and should be in ASCII. Like all other strings, it is terminated with a zero byte.

All packets other than duplicate ACKs (explained subsequently) and those used for termination are to be acknowledged. Any packet can be acknowledged by an error packet. If there are no errors, then the following conventions apply. A WRQ or a data packet is acknowledged by an ACK packet. When a RRQ is sent, the other side responds (in the absence of error) by beginning to transfer the file; thus, the first data block serves as an

Table 2.4 TFTP Error Codes

Value	Meaning
0	Not defined, see error message (if any)
1	File not found
2	Access violation
3	Disk full or allocation exceeded
4	Illegal TFTP operation
5	Unknown transfer ID
6	File already exists
7	No such user

acknowledgment of the RRQ packet. Unless a file transfer is complete, each ACK packet from one side is followed by a data packet from the other, so that the data packet functions as an acknowledgment. An error packet can be acknowledged by any other kind of packet, depending on the circumstance.

Figure 2.15 shows a TFTP data packet in context. When such a packet is handed down to UDP, UDP adds a header to form a UDP segment. This is then passed to IP, which adds an IP header to form an IP datagram.

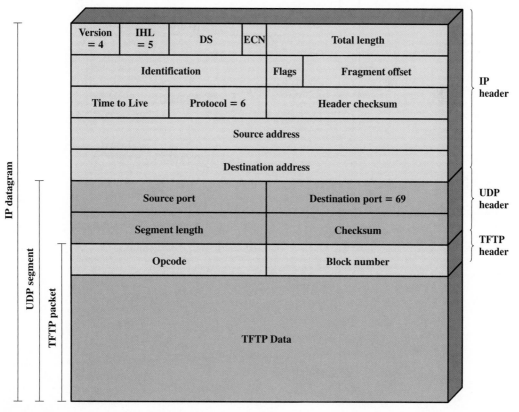

Figure 2.15   A TFTP Packet in Context

Overview of a Transfer

The example illustrated in Figure 2.16 is of a simple file transfer operation from A to B. No errors occur and the details of the option specification are not explored.

The operation begins when the TFTP module in system A sends a write request (WRQ) to the TFTP module in system B. The WRQ packet is carried as the body of a UDP segment. The write request includes the name of the file (in this case, XXX) and a mode of octet, or raw data. In the UDP header, the destination port number is 69, which alerts the receiving UDP entity that this message is intended for the TFTP application. The source port number is a TID selected by A, in this case 1511. System B is prepared to accept the file and so responds with an ACK with a block number of 0. In the UDP header, the destination port is 1511, which enables the UDP entity at A to route the incoming packet to the TFTP module, which can match this TID with the TID in the WRQ. The source port is a TID selected by B for this file transfer, in this case 1660.

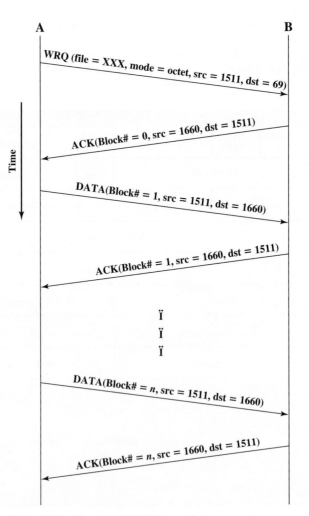

Figure 2.16 Example TFTP Operation

Following this initial exchange, the file transfer proceeds. The transfer consists of one or more data packets from A, each of which is acknowledged by B. The final data packet contains less than 512 bytes of data, which signals the end of the transfer.

Errors and Delays

If TFTP operates over a network or internet (as opposed to a direct data link), it is possible for packets to be lost. Because TFTP operates over UDP, which does not provide a reliable delivery service, there needs to be some mechanism in TFTP to deal with lost packets. TFTP uses the common technique of a timeout mechanism. Suppose that A sends a packet to B that requires an acknowledgment (i.e., any packet other than duplicate ACKs and those used for termination). When A has transmitted the packet, it starts a timer. If the timer expires before the acknowledgment is received from B, A retransmits the same packet. If in fact the original packet was lost, then the retransmission will be the first copy of this packet received by B. If the original packet was not lost but the acknowledgment from B was lost, then B will receive two copies of the same packet from A and simply acknowledges both copies. Because of the use of block numbers, this causes no confusion. The only exception to this rule is for duplicate ACK packets. The second ACK is ignored.

Syntax, Semantics, and Timing

In Section 2.1, it was mentioned that the key features of a protocol can be classified as syntax, semantics, and timing. These categories are easily seen in TFTP. The formats of the various TFTP packets form the **syntax** of the protocol. The **semantics** of the protocol are shown in the definitions of each of the packet types and the error codes. Finally, the sequence in which packets are exchanged, the use of block numbers, and the use of timers are all aspects of the **timing** of TFTP.

DATA TRANSMISSION

What we've got here is failure to communicate

—Paul Newman, *Cool Hand Luke*

KEY POINTS

◆ All of the forms of information that are discussed in this book (voice, data, image, video) can be represented by electromagnetic signals. Depending on the transmission medium and the communications environment, either analog or digital signals can be used to convey information.

◆ Any electromagnetic signal, analog or digital, is made up of a number of constituent frequencies. A key parameter that characterizes the signal is bandwidth, which is the width of the range of frequencies that comprises the signal. In general, the greater the bandwidth of the signal, the greater its information-carrying capacity.

◆ A major problem in designing a communications facility is transmission impairment. The most significant impairments are attenuation, attenuation distortion, delay distortion, and the various types of noise. The various forms of noise include thermal noise, intermodulation noise, crosstalk, and impulse noise. For analog signals, transmission impairments introduce random effects that degrade the quality of the received information and may affect intelligibility. For digital signals, transmission impairments may cause bit errors at the receiver.

◆ The designer of a communications facility must deal with four factors: the bandwidth of the signal, the data rate that is used for digital information, the amount of noise and other impairments, and the level of error rate that is acceptable. The bandwidth is limited by the transmission medium and the desire to avoid interference with other nearby signals. Because bandwidth is a scarce resource, we would like to maximize the data rate that is achieved in a given bandwidth. The data rate is limited by the bandwidth, the presence of impairments, and the error rate that is acceptable.

The successful transmission of data depends principally on two factors: the quality of the signal being transmitted and the characteristics of the transmission medium. The objective of this chapter and the next is to provide the reader with an intuitive feeling for the nature of these two factors.

The first section presents some concepts and terms from the field of electrical engineering. This should provide sufficient background to deal with the remainder of the chapter. Section 3.2 clarifies the use of the terms *analog* and *digital*. Either analog or digital data may be transmitted using either analog or digital signals. Furthermore, it is common for intermediate processing to be performed between source and destination, and this processing has either an analog or digital character.

63

Section 3.3 looks at the various impairments that may introduce errors into the data during transmission. The chief impairments are attenuation, attenuation distortion, delay distortion, and the various forms of noise. Finally, we look at the important concept of channel capacity.

3.1 CONCEPTS AND TERMINOLOGY

In this section we introduce some concepts and terms that will be referred to throughout the rest of the chapter and, indeed, throughout Part Two.

Transmission Terminology

Data transmission occurs between transmitter and receiver over some transmission medium. Transmission media may be classified as guided or unguided. In both cases, communication is in the form of electromagnetic waves. With **guided media**, the waves are guided along a physical path; examples of guided media are twisted pair, coaxial cable, and optical fiber. **Unguided media**, also called **wireless**, provide a means for transmitting electromagnetic waves but do not guide them; examples are propagation through air, vacuum, and seawater.

The term **direct link** is used to refer to the transmission path between two devices in which signals propagate directly from transmitter to receiver with no intermediate devices, other than amplifiers or repeaters used to increase signal strength. Note that this term can apply to both guided and unguided media.

A guided transmission medium is **point to point** if it provides a direct link between two devices and those are the only two devices sharing the medium. In a **multipoint** guided configuration, more than two devices share the same medium.

A transmission may be simplex, half duplex, or full duplex. In **simplex** transmission, signals are transmitted in only one direction; one station is transmitter and the other is receiver. In **half-duplex** operation, both stations may transmit, but only one at a time. In **full-duplex** operation, both stations may transmit simultaneously. In the latter case, the medium is carrying signals in both directions at the same time. How this can be is explained in due course. We should note that the definitions just given are the ones in common use in the United States (ANSI definitions). Elsewhere (ITU-T definitions), the term *simplex* is used to correspond to *half duplex* as defined previously, and *duplex* is used to correspond to *full duplex* as just defined.

Frequency, Spectrum, and Bandwidth

In this book, we are concerned with electromagnetic signals used as a means to transmit data. At point 3 in Figure 1.5, a signal is generated by the transmitter and transmitted over a medium. The signal is a function of time, but it can also be expressed as a function of frequency; that is, the signal consists of components of different frequencies. It turns out that the **frequency domain** view of a signal is more important to an understanding of data transmission than a **time domain** view. Both views are introduced here.

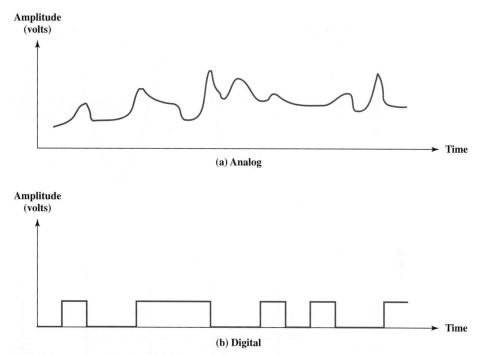

Figure 3.1   Analog and Digital Waveforms

TIME DOMAIN CONCEPTS Viewed as a function of time, an electromagnetic signal can be either analog or digital. An **analog signal** is one in which the signal intensity varies in a smooth, or **continuous**, fashion over time. In other words, there are no breaks or discontinuities in the signal.[1] A **digital signal** is one in which the signal intensity maintains a constant level for some period of time and then abruptly changes to another constant level, in a **discrete** fashion.[2] Figure 3.1 shows an example of each kind of signal. The analog signal might represent speech, and the digital signal might represent binary 1s and 0s.

The simplest sort of signal is a **periodic signal**, in which the same signal pattern repeats over time. Figure 3.2 shows an example of a periodic continuous signal (sine wave) and a periodic discrete signal (square wave). Mathematically, a signal $s(t)$ is defined to be periodic if and only if

$$s(t + T) = s(t) \qquad -\infty < t < +\infty$$

where the constant T is the period of the signal (T is the smallest value that satisfies the equation). Otherwise, a signal is **aperiodic**.

The sine wave is the fundamental periodic signal. A general sine wave can be represented by three parameters: peak amplitude (A), frequency (f), and phase (ϕ).

---

[1]A mathematical definition: a signal $s(t)$ is continuous if $\lim\limits_{t \to a} s(t) = s(a)$ for all a.

[2]This is an idealized definition. In fact, the transition from one voltage level to another will not be instantaneous, but there will be a small transition period. Nevertheless, an actual digital signal approximates closely the ideal model of constant voltage levels with instantaneous transitions.

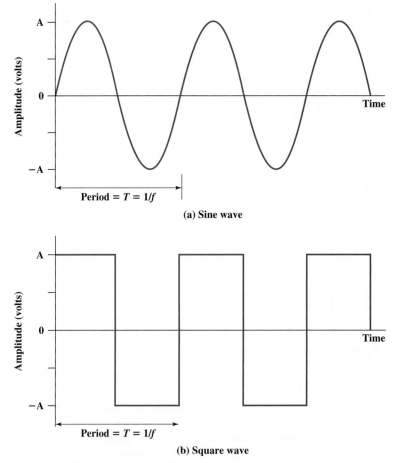

Figure 3.2   Examples of Periodic Signals

The **peak amplitude** is the maximum value or strength of the signal over time; typically, this value is measured in volts. The **frequency** is the rate [in cycles per second, or hertz (Hz)] at which the signal repeats. An equivalent parameter is the **period** (*T*) of a signal, which is the amount of time it takes for one repetition; therefore, *T* = 1/*f*. **Phase** is a measure of the relative position in time within a single period of a signal, as is illustrated subsequently. More formally, for a periodic signal *f*(*t*), phase is the fractional part *t*/*T* of the period *T* through which *t* has advanced relative to an arbitrary origin. The origin is usually taken as the last previous passage through zero from the negative to the positive direction.

The general sine wave can be written

$$s(t) = A \sin(2\pi ft + \phi)$$

A function with the form of the preceding equation is known as a **sinusoid**. Figure 3.3 shows the effect of varying each of the three parameters. In part (a) of the figure, the frequency is 1 Hz; thus the period is *T* = 1 second. Part (b) has the same frequency

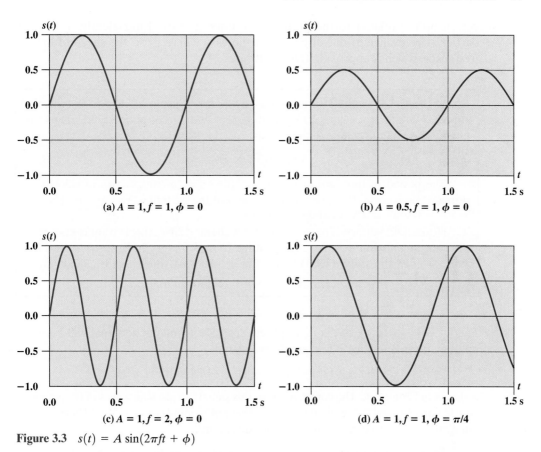

Figure 3.3 $s(t) = A \sin(2\pi f t + \phi)$

and phase but a peak amplitude of 0.5. In part (c) we have $f = 2$, which is equivalent to $T = 0.5$. Finally, part (d) shows the effect of a phase shift of $\pi/4$ radians, which is 45 degrees (2π radians $= 360° = 1$ period).

In Figure 3.3, the horizontal axis is time; the graphs display the value of a signal at a given point in space as a function of time. These same graphs, with a change of scale, can apply with horizontal axes in space. In this case, the graphs display the value of a signal at a given point in time as a function of distance. For example, for a sinusoidal transmission (e.g., an electromagnetic radio wave some distance from a radio antenna, or sound some distance from a loudspeaker), at a particular instant of time, the intensity of the signal varies in a sinusoidal way as a function of distance from the source.[3]

There is a simple relationship between the two sine waves, one in time and one in space. The **wavelength** (λ) of a signal is the distance occupied by a single cycle, or, put another way, the distance between two points of corresponding phase of two consecutive cycles. Assume that the signal is traveling with a velocity v. Then the

---

[3]An electromagnetic signal attenuates as it propagates, as a function of distance from the source of the signal. This effect is ignored in Figure 3.3.

wavelength is related to the period as follows: $\lambda = vT$. Equivalently, $\lambda f = v$. Of particular relevance to this discussion is the case where $v = c$, the speed of light in free space, which is approximately 3×10^8 m/s.

EXAMPLE 3.1 In the United States, ordinary household current is typically supplied at a frequency of 60 Hz with a peak voltage of about 170 V. Thus the power line voltage can be expressed as

$$170 \sin(2\pi \times 60 \times t)$$

The period of this current is $1/60 = 0.0167$ s $= 16.7$ ms. A typical velocity of propagation is about 0.9 c, so the wavelength of the current is $\lambda = vT = 0.9 \times 3 \times 10^8 \times 0.0167 = 4.5 \times 10^6$ m $= 4500$ km.

Household voltage is normally stated as being 120 V. This is what is known as the root mean square (square the voltage to make everything positive, find the average, take the square root) value. For a sine wave, the value is calculated as $\sqrt{(A^2 - 0)/2} = 0.707A$. In this case, $0.707 \times 170 = 120$.

FREQUENCY DOMAIN CONCEPTS In practice, an electromagnetic signal will be made up of many frequencies. For example, the signal

$$s(t) = (4/\pi) \times [\sin(2\pi ft) + (1/3) \sin(2\pi(3f)t)]$$

is shown in Figure 3.4c. The components of this signal are just sine waves of frequencies f and $3f$; parts (a) and (b) of the figure show these individual components.[4] There are two interesting points that can be made about this figure:

- The second frequency is an integer multiple of the first frequency. When all of the frequency components of a signal are integer multiples of one frequency, the latter frequency is referred to as the **fundamental frequency**. Each multiple of the fundamental frequency is referred to as a **harmonic frequency** of the signal.
- The period of the total signal is equal to the period of the fundamental frequency. The period of the component $\sin(2\pi ft)$ is $T = 1/f$, and the period of $s(t)$ is also T, as can be seen from Figure 3.4c.

It can be shown, using a discipline known as Fourier analysis, that any signal is made up of components at various frequencies, in which each component is a sinusoid. By adding together enough sinusoidal signals, each with the appropriate amplitude, frequency, and phase, any electromagnetic signal can be constructed. Put another way, any electromagnetic signal can be shown to consist of a collection of periodic analog signals (sine waves) at different amplitudes, frequencies, and phases. The importance of being able to look at a signal from the frequency perspective (frequency domain) rather than a time perspective (time domain) should become clear as the discussion proceeds. For the interested reader, the subject of Fourier analysis is introduced in Appendix A.

---

[4]The scaling factor of $4/\pi$ is used to produce a wave whose peak amplitude is close to 1.

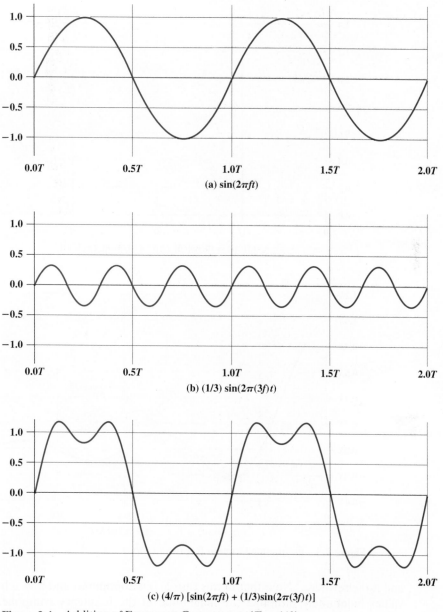

(a) $\sin(2\pi ft)$

(b) $(1/3)\,\sin(2\pi(3f)t)$

(c) $(4/\pi)\,[\sin(2\pi ft) + (1/3)\sin(2\pi(3f)t)]$

Figure 3.4 Addition of Frequency Components ($T = 1/f$)

So we can say that for each signal, there is a time domain function $s(t)$ that specifies the amplitude of the signal at each instant in time. Similarly, there is a frequency domain function $S(f)$ that specifies the peak amplitude of the constituent frequencies of the signal. Figure 3.5a shows the frequency domain function for the signal of Figure 3.4c. Note that, in this case, $S(f)$ is discrete. Figure 3.5b shows the frequency domain function for a single square pulse that has the value 1 between $-X/2$ and $X/2$,

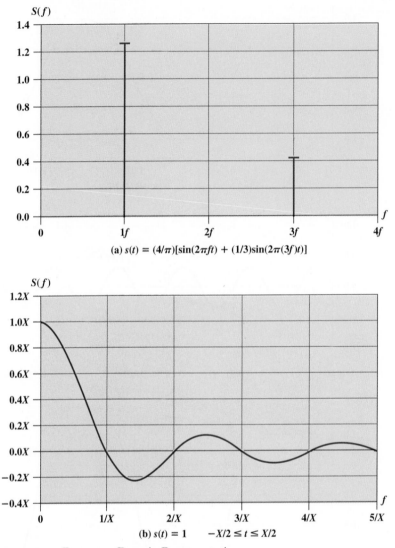

(a) $s(t) = (4/\pi)[\sin(2\pi ft) + (1/3)\sin(2\pi(3f)t)]$

(b) $s(t) = 1$ $\quad -X/2 \le t \le X/2$

Figure 3.5 Frequency Domain Representations

and is 0 elsewhere.[5] Note that in this case $S(f)$ is continuous and that it has nonzero values indefinitely, although the magnitude of the frequency components rapidly shrinks for larger f. These characteristics are common for real signals.

The **spectrum** of a signal is the range of frequencies that it contains. For the signal of Figure 3.4c, the spectrum extends from f to $3f$. The **absolute bandwidth** of a signal is the width of the spectrum. In the case of Figure 3.4c, the bandwidth is $3f - f = 2f$ Many signals, such as that of Figure 3.5b, have an infinite bandwidth. However, most of

---

[5]In fact, the function $S(f)$ for this case is symmetric around $f = 0$ and so has values for negative frequencies. The presence of negative frequencies is a mathematical artifact whose explanation is beyond the scope of this book.

the energy in the signal is contained in a relatively narrow band of frequencies. This band is referred to as the **effective bandwidth**, or just **bandwidth**.

One final term to define is **dc component**. If a signal includes a component of zero frequency, that component is a direct current (dc) or constant component. For example, Figure 3.6 shows the result of adding a dc component to the signal of Figure 3.4c. With no dc component, a signal has an average amplitude of zero, as seen in the time domain. With a dc component, it has a frequency term at $f = 0$ and a nonzero average amplitude.

RELATIONSHIP BETWEEN DATA RATE AND BANDWIDTH We have said that effective bandwidth is the band within which most of the signal energy is concentrated. The meaning of the term *most* in this context is somewhat arbitrary. The important issue here is that, although a given waveform may contain frequencies over a very broad range, as a practical matter any transmission system (transmitter plus medium plus receiver) will be able to accommodate only a limited band of frequencies. This, in turn, limits the data rate that can be carried on the transmission medium.

To try to explain these relationships, consider the square wave of Figure 3.2b. Suppose that we let a positive pulse represent binary 0 and a negative pulse represent binary 1. Then the waveform represents the binary stream 0101. . . . The duration of

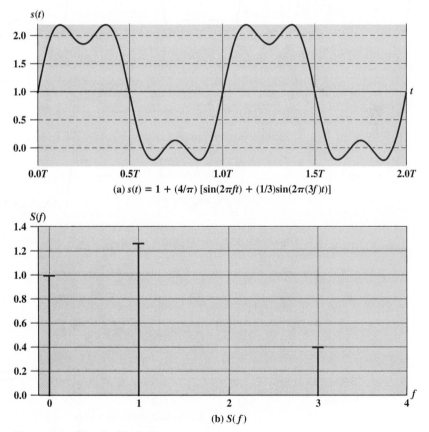

(a) $s(t) = 1 + (4/\pi)\,[\sin(2\pi f t) + (1/3)\sin(2\pi(3f)t)]$

(b) $S(f)$

Figure 3.6   Signal with dc Component

each pulse is $1/(2f)$; thus the data rate is $2f$ bits per second (bps). What are the frequency components of this signal? To answer this question, consider again Figure 3.4. By adding together sine waves at frequencies f and $3f$, we get a waveform that begins to resemble the original square wave. Let us continue this process by adding a sine wave of frequency $5f$, as shown in Figure 3.7a, and then adding a sine wave of frequency $7f$, as shown in Figure 3.7b. As we add additional odd multiples of f, suitably scaled, the resulting waveform approaches that of a square wave more and more closely.

Indeed, it can be shown that the frequency components of the square wave with amplitudes A and $-A$ can be expressed as follows:

$$s(t) = A \times \frac{4}{\pi} \times \sum_{k\,\text{odd},k=1}^{\infty} \frac{\sin(2\pi kft)}{k}$$

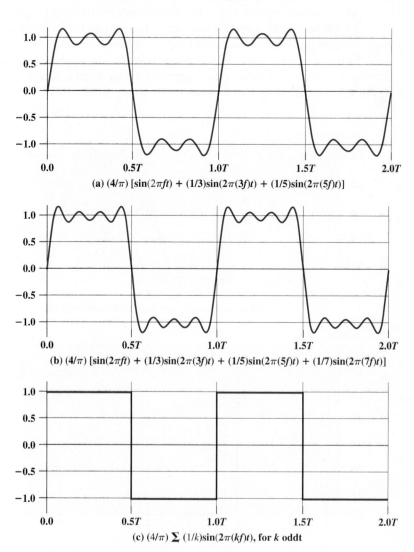

(a) $(4/\pi)\,[\sin(2\pi ft) + (1/3)\sin(2\pi(3f)t) + (1/5)\sin(2\pi(5f)t)]$

(b) $(4/\pi)\,[\sin(2\pi ft) + (1/3)\sin(2\pi(3f)t) + (1/5)\sin(2\pi(5f)t) + (1/7)\sin(2\pi(7f)t)]$

(c) $(4/\pi)\,\Sigma\,(1/k)\sin(2\pi(kf)t)$, for k oddt

Figure 3.7 Frequency Components of Square Wave ($T = 1/f$)

Thus, this waveform has an infinite number of frequency components and hence an infinite bandwidth. However, the peak amplitude of the kth frequency component, kf, is only $1/k$, so most of the energy in this waveform is in the first few frequency components. What happens if we limit the bandwidth to just the first three frequency components? We have already seen the answer, in Figure 3.7a. As we can see, the shape of the resulting waveform is reasonably close to that of the original square wave.

EXAMPLE 3.2 We can use Figures 3.4 and 3.7 to illustrate the relationship between data rate and bandwidth. Suppose that we are using a digital transmission system that is capable of transmitting signals with a bandwidth of 4 MHz. Let us attempt to transmit a sequence of alternating 1s and 0s as the square wave of Figure 3.7c. What data rate can be achieved? We look at three cases.

Case I. Let us approximate our square wave with the waveform of Figure 3.7a, which consists of the fundamental frequency and two harmonics. Although this waveform is a "distorted" square wave, it is sufficiently close to the square wave that a receiver should be able to discriminate between a binary 0 and a binary 1. If we let $f = 10^6$ cycles/second = 1 MHz, then the bandwidth of the signal

$$s(t) = \frac{4}{\pi} \times \left[\sin\big((2\pi \times 10^6)t\big) + \frac{1}{3}\sin\big((2\pi \times 3 \times 10^6)t\big) \right.$$
$$\left. + \frac{1}{5}\sin\big((2\pi \times 5 \times 10^6)t\big) \right]$$

is $(5 \times 10^6) - 10^6 = 4$ MHz. Note that for $f = 1$ MHz, the period of the fundamental frequency is $T = 1/10^6 = 10^{-6} = 1$ μs. If we treat this waveform as a bit string of 1s and 0s, 1 bit occurs every 0.5 μs, for a data rate of $2 \times 10^6 = 2$ Mbps. Thus, for a bandwidth of 4 MHz, a data rate of 2 Mbps is achieved.

Case II. Now suppose that we have a bandwidth of 8 MHz. Let us look again at Figure 3.7a, but now with $f = 2$ MHz. Using the same line of reasoning as before, the bandwidth of the signal is $(5 \times 2 \times 10^6) - (2 \times 10^6) = 8$ MHz. But in this case $T = 1/f = 0.5$ μs. As a result, 1 bit occurs every 0.25 μs for a data rate of 4 Mbps. Thus, other things being equal, by doubling the bandwidth, we double the potential data rate.

Case III. Now suppose that the waveform of Figure 3.4c is considered adequate for approximating a square wave. That is, the difference between a positive and negative pulse in Figure 3.4c is sufficiently distinct that the waveform can be successfully used to represent a sequence of 1s and 0s. Assume as in Case II that $f = 2$ MHz and $T = 1/f = 0.5$ μs, so that 1 bit occurs every 0.25 μs for a data rate of 4 Mbps. Using the waveform of Figure 3.4c, the bandwidth of the signal is $(3 \times 2 \times 10^6) - (2 \times 10^6) = 4$ MHz. Thus, a given bandwidth can support various data rates depending on the ability of the receiver to discern the difference between 0 and 1 in the presence of noise and other impairments.

To summarize,
Case I: Bandwidth = 4 MHz; data rate = 2 Mbps
Case II: Bandwidth = 8 MHz; data rate = 4 Mbps
Case III: Bandwidth = 4 MHz; data rate = 4 Mbps

We can draw the following conclusions from the preceding example. In general, any digital waveform will have infinite bandwidth. If we attempt to transmit this waveform as a signal over any medium, the transmission system will limit the bandwidth that can be transmitted. Furthermore, for any given medium, the greater the bandwidth transmitted, the greater the cost. Thus, on the one hand, economic and practical reasons dictate that digital information be approximated by a signal of limited bandwidth. On the other hand, limiting the bandwidth creates distortions, which makes the task of interpreting the received signal more difficult. The more limited the bandwidth, the greater the distortion, and the greater the potential for error by the receiver.

One more illustration should serve to reinforce these concepts. Figure 3.8 shows a digital bit stream with a data rate of 2000 bits per second. With a bandwidth of 2500 Hz, or even 1700 Hz, the representation is quite good. Furthermore, we can

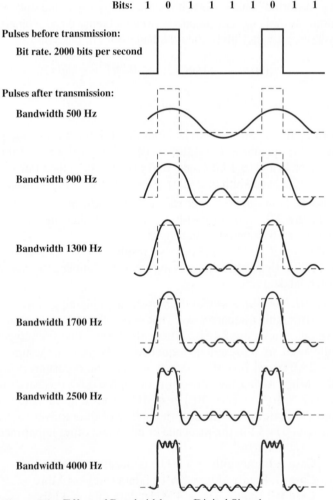

Figure 3.8 Effect of Bandwidth on a Digital Signal

generalize these results. If the data rate of the digital signal is W bps, then a very good representation can be achieved with a bandwidth of $2W$ Hz. However, unless noise is very severe, the bit pattern can be recovered with less bandwidth than this (see the discussion of channel capacity in Section 3.4).

Thus, there is a direct relationship between data rate and bandwidth: The higher the data rate of a signal, the greater is its required effective bandwidth. Looked at the other way, the greater the bandwidth of a transmission system, the higher is the data rate that can be transmitted over that system.

Another observation worth making is this: If we think of the bandwidth of a signal as being centered about some frequency, referred to as the **center frequency**, then the higher the center frequency, the higher the potential bandwidth and therefore the higher the potential data rate. For example, if a signal is centered at 2 MHz, its maximum potential bandwidth is 4 MHz.

We return to a discussion of the relationship between bandwidth and data rate in Section 3.4, after a consideration of transmission impairments.

3.2 ANALOG AND DIGITAL DATA TRANSMISSION

The terms *analog* and *digital* correspond, roughly, to *continuous* and *discrete*, respectively. These two terms are used frequently in data communications in at least three contexts: data, signaling, and transmission.

Briefly, we define **data** as entities that convey meaning, or information. **Signals** are electric or electromagnetic representations of data. **Signaling** is the physical propagation of the signal along a suitable medium. **Transmission** is the communication of data by the propagation and processing of signals. In what follows, we try to make these abstract concepts clear by discussing the terms *analog* and *digital* as applied to data, signals, and transmission.

Analog and Digital Data

The concepts of analog and digital data are simple enough. Analog data take on continuous values in some interval. For example, voice and video are continuously varying patterns of intensity. Most data collected by sensors, such as temperature and pressure, are continuous valued. Digital data take on discrete values; examples are text and integers.

The most familiar example of analog data is **audio**, which, in the form of acoustic sound waves, can be perceived directly by human beings. Figure 3.9 shows the acoustic spectrum for human speech and for music.[6] Frequency components of typical speech may be found between approximately 100 Hz and 7 kHz. Although much of the energy in speech is concentrated at the lower frequencies, tests have shown that frequencies below 600 or 700 Hz add very little to the intelligibility of speech to the human ear. Typical speech has a dynamic range of about 25 dB;[7] that is,

---

[6]Note the use of a log scale for the *x*-axis. Because the *y*-axis is in units of decibels, it is effectively a log scale also. A basic review of log scales is in the math refresher document at the Computer Science Student Resource Site at WilliamStallings.com/StudentSupport.html.

[7]The concept of decibels is explained in Appendix 3A.

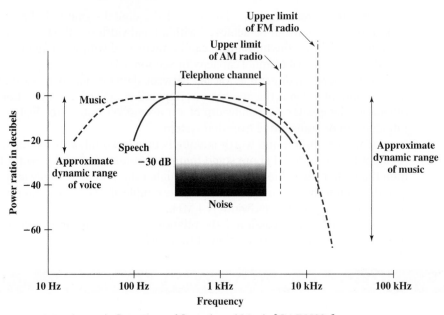

Figure 3.9 Acoustic Spectrum of Speech and Music [CARN99a]

the power produced by the loudest shout may be as much as 300 times greater than the least whisper. Figure 3.9 also shows the acoustic spectrum and dynamic range for music.

Another common example of analog data is **video**. Here it is easier to characterize the data in terms of the TV screen (destination) rather than the original scene (source) recorded by the TV camera. To produce a picture on the screen, an electron beam scans across the surface of the screen from left to right and top to bottom. For black-and-white television, the amount of illumination produced (on a scale from black to white) at any point is proportional to the intensity of the beam as it passes that point. Thus at any instant in time the beam takes on an analog value of intensity to produce the desired brightness at that point on the screen. Further, as the beam scans, the analog value changes. Thus the video image can be thought of as a time-varying analog signal.

Figure 3.10 depicts the scanning process. At the end of each scan line, the beam is swept rapidly back to the left (horizontal retrace). When the beam reaches the bottom, it is swept rapidly back to the top (vertical retrace). The beam is turned off (blanked out) during the retrace intervals.

To achieve adequate resolution, the beam produces a total of 483 horizontal lines at a rate of 30 complete scans of the screen per second. Tests have shown that this rate will produce a sensation of flicker rather than smooth motion. To provide a flicker-free image without increasing the bandwidth requirement, a technique known as **interlacing** is used. As Figure 3.10 shows, the odd numbered scan lines and the even numbered scan lines are scanned separately, with odd and even fields alternating on successive scans. The odd field is the scan from A to B and the even field is the scan from C to D. The beam reaches the middle of the screen's lowest line

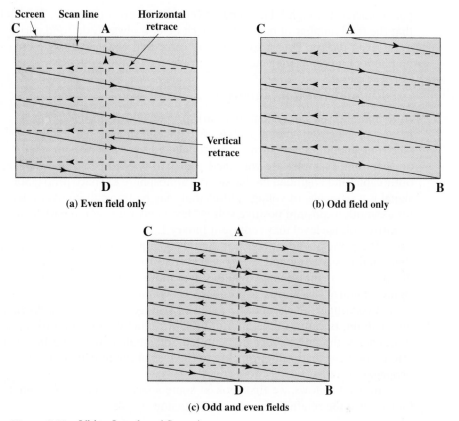

Figure 3.10   Video Interlaced Scanning

after 241.5 lines. At this point, the beam is quickly repositioned at the top of the screen and recommences in the middle of the screen's topmost visible line to produce an additional 241.5 lines interlaced with the original set. Thus the screen is refreshed 60 times per second rather than 30, and flicker is avoided.

A familiar example of digital data is **text** or character strings. While textual data are most convenient for human beings, they cannot, in character form, be easily stored or transmitted by data processing and communications systems. Such systems are designed for binary data. Thus a number of codes have been devised by which characters are represented by a sequence of bits. Perhaps the earliest common example of this is the Morse code. Today, the most commonly used text code is the International Reference Alphabet (IRA).[8] Each character in this code is represented by a unique 7-bit pattern; thus 128 different characters can be represented. This is a larger number than is necessary, and some of the patterns represent invisible *control characters*. IRA-encoded characters are almost always stored and transmitted using 8 bits

---

[8]IRA is defined in ITU-T Recommendation T.50 and was formerly known as International Alphabet Number 5 (IA5). The U.S. national version of IRA is referred to as the American Standard Code for Information Interchange (ASCII). Appendix E provides a description and table of the IRA code.

per character. The eighth bit is a parity bit used for error detection. This bit is set such that the total number of binary 1s in each octet is always odd (odd parity) or always even (even parity). Thus a transmission error that changes a single bit, or any odd number of bits, can be detected.

Analog and Digital Signals

In a communications system, data are propagated from one point to another by means of electromagnetic signals. An **analog signal** is a continuously varying electromagnetic wave that may be propagated over a variety of media, depending on spectrum; examples are wire media, such as twisted pair and coaxial cable; fiber optic cable; and unguided media, such as atmosphere or space propagation. A **digital signal** is a sequence of voltage pulses that may be transmitted over a wire medium; for example, a constant positive voltage level may represent binary 0 and a constant negative voltage level may represent binary 1.

The principal advantages of digital signaling are that it is generally cheaper than analog signaling and is less susceptible to noise interference. The principal disadvantage is that digital signals suffer more from attenuation than do analog signals. Figure 3.11 shows a sequence of voltage pulses, generated by a source using two voltage levels, and the received voltage some distance down a conducting medium. Because of the attenuation, or reduction, of signal strength at higher frequencies, the pulses become rounded and smaller. It should be clear that this attenuation can lead rather quickly to the loss of the information contained in the propagated signal.

In what follows, we first look at some specific examples of signal types and then discuss the relationship between data and signals.

Examples Let us return to our three examples of the preceding subsection. For each example, we will describe the signal and estimate its bandwidth.

The most familiar example of analog information is **audio**, or acoustic, information, which, in the form of sound waves, can be perceived directly by human beings. One form of acoustic information, of course, is human speech. This form of information is easily converted to an electromagnetic signal for transmission (Figure 3.12). In essence, all of the sound frequencies, whose amplitude is measured in terms of loudness, are converted into electromagnetic frequencies, whose amplitude is measured in volts. The telephone handset contains a simple mechanism for making such a conversion.

In the case of acoustic data (voice), the data can be represented directly by an electromagnetic signal occupying the same spectrum. However, there is a need to compromise between the fidelity of the sound as transmitted electrically and the cost of transmission, which increases with increasing bandwidth. As mentioned, the

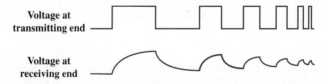

Figure 3.11 Attenuation of Digital Signals

In this graph of a typical analog signal, the variations in amplitude and frequency convey the gradations of loudness and pitch in speech or music. Similar signals are used to transmit television pictures, but at much higher frequencies.

Figure 3.12 Conversion of Voice Input to Analog Signal

spectrum of speech is approximately 100 Hz to 7 kHz, although a much narrower bandwidth will produce acceptable voice reproduction. The standard spectrum for a voice channel is 300 to 3400 Hz. This is adequate for speech transmission, minimizes required transmission capacity, and allows the use of rather inexpensive telephone sets. The telephone transmitter converts the incoming acoustic voice signal into an electromagnetic signal over the range 300 to 3400 Hz. This signal is then transmitted through the telephone system to a receiver, which reproduces it as acoustic sound.

Now let us look at the **video** signal. To produce a video signal, a TV camera, which performs similar functions to the TV receiver, is used. One component of the camera is a photosensitive plate, upon which a scene is optically focused. An electron beam sweeps across the plate from left to right and top to bottom, in the same fashion as depicted in Figure 3.10 for the receiver. As the beam sweeps, an analog electric signal is developed proportional to the brightness of the scene at a particular spot. We mentioned that a total of 483 lines are scanned at a rate of 30 complete scans per second. This is an approximate number taking into account the time lost during the vertical retrace interval. The actual U.S. standard is 525 lines, but of these about 42 are lost during vertical retrace. Thus the horizontal scanning frequency is (525 lines) × (30 scan/s) = 15,750 lines per second, or 63.5 μs/line. Of the 63.5 μs, about 11 μs are allowed for horizontal retrace, leaving a total of 52.5 μs per video line.

Now we are in a position to estimate the bandwidth required for the video signal. To do this we must estimate the upper (maximum) and lower (minimum) frequency of the band. We use the following reasoning to arrive at the maximum frequency: The maximum frequency would occur during the horizontal scan if the scene were alternating between black and white as rapidly as possible. We can estimate this maximum value by considering the resolution of the video image. In the vertical dimension, there are 483 lines, so the maximum vertical resolution would be 483. Experiments have shown that the actual subjective resolution is about 70% of that number, or about 338 lines. In the interest of a balanced picture, the horizontal and vertical resolutions should be about the same. Because the ratio of width to height of a TV screen is 4 : 3, the horizontal resolution should be about 4/3 × 338 = 450 lines. As a worst case, a scanning line would be made up of 450 elements alternating black and white. The scan would result in a wave, with each cycle of the wave consisting of one higher (black) and one lower (white) voltage level. Thus, there would be 450/2 = 225 cycles of the wave in

52.5 μs, for a maximum frequency of about 4.2 MHz. This rough reasoning, in fact, is fairly accurate. The lower limit is a dc or zero frequency, where the dc component corresponds to the average illumination of the scene (the average value by which the brightness exceeds the reference black level). Thus the bandwidth of the video signal is approximately 4 MHz $-$ 0 = 4 MHz.

The foregoing discussion did not consider color or audio components of the signal. It turns out that, with these included, the bandwidth remains about 4 MHz.

Finally, the third example described is the general case of **binary data**. Binary data is generated by terminals, computers, and other data processing equipment and then converted into digital voltage pulses for transmission, as illustrated in Figure 3.13. A commonly used signal for such data uses two constant (dc) voltage levels: one level for binary 1 and one level for binary 0. (In Chapter 5, we shall see that this is but one alternative, referred to as nonreturn to zero (NRZ).) Again, we are interested in the bandwidth of such a signal. This will depend, in any specific case, on the exact shape of the waveform and the sequence of 1s and 0s. We can obtain some understanding by considering Figure 3.8 (compare with Figure 3.7). As can be seen, the greater the bandwidth of the signal, the more faithfully it approximates a digital pulse stream.

Data and Signals   In the foregoing discussion, we have looked at analog signals, used to represent analog data, and digital signals, used to represent digital data. Generally, analog data are a function of time and occupy a limited frequency spectrum; such data can be represented by an electromagnetic signal occupying the same spectrum. Digital data can be represented by digital signals, with a different voltage level for each of the two binary digits.

As Figure 3.14 illustrates, these are not the only possibilities. Digital data can also be represented by analog signals by use of a modem (modulator/demodulator). The modem converts a series of binary (two-valued) voltage pulses into an analog signal by encoding the digital data onto a carrier frequency. The resulting signal occupies a certain spectrum of frequency centered about the carrier and may be propagated across a medium suitable for that carrier. The most common modems represent digital data in the voice spectrum and hence allow those data to be propagated over ordinary voice-grade telephone lines. At the other end of the line, another modem demodulates the signal to recover the original data.

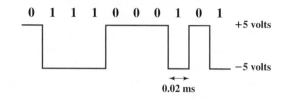

User input at a PC is converted into a stream of binary digits (1s and 0s). In this graph of a typical digital signal, binary one is represented by -5 volts and binary zero is represented by $+5$ volts. The signal for each bit has a duration of 0.02 ms, giving a data rate of 50,000 bits per second (50 kbps).

Figure 3.13   Conversion of PC Input to Digital Signal

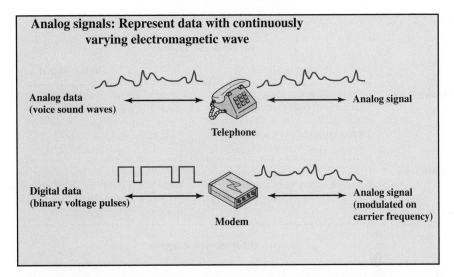

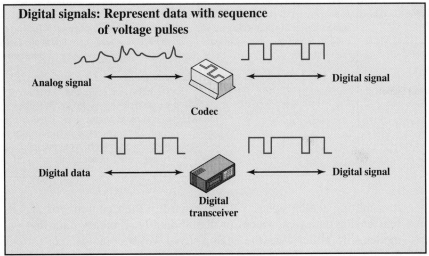

Figure 3.14   Analog and Digital Signaling of Analog and Digital Data

In an operation very similar to that performed by a modem, analog data can be represented by digital signals. The device that performs this function for voice data is a codec (coder-decoder). In essence, the codec takes an analog signal that directly represents the voice data and approximates that signal by a bit stream. At the receiving end, the bit stream is used to reconstruct the analog data.

Thus, Figure 3.14 suggests that data may be encoded into signals in a variety of ways. We will return to this topic in Chapter 5.

Analog and Digital Transmission

Both analog and digital signals may be transmitted on suitable transmission media. The way these signals are treated is a function of the transmission system. Table 3.1 summarizes the methods of data transmission. **Analog transmission** is a means of

Table 3.1 Analog and Digital Transmission

(a) Data and Signals

	Analog Signal	Digital Signal
Analog Data	Two alternatives: (1) signal occupies the same spectrum as the analog data; (2) analog data are encoded to occupy a different portion of spectrum.	Analog data are encoded using a codec to produce a digital bit stream.
Digital Data	Digital data are encoded using a modem to produce analog signal.	Two alternatives: (1) signal consists of two voltage levels to represent the two binary values; (2) digital data are encoded to produce a digital signal with desired properties.

(b) Treatment of Signals

	Analog Transmission	Digital Transmission
Analog Signal	Is propagated through amplifiers; same treatment whether signal is used to represent analog data or digital data.	Assumes that the analog signal represents digital data. Signal is propagated through repeaters; at each repeater, digital data are recovered from inbound signal and used to generate a new analog outbound signal.
Digital Signal	Not used	Digital signal represents a stream of 1s and 0s, which may represent digital data or may be an encoding of analog data. Signal is propagated through repeaters; at each repeater, stream of 1s and 0s is recovered from inbound signal and used to generate a new digital outbound signal.

transmitting analog signals without regard to their content; the signals may represent analog data (e.g., voice) or digital data (e.g., binary data that pass through a modem). In either case, the analog signal will become weaker (attenuate) after a certain distance. To achieve longer distances, the analog transmission system includes amplifiers that boost the energy in the signal. Unfortunately, the amplifier also boosts the noise components. With amplifiers cascaded to achieve long distances, the signal becomes more and more distorted. For analog data, such as voice, quite a bit of distortion can be tolerated and the data remain intelligible. However, for digital data, cascaded amplifiers will introduce errors.

Digital transmission, in contrast, assumes a binary content to the signal. A digital signal can be transmitted only to a limited distance before attenuation, noise, and other impairments endanger the integrity of the data. To achieve greater distances, repeaters are used. A repeater receives the digital signal, recovers the pattern of 1s and 0s, and retransmits a new signal. Thus the attenuation is overcome.

The same technique may be used with an analog signal if it is assumed that the signal carries digital data. At appropriately spaced points, the transmission system has repeaters rather than amplifiers. The repeater recovers the digital data from the analog signal and generates a new, clean analog signal. Thus noise is not cumulative.

The question naturally arises as to which is the preferred method of transmission. The answer being supplied by the telecommunications industry and its customers is digital. Both long-haul telecommunications facilities and intrabuilding services have moved to digital transmission and, where possible, digital signaling techniques. The most important reasons are the following:

- **Digital technology:** The advent of large-scale integration (LSI) and very-large-scale integration (VLSI) technology has caused a continuing drop in the cost and size of digital circuitry. Analog equipment has not shown a similar drop.

- **Data integrity:** With the use of repeaters rather than amplifiers, the effects of noise and other signal impairments are not cumulative. Thus it is possible to transmit data longer distances and over lower quality lines by digital means while maintaining the integrity of the data.

- **Capacity utilization:** It has become economical to build transmission links of very high bandwidth, including satellite channels and optical fiber. A high degree of multiplexing is needed to utilize such capacity effectively, and this is more easily and cheaply achieved with digital (time division) rather than analog (frequency division) techniques. This is explored in Chapter 8.

- **Security and privacy** Encryption techniques can be readily applied to digital data and to analog data that have been digitized.

- **Integration:** By treating both analog and digital data digitally, all signals have the same form and can be treated similarly. Thus economies of scale and convenience can be achieved by integrating voice, video, and digital data.

3.3 TRANSMISSION IMPAIRMENTS

With any communications system, the signal that is received may differ from the signal that is transmitted, due to various transmission impairments. For analog signals, these impairments introduce various random modifications that degrade the signal quality. For digital signals, bit errors may be introduced, such that a binary 1 is transformed into a binary 0 or vice versa. In this section, we examine the various impairments and how they may affect the information-carrying capacity of a communication link; Chapter 5 looks at measures that can be taken to compensate for these impairments.

The most significant impairments are

- Attenuation and attenuation distortion
- Delay distortion
- Noise

Attenuation

The strength of a signal falls off with distance over any transmission medium. For guided media (e.g., twisted-pair wire, optical fiber), this reduction in strength, or attenuation, is generally exponential and thus is typically expressed as a constant number of decibels per unit distance.[9] For unguided media (wireless transmission), attenuation is a more complex function of distance and the makeup of the atmosphere. Attenuation introduces three considerations for the transmission engineer.

1. A received signal must have sufficient strength so that the electronic circuitry in the receiver can detect and interpret the signal.
2. The signal must maintain a level sufficiently higher than noise to be received without error.
3. Attenuation is greater at higher frequencies, and this causes distortion.

The first and second considerations are dealt with by attention to signal strength and the use of amplifiers or repeaters. For a point-to-point link, the signal strength of the transmitter must be strong enough to be received intelligibly, but not so strong as to overload the circuitry of the transmitter or receiver, which would cause distortion. Beyond a certain distance, the attenuation becomes unacceptably great, and repeaters or amplifiers are used to boost the signal at regular intervals. These problems are more complex for multipoint lines where the distance from transmitter to receiver is variable.

The third consideration, known as attenuation distortion, is particularly noticeable for analog signals. Because attenuation is different for different frequencies, and the signal is made up of a number of components at different frequencies, the received signal is not only reduced in strength but is also distorted. To overcome this problem, techniques are available for equalizing attenuation across a band of frequencies. This is commonly done for voice-grade telephone lines by using loading coils that change the electrical properties of the line; the result is to smooth out attenuation effects. Another approach is to use amplifiers that amplify high frequencies more than lower frequencies.

An example is provided in Figure 3.15a, which shows attenuation as a function of frequency for a typical leased line. In the figure, attenuation is measured relative to the attenuation at 1000 Hz. Positive values on the y-axis represent attenuation greater than that at 1000 Hz. A 1000-Hz tone of a given power level is applied to the input, and the power, P_{1000}, is measured at the output. For any other frequency f, the procedure is repeated and the relative attenuation in decibels is[10]

$$N_f = -10 \log_{10} \frac{P_f}{P_{1000}}$$

The solid line in Figure 3.15a shows attenuation without equalization. As can be seen, frequency components at the upper end of the voice band are attenuated much more than those at lower frequencies. It should be clear that this will result in a distortion of the received speech signal. The dashed line shows the effect of equalization. The flattened response curve improves the quality of voice signals. It also allows higher data rates to be used for digital data that are passed through a modem.

---

[9]Standards documents generally use the term *insertion loss* when referring to losses associated with cabling, because it is more descriptive of a loss caused by the insertion of a link between transmitter and receiver. Because it remains a more familiar term, we generally use *attenuation* in this book.

[10]In the remainder of this book, unless otherwise indicated, we use $\log(x)$ to mean $\log_{10}(x)$.

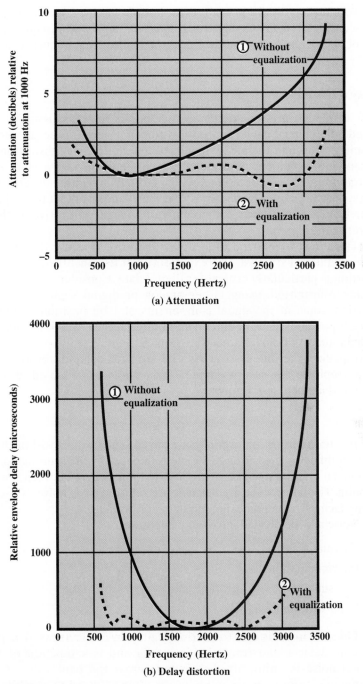

Figure 3.15   Attenuation and Delay Distortion Curves for a Voice Channel

Attenuation distortion can present less of a problem with digital signals. As we have seen, the strength of a digital signal falls off rapidly with frequency (Figure 3.5b); most of the content is concentrated near the fundamental frequency or bit rate of the signal.

Delay Distortion

Delay distortion is a phenomenon that occurs in transmission cables (such as twisted pair, coaxial cable, and optical fiber); it does not occur when signals are transmitted through the air by means of antennas. Delay distortion is caused by the fact that the velocity of propagation of a signal through a cable is different for different frequencies. For a signal with a given bandwidth, the velocity tends to be highest near the center frequency of the signal and to fall off toward the two edges of the band. Thus, various components of a signal will arrive at the receiver at different times.

This effect is referred to as delay distortion because the received signal is distorted due to varying delays experienced at its constituent frequencies. Delay distortion is particularly critical for digital data. Consider that a sequence of bits is being transmitted, using either analog or digital signals. Because of delay distortion, some of the signal components of 1 bit position will spill over into other bit positions, causing **intersymbol interference**, which is a major limitation to maximum bit rate over a transmission channel.

Equalizing techniques can also be used for delay distortion. Again using a leased telephone line as an example, Figure 3.15b shows the effect of equalization on delay as a function of frequency.

Noise

For any data transmission event, the received signal will consist of the transmitted signal, modified by the various distortions imposed by the transmission system, plus additional unwanted signals that are inserted somewhere between transmission and reception. The latter, undesired signals are referred to as **noise**. Noise is the major limiting factor in communications system performance.

Noise may be divided into four categories:

- Thermal noise
- Intermodulation noise
- Crosstalk
- Impulse noise

Thermal noise is due to thermal agitation of electrons. It is present in all electronic devices and transmission media and is a function of temperature. Thermal noise is uniformly distributed across the bandwidths typically used in communications systems and hence is often referred to as **white noise**. Thermal noise cannot be eliminated and therefore places an upper bound on communications system performance. Because of the weakness of the signal received by satellite earth stations, thermal noise is particularly significant for satellite communication.

The amount of thermal noise to be found in a bandwidth of 1 Hz in any device or conductor is

$$N_0 = kT(\text{W/Hz})$$

where[11]

N_0 = noise power density in watts per 1 Hz of bandwidth

k = Boltzmann's constant = 1.38×10^{-23} J/K

T = temperature, in kelvins (absolute temperature) where the symbol K is used to represent 1 kelvin

---

EXAMPLE 3.3 Room temperature is usually specified as $T = 17°C$, or 290 K. At this temperature, the thermal noise power density is

$$N_0 = (1.38 \times 10^{-23}) \times 290 = 4 \times 10^{-21}\,\text{W/H}_Z = -204\,\text{dBW/H}_Z$$

where dBW is the decibel-watt, defined in Appendix 3A.

The noise is assumed to be independent of frequency. Thus the thermal noise in watts present in a bandwidth of B hertz can be expressed as

$$N = kTB$$

or, in decibel-watts,

$$N = 10 \log k + 10 \log T + 10 \log B$$
$$= -228.6\,\text{dBW} + 10 \log T + 10 \log B$$

EXAMPLE 3.4 Given a receiver with an effective noise temperature of 294 K and a 10-MHz bandwidth, the thermal noise level at the receiver's output is

$$N = -228.6\,\text{dBW} + 10 \log(294) + 10 \log 10^7$$
$$= -228.6 + 24.7 + 70$$
$$= -133.9\,\text{dBW}$$

When signals at different frequencies share the same transmission medium, the result may be **intermodulation noise**. The effect of intermodulation noise is to produce signals at a frequency that is the sum or difference of the two original frequencies or multiples of those frequencies. For example, if two signals, one at 4000 Hz and one at 8000 Hz, share the same transmission facility, they might produce energy at 12,000 Hz. This noise could interfere with an intended signal at 12,000 Hz.

Intermodulation noise is produced by nonlinearities in the transmitter, receiver, and/or intervening transmission medium. Ideally, these components behave as linear systems; that is, the output is equal to the input times a constant. However, in any real system, the output is a more complex function of the input. Excessive nonlinearity can be caused by component malfunction or overload from excessive signal strength. It is under these circumstances that the sum and difference frequency terms occur.

---

[11]A joule (J) is the International System (SI) unit of electrical, mechanical, and thermal energy. A watt is the SI unit of power, equal to one joule per second. The kelvin (K) is the SI unit of thermodynamic temperature. For a temperature in kelvins of T, the corresponding temperature in degrees Celsius is equal to $T - 273.15$.

Crosstalk has been experienced by anyone who, while using the telephone, has been able to hear another conversation; it is an unwanted coupling between signal paths. It can occur by electrical coupling between nearby twisted pairs or, rarely, coax cable lines carrying multiple signals. Crosstalk can also occur when microwave antennas pick up unwanted signals; although highly directional antennas are used, microwave energy does spread during propagation. Typically, crosstalk is of the same order of magnitude as, or less than, thermal noise.

All of the types of noise discussed so far have reasonably predictable and relatively constant magnitudes. Thus it is possible to engineer a transmission system to cope with them. **Impulse noise**, however, is noncontinuous, consisting of irregular pulses or noise spikes of short duration and of relatively high amplitude. It is generated from a variety of causes, including external electromagnetic disturbances, such as lightning, and faults and flaws in the communications system.

Impulse noise is generally only a minor annoyance for analog data. For example, voice transmission may be corrupted by short clicks and crackles with no loss of intelligibility. However, impulse noise is the primary source of error in digital data communication. For example, a sharp spike of energy of 0.01s duration would not destroy any voice data but would wash out about 560 bits of digital data being transmitted at 56 kbps. Figure 3.16 is an example of the effect of noise on a digital signal.

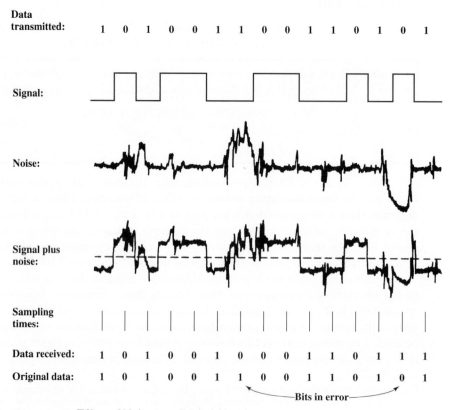

Figure 3.16 Effect of Noise on a Digital Signal

Here the noise consists of a relatively modest level of thermal noise plus occasional spikes of impulse noise. The digital data can be recovered from the signal by sampling the received waveform once per bit time. As can be seen, the noise is occasionally sufficient to change a 1 to a 0 or a 0 to a 1.

3.4 CHANNEL CAPACITY

We have seen that there are a variety of impairments that distort or corrupt a signal. For digital data, the question that then arises is to what extent these impairments limit the data rate that can be achieved. The maximum rate at which data can be transmitted over a given communication path, or channel, under given conditions, is referred to as the **channel capacity**.

There are four concepts here that we are trying to relate to one another.

- **Data rate:** The rate, in bits per second (bps), at which data can be communicated
- **Bandwidth:** The bandwidth of the transmitted signal as constrained by the transmitter and the nature of the transmission medium, expressed in cycles per second, or hertz
- **Noise:** The average level of noise over the communications path
- **Error rate:** The rate at which errors occur, where an error is the reception of a 1 when a 0 was transmitted or the reception of a 0 when a 1 was transmitted

The problem we are addressing is this: Communications facilities are expensive, and, in general, the greater the bandwidth of a facility, the greater the cost. Furthermore, all transmission channels of any practical interest are of limited bandwidth. The limitations arise from the physical properties of the transmission medium or from deliberate limitations at the transmitter on the bandwidth to prevent interference from other sources. Accordingly, we would like to make as efficient use as possible of a given bandwidth. For digital data, this means that we would like to get as high a data rate as possible at a particular limit of error rate for a given bandwidth. The main constraint on achieving this efficiency is noise.

Nyquist Bandwidth

To begin, let us consider the case of a channel that is noise free. In this environment, the limitation on data rate is simply the bandwidth of the signal. A formulation of this limitation, due to Nyquist, states that if the rate of signal transmission is $2B$, then a signal with frequencies no greater than B is sufficient to carry the signal rate. The converse is also true: Given a bandwidth of B, the highest signal rate that can be carried is $2B$. This limitation is due to the effect of intersymbol interference, such as is produced by delay distortion. The result is useful in the development of digital-to-analog encoding schemes and is, in essence, based on the same derivation as that of the sampling theorem, described in Appendix F.

Note that in the preceding paragraph, we referred to signal rate. If the signals to be transmitted are binary (two voltage levels), then the data rate that can be supported by B Hz is $2B$ bps. However, as we shall see in Chapter 5, signals with more than two levels can be used; that is, each signal element can represent more than 1 bit. For example, if four possible voltage levels are used as signals, then each signal element can represent 2 bits. With multilevel signaling, the Nyquist formulation becomes

$$C = 2B \log_2 M$$

where M is the number of discrete signal or voltage levels.

So, for a given bandwidth, the data rate can be increased by increasing the number of different signal elements. However, this places an increased burden on the receiver: Instead of distinguishing one of two possible signal elements during each signal time, it must distinguish one of M possible signal elements. Noise and other impairments on the transmission line will limit the practical value of M.

> **EXAMPLE 3.5** Consider a voice channel being used, via modem, to transmit digital data. Assume a bandwidth of 3100 Hz. Then the Nyquist capacity, C, of the channel is $2B = 6200$ bps. For $M = 8$, a value used with some modems, C becomes 18,600 bps for a bandwidth of 3100 Hz.

Shannon Capacity Formula

Nyquist's formula indicates that, all other things being equal, doubling the bandwidth doubles the data rate. Now consider the relationship among data rate, noise, and error rate. The presence of noise can corrupt 1 or more bits. If the data rate is increased, then the bits become "shorter" so that more bits are affected by a given pattern of noise.

Figure 3.16 illustrates this relationship. If the data rate is increased, then more bits will occur during the interval of a noise spike, and hence more errors will occur.

All of these concepts can be tied together neatly in a formula developed by the mathematician Claude Shannon. As we have just illustrated, the higher the data rate, the more damage that unwanted noise can do. For a given level of noise, we would expect that a greater signal strength would improve the ability to receive data correctly in the presence of noise. The key parameter involved in this reasoning is the **signal-to-noise ratio** (SNR, or S/N),[12] which is the ratio of the power in a signal to the power contained in the noise that is present at a particular point in the transmission. Typically, this ratio is measured at a receiver, because it is at this point that an attempt is made to process the signal and recover the data. For convenience, this ratio is often reported in decibels:

$$\text{SNR}_{dB} = 10 \log_{10} \frac{\text{signal power}}{\text{noise power}}$$

This expresses the amount, in decibels, that the intended signal exceeds the noise level. A high SNR will mean a high-quality signal and a low number of required intermediate repeaters.

---

[12]Some of the literature uses SNR; others use S/N. Also, in some cases the dimensionless quantity is referred to as SNR or S/N and the quantity in decibels is referred to as SNR_{dB} or $(\text{S/N})_{dB}$. Others use just SNR or S/N to mean the dB quantity. This text uses SNR and SNR_{dB}.

The signal-to-noise ratio is important in the transmission of digital data because it sets the upper bound on the achievable data rate. Shannon's result is that the maximum channel capacity, in bits per second, obeys the equation

$$C = B \log_2 (1 + SNR) \tag{3.1}$$

where C is the capacity of the channel in bits per second and B is the bandwidth of the channel in hertz.[13] The Shannon formula represents the theoretical maximum that can be achieved. In practice, however, only much lower rates are achieved. One reason for this is that the formula assumes white noise (thermal noise). Impulse noise is not accounted for, nor are attenuation distortion and delay distortion. Even in an ideal white noise environment, present technology still cannot achieve Shannon capacity due to encoding issues, such as coding length and complexity.

The capacity indicated in the preceding equation is referred to as the error-free capacity. Shannon proved that if the actual information rate on a channel is less than the error-free capacity, then it is theoretically possible to use a suitable signal code to achieve error-free transmission through the channel. Shannon's theorem unfortunately does not suggest a means for finding such codes, but it does provide a yardstick by which the performance of practical communication schemes may be measured.

Several other observations concerning the preceding equation may be instructive. For a given level of noise, it would appear that the data rate could be increased by increasing either signal strength or bandwidth. However, as the signal strength increases, the effects of nonlinearities in the system also increase, leading to an increase in intermodulation noise. Note also that, because noise is assumed to be white, the wider the bandwidth, the more noise is admitted to the system. Thus, as B increases, SNR decreases.

EXAMPLE 3.6 Let us consider an example that relates the Nyquist and Shannon formulations. Suppose that the spectrum of a channel is between 3 MHz and 4 MHz and SNR_{dB} = 24 dB. Then

$$B = 4\,MH_Z - 3\,MH_Z = 1\,MH_Z$$
$$SNR_{dB} = 24\,dB = 10 \log_{10}(SNR)$$
$$SNR = 251$$

Using Shannon's formula,

$$C = 10^6 \times \log_2(1 + 251) \approx 10^6 \times 8 = 8\,Mbps$$

This is a theoretical limit and, as we have said, is unlikely to be reached. But assume we can achieve the limit. Based on Nyquist's formula, how many signaling levels are required? We have

---

[13] An intuitive proof of Shannon's equation is contained in a document in the premium content section of this book's Web site.

$$C = 2B \log_2 M$$
$$8 \times 10^6 = 2 \times (10^6) \times \log_2 M$$
$$4 = \log_2 M$$
$$M = 16$$

The Expression E_b/N_0

Finally, we mention a parameter related to SNR that is more convenient for determining digital data rates and error rates and that is the standard quality measure for digital communication system performance. The parameter is the ratio of signal energy per bit to noise power density per hertz, E_b/N_0. Consider a signal, digital or analog, that contains binary digital data transmitted at a certain bit rate R. Recalling that 1 watt = 1 J/s, the energy per bit in a signal is given by $E_b = ST_b$, where S is the signal power and T_b is the time required to send 1 bit. The data rate R is just $R = 1/T_b$. Thus

$$\frac{E_b}{N_0} = \frac{S/R}{N_0} = \frac{S}{kTR}$$

or, in decibel notation,

$$\left(\frac{E_b}{N_0}\right)_{dB} = S_{dBW} - 10 \log R - 10 \log k - 10 \log T$$
$$= S_{dBW} - 10 \log R + 228.6 \text{ dBW} - 10 \log T$$

The ratio E_b/N_0 is important because the bit error rate for digital data is a (decreasing) function of this ratio. Given a value of E_b/N_0 needed to achieve a desired error rate, the parameters in the preceding formula may be selected. Note that as the bit rate R increases, the transmitted signal power, relative to noise, must increase to maintain the required E_b/N_0.

Let us try to grasp this result intuitively by considering again Figure 3.16. The signal here is digital, but the reasoning would be the same for an analog signal. In several instances, the noise is sufficient to alter the value of a bit. If the data rate were doubled, the bits would be more tightly packed together, and the same passage of noise might destroy 2 bits. Thus, for constant signal to noise ratio, an increase in data rate increases the error rate.

The advantage of E_b/N_0 over SNR is that the latter quantity depends on the bandwidth.

EXAMPLE 3.7 For binary phase-shift keying (defined in Chapter 5), $E_b/N_0 = 8.4$ dB is required for a bit error rate of 10^{-4} (1 bit error out of every 10,000). If the effective noise temperature is 290 K (room temperature) and the data rate is 2400 bps, what received signal level is required?

We have

$$8.4 = S(\text{dBW}) - 10 \log 2400 + 228.6 \text{ dBW} - 10 \log 290$$
$$= S(\text{dBW}) - (10)(3.38) + 228.6 - (10)(2.46)$$
$$S = -161.8 \text{ dBW}$$

We can relate E_b/N_0 to SNR as follows. We have

$$\frac{E_b}{N_0} = \frac{S}{N_0 R}$$

The parameter N_0 is the noise power density in watts/hertz. Hence, the noise in a signal with bandwidth B is $N = N_0 B$. Substituting, we have

$$\frac{E_b}{N_0} = \frac{S}{N} \frac{B}{R} \tag{3.2}$$

Another formulation of interest relates E_b/N_0 to spectral efficiency. Shannon's result (Equation 3.1) can be rewritten as:

$$\frac{S}{N} = 2^{C/B} - 1$$

Using Equation (3.2), and equating R with C, we have

$$\frac{E_b}{N_0} = \frac{B}{C} 2 2^{C/B} - 1$$

This is a useful formula that relates the achievable spectral efficiency C/B to E_b/N_0.

EXAMPLE 3.8 Suppose we want to find the minimum E_b/N_0 required to achieve a spectral efficiency of 6 bps/Hz. Then $E_b/N_0 = (1/6)(2^6 - 1) = 10.5 = 10.21$ dB.

3.5 RECOMMENDED READING AND WEB SITE

There are many books that cover the fundamentals of analog and digital transmission. [COUC07] is quite thorough. Other good reference works are [FREE05], which includes some of the examples used in this chapter, and [HAYK09].

COUC07 Couch, L. *Digital and Analog Communication Systems.* Upper Saddle River, NJ: Prentice Hall, 2007.

FREE05 Freeman, R. *Fundamentals of Telecommunications.* New York: Wiley, 2005.

HAYK09 Haykin, S. *Communication Systems.* New York: Wiley, 2009.

Recommended Web site:

- **Fourier series synthesis:** An excellent visualization tool for Fourier series

3.6 KEY TERMS, REVIEW QUESTIONS, AND PROBLEMS

Key Terms

absolute bandwidth	digital transmission	peak amplitude
analog data	direct link	period
analog signal	discrete	periodic signal
analog transmission	effective bandwidth	point-to-point link
aperiodic	frequency	phase
attenuation	frequency domain	signal
attenuation distortion	full duplex	signal-to-noise ratio (SNR)
audio	fundamental frequency	signaling
bandwidth	gain	simplex
binary data	guided media	sinusoid
center frequency	half duplex	spectrum
channel capacity	harmonic frequency	text
continuous	impulse noise	thermal noise
crosstalk	interlacing	time domain
data	intermodulation noise	transmission
dc component	intersymbol interference	unguided media
decibel (dB)	loss	video
delay distortion	multipoint link	wavelength
digital data	noise	white noise
digital signal	Nyquist bandwidth	wireless

Review Questions

3.1 Differentiate between guided media and unguided media.
3.2 Differentiate between an analog and a digital electromagnetic signal.
3.3 What are three important characteristics of a periodic signal?
3.4 How many radians are there in a complete circle of 360 degrees?
3.5 What is the relationship between the wavelength and frequency of a sine wave?
3.6 Define *fundamental frequency*.
3.7 What is the relationship between a signal's spectrum and its bandwidth?
3.8 What is attenuation?
3.9 Define *channel capacity*.
3.10 What key factors affect channel capacity?

Problems

3.1 **a.** For multipoint configuration, only one device at a time can transmit. Why?
   b. There are two methods of enforcing the rule that only one device can transmit. In the centralized method, one station is in control and can either transmit or allow a specified other station to transmit. In the decentralized method, the stations jointly cooperate in taking turns. What do you see as the advantages and disadvantages of the two methods?
3.2 A signal has a fundamental frequency of 1000 Hz. What is its period?

3.3 Express the following in the simplest form you can:
  a. $\sin(2\pi ft - \pi) + \sin(2\pi ft + \pi)$
  b. $\sin(2\pi ft) + \sin(2\pi ft - \pi)$

3.4 Sound may be modeled as sinusoidal functions. Compare the relative frequency and wavelength of musical notes. Use 330 m/s as the speed of sound and the following frequencies for the musical scale.

Note	C	D	E	F	G	A	B	C
Frequency	264	297	330	352	396	440	495	528

3.5 If the solid curve in Figure 3.17 represents $\sin(2\pi t)$, what does the dotted curve represent? That is, the dotted curve can be written in the form $A \sin(2\pi ft + \phi)$; what are A, f, and ϕ?

3.6 Decompose the signal $(1 + 0.1 \cos 5t) \cos 100t$ into a linear combination of sinusoidal functions, and find the amplitude, frequency, and phase of each component. *Hint:* Use the identity for $\cos a \cos b$.

3.7 Find the period of the function $f(t) = (10 \cos t)^2$.

3.8 Consider two periodic functions $f_1(t)$ and $f_2(t)$, with periods T_1 and T_2, respectively. Is it always the case that the function $f(t) = f_1(t) + f_2(t)$ is periodic? If so, demonstrate this fact. If not, under what conditions is $f(t)$ periodic?

3.9 Figure 3.4 shows the effect of eliminating higher-harmonic components of a square wave and retaining only a few lower harmonic components. What would the signal look like in the opposite case—that is, retaining all higher harmonics and eliminating a few lower harmonics?

3.10 Figure 3.5b shows the frequency domain function for a single square pulse. The single pulse could represent a digital 1 in a communication system. Note that an infinite number of higher frequencies of decreasing magnitudes is needed to represent the single pulse. What implication does that have for a real digital transmission system?

3.11 IRA is a 7-bit code that allows 128 characters to be defined. In the 1970s, many newspapers received stories from the wire services in a 6-bit code called TTS. This code carried upper- and lower-case characters as well as many special characters and formatting commands. The typical TTS character set allowed over 100 characters to be defined. How do you think this could be accomplished?

3.12 For a video signal, what increase in horizontal resolution is possible if a bandwidth of 5 MHz is used? What increase in vertical resolution is possible? Treat the two questions separately; that is, the increased bandwidth is to be used to increase either horizontal or vertical resolution, but not both.

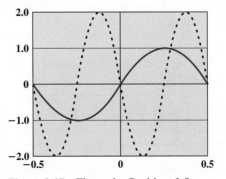

Figure 3.17   Figure for Problem 3.5

3.13 a. Suppose that a digitized TV picture is to be transmitted from a source that uses a matrix of 480×500 picture elements (pixels), where each pixel can take on one of 32 intensity values. Assume that 30 pictures are sent per second. (This digital source is roughly equivalent to broadcast TV standards that have been adopted.) Find the source rate R (bps).

b. Assume that the TV picture is to be transmitted over a channel with 4.5-MHz bandwidth and a 35-dB signal-to-noise ratio. Find the capacity of the channel (bps).

c. Discuss how the parameters given in part (a) could be modified to allow transmission of color TV signals without increasing the required value for R.

3.14 Given an amplifier with an effective noise temperature of 10,000 K and a 10-MHz bandwidth, what thermal noise level, in dBW, may we expect at its output?

3.15 What is the channel capacity for a teleprinter channel with a 300-Hz bandwidth and a signal-to-noise ratio of 3 dB, where the noise is white thermal noise?

3.16 A digital signaling system is required to operate at 9600 bps.

a. If a signal element encodes a 4-bit word, what is the minimum required bandwidth of the channel?

b. Repeat part (a) for the case of 8-bit words.

3.17 What is the thermal noise level of a channel with a bandwidth of 10 kHz carrying 1000 watts of power operating at 50°C?

3.18 Given the narrow (usable) audio bandwidth of a telephone transmission facility, a nominal SNR of 56 dB (400,000), and a certain level of distortion

a. What is the theoretical maximum channel capacity (kbps) of traditional telephone lines?

b. What can we say about the actual maximum channel capacity?

3.19 Study the works of Shannon and Nyquist on channel capacity. Each places an upper limit on the bit rate of a channel based on two different approaches. How are the two related?

3.20 Consider a channel with a 1 MHz capacity and an SNR of 63.

a. What is the upper limit to the data rate that the channel can carry?

b. The result of part (a) is the upper limit. However, as a practical matter, better error performance will be achieved at a lower data rate. Assume we choose a data rate of 2/3 as the maximum theoretical limit. How many signal levels are needed to achieve this data rate?

3.21 Given a channel with an intended capacity of 20 Mbps, the bandwidth of the channel is 3 MHz. Assuming white thermal noise, what signal-to-noise ratio is required to achieve this capacity?

3.22 The square wave of Figure 3.7c, with $T = 1$ ms, is passed through a lowpass filter that passes frequencies up to 8 kHz with no attenuation.

a. Find the power in the output waveform.

b. Assuming that at the filter input there is a thermal noise voltage with $N_0 = 0.1$ μW/Hz, find the output signal to noise ratio in dB.

3.23 If the received signal level for a particular digital system is –151 dBW and the receiver system effective noise temperature is 1500 K, what is E_b/N_0 for a link transmitting 2400 bps?

3.24 Fill in the missing elements in the following table of approximate power ratios for various dB levels.

Decibels	1	2	3	4	5	6	7	8	9	10
Losses			0.5							0.1
Gains			2							10

3.25 If an amplifier has a 30-dB voltage gain, what voltage ratio does the gain represent?

3.26 An amplifier has an output of 20 W. What is its output in dBW?

APPENDIX 3A   DECIBELS AND SIGNAL STRENGTH

An important parameter in any transmission system is the signal strength. As a signal propagates along a transmission medium, there will be a loss, or *attenuation*, of signal strength. To compensate, amplifiers may be inserted at various points to impart a gain in signal strength.

It is customary to express gains, losses, and relative levels in decibels because

- Signal strength often falls off exponentially, so loss is easily expressed in terms of the decibel, which is a logarithmic unit.
- The net gain or loss in a cascaded transmission path can be calculated with simple addition and subtraction.

The decibel is a measure of the ratio between two signal levels. The decibel gain is given by:

$$G_{dB} = 10 \log_{10} \frac{P_{out}}{P_{in}}$$

where

G_{dB} = gain, in decibels
P_{in} = input power level
P_{out} = output power level
$\log_{10}$ = logarithm to the base 10

Table 3.2 shows the relationship between decibel values and powers of 10. The table also includes the decibel values for 2 and 1/2.

There is some inconsistency in the literature over the use of the terms **gain** and **loss**. If the value of G_{dB} is positive, this represents an actual gain in power. For example, a gain of 3 dB means that the power has approximately doubled. If the value of G_{dB} is negative, this represents an actual loss in power. For example, a gain of –3 dB means that the power has approximately halved, and this is a loss of power. Normally, this is expressed by saying there is a loss of 3 dB. However, some of the literature would say that this is a loss of –3 dB. It makes more sense to say that a negative gain corresponds to a positive loss. Therefore, we define a decibel loss as:

$$L_{dB} = -10 \log_{10} \frac{P_{out}}{P_{in}} = 10 \log_{10} \frac{P_{in}}{P_{out}} \tag{3.3}$$

Table 3.2   Decibel Values

Power Ratio	dB	Power Ratio	dB
2	3.01	0.5	–3.01
10^1	10	10^{-1}	–10
10^2	20	10^{-2}	–20
10^3	30	10^{-3}	–30
10^4	40	10^{-4}	–40
10^5	50	10^{-5}	–50
10^6	60	10^{-6}	–60

EXAMPLE 3.9 If a signal with a power level of 10 mW is inserted onto a transmission line and the measured power some distance away is 5 mW, the loss can be expressed as

$$L_{dB} = 10 \log(10/5) = 10(0.301) = 3.01 \text{ dB}.$$

Note that the decibel is a measure of relative, not absolute, difference. A loss from 1000 mW to 500 mW is also a loss of approximately 3 dB.

The decibel is also used to measure the difference in voltage, taking into account that power is proportional to the square of the voltage:

$$P = \frac{V^2}{R}$$

where

> P = power dissipated across resistance R
> V = voltage across resistance R

Thus,

$$L_{dB} = 10 \log \frac{P_{in}}{P_{out}} = 10 \log \frac{V_{in}^2/R}{V_{out}^2/R} = 20 \log \frac{V_{in}}{V_{out}}$$

EXAMPLE 3.10 Decibels are useful in determining the gain or loss over a series of transmission elements. Consider a series in which the input is at a power level of 4 mW, the first element is a transmission line with a 12-dB loss (−12-dB gain), the second element is an amplifier with a 35-dB gain, and the third element is a transmission line with a 10-dB loss. The net gain is (−12 + 35 − 10) = 13 dB. To calculate the output power P_{out}:

$$G_{dB} = 13 = 10 \log(P_{out}/4 \text{ mW})$$
$$P_{out} = 4 \times 10^{1.3} \text{ mW} = 79.8 \text{ mW}$$

Decibel values refer to relative magnitudes or changes in magnitude, not to an absolute level. It is convenient to be able to refer to an absolute level of power or voltage in decibels so that gains and losses with reference to an initial signal level may be calculated easily. The **dBW (decibel-watt)** is used extensively in microwave applications. The value of 1 W is selected as a reference and defined to be 0 dBW. The absolute decibel level of power in dBW is defined as:

$$\text{Power}_{dBW} = 10 \log \frac{\text{Power}_W}{1 \text{ W}}$$

EXAMPLE 3.11 A power of 1000 W is 30 dBW, and a power of 1 mW is −30 dBW.

Another common unit is the **dBm (decibel-milliwatt)**, which uses 1 mW as the reference. Thus 0 dBm = 1 mW. The formula is:

$$\text{Power}_{\text{dBm}} = 10 \log \frac{\text{Power}_{\text{mW}}}{1 \text{ mW}}$$

Note the following relationships:

$$+30 \text{ dBm} = 0 \text{ dBW}$$
$$0 \text{ dBm} = -30 \text{ dBW}$$

A unit in common use in cable television and broadband LAN applications is the **dBmV (decibel-millivolt)**. This is an absolute unit with 0 dBmV equivalent to 1 mV. Thus,

$$\text{Voltage}_{\text{dBmV}} = 20 \log \frac{\text{Voltage}_{\text{mV}}}{1 \text{ mV}}$$

In this case, the voltage levels are assumed to be across a 75-Ω resistance.

CHAPTER 4

TRANSMISSION MEDIA

Communication channels in the animal world include touch, sound, sight, and scent. Electric eels even use electric pulses. Ravens also are very expressive. By a combination voice, patterns of feather erection and body posture ravens communicate so clearly that an experienced observer can identify anger, affection, hunger, curiosity, playfulness, fright, boldness, and depression.

— Mind of the Raven, Bernd Heinrich

KEY POINTS

- ◆ The transmission media that are used to convey information can be classified as guided or unguided. Guided media provide a physical path along which the signals are propagated; these include twisted pair, coaxial cable, and optical fiber. Unguided media employ an antenna for transmitting through air, vacuum, or water.

- ◆ Traditionally, twisted pair has been the workhorse for communications of all sorts. Higher data rates over longer distances can be achieved with coaxial cable, and so coaxial cable has often been used for high-speed local area network and for high-capacity long-distance trunk applications. However, the tremendous capacity of optical fiber has made this medium more attractive than coaxial cable, and thus optical fiber has taken over much of the market for high-speed LANs and for long-distance applications.

- ◆ Unguided transmission techniques commonly used for information communications include broadcast radio, terrestrial microwave, and satellite. Infrared transmission is used in some LAN applications.

In a data transmission system, the **transmission medium** is the physical path between transmitter and receiver. Recall from Chapter 3 that for **guided media**, electromagnetic waves are guided along a solid medium, such as copper twisted pair, copper coaxial cable, and optical fiber. For **unguided media**, wireless transmission occurs through the atmosphere, outer space, or water.

The characteristics and quality of a data transmission are determined both by the characteristics of the medium and the characteristics of the signal. In the case of guided media, the medium itself is more important in determining the limitations of transmission.

For unguided media, the bandwidth of the signal produced by the transmitting antenna is more important than the medium in determining transmission characteristics. One key property of signals transmitted by antenna is directionality. In general, signals at lower frequencies are omnidirectional; that is, the signal propagates in all directions from the antenna. At higher frequencies, it is possible to focus the signal into a directional beam.

Data rate and distance are the key considerations in data transmission system design, with emphasis placed on achieving the highest data rates over

101

the longest distances. A number of design factors relating to the transmission medium and the signal determine the data rate and distance:

- **Bandwidth:** All other factors remaining constant, the greater the bandwidth of a signal, the higher the data rate that can be achieved.

- **Transmission impairments:** Impairments, such as attenuation, limit the distance. For guided media, twisted pair generally suffers more impairment than coaxial cable, which in turn suffers more than optical fiber.

- **Interference:** Interference from competing signals in overlapping frequency bands can distort or cancel out a signal. Interference is of particular concern for unguided media, but is also a problem with guided media. For guided media, interference can be caused by emanations coupling from nearby cables (alien crosstalk) or adjacent conductors under the same cable sheath (internal crosstalk). For example, twisted pairs are often bundled together and conduits often carry multiple cables. Interference can also be caused by electromagnetic coupling from unguided transmissions. Proper shielding of a guided medium can minimize this problem.

- **Number of receivers:** A guided medium can be used to construct a point-to-point link or a shared link with multiple attachments. In the latter case, each attachment introduces some attenuation and distortion on the line, limiting distance and/or data rate.

Figure 4.1 depicts the electromagnetic spectrum and indicates the frequencies at which various guided media and unguided transmission techniques operate. In this chapter we examine these guided and unguided alternatives. In all cases, we describe the systems physically, briefly discuss applications, and summarize key transmission characteristics.

4.1 GUIDED TRANSMISSION MEDIA

For guided transmission media, the transmission capacity, in terms of either data rate or bandwidth, depends critically on the distance and on whether the medium is point-to-point or multipoint. Table 4.1 indicates the characteristics typical for the common guided media for long-distance point-to-point applications; we defer a discussion of the use of these media for LANs to Part Four.

The three guided media commonly used for data transmission are twisted pair, coaxial cable, and optical fiber (Figure 4.2). We examine each of these in turn.

Twisted Pair

The least expensive and most widely used guided transmission medium is twisted pair.

PHYSICAL DESCRIPTION A twisted pair consists of two insulated copper wires arranged in a regular spiral pattern. A wire pair acts as a single communication link. Typically, a number of these pairs are bundled together into a cable by wrapping them in a tough protective sheath, or jacket. Over longer distances, cables may contain hundreds of pairs. The twisting tends to decrease the crosstalk interference

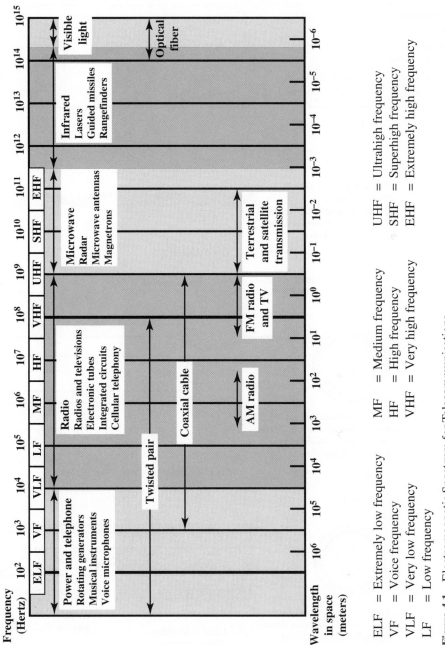

Figure 4.1 Electromagnetic Spectrum for Telecommunications

ELF = Extremely low frequency

VF = Voice frequency

VLF = Very low frequency

LF = Low frequency

MF = Medium frequency

HF = High frequency

VHF = Very high frequency

UHF = Ultrahigh frequency

SHF = Superhigh frequency

EHF = Extremely high frequency

Table 4.1   Point-to-Point Transmission Characteristics of Guided Media

	Frequency Range	**Typical Attenuation**	**Typical Delay**	**Repeater Spacing**
Twisted pair (with loading)	0 to 3.5 kHz	0.2 dB/km @ 1 kHz	50 μs/km	2 km
Twisted pairs (multipair cables)	0 to 1 MHz	0.7 dB/km @ 1 kHz	5 μs/km	2 km
Coaxial cable	0 to 500 MHz	7 dB/km @ 10 MHz	4 μs/km	1 to 9 km
Optical fiber	186 to 370 THz	0.2 to 0.5 dB/km	5 μs/km	40 km

THz = terahertz = 10^{12} Hz

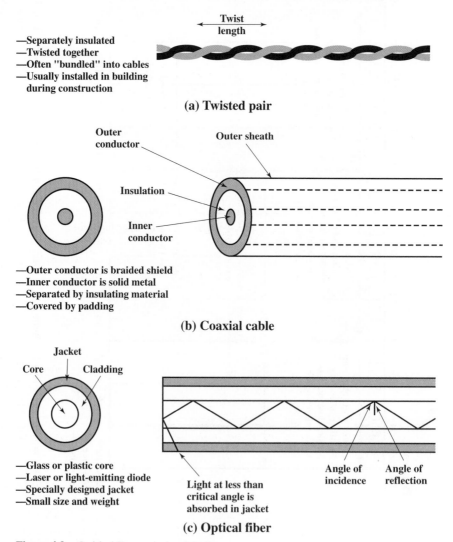

—Separately insulated
—Twisted together
—Often "bundled" into cables
—Usually installed in building
  during construction

(a) Twisted pair

—Outer conductor is braided shield
—Inner conductor is solid metal
—Separated by insulating material
—Covered by padding

(b) Coaxial cable

—Glass or plastic core
—Laser or light-emitting diode
—Specially designed jacket
—Small size and weight

(c) Optical fiber

Figure 4.2   Guided Transmission Media

between adjacent pairs in a cable. Neighboring pairs in a bundle typically have somewhat different twist lengths to reduce the crosstalk interference. On long-distance links, the twist length typically varies from 5 to 15 cm. The wires in a pair have thicknesses of from 0.4 to 0.9 mm.

APPLICATIONS By far the most common guided transmission medium for both analog and digital signals is twisted pair. It is the most commonly used medium in the telephone network and is the workhorse for communications within buildings.

In the telephone system, individual residential telephone sets are connected to the local telephone exchange, or "end office," by twisted-pair wire. These are referred to as **subscriber loops**. Within an office building, each telephone is also connected to a twisted pair, which goes to the in-house private branch exchange (PBX) system or to a Centrex facility at the end office. These twisted-pair installations were designed to support voice traffic using analog signaling. However, by means of a modem, these facilities can handle digital data traffic at modest data rates.

Twisted pair is also the most common medium used for digital signaling. For connections to a digital data switch or digital PBX within a building, a data rate of 64 kbps is common. Ethernet operating over twisted-pair cabling is commonly used within a building for local area networks supporting personal computers. Data rates for Ethernet products are typically in the neighborhood of 100 Mbps to 1 Gbps. Emerging twisted-pair cabling Ethernet technology can support data rates of 10 Gbps. For long-distance applications, twisted pair can be used at data rates of 4 Mbps or more.

Twisted pair is much less expensive than the other commonly used guided transmission media (coaxial cable, optical fiber) and is easier to work with.

TRANSMISSION CHARACTERISTICS Twisted pair may be used to transmit both analog and digital transmission. For analog signals, amplifiers are required for about every 5 to 6 km. For digital transmission (using either analog or digital signals), repeaters are required every 2 or 3 km.

Compared to other commonly used guided transmission media (coaxial cable, optical fiber), twisted pair is limited in distance, bandwidth, and data rate. As Figure 4.3a shows, the attenuation for twisted pair is a very strong function of frequency. Twisted-pair cabling is also susceptible to signal reflections, or return loss, caused by impedance mismatches along the length of the transmission line and crosstalk from adjacent twisted-pairs or twisted-pair cables. Due to the well-controlled geometry of the twisted pair itself (pairs are manufactured with a unique and precise twist rate that varies from pair to pair within a cable) and the media's differential mode transmission scheme (discussed in Chapter 5), twisted-pair cabling used for data transmission is highly immune to interference from low frequency (i.e., 60 Hz) disturbers. Note that twisted-pair cabling is usually run separately from cables transmitting ac power in order to comply with local safety codes, which protect low-voltage telecommunications installers from high-voltage applications. The possibility of electromagnetic interference from high frequency (i.e., greater than 30 MHz) disturbers such as walkie-talkies and other wireless transmitters can be alleviated by using shielded twisted-pair cabling.

For point-to-point analog signaling, a bandwidth of up to about 1 MHz is possible. This accommodates a number of voice channels. For long-distance digital point-to-point signaling, data rates of up to a few Mbps are possible. Ethernet data rates of up to 10 Gbps can be achieved over 100 m of twisted-pair cabling.

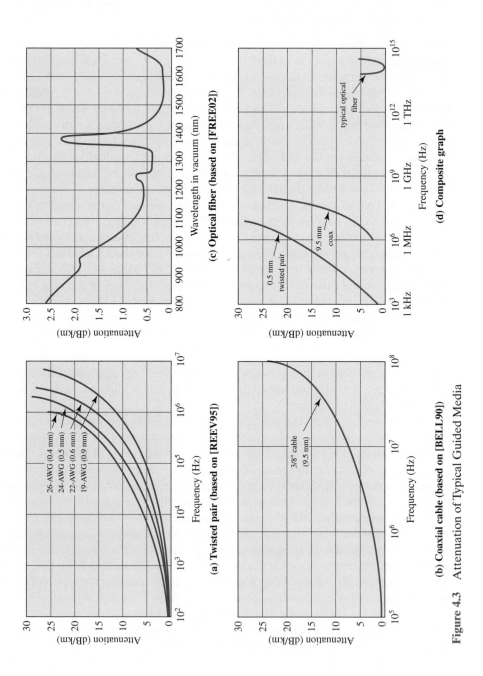

Figure 4.3 Attenuation of Typical Guided Media

Unshielded and Shielded Twisted Pair Twisted pair comes in two varieties: unshielded and shielded. As the name implies, **unshielded twisted pair (UTP)** consists of one or more twisted-pair cables, typically enclosed within an overall thermoplastic jacket, which provides no electromagnetic shielding. The most common form of UTP is ordinary voice-grade telephone wire, which is pre-wired in residential and office buildings. For data transmission purposes, UTP may vary from voice-grade to very high-speed cable for local area networks (LANs). For high-speed LANs, UTP typically has four pairs of wires inside the jacket, with each pair twisted with a different number of twists per centimeter to help eliminate interference between adjacent pairs. The tighter the twisting, the higher the supported transmission rate, and the greater the cost per meter.

Unshielded twisted pair is subject to external electromagnetic interference, including interference from nearby twisted pair and from noise generated in the environment. In an environment with a number of sources of potential interference (e.g., electric motors, wireless devices, and RF transmitters), **shielded twisted pair (STP)** may be a preferred solution. Shielded twisted pair cable is manufactured in three different configurations:

1. Each pair of wires is individually shielded with metallic foil, generally referred to as foil twisted pair (FTP).

2. There is a foil or braid shield inside the jacket covering all wires (as a group). This configuration is sometimes designated as screened twisted pair (F/UTP).

3. There is a shield around each individual pair, as well as around the entire group of wires. This is referred to as fully shielded twisted pair or shielded/foil twisted pair (S/FTP).

The shielding reduces interference and provides better performance at higher data rates. However, it may be more expensive and installers familiar with UTP technology may be reluctant to work with a new media type.

Categories of Twisted Pair for Data Transmission In 1991, the Electronic Industries Association published standard ANSI/EIA/TIA-568, *Commercial Building Telecommunications Cabling Standard*, which specifies the use of voice- and data-grade UTP and F/UTP cabling for in-building data applications. At that time, the specification was felt to be adequate for the range of frequencies and data rates found in office environments. With continuing advances in cable and connector design and test methods, this standard has undergone a number of iterations to provide support for higher data rates using higher-quality cable and connectors. The current version is the responsibility of the Telecommunications Industry Association, and was issued in 2009 as four American National Standards Institute (ANSI) standards:

- **ANSI/TIA-568-C.0 Generic Telecommunications Cabling for Customer Premises:** Enables the planning and installation of a structured cabling system for all types of customer premises.

- **ANSI/TIA-568-C.1 Commercial Building Telecommunications Cabling Standard:** Enables the planning and installation of a structured cabling system for commercial buildings.

- **ANSI/TIA-568-C.2 Balanced Twisted-Pair Telecommunications Cabling and Components Standards:** Specifies minimum requirements for balanced twisted-pair telecommunications cabling (e.g., channels and permanent links) and components (e.g., cable, connectors, connecting hardware, patch cords, equipment cords, work area cords, and jumpers) that are used up to and including the telecommunications outlet/connector and between buildings in a campus environment. This standard also specifies field test procedures and applicable laboratory reference measurement procedures for all transmission parameters.

- **ANSI/TIA-568-C.3 Optical Fiber Cabling Components Standard:** Specifies cable and component transmission performance requirements for premises optical fiber cabling.

The 568-C standards identify a number of categories of cabling and associated components that can be used for premises and campus-wide data distribution. An overlapping standard, jointly issued by the International Standards Organization and the International Electrotechnical Commission (IEC), known as ISO/IEC 11801, second edition, identifies a number of classes of cabling and associated components, which correspond to the 568-C categories.

Table 4.2 summarizes key characteristics of the various categories and classes recognized in the current standards. The categories listed in the table are the following:

- **Category 5e/Class D:** This specification was first published in 2000 in order to address the transmission performance characterization required by applications such as 1-Gbps Ethernet that utilize bidirectional and full four-pair transmission schemes (described in Chapter 16).

- **Category 6/Class E:** In recent years, the majority of structured cabling specified for new buildings has been category 6/class E. This category provides a greater performance margin (also called performance headroom) than category 5e to ensure that the cabling plant could withstand the rigors of the cabling environment and still support 1-Gbps Ethernet when it was time for an application upgrade from 100-Mbps Ethernet. This category was published in 2002, with a targeted lifetime of 10 years, so its use is likely to decline rapidly in new installations.

- **Category 6A/Class E_A:** This specification is targeted at 10-Gbps Ethernet applications.

- **Category 7/Class F:** This specification uses fully shielded twisted pair (i.e., cabling with an overall shield and individually shielded pairs). The advantage of this category over lower grades of cabling is that the use of both an overall shield and a foil shield around individual pairs dramatically decreases internal pair-to-pair crosstalk and external alien crosstalk. This class is targeted for support of next-generation applications beyond 10-Gbps Ethernet.

- **Category 7A/Class F_A:** The requirements for this class are based on class F cabling requirements. The main enhancement is to extend the frequency bandwidth to 1 GHz. This enhancement enables support of all channels of broadband video (e.g., CATV) that operate up to 862 MHz. It is likely that all fully shielded cabling solutions specified in the near future will be class F_A.

Table 4.2 Twisted Pair Categories and Classes

	Category 5e Class D	Category 6 Class E	Category 6A Class E$_A$	Category 7 Class F	Category 7$_A$ Class F$_A$
Bandwidth	100 MHz	250 MHz	500 MHz	600 MHz	1,000 MHz
Cable type	UTP	UTP/FTP	UTP/FTP	S/FTP	S/FTP
Insertion loss (dB)	24	21.3	20.9	20.8	20.3
NEXT loss (dB)	30.1	39.9	39.9	62.9	65
ACR (dB)	6.1	18.6	19	42.1	44.1

UTP = Unshielded twisted pair
FTP = Foil twisted pair
S/FTP = Shielded/foil twisted pair

Table 4.2 includes three key performance parameters. **Insertion loss** in this context refers to the amount of **attenuation** across the link from the transmitting system to the receiving system. Thus, lower dB values are better. The table shows the amount of attenuation at a frequency of 100 MHz. This is the standard frequency used in tables comparing various classes of twisted pair. However, attenuation is an increasing function of frequency, and the 568 standards specify that attenuation at various frequencies. In accordance with ANSI/TIA-568-C.2 and ISO/IEC 11801 2nd edition, all transmission characteristics are specified as a worst case value for a 100 m length. While cabling lengths may be less than 100 m, no provisions are provided in the standards for the scaling of the specified limits. Attenuation in decibels is a linear function of distance, so attenuation for shorter or longer distances is easily calculated. In practice, as is shown in Chapter 16, distances much less than 100 m are typical for Ethernet at data rates of 1 GB and above.

Near-end crosstalk (NEXT) loss as it applies to twisted- pair wiring systems is the coupling of the signal from one pair of conductors to another pair. These conductors may be the metal pins in a connector or wire pairs in a cable. The near end refers to coupling that takes place when the transmit signal entering the link couples back to the receive conductor pair at that same end of the link (i.e., the near-end transmitted signal is picked up by the near- receive pair). We can think of this as noise introduced into the system, so higher dB loss values are better; that is, greater NEXT loss magnitudes are associated with less crosstalk noise. Figure 4.4 illustrates the relationship between NEXT loss and insertion loss at system A. A transmitted signal from system B, with a transmitted signal power of P_t is received at A with a reduced signal power of P_r. At the same time, system A is transmitting to signal B, and we assume that the transmission is at the same transmit signal power of P_t. Due to crosstalk, a certain level of signal from A's transmitter is induced on the receive wire pair at A with a power level of P_c; this is the crosstalk signal. Clearly, we need to have $P_r > P_c$ to be able to intelligibly receive the intended signal, and the greater the difference between P_r and P_c, the better. Unlike insertion loss, NEXT loss does not vary as a function of the length of the link, because, as Figure 4.4 indicates, NEXT loss is an end phenomenon. NEXT loss varies as a function of frequency, with losses increasing as a function of frequency. That is, the amount of signal power from the near-end transmitter that couples over to an adjacent transmission line increases as a function of frequency.

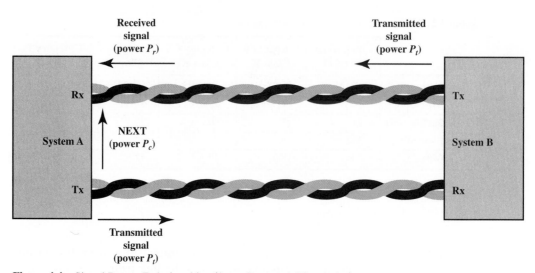

Figure 4.4 Signal Power Relationships (from System A Viewpoint)

For Table 4.2, insertion loss and NEXT loss are defined using the same form as Equation (3.3):

$$A_{dB} = 10 \log_{10}\frac{P_t}{P_r} \qquad NEXT_{dB} = 10 \log_{10}\frac{P_t}{P_c}$$

Note that NEXT loss is defined in terms of the amount of signal loss between the local transmitter and the local receiver. Thus, smaller values of NEXT loss correspond to increasing amount of crosstalk.

Another important parameter used in the 11801, second edition specification, is the **attenuation-to-crosstalk ratio (ACR)**, which is defined as $ACR_{dB} = NEXT_{dB} - A_{dB}$. ACR is a measure of how much larger the received signal strength is compared to the crosstalk on the same pair. A positive value is required for successful operation. To see that this is so, consider the following derivation. We want $NEXT_{dB} > A_{dB}$. This implies

$$10 \log_{10}\frac{P_t}{P_c} > 10 \log_{10}\frac{P_t}{P_r}$$
$$\log_{10}P_t - \log_{10}P_c > \log_{10}P_t - \log_{10}P_r$$
$$\log_{10}P_r > \log_{10}P_c$$
$$P_r > P_c$$

which is the desired condition.

EXAMPLE 4.1 Figure 4.5 Shows attenuation (insertion loss) and NEXT loss as a function of frequency for category 6A twisted pair. As usual, a link of 100 m is assumed. The figure suggests that above a frequency of about 250 MHz, communication is impractical. Yet Table 4.2 indicates that category 6A is specified to operate up to 500 MHz. The explanation is that the 10-Gbps application employs crosstalk cancellation, which effectively provides a positive ACR margin out to 500 MHz. The standard indicates a worst-case situation, and engineering practices, such as crosstalk cancellation, are used to overcome the worst-case limitations.

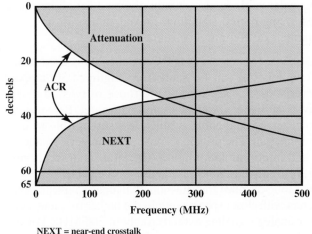

NEXT = near-end crosstalk
ACR = attenuation-to-crosstalk ratio

Figure 4.5   Category 6A Channel Requirements

Coaxial Cable

PHYSICAL DESCRIPTION Coaxial cable, like twisted pair, consists of two conductors, but is constructed differently to permit it to operate over a wider range of frequencies. It consists of a hollow outer cylindrical conductor that surrounds a single inner wire conductor (Figure 4.2b). The inner conductor is held in place by either regularly spaced insulating rings or a solid dielectric material. The outer conductor is covered with a jacket or shield. A single coaxial cable has a diameter of from 1 to 2.5 cm. Coaxial cable can be used over longer distances and support more stations on a shared line than twisted pair.

APPLICATIONS Coaxial cable is a versatile transmission medium, used in a wide variety of applications. The most important of these are

- Television distribution
- Long-distance telephone transmission
- Short-run computer system links
- Local area networks

Coaxial cable is widely used as a means of distributing TV signals to individual homes—cable TV. From its modest beginnings as Community Antenna Television (CATV), designed to provide service to remote areas, cable TV reaches almost as many homes and offices as the telephone. A cable TV system can carry dozens or even hundreds of TV channels at ranges up to a few tens of kilometers.

Coaxial cable has traditionally been an important part of the long-distance telephone network. Today, it faces increasing competition from optical fiber, terrestrial microwave, and satellite. Using frequency division multiplexing (FDM, see Chapter 8), a coaxial cable can carry over 10,000 voice channels simultaneously.

Coaxial cable is also commonly used for short-range connections between devices. Using digital signaling, coaxial cable can be used to provide high-speed I/O channels on computer systems.

TRANSMISSION CHARACTERISTICS Coaxial cable is used to transmit both analog and digital signals. As can be seen from Figure 4.3b, coaxial cable has frequency characteristics that are superior to those of twisted pair and can hence be used effectively at higher frequencies and data rates. Because of its shielded, concentric construction, coaxial cable is much less susceptible to interference and crosstalk than twisted pair. The principal constraints on performance are attenuation, thermal noise, and intermodulation noise. The latter is present only when several channels (FDM) or frequency bands are in use on the cable.

For long-distance transmission of analog signals, amplifiers are needed every few kilometers, with closer spacing required if higher frequencies are used. The usable spectrum for analog signaling extends to about 500 MHz. For digital signaling, repeaters are needed every kilometer or so, with closer spacing needed for higher data rates.

Optical Fiber

PHYSICAL DESCRIPTION An optical fiber is a thin (2 to 125 μm), flexible medium capable of guiding an optical ray. Various glasses and plastics can be used to make optical fibers. The lowest losses have been obtained using fibers of ultrapure fused silica. Ultrapure fiber is difficult to manufacture; higher-loss multicomponent glass fibers are more economical and still provide good performance. Plastic fiber is even less costly and can be used for short-haul links, for which moderately high losses are acceptable.

An optical fiber cable has a cylindrical shape and consists of three concentric sections: the core, the cladding, and the jacket (Figure 4.2c). The **core** is the innermost section and consists of one or more very thin strands, or fibers, made of glass or plastic; the core has a diameter in the range of 8 to 50 μm. Each fiber is surrounded by its own **cladding**, a glass or plastic coating that has optical properties different from those of the core and a diameter of 125 μm. The interface between the core and cladding acts as a reflector to confine light that would otherwise escape the core. The outermost layer, surrounding one or a bundle of cladded fibers, is the **jacket**. The jacket is composed of plastic and other material layered to protect against moisture, abrasion, crushing, and other environmental dangers.

APPLICATIONS Optical fiber already enjoys considerable use in long-distance telecommunications, and its use in military applications is growing. The continuing improvements in performance and decline in prices, together with the inherent advantages of optical fiber, have made it increasingly attractive for local area networking. The following characteristics distinguish optical fiber from twisted pair or coaxial cable:

- **Greater capacity:** The potential bandwidth, and hence data rate, of optical fiber is immense; data rates of hundreds of Gbps over tens of kilometers have been demonstrated. Compare this to the practical maximum of hundreds of Mbps over about 1 km for coaxial cable and just a few Mbps over 1 km or up to 100 Mbps to 10 Gbps over a few tens of meters for twisted pair.

- **Smaller size and lighter weight:** Optical fibers are considerably thinner than coaxial cable or bundled twisted-pair cable—at least an order of magnitude thinner for comparable information transmission capacity. For cramped conduits in buildings and underground along public rights-of-way, the advantage of small size is considerable. The corresponding reduction in weight reduces structural support requirements.

- **Lower attenuation:** Attenuation is significantly lower for optical fiber than for coaxial cable or twisted pair (Figure 4.3c) and is constant over a wide range.

- **Electromagnetic isolation:** Optical fiber systems are not affected by external electromagnetic fields. Thus the system is not vulnerable to interference, impulse noise, or crosstalk. By the same token, fibers do not radiate energy, so there is little interference with other equipment and there is a high degree of security from eavesdropping. In addition, fiber is inherently difficult to tap.

- **Greater repeater spacing:** Fewer repeaters mean lower cost and fewer sources of error. The performance of optical fiber systems from this point of view has been steadily improving. Repeater spacing in the tens of kilometers for optical fiber is common, and repeater spacings of hundreds of kilometers have been demonstrated. Coaxial and twisted-pair systems generally have repeaters every few kilometers.

Five basic categories of application have become important for optical fiber:

- Long-haul trunks
- Metropolitan trunks
- Rural exchange trunks
- Subscriber loops
- Local area networks

Long-haul fiber transmission is becoming increasingly common in the telephone network. Long-haul routes average about 1500 km in length and offer high capacity (typically 20,000 to 60,000 voice channels). These systems compete economically with microwave and have so underpriced coaxial cable in many developed countries that coaxial cable is rapidly being phased out of the telephone network in such countries. Undersea optical fiber cables have also enjoyed increasing use.

Metropolitan trunking circuits have an average length of 12 km and may have as many as 100,000 voice channels in a trunk group. Most facilities are installed in underground conduits and are repeaterless, joining telephone exchanges in a metropolitan or city area. Included in this category are routes that link long-haul microwave facilities that terminate at a city perimeter to the main telephone exchange building downtown.

Rural exchange trunks have circuit lengths ranging from 40 to 160 km and link towns and villages. In the United States, they often connect the exchanges of different telephone companies. Most of these systems have fewer than 5000 voice channels. The technology used in these applications competes with microwave facilities.

Subscriber loop circuits are fibers that run directly from the central exchange to a subscriber. These facilities are beginning to displace twisted pair and coaxial cable links as the telephone networks evolve into full-service networks capable of handling not only voice and data, but also image and video. The initial penetration of optical fiber in this application has been for the business subscriber, but fiber transmission into the home is now a significant presence in many areas.

A final important application of optical fiber is for local area networks. Standards have been developed and products introduced for optical fiber networks that have a total capacity of 100 Mbps to 10 Gbps and can support hundreds or even thousands of stations in a large office building or a complex of buildings.

The advantages of optical fiber over twisted-pair and coaxial cable become more compelling as the demand for all types of information (voice, data, image, video) increases.

TRANSMISSION CHARACTERISTICS Optical fiber transmits a signal-encoded beam of light by means of **total internal reflection**. Total internal reflection can occur in any transparent medium that has a higher index of refraction than the surrounding medium. In effect, the optical fiber acts as a waveguide for frequencies in the range of about 10^{14} to 10^{15} Hz; this covers portions of the infrared and visible spectra.

Figure 4.6 shows the principle of optical fiber transmission. Light from a source enters the cylindrical glass or plastic core. Rays at shallow angles are reflected and propagated along the fiber; other rays are absorbed by the surrounding material. This form of propagation is called **step-index multimode**, referring to the variety of angles that reflect. With multimode transmission, multiple propagation paths exist, each with a different path length and hence time to traverse the fiber. This causes signal elements (light pulses) to spread out in time, which limits the rate at which data can be accurately received. Put another way, the need to leave spacing between the pulses limits data rate. This type of fiber is best suited for transmission over very short distances. When the fiber core radius is reduced, fewer angles will reflect. By reducing the radius of the core to the order of a wavelength, only a single

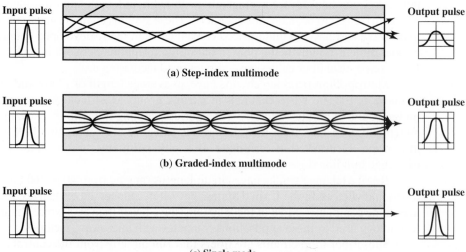

(a) Step-index multimode

(b) Graded-index multimode

(c) Single mode

Figure 4.6 Optical Fiber Transmission Modes

angle or mode can pass: the axial ray. This **single-mode** propagation provides superior performance for the following reason. Because there is a single transmission path with single-mode transmission, the distortion found in multimode cannot occur. Single mode is typically used for long-distance applications, including telephone and cable television. Finally, by varying the index of refraction of the core, a third type of transmission, known as **graded-index multimode**, is possible. This type is intermediate between the other two in characteristics. The higher refractive index (discussed subsequently) at the center makes the light rays moving down the axis advance more slowly than those near the cladding. Rather than zig-zagging off the cladding, light in the core curves helically because of the graded index, reducing its travel distance. The shortened path and higher speed allows light at the periphery to arrive at a receiver at about the same time as the straight rays in the core axis. Graded-index fibers are often used in local area networks.

Two different types of light source are used in fiber optic systems: the light-emitting diode (LED) and the injection laser diode (ILD). Both are semiconductor devices that emit a beam of light when a voltage is applied. The LED is less costly, operates over a greater temperature range, and has a longer operational life. The ILD, which operates on the laser principle, is more efficient and can sustain greater data rates.

There is a relationship among the wavelength employed, the type of transmission, and the achievable data rate. Both single mode and multimode can support several different wavelengths of light and can employ laser or LED light sources. In optical fiber, based on the attenuation characteristics of the medium and on properties of light sources and receivers, four transmission windows are appropriate, shown in Table 4.3.

Note the tremendous bandwidths available. For the four windows, the respective bandwidths are 33 THz, 12 THz, 4 THz, and 7 THz.[1] This is several orders of magnitude greater than the bandwidth available in the radio-frequency spectrum.

One confusing aspect of reported attenuation figures for fiber optic transmission is that, invariably, fiber optic performance is specified in terms of wavelength rather than frequency. The wavelengths that appear in graphs and tables are the wavelengths corresponding to transmission in a vacuum. However, on the fiber, the

Table 4.3 Frequency Utilization for Fiber Applications

Wavelength (in vacuum) range (nm)	Frequency Range (THz)	Band Label	Fiber Type	Application
820 to 900	366 to 333		Multimode	LAN
1280 to 1350	234 to 222	S	Single mode	Various
1528 to 1561	196 to 192	C	Single mode	WDM
1561 to 1620	192 to 185	L	Single mode	WDM

WDM = wavelength division multiplexing (see Chapter 8)

---

[1]1 THz = 10^{12} Hz. For a definition of numerical prefixes in common use, see the supporting document at William Stallings.com.

velocity of propagation is less than the speed of light in a vacuum (c); the result is that although the frequency of the signal is unchanged, the wavelength is changed.

EXAMPLE 4.2 For a wavelength in vacuum of 1550 nm, the corresponding frequency is $f = c/\lambda = (3 \times 10^8)/(1550 \times 10^{-9}) = 193.4 \times 10^{12} = 193.4$ THz. For a typical single-mode fiber, the velocity of propagation is approximately $v = 2.04 \times 10^8$. In this case, a frequency of 193.4 THz corresponds to a wavelength of $\lambda = v/f = (2.04 \times 10^8)/(193.4 \times 10^{12}) = 1055$ nm. Therefore, on this fiber, when a wavelength of 1550 nm is cited, the actual wavelength on the fiber is 1055 nm.

The four transmission windows are in the infrared portion of the frequency spectrum, below the visible-light portion, which is 400 to 700 nm. The loss is lower at higher wavelengths, allowing greater data rates over longer distances. Many local applications today use 850-nm LED light sources. Although this combination is relatively inexpensive, it is generally limited to data rates under 100 Mbps and distances of a few kilometers. To achieve higher data rates and longer distances, a 1300-nm LED or laser source is needed. The highest data rates and longest distances require 1500-nm laser sources.

Figure 4.3c shows attenuation versus wavelength for a typical optical fiber. The unusual shape of the curve is due to the combination of a variety of factors that contribute to attenuation. The two most important of these are absorption and scattering. In this context, the term *scattering* refers to the change in direction of light rays after they strike small particles or impurities in the medium.

4.2 WIRELESS TRANSMISSION

Three general ranges of frequencies are of interest in our discussion of wireless transmission. Frequencies in the range of about 1 GHz (gigahertz = 10^9 hertz) to 40 GHz are referred to as **microwave frequencies**. At these frequencies, highly directional beams are possible, and microwave is quite suitable for point-to-point transmission. Microwave is also used for satellite communications. Frequencies in the range of 30 MHz to 1 GHz are suitable for omnidirectional applications. We refer to this range as the **radio** range.

Another important frequency range, for local applications, is the infrared portion of the spectrum. This covers, roughly, from 3×10^{11} to 2×10^{14} Hz. Infrared is useful to local point-to-point and multipoint applications within confined areas, such as a single room.

For unguided media, transmission and reception are achieved by means of an antenna. Before looking at specific categories of wireless transmission, we provide a brief introduction to antennas.

Antennas

An antenna can be defined as an electrical conductor or system of conductors used either for radiating electromagnetic energy or for collecting electromagnetic energy. For transmission of a signal, radio-frequency electrical energy from the transmitter is converted into electromagnetic energy by the antenna and radiated into the surrounding environment (atmosphere, space, water). For reception of a signal, electromagnetic energy impinging on the antenna is converted into radio-frequency electrical energy and fed into the receiver.

In two-way communication, the same antenna can be and often is used for both transmission and reception. This is possible because any antenna transfers energy from the surrounding environment to its input receiver terminals with the same efficiency that it transfers energy from the output transmitter terminals into the surrounding environment, assuming that the same frequency is used in both directions. Put another way, antenna characteristics are essentially the same whether an antenna is sending or receiving electromagnetic energy.

An antenna radiates power in all directions but, typically, does not perform equally well in all directions. A common way to characterize the performance of an antenna is the radiation pattern, which is a graphical representation of the radiation properties of an antenna as a function of space coordinates. The simplest pattern is produced by an idealized antenna known as the isotropic antenna. An **isotropic antenna** is a point in space that radiates power in all directions equally. The actual radiation pattern for the isotropic antenna is a sphere with the antenna at the center.

PARABOLIC REFLECTIVE ANTENNA An important type of antenna is the **parabolic reflective antenna**, which is used in terrestrial microwave and satellite applications. A parabola is the locus of all points equidistant from a fixed line and a fixed point not on the line. The fixed point is called the *focus* and the fixed line is called the *directrix* (Figure 4.7a). If a parabola is revolved about its axis, the surface generated is called a *paraboloid*. A cross section through the paraboloid parallel to its axis forms a parabola and a cross section perpendicular to the axis forms a circle. Such surfaces are used in automobile headlights, optical and radio telescopes, and microwave antennas because of the following property: If a source

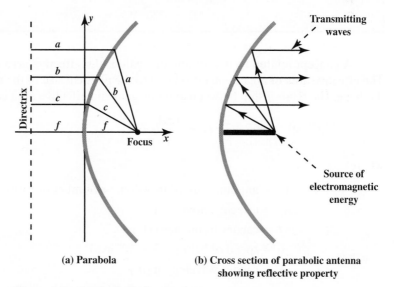

(a) Parabola

(b) Cross section of parabolic antenna showing reflective property

Figure 4.7 Parabolic Reflective Antenna

of electromagnetic energy (or sound) is placed at the focus of the paraboloid, and if the paraboloid is a reflecting surface, then the wave bounces back in lines parallel to the axis of the paraboloid; Figure 4.7b shows this effect in cross section. In theory, this effect creates a parallel beam without dispersion. In practice, there is some dispersion, because the source of energy must occupy more than one point. The larger the diameter of the antenna, the more tightly directional is the beam. On reception, if incoming waves are parallel to the axis of the reflecting paraboloid, the resulting signal is concentrated at the focus.

ANTENNA GAIN **Antenna gain** is a measure of the directionality of an antenna. Antenna gain is defined as the power output, in a particular direction, compared to that produced in any direction by a perfect omnidirectional antenna (isotropic antenna). Specifically, $G_{dB} = 10 \log (P_2/P_1)$, where G is the antenna gain, P_1 is the radiated power of the directional antenna, and P_2 is the radiated power from the reference antenna. For example, if an antenna has a gain of 3 dB, that antenna improves upon the isotropic antenna in that direction by 3 dB, or a factor of 2. The increased power radiated in a given direction is at the expense of other directions. In effect, increased power is radiated in one direction by reducing the power radiated in other directions. It is important to note that antenna gain does not refer to obtaining more output power than input power but rather to directionality.

EXAMPLE 4.3 Consider a directional antenna that has a gain of 6 dB over a reference antenna and that radiates 700 W. How much power must the reference antenna radiate to provide the same signal power in the preferred direction? To solve, we have

$$6 = 10 \ \log(P_2/700)$$
$$P_2/700 = 10^{0.6} = 3.98$$
$$P_2 = 2786 \, \text{W}$$

A concept related to that of antenna gain is the **effective area** of an antenna. The effective area of an antenna is related to the physical size of the antenna and to its shape. The relationship between antenna gain and effective area is:

$$G = \frac{4\pi A_e}{\lambda^2} = \frac{4\pi f^2 A_e}{c^2} \tag{4.1}$$

where

$$G = \text{antenna gain (dimensionless number or ratio)}$$
$$A_e = \text{effective area (m}^2\text{)}$$
$$f = \text{carrier frequency (Hz)}$$
$$c = \text{speed of light } (\approx 3 \times 10^8 \text{ m/s})$$
$$\lambda = \text{carrier wavelength (m)}$$

Expressed in decibels, we have $G_{dB} = 10 \log G$

For example, the effective area of an ideal isotropic antenna is $\lambda^2/4\pi$, with a power gain of 1; the effective area of a parabolic antenna with a face area of A is $0.56A$, with a power gain of $7A/\lambda^2$.

EXAMPLE 4.4 For a parabolic reflective antenna with a diameter of 2 m, operating at 12 GHz, what are the effective area and the antenna gain? We have an area of $A \times \pi r^2 = \pi$ and an effective area of $A_e = 0.56\pi$. The wavelength is $\lambda = c/f = (3 \times 10^8)/(12 \times 10^9) = 0.025$ m. Then

$$G = (7A)/\lambda^2 = (7 \times \pi)/(0.025)^2 = 35{,}186$$
$$G_{dB} = 10 \log 35{,}186 = 45.46 \text{ dB}$$

Terrestrial Microwave

PHYSICAL DESCRIPTION The most common type of microwave antenna is the parabolic "dish." A typical size is about 3 m in diameter. The antenna is fixed rigidly and focuses a narrow beam to achieve line-of-sight transmission to the receiving antenna. Microwave antennas are usually located at substantial heights above ground level to extend the range between antennas and to be able to transmit over intervening obstacles. To achieve long-distance transmission, a series of microwave relay towers is used, and point-to-point microwave links are strung together over the desired distance.

APPLICATIONS The primary use for terrestrial microwave systems is in long-haul telecommunications service, as an alternative to coaxial cable or optical fiber. The microwave facility requires far fewer amplifiers or repeaters than coaxial cable over the same distance, but requires line-of-sight transmission. Microwave is commonly used for both voice and television transmission.

Another increasingly common use of microwave is for short point-to-point links between buildings. This can be used for closed-circuit TV or as a data link between local area networks. Short-haul microwave can also be used for the so-called bypass application. A business can establish a microwave link to a long-distance telecommunications facility in the same city, bypassing the local telephone company.

Another important use of microwave is in cellular systems, examined in Chapter 14.

TRANSMISSION CHARACTERISTICS Microwave transmission covers a substantial portion of the electromagnetic spectrum. Common frequencies used for transmission are in the range 1 to 40 GHz. The higher the frequency used, the higher the potential bandwidth, and therefore the higher the potential data rate. Table 4.4 indicates bandwidth and data rate for some typical systems.

As with any transmission system, a main source of loss is attenuation. For microwave (and radio frequencies), the loss can be expressed as

$$L = 10 \log\left(\frac{4\pi d}{\lambda}\right)^2 \text{ dB} \qquad \textbf{(4.2)}$$

Table 4.4 Typical Digital Microwave Performance

Band (GHz)	Bandwidth (MHz)	Data Rate (Mbps)
2	7	12
6	30	90
11	40	135
18	220	274

where d is the distance and λ is the wavelength, in the same units. Thus, loss varies as the square of the distance. In contrast, for twisted-pair and coaxial cable, loss varies exponentially with distance (linear in decibels). Thus repeaters or amplifiers may be placed farther apart for microwave systems—10 to 100 km is typical. Attenuation is increased with rainfall. The effects of rainfall become especially noticeable above 10 GHz. Another source of impairment is interference. With the growing popularity of microwave, transmission areas overlap and interference is always a danger. Thus the assignment of frequency bands is strictly regulated.

The most common bands for long-haul telecommunications are the 4-GHz to 6-GHz bands. With increasing congestion at these frequencies, the 11-GHz band is now coming into use. The 12-GHz band is used as a component of cable TV systems. Microwave links are used to provide TV signals to local CATV installations; the signals are then distributed to individual subscribers via coaxial cable. Higher-frequency microwave is being used for short point-to-point links between buildings; typically, the 22-GHz band is used. The higher microwave frequencies are less useful for longer distances because of increased attenuation but are quite adequate for shorter distances. In addition, at the higher frequencies, the antennas are smaller and cheaper.

Satellite Microwave

PHYSICAL DESCRIPTION A communication satellite is, in effect, a microwave relay station. It is used to link two or more ground-based microwave transmitter/receivers, known as **earth stations**, or ground stations. The satellite receives transmissions on one frequency band (**uplink**), amplifies or repeats the signal, and transmits it on another frequency (**downlink**). A single orbiting satellite will operate on a number of frequency bands, called **transponder channels**, or simply **transponders**.

Figure 4.8 depicts in a general way two common configurations for satellite communication. In the first, the satellite is being used to provide a point-to-point link between two distant ground-based antennas. In the second, the satellite provides communications between one ground-based transmitter and a number of ground-based receivers.

For a communication satellite to function effectively, it is generally required that it remain stationary with respect to its position over the Earth. Otherwise, it would not be within the line of sight of its earth stations at all times. To remain stationary, the satellite must have a period of rotation equal to the Earth's period of rotation. This match occurs at a height of 35,863 km at the equator.

Two satellites using the same frequency band, if close enough together, interfere with each other. To avoid this, current standards require a 4° spacing (angular

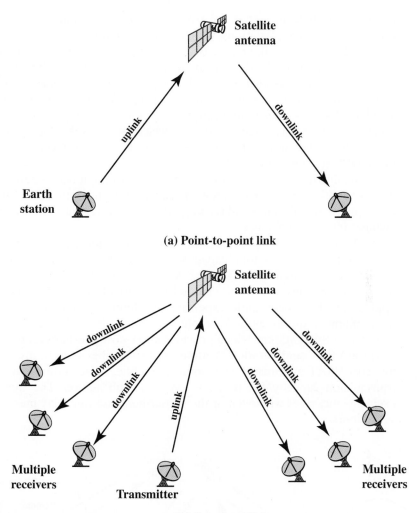

Figure 4.8 Satellite Communication Configurations

displacement as measured from the Earth) in the 4/6-GHz band and a 3° spacing at 12/14 GHz. Thus the number of possible satellites is quite limited.

APPLICATIONS Among the most important applications for satellites:

- Television distribution
- Long-distance telephone transmission
- Private business networks
- Global positioning

Because of their broadcast nature, satellites are well suited to television distribution and are being used extensively in the United States and throughout the world for this purpose. In its traditional use, a network provides programming from a central location. Programs are transmitted to the satellite and then broadcast down to a number of stations, which then distribute the programs to individual viewers. One network, the Public Broadcasting Service (PBS), distributes its television programming almost exclusively by the use of satellite channels. Other commercial networks also make substantial use of satellite, and cable television systems are receiving an ever-increasing proportion of their programming from satellites. The most recent application of satellite technology to television distribution is direct broadcast satellite (DBS), in which satellite video signals are transmitted directly to the home user. The decreasing cost and size of receiving antennas have made DBS economically feasible.

Satellite transmission is also used for point-to-point trunks between telephone exchange offices in public telephone networks. It is the optimum medium for high-usage international trunks and is competitive with terrestrial systems for many long-distance intranational links.

There are a number of business data applications for satellite. The satellite provider can divide the total capacity into a number of channels and lease these channels to individual business users. A user equipped with the antennas at a number of sites can use a satellite channel for a private network. Traditionally, such applications have been quite expensive and limited to larger organizations with high-volume requirements. A recent development is the very small aperture terminal (VSAT) system, which provides a low-cost alternative. Figure 4.9 depicts a typical VSAT configuration. A number of subscriber stations are equipped with low-cost VSAT antennas. Using some discipline, these stations share a satellite transmission capacity for transmission to a hub station. The hub station can exchange messages with each of the subscribers and can relay messages between subscribers.

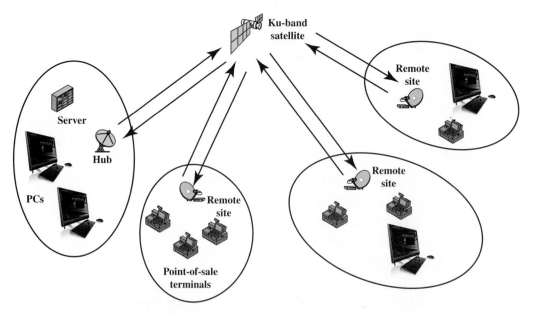

Figure 4.9   Typical VSAT Configuration

A final application of satellites, which has become pervasive, is worthy of note. The Navstar Global Positioning System, or GPS for short, consists of three segments or components:

- A constellation of satellites (currently 27) orbiting about 20,000 km above the Earth's surface, which transmit ranging signals on two frequencies in the microwave part of the radio spectrum
- A control segment which maintains GPS through a system of ground monitor stations and satellite upload facilities
- The user receivers—both civil and military

Each satellite transmits a unique digital code sequence of 1s and 0s, precisely timed by an atomic clock, which is picked up by a GPS receiver's antenna and matched with the same code sequence generated inside the receiver. By lining up or matching the signals, the receiver determines how long it takes the signals to travel from the satellite to the receiver. These timing measurements are converted to distances using the speed of light. Measuring distances to four or more satellites simultaneously and knowing the exact locations of the satellites (included in the signals transmitted by the satellites), the receiver can determine its latitude, longitude, and height while at the same time synchronizing its clock with the GPS time standard which also makes the receiver a precise time piece.

TRANSMISSION CHARACTERISTICS The optimum frequency range for satellite transmission is in the range 1 to 10 GHz. Below 1 GHz, there is significant noise from natural sources, including galactic, solar, and atmospheric noise, and human-made interference from various electronic devices. Above 10 GHz, the signal is severely attenuated by atmospheric absorption and precipitation.

Most satellites providing point-to-point service today use a frequency bandwidth in the range 5.925 to 6.425 GHz for transmission from Earth to satellite (uplink) and a bandwidth in the range 3.7 to 4.2 GHz for transmission from satellite to Earth (downlink). This combination is referred to as the 4/6-GHz band. Note that the uplink and downlink frequencies differ. For continuous operation without interference, a satellite cannot transmit and receive on the same frequency. Thus signals received from a ground station on one frequency must be transmitted back on another.

The 4/6 GHz band is within the optimum zone of 1 to 10 GHz but has become saturated. Other frequencies in that range are unavailable because of sources of interference operating at those frequencies, usually terrestrial microwave. Therefore, the 12/14-GHz band has been developed (uplink: 14 to 14.5 GHz; downlink: 11.7 to 12.2 GHz). At this frequency band, attenuation problems must be overcome. However, smaller and cheaper earth-station receivers can be used. It is anticipated that this band will also saturate, and use is projected for the 20/30-GHz band (uplink: 27.5 to 30.0 GHz; downlink: 17.7 to 20.2 GHz). This band experiences even greater attenuation problems but will allow greater bandwidth (2500 MHz versus 500 MHz) and even smaller and cheaper receivers.

Several properties of satellite communication should be noted. First, because of the long distances involved, there is a propagation delay of about a quarter second from transmission from one earth station to reception by another earth station. This delay is noticeable in ordinary telephone conversations. It also introduces problems in the areas of error control and flow control, which we discuss in later chapters. Second, satellite microwave is inherently a broadcast facility. Many stations can transmit to the satellite, and a transmission from a satellite can be received by many stations.

Broadcast Radio

PHYSICAL DESCRIPTION The principal difference between broadcast radio and microwave is that the former is omnidirectional and the latter is directional. Thus broadcast radio does not require dish-shaped antennas, and the antennas need not be rigidly mounted to a precise alignment.

APPLICATIONS **Radio** is a general term used to encompass frequencies in the range of 3 kHz to 300 GHz. We are using the informal term **broadcast radio** to cover the VHF and part of the UHF band: 30 MHz to 1 GHz. This range covers FM radio and UHF and VHF television. This range is also used for a number of data networking applications.

TRANSMISSION CHARACTERISTICS The range 30 MHz to 1 GHz is an effective one for broadcast communications. Unlike the case for lower-frequency electromagnetic waves, the ionosphere is transparent to radio waves above 30 MHz. Thus transmission is limited to the line of sight, and distant transmitters will not interfere with each other due to reflection from the atmosphere. Unlike the higher frequencies of the microwave region, broadcast radio waves are less sensitive to attenuation from rainfall.

As with microwave, the amount of attenuation due to distance obeys Equation (4.2), namely $10 \log\left(\frac{4\pi d}{\lambda}\right)^2$ dB. Because of the longer wavelength, radio waves suffer relatively less attenuation.

A prime source of impairment for broadcast radio waves is multipath interference. Reflection from land, water, and natural or human-made objects can create multiple paths between antennas.

Infrared

Infrared communications is achieved using transmitters/receivers (transceivers) that modulate noncoherent infrared light. Transceivers must be within the line of sight of each other either directly or via reflection from a light-colored surface such as the ceiling of a room.

One important difference between infrared and microwave transmission is that the former does not penetrate walls. Thus the security and interference problems encountered in microwave systems are not present. Furthermore, there is no frequency allocation issue with infrared, because no licensing is required.

4.3 WIRELESS PROPAGATION

A signal radiated from an antenna travels along one of three routes: ground wave, sky wave, or line of sight (LOS). Table 4.5 shows in which frequency range each predominates. In this book, we are almost exclusively concerned with LOS communication, but a short overview of each mode is given in this section.

Table 4.5 Frequency Bands

Band	Frequency Range	Free-Space Wavelength Range	Propagation Characteristics	Typical Use
ELF (extremely low frequency)	30 to 300 Hz	10,000 to 1000 km	GW	Power line frequencies; used by some home control systems
VF (voice frequency)	300 to 3000 Hz	1000 to 100 km	GW	Used by the telephone system for analog subscriber lines
VLF (very low frequency)	3 to 30 kHz	100 to 10 km	GW; low attenuation day and night; high atmospheric noise level	Long-range navigation; submarine communication
LF (low frequency)	30 to 300 kHz	10 to 1 km	GW; slightly less reliable than VLF; absorption in daytime	Long-range navigation; marine communication radio beacons
MF (medium frequency)	300 to 3000 kHz	1,000 to 100 m	GW and night SW; attenuation low at night, high in day; atmospheric noise	Maritime radio; direction finding; AM broadcasting
HF (high frequency)	3 to 30 MHz	100 to 10 m	SW; quality varies with time of day, season, and frequency	Amateur radio; military communication
VHF (very high frequency)	30 to 300 MHz	10 to 1 m	LOS; scattering because of temperature inversion; cosmic noise	VHF television; FM broadcast and two-way radio, AM aircraft communication; aircraft navigational aids
UHF (ultra high frequency)	300 to 3000 MHz	100 to 10 cm	LOS; cosmic noise	UHF television; cellular telephone; radar; microwave links; personal communications systems
SHF (super high frequency)	3 to 30 GHz	10 to 1 cm	LOS; rainfall attenuation above 10 GHz; atmospheric attenuation due to oxygen and water vapor	Satellite communication; radar; terrestrial microwave links; wireless local loop
EHF (extremely high frequency)	30 to 300 GHz	10 to 1 mm	LOS; atmospheric attenuation due to oxygen and water vapor	Experimental; wireless local loop; radio astronomy
Infrared	300 GHz to 400 THz	1 mm to 770 nm	LOS	Infrared LANs; consumer electronic applications
Visible light	400 to 900 THz	770 to 330 nm	LOS	Optical communication

125

Ground Wave Propagation

Ground wave propagation (Figure 4.10a) more or less follows the contour of the Earth and can propagate considerable distances, well over the visual horizon. This effect is found in frequencies up to about 2 MHz. Several factors account for the tendency of electromagnetic wave in this frequency band to follow the Earth's curvature. One factor is that the electromagnetic wave induces a current in the

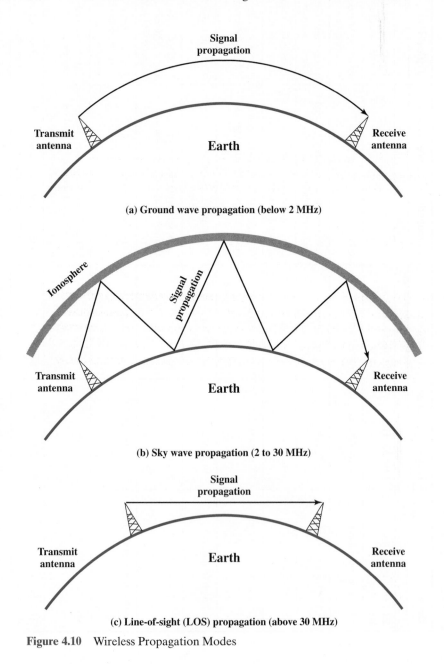

(a) Ground wave propagation (below 2 MHz)

(b) Sky wave propagation (2 to 30 MHz)

(c) Line-of-sight (LOS) propagation (above 30 MHz)

Figure 4.10   Wireless Propagation Modes

Earth's surface, the result of which is to slow the wavefront near the Earth, causing the wavefront to tilt downward and hence follow the Earth's curvature. Another factor is diffraction, which is a phenomenon having to do with the behavior of electromagnetic waves in the presence of obstacles. Electromagnetic waves in this frequency range are scattered by the atmosphere in such a way that they do not penetrate the upper atmosphere.

The best-known example of ground wave communication is AM radio.

Sky Wave Propagation

Sky wave propagation is used for amateur radio and international broadcasts such as *BBC* and *Voice of America*. With sky wave propagation, a signal from an earth-based antenna is reflected from the ionized layer of the upper atmosphere (ionosphere) back down to Earth. Although it appears the wave is reflected from the ionosphere as if the ionosphere were a hard reflecting surface, the effect is in fact caused by refraction. Refraction is described subsequently.

A sky wave signal can travel through a number of hops, bouncing back and forth between the ionosphere and the Earth's surface (Figure 4.10b). With this propagation mode, a signal can be picked up thousands of kilometers from the transmitter.

Line-of-Sight Propagation

Above 30 MHz, neither ground wave nor sky wave propagation modes operate, and communication must be by line of sight (Figure 4.10c). For satellite communication, a signal above 30 MHz is not reflected by the ionosphere and therefore a signal can be transmitted between an earth station and a satellite overhead that is not beyond the horizon. For ground-based communication, the transmitting and receiving antennas must be within an *effective* line of sight of each other. The term *effective* is used because microwaves are bent or refracted by the atmosphere. The amount and even the direction of the bend depend on conditions, but generally microwaves are bent with the curvature of the Earth and will therefore propagate farther than the optical line of sight.

REFRACTION Before proceeding, a brief discussion of refraction is warranted. Refraction occurs because the velocity of an electromagnetic wave is a function of the density of the medium through which it travels. In a vacuum, an electromagnetic wave (such as light or a radio wave) travels at approximately 3×10^8 m/s. This is the constant, c, commonly referred to as the speed of light, but actually referring to the speed of light in a vacuum.[2] In air, water, glass, and other transparent or partially transparent media, electromagnetic waves travel at speeds less than c.

When an electromagnetic wave moves from a medium of one density to a medium of another density, its speed changes. The effect is to cause a one-time bending of the direction of the wave at the boundary between the two media.

---

[2]The exact value is 299,792,458 m/s.

Moving from a less dense to a more dense medium, the wave bends toward the more dense medium. This phenomenon is easily observed by partially immersing a stick in water.

The **index of refraction**, or **refractive index**, of one medium relative to another is the sine of the angle of incidence divided by the sine of the angle of refraction. The index of refraction is also equal to the ratio of the respective velocities in the two media. The absolute index of refraction of a medium is calculated in comparison with that of a vacuum. Refractive index varies with wavelength, so that refractive effects differ for signals with different wavelengths.

Although an abrupt, one-time change in direction occurs as a signal moves from one medium to another, a continuous, gradual bending of a signal occurs if it is moving through a medium in which the index of refraction gradually changes. Under normal propagation conditions, the refractive index of the atmosphere decreases with height so that radio waves travel more slowly near the ground than at higher altitudes. The result is a slight bending of the radio waves toward the earth.

OPTICAL AND RADIO LINE OF SIGHT   With no intervening obstacles, the optical line of sight can be expressed as

$$d = 3.57\sqrt{h}$$

where d is the distance between an antenna and the horizon in kilometers and h is the antenna height in meters. The effective, or radio, line of sight to the horizon is expressed as (Figure 4.11)

$$d = 3.57\sqrt{Kh}$$

where K is an adjustment factor to account for the refraction. A good rule of thumb is $K = 4/3$. Thus, the maximum distance between two antennas for LOS propagation is $3.57\left(\sqrt{Kh_1} + \sqrt{Kh_2}\right)$, where h_1 and h_2 are the heights of the two antennas.

EXAMPLE 4.5 The maximum distance between two antennas for LOS transmission if one antenna is 100 m high and the other is at ground level is:

$$d = 3.57\sqrt{Kh} = 3.57\sqrt{133} = 41 \text{ km}$$

Now suppose that the receiving antenna is 10 m high. To achieve the same distance, how high must the transmitting antenna be? The result is:

$$41 = 3.57\left(\sqrt{Kh_1} + \sqrt{13.3}\right)$$

$$\sqrt{Kh_1} = \frac{41}{3.57} - \sqrt{13.3} = 7.84$$

$$h_1 = 7.84^2/1.33 = 46.2 \text{ m}$$

This is a savings of over 50 m in the height of the transmitting antenna. This example illustrates the benefit of raising receiving antennas above ground level to reduce the necessary height of the transmitter.

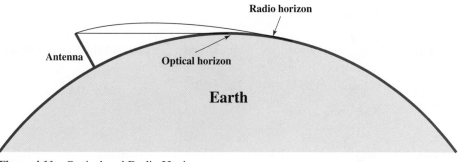

Figure 4.11   Optical and Radio Horizons

4.4   LINE-OF-SIGHT TRANSMISSION

Section 3.3 discusses various transmission impairments common to both guided and wireless transmission. In this section, we extend the discussion to examine some impairments specific to wireless line-of-sight transmission.

Free Space Loss

For any type of wireless communication the signal disperses with distance. Therefore, an antenna with a fixed area receives less signal power the farther it is from the transmitting antenna. For satellite communication this is the primary mode of signal loss. Even if no other sources of attenuation or impairment are assumed, a transmitted signal attenuates over distance because the signal is being spread over a larger and larger area. This form of attenuation is known as **free space loss**, which can be expressed in terms of the ratio of the radiated power P_t to the power P_r received by the antenna or, in decibels, by taking 10 times the log of that ratio. For the ideal isotropic antenna, free space loss is

$$\frac{P_t}{P_r} = \frac{(4\pi d)^2}{\lambda^2} = \frac{(4\pi f d)^2}{c^2} \tag{4.3}$$

where

$$P_t = \text{signal power at the transmitting antenna}$$
$$P_r = \text{signal power at the receiving antenna}$$
$$\lambda = \text{carrier wavelength}$$
$$d = \text{propagation distance between antennas}$$
$$c = \text{speed of light } (3 \times 10^8 \text{ m/s})$$

where d and λ are in the same units (e.g., meters).

This can be recast as:[3]

$$L_{dB} = 10 \log \frac{P_t}{P_r} = 10 \log\left(\frac{4\pi d}{\lambda^2}\right)^2 = 20 \log\left(\frac{4\pi d}{\lambda}\right) \text{ substituting from Equation (4.3)}$$

$$L_{dB} = -20 \log(\lambda) + 20 \log(d) + 21.98 \text{ dB}$$

And using $\lambda f = c$.

$$L_{dB} = 20 \log\left(\frac{4\pi f d}{c}\right) = 20 \log(f) + 20 \log(d) - 147.56 \text{ dB} \tag{4.4}$$

Figure 4.12 illustrates the free space loss equation.

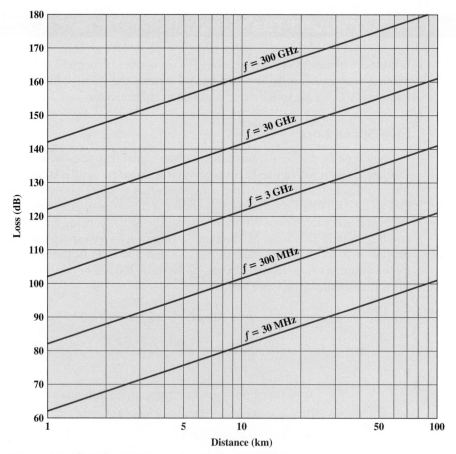

Figure 4.12   Free Space Loss

[3]As was mentioned in Appendix 3A, there is some inconsistency in the literature over the use of the terms *gain* and *loss*. Equation (4.4) follows the convention of Equation (3.3).

For other antennas, we must take into account the gain of the antenna, which yields the following free space loss equation:

$$\frac{P_t}{P_r} = \frac{(4\pi)^2(d)^2}{G_r G_t \lambda^2} = \frac{(\lambda d)^2}{A_r A_t} = \frac{(cd)^2}{f^2 A_r A_t}$$

where

G_t = gain of the transmitting antenna

G_r = gain of the receiving antenna

A_t = effective area of the transmitting antenna

A_r = effective area of the receiving antenna

The third fraction is derived from the second fraction using the relationship between antenna gain and effective area defined in Equation (4.1). We can recast the loss equation as:

$$\begin{aligned} L_{dB} &= 20\log(\lambda) + 20\log(d) - 10\log(A_t A_r) \\ &= -20\log(f) + 20\log(d) - 10\log(A_t A_r) + 169.54 \text{ dB} \end{aligned} \quad \textbf{(4.5)}$$

Thus, for the same antenna dimensions and separation, the longer the carrier wavelength (lower the carrier frequency f), the higher is the free space path loss. It is interesting to compare Equations (4.4) and (4.5). Equation (4.4) indicates that as the frequency increases, the free space loss also increases, which would suggest that at higher frequencies, losses become more burdensome. However, Equation (4.5) shows that we can easily compensate for this increased loss with antenna gains. In fact, there is a net gain at higher frequencies, other factors remaining constant. Equation (4.4) shows that at a fixed distance an increase in frequency results in an increased loss measured by $20\log(f)$. However, if we take into account antenna gain and fix antenna area, then the change in loss is measured by $-20\log(f)$; that is, there is actually a decrease in loss at higher frequencies.

EXAMPLE 4.6 Determine the isotropic free space loss at 4 GHz for the shortest path to a synchronous satellite from Earth (35,863 km). At 4 GHz, the wavelength is $(3 \times 10^8)/(4 \times 10^9) = 0.075$ m. Then

$$L_{dB} = -20\log(0.075) + 20\log(35.853 \times 10^6) + 21.98 = 195.6 \text{ dB}$$

Now consider the antenna gain of both the satellite- and ground-based antennas. Typical values are 44 dB and 48 dB, respectively. The free space loss is

$$L_{dB} = 195.6 - 44 - 48 = 103.6 \text{ dB}$$

Now assume a transmit power of 250 W at the earth station. What is the power received at the satellite antenna? A power of 250 W translates into 24 dBW, so the power at the receiving antenna is $24 - 103.6 = -79.6$ dBW.

Atmospheric Absorption

An additional loss between the transmitting and receiving antennas is atmospheric absorption. Water vapor and oxygen contribute most to attenuation. A peak attenuation occurs in the vicinity of 22 GHz due to water vapor. At frequencies below 15 GHz, the attenuation is less. The presence of oxygen results in an absorption peak in the vicinity of 60 GHz but contributes less at frequencies below 30 GHz. Rain and fog (suspended water droplets) cause scattering of radio waves that results in attenuation. In this context, the term *scattering* refers to the production of waves of changed direction or frequency when radio waves encounter matter. This can be a major cause of signal loss. Thus, in areas of significant precipitation, either path lengths have to be kept short or lower-frequency bands should be used.

Multipath

For wireless facilities where there is a relatively free choice of where antennas are to be located, they can be placed so that if there are no nearby interfering obstacles, there is a direct line-of-sight path from transmitter to receiver. This is generally the case for many satellite facilities and for point-to-point microwave. In other cases, such as mobile telephony, there are obstacles in abundance. The signal can be reflected by such obstacles so that multiple copies of the signal with varying delays can be received. In fact, in extreme cases, there may be no direct signal. Depending on the differences in the path lengths of the direct and reflected waves, the composite signal can be either larger or smaller than the direct signal. Reinforcement and cancellation of the signal resulting from the signal following multiple paths can be controlled for communication between fixed, well-sited antennas, and between satellites and fixed ground stations. One exception is when the path goes across water, where the wind keeps the reflective surface of the water in motion. For mobile telephony and communication to antennas that are not well sited, multipath considerations can be paramount.

Figure 4.13 illustrates in general terms the types of multipath interference typical in terrestrial, fixed microwave and in mobile communications. For fixed microwave, in addition to the direct line of sight, the signal may follow a curved path through the atmosphere due to refraction and the signal may also reflect from the ground. For mobile communications, structures and topographic features provide reflection surfaces.

Refraction

Radio waves are refracted (or bent) when they propagate through the atmosphere. The refraction is caused by changes in the speed of the signal with altitude or by other spatial changes in the atmospheric conditions. Normally, the speed of the signal increases with altitude, causing radio waves to bend downward. However, on occasion, weather conditions may lead to variations in speed with height that differ significantly from the typical variations. This may result in a situation in which only a fraction or no part of the line-of-sight wave reaches the receiving antenna.

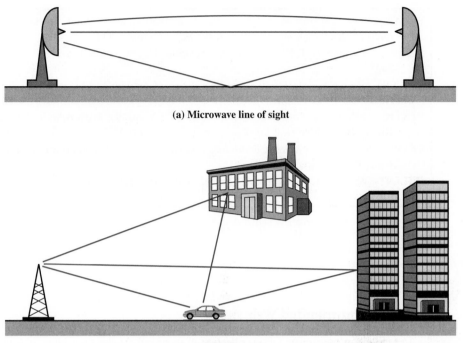

(a) Microwave line of sight

(b) Mobile radio

Figure 4.13   Examples of Multipath Interference

4.5   RECOMMENDED READING AND WEB SITES

Detailed descriptions of the transmission characteristics of the transmission media discussed in this chapter can be found in [FREE98b]. A less technical but excellent resource is [OLIV09]. [REEV95] provides an excellent treatment of twisted pair and optical fiber. [BORE97] is a thorough treatment of optical fiber transmission components. Another good paper on the subject is [WILL97]. [RAMA06] surveys optical network technologies. [FREE02] is a detailed technical reference on optical fiber. [STAL00] discusses the characteristics of transmission media for LANs in greater detail.

For a more thorough treatment on wireless transmission and propagation, see [STAL05] and [RAPP02]. [FREE07] is an excellent detailed technical reference on wireless topics.

BORE97   Borella, M., et al. "Optical Components for WDM Lightwave Networks." *Proceedings of the IEEE,* August 1997.

FREE98b   Freeman, R. *Telecommunication Transmission Handbook.* New York: Wiley, 1998.

FREE02   Freeman, R. *Fiber-Optic Systems for Telecommunications.* New York: Wiley, 2002.

FREE07   Freeman, R. *Radio System Design for Telecommunications.* New York: Wiley, 2007.

OLIV09   Oliviero, A., and Woodward, B. *Cabling: The Complete Guide to Copper and Fiber-Optic Networking.* Indianapolis: Sybex, 2009.

RAMA06 Ramaswami, R. "Optical Network Technologies: What Worked and What Didn't." *IEEE Communications Magazine*, September 2006.

RAPP02 Rappaport, T. *Wireless Communications.* Upper Saddle River, NJ: Prentice Hall, 2002.

REEV95 Reeve, W. *Subscriber Loop Signaling and Transmission Handbook.* Piscataway, NJ: IEEE Press, 1995.

STAL00 Stallings, W. *Local and Metropolitan Area Networks,* Sixth Edition. Upper Saddle River, NJ: Prentice Hall, 2000.

STAL05 Stallings, W. *Wireless Communications and Networks*, Second Edition. Upper Saddle River, NJ: Prentice Hall, 2005.

WILL97 Willner, A. "Mining the Optical Bandwidth for a Terabit per Second." *IEEE Spectrum*, April 1997.

Recommended Web sites:

- **Siemon company:** Good collection of technical articles on cabling, plus information about cabling standards
- **Wireless developer network:** News, tutorials, and discussions on wireless topics
- **About antennas:** Good source of information and links
- **U.S. frequency allocation chart:** Chart plus background paper

4.6 KEY TERMS, REVIEW QUESTIONS, AND PROBLEMS

Key Terms

antenna	global positioning system (GPS)	optical fiber
antenna gain	graded-index multimode	optical LOS
atmospheric absorption	ground wave propagation	parabolic reflective antenna
attenuation	guided media	radio
attenuation-to-crosstalk ratio (ACR)	index of refraction	radio LOS
broadcast radio	infrared	reflection
cladding	insertion loss	refraction
core	isotropic antenna	refractive index
coaxial cable	jacket	scattering
directional antenna	line of sight (LOS)	satellite
downlink	microwave frequencies	shielded twisted pair (STP)
earth stations	multipath	single-mode
effective area	near-end crosstalk (NEXT) loss	sky wave propagation
free space loss	omnidirectional antenna	step-index multimode
		subscriber loops

terrestrial microwave	transponders	uplink
total internal reflection	twisted pair	wavelength division
transmission medium	unguided media	multiplexing (WDM)
transponder channels	unshielded twisted pair (UTP)	wireless transmission

Review Questions

4.1 Why are the wires twisted in twisted-pair copper wire?

4.2 What are some major limitations of twisted-pair wire?

4.3 What is the difference between unshielded twisted pair and shielded twisted pair?

4.4 Describe the components of optical fiber cable.

4.5 What are some major advantages and disadvantages of microwave transmission?

4.6 What is direct broadcast satellite (DBS)?

4.7 Why must a satellite have distinct uplink and downlink frequencies?

4.8 Indicate some significant differences between broadcast radio and microwave.

4.9 What two functions are performed by an antenna?

4.10 What is an isotropic antenna?

4.11 What is the advantage of a parabolic reflective antenna?

4.12 What factors determine antenna gain?

4.13 What is the primary cause of signal loss in satellite communications?

4.14 What is refraction?

4.15 What is the difference between diffraction and scattering?

Problems

4.1 Suppose that data are stored on 8.54-Gbyte single-sided, double-layer DVDs that weigh 15 g each. Suppose that an Eurostar rail service train, London to Paris via Chunnel, carries 10^4 kg of these DVDs. The great circle distance of the line is 640 km and the traveling time is 2 hours, 15 minutes. What is the data transmission rate in bits per second of this system?

4.2 A telephone line is known to have a loss of 20 dB. The input signal power is measured as 0.5 W, and the output noise level is measured as 4.5 μW. Using this information, calculate the output signal-to-noise ratio in dB.

4.3 Given a 100-watt power source, what is the maximum allowable length for the following transmission media if a signal of 1 watt is to be received?

    a. 24-gauge (0.5 mm) twisted pair operating at 300 kHz

    b. 24-gauge (0.5 mm) twisted pair operating at 1 MHz

    c. 0.375-inch (9.5 mm) coaxial cable operating at 1 MHz

    d. 0.375-inch (9.5 mm) coaxial cable operating at 25 MHz

    e. optical fiber operating at its optimal frequency

4.4 Coaxial cable is a two-wire transmission system. What is the advantage of connecting the outer conductor to ground?

4.5 Show that doubling the transmission frequency or doubling the distance between transmitting antenna and receiving antenna attenuates the power received by 6 dB.

4.6 It turns out that the depth in the ocean to which airborne electromagnetic signals can be detected grows with the wavelength. Therefore, the military got the idea of using very long wavelengths corresponding to about 30 Hz to communicate with submarines throughout the world. It is desirable to have an antenna that is about one-half wavelength long. How long would that be?

4.7   The audio power of the human voice is concentrated at about 300 Hz. Antennas of the appropriate size for this frequency are impracticably large, so that to send voice by radio the voice signal must be used to modulate a higher (carrier) frequency for which the natural antenna size is smaller.

    a.   What is the length of an antenna one-half wavelength long for sending radio at 300 Hz?

    b.   An alternative is to use a modulation scheme, as described in Chapter 5, for transmitting the voice signal by modulating a carrier frequency, so that the bandwidth of the signal is a narrow band centered on the carrier frequency. Suppose we would like a half-wave antenna to have a length of 1 m. What carrier frequency would we use?

4.8   Stories abound of people who receive radio signals in fillings in their teeth. Suppose you have one filling that is 2.5 mm (0.0025 m) long that acts as a radio antenna. That is, it is equal in length to one-half the wavelength. What frequency do you receive?

4.9   You are communicating between two satellites. The transmission obeys the free space law. The signal is too weak. Your vendor offers you two options. The vendor can use a higher frequency that is twice the current frequency or can double the effective area of both of the antennas. Which will offer you more received power or will both offer the same improvement, all other factors remaining equal? How much improvement in the received power do you obtain from the best option?

4.10   In satellite communications, different frequency bands are used for the uplink and the downlink. Discuss why this pattern occurs.

4.11   For radio transmission in free space, signal power is reduced in proportion to the square of the distance from the source, whereas in wire transmission, the attenuation is a fixed number of dB per kilometer. The following table is used to show the dB reduction relative to some reference for free space radio and uniform wire. Fill in the missing numbers to complete the table.

Distance (km)	Radio (dB)	Wire (dB)
1	−6	−3
2		
4		
8		
16		

4.12   Section 4.2 states that if a source of electromagnetic energy is placed at the focus of the paraboloid, and if the paraboloid is a reflecting surface, then the wave will bounce back in lines parallel to the axis of the paraboloid. To demonstrate this, consider the parabola $y^2 = 2px$ shown in Figure 4.14. Let $P(x_1, y_1)$ be a point on the parabola, and PF be the line from P to the focus. Construct the line L through P parallel to the x-axis and the line M tangent to the parabola at P. The angle between L and M is β, and the angle between PF and M is α. The angle α is the angle at which a ray from F strikes the parabola at P. Because the angle of incidence equals the angle of reflection, the ray reflected from P must be at an angle α to M. Thus, if we can show that $\alpha = \beta$, we have demonstrated that rays reflected from the parabola starting at F will be parallel to the x-axis.

    a.   First show that $\tan \beta = (p/y_1)$. *Hint:* Recall from trigonometry that the slope of a line is equal to the tangent of the angle the line makes with the positive x-direction. Also recall that the slope of the line tangent to a curve at a given point is equal to the derivative of the curve at that point.

    b.   Now show that $\tan \alpha = (p/y_1)$, which demonstrates that $\alpha = \beta$. *Hint:* Recall from trigonometry that the formula for the tangent of the difference between two angles α_1 and α_2 is $\tan(\alpha_2 - \alpha_1) = (\tan \alpha_2 - \tan \alpha_1)/(1 + \tan \alpha_2 \times \tan \alpha_1)$.

4.13   It is often more convenient to express distance in km rather than m and frequency in MHz rather than Hz. Rewrite Equation (4.4) using these dimensions.

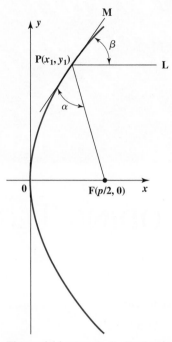

Figure 4.14   Parabolic Reflection

4.14   Suppose a transmitter produces 50 W of power.
  a.   Express the transmit power in units of dBm and dBW.
  b.   If the transmitter's power is applied to a unity gain antenna with a 900 MHz carrier frequency, what is the received power in dBm at a free space distance of 100 m?
  c.   Repeat (b) for a distance of 10 km.
  d.   Repeat (c) but assume a receiver antenna gain of 2.

4.15   A microwave transmitter has an output of 0.1 W at 2 GHz. Assume that this transmitter is used in a microwave communication system where the transmitting and receiving antennas are parabolas, each 1.2 m in diameter.
  a.   What is the gain of each antenna in decibels?
  b.   Taking into account antenna gain, what is the effective radiated power of the transmitted signal?
  c.   If the receiving antenna is located 24 km from the transmitting antenna over a free space path, find the available signal power out of the receiving antenna in dBm units.

4.16   Section 4.3 states that with no intervening obstacles, the optical line of sight can be expressed as $d = 3.57\sqrt{h}$, where d is the distance between an antenna and the horizon in kilometers and h is the antenna height in meters. Using a value for the Earth's radius of 6370 km, derive this equation. *Hint:* Assume that the antenna is perpendicular to the Earth's surface, and note that the line from the top of the antenna to the horizon forms a tangent to the Earth's surface at the horizon. Draw a picture showing the antenna, the line of sight, and the Earth's radius to help visualize the problem.

4.17   Determine the height of an antenna for a TV station that must be able to reach customers up to 80 km away.

4.18   Suppose a ray of visible light passes from the atmosphere into water at an angle to the horizontal of 30°. What is the angle of the ray in the water? *Note:* At standard atmospheric conditions at the Earth's surface, a reasonable value for refractive index is 1.0003. A typical value of refractive index for water is 4/3.

CHAPTER 5

SIGNAL ENCODING TECHNIQUES

Even the natives have difficulty mastering this peculiar vocabulary.

— *The Golden Bough,* Sir James George Frazer

KEY POINTS

◆ Both analog and digital information can be encoded as either analog or digital signals. The particular encoding that is chosen depends on the specific requirements to be met and the media and communications facilities available.

◆ **Digital data, digital signals:** The simplest form of digital encoding of digital data is to assign one voltage level to binary one and another to binary zero. More complex encoding schemes are used to improve performance, by altering the spectrum of the signal and providing synchronization capability.

◆ **Digital data, analog signal:** A modem converts digital data to an analog signal so that it can be transmitted over an analog line. The basic techniques are amplitude shift keying (ASK), frequency shift keying (FSK), and phase shift keying (PSK). All involve altering one or more characteristics of a carrier frequency to represent binary data.

◆ **Analog data, digital signals:** Analog data, such as voice and video, are often digitized to be able to use digital transmission facilities. The simplest technique is pulse code modulation (PCM), which involves sampling the analog data periodically and quantizing the samples.

◆ **Analog data, analog signals:** Analog data are modulated by a carrier frequency to produce an analog signal in a different frequency band, which can be utilized on an analog transmission system. The basic techniques are amplitude modulation (AM), frequency modulation (FM), and phase modulation (PM).

In Chapter 3 a distinction was made between analog and digital data, and analog and digital signals. Figure 3.14 suggested that either form of data could be encoded into either form of signal.

Figure 5.1 is another depiction that emphasizes the process involved. For **digital signaling**, a data source $g(t)$, which may be either digital or analog, is encoded into a digital signal $x(t)$. The actual form of $x(t)$ depends on the encoding technique and is chosen to optimize use of the transmission medium. For example, the encoding may be chosen to conserve bandwidth or to minimize errors.

The basis for **analog signaling** is a continuous constant-frequency signal known as the **carrier signal**. The frequency of the carrier signal is chosen to be compatible with the transmission medium being used. Data may be transmitted using a

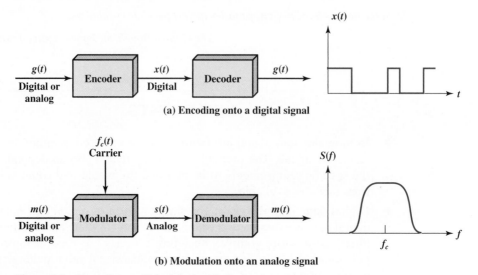

Figure 5.1   Encoding and Modulation Techniques

carrier signal by modulation. **Modulation** is the process of encoding source data onto a carrier signal with frequency f_c. All modulation techniques involve operation on one or more of the three fundamental frequency domain parameters: amplitude, frequency, and phase.

The input signal $m(t)$ may be analog or digital and is called the modulating signal or **baseband signal**. The result of modulating the carrier signal is called the modulated signal $s(t)$. As Figure 5.1b indicates, $s(t)$ is a bandlimited (bandpass) signal. The location of the bandwidth on the spectrum is related to f_c and is often centered on f_c. Again, the actual form of the encoding is chosen to optimize some characteristics of the transmission.

Each of the four possible combinations depicted in Figure 5.1 is in widespread use. The reasons for choosing a particular combination for any given communication task vary. We list here some representative reasons:

- **Digital data, digital signal:** In general, the equipment for encoding digital data into a digital signal is less complex and less expensive than digital-to-analog modulation equipment.
- **Analog data, digital signal:** Conversion of analog data to digital form permits the use of modern digital transmission and switching equipment. The advantages of the digital approach were outlined in Section 3.2.
- **Digital data, analog signal:** Some transmission media, such as optical fiber and unguided media, will only propagate analog signals.
- **Analog data, analog signal:** Analog data in electrical form can be transmitted as baseband signals easily and cheaply. This is done with voice transmission over voice-grade lines. One common use of modulation is to shift the bandwidth of a

baseband signal to another portion of the spectrum. In this way multiple signals, each at a different position on the spectrum, can share the same transmission medium. This is known as frequency division multiplexing.

We now examine the techniques involved in each of these four combinations.

5.1 DIGITAL DATA, DIGITAL SIGNALS

A digital signal is a sequence of discrete, discontinuous voltage pulses. Each pulse is a signal element. Binary data are transmitted by encoding each data bit into signal elements. In the simplest case, there is a one-to-one correspondence between bits and signal elements. An example is shown in Figure 3.16, in which binary 1 is represented by a lower voltage level and binary 0 by a higher voltage level. We show in this section that a variety of other encoding schemes are also used.

First, we define some terms. If the signal elements all have the same algebraic sign, that is, all positive or negative, then the signal is **unipolar**. In **polar** signaling, one logic state is represented by a positive voltage level, and the other by a negative voltage level. The **data signaling rate**, or just **data rate**, of a signal is the rate, in bits per second, that data are transmitted. The duration or length of a bit is the amount of time it takes for the transmitter to emit the bit; for a data rate R, the bit duration is $1/R$. The **modulation rate**, in contrast, is the rate at which the signal level is changed. This will depend on the nature of the digital encoding, as explained later. The modulation rate is expressed in baud, which means signal elements per second. Finally, the terms *mark* and *space*, for historical reasons, refer to the binary digits 1 and 0, respectively. Table 5.1 summarizes key terms; these should be clearer when we see an example later in this section.

The tasks involved in interpreting digital signals at the receiver can be summarized by again referring to Figure 3.16. First, the receiver must know the timing of each bit; that is, the receiver must know with some accuracy when a bit begins and ends. Second, the receiver must determine whether the signal level for each bit position is high (0) or low (1). In Figure 3.16, these tasks are performed by sampling each bit position in the middle of the interval and comparing the value to a threshold. Because of noise and other impairments, there will be errors, as shown.

Table 5.1 Key Data Transmission Terms

Term	Units	Definition
Data element	Bits	A single binary one or zero
Data rate	Bits per second (bps)	The rate at which data elements are transmitted
Signal element	Digital: a voltage pulse of constant amplitude	That part of a signal that occupies the shortest interval of a signaling code
	Analog: a pulse of constant frequency, phase, and amplitude	
Signaling rate or modulation rate	Signal elements per second (baud)	The rate at which signal elements are transmitted

What factors determine how successful the receiver will be in interpreting the incoming signal? We saw in Chapter 3 that three factors are important: the signal-to-noise ratio (SNR), the data rate, and the bandwidth. With other factors held constant, the following statements are true:

- An increase in data rate increases bit error rate (BER).[1]
- An increase in SNR decreases bit error rate.
- An increase in bandwidth allows an increase in data rate.

There is another factor that can be used to improve performance, and that is the encoding scheme. The encoding scheme is simply the mapping from data bits to signal elements. A variety of approaches have been tried. In what follows, we describe some of the more common ones; they are defined in Table 5.2.

Table 5.2 Definition of Digital Signal Encoding Formats

Nonreturn to Zero-Level (NRZ-L)
0 = high level
1 = low level
Nonreturn to Zero Inverted (NRZI)
0 = no transition at beginning of interval (one bit time)
1 = transition at beginning of interval
Bipolar-AMI
0 = no line signal
1 = positive or negative level, alternating for successive ones
Pseudoternary
0 = positive or negative level, alternating for successive zeros
1 = no line signal
Manchester
0 = transition from high to low in middle of interval
1 = transition from low to high in middle of interval
Differential Manchester
Always a transition in middle of interval
0 = transition at beginning of interval
1 = no transition at beginning of interval
B8ZS
Same as bipolar AMI, except that any string of eight zeros is replaced by a string with two code violations
HDB3
Same as bipolar AMI, except that any string of four zeros is replaced by a string with one code violation

---

[1]The BER is the most common measure of error performance on a data circuit and is defined as the probability that a bit is received in error. It is also called the bit error ratio. This latter term is clearer, because the term *rate* typically refers to some quantity that varies with time. Unfortunately, most books and standards documents refer to the R in BER as *rate*.

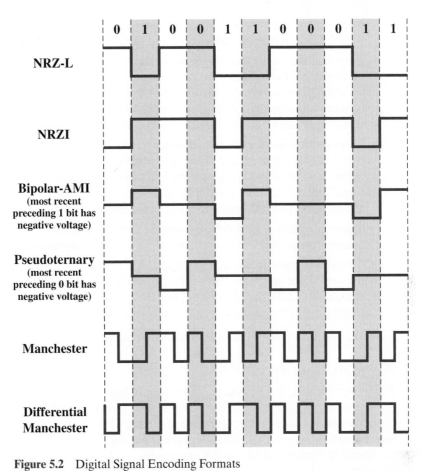

Figure 5.2   Digital Signal Encoding Formats

EXAMPLE 5.1 Figure 5.2 shows the signal encoding for the binary sequence 01001100011 using six different signal encoding schemes.

Before describing these techniques, let us consider the following ways of evaluating or comparing the various techniques.

- **Signal spectrum:** Several aspects of the signal spectrum are important. A lack of high-frequency components means that less bandwidth is required for transmission. In addition, lack of a direct-current (dc) component is also desirable. With a dc component to the signal, there must be direct physical attachment of transmission components. With no dc component, ac coupling via transformer is possible; this provides excellent electrical isolation, reducing interference. Finally, the magnitude of the effects of signal distortion and interference depend on the spectral properties of the transmitted signal. In practice, it usually happens that the transmission characteristics of a channel are worse near the band edges. Therefore, a good signal design should concentrate the transmitted power in the middle of the transmission bandwidth. In such a case, a smaller distortion should be present in the received signal. To meet this objective, codes can be designed with the aim of shaping the spectrum of the transmitted signal.

- **Clocking:** We mentioned the need to determine the beginning and end of each bit position. This is no easy task. One rather expensive approach is to provide a separate clock lead to synchronize the transmitter and receiver. The alternative is to provide some synchronization mechanism that is based on the transmitted signal. This can be achieved with suitable encoding, as explained subsequently.

- **Error detection:** We will discuss various error-detection techniques in Chapter 6 and show that these are the responsibility of a layer of logic above the signaling level that is known as data link control. However, it is useful to have some error detection capability built into the physical signaling encoding scheme. This permits errors to be detected more quickly.

- **Signal interference and noise immunity:** Certain codes exhibit superior performance in the presence of noise. Performance is usually expressed in terms of a BER.

- **Cost and complexity:** Although digital logic continues to drop in price, this factor should not be ignored. In particular, the higher the signaling rate to achieve a given data rate, the greater the cost. We shall see that some codes require a signaling rate that is greater than the actual data rate.

We now turn to a discussion of various techniques.

Nonreturn to Zero (NRZ)

The most common, and easiest, way to transmit digital signals is to use two different voltage levels for the two binary digits. Codes that follow this strategy share the property that the voltage level is constant during a bit interval; there is no transition (no return to a zero voltage level). For example, the absence of voltage can be used to represent binary 0, with a constant positive voltage used to represent binary 1. More commonly, a negative voltage represents one binary value and a positive voltage represents the other. This latter code, known as **Nonreturn to Zero-Level (NRZ-L)**, is illustrated[2] in Figure 5.2. NRZ-L is typically the code used to generate or interpret digital data by terminals and other devices. If a different code is to be used for transmission, it is generated from an NRZ-L signal by the transmission system [in terms of Figure 5.1, NRZ-L is $g(t)$ and the encoded signal is $x(t)$].

A variation of NRZ is known as **NRZI** (Nonreturn to Zero, invert on ones). As with NRZ-L, NRZI maintains a constant voltage pulse for the duration of a bit time. The data themselves are encoded as the presence or absence of a signal transition at the beginning of the bit time. A transition (low to high or high to low) at the beginning of a bit time denotes a binary 1 for that bit time; no transition indicates a binary 0.

NRZI is an example of **differential encoding**. In differential encoding, the information to be transmitted is represented in terms of the changes between successive signal elements rather than the signal elements themselves. The encoding of the current bit is determined as follows: If the current bit is a binary 0, then

---

[2]In this figure, a negative voltage is equated with binary 1 and a positive voltage with binary 0. This is the opposite of the definition used in virtually all other textbooks. The definition here conforms to the use of NRZ-L in data communications interfaces and the standards that govern those interfaces.

the current bit is encoded with the same signal as the preceding bit; if the current bit is a binary 1, then the current bit is encoded with a different signal than the preceding bit. One benefit of differential encoding is that it may be more reliable to detect a transition in the presence of noise than to compare a value to a threshold. Another benefit is that with a complex transmission layout, it is easy to lose the sense of the polarity of the signal. For example, on a multidrop twisted-pair line, if the leads from an attached device to the twisted pair are accidentally inverted, all 1s and 0s for NRZ-L will be inverted. This does not happen with differential encoding.

The NRZ codes are the easiest to engineer and, in addition, make efficient use of bandwidth. This latter property is illustrated in Figure 5.3, which compares the spectral density of various encoding schemes. In the figure, frequency is normalized to the data rate. Most of the energy in NRZ and NRZI signals is between dc and half the bit rate. For example, if an NRZ code is used to generate a signal with data rate of 9600 bps, most of the energy in the signal is concentrated between dc and 4800 Hz.

The main limitations of NRZ signals are the presence of a dc component and the lack of synchronization capability. To picture the latter problem, consider that with a long string of 1s or 0s for NRZ-L or a long string of 0s for NRZI, the output is a constant voltage over a long period of time. Under these circumstances, any drift between the clocks of transmitter and receiver will result in loss of synchronization between the two.

Because of their simplicity and relatively low-frequency response characteristics, NRZ codes are commonly used for digital magnetic recording. However, their limitations make these codes unattractive for signal transmission applications.

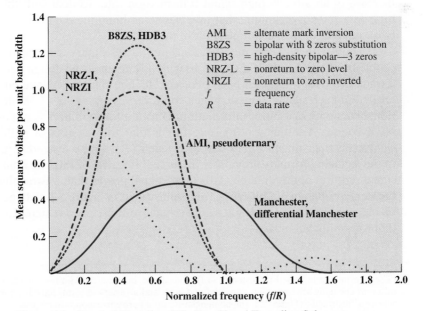

Figure 5.3 Spectral Density of Various Signal Encoding Schemes

Multilevel Binary

A category of encoding techniques that are known as multilevel binary addresses some of the deficiencies of the NRZ codes. These codes use more than two signal levels. Two examples of this scheme are illustrated in Figure 5.2, bipolar-AMI (alternate mark inversion) and pseudoternary.[3]

In the case of the **bipolar-AMI** scheme, a binary 0 is represented by no line signal, and a binary 1 is represented by a positive or negative pulse. The binary 1 pulses must alternate in polarity. There are several advantages to this approach. First, there will be no loss of synchronization if a long string of 1s occurs. Each 1 introduces a transition, and the receiver can resynchronize on that transition. A long string of 0s would still be a problem. Second, because the 1 signals alternate in voltage from positive to negative, there is no net dc component. Also, the bandwidth of the resulting signal is considerably less than the bandwidth for NRZ (Figure 5.3). Finally, the pulse alternation property provides a simple means of error detection. Any isolated error, whether it deletes a pulse or adds a pulse, causes a violation of this property.

The comments of the previous paragraph also apply to **pseudoternary**. In this case, it is the binary 1 that is represented by the absence of a line signal, and the binary 0 by alternating positive and negative pulses. There is no particular advantage of one technique versus the other, and each is the basis of some applications.

Although a degree of synchronization is provided with these codes, a long string of 0s in the case of AMI or 1s in the case of pseudoternary still presents a problem. Several techniques have been used to address this deficiency. One approach is to insert additional bits that force transitions. This technique is used in ISDN (integrated services digital network) for relatively low data rate transmission. Of course, at a high data rate, this scheme is expensive, because it results in an increase in an already high signal transmission rate. To deal with this problem at high data rates, a technique that involves scrambling the data is used. We examine two examples of this technique later in this section.

Thus, with suitable modification, multilevel binary schemes overcome the problems of NRZ codes. Of course, as with any engineering design decision, there is a trade-off. With multilevel binary coding, the line signal may take on one of three levels, but each signal element, which could represent $\log_2 3 = 1.58$ bits of information, bears only one bit of information. Thus multilevel binary is not as efficient as NRZ coding. Another way to state this is that the receiver of multilevel binary signals has to distinguish between three levels $(+A, -A, 0)$ instead of just two levels in the signaling formats previously discussed. Because of this, the multilevel binary signal requires approximately 3 dB more signal power than a two-valued signal for the same probability of bit error. This is illustrated in Figure 5.4. Put another way, the bit error rate for NRZ codes, at a given signal-to-noise ratio, is significantly less than that for multilevel binary.

---

[3]These terms are not used consistently in the literature. In some books, these two terms are used for different encoding schemes than those defined here, and a variety of terms have been used for the two schemes illustrated in Figure 5.2. The nomenclature used here corresponds to the usage in various ITU-T standards documents.

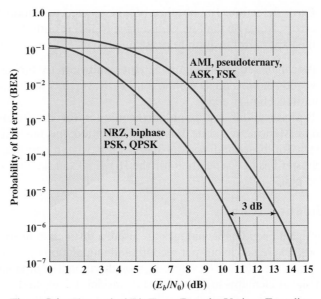

Figure 5.4 Theoretical Bit Error Rate for Various Encoding Schemes

Biphase

There is another set of coding techniques, grouped under the term *biphase*, that overcomes the limitations of NRZ codes. Two of these techniques, Manchester and differential Manchester, are in common use.

In the **Manchester** code, there is a transition at the middle of each bit period. The midbit transition serves as a clocking mechanism and also as data: A low-to-high transition represents a 1, and a high-to-low transition represents a 0.[4] In **differential Manchester**, the midbit transition is used only to provide clocking. The encoding of a 0 is represented by the presence of a transition at the beginning of a bit period, and a 1 is represented by the absence of a transition at the beginning of a bit period. Differential Manchester has the added advantage of employing differential encoding.

All of the biphase techniques require at least one transition per bit time and may have as many as two transitions. Thus, the maximum modulation rate is twice that for NRZ; this means that the bandwidth required is correspondingly greater. On the other hand, the biphase schemes have several advantages:

- **Synchronization:** Because there is a predictable transition during each bit time, the receiver can synchronize on that transition. For this reason, the biphase codes are known as self-clocking codes.

- **No dc component:** Biphase codes have no dc component, yielding the benefits described earlier.

---

[4]The definition of Manchester presented here is the opposite of that used in a number of respectable textbooks, in which a low-to-high transition represents a binary 0 and a high-to-low transition represents a binary 1. Here, we conform to industry practice and to the definition used in the various LAN standards, such as IEEE 802.3.

- **Error detection:** The absence of an expected transition can be used to detect errors. Noise on the line would have to invert both the signal before and after the expected transition to cause an undetected error.

As can be seen from Figure 5.3, the bandwidth for biphase codes is reasonably narrow and contains no dc component. However, it is wider than the bandwidth for the multilevel binary codes.

Biphase codes are popular techniques for data transmission. The more common Manchester code has been specified for the IEEE 802.3 (Ethernet) standard for baseband coaxial cable and twisted-pair bus LANs. Differential Manchester has been specified for the IEEE 802.5 token ring LAN, using shielded twisted pair.

Modulation Rate

When signal-encoding techniques are used, a distinction needs to be made between data rate (expressed in bits per second) and modulation rate (expressed in baud). The data rate, or bit rate, is $1/T_b$, where $T_b =$ bit duration. The modulation rate is the rate at which signal elements are generated. Consider, for example, Manchester encoding. The minimum size signal element is a pulse of one-half the duration of a bit interval. For a string of all binary zeroes or all binary ones, a continuous stream of such pulses is generated. Hence, the maximum modulation rate for Manchester is $2/T_b$. This situation is illustrated in Figure 5.5, which shows the transmission of a stream of binary 1s at a data rate of 1 Mbps using NRZI and Manchester. In general,

$$D = \frac{R}{L} = \frac{R}{\log_2 M} \qquad \text{(5.1)}$$

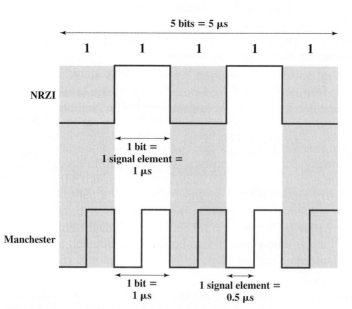

Figure 5.5 A Stream of Binary Ones at 1 Mbps

Table 5.3 Normalized Signal Transition Rate of Various Digital Signal Encoding Schemes

	Minimum	101010 . . .	Maximum
NRZ-L	0 (all 0s or 1s)	1.0	1.0
NRZI	0 (all 0s)	0.5	1.0 (all 1s)
Bipolar-AMI	0 (all 0s)	1.0	1.0
Pseudoternary	0 (all 1s)	1.0	1.0
Manchester	1.0 (1010 . . .)	1.0	2.0 (all 0s or 1s)
Differential Manchester	1.0 (all 1s)	1.5	2.0 (all 0s)

where

$$D = \text{modulation rate, baud}$$
$$R = \text{data rate, bps}$$
$$M = \text{number of different signal elements} = 2^L$$
$$L = \text{number of bits per signal element}$$

One way of characterizing the modulation rate is to determine the average number of transitions that occur per bit time. In general, this will depend on the exact sequence of bits being transmitted. Table 5.3 compares transition rates for various techniques. It indicates the signal transition rate in the case of a data stream of alternating 1s and 0s, and for the data stream that produces the minimum and maximum modulation rate.

EXAMPLE 5.2 For the 11-bit binary string 01001100011 (Figure 5.2) the number of transitions for the encoding schemes discussed in this section is:

NRZ-L	5	Pseudoternary	8
NRZI	5	Manchester	16
Bipolar-AMI	7	Differential Manchester	16

Scrambling Techniques

Although the biphase techniques have achieved widespread use in local area network applications at relatively high data rates (up to 10 Mbps), they have not been widely used in long-distance applications. The principal reason for this is that they require a high signaling rate relative to the data rate. This sort of inefficiency is more costly in a long-distance application.

Another approach is to make use of some sort of scrambling scheme. The idea behind this approach is simple: Sequences that would result in a constant voltage level on the line are replaced by filling sequences that will provide sufficient transitions for the receiver's clock to maintain synchronization. The filling sequence must be recognized by the receiver and replaced with the original data sequence.

The filling sequence is the same length as the original sequence, so there is no data rate penalty. The design goals for this approach can be summarized as follows:

- No dc component
- No long sequences of zero-level line signals
- No reduction in data rate
- Error-detection capability

We now look at two scrambling techniques that are commonly used in long-distance transmission services: B8ZS and HDB3.

The **bipolar with 8-zeros substitution (B8ZS)** coding scheme is commonly used in North America. The coding scheme is based on a bipolar-AMI. We have seen that the drawback of the AMI code is that a long string of zeros may result in loss of synchronization. To overcome this problem, the encoding is amended with the following rules:

- If an octet of all zeros occurs and the last voltage pulse preceding this octet was positive, then the eight zeros of the octet are encoded as $000+-0-+$.
- If an octet of all zeros occurs and the last voltage pulse preceding this octet was negative, then the eight zeros of the octet are encoded as $000-+0+-$.

This technique forces two code violations (signal patterns not allowed in AMI) of the AMI code, an event unlikely to be caused by noise or other transmission impairment. The receiver recognizes the pattern and interprets the octet as consisting of all zeros.

A coding scheme that is commonly used in Europe and Japan is known as the **high-density bipolar-3 zeros (HDB3)** code (Table 5.4). As before, it is based on the use of AMI encoding. In this case, the scheme replaces strings of four zeros with sequences containing one or two pulses. In each case, the fourth zero is replaced with a code violation. In addition, a rule is needed to ensure that successive violations are of alternate polarity so that no dc component is introduced. Thus, if the last violation was positive, this violation must be negative and vice versa. Table 5.4 shows that this condition is tested for by determining (1) whether the number of pulses since the last violation is even or odd and (2) the polarity of the last pulse before the occurrence of the four zeros.

EXAMPLE 5.3 Figure 5.6 shows the signal encoding for the binary sequence 1100000000110000010 using AMI, and then scrambled using B8ZS and HDB3. The original sequence includes a continuous strings of eight zeros and five zeros. B8ZS eliminates the string of eight zeros. HDB3 eliminates both strings. The total number of transitions for this sequence is 7 for Bipolar AMI, 12 for B8ZS, and 14 for HDB3.

Table 5.4   HDB3 Substitution Rules

Polarity of Preceding Pulse	Number of Bipolar Pulses (ones) since Last Substitution	
	Odd	**Even**
−	000−	+00+
+	000+	−00−

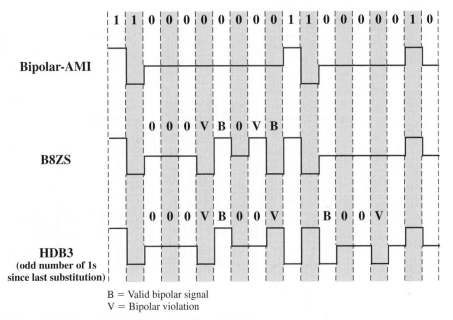

B = Valid bipolar signal
V = Bipolar violation

Figure 5.6 Encoding Rules for B8ZS and HDB3

Figure 5.3 shows the spectral properties of these two codes. As can be seen, neither has a dc component. Most of the energy is concentrated in a relatively sharp spectrum around a frequency equal to one-half the data rate. Thus, these codes are well suited to high data rate transmission.

5.2 DIGITAL DATA, ANALOG SIGNALS

We turn now to the case of transmitting digital data using analog signals. The most familiar use of this transformation is for transmitting digital data through the public telephone network. The telephone network was designed to receive, switch, and transmit analog signals in the voice-frequency range of about 300 to 3400 Hz. It is not at present suitable for handling digital signals from the subscriber locations (although this is beginning to change). Thus digital devices are attached to the network via a modem (modulator-demodulator), which converts digital data to analog signals, and vice versa.

For the telephone network, modems are used that produce signals in the voice-frequency range. The same basic techniques are used for modems that produce signals at higher frequencies (e.g., microwave). This section introduces these techniques and provides a brief discussion of the performance characteristics of the alternative approaches.

We mentioned that modulation involves operation on one or more of the three characteristics of a carrier signal: amplitude, frequency, and phase. Accordingly, there are three basic encoding or modulation techniques for transforming digital data into analog signals, as illustrated in Figure 5.7: amplitude shift keying (ASK), frequency shift keying (FSK), and phase shift keying (PSK). In all these cases, the resulting signal occupies a bandwidth centered on the carrier frequency.

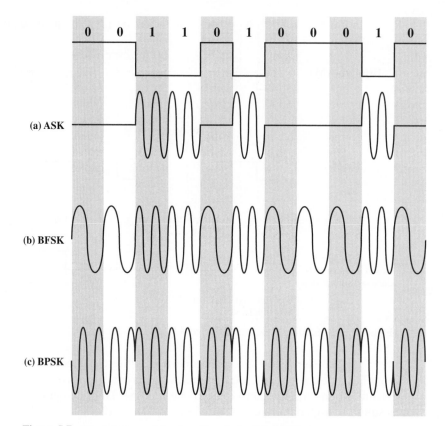

Figure 5.7 Modulation of Analog Signals for Digital Data

Amplitude Shift Keying

In ASK, the two binary values are represented by two different amplitudes of the carrier frequency. Commonly, one of the amplitudes is zero; that is, one binary digit is represented by the presence, at constant amplitude, of the carrier, the other by the absence of the carrier (Figure 5.7a). The resulting transmitted signal for one bit time is

$$\textbf{ASK}\quad s(t) = \begin{cases} A\cos(2\pi f_c t) & \text{binary 1} \\ 0 & \text{binary 0} \end{cases} \tag{5.2}$$

where the carrier signal is $A\cos(2\pi f_c t)$. ASK is susceptible to sudden gain changes and is a rather inefficient modulation technique. On voice-grade lines, it is typically used only up to 1200 bps.

The ASK technique is used to transmit digital data over optical fiber. For LED (light-emitting diode) transmitters, Equation (5.2) is valid. That is, one signal element is represented by a light pulse while the other signal element is represented by the absence of light. Laser transmitters normally have a fixed "bias" current that causes the device to emit a low light level. This low level represents one signal element, while a higher-amplitude lightwave represents another signal element.

Frequency Shift Keying

The most common form of FSK is binary FSK (BFSK), in which the two binary values are represented by two different frequencies near the carrier frequency (Figure 5.7b). The resulting transmitted signal for one bit time is

$$\textbf{BFSK} \qquad s(\text{t}) = \begin{cases} A \cos(2\pi f_1 t) & \text{binary 1} \\ A \cos(2\pi f_2 t) & \text{binary 0} \end{cases} \qquad \textbf{(5.3)}$$

where f_1 and f_2 are typically offset from the carrier frequency f_c by equal but opposite amounts.

Figure 5.8 shows an example of the use of BFSK for full-duplex operation over a voice-grade line. The figure is a specification for the Bell System 108 series modems. Recall that a voice-grade line will pass frequencies in the approximate range 300 to 3400 Hz, and that *full duplex* means that signals are transmitted in both directions at the same time. To achieve full-duplex transmission, this bandwidth is split. In one direction (transmit or receive), the frequencies used to represent 1 and 0 are centered on 1170 Hz, with a shift of 100 Hz on either side. The effect of alternating between those two frequencies is to produce a signal whose spectrum is indicated as the shaded area on the left in Figure 5.8. Similarly, for the other direction (receive or transmit) the modem uses frequencies shifted 100 Hz to each side of a center frequency of 2125 Hz. This signal is indicated by the shaded area on the right in Figure 5.8. Note that there is little overlap and thus little interference.

BFSK is less susceptible to error than ASK. On voice-grade lines, it is typically used up to 1200 bps. It is also commonly used for high-frequency (3 to 30 MHz) radio transmission. It can also be used at even higher frequencies on local area networks that use coaxial cable.

A signal that is more bandwidth efficient, but also more susceptible to error, is multiple FSK (MFSK), in which more than two frequencies are used. In this case each signaling element represents more than one bit. The transmitted MFSK signal for one signal element time can be defined as follows:

$$\textbf{MFSK} \qquad s_i(t) = A \cos 2\pi f_i t, \qquad 1 \le i \le M \qquad \textbf{(5.4)}$$

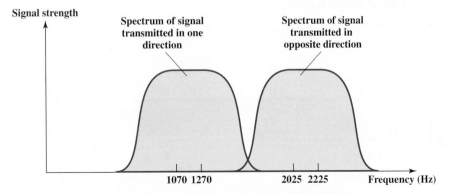

Figure 5.8 Full-Duplex FSK Transmission on a Voice-Grade Line

where

$$f_i = f_c + (2i - 1 - M)f_d$$

f_c = the carrier frequency

f_d = the difference frequency

M = number of different signal elements = 2^L

L = number of bits per signal element

To match the data rate of the input bit stream, each output signal element is held for a period of $T_s = LT$ seconds, where T is the bit period (data rate = $1/T$). Thus, one signal element, which is a constant-frequency tone, encodes L bits. The total bandwidth required is $2Mf_d$. It can be shown that the minimum frequency separation required is $2f_d = 1/T_s$. Therefore, the modulator requires a bandwidth of $W_d = 2Mf_d = M/T_s$.

EXAMPLE 5.4 With f_c = 250 kHz, f_d = 25 kHz, and M = 8 (L = 3 bits), we have the following frequency assignments for each of the eight possible 3-bit data combinations:

f_1 = 75 kHz 000 f_2 =125 kHz 001 f_3 = 175 kHz 010 f_4 = 225 kHz 011
f_5 = 275 kHz 100 f_6 = 325 kHz 101 f_7 = 375 kHz 110 f_8 = 425 kHz 111

This scheme can support a data rate of $1/T = 2Lf_d$ = 150 kbps.

EXAMPLE 5.5 Figure 5.9 shows an example of MFSK with M = 4. An input bit stream of 20 bits is encoded 2 bits at a time, with each of the four possible 2-bit combinations transmitted as a different frequency. The display in the figure shows the frequency transmitted (y axis) as a function of time (x axis). Each column represents a time unit T_s in which a single 2-bit signal element is transmitted. The shaded rectangle in the column indicates the frequency transmitted during that time unit.

Phase Shift Keying

In PSK, the phase of the carrier signal is shifted to represent data.

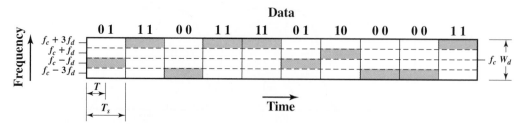

Figure 5.9   MFSK Frequency Use (M = 4)

Two-Level PSK The simplest scheme uses two phases to represent the two binary digits (Figure 5.7c) and is known as binary phase shift keying. The resulting transmitted signal for one bit time is

$$\textbf{BPSK} \quad s(t) = \begin{cases} A \cos(2\pi f_c t) \\ A \cos(2\pi f_c t + \pi) \end{cases} = \begin{cases} A \cos(2\pi f_c t) & \text{binary 1} \\ -A \cos(2\pi f_c t) & \text{binary 0} \end{cases} \quad \textbf{(5.5)}$$

Because a phase shift of 180° (π) is equivalent to flipping the sine wave or multiplying it by -1, the rightmost expressions in Equation (5.5) can be used. This leads to a convenient formulation. If we have a bit stream, and we define $d(t)$ as the discrete function that takes on the value of $+1$ for one bit time if the corresponding bit in the bit stream is 1 and the value of -1 for one bit time if the corresponding bit in the bit stream is 0, then we can define the transmitted signal as

$$\textbf{BPSK} \qquad s_d(t) = A\, d(t) \cos(2\pi f_c t) \qquad\qquad \textbf{(5.6)}$$

An alternative form of two-level PSK is differential PSK (DPSK). Figure 5.10 shows an example. In this scheme, a binary 0 is represented by sending a signal burst of the same phase as the previous signal burst sent. A binary 1 is represented by sending a signal burst of opposite phase to the preceding one. This term *differential* refers to the fact that the phase shift is with reference to the previous bit transmitted rather than to some constant reference signal. In differential encoding, the information to be transmitted is represented in terms of the changes between successive data symbols rather than the signal elements themselves. DPSK avoids the requirement for an accurate local oscillator phase at the receiver that is matched with the transmitter. As long as the preceding phase is received correctly, the phase reference is accurate.

Four-Level PSK More efficient use of bandwidth can be achieved if each signaling element represents more than one bit. For example, instead of a phase shift of 180°, as allowed in BPSK, a common encoding technique known as quadrature phase shift keying (QPSK) uses phase shifts separated by multiples of $\pi/2$ (90°).

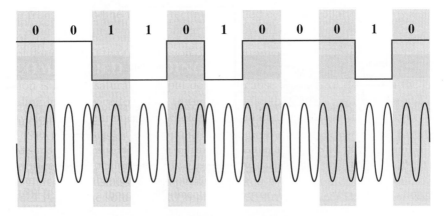

Figure 5.10 Differential Phase—Shift Keying (DPSK)

QPSK $\quad s(t) = \begin{cases} A\cos\left(2\pi f_c t + \dfrac{\pi}{4}\right) & 11 \\[2mm] A\cos\left(2\pi f_c t + \dfrac{3\pi}{4}\right) & 01 \\[2mm] A\cos\left(2\pi f_c t - \dfrac{3\pi}{4}\right) & 00 \\[2mm] A\cos\left(2\pi f_c t - \dfrac{\pi}{4}\right) & 10 \end{cases}$ **(5.7)**

Thus each signal element represents two bits rather than one.

Figure 5.11 shows the QPSK modulation scheme in general terms. The input is a stream of binary digits with a data rate of $R = 1/T_b$, where T_b is the width of each bit. This stream is converted into two separate bit streams of $R/2$ bps each, by taking alternate bits for the two streams. The two data streams are referred to as the I (in-phase) and Q (quadrature phase) streams. In the diagram, the upper stream is modulated on a carrier of frequency f_c by multiplying the bit stream by the carrier. For convenience of modulator structure we map binary 1 to $\sqrt{1/2}$ and binary 0 to $-\sqrt{1/2}$. Thus, a binary 1 is represented by a scaled version of the carrier wave and a binary 0 is represented by a scaled version of the negative of the carrier wave, both at a constant amplitude. This same carrier wave is shifted by 90° and used for modulation of the lower binary stream. The two modulated signals are then added together and transmitted. The transmitted signal can be expressed as follows:

QPSK $\quad s(t) = \dfrac{1}{\sqrt{2}}I(t)\cos 2\pi f_c t - \dfrac{1}{\sqrt{2}}Q(t)\sin 2\pi f_c t$

Figure 5.12 shows an example of QPSK coding. Each of the two modulated streams is a BPSK signal at half the data rate of the original bit stream. Thus, the

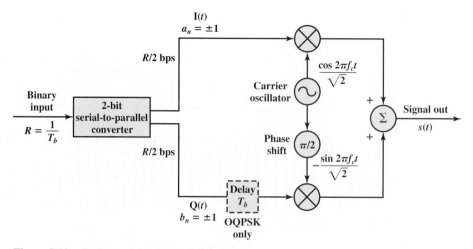

Figure 5.11 QPSK and OQPSK Modulators

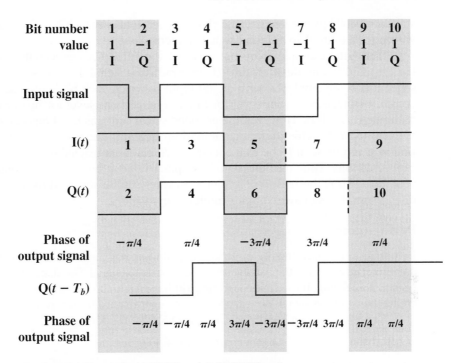

Figure 5.12 Example of QPSK and OQPSK Waveforms

combined signals have a symbol rate that is half the input bit rate. Note that from one symbol time to the next, a phase change of as much as 180° (π) is possible.

Figure 5.11 also shows a variation of QPSK known as offset QPSK (OQPSK), or orthogonal QPSK. The difference is that a delay of one bit time is introduced in the Q stream, resulting in the following signal:

$$s(t) = \frac{1}{\sqrt{2}} I(t) \cos 2\pi f_c t - \frac{1}{\sqrt{2}} Q(t - T_b) \sin 2\pi f_c t$$

Because OQPSK differs from QPSK only by the delay in the Q stream, its spectral characteristics and bit-error performance are the same as that of QPSK. From Figure 5.12, we can observe that only one of two bits in the pair can change sign at any time and thus the phase change in the combined signal never exceeds 90° ($\pi/2$). This can be an advantage because physical limitations on phase modulators make large phase shifts at high transition rates difficult to perform. OQPSK also provides superior performance when the transmission channel (including transmitter and receiver) has significant nonlinear components. The effect of nonlinearities is a spreading of the signal bandwidth, which may result in adjacent channel interference. It is easier to control this spreading if the phase changes are smaller, hence the advantage of OQPSK over QPSK.

MULTILEVEL PSK The use of multiple levels can be extended beyond taking bits two at a time. It is possible to transmit bits three at a time using eight different phase angles. Further, each angle can have more than one amplitude. For example, a standard 9600 bps modem uses 12 phase angles, four of which have two amplitude values, for a total of 16 different signal elements.

This latter example points out very well the difference between the data rate R (in bps) and the modulation rate D (in baud) of a signal. Let us assume that this scheme is being employed with digital input in which each bit is represented by a constant voltage pulse, one level for binary one and one level for binary zero. The data rate is $R = 1/T_b$. However, the encoded signal contains L = 4 bits in each signal element using $M = 16$ different combinations of amplitude and phase. The modulation rate can be seen to be $R/4$, because each change of signal element communicates four bits. Thus the line signaling speed is 2400 baud, but the data rate is 9600 bps. This is the reason that higher bit rates can be achieved over voice-grade lines by employing more complex modulation schemes.

Performance

In looking at the performance of various digital-to-analog modulation schemes, the first parameter of interest is the bandwidth of the modulated signal. This depends on a variety of factors, including the definition of bandwidth used and the filtering technique used to create the bandpass signal. We will use some straightforward results from [COUC07].

The transmission bandwidth B_T for ASK is of the form

$$\textbf{ASK} \quad B_T = (1 + r)R \tag{5.8}$$

where R is the bit rate and r is related to the technique by which the signal is filtered to establish a bandwidth for transmission; typically $0 < r < 1$. Thus the bandwidth is directly related to the bit rate. The preceding formula is also valid for PSK and, under certain assumptions, FSK.

With multilevel PSK (MPSK), significant improvements in bandwidth can be achieved. In general

$$\textbf{MPSK} \quad B_T = \left(\frac{1 + r}{L}\right)R = \left(\frac{1 + r}{\log_2 M}\right)R \tag{5.9}$$

where L is the number of bits encoded per signal element and M is the number of different signal elements.

For multilevel FSK (MFSK), we have

$$\textbf{MFSK} \quad B_T = \left(\frac{(1 + r)M}{\log_2 M}\right)R \tag{5.10}$$

Table 5.5 shows the ratio of data rate, R, to transmission bandwidth for various schemes. This ratio is also referred to as the **bandwidth efficiency**. As the name suggests, this parameter measures the efficiency with which bandwidth can be used to transmit data. The advantage of multilevel signaling methods now becomes clear.

Of course, the preceding discussion refers to the spectrum of the input signal to a communications line. Nothing has yet been said of performance in the presence of noise. Figure 5.4 summarizes some results based on reasonable assumptions concerning the transmission system [COUC07]. Here bit error rate is plotted as a function of the ratio E_b/N_0 defined in Chapter 3. Of course, as that ratio increases, the bit error rate drops. Further, DPSK and BPSK are about 3 dB superior to ASK and BFSK.

Table 5.5   Bandwidth Efficiency (R/B_T) for Various Digital-to-Analog Encoding Schemes

	$r = 0$	$r = 0.5$	$r = 1$
ASK	1.0	0.67	0.5
Multilevel FSK			
M = 4, L = 2	0.5	0.33	0.25
M = 8, L = 3	0.375	0.25	0.1875
M = 16, L = 4	0.25	0.167	0.125
M = 32, L = 5	0.156	0.104	0.078
PSK	1.0	0.67	0.5
Multilevel PSK			
M = 4, L = 2	2.00	1.33	1.00
M = 8, L = 3	3.00	2.00	1.50
M = 16, L = 4	4.00	2.67	2.00
M = 32, L = 5	5.00	3.33	2.50

Figure 5.13 shows the same information for various levels of M for MFSK and MPSK. There is an important difference. For MFSK, the error probability for a given value of E_b/N_0 decreases as M increases, while the opposite is true for MPSK. On the other hand, comparing Equations (5.9) and (5.10), the bandwidth efficiency of MFSK decreases as M increases, while the opposite is true of MPSK. Thus, in both cases, there is a trade-off between bandwidth efficiency and error performance: An increase in bandwidth efficiency results in an increase in error probability. The fact that these trade-offs move in opposite directions with respect to the number of levels M for MFSK and MPSK can be derived from the underlying equations. A discussion of the reasons for this difference is beyond the scope of this book. See [SKLA01] for a full treatment.

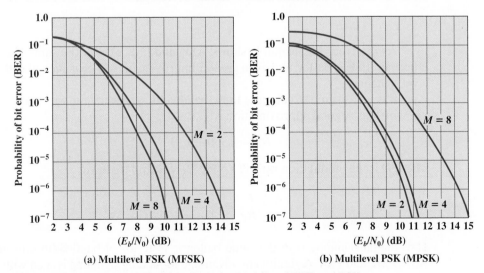

(a) Multilevel FSK (MFSK)   **(b) Multilevel PSK (MPSK)**

Figure 5.13   Theoretical Bit Error Rate for Multilevel FSK and PSK

EXAMPLE 5.6 What is the bandwidth efficiency for FSK, ASK, PSK, and QPSK for a bit error rate of 10^{-7} on a channel with an SNR of 12 dB?

Using Equation (3.2), we have

$$\left(\frac{E_b}{N_0}\right)_{dB} = 12\,dB - \left(\frac{R}{B_T}\right)_{dB}$$

For FSK and ASK, from Figure 5.4,

$$\left(\frac{E_b}{N_0}\right)_{dB} = 14.2\,dB$$

$$\left(\frac{R}{B_T}\right)_{dB} = -2.2\,dB$$

$$\frac{R}{B_T} = 0.6$$

For PSK, from Figure 5.4

$$\left(\frac{E_b}{N_0}\right)_{dB} = 11.2\,dB$$

$$\left(\frac{R}{B_T}\right)_{dB} = 0.8dB$$

$$\frac{R}{B_T} = 1.2$$

The result for QPSK must take into account that the baud rate $D = R/2$. Thus

$$\frac{R}{B_T} = 2.4$$

As the preceding example shows, ASK and FSK exhibit the same bandwidth efficiency; PSK is better, and even greater improvement can be achieved with multilevel signaling.

It is worthwhile to compare these bandwidth requirements with those for digital signaling. A good approximation is

$$B_T = 0.5(1 + r)D$$

where D is the modulation rate. For NRZ, $D = R$, and we have

$$\frac{R}{B_T} = \frac{2}{1 + r}$$

Thus digital signaling is in the same ballpark, in terms of bandwidth efficiency, as ASK, FSK, and PSK. A significant advantage for analog signaling is seen with multilevel techniques.

Quadrature Amplitude Modulation

Quadrature amplitude modulation (QAM) is a popular analog signaling technique that is used in the asymmetric digital subscriber line (ADSL) and in cable modems, described in Chapter 8, and in some wireless standards. This modulation technique is a combination of ASK and PSK. QAM can also be considered a logical extension of QPSK. QAM takes advantage of the fact that it is possible to send two different signals simultaneously on the same carrier frequency, by using two copies of the carrier frequency, one shifted by 90° with respect to the other. For QAM, each carrier is ASK modulated. The two independent signals are simultaneously transmitted over the same medium. At the receiver, the two signals are demodulated and the results combined to produce the original binary input.

Figure 5.14 shows the QAM modulation scheme in general terms. The input is a stream of binary digits arriving at a rate of R bps. This stream is converted into two separate bit streams of $R/2$ bps each, by taking alternate bits for the two streams. In the diagram, the upper stream is ASK modulated on a carrier of frequency f_c by multiplying the bit stream by the carrier. Thus, a binary zero is represented by the absence of the carrier wave and a binary one is represented by the presence of the carrier wave at a constant amplitude. This same carrier wave is shifted by 90° and used for ASK modulation of the lower binary stream. The two modulated signals are then added together and transmitted. The transmitted signal can be expressed as follows:

$$\textbf{QAM} \qquad s(t) = d_1(t)\cos 2\pi f_c t + d_2(t)\sin 2\pi f_c t$$

If two-level ASK is used, then each of the two streams can be in one of two states and the combined stream can be in one of $4 = 2 \times 2$ states. This is essentially QPSK. If four-level ASK is used (i.e., four different amplitude levels), then the combined stream can be in one of $16 = 4 \times 4$ states. Systems using 64 and even 256 states have been implemented. The greater the number of states, the higher the data rate that is possible within a given bandwidth. Of course, as discussed previously, the greater the number of states, the higher the potential error rate due to noise and attenuation.

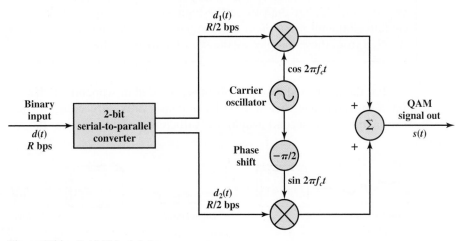

Figure 5.14 QAM Modulator

5.3 ANALOG DATA, DIGITAL SIGNALS

In this section we examine the process of transforming analog data into digital signals. Strictly speaking, it might be more correct to refer to this as a process of converting analog data into digital data; this process is known as digitization. Once analog data have been converted into digital data, a number of things can happen. The three most common outcomes are the following:

1. The digital data can be transmitted using NRZ-L. In this case, we have in fact gone directly from analog data to a digital signal.

2. The digital data can be encoded as a digital signal using a code other than NRZ-L. Thus an extra step is required.

3. The digital data can be converted into an analog signal, using one of the modulation techniques discussed in Section 5.2.

This last, seemingly curious, procedure is illustrated in Figure 5.15, which shows voice data that are digitized and then converted to an analog ASK signal. This allows digital transmission in the sense defined in Chapter 3. The voice data, because they have been digitized, can be treated as digital data, even though transmission requirements (e.g., use of microwave) dictate that an analog signal be used.

The device used for converting analog data into digital form for transmission, and subsequently recovering the original analog data from the digital, is known as a **codec** (coder-decoder). In this section we examine the two principal techniques used in codecs: pulse code modulation and delta modulation. The section closes with a discussion of comparative performance.

Pulse Code Modulation

Pulse code modulation (PCM) is based on the sampling theorem:

> **SAMPLING THEOREM:** If a signal $f(t)$ is sampled at regular intervals of time and at a rate higher than twice the highest signal frequency, then the samples contain all the information of the original signal. The function $f(t)$ may be reconstructed from these samples by the use of a lowpass filter.

For the interested reader, a proof is provided in Appendix F. If voice data are limited to frequencies below 4000 Hz, a conservative procedure for intelligibility, 8000 samples per second would be sufficient to characterize the voice signal

Analog data   Digital data   Analog signal
(voice)   (ASK)

Figure 5.15 Digitizing Analog Data

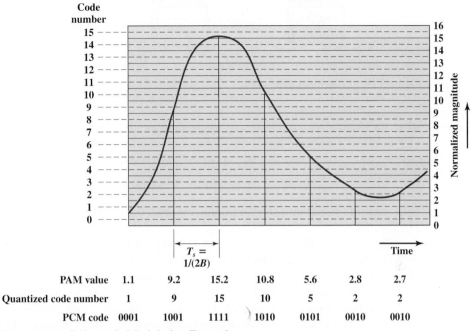

PAM value	1.1	9.2	15.2	10.8	5.6	2.8	2.7
Quantized code number	1	9	15	10	5	2	2
PCM code	0001	1001	1111	1010	0101	0010	0010

Figure 5.16 Pulse code Modulation Example

completely. Note, however, that these are analog samples, called **pulse amplitude modulation (PAM)** samples. To convert to digital, each of these analog samples must be assigned a binary code.

EXAMPLE 5.7 Figure 5.16 shows an example in which the original signal is assumed to be bandlimited with a bandwidth of B. PAM samples are taken at a rate of $2B$, or once every $T_s = 1/2B$ seconds. Each PAM sample is approximated by being *quantized* into one of 16 different levels. Each sample can then be represented by 4 bits. The resulting digital code for this analog signal is 0001100111111010010100100010.

Because the quantized values are only approximations, it is impossible to recover the original signal exactly. By using an 8-bit sample, which allows 256 quantizing levels, the quality of the recovered voice signal is comparable with that achieved via analog transmission. Note that this implies that a data rate of 8000 samples per second $\times$ 8 bits per sample = 64 kbps is needed for a single voice signal.

Thus, PCM starts with a continuous-time, continuous-amplitude (analog) signal, from which a digital signal is produced (Figure 5.17). The digital signal consists of blocks of n bits, where each n-bit number is the amplitude of a PCM pulse. On reception, the process is reversed to reproduce the analog signal. Notice, however, that this process violates the terms of the sampling theorem. By quantizing the PAM

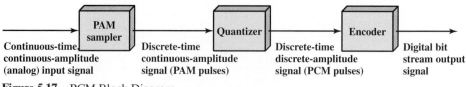

Figure 5.17 PCM Block Diagram

pulse, the original signal is now only approximated and cannot be recovered exactly. This effect is known as **quantizing error** or **quantizing noise**. The signal-to-noise ratio for quantizing noise can be expressed as [GIBS93]

$$\mathrm{SNR_{dB}} = 20 \log 2^n + 1.76 \text{ dB} = 6.02n + 1.76 \text{ dB}$$

Thus each additional bit used for quantizing increases SNR by about 6 dB, which is a factor of 4.

Typically, the PCM scheme is refined using a technique known as nonlinear encoding, which means, in effect, that the quantization levels are not equally spaced. The problem with equal spacing is that the mean absolute error for each sample is the same, regardless of signal level. Consequently, lower amplitude values are relatively more distorted. By using a greater number of quantizing steps for signals of low amplitude, and a smaller number of quantizing steps for signals of large amplitude, a marked reduction in overall signal distortion is achieved (e.g., see Figure 5.18).

The same effect can be achieved by using uniform quantizing but companding (compressing-expanding) the input analog signal. Companding is a process that compresses the intensity range of a signal by imparting more gain to weak signals than to strong signals on input. At output, the reverse operation is performed. Figure 5.19 shows typical companding functions. Note that the effect on the input side is to compress the sample so that the higher values are reduced with respect to the lower values. Thus, with a fixed number of quantizing levels, more levels are

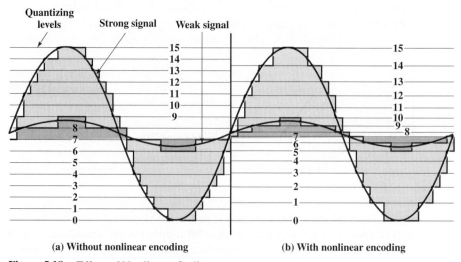

(a) Without nonlinear encoding   (b) With nonlinear encoding

Figure 5.18 Effect of Nonlinear Coding

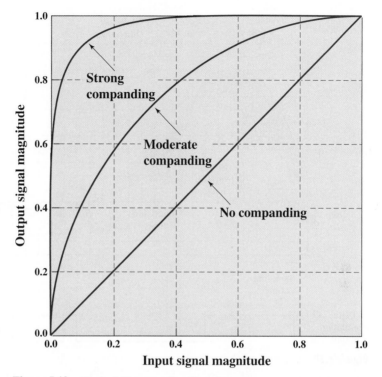

Figure 5.19   Typical Companding Functions

available for lower-level signals. On the output side, the compander expands the samples so the compressed values are restored to their original values.

Nonlinear encoding can significantly improve the PCM SNR. For voice signals, improvements of 24 to 30 dB have been achieved.

Delta Modulation (DM)

A variety of techniques have been used to improve the performance of PCM or to reduce its complexity. One of the most popular alternatives to PCM is delta modulation (DM).

With delta modulation, an analog input is approximated by a staircase function that moves up or down by one quantization level (δ) at each sampling interval (T_s). The important characteristic of this staircase function is that its behavior is binary: At each sampling time, the function moves up or down a constant amount δ. Thus, the output of the delta modulation process can be represented as a single binary digit for each sample. In essence, a bit stream is produced by approximating the derivative of an analog signal rather than its amplitude: A 1 is generated if the staircase function is to go up during the next interval; a 0 is generated otherwise.

EXAMPLE 5.8 Figure 5.20 shows an example, with the staircase function overlaid on the original analog waveform. The resulting digital code for this analog signal is 0111111100000000001010101110.

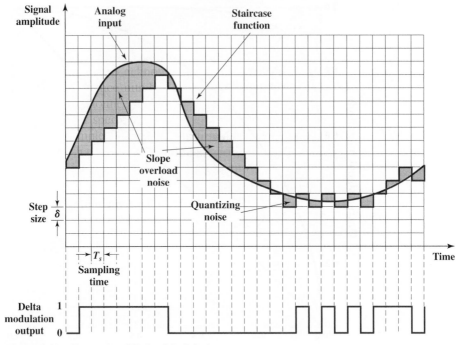

Figure 5.20   Example of Delta Modulation

The transition (up or down) that occurs at each sampling interval is chosen so that the staircase function tracks the original analog waveform as closely as possible. Figure 5.21 illustrates the logic of the process, which is essentially a feedback mechanism. For transmission, the following occurs: At each sampling time, the analog input is compared to the most recent value of the approximating staircase function. If the value of the sampled waveform exceeds that of the staircase function, a 1 is generated; otherwise, a 0 is generated. Thus, the staircase is always changed in the direction of the input signal. The output of the DM process is therefore a binary sequence that can be used at the receiver to reconstruct the staircase function. The staircase function can then be smoothed by some type of integration process or by passing it through a lowpass filter to produce an analog approximation of the analog input signal.

There are two important parameters in a DM scheme: the size of the step assigned to each binary digit, δ, and the sampling rate. As Figure 5.20 illustrates, δ must be chosen to produce a balance between two types of errors or noise. When the analog waveform is changing very slowly, there will be quantizing noise. This noise increases as δ is increased. On the other hand, when the analog waveform is changing more rapidly than the staircase can follow, there is slope overload noise. This noise increases as δ is decreased.

It should be clear that the accuracy of the scheme can be improved by increasing the sampling rate. However, this increases the data rate of the output signal.

The principal advantage of DM over PCM is the simplicity of its implementation. In general, PCM exhibits better SNR characteristics at the same data rate.

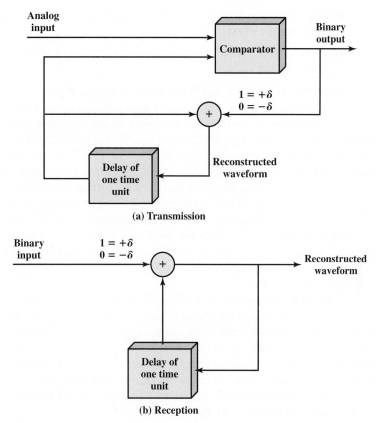

Figure 5.21   Delta Modulation

Performance

Good voice reproduction via PCM can be achieved with 128 quantization levels, or 7-bit coding ($2^7 = 128$). A voice signal, conservatively, occupies a bandwidth of 4 kHz. Thus, according to the sampling theorem, samples should be taken at a rate of 8000 samples per second. This implies a data rate of $8000 \times 7 = 56$ kbps for the PCM-encoded digital data.

Consider what this means from the point of view of bandwidth requirement. An analog voice signal occupies 4 kHz. Using PCM this 4-kHz analog signal can be converted into a 56-kbps digital signal. But using the Nyquist criterion from Chapter 3, this digital signal could require on the order of 28 kHz of bandwidth. Even more severe differences are seen with higher bandwidth signals. For example, a common PCM scheme for color television uses 10-bit codes, which works out to 92 Mbps for a 4.6-MHz bandwidth signal. In spite of these numbers, digital techniques continue to grow in popularity for transmitting analog data. The principal reasons for this are the following:

- Repeaters are used instead of amplifiers, so there is no cumulative noise.
- As we shall see, time division multiplexing (TDM) is used for digital signals instead of the frequency division multiplexing (FDM) used for analog signals.

> With TDM, there is no intermodulation noise, whereas we have seen that this is a concern for FDM.

- The conversion to digital signaling allows the use of the more efficient digital switching techniques.

Furthermore, techniques have been developed to provide more efficient codes. In the case of voice, a reasonable goal appears to be in the neighborhood of 4 kbps. With video, advantage can be taken of the fact that from frame to frame, most picture elements will not change. Interframe coding techniques should allow the video requirement to be reduced to about 15 Mbps, and for slowly changing scenes, such as found in a video teleconference, down to 64 kbps or less.

As a final point, we mention that in many instances, the use of a telecommunications system will result in both digital-to-analog and analog-to-digital processing. The overwhelming majority of local terminations into the telecommunications network is analog, and the network itself uses a mixture of analog and digital techniques. Thus digital data at a user's terminal may be converted to analog by a modem, subsequently digitized by a codec, and perhaps suffer repeated conversions before reaching its destination.

Thus, telecommunication facilities handle analog signals that represent both voice and digital data. The characteristics of the waveforms are quite different. Whereas voice signals tend to be skewed to the lower portion of the bandwidth (Figure 3.9), analog encoding of digital signals has a more uniform spectral content over the bandwidth and therefore contains more high-frequency components. Studies have shown that, because of the presence of these higher frequencies, PCM-related techniques are preferable to DM-related techniques for digitizing analog signals that represent digital data.

5.4 ANALOG DATA, ANALOG SIGNALS

Modulation has been defined as the process of combining an input signal $m(t)$ and a carrier at frequency f_c to produce a signal $s(t)$ whose bandwidth is (usually) centered on f_c. For digital data, the motivation for modulation should be clear: When only analog transmission facilities are available, modulation is required to convert the digital data to analog form. The motivation when the data are already analog is less clear. After all, voice signals are transmitted over telephone lines at their original spectrum (referred to as baseband transmission). There are two principal reasons for analog modulation of analog signals:

- A higher frequency may be needed for effective transmission. For unguided transmission, it is virtually impossible to transmit baseband signals; the required antennas would be many kilometers in diameter.

- Modulation permits frequency division multiplexing, an important technique explored in Chapter 8.

In this section we look at the principal techniques for modulation using analog data: amplitude modulation (AM), frequency modulation (FM), and phase modulation (PM). As before, the three basic characteristics of a signal are used for modulation.

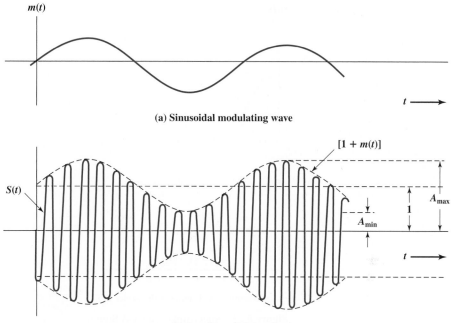

(a) Sinusoidal modulating wave

(b) Resulting AM signal

Figure 5.22   Amplitude Modulation

Amplitude Modulation

Amplitude modulation (AM) is the simplest form of modulation and is depicted in Figure 5.22. Mathematically, the process can be expressed as

$$\text{AM} \qquad s(t) = [1 + n_a x(t)]\cos 2\pi f_c t \qquad\qquad (5.11)$$

where $\cos 2\pi f_c t$ is the carrier and $x(t)$ is the input signal (carrying data), both normalized to unity amplitude. The parameter n_a, known as the **modulation index**, is the ratio of the amplitude of the input signal to the carrier. Corresponding to our previous notation, the input signal is $m(t) = n_a x(t)$. The "1" in the Equation (5.11) is a dc component that prevents loss of information, as explained subsequently. This scheme is also known as double sideband transmitted carrier (DSBTC).

EXAMPLE 5.9   Derive an expression for $s(t)$ if $x(t)$ is the amplitude-modulating signal $\cos 2\pi f_m t$. We have

$$s(t) = [1 + n_a \cos 2\pi f_m t]\cos 2\pi f_c t$$

By trigonometric identity, this may be expanded to

$$s(t) = \cos 2\pi f_c t + \frac{n_a}{2}\cos 2\pi(f_c - f_m)t + \frac{n_a}{2}\cos 2\pi(f_c + f_m)t$$

The resulting signal has a component at the original carrier frequency plus a pair of components each spaced f_m Hz from the carrier.

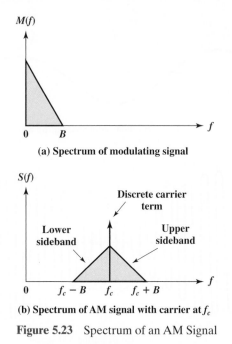

(a) Spectrum of modulating signal

(b) Spectrum of AM signal with carrier at f_c

Figure 5.23   Spectrum of an AM Signal

From Equation (5.11) and Figure 5.22, it can be seen that AM involves the multiplication of the input signal by the carrier. The envelope of the resulting signal is $[1 + n_a x(t)]$ and, as long as $n_a < 1$, the envelope is an exact reproduction of the original signal. If $n_a > 1$, the envelope will cross the time axis and information is lost.

It is instructive to look at the spectrum of the AM signal. An example is shown in Figure 5.23. The spectrum consists of the original carrier plus the spectrum of the input signal translated to f_c. The portion of the spectrum for $|f| > |f_c|$ is the *upper sideband*, and the portion of the spectrum for $|f| < |f_c|$ is *lower sideband*. Both the upper and lower sidebands are replicas of the original spectrum $M(f)$, with the lower sideband being frequency reversed.

EXAMPLE 5.10 Consider a voice signal with a bandwidth that extends from 300 to 3000 Hz being modulated on a 60-kHz carrier. The resulting signal contains an upper sideband of 60.3 to 63 kHz, a lower sideband of 57 to 59.7 kHz, and the 60-kHz carrier. If the carrier has an amplitude of 50 V and the audio signal has an amplitude of 20 V, then the modulation index is $n_a = 20/50 = 0.4$.

An important relationship is

$$P_t = P_c\left(1 + \frac{n_a^2}{2}\right)$$

where P_t is the total transmitted power in $s(t)$ and P_c is the transmitted power in the carrier. We would like n_a as large as possible so that most of the signal power is used to carry information. However, n_a must remain below 1.

EXAMPLE 5.11 Determine the power content of the carrier and each of the sidebands for an AM signal having a modulation index of 0.8 and a total power of 2500 W. Using the preceding equation, we have

$$2500 = P_c(1 + (0.8)^2/2) = 1.32 \ P_c$$
$$P_c = 1893.9 \ \text{W}$$

The remaining power is split evenly between the two sidebands, so that each sideband has a power content of $(2500 - 1893.9)/2 = 303$ W

It should be clear that $s(t)$ contains unnecessary components, because each of the sidebands contains the complete spectrum of $m(t)$. A popular variant of AM, known as single sideband (SSB), takes advantage of this fact by sending only one of the sidebands, eliminating the other sideband and the carrier. The principal advantages of this approach are as follows:

- Only half the bandwidth is required, that is, $B_T = B$, where B is the bandwidth of the original signal. For DSBTC, $B_T = 2B$.
- Less power is required because no power is used to transmit the carrier or the other sideband. Another variant is double sideband suppressed carrier (DSBSC), which filters out the carrier frequency and sends both sidebands. This saves some power but uses as much bandwidth as DSBTC.

The disadvantage of suppressing the carrier is that the carrier can be used for synchronization purposes. For example, suppose that the original analog signal is an ASK waveform encoding digital data. The receiver needs to know the starting point of each bit time to interpret the data correctly. A constant carrier provides a clocking mechanism by which to time the arrival of bits. A compromise approach is vestigial sideband (VSB), which uses one sideband and a reduced-power carrier.

Angle Modulation

Frequency modulation (FM) and phase modulation (PM) are special cases of angle modulation. The modulated signal is expressed as

$$\textbf{Angle Modulation} \qquad s(t) = A_c \cos[2\pi f_c t + \phi(t)] \qquad \textbf{(5.12)}$$

For phase modulation, the phase is proportional to the modulating signal:

$$\textbf{PM} \qquad \phi(t) = n_p m(t) \qquad \textbf{(5.13)}$$

where n_p is the phase modulation index.

For frequency modulation, the derivative of the phase is proportional to the modulating signal:

$$\textbf{FM} \qquad \phi'(t) = n_f m(t) \qquad \textbf{(5.14)}$$

where n_f is the frequency modulation index and $\phi'(t)$ is the derivative of $\phi(t)$.

For those who wish a more detailed mathematical explanation of the preceding, consider the following. The phase of $s(t)$ at any instant is just $2\pi f_c t + \phi(t)$. The instantaneous phase deviation from the carrier signal is $\phi(t)$. In PM, this instantaneous phase deviation is proportional to $m(t)$. Because frequency can be defined as the rate of change of phase of a signal, the instantaneous frequency of $s(t)$ is

$$2\pi f_i(t) = \frac{d}{dt}[2\pi f_c t + \phi(t)]$$

$$f_i(t) = f_c + \frac{1}{2\pi}\phi'(t)$$

and the instantaneous frequency deviation from the carrier frequency is $\phi'(t)$, which in FM is proportional to $m(t)$.

Figure 5.24 illustrates amplitude, phase, and frequency modulation by a sine wave. The shapes of the FM and PM signals are very similar. Indeed, it is impossible to tell them apart without knowledge of the modulation function.

Several observations about the FM process are in order. The peak deviation ΔF can be seen to be

$$\Delta F = \frac{1}{2\pi}n_f A_m \quad \text{Hz}$$

where A_m is the maximum value of $m(t)$. Thus an increase in the magnitude of $m(t)$ will increase ΔF, which, intuitively, should increase the transmitted bandwidth B_T. However, as should be apparent from Figure 5.24, this will not increase the average power level of the FM signal, which is $A_c^2/2$. This is distinctly different from AM, where the level of modulation affects the power in the AM signal but does not affect its bandwidth.

EXAMPLE 5.12 Derive an expression for $s(t)$ if $\phi(t)$ is the phase-modulating signal $n_p \cos 2\pi f_m t$. Assume that $A_c = 1$. This can be seen directly to be

$$s(t) = \cos[2\pi f_c t + n_p \cos 2\pi f_m t]$$

The instantaneous phase deviation from the carrier signal is $n_p \cos 2\pi f_m t$. The phase angle of the signal varies from its unmodulated value in a simple sinusoidal fashion, with the peak phase deviation equal to n_p.

The preceding expression can be expanded using Bessel's trigonometric identities:

$$s(t) = \sum_{n=-\infty}^{\infty} J_n(n_p) \cos\left(2\pi f_c t + 2\pi n f_m t + \frac{n\pi}{2}\right)$$

where, $J_n(n_p)$ is the nth-order Bessel function of the first kind. Using the property

$$J_{-n}(x) = (-1)^n J_n(x)$$

this can be rewritten as

$$s(t) = J_0(n_p) \cos 2\pi f_c t + \sum_{n=1}^{\infty} J_n(n_p)\left[\cos\left(2\pi(f_c + n f_m)t + \frac{n\pi}{2}\right)\right.$$
$$\left. + \cos\left(2\pi(f_c - n f_m)t + \frac{(n+2)\pi}{2}\right)\right]$$

The resulting signal has a component at the original carrier frequency plus a set of sidebands displaced from f_c by all possible multiples of f_m. For $n_p \ll 1$, the higher-order terms fall off rapidly.

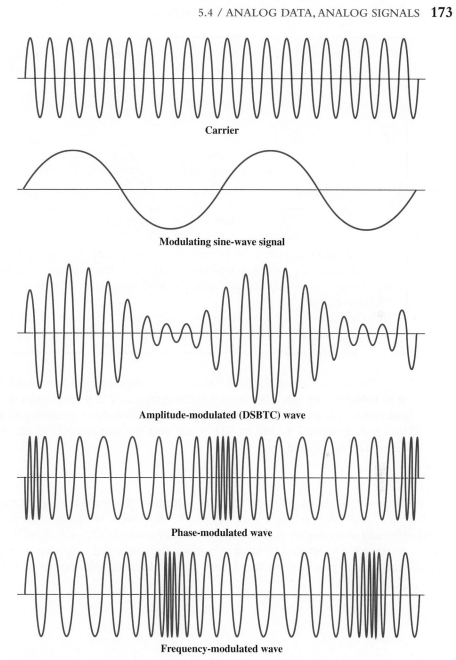

Carrier

Modulating sine-wave signal

Amplitude-modulated (DSBTC) wave

Phase-modulated wave

Frequency-modulated wave

Figure 5.24   Amplitude, Phase, and Frequency Modulation of a Sine-Wave Carrier by a Sine-Wave Signal

EXAMPLE 5.13 Derive an expression for $s(t)$ if $\phi'(t)$ is the frequency modulating signal $-n_f \sin 2\pi f_m t$. The form of $\phi'(t)$ was chosen for convenience. We have

$$\phi(t) = -\int n_f \sin 2\pi f_m t \, dt = \frac{n_f}{2\pi f_m} \cos 2\pi f_m t$$

Thus

$$s(t) = \cos\left[2\pi f_c t + \frac{n_f}{2\pi f_m} \cos 2\pi f_m t\right]$$

$$= \cos\left[2\pi f_c t + \frac{\Delta F}{f_m} \cos 2\pi f_m t\right]$$

The instantaneous frequency deviation from the carrier signal is $-n_f \sin 2\pi f_m t$. The frequency of the signal varies from its unmodulated value in a simple sinusoidal fashion, with the peak frequency deviation equal to n_f radians/second.

The equation for the FM signal has the identical form as for the PM signal, with $\Delta F/f_m$ substituted for n_p. Thus the Bessel expansion is the same.

As with AM, both FM and PM result in a signal whose bandwidth is centered at f_c. However, we can now see that the magnitude of that bandwidth is very different. Amplitude modulation is a linear process and produces frequencies that are the sum and difference of the carrier signal and the components of the modulating signal. Hence, for AM,

$$B_T = 2B$$

However, angle modulation includes a term of the form $\cos(\phi(t))$, which is nonlinear and will produce a wide range of frequencies. In essence, for a modulating sinusoid of frequency f_m, $s(t)$ will contain components at $f_c + f_m, f_c + 2f_m$, and so on. In the most general case, infinite bandwidth is required to transmit an FM or PM signal. As a practical matter, a very good rule of thumb, known as Carson's rule [COUC07], is

$$B_T = 2(\beta + 1)B$$

where

$$\beta = \begin{cases} n_p A_m & \text{for PM} \\ \dfrac{\Delta F}{B} = \dfrac{n_f A_m}{2\pi B} & \text{for FM} \end{cases}$$

We can rewrite the formula for FM as

$$B_T = 2\Delta F + 2B \tag{5.15}$$

Thus both FM and PM require greater bandwidth than AM.

5.5 RECOMMENDED READING

It is difficult, for some reason, to find solid treatments of digital-to-digital encoding schemes. Useful accounts include [SKLA01] and [BERG96].

There are many good references on analog modulation schemes for digital data. Good choices are [COUC07], [XION00], and [PROA05]; these three also provide comprehensive treatment of digital and analog modulation schemes for analog data.

An instructive treatment of the concepts of bit rate, baud, and bandwidth is [FREE98]. A recommended tutorial that expands on the concepts treated in the past few chapters relating to bandwidth efficiency and encoding schemes is [SKLA93].

BERG96 Bergmans, J. *Digital Baseband Transmission and Recording.* Boston: Kluwer, 1996.

COUC07 Couch, L. *Digital and Analog Communication Systems.* Upper Saddle River, NJ: Prentice Hall, 2007.

FREE98 Freeman, R. "Bits, Symbols, Baud, and Bandwidth." *IEEE Communications Magazine,* April 1998.

PROA05 Proakis, J. *Fundamentals of Communication Systems.* Upper Saddle River, NJ: Prentice Hall, 2005.

SKLA93 Sklar, B. "Defining, Designing, and Evaluating Digital Communication Systems." *IEEE Communications Magazine,* November 1993.

SKLA01 Sklar, B. *Digital Communications: Fundamentals and Applications.* Englewood Cliffs, NJ: Prentice Hall, 2001.

XION00 Xiong, F. *Digital Modulation Techniques.* Boston: Artech House, 2000.

5.6 KEY TERMS, REVIEW QUESTIONS, AND PROBLEMS

Key Terms

alternate mark inversion (AMI)	data signaling rate	nonreturn to zero, inverted (NRZI)
amplitude modulation (AM)	delta modulation (DM)	nonreturn to zero-level (NRZ-L)
amplitude shift keying (ASK)	differential encoding	phase modulation (PM)
analog signaling	differential Manchester	phase shift keying (PSK)
angle modulation	differential PSK (DPSK)	polar
bandwidth efficiency	digital signaling	pseudoternary
baseband signal	frequency modulation (FM)	pulse amplitude modulation (PAM)
biphase	frequency shift keying (FSK)	pulse code modulation (PCM)
bipolar-AMI	high-density bipolar-3 zeros (HDB3)	quadrature amplitude modulation (QAM)
bipolar with 8-zeros substitution (B8ZS)	Manchester	quadrature PSK (QPSK)
bit error rate (BER)	Modulation	quantizing error
carrier frequency	modulation index	quantizing noise
carrier signal	modulation rate	scrambling
codec	multilevel binary	unipolar
data rate	nonreturn to zero (NRZ)	

Review Questions

5.1 List and briefly define important factors that can be used in evaluating or comparing the various digital-to-digital encoding techniques.

5.2 What is differential encoding?

5.3 Explain the difference between NRZ-L and NRZI.

5.4 Describe two multilevel binary digital-to-digital encoding techniques.

5.5 Define biphase encoding and describe two biphase encoding techniques.

5.6 Explain the function of scrambling in the context of digital-to-digital encoding techniques.

5.7 What function does a modem perform?

5.8 How are binary values represented in amplitude shift keying, and what is the limitation of this approach?

5.9 What is the difference between QPSK and offset QPSK?

5.10 What is QAM?

5.11 What does the sampling theorem tell us concerning the rate of sampling required for an analog signal?

5.12 What are the differences among angle modulation, PM, and FM?

Problems

5.1 Which of the signals of Table 5.2 use differential encoding?

5.2 Develop algorithms for generating each of the codes of Table 5.2 from NRZ-L.

5.3 A modified NRZ code known as enhanced-NRZ (E-NRZ) is sometimes used for high-density magnetic tape recording. E-NRZ encoding entails separating the NRZ-L data stream into 7-bit words; inverting bits 2, 3, 6, and 7; and adding one parity bit to each word. The parity bit is chosen to make the total number of 1s in the 8-bit word an odd count. What are the advantages of E-NRZ over NRZ-L? Any disadvantages?

5.4 Develop a state diagram (finite state machine) representation of pseudoternary coding.

5.5 Consider the following signal encoding technique. Binary data are presented as input, a_m, for m = 1, 2, 3, ... Two levels of processing occur. First, a new set of binary numbers are produced:

$$b_0 = 0$$
$$b_m = (a_m + b_{m-1})\bmod 2$$

These are then encoded as

$$c_m = b_m - b_{m-1}$$

On reception, the original data are recovered by

$$a_m = c_m \bmod 2$$

a. Verify that the received values of a_m equal the transmitted values of a_m.
b. What sort of encoding is this?

5.6 For the bit stream 01001110, sketch the waveforms for each of the codes of Table 5.2. Assume that: the signal level for the preceding bit for NRZI was high; the most recent preceding 1 bit (AMI) has a negative voltage; and the most recent preceding 0 bit (pseudoternary) has a negative voltage.

5.7 The waveform of Figure 5.25 belongs to a Manchester-encoded binary data stream. Determine the beginning and end of bit periods (i.e., extract clock information) and give the data sequence.

Figure 5.25 A Manchester Stream

5.8 Consider a stream of binary data consisting of a long sequence of 1s followed by a zero followed by a long string of 1s, with the same assumptions as Problem 5.6. Draw the waveform for this sequence using
   a. NRZ-L
   b. Bipolar-AMI
   c. Pseudoternary

5.9 The bipolar-AMI waveform representing the binary sequence 0100101011 is transmitted over a noisy channel. The received waveform is shown in Figure 5.26; it contains a single error. Locate the position of this error and explain your answer.

5.10 One positive side-effect of bipolar encoding is that a bipolar violation (two consecutive + pulses or two consecutive −pulses separated by any number of zeros) indicates to the receiver that an error has occurred in transmission. Unfortunately, upon the receipt of such a violation, the receiver does not know which bit is in error (only that an error has occurred). The received bipolar sequence

$$+ - 0 + - 0 - +$$

has one bipolar violation. Construct two scenarios (each of which involves a different transmitted bit stream with one transmitted bit being converted via an error) that will produce this same received bit pattern.

5.11 Given the bit pattern 01100, encode this data using ASK, BFSK, and BPSK.

5.12 A sine wave is to be used for two different signaling schemes: (a) PSK; (b) QPSK. The duration of a signal element is 10^{-5} s. If the received signal is of the following form:

$$s(t) = 0.005 \sin(2\pi 10^6 t + \theta)\,\text{V}$$

and if the measured noise power at the receiver is 2.5×10^{-8} watts, determine the E_b/N_0 (in dB) for each case.

5.13 Derive an expression for baud rate D as a function of bit rate R for QPSK using the digital encoding techniques of Table 5.2.

5.14 What SNR is required to achieve a bandwidth efficiency of 1.0 for ASK, FSK, PSK, and QPSK? Assume that the required bit error rate is 10^{-6}.

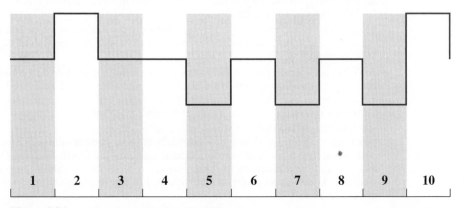

Figure 5.26 A Received Bipolar-AMI Waveform

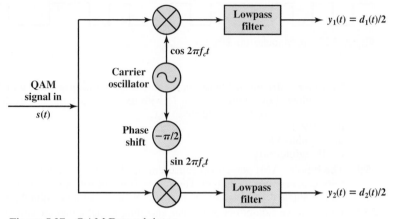

Figure 5.27 QAM Demodulator

5.15 An NRZ-L signal is passed through a filter with $r = 0.5$ and then modulated onto a carrier. The data rate is 2400 bps. Evaluate the bandwidth for ASK and FSK. For FSK assume that the two frequencies used are 50 kHz and 55 kHz.

5.16 Assume that a telephone line channel is equalized to allow bandpass data transmission over a frequency range of 600 to 3000 Hz. The available bandwidth is 2400 Hz. For $r = 1$, evaluate the required bandwidth for 2400 bps QPSK and 4800-bps, eight-level multilevel signaling. Is the bandwidth adequate?

5.17 Figure 5.27 shows the QAM demodulator corresponding to the QAM modulator of Figure 5.14. Show that this arrangement does recover the two signals $d_1(t)$ and $d_2(t)$, which can be combined to recover the original input.

5.18 Why should PCM be preferable to DM for encoding analog signals that represent digital data?

5.19 Are the modem and the codec functional inverses (i.e., could an inverted modem function as a codec, or vice versa)?

5.20 A signal is quantized using 10-bit PCM. Find the signal-to-quantization noise ratio.

5.21 Consider an audio signal with spectral components in the range 300 to 3000 Hz. Assume that a sampling rate of 7000 samples per second will be used to generate a PCM signal.
   a. For SNR = 30 dB, what is the number of uniform quantization levels needed?
   b. What data rate is required?

5.22 Find the step size δ required to prevent slope overload noise as a function of the frequency of the highest-frequency component of the signal. Assume that all components have amplitude A.

5.23 A PCM encoder accepts a signal with a full-scale voltage of 10 V and generates 8-bit codes using uniform quantization. The maximum normalized quantized voltage is $1 - 2^{-8}$. Determine: (a) normalized step size, (b) actual step size in volts, (c) actual maximum quantized level in volts, (d) normalized resolution, (e) actual resolution, and (f) percentage resolution.

5.24 The analog waveform shown in Figure 5.28 is to be delta modulated. The sampling period and the step size are indicated by the grid on the figure. The first DM output and the staircase function for this period are also shown. Show the rest of the staircase function and give the DM output. Indicate regions where slope overload distortion exists.

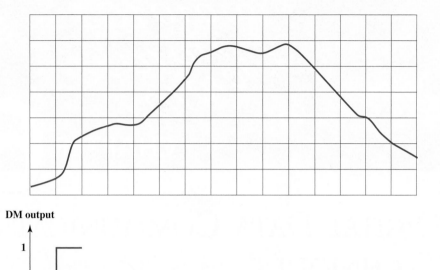

DM output

Figure 5.28   Delta Modulation Example

5.25   Consider the angle-modulated signal

$$s(t) = 10 \cos [(10^8)\pi t + 5 \sin 2\pi(10^3)t]$$

Find the maximum phase deviation and the maximum frequency deviation.

5.26   Consider the angle-modulated signal

$$s(t) = 10 \cos [2\pi(10^6)t + 0.1 \sin (10^3) \pi t]$$

  a. Express $s(t)$ as a PM signal with $n_p = 10$.
  b. Express s(t) as an FM signal with $n_f = 10 \pi$.

5.27   Let $m_1(t)$ and $m_2(t)$ be message signals and let $s_1(t)$ and $s_2(t)$ be the corresponding modulated signals using a carrier frequency of f_c.
  a. Show that if simple AM modulation is used, then $m_1(t) + m_2(t)$ produces a modulated signal equal that is a linear combination of $s_1(t)$ and $s_2(t)$. This is why AM is sometimes referred to as linear modulation.
  b. Show that if simple PM modulation is used, then $m_1(t) + m_2(t)$ produces a modulated signal that is not a linear combination of $s_1(t)$ and s$_2(t)$. This is why angle modulation is sometimes referred to as nonlinear modulation.

DIGITAL DATA COMMUNICATION TECHNIQUES

A conversation forms a two-way communication link; there is a measure of symmetry between the two parties, and messages pass to and fro. There is a continual stimulus-response, cyclic action; remarks call up other remarks, and the behavior of the two individuals becomes concerted, co-operative, and directed toward some goal. This is true communication.

—On Human Communication, Colin Cherry

KEY POINTS

◆ The transmission of a stream of bits from one device to another across a transmission link involves a great deal of cooperation and agreement between the two sides. One of the most fundamental requirements is **synchronization**. The receiver must know the rate at which bits are being received so that it can sample the line at appropriate intervals to determine the value of each received bit. Two techniques are in common use for this purpose. In **asynchronous transmission**, each character of data is treated independently. Each character begins with a start bit that alerts the receiver that a character is arriving. The receiver samples each bit in the character and then looks for the beginning of the next character. This technique would not work well for long blocks of data because the receiver's clock might eventually drift out of synchronization with the transmitter's clock. However, sending data in large blocks is more efficient than sending data one character at a time. For large blocks, **synchronous transmission** is used. Each block of data is formatted as a frame that includes a starting and an ending flag. Some form of synchronization, such as the use of Manchester encoding, is employed.

◆ **Error detection** is performed by calculating an error-detecting code that is a function of the bits being transmitted. The code is appended to the transmitted bits. The receiver calculates the code based on the incoming bits and compares it to the incoming code to check for errors.

◆ **Error correction** operates in a fashion similar to error detection but is capable of correcting certain errors in a transmitted bit stream.

The preceding three chapters have been concerned primarily with the attributes of data transmission, such as the characteristics of data signals and transmission media, the encoding of signals, and transmission performance. In this chapter, we shift our emphasis from data transmission to data communications.

For two devices linked by a transmission medium to exchange data, a high degree of cooperation is required. Typically, data are transmitted one bit at a time over the medium. The timing (rate, duration, spacing) of these bits must be the same for transmitter and receiver. Two common techniques for controlling this timing—asynchronous and synchronous—are explored in Section 6.1. Next, we look at the problem of bit errors. As we have seen, data transmission is not an error-free process, and some means of accounting for these errors is needed. After a brief discussion of the distinction between single-bit errors and burst errors, the chapter turns to two approaches to dealing with errors: error detection and error correction.

Next, the chapter provides an overview of the types of line configurations in common use. To supplement the material in this chapter, Appendix G looks at the physical interface between data transmitting devices and the transmission line. Typically, digital data devices do not attach to and signal across the medium directly. Instead, this process is mediated through a standardized interface that provides considerable control over the interaction between the transmitting/receiving devices and the transmission line.

6.1 ASYNCHRONOUS AND SYNCHRONOUS TRANSMISSION

In this book, we are primarily concerned with serial transmission of data; that is, data are transferred over a single signal path rather than a parallel set of lines, as is common with I/O devices and internal computer signal paths. With serial transmission, signaling elements are sent down the line one at a time. Each signaling element may be

- **Less than one bit:** This is the case, for example, with Manchester coding.
- **One bit:** NRZ-L and FSK are digital and analog examples, respectively.
- **More than one bit:** QPSK is an example.

For simplicity in the following discussion, we assume one bit per signaling element unless otherwise stated. The discussion is not materially affected by this simplification.

Recall from Figure 3.16 that the reception of digital data involves sampling the incoming signal once per bit time to determine the binary value. One of the difficulties encountered in such a process is that various transmission impairments will corrupt the signal so that occasional errors will occur. This problem is compounded by a timing difficulty: In order for the receiver to sample the incoming bits properly, it must know the arrival time and duration of each bit that it receives.

Suppose that the sender simply transmits a stream of data bits. The sender has a clock that governs the timing of the transmitted bits. For example, if data are to be transmitted at 1 million bits per second (1 Mbps), then one bit will be transmitted every $1/10^6 = 1$ microsecond (μs), as measured by the sender's clock. Typically, the receiver will attempt to sample the medium at the center of each bit time. The receiver will time its samples at intervals of one bit time. In our example, the sampling would occur once every 1 μs. If the receiver times its samples based on its own clock, then there will be a problem if the transmitter's and receiver's clocks are not precisely aligned. If there is a drift of 1% (the receiver's clock is 1% faster or slower than the transmitter's clock), then the first sampling will be 0.01 of a bit time (0.01 μs) away from the center of the bit (center of bit is 0.5 μs from beginning and end of bit). After 50 or more samples, the receiver may be in error because it is sampling in the wrong bit time ($50 \times .01 = 0.5$ μs). For smaller timing differences, the error would occur later, but eventually the receiver will be out of step with the transmitter if the transmitter sends a sufficiently long stream of bits and if no steps are taken to synchronize the transmitter and receiver.

Asynchronous Transmission

Two approaches are common for achieving the desired synchronization. The first is called, oddly enough, asynchronous transmission. The strategy with this scheme is to avoid the timing problem by not sending long, uninterrupted streams of bits. Instead, data are transmitted one character at a time, where each character is 5 to 8 bits in length.[1] Timing or synchronization must only be maintained within each character; the receiver has the opportunity to resynchronize at the beginning of each new character.

Figure 6.1 illustrates this technique. When no character is being transmitted, the line between transmitter and receiver is in an *idle* state. The definition of *idle* is equivalent to the signaling element for binary 1. Thus, for NRZ-L signaling (see Figure 5.2), which is common for asynchronous transmission, idle would be the presence of a negative voltage on the line. The beginning of a character is signaled by a *start bit* with a value of binary 0. This is followed by the 5 to 8 bits that actually make up the character. The bits of the character are transmitted beginning with the least significant bit. For example, for IRA characters, the data bits are usually followed by a parity bit, which therefore is in the most significant bit position. The parity bit is set by the transmitter such that the total number of ones in the character, including the parity bit, is even (even parity) or odd (odd parity), depending on the convention being used. The receiver uses this bit for error detection, as discussed in Section 6.3. The final element is a *stop element*, which is a binary 1. A minimum length for the stop element is specified, and this is usually 1, 1.5, or 2 times the duration of an ordinary bit. No maximum value is specified. Because the stop element is the same as the idle state, the transmitter will continue to transmit the stop element until it is ready to send the next character.

The timing requirements for this scheme are modest. For example, IRA characters are typically sent as 8-bit units, including the parity bit. If the receiver is 5% slower or faster than the transmitter, the sampling of the eighth character bit will be displaced by 45% and still be correctly sampled.

---

[1]The number of bits that comprise a character depends on the code used. We have already described one common example, the IRA code, which uses 7 bits per character. Another common code is the Extended Binary Coded Decimal Interchange Code (EBCDIC), which is an 8-bit character code used on IBM mainframes.

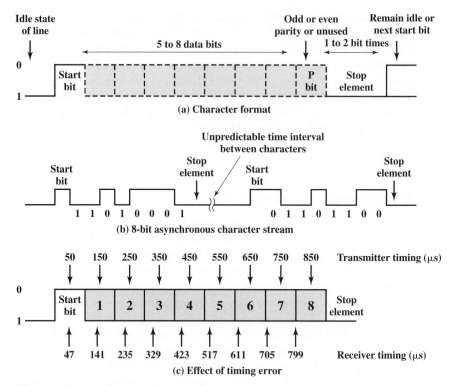

Figure 6.1 Asynchronous Transmission

EXAMPLE 6.1 Figure 6.1c shows the effects of a timing error of sufficient magnitude to cause an error in reception. In this example we assume a data rate of 10,000 bits per second (10 kbps); therefore, each bit is of 0.1 millisecond (ms), or 100 μs, duration. Assume that the receiver is fast by 6%, or 6 μs per bit time. Thus, the receiver samples the incoming character every 94 μs (based on the transmitter's clock). As can be seen, the last sample is erroneous.

An error such as just described actually results in two errors. First, the last sampled bit is incorrectly received. Second, the bit count may now be out of alignment. If bit 7 is a 1 and bit 8 is a 0, bit 8 could be mistaken for a start bit. This condition is termed a *framing error*, as the character plus start bit and stop element are sometimes referred to as a frame. A framing error can also occur if some noise condition causes the false appearance of a start bit during the idle state.

Asynchronous transmission is simple and cheap but requires an overhead of 2 to 3 bits per character. For example, for an 8-bit character with no parity bit, using a 1-bit-long stop element, 2 out of every 10 bits convey no information but are there merely for synchronization; thus the overhead is 20%. Of course, the percentage overhead could be reduced by sending larger blocks of bits between the start bit and stop element. However, as Figure 6.1c indicates, the larger the block of bits, the greater the cumulative timing error. To achieve greater efficiency, a different form of synchronization, known as synchronous transmission, is used.

Synchronous Transmission

With synchronous transmission, a block of bits is transmitted in a steady stream without start and stop codes. The block may be many bits in length. To prevent timing drift between transmitter and receiver, their clocks must somehow be synchronized. One possibility is to provide a separate clock line between transmitter and receiver. One side (transmitter or receiver) pulses the line regularly with one short pulse per bit time. The other side uses these regular pulses as a clock. This technique works well over short distances, but over longer distances the clock pulses are subject to the same impairments as the data signal, and timing errors can occur. The other alternative is to embed the clocking information in the data signal. For digital signals, this can be accomplished with Manchester or differential Manchester encoding. For analog signals, a number of techniques can be used; for example, the carrier frequency itself can be used to synchronize the receiver based on the phase of the carrier.

With synchronous transmission, there is another level of synchronization required, to allow the receiver to determine the beginning and end of a block of data. To achieve this, each block begins with a *preamble* bit pattern and generally ends with a *postamble* bit pattern. In addition, other bits are added to the block that conveys control information used in the data link control procedures discussed in Chapter 7. The data plus preamble, postamble, and control information are called a **frame**. The exact format of the frame depends on which data link control procedure is being used.

Figure 6.2 shows, in general terms, a typical frame format for synchronous transmission. Typically, the frame starts with a preamble called a flag, which is 8 bits long. The same flag is used as a postamble. The receiver looks for the occurrence of the flag pattern to signal the start of a frame. This is followed by some number of control fields (containing data link control protocol information), then a data field (variable length for most protocols), more control fields, and finally the flag is repeated.

For sizable blocks of data, synchronous transmission is far more efficient than asynchronous. Asynchronous transmission requires 20% or more overhead. The control information, preamble, and postamble in synchronous transmission are typically less than 100 bits.

Figure 6.2 Synchronous Frame Format

> **EXAMPLE 6.2** One of the more common schemes, high-level data link control (HDLC), described in Chapter 7, contains 48 bits of control, preamble, and postamble. Thus, for a 1000-character block of data, each frame consists of 48 bits of overhead and $1000 \times 8 = 8000$ bits of data, for a percentage overhead of only $48/8048 \times 100\% = 0.6\%$.

6.2 TYPES OF ERRORS

In digital transmission systems, an error occurs when a bit is altered between transmission and reception; that is, a binary 1 is transmitted and a binary 0 is received, or a binary 0 is transmitted and a binary 1 is received. Two general types of errors can occur: single-bit errors and burst errors. A single-bit error is an isolated error condition that alters 1one bit but does not affect nearby bits. A burst error of length B is a contiguous sequence of B bits in which the first and last bits and any number of intermediate bits are received in error. More precisely, IEEE Std 100 and ITU-T Recommendation Q.9 both define an error burst as follows:

> **Error burst:** A group of bits in which two successive erroneous bits are always separated by less than a given number x of correct bits. The last erroneous bit in the burst and the first erroneous bit in the following burst are accordingly separated by x correct bits or more.

Thus, in an error burst, there is a cluster of bits in which a number of errors occur, although not necessarily all of the bits in the cluster suffer an error.

A single-bit error can occur in the presence of white noise, when a slight random deterioration of the signal-to-noise ratio is sufficient to confuse the receiver's decision of a single bit. Burst errors are more common and more difficult to deal with. Burst errors can be caused by impulse noise, which was described in Chapter 3. Another cause is fading in a mobile wireless environment; fading is described in Chapter 14.

Note that the effects of burst errors are greater at higher data rates.

> **EXAMPLE 6.3** An impulse noise event or a fading event of 1 μs occurs. At a data rate of 10 Mbps, there is a resulting error burst of 10 bits. At a data rate of 100 Mbps, there is an error burst of 100 bits.

6.3 ERROR DETECTION

Regardless of the design of the transmission system, there will be errors, resulting in the change of one or more bits in a transmitted frame. In what follows, we assume that data are transmitted as one or more contiguous sequences of bits, called frames. We define these probabilities with respect to errors in transmitted frames:

P_b: Probability that a bit is received in error; also known as the bit error rate (BER)

P_1: Probability that a frame arrives with no bit errors

P_2: Probability that, with an error-detecting algorithm in use, a frame arrives with one or more undetected errors

P_3: Probability that, with an error-detecting algorithm in use, a frame arrives with one or more detected bit errors but no undetected bit errors

First consider the case in which no means are taken to detect errors. Then the probability of detected errors (P_3) is zero. To express the remaining probabilities, assume the probability that any bit is in error (P_b) is constant and independent for each bit. Then we have

$$P_1 = (1 - P_b)^F$$
$$P_2 = 1 - P_1$$

where F is the number of bits per frame. In words, the probability that a frame arrives with no bit errors decreases when the probability of a single bit error increases, as you would expect. Also, the probability that a frame arrives with no bit errors decreases with increasing frame length; the longer the frame, the more bits it has and the higher the probability that one of these is in error.

EXAMPLE 6.4 A defined objective for ISDN (integrated services digital network) connections is that the BER on a 64-kbps channel should be less than 10^{-6} on at least 90% of observed 1-minute intervals. Suppose now that we have the rather modest user requirement that on average one frame with an undetected bit error should occur per day on a continuously used 64-kbps channel, and let us assume a frame length of 1000 bits. The number of frames that can be transmitted in a day comes out to 5.529×10^6, which yields a desired frame error rate of $P_2 = 1/(5.529 \times 10^6) = 0.18 \times 10^{-6}$. But if we assume a value of P_b of 10^{-6}, then $P_1 = (0.999999)^{1000} = 0.999$ and therefore $P_2 = 10^{-3}$, which is about three orders of magnitude too large to meet our requirement.

This is the kind of result that motivates the use of error-detecting techniques. All of these techniques operate on the following principle (Figure 6.3). For a given frame of bits, additional bits that constitute an **error-detecting code** are added by the transmitter. This code is calculated as a function of the other transmitted bits. Typically, for a data block of k bits, the error-detecting algorithm yields an error-detecting code of $n - k$ bits, where $(n - k) < k$. The error-detecting code, also referred to as the **check bits**, is appended to the data block to produce a frame of n bits, which is then transmitted. The receiver separates the incoming frame into the k bits

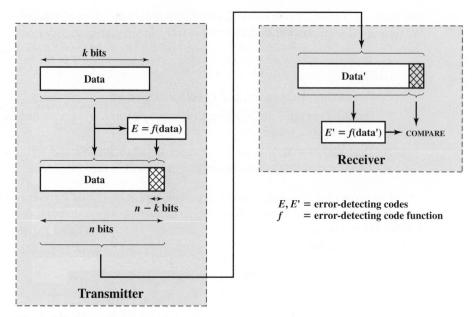

Figure 6.3   Error Detection Process

of data and $(n - k)$ bits of the error-detecting code. The receiver performs the same error-detecting calculation on the data bits and compares this value with the value of the incoming error-detecting code. A detected error occurs if and only if there is a mismatch. Thus P_3 is the probability that a frame contains errors and that the error-detecting scheme will detect that fact. P_2 is known as the residual error rate and is the probability that an error will be undetected despite the use of an error-detecting scheme.

Parity Check

The simplest error-detecting scheme is to append a parity bit to the end of a block of data. A typical example is character transmission, in which a parity bit is attached to each 7-bit IRA character. The value of this bit is selected so that the character has an even number of 1s (even parity) or an odd number of 1s (odd parity).

EXAMPLE 6.5 If the transmitter is transmitting an IRA character G (1110001) and using odd parity, it will append a 1 and transmit 11110001.[2] The receiver examines the received character and, if the total number of 1s is odd, assumes that no error has occurred. If one bit (or any odd number of bits) is erroneously inverted during transmission (e.g., 11100001), then the receiver will detect an error.

---

[2]Recall from our discussion in Section 5.1 that the least significant bit of a character is transmitted first and that the parity bit is the most significant bit.

Note, however, that if two (or any even number) of bits are inverted due to error, an undetected error occurs. Typically, even parity is used for synchronous transmission and odd parity for asynchronous transmission.

The use of the parity bit is not foolproof, as noise impulses are often long enough to destroy more than one bit, particularly at high data rates.

Cyclic Redundancy Check (CRC)

One of the most common, and one of the most powerful, error-detecting codes is the cyclic redundancy check (CRC), which can be described as follows. Given a k-bit block of bits, or message, the transmitter generates an $(n - k)$-bit sequence, known as a frame check sequence (FCS), such that the resulting frame, consisting of n bits, is exactly divisible by some predetermined number. The receiver then divides the incoming frame by that number and, if there is no remainder, assumes there was no error.[3]

To clarify this, we present the procedure in three equivalent ways: modulo 2 arithmetic, polynomials, and digital logic.

MODULO 2 ARITHMETIC Modulo 2 arithmetic uses binary addition with no carries, which is just the exclusive-OR (XOR) operation. Binary subtraction with no carries is also interpreted as the XOR operation: For example

$$
\begin{array}{ccc}
\begin{array}{r} 1111 \\ +1010 \\ \hline 0101 \end{array} &
\begin{array}{r} 1111 \\ -0101 \\ \hline 1010 \end{array} &
\begin{array}{r} 11001 \\ \times 11 \\ \hline 11001 \\ 11001 \\ \hline 101011 \end{array}
\end{array}
$$

Now define

$T = n$-bit frame to be transmitted

$D = k$-bit block of data, or message, the first k bits of T

$F = (n - k)$-bit FCS, the last $(n - k)$ bits of T

$P = $ pattern of $n - k + 1$ bits; this is the predetermined divisor

We would like T/P to have no remainder. It should be clear that

$$ T = 2^{n-k}D + F $$

That is, by multiplying D by 2^{n-k}, we have in effect shifted it to the left by $n - k$ bits and padded out the result with zeroes. Adding F yields the concatenation of D and

---

[3]This procedure is slightly different from that of Figure 6.3. As shall be seen, the CRC process could be implemented as follows. The receiver could perform a division operation on the incoming k data bits and compare the result to the incoming $(n - k)$ check bits.

F, which is T. We want T to be exactly divisible by P. Suppose that we divide $2^{n-k}D$ by P:

$$\frac{2^{n-k}D}{P} = Q + \frac{R}{P} \tag{6.1}$$

There is a quotient and a remainder. Because division is modulo 2, the remainder is always at least 1one bit shorter than the divisor. We will use this remainder as our FCS. Then

$$T = 2^{n-k}D + R \tag{6.2}$$

Does this R satisfy our condition that T/P has no remainder? To see that it does, consider:

$$\frac{T}{P} = \frac{2^{n-k}D + R}{P} = \frac{2^{n-k}D}{P} + \frac{R}{P}$$

Substituting Equation (6.1), we have

$$\frac{T}{P} = Q + \frac{R}{P} + \frac{R}{P}$$

However, any binary number added to itself modulo 2 yields zero. Thus

$$\frac{T}{P} = Q + \frac{R + R}{P} = Q$$

There is no remainder, and therefore T is exactly divisible by P. Thus, the FCS is easily generated: Simply divide $2^{n-k}D$ by P and use the $(n - k)$-bit remainder as the FCS. On reception, the receiver will divide T by P and will get no remainder if there have been no errors.

EXAMPLE 6.6

1. Given

$$\text{Message } D = 1010001101 \text{ (10 bits)}$$
$$\text{Pattern } P = 110101 \text{ (6 bits)}$$
$$\text{FCS } R = \text{ to be calculated (5 bits)}$$

Thus, $n = 15$, $k = 10$, and $(n - k) = 5$.

2. The message is multiplied by 2^5, yielding 101000110100000.
3. This product is divided by P:

```
                                    1  1  0  1  0  1  0  1  1  0  ← Q
    P →  1  1  0  1  0  1 / 1  0  1  0  0  0  1  1  0  1  0  0  0  0  0  ← 2ⁿ⁻ᵏD
                           1  1  0  1  0  1
                              1  1  1  0  1  1
                              1  1  0  1  0  1
                                 1  1  1  0  1  0
                                 1  1  0  1  0  1
                                    1  1  1  1  1  0
                                    1  1  0  1  0  1
                                       1  0  1  1  0  0
                                       1  1  0  1  0  1
                                          1  1  0  0  1  0
                                          1  1  0  1  0  1
                                             0  1  1  1  0  ← R
```

4. The remainder is added to $2^5 D$ to give $T = 101000110101110$, which is transmitted.

5. If there are no errors, the receiver receives T intact. The received frame is divided by P:

```
                                    1  1  0  1  0  1  0  1  1  0  ← Q
    P →  1  1  0  1  0  1 / 1  0  1  0  0  0  1  1  0  1  0  1  1  1  0  ← T
                           1  1  0  1  0  1
                              1  1  1  0  1  1
                              1  1  0  1  0  1
                                 1  1  1  0  1  0
                                 1  1  0  1  0  1
                                    1  1  1  1  1  0
                                    1  1  0  1  0  1
                                       1  0  1  1  1  1
                                       1  1  0  1  0  1
                                          1  1  0  1  0  1
                                          1  1  0  1  0  1
                                                   0  ← R
```

Because there is no remainder, it is assumed that there have been no errors.

The pattern P is chosen to be one bit longer than the desired FCS, and the exact bit pattern chosen depends on the type of errors expected. At minimum, both the high- and low-order bits of P must be 1.

There is a concise method for specifying the occurrence of one or more errors. An error results in the reversal of a bit. This is equivalent to taking the XOR of the bit and 1 (modulo 2 addition of 1 to the bit): $0 + 1 = 1$; $1 + 1 = 0$. Thus, the errors in an n-bit frame can be represented by an n-bit field with 1s in each error position. The resulting frame T_r can be expressed as

$$T_r = T \oplus E$$

where

T = transmitted frame
E = error pattern with 1s in positions where errors occur
T_r = received frame
$\oplus$ = bitwise exclusive-OR (XOR)

If there is an error ($E \neq 0$), the receiver will fail to detect the error if and only if T_r is divisible by P, which is equivalent to E divisible by P. Intuitively, this seems an unlikely occurrence.

POLYNOMIALS A second way of viewing the CRC process is to express all values as polynomials in a dummy variable X, with binary coefficients. The coefficients correspond to the bits in the binary number. Thus, for $D = 110011$, we have $D(X) = X^5 + X^4 + X + 1$, and for $P = 11001$, we have $P(X) = X^4 + X^3 + 1$. Arithmetic operations are again modulo 2. The CRC process can now be described as

$$\frac{X^{n-k}D(X)}{P(X)} = Q(X) + \frac{R(X)}{P(X)}$$

$$T(X) = X^{n-k}D(X) + R(X)$$

Compare these equations with Equations (6.1) and (6.2).

EXAMPLE 6.7 Using the preceding example, for $D = 1010001101$, we have $D(X) = X^9 + X^7 + X^3 + X^2 + 1$, and for $P = 110101$, we have $P(X) = X^5 + X^4 + X^2 + 1$. We should end up with $R = 01110$, which corresponds to $R(X) = X^3 + X^2 + X$. Figure 6.4 shows the polynomial division that corresponds to the binary division in the preceding example.

An m-bit CRC is typically generated by a polynomial of the form

$$P(X) = q(X) \text{ or}$$
$$P(X) = (X + 1)q(X)$$

Where $q(X)$ is a special type of polynomial, called a primitive polynomial.[4]

---

[4]A document at this book's access-controlled Web site provides an explanation of primitive polynomials.

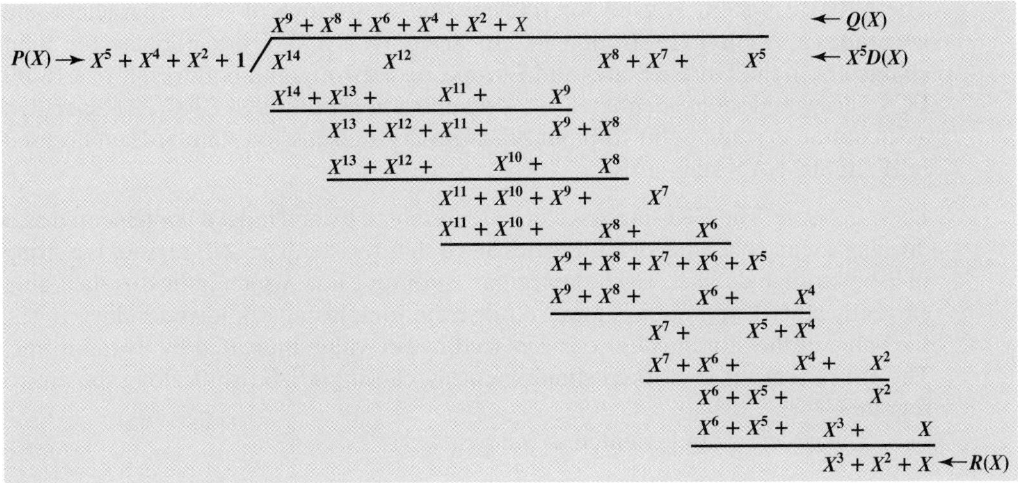

$$\frac{X^9 + X^8 + X^6 + X^4 + X^2 + X}{P(X) \rightarrow X^5 + X^4 + X^2 + 1 / X^{14} \qquad X^{12} \qquad\qquad X^8 + X^7 + \qquad X^5} \quad \leftarrow Q(X)$$

Figure 6.4 shows the long division layout:

$$P(X) \rightarrow X^5 + X^4 + X^2 + 1 \overline{)\, X^{14} \qquad X^{12} \qquad\qquad X^8 + X^7 + \quad X^5\,} \leftarrow X^5 D(X)$$

$$X^{14} + X^{13} + \quad X^{11} + \quad X^9$$
$$\overline{X^{13} + X^{12} + X^{11} + \quad X^9 + X^8}$$
$$X^{13} + X^{12} + \quad X^{10} + \quad X^8$$
$$\overline{X^{11} + X^{10} + X^9 + \quad X^7}$$
$$X^{11} + X^{10} + \quad X^8 + \quad X^6$$
$$\overline{X^9 + X^8 + X^7 + X^6 + X^5}$$
$$X^9 + X^8 + \quad X^6 + \quad X^4$$
$$\overline{X^7 + \quad X^5 + X^4}$$
$$X^7 + X^6 + \quad X^4 + \quad X^2$$
$$\overline{X^6 + X^5 + \quad X^2}$$
$$X^6 + X^5 + \quad X^3 + \quad X$$
$$\overline{X^3 + X^2 + X} \quad \leftarrow R(X)$$

Figure 6.4 Example of Polynomial Division

An error $E(X)$ will only be undetectable if it is divisible by $P(X)$. It can be shown [PETE61, RAMA88] that all of the following errors are not divisible by a suitably chosen $P(X)$ and hence are detectable:

- All single-bit errors, if $P(X)$ has more than one nonzero term
- All double-bit errors, as long as $P(X)$ is of one of the two forms shown above
- Any odd number of errors, as long as $P(X)$ contains a factor $(X + 1)$
- Any burst error for which the length of the burst is less than or equal to $n - k$; that is, less than or equal to the length of the FCS
- A fraction of error bursts of length $n - k + 1$; the fraction equals $1 - 2^{-(n-k-1)}$
- A fraction of error bursts of length greater than $n - k + 1$; the fraction equals $1 - 2^{-(n-k)}$

In addition, it can be shown that if all error patterns are considered equally likely, then for a burst error of length $r + 1$, the probability of an undetected error ($E(X)$ is divisible by $P(X)$) is $1/2^{r-1}$, and for a longer burst, the probability is $1/2^r$, where r is the length of the FCS.

Four versions of $P(X)$ are widely used:

$$\text{CRC-12} = X^{12} + X^{11} + X^3 + X^2 + X + 1 = (X + 1)(X^{11} + X^2 + 1)$$

$$\text{CRC-ANSI} = X^{16} + X^{15} + X^2 + 1 = (X + 1)(X^{15} + X + 1)$$

$$\text{CRC-CCITT} = X^{16} + X^{12} + X^5 + 1 = (X + 1)(X^{15} + X^{14} + X^{13} + X^{12} + X^4 + X^3 + X^2 + X + 1)$$

$$\text{IEEE-802} = X^{32} + X^{26} + X^{23} + X^{22} + X^{16} + X^{12} + X^{11} + X^{10} + X^8 + X^7 + X^5 + X^4 + X^2 + X + 1$$

The CRC-12 system is used for transmission of streams of 6-bit characters and generates a 12-bit FCS. Both CRC-16 and CRC-CCITT are popular for 8-bit characters, in the United States and Europe, respectively, and both result in a 16-bit FCS. This would seem adequate for most applications, although CRC-32 is specified as an option in some point-to-point synchronous transmission standards and is used in IEEE 802 LAN standards.

DIGITAL LOGIC The CRC process can be represented by, and indeed implemented as, a dividing circuit consisting of XOR gates and a shift register. The shift register is a string of 1-bit storage devices. Each device has an output line, which indicates the value currently stored, and an input line. At discrete time instants, known as clock times, the value in the storage device is replaced by the value indicated by its input line. The entire register is clocked simultaneously, causing a 1-bit shift along the entire register.

The circuit is implemented as follows:

1. The register contains $n - k$ bits, equal to the length of the FCS.
2. There are up to $n - k$ XOR gates.
3. The presence or absence of a gate corresponds to the presence or absence of a term in the divisor polynomial, $P(X)$, excluding the terms 1 and X^{n-k}.

EXAMPLE 6.8 The architecture of a CRC circuit is best explained by first considering an example, which is illustrated in Figure 6.5. In this example, we use:

$$\text{Data } D = 1010001101; \quad D(X) = X^9 + X^7 + X^3 + X^2 + 1$$
$$\textit{Divisor } P = 110101; \quad P(X) = X^5 + X^4 + X^2 + 1$$

which were used earlier in the discussion.

Figure 6.5a shows the shift-register implementation. The process begins with the shift register cleared (all zeros). The message, or dividend, is then entered one bit at a time, starting with the most significant bit. Figure 6.5b is a table that shows the step-by-step operation as the input is applied one bit at a time. Each row of the table shows the values currently stored in the five shift-register elements. In addition, the row shows the values that appear at the outputs of the three XOR circuits. Finally, the row shows the value of the next input bit, which is available for the operation of the next step.

Note that the XOR operation affects C_4, C_2, and C_0 on the next shift. This is identical to the binary long division process illustrated earlier. The process continues through all the bits of the message. To produce the proper output, two switches are used. The input data bits are fed in with both switches in the A position. As a result, for the first 10 steps, the input bits are fed into the shift register and also used as output bits. After the last data bit is processed, the shift register contains the remainder (FCS) (shown shaded). As soon as the last data bit is provided to the shift register, both switches are set to the B position.

This has two effects: (1) all of the XOR gates become simple pass-throughs; no bits are changed, and (2) as the shifting process continues, the 5 CRC bits are output.

At the receiver, the same logic is used. As each bit of M arrives, it is inserted into the shift register. If there have been no errors, the shift register should contain the bit pattern for R at the conclusion of M. The transmitted bits of R now begin to arrive, and the effect is to zero out the register so that, at the conclusion of reception, the register contains all 0s.

Figure 6.6 indicates the general architecture of the shift-register implementation of a CRC for the polynomial $P(X) = \sum_{i=0}^{n-k} A_i X^i$, where $A_0 = A_{n-k} = 1$ and all other A_i equal either 0 or 1.[5]

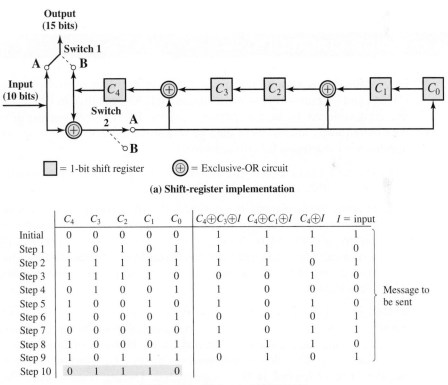

(a) Shift-register implementation

	C_4	C_3	C_2	C_1	C_0	$C_4{\oplus}C_3{\oplus}I$	$C_4{\oplus}C_1{\oplus}I$	$C_4{\oplus}I$	I = input	
Initial	0	0	0	0	0	1	1	1	1	
Step 1	1	0	1	0	1	1	1	1	0	
Step 2	1	1	1	1	1	1	1	0	1	
Step 3	1	1	1	1	0	0	0	1	0	
Step 4	0	1	0	0	1	1	0	0	0	Message to
Step 5	1	0	0	1	0	1	0	1	0	be sent
Step 6	1	0	0	0	1	0	0	0	1	
Step 7	0	0	0	1	0	1	0	1	1	
Step 8	1	0	0	0	1	1	1	1	0	
Step 9	1	0	1	1	1	0	1	0	1	
Step 10	0	1	1	1	0					

(b) **Example with input of 1010001101**

Figure 6.5   Circuit with Shift Registers for Dividing by the Polynomial $X^5 + X^4 + X^2 + 1$

[5]It is common for the CRC register to be shown shifting to the right, which is the reverse of the analogy to binary division. Because binary numbers are usually shown with the most significant bit on the left, a left-shifting register, as is used here, is more appropriate.

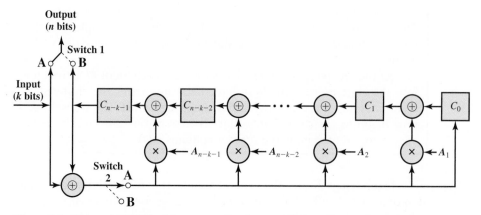

Figure 6.6 General CRC Architecture to Implement Divisor $(1 + A_1X + A_2X + \cdots + A_{n-1}X^{n-k-1} + X^{n-k})$

6.4 ERROR CORRECTION

Error detection is a useful technique, found in data link control protocols, such as HDLC, and in transport protocols, such as TCP. As explained in Chapter 7, an error-detecting code can be used as part of a protocol that corrects errors in transmitted data by requiring the blocks of data be retransmitted. For wireless applications this approach is inadequate for two reasons:

1. The bit error rate on a wireless link can be quite high, which would result in a large number of retransmissions.

2. In some cases, especially satellite links, the propagation delay is very long compared to the transmission time of a single frame. The result is a very inefficient system. As is discussed in Chapter 7, the common approach to retransmission is to retransmit the frame in error plus all subsequent frames. With a long data link, an error in a single frame necessitates retransmitting many frames.

Instead, it would be desirable to enable the receiver to correct errors in an incoming transmission on the basis of the bits in that transmission. Figure 6.7 shows in general how this is done. On the transmission end, each k-bit block of data is mapped into an n-bit block $(n > k)$ called a **codeword**, using an FEC (forward error correction) encoder. The codeword is then transmitted. During transmission, the signal is subject to impairments, which may produce bit errors in the signal. At the receiver, the incoming signal is demodulated to produce a bit string that is similar to the original codeword but may contain errors. This block is passed through an FEC decoder, with one of four possible outcomes:

1. If there are no bit errors, the input to the FEC decoder is identical to the original codeword, and the decoder produces the original data block as output.

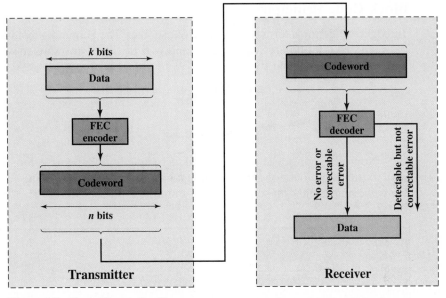

Figure 6.7   Error Correction Process

2. For certain error patterns, it is possible for the decoder to detect and correct those errors. Thus, even though the incoming data block differs from the transmitted codeword, the FEC decoder is able to map this block into the original data block.

3. For certain error patterns, the decoder can detect but not correct the errors. In this case, the decoder simply reports an uncorrectable error.

4. For certain, typically rare, error patterns, the decoder does not detect that any errors have occurred and maps the incoming n-bit data block into a k-bit block that differs from the original k-bit block.

How is it possible for the decoder to correct bit errors? In essence, error correction works by adding redundancy to the transmitted message. The redundancy makes it possible for the receiver to deduce what the original message was, even in the face of a certain level of error rate. In this section we look at a widely used form of error-correcting code known as a block error-correcting code. Our discussion only deals with basic principles; a discussion of specific error-correcting codes is beyond our scope.

Before proceeding, we note that in many cases, the error-correcting code follows the same general layout as shown for error-detecting codes in Figure 6.3. That is, the FEC algorithm takes as input a k-bit block and adds $(n - k)$ check bits to that block to produce an n-bit block; all of the bits in the original k-bit block show up in the n-bit block. For some FEC algorithms, the FEC algorithm maps the k-bit input into an n-bit codeword in such a way that the original k bits do not appear in the codeword.

Block Code Principles

To begin, we define a term that shall be of use to us. The **Hamming distance** $d(v_1, v_2)$ between two n-bit binary sequences v_1 and v_2 is the number of bits in which v_1 and v_2 disagree. For example, if

$$v_1 = 011011, \quad v_2 = 110001$$

then

$$d(v_1, v_2) = 3$$

Now let us consider the block code technique for error correction. Suppose we wish to transmit blocks of data of length k bits. Instead of transmitting each block as k bits, we map each k-bit sequence into a unique n-bit codeword.

EXAMPLE 6.9

For $k = 2$ and $n = 5$, we can make the following assignment:

Data Block	Codeword
00	00000
01	00111
10	11001
11	11110

Now, suppose that a codeword block is received with the bit pattern 00100. This is not a valid codeword, and so the receiver has detected an error. Can the error be corrected? We cannot be sure which data block was sent because 1, 2, 3, 4, or even all 5 of the bits that were transmitted may have been corrupted by noise. However, notice that it would require only a single-bit change to transform the valid codeword 00000 into 00100. It would take two bit changes to transform 00111 to 00100, three bit changes to transform 11110 to 00100, and it would take four bit changes to transform 11001 into 00100. Thus, we can deduce that the most likely codeword that was sent was 00000 and that therefore the desired data block is 00. This is error correction. In terms of Hamming distances, we have

$$d(00000, 00100) = 1; \quad d(00111, 00100) = 2;$$
$$d(11001, 00100) = 4; \quad d(11110, 00100) = 3$$

So the rule we would like to impose is that if an invalid codeword is received, then the valid codeword that is closest to it (minimum distance) is selected. This will only work if there is a unique valid codeword at a minimum distance from each invalid codeword.

For our example, it is not true that for every invalid codeword there is one and only one valid codeword at a minimum distance. There are $2^5 = 32$ possible codewords of which 4 are valid, leaving 28 invalid codewords. For the invalid codewords, we have the following:

Invalid Codeword	Minimum Distance	Valid Codeword	Invalid Codeword	Minimum Distance	Valid Codeword
00001	1	00000	10000	1	00000
00010	1	00000	10001	1	11001
00011	1	00111	10010	2	00000 or 11110
00100	1	00000	10011	2	00111 or 11001
00101	1	00111	10100	2	00000 or 11110
00110	1	00111	10101	2	00111 or 11001
01000	1	00000	10110	1	11110
01001	1	11001	10111	1	00111
01010	2	00000 or 11110	11000	1	11001
01011	2	00111 or 11001	11010	1	11110
01100	2	00000 or 11110	11011	1	11001
01101	2	00111 or 11001	11100	1	11110
01110	1	11110	11101	1	11001
01111	1	00111	11111	1	11110

There are eight cases in which an invalid codeword is at a distance 2 from two different valid codewords. Thus, if one such invalid codeword is received, an error in 2 bits could have caused it and the receiver has no way to choose between the two alternatives. An error is detected but cannot be corrected. However, in every case in which a single-bit error occurs, the resulting codeword is of distance 1 from only one valid codeword and the decision can be made. This code is therefore capable of correcting all single-bit errors but cannot correct double-bit errors. Another way to see this is to look at the pairwise distances between valid codewords:

$$d(00000, 00111) = 3; \quad d(00000, 11001) = 3; \quad d(00000, 11110) = 4;$$
$$d(00111, 11001) = 4; \quad d(00111, 11110) = 3; \quad d(11001, 11110) = 3$$

The minimum distance between valid codewords is 3. Therefore, a single-bit error will result in an invalid codeword that is a distance 1 from the original valid codeword but a distance at least 2 from all other valid codewords. As a result, the code can always correct a single-bit error. Note that the code also will always detect a double-bit error.

The preceding example illustrates the essential properties of a block error-correcting code. An (n, k) block code encodes k data bits into n-bit codewords. Typically, each valid codeword reproduces the original k data bits and adds to them $(n - k)$ check bits to form the n-bit codeword. Thus the design of a block code is equivalent to the design of a function of the form $\mathbf{v_c} = f(\mathbf{v_d})$, where $\mathbf{v_d}$ is a vector of k data bits and $\mathbf{v_c}$ is a vector of n codeword bits.

With an (n, k) block code, there are 2^k valid codewords out of a total of 2^n possible codewords. The ratio of redundant bits to data bits, $(n - k)/k$, is called the **redundancy** of the code, and the ratio of data bits to total bits, k/n, is called the **code rate**. The code rate is a measure of how much additional bandwidth is required to carry data at the same data rate as without the code. For example, a code rate of 1/2 requires double the transmission capacity of an uncoded system to maintain the same data rate. Our example has a code rate of 2/5 and so requires 2.5 times the capacity of an uncoded system. For example, if the data rate input to the encoder is 1 Mbps, then the output from the encoder must be at a rate of 2.5 Mbps to keep up.

For a code consisting of the codewords $\mathbf{w}_1, \mathbf{w}_2, \ldots, \mathbf{w}_s$, where $s = 2^n$, the minimum distance d_{min} of the code is defined as

$$d_{min} = \min_{i \neq j} [d(\mathbf{w}_i, \mathbf{w}_j)]$$

It can be shown that the following conditions hold. For a given positive integer t, if a code satisfies $d_{min} \geq (2t + 1)$, then the code can correct all bit errors up to and including errors of t bits. If $d_{min} \geq 2t$, then all errors $\leq (t - 1)$ bits can be corrected and errors of t bits can be detected but not, in general, corrected. Conversely, any code for which all errors of magnitude $\leq t$ are corrected must satisfy $d_{min} \geq (2t + 1)$, and any code for which all errors of magnitude $\leq (t - 1)$ are corrected and all errors of magnitude t are detected must satisfy $d_{min} \geq 2t$.

Another way of putting the relationship between d_{min} and t is to say that the maximum number of guaranteed correctable errors per codeword satisfies

$$t = \left\lfloor \frac{d_{min} - 1}{2} \right\rfloor$$

where $\lfloor x \rfloor$ means the largest integer not to exceed x (e.g., $\lfloor 6.3 \rfloor = 6$). Furthermore, if we are concerned only with error detection and not error correction, then the number of errors, t, that can be detected satisfies

$$t = d_{min} - 1$$

To see this, consider that if d_{min} errors occur, this could change one valid codeword into another. Any number of errors less than d_{min} cannot result in another valid codeword.

The design of a block code involves a number of considerations.

1. For given values of n and k, we would like the largest possible value of d_{min}.
2. The code should be relatively easy to encode and decode, requiring minimal memory and processing time.
3. We would like the number of extra bits $(n - k)$ to be small, to reduce bandwidth.
4. We would like the number of extra bits $(n - k)$ to be large, to reduce error rate.

Clearly, the last two objectives are in conflict, and trade-offs must be made.

It is instructive to examine Figure 6.8, based on [LEBO98]. The literature on error-correcting codes frequently includes graphs of this sort to demonstrate the effectiveness of various encoding schemes. Recall from Chapter 5 that coding can be

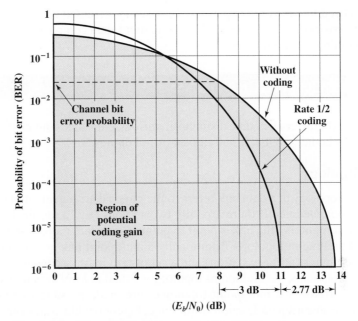

Figure 6.8 How Coding Improves System Performance

used to reduce the required E_b/N_0 value to achieve a given bit error rate.[6] The coding discussed in Chapter 5 has to do with the definition of signal elements to represent bits. The coding discussed in this chapter also has an effect on E_b/N_0. In Figure 6.8, the curve on the right is for an uncoded modulation system; the shaded region represents the area in which improvement can be achieved. In this region, a smaller BER (bit error rate) is achieved for a given E_b/N_0, and conversely, for a given BER, a smaller E_b/N_0 is required. The other curve is a typical result of a code rate of one-half (equal number of data and check bits). Note that at an error rate of 10^{-16}, the use of coding allows a reduction in E_b/N_0 of 2.77 dB. This reduction is referred to as the **coding gain**, which is defined as the reduction, in decibels, in the required E_b/N_0 to achieve a specified BER of an error-correcting coded system compared to an uncoded system using the same modulation.

It is important to realize that the BER for the second rate 1/2 curve refers to the rate of uncorrected errors and that the E_b value refers to the energy per data bit. Because the rate is 1/2, there are 2two bits on the channel for each data bit, and the energy per coded bit is half that of the energy per data bit, or a reduction of 3 dB to a value of 8 dB. If we look at the energy per coded bit for this system, then we see that the channel bit error rate is about 2.4×10^{-2}, or 0.024.

Finally, note that below a certain threshold of E_b/N_0, the coding scheme actually degrades performance. In our example of Figure 6.8, the threshold occurs at about 5.4 dB. Below the threshold, the extra check bits add overhead to the system

---

[6]E_b/N_0 is the ratio of signal energy per bit to noise power density per Hz; it is defined and discussed in Chapter 3.

that reduces the energy per data bit causing increased errors. Above the threshold, the error-correcting power of the code more than compensates for the reduced E_b, resulting in a coding gain.

6.5 LINE CONFIGURATIONS

Two characteristics that distinguish various data link configurations are topology and whether the link is half duplex or full duplex.

Topology

The topology of a data link refers to the physical arrangement of stations on a transmission medium. If there are only two stations (e.g., a terminal and a computer or two computers), the link is point to point. If there are more than two stations, then it is a multipoint topology. Traditionally, a multipoint link has been used in the case of a computer (primary station) and a set of terminals (secondary stations). In today's environments, the multipoint topology is found in local area networks.

Traditional multipoint topologies are made possible when the terminals are only transmitting a fraction of the time. Figure 6.9 illustrates the advantages of the multipoint configuration. If each terminal has a point-to-point link to its computer, then the computer must have one I/O port for each terminal. Also there is a separate transmission line from the computer to each terminal. In a multipoint configuration, the computer needs only a single I/O port and a single transmission line, which saves costs.

Full Duplex and Half Duplex

Data exchanges over a transmission line can be classified as full duplex or half duplex. With **half-duplex transmission**, only one of two stations on a point-to-point link may transmit at a time. This mode is also referred to as *two-way alternate*, suggestive of the fact that two stations must alternate in transmitting. This can be compared to a one-lane, two-way bridge. This form of transmission is often used for terminal-to-computer interaction. While a user is entering and transmitting data, the computer is prevented from sending data to the terminal, which would appear on the terminal screen and cause confusion.

For **full-duplex transmission**, two stations can simultaneously send and receive data from each other. Thus, this mode is known as *two-way simultaneous* and may be compared to a two-lane, two-way bridge. For computer-to-computer data exchange, this form of transmission is more efficient than half-duplex transmission.

With digital signaling, which requires guided transmission, full-duplex operation usually requires two separate transmission paths (e.g., two twisted pairs), while half duplex requires only one. For analog signaling, it depends on frequency: If a station transmits and receives on the same frequency, it must operate in half-duplex mode for wireless transmission, although it may operate in full-duplex mode for guided transmission using two separate transmission lines. If a station transmits on one frequency and receives on another, it may operate in full-duplex

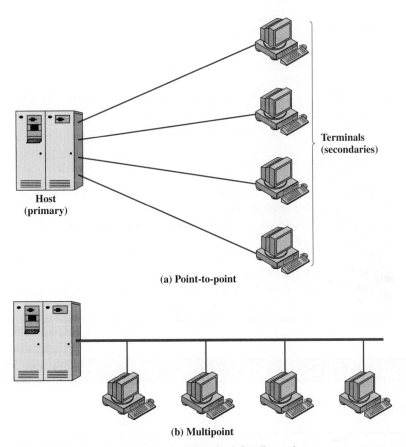

(a) Point-to-point

(b) Multipoint

Figure 6.9   Traditional Computer/Terminal Configurations

mode for wireless transmission and in full-duplex mode with a single line for guided transmission.

It is possible to transmit digital signals simultaneously in both directions on a single transmission line using a technique called echo cancellation. This is a signal-processing technique, whose explanation is beyond the scope of this book.

6.6   RECOMMENDED READING

The classic treatment of error-detecting codes and CRC is [PETE61]. [RAMA88] is an excellent tutorial on CRC.

[STAL05] discusses most of the widely used error-correcting codes. [ADAM91] provides comprehensive treatment of error-correcting codes. [SKLA01] contains a clear, well-written section on the subject. Two useful survey articles are [BERL87] and [BHAR83]. A quite readable theoretical and mathematical treatment of error-correcting codes is [ASH90]. [LIN04] is a thorough treatment of both error-detecting and error correction codes.

[FREE98b] provides good coverage of many physical layer interface standards.

ADAM91 Adamek, J. *Foundations of Coding.* New York: Wiley, 1991.

ASH90 Ash, R. *Information Theory.* New York: Dover, 1990.

BERL87 Berlekamp, E.; Peile, R.; and Pope, S. "The Application of Error Control to Communications." *IEEE Communications Magazine*, April 1987.

BHAR83 Bhargava, V. "Forward Error Correction Schemes for Digital Communications." *IEEE Communications Magazine*, January 1983.

FREE98b Freeman, R. *Telecommunication Transmission Handbook.* New York: Wiley, 1998.

LIN04 Lin, S., and Costello, D. *Error Control Coding.* Upper Saddle River, NJ: Prentice Hall, 2004.

PETE61 Peterson, W., and Brown, D. "Cyclic Codes for Error Detection." *Proceedings of the IEEE*, January 1961.

RAMA88 Ramabadran, T., and Gaitonde, S. "A Tutorial on CRC Computations." *IEEE Micro*, August 1988.

SKLA01 Sklar, B. *Digital Communications: Fundamentals and Applications.* Upper Saddle River, NJ: Prentice Hall, 2001.

STAL05 Stallings, W. *Wireless Communications and Networks*, Second Edition. Upper Saddle River, NJ: Prentice Hall, 2005.

6.7 KEY TERMS, REVIEW QUESTIONS, AND PROBLEMS

Key Terms

asynchronous transmission	error detection	interchange circuits
check bits	error-detecting code	Integrated Services Digital
codeword	forward error correction (FEC)	Network (ISDN)
code rate	frame	modem
coding gain	frame check sequence (FCS)	parity bit
cyclic code	full duplex	parity check
cyclic redundancy check (CRC)	full-duplex transmission	point-to-point
EIA-232	half duplex	redundancy
error correction	half-duplex transmission	synchronization
error-correcting code (ECC)	Hamming distance	synchronous transmission

Review Questions

6.1 How is the transmission of a single character differentiated from the transmission of the next character in asynchronous transmission?

6.2 What is a major disadvantage of asynchronous transmission?

6.3 How is synchronization provided for synchronous transmission?

6.4 What is a parity bit?

6.5 What is the CRC?

6.6 Why would you expect a CRC to detect more errors than a parity bit?

6.7 List three different ways in which the CRC algorithm can be described.

6.8 Is it possible to design an ECC that will correct some double-bit errors but not all double-bit errors? Why or why not?

6.9 In an (n, k) block ECC, what do n and k represent?

Problems

6.1 Suppose a file of 10,000 bytes is to be sent over a line at 2400 bps.
  a. Calculate the overhead in bits and time in using asynchronous communication. Assume one start bit and a stop element of length one bit, and 8 bits to send the byte itself for each character. The 8-bit character consists of all data bits, with no parity bit.
  b. Calculate the overhead in bits and time using synchronous communication. Assume that the data are sent in frames. Each frame consists of 1000 characters = 8000 bits and an overhead of 48 control bits per frame.
  c. What would the answers to parts (a) and (b) be for a file of 100,000 characters?
  d. What would the answers to parts (a) and (b) be for the original file of 10,000 characters except at a data rate of 9600 bps?

6.2 A data source produces 7-bit IRA characters. Derive an expression of the maximum effective data rate (rate of IRA data bits) over an x-bps line for the following:
  a. Asynchronous transmission, with a 1.5-unit stop element and a parity bit.
  b. Synchronous transmission, with a frame consisting of 48 control bits and 128 information bits. The information field contains 8-bit (parity included) IRA characters.
  c. Same as part (b), except that the information field is 1024 bits.

6.3 Demonstrate by example (write down a few dozen arbitrary bit patterns; assume one start bit and a stop element of length one bit) that a receiver that suffers a framing error on asynchronous transmission will eventually become realigned.

6.4 Suppose that a sender and receiver use asynchronous transmission and agree not to use any stop elements. Could this work? If so, explain any necessary conditions.

6.5 An asynchronous transmission scheme uses 8 data bits, an even parity bit, and a stop element of length 2 bits. What percentage of clock inaccuracy can be tolerated at the receiver with respect to the framing error? Assume that the bit samples are taken at the middle of the clock period. Also assume that at the beginning of the start bit the clock and incoming bits are in phase.

6.6 Suppose that a synchronous serial data transmission is clocked by two clocks (one at the sender and one at the receiver) that each have a drift of 1 minute in one year. How long a sequence of bits can be sent before possible clock drift could cause a problem? Assume that a bit waveform will be good if it is sampled within 40% of its center and that the sender and receiver are resynchronized at the beginning of each frame. Note that the transmission rate is not a factor, as both the bit period and the absolute timing error decrease proportionally at higher transmission rates.

6.7 Would you expect that the inclusion of a parity bit with each character would change the probability of receiving a correct message?

6.8 Two communicating devices are using a single-bit even parity check for error detection. The transmitter sends the byte 10101010 and, because of channel noise, the receiver gets the byte 10011010. Will the receiver detect the error? Why or why not?

6.9 What is the purpose of using modulo 2 arithmetic rather than binary arithmetic in computing an FCS?

6.10 Consider a frame consisting of two characters of four bits each. Assume that the probability of bit error is 10^{-3} and that it is independent for each bit.
  a. What is the probability that the received frame contains at least one error?
  b. Now add a parity bit to each character. What is the probability?

6.11 Using the CRC-CCITT polynomial, generate the 16-bit CRC code for a message consisting of a 1 followed by 15 0s.
   a. Use long division.
   b. Use the shift-register mechanism shown in Figure 6.6.

6.12 Explain in words why the shift-register implementation of CRC will result in all 0s at the receiver if there are no errors. Demonstrate by example.

6.13 For $P = 110011$ and $M = 11100011$, find the CRC.

6.14 A CRC is constructed to generate a 4-bit FCS for an 11-bit message. The generator polynomial is $X^4 + X^3 + 1$.
   a. Draw the shift-register circuit that would perform this task (see Figure 6.6).
   b. Encode the data bit sequence 10011011100 (leftmost bit is the least significant) using the generator polynomial and give the codeword.
   c. Now assume that bit 7 (counting from the LSB) in the codeword is in error and show that the detection algorithm detects the error.

6.15 **a.** In a CRC error-detecting scheme, choose $P(X) = X^4 + X + 1$. Encode the bits 10010011011.
   b. Suppose the channel introduces an error pattern 100010000000000 (i.e., a flip from 1 to 0 or from 0 to 1 in position 1 and 5). What is received? Can the error be detected?
   c. Repeat part (b) with error pattern 100110000000000.

6.16 A modified CRC procedure is commonly used in communications standards. It is defined as follows:

$$\frac{X^{16}D(X) + X^kL(X)}{P(X)} = Q + \frac{R(X)}{P(X)}$$

$$FCS = L(X) + R(X)$$

where

$$L(X) = X^{15} + X^{14} + X^{13} + \cdots + X + 1$$

and k is the number of bits being checked (address, control, and information fields).
   a. Describe in words the effect of this procedure.
   b. Explain the potential benefits.
   c. Show a shift-register implementation for $P(X) = X^{16} + X^{12} + X^5 + 1$.

6.17 Calculate the Hamming pairwise distances among the following codewords:
   a. 00000, 10101, 01010
   b. 000000, 010101, 101010, 110110

6.18 Section 6.4 discusses block error-correcting codes that make a decision on the basis of minimum distance. That is, given a code consisting of s equally likely codewords of length n, for each received sequence $\mathbf{v}$, the receiver selects the codeword $\mathbf{w}$ for which the distance $d(\mathbf{w}, \mathbf{v})$ is a minimum. We would like to prove that this scheme is "ideal" in the sense that the receiver always selects the codeword for which the probability of $\mathbf{w}$ given $\mathbf{v}$, $p(\mathbf{w}|\mathbf{v})$, is a maximum. Because all codewords are assumed equally likely, the codeword that maximizes $p(\mathbf{w}|\mathbf{v})$ is the same as the codeword that maximizes $p(\mathbf{v}|\mathbf{w})$.
   a. In order that $\mathbf{w}$ be received as $\mathbf{v}$, there must be exactly $d(\mathbf{w}, \mathbf{v})$ errors in transmission, and these errors must occur in those bits where $\mathbf{w}$ and $\mathbf{v}$ disagree. Let β be the probability that a given bit is transmitted incorrectly and n be the length of a codeword. Write an expression for $p(\mathbf{v}|\mathbf{w})$ as a function of β, $d(\mathbf{w}, \mathbf{v})$, and n. *Hint:* the number of bits in error is $d(\mathbf{w}, \mathbf{v})$ and the number of bits not in error is $n - d(\mathbf{w}, \mathbf{v})$.
   b. Now compare $p(\mathbf{v}|\mathbf{w}_1)$ and $p(\mathbf{v}|\mathbf{w}_2)$ for two different codewords $\mathbf{w}_1$ and $\mathbf{w}_2$ by calculating $p(\mathbf{v}|\mathbf{w}_1)/p(\mathbf{v}|\mathbf{w}_2)$.

    c. Assume that $0 < \beta < 0.5$ and show that $p(\mathbf{v}|\mathbf{w}_1) > p(\mathbf{v}|\mathbf{w}_2)$ if and only if $d(\mathbf{v}, \mathbf{w}_1) < d(\mathbf{v}, \mathbf{w}_2)$. This proves that the codeword $\mathbf{w}$ that gives the largest value of $p(\mathbf{v}|\mathbf{w})$ is that word whose distance from $\mathbf{v}$ is a minimum.

6.19 Section 6.4 states that for a given positive integer t, if a code satisfies $d_{min} \geq 2t + 1$, then the code can correct all bit errors up to and including errors of t bits. Prove this assertion. *Hint:* Start by observing that for a codeword $\mathbf{w}$ to be decoded as another codeword $\mathbf{w}'$, the received sequence must be at least as close to $\mathbf{w}'$ as to $\mathbf{w}$.

Note: The remaining problems concern material in Appendix G.

6.20 Draw a timing diagram showing the state of all EIA-232 leads between two DTE-DCE pairs during the course of a data call on the switched telephone network.

6.21 Explain the operation of each null modem connection in Figure G.5.

6.22 For the V.24/EIA-232 Remote Loopback circuit to function properly, what circuits must be logically connected?

CHAPTER 7

DATA LINK CONTROL PROTOCOLS

"Great and enlightened one," said Ten-teh, as soon as his stupor was lifted, "has this person delivered his message competently, for his mind was still a seared vision of snow and sand and perchance his tongue has stumbled?"

"Bend your ears to the wall," replied the Emperor, "and be assured."

—Kai Lung's Golden Hours, Earnest Bramah

KEY POINTS

- ◆ Because of the possibility of transmission errors, and because the receiver of data may need to regulate the rate at which data arrive, synchronization and interfacing techniques are insufficient by themselves. It is necessary to impose a layer of control in each communicating device that provides functions such as flow control, error detection, and error control. This layer of control is known as a **data link control protocol**.

- ◆ **Flow control** enables a receiver to regulate the flow of data from a sender so that the receiver's buffers do not overflow.

- ◆ In a data link control protocol, **error control** is achieved by retransmission of damaged frames that have not been acknowledged or for which the other side requests a retransmission.

- ◆ High-level data link control (HDLC) is a widely used data link control protocol. It contains virtually all of the features found in other data link control protocols.

Our discussion so far has concerned *sending signals over a transmission link.* For effective digital data communications, much more is needed to control and manage the exchange. In this chapter, we shift our emphasis to that of *sending data over a data communications link.* To achieve the necessary control, a layer of logic is added above the physical layer discussed in Chapter 6; this logic is referred to as **data link control** or a **data link control protocol**. When a data link control protocol is used, the transmission medium between systems is referred to as a **data link**.

To see the need for data link control, we list some of the requirements and objectives for effective data communication between two directly connected transmitting-receiving stations:

- • **Frame synchronization:** Data are sent in blocks called frames. The beginning and end of each frame must be recognizable. We briefly introduced this topic with the discussion of synchronous frames (Figure 6.2).

- • **Flow control:** The sending station must not send frames at a rate faster than the receiving station can absorb them.

- • **Error control:** Bit errors introduced by the transmission system should be corrected.

209

- **Addressing:** On a shared link, such as a local area network (LAN), the identity of the two stations involved in a transmission must be specified.
- **Control and data on same link:** It is usually not desirable to have a physically separate communications path for control information. Accordingly, the receiver must be able to distinguish control information from the data being transmitted.
- **Link management:** The initiation, maintenance, and termination of a sustained data exchange require a fair amount of coordination and cooperation among stations. Procedures for the management of this exchange are required.

None of these requirements is satisfied by the techniques described in Chapter 6. We shall see in this chapter that a data link protocol that satisfies these requirements is a rather complex affair. We begin by looking at two key mechanisms that are part of data link control: flow control and error control. Following this background we look at the most important example of a data link control protocol: HDLC (high level data link control). This protocol is important for two reasons: First, it is a widely used standardized data link control protocol. Second, HDLC serves as a baseline from which virtually all other important data link control protocols are derived. Finally, an appendix to this chapter addresses some performance issues relating to data link control.

7.1 FLOW CONTROL

Flow control is a technique for assuring that a transmitting entity does not overwhelm a receiving entity with data. The receiving entity typically allocates a data buffer of some maximum length for a transfer. When data are received, the receiver must do a certain amount of processing before passing the data to the higher-level software. In the absence of flow control, the receiver's buffer may fill up and overflow while it is processing old data.

To begin, we examine mechanisms for flow control in the absence of errors. The model we will use is depicted in Figure 7.1a, which is a vertical time sequence diagram. It has the advantages of showing time dependencies and illustrating the correct send–receive relationship. Each arrow represents a single frame transiting a data link between two stations. The data are sent in a sequence of frames, with each frame containing a portion of the data and some control information. The time it takes for a station to emit all of the bits of a frame onto the medium is the **transmission time**; this is proportional to the length of the frame. The **propagation time** is the time it takes for a bit to traverse the link between source and destination. For this section, we assume that all frames that are transmitted are successfully received; no frames are lost and none arrive with errors. Furthermore, frames arrive in the same order in which they are sent. However, each transmitted frame suffers an arbitrary and variable amount of delay before reception.[1]

---

[1]On a direct point-to-point link, the amount of delay is fixed rather than variable. However, a data link control protocol can be used over a network connection, such as a circuit-switched or ATM network, in which case the delay may be variable.

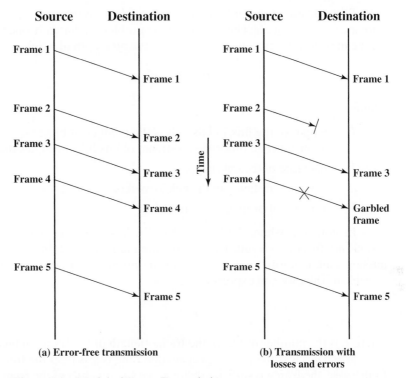

Figure 7.1   Model of Frame Transmission

Stop-and-Wait Flow Control

The simplest form of flow control, known as stop-and-wait flow control, works as follows. A source entity transmits a frame. After the destination entity receives the frame, it indicates its willingness to accept another frame by sending back an acknowledgment to the frame just received. The source must wait until it receives the acknowledgment before sending the next frame. The destination can thus stop the flow of data simply by withholding acknowledgment. This procedure works fine and, indeed, can hardly be improved upon when a message is sent in a few large frames. However, it is often the case that a source will break up a large block of data into smaller blocks and transmit the data in many frames. This is done for the following reasons:

- The buffer size of the receiver may be limited.
- The longer the transmission, the more likely that there will be an error, necessitating retransmission of the entire frame. With smaller frames, errors are detected sooner, and a smaller amount of data needs to be retransmitted.
- On a shared medium, such as a LAN, it is usually desirable not to permit one station to occupy the medium for an extended period, thus causing long delays at the other sending stations.

With the use of multiple frames for a single message, the stop-and-wait proce-dure may be inadequate. The essence of the problem is that only one frame at a time can be in transit. To explain we first define the **bit length of a link** as follows:

$$B = R \times \frac{d}{V} \tag{7.1}$$

where

$B =$ length of the link in bits; this is the number of bits present on the link at an instance in time when a stream of bits fully occupies the link

$R =$ data rate of the link, in bps

$d =$ length, or distance, of the link in meters

$V =$ velocity of propagation, in m/s

In situations where the bit length of the link is greater than the frame length, serious inefficiencies result. This is illustrated in Figure 7.2. In the figure, the trans-mission time is normalized to one, and the propagation delay is expressed as the variable a. Thus, we can express a as

$$a = \frac{B}{L} \tag{7.2}$$

where L is the number of bits in the frame (length of the frame in bits).

When a is less than 1, the propagation time is less than the transmission time. In this case, the frame is sufficiently long that the first bits of the frame have arrived

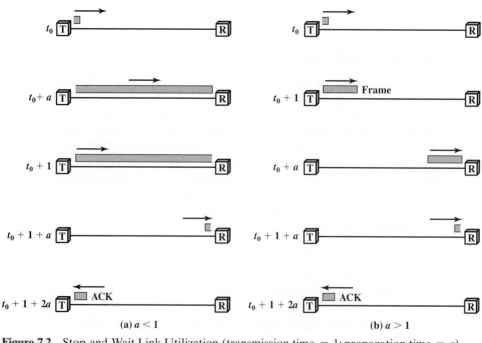

Figure 7.2 Stop-and-Wait Link Utilization (transmission time $= 1$; propagation time $= a$)

at the destination before the source has completed the transmission of the frame. When a is greater than 1, the propagation time is greater than the transmission time. In this case, the sender completes transmission of the entire frame before the leading bits of that frame arrive at the receiver. Put another way, larger values of a are consistent with higher data rates and/or longer distances between stations. Appendix 7A discusses a and data link performance.

Both parts of Figure 7.2 (a and b) consist of a sequence of snapshots of the transmission process over time. In both cases, the first four snapshots show the process of transmitting a frame containing data, and the last snapshot shows the return of a small acknowledgment frame. Note that for $a > 1$, the line is always underutilized and even for $a < 1$, the line is inefficiently utilized. In essence, for very high data rates, for very long distances between sender and receiver, stop-and-wait flow control provides inefficient line utilization.

EXAMPLE 7.1 Consider a 200-m optical fiber link operating at 1 Gbps. The velocity of propagation of optical fiber is typically about 2×10^8 m/s. Using Equation (7.1), $B = (10^9 \times 200)/(2 \times 10^8) = 1000$ bits. Assume a frame of 1000 octets, or 8000 bits, is transmitted. Using Equation (7.2), $a = (1000/8000) = 0.125$. Using Figure 7.2a as a guide, assume transmission starts at time $t = 0$. After 1 μs (a normalized time of 0.125 frame times), the leading edge (first bit) of the frame has reached R, and the first 1000 bits of the frame are spread out across the link. At time $t = 8$ μs, the trailing edge (final bit) of the frame has just been emitted by T, and the final 1000 bits of the frame are spread out across the link. At $t = 9$ μs, the final bit of the frame arrives at R. R now sends back an ACK frame. If we assume the frame transmission time is negligible (very small ACK frame) and that the ACK is sent immediately, the ACK arrives at T at $t = 10$ μs. At this point, T can begin transmitting a new frame. The actual transmission time for the frame was 8 μs, but the total time to transmit the first frame and receive an ACK is 10 μs.

Now consider a 1-Mbps link between two ground stations that communicate via a satellite relay. A geosynchronous satellite has an altitude of roughly 36,000 km. Then $B = (10^6 \times 2 \times 36,000,000)/(3 \times 10^8) = 240,000$ bits. For a frame length of 8000 bits, $a = (240,000/8000) = 30$. Using Figure 7.2b as a guide, we can work through the same steps as before. In this case, it takes 240 ms for the leading edge of the frame to arrive and an additional 8 ms for the entire frame to arrive. The ACK arrives back at T at $t = 488$ ms. The actual transmission time for the first frame was 8 ms, but the total time to transmit the first frame and receive an ACK is 488 ms.

Sliding-Window Flow Control

The essence of the problem described so far is that only one frame at a time can be in transit. In situations where the bit length of the link is greater than the frame length ($a > 1$), serious inefficiencies result. Efficiency can be greatly improved by allowing multiple frames to be in transit at the same time.

Let us examine how this might work for two stations, A and B, connected via a full-duplex link. Station B allocates buffer space for W frames. Thus, B can accept W frames, and A is allowed to send W frames without waiting for any acknowledgments. To keep track of which frames have been acknowledged, each is labeled with a sequence number. B acknowledges a frame by sending an acknowledgment that includes the sequence number of the next frame expected. This acknowledgment also implicitly announces that B is prepared to receive the next W frames, beginning with the number specified. This scheme can also be used to acknowledge multiple frames. For example, B could receive frames 2, 3, and 4 but withhold acknowledgment until frame 4 has arrived. By then returning an acknowledgment with sequence number 5, B acknowledges frames 2, 3, and 4 at one time. A maintains a list of sequence numbers that it is allowed to send, and B maintains a list of sequence numbers that it is prepared to receive. Each of these lists can be thought of as a *window* of frames. The operation is referred to as **sliding-window flow control**.

Several additional comments need to be made. Because the sequence number to be used occupies a field in the frame, it is limited to a range of values. For example, for a 3-bit field, the sequence number can range from 0 to 7. Accordingly, frames are numbered modulo 8; that is, after sequence number 7, the next number is 0. In general, for a k-bit field the range of sequence numbers is 0 through $2^k - 1$, and frames are numbered modulo 2^k. As will be shown subsequently, the maximum window size is $2^k - 1$.

Figure 7.3 is a useful way of depicting the sliding-window process. It assumes the use of a 3-bit sequence number, so that frames are numbered sequentially from

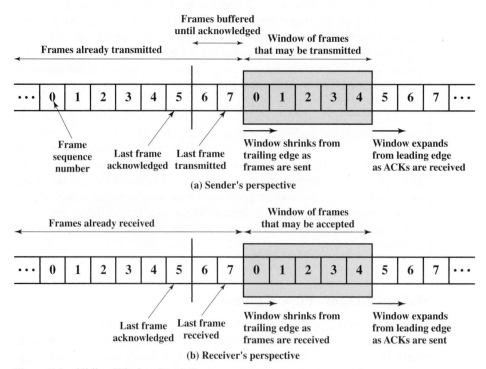

Figure 7.3   Sliding-Window Depiction

0 through 7, and then the same numbers are reused for subsequent frames. The shaded rectangle indicates the frames that may be sent; in this figure, the sender may transmit five frames, beginning with frame 0. Each time a frame is sent, the shaded window shrinks; each time an acknowledgment is received, the shaded window grows. Frames between the vertical bar and the shaded window have been sent but not yet acknowledged. As we shall see, the sender must buffer these frames in case they need to be retransmitted.

The window size need not be the maximum possible size for a given sequence number length. For example, using a 3-bit sequence number, a window size of 5 could be configured for the stations using the sliding-window flow control protocol.

EXAMPLE 7.2 An example is shown in Figure 7.4. The example assumes a 3-bit sequence number field and a maximum window size of seven frames. Initially, A and B have windows indicating that A may transmit seven frames, beginning with frame 0 (F0). After transmitting three frames (F0, F1, F2) without acknowledgment, A has shrunk its window to four frames and maintains a copy of the three transmitted frames. The window indicates that A may transmit four frames, beginning with frame number 3. B then transmits an RR (receive ready) 3, which means "I have received all frames up through frame number 2 and am ready to receive frame number 3; in fact, I am prepared to receive seven frames, beginning with frame number 3." With this acknowledgment, A is back up to permission to transmit seven frames, still beginning with frame 3; also A may discard the buffered frames that have now been acknowledged. A proceeds to transmit frames 3, 4, 5, and 6. B returns RR 4, which acknowledges F3, and allows transmission of F4 through the next instance of F2. By the time this RR reaches A, it has already transmitted F4, F5, and F6, and therefore A may only open its window to permit sending four frames beginning with F7.

The mechanism so far described provides a form of flow control: The receiver must only be able to accommodate seven frames beyond the one it has last acknowledged. Most data link control protocols also allow a station to cut off the flow of frames from the other side by sending a Receive Not Ready (RNR) message, which acknowledges former frames but forbids transfer of future frames. Thus, RNR 5 means, "I have received all frames up through number 4 but am unable to accept any more at this time." At some subsequent point, the station must send a normal acknowledgment to reopen the window.

So far, we have discussed transmission in one direction only. If two stations exchange data, each needs to maintain two windows, one for transmit and one for receive, and each side needs to send the data and acknowledgments to the other. To provide efficient support for this requirement, a feature known as **piggybacking** is typically provided. Each **data frame** includes a field that holds the sequence number of that frame plus a field that holds the sequence number used for acknowledgment.

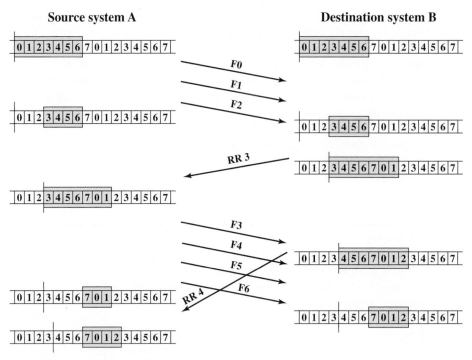

Figure 7.4   Example of a Sliding-Window Protocol

Thus, if a station has data to send and an acknowledgment to send, it sends both together in one frame, saving communication capacity. Of course, if a station has an acknowledgment but no data to send, it sends a separate **acknowledgment frame**, such as RR or RNR. If a station has data to send but no new acknowledgment to send, it must repeat the last acknowledgment sequence number that it sent. This is because the data frame includes a field for the acknowledgment number, and some value must be put into that field. When a station receives a duplicate acknowledgment, it simply ignores it.

Sliding-window flow control is potentially much more efficient than stop-and-wait flow control. The reason is that, with sliding-window flow control, the transmission link is treated as a pipeline that may be filled with frames in transit. In contrast, with stop-and-wait flow control, only one frame may be in the pipe at a time. Appendix 7A quantifies the improvement in efficiency.

EXAMPLE 7.3 Let us consider the use of sliding-window flow control for the two configurations of Example 7.1. As was calculated in Example 7.1, it takes 10 μs for an ACK to the first frame to be received. It takes 8 μs to transmit one frame, so the sender can transmit one frame and part of a second frame by the time the ACK to the first frame is received. Thus, a window size of 2 is adequate to enable the sender to transmit frames continuously, or at a rate of one frame every 8 μs. With stop-and-wait, a rate of only one frame per 10 μs is possible.

For the satellite configuration, it takes 488 ms for an ACK to the first frame to be received. It takes 8 ms to transmit one frame, so the sender can transmit 61 frames by the time the ACK to the first frame is received. With a window field of 6 bits or more, the sender can transmit continuously, or at a rate of one frame every 8 ms. If the window size is 7, using a 3-bit window field, then the sender can only send 7 frames and then must wait for an ACK before sending more. In this case, the sender can transmit at a rate of 7 frames per 488 ms, or about one frame every 70 ms. With stop-and-wait, a rate of only one frame per 488 ms is possible.

7.2 ERROR CONTROL

Error control refers to mechanisms to detect and correct errors that occur in the transmission of frames. The model that we will use, which covers the typical case, is illustrated in Figure 7.1b. As before, data are sent as a sequence of frames; frames arrive in the same order in which they are sent; and each transmitted frame suffers an arbitrary and potentially variable amount of delay before reception. In addition, we admit the possibility of two types of errors:

- **Lost frame:** A frame fails to arrive at the other side. In the case of a network, the network may simply fail to deliver a frame. In the case of a direct point-to-point data link, a noise burst may damage a frame to the extent that the receiver is not aware that a frame has been transmitted.
- **Damaged frame:** A recognizable frame does arrive, but some of the bits are in error (have been altered during transmission).

The most common techniques for error control are based on some or all of the following ingredients:

- **Error detection:** The destination detects frames that are in error, using the techniques described in the preceding chapter, and discards those frames.
- **Positive acknowledgment:** The destination returns a positive acknowledgment to successfully received, error-free frames.
- **Retransmission after timeout:** The source retransmits a frame that has not been acknowledged after a predetermined amount of time.
- **Negative acknowledgment and retransmission:** The destination returns a negative acknowledgment to frames in which an error is detected. The source retransmits such frames.

Collectively, these mechanisms are all referred to as **automatic repeat request (ARQ)**. The effect of ARQ is to turn a potentially unreliable data link into a reliable one. Three versions of ARQ have been standardized:

- Stop-and-wait ARQ
- Go-back-N ARQ
- Selective-reject ARQ

All of these forms are based on the use of the flow control techniques discussed in Section 7.1. We examine each in turn.

Stop-and-Wait ARQ

Stop-and-wait ARQ is based on the stop-and-wait flow control technique outlined previously. The source station transmits a single frame and then must await an acknowledgment (ACK). No other data frames can be sent until the destination station's reply arrives at the source station.

Two sorts of errors could occur. First, the frame that arrives at the destination could be damaged. The receiver detects this by using the error-detection technique referred to earlier and simply discards the frame. To account for this possibility, the source station is equipped with a timer. After a frame is transmitted, the source station waits for an acknowledgment. If no acknowledgment is received by the time that the timer expires, then the same frame is sent again. Note that this method requires that the transmitter maintain a copy of a transmitted frame until an acknowledgment is received for that frame.

The second sort of error is a damaged acknowledgment. Consider the following situation. Station A sends a frame. The frame is received correctly by station B, which responds with an acknowledgment. The ACK is damaged in transit and is not recognizable by A, which will therefore time out and resend the same frame. This duplicate frame arrives and is accepted by B. B has therefore accepted two copies of the same frame as if they were separate. To avoid this problem, frames are alternately labeled with 0 or 1, and positive acknowledgments are of the form ACK0 and ACK1. In keeping with the sliding-window convention, an ACK0 acknowledges receipt of a frame numbered 1 and indicates that the receiver is ready for a frame numbered 0.

Figure 7.5 gives an example of the use of stop-and-wait ARQ, showing the transmission of a sequence of frames from source A to destination B.[2] The figure shows the two types of errors just described. The third frame transmitted by A is lost or damaged and therefore B does not return an ACK. A times out and retransmits the frame. Later, A transmits a frame labeled 1 but the ACK0 for that frame is lost. A times out and retransmits the same frame. When B receives two frames in a row with the same label, it discards the second frame but sends back an ACK0 to each.

The principal advantage of stop-and-wait ARQ is its simplicity. Its principal disadvantage, as discussed in Section 7.1, is that stop-and-wait is an inefficient mechanism. The sliding-window flow control technique can be adapted to provide more efficient line use; in this context, it is sometimes referred to as *continuous ARQ*.

Go-Back-N ARQ

The form of error control based on sliding-window flow control that is most commonly used is called go-back-N ARQ. In this method, a station may send a series of frames sequentially numbered modulo some maximum value. The number of unacknowledged frames outstanding is determined by window size, using the

---

[2]This figure indicates the time required to transmit a frame. For simplicity, other figures in this chapter do not show this time.

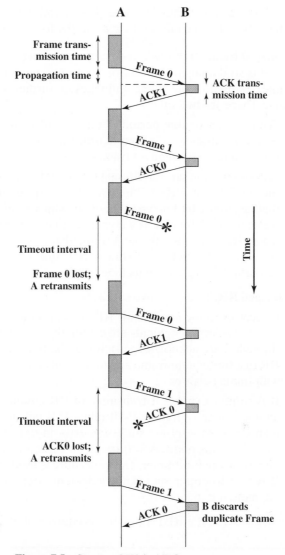

Figure 7.5   Stop-and-Wait ARQ

sliding-window flow control technique. While no errors occur, the destination will acknowledge incoming frames as usual (RR = receive ready, or piggybacked acknowledgment). If the destination station detects an error in a frame, it may send a negative acknowledgment (REJ = reject) for that frame, as explained in the following rules. The destination station will discard that frame and all future incoming frames until the frame in error is correctly received. Thus, the source station, when it receives a REJ, must retransmit the frame in error plus all succeeding frames that were transmitted in the interim.

Suppose that station A is sending frames to station B. After each transmission, A sets an acknowledgment timer for the frame just transmitted. Suppose that B has previously successfully received frame $(i - 1)$ and A has just transmitted frame i. The go-back-N technique takes into account the following contingencies:

1. **Damaged frame.** If the received frame is invalid (i.e., B detects an error, or the frame is so damaged that B does not even perceive that it has received a frame), B discards the frame and takes no further action as the result of that frame. There are two subcases:

   a. Within a reasonable period of time, A subsequently sends frame $(i + 1)$. B receives frame $(i + 1)$ out of order and sends a REJ i. A must retransmit frame i and all subsequent frames.

   b. A does not soon send additional frames. B receives nothing and returns neither an RR nor a REJ. When A's timer expires, it transmits an RR frame that includes a bit known as the P bit, which is set to 1. B interprets the RR frame with a P bit of 1 as a command that must be acknowledged by sending an RR indicating the next frame that it expects, which is frame i. When A receives the RR, it retransmits frame i. Alternatively, A could just retransmit frame i when its timer expires.

2. **Damaged RR.** There are two subcases:

   a. B receives frame i and sends RR $(i + 1)$, which suffers an error in transit. Because acknowledgments are cumulative (e.g., RR 6 means that all frames through 5 are acknowledged), it may be that A will receive a subsequent RR to a subsequent frame and that it will arrive before the timer associated with frame i expires.

   b. If A's timer expires, it transmits an RR command as in Case 1b. It sets another timer, called the P-bit timer. If B fails to respond to the RR command, or if its response suffers an error in transit, then A's P-bit timer will expire. At this point, A will try again by issuing a new RR command and restarting the P-bit timer. This procedure is tried for a number of iterations. If A fails to obtain an acknowledgment after some maximum number of attempts, it initiates a reset procedure.

3. **Damaged REJ.** If a REJ is lost, this is equivalent to Case 1b.

EXAMPLE 7.4 Figure 7.6a is an example of the frame flow for go-back-N ARQ. Because of the propagation delay on the line, by the time that an acknowledgment (positive or negative) arrives back at the sending station, it has already sent at least one additional frame beyond the one being acknowledged. In this example, frame 4 is damaged. Frames 5 and 6 are received out of order and are discarded by B. When frame 5 arrives, B immediately sends a REJ 4. When the REJ to frame 4 is received, not only frame 4 but frames 5 and 6 must be retransmitted. Note that the transmitter must keep a copy of all unacknowledged frames. Figure 7.6a also shows an example of retransmission after timeout. No acknowledgment is received for frame 5 within the timeout period, so A issues an RR to determine the status of B.

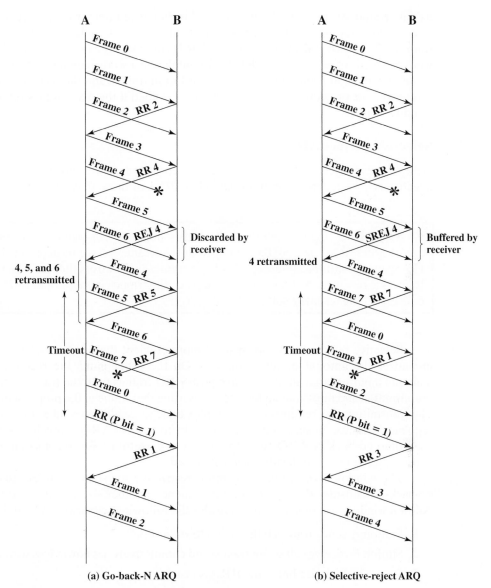

Figure 7.6 Sliding-Window ARQ Protocols

In Section 7.1, we mentioned that for a k-bit sequence number field, which provides a sequence number range of 2^k, the maximum window size is limited to $2^k - 1$. This has to do with the interaction between error control and acknowledgment. Consider that if data are being exchanged in both directions, station B must send piggybacked acknowledgments to station A's frames in the data frames being transmitted by B, even if the acknowledgment has already been sent. As we have mentioned, this is because B must put some number in the acknowledgment field of its data frame. As an example, assume a 3-bit sequence number (sequence number space = 8). Suppose a station sends frame 0 and gets back an RR 1 and then sends frames $1, 2, 3, 4, 5, 6, 7, 0$ and gets another RR 1. This could mean that all eight frames were received correctly and the RR 1 is a cumulative acknowledgment. It could also mean that all eight frames were damaged or lost in transit, and the receiving station is repeating its previous RR 1. The problem is avoided if the maximum window size is limited to 7 ($2^3 - 1$).

Selective–Reject ARQ

With selective-reject ARQ, the only frames retransmitted are those that receive a negative acknowledgment, in this case called SREJ, or those that time out.

EXAMPLE 7.5 Figure 7.6b illustrates this scheme. When frame 5 is received out of order, B sends a SREJ 4, indicating that frame 4 has not been received. However, B continues to accept incoming frames and buffers them until a valid frame 4 is received. At that point, B can place the frames in the proper order for delivery to higher-layer software.

Selective reject would appear to be more efficient than go-back-N, because it minimizes the amount of retransmission. On the other hand, the receiver must maintain a buffer large enough to save post-SREJ frames until the frame in error is retransmitted and must contain logic for reinserting that frame in the proper sequence. The transmitter, too, requires more complex logic to be able to send a frame out of sequence. Because of such complications, selective-reject ARQ is much less widely used than go-back-N ARQ. Selective reject is a useful choice for a satellite link because of the long propagation delay involved.

The window size limitation is more restrictive for selective-reject than for go-back-N. Consider the case of a 3-bit sequence number size for selective-reject. Allow a window size of seven, and consider the following scenario [TANE03]:

1. Station A sends frames 0 through 6 to station B.
2. Station B receives all seven frames and cumulatively acknowledges with RR 7.
3. Because of a noise burst, the RR 7 is lost.
4. A times out and retransmits frame 0.
5. B has already advanced its receive window to accept frames $7, 0, 1, 2, 3, 4$, and 5. Thus it assumes that frame 7 has been lost and that this is a new frame 0, which it accepts.

The problem with the preceding scenario is that there is an overlap between the sending and receiving windows. To overcome the problem, the maximum window size should be no more than half the range of sequence numbers. In the preceding scenario, if only four unacknowledged frames may be outstanding, no confusion can result. In general, for a k-bit sequence number field, which provides a sequence number range of 2^k, the maximum window size is limited to 2^{k-1}.

7.3 HIGH-LEVEL DATA LINK CONTROL (HDLC)

The most important data link control protocol is HDLC (ISO 3009, ISO 4335). Not only is HDLC widely used, but it is the basis for many other important data link control protocols, which use the same or similar formats and the same mechanisms as employed in HDLC.

Basic Characteristics

To satisfy a variety of applications, HDLC defines three types of stations, two link configurations, and three data transfer modes of operation. The three station types are:

- **Primary station:** Responsible for controlling the operation of the link. Frames issued by the primary are called commands.
- **Secondary station:** Operates under the control of the primary station. Frames issued by a secondary are called responses. The primary maintains a separate logical link with each secondary station on the line.
- **Combined station:** Combines the features of primary and secondary. A combined station may issue both commands and responses.

  The two link configurations are

- **Unbalanced configuration:** Consists of one primary and one or more secondary stations and supports both full-duplex and half-duplex transmission.
- **Balanced configuration:** Consists of two combined stations and supports both full-duplex and half-duplex transmission.

  The three data transfer modes are

- **Normal response mode (NRM):** Used with an unbalanced configuration. The primary may initiate data transfer to a secondary, but a secondary may only transmit data in response to a command from the primary.
- **Asynchronous balanced mode (ABM):** Used with a balanced configuration. Either combined station may initiate transmission without receiving permission from the other combined station.
- **Asynchronous response mode (ARM):** Used with an unbalanced configuration. The secondary may initiate transmission without explicit permission of the primary. The primary still retains responsibility for the line, including initialization, error recovery, and logical disconnection.

NRM is used on multidrop lines, in which a number of terminals are connected to a host computer. The computer polls each terminal for input. NRM is also sometimes used on point-to-point links, particularly if the link connects a terminal or other peripheral to a computer. ABM is the most widely used of the three modes; it makes more efficient use of a full-duplex point-to-point link because there is no polling overhead. ARM is rarely used; it is applicable to some special situations in which a secondary may need to initiate transmission.

Frame Structure

HDLC uses synchronous transmission. All transmissions are in the form of frames, and a single frame format suffices for all types of data and control exchanges.

Figure 7.7 depicts the structure of the HDLC frame. The flag, address, and control fields that precede the information field are known as a **header**. The frame check sequence and flag fields following the data field are referred to as a **trailer**.

FLAG FIELDS Flag fields delimit the frame at both ends with the unique pattern 01111110. A single flag may be used as the closing flag for one frame and the opening flag for the next. On both sides of the user-network interface, receivers are continuously hunting for the flag sequence to synchronize on the start of a frame. While receiving a frame, a station continues to hunt for that sequence to determine the end of the frame. Because the protocol allows the presence of arbitrary bit patterns (i.e., there are no restrictions on the content of the various fields imposed by the link protocol), there is no assurance that the pattern 01111110 will not appear somewhere inside the frame, thus destroying synchronization. To avoid this problem, a procedure known as **bit stuffing** is used. For all bits between the starting and ending

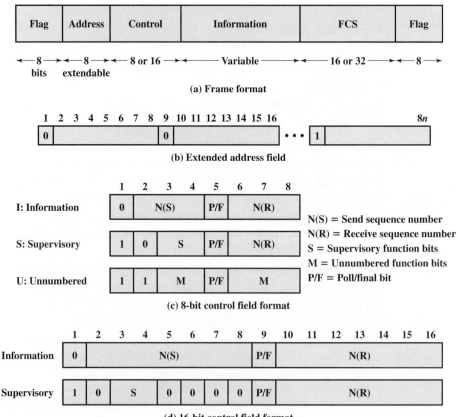

Figure 7.7 HDLC frame structure

Original pattern:

111111111111011111101111110

After bit-stuffing:

111110011111011011111010110111111010

Figure 7.8   Bit Stuffing

flags, the transmitter inserts an extra 0 bit after each occurrence of five 1s in the frame. After detecting a starting flag, the receiver monitors the bit stream. When a pattern of five 1s appears, the sixth bit is examined. If this bit is 0, it is deleted. If the sixth bit is a 1 and the seventh bit is a 0, the combination is accepted as a flag. If the sixth and seventh bits are both 1, the sender is indicating an abort condition.

With the use of bit stuffing, arbitrary bit patterns can be inserted into the data field of the frame. This property is known as **data transparency**.

Figure 7.8 shows an example of bit stuffing. Note that in the first two cases, the extra 0 is not strictly necessary for avoiding a flag pattern but is necessary for the operation of the algorithm.

ADDRESS FIELD   The address field identifies the secondary station that transmitted or is to receive the frame. This field is not needed for point-to-point links but is always included for the sake of uniformity. The address field is usually 8 bits long but, by prior agreement, an extended format may be used in which the actual address length is a multiple of 7 bits. The leftmost bit of each octet is 1 or 0 according as it is or is not the last octet of the address field. The remaining 7 bits of each octet form part of the address. The single-octet address of 11111111 is interpreted as the all-stations address in both basic and extended formats. It is used to allow the primary to broadcast a frame for reception by all secondaries.

CONTROL FIELD   HDLC defines three types of frames, each with a different control field format. **Information frames** (I-frames) carry the data to be transmitted for the user (the logic above HDLC that is using HDLC). Additionally, flow and error control data, using the ARQ mechanism, are piggybacked on an information frame. **Supervisory frames** (S-frames) provide the ARQ mechanism when piggybacking is not used. **Unnumbered frames** (U-frames) provide supplemental link control functions. The first one or two bits of the control field serves to identify the frame type. The remaining bit positions are organized into subfields as indicated in Figures 7.7c and d. Their use is explained in the discussion of HDLC operation later in this chapter.

All of the control field formats contain the poll/final (P/F) bit. Its use depends on context. Typically, in command frames, it is referred to as the P bit and is set to 1 to solicit (poll) a response frame from the peer HDLC entity. In response frames, it is referred to as the F bit and is set to 1 to indicate the response frame transmitted as a result of a soliciting command.

Note that the basic control field for S- and I-frames uses 3-bit sequence numbers. With the appropriate set-mode command, an extended control field can be used for S- and I-frames that employs 7-bit sequence numbers. U-frames always contain an 8-bit control field.

INFORMATION FIELD The information field is present only in I-frames and some U-frames. The field can contain any sequence of bits but must consist of an integral number of octets. The length of the information field is variable up to some system-defined maximum.

FRAME CHECK SEQUENCE FIELD The frame check sequence (FCS) is an error-detecting code calculated from the remaining bits of the frame, exclusive of flags. The normal code is the 16-bit CRC-CCITT defined in Section 6.3. An optional 32-bit FCS, using CRC-32, may be employed if the frame length or the line reliability dictates this choice.

Operation

HDLC operation consists of the exchange of I-frames, S-frames, and U-frames between two stations. The various commands and responses defined for these frame types are listed in Table 7.1. In describing HDLC operation, we will discuss these three types of frames.

The operation of HDLC involves three phases. First, one side or another initializes the data link so that frames may be exchanged in an orderly fashion. During this phase, the options that are to be used are agreed upon. After initialization, the two sides exchange user data and the control information to exercise flow and error control. Finally, one of the two sides signals the termination of the operation.

INITIALIZATION Either side may request initialization by issuing one of the six set-mode commands. This command serves three purposes:

1. It signals the other side that initialization is requested.
2. It specifies which of the three modes (NRM, ABM, ARM) is requested.
3. It specifies whether 3- or 7-bit sequence numbers are to be used.

If the other side accepts this request, then the HDLC module on that end transmits an unnumbered acknowledged (UA) frame back to the initiating side. If the request is rejected, then a disconnected mode (DM) frame is sent.

DATA TRANSFER When the initialization has been requested and accepted, then a logical connection is established. Both sides may begin to send user data in I-frames, starting with sequence number 0. The N(S) and N(R) fields of the I-frame are sequence numbers that support flow control and error control. An HDLC module sending a sequence of I-frames will number them sequentially, modulo 8 or 128, depending on whether 3- or 7-bit sequence numbers are used, and place the sequence number in N(S). N(R) is the acknowledgment for I-frames received; it enables the HDLC module to indicate which number I-frame it expects to receive next.

S-frames are also used for flow control and error control. The receive ready (RR) frame acknowledges the last I-frame received by indicating the next I-frame expected. The RR is used when there is no reverse user data traffic (I-frames) to carry an acknowledgment. Receive not ready (RNR) acknowledges an I-frame, as with RR, but also asks the peer entity to suspend transmission of I-frames. When the entity that issued RNR is again ready, it sends an RR. REJ initiates the go-back-N ARQ.

Table 7.1   HDLC Commands and Responses

Name	Command/ Response	Description
Information (I)	C/R	Exchange user data
Supervisory (S)		
Receive ready (RR)	C/R	Positive acknowledgment; ready to receive I-frame
Receive not ready (RNR)	C/R	Positive acknowledgment; not ready to receive
Reject (REJ)	C/R	Negative acknowledgment; go back N
Selective reject (SREJ)	C/R	Negative acknowledgment; selective reject
Unnumbered (U)		
Set normal response/extended mode (SNRM/SNRME)	C	Set mode; extended = 7-bit sequence numbers
Set asynchronous response/ extended mode (SARM/SARME)	C	Set mode; extended = 7-bit sequence numbers
Set asynchronous balanced/ extended mode (SABM, SABME)	C	Set mode; extended = 7-bit sequence numbers
Set initialization mode (SIM)	C	Initialize link control functions in addressed station
Disconnect (DISC)	C	Terminate logical link connection
Unnumbered Acknowledgment (UA)	R	Acknowledge acceptance of one of the set-mode commands
Disconnected mode (DM)	R	Responder is in disconnected mode
Request disconnect (RD)	R	Request for DISC command
Request initialization mode (RIM)	R	Initialization needed; request for SIM command
Unnumbered information (UI)	C/R	Used to exchange control information
Unnumbered poll (UP)	C	Used to solicit control information
Reset (RSET)	C	Used for recovery; resets $N(R), N(S)$
Exchange identification (XID)	C/R	Used to request/report status
Test (TEST)	C/R	Exchange identical information fields for testing
Frame reject (FRMR)	R	Report receipt of unacceptable frame

It indicates that the last I-frame received has been rejected and that retransmission of all I-frames beginning with number $N(R)$ is required. Selective reject (SREJ) is used to request retransmission of just a single frame.

DISCONNECT Either HDLC module can initiate a disconnect, either on its own initiative if there is some sort of fault, or at the request of its higher-layer user. HDLC issues a disconnect by sending a disconnect (DISC) frame. The remote entity must accept the disconnect by replying with a UA and informing its layer 3 user that the connection has been terminated. Any outstanding unacknowledged I-frames may be lost, and their recovery is the responsibility of higher layers.

EXAMPLES OF OPERATION To better understand HDLC operation, several examples are presented in Figure 7.9. In the example diagrams, each arrow includes a legend that specifies the frame name, the setting of the P/F bit, and, where appropriate, the values of N(R) and N(S). The setting of the P or F bit is 1 if the designation is present and 0 if absent.

Figure 7.9a shows the frames involved in link setup and disconnect. The HDLC protocol entity for one side issues an SABM command to the other side and

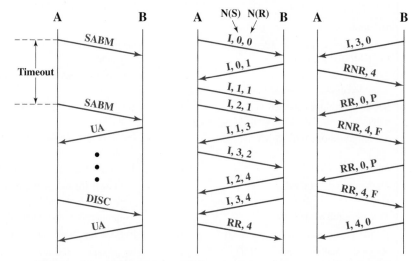

(a) Link setup and disconnect (b) Two-way data exchange (c) Busy condition

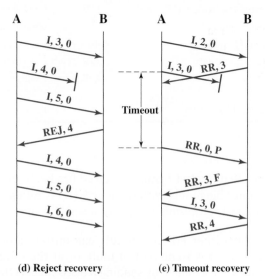

(d) Reject recovery (e) Timeout recovery

Figure 7.9   Examples of HDLC Operation

starts a timer. The other side, upon receiving the SABM, returns a UA response and sets local variables and counters to their initial values. The initiating entity receives the UA response, sets its variables and counters, and stops the timer. The logical connection is now active, and both sides may begin transmitting frames. Should the timer expire without a response to an SABM, the originator will repeat the SABM, as illustrated. This would be repeated until a UA or DM is received or until, after a given number of tries, the entity attempting initiation gives up and reports failure to a management entity. In such a case, higher-layer intervention is necessary. The same figure (Figure 7.9a) shows the disconnect procedure. One side issues a DISC command, and the other responds with a UA response.

Figure 7.9b illustrates the full-duplex exchange of I-frames. When an entity sends a number of I-frames in a row with no incoming data, then the receive sequence number is simply repeated (e.g., I,1,1; I,2,1 in the A-to-B direction). When an entity receives a number of I-frames in a row with no outgoing frames, then the receive sequence number in the next outgoing frame must reflect the cumulative activity (e.g., I,1,3 in the B-to-A direction). Note that, in addition to I-frames, data exchange may involve supervisory frames.

Figure 7.9c shows an operation involving a busy condition. Such a condition may arise because an HDLC entity is not able to process I-frames as fast as they are arriving, or the intended user is not able to accept data as fast as they arrive in I-frames. In either case, the entity's receive buffer fills up and it must halt the incoming flow of I-frames, using an RNR command. In this example, A issues an RNR, which requires B to halt transmission of I-frames. The station receiving the RNR will usually poll the busy station at some periodic interval by sending an RR with the P bit set. This requires the other side to respond with either an RR or an RNR. When the busy condition has cleared, A returns an RR, and I-frame transmission from B can resume.

An example of error recovery using the REJ command is shown in Figure 7.9d. In this example, A transmits I-frames numbered 3, 4, and 5. Number 4 suffers an error and is lost. When B receives I-frame number 5, it discards this frame because it is out of order and sends an REJ with an N(R) of 4. This causes A to initiate retransmission of I-frames previously sent, beginning with frame 4. A may continue to send additional frames after the retransmitted frames.

An example of error recovery using a timeout is shown in Figure 7.9e. In this example, A transmits I-frame number 3 as the last in a sequence of I-frames. The frame suffers an error. B detects the error and discards it. However, B cannot send an REJ, because there is no way to know if this was an I-frame. If an error is detected in a frame, all of the bits of that frame are suspect, and the receiver has no way to act upon it. A, however, would have started a timer as the frame was transmitted. This timer has a duration long enough to span the expected response time. When the timer expires, A initiates recovery action. This is usually done by polling the other side with an RR command with the P bit set, to determine the status of the other side. Because the poll demands a response, the entity will receive a frame containing an N(R) field and be able to proceed. In this case, the response indicates that frame 3 was lost, which A retransmits.

These examples are not exhaustive. However, they should give the reader a good feel for the behavior of HDLC.

7.4 RECOMMENDED READING

An excellent and very detailed treatment of flow control and error control is to be found in [BERT92]. [FIOR95] points out some of the real-world reliability problems with HDLC.

There is a large body of literature on the performance of ARQ link control protocols. Three classic papers, well worth reading, are [BENE64], [KONH80], and [BUX80]. A readable survey with simplified performance results is [LIN84]. A more thorough treatment can be found in [LIN04]. A more recent analysis is [ZORZ96].

[KLEI92] and [KLEI93] are two key papers that look at the implications of gigabit data rates on performance.

BENE64   Benice, R. "An Analysis of Retransmission Systems." *IEEE Transactions on Communication Technology*, December 1964.

BERT92   Bertsekas, D., and Gallager, R. *Data Networks*. Englewood Cliffs, NJ: Prentice Hall, 1992.

BUX80   Bux, W.; Kummerle, K.; and Truong, H. "Balanced HDLC Procedures: A Performance Analysis." *IEEE Transactions on Communications*, November 1980.

FIOR95   Fiorini, D.; Chiani, M.; Tralli, V.; and Salati, C. "Can We Trust HDLC?" *ACM Computer Communications Review*, October 1995.

KLEI92   Kleinrock, L. "The Latency/Bandwidth Tradeoff in Gigabit Networks." *IEEE Communications Magazine*, April 1992.

KLEI93   Kleinrock, L. "On the Modeling and Analysis of Computer Networks." *Proceedings of the IEEE*, August 1993.

KONH80   Konheim, A. "A Queuing Analysis of Two ARQ Protocols." *IEEE Transactions on Communications*, July 1980.

LIN84   Lin, S.; Costello, D.; and Miller, M. "Automatic-Repeat-Request Error-Control Schemes." *IEEE Communications Magazine*, December 1984.

LIN04   Lin, S., and Costello, D. *Error Control Coding*. Upper Saddle River, NJ: Prentice Hall, 2004.

ZORZ96   Zorzi, M., and Rao, R. "On the Use of Renewal Theory in the Analysis of ARQ Protocols." *IEEE Transactions on Communications*, September 1996.

7.5 KEY TERMS, REVIEW QUESTIONS, AND PROBLEMS

Key Terms

automatic repeat request (ARQ)	flag field	piggybacking
acknowledgment frame	flow control	selective-reject ARQ
data frame	frame	sliding-window flow control
data link	frame synchronization	stop-and-wait ARQ
data link control protocol	go-back-N ARQ	stop-and-wait flow control
data transparency	header	trailer
error control	high-level data link control (HDLC)	

Review Questions

7.1 List and briefly define some of the requirements for effective communications over a data link.

7.2 Define *flow control*.

7.3 Describe stop-and-wait flow control.

7.4 What are reasons for breaking up a long data transmission into a number of frames?

7.5 Describe sliding-window flow control.

7.6 What is the advantage of sliding-window flow control compared to stop-and-wait flow control?

7.7 What is piggybacking?

7.8 Define *error control*.

7.9 List common ingredients for error control for a link control protocol.

7.10 Describe automatic repeat request (ARQ).

7.11 List and briefly define three versions of ARQ.

7.12 What are the station types supported by HDLC? Describe each.

7.13 What are the transfer modes supported by HDLC? Describe each.

7.14 What is the purpose of the flag field?

7.15 Define *data transparency*.

7.16 What are the three frame types supported by HDLC? Describe each.

Problems

7.1 Consider a half-duplex point-to-point link using a stop-and-wait scheme, in which a series of messages is sent, with each message segmented into a number of frames. Ignore errors and frame overhead.

    a. What is the effect on line utilization of increasing the message size so that fewer messages will be required? Other factors remain constant.

    b. What is the effect on line utilization of increasing the number of frames for a constant message size?

    c. What is the effect on line utilization of increasing frame size?

7.2 The number of bits on a transmission line that are in the process of actively being transmitted (i.e., the number of bits that have been transmitted but have not yet been received) is referred to as the *bit length* of the line. Plot the line distance versus the transmission speed for a bit length of 1000 bits. Assume a propagation velocity of 2×10^8 m/s.

7.3 A channel has a data rate of 4 kbps and a propagation delay of 20 ms. For what range of frame sizes does stop-and-wait give an efficiency of at least 50%?

7.4 Consider the use of 1000-bit frames on a 1-Mbps satellite channel with a 270-ms delay. What is the maximum link utilization for

    a. Stop-and-wait flow control?

    b. Continuous flow control with a window size of 7?

    c. Continuous flow control with a window size of 127?

    d. Continuous flow control with a window size of 255?

7.5 In Figure 7.10 frames are generated at node A and sent to node C through node B. Determine the minimum data rate required between nodes B and C so that the buffers of node B are not flooded, based on the following:

- The data rate between A and B is 100 kbps.
- The propagation delay is 5 μs/km for both lines.
- There are full duplex lines between the nodes.
- All data frames are 1000 bits long; ACK frames are separate frames of negligible length.

Figure 7.10 Configuration for Problem 7.5

- Between A and B, a sliding-window protocol with a window size of 3 is used.
- Between B and C, stop-and-wait is used.
- There are no errors.

Hint: In order not to flood the buffers of B, the average number of frames entering and leaving B must be the same over a long interval.

7.6 A channel has a data rate of R bps and a propagation delay of t s/km. The distance between the sending and receiving nodes is L kilometers. Nodes exchange fixed-size frames of B bits. Find a formula that gives the minimum sequence field size of the frame as a function of R, t, B, and L (considering maximum utilization). Assume that ACK frames are negligible in size and the processing at the nodes is instantaneous.

7.7 No mention was made of reject (REJ) frames in the stop-and-wait ARQ discussion. Why is it not necessary to have REJ0 and REJ1 for stop-and-wait ARQ?

7.8 Suppose that a selective-reject ARQ is used where $W = 4$. Show, by example, that a 3-bit sequence number is needed.

7.9 Using the same assumptions that are used for Figure 7.13 in Appendix 7A, plot line utilization as a function of P, the probability that a single frame is in error for the following error-control techniques:
  a. Stop-and-wait
  b. Go-back-N with $W = 7$
  c. Go-back-N with $W = 127$
  d. Selective reject with $W = 7$
  e. Selective reject with $W = 127$

Do all of the preceding for the following values of a: 0.1, 1, 10, 100. Draw conclusions about which technique is appropriate for various ranges of a.

7.10 Two neighboring nodes (A and B) use a sliding-window protocol with a 3-bit sequence number. As the ARQ mechanism, go-back-N is used with a window size of 4. Assuming A is transmitting and B is receiving, show the window positions for the following succession of events:
  a. Before A sends any frames
  b. After A sends frames 0, 1, 2 and receives acknowledgment from B for 0 and 1
  c. After A sends frames 3, 4, and 5 and B acknowledges 4 and the ACK is received by A

7.11 Out-of-sequence acknowledgment cannot be used for selective-reject ARQ. That is, if frame i is rejected by station X, all subsequent I-frames and RR frames sent by X must have $N(R) = i$ until frame i is successfully received, even if other frames with $N(S) > i$ are successfully received in the meantime. One possible refinement is the following: $N(R) = j$ in an I-frame or an RR frame is interpreted to mean that frame $j - 1$ and all preceding frames are accepted except for those that have been explicitly rejected using an SREJ frame. Comment on any possible drawback to this scheme.

7.12 The ISO standard for HDLC procedures (ISO 4335) includes the following definitions: (1) an REJ condition is considered cleared upon the receipt of an incoming I-frame with an $N(S)$ equal to the $N(R)$ of the outgoing REJ frame; and (2) a SREJ condition is considered cleared upon the receipt of an I-frame with an $N(S)$ equal to the $N(R)$ of the SREJ frame. The standard includes rules concerning the relationship between REJ and SREJ frames. These rules indicate what is allowable (in terms of transmitting REJ and SREJ frames) if an REJ condition has not yet been cleared and what is allowable if an SREJ condition has not yet been cleared. Deduce the rules and justify your answer.

7.13 Two stations communicate via a 1-Mbps satellite link with a propagation delay of 270 ms. The satellite serves merely to retransmit data received from one station to another, with negligible switching delay. Using HDLC frames of 1024 bits with 3-bit sequence numbers, what is the maximum possible data throughput; that is, what is the throughput of data bits carried in HDLC frames?

7.14 It is clear that bit stuffing is needed for the address, data, and FCS fields of an HDLC frame. Is it needed for the control field?

7.15 Because of the provision that a single flag can be used as both an ending and a starting flag, a single-bit error can cause problems.
  a. Explain how a single-bit error can merge two frames into one.
  b. Explain how a single-bit error can split a single frame into two frames.

7.16 Suggest improvements to the bit stuffing-algorithm to overcome the problems of single-bit errors described in the preceding problem.

7.17 Using the example bit string of Figure 7.8, show the signal pattern on the line using NRZ-L coding. Does this suggest a side benefit of bit stuffing?

7.18 Assume that the primary HDLC station in NRM has sent six I-frames to a secondary. The primary's N(S) count was three (011 binary) prior to sending the six frames. If the poll bit is on in the sixth frame, what will be the N(R) count back from the secondary after the last frame? Assume error-free operation.

7.19 Consider that several physical links connect two stations. We would like to use a "multilink HDLC" that makes efficient use of these links by sending frames on a FIFO basis on the next available link. What enhancements to HDLC are needed?

7.20 A World Wide Web server is usually set up to receive relatively small messages from its clients but to transmit potentially very large messages to them. Explain, then, which type of ARQ protocol (selective reject, go-back-N) would provide less of a burden to a particularly popular WWW server.

APPENDIX 7A PERFORMANCE ISSUES

In this appendix, we examine some of the performance issues related to the use of sliding-window flow control.

Stop-and-Wait Flow Control

Let us determine the maximum potential efficiency of a half-duplex point-to-point line using the stop-and-wait scheme described in Section 7.1. Suppose that a long message is to be sent as a sequence of frames $F_1, F_2, ..., F_n$, in the following fashion:

- Station S_1 sends F_1.
- Station S_2 sends an acknowledgment.
- Station S_1 sends F_2.
- Station S_2 sends an acknowledgment.
- Station S_1 sends F_n.
- Station S_2 sends an acknowledgment.

The total time to send the data, T, can be expressed as $T = nT_F$, where T_F is the time to send one frame and receive an acknowledgment. We can express T_F as follows:

$$T_F = t_{prop} + t_{frame} + t_{proc} + t_{prop} + t_{ack} + t_{proc}$$

where

t_{prop} = propagation time from S_1 to S_2

t_{frame} = time to transmit a frame (time for the transmitter to send out all of the bits of the frame)

t_{proc} = processing time at each station to react to an incoming event

t_{ack} = time to transmit an acknowledgment

Let us assume that the processing time is relatively negligible, and that the acknowledgment frame is very small compared to a data frame, both of which are reasonable assumptions. Then we can express the total time to send the data as

$$T = n(2t_{prop} + t_{frame})$$

Of that time, only $n \times t_{frame}$ is actually spent transmitting data and the rest is overhead. The utilization, or efficiency, of the line is

$$U = \frac{n \times t_{frame}}{n(2t_{prop} + t_{frame})} = \frac{t_{frame}}{2t_{prop} + t_{frame}} \qquad (7.3)$$

It is useful to define the parameter $a = t_{prop}/t_{frame}$ (see Figure 7.2). Then

$$U = \frac{1}{1 + 2a} \qquad (7.4)$$

This is the maximum possible utilization of the link. Because the frame contains overhead bits, actual utilization is lower. The parameter a is constant if both t_{prop} and t_{frame} are constants, which is typically the case: Fixed-length frames are often used for all except the last frame in a sequence, and the propagation delay is constant for point-to-point links.

To get some insight into Equation (7.4), let us derive a different expression for a. We have

$$a = \frac{\text{Propagation Time}}{\text{Transmission Time}} \qquad (7.5)$$

The propagation time is equal to the distance d of the link divided by the velocity of propagation V. For unguided transmission through air or space, V is the speed of light, approximately 3×10^8 m/s. For guided transmission, V is approximately 0.67 times the speed of light for optical fiber and copper media. The transmission time is equal to the length of the frame in bits, L, divided by the data rate R. Therefore,

$$a = \frac{d/V}{L/R} = \frac{Rd}{VL}$$

Thus, for fixed-length frames, a is proportional to the data rate times the length of the medium. A useful way of looking at a is that it represents the length of the medium in bits $[R \times (d/v)]$ compared to the frame length (L).

With this interpretation in mind, Figure 7.2 illustrates Equation (7.4). In this figure, transmission time is normalized to 1 and hence the propagation time, by Equation (7.5), is a. For the case of $a < 1$, the link's bit length is less than that of the frame. The station T begins transmitting a frame at time t_0. At $t_0 + a$, the leading edge of the frame reaches the receiving station R, while T is still in the process of transmitting the frame. At $t_0 + 1$, T completes transmission. At $t_0 + 1 + a$, R has received the entire frame and immediately transmits a small acknowledgment frame. This acknowledgment arrives back at T at $t_0 + 1 + 2a$.

Total elapsed time: $1 + 2a$. Total transmission time: 1. Hence utilization is $1/(1 + 2a)$. The same result is achieved with $a > 1$, as illustrated in Figure 7.2.

EXAMPLE 7.6 First, consider a wide area network using asynchronous transfer mode (described in Part Three), with the two stations a thousand kilometers apart. The standard ATM frame size (called a cell) is 424 bits and one of the standardized data rates is 155.52 Mbps. Thus, transmission time equals $424/(155.52 \times 10^6) = 2.7 \times 10^{-6}$ s. If we assume an optical fiber link, then the propagation time is $(10^6 \text{ m})/(2 \times 10^8 \text{ m/s}) = 0.5 \times 10^{-2}$ s. Thus, $a = (0.5 \times 10^{-2})/(2.7 \times 10^{-6}) \approx 1850$, and efficiency is only $1/3701 = 0.00027$.

At the other extreme, in terms of distance, is the local area network. Distances range from 0.1 to 10 km, with data rates of 10 Mbps to 1 Gbps; higher data rates tend to be associated with shorter distances. Using a value of $V = 2 \times 10^8$ m/s, a frame size of 1000 bits, and a data rate of 10 Mbps, the value of a is in the range of 0.005 to 0.5. This yields a utilization in the range of 0.5 to 0.99. For a 100-Mbps LAN, given the shorter distances, comparable utilizations are possible.

We can see that LANs are typically quite efficient, whereas high-speed WANs are not. As a final example, let us consider digital data transmission via modem over a voice-grade line. A typical data rate is 56 kbps. Again, let us consider a 1000-bit frame. The link distance can be anywhere from a few tens of meters to thousands of kilometers. If we pick, say, as a short distance $d = 1000$ m, then $a = (56,000 \text{ bps} \times 1000 \text{ m})/(2 \times 10^8 \text{ m/s} \times 1000 \text{ bits}) = 2.8 \times 10^{-4}$, and utilization is effectively 1.0. Even in a long-distance case, such as $d = 5000$ km, we have $a = (56,000 \times 5 \times 10^6)/(2 \times 10^8 \times 1000 \text{ bits}) = 1.4$ and efficiency equals 0.26.

Error-Free Sliding-Window Flow Control

For sliding-window flow control, the throughput on the line depends on both the window size W and the value of a. For convenience, let us again normalize frame transmission time to a value of 1; thus, the propagation time is a. Figure 7.11 illustrates the efficiency of a full duplex point-to-point line.[3] Station A begins to emit a sequence of frames at time $t = 0$. The leading edge of the first frame reaches station B at $t = a$. The first frame is entirely absorbed by $t = a + 1$. Assuming negligible processing time, B can immediately acknowledge the first frame (ACK). Let us also assume that the acknowledgment frame is so small that transmission time is negligible. Then the ACK reaches A at $t = 2a + 1$. To evaluate performance, we need to consider two cases:

- **Case 1:** $W \geq 2a + 1$. The acknowledgment for frame 1 reaches A before A has exhausted its window. Thus, A can transmit continuously with no pause and normalized throughput is 1.0.
- **Case 2:** $W < 2a + 1$. A exhausts its window at $t = W$ and cannot send additional frames until $t = 2a + 1$. Thus, normalized throughput is W time units out of a period of $(2a + 1)$ time units.

---

[3]For simplicity, we assume that a is an integer, so that an integer number of frames exactly fills the line. The argument does not change for noninteger values of a.

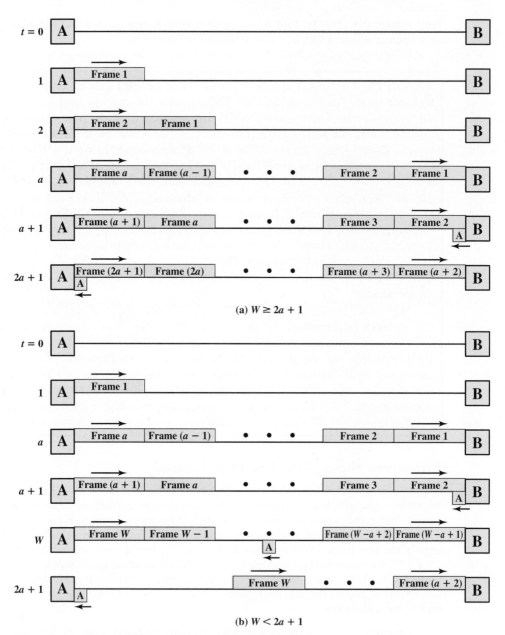

Figure 7.11 Timing of Sliding-Window Protocol

Therefore, we can express the utilization as

$$U = \begin{cases} 1 & W \geq 2a + 1 \\ \dfrac{W}{2a + 1} & W < 2a + 1 \end{cases} \tag{7.6}$$

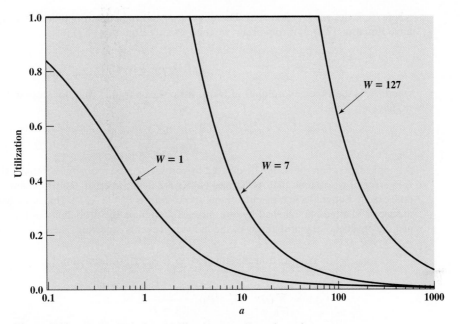

Figure 7.12   Sliding-Window Utilization as a Function of *a*

Typically, the sequence number is provided for in an *n*-bit field and the maximum window size is $W = 2^n - 1$ (not 2^n; this is explained in Section 7.2). Figure 7.12 shows the maximum utilization achievable for window sizes of 1, 7, and 127 as a function of *a*. A window size of 1 corresponds to stop and wait. A window size of 7 (3 bits) is adequate for many applications. A window size of 127 (7 bits) is adequate for larger values of *a*, such as may be found in high-speed WANs.

ARQ

We have seen that sliding-window flow control is more efficient than stop-and-wait flow control. We would expect that when error control functions are added that this would still be true: that is, that go-back-N and selective-reject ARQ are more efficient than stop-and-wait ARQ. Let us develop some approximations to determine the degree of improvement to be expected.

First, consider stop-and-wait ARQ. With no errors, the maximum utilization is $1/(1 + 2a)$ as shown in Equation (7.4). We want to account for the possibility that some frames are repeated because of bit errors. To start, note that the utilization *U* can be defined as

$$U = \frac{T_f}{T_t} \tag{7.7}$$

where

    T_f = time for transmitter to emit a single frame

    T_t = total time that line is engaged in the transmission of a single frame

For error-free operation using stop-and-wait ARQ:

$$U = \frac{T_f}{T_f + 2T_p}$$

where T_p is the propagation time. Dividing by T_f and remembering that $a = T_p/T_f$, we again have Equation (7.4). If errors occur, we must modify Equation (7.7) to

$$U = \frac{T_f}{N_r T_t}$$

where N_r is the expected number of transmissions of a frame. Thus, for stop-and-wait ARQ, we have

$$U = \frac{1}{N_r(1 + 2a)}$$

A simple expression for N_r can be derived by considering the probability P that a single frame is in error. If we assume that ACKs and NAKs are never in error, the probability that it will take exactly k attempts to transmit a frame successfully is $P^{k-1}(1 - P)$. That is, we have $(k - 1)$ unsuccessful attempts followed by one successful attempt; the probability of this occurring is just the product of the probability of the individual events occurring. Then,[4]

$$N_r = E[\text{transmissions}] = \sum_{i=1}^{\infty} (i \times \Pr[i \text{ transmissions}])$$

$$= \sum_{i=1}^{\infty} (iP^{i-1}(1 - P)) = \frac{1}{1 - P}$$

So we have

Stop-and-Wait:	$U = \dfrac{1 - P}{1 + 2a}$

For the sliding-window protocol, Equation (7.6) applies for error-free operation. For selective-reject ARQ, we can use the same reasoning as applied to stop-and-wait ARQ. That is, the error-free equations must be divided by N_r. Again, $N_r = 1/(1 - P)$. So

Selective-Reject:	$U = \begin{cases} 1 - P & W \geq 2a + 1 \\ \dfrac{W(1 - P)}{2a + 1} & W < 2a + 1 \end{cases}$

The same reasoning applies for go-back-N ARQ, but we must be more careful in approximating N_r. Each error generates a requirement to retransmit K frames rather than just one frame. Thus

$$N_r = E[\text{number of transmitted frames to successfully transmit one frame}]$$

$$= \sum_{i=1}^{\infty} f(i)P^{i-1}(1 - P)$$

where $f(i)$ is the total number of frames transmitted if the original frame must be transmitted i times. This can be expressed as

$$f(i) = 1 + (i - 1)K$$

$$= (1 - K) + Ki$$

---

[4]This derivation uses the equality $\sum_{i=1}^{\infty}(iX^{i-1}) = \dfrac{1}{(1 - X)^2}$ for $(-1 < X < 1)$.

Substituting yields[5]

$$N_r = (1 - K)\sum_{i=1}^{\infty} P^{i-1}(1 - P) + K\sum_{i=1}^{\infty} iP^{i-1}(1 - P)$$

$$= 1 - K + \frac{K}{1 - P}$$

$$= \frac{1 - P + KP}{1 - P}$$

By studying Figure 7.11, the reader should conclude that K is approximately equal to $(2a + 1)$ for $W \geq (2a + 1)$, and $K = W$ for $W < (2a + 1)$. Thus

Go-back-N:	$U = \begin{cases} \dfrac{1 - P}{1 + 2aP} & W \geq 2a + 1 \\[2ex] \dfrac{W(1 - P)}{(2a + 1)(1 - P + WP)} & W < 2a + 1 \end{cases}$

Note that for $W = 1$, both selective-reject and go-back-N ARQ reduce to stop and wait. Figure 7.13[6] compares these three error control techniques for a value of $P = 10^{-3}$. This figure and the equations are only approximations. For example, we have ignored errors in acknowledgment frames and, in the case of go-back-N, errors in retransmitted frames other than the frame initially in error. However, the results do give an indication of the relative performance of the three techniques.

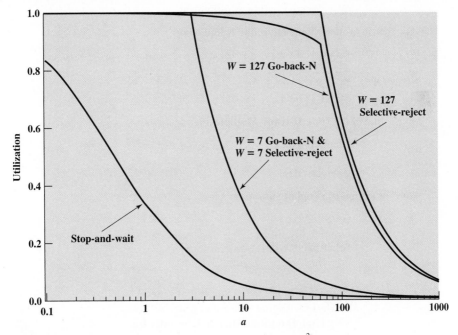

Figure 7.13 ARQ Utilization as a Function of a ($P = 10^{-3}$)

---

[5]This derivation uses the equality $\sum_{i=1}^{\infty} X^{i-1} = \dfrac{1}{1 - X}$ for $(-1 < X < 1)$.

[6]For $W = 7$, the curves for go-back-N and selective-reject are so close that they appear to be identical in the figure.

MULTIPLEXING

It was impossible to get a conversation going, everybody was talking too much.

Yogi Berra

KEY POINTS

◆ To make efficient use of high-speed telecommunications lines, some form of multiplexing is used. Multiplexing allows several transmission sources to share a larger transmission capacity. The two common forms of multiplexing are frequency division multiplexing (FDM) and time division multiplexing (TDM).

◆ **Frequency division multiplexing** can be used with analog signals. A number of signals are carried simultaneously on the same medium by allocating to each signal a different frequency band. Modulation equipment is needed to move each signal to the required frequency band, and multiplexing equipment is needed to combine the modulated signals.

◆ **Synchronous time division multiplexing** can be used with digital signals or analog signals carrying digital data. In this form of multiplexing, data from various sources are carried in repetitive frames. Each frame consists of a set of time slots, and each source is assigned one or more time slots per frame. The effect is to interleave bits of data from the various sources.

◆ **Statistical time division multiplexing** provides a generally more efficient service than synchronous TDM for the support of terminals. With statistical TDM, time slots are not preassigned to particular data sources. Rather, user data are buffered and transmitted as rapidly as possible using available time slots.

In Chapter 7, we described efficient techniques for utilizing a data link under heavy load. Specifically, with two devices connected by a point-to-point link, it is generally desirable to have multiple frames outstanding so that the data link does not become a bottleneck between the stations. Now consider the opposite problem. Typically, two communicating stations will not utilize the full capacity of a data link. For efficiency, it should be possible to share that capacity. A generic term for such sharing is **multiplexing**.

A common application of multiplexing is in long-haul communications. Trunks on long-haul networks are high-capacity fiber, coaxial, or microwave links. These links can carry large numbers of voice and data transmissions simultaneously using multiplexing.

Figure 8.1 depicts the multiplexing function in its simplest form. There are *n* inputs to a multiplexer. The multiplexer is connected by a single data

241

Figure 8.1 Multiplexing

link to a demultiplexer. The link is able to carry n separate channels of data. The multiplexer combines (multiplexes) data from the n input lines and transmits over a higher-capacity data link. The demultiplexer accepts the multiplexed data stream, separates (demultiplexes) the data according to channel, and delivers data to the appropriate output lines.

The widespread use of multiplexing in data communications can be explained by the following:

- The higher the data rate, the more cost-effective the transmission facility. That is, for a given application and over a given distance, the cost per kbps declines with an increase in the data rate of the transmission facility. Similarly, the cost of transmission and receiving equipment, per kbps, declines with increasing data rate.

- Most individual data communicating devices require relatively modest data rate support. For example, for many terminal and personal computer applications that do not involve Web access or intensive graphics, a data rate of between 9600 bps and 64 kbps is generally adequate.

The preceding statements were phrased in terms of data communicating devices. Similar statements apply to voice communications. That is, the greater the capacity of a transmission facility, in terms of voice channels, the less the cost per individual voice channel, and the capacity required for a single voice channel is modest.

This chapter concentrates on three types of multiplexing techniques. The first, frequency division multiplexing (FDM), is the most heavily used and is familiar to anyone who has ever used a radio or television set. The second is a particular case of time division multiplexing (TDM) known as synchronous TDM. This is commonly used for multiplexing digitized voice streams and data streams. The third type seeks to improve on the efficiency of synchronous TDM by adding complexity to the multiplexer. It is known by a variety of names, including statistical TDM, asynchronous TDM, and intelligent TDM. This book uses the term *statistical TDM*, which highlights one of its chief properties. Finally, we look at the digital subscriber line, which combines FDM and synchronous TDM technologies.

8.1   FREQUENCY DIVISION MULTIPLEXING

Characteristics

FDM is possible when the useful bandwidth of the transmission medium exceeds the required bandwidth of signals to be transmitted. A number of signals can be carried simultaneously if each signal is modulated onto a different carrier frequency and the carrier frequencies are sufficiently separated that the bandwidths of the signals do not significantly overlap. A general case of FDM is shown in Figure 8.2a.

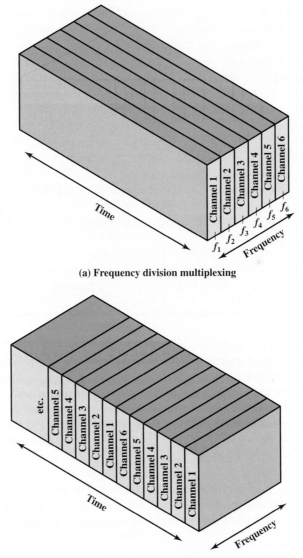

(a) Frequency division multiplexing

(b) Time division multiplexing

Figure 8.2   FDM and TDM

Six signal sources are fed into a multiplexer, which modulates each signal onto a different frequency $(f_1, \ldots, f_6)$. Each modulated signal requires a certain bandwidth centered on its carrier frequency, referred to as a **channel**. To prevent interference, the channels are separated by guard bands, which are unused portions of the spectrum.

The composite signal transmitted across the medium is analog. Note, however, that the input signals may be either digital or analog. In the case of digital input, the input signals must be passed through modems to be converted to analog. In either case, each input analog signal must then be modulated to move it to the appropriate frequency band.

EXAMPLE 8.1 A familiar example of FDM is broadcast and cable television. The television signal discussed in Chapter 3 fits comfortably into a 6-MHz bandwidth. Figure 8.3 depicts the transmitted TV signal and its bandwidth. The black-and-white video signal is amplitude-modulated on a carrier signal f_{cv}. Because the baseband video signal has a bandwidth of 4 MHz, we would expect the modulated signal to have a bandwidth of 8 MHz centered on f_{cv}. To conserve bandwidth, the signal is passed through a sideband filter so that most of the lower sideband is suppressed. The resulting signal extends from about $f_{cv} - 0.75$ MHz to $f_{cv} + 4.2$ MHz. A separate color carrier, f_{cc}, is used to transmit color information. This is spaced far enough from f_{cv} that there is essentially no interference. Finally, the audio portion of the signal is modulated on f_{ca}, outside the effective bandwidth of the other two signals. A bandwidth of 50 kHz is allocated for the audio signal. The composite signal fits into a 6-MHz bandwidth with the video, color, and audio signal carriers at 1.25 MHz, 4.799545 MHz, and 5.75 MHz above the lower edge of the band, respectively. Thus, multiple TV signals can be frequency division multiplexed on a cable, each with a bandwidth of 6 MHz. Given the enormous bandwidth of coaxial cable (as much as 500 MHz), dozens of TV signals can be simultaneously carried using FDM. Of course, using radio-frequency propagation through the atmosphere is also a form of FDM.

A generic depiction of an FDM system is shown in Figure 8.4. A number of analog or digital signals $[m_i(t), i = 1, n]$ are to be multiplexed onto the same transmission medium. Each signal $m_i(t)$ is modulated onto a carrier f_i; because multiple carriers are to be used, each is referred to as a **subcarrier**. Any type of modulation may be used. The resulting analog, modulated signals are then summed to produce a composite baseband[1] signal $m_b(t)$. Figure 8.4b shows the result. The spectrum of signal $m_i(t)$ is shifted to be centered on f_i. For this scheme to work, f_i must be chosen so that the bandwidths of the various signals do not significantly overlap. Otherwise, it will be impossible to recover the original signals.

The composite signal may then be shifted as a whole to another carrier frequency by an additional modulation step. We will see examples of this later. This second modulation step need not use the same modulation technique as the first.

---

[1]The term *baseband* is used to designate the band of frequencies of the signal delivered by the source and potentially used as a modulating signal. Typically, the spectrum of a baseband signal is significant in a band that includes or is in the vicinity of $f = 0$.

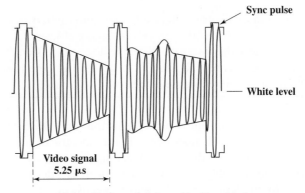

(a) Amplitude modulation with video signal

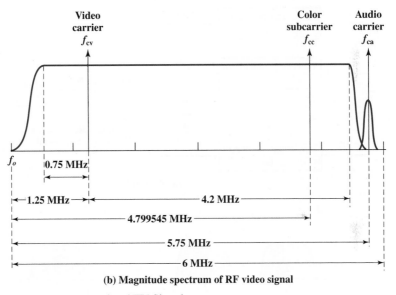

(b) Magnitude spectrum of RF video signal

Figure 8.3   Transmitted TV Signal

The FDM signal $s(t)$ has a total bandwidth B, where $B > \sum_{i=1}^{n} B_i$. This analog signal may be transmitted over a suitable medium. At the receiving end, the FDM signal is demodulated to retrieve $m_b(t)$, which is then passed through n bandpass filters, each filter centered on f_i and having a bandwidth B_i, for $1 \le i \le n$. In this way, the signal is again split into its component parts. Each component is then demodulated to recover the original signal.

EXAMPLE 8.2 Let us consider a simple example of transmitting three voice signals simultaneously over a medium. As was mentioned, the bandwidth of a voice signal is generally taken to be 4 kHz, with an effective spectrum of 300 to 3400 Hz (Figure 8.5a). If such a signal is used to amplitude-modulate a 64-kHz carrier, the spectrum of Figure 8.5b results. The modulated signal has a bandwidth of 8 kHz, extending from 60 to 68 kHz. To make efficient use of bandwidth, we elect to transmit only the lower sideband. If three voice signals are used to modulate carriers at 64 kHz, 68 kHz, and 72 kHz, and only the lower sideband of each is taken, the spectrum of Figure 8.5c results.

Figure 8.5 points out two problems that an FDM system must cope with. The first is crosstalk, which may occur if the spectra of adjacent component signals overlap significantly. In the case of voice signals, with an effective bandwidth of only 3100 Hz (300 to 3400), a 4-kHz bandwidth is adequate. The spectra of signals produced by modems for voiceband transmission also fit well in this bandwidth.

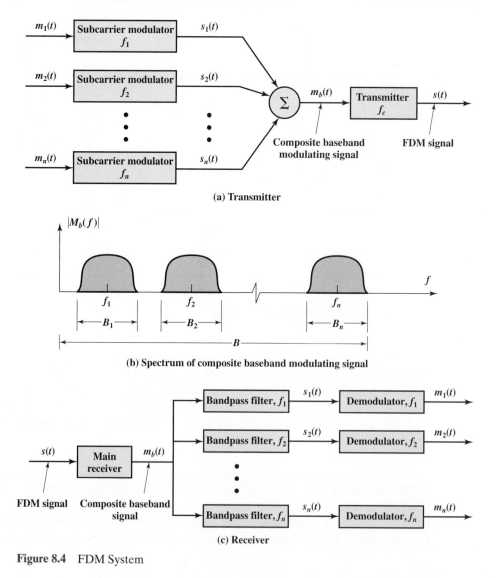

(a) Transmitter

(b) Spectrum of composite baseband modulating signal

(c) Receiver

Figure 8.4 FDM System

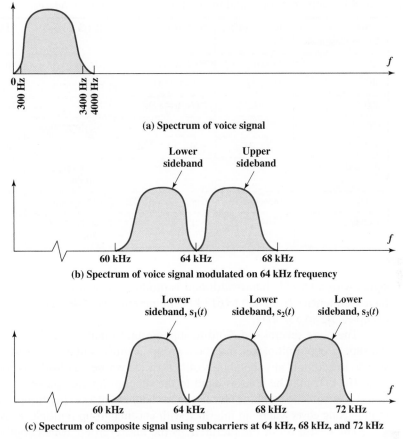

(a) Spectrum of voice signal

(b) Spectrum of voice signal modulated on 64 kHz frequency

(c) Spectrum of composite signal using subcarriers at 64 kHz, 68 kHz, and 72 kHz

Figure 8.5 FDM of Three Voiceband Signals

Another potential problem is intermodulation noise, which was discussed in Chapter 3. On a long link, the nonlinear effects of amplifiers on a signal in one channel could produce frequency components in other channels.

Analog Carrier Systems

The long-distance carrier system provided in the United States and throughout the world is designed to transmit voiceband signals over high-capacity transmission links, such as coaxial cable and microwave systems. The earliest, and still a very common, technique for utilizing high-capacity links is FDM. In the United States, AT&T has designated a hierarchy of FDM schemes to accommodate transmission systems of various capacities. A similar, but unfortunately not identical, system has been adopted internationally under the auspices of ITU-T (Table 8.1).

At the first level of the AT&T hierarchy, 12 voice channels are combined to produce a group signal with a bandwidth of 12×4 kHz = 48 kHz, in the range 60 to 108 kHz. The signals are produced in a fashion similar to that described previously, using subcarrier frequencies of from 64 to 108 kHz in increments of 4 kHz. The next basic building block is the 60-channel supergroup, which is formed by frequency division multiplexing five group signals. At this step, each group is treated as a single

Table 8.1 North American and International FDM Carrier Standards

Number of Voice Channels	Bandwidth	Spectrum	AT&T	ITU-T
12	48 kHz	60–108 kHz	Group	Group
60	240 kHz	312–552 kHz	Supergroup	Supergroup
300	1.232 MHz	812–2044 kHz		Mastergroup
600	2.52 MHz	564–3084 kHz	Mastergroup	
900	3.872 MHz	8.516–12.388 MHz		Supermaster group
$N \times 600$			Mastergroup multiplex	
3,600	16.984 MHz	0.564–17.548 MHz	Jumbogroup	
10,800	57.442 MHz	3.124–60.566 MHz	Jumbogroup multiplex	

signal with a 48-kHz bandwidth and is modulated by a subcarrier. The subcarriers have frequencies from 420 to 612 kHz in increments of 48 kHz. The resulting signal occupies 312 to 552 kHz.

There are several variations to supergroup formation. Each of the five inputs to the supergroup multiplexer may be a group channel containing 12 multiplexed voice signals. In addition, any signal up to 48 kHz wide whose bandwidth is contained within 60 to 108 kHz may be used as input to the supergroup multiplexer. As another variation, it is possible to combine 60 voiceband channels into a supergroup. This may reduce multiplexing costs where an interface with existing group multiplexer is not required.

The next level of the hierarchy is the mastergroup, which combines 10 supergroup inputs. Again, any signal with a bandwidth of 240 kHz in the range 312 to 552 kHz can serve as input to the mastergroup multiplexer. The mastergroup has a bandwidth of 2.52 MHz and can support 600 voice frequency (VF) channels. Higher-level multiplexing is defined above the mastergroup, as shown in Table 8.1.

Note that the original voice or data signal may be modulated many times. For example, a data signal may be encoded using QPSK to form an analog voice signal. This signal could then be used to modulate a 76-kHz carrier to form a component of a group signal. This group signal could then be used to modulate a 516-kHz carrier to form a component of a supergroup signal. Each stage can distort the original data; this is so, for example, if the modulator/multiplexer contains nonlinearities or introduces noise.

Wavelength Division Multiplexing

The true potential of optical fiber is fully exploited when multiple beams of light at different frequencies are transmitted on the same fiber. This is a form of frequency division multiplexing but is commonly called **wavelength division multiplexing (WDM)**. With WDM, the light streaming through the fiber consists of many colors, or wavelengths, each carrying a separate channel of data. In 1997, a landmark was reached when Bell Laboratories was able to demonstrate a WDM system with 100 beams each operating at 10 Gbps, for a total data rate of 1 trillion bits per second

Table 8.2 ITU WDM Channel Spacing (G.692)

Frequency (THz)	Wavelength in Vacuum (nm)	50 GHz	100 GHz	200 GHz
196.10	1528.77	X	X	X
196.05	1529.16	X		
196.00	1529.55	X	X	
195.95	1529.94	X		
195.90	1530.33	X	X	X
195.85	1530.72	X		
195.80	1531,12	X	X	
195.75	1531.51	X		
195.70	1531.90	X	X	X
195.65	1532.29	X		
195.60	1532.68	X	X	
. . .	. . .			
192.10	1560.61	X	X	X

(also referred to as 1 terabit per second or 1 Tbps). Commercial systems with 160 channels of 10 Gbps are now available. In a lab environment, Alcatel has carried 256 channels at 39.8 Gbps each, a total of 10.1 Tbps, over a 100-km span.

A typical WDM system has the same general architecture as other FDM systems. A number of sources generate a laser beam at different wavelengths. These are sent to a multiplexer, which consolidates the sources for transmission over a single fiber line. Optical amplifiers, typically spaced tens of kilometers apart, amplify all of the wavelengths simultaneously. Finally, the composite signal arrives at a demultiplexer, where the component channels are separated and sent to receivers at the destination point.

Most WDM systems operate in the 1550-nm range. In early systems, 200 GHz was allocated to each channel, but today most WDM systems use 50-GHz spacing. The channel spacing defined in ITU-T G.692, which accommodates 80 50-GHz channels, is summarized in Table 8.2.

The term **dense wavelength division multiplexing (DWDM)** is often seen in the literature. There is no official or standard definition of this term. The term connotes the use of more channels, more closely spaced, than ordinary WDM. In general, a channel spacing of 200 GHz or less could be considered dense.

8.2 SYNCHRONOUS TIME DIVISION MULTIPLEXING

Characteristics

Synchronous time division multiplexing is possible when the achievable data rate (sometimes, unfortunately, called bandwidth) of the medium exceeds the data rate of digital signals to be transmitted. Multiple digital signals (or analog signals carrying digital data) can be carried on a single transmission path by interleaving portions of each signal in time. The interleaving can be at the bit level or in blocks of bytes or larger quantities. For example, the multiplexer in Figure 8.2b has six inputs that might each be, say, 9.6 kbps. A single line with a capacity of at least 57.6 kbps (plus overhead capacity) could accommodate all six sources.

A generic depiction of a synchronous TDM system is provided in Figure 8.6. A number of signals $[m_i(t), i = 1, n]$ are to be multiplexed onto the same transmission medium. The signals carry digital data and are generally digital signals. The incoming data from each source are briefly buffered. Each buffer is typically one bit or one character in length. The buffers are scanned sequentially to form a composite digital data stream $m_c(t)$. The scan operation is sufficiently rapid so that each buffer is emptied before more data can arrive. Thus, the data rate of $m_c(t)$ must at least equal the sum of the data rates of the $m_i(t)$. The digital signal $m_c(t)$ may be transmitted directly,

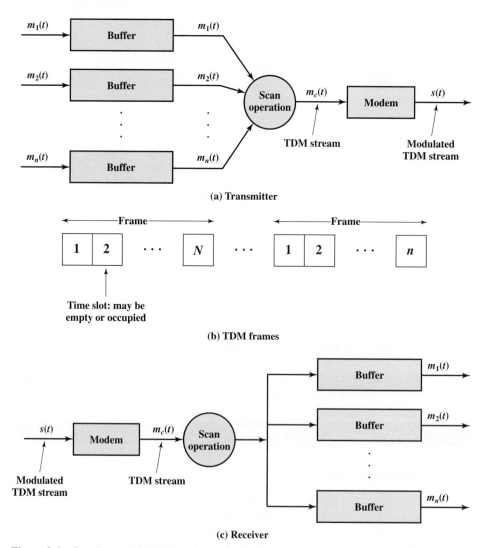

Figure 8.6 Synchronous TDM System

or passed through a modem so that an analog signal is transmitted. In either case, transmission is typically synchronous.

The transmitted data may have a format something like Figure 8.6b. The data are organized into **frames**. Each frame contains a cycle of time slots. In each frame, one or more slots are dedicated to each data source. The sequence of slots dedicated to one source, from frame to frame, is called a **channel**. The slot length equals the transmitter buffer length, typically a bit or a byte (character).

The byte-interleaving technique is used with asynchronous and synchronous sources. Each time slot contains one character of data. Typically, the start and stop bits of each character are eliminated before transmission and reinserted by the receiver, thus improving efficiency. The bit-interleaving technique is used with synchronous sources and may also be used with asynchronous sources. Each time slot contains just one bit.

At the receiver, the interleaved data are demultiplexed and routed to the appropriate destination buffer. For each input source $m_i(t)$, there is an identical output destination that will receive the output data at the same rate at which it was generated.

Synchronous TDM is called synchronous not because synchronous transmission is used, but because the time slots are preassigned to sources and fixed. The time slots for each source are transmitted whether or not the source has data to send. This is, of course, also the case with FDM. In both cases, capacity is wasted to achieve simplicity of implementation. Even when fixed assignment is used, however, it is possible for a synchronous TDM device to handle sources of different data rates. For example, the slowest input device could be assigned one slot per cycle, while faster devices are assigned multiple slots per cycle.

TDM Link Control

The reader will note that the transmitted data stream depicted in Figure 8.6b does not contain the headers and trailers that we have come to associate with synchronous transmission. The reason is that the control mechanisms provided by a data link protocol are not needed. It is instructive to ponder this point, and we do so by considering two key data link control mechanisms: flow control and error control. It should be clear that, as far as the multiplexer and demultiplexer (Figure 8.1) are concerned, flow control is not needed. The data rate on the multiplexed line is fixed, and the multiplexer and demultiplexer are designed to operate at that rate. But suppose that one of the individual output lines attaches to a device that is temporarily unable to accept data. Should the transmission of TDM frames cease? Clearly not, because the remaining output lines are expecting to receive data at predetermined times. The solution is for the saturated output device to cause the flow of data from the corresponding input device to cease. Thus, for a while, the channel in question will carry empty slots, but the frames as a whole will maintain the same transmission rate.

The reasoning for error control is the same. It would not do to request retransmission of an entire TDM frame because an error occurs on one channel. The devices using the other channels do not want a retransmission nor would they know that a retransmission has been requested by some other device on another channel. Again, the solution is to apply error control on a per-channel basis.

Flow control and error control can be provided on a per-channel basis by using a data link control protocol such as HDLC on a per-channel basis.

(a) Configuration

Input₁·········· F_1 f_1 f_1 d_1 d_1 d_1 C_1 A_1 F_1 f_1 f_1 d_1 d_1 d_1 C_1 A_1 F_1

Input₂···F_2 f_2 f_2 d_2 d_2 d_2 d_2 C_2 A_2 F_2 f_2 f_2 d_2 d_2 d_2 d_2 C_2 A_2 F_2

(b) Input data streams

··· f_2 F_1 d_2 f_1 d_2 f_1 d_2 d_1 d_2 d_1 C_2 d_1 A_2 C_1 F_2 A_1 f_2 F_1 f_2 f_1 d_2 f_1 d_2 d_1 d_2 d_1 d_2 d_1 C_2 C_1 A_2 A_1 F_2 F_1

(c) Multiplexed data stream

Legend: F = flag field   d = one octet of data field
         A = address field   f = one octet of FCS field
         C = control field

Figure 8.7 Use of Data Link Control on TDM Channels

EXAMPLE 8.3 Figure 8.7 provides a simplified example. We assume two data sources, each using HDLC. One is transmitting a stream of HDLC frames containing three octets of data each, and the other is transmitting HDLC frames containing four octets of data. For clarity, we assume that character-interleaved multiplexing is used, although bit interleaving is more typical. Notice what is happening. The octets of the HDLC frames from the two sources are shuffled together for transmission over the multiplexed line. The reader may initially be uncomfortable with this diagram, because the HDLC frames have lost their integrity in some sense. For example, each frame check sequence (FCS) on the line applies to a disjointed set of bits. Even the FCS is not in one piece. However, the pieces are reassembled correctly before they are seen by the device on the other end of the HDLC protocol. In this sense, the multiplexing/demultiplexing operation is transparent to the attached stations; to each communicating pair of stations, it appears that they have a dedicated link.

One refinement is needed in Figure 8.7. Both ends of the line need to be a combination multiplexer/demultiplexer with a full-duplex line in between. Then each channel consists of two sets of slots, one traveling in each direction. The individual devices attached at each end can, in pairs, use HDLC to control their own channel. The multiplexer/demultiplexers need not be concerned with these matters.

FRAMING We have seen that a link control protocol is not needed to manage the overall TDM link. There is, however, a basic requirement for framing. Because we are not providing flag or SYNC characters to bracket TDM frames, some means is needed to assure frame synchronization. It is clearly important to maintain framing synchronization because, if the source and destination are out of step, data on all channels are lost.

Perhaps the most common mechanism for framing is known as added-digit framing. In this scheme, typically, one control bit is added to each TDM frame.

An identifiable pattern of bits, from frame to frame, is used as a "control channel." A typical example is the alternating bit pattern, 101010. . . . This is a pattern unlikely to be sustained on a data channel. Thus, to synchronize, a receiver compares the incoming bits of one frame position to the expected pattern. If the pattern does not match, successive bit positions are searched until the pattern persists over multiple frames. Once framing synchronization is established, the receiver continues to monitor the framing bit channel. If the pattern breaks down, the receiver must again enter a framing search mode.

PULSE STUFFING Perhaps the most difficult problem in the design of a synchronous time division multiplexer is that of synchronizing the various data sources. If each source has a separate clock, any variation among clocks could cause loss of synchronization. Also, in some cases, the data rates of the input data streams are not related by a simple rational number. For both these problems, a technique known as pulse stuffing is an effective remedy. With pulse stuffing, the outgoing data rate of the multiplexer, excluding framing bits, is higher than the sum of the maximum instantaneous incoming rates. The extra capacity is used by stuffing extra dummy bits or pulses into each incoming signal until its rate is raised to that of a locally generated clock signal. The stuffed pulses are inserted at fixed locations in the multiplexer frame format so that they may be identified and removed at the demultiplexer.

EXAMPLE 8.4 An example, from [COUC07], illustrates the use of synchronous TDM to multiplex digital and analog sources (Figure 8.8). Consider that there are 11 sources to be multiplexed on a single link:

Source 1:	Analog, 2-kHz bandwidth
Source 2:	Analog, 4-kHz bandwidth
Source 3:	Analog, 2-kHz bandwidth
Sources 4–11:	Digital, 7200 bps synchronous

As a first step, the analog sources are converted to digital using pulse code modulation (PCM). Recall from Chapter 5 that PCM is based on the sampling theorem, which dictates that a signal be sampled at a rate equal to twice its bandwidth. Thus, the required sampling rate is 4000 samples per second for sources 1 and 3, and 8000 samples per second for source 2. These samples, which are analog (PAM), must then be quantized or digitized. Let us assume that 4 bits are used for each analog sample. For convenience, these three sources will be multiplexed first, as a unit. At a scan rate of 4 kHz, one PAM sample each is taken from sources 1 and 3, and two PAM samples are taken from source 2 per scan. These four samples are interleaved and converted to 4-bit PCM samples. Thus, a total of 16 bits is generated at a rate of 4000 times per second, for a composite bit rate of 64 kbps.

For the digital sources, pulse stuffing is used to raise each source to a rate of 8 kbps, for an aggregate data rate of 64 kbps. A frame can consist of multiple cycles of 32 bits, each containing 16 PCM bits and two bits from each of the eight digital sources.

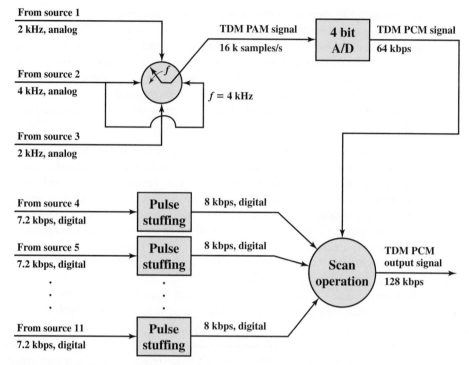

Figure 8.8   TDM of Analog and Digital Sources

Digital Carrier Systems

The long-distance carrier system provided in the United States and throughout the world was designed to transmit voice signals over high-capacity transmission links, such as optical fiber, coaxial cable, and microwave. Part of the evolution of these telecommunications networks to digital technology has been the adoption of synchronous TDM transmission structures. In the United States, AT&T developed a hierarchy of TDM structures of various capacities; this structure is used in Canada and Japan as well as the United States. A similar, but unfortunately not identical, hierarchy has been adopted internationally under the auspices of ITU-T (Table 8.3).

Table 8.3   North American and International TDM Carrier Standards

North American			International (ITU-T)		
Designation	**Number of Voice Channels**	**Data Rate (Mbps)**	**Level**	**Number of Voice Channels**	**Data Rate (Mbps)**
DS-1	24	1.544	1	30	2.048
DS-1C	48	3.152	2	120	8.448
DS-2	96	6.312	3	480	34.368
DS-3	672	44.736	4	1920	139.264
DS-4	4032	274.176	5	7680	565.148

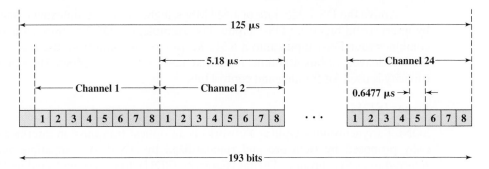

Notes:
1. The first bit is a framing bit, used for synchronization.
2. Voice channels:
   ·8-bit PCM used on five of six frames.
   ·7-bit PCM used on every sixth frame; bit 8 of each channel is a signaling bit.
3. Data channels:
   ·Channel 24 is used for signaling only in some schemes.
   ·Bits 1–7 used for 56-kbps service.
   ·Bits 2–7 used for 9.6-kbps, 4.8-kbps, and 2.4-kbps service.

Figure 8.9   DS-1 Transmission Format

The basis of the TDM hierarchy (in North America and Japan) is the DS-1 transmission format (Figure 8.9), which multiplexes 24 channels. Each frame contains 8 bits per channel plus a framing bit for $24 \times 8 + 1 = 193$ bits. For voice transmission, the following rules apply. Each channel contains one word of digitized voice data. The original analog voice signal is digitized using pulse code modulation (PCM) at a rate of 8000 samples per second. Therefore, each channel slot and hence each frame must repeat 8000 times per second. With a frame length of 193 bits, we have a data rate of $8000 \times 193 = 1.544$ Mbps. For five of every six frames, 8-bit PCM samples are used. For every sixth frame, each channel contains a 7-bit PCM word plus a *signaling bit*. The signaling bits form a stream for each voice channel that contains network control and routing information. For example, control signals are used to establish a connection or terminate a call.

The same DS-1 format is used to provide digital data service. For compatibility with voice, the same 1.544-Mbps data rate is used. In this case, 23 channels of data are provided. The twenty-fourth channel position is reserved for a special sync byte, which allows faster and more reliable reframing following a framing error. Within each channel, 7 bits per frame are used for data, with the eighth bit used to indicate whether the channel, for that frame, contains user data or system control data. With 7 bits per channel, and because each frame is repeated 8000 times per second, a data rate of 56 kbps can be provided per channel. Lower data rates are provided using a technique known as subrate multiplexing. For this technique, an additional bit is robbed from each channel to indicate which subrate multiplexing rate is being provided. This leaves a total capacity per channel of $6 \times 8000 = 48$ kbps. This capacity is used to multiplex five 9.6-kbps channels, ten 4.8-kbps channels, or twenty 2.4-kbps channels. For example, if channel 2 is used to provide 9.6-kbps service, then up to five data subchannels share this channel. The data for each subchannel appear as six bits in channel 2 every fifth frame.

Finally, the DS-1 format can be used to carry a mixture of voice and data channels. In this case, all 24 channels are utilized; no sync byte is provided.

Above the DS-1 data rate of 1.544 Mbps, higher-level multiplexing is achieved by interleaving bits from DS-1 inputs. For example, the DS-2 transmission system combines four DS-1 inputs into a 6.312-Mbps stream. Data from the four sources are interleaved 12 bits at a time. Note that $1.544 \times 4 = 6.176$ Mbps. The remaining capacity is used for framing and control bits.

Sonet/SDH

SONET (Synchronous Optical Network) is an optical transmission interface originally proposed by BellCore and standardized by ANSI. A compatible version, referred to as Synchronous Digital Hierarchy (SDH), has been published by ITU-T in Recommendation G.707.[2] SONET is intended to provide a specification for taking advantage of the high-speed digital transmission capability of optical fiber.

SIGNAL HIERARCHY The SONET specification defines a hierarchy of standardized digital data rates (Table 8.4). The lowest level, referred to as STS-1 (Synchronous Transport Signal level 1) or OC-1 (Optical Carrier level 1),[3] is 51.84 Mbps. This rate can be used to carry a single DS-3 signal or a group of lower-rate signals, such as DS1, DS1C, DS2, plus ITU-T rates (e.g., 2.048 Mbps).

Multiple STS-1 signals can be combined to form an STS-N signal. The signal is created by interleaving bytes from N STS-1 signals that are mutually synchronized.

For the ITU-T Synchronous Digital Hierarchy, the lowest rate is 155.52 Mbps, which is designated STM-1. This corresponds to SONET STS-3.

FRAME FORMAT The basic SONET building block is the STS-1 frame, which consists of 810 octets and is transmitted once every 125 μs, for an overall data rate of 51.84 Mbps (Figure 8.10a). The frame can logically be viewed as a matrix of 9 rows of 90 octets each, with transmission being one row at a time, from left to right and top to bottom.

The first three columns (3 octets $\times$ 9 rows $= 27$ octets) of the frame are devoted to overhead octets. Nine octets are devoted to section-related overhead and 18 octets are devoted to line overhead. Figure 8.11a shows the arrangement of overhead octets, and Table 8.5 defines the various fields.

Table 8.4 SONET/SDH Signal Hierarchy

SONET Designation	ITU-T Designation	Data Rate	Payload Rate (Mbps)
STS-1/OC-1		51.84 Mbps	50.112 Mbps
STS-3/OC-3	STM-1	155.52 Mbps	150.336 Mbps
STS-12/OC-12	STM-4	622.08 Mbps	601.344 Mbps
STS-48/OC-48	STM-16	2.48832 Gbps	2.405376 Gbps
STS-192/OC-192	STM-64	9.95328 Gbps	9.621504 Gbps
STS-768	STM-256	39.81312 Gbps	38.486016 Gbps
STS-3072		159.25248 Gbps	153.944064 Gbps

---

[2]In what follows, we will use the term *SONET* to refer to both specifications. Where differences exist, these will be addressed.

[3]An OC-N rate is the optical equivalent of an STS-N electrical signal. End-user devices transmit and receive electrical signals; these must be converted to and from optical signals for transmission over optical fiber.

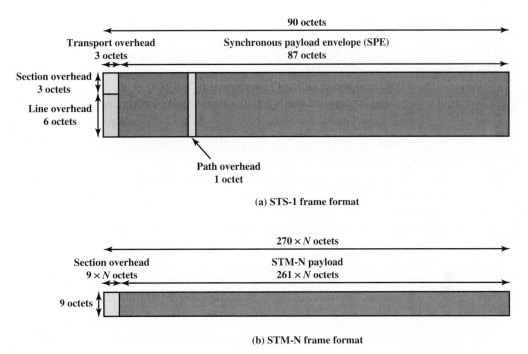

Figure 8.10   SONET/SDH Frame Formats

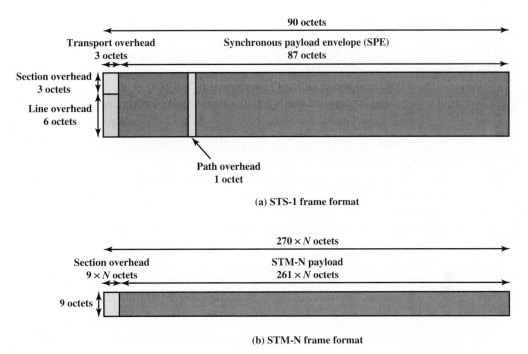

Figure 8.11   SONET STS-1 Overhead Octets

Table 8.5 STS-1 Overhead Bits

Section Overhead	
A1, A2:	Framing bytes = F6,28 hex; used to indicate the beginning of the frame.
J0/Z0:	Allows two connected sections to verify the connections between them by transmitting a sixteen-byte message. This message is transmitted in sixteen consecutive frames with first byte (J0) carried in first frame, second byte in second frame and so on (Z0).
B1:	Bit-interleaved parity byte providing even parity over previous STS-N frame after scrambling; the ith bit of this octet contains the even parity value calculated from the ith bit position of all octets in the previous frame.
E1:	Section level 64-kbps PCM orderwire; optional 64-kbps voice channel to be used between section terminating equipment, hubs, and remote terminals.
F1:	64-kbps channel set aside for user purposes.
D1-D3:	192-kbps data communications channel for alarms, maintenance, control, and administration between sections.
Line Overhead	
H1-H3:	Pointer bytes used in frame alignment and frequency adjustment of payload data.
B2:	Bit-interleaved parity for line level error monitoring.
K1, K2:	Two bytes allocated for signaling between line level automatic protection switching equipment; uses a bit-oriented protocol that provides for error protection and management of the SONET optical link.
D4-D12:	576-kbps data communications channel for alarms, maintenance, control, monitoring, and administration at the line level.
S1/Z1:	In the first STS-1 of an STS-N signal, used for transporting synchronization message (S1). Undefined in the second through Nth STS-1 (Z1)
M0/M1:	Remote error indication in first STS-1 (M0) and third frames
E2:	64-kbps PCM voice channel for line level orderwire.
Path Overhead	
J1:	64-kbps channel used to send repetitively a 64-octet fixed-length string so a receiving terminal can continuously verify the integrity of a path; the contents of the message are user programmable.
B3:	Bit-interleaved parity at the path level, calculated over all bits of the previous SPE.
C2:	STS path signal label to designate equipped versus unequipped STS signals. *Unequipped* means the line connection is complete but there is no path data to send. For equipped signals, the label can indicate the specific STS payload mapping that might be needed in receiving terminals to interpret the payloads.
G1:	Status byte sent from path terminating equipment back to path originating equipment to convey status of terminating equipment and path error performance.
F2:	64-kbps channel for path user.
H4:	Multiframe indicator for payloads needing frames that are longer than a single STS frame; multiframe indicators are used when packing lower rate channels (virtual tributaries) into the SPE.
Z3-Z5:	Reserved for future use.

The remainder of the frame is payload. The payload includes a column of path overhead, which is not necessarily in the first available column position; the line overhead contains a pointer that indicates where the path overhead starts. Figure 8.11b shows the arrangement of path overhead octets, and Table 8.5 defines these.

Figure 8.10b shows the general format for higher-rate frames, using the ITU-T designation.

8.3   STATISTICAL TIME DIVISION MULTIPLEXING

Characteristics

In a synchronous time division multiplexer, it is often the case that many of the time slots in a frame are wasted. A typical application of a synchronous TDM involves linking a number of terminals to a shared computer port. Even if all terminals are actively in use, most of the time there is no data transfer at any particular terminal.

An alternative to synchronous TDM is statistical TDM. The statistical multiplexer exploits this common property of data transmission by dynamically allocating time slots on demand. As with a synchronous TDM, the statistical multiplexer has a number of I/O lines on one side and a higher speed multiplexed line on the other. Each I/O line has a buffer associated with it. In the case of the statistical multiplexer, there are n I/O lines, but only k, where $k < n$, time slots available on the TDM frame. For input, the function of the multiplexer is to scan the input buffers, collecting data until a frame is filled, and then send the frame. On output, the multiplexer receives a frame and distributes the slots of data to the appropriate output buffers.

Because statistical TDM takes advantage of the fact that the attached devices are not all transmitting all of the time, the data rate on the multiplexed line is less than the sum of the data rates of the attached devices. Thus, a statistical multiplexer can use a lower data rate to support as many devices as a synchronous multiplexer. Alternatively, if a statistical multiplexer and a synchronous multiplexer both use a link of the same data rate, the statistical multiplexer can support more devices.

Figure 8.12 contrasts statistical and synchronous TDM. The figure depicts four data sources and shows the data produced in four time epochs (t_0, t_1, t_2, t_3). In the case of the synchronous multiplexer, the multiplexer has an effective output rate of four times the data rate of any of the input devices. During each epoch, data are collected from all four sources and sent out. For example, in the first epoch, sources C and D produce no data. Thus, two of the four time slots transmitted by the multiplexer are empty.

In contrast, the statistical multiplexer does not send empty slots if there are data to send. Thus, during the first epoch, only slots for A and B are sent. However, the positional significance of the slots is lost in this scheme. It is not known ahead of time which source's data will be in any particular slot. Because data arrive from and are distributed to I/O lines unpredictably, address information is required to assure proper delivery. Thus, there is more overhead per slot for statistical TDM because each slot carries an address as well as data.

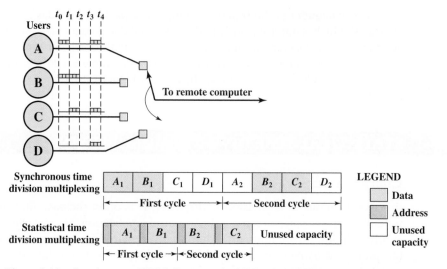

Figure 8.12 Synchronous TDM Compared with Statistical TDM

The frame structure used by a statistical multiplexer has an impact on performance. Clearly, it is desirable to minimize overhead bits to improve throughput. Typically, a statistical TDM system will use a synchronous protocol such as HDLC. Within the HDLC frame, the data frame must contain control bits for the multiplexing operation. Figure 8.13 shows two possible formats. In the first case, only one source of data is included per frame. That source is identified by an address. The length of the data field is variable, and its end is marked by the end of the overall frame. This scheme can work well under light load but is quite inefficient under heavy load.

A way to improve efficiency is to allow multiple data sources to be packaged in a single frame. Now, however, some means is needed to specify the length of data for each source. Thus, the statistical TDM subframe consists of a sequence of data fields, each labeled with an address and a length. Several techniques can be used to make this approach even more efficient. The address field can be reduced by using

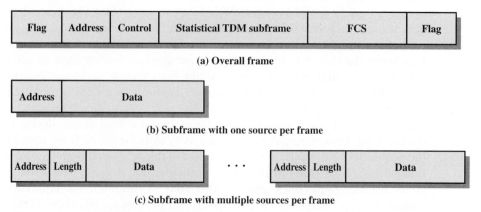

Figure 8.13 Statistical TDM Frame Formats

relative addressing. That is, each address specifies the number of the current source relative to the previous source, modulo the total number of sources. So, for example, instead of an 8-bit address field, a 4-bit field might suffice.

Another refinement is to use a 2-bit label with the length field. A value of 00, 01, or 10 corresponds to a data field of 1, 2, or 3 bytes; no length field is necessary. A value of 11 indicates that a length field is included.

Yet another approach is to multiplex one character from each data source that has a character to send in a single data frame. In this case the frame begins with a bit map that has a bit length equal to the number of sources. For each source that transmits a character during a given frame, the corresponding bit is set to one.

Performance

We have said that the data rate of the output of a statistical multiplexer is less than the sum of the data rates of the inputs. This is allowable because it is anticipated that the average amount of input is less than the capacity of the multiplexed line. The difficulty with this approach is that, while the average aggregate input may be less than the multiplexed line capacity, there may be peak periods when the input exceeds capacity. The solution to this problem is to include a buffer in the multiplexer to hold temporary excess input.

> **EXAMPLE 8.5** Table 8.6 gives an example of the behavior of such systems. We assume 10 sources, each capable of 1000 bps, and we assume that the average input per source is 50% of its maximum. Thus, on average, the input load is 5000 bps. Two cases are shown: multiplexers of output capacity 5000 bps and 7000 bps. The entries in the table show the number of bits input from the 10 devices each millisecond and the output from the multiplexer. When the input exceeds the output, backlog develops that must be buffered.

There is a trade-off between the size of the buffer used and the data rate of the line. We would like to use the smallest possible buffer and the smallest possible data rate, but a reduction in one requires an increase in the other. Note that we are not so much concerned with the cost of the buffer—memory is cheap—as we are with the fact that the more buffering there is, the longer the delay. Thus, the trade-off is really one between system response time and the speed of the multiplexed line. In this section, we present some approximate measures that examine this trade-off. These are sufficient for most purposes.

Let us define the following parameters for a statistical time division multiplexer:

I = number of input sources

R = data rate of each source, bps

M = effective capacity of multiplexed line, bps

α = mean fraction of time each source is transmitting, $0 < \alpha < 1$

$K = \dfrac{M}{IR}$ = ratio of multiplexed line capacity to total maximum input

Table 8.6 Example of Statistical Multiplexer Performance

Input[a]	Capacity = 5000 bps		Capacity = 7000 bps	
	Output	Backlog	Output	Backlog
6	5	1	6	0
9	5	5	7	2
3	5	3	5	0
7	5	5	7	0
2	5	2	2	0
2	4	0	2	0
2	2	0	2	0
3	3	0	3	0
4	4	0	4	0
6	5	1	6	0
1	2	0	1	0
10	5	5	7	3
7	5	7	7	3
5	5	7	7	1
8	5	10	7	2
3	5	8	5	0
6	5	9	6	0
2	5	6	2	0
9	5	10	7	2
5	5	10	7	0

[a]Input = 10 sources, 1000 bps/source; average input rate = 50% of maximum.

We have defined M taking into account the overhead bits introduced by the multiplexer. That is, M represents the maximum rate at which data bits can be transmitted.

The parameter K is a measure of the compression achieved by the multiplexer. For example, for a given data rate M, if $K = 0.25$, there are four times as many devices being handled as by a synchronous time division multiplexer using the same link capacity. The value of K can be bounded:

$$\alpha < K < 1$$

A value of $K = 1$ corresponds to a synchronous time division multiplexer, because the system has the capacity to service all input devices at the same time. If $K < \alpha$, the input will exceed the multiplexer's capacity.

Some results can be obtained by viewing the multiplexer as a single-server queue. A queuing situation arises when a "customer" arrives at a service facility and, finding it busy, is forced to wait. The delay incurred by a customer is the time spent waiting in the queue plus the time for the service. The delay depends on the pattern of arriving traffic and the characteristics of the server. Table 8.7 summarizes results

Table 8.7   Single-Server Queues with Constant Service Times and Poisson (Random) Arrivals

Parameters
λ = mean number of arrivals per second
T_s = service time for each arrival
ρ = utilization; fraction of time server is busy
N = mean number of items in system (waiting and being served)
T_r = residence time; mean time an item spends in system (waiting and being served)
σ_r = standard deviation of T_r

Formulas
$\rho = \lambda T_s$
$N = \dfrac{\rho^2}{2(1 - \rho)} + \rho$
$T_r = \dfrac{T_s(2 - \rho)}{2(1 - \rho)}$
$\sigma_r = \dfrac{1}{1 - \rho}\sqrt{\rho - \dfrac{3\rho^2}{2} + \dfrac{5\rho^3}{6} - \dfrac{\rho^4}{12}}$

for the case of random (Poisson) arrivals and constant service time. See Appendix H for details. This model is easily related to the statistical multiplexer:

$$\lambda = \alpha IR$$

$$T_s = \frac{1}{M}$$

The average arrival rate λ, in bps, is the total potential input (IR) times the fraction of time α that each source is transmitting. The service time T_s, in seconds, is the time it takes to transmit 1one bit, which is $1/M$. Note that

$$\rho = \lambda T_s = \frac{\alpha IR}{M} = \frac{\alpha}{K} = \frac{\lambda}{M}$$

The parameter ρ is the utilization or fraction of total link capacity being used. For example, if the capacity M is 50 kbps and $\rho = 0.5$, the load on the system is 25 kbps. The parameter N in Table 8.7 is a measure of the amount of buffer space being used in the multiplexer. Finally, T_r is a measure of the average delay encountered by an input source.

Figure 8.14 gives some insight into the nature of the trade-off between system response time and the speed of the multiplexed line. It assumes that data are being transmitted in 1000-bit frames. Figure 8.14a shows the average number of frames that must be buffered as a function of the average utilization of the multiplexed line. The utilization is expressed as a percentage of the total line capacity. Thus, if the average input load is 5000 bps, the utilization is 100% for a line capacity of 5000 bps and about 71% for a line capacity of 7000 bps. Figure 8.14b shows the average delay experienced by a frame as a function of utilization and data rate. Note that as the

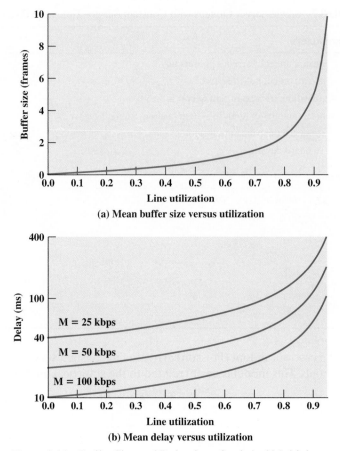

Figure 8.14 Buffer Size and Delay for a Statistical Multiplexer

utilization rises, so do the buffer requirements and the delay. A utilization above 80% is clearly undesirable.

Note that the average buffer size being used depends only on ρ, and not directly on M. For example, consider the following two cases:

Case I	Case II
$I = 10$	$I = 100$
$R = 100$ bps	$R = 100$ bps
$\alpha = 0.4$	$\alpha = 0.4$
$M = 500$ bps	$M = 5000$ bps

In both cases, the value of ρ is 0.8 and the mean buffer size is $N = 2.4$. Thus, proportionately, a smaller amount of buffer space per source is needed for multiplexers that handle a larger number of sources. Figure 8.14b also shows that the average delay will be smaller as the link capacity increases, for constant utilization.

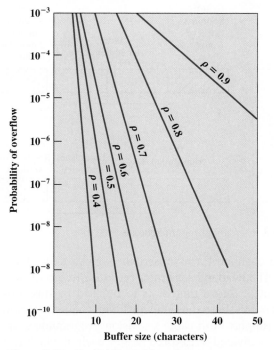

Figure 8.15   Probability of Overflow as a Function of Buffer Size

So far, we have been considering average queue length, and hence the average amount of buffer capacity needed. Of course, there will be some fixed upper bound on the buffer size available. The variance of the queue size grows with utilization. Thus, at a higher level of utilization, a larger buffer is needed to hold the backlog. Even so, there is always a finite probability that the buffer will overflow. Figure 8.15 shows the strong dependence of overflow probability on utilization. This figure and Figure 8.14 suggest that utilization above about 0.8 is undesirable.

Cable Modem

A cable modem is a device that allows a user to access the Internet and other online services through a cable TV network. To support data transfer to and from a cable modem, a cable TV provider dedicates two 6-MHz channels, one for transmission in each direction. Each channel is shared by a number of subscribers, and so some scheme is needed for allocating capacity on each channel for transmission. Typically, a form of statistical TDM is used, as illustrated in Figure 8.16. In the downstream direction, cable **headend** to subscriber, a cable scheduler delivers data in the form of small packets. Because the channel is shared by a number of subscribers, if more than one subscriber is active, each subscriber gets only a fraction of the downstream capacity. An individual cable modem subscriber may experience access speeds from 500 kbps to 1.5 Mbps or more, depending on the network architecture and traffic load. The downstream direction is also used to grant time slots to subscribers. When a subscriber has data to transmit, it must first request time slots on the shared

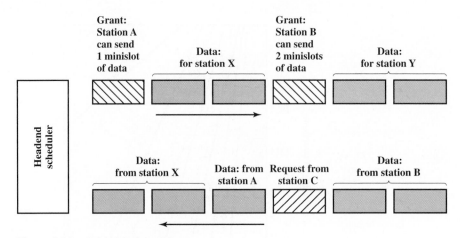

Figure 8.16 Cable Modem Scheme

upstream channel. Each subscriber is given dedicated time slots for this request purpose. The headend scheduler responds to a request packet by sending back an assignment of future time slots to be used by this subscriber. Thus, a number of subscribers can share the same upstream channel without conflict.

To support both cable television programming and data channels, the cable spectrum is divided in to three ranges, each of which is further divided into 6-MHz channels. In North America, the spectrum division is as follows:

- User-to-network data (upstream): 5–40 MHz
- Television delivery (downstream): 50–550 MHz
- Network to user data (downstream): 550–750 MHz

Figure 8.17 shows a typical cable modem configuration at a residential or office location. At the interface to the external cable, a one-to-two splitter enables the subscriber to continue to receive cable television service through numerous FDM 6-MHz channels, while simultaneously supporting data channels to one or more computers in a local area network. The inbound channel first goes through a radio frequency (RF) tuner that selects and demodulates the data channel down to a spectrum of 0 to 6 MHz. This channel provides a data stream encoded using 64-QAM (quadrature amplitude modulation) or 256-QAM. The QAM demodulator extracts the encoded data stream and converts it to a digital signal that it passes to the media access control (MAC) module. In the outbound direction, a data stream is modulated using either QPSK (quadrature phase shift keying) or 16-QAM.

8.4 ASYMMETRIC DIGITAL SUBSCRIBER LINE

In the implementation and deployment of a high-speed wide area public digital network, the most challenging part is the link between subscriber and network: the digital subscriber line. With billions of potential endpoints worldwide, the prospect of installing new cable for each new customer is daunting. Instead, network designers

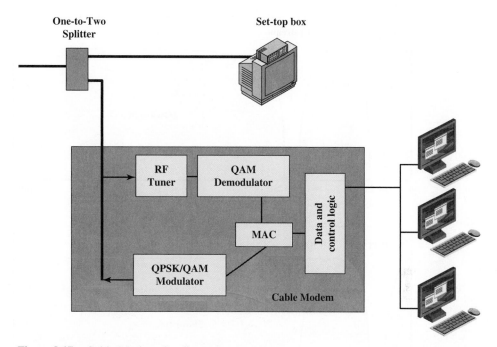

Figure 8.17 Cable Modem Configuration

have sought ways of exploiting the installed base of twisted-pair wire that links virtually all residential and business customers to telephone networks. These links were installed to carry voice-grade signals in a bandwidth from zero to 4 kHz. However, the wires are capable of transmitting signals over a far broader spectrum—1 MHz or more.

ADSL is the most widely publicized of a family of new modem technologies designed to provide high-speed digital data transmission over ordinary telephone wire. ADSL is now being offered by a number of carriers and is defined in an ANSI standard. In this following section, we first look at the overall design of ADSL and then examine the key underlying technology, known as DMT.

ADSL Design

The term *asymmetric* refers to the fact that ADSL provides more capacity downstream (from the carrier's central office to the customer's site) than upstream (from customer to carrier). ADSL was originally targeted at the expected need for video on demand and related services. This application has not materialized. However, since the introduction of ADSL technology, the demand for high-speed access to the Internet has grown. Typically, the user requires far higher capacity for downstream than for upstream transmission. Most user transmissions are in the form of keyboard strokes or transmission of short e-mail messages, whereas incoming traffic, especially Web traffic, can involve large amounts of data and include images or even video. Thus, ADSL provides a perfect fit for the Internet requirement.

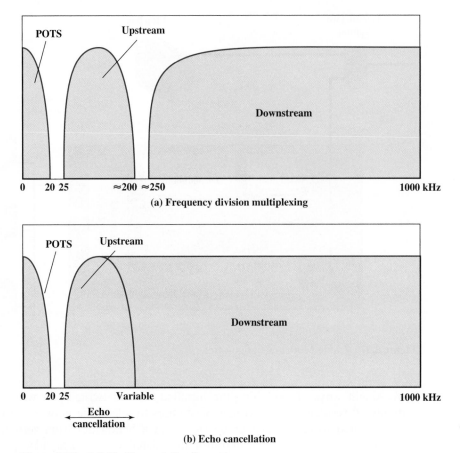

Figure 8.18 ADSL Channel Configuration

ADSL uses frequency division multiplexing in a novel way to exploit the 1-MHz capacity of twisted pair. There are three elements of the ADSL strategy (Figure 8.18):

- Reserve lowest 25 kHz for voice, known as POTS (plain old telephone service). The voice is carried only in the 0 to 4 kHz band; the additional bandwidth is to prevent crosstalk between the voice and data channels.
- Use either echo cancellation[4] or FDM to allocate two bands, a smaller upstream band and a larger downstream band.
- Use FDM within the upstream and downstream bands. In this case, a single bit stream is split into multiple parallel bit streams and each portion is carried in a separate frequency band.

When echo cancellation is used, the entire frequency band for the upstream channel overlaps the lower portion of the downstream channel. This has two advantages compared to the use of distinct frequency bands for upstream and downstream.

---

[4]Echo cancellation is a signal-processing technique that allows transmission of digital signals in both directions on a single transmission line simultaneously. In essence, a transmitter must subtract the echo of its own transmission from the incoming signal to recover the signal sent by the other side.

- The higher the frequency, the greater the attenuation. With the use of echo cancellation, more of the downstream bandwidth is in the "good" part of the spectrum.

- The echo cancellation design is more flexible for changing upstream capacity. The upstream channel can be extended upward without running into the downstream; instead, the area of overlap is extended.

The disadvantage of the use of echo cancellation is the need for echo cancellation logic on both ends of the line.

The ADSL scheme provides a range of up to 5.5 km, depending on the diameter of the cable and its quality. This is sufficient to cover about 95% of all U.S. subscriber lines and should provide comparable coverage in other nations.

Discrete Multitone

Discrete multitone (DMT) uses multiple carrier signals at different frequencies, sending some of the bits on each channel. The available transmission band (upstream or downstream) is divided into a number of 4-kHz subchannels. On initialization, the DMT modem sends out test signals on each subchannel to determine the signal-to-noise ratio. The modem then assigns more bits to channels with better signal transmission qualities and less bits to channels with poorer signal transmission qualities. Figure 8.19 illustrates this process. Each subchannel can carry a data rate of from 0 to 60 kbps. The figure shows a typical situation in which there is increasing attenuation and hence decreasing signal-to-noise ratio at higher frequencies. As a result, the higher-frequency subchannels carry less of the load.

Figure 8.20 provides a general block diagram for DMT transmission. After initialization, the bit stream to be transmitted is divided into a number of sub-streams, one for each subchannel that will carry data. The sum of the data rates of the substreams is equal to the total data rate. Each substream is then converted to an analog signal using quadrature amplitude modulation, described in Chapter 5. This scheme works easily because of QAM's ability to assign different numbers of bits per transmitted signal. Each QAM signal occupies a distinct frequency band, so these signals can be combined by simple addition to produce the composite signal for transmission.

Present ADSL/DMT designs employ 256 downstream subchannels. In theory, with each 4-kHz subchannel carrying 60 kbps, it would be possible to transmit at a rate of 15.36 Mbps. In practice, transmission impairments prevent attainment of this data rate. Current implementations operate at from 1.5 to 9 Mbps, depending on line distance and quality.

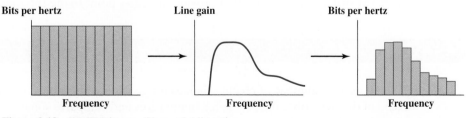

Figure 8.19   DMT Bits per Channel Allocation

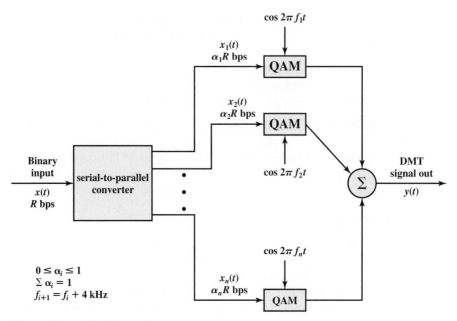

Figure 8.20 DMT Transmitter

Broadband Access Configuration

Figure 8.21 shows a typical configuration for broadband service using DSL. The DSL link is between the provider central office and the residential or business premises. On the customer side, a splitter allows simultaneous telephone and data service. The data service makes use of a DSL modem, sometimes referred to as a G.DMT modem, because the modem conforms to the ITU-T G.992.1 recommendation for DMT over DSL. The DSL data signal can be further divided into a video stream and a data stream. The latter connects the modem to either a single local computer or to a wireless modem/router, which enables the customer to support a wireless local area network.

On the provider side, a splitter is also used to separate the telephone service from the Internet service. The voice traffic is connected to the public switched telephone network (PSTN), thus providing the same service as an ordinary telephone line to the subscriber. The data traffic connects to a DSL access multiplexer (DSLAM), which multiplexes multiple customer DSL connections on to a single high-speed asynchronous transfer mode line. The ATM line connects via one or more ATM switches to a router that provides an entry point to the Internet.

8.5 xDSL

ADSL is one of a number of recent schemes for providing high-speed digital transmission of the subscriber line. Table 8.8 summarizes and compares some of the most important of these new schemes, which collectively are referred to as xDSL.

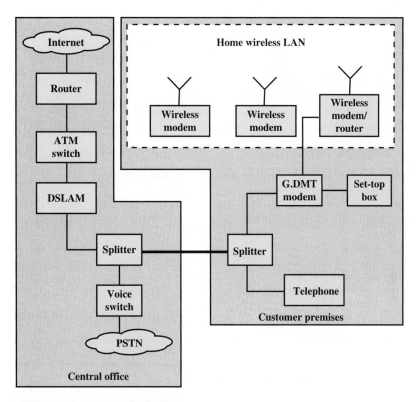

ATM = asynchronous transfer mode
DSLAM = digital subscriber line access multiplexer
PSTN = public switched telephone network
G.DMT = G.992.1 discrete multitone

Figure 8.21 DSL Broadband Access

Table 8.8 Comparison of xDSL Alternatives

	ADSL	HDSL	SDSL	VDSL
Data Rate	1.5–9 Mbps downstream	1.544 or 2.048 Mbps	1.544 or 2.048 Mbps	13–52 Mbps downstream
	16–640 kbps upstream			1.5–2.3 Mbps upstream
Mode	Asymmetric	Symmetric	Symmetric	Asymmetric
Copper Pairs	1	2	1	1
Range (24-Gauge UTP)	3.7–5.5 km	3.7 km	3.0 km	1.4 km
Signaling	Analog	Digital	Digital	Analog
Line Code	CAP/DMT	2B1Q	2B1Q	DMT
Frequency	1–5 MHz	196 kHz	196 kHz	≥10 MHz
Bits/Cycle	Varies	4	4	Varies

UTP = unshielded twisted pair

High Data Rate Digital Subscriber Line

HDSL was developed in the late 1980s by BellCore to provide a more cost-effective means of delivering a T1 data rate (1.544 Mbps). The standard T1 line uses alternate mark inversion (AMI) coding, which occupies a bandwidth of about 1.5 MHz. Because such high frequencies are involved, the attenuation characteristics limit the use of T1 to a distance of about 1 km between repeaters. Thus, for many subscriber lines one or more repeaters are required, which adds to the installation and maintenance expense.

HDSL uses the 2B1Q coding scheme to provide a data rate of up to 2 Mbps over two twisted-pair lines within a bandwidth that extends only up to about 196 kHz. This enables a range of about 3.7 km to be achieved.

Single-Line Digital Subscriber Line

Although HDSL is attractive for replacing existing T1 lines, it is not suitable for residential subscribers because it requires two twisted pair, whereas the typical residential subscriber has a single twisted pair. SDSL was developed to provide the same type of service as HDSL but over a single twisted-pair line. As with HDSL, 2B1Q coding is used. Echo cancellation is used to achieve full-duplex transmission over a single pair.

Very High Data Rate Digital Subscriber Line

One of the newest xDSL schemes is VDSL. As of this writing, many of the details of this signaling specification remain to be worked out. The objective is to provide a scheme similar to ADSL at a much higher data rate by sacrificing distance. The likely signaling technique is DMT/QAM.

VDSL does not use echo cancellation but provides separate bands for different services, with the following tentative allocation:

- POTS: 0–4 kHz
- ISDN: 4–80 kHz
- Upstream: 300–700 kHz
- Downstream: ≥1 MHz

8.6 RECOMMENDED READING AND WEB SITES

A discussion of FDM and TDM carrier systems can be found in [FREE98b]. SONET is treated in greater depth in [STAL99] and in [TEKT01]. Useful articles on SONET are [BALL89] and [BOEH90]. A good overview of WDM is [MUKH00].

Two good articles on cable modems are [FELL01] and [CICI01].

[MAXW96] provides a useful a discussion of ADSL. Recommended treatments of xDSL are [HAWL97] and [HUMP97].

BALL89 Ballart, R., and Ching, Y. "SONET: Now It's the Standard Optical Network." *IEEE Communications Magazine*, March 1989.

BOEH90 Boehm, R. "Progress in Standardization of SONET." *IEEE LCS*, May 1990.

CICI01 Ciciora, W. "The Cable Modem Traffic Jam." *IEEE Spectrum*, June 2001.

FELL01 Fellows, D., and Jones, D. "DOCSIS Cable Modem Technology." *IEEE Communications Magazine*, March 2001.

FREE98b Freeman, R. *Telecommunications Transmission Handbook.* New York: Wiley, 1998.

HAWL97 Hawley, G. "Systems Considerations for the Use of xDSL Technology for Data Access." *IEEE Communications Magazine*, March 1997.

HUMP97 Humphrey, M., and Freeman, J. "How xDSL Supports Broadband Services to the Home." *IEEE Network*, January/March 1997.

MAXW96 Maxwell, K. "Asymmetric Digital Subscriber Line: Interim Technology for the Next Forty Years." *IEEE Communications Magazine*, October 1996.

MUKH00 Mukherjee, B. "WDM Optical Communication Networks: Progress and Challenges." *IEEE Journal on Selected Areas in Communications*, October 2000.

STAL99 Stallings, W. *ISDN and Broadband ISDN, with Frame Relay and ATM.* Upper Saddle River, NJ: Prentice Hall, 1999.

TEKT01 Tektronix. *SONET Telecommunications Standard Primer.* Tektronix White Paper, 2001, www.tektronix.com/optical.

Recommended Web sites:

- **Broadband Forum:** Includes a FAQ and technical information about ADSL and other xDSL technologies
- **SONET Home Page:** Useful links, tutorials, white papers, FAQs

8.7 KEY TERMS, REVIEW QUESTIONS, AND PROBLEMS

Key Terms

ADSL	downstream	SONET
baseband	echo cancellation	statistical TDM
cable modem	frame	subcarrier
channel	frequency division	synchronous TDM
demultiplexer	multiplexing (FDM)	time division multiplexing
dense wavelength division	headend	(TDM)
multiplexing (DWDM)	multiplexer	upstream
dense WDM	multiplexing	wavelength division
digital carrier system	pulse stuffing	multiplexing (WDM)
discrete multitone	SDH	

Review Questions

8.1 Why is multiplexing so cost-effective?

8.2 How is interference avoided by using frequency division multiplexing?

8.3 What is echo cancellation?

8.4 Define *upstream* and *downstream* with respect to subscriber lines.

8.5 Explain how synchronous time division multiplexing (TDM) works.

8.6 Why is a statistical time division multiplexer more efficient than a synchronous time division multiplexer?

8.7 Using Table 8.3 as a guide, indicate the major difference between North American and international TDM carrier standards.

8.8 Using Figure 8.14 as a guide, indicate the relationship between buffer size and line utilization.

Problems

8.1 The information in four analog signals is to be multiplexed and transmitted over a telephone channel that has a 400- to 3100-Hz bandpass. Each of the analog baseband signals is bandlimited to 500 Hz. Design a communication system (block diagram) that will allow the transmission of these four sources over the telephone channel using

a. Frequency division multiplexing with SSB (single sideband) subcarriers
b. Time division multiplexing using PCM; assume 4-bit samples

Show the block diagrams of the complete system, including the transmission, channel, and reception portions. Include the bandwidths of the signals at the various points in the systems.

8.2 To paraphrase Lincoln: ". . . all of the channel some of the time, some of the channel all of the time. . . ." Refer to Figure 8.2 and relate the preceding to the figure.

8.3 Consider a transmission system using frequency division multiplexing. What cost factors are involved in adding one more pair of stations to the system?

8.4 In synchronous TDM, it is possible to interleave bits, one bit from each channel participating in a cycle. If the channel is using a self-clocking code to assist synchronization, might this bit interleaving introduce problems because there is not a continuous stream of bits from one source?

8.5 Why is it that the start and stop bits can be eliminated when character interleaving is used in synchronous TDM?

8.6 Explain in terms of data link control and physical layer concepts how error and flow control are accomplished in synchronous time division multiplexing.

8.7 One of the 193 bits in the DS-1 transmission format is used for frame synchronization. Explain its use.

8.8 In the DS-1 format, what is the control signal data rate for each voice channel?

8.9 Twenty-four voice signals are to be multiplexed and transmitted over twisted pair. What is the bandwidth required for FDM? Assuming a bandwidth efficiency (ratio of data rate to transmission bandwidth, as explained in Chapter 5) of 1 bps/Hz, what is the bandwidth required for TDM using PCM?

8.10 Draw a block diagram similar to Figure 8.8 for a TDM PCM system that will accommodate four 300-bps, synchronous, digital inputs and one analog input with a bandwidth of 500 Hz. Assume that the analog samples will be encoded into 4-bit PCM words.

8.11 A character-interleaved time division multiplexer is used to combine the data streams of a number of 110-bps asynchronous terminals for data transmission over a 2400-bps digital line. Each terminal sends asynchronous characters consisting of 7 data bits, 1 parity bit, 1 start bit, and 2 stop bits. Assume that one synchronization character is sent every 19 data characters and, in addition, at least 3% of the line capacity is reserved for pulse stuffing to accommodate speed variations from the various terminals.

    a. Determine the number of bits per character.
    b. Determine the number of terminals that can be accommodated by the multiplexer.
    c. Sketch a possible framing pattern for the multiplexer.

8.12 Find the number of the following devices that could be accommodated by a T1-type TDM line if 1% of the T1 line capacity is reserved for synchronization purposes.

    a. 110-bps teleprinter terminals
    b. 300-bps computer terminals
    c. 1200-bps computer terminals
    d. 9600-bps computer output ports
    e. 64-kbps PCM voice-frequency lines

How would these numbers change if each of the sources were transmitting an average of 10% of the time and a statistical multiplexer was used?

8.13 Ten 9600-bps lines are to be multiplexed using TDM. Ignoring overhead bits in the TDM frame, what is the total capacity required for synchronous TDM? Assuming that we wish to limit average TDM link utilization to 0.8, and assuming that each TDM link is busy 50% of the time, what is the capacity required for statistical TDM?

8.14 A synchronous nonstatistical TDM is to be used to combine four 4.8-kbps and one 9.6-kbps signals for transmission over a single leased line. For framing, a block of 7 bits (pattern 1011101) is inserted for each 48 data bits. The reframing algorithm (at the receiving demultiplex) is as follows:

    1. Arbitrarily select a bit position.
    2. Consider the block of 7 contiguous bits starting with that position.
    3. Observe that block of 7 bits each frame for 12 consecutive frames.
    4. If 10 of the 12 blocks match the framing pattern the system is "in-frame"; if not advance one bit position and return to step 2.

        a. Draw the multiplexed bit stream (note that the 9.6 kbps input may be treated as two 4.8-kbps inputs).
        b. What is the percentage overhead in the multiplexed bit stream?
        c. What is the multiplexed output bit rate?
        d. What is the minimum reframe time? What is the maximum reframe time? What is the average reframe time?

8.15 A company has two locations: a headquarters and a factory about 25 km away. The factory has four 300-bps terminals that communicate with the central computer facilities over leased voice-grade lines. The company is considering installing TDM equipment so that only one line will be needed. What cost factors should be considered in the decision?

8.16 In synchronous TDM, the I/O lines serviced by the two multiplexers may be either synchronous or asynchronous although the channel between the two multiplexers must be synchronous. Is there any inconsistency in this? Why or why not?

8.17 Assume that you are to design a TDM carrier, say DS-489, to support 30 voice channels using 6-bit samples and a structure similar to DS-1. Determine the required bit rate.

8.18 For a statistical time division multiplexer, define the following parameters:

$$F = \text{frame length, bits}$$
$$OH = \text{overhead in a frame, bits}$$
$$L = \text{load of data in the frame, bps}$$
$$C = \text{capacity of link, bps}$$

    a. Express F as a function of the other parameters. Explain why F can be viewed as a variable rather than a constant.
    b. Plot F versus L for $C = 9.6$ kbps and values of $OH = 40, 80, 120$. Comment on the results and compare to Figure 8.14.
    c. Plot F versus L for $OH = 40$ and values of $C = 9.6$ kbps and 8.2 kbps. Comment on the results and compare to Figure 8.14.

8.19 In statistical TDM, there may be a length field. What alternative could there be to the inclusion of a length field? What problem might this solution cause and how could it be solved?

SPREAD SPECTRUM

All creative people want to do the unexpected.

> — *Ecstasy and Me: My Life as a Woman,* Hedy Lamarr

KEY POINTS

◆ Spread spectrum is an important form of encoding for wireless communications. The use of spread spectrum makes jamming and interception more difficult and provides improved reception.

◆ The basic idea of spread spectrum is to modulate the signal so as to increase significantly the bandwidth (spread the spectrum) of the signal to be transmitted.

◆ **Frequency-hopping spread spectrum** is a form of spread spectrum in which the signal is broadcast over a seemingly random series of radio frequencies, hopping from frequency to frequency at fixed intervals.

◆ **Direct sequence spread spectrum** is a form of spread spectrum in which each bit in the original signal is represented by multiple bits in the transmitted signal, using a spreading code.

◆ **Code division multiple access** exploits the nature of spread spectrum transmission to enable multiple users to independently use the same bandwidth with very little interference.

Spread spectrum is an important form of encoding for wireless communications. This technique does not fit neatly into the categories defined in Chapter 5, as it can be used to transmit either analog or digital data, using an analog signal.

The spread spectrum technique was developed initially for military and intelligence requirements. The essential idea is to spread the information signal over a wider bandwidth to make jamming and interception more difficult. The first type of spread spectrum developed is known as frequency hopping.[1] A more recent type of spread spectrum is direct sequence. Both of these techniques are used in various wireless communications standards and products.

After a brief overview, we look at these two spread spectrum techniques. We then examine a multiple access technique based on spread spectrum.

---

[1]Spread spectrum (using frequency hopping) was invented, believe it or not, by Hollywood screen siren Hedy Lamarr in 1940 at the age of 26. She and a partner who later joined her effort were granted a patent in 1942 (U.S. Patent 2,292,387; August 11, 1942). Lamarr considered this her contribution to the war effort and never profited from her invention.

9.1   THE CONCEPT OF SPREAD SPECTRUM

Figure 9.1 highlights the key characteristics of any spread spectrum system. Input is fed into a channel encoder that produces an analog signal with a relatively narrow bandwidth around some center frequency. This signal is further modulated using a sequence of digits known as a spreading code or spreading sequence. Typically, but not always, the spreading code is generated by a pseudonoise, or pseudorandom number, generator. The effect of this modulation is to increase significantly the bandwidth (spread the spectrum) of the signal to be transmitted. On the receiving end, the same digit sequence is used to demodulate the spread spectrum signal. Finally, the signal is fed into a channel decoder to recover the data.

Several things can be gained from this apparent waste of spectrum:

- The signals gains immunity from various kinds of noise and multipath distortion. The earliest applications of spread spectrum were military, where it was used for its immunity to jamming.

- It can also be used for hiding and encrypting signals. Only a recipient who knows the spreading code can recover the encoded information.

- Several users can independently use the same higher bandwidth with very little interference. This property is used in cellular telephony applications, with a technique known as code division multiplexing (CDM) or code division multiple access (CDMA).

A comment about pseudorandom numbers is in order. These numbers are generated by an algorithm using some initial value called the seed. The algorithm is deterministic and therefore produces sequences of numbers that are not statistically random. However, if the algorithm is good, the resulting sequences will pass many reasonable tests of randomness. Such numbers are often referred to as pseudorandom numbers.[2] The important point is that unless you know the algorithm and the seed, it is impractical to predict the sequence. Hence, only a receiver that shares this information with a transmitter will be able to decode the signal successfully.

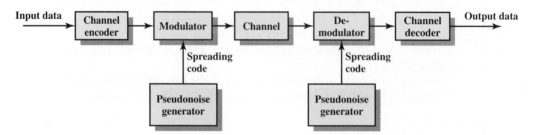

Figure 9.1   General Model of Spread Spectrum Digital Communication System

---

[2]See [STAL05] for a more detailed discussion of pseudorandom numbers.

9.2 FREQUENCY-HOPPING SPREAD SPECTRUM

With frequency-hopping spread spectrum (FHSS), the signal is broadcast over a seemingly random series of radio frequencies, hopping from frequency to frequency at fixed intervals. A receiver, hopping between frequencies in synchronization with the transmitter, picks up the message. Would-be eavesdroppers hear only unintelligible blips. Attempts to jam the signal on one frequency succeed only at knocking out a few bits of it.

Basic Approach

In FHSS, a number of channels are allocated for the frequency-hopping (FH) signal. Typically, there are 2^k carrier frequencies forming 2^k channels. The spacing between carrier frequencies and hence the width of each channel usually corresponds to the bandwidth of the input signal. The transmitter operates in one channel at a time for a fixed interval; for example, the IEEE 802.11 standard uses a 300-ms interval. During that interval, some number of bits (possibly a fraction of a bit, as discussed subsequently) is transmitted using some encoding scheme. A spreading code dictates the sequence of channels used. Both transmitter and receiver use the same code to tune into a sequence of channels in synchronization.

EXAMPLE 9.1 Figure 9.2 shows an example of a frequency-hopping signal using 8 frequencies. The numbers along the top of Figure 9.2a indicate the sequence in which the 8 frequencies are used for transmission; this is the spreading code. Figure 9.2b illustrates the frequency used as a function of time. Each frequency is used for a fixed time interval. After 8 time intervals, the sequence repeats.

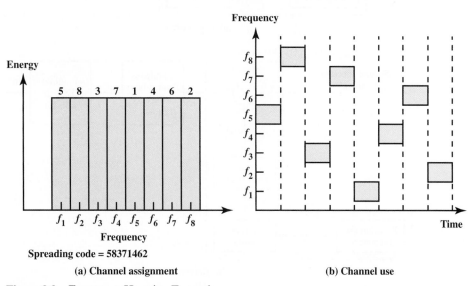

(a) Channel assignment

Spreading code = 58371462

(b) Channel use

Figure 9.2 Frequency Hopping Example

A typical block diagram for a frequency-hopping system is shown in Figure 9.3. For transmission, binary data are fed into a modulator using some digital-to-analog encoding scheme, such as frequency shift keying (FSK) or binary phase shift keying (BPSK). The resulting signal is centered on some base frequency. A pseudonoise (PN), or pseudorandom number, source serves as an index into a table of frequencies; this is the spreading code referred to previously. Each k bits of the PN source specifies one of the 2^k carrier frequencies. At each successive interval (each k PN bits), a new carrier frequency is selected. This frequency is then modulated by the signal produced from the initial modulator to produce a new signal with the same shape but now centered on the selected carrier frequency. On reception, the spread spectrum signal is demodulated using the same sequence of PN-derived frequencies and then demodulated to produce the output data.

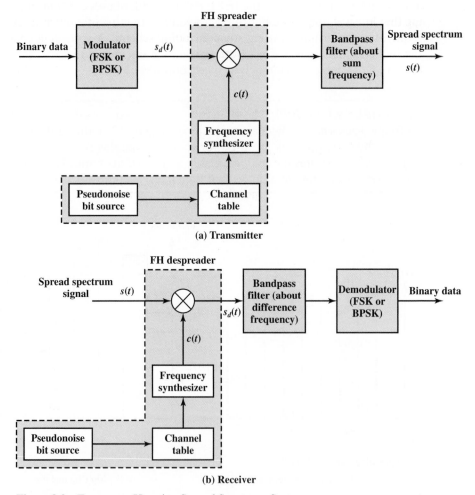

Figure 9.3 Frequency-Hopping Spread Spectrum System

Figure 9.3 indicates that the two signals are multiplied. Let us give an example of how this works, using BFSK as the data modulation scheme. We can define the FSK input to the FHSS system as [compare to Equation (5.3)]:

$$s_d(t) = A \cos(2\pi(f_0 + 0.5(b_i + 1)\Delta f)t) \qquad \text{for } iT < t < (i + 1)T \qquad \textbf{(9.1)}$$

where

A = amplitude of signal

f_0 = base frequency

b_i = value of the ith bit of data ($+1$ for binary 1, -1 for binary 0)

Δf = frequency separation

T = bit duration; data rate $= 1/T$

Thus, during the ith bit interval, the frequency of the data signal is f_0 if the data bit is -1 and $f_0 + \Delta f$ if the data bit is $+1$.

The frequency synthesizer generates a constant-frequency tone whose frequency hops among a set of 2^k frequencies, with the hopping pattern determined by k bits from the PN sequence. For simplicity, assume the duration of one hop is the same as the duration of one bit and we ignore phase differences between the data signal $s_d(t)$ and the spreading signal, also called a **chipping signal**, $c(t)$. Then the product signal during the ith hop (during the ith bit) is

$$p(t) = s_d(t)c(t) = A \cos(2\pi(f_0 + 0.5(b_i + 1)\Delta f)t) \cos(2\pi f_i t)$$

where f_i is the frequency of the signal generated by the frequency synthesizer during the ith hop. Using the trigonometric identity[3] $\cos(x)\cos(y) = (1/2)(\cos(x + y) + \cos(x - y))$, we have

$$p(t) = 0.5A[\cos(2\pi(f_0 + 0.5(b_i + 1)\Delta f + f_i)t) + \cos(2\pi(f_0 + 0.5(b_i + 1)\Delta f - f_i)t)]$$

A bandpass filter (Figure 9.3) is used to block the difference frequency and pass the sum frequency, yielding an FHSS signal of

$$s(t) = 0.5A \cos(2\pi(f_0 + 0.5(b_i + 1)\Delta f + f_i)t) \qquad \textbf{(9.2)}$$

Thus, during the ith bit interval, the frequency of the data signal is $f_0 + f_i$ if the data bit is -1 and $f_0 + f_i + \Delta f$ if the data bit is $+1$.

At the receiver, a signal of the form $s(t)$ just defined will be received. This is multiplied by a replica of the spreading signal to yield a product signal of the form

$$p(t) = s(t)c(t) = 0.5A \cos(2\pi(f_0 + 0.5(b_i + 1)\Delta f + f_i)t) \cos(2\pi f_i t)$$

Again using the trigonometric identity, we have

$$p(t) = s(t)c(t) = 0.25A[\cos(2\pi(f_0 + 0.5(b_i + 1)\Delta f + f_i + f_i)t) \\ + \cos(2\pi(f_0 + 0.5(b_i + 1)\Delta f)t)]$$

---

[3]See the math refresher document at WilliamStallings.com/StudentSupport.html for a summary of trigonometric identities.

A bandpass filter (Figure 9.3) is used to block the sum frequency and pass the difference frequency, yielding a signal of the form of $s_d(t)$, defined in Equation (9.1):

$$0.25A \cos(2\pi(f_0 + 0.5(b_i + 1)\Delta f)t)$$

FHSS Using MFSK

A common modulation technique used in conjunction with FHSS is multiple FSK (MFSK). Recall from Chapter 5 that MFSK uses $M = 2^L$ different frequencies to encode the digital input L bits at a time. The transmitted signal is of the form (Equation 5.4):

$$s_i(t) = A \cos 2\pi f_i t, \qquad 1 \le i \le M$$

where

$f_i = f_c + (2i - 1 - M)f_d$

f_c = denotes the carrier frequency

f_d = denotes the difference frequency

M = number of different signal elements $= 2^L$

L = number of bits per signal element

For FHSS, the MFSK signal is translated to a new frequency every T_c seconds by modulating the MFSK signal with the FHSS carrier signal. The effect is to translate the MFSK signal into the appropriate FHSS channel. For a data rate of R, the duration of a bit is $T = 1/R$ seconds and the duration of a signal element is $T_s = LT$ seconds. If T_c is greater than or equal to T_s, the spreading modulation is referred to as slow-frequency-hop spread spectrum; otherwise it is known as fast-frequency-hop spread spectrum.[4] To summarize,

Slow-frequency-hop spread spectrum	$T_c \ge T_s$
Fast-frequency-hop spread spectrum	$T_c < T_s$

EXAMPLE 9.2 Figure 9.4 shows an example of slow FHSS, using the MFSK example from Figure 5.9. Here we have $M = 4$, which means that four different frequencies are used to encode the data input 2 bits at a time. Each signal element is a discrete frequency tone, and the total MFSK bandwidth is $W_d = Mf_d$. We use an FHSS scheme with $k = 2$. That is, there are $4 = 2^k$ different channels, each of width W_d. The total FHSS bandwidth is $W_s = 2^k W_d$. Each 2 bits of the PN sequence is used to select one of the four channels. That channel is held for a duration of two signal elements, or four bits ($T_c = 2T_s = 4T$).

---

[4]Some authors use a somewhat different definition (e.g., [PICK82]) of multiple hops per bit for fast frequency hop, multiple bits per hop for slow frequency hop, and one hop per bit if neither fast nor slow. The more common definition, which we use, relates hops to signal elements rather than bits.

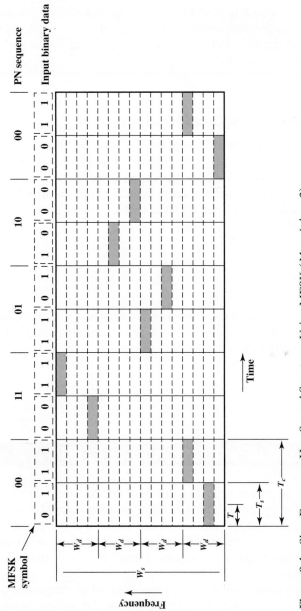

Figure 9.4 Slow Frequency Hop Spread Spectrum Using MFSK ($M = 4, k = 2$)

EXAMPLE 9.3 Figure 9.5 shows an example of fast FHSS, using the same MFSK example. Again, $M = 4$ and $k = 2$. In this case, however, each signal element is represented by two frequency tones. Again, $W_d = Mf_d$ and $W_s = 2^k W_d$. In this example $T_s = 2T_c = 2T$. In general, fast FHSS provides improved performance compared to slow FHSS in the face of noise or jamming. For example, if three or more frequencies (chips) are used for each signal element, the receiver can decide which signal element was sent on the basis of a majority of the chips being correct.

FHSS Performance Considerations

Typically, a large number of frequencies is used in FHSS so that W_s is much larger than W_d. One benefit of this is that a large value of k results in a system that is quite resistant to jamming. For example, suppose we have an MFSK transmitter with bandwidth W_d and a noise jammer of the same bandwidth and fixed power S_j on the signal carrier frequency. Then we have a ratio of signal energy per bit to noise power density per Hertz of

$$\frac{E_b}{N_j} = \frac{E_b W_d}{S_j}$$

If frequency hopping is used, the jammer must jam all 2^k frequencies. With a fixed power, this reduces the jamming power in any one frequency band to $S_j/2^k$. The gain in signal-to-noise ratio, or processing gain, is

$$G_P = 2^k = \frac{W_s}{W_d} \tag{9.3}$$

9.3 DIRECT SEQUENCE SPREAD SPECTRUM

With direct sequence spread spectrum (DSSS), each bit in the original signal is represented by multiple bits in the transmitted signal, using a spreading code. The spreading code spreads the signal across a wider frequency band in direct proportion to the number of bits used. Therefore, a 10-bit spreading code spreads the signal across a frequency band that is 10 times greater than a 1-bit spreading code.

One technique with direct sequence spread spectrum is to combine the digital information stream with the spreading code bit stream using an exclusive-OR (XOR). The XOR obeys the following rules:

$$0 \oplus 0 = 0 \qquad 0 \oplus 1 = 1 \qquad 1 \oplus 0 = 1 \qquad 1 \oplus 1 = 0$$

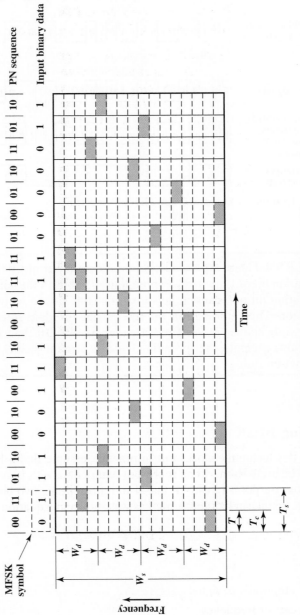

Figure 9.5 Fast Frequency Hop Spread Spectrum Using MFSK ($M = 4$, $k = 2$)

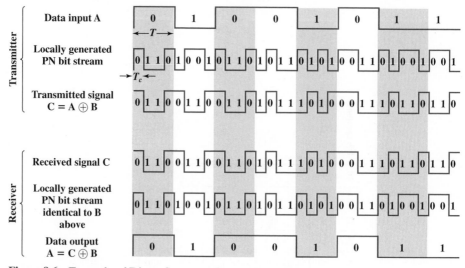

Figure 9.6 Example of Direct Sequence Spread Spectrum

EXAMPLE 9.4 Figure 9.6 uses DSSS on a data input of 01001011. Note that an information bit of 1 inverts the spreading code bits in the combination, while an information bit of 0 causes the spreading code bits to be transmitted without inversion. The combination bit stream has the data rate of the original spreading code sequence, so it has a wider bandwidth than the information stream. In this example, the spreading code bit stream is clocked at four times the information rate.

DSSS Using BPSK

To see how this technique works out in practice, assume that a BPSK modulation scheme is to be used. Rather than represent binary data with 1 and 0, it is more convenient for our purposes to use +1 and −1 to represent the two binary digits. In that case, a BPSK signal can be represented as was shown in Equation (5.6):

$$s_d(t) = A\ d(t)\ \cos(2\pi f_c t) \tag{9.4}$$

where

$\quad A$ = amplitude of signal

$\quad f_c$ = carrier frequency

$\quad d(t)$ = the discrete function that takes on the value of +1 for one
$\qquad\qquad$ bit time if the corresponding bit in the bit stream is 1 and the
$\qquad\qquad$ value of −1 for one bit time if the corresponding bit in the bit
$\qquad\qquad$ stream is 0

To produce the DSSS signal, we multiply the preceding by $c(t)$, which is the PN sequence taking on values of +1 and –1:

$$s(t) = A\ d(t)c(t) \cos(2\pi f_c t) \qquad (9.5)$$

At the receiver, the incoming signal is multiplied again by $c(t)$. But $c(t) \times c(t) = 1$ and therefore the original signal is recovered:

$$s(t)c(t) = A\ d(t)c(t)c(t) \cos(2\pi f_c t) = s_d(t)$$

Equation (9.5) can be interpreted in two ways, leading to two different implementations. The first interpretation is to first multiply $d(t)$ and $c(t)$ together and then perform the BPSK modulation. That is the interpretation we have been discussing. Alternatively, we can first perform the BPSK modulation on the data stream $d(t)$ to generate the data signal $s_d(t)$. This signal can then be multiplied by $c(t)$.

An implementation using the second interpretation is shown in Figure 9.7.

EXAMPLE 9.5 Figure 9.8 uses the approach of Figure 9.7 on an input data of 1010, which is represented as +1 −1 +1 −1. The spreading code bit stream is clocked at three times the information rate.

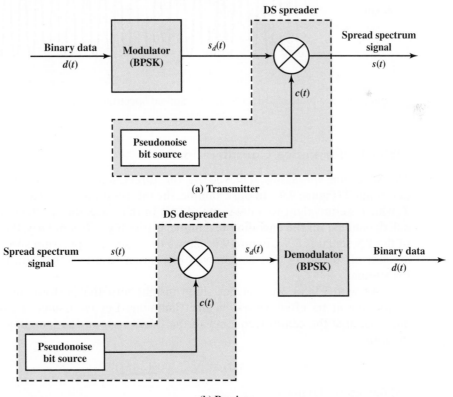

(a) Transmitter

(b) Receiver

Figure 9.7   Direct Sequence Spread Spectrum System

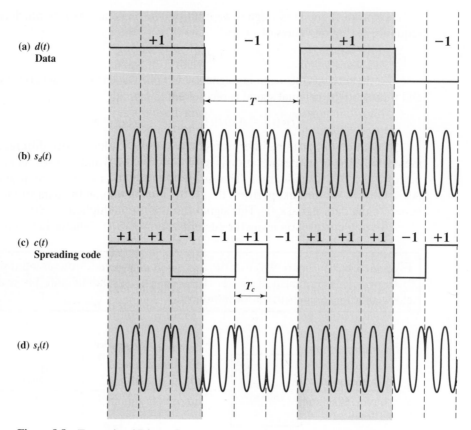

Figure 9.8 Example of Direct-Sequence Spread Spectrum Using BPSK

DSSS Performance Considerations

The spectrum spreading achieved by the direct sequence technique is easily determined (Figure 9.9). In our example, the information signal has a bit width of T, which is equivalent to a data rate of $1/T$. In that case, the spectrum of the signal, depending on the encoding technique, is roughly $2/T$. Similarly, the spectrum of the PN signal is $2/T_c$. Figure 9.9c shows the resulting spectrum spreading. The amount of spreading that is achieved is a direct result of the data rate of the PN stream.

As with FHSS, we can get some insight into the performance of DSSS by looking at its effectiveness against jamming. Let us assume a simple jamming signal at the center frequency of the DSSS system. The jamming signal has the form

$$s_j(t) = \sqrt{2S_j} \cos(2\pi f_c t)$$

and the received signal is

$$s_r(t) = s(t) + s_j(t) + n(t)$$

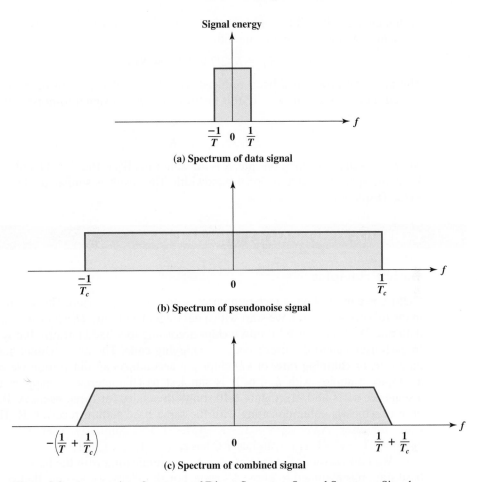

Figure 9.9   Appropriate Spectrum of Direct Sequence Spread Spectrum Signal

where

$s(t)$ = transmitted signal

$s_j(t)$ = jamming signal

$n(t)$ = additive white noise

S_j = jammer signal power

The despreader at the receiver multiplies $s_r(t)$ by $c(t)$, so the signal component due to the jamming signal is

$$y_j(t) = \sqrt{2S_j}c(t)\cos(2\pi f_c t)$$

This is simply a BPSK modulation of the carrier tone. Thus, the carrier power S_j is spread over a bandwidth of approximately $2/T_c$. However, the BPSK demodulator (Figure 9.7) following the DSSS despreader includes a bandpass filter matched to the BPSK data, with bandwidth of $2/T$. Thus, most of the jamming power is filtered.

Although a number of factors come into play, as an approximation, we can say that the jamming power passed by the filter is

$$S_{iF} = S_j(2/T)/(2/T_c) = S_j(T_c/T)$$

The jamming power has been reduced by a factor of (T_c/T) through the use of spread spectrum. The inverse of this factor is the gain in signal-to-noise ratio:

$$G_P = \frac{T}{T_c} = \frac{R_c}{R} \approx \frac{W_s}{W_d} \tag{9.6}$$

where R_c is the spreading bit rate, R is the data rate, W_d is the signal bandwidth, and W_s is the spread spectrum signal bandwidth. The result is similar to the result for FHSS (Equation 9.3).

9.4   CODE DIVISION MULTIPLE ACCESS

Basic Principles

CDMA is a multiplexing technique used with spread spectrum. The scheme works in the following manner. We start with a data signal with rate D, which we call the bit data rate. We break each bit into k **chips** according to a fixed pattern that is specific to each user, called the user's code, or **chipping code**. The new channel has a chip data rate, or **chipping rate**, of kD chips per second. As an illustration we consider a simple example[5] with $k = 6$. It is simplest to characterize a chipping code as a sequence of 1s and –1s. Figure 9.10 shows the codes for three users, A, B, and C, each of which is communicating with the same base station receiver, R. Thus, the code for user A is $c_A = <1, -1, -1, 1, -1, 1>$. Similarly, user B has code $c_B = <1, 1, -1, -1, 1, 1>$, and user C has $c_C = <1, 1, -1, 1, 1, -1>$.

We now consider the case of user A communicating with the base station. The base station is assumed to know A's code. For simplicity, we assume that communication is already synchronized so that the base station knows when to look for codes. If A wants to send a 1 bit, A transmits its code as a chip pattern $<1, -1, -1, 1, -1, 1>$. If a 0 bit is to be sent, A transmits the complement (1s and –1s reversed) of its code, $<-1, 1, 1, -1, 1, -1>$. At the base station the receiver decodes the chip patterns. In our simple version, if the receiver R receives a chip pattern $d = <d1, d2, d3, d4, d5, d6>$, and the receiver is seeking to communicate with a user u so that it has at hand u's code, $<c1, c2, c3, c4, c5, c6>$, the receiver performs electronically the following decoding function:

$$S_u(d) = d1 \times c1 + d2 \times c2 + d3 \times c3 + d4 \times c4 + d5 \times c5 + d6 \times c6$$

The subscript u on S simply indicates that u is the user that we are interested in. Let's suppose the user u is actually A and see what happens. If A sends a 1 bit, then d is $<1, -1, -1, 1, -1, 1>$ and the preceding computation using S_A becomes

$$S_A(1, -1, -1, 1, -1, 1) = 1 \times 1 + (-1) \times (-1) + (-1) \times (-1)$$
$$+ 1 \times 1 + (-1) \times (-1) + 1 \times 1 = 6$$

---

[5]This example was provided by Professor Richard Van Slyke of the Polytechnic University of Brooklyn.

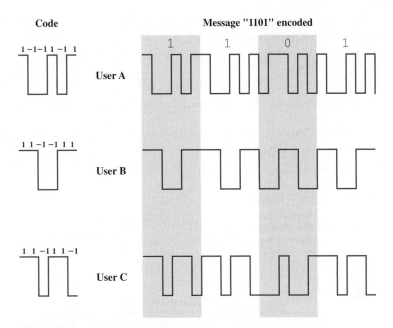

Figure 9.10 CDMA Example

If A sends a 0 bit that corresponds to $d = <-1, 1, 1, -1, 1, -1>$, we get

$$S_A(-1, 1, 1, -1, 1, -1) = -1 \times 1 + 1 \times (-1) + 1 \times (-1) + (-1) \times 1$$
$$+ 1 \times (-1) + (-1) \times 1 = -6$$

Please note that it is always the case that $-6 \leq S_A(d) \leq 6$ no matter what sequence of -1s and 1s that d is, and that the only d's resulting in the extreme values of 6 and -6 are A's code and its complement, respectively. So if S_A produces a $+6$, we say that we have received a 1 bit from A; if S_A produces a -6, we say that we have received a 0 bit from user A; otherwise, we assume that someone else is sending information or there is an error. So why go through all this? The reason becomes clear if we see what happens if user B is sending and we try to receive it with S_A, that is, we are decoding with the wrong code, A's. If B sends a 1 bit, then $d = <1, 1, -1, -1, 1, 1>$. Then

$$S_A(1, 1, -1, -1, 1, 1) = 1 \times 1 + 1 \times (-1) + (-1) \times (-1) + (-1) \times 1$$
$$+ 1 \times (-1) + 1 \times 1 = 0$$

Thus, the unwanted signal (from B) does not show up at all. You can easily verify that if B had sent a 0 bit, the decoder would produce a value of 0 for S_A again. This means that if the decoder is linear and if A and B transmit signals s_A and s_B, respectively, at the same time, then $S_A(s_A + s_B) = S_A(s_A) + S_A(s_B) = S_A(s_A)$ since the decoder ignores B when it is using A's code. The codes of A and B that have the property that $S_A(c_B) = S_B(c_A) = 0$ are called **orthogonal**.[6] Such codes are very nice

---

[6]See Appendix N for a discussion of orthogonality of chipping codes.

to have but there are not all that many of them. More common is the case when $S_X(c_Y)$ is small in absolute value when $X \neq Y$. Then it is easy to distinguish between the two cases when $X = Y$ and when $X \neq Y$. In our example $S_A(c_C) = S_C(c_A) = 0$, but $S_B(c_C) = S_C(c_B) = 2$. In the latter case the C signal would make a small contribution to the decoded signal instead of 0. Using the decoder, S_u, the receiver can sort out transmission from u even when there may be other users broadcasting in the same cell.

Table 9.1 summarizes the example from the preceding discussion.

In practice, the CDMA receiver can filter out the contribution from unwanted users or they appear as low-level noise. However, if there are many users competing

Table 9.1 CDMA Example

(a) User's codes

User A	1	−1	−1	1	−1	1
User B	1	1	−1	−1	1	1
User C	1	1	−1	1	1	−1

(b) Transmission from A

Transmit (data bit = 1)	1	−1	−1	1	−1	1	
Receiver codeword	1	−1	−1	1	−1	1	
Multiplication	1	1	1	1	1	1	= 6

Transmit (data bit = 0)	−1	1	1	−1	1	−1	
Receiver codeword	1	−1	−1	1	−1	1	
Multiplication	−1	−1	−1	−1	−1	−1	= −6

(c) Transmission from B, receiver attempts to recover A's transmission

Transmit (data bit = 1)	1	1	−1	−1	1	1	
Receiver codeword	1	−1	−1	1	−1	1	
Multiplication	1	−1	1	−1	−1	1	= 0

(d) Transmission from C, receiver attempts to recover B's transmission

Transmit (data bit = 1)	1	1	−1	1	1	−1	
Receiver codeword	1	1	−1	−1	1	1	
Multiplication	1	1	1	1	1	−1	= 2

(e) Transmission from B and C, receiver attempts to recover B's transmission

B (data bit = 1)	1	1	−1	−1	1	1	
C (data bit = 1)	1	1	−1	1	1	−1	
Combined signal	2	2	−2	0	2	0	
Receiver codeword	1	1	−1	−1	1	1	
Multiplication	2	2	2	0	2	0	= 8

for the channel with the user the receiver is trying to listen to, or if the signal power of one or more competing signals is too high, perhaps because it is very near the receiver (the "near/far" problem), the system breaks down.

CDMA for Direct Sequence Spread Spectrum

Let us now look at CDMA from the viewpoint of a DSSS system using BPSK. Figure 9.11 depicts a configuration in which there are n users, each transmitting using a different, orthogonal, PN sequence (compare Figure 9.7). For each user, the data stream to be transmitted, $d_i(t)$, is BPSK modulated to produce a signal with a bandwidth of W_s and then multiplied by the spreading code for that user, $c_i(t)$. All of the signals, plus noise, are received at the receiver's antenna. Suppose that the receiver is attempting to recover the data of user 1. The incoming signal is multiplied by the spreading code of user 1 and then demodulated. The effect of this is to narrow the bandwidth of that portion of the incoming signal corresponding to user 1 to the original bandwidth of the unspread signal, which is proportional to the data rate. Incoming signals from other users are not despread by the spreading code from user 1 and hence retain their bandwidth of W_s. Thus the unwanted signal energy remains spread over a large bandwidth and the wanted signal is concentrated in a narrow bandwidth. The bandpass filter at the demodulator can therefore recover the desired signal.

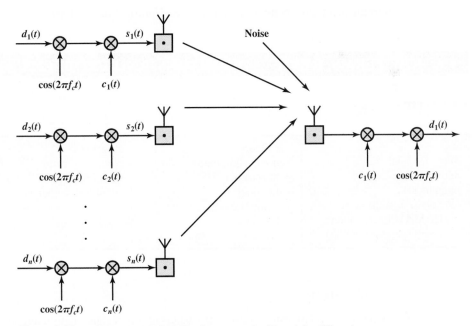

Figure 9.11 CDMA in a DSSS Environment for Receiving User 1

9.5   RECOMMENDED READING AND WEB SITE

Both [IPAT05] and [TORR05] provide comprehensive treatment of spread spectrum. [TANT98] contains reprints of many important papers in the field, including [PICK82], which provides an excellent introduction to spread spectrum.

IPAT05   Ipatov, V. *Spread Spectrum and CDMA: Principles and Applications.* New York: Wiley, 2005.

PICK82   Pickholtz, R.; Schilling, D.; and Milstein, L. "Theory of Spread Spectrum Communications—A Tutorial." *IEEE Transactions on Communications,* May 1982. Reprinted in [TANT98].

TANT98   Tantaratana, S., and Ahmed, K., eds. *Wireless Applications of Spread Spectrum Systems: Selected Readings.* Piscataway, NJ: IEEE Press, 1998.

TORR05   Torrieri, D. *Principles of Spread-Spectrum Communication Systems.* New York: Springer, 2005.

Recommended Web site:

- **Spread spectrum scene:** Excellent source of information and links

9.6   KEY TERMS, REVIEW QUESTIONS, AND PROBLEMS

Key Terms

chip
chipping signal
chipping code
chipping rate
code division multiple access
   (CDMA) direct sequence
   spread spectrum (DSSS)
	fast FHSS
	frequency-hopping spread
	   spectrum (FHSS)
	orthogonal
	pseudonoise (PN)
		slow FHSS
		spread spectrum
		spreading code
		spreading sequence

Review Questions

9.1   What is the relationship between the bandwidth of a signal before and after it has been encoded using spread spectrum?

9.2   List three benefits of spread spectrum.

9.3   What is frequency-hopping spread spectrum?

9.4   Explain the difference between slow FHSS and fast FHSS.

9.5 What is direct sequence spread spectrum?

9.6 What is the relationship between the bit rate of a signal before and after it has been encoded using DSSS?

9.7 What is CDMA?

Problems

9.1 Assume we wish to transmit a 56-kbps data stream using spread spectrum.
  a. Find the channel bandwidth required to achieve a 56-kbps channel capacity when SNR = 0.1, 0.01, and 0.001.
  b. In an ordinary (not spread spectrum) system, a reasonable goal for bandwidth efficiency might be 1 bps/Hz. That is, to transmit a data stream of 56 kbps, a bandwidth of 56 kHz is used. In this case, what is the minimum SNR that can be endured for transmission without appreciable errors? Compare to the spread spectrum case.
  Hint: Review the discussion of channel capacity in Section 3.4.

9.2 An FHSS system employs a total bandwidth of W_s = 400 MHz and an individual channel bandwidth of 100 Hz. What is the minimum number of PN bits required for each frequency hop?

9.3 An FHSS system using MFSK with M = 4 employs 1000 different frequencies. What is the processing gain?

9.4 The following table illustrates the operation of an FHSS system for one complete period of the PN sequence.

Time	0	1	2	3	4	5	6	7	8	9	10	11
Input data	0	1	1	1	1	1	1	0	0	0	1	0
Frequency	f_1		f_3		f_{23}		f_{22}		f_8		f_{10}	
PN sequence	001				110				011			

Time	12	13	14	15	16	17	18	19
Input data	0	1	1	1	1	0	1	0
Frequency	f_1		f_3		f_2		f_2	
PN sequence	001				001			

  a. What is the period of the PN sequence, in terms of bits in the sequence?
  b. The system makes use of a form of FSK. What form of FSK is it?
  c. What is the number of bits per signal element?
  d. What is the number of FSK frequencies?
  e. What is the length of a PN sequence per hop?
  f. Is this a slow or fast FH system?
  g. What is the total number of possible carrier frequencies?
  h. Show the variation of the base, or demodulated, frequency with time.

9.5 The following table illustrates the operation of a FHSS system using the same PN sequence as Problem 9.4.

Time	0	1	2	3	4	5	6	7	8	9	10	11
Input data	0	1	1	1	1	1	1	0	0	0	1	0
Frequency	f_1	f_{21}	f_{11}	f_3	f_3	f_3	f_{22}	f_{10}	f_0	f_0	f_2	f_{22}
PN sequence	001	110	011	001	001	001	110	011	001	001	001	110

Time	12	13	14	15	16	17	18	19
Input data	0	1	1	1	1	0	1	0
Frequency	f_9	f_1	f_3	f_3	f_{22}	f_{10}	f_2	f_2
PN sequence	011	001	001	001	110	011	001	001

   a. What is the period of the PN sequence?
   b. The system makes use of a form of FSK. What form of FSK is it?
   c. What is the number of bits per signal element?
   d. What is the number of FSK frequencies?
   e. What is the length of a PN sequence per hop?
   f. Is this a slow or fast FH system?
   g. What is the total number of possible carrier frequencies?
   h. Show the variation of the base, or demodulated, frequency with time.

9.6 Consider an MFSK scheme with $f_c = 250$ kHz, $f_d = 25$ kHz, and $M = 8$ ($L = 3$ bits)

   a. Make a frequency assignment for each of the eight possible 3-bit data combinations.
   b. We wish to apply FHSS to this MFSK scheme with $k = 2$; that is, the system will hop among four different carrier frequencies. Expand the results of part (a) to show the $4 \times 8 = 32$ frequency assignments.

9.7 Figure 9.12 depicts a simplified scheme for CDMA encoding and decoding. There are seven logical channels, all using DSSS with a spreading code of 7 bits. Assume that all sources are synchronized. If all seven sources transmit a data bit, in the form of a 7-bit sequence, the signals from all sources combine at the receiver so that two positive or two negative values reinforce and a positive and negative value cancel. To decode a given channel, the receiver multiplies the incoming composite signal by the spreading code for that channel, sums the result, and assigns binary 1 for a positive value and binary 0 for a negative value.

   a. What are the spreading codes for the seven channels?
   b. Determine the receiver output measurement for channel 1 and the bit value assigned.
   c. Repeat part (b) for channel 2.

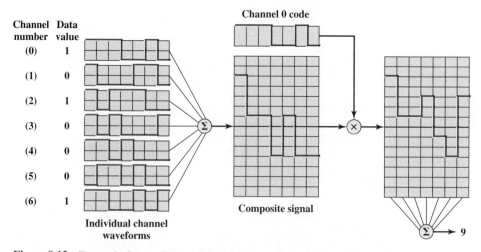

Figure 9.12 Example Seven-Channel CDMA Encoding and Decoding

9.8 By far, the most widely used technique for pseudorandom number generation is the linear congruential method. The algorithm is parameterized with four numbers, as follows:

m	the modulus	$m > 0$
a	the multiplier	$0 \le a < m$
c	the increment	$0 \le c < m$
X_0	the starting value, or seed	$0 \le X_0 < m$

The sequence of pseudorandom numbers $\{X_n\}$ is obtained via the following iterative equation:

$$X_{n+1} = (aX_n + c) \bmod m$$

If m, a, c, and X_0 are integers, then this technique will produce a sequence of integers with each integer in the range $0 \le X_n < m$. An essential characteristic of a pseudorandom number generator is that the generated sequence should appear random. Although the sequence is not random, because it is generated deterministically, there is a variety of statistical tests that can be used to assess the degree to which a sequence exhibits randomness. Another desirable characteristic is that the function should be a full-period generating function. That is, the function should generate all the numbers between 0 and m before repeating.

With the linear congruential algorithm, a choice of parameters that provides a full period does not necessarily provide a good randomization. For example, consider the two generators:

$$X_{n+1} = (6X_n) \bmod 13$$

$$X_{n+1} = (7X_n) \bmod 13$$

Write out the two sequences to show that both are full period. Which one appears more random to you?

9.9 We would like m to be very large so that there is the potential for producing a long series of distinct random numbers. A common criterion is that m be nearly equal to the maximum representable nonnegative integer for a given computer. Thus, a value of m near to or equal to 2^{31} is typically chosen. Many experts recommend a value of $2^{31} - 1$. You may wonder why one should not simply use 2^{31}, because this latter number can be represented with no additional bits, and the mod operation should be easier to perform. In general, the modulus $2^k - 1$ is preferable to 2^k. Why is this so?

9.10 In any use of pseudorandom numbers, whether for encryption, simulation, or statistical design, it is dangerous to trust blindly the random number generator that happens to be available in your computer's system library. [PARK88] found that many contemporary textbooks and programming packages make use of flawed algorithms for pseudorandom number generation. This exercise will enable you to test your system.

The test is based on a theorem attributed to Ernesto Cesaro (see [KNUT98] for a proof), which states that the probability is equal to $\frac{6}{\pi^2}$ that the greatest common divisor of two randomly chosen integers is 1. Use this theorem in a program to determine statistically the value of π. The main program should call three subprograms: the random number generator from the system library to generate the random integers, a subprogram to calculate the greatest common divisor of two integers using Euclid's algorithm, and a subprogram that calculates square roots. If these latter two programs are not available, you will have to write them as well. The main program should loop through a large number of random numbers to give an estimate of the aforementioned probability. From this, it is a simple matter to solve for your estimate of π.

If the result is close to 3.14, congratulations! If not, then the result is probably low, usually a value of around 2.7. Why would such an inferior result be obtained?

CIRCUIT SWITCHING AND PACKET SWITCHING

He got into a District Line train at Wimbledon Park, changed on to the Victoria Line at Victoria and on to the Jubilee Line at Green Park for West Hampstead. It was a long and awkward journey but he enjoyed it.

—*King Solomon's Carpet,* Barbara Vine (Ruth Rendell)

KEY POINTS

- ◆ Circuit switching is used in public telephone networks and is the basis for private networks built on leased lines and using on-site circuit switches. Circuit switching was developed to handle voice traffic but can also handle digital data, although this its latter use is often inefficient.

- ◆ With circuit switching, a dedicated path is established between two stations for communication. Switching and transmission resources within the network are reserved for the exclusive use of the circuit for the duration of the connection. The connection is transparent: Once it is established, it appears to attached devices as if there were a direct connection.

- ◆ Packet switching was designed to provide a more efficient facility than circuit switching for bursty data traffic. With packet switching, a station transmits data in small blocks, called packets. Each packet contains some portion of the user data plus control information needed for proper functioning of the network.

- ◆ A key distinguishing element of packet-switching networks is whether the internal operation is datagram or virtual circuit. With internal virtual circuits, a route is defined between two endpoints and all packets for that virtual circuit follow the same route. With internal datagrams, each packet is treated independently, and packets intended for the same destination may follow different routes.

Part Two describes how information can be encoded and transmitted over a communications link. We now turn to the broader discussion of networks, which can be used to interconnect many devices. The chapter begins with a general discussion of switched communications networks. The remainder of the chapter focuses on wide area networks and, in particular, on traditional approaches to wide area network design: circuit switching and packet switching.

Since the invention of the telephone, circuit switching has been the dominant technology for voice communications, and it has remained so well into the digital era. This chapter looks at the key characteristics of a circuit-switching network.

Around 1970, research began on a new form of architecture for long-distance digital data communications: packet switching. Although the technology of packet switching has evolved substantially since that time, it is remarkable that (1) the basic technology of packet switching is fundamentally the same today as it was in the early 1970s networks, and (2) packet switching remains one of the few effective technologies for long-distance data communications.

This chapter provides an overview of packet-switching technology. We will see, in this chapter and later in this part, that many of the advantages of packet switching (flexibility, resource sharing, robustness, responsiveness) come with a cost. The packet-switching network is a distributed collection of packet-switching nodes. Ideally, all packet-switching nodes would always know the state of the entire network. Unfortunately, because the nodes are distributed, there is a time delay between a change in status in one portion of the network and knowledge of that change elsewhere. Furthermore, there is overhead involved in communicating status information. As a result, a packet-switching network can never perform "perfectly," and elaborate algorithms are used to cope with the time delay and overhead penalties of network operation. These same issues will appear again when we discuss internetworking in Part Five.

10.1 SWITCHED COMMUNICATIONS NETWORKS

For transmission of data[1] beyond a local area, communication is typically achieved by transmitting data from source to destination through a network of intermediate switching nodes; this switched network design is typically used to implement LANs as well. The switching nodes are not concerned with the content of the data; rather, their purpose is to provide a switching facility that will move the data from node to node until they reach their destination. Figure 10.1 illustrates a simple network. The devices attached to the network may be referred to as *stations*. The stations may be computers, terminals, telephones, or other communicating devices. We refer to the switching devices whose purpose is to provide communication as *nodes*. Nodes are connected to one another in some topology by transmission links. Each station attaches to a node, and the collection of nodes is referred to as a *communications network*.

In a *switched communication network*, data entering the network from a station are routed to the destination by being switched from node to node.

---

[1]We use this term here in a very general sense, to include voice, image, and video, as well as ordinary data (e.g., numerical, text).

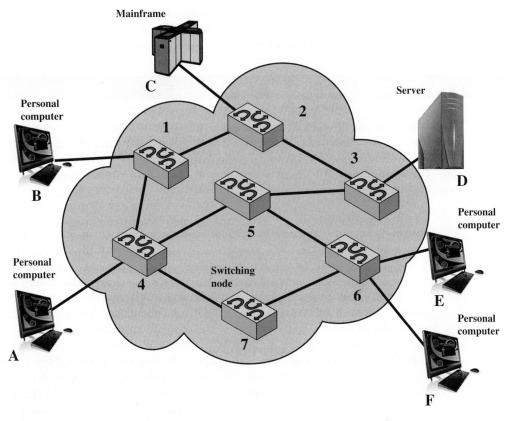

Figure 10.1 Simple Switching Network

EXAMPLE 10.1 In Figure 10.1, data from station A intended for station F are sent to node 4. They may then be routed via nodes 5 and 6 or nodes 7 and 6 to the destination. Several observations are in order:

1. Some nodes connect only to other nodes (e.g., 5 and 7). Their sole task is the internal (to the network) switching of data. Other nodes have one or more stations attached as well; in addition to their switching functions, such nodes accept data from and deliver data to the attached stations.

2. Node–station links are generally dedicated point-to-point links. Node–node links are usually multiplexed, using either frequency division multiplexing or time division multiplexing.

3. Usually, the network is not fully connected; that is, there is not a direct link between every possible pair of nodes. However, it is always desirable to have more than one possible path through the network for each pair of stations. This enhances the reliability of the network.

Two different technologies are used in wide area switched networks: circuit switching and packet switching. These two technologies differ in the way the nodes switch information from one link to another on the way from source to destination.

10.2 CIRCUIT-SWITCHING NETWORKS

Communication via circuit switching implies that there is a dedicated communication path between two stations. That path is a connected sequence of links between network nodes. On each physical link, a logical channel is dedicated to the connection. Communication via circuit switching involves three phases, which can be explained with reference to Figure 10.1.

1. **Circuit establishment**. Before any signals can be transmitted, an end-to-end (station-to-station) circuit must be established. For example, station A sends a request to node 4 requesting a connection to station E. Typically, the link from A to 4 is a dedicated line, so that part of the connection already exists. Node 4 must find the next leg in a route leading to E. Based on routing information and measures of availability and perhaps cost, node 4 selects the link to node 5, allocates a free channel (using FDM or TDM) on that link, and sends a message requesting connection to E. So far, a dedicated path has been established from A through 4 to 5. Because a number of stations may attach to 4, it must be able to establish internal paths from multiple stations to multiple nodes. How this is done is discussed later in this section. The remainder of the process proceeds similarly. Node 5 allocates a channel to node 6 and internally ties that channel to the channel from node 4. Node 6 completes the connection to E. In completing the connection, a test is made to determine if E is busy or is prepared to accept the connection.

2. **Data transfer**. Data can now be transmitted from A through the network to E. The transmission may be analog or digital, depending on the nature of the network. As the carriers evolve to fully integrated digital networks, the use of digital (binary) transmission for both voice and data is becoming the dominant method. The path is A-4 link, internal switching through 4, 4-5 channel, internal switching through 5, 5-6 channel, internal switching through 6, 6-E link. Generally, the connection is full duplex.

3. **Circuit disconnect**. After some period of data transfer, the connection is terminated, usually by the action of one of the two stations. Signals must be propagated to nodes 4, 5, and 6 to deallocate the dedicated resources.

Note that the connection path is established before data transmission begins. Thus, channel capacity must be reserved between each pair of nodes in the path, and each node must have available internal switching capacity to handle the requested connection. The switches must have the intelligence to make these allocations and to devise a route through the network.

Circuit switching can be rather inefficient. Channel capacity is dedicated for the duration of a connection, even if no data are being transferred. For a voice connection, utilization may be rather high, but it still does not approach 100%. For a

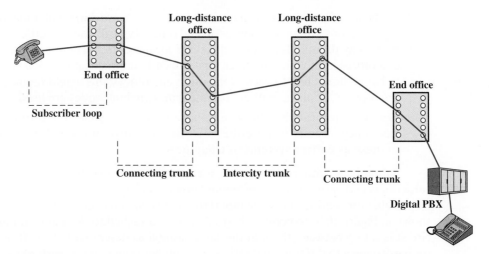

Figure 10.2 Example Connection Over a Public Circuit-Switching Network

client/server or terminal-to-computer connection, the capacity may be idle during most of the time of the connection. In terms of performance, there is a delay prior to signal transfer for call establishment. However, once the circuit is established, the network is effectively transparent to the users. Information is transmitted at a fixed data rate with no delay other than the propagation delay through the transmission links. The delay at each node is negligible.

Circuit switching was developed to handle voice traffic but is now also used for data traffic. The best-known example of a circuit-switching network is the public telephone network (Figure 10.2). This is actually a collection of national networks interconnected to form the international service. Although originally designed and implemented to service analog telephone subscribers, it handles substantial data traffic via modem and is gradually being converted to a digital network. Another well-known application of circuit switching is the private branch exchange (PBX), used to interconnect telephones within a building or office. Circuit switching is also used in private networks. Typically, such a network is set up by a corporation or other large organization to interconnect its various sites. Such a network usually consists of PBX systems at each site interconnected by dedicated, leased lines obtained from one of the carriers, such as AT&T. A final common example of the application of circuit switching is the data switch. The data switch is similar to the PBX but is designed to interconnect digital data processing devices, such as terminals and computers.

A public telecommunications network can be described using four generic architectural components:

- **Subscribers:** The devices that attach to the network. It is still the case that most subscriber devices to public telecommunications networks are telephones, but the percentage of data traffic increases year by year.

- **Subscriber line:** The link between the subscriber and the network, also referred to as the *subscriber loop* or *local loop*. Almost all local loop connections use twisted-pair wire. The length of a local loop is typically in a range from a few kilometers to a few tens of kilometers.

- **Exchanges:** The switching centers in the network. A switching center that directly supports subscribers is known as an end office. Typically, an end office will support many thousands of subscribers in a localized area. There are over 19,000 end offices in the United States, so it is clearly impractical for each end office to have a direct link to each of the other end offices; this would require on the order of 2×10^8 links. Rather, intermediate switching nodes are used.

- **Trunks:** The branches between exchanges. Trunks carry multiple voice-frequency circuits using either FDM or synchronous TDM. We referred to these as carrier systems in Chapter 8.

Subscribers connect directly to an end office, which switches traffic between subscribers and between a subscriber and other exchanges. The other exchanges are responsible for routing and switching traffic between end offices. This distinction is shown in Figure 10.3. To connect two subscribers attached to the same end office, a circuit is set up between them in the same fashion as described before. If two subscribers connect to different end offices, a circuit between them consists of a chain of circuits through one or more intermediate offices. In the figure, a connection is established between lines a and b by simply setting up the connection through the end office. The connection between c and d is more complex. In c's end office, a connection is established between line c and one channel on a TDM trunk to the intermediate switch. In the intermediate switch, that channel is connected to a channel on a TDM trunk to d's end office. In that end office, the channel is connected to line d.

Circuit-switching technology has been driven by those applications that handle voice traffic. One of the key requirements for voice traffic is that there must be virtually no transmission delay and certainly no variation in delay. A constant signal transmission rate must be maintained, because transmission and reception occur at the same signal rate. These requirements are necessary to allow normal human conversation. Further, the quality of the received signal must be sufficiently high to provide, at a minimum, intelligibility.

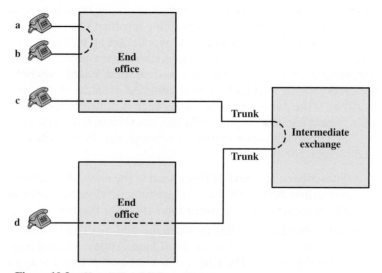

Figure 10.3 Circuit Establishment

Circuit switching achieved its widespread, dominant position because it is well suited to the analog transmission of voice signals. In today's digital world, its inefficiencies are more apparent. However, despite its inefficiencies, circuit switching will remain an attractive choice for both local area and wide area networking. One of its key strengths is that it is transparent. Once a circuit is established, it appears as a direct connection to the two attached stations; no special networking logic is needed at the station.

10.3 CIRCUIT-SWITCHING CONCEPTS

The technology of circuit switching is best approached by examining the operation of a single circuit-switching node. A network built around a single circuit-switching node consists of a collection of stations attached to a central switching unit. The central switch establishes a dedicated path between any two devices that wish to communicate. Figure 10.4 depicts the major elements of such a one-node network. The dotted lines inside the switch symbolize the connections that are currently active.

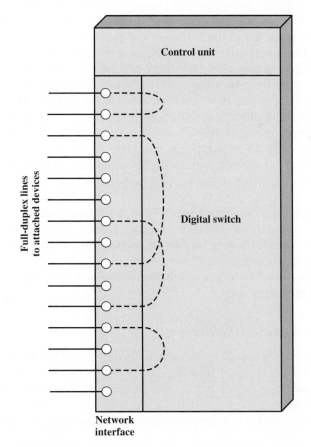

Figure 10.4 Elements of a Circuit-Switch Node

The heart of a modern system is a **digital switch**. The function of the digital switch is to provide a transparent signal path between any pair of attached devices. The path is transparent in that it appears to the attached pair of devices that there is a direct connection between them. Typically, the connection must allow full-duplex transmission.

The **network interface** element represents the functions and hardware needed to connect digital devices, such as data processing devices and digital telephones, to the network. Analog telephones can also be attached if the network interface contains the logic for converting to digital signals. Trunks to other digital switches carry TDM signals and provide the links for constructing multiple-node networks.

The **control unit** performs three general tasks. First, it establishes connections. This is generally done on demand, that is, at the request of an attached device. To establish the connection, the control unit must handle and acknowledge the request, determine if the intended destination is free, and construct a path through the switch. Second, the control unit must maintain the connection. Because the digital switch uses time division principles, this may require ongoing manipulation of the switching elements. However, the bits of the communication are transferred transparently (from the point of view of the attached devices). Third, the control unit must tear down the connection, either in response to a request from one of the parties or for its own reasons.

An important characteristic of a circuit-switching device is whether it is blocking or nonblocking. Blocking occurs when the network is unable to connect two stations because all possible paths between them are already in use. A blocking network is one in which such blocking is possible. Hence a nonblocking network permits all stations to be connected (in pairs) at once and grants all possible connection requests as long as the called party is free. When a network is supporting only voice traffic, a blocking configuration is generally acceptable, because it is expected that most phone calls are of short duration and that therefore only a fraction of the telephones will be engaged at any time. However, when data processing devices are involved, these assumptions may be invalid. For example, for a data entry application, a terminal may be continuously connected to a computer for hours at a time. Hence, for data applications, there is a requirement for a nonblocking or "nearly nonblocking" (very low probability of blocking) configuration.

We turn now to an examination of the switching techniques internal to a single circuit-switching node.

Space Division Switching

Space division switching was originally developed for the analog environment and has been carried over into the digital realm. The fundamental principles are the same, whether the switch is used to carry analog or digital signals. As its name implies, a space division switch is one in which the signal paths are physically separate from one another (divided in space). Each connection requires the establishment of a physical path through the switch that is dedicated solely to the transfer of signals between the two endpoints. The basic building block of the switch is a metallic crosspoint or semiconductor gate that can be enabled and disabled by a control unit.

EXAMPLE 10.2 Figure 10.5 shows a simple crossbar matrix with 10 full-duplex I/O lines. The matrix has 10 inputs and 10 outputs; each station attaches to the matrix via one input and one output line. Interconnection is possible between any two lines by enabling the appropriate crosspoint. Note that a total of 100 crosspoints is required.

The crossbar switch has a number of limitations:

- The number of crosspoints grows with the square of the number of attached stations. This is costly for a large switch.
- The loss of a crosspoint prevents connection between the two devices whose lines intersect at that crosspoint.
- The crosspoints are inefficiently utilized; even when all of the attached devices are active, only a small fraction of the crosspoints are engaged.

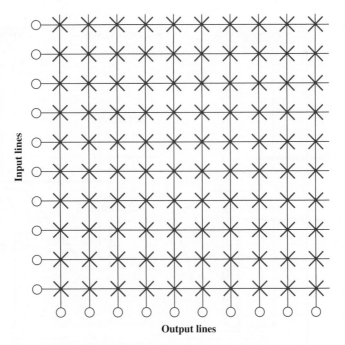

Figure 10.5 Space Division Switch

To overcome these limitations, multiple-stage switches are employed.

> **EXAMPLE 10.3** Figure 10.6 is an example of a three-stage switch.

A multiple-stage switch has two advantages over a single-stage crossbar matrix:

- The number of crosspoints is reduced, increasing crossbar utilization. In Examples 10.2 and 10.3, the total number of crosspoints for 10 stations is reduced from 100 to 48.
- There is more than one path through the network to connect two endpoints, increasing reliability.

Of course, a multistage network requires a more complex control scheme. To establish a path in a single-stage network, it is only necessary to enable a single gate. In a multistage network, a free path through the stages must be determined and the appropriate gates enabled.

A consideration with a multistage space division switch is that it may be blocking. It should be clear from Figure 10.5 that a single-stage crossbar matrix is nonblocking; that is, a path is always available to connect an input to an output. That this may not be the case with a multiple-stage switch can be seen in Figure 10.6. The heavier lines indicate the lines that are already in use. In this state, input line 10, for example, cannot be connected to output line 3, 4, or 5, even though all of these output lines are available.

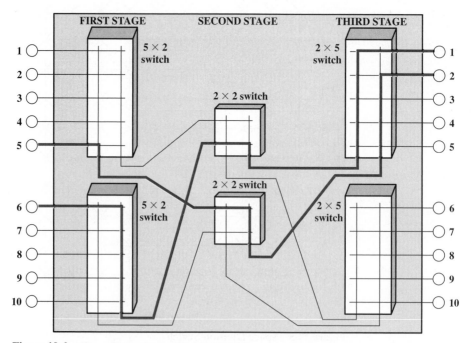

Figure 10.6 Three-Stage Space Division Switch

A multiple-stage switch can be made nonblocking by increasing the number or size of the intermediate switches, but of course this increases the cost.

Time Division Switching

The technology of switching has a long history, most of it covering an era when analog signal switching predominated. With the advent of digitized voice and synchronous time division multiplexing techniques, both voice and data can be transmitted via digital signals. This has led to a fundamental change in the design and technology of switching systems. Instead of the relatively dumb space division approach, modern digital systems rely on intelligent control of space and time division elements.

Virtually all modern circuit switches use digital time division techniques for establishing and maintaining "circuits." Time division switching involves the partitioning of a lower-speed bit stream into pieces that share a higher-speed stream with other bit streams. The individual pieces, or slots, are manipulated by control logic to route data from input to output. There are a number of variations on this basic concept, which are beyond the scope of this book

10.4 SOFTSWITCH ARCHITECTURE

The latest trend in the development of circuit-switching technology is generally referred to as the softswitch. In essence, a softswitch is a general-purpose computer running specialized software that turns it into a smart phone switch. Softswitches cost significantly less than traditional circuit switches and can provide more functionality. In particular, in addition to handling the traditional circuit-switching functions, a softswitch can convert a stream of digitized voice bits into packets. This opens up a number of options for transmission, including the increasingly popular voice over IP (Internet Protocol) approach.

In any telephone network switch, the most complex element is the software that controls call processing. This software performs call routing and implements call-processing logic for hundreds of custom-calling features. Typically, this software runs on a proprietary processor that is integrated with the physical circuit-switching hardware. A more flexible approach is to physically separate the call-processing function from the hardware-switching function. In softswitch terminology, the physical-switching function is performed by a **media gateway (MG)** and the call-processing logic resides in a **media gateway controller (MGC)**.

Figure 10.7 contrasts the architecture of a traditional telephone network circuit switch with the softswitch architecture. In the latter case, the MG and MGC are distinct entities and may be provided by different vendors. To facilitate interoperability, ITU-T has issued a standard for a media gateway control protocol between the MG and MGC: H.248.1 (*Gateway Control Protocol, Version 3*, 2005). RFC 2805 (*Media Gateway Control Protocol Architecture and Requirements*, 2000) provides an overview of media gateway concepts.

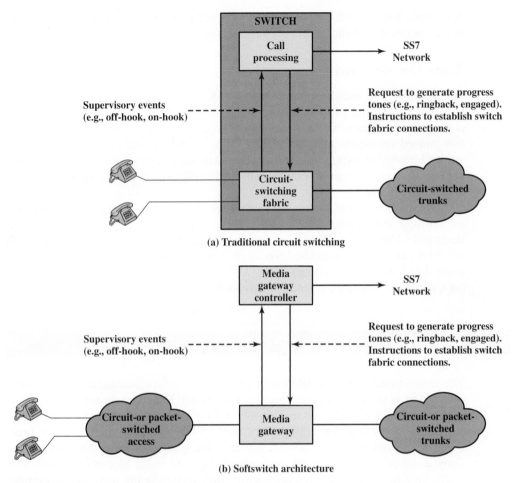

Figure 10.7 Comparison between Traditional Circuit Switching and Softswitch

10.5 PACKET-SWITCHING PRINCIPLES

The long-haul circuit-switching telecommunications network was originally designed to handle voice traffic, and the majority of traffic on these networks continues to be voice. A key characteristic of circuit-switching networks is that resources within the network are dedicated to a particular call. For voice connections, the resulting circuit will enjoy a high percentage of utilization because, most of the time, one party or the other is talking. However, as the circuit-switching network began to be used increasingly for data connections, two shortcomings became apparent:

- In a typical user/host data connection (e.g., personal computer user logged on to a database server), much of the time the line is idle. Thus, with data connections, a circuit-switching approach is inefficient.

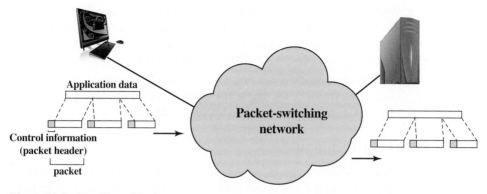

Figure 10.8   The Use of Packets

- In a circuit-switching network, the connection provides for transmission at a constant data rate. Thus, each of the two devices that are connected must transmit and receive at the same data rate as the other. This limits the utility of the network in interconnecting a variety of host computers and workstations.

To understand how packet switching addresses these problems, let us briefly summarize packet-switching operation. Data are transmitted in short packets. A typical upper bound on packet length is 1000 octets (bytes). If a source has a longer message to send, the message is broken up into a series of packets (Figure 10.8). Each packet contains a portion (or all for a short message) of the user's data plus some control information. The control information, at a minimum, includes the information that the network requires to be able to route the packet through the network and deliver it to the intended destination. At each node en route, the packet is received, stored briefly, and passed on to the next node.

Let us return to Figure 10.1, but now assume that it depicts a simple packet-switching network. Consider a packet to be sent from station A to station E. The packet includes control information that indicates that the intended destination is E. The packet is sent from A to node 4. Node 4 stores the packet, determines the next leg of the route (say 5), and queues the packet to go out on that link (the 4-5 link). When the link is available, the packet is transmitted to node 5, which forwards the packet to node 6, and finally to E. This approach has a number of advantages over circuit switching:

- Line efficiency is greater, because a single node-to-node link can be dynamically shared by many packets over time. The packets are queued up and transmitted as rapidly as possible over the link. By contrast, with circuit switching, time on a node-to-node link is preallocated using synchronous time division multiplexing. Much of the time, such a link may be idle because a portion of its time is dedicated to a connection that is idle.
- A packet-switching network can perform data-rate conversion. Two stations of different data rates can exchange packets because each connects to its node at its proper data rate.

- When traffic becomes heavy on a circuit-switching network, some calls are blocked; that is, the network refuses to accept additional connection requests until the load on the network decreases. On a packet-switching network, packets are still accepted, but delivery delay increases.

- Priorities can be used. If a node has a number of packets queued for transmission, it can transmit the higher-priority packets first. These packets will therefore experience less delay than lower-priority packets.

Switching Technique

If a station has a message to send through a packet-switching network that is of length greater than the maximum packet size, it breaks the message up into packets and sends these packets, one at a time, to the network. A question arises as to how the network will handle this stream of packets as it attempts to route them through the network and deliver them to the intended destination. Two approaches are used in contemporary networks: datagram and virtual circuit.

In the **datagram** approach, each packet is treated independently, with no reference to packets that have gone before. This approach is illustrated in Figure 10.9, which shows a time sequence of snapshots of the progress of three packets through the network. Each node chooses the next node on a packet's path, taking into account information received from neighboring nodes on traffic, line failures, and so on. So the packets, each with the same destination address, do not all follow the same route, and they may arrive out of sequence at the exit point. In this example, the exit node restores the packets to their original order before delivering them to the destination. In some datagram networks, it is up to the destination rather than the exit node to do the reordering. Also, it is possible for a packet to be destroyed in the network. For example, if a packet-switching node crashes momentarily, all of its queued packets may be lost. Again, it is up to either the exit node or the destination to detect the loss of a packet and decide how to recover it. In this technique, each packet, treated independently, is referred to as a datagram.

In the **virtual circuit** approach, a preplanned route is established before any packets are sent. Once the route is established, all the packets between a pair of communicating parties follow this same route through the network. This is illustrated in Figure 10.10. Because the route is fixed for the duration of the logical connection, it is somewhat similar to a circuit in a circuit-switching network and is referred to as a virtual circuit. Each packet contains a virtual circuit identifier as well as data. Each node on the preestablished route knows where to direct such packets; no routing decisions are required. At any time, each station can have more than one virtual circuit to any other station and can have virtual circuits to more than one station.

So the main characteristic of the virtual circuit technique is that a route between stations is set up prior to data transfer. Note that this does not mean that this is a dedicated path, as in circuit switching. A transmitted packet is buffered at each node, and queued for output over a line, while other packets on other virtual circuits may share the use of the line. The difference from the datagram approach is that, with virtual circuits, the node need not make a routing decision for each packet. It is made only once for all packets using that virtual circuit.

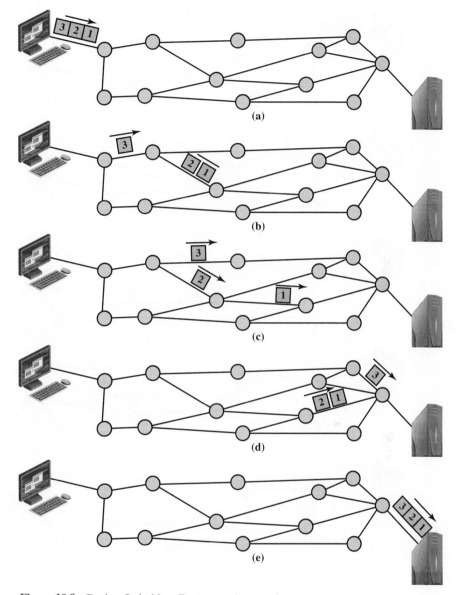

Figure 10.9   Packet Switching: Datagram Approach

If two stations wish to exchange data over an extended period of time, there are certain advantages to virtual circuits. First, the network may provide services related to the virtual circuit, including sequencing and error control. Sequencing refers to the fact that, because all packets follow the same route, they arrive in the original order. Error control is a service that assures not only that packets arrive in proper sequence, but also that all packets arrive correctly. For example, if a packet in a sequence from node 4 to node 6 fails to arrive at node 6, or arrives with an error, node 6 can request a retransmission of that packet from node 4. Another advantage

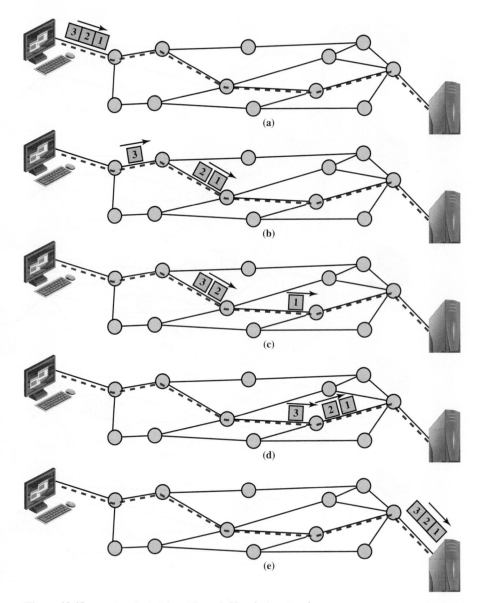

Figure 10.10 Packet Switching: Virtual-Circuit Approach

is that packets should transit the network more rapidly with a virtual circuit; it is not necessary to make a routing decision for each packet at each node.

One advantage of the datagram approach is that the call setup phase is avoided. Thus, if a station wishes to send only one or a few packets, datagram delivery will be quicker. Another advantage of the datagram service is that, because it is more primitive, it is more flexible. For example, if congestion develops in one part of the network, incoming datagrams can be routed away from the congestion. With the use of virtual circuits, packets follow a predefined route, and thus it is more difficult for the network to adapt to congestion. A third advantage is that datagram delivery is inherently more reliable. With the use of virtual circuits, if a node fails, all virtual circuits that pass through that node are lost. With datagram delivery, if a node fails, subsequent packets may find an alternate route that bypasses that node. A datagram-style of operation is common in internetworks, discussed in Part Five.

Packet Size

There is a significant relationship between packet size and transmission time, as shown in Figure 10.11. In this example, it is assumed that there is a virtual circuit from station X through nodes a and b to station Y. The message to be sent comprises

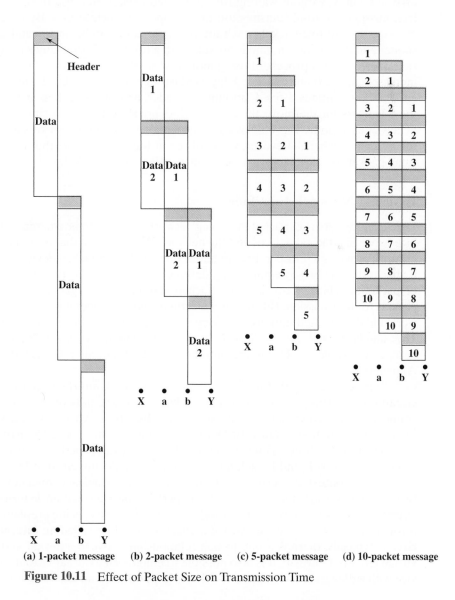

(a) 1-packet message   (b) 2-packet message   (c) 5-packet message   (d) 10-packet message

Figure 10.11   Effect of Packet Size on Transmission Time

40 octets, and each packet contains 3 octets of control information, which is placed at the beginning of each packet and is referred to as a header. If the entire message is sent as a single packet of 43 octets (3 octets of header plus 40 octets of data), then the packet is first transmitted from station X to node a (Figure 10.11a). When the entire packet is received, it can then be transmitted from a to b. When the entire packet is received at node b, it is then transferred to station Y. Ignoring switching time, total transmission time is 129 octet-times (43 octets × 3 packet transmissions).

Suppose now that we break up the message into two packets, each containing 20 octets of the message and, of course, 3 octets each of header, or control information. In this case, node a can begin transmitting the first packet as soon as it has arrived from X, without waiting for the second packet. Because of this overlap in transmission, the total transmission time drops to 92 octet-times. By breaking the message up into five packets, each intermediate node can begin transmission even sooner and the savings in time is greater, with a total of 77 octet-times for transmission. However, this process of using more and smaller packets eventually results in increased, rather than reduced, delay as illustrated in Figure 10.11d. This is because each packet contains a fixed amount of header, and more packets mean more of these headers. Furthermore, the example does not show the processing and queuing delays at each node. These delays are also greater when more packets are handled for a single message. However, we shall see in the next chapter that an extremely small packet size (53 octets) can result in an efficient network design.

External Network Interface

One technical aspect of packet-switching networks remains to be examined: the interface between attached devices and the network. We have seen that a circuit-switching network provides a transparent communications path for attached devices that makes it appear that the two communicating stations have a direct link. However, in the case of packet-switching networks, the attached stations must organize their data into packets for transmission. This requires a certain level of cooperation between the network and the attached stations. This cooperation is embodied in an interface standard. The standard used for traditional packet-switching networks is X.25, which is described in Appendix U. Another interface standard is frame relay, also discussed in Appendix U.

Typically, standards for packet-switching network interfaces define a virtual circuit service. This service enables any subscriber to the network to set up logical connections, called virtual circuits, to other subscribers. An example is shown in Figure 10.12 (compare Figure 10.1). In this example, station A has a virtual circuit connection to C; station B has two virtual circuits established, one to C and one to D; and stations E and F each have a virtual circuit connection to D.

In this context, the term *virtual circuit* refers to the logical connection between two stations through the network; this is perhaps best termed an **external virtual circuit**. Earlier, we used the term *virtual circuit* to refer to a specific preplanned route through the network between two stations; this could be called an **internal virtual circuit**. Typically, there is a one-to-one relationship between external and internal virtual circuits. However, it is also possible to employ an external virtual circuit service with a datagram-style network. What is important for an external virtual circuit

This is because circuit switching is an essentially transparent process, providing a constant data rate across the network. Packet switching involves some delay at each node in the path. Worse, this delay is variable and will increase with increased load.

Datagram packet switching does not require a call setup. Thus, for short messages, it will be faster than virtual circuit packet switching and perhaps circuit switching. However, because each individual datagram is routed independently, the processing for each datagram at each node may be longer than for virtual circuit packets. Thus, for long messages, the virtual circuit technique may be superior.

Figure 10.13 is intended only to suggest what the relative performance of the techniques might be; actual performance depends on a host of factors, including the size of the network, its topology, the pattern of load, and the characteristics of typical exchanges.

OTHER CHARACTERISTICS Besides performance, there are a number of other characteristics that may be considered in comparing the techniques we have been discussing. Table 10.1 summarizes the most important of these. Most of these characteristics have already been discussed. A few additional comments follow.

As was mentioned, circuit switching is essentially a transparent service. Once a connection is established, a constant data rate is provided to the connected stations. This is not the case with packet switching, which typically introduces variable delay,

Table 10.1   Comparison of Communication Switching Techniques

Circuit Switching	Datagram Packet Switching	Virtual Circuit Packet Switching
Dedicated transmission path	No dedicated path	No dedicated path
Continuous transmission of data	Transmission of packets	Transmission of packets
Fast enough for interactive	Fast enough for interactive	Fast enough for interactive
Messages are not stored	Packets may be stored until delivered	Packets stored until delivered
The path is established for entire conversation	Route established for each packet	Route established for entire conversation
Call setup delay; negligible transmission delay	Packet transmission delay	Call setup delay; packet transmission delay
Busy signal if called party busy	Sender may be notified if packet not delivered	Sender notified of connection denial
Overload may block call setup; no delay for established calls	Overload increases packet delay	Overload may block call setup; increases packet delay
Electromechanical or computerized switching nodes	Small switching nodes	Small switching nodes
User responsible for message loss protection	Network may be responsible for individual packets	Network may be responsible for packet sequences
Usually no speed or code conversion	Speed and code conversion	Speed and code conversion
Fixed bandwidth	Dynamic use of bandwidth	Dynamic use of bandwidth
No overhead bits after call setup	Overhead bits in each packet	Overhead bits in each packet

so that data arrive in a choppy manner. Indeed, with datagram packet switching, data may arrive in a different order than they were transmitted.

An additional consequence of transparency is that there is no overhead required to accommodate circuit switching. Once a connection is established, the analog or digital data are passed through, as is, from source to destination. For packet switching, analog data must be converted to digital before transmission; in addition, each packet includes overhead bits, such as the destination address.

10.6 RECOMMENDED READING

As befits its age, circuit switching has inspired a voluminous literature. Two good books on the subject are [BELL00] and [FREE04].

The literature on packet switching is enormous. Books with good treatments of this subject include [BERT92] and [SPRA91]. [ROBE78] is a classic paper on how packet-switching technology evolved. [BARA02] and [HEGG84] are also interesting.

BARA02   Baran, P. "The Beginnings of Packet Switching: Some Underlying Concepts." *IEEE Communications Magazine*, July 2002.

BELL00   Bellamy, J. *Digital Telephony*. New York: Wiley, 2000.

BERT92   Bertsekas, D., and Gallager, R. *Data Networks*. Englewood Cliffs, NJ: Prentice Hall, 1992.

FREE04   Freeman, R. *Telecommunication System Engineering*. New York: Wiley, 2004.

HEGG84   Heggestad, H. "An Overview of Packet Switching Communications." *IEEE Communications Magazine*, April 1984.

ROBE78   Roberts, L. "The Evolution of Packet Switching." *Proceedings of the IEEE*, November 1978.

SPRA91   Spragins, J.; Hammond, J.; and Pawlikowski, K. *Telecommunications Protocols and Design*. Reading, MA: Addison-Wesley, 1991.

10.7 KEY TERMS, REVIEW QUESTIONS, AND PROBLEMS

Key Terms

circuit switching	frame relay	subscriber
circuit-switching network	internal virtual circuit	subscriber line
crossbar matrix	local loop	subscriber loop
datagram	media gateway controller	time division switching
digital switch	packet switching	trunk
exchange	softswitch	virtual circuit
external virtual circuit	space division switching	

Review Questions

10.1 Why is it useful to have more than one possible path through a network for each pair of stations?

10.2 What are the four generic architectural components of a public communications network? Define each term.

10.3 What is the principal application that has driven the design of circuit-switching networks?

10.4 What are the advantages of packet switching compared to circuit switching?

10.5 Explain the difference between datagram and virtual circuit operation.

10.6 What is the significance of packet size in a packet-switching network?

10.7 What types of delay are significant in assessing the performance of a packet-switching network?

Problems

10.1 Consider a simple telephone network consisting of two end offices and one intermediate switch with a 1-MHz full-duplex trunk between each end office and the intermediate switch. Assume a 4-kHz channel for each voice call. The average telephone is used to make four calls per 8-hour workday, with a mean call duration of six minutes. Ten percent of the calls are long distance. What is the maximum number of telephones an end office can support?

10.2 **a.** If a crossbar matrix has n input lines and m output lines, how many crosspoints are required?

  b. How many crosspoints would be required if there were no distinction between input and output lines (i.e., if any line could be interconnected to any other line serviced by the crossbar)?

  c. Show the minimum configuration.

10.3 Consider a three-stage switch such as Figure 10.6. Assume that there are a total of N input lines and N output lines for the overall three-stage switch. If n is the number of input lines to a stage 1 crossbar and the number of output lines to a stage 3 crossbar, then there are N/n stage 1 crossbars and N/n stage 3 crossbars. Assume each stage 1 crossbar has one output line going to each stage 2 crossbar, and each stage 2 crossbar has one output line going to each stage 3 crossbar. For such a configuration it can be shown that, for the switch to be nonblocking, the number of stage 2 crossbar matrices must equal $2n - 1$.

  a. What is the total number of crosspoints among all the crossbar switches?

  b. For a given value of N, the total number of crosspoints depends on the value of n. That is, the value depends on how many crossbars are used in the first stage to handle the total number of input lines. Assuming a large number of input lines to each crossbar (large value of n), what is the minimum number of crosspoints for a nonblocking configuration as a function of n?

  c. For a range of N from 10^2 to 10^6, plot the number of crosspoints for a single-stage $N \times N$ switch and an optimum three-stage crossbar switch.

10.4 Explain the flaw in the following reasoning: Packet switching requires control and address bits to be added to each packet. This introduces considerable overhead in packet switching. In circuit switching, a transparent circuit is established. No extra bits are needed. Therefore, there is no overhead in circuit switching. Because there is no overhead in circuit switching, line utilization must be more efficient than in packet switching.

10.5 Define the following parameters for a switching network:

N = number of hops between two given end systems
L = message length in bits
B = data rate, in bits per second (bps), on all links
P = fixed packet size, in bits
H = overhead (header) bits per packet
S = call setup time (circuit switching or virtual circuit) in seconds
D = propagation delay per hop in seconds

a. For $N = 4$, $L = 3200$, $B = 9600$, $P = 1024$, $H = 16$, $S = 0.2$, $D = 0.001$, compute the end-to-end delay for circuit switching, virtual circuit packet switching, and datagram packet switching. Assume that there are no acknowledgments. Ignore processing delay at the nodes.

b. Derive general expressions for the three techniques of part (a), taken two at a time (three expressions in all), showing the conditions under which the delays are equal.

10.6 What value of P, as a function of N, L, and H, results in minimum end-to-end delay on a datagram network? Assume that L is much larger than P, and D is zero.

10.7 Assuming no malfunction in any of the stations or nodes of a network, is it possible for a packet to be delivered to the wrong destination?

ASYNCHRONOUS TRANSFER MODE

One man had a vision of railways that would link all the mainline railroad termini. His name was Charles Pearson and, though born the son of an upholsterer, he became Solicitor to the city of London. There had previously been a plan for gaslit subway streets through which horse-drawn traffic could pass. This was rejected on the grounds that such sinister tunnels would become lurking places for thieves. Twenty years before his system was built, Pearson envisaged a line running through "a spacious archway," well-lit and well-ventilated.

His was a scheme for trains in a drain.

—King Solomon's Carpet, Barbara Vine (Ruth Rendell)

KEY POINTS

◆ ATM is a streamlined packet transfer interface. ATM makes use of fixed-size packets, called cells. The use of a fixed size and fixed format results in an efficient scheme for transmission over high-speed networks.

◆ Some form of transmission structure must be used to transport ATM cells. One option is the use of a continuous stream of cells, with no multiplex frame structure imposed at the interface. Synchronization is on a cell-by-cell basis. The second option is to place the cells in a synchronous time-division multiplex envelope. In this case, the bit stream at the interface has an external frame based on the Synchronous Digital Hierarchy (SDH).

◆ ATM provides both real-time and non-real-time services. An ATM-based network can support a wide range of traffic, including synchronous TDM streams such as T-1, using the constant bit rate (CBR) service; compressed voice and video, using the real-time variable bit rate (rt-VBR) service; traffic with specific quality-of-service requirements, using the non-real-time VBR (nrt-VBR) service; and IP-based traffic, using the available bit rate (ABR), unspecified bit rate (UBR), and guaranteed frame rate (GFR) services.

Asynchronous transfer mode (ATM), also known as cell relay, takes advantage of the reliability and fidelity of modern digital facilities to provide a very high speed form of packet switching.

We begin this chapter with an overview of the current status of ATM as a networking technology. This is followed by an examination of the details of the ATM protocol and formats. Next, we look at the manner in which ATM cells are actually packaged for transmission across the user–network interface. Finally, we examine the various service categories defined for ATM transmission.

A discussion of ATM quality of service (QoS) and traffic management aspects are provided in Chapter 13. Appendix I addresses the requirement for mapping various applications onto ATM by means of the ATM adaptation layer (AAL).

11.1 THE ROLE OF ATM

Asynchronous transfer mode is a switching and multiplexing technology that employs small, fixed-length packets, called **cells**. A fixed-size packet was chosen to ensure that the switching and multiplexing function could be carried out efficiently, with little delay variation. A small cell size was chosen primarily to support delay-intolerant interactive voice service with a small packetization delay. ATM is a connection-oriented packet-switching technology that was designed to provide the performance of a circuit-switching network and the flexibility and efficiency of a packet-switching network. A major thrust of the ATM standardization effort was to provide a powerful set of tools for supporting a rich QoS capability and a powerful traffic management capability. ATM was intended to provide a unified networking standard for both circuit-switched and packet-switched traffic, and to support data, voice, and video with appropriate QoS mechanisms. With ATM, the user can select the desired level of service and obtain guaranteed service quality. Internally, the ATM network makes reservations and preplans routes so that transmission allocation is based on priority and QoS characteristics.

The International Telecommunication Union Telecommunication Standardization Sector (ITU-T) is the lead organization in developing ATM standards. In addition, the ATM Forum (now part of the Broadband Forum) was founded to ensure interoperability among public and private ATM implementations.

ATM was intended to be a universal networking technology, with much of the switching and routing capability implemented in hardware, and with the ability to support IP-based networks and circuit-switched networks. It was also anticipated that ATM would be used to implement local area networks. ATM never achieved this comprehensive deployment. However, ATM remains an important technology. ATM is commonly used by telecommunications providers to implement wide-area networks. Many DSL implementations use ATM over the basic DSL hardware for multiplexing and switching, and ATM is used as a backbone network technology in numerous IP networks and portions of the Internet.

A number of factors have led to this lesser role for ATM. IP, with its many associated protocols, provides an integrative technology that is more scalable and less complex than ATM. In addition, the need to use small fixed-sized cells to reduce jitter has disappeared as transport speeds have increased. The development of voice and video over IP protocols has provided an integration capability at the IP level.

Perhaps the most significant development related to the reduced role for ATM is the widespread acceptance of Multiprotocol Label Switching (MPLS). MPLS is a layer-2 connection-oriented packet-switching protocol that, as the name suggests, can provide a switching service for a variety of protocols and applications, including IP, voice, and video. We introduce MPLS in Chapter 21.

It remains worthwhile to study ATM for two reasons. First, ATM is still commonly deployed in wide-area networks and DSL broadband access configurations. Second, many of the concepts in ATM have been adopted in the MPLS standards.

11.2 PROTOCOL ARCHITECTURE

Asynchronous transfer mode is in some ways similar to packet switching using X.25 and to frame relay. Like packet switching and frame relay, ATM involves the transfer of data in discrete chunks. Also, like packet switching and frame relay, ATM allows multiple logical connections to be multiplexed over a single physical interface. In the case of ATM, the information flow on each logical connection is organized into fixed-size packets, called *cells*.

ATM is a streamlined protocol with minimal error and flow control capabilities. This reduces the overhead of processing ATM cells and reduces the number of overhead bits required with each cell, thus enabling ATM to operate at high data rates. Further, the use of fixed-size cells simplifies the processing required at each ATM node, again supporting the use of ATM at high data rates.

The standards issued for ATM by ITU-T are based on the protocol architecture shown in Figure 11.1, which illustrates the basic architecture for an interface between user and network. The physical layer involves the specification of a transmission medium and a signal-encoding scheme. The data rates specified at the physical layer range from 25.6 to 622.08 Mbps. Other data rates, both higher and lower, are possible.

Two layers of the protocol architecture relate to ATM functions. There is an ATM layer common to all services that provides packet transfer capabilities, and an ATM adaptation layer (AAL) that is service dependent. The ATM layer defines the transmission of data in fixed-size cells and defines the use of logical connections. The use of ATM creates the need for an adaptation layer to support information transfer protocols not based on ATM. The AAL maps higher-layer information into ATM cells to be transported over an ATM network, then collects information from ATM cells for delivery to higher layers. Figure 11.2 illustrates the relationship between the AAL and ATM layers. AAL is employed only in end systems that use an ATM network. The AAL data and control information is transferred between end systems inside ATM cells. The individual ATM switches in the network deal only with the cells and are not concerned with cell payload.

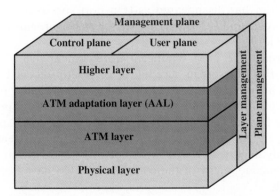

Figure 11.1   ATM Protocol Architecture

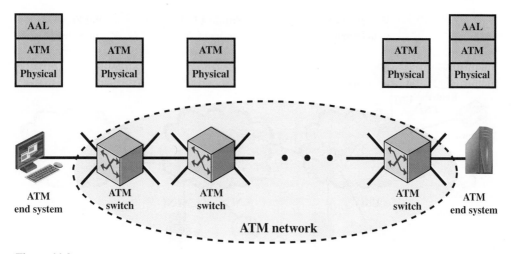

Figure 11.2   ATM Protocol Layers

The protocol reference model involves three separate planes:

- **User plane:** Provides for user information transfer, along with associated controls (e.g., flow control, error control)
- **Control plane:** Performs call control and connection control functions
- **Management plane:** Includes plane management, which performs management functions related to a system as a whole and provides coordination between all the planes, and layer management, which performs management functions relating to resources and parameters residing in its protocol entities

ATM Network Interfaces

An ATM network consists of a set of ATM switches interconnected by point-to-point ATM links, called *interfaces*. An ATM switch supports two types of interfaces: user–network interface (UNI) and network node interface (NNI). An interface specification includes a definition of link types allowed, addressing formats, cell format, and control signaling protocols.

As shown in Figure 11.3, the UNI connects an end system to an ATM switch. An end system can be an end-user device, such as a telephone, workstation, video camera or display, and server. An end system can also be a network device, such as an IP router, a local area network switch, or a telephone switch. Note that the UNI specification is used between a public ATM network and a private ATM network. In this case, the ATM switch in the private network that has a direct link to an ATM switch in the public network is considered an end system by the public ATM network.

The NNI connects two ATM switches in the same network. An additional specification, the broadband intercarrier interface (B-ICI), connects two public

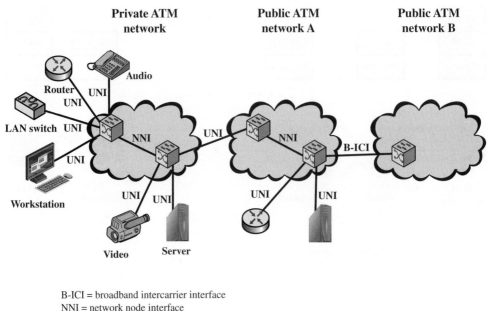

B-ICI = broadband intercarrier interface
NNI = network node interface
UNI = user–network interface

Figure 11.3 ATM Interfaces

switches from different service providers. These interfaces include definition of routing and quality of service functionality.

11.3 ATM LOGICAL CONNECTIONS

Logical connections in ATM are referred to as **virtual channel connections (VCCs)**. A VCC is analogous to a virtual circuit in X.25; it is the basic unit of switching in an ATM network. A VCC is set up between two end users through the network, and a variable-rate, full-duplex flow of fixed-size cells is exchanged over the connection. VCCs are also used for user–network exchange (control signaling) and network–network exchange (network management and routing).

For ATM, a second sublayer of processing has been introduced that deals with the concept of virtual path (Figure 11.4). A **virtual path connection (VPC)** is a

Figure 11.4 ATM Connection Relationships

bundle of VCCs that have the same endpoints. Thus, all of the cells flowing over all of the VCCs in a single VPC are switched together.

The virtual path concept was developed in response to a trend in high-speed networking in which the control cost of the network is becoming an increasingly higher proportion of the overall network cost. The virtual path technique helps contain the control cost by grouping connections sharing common paths through the network into a single unit. Network management actions can then be applied to a small number of groups of connections instead of a large number of individual connections.

Several advantages can be listed for the use of virtual paths:

- **Simplified network architecture:** Network transport functions can be separated into those related to an individual logical connection (virtual channel) and those related to a group of logical connections (virtual path).
- **Increased network performance and reliability:** The network deals with fewer, aggregated entities.
- **Reduced processing and short connection setup time:** Much of the work is done when the virtual path is set up. By reserving capacity on a virtual path connection in anticipation of later call arrivals, new virtual channel connections can be established by executing simple control functions at the endpoints of the virtual path connection; no call processing is required at transit nodes. Thus, the addition of new virtual channels to an existing virtual path involves minimal processing.
- **Enhanced network services:** The virtual path is used internal to the network but is also visible to the end user. Thus, the user may define closed user groups or closed networks of virtual channel bundles.

Figure 11.5 suggests in a general way the call establishment process using virtual channels and virtual paths. The process of setting up a virtual path connection is decoupled from the process of setting up an individual virtual channel connection:

- The virtual path control mechanisms include calculating routes, allocating capacity, and storing connection state information.
- To set up a virtual channel, there must first be a virtual path connection to the required destination node with sufficient available capacity to support the virtual channel, with the appropriate quality of service. A virtual channel is set up by storing the required state information (virtual channel/virtual path mapping).

The terminology of virtual paths and virtual channels used in the standard is a bit confusing and is summarized in Table 11.1. Whereas many network-layer protocols relate only to the user–network interface, the concepts of virtual path and virtual channel are defined in the ITU-T Recommendations with reference to both the user–network interface and the internal network operation.

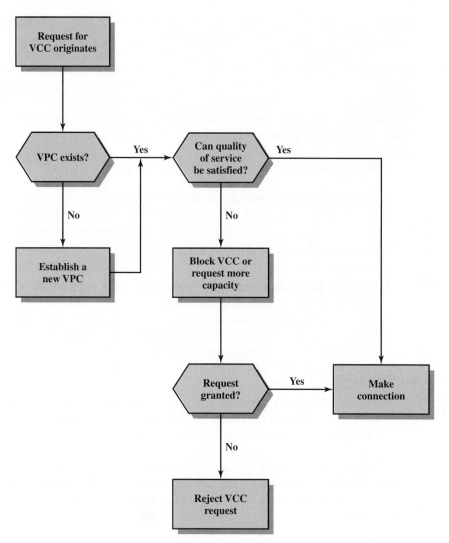

Figure 11.5 Call Establishment Using Virtual Paths

Virtual Channel Connection Uses

The endpoints of a VCC may be end users, network entities, or an end user and a network entity. In all cases, cell sequence integrity is preserved within a VCC: That is, cells are delivered in the same order in which they are sent. Let us consider examples of the three uses of a VCC:

- **Between end users:** Can be used to carry end-to-end user data; can also be used to carry control signaling between end users, as explained later. A VPC between end users provides them with an overall capacity; the VCC organization of the VPC is up to the two end users, provided the set of VCCs does not exceed the VPC capacity.

Table 11.1 Virtual Path/Virtual Channel Terminology

Virtual Channel (VC)	A generic term used to describe unidirectional transport of ATM cells associated by a common unique identifier value.
Virtual Channel Link	A means of unidirectional transport of ATM cells between a point where a VCI value is assigned and the point where that value is translated or terminated.
Virtual Channel Identifier (VCI)	A unique numerical tag that identifies a particular VC link for a given VPC.
Virtual Channel Connection (VCC)	A concatenation of VC links that extends between two points where ATM service users access the ATM layer. VCCs are provided for the purpose of user–user, user–network, or network–network information transfer. Cell sequence integrity is preserved for cells belonging to the same VCC.
Virtual Path	A generic term used to describe unidirectional transport of ATM cells belonging to virtual channels that are associated by a common unique identifier value.
Virtual Path Link	A group of VC links, identified by a common value of VPI, between a point where a VPI value is assigned and the point where that value is translated or terminated.
Virtual Path Identifier (VPI)	Identifies a particular VP link.
Virtual Path Connection (VPC)	A concatenation of VP links that extends between the point where the VCI values are assigned and the point where those values are translated or removed, i.e., extending the length of a bundle of VC links that share the same VPI. VPCs are provided for the purpose of user–user, user–network, or network–network information transfer.

- **Between an end user and a network entity:** Used for user-to-network control signaling, as discussed subsequently. A user-to-network VPC can be used to aggregate traffic from an end user to a network exchange or network server.
- **Between two network entities:** Used for network traffic management and routing functions. A network-to-network VPC can be used to define a common route for the exchange of network management information.

Virtual Path/Virtual Channel Characteristics

ITU-T Recommendation I.150 lists the following as characteristics of virtual channel connections:

- **Quality of service (QoS):** A user of a VCC is provided with a QoS specified by parameters such as cell loss ratio (ratio of cells lost to cells transmitted) and cell delay variation.
- **Switched and semipermanent virtual channel connections:** A switched VCC is an on-demand connection, which requires a call control signaling for setup and tearing down. A semipermanent VCC is one that is of long duration and is set up by configuration or network management action.

- **Cell sequence integrity:** The sequence of transmitted cells within a VCC is preserved.

- **Traffic parameter negotiation and usage monitoring:** Traffic parameters can be negotiated between a user and the network for each VCC. The network monitors the input of cells to the VCC, to ensure that the negotiated parameters are not violated.

The types of traffic parameters that can be negotiated include average rate, peak rate, burstiness, and peak duration. The network may need a number of strategies to deal with congestion and to manage existing and requested VCCs. At the crudest level, the network may simply deny new requests for VCCs to prevent congestion. Additionally, cells may be discarded if negotiated parameters are violated or if congestion becomes severe. In an extreme situation, existing connections might be terminated.

I.150 also lists characteristics of VPCs. The first four characteristics listed are identical to those for VCCs. That is, QoS; switched and semipermanent VPCs; cell sequence integrity; and traffic parameter negotiation and usage monitoring are all also characteristics of a VPC. There are a number of reasons for this duplication. First, this provides some flexibility in how the network service manages the requirements placed upon it. Second, the network must be concerned with the overall requirements for a VPC, and within a VPC may negotiate the establishment of virtual channels with given characteristics. Finally, once a VPC is set up, it is possible for the end users to negotiate the creation of new VCCs. The VPC characteristics impose a discipline on the choices that the end users may make.

In addition, a fifth characteristic is listed for VPCs:

- **Virtual channel identifier restriction within a VPC:** One or more virtual channel identifiers, or numbers, may not be available to the user of the VPC but may be reserved for network use. Examples include VCCs used for network management.

Control Signaling

In ATM, a mechanism is needed for the establishment and release of VPCs and VCCs. The exchange of information involved in this process is referred to as control signaling and takes place on separate connections from those that are being managed.

For VCCs, I.150 specifies four methods for providing an establishment/release facility. One or a combination of these methods will be used in any particular network:

1. **Semipermanent VCCs** may be used for user-to-user exchange. In this case, no control signaling is required.

2. If there is no preestablished call control signaling channel, then one must be set up. For that purpose, a control signaling exchange must take place between the user and the network on some channel. Hence we need a permanent channel, probably of low data rate, that can be used to set up VCCs that can be used

for call control. Such a channel is called a **meta-signaling channel**, as the channel is used to set up signaling channels.

3. The meta-signaling channel can be used to set up a VCC between the user and the network for call control signaling. This **user-to-network signaling virtual channel** can then be used to set up VCCs to carry user data.

4. The meta-signaling channel can also be used to set up a **user-to-user signaling virtual channel**. Such a channel must be set up within a preestablished VPC. It can then be used to allow the two end users, without network intervention, to establish and release user-to-user VCCs to carry user data.

For VPCs, three methods are defined in I.150:

1. A VPC can be established on a **semipermanent** basis by prior agreement. In this case, no control signaling is required.

2. VPC establishment/release may be **customer controlled**. In this case, the customer uses a signaling VCC to request the VPC from the network.

3. VPC establishment/release may be **network controlled**. In this case, the network establishes a VPC for its own convenience. The path may be network-to-network, user-to-network, or user-to-user.

ATM signaling protocols can be classified by the type of ATM network interface, as follows:

- **UNI signaling:** Used between an ATM end system and ATM switch across UNI links. UNI signaling in ATM defines the protocol by which switched VCCs are set up dynamically by the ATM devices in the network.

- **NNI signaling:** Used between ATM switches across NNI links. NNI signaling includes both signaling and routing.

11.4 ATM CELLS

The asynchronous transfer mode makes use of fixed-size cells, consisting of a 5-octet header and a 48-octet information field. There are several advantages to the use of small, fixed-size cells. First, the use of small cells may reduce queuing delay for a high-priority cell, because it waits less if it arrives slightly behind a lower-priority cell that has gained access to a resource (e.g., the transmitter). Second, it appears that fixed-size cells can be switched more efficiently, which is important for the very high data rates of ATM [PARE88]. With fixed-size cells, it is easier to implement the switching mechanism in hardware.

Header Format

Figure 11.6a shows the cell header format at the user–network interface. Figure 11.6b shows the cell header format internal to the network.

The **generic flow control (GFC)** field does not appear in the cell header internal to the network, but only at the user–network interface. Hence, it can be used for control of cell flow only at the local user–network interface. The field could be used

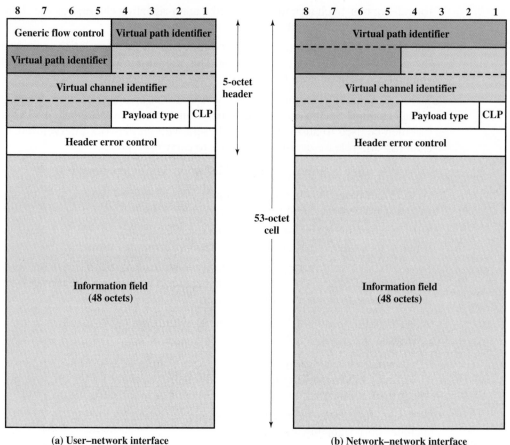

(a) User–network interface   (b) Network–network interface

Figure 11.6   ATM Cell Format

to assist the customer in controlling the flow of traffic for different qualities of service. In any case, the GFC mechanism is used to alleviate short-term overload conditions in the network.

I.150 lists as a requirement for the GFC mechanism that all terminals be able to get access to their assured capacities. This includes all constant-bit-rate (CBR) terminals as well as the variable-bit-rate (VBR) terminals that have an element of guaranteed capacity (CBR and VBR are explained in Section 11.6). The current GFC mechanism is described in a subsequent subsection.

The **virtual path identifier (VPI)** constitutes a routing field for the network. It is 8 bits at the user–network interface and 12 bits at the network–network interface. The latter allows support for an expanded number of VPCs internal to the network, to include those supporting subscribers and those required for network management. The **virtual channel identifier (VCI)** is used for routing to and from the end user.

The **payload type (PT)** field indicates the type of information in the information field. Table 11.2 shows the interpretation of the PT bits. A value of 0 in the first bit indicates user information (i.e., information from the next higher layer). In this

Table 11.2 Payload Type (PT) Field Coding

PT Coding	Interpretation		
0 0 0	User data cell,	congestion not experienced,	SDU-type = 0
0 0 1	User data cell,	congestion not experienced,	SDU-type = 1
0 1 0	User data cell,	congestion experienced,	SDU-type = 0
0 1 1	User data cell,	congestion experienced,	SDU-type = 1
1 0 0	OAM segment associated cell		
1 0 1	OAM end-to-end associated cell		
1 1 0	Resource management cell		
1 1 1	Reserved for future function		

SDU = Service Data Unit
OAM = Operations, Administration, and Maintenance

case, the second bit indicates whether congestion has been experienced; the third bit, known as the Service Data Unit (SDU)[1] type bit, is a one-bit field that can be used to discriminate two types of ATM SDUs associated with a connection. The term *SDU* refers to the 48-octet payload of the cell. A value of 1 in the first bit of the Payload Type field indicates that this cell carries network management or maintenance information. This indication allows the insertion of network-management cells onto a user's VCC without impacting the user's data. Thus, the PT field can provide inband control information.

The **Cell Loss Priority (CLP)** bit is used to provide guidance to the network in the event of congestion. A value of 0 indicates a cell of relatively higher priority, which should not be discarded unless no other alternative is available. A value of 1 indicates that this cell is subject to discard within the network. The user might employ this field so that extra cells (beyond the negotiated rate) may be inserted into the network, with a CLP of 1, and delivered to the destination if the network is not congested. The network may set this field to 1 for any data cell that is in violation of an agreement concerning traffic parameters between the user and the network. In this case, the switch that does the setting realizes that the cell exceeds the agreed traffic parameters but that the switch is capable of handling the cell. At a later point in the network, if congestion is encountered, this cell has been marked for discard in preference to cells that fall within agreed traffic limits.

The **header error control (HEC)** field is used for both error control and synchronization, as explained subsequently.

Generic Flow Control

I.150 specifies the use of the GFC field to control traffic flow at the user–network interface (UNI) in order to alleviate short-term overload conditions. The actual flow control mechanism is defined in I.361. GFC flow control is part of a proposed

---

[1]This is the term used in ATM Forum documents. In ITU-T documents, this bit is referred to as the ATM-user-to-ATM-user (AAU) indication bit. The meaning is the same.

controlled cell transfer (CCT) capability intended to meet the requirements of non-ATM LANs connected to a wide area ATM network [LUIN97]. In particular, CCT is intended to provide good service for high-volume bursty traffic with variable-length messages. In the remainder of this subsection, we examine the GFC mechanism, as so far standardized.

When the equipment at the UNI is configured to support the GFC mechanism, two sets of procedures are used: uncontrolled transmission and controlled transmission. In essence, every connection is identified as either subject to flow control or not. Of those subject to flow control, there may be one group of controlled connections (Group A) that is the default, or controlled traffic may be classified into two groups of controlled connections (Group A and Group B); these are known, respectively, as the one-queue and two-queue models. Flow control is exercised in the direction from the subscriber to the network by the network side.

First, we consider the operation of the GFC mechanism when there is only one group of controlled connections. The controlled equipment, called terminal equipment (TE), initializes two variables: TRANSMIT is a flag initialized to SET (1), and GO_CNTR, which is a credit counter, is initialized to 0. A third variable, GO_VALUE, is either initialized to 1 or set to some larger value at configuration time. The rules for transmission by the controlled device are as follows:

1. If TRANSMIT = 1, cells on uncontrolled connections may be sent at any time. If TRANSMIT = 0, no cells may be sent on either controlled or uncontrolled connections.

2. If a HALT signal is received from the controlling equipment, TRANSMIT is set to 0 and remains at zero until a NO_HALT signal is received, at which time TRANSMIT is set to 1.

3. If TRANSMIT = 1 and there is no cell to transmit on any uncontrolled connections, then
   - —If GO_CNTR > 0, then the TE may send a cell on a controlled connection. The TE marks that cell as a cell on a controlled connection and decrements GO_CNTR.
   - —If GO_CNTR = 0, then the TE may not send a cell on a controlled connection.

4. The TE sets GO_CNTR to GO_VALUE upon receiving a SET signal; a null signal has no effect on GO_CNTR.

The HALT signal is used logically to limit the effective ATM data rate and should be cyclic. For example, to reduce the data rate over a link by half, the HALT command is issued by the controlling equipment so as to be in effect 50% of the time. This is done in a predictable, regular pattern over the lifetime of the physical connection.

For the two-queue model, there are two counters, each with a current counter value and an initialization value: GO_CNTR_A, GO_VALUE_A, GO_CNTR_B, and GO_VALUE_B. This enables the network to control two separate groups of connections.

Table 11.3 summarizes the rules for setting GFC bits.

Table 11.3 Generic Flow Control (GFC) Field Coding

	Uncontrolled	Controlling → Controlled		Controlled → Controlling	
		1-Queue Model	**2-Queue Model**	**1-Queue Model**	**2-Queue Model**
First bit	0	HALT(1)/ NO_HALT(0)	HALT(1)/ NO_HALT(0)	0	0
Second bit	0	SET(1)/ NULL(0)	SET(1)/ NULL(0) for Group A	cell belongs to controlled(1)/ uncontrolled(0)	cell belongs to Group A(1)/ or not (0)
Third bit	0	0	SET(1)/ NULL(0) for Group B	0	cell belongs to Group B(1)/ or not (0)
Fourth bit	0	0	0	equipment is uncontrolled(0)/ controlled(1)	equipment is uncontrolled(0)/ controlled(1)

Header Error Control

Each ATM cell includes an 8-bit HEC field that is calculated based on the remaining 32 bits of the header. The polynomial used to generate the code is $X^8 + X^2 + X + 1$. In most existing protocols that include an error control field, such as HDLC, the data that serve as input to the error code calculation are in general much longer than the size of the resulting error code. This allows for error detection. In the case of ATM, the input to the calculation is only 32 bits, compared to 8 bits for the code. The fact that the input is relatively short allows the code to be used not only for error detection but also, in some cases, for actual error correction. This is because there is sufficient redundancy in the code to recover from certain error patterns.

Figure 11.7 depicts the operation of the HEC algorithm at the receiver. At initialization, the receiver's error correction algorithm is in the default mode for single-bit error correction. As each cell is received, the HEC calculation and comparison is performed. As long as no errors are detected, the receiver remains in error correction mode. When an error is detected, the receiver will correct the error

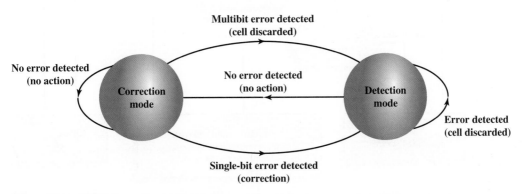

Figure 11.7 HEC Operation at Receiver

if it is a single-bit error or will detect that a multibit error has occurred. In either case, the receiver now moves to detection mode. In this mode, no attempt is made to correct errors. The reason for this change is a recognition that a noise burst or other event might cause a sequence of errors, a condition for which the HEC is insufficient for error correction. The receiver remains in detection mode as long as errored cells are received. When a header is examined and found not to be in error, the receiver switches back to correction mode. The flowchart of Figure 11.8 shows the consequence of errors in the cell header.

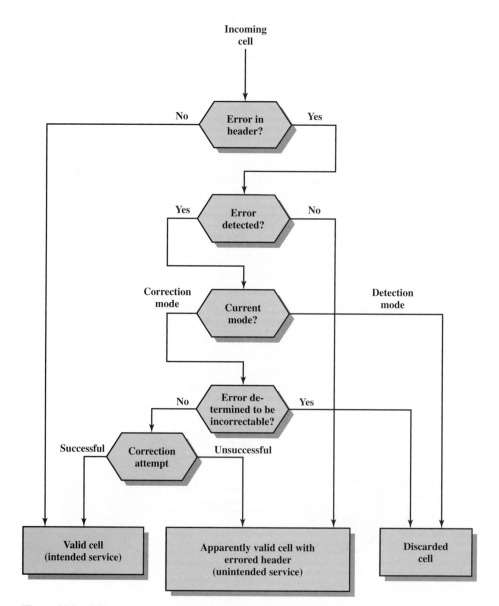

Figure 11.8 Effect of Error in Cell Header

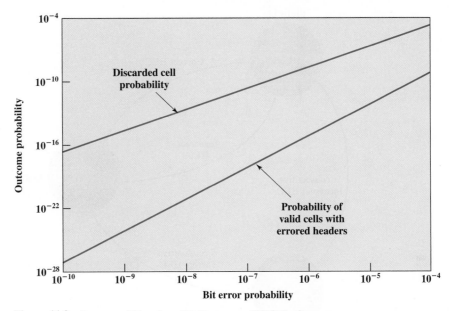

Figure 11.9 Impact of Random Bit Errors on HEC Performance

The error-protection function provides both recovery from single-bit header errors and a low probability of the delivery of cells with errored headers under bursty error conditions. The error characteristics of fiber-based transmission systems appear to be a mix of single-bit errors and relatively large burst errors. For some transmission systems, the error correction capability, which is more time-consuming, might not be invoked.

Figure 11.9, based on one in ITU-T I.432, indicates how random bit errors impact the probability of occurrence of discarded cells and valid cells with errored headers when HEC is employed.

11.5 TRANSMISSION OF ATM CELLS

I.432 specifies that ATM cells may be transmitted at one of several data rates: 622.08 Mbps, 155.52 Mbps, 51.84 Mbps, or 25.6 Mbps. We need to specify the transmission structure that will be used to carry this payload. Two approaches are defined in I.432: a cell-based physical layer and an SDH-based physical layer.[2] We examine each of these approaches in turn.

Cell-Based Physical Layer

For the cell-based physical layer, no framing is imposed. The interface structure consists of a continuous stream of 53-octet cells. Because there is no external frame imposed in the cell-based approach, some form of synchronization is needed.

---

[2]The SDH-based approach is not defined for 25.6 Mbps.

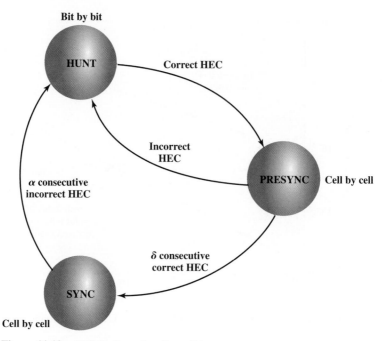

Figure 11.10   Cell Delineation State Diagram

Synchronization is achieved on the basis of the HEC field in the cell header. The procedure is as follows (Figure 11.10):

1. In the HUNT state, a cell delineation algorithm is performed bit by bit to determine if the HEC coding law is observed (i.e., match between received HEC and calculated HEC). Once a match is achieved, it is assumed that one header has been found, and the method enters the PRESYNC state.

2. In the PRESYNC state, a cell structure is now assumed. The cell delineation algorithm is performed cell by cell until the encoding law has been confirmed consecutively δ times.

3. In the SYNC state, the HEC is used for error detection and correction (see Figure 11.7). Cell delineation is assumed to be lost if the HEC coding law is recognized consecutively as incorrect α times.

The values of α and δ are design parameters. Greater values of δ result in longer delays in establishing synchronization but in greater robustness against false delineation. Greater values of α result in longer delays in recognizing a misalignment but in greater robustness against false misalignment. Figures 11.11 and 11.12, based on I.432, show the impact of random bit errors on cell delineation performance for various values of α and δ. The first figure shows the average amount of time that the receiver will maintain synchronization in the face of errors, with α as a parameter. The second figure shows the average amount of time to acquire synchronization as a function of error rate, with δ as a parameter.

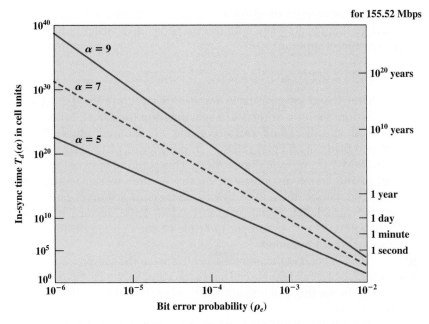

Figure 11.11 Impact of Random Bit Errors on Cell-Delineation Performance

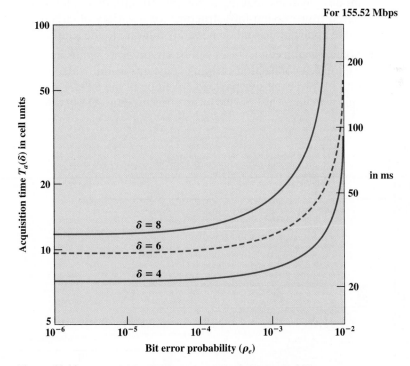

Figure 11.12 Acquisition Time versus Bit-Error Probability

The advantage of using a cell-based transmission scheme is the simplified interface that results when both transmission and transfer mode functions are based on a common structure.

SDH-Based Physical Layer

The SDH-based physical layer imposes a structure on the ATM cell stream. In this section, we look at the I.432 specification for 155.52 Mbps; similar structures are used at other data rates. For the SDH-based physical layer, framing is imposed using the STM-1 (STS-3) frame. Figure 11.13 shows the payload portion of an STM-1 frame (see Figure 8.11). This payload may be offset from the beginning of the frame, as indicated by the pointer in the section overhead of the frame. As can be seen, the payload consists of a 9-octet path overhead portion and the remainder, which contains ATM cells. Because the payload capacity (2340 octets) is not an integer multiple of the cell length (53 octets), a cell may cross a payload boundary.

The H4 octet in the path overhead is set at the sending side to indicate the next occurrence of a cell boundary. That is, the value in the H4 field indicates the number of octets to the first cell boundary following the H4 octet. The permissible range of values is 0 to 52.

The advantages of the SDH-based approach include:

- It can be used to carry either ATM-based or STM-based (synchronous transfer mode) payloads, making it possible to initially deploy a high-capacity fiber-based transmission infrastructure for a variety of circuit-switched and dedicated applications and then readily migrate to the support of ATM.

- Some specific connections can be circuit switched using an SDH channel. For example, a connection carrying constant-bit-rate video traffic can be mapped into its own exclusive payload envelope of the STM-1 signal, which can be circuit switched. This may be more efficient than ATM switching.

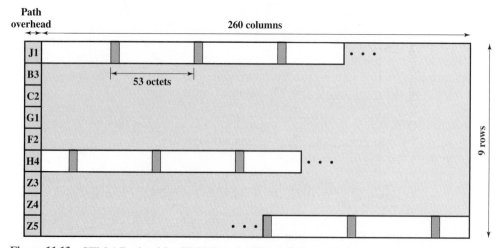

Figure 11.13   STM-1 Payload for SDH-Based ATM Cell Transmission

- Using SDH synchronous multiplexing techniques, several ATM streams can be combined to build interfaces with higher bit rates than those supported by the ATM layer at a particular site. For example, four separate ATM streams, each with a bit rate of 155 Mbps (STM-1), can be combined to build a 622-Mbps (STM-4) interface. This arrangement may be more cost effective than one using a single 622-Mbps ATM stream.

11.6 ATM SERVICE CATEGORIES

An ATM network is designed to be able to transfer many different types of traffic simultaneously, including real-time flows such as voice, video, and bursty TCP flows. Although each such traffic flow is handled as a stream of 53-octet cells traveling through a virtual channel, the way in which each data flow is handled within the network depends on the characteristics of the traffic flow and the requirements of the application. For example, real-time video traffic must be delivered within minimum variation in delay.

We examine the way in which an ATM network handles different types of traffic flows in Chapter 13. In this section, we summarize ATM service categories, which are used by an end system to identify the type of service required. The following service categories have been defined by the ATM Forum:

- **Real-Time Service**
  - —Constant bit rate (CBR)
  - —Real-time variable bit rate (rt-VBR)
- **Non-Real-Time Service**
  - —Non-real-time variable bit rate (nrt-VBR)
  - —Available bit rate (ABR)
  - —Unspecified bit rate (UBR)
  - —Guaranteed frame rate (GFR)

Real-Time Services

The most important distinction among applications concerns the amount of delay and the variability of delay, referred to as jitter, that the application can tolerate. Real-time applications typically involve a flow of information to a user that is intended to reproduce that flow at a source. For example, a user expects a flow of audio or video information to be presented in a continuous, smooth fashion. A lack of continuity or excessive loss results in significant loss of quality. Applications that involve interaction between people have tight constraints on delay. Typically, any delay above a few hundred milliseconds becomes noticeable and annoying. Accordingly, the demands in the ATM network for switching and delivery of real-time data are high.

CONSTANT BIT RATE (CBR) The CBR service is perhaps the simplest service to define. It is used by applications that require a fixed data rate that is continuously available during the connection lifetime and a relatively tight upper bound on transfer delay. CBR is commonly used for uncompressed audio and video information. Example of CBR applications include

- Videoconferencing
- Interactive audio (e.g., telephony)
- Audio/video distribution (e.g., television, distance learning, pay-per-view)
- Audio/video retrieval (e.g., video-on-demand, audio library)

REAL-TIME VARIABLE BIT RATE (RT-VBR) The rt-VBR category is intended for time-sensitive applications; that is, those requiring tightly constrained delay and delay variation. The principal difference between applications appropriate for rt-VBR and those appropriate for CBR is that rt-VBR applications transmit at a rate that varies with time. Equivalently, an rt-VBR source can be characterized as somewhat bursty. For example, the standard approach to video compression results in a sequence of image frames of varying sizes. Because real-time video requires a uniform frame transmission rate, the actual data rate varies.

The rt-VBR service allows the network more flexibility than CBR. The network is able to statistically multiplex a number of connections over the same dedicated capacity and still provide the required service to each connection.

Non-Real-Time Services

Non-real-time services are intended for applications that have bursty traffic characteristics and do not have tight constraints on delay and delay variation. Accordingly, the network has greater flexibility in handling such traffic flows and can make greater use of statistical multiplexing to increase network efficiency.

NON-REAL-TIME VARIABLE BIT RATE-(NRT-VBR) For some non-real-time applications, it is possible to characterize the expected traffic flow so that the network can provide substantially improved QoS in the areas of loss and delay. Such applications can use the nrt-VBR service. With this service, the end system specifies a peak cell rate, a sustainable or average cell rate, and a measure of how bursty or clumped the cells may be. With this information, the network can allocate resources to provide relatively low delay and minimal cell loss.

The nrt-VBR service can be used for data transfers that have critical response-time requirements. Examples include airline reservations, banking transactions, and process monitoring.

UNSPECIFIED BIT RATE (UBR) At any given time, a certain amount of the capacity of an ATM network is consumed in carrying CBR and the two types of VBR traffic. Additional capacity is available for one or both of the following reasons: (1) Not all of the total resources have been committed to CBR and VBR traffic, and (2) the bursty nature of VBR traffic means that at some times less than the committed capacity is being used. All of this unused capacity could be made available for the UBR service. This service is suitable for applications that can tolerate variable delays and some cell losses, which is typically true of TCP-based traffic. With UBR, cells are forwarded on a first-in-first-out (FIFO) basis using the capacity not consumed by other services; both delays and variable losses are possible. No initial commitment is made to a UBR source and no feedback concerning congestion is provided; this is referred to as a **best-effort service**. Examples of UBR applications include:

- Text/data/image transfer, messaging, distribution, retrieval
- Remote terminal (e.g., telecommuting)

AVAILABLE BIT RATE (ABR) Bursty applications that use a reliable end-to-end protocol such as TCP can detect congestion in a network by means of increased round-trip delays and packet discarding. This is discussed in Chapter 22. However, TCP has no mechanism for causing the resources within the network to be shared fairly among many TCP connections. Further, TCP does not minimize congestion as efficiently as is possible using explicit information from congested nodes within the network.

To improve the service provided to bursty sources that would otherwise use UBR, the ABR service has been defined. An application using ABR specifies a peak cell rate (PCR) that it will use and a minimum cell rate (MCR) that it requires. The network allocates resources so that all ABR applications receive at least their MCR capacity. Any unused capacity is then shared in a fair and controlled fashion among all ABR sources. The ABR mechanism uses explicit feedback to sources to assure that capacity is fairly allocated. Any capacity not used by ABR sources remains available for UBR traffic.

An example of an application using ABR is LAN interconnection. In this case, the end systems attached to the ATM network are routers.

Figure 11.14 suggests how a network allocates resources during a steady-state period of time (no additions or deletions of virtual channels).

GUARANTEED FRAME RATE (GFR) The most recent addition to the set of ATM service categories is GFR, which is designed specifically to support IP backbone subnetworks. GFR provides better service than UBR for frame-based traffic, including IP and Ethernet. A major goal of GFR is to optimize the handling of frame-based traffic that passes from a LAN through a router onto an ATM backbone network. Such ATM networks are increasingly being used in large enterprise, carrier, and Internet service provider networks to consolidate and extend IP services over the wide area. While ABR is also an ATM service meant to provide a greater measure of guaranteed packet performance over ATM backbones, ABR is relatively difficult to implement between routers over an ATM network.

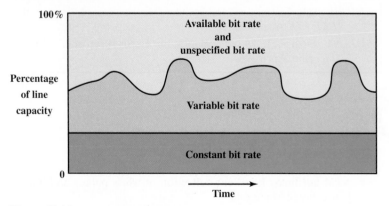

Figure 11.14   ATM Bit Rate Services

With the increased emphasis on using ATM to support IP-based traffic, especially traffic that originates on Ethernet LANs, GFR may offer the most attractive alternative for providing ATM service.

One of the techniques used by GFR to provide improved performance compared to UBR is to require that network elements be aware of frame or packet boundaries. Thus, when congestion requires the discard of cells, network elements must discard all of the cells that comprise a single frame. GFR also allows a user to reserve capacity for each GFR VC. The user is guaranteed that this minimum capacity will be supported. Additional frames may be transmitted if the network is not congested.

11.7 RECOMMENDED READING AND WEB SITE

[IBM95] provides a detailed treatment of ATM technology. [MCDY99] and [BLAC99] also provide good coverage of ATM. The virtual path/virtual channel approach of ATM is examined in [SATO90], [SATO91], and [BURG91].

[GARR96] provides a rationale for the ATM service categories and discuss the traffic management implications of each. [ARMI93] and [SUZU94] discuss AAL and compare types 3/4 and 5.

ARMI93   Armitage, G., and Adams, K. "Packet Reassembly During Cell Loss." *IEEE Network*, September 1993.

BLAC99   Black, U. *ATM Volume I: Foundation for Broadband Networks*. Upper Saddle River, NJ: Prentice Hall, 1999.

BURG91   Burg, J., and Dorman, D. "Broadband ISDN Resource Management: The Role of Virtual Paths." *IEEE Communications Magazine*, September 1991.

GARR96   Garrett, M. "A Service Architecture for ATM: From Applications to Scheduling." *IEEE Network*, May/June 1996.

IBM95   IBM International Technical Support Organization. *Asynchronous Transfer Mode (ATM) Technical Overview*. IBM Redbook SG24-4625-00, 1995, www.redbooks.ibm.com

MCDY99   McDysan, D., and Spohn, D. *ATM: Theory and Application*. New York: McGraw-Hill, 1999.

SATO90   Sato, K.; Ohta, S.; and Tokizawa, I. "Broad-band ATM Network Architecture Based on Virtual Paths." *IEEE Transactions on Communications*, August 1990.

SATO91   Sato, K.; Ueda, H.; and Yoshikai, M. "The Role of Virtual Path Crossconnection." *IEEE LTS*, August 1991.

SUZU94   Suzuki, T. "ATM Adaptation Layer Protocol." *IEEE Communications Magazine*, April 1994.

Recommended Web site:

- **ATM hot links:** Excellent collection of white papers and links maintained by the University of Minnesota.

11.8 KEY TERMS, REVIEW QUESTIONS, AND PROBLEMS

Key Terms

asynchronous transfer mode (ATM)	header error control (HEC)	virtual channel
ATM adaptation layer (AAL)	non-real-time variable bit rate (nrt-VBR)	virtual channel connection (VCC)
available bit rate (ABR)	payload type (PT)	virtual channel identifier (VCI)
cell	real-time variable bit rate (rt-VBR)	virtual path
cell loss priority (CLP)	service data unit (SDU)	virtual path connection (VPC)
constant bit rate (CBR)	unspecified bit rate (UBR)	virtual path identifier (VPI)
generic flow control (GFC)	variable bit rate (VBR)	
guaranteed frame rate (GFR)		

Review Questions

11.1 How does ATM differ from frame relay?

11.2 What are the relative advantages and disadvantages of ATM compared to frame relay?

11.3 What is the difference between a virtual channel and a virtual path?

11.4 What are the advantages of the use of virtual paths?

11.5 What are the characteristics of a virtual channel connection?

11.6 What are the characteristics of a virtual path connection?

11.7 List and briefly explain the fields in an ATM cell.

11.8 Briefly explain two methods for transmitting ATM cells.

11.9 List and briefly define the ATM service categories.

Problems

11.1 List all 16 possible values of the GFC field and the interpretation of each value (some values are illegal).

11.2 Although ATM does not include any end-to-end error detection and control functions on the user data, it is provided with a HEC field to detect and correct header errors. Let us consider the value of this feature. Suppose that the bit error rate of the transmission system is B. If errors are uniformly distributed, then the probability of an error in the header is

$$\frac{h}{h + i} \times B$$

and the probability of error in the data field is

$$\frac{i}{h + i} \times B$$

where h is the number of bits in the header and i is the number of bits in the data field.

a. Suppose that errors in the header are not detected and not corrected. In that case, a header error may result in a misrouting of the cell to the wrong destination; therefore, i bits will arrive at an incorrect destination, and i bits will not arrive at the correct destination. What is the overall bit error rate $B1$? Find an expression for the multiplication effect on the bit error rate: $M1 = B1/B$.

  b. Now suppose that header errors are detected but not corrected. In that case, i bits will not arrive at the correct destination. What is the overall bit error rate $B2$? Find an expression for the multiplication effect on the bit error rate: $M2 = B2/B$.

  c. Now suppose that header errors are detected and corrected. What is the overall bit error rate $B3$? Find an expression for the multiplication effect on the bit error rate: $M3 = B3/B$.

  d. Plot $M1$, $M2$, and $M3$ as a function of header length, for $i = 48 \times 8 = 384$ bits. Comment on the results.

11.3 One key design decision for ATM was whether to use fixed or variable length cells. Let us consider this decision from the point of view of efficiency. We can define transmission efficiency as

$$N = \frac{\text{Number of information octets}}{\text{Number of information octets} + \text{Number of overhead octets}}$$

  a. Consider the use of fixed-length packets. In this case the overhead consists of the header octets. Define

  L = Data field size of the cell in octets

  H = Header size of the cell in octets

  X = Number of information octets to be transmitted as a single message

  Derive an expression for N. *Hint:* The expression will need to use the operator $\lceil \cdot \rceil$, where $\lceil Y \rceil$ = the smallest integer greater than or equal to Y.

  b. If cells have variable length, then overhead is determined by the header, plus the flags to delimit the cells or an additional length field in the header. Let Hv = additional overhead octets required to enable the use of variable-length cells. Derive an expression for N in terms of X, H, and Hv.

  c. Let $L = 48$, $H = 5$, and $Hv = 2$. Plot N versus message size for fixed- and variable-length cells. Comment on the results.

11.4 Another key design decision for ATM is the size of the data field for fixed-size cells. Let us consider this decision from the point of view of efficiency and delay.

  a. Assume that an extended transmission takes place, so that all cells are completely filled. Derive an expression for the efficiency N as a function of H and L.

  b. Packetization delay is the delay introduced into a transmission stream by the need to buffer bits until an entire packet is filled before transmission. Derive an expression for this delay as a function of L and the data rate R of the source.

  c. Common data rates for voice coding are 32 kbps and 64 kbps. Plot packetization delay as a function of L for these two data rates; use a left-hand y axis with a maximum value of 2 ms. On the same graph, plot transmission efficiency as a function of L; use a right-hand y-axis with a maximum value of 100%. Comment on the results.

11.5 Consider compressed video transmission in an ATM network. Suppose standard ATM cells must be transmitted through 5 switches. The data rate is 43 Mbps.

  a. What is the transmission time for one cell through one switch?

  b. Each switch may be transmitting a cell from other traffic all of which we assume to have lower (non-preemptive for the cell) priority. If the switch is busy transmitting a cell, our cell has to wait until the other cell completes transmission. If the switch is free our cell is transmitted immediately. What is the maximum time from when a typical video cell arrives at the first switch (and possibly waits) until it is finished being transmitted by the fifth and last one? Assume that you can ignore propagation time, switching time, and everything else but the transmission time and the time spent waiting for another cell to clear a switch.

  c. Now suppose we know that each switch is utilized 60% of the time with the other low- priority traffic. By this we mean that with probability 0.6 when we look at a switch it is busy. Suppose that if there is a cell being transmitted by a switch, the average delay spent waiting for a cell to finish transmission is one-half a cell transmission time. What is the average time from the input of the first switch to clearing the fifth?

d. However, the measure of most interest is not delay but jitter, which is the variability in the delay. Use parts (b) and (c) to calculate the maximum and average variability, respectively, in the delay.

In all cases assume that the various random events are independent of one another; for example, we ignore the burstiness typical of such traffic.

11.6 In order to support IP service over an ATM network, IP datagrams must first be segmented into a number of ATM cells before sending them over the ATM network. As ATM does not provide cell loss recovery, the loss of any of these cells will result in the loss of the entire IP packet. Given:

$$PC = \text{cell loss rate in the ATM network}$$

$$n = \text{number of cells required to transmit a single IP datagram}$$

$$PP = \text{IP-packet loss rate}$$

a. Derive an expression for PP, and comment on the resulting expression.

b. What ATM service would you use to get the best possible performance?

Note: The following problems deal with AAL, covered in Appendix I

11.7 Suppose that AAL 3/4 is being used and that the receiver is in an idle state (no incoming cells). Then, a block of user data is transmitted as a sequence of SAR-PDUs.

a. Suppose that the BOM SAR-PDU is lost. What happens at the receiving end?

b. Suppose that one of the COM SAR-PDUs is lost. What happens at the receiving end?

c. Suppose that 16 consecutive COM SAR-PDUs are lost. What happens at the receiving end?

d. Suppose that a multiple of 16 consecutive COM SAR-PDUs are lost. What happens at the receiving end?

11.8 Again using AAL 3/4, suppose that the receiver is in an idle state and that two blocks of user data are transmitted as two separate sequences of SAR-PDUs.

a. Suppose that the EOM SAR-PDU of the first sequence is lost. What happens at the receiving end?

b. Suppose that the EOM SAR-PDU of the first sequence and the BOM SAR-PDU of the second sequence are both lost. What happens at the receiving end?

11.9 Suppose that AAL 5 is being used and that the receiver is in an idle state (no incoming cells). Then, a block of user data is transmitted as a sequence of SAR-PDUs.

a. Suppose that a single-bit error in one of the SAR-PDUs occurs. What happens at the receiving end?

b. Suppose that one of the cells with SDU type bit = 0 is lost. What happens at the receiving end?

c. Suppose that one of the cells with SDU type bit = 1 is lost. What happens at the receiving end?

ROUTING IN SWITCHED DATA NETWORKS

"I tell you," went on Syme with passion, *"that every time a train comes in I feel that it has broken past batteries of besiegers, and that man has won a battle against chaos. You say contemptuously that when one has left Sloane Square one must come to Victoria. I say that one might do a thousand things instead, and that whenever I really come there I have the sense of hairbreadth escape. And when I hear the guard shout out the word 'Victoria', it is not an unmeaning word. It is to me the cry of a herald announcing conquest. It is to me indeed 'Victoria'; it is the victory of Adam."*

— *The Man Who Was Thursday*, G.K. Chesterton

KEY POINTS

◆ A variety of routing algorithms have been developed for packet-switching, frame relay, and ATM networks, and for the Internet and internetworks. These algorithms share many common principles.

◆ Routing schemes can be categorized based on a number of factors, such as what criterion is used to determine the best route between two nodes, what strategy is used for obtaining information needed to determine route, and whether a distributed or centralized algorithm is used.

◆ The routing function attempts to find the least-cost route through the network, with cost based on number of hops, expected delay, or other metrics. Adaptive routing algorithms typically rely on the exchange of information about traffic conditions among nodes.

A key design issue in switched networks, including packet-switching, frame relay, and ATM networks, and with internets, is that of routing. In general terms, the routing function seeks to design routes through the network for individual pairs of communicating end nodes such that the network is used efficiently.

This chapter begins with a brief overview of issues involved in routing design. Next, we look at the routing function in packet-switching networks and then examine least-cost algorithms that are a central part of routing in switched networks. These topics cover issues that are relevant to routing in internets as well as packet-switching networks.

12.1 ROUTING IN PACKET-SWITCHING NETWORKS

One of the most complex and crucial design aspects of switched data networks is routing. This section surveys key characteristic that can be used to classify routing strategies. The principles described in this section are also applicable to internetwork routing, discussed in Part Five.

Characteristics

The primary function of a packet-switching network is to accept packets from a source station and deliver them to a destination station. To accomplish this, a path or route through the network must be determined; generally, more than one route is possible. Thus, a routing function must be performed. The requirements for this function include the following:

- Correctness
- Simplicity
- Robustness
- Stability
- Fairness
- Optimality
- Efficiency

The first two items on the list, correctness and simplicity, are self-explanatory. Robustness has to do with the ability of the network to deliver packets via some route in the face of localized failures and overloads. Ideally, the network can react to such contingencies without the loss of packets or the breaking of virtual circuits. The designer who seeks robustness must cope with the competing requirement for stability. Techniques that react to changing conditions have an unfortunate tendency to either react too slowly to events or to experience unstable swings from one extreme to another. For example, the network may react to congestion in one area by shifting most of the load to a second area. Now the second area is overloaded and the first is underutilized, causing a second shift. During these shifts, packets may travel in loops through the network.

A trade-off also exists between fairness and optimality. Some performance criteria may give higher priority to the exchange of packets between nearby stations compared to an exchange between distant stations. This policy may maximize average throughput but will appear unfair to the station that primarily needs to communicate with distant stations.

Finally, any routing technique involves some processing overhead at each node and often a transmission overhead as well, both of which impair network efficiency. The penalty of such overhead needs to be less than the benefit accrued based on some reasonable metric, such as increased robustness or fairness.

With these requirements in mind, we are in a position to assess the various design elements that contribute to a routing strategy. Table 12.1 lists these elements. Some of these categories overlap or are dependent on one another. Nevertheless, an examination of this list serves to clarify and organize routing concepts.

PERFORMANCE CRITERIA The selection of a route is generally based on some performance criterion. The simplest criterion is to choose the minimum-hop route (one that passes through the least number of nodes) through the network.[1] This is

---

[1] The term *hop* is used somewhat loosely in the literature. The more common definition, which we use, is that the number of hops along a path from a given source to a given destination is the number of links between network nodes (packet-switching nodes, ATM switches, routers, etc.) that a packet traverses along that path. Sometimes the number of hops is defined to include the link between the source station and the network and the link between the destination station and the network. This latter definition produces a value 2 greater than the definition we use.

Table 12.1   Elements of Routing Techniques for Packet-Switching Networks

Performance Criteria	Network Information Source
Number of hops	None
Cost	Local
Delay	Adjacent node
Throughput	Nodes along route
	All nodes
Decision Time	
Packet (datagram)	**Network Information Update Timing**
Session (virtual circuit)	Continuous
	Periodic
Decision Place	
Each node (distributed)	Major load change
Central node (centralized)	Topology change
Originating node (source)	

an easily measured criterion and should minimize the consumption of network resources. A generalization of the minimum-hop criterion is least-cost routing. In this case, a cost is associated with each link, and, for any pair of attached stations, the route through the network that accumulates the least cost is sought.

> **EXAMPLE 12.1** Figure 12.1 illustrates a network in which the two arrowed lines between a pair of nodes represent a link between these nodes, and the corresponding numbers represent the current link cost in each direction. The shortest path (fewest hops) from node 1 to node 6 is 1-3-6 (cost = 5 + 5 = 10), but the least-cost path is 1-4-5-6 (cost = 1 + 1 + 2 = 4).

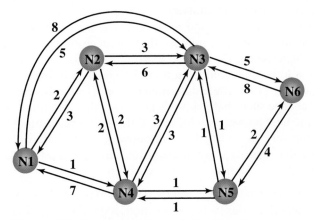

Figure 12.1   Example of Network Configuration

Costs are assigned to links to support one or more design objectives. For example, the cost could be inversely related to the data rate (i.e., the higher the data rate on a link, the lower the assigned cost of the link) or the current queuing delay on the link. In the first case, the least-cost route should provide the highest throughput. In the second case, the least-cost route should minimize delay.

In either the minimum-hop or least-cost approach, the algorithm for determining the optimum route for any pair of stations is relatively straightforward, and the processing time would be about the same for either computation. Because the least-cost criterion is more flexible, this is more common than the minimum-hop criterion.

Several least-cost routing algorithms are in common use. These are described in Section 12.3.

DECISION TIME AND PLACE Routing decisions are made on the basis of some performance criterion. Two key characteristics of the decision are the time and place that the decision is made.

Decision time is determined by whether the routing decision is made on a packet or virtual circuit basis. When the internal operation of the network is datagram, a routing decision is made individually for each packet. For internal virtual circuit operation, a routing decision is made at the time the virtual circuit is established. In the simplest case, all subsequent packets using that virtual circuit follow the same route. In more sophisticated network designs, the network may dynamically change the route assigned to a particular virtual circuit in response to changing conditions (e.g., overload or failure of a portion of the network).

The term *decision place* refers to which node or nodes in the network are responsible for the routing decision. Most common is distributed routing, in which each node has the responsibility of selecting an output link for routing packets as they arrive. For centralized routing, the decision is made by some designated node, such as a network control center. The danger of this latter approach is that the loss of the network control center may block operation of the network. The distributed approach is perhaps more complex but is also more robust. A third alternative, used in some networks, is source routing. In this case, the routing decision is actually made by the source station rather than by a network node and is then communicated to the network. This allows the user to dictate a route through the network that meets criteria local to that user.

The decision time and decision place are independent design variables. For example, in Figure 12.1, suppose that the decision place is each node and that the values depicted are the costs at a given instant in time: The costs may change. If a packet is to be delivered from node 1 to node 6, it might follow the route 1-4-5-6, with each leg of the route determined locally by the transmitting node. Now let the values change such that 1-4-5-6 is no longer the optimum route. In a datagram network, the next packet may follow a different route, again determined by each node along the way. In a virtual circuit network, each node will remember the routing decision that was made when the virtual circuit was established, and simply pass on the packets without making a new decision.

NETWORK INFORMATION SOURCE AND UPDATE TIMING Most routing strategies require that decisions be based on knowledge of the topology of the network, traffic load, and link cost. Surprisingly, some strategies use no such information and yet manage to get packets through; flooding and some random strategies (discussed later) are in this category.

With distributed routing, in which the routing decision is made by each node, the individual node may make use of only local information, such as the cost of each outgoing link. Each node might also collect information from adjacent (directly connected) nodes, such as the amount of congestion experienced at that node. Finally, there are algorithms in common use that allow the node to gain information from all nodes on any potential route of interest. In the case of centralized routing, the central node typically makes use of information obtained from all nodes.

A related concept is that of information update timing, which is a function of both the information source and the routing strategy. Clearly, if no information is used (as in flooding), there is no information to update. If only local information is used, the update is essentially continuous. That is, an individual node always knows its local conditions. For all other information source categories (adjacent nodes, all nodes), update timing depends on the routing strategy. For a fixed strategy, the information is never updated. For an adaptive strategy, information is updated from time to time to enable the routing decision to adapt to changing conditions.

As you might expect, the more information available, and the more frequently it is updated, the more likely the network is to make good routing decisions. On the other hand, the transmission of that information consumes network resources.

Routing Strategies

A large number of routing strategies have evolved for dealing with the routing requirements of packet-switching networks. Many of these strategies are also applied to internetwork routing, which we cover in Part Five. In this section, we survey four key strategies: fixed, flooding, random, and adaptive.

FIXED ROUTING   For fixed routing, a single, permanent route is configured for each source–destination pair of nodes in the network. Either of the least-cost routing algorithms described in Section 12.3 could be used. The routes are fixed, or at least only change when there is a change in the topology of the network. Thus, the link costs used in designing routes cannot be based on any dynamic variable such as traffic. They could, however, be based on expected traffic or capacity.

> **EXAMPLE 12.2** Figure 12.2 suggests how fixed routing might be implemented for the network in Figure 12.1, with the associated link costs shown in Figure 12.1. A central routing matrix is created, to be stored perhaps at a network control center. The matrix shows, for each source–destination pair of nodes, the identity of the next node on the route.

Note that it is not necessary to store the complete route for each possible pair of nodes. Rather, it is sufficient to know, for each pair of nodes, the identity of the first node on the route. To see this, suppose that the least-cost route from X to Y begins with the X-A link. Call the remainder of the route R_1; this is the part from A to Y.

Central routing directory

From node

		1	2	3	4	5	6
	1	—	1	5	2	4	5
	2	2	—	5	2	4	5
To	3	4	3	—	5	3	5
node	4	4	4	5	—	4	5
	5	4	4	5	5	—	5
	6	4	4	5	5	6	—

Node 1 directory

Destination	Next node
2	2
3	4
4	4
5	4
6	4

Node 2 directory

Destination	Next node
1	1
3	3
4	4
5	4
6	4

Node 3 directory

Destination	Next node
1	5
2	5
4	5
5	5
6	5

Node 4 directory

Destination	Next node
1	2
2	2
3	5
5	5
6	5

Node 5 directory

Destination	Next node
1	4
2	4
3	3
4	4
6	6

Node 6 directory

Destination	Next node
1	5
2	5
3	5
4	5
5	5

Figure 12.2 Fixed Routing (using Figure 12.1)

Define R_2 as the least-cost route from A to Y. Now, if the cost of R_1 is greater than that of R_2, then the X-Y route can be improved by using R_2 instead. If the cost of R_1 is less than R_2, then R_2 is not the least-cost route from A to Y. Therefore, $R_1 = R_2$. Thus, at each point along a route, it is only necessary to know the identity of the next node, not the entire route. In our example, the route from node 1 to node 6 begins by going through node 4. Again consulting the matrix, the route from node 4 to node 6 goes through node 5. Finally, the route from node 5 to node 6 is a direct link to node 6. Thus, the complete route from node 1 to node 6 is 1-4-5-6.

From this overall matrix, routing tables can be developed and stored at each node. From the reasoning in the preceding paragraph, it follows that each node need only store a single column of the routing directory. The node's directory shows the next node to take for each destination.

With fixed routing, there is no difference between routing for datagrams and virtual circuits. All packets from a given source to a given destination follow the same route. The advantage of fixed routing is its simplicity, and it should work well in a reliable network with a stable load. Its disadvantage is its lack of flexibility. It does not react to network congestion or failures.

A refinement to fixed routing that would accommodate link and node outages would be to supply the nodes with an alternate next node for each destination. For example, the alternate next nodes in the node 1 directory might be 4, 3, 2, 3, 3.

FLOODING   Another simple routing technique is flooding. This technique requires no network information whatsoever and works as follows. A packet is sent by a source node to every one of its neighbors. At each node, an incoming packet is retransmitted on all outgoing links except for the link on which it arrived. For example, if node 1 in Figure 12.1 has a packet to send to node 6, it sends a copy of that packet (with a destination address of 6) to nodes 2, 3, and 4. Node 2 will send a copy to nodes 3 and 4. Node 4 will send a copy to nodes 2, 3, and 5. And so it goes. Eventually, a number of copies of the packet will arrive at node 6. The packet must have some unique identifier (e.g., source node and sequence number, or virtual circuit number and sequence number) so that node 6 knows to discard all but the first copy.

Unless something is done to stop the incessant retransmission of packets, the number of packets in circulation just from a single source packet grows without bound. One way to prevent this is for each node to remember the identity of those packets it has already retransmitted. When duplicate copies of the packet arrive, they are discarded. A simpler technique is to include a hop count field with each packet. The count can originally be set to some maximum value, such as the diameter (length of the longest minimum-hop path through the network)[2] of the network. Each time a node passes on a packet, it decrements the count by one. When the count reaches zero, the packet is discarded.

EXAMPLE 12.3   An example of the latter tactic is shown in Figure 12.3. The label on each packet in the figure indicates the current value of the hop count field in that packet. A packet is to be sent from node 1 to node 6 and is assigned a hop count of 3. On the first hop, three copies of the packet are created, and the hop count is decrement to 2. For the second hop of all these copies, a total of nine copies are created. One of these copies reaches node 6, which recognizes that it is the intended destination and does not retransmit. However, the other nodes generate a total of 22 new copies for their third and final hop. Each packet now has a hop count of 1. Note that if a node is not keeping track of packet identifier, it may generate multiple copies at this third stage. All packets received from the third hop are discarded, because the hop count is exhausted. In all, node 6 has received four additional copies of the packet.

---

[2]For each pair of end systems attached to the network, there is a minimum-hop path. The length of the longest such minimum-hop path is the diameter of the network.

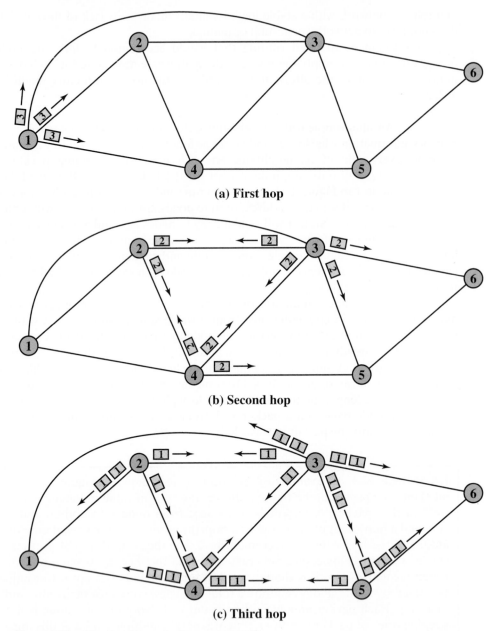

Figure 12.3 Flooding Example (hop count = 3)

The flooding technique has three remarkable properties:

- All possible routes between source and destination are tried. Thus, no matter what link or node outages have occurred, a packet will always get through if at least one path between source and destination exists.

- Because all routes are tried, at least one copy of the packet to arrive at the destination will have used a minimum-hop route.
- All nodes that are directly or indirectly connected to the source node are visited.

Because of the first property, the flooding technique is highly robust and could be used to send emergency messages. An example application is a military network that is subject to extensive damage. Because of the second property, flooding might be used initially to set up the route for a virtual circuit. The third property suggests that flooding can be useful for the dissemination of important information to all nodes; we will see that it is used in some schemes to disseminate routing information.

The principal disadvantage of flooding is the high traffic load that it generates, which is directly proportional to the connectivity of the network. Another disadvantage is that every node sees the routing data, which may create a security concern.

RANDOM ROUTING Random routing has the simplicity and robustness of flooding with far less traffic load. With random routing, a node selects only one outgoing path for retransmission of an incoming packet. The outgoing link is chosen at random, excluding the link on which the packet arrived. If all links are equally likely to be chosen, then a node may simply utilize outgoing links in a round-robin fashion.

A refinement of this technique is to assign a probability to each outgoing link and to select the link based on that probability. The probability could be based on data rate, in which case we have:

$$P_i = \frac{R_i}{\sum_j R_j}$$

where

P_i = probability of selecting link i

R_i = data rate on link i

The sum is taken over all candidate outgoing links. This scheme should provide good traffic distribution. Note that the probabilities could also be based on fixed link costs.

Like flooding, random routing requires the use of no network information. Because the route taken is random, the actual route will typically be neither the least-cost route nor the minimum-hop route. Thus, the network must carry a higher-than-optimum traffic load, although not nearly as high as for flooding.

ADAPTIVE ROUTING In virtually all packet-switching networks, some sort of adaptive routing technique is used. That is, the routing decisions that are made change as conditions on the network change. The principal conditions that influence routing decisions are given:

- **Failure:** When a node or link fails, it can no longer be used as part of a route.
- **Congestion:** When a particular portion of the network is heavily congested, it is desirable to route packets around rather than through the area of congestion.

For adaptive routing to be possible, information about the state of the network must be exchanged among the nodes. There are several drawbacks associated with the use of adaptive routing, compared to fixed routing:

- The routing decision is more complex; therefore, the processing burden on network nodes increases.

- In most cases, adaptive strategies depend on status information that is collected at one place but used at another. There is a trade-off here between the quality of the information and the amount of overhead. The more information that is exchanged, and the more frequently it is exchanged, the better will be the routing decisions that each node makes. On the other hand, this information is itself a load on the constituent networks, causing a performance degradation.

- An adaptive strategy may react too quickly, causing congestion-producing oscillation, or too slowly, being irrelevant.

Despite these real dangers, adaptive routing strategies are by far the most prevalent, for two reasons:

- An adaptive routing strategy can improve performance, as seen by the network user.

- An adaptive routing strategy can aid in congestion control, which is discussed in Chapter 13. Because an adaptive routing strategy tends to balance loads, it can delay the onset of severe congestion.

These benefits may or may not be realized, depending on the soundness of the design and the nature of the load. By and large, adaptive routing is an extraordinarily complex task to perform properly. As demonstration of this, most major packet-switching networks, such as ARPANET and its successors, and many commercial networks, have endured at least one major overhaul of their routing strategy.

A convenient way to classify adaptive routing strategies is on the basis of information source: local, adjacent nodes, all nodes. An example of an adaptive routing strategy that relies only on local information is one in which a node routes each packet to the outgoing link with the shortest queue length, Q. This would have the effect of balancing the load on outgoing links. However, some outgoing links may not be headed in the correct general direction. We can improve matters by also taking into account preferred direction, much as with random routing. In this case, each link emanating from the node would have a bias B_i, for each destination i, such that lower values of B_i indicate more preferred directions. For each incoming packet headed for node i, the node would choose the outgoing link that minimizes $Q + B_i$. Thus a node would tend to send packets in the right direction, with a concession made to current traffic delays.

EXAMPLE 12.4 Figure 12.4 shows the status of node 4 of Figure 12.1 at a certain point in time. Node 4 has links to four other nodes. Packets have been arriving and a backlog has built up, with a queue of packets waiting for each of the outgoing links. A packet arrives from node 1 destined for node 6. To which outgoing link should the packet be routed? Based on current queue lengths and the values of bias (B_6) for each outgoing link, the minimum value of $Q + B_6$ is 4, on the link to node 3. Thus, node 4 routes the packet through node 3.

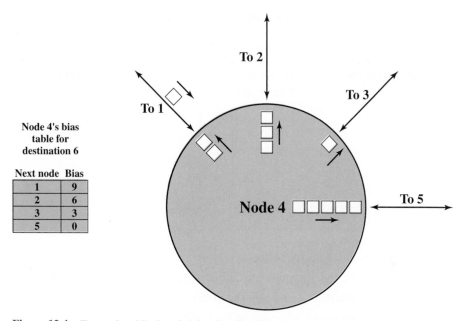

Node 4's bias
table for
destination 6

Next node	Bias
1	9
2	6
3	3
5	0

Figure 12.4   Example of Isolated Adaptive Routing

Adaptive schemes based only on local information are rarely used because they do not exploit easily available information. Strategies based on information from adjacent nodes or all nodes are commonly found. Both take advantage of information that each node has about delays and outages that it experiences. Such adaptive strategies can be either distributed or centralized. In the distributed case, each node exchanges delay information with other nodes. Based on incoming information, a node tries to estimate the delay situation throughout the network, and applies a least-cost routing algorithm. In the centralized case, each node reports its link delay status to a central node, which designs routes based on this incoming information and sends the routing information back to the nodes.

12.2 EXAMPLES: ROUTING IN ARPANET

In this section, we look at several examples of routing strategies. All of these were initially developed for ARPANET, which is a packet-switching network that was the foundation of the present-day Internet. It is instructive to examine these strategies for several reasons. First, these strategies and similar ones are also used in other packet-switching networks, including a number of networks on the Internet. Second, routing schemes based on the ARPANET work have also been used for internetwork routing in the Internet and in private internetworks. And finally, the ARPANET routing scheme evolved in a way that illuminates some of the key design issues related to routing algorithms.

First Generation—Distance Vector Routing

The original routing algorithm, designed in 1969, was a distributed adaptive algorithm using estimated delay as the performance criterion and a version of the Bellman-Ford algorithm (Section 12.3). The approach used is referred to as **distance-vector routing**. For this algorithm, each node maintains two vectors:

$$D_i = \begin{bmatrix} d_{i1} \\ \bullet \\ \bullet \\ \bullet \\ d_{iN} \end{bmatrix} \qquad S_i = \begin{bmatrix} s_{i1} \\ \bullet \\ \bullet \\ \bullet \\ s_{iN} \end{bmatrix}$$

Where

D_i = delay vector for node i

d_{ij} = current estimate of minimum delay from node i to node j $(d_{ii} = 0)$

N = number of nodes in the network

S_i = successor node vector for node i

s_{ij} = the next node in the current minimum-delay route from i to j

Periodically (every 128 ms), each node exchanges its delay vector with all of its neighbors. On the basis of all incoming delay vectors, a node k updates both of its vectors as follows:

$$d_{kj} = \min_{i \in A} [d_{ij} + l_{ki}]$$

$s_{kj} = i$ using i that minimizes the preceding expression

where

A = set of neighbor nodes for k

l_{ki} = current estimate of delay from k to i

EXAMPLE 12.5 Figure 12.5 shows the data structures of the original ARPANET algorithm, using the network of Figure 12.6. This is the same network as that of Figure 12.1, with some of the link costs having different values (and assuming the same cost in both directions). Figure 12.5a shows the routing table for node 1 at an instant in time that reflects the link costs of Figure 12.6. For each destination, a delay is specified, and the next node on the route that produces that delay. At some point, the link costs change to those of Figure 12.1. Assume that node 1's neighbors (nodes 2, 3, and 4) learn of the change before node 1. Each of these nodes updates its delay vector and sends a copy to all of its neighbors, including node 1 (Figure 12.5b). Node 1 discards its current routing table and builds a new one, based solely on the incoming delay vector and its own estimate of link delay to each of its neighbors. The result is shown in Figure 12.5c.

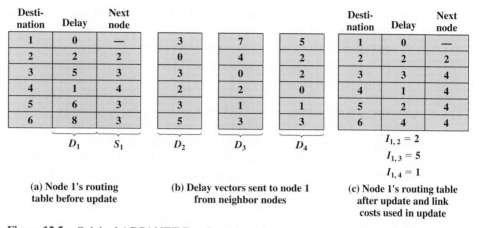

Desti-nation	Delay	Next node
1	0	—
2	2	2
3	5	3
4	1	4
5	6	3
6	8	3

D_1 S_1

3	7	5
0	4	2
3	0	2
2	2	0
3	1	1
5	3	3

D_2 D_3 D_4

Desti-nation	Delay	Next node
1	0	—
2	2	2
3	3	4
4	1	4
5	2	4
6	4	4

$I_{1,2} = 2$
$I_{1,3} = 5$
$I_{1,4} = 1$

(a) Node 1's routing table before update

(b) Delay vectors sent to node 1 from neighbor nodes

(c) Node 1's routing table after update and link costs used in update

Figure 12.5   Original ARPANET Routing Algorithm

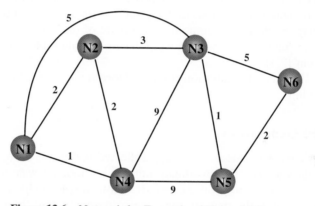

Figure 12.6   Network for Example of Figure 12.5a

The estimated link delay is simply the queue length for that link. Thus, in building a new routing table, the node will tend to favor outgoing links with shorter queues. This tends to balance the load on outgoing links. However, because queue lengths vary rapidly with time, the distributed perception of the shortest route could change while a packet is en route. This could lead to a thrashing situation in which a packet continues to seek out areas of low congestion rather than aiming at the destination.

Second Generation—Link-State Routing

After some years of experience and several minor modifications, the original routing algorithm was replaced by a quite a different one in 1979 [MCQU80]. The major shortcomings of the old algorithm were these:

- The algorithm did not consider line speed, merely queue length. Thus, higher-capacity links were not given the favored status they deserved.

- Queue length is, in any case, an artificial measure of delay, because some variable amount of processing time elapses between the arrival of a packet at a node and its placement in an outbound queue.
- The algorithm was not very accurate. In particular, it responded slowly to congestion and delay increases.

The new algorithm is also a distributed adaptive one, using delay as the performance criterion, but the differences are significant. Rather than using queue length as a surrogate for delay, the delay is measured directly. At a node, each incoming packet is timestamped with an arrival time. A departure time is recorded when the packet is transmitted. If a positive acknowledgment is returned, the delay for that packet is recorded as the departure time minus the arrival time plus transmission time and propagation delay. The node must therefore know link data rate and propagation time. If a negative acknowledgment comes back, the departure time is updated and the node tries again, until a measure of successful transmission delay is obtained.

Every 10 s, the node computes the average delay on each outgoing link. If there are any significant changes in delay, the information is sent to all other nodes using flooding. Each node maintains an estimate of delay on every network link. When new information arrives, it recomputes its routing table using Dijkstra's algorithm (Section 12.3).

The second-generation routing algorithm is referred to as a **link-state routing** algorithm.

Third Generation

Experience with this new strategy indicated that it was more responsive and stable than the old one. The overhead induced by flooding was moderate because each node does this at most once every 10 s. However, as the load on the network grew, a shortcoming in the new strategy began to appear, and the strategy was revised in 1987 [KHAN89].

The problem with the second strategy is the assumption that the measured packet delay on a link is a good predictor of the link delay encountered after all nodes reroute their traffic based on this reported delay. Thus, it is an effective routing mechanism only if there is some correlation between the reported values and those actually experienced after rerouting. This correlation tends to be rather high under light and moderate traffic loads. However, under heavy loads, there is little correlation. Therefore, immediately after all nodes have made routing updates, the routing tables are obsolete!

As an example, consider a network that consists of two regions with only two links, A and B, connecting the two regions (Figure 12.7). Each route between two nodes in different regions must pass through one of these links. Assume that a situation develops in which most of the traffic is on link A. This will cause the link delay on A to be significant, and at the next opportunity, this delay value will be reported to all other nodes. These updates will arrive at all nodes at about the same time, and all will update their routing tables immediately. It is likely that this new delay value

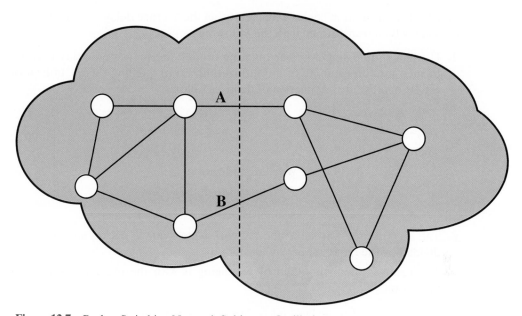

Figure 12.7   Packet-Switching Network Subject to Oscillations

for link A will be high enough to make link B the preferred choice for most, if not all, interregion routes. Because all nodes adjust their routes at the same time, most or all interregion traffic shifts at the same time to link B. Now the link delay value on B will become high, and there will be a subsequent shift to link A. This oscillation will continue until the traffic volume subsides.

There are a number of reasons why this oscillation is undesirable:

- A significant portion of available capacity is unused at just the time when it is needed most: under heavy traffic load.

- The overutilization of some links can lead to the spread of congestion within the network (this will be seen in the discussion of congestion in Chapter 13).

- The large swings in measured delay values result in the need for more frequent routing update messages. This increases the load on the network at just the time when the network is already stressed.

The ARPANET designers concluded that the essence of the problem was that every node was trying to obtain the best route for all destinations, and that these efforts conflicted. It was concluded that under heavy loads, the goal of routing should be to give the average route a good path instead of attempting to give all routes the best path.

The designers decided that it was unnecessary to change the overall routing algorithm. Rather, it was sufficient to change the function that calculates link costs. This was done in such a way as to damp routing oscillations and reduce routing overhead. The calculation begins with measuring the average delay over the last 10 s. This value is then transformed with the following steps:

1. Using a simple single-server queuing model, the measured delay is transformed into an estimate of link utilization. From queuing theory, utilization can be expressed as a function of delay as follows:

$$\rho = \frac{2(T_s - T)}{T_s - 2T}$$

where

$$\rho = \text{link utilization}$$
$$T = \text{measured delay}$$
$$T_s = \text{service time}$$

2. The service time was set at the network-wide average packet size (600 bits) divided by the data rate of the link.

3. The result is then smoothed by averaging it with the previous estimate of utilization:

$$U(n + 1) = 0.5 \times \rho(n + 1) + 0.5 \times U(n)$$

where

$$U(n) = \text{average utilization calculated at sampling time } n$$
$$\rho(n) = \text{link utilization measured at sampling time } n$$

Averaging increases the period of routing oscillations, thus reducing routing overhead.

4. The link cost is then set as a function of average utilization that is designed to provide a reasonable estimate of cost while avoiding oscillation. Figure 12.8 indicates the way in which the estimate of utilization is converted into a cost value. The final cost value is, in effect, a transformed value of delay.

In Figure 12.8, delay is normalized to the value achieved on an idle line, which is just propagation delay plus transmission time. One curve on the figure indicates the way in which the actual delay rises as a function of utilization; the increase in delay is due to queuing delay at the node. For the revised algorithm, the cost value is kept at the minimum value until a given level of utilization is reached. This feature has the effect of reducing routing overhead at low traffic levels. Above a certain level of utilization, the cost level is allowed to rise to a maximum value that is equal to three times the minimum value. The effect of this maximum value is to dictate that traffic should not be routed around a heavily utilized line by more than two additional hops.

Note that the minimum threshold is set higher for satellite links. This encourages the use of terrestrial links under conditions of light traffic, because the terrestrial links have much lower propagation delay. Note also that the actual delay curve is much steeper than the transformation curves at high utilization levels. It is this steep rise in link cost that causes all of the traffic on a link to be shed, which in turn causes routing oscillations.

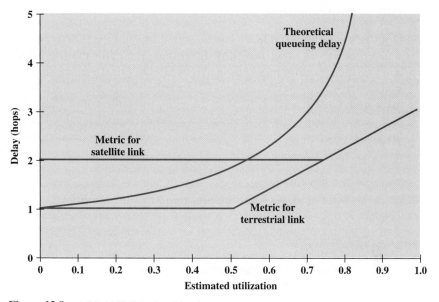

Figure 12.8   ARPANET Delay Metrics

In summary, the revised cost function is keyed to utilization rather than delay. The function acts similar to a delay-based metric under light loads and to a capacity-based metric under heavy loads.

12.3 LEAST-COST ALGORITHMS

Virtually all packet-switching networks and all internets base their routing decision on some form of least-cost criterion. If the criterion is to minimize the number of hops, each link has a value of 1. More typically, the link value is inversely proportional to the link capacity, proportional to the current load on the link, or some combination. In any case, these link or hop costs are used as input to a least-cost routing algorithm, which can be simply stated as:

> Given a network of nodes connected by bidirectional links, where each link has a cost associated with it in each direction, define the cost of a path between two nodes as the sum of the costs of the links traversed. For each pair of nodes, find a path with the least cost.

Note that the cost of a link may differ in its two directions. This would be true, for example, if the cost of a link equaled the length of the queue of packets awaiting transmission from each of the two nodes on the link.

Most least-cost routing algorithms in use in packet-switching networks and internets are variations of one of two common algorithms, known as Dijkstra's algorithm and the Bellman-Ford algorithm. This section provides a summary of these two algorithms.

Dijkstra's Algorithm

Dijkstra's algorithm [DIJK59] can be stated as: Find the shortest paths from a given source node to all other nodes by developing the paths in order of increasing path length. The algorithm proceeds in stages. By the kth stage, the shortest paths to the k nodes closest to (least cost away from) the source node have been determined; these nodes are in a set T. At stage $(k + 1)$, the node not in T that has the shortest path from the source node is added to T. As each node is added to T, its path from the source is defined. The algorithm can be formally described as follows. Define:

N = set of nodes in the network

s = source node

T = set of nodes so far incorporated by the algorithm

$w(i, j)$ = link cost from node i to node j; $w(i, i)$ = 0; $w(i, j)$ = ∞ if the two nodes are not directly connected; $w(i, j) \geq 0$ if the two nodes are directly connected

$L(n)$ = cost of the least-cost path from node s to node n that is currently known to the algorithm; at termination, this is the cost of the least-cost path in the graph from s to n

The algorithm has three steps; steps 2 and 3 are repeated until $T = N$. That is, steps 2 and 3 are repeated until final paths have been assigned to all nodes in the network:

1. **[Initialization]**

   $T = \{s\}$ i.e., the set of nodes so far incorporated consists of only the source node

   $L(n) = w(s, n)$ for $n \neq s$ i.e., the initial path costs to neighboring nodes are simply the link costs

2. **[Get Next Node]** Find the neighboring node not in T that has the least-cost path from node s and incorporate that node into T. Also incorporate the edge that is incident on that node and a node in T that contributes to the path. This can be expressed as:

   $$\text{Find } x \notin T \text{ such that } L(x) = \min_{j \notin T} L(j)$$

   Add x to T; add to T the edge that is incident on x and that contributes the least-cost component to $L(x)$, that is, the last hop in the path.

3. **[Update Least-Cost Paths]**

   $$L(n) = \min [L(n), L(x) + w(x, n)] \text{ for all } n \notin T$$

   If the latter term is the minimum, the path from s to n is now the path from s to x concatenated with the edge from x to n.

The algorithm terminates when all nodes have been added to T. At termination, the value $L(x)$ associated with each node x is the cost (length) of the least-cost path from s to x. In addition, T defines the least-cost path from s to each other node.

One iteration of steps 2 and 3 adds one new node to T and defines the least-cost path from s to that node. That path passes only through nodes that are in T.

To see this, consider the following line of reasoning. After k iterations, there are k nodes in T, and the least-cost path from s to each of these nodes has been defined. Now consider all possible paths from s to nodes not in T. Among those paths, there is one of least cost that passes exclusively through nodes in T (see Problem 12.4), ending with a direct link from some node in T to a node not in T. This node is added to T and the associated path is defined as the least-cost path for that node.

> **EXAMPLE 12.6** Table 12.2a and Figure 12.9 show the result of applying this algorithm to the graph of Figure 12.1, using $s = 1$. The shaded edges define the spanning tree for the graph. The values in each circle are the current estimates of $L(x)$ for each node x. A node is shaded when it is added to T. Note that at each step the path to each node plus the total cost of that path is generated. After the final iteration, the least-cost path to each node and the cost of that path have been developed. The same procedure can be used with node 2 as source node, and so on.

Bellman–Ford Algorithm

The Bellman-Ford algorithm [FORD62] can be stated as: Find the shortest paths from a given source node subject to the constraint that the paths contain at most one link, then find the shortest paths with a constraint of paths of at most two links,

Table 12.2 Example of Least-Cost Routing Algorithms (using Figure 12.1)

(a) Dijkstra'a Algorithm ($s = 1$)

Iteration	T	$L(2)$	Path	$L(3)$	Path	$L(4)$	Path	$L(5)$	Path	$L(6)$	Path
1	{1}	2	1-2	5	1-3	1	1-4	∞	—	∞	—
2	{1, 4}	2	1-2	4	1-4-3	1	1-4	2	1-4-5	∞	—
3	{1, 2, 4}	2	1-2	4	1-4-3	1	1-4	2	1-4-5	∞	—
4	{1, 2, 4, 5}	2	1-2	3	1-4-5-3	1	1-4	2	1-4-5	4	1-4-5-6
5	{1, 2, 3, 4, 5}	2	1-2	3	1-4-5-3	1	1-4	2	1-4-5	4	1-4-5-6
6	{1, 2, 3, 4, 5, 6}	2	1-2	3	1-4-5-3	1	1-4	2	1-4-5	4	1-4-5-6

(b) Bellman-Ford Algorithm ($s = 1$)

h	$L_h(2)$	Path	$L_h(3)$	Path	$L_h(4)$	Path	$L_h(5)$	Path	$L_h(6)$	Path
0	∞	—	∞	—	∞	—	∞	—	∞	—
1	2	1-2	5	1-3	1	1-4	∞	—	∞	—
2	2	1-2	4	1-4-3	1	1-4	2	1-4-5	10	1-3-6
3	2	1-2	3	1-4-5-3	1	1-4	2	1-4-5	4	1-4-5-6
4	2	1-2	3	1-4-5-3	1	1-4	2	1-4-5	4	1-4-5-6

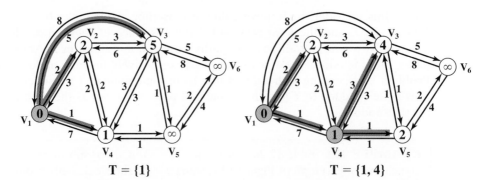

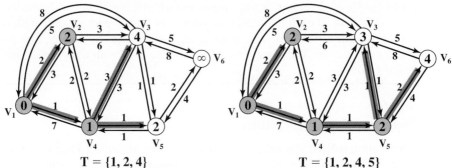

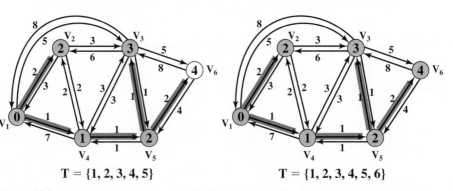

Figure 12.9 Dijkstra's Algorithm Applied to Graph of Figure 12.1

and so on. This algorithm also proceeds in stages. The algorithm can be formally described as follows. Define:

s = source node

$w(i, j)$ = link cost from node i to node j; $w(i, i) = 0$; $w(i, j) = \infty$ if the two nodes are not directly connected; $w(i, j) \geq 0$ if the two nodes are directly connected

h = maximum number of links in a path at the current stage of the algorithm

$L_h(n)$ = cost of the least-cost path from node s to node n under the constraint of no more than h links

1. **[Initialization]**
$$L_0(n) = \infty, \text{for all } n \neq s$$
$$L_h(s) = 0, \text{for all } h$$

2. **[Update]**

For each successive $h \geq 0$:

For each $n \neq s$, compute

$$L_{h+1}(n) = \min_j[L_h(j) + w(j, n)]$$

Connect n with the predecessor node j that achieves the minimum, and eliminate any connection of n with a different predecessor node formed during an earlier iteration. The path from s to n terminates with the link from j to n.

For the iteration of step 2 with $h = K$, and for each destination node n, the algorithm compares potential paths from s to n of length $K + 1$ with the path that existed at the end of the previous iteration. If the previous, shorter, path has less cost, then that path is retained. Otherwise a new path with length $K + 1$ is defined from s to n; this path consists of a path of length K from s to some node j, plus a direct hop from node j to node n. In this case, the path from s to j that is used is the K-hop path for j defined in the previous iteration (see Problem 12.5).

EXAMPLE 12.7 Table 12.2b and Figure 12.10 show the result of applying this algorithm to Figure 12.1, using $s = 1.$s At each step, the least-cost paths with a maximum number of links equal to h are found. After the final iteration, the least-cost path to each node and the cost of that path have been developed. The same procedure can be used with node 2 as source node, and so on. Note that the results agree with those obtained using Dijkstra's algorithm.

Comparison

One interesting comparison can be made between these two algorithms, having to do with what information needs to be gathered. Consider first the Bellman-Ford algorithm. In step 2, the calculation for node n involves knowledge of the link cost to all neighboring nodes to node n [i.e., $w(j, n)$] plus the total path cost to each of those neighboring nodes from a particular source node s [i.e., $L_h(j)$]. Each node can maintain a set of costs and associated paths for every other node in the network and exchange this information with its direct neighbors from time to time. Each node can therefore use the expression in step 2 of the Bellman-Ford algorithm, based only on information from its neighbors and knowledge of its link costs, to update its costs and paths. On the other hand, consider Dijkstra's algorithm. Step 3 appears to require that each node must have complete topological information about the network. That is, each node must know the link costs of all links in the network. Thus, for this algorithm, information must be exchanged with all other nodes.

In general, evaluation of the relative merits of the two algorithms should consider the processing time of the algorithms and the amount of information that must be collected from other nodes in the network or internet. The evaluation will depend on the implementation approach and the specific implementation.

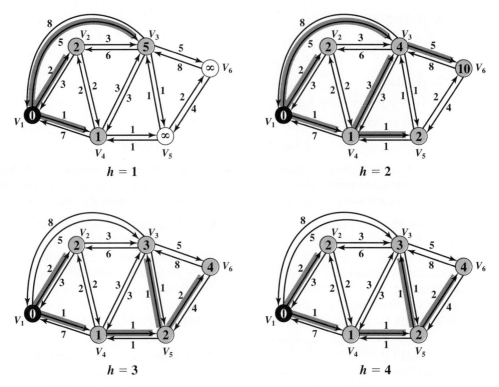

Figure 12.10 Bellman-Ford Algorithm Applied to Graph of Figure 12.1

A final point: Both algorithms are known to converge under static conditions of topology and link costs, and both will converge to the same solution. If the link costs change over time, the algorithm will attempt to catch up with these changes. However, if the link cost depends on traffic, which in turn depends on the routes chosen, then a feedback condition exists, and instabilities may result.

12.4 RECOMMENDED READING

[MAXE90] is a useful survey of routing algorithms. Another survey, with numerous examples, is [SCHW80].

[CORM09] contains a detailed analysis of the least-cost algorithms discussed in this chapter. [BERT92] also discusses these algorithms in detail.

BERT92 Bertsekas, D., and Gallager, R. *Data Networks*. Upper Saddle River, NJ: Prentice Hall, 1992.

CORM09 Cormen, T., et al. *Introduction to Algorithms*. Cambridge, MA: MIT Press, 2009.

MAXE90 Maxemchuk, N., and Zarki, M. "Routing and Flow Control in High-Speed Wide-Area Networks." *Proceedings of the IEEE*, January 1990,

SCHW80 Schwartz, M., and Stern, T. "Routing Techniques Used in Computer Communication Networks." *IEEE Transactions on Communications*, April 1980.

12.5 KEY TERMS, REVIEW QUESTIONS, AND PROBLEMS

Key Terms

adaptive routing	distance-vector	link-state routing
Bellman-Ford algorithm	flooding	random routing
Dijkstra's algorithm	least-cost algorithms	routingfixed routing

Review Questions

12.1 What are the key requirements for a routing function for a packet-switching network?

12.2 What is fixed routing?

12.3 What is flooding?

12.4 What are the advantages and disadvantages of adaptive routing?

12.5 What is a least-cost algorithm?

12.6 What is the essential difference between Dijkstra's algorithm and the Bellman-Ford algorithm?

Problems

12.1 Consider a packet-switching network of N nodes, connected by the following topologies:

a. Star: one central node with no attached station; all other nodes attach to the central node.

b. Loop: each node connects to two other nodes to form a closed loop.

c. Fully connected: each node is directly connected to all other nodes.

For each case, give the average number of hops between stations.

12.2 Consider a binary tree topology for a packet-switching network. The root node connects to two other nodes. All intermediate nodes connect to one node in the direction toward the root, and two in the direction away from the root. At the bottom are nodes with just one link back toward the root. If there are $2^N - 1$ nodes, derive an expression for the mean number of hops per packet for large N, assuming that trips between all node pairs are equally likely. *Hint:* You will find the following equalities useful:

$$\sum_{i=1}^{\infty} X^i = \frac{X}{1 - X}; \sum_{i=1}^{\infty} iX^i = \frac{X}{(1 - X)^2}$$

12.3 Dijkstra's algorithm, for finding the least-cost path from a specified node s to a specified node t, can be expressed in the following program:

```
for n := 1 to N do
    begin
        L[n] := ∞; final[n] := false; {all nodes are temporarily labeled with ∞}
        pred[n] := 1
    end;
L[s] := 0; final[s] := true;   {node s is permanently labeled with 0}
recent := s;                   {the most recent node to be permanently labeled is s}
```

```
                    path := true;
                    {initialization over }

                    while final[t] = false do
                    begin
                        for n := 1 to N do {find new label}
                            if (w[recent, n] < ∞) AND (NOT final[n]) then
                            {for every immediate successor of recent that is not permanently labeled, do }
                                begin {update temporary labels}
                                    newlabel := L[recent] + w[recent,n];
                                    if newlabel < L[n] then

                                            begin L[n] := newlabel; pred[n] := recent end
                                            {relabel n if there is a shorter path via node recent and make
                                            recent the predecessor of n on the shortest path from s}

                            end;
                        temp := ∞;
                        for x := 1 to N do {find node with smallest temporary label}
                            if (NOT final[x]) AND (L[x] < temp) then
                                    begin y := x; temp :=L[x] end;
                            if temp < ∞ then {there is a path} then
                                begin final[y] := true; recent := y end
                                {y, the next closest node to s gets permanently labeled}
                            else begin path := false; final[t] := true end
                    end
```

In this program, each node is assigned a temporary label initially. As a final path
to a node is determined, it is assigned a permanent label equal to the cost of the path
from s. Write a similar program for the Bellman-Ford algorithm. *Hint:* The
Bellman-Ford algorithm is often called a label-correcting method, in contrast to
Dijkstra's label-setting method.

12.4 In the discussion of Dijkstra's algorithm in Section 12.3, it is asserted that at each iteration, a new node is added to T and that the least-cost path for that new node passes
only through nodes already in T. Demonstrate that this is true. *Hint:* Begin at the
beginning. Show that the first node added to T must have a direct link to the source
node. Then show that the second node to T must either have a direct link to the
source node or a direct link to the first node added to T, and so on. Remember that
all link costs are assumed nonnegative.

12.5 In the discussion of the Bellman-Ford algorithm, it is asserted that at the iteration for
which $h = K$, if any path of length $K + 1$ is defined, the first K hops of that path form
a path defined in the previous iteration. Demonstrate that this is true.

12.6 In step 3 of Dijkstra's algorithm, the least-cost path values are only updated for nodes
not yet in T. Is it possible that a lower-cost path could be found to a node already in
T? If so, demonstrate by example. If not, provide reasoning as to why not.

12.7 Using Dijkstra's algorithm, generate a least-cost route to all other nodes for nodes 2
through 6 of Figure 12.1. Display the results as in Table 12.2a.

12.8 Repeat Problem 12.7 using the Bellman-Ford algorithm.

12.9 Apply Dijkstra's routing algorithm to the networks in Figure 12.11. Provide a table
similar to Table 12.2a and a figure similar to Figure 12.9.

12.10 Repeat Problem 12.9 using the Bellman-Ford algorithm.

12.11 Will Dijkstra's algorithm and the Bellman-Ford algorithm always yield the same solutions? Why or why not?

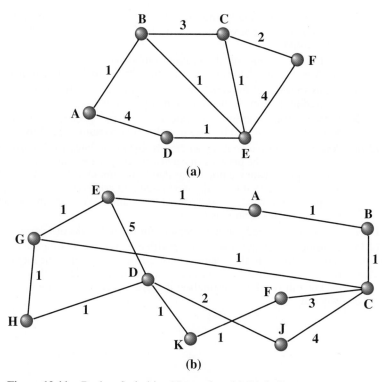

Figure 12.11   Packet-Switching Networks with Link Costs

12.12 Both Dijkstra's algorithm and the Bellman-Ford algorithm find the least-cost paths from one node to all other nodes. The Floyd-Warshall algorithm finds the least-cost paths between all pairs of nodes together. Define:

N = set of nodes in the network

$w(i, j)$ = link cost from node i to node j; $w(i, i) = 0$; $w(i, j) = \infty$ if the two nodes are not directly connected

$L_n(i, j)$ = cost of the least-cost path from node i to node j with the constraint that only nodes $1, 2, \ldots, n$ can be used as intermediate nodes on paths

The algorithm has the following steps:

1. Initialize:

$$L_0(i, j) = w(i, j), \text{for all } i, j, \; i \neq j$$

2. For $n = 0, 1, \ldots, N - 1$

$$L_{n+1}(i, j) = \min[L_n(i, j), L_n(i, n + 1) + L_n(n + 1, j)] \quad \text{for all } i \neq j$$

Explain the algorithm in words. Use induction to demonstrate that the algorithm works.

12.13 In Figure 12.3, node 1 sends a packet to node 6 using flooding. Counting the transmission of one packet across one link as a load of one, what is the total load generated if:

    a. Each node discards duplicate incoming packets?

    b. A hop count field is used and is initially set to 5, and no duplicate is discarded?

12.14 It was shown that flooding can be used to determine the minimum-hop route. Can it be used to determine the minimum delay route?

12.15 With random routing, only one copy of the packet is in existence at a time. Nevertheless, it would be wise to utilize a hop count field. Why?

12.16 Another adaptive routing scheme is known as backward learning. As a packet is routed through the network, it carries not only the destination address, but the source address plus a running hop count that is incremented for each hop. Each node builds a routing table that gives the next node and hop count for each destination. How is the packet information used to build the table? What are the advantages and disadvantages of this technique?

12.17 Build a centralized routing directory for the networks of Figure 12.11.

12.18 Consider a system using flooding with a hop counter. Suppose that the hop counter is originally set to the "diameter" of the network. When the hop count reaches zero, the packet is discarded except at its destination. Does this always ensure that a packet will reach its destination if there exists at least one operable path? Why or why not?

CHAPTER 13

CONGESTION CONTROL IN DATA NETWORKS

We were doing very well, up to the kind of sum when a bath is filling at the rate of so many gallons and two holes are letting the water out, and please to say how long it will take to fill the bath, when my mother put down the socks she was darning and clicked her tongue in impatience.

"Filling up an old bath with holes in it, indeed. Who would be such a fool?"

"A sum it is, girl," my father said. "A sum. A problem for the mind."

"Filling the boy with old nonsense," Mama said.

"Not nonsense, Beth," my father said. "A sum, it is. The water pours in and takes so long. It pours out and takes so long. How long to fill? That is all."

"But who would pour water into an old bath with holes?" my mother said. "Who would think to do it, but a lunatic?"

— *How Green Was My Valley*, Richard Llewellyn

KEY POINTS

♦ Congestion occurs when the number of packets being transmitted through a network begins to approach the packet-handling capacity of the network. The objective of congestion control is to maintain the number of packets within the network below the level at which performance falls off dramatically.

♦ The lack of flow control mechanisms built into the ATM and frame relay protocols makes congestion control difficult. A variety of techniques have been developed to cope with congestion and to give different quality-of-service guarantees to different types of traffic.

♦ ATM networks establish a traffic contract with each user that specifies the characteristics of the expected traffic and the type of service that the network will provide. The network implements congestion control techniques in such a way as to protect the network from congestion while meeting the traffic contracts.

♦ An ATM network monitors the cell flow from each incoming source and may discard or label for potential discard cells that exceed the agreed traffic contract. In addition, the network may shape the traffic coming from users by temporarily buffering cells to smooth out traffic flows.

A key design issue that must be confronted both with data networks, such as packet-switching, frame relay, and ATM networks, and also with internets, is that of congestion control. The phenomenon of congestion is a complex one, as is the subject of congestion control. In very general terms, congestion occurs when the number of packets[1] being transmitted through a network begins to approach

---

[1]In this chapter we use the term *packet* in a broad sense, to include packets in a packet-switching network, frames in a frame relay network, cells in an ATM network, or IP datagrams in an internet.

378

the packet-handling capacity of the network. The objective of congestion control is to maintain the number of packets within the network below the level at which performance falls off dramatically.

To understand the issues involved in congestion control, we need to look at some results from queuing theory.[2] In essence, a data network or internet is a network of queues. At each node (data network switch, internet router), there is a queue of packets for each outgoing channel. If the rate at which packets arrive and queue up exceeds the rate at which packets can be transmitted, the queue size grows without bound and the delay experienced by a packet goes to infinity. Even if the packet arrival rate is less than the packet transmission rate, queue length will grow dramatically as the arrival rate approaches the transmission rate. As a rule of thumb, when the line for which packets are queuing becomes more than 80% utilized, the queue length grows at an alarming rate. This growth in queue length means that the delay experienced by a packet at each node increases. Further, since the size of any queue is finite, as queue length grows, eventually the queue must overflow.

This chapter focuses on congestion control in switched data networks, including packet-switching and ATM networks. Congestion control in frame relay networks is discussed in Appendix U. The principles examined here are also applicable to internetworks. In Part Five, we look at additional congestion control mechanisms in our discussion of internetwork operation and TCP congestion control.

13.1 EFFECTS OF CONGESTION

Consider the queuing situation at a single packet switch or router, such as is illustrated in Figure 13.1. Any given node has a number of I/O ports[3] attached to it: one or more to other nodes, and zero or more to end systems. On each port, packets arrive and depart. We can consider that there are two buffers, or queues, at each port, one to accept arriving packets, and one to hold packets that are waiting to depart. In practice, there might be two fixed-size buffers associated with each port, or there might be a pool of memory available for all buffering activities. In the latter case, we can think of each port having two variable-size buffers associated with it, subject to the constraint that the sum of all buffer sizes is a constant.

In any case, as packets arrive, they are stored in the input buffer of the corresponding port. The node examines each incoming packet, makes a routing decision, and then moves the packet to the appropriate output buffer. Packets queued for output are transmitted as rapidly as possible; this is, in effect, statistical time division multiplexing. If packets arrive too fast for the node to process them (make routing decisions) or faster than packets can be cleared from the outgoing buffers, then eventually packets will arrive for which no memory is available.

---

[2]Appendix H provides an overview of queuing analysis.

[3]In the case of a switch of a packet-switching, frame relay, or ATM network, each I/O port connects to a transmission link that connects to another node or end system. In the case of a router of an internet, each I/O port connects to either a direct link to another node or to a subnetwork.

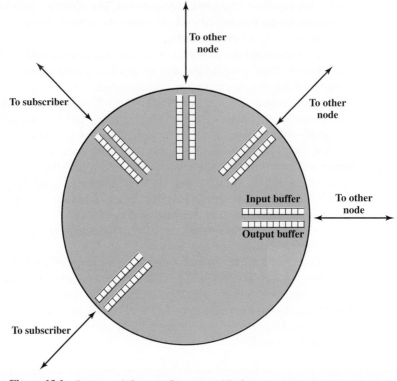

Figure 13.1   Input and Output Queues at Node

When such a saturation point is reached, one of two general strategies can be adopted. The first such strategy is to discard any incoming packet for which there is no available buffer space. The alternative is for the node that is experiencing these problems to exercise some sort of flow control over its neighbors so that the traffic flow remains manageable. But, as Figure 13.2 illustrates, each of a

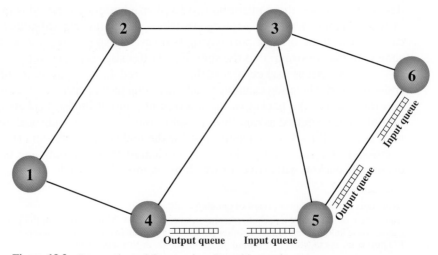

Figure 13.2   Interaction of Queues in a Data Network

node's neighbors is also managing a number of queues. If node 6 restrains the flow of packets from node 5, this causes the output buffer in node 5 for the port to node 6 to fill up. Thus, congestion at one point in the network can quickly propagate throughout a region or the entire network. While flow control is indeed a powerful tool, we need to use it in such a way as to manage the traffic on the entire network.

Ideal Performance

Figure 13.3 suggests the ideal goal for network utilization. The top graph plots the steady-state total throughput (number of packets delivered to destination end systems) through the network as a function of the offered load (number of packets transmitted by source end systems), both normalized to the maximum theoretical throughput of the network. For example, if a network consists of a single node with two full-duplex 1-Mbps links, then the theoretical capacity of the network is 2 Mbps, consisting of a 1-Mbps flow in each direction. In the ideal case, the throughput of the network increases to accommodate load up to an offered load equal to the full capacity of the network; then normalized throughput remains at 1.0 at higher input loads. Note, however, what happens to the end-to-end delay experienced by the average packet even with this

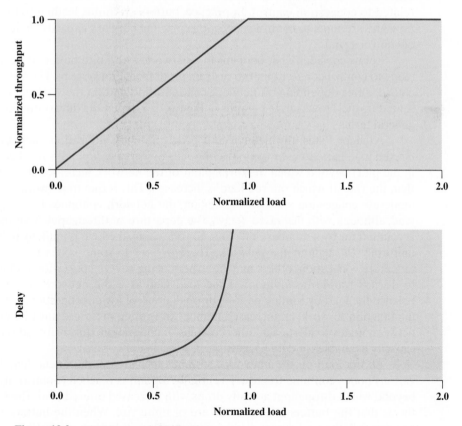

Figure 13.3   Ideal Network Utilization

assumption of ideal performance. At negligible load, there is some small constant amount of delay that consists of the propagation delay through the network from source to destination plus processing delay at each node. As the load on the network increases, queuing delays at each node are added to this fixed amount of delay. When the load exceeds the network capacity, delays increase without bound.

Here is a simple intuitive explanation of why delay must go to infinity. Suppose that each node in the network is equipped with buffers of infinite size and suppose that the input load exceeds network capacity. Under ideal conditions, the network will continue to sustain a normalized throughput of 1.0. Therefore, the rate of packets leaving the network is 1.0. Because the rate of packets entering the network is greater than 1.0, internal queue sizes grow. In the steady state, with input greater than output, these queue sizes grow without bound and therefore queuing delays grow without bound.

It is important to grasp the meaning of Figure 13.3 before looking at real-world conditions. This figure represents the ideal, but unattainable, goal of all traffic and congestion control schemes. No scheme can exceed the performance depicted in Figure 13.3.

Practical Performance

The ideal case reflected in Figure 13.3 assumes infinite buffers and no overhead related to congestion control. In practice, buffers are finite, leading to buffer over-flow, and attempts to control congestion consume network capacity in the exchange of control signals.

Let us consider what happens in a network with finite buffers if no attempt is made to control congestion or to restrain input from end systems. The details will, of course, differ depending on network configuration and on the statistics of the presented traffic. However, the graphs in Figure 13.4 depict the devastating outcome in general terms.

At light loads, throughput, and hence network utilization, increases as the offered load increases. As the load continues to increase, a point is reached (point A in the plot) beyond which the throughput of the network increases at a rate slower than the rate at which offered load is increased. This is due to network entry into a moderate congestion state. In this region, the network continues to cope with the load, although with increased delays. The departure of throughput from the ideal is accounted for by a number of factors. For one thing, the load is unlikely to be spread uniformly throughout the network. Therefore, while some nodes may experience moderate congestion, others may be experiencing severe congestion and may need to discard traffic. In addition, as the load increases, the network will attempt to balance the load by routing packets through areas of lower congestion. For the routing function to work, an increased number of routing messages must be exchanged between nodes to alert each other to areas of congestion; this overhead reduces the capacity available for data packets.

As the load on the network continues to increase, the queue lengths of the various nodes continue to grow. Eventually, a point is reached (point B in the plot) beyond which throughput actually drops with increased offered load. The reason for this is that the buffers at each node are of finite size. When the buffers at a node become full, the node must discard packets. Thus, the sources must retransmit the

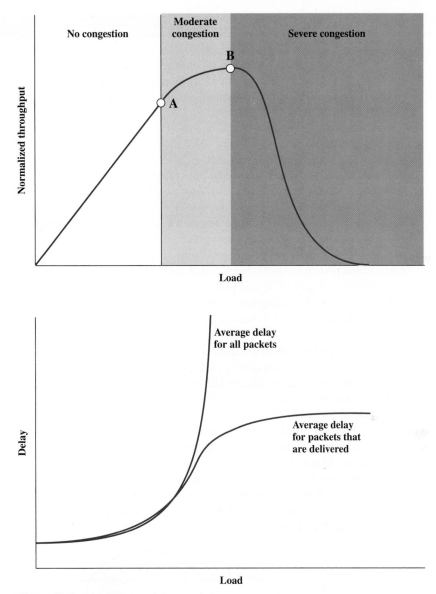

Figure 13.4   The Effects of Congestion

discarded packets in addition to new packets. This only exacerbates the situation: As more and more packets are retransmitted, the load on the system grows, and more buffers become saturated. While the system is trying desperately to clear the backlog, users are pumping old and new packets into the system. Even successfully delivered packets may be retransmitted because it takes too long, at a higher layer (e.g., transport layer), to acknowledge them: The sender assumes the packet did not get through and retransmits. Under these circumstances, the effective capacity of the system declines to zero.

13.2 CONGESTION CONTROL

In this book, we discuss various techniques for controlling congestion in packet-switching, frame relay, and ATM networks, and in IP-based internets. To give context to this discussion, Figure 13.5 provides a general depiction of important congestion control techniques.

Backpressure

We have already made reference to backpressure as a technique for congestion control. This technique produces an effect similar to backpressure in fluids flowing down a pipe. When the end of a pipe is closed (or restricted), the fluid pressure backs up the pipe to the point of origin, where the flow is stopped (or slowed).

Backpressure can be exerted on the basis of links or logical connections (e.g., virtual circuits). Referring again to Figure 13.2, if node 6 becomes congested (buffers fill up), then node 6 can slow down or halt the flow of all packets from node 5 (or node 3, or both nodes 5 and 3). If this restriction persists, node 5 will need to slow down or halt traffic on its incoming links. This flow restriction propagates backward (against the flow of data traffic) to sources, which are restricted in the flow of new packets into the network.

Backpressure can be selectively applied to logical connections, so that the flow from one node to the next is only restricted or halted on some connections, generally the ones with the most traffic. In this case, the restriction propagates back along the connection to the source.

Backpressure is of limited utility. It can be used in a connection-oriented network that allows hop-by-hop (from one node to the next) flow control. X.25-based packet-switching networks typically provide this feature. However, neither frame relay nor ATM has any capability for restricting flow on a hop-by-hop basis. In the case of IP-based internets, there have traditionally been no built-in facilities for regulating the flow of data from one router to the next along a path through the internet. Recently, some flow-based schemes have been developed; this topic is introduced in Part Five.

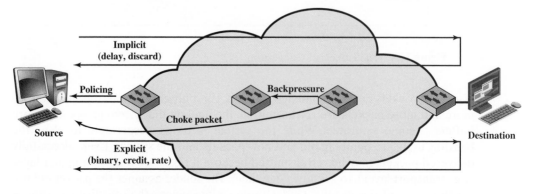

Figure 13.5   Mechanisms for Congestion Control

Choke Packet

A choke packet is a control packet generated at a congested node and transmitted back to a source node to restrict traffic flow. An example of a choke packet is the ICMP (Internet Control Message Protocol) Source Quench packet. Either a router or a destination end system may send this message to a source end system, requesting that it reduce the rate at which it is sending traffic to the internet destination. On receipt of a source quench message, the source host should cut back the rate at which it is sending traffic to the specified destination until it no longer receives source quench messages. The source quench message can be used by a router or host that must discard IP datagrams because of a full buffer. In that case, the router or host will issue a source quench message for every datagram that it discards. In addition, a system may anticipate congestion and issue source quench messages when its buffers approach capacity. In that case, the datagram referred to in the source quench message may well be delivered. Thus, receipt of a source quench message does not imply delivery or nondelivery of the corresponding datagram.

The choke package is a relatively crude technique for controlling congestion. More sophisticated forms of explicit congestion signaling are discussed subsequently.

Implicit Congestion Signaling

When network congestion occurs, two things may happen: (1) The transmission delay for an individual packet from source to destination increases, so that it is noticeably longer than the fixed propagation delay, and (2) packets are discarded. If a source is able to detect increased delays and packet discards, then it has implicit evidence of network congestion. If all sources can detect congestion and, in response, reduce flow on the basis of congestion, then the network congestion will be relieved. Thus, congestion control on the basis of implicit signaling is the responsibility of end systems and does not require action on the part of network nodes.

Implicit signaling is an effective congestion control technique in connectionless, or datagram, configurations, such as datagram packet-switching networks and IP-based internets. In such cases, there are no logical connections through the internet on which flow can be regulated. However, between the two end systems, logical connections can be established at the TCP level. TCP includes mechanisms for acknowledging receipt of TCP segments and for regulating the flow of data between source and destination on a TCP connection. TCP congestion control techniques based on the ability to detect increased delay and segment loss are discussed in Chapter 22.

Implicit signaling can also be used in connection-oriented networks. For example, in frame relay networks, the LAPF control protocol, which is end to end, includes facilities similar to those of TCP for flow and error control. LAPF control is capable of detecting lost frames and adjusting the flow of data accordingly.

Explicit Congestion Signaling

It is desirable to use as much of the available capacity in a network as possible but still react to congestion in a controlled and fair manner. This is the purpose of explicit congestion avoidance techniques. In general terms, for explicit congestion avoidance, the network alerts end systems to growing congestion within the network and the end systems take steps to reduce the offered load to the network.

Typically, explicit congestion control techniques operate over connection-oriented networks and control the flow of packets over individual connections. Explicit congestion signaling approaches can work in one of two directions:

- **Backward:** Notifies the source that congestion avoidance procedures should be initiated where applicable for traffic in the opposite direction of the received notification. It indicates that the packets that the user transmits on this logical connection may encounter congested resources. Backward information is transmitted either by altering bits in a header of a data packet headed for the source to be controlled or by transmitting separate control packets to the source.

- **Forward:** Notifies the user that congestion avoidance procedures should be initiated where applicable for traffic in the same direction as the received notification. It indicates that this packet, on this logical connection, has encountered congested resources. Again, this information may be transmitted either as altered bits in data packets or in separate control packets. In some schemes, when a forward signal is received by an end system, it echoes the signal back along the logical connection to the source. In other schemes, the end system is expected to exercise flow control upon the source end system at a higher layer (e.g., TCP).

We can divide explicit congestion signaling approaches into three general categories:

- **Binary:** A bit is set in a data packet as it is forwarded by the congested node. When a source receives a binary indication of congestion on a logical connection, it may reduce its traffic flow.

- **Credit based:** These schemes are based on providing an explicit credit to a source over a logical connection. The credit indicates how many octets or how many packets the source may transmit. When the credit is exhausted, the source must await additional credit before sending additional data. Credit-based schemes are common for end-to-end flow control, in which a destination system uses credit to prevent the source from overflowing the destination buffers, but credit-based schemes have also been considered for congestion control.

- **Rate based:** These schemes are based on providing an explicit data rate limit to the source over a logical connection. The source may transmit data at a rate up to the set limit. To control congestion, any node along the path of the connection can reduce the data rate limit in a control message to the source.

13.3 TRAFFIC MANAGEMENT

There are a number of issues related to congestion control that might be included under the general category of traffic management. In its simplest form, congestion control is concerned with efficient use of a network at high load. The various mechanisms discussed in the previous section can be applied as the situation arises, without regard to the particular source or destination affected. When a node is saturated and must discard packets, it can apply some simple rule, such as discard the most recent arrival. However, other considerations can be used to refine the application of congestion control techniques and discard policy. We briefly introduce several of those areas here.

Fairness

As congestion develops, flows of packets between sources and destinations will experience increased delays and, with high congestion, packet losses. In the absence of other requirements, we would like to assure that the various flows suffer from congestion equally. Simply to discard on a last-in-first-discarded basis may not be fair. As an example of a technique that might promote fairness, a node can maintain a separate queue for each logical connection or for each source-destination pair. If all of the queue buffers are of equal length, then the queues with the highest traffic load will suffer discards more often, allowing lower-traffic connections a fair share of the capacity.

Quality of Service

We might wish to treat different traffic flows differently. For example, as [JAIN92] points out, some applications, such as voice and video, are delay sensitive but loss insensitive. Others, such as file transfer and electronic mail, are delay insensitive but loss sensitive. Still others, such as interactive graphics or interactive computing applications, are delay sensitive and loss sensitive. Also, different traffic flows have different priorities; for example, network management traffic, particularly during times of congestion or failure, is more important than application traffic.

It is particularly important during periods of congestion that traffic flows with different requirements be treated differently and provided a different quality of service (QoS). For example, a node might transmit higher-priority packets ahead of lower-priority packets in the same queue. Or a node might maintain different queues for different QoS levels and give preferential treatment to the higher levels.

Reservations

One way to avoid congestion and also to provide assured service to applications is to use a reservation scheme. Such a scheme is an integral part of ATM networks. When a logical connection is established, the network and the user enter into a traffic contract, which specifies a data rate and other characteristics of the traffic flow. The network agrees to give a defined QoS so long as the traffic flow is within contract parameters; excess traffic is either discarded or handled on a best-effort basis, subject to discard. If the current outstanding reservations are such that the network resources are inadequate to meet the new reservation, then the new reservation is denied. A similar type of scheme has now been developed for IP-based internets (RSVP, which is discussed in Chapter 20).

One aspect of a reservation scheme is traffic policing (Figure 13.5). A node in the network, typically the node to which the end system attaches, monitors the traffic flow and compares it to the traffic contract. Excess traffic is either discarded or marked to indicate that it is liable to discard or delay.

13.4 CONGESTION CONTROL IN PACKET-SWITCHING NETWORKS

A number of control mechanisms for congestion control in packet-switching networks have been suggested and tried. The following are examples:

1. Send a control packet from a congested node to some or all source nodes. This choke packet will have the effect of stopping or slowing the rate of transmission from sources and hence limit the total number of packets in the network. This approach requires additional traffic on the network during a period of congestion.

2. Rely on routing information. Routing algorithms, such as ARPANET's, provide link delay information to other nodes, which influences routing decisions. This information could also be used to influence the rate at which new packets are produced. Because these delays are being influenced by the routing decision, they may vary too rapidly to be used effectively for congestion control.

3. Make use of an end-to-end probe packet. Such a packet could be timestamped to measure the delay between two particular endpoints. This has the disadvantage of adding overhead to the network.

4. Allow packet-switching nodes to add congestion information to packets as they go by. There are two possible approaches here. A node could add such information to packets going in the direction opposite of the congestion. This information quickly reaches the source node, which can reduce the flow of packets into the network. Alternatively, a node could add such information to packets going in the same direction as the congestion. The destination either asks the source to adjust the load or returns the signal back to the source in the packets (or acknowledgments) going in the reverse direction.

13.5 ATM TRAFFIC MANAGEMENT

Because of their high speed and small cell size, ATM networks present difficulties in effectively controlling congestion not found in other types of data networks. The complexity of the problem is compounded by the limited number of overhead bits available for exerting control over the flow of user cells. This area is currently the subject of intense research, and approaches to traffic and congestion control are still evolving. ITU-T has defined a restricted initial set of traffic and congestion control capabilities aiming at simple mechanisms and realistic network efficiency; these are specified in I.371. The ATM Forum has published a somewhat more advanced version of this set in its Traffic Management Specification 4.0. This section focuses on the ATM Forum specifications.

We begin with an overview of the congestion problem and the framework adopted by ITU-T and the ATM Forum. We then discuss some of the specific techniques that have been developed for traffic management and congestion control.

Requirements for ATM Traffic and Congestion Control

Both the types of traffic patterns imposed on ATM networks and the transmission characteristics of those networks differ markedly from those of other switching networks. Most packet-switching and frame relay networks carry non-real-time data traffic. Typically, the traffic on individual virtual circuits or frame relay connections is bursty in nature, and the receiving system expects to receive incoming traffic on each connection in a bursty fashion. As a result,

- The network does not need to replicate the exact timing pattern of incoming traffic at the exit node.
- Therefore, simple statistical multiplexing can be used to accommodate multiple logical connections over the physical interface between user and network. The average data rate required by each connection is less than the burst rate for that connection, and the user–network interface (UNI) need only be designed for a capacity somewhat greater than the sum of the average data rates for all connections.

A number of tools are available for control of congestion in packet-switched and frame relay networks, some of which are discussed elsewhere in this chapter and in Appendix U. These types of congestion control schemes are inadequate for ATM networks. [GERS91] cites the following reasons:

- The majority of traffic is not amenable to flow control. For example, voice and video traffic sources cannot stop generating cells even when the network is congested.
- Feedback is slow due to the drastically reduced cell transmission time compared to propagation delays across the network.
- ATM networks typically support a wide range of applications requiring capacity ranging from a few kbps to several hundred Mbps. Relatively simple-minded congestion control schemes generally end up penalizing one end or the other of that spectrum.
- Applications on ATM networks may generate very different traffic patterns (e.g., constant bit rate versus variable bit rate sources). Again, it is difficult for conventional congestion control techniques to handle fairly such variety.
- Different applications on ATM networks require different network services (e.g., delay-sensitive service for voice and video, and loss-sensitive service for data).
- The very high speeds in switching and transmission make ATM networks more volatile in terms of congestion and traffic control. A scheme that relies heavily on reacting to changing conditions will produce extreme and wasteful fluctuations in routing policy and flow control.

Two key performance issues that relate to the preceding points are latency/speed effects and cell delay variation, topics to which we now turn.

Latency/Speed Effects

Consider the transfer of ATM cells over a network at a data rate of 150 Mbps. At that rate, it takes $(53 \times 8 \text{ bits})/(150 \times 10^6 \text{ bps}) \approx 2.8 \times 10^{-6}$ s to insert a single cell onto the network. The time it takes to transfer the cell from the source to the destination user will depend on the number of intermediate ATM switches, the switching time at each switch, and the propagation time along all links in the path from source to destination. For simplicity, ignore ATM switching delays and assume propagation at the two-thirds the speed of light. Then, if source and destination are on opposite coasts of the United States, the round-trip propagation delay is about 48×10^{-3} s.

With these conditions in place, suppose that source A is performing a long file transfer to destination B and that implicit congestion control is being used (i.e., there are no explicit congestion notifications; the source deduces the presence of congestion by the loss of data). If the network drops a cell due to congestion, B can return a reject message to A, which must then retransmit the dropped cell and possibly all subsequent cells. But by the time the notification gets back to A, it has transmitted an additional N cells, where

$$ N = \frac{48 \times 10^{-3} \text{ s}}{2.8 \times 10^{-6} \text{ s/cell}} = 1.7 \times 10^4 \text{ cells} = 7.2 \times 10^6 \text{ bits} $$

Over 7 megabits have been transmitted before A can react to the congestion indication.

This calculation helps to explain why the techniques that are satisfactory for more traditional networks break down when dealing with ATM WANs.

Cell Delay Variation

For an ATM network, voice and video signals can be digitized and transmitted as a stream of cells. A key requirement, especially for voice, is that the delay across the network be short. Generally, this will be the case for ATM networks. As we have discussed, ATM is designed to minimize the processing and transmission overhead internal to the network so that very fast cell switching and routing is possible.

There is another important requirement that to some extent conflicts with the preceding requirement, namely that the rate of delivery of cells to the destination user must be constant. It is inevitable that there will be some variability in the rate of delivery of cells due both to effects within the network and at the source UNI; we summarize these effects presently. First, let us consider how the destination user might cope with variations in the delay of cells as they transit from source user to destination user.

A general procedure for achieving a constant bit rate (CBR) is illustrated in Figure 13.6. Let $D(i)$ represent the end-to-end delay experienced by the ith cell. The destination system does not know the exact amount of this delay: There is no time-stamp information associated with each cell and, even if there were, it is impossible to keep source and destination clocks perfectly synchronized. When the first cell on a connection arrives at time t_0, the target user delays the cell an additional amount $V(0)$ prior to delivery to the application. $V(0)$ is an estimate of the amount of cell delay variation that this application can tolerate and that is likely to be produced by the network.

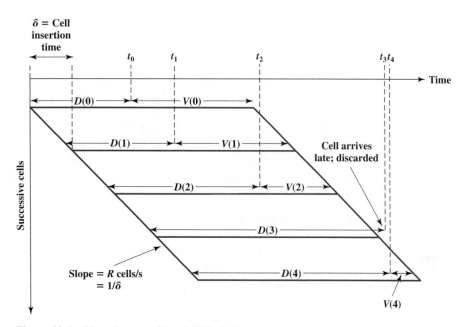

Figure 13.6   Time Reassembly of CBR Cells

Subsequent cells are delayed so that they are delivered to the user at a constant rate of R cells per second. The time between delivery of cells to the target application (time between the start of delivery of one cell and the start of delivery of the next cell) is therefore $\delta = 1/R$. To achieve a constant rate, the next cell is delayed a variable amount $V(1)$ to satisfy:

$$t_1 + V(1) = t_0 + V(0) + \delta$$

So,

$$V(1) = V(0) - [t_1 - (t_0 + \delta)]$$

In general,

$$V(i) = V(0) - [t_i - (t_0 + i \times \delta)]$$

which can also be expressed as

$$V(i) = V(i - 1) - [t_i - (t_{i-1} + \delta)]$$

If the computed value of $V(i)$ is negative, then that cell is discarded. The result is that data is delivered to the higher layer at a constant bit rate, with occasional gaps due to dropped cells.

The amount of the initial delay $V(0)$, which is also the average delay applied to all incoming cells, is a function of the anticipated cell delay variation. To minimize this delay, a subscriber will therefore request a minimal cell delay variation from the network provider. This leads to a trade-off: Cell delay variation can be reduced by increasing the data rate at the UNI relative to the load and by increasing resources within the network.

NETWORK CONTRIBUTION TO CELL DELAY VARIATION One component of cell delay variation is due to events within the network. For packet-switching networks, packet delay variation can be considerable due to queuing effects at each of the intermediate switching nodes and the processing time required to analyze packet headers and perform routing. To a much lesser extent, this is also true of frame delay variation in frame relay networks. In the case of ATM networks, cell delay variations due to network effects are likely to be even less than for frame relay. The principal reasons for this are the following:

- The ATM protocol is designed to minimize processing overhead at intermediate switching nodes. The cells are fixed size with fixed header formats, and there is no flow control or error control processing required.
- To accommodate the high speeds of ATM networks, ATM switches have had to be designed to provide extremely high throughput. Thus, the processing time for an individual cell at a node is negligible.

The only factor that could lead to noticeable cell delay variation within the network is congestion. If the network begins to become congested, either cells must be discarded or there will be a buildup of queuing delays at affected switches. Thus, it is important that the total load accepted by the network at any time not be such as to cause congestion.

CELL DELAY VARIATION AT THE UNI Even if an application generates data for transmission at a constant bit rate, cell delay variation can occur at the source due to the processing that takes place at the three layers of the ATM model.

Figure 13.7 illustrates the potential causes of cell delay variation. In this example, ATM connections A and B support user data rates of X and Y Mbps, respectively $(X > Y)$. At the AAL level, data are segmented into 48-octet blocks. Note that on a time diagram, the blocks appear to be of different sizes for the two connections; specifically, the time required to generate a 48-octet block of data, in microseconds, is

$$\text{Connection A: } \frac{48 \times 8}{X}$$
$$\text{Connection B: } \frac{48 \times 8}{Y}$$

The ATM layer encapsulates each segment into a 53-octet cell. These cells must be interleaved and delivered to the physical layer to be transmitted at the data rate of the physical link. Delay is introduced into this interleaving process: If two cells from different connections arrive at the ATM layer at overlapping times, one of the cells must be delayed by the amount of the overlap. In addition, the ATM layer is generating OAM (operation and maintenance) cells that must also be interleaved with user cells.

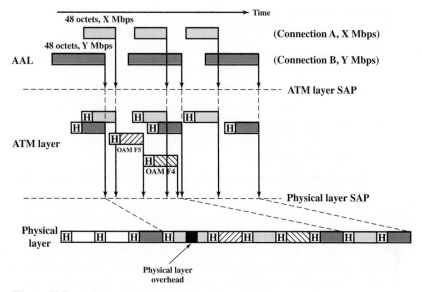

Figure 13.7   Origins of Cell Delay Variation (I.371)

At the physical layer, there is opportunity for the introduction of further cell delays. For example, if cells are transmitted in SDH (synchronous digital hierarchy) frames, overhead bits for those frames will be inserted onto the physical link, delaying bits from the ATM layer.

None of the delays just listed can be predicted in any detail, and none follow any repetitive pattern. Accordingly, there is a random element to the time interval between reception of data at the ATM layer from the AAL and the transmission of that data in a cell across the UNI.

Traffic and Congestion Control Framework

I.371 lists the following objectives of ATM layer traffic and congestion control:

- ATM layer traffic and congestion control should support a set of ATM layer QoS classes sufficient for all foreseeable network services; the specification of these QoS classes should be consistent with network performance parameters currently under study.

- ATM layer traffic and congestion control should not rely on AAL protocols that are network service specific, nor on higher-layer protocols that are application specific. Protocol layers above the ATM layer may make use of information provided by the ATM layer to improve the utility those protocols can derive from the network.

- The design of an optimum set of ATM layer traffic controls and congestion controls should minimize network and end-system complexity while maximizing network utilization.

To meet these objectives, ITU-T and the ATM Forum have defined a collection of traffic and congestion control functions that operate across a spectrum of timing intervals. Table 13.1 lists these functions with respect to the response times within which they operate. Four levels of timing are considered:

- **Cell insertion time:** Functions at this level react immediately to cells as they are transmitted.
- **Round-trip propagation time:** At this level, the network responds within the lifetime of a cell in the network and may provide feedback indications to the source.
- **Connection duration:** At this level, the network determines whether a new connection at a given QoS can be accommodated and what performance levels will be agreed to.
- **Long term:** These are controls that affect more than one ATM connection and are established for long-term use.

The essence of the traffic control strategy is based on (1) determining whether a given new ATM connection can be accommodated and (2) agreeing with the subscriber on the performance parameters that will be supported. In effect, the subscriber and the network enter into a traffic contract: The network agrees to support traffic at a certain level of performance on this connection, and the subscriber agrees not to exceed traffic parameter limits. Traffic control functions are concerned with establishing these traffic parameters and enforcing them. Thus, they are concerned with congestion avoidance. If traffic control fails in certain instances, then congestion may occur. At this point, congestion control functions are invoked to respond to and recover from the congestion.

Traffic Management and Congestion Control Techniques

ITU-T and the ATM Forum have defined a range of traffic management functions to maintain the quality of service of ATM connections. ATM traffic management function refers to the set of actions taken by the network to avoid congestion conditions or to minimize congestion effects. In this subsection, we highlight the following techniques:

- Resource management using virtual paths
- Connection admission control

Table 13.1   Traffic Control and Congestion Control Functions

Response Time	Traffic Control Functions	Congestion Control Functions
Long Term	• Resource management using virtual paths	
Connection Duration	• Connection admission control (CAC)	
Round-Trip Propagation Time	• Fast resource management	• Explicit forward congestion indication (EFCI) • ABR flow control
Cell Insertion Time	• Usage parameter control (UPC) • Priority control • Traffic shaping	• Selective cell discard

- Usage parameter control
- Selective cell discard
- Traffic shaping

RESOURCE MANAGEMENT USING VIRTUAL PATHS The essential concept behind network resource management is to allocate network resources in such a way as to separate traffic flows according to service characteristics. So far, the only specific traffic control function based on network resource management defined by the ATM Forum deals with the use of virtual paths.

As discussed in Chapter 11, a virtual path connection (VPC) provides a convenient means of grouping similar virtual channel connections (VCCs). The network provides aggregate capacity and performance characteristics on the virtual path, and these are shared by the virtual connections. There are three cases to consider:

- **User-to-user application:** The VPC extends between a pair of UNIs. In this case the network has no knowledge of the QoS of the individual VCCs within a VPC. It is the user's responsibility to assure that the aggregate demand from the VCCs can be accommodated by the VPC.

- **User-to-network application:** The VPC extends between a UNI and a network node. In this case, the network is aware of the QoS of the VCCs within the VPC and has to accommodate them.

- **Network-to-network application:** The VPC extends between two network nodes. Again, in this case, the network is aware of the QoS of the VCCs within the VPC and has to accommodate them.

The QoS parameters that are of primary concern for network resource management are cell loss ratio, cell transfer delay, and cell delay variation, all of which are affected by the amount of resources devoted to the VPC by the network. If a VCC extends through multiple VPCs, then the performance on that VCC depends on the performances of the consecutive VPCs and on how the connection is handled at any node that performs VCC-related functions. Such a node may be a switch, concentrator, or other network equipment. The performance of each VPC depends on the capacity of that VPC and the traffic characteristics of the VCCs contained within the VPC. The performance of each VCC-related function depends on the switching/processing speed at the node and on the relative priority with which various cells are handled.

Figure 13.8 gives an example. VCCs 1 and 2 experience a performance that depends on VPCs b and c and on how these VCCs are handled by the intermediate nodes. This may differ from the performance experienced by VCCs 3, 4, and 5.

There are a number of alternatives for the way in which VCCs are grouped and the type of performance they experience. If all of the VCCs within a VPC are handled similarly, then they should experience similar expected network performance, in terms of cell loss ratio, cell transfer delay, and cell delay variation. Alternatively, when different VCCs within the same VPC require different QoS, the VPC performance objective agreed by network and subscriber should be set suitably for the most demanding VCC requirement.

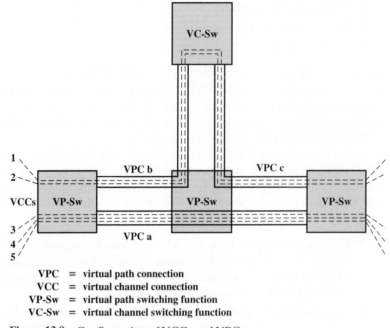

VPC = virtual path connection
VCC = virtual channel connection
VP-Sw = virtual path switching function
VC-Sw = virtual channel switching function

Figure 13.8 Configuration of VCCs and VPCs

In either case, with multiple VCCs within the same VPC, the network has two general options for allocating capacity to the VPC:

- **Aggregate peak demand:** The network may set the capacity (data rate) of the VPC equal to the total of the peak data rates of all of the VCCs within the VPC. The advantage of this approach is that each VCC can be given a QoS that accommodates its peak demand. The disadvantage is that most of the time, the VPC capacity will not be fully utilized and therefore the network will have underutilized resources.

- **Statistical multiplexing:** If the network sets the capacity of the VPC to be greater than or equal to the average data rates of all the VCCs but less than the aggregate peak demand, then a statistical multiplexing service is supplied. With statistical multiplexing, VCCs experience greater cell delay variation and greater cell transfer delay. Depending on the size of buffers used to queue cells for transmission, VCCs may also experience greater cell loss ratio. This approach has the advantage of more efficient utilization of capacity and is attractive if the VCCs can tolerate the lower QoS.

When statistical multiplexing is used, it is preferable to group VCCs into VPCs on the basis of similar traffic characteristics and similar QoS requirements. If dissimilar VCCs share the same VPC and statistical multiplexing is used, it is difficult to provide fair access to both high-demand and low-demand traffic streams.

CONNECTION ADMISSION CONTROL Connection admission control is the first line of defense for the network in protecting itself from excessive loads. In essence, when a user requests a new VPC or VCC, the user must specify (implicitly or explicitly) the traffic characteristics in both directions for that connection. The user selects traffic characteristics by selecting a QoS from among the QoS classes that the network provides. The network accepts the connection only if it can commit the resources necessary to support that traffic level while at the same time maintaining the agreed QoS of existing connections. By accepting the connection, the network forms a *traffic contract* with the user. Once the connection is accepted, the network continues to provide the agreed QoS as long as the user complies with the traffic contract.

The traffic contract may consist of the four parameters defined in Table 13.2: peak cell rate (PCR), cell delay variation (CDV), sustainable cell rate (SCR), and burst tolerance. Only the first two parameters are relevant for a constant-bit-rate (CBR) source; all four parameters may be used for variable-bit-rate (VBR) sources.

As the name suggests, the peak cell rate is the maximum rate at which cells are generated by the source on this connection. However, we need to take into account the cell delay variation. Although a source may be generating cells at a constant peak rate, cell delay variations introduced by various factors (see Figure 13.7) will affect the timing, causing cells to clump up and gaps to occur. Thus, a source may temporarily exceed the peak cell rate due to clumping. For the network to properly allocate resources to this connection, it must know not only the peak cell rate but also the CDV.

The exact relationship between peak cell rate and CDV depends on the operational definitions of these two terms. The standards provide these definitions in terms of a cell rate algorithm. Because this algorithm can be used for usage parameter control, we defer a discussion until the next subsection.

The PCR and CDV must be specified for every connection. As an option for variable-bit rate sources, the user may also specify a sustainable cell rate and burst tolerance. These parameters are analogous to PCR and CDV, respectively, but apply to an average rate of cell generation rather than a peak rate. The user can describe the future flow of cells in greater detail by using the SCR and burst tolerance as well as the PCR and CDV. With this additional information, the network may be able to

Table 13.2 Traffic Parameters Used in Defining VCC/VPC Quality of Service

Parameter	Description	Traffic Type
Peak Cell Rate (PCR)	An upper bound on the traffic that can be submitted on an ATM connection.	CBR, VBR
Cell Delay Variation (CDV)	An upper bound on the variability in the pattern of cell arrivals observed at a single measurement point with reference to the peak cell rate.	CBR, VBR
Sustainable Cell Rate (SCR)	An upper bound on the average rate of an ATM connection, calculated over the duration of the connection.	VBR
Burst Tolerance	An upper bound on the variability in the pattern of cell arrivals observed at a single measurement point with reference to the sustainable cell rate.	VBR

CBR = constant bit rate
VBR = variable bit rate

utilize the network resources more efficiently. For example, if a number of VCCs are statistically multiplexed over a VPC, knowledge of both average and peak cell rates enables the network to allocate buffers of sufficient size to handle the traffic efficiently without cell loss.

For a given connection (VPC or VCC) the four traffic parameters may be specified in several ways, as illustrated in Table 13.3. Parameter values may be implicitly defined by default rules set by the network operator. In this case, all connections are assigned the same values, or all connections of a given class are assigned the same values for that class. The network operator may also associate parameter values with a given subscriber and assign these at the time of subscription. Finally, parameter values tailored to a particular connection may be assigned at connection time. In the case of a permanent virtual connection, these values are assigned by the network when the connection is set up. For a switched virtual connection, the parameters are negotiated between the user and the network via a signaling protocol.

Another aspect of quality of service that may be requested or assigned for a connection is cell loss priority. A user may request two levels of cell loss priority for an ATM connection; the priority of an individual cell is indicated by the user through the CLP bit in the cell header (Figure 11.6). When two priority levels are used, the traffic parameters for both cell flows must be specified. Typically, this is done by specifying a set of traffic parameters for high-priority traffic (CLP = 0) and a set of traffic parameters for all traffic (CLP = 0 or 1). Based on this breakdown, the network may be able to allocate resources more efficiently.

USAGE PARAMETER CONTROL   Once a connection has been accepted by the connection admission control function, the usage parameter control (UPC) function of the network monitors the connection to determine whether the traffic conforms to the traffic contract. The main purpose of usage parameter control is to protect network resources from an overload on one connection that would adversely affect the QoS on other connections by detecting violations of assigned parameters and taking appropriate actions.

Table 13.3   Procedures Used to Set Values of Traffic Contract Parameters

	Explicitly Specified Parameters		**Implicitly Specified Parameters**
	Parameter Values Set at Connection-Setup Time	**Parameter Values Specified at Subscription Time**	**Parameter Values Set Using Default Rules**
	Requested by User/NMS	**Assigned by Network Operator**	
SVC	signaling	by subscription	network-operator default rules
PVC	NMS	by subscription	network-operator default rules

SVC = switched virtual connection
PVC = permanent virtual connection
NMS = network management system

Usage parameter control can be done at both the virtual path and virtual channel levels. Of these, the more important is VPC-level control, because network resources are, in general, initially allocated on the basis of virtual paths, with the virtual path capacity shared among the member virtual channels.

There are two separate functions encompassed by usage parameter control:

- Control of peak cell rate and the associated cell delay variation (CDV)
- Control of sustainable cell rate and the associated burst tolerance

Let us first consider the peak cell rate and the associated cell delay variation. In simple terms, a traffic flow is compliant if the peak rate of cell transmission does not exceed the agreed peak cell rate, subject to the possibility of cell delay variation within the agreed bound. I.371 defines an algorithm, the peak cell rate algorithm, that monitors compliance. The algorithm operates on the basis of two parameters: a peak cell rate R and a CDV tolerance limit of τ. Then $T = 1/R$ is the interarrival time between cells if there were no CDV. With CDV, T is the average interarrival time at the peak rate. The algorithm has been defined to monitor the rate at which cells arrive and to assure that the interarrival time is not too short to cause the flow to exceed the peak cell rate by an amount greater than the tolerance limit.

The same algorithm, with different parameters, can be used to monitor the sustainable cell rate and the associated burst tolerance. In this case, the parameters are the sustainable cell rate R_s and a burst tolerance τ_s.

The cell rate algorithm is rather complex; details can be found in Appendix J; the technique is known as the **leaky bucket algorithm**. The algorithm simply defines a way to monitor compliance with the traffic contract. To perform usage parameter control, the network must act on the results of the algorithm. The simplest strategy is that compliant cells are passed along and noncompliant cells are discarded at the point of the UPC function.

At the network's option, cell tagging may also be used for noncompliant cells. In this case, a noncompliant cell may be tagged with CLP = 1 (low priority) and passed. Such cells are then subject to discard at a later point in the network, should congestion be encountered.

If the user has negotiated two levels of cell loss priority for a network, then the situation is more complex. Recall that the user may negotiate a traffic contract for high-priority traffic (CLP = 0) and a separate contract for aggregate traffic (CLP 0 or 1). The following rules apply:

1. A cell with CLP = 0 that conforms to the traffic contract for CLP = 0 passes.
2. A cell with CLP = 0 that is noncompliant for (CLP = 0) traffic but compliant for (CLP 0 or 1) traffic is tagged and passed.
3. A cell with CLP = 0 that is noncompliant for (CLP = 0) traffic and noncompliant for (CLP 0 or 1) traffic is discarded.
4. A cell with CLP = 1 that is compliant for (CLP = 0 or 1) traffic is passed.
5. A cell with CLP = 1 that is noncompliant for (CLP 0 or 1) traffic is discarded.

SELECTIVE CELL DISCARD Selective cell discard comes into play when the network, at some point beyond the UPC function, discards (CLP = 1) cells. The objective is to

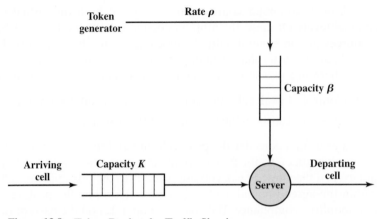

Figure 13.9 Token Bucket for Traffic Shaping

discard lower-priority cells during congestion to protect the performance for higher-priority cells. Note that the network has no way to discriminate between cells that were labeled as lower priority by the source and cells that were tagged by the UPC function.

TRAFFIC SHAPING The UPC algorithm is referred to as a form of **traffic policing**. Traffic policing occurs when a flow of data is regulated so that cells (or frames or packets) that exceed a certain performance level are discarded or tagged. It may be desirable to supplement a traffic-policing policy with a **traffic-shaping** policy. Traffic shaping is used to smooth out a traffic flow and reduce cell clumping. This can result in a fairer allocation of resources and a reduced average delay time.

A simple approach to traffic shaping is to use a form of the UPC algorithm known as token bucket. In contrast to the UPC algorithm, which simply monitors the traffic and tags or discards noncompliant cells, a traffic-shaping token bucket controls the flow of compliant cells.

Figure 13.9 illustrates the basic principle of the token bucket. A token generator produces tokens at a rate of ρ tokens per second and places these in the token bucket, which has a maximum capacity of β tokens. Cells arriving from the source are placed in a buffer with a maximum capacity of K cells. To transmit a cell through the server, one token must be removed from the bucket. If the token bucket is empty, the cell is queued waiting for the next token. The result of this scheme is that if there is a backlog of cells and an empty bucket, then cells are emitted at a smooth flow of ρ cells per second with no cell delay variation until the backlog is cleared. Thus, the token bucket smoothes out bursts of cells.

13.6 ATM–GFR TRAFFIC MANAGEMENT

GFR (guaranteed frame rate) provides a service that is as simple as UBR (unspecified bit rate) from the end system's point of view while placing a relatively modest requirement on the ATM network elements in terms of processing complexity and overhead. In essence, with GFR, an end system does no policing or shaping of the traffic it transmits but may transmit at the line rate of the ATM adapter. As with

UBR, there is no guarantee of frame delivery. It is up to a higher layer, such as TCP, to react to congestion that results in dropped frames by employing the window management and congestion control techniques discussed in Part Five. Unlike UBR, GFR allows the user to reserve a certain amount of capacity, in terms of a cell rate, for each GFR virtual channel (VC). A GFR reservation assures an application that it may transmit at a minimum rate without losses. If the network is not congested, the user will be able to transmit at a higher rate.

A distinctive characteristic of GFR is that it requires the network to recognize frames as well as cells. When congestion occurs, the network discards entire frames rather than individual cells. Further, GFR requires that all of the cells of a frame have the same CLP bit setting. The CLP = 1 AAL5 frames are treated as lower-priority frames that are to be transmitted on a best-effort basis. The minimum guaranteed capacity applies to the CLP = 0 frames.

The GFR traffic contract consists of the following parameters:

- Peak cell rate (PCR)
- Minimum cell rate (MCR)
- Maximum burst size (MBS)
- Maximum frame size (MFS)
- Cell delay variation tolerance (CDVT)

Mechanisms for Supporting Rate Guarantees

There are three basic approaches that can be used by the network to provide per-VC guarantees for GFR and to enable a number of users to efficiently use and fairly share the available network capacity [GOYA98]:

- Tagging and policing
- Buffer management
- Scheduling

These approaches can be combined in various ways in an ATM network elements to yield a number of possible GFR implementations. Figure 13.10 illustrates their use.

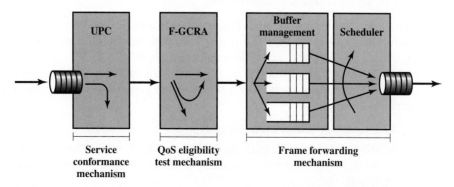

Figure 13.10 The Fundamental Components of a GFR Mechanism [ANDR99]

TAGGING AND POLICING Tagging is used to discriminate between frames that conform to the GFR traffic contract and those that do not. The network element doing the conformance checking sets CLP = 1 on all cells of each frame that does not conform. Because tagged cells are assumed to be in violation of the traffic contract, they are given a lower quality of service than untagged cells by subsequent mechanisms, such as buffer management and scheduling. Tagging can be done by the network, especially the network element at the ingress to the ATM network. But tagging may also be done by the source end system to indicate less important frames.

The network, at either the ingress network element or at other ATM switching elements, may also choose to discard cells of nonconforming frames (i.e., cells with CLP = 1). Cell discard is considered a policing function.

BUFFER MANAGEMENT Buffer management mechanisms have to do with the way in which cells are treated that have been buffered at a network switch or that arrive at a network switch and must be buffered prior to forwarding. When a congestion condition exists, as reflected by high buffer occupancy, a network element will discard tagged cells in preference to untagged cells. In particular, a network element may discard a tagged cell that is already in a buffer to make room for an incoming untagged cell. To provide fair and efficient use of buffer resources, a network element may perform per-VC buffering, dedicating a certain amount of buffer space to individual VCs. Then, on the basis of the traffic contracts for each VC and the buffer occupancy per VC, the network element can make decisions concerning cell discard. That is, cell discard can be based on queue-specific occupancy thresholds.

SCHEDULING A scheduling function, at minimum, can give preferential treatment to untagged cells over tagged cells. A network can also maintain separate queues for each VC and make per-VC scheduling decisions. Thus, within each queue, a first-come, first-served discipline can be used, perhaps modified to give higher priority for scheduling to CLP = 0 frames. Scheduling among the queues enables the network element to control the outgoing rate of individual VCs and thus ensure that individual VCs receive a fair allocation of capacity while meeting traffic contract requirements for minimum cell rate for each VC.

GFR Conformance Definition

The first function indicated in Figure 13.10 is a UPC function. UPC monitors each active VC to ensure that the traffic on each connection conforms to the traffic contract, and tags or discards nonconforming cells.

A frame is conforming if all of its cells are conforming, and is nonconforming if one or more cells are nonconforming. Three conditions must be met for a cell to be conforming:

1. The rate of cells must be within the cell rate contract.
2. All cells of a frame must have the same CLP value. Thus, the CLP bit of the current cell must have the same value as the CLP bit of the first cell of the frame.

3. The frame containing this cell must satisfy the MFS parameter. This condition can be met by performing the following test on each cell: The cell either is the last cell of the frame or the number of cells in the frame up to and including this cell is less than MFS.

QoS Eligibility Test Mechanism

The first two boxes in Figure 13.10 show what amounts to a two-stage filtering process. First, frames are tested for conformance to the traffic contract. Frames that do not conform may be discarded immediately. If a nonconforming frame is not discarded, its cells are tagged (CLP = 1), making them vulnerable to discard later on in the network. This first stage is therefore looking at an upper bound on traffic and penalizing cells that push the traffic flow above the upper bound.

The second stage of filtering determines which frames are eligible for QoS guarantees under the GFR contract for a given VC. This stage is looking at a lower bound on traffic; over a given period of time, those frames that constitute a traffic flow below the defined threshold are designated as eligible for QoS handling.

Therefore, the frames transmitted on a GFR VC fall into three categories:

- **Nonconforming frame:** Cells of this frame will be tagged or discarded.
- **Conforming but ineligible frames:** Cells will receive a best-effort service.
- **Conforming and eligible frames:** Cells will receive a guarantee of delivery.

To determine eligibility, a form of the cell rate algorithm referred to in Section 13.5 is used. A network may discard or tag any cells that are not eligible. However, TM 4.1 states that it is expected that an implementation will attempt to deliver conforming but ineligible traffic on the basis of available resources, with each GFR connection being provided at each link with a fair share of the local residual bandwidth. The specification does not attempt to define a criterion by which to determine if a given implementation meets the aforementioned expectation.

13.7 RECOMMENDED READING

[YANG95] is a comprehensive survey of congestion control techniques. [JAIN90] and [JAIN92] provide excellent discussions of the requirements for congestion control, the various approaches that can be taken, and performance considerations. An excellent discussion of data network performance issues is provided by [KLEI93]. While somewhat dated, the definitive reference on flow control is [GERL80].

[GARR96] provides a rationale for the ATM service categories and discusses the traffic management implications of each. [MCDY99] contains a thorough discussion of ATM traffic control for CBR and VBR. Two excellent treatments of ATM traffic characteristics and performance are [GIRO99] and [SCHW96].

[ANDR99] provides a clear, detailed description of GFR. Another useful description is [BONA01].

ANDR99   Andrikopoulos, I.; Liakopoulous, A.; Pavlou, G.; and Sun, Z. "Providing Rate Guarantees for Internet Application Traffic Across ATM Networks." *IEEE Communications Surveys*, Third Quarter 1999, http://www.comsoc.org/pubs/surveys.

BONA01   Bonaventure, O., and Nelissen, J. "Guaranteed Frame Rate: A Better Service for TCP/IP in ATM Networks." *IEEE Network*, January/February 2001.

GARR96   Garrett, M. "A Service Architecture for ATM: From Applications to Scheduling." *IEEE Network*, May/June 1996.

GERL80   Gerla, M., and Kleinrock, L. "Flow Control: A Comparative Survey." *IEEE Transactions on Communications*, April 1980.

GIRO99   Giroux, N., and Ganti, S. *Quality of Service in ATM Networks.* Upper Saddle River, NJ: Prentice Hall, 1999.

JAIN90   Jain, R. "Congestion Control in Computer Networks: Issues and Trends." *IEEE Network Magazine*, May 1990.

JAIN92   Jain, R. "Myths About Congestion Management in High-Speed Networks." *Internetworking: Research and Experience*, Volume 3, 1992.

KLEI93   Kleinrock, L. "On the Modeling and Analysis of Computer Networks." *Proceedings of the IEEE*, August 1993.

MCDY99   McDysan, D., and Spohn, D. *ATM: Theory and Application.* New York: McGraw-Hill, 1999.

SCHW96   Schwartz, M. *Broadband Integrated Networks.* Upper Saddle River, NJ: Prentice Hall PTR, 1996.

YANG95   Yang, C., and Reddy, A. "A Taxonomy for Congestion Control Algorithms in Packet Switching Networks." *IEEE Network*, July/August 1995.

13.8 KEY TERMS, REVIEW QUESTIONS, AND PROBLEMS

Key Terms

backpressure	explicit congestion signaling	reservations
cell delay variation	implicit congestion signaling	traffic management
choke packet	quality of service (QoS)	traffic policing
congestion	leaky bucket algorithm	traffic-shaping
congestion control		

Review Questions

13.1   When a node experiences saturation with respect to incoming packets, what general strategies may be used?

13.2   Why is it that when the load exceeds the network capacity, delay tends to infinity?

13.3   Give a brief explanation of each of the congestion control techniques illustrated in Figure 13.5.

13.4   What is the difference between backward and forward explicit congestion signaling?

13.5   Briefly explain the three general approaches to explicit congestion signaling.

13.6   What is the significance of cell delay variation in an ATM network?

13.7 What functions are included in ATM usage parameter control?

13.8 What is the difference between traffic policing and traffic shaping?

Problems

13.1 A proposed congestion control technique is known as isarithmic control. In this method, the total number of frames in transit is fixed by inserting a fixed number of permits into the network. These permits circulate at random through the frame relay network. Whenever a frame handler wants to relay a frame just given to it by an attached user, it must first capture and destroy a permit. When the frame is delivered to the destination user by the frame handler to which it attaches, that frame handler reissues the permit. List three potential problems with this technique.

13.2 In the discussion of latency/speed effects in Section 13.5, an example was given in which over 7 megabits were transmitted before the source could react. But isn't a sliding-window flow control technique, such as described for HDLC, designed to cope with long propagation delays?

13.3 When the sustained traffic through a packet-switching node exceeds the node's capacity, the node must discard packets. Buffers only defer the congestion problem; they do not solve it. Consider the packet-switching network in Figure 13.11. Five stations attach to one of the network's nodes. The node has a single link to the rest of the network with a normalized throughput capacity of $C = 1.0$. Senders 1 through 5 are sending at average sustained rates of r_i of 0.1, 0.2, 0.3, 0.4, and 0.5 respectively. Clearly the node is overloaded. To deal with the congestion, the node discards packets from sender i with a probability of p_i.

  a. Show the relationship among p_i, r_i, and C so that the rate of undiscarded packets does not exceed C.

  The node establishes a discard policy by assigning values to the p_i such that the relationship derived in part (a) of this problem is satisfied. For each of the following policies, verify that the relationship is satisfied and describe in words the policy from the point of view of the senders.

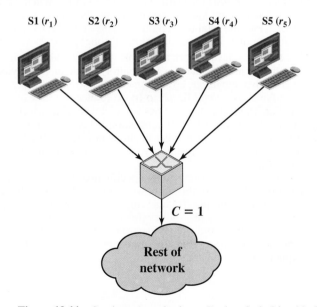

Figure 13.11 Stations Attached to a Packet-Switching Node

b. $p_1 = 0.333; p_2 = 0.333; p_3 = 0.333; p_4 = 0.333; p_5 = 0.333$
c. $p_1 = 0.091; p_2 = 0.182; p_3 = 0.273; p_4 = 0.364; p_5 = 0.455$
d. $p_1 = 0.0; p_2 = 0.0; p_3 = 0.222; p_4 = 0.417; p_5 = 0.533$
e. $p_1 = 0.0; p_2 = 0.0; p_3 = 0.0; p_4 = 0.0; p_5 = 1.0$

13.4 Compare sustainable cell rate and burst tolerance, as used in ATM networks, with committed information rate and excess burst size, as used in frame relay networks (see Appendix U). Do the respective terms represent the same concepts?

13.5 A congestion control scheme used with ATM (Available Bit Rate) is to decrease the allowable data rate in response to congestion with the following equation.

$$\text{Ratenew} = \text{Rateold} - \text{Rateold} \times \text{RDF},$$

Where RDF is the rate decrease factor,
a. Discuss how fast/slow does the sender respond to congestion for the various values of RDF.
b. If the equation was changed to Ratenew = Rateold − Rateold × α, do you think the response will be better or worse and why?

Note: the following two problems refer to Appendix J.

13.6 a. Demonstrate that Equation (J.1) is correct.
b. Demonstrate that Equation (J.2) is correct.
c. Demonstrate that Equation (J.3) is correct.

13.7 Show that over any closed interval of length t, the number of cells, $N(t)$, that can be emitted with spacing no less than T and still be in conformance with $GCRA(T_s, \tau_s)$ is bounded by:

$$N(t) \leq \min\left(\left\lfloor 1 + \frac{t + \tau_s}{T_s} \right\rfloor, \left\lfloor 1 + \frac{t}{T} \right\rfloor\right)$$

Note: the following two problems refer to Appendix V.

13.8 Consider the frame relay network depicted in Figure V.6. C is the capacity of a link in frames per second. Node A presents a constant load of 0.8 frames per second destined for A'. Node B presents a load λ destined for B'. Node S has a common pool of buffers that it uses for traffic both to A' and B'. When the buffer is full, frames are discarded, and are later retransmitted by the source node. S has a throughput capacity of 2. Plot the total throughput (i.e., the sum of A-A' and B-B' delivered traffic) as a function of λ. What fraction of the throughput is A-A' traffic for $\lambda > 1$?

13.9 For a frame relay network to be able to detect and then signal congestion, it is necessary for each frame handler to monitor its queuing behavior. If queue lengths begin to grow to a dangerous level, then either forward or backward explicit notification or a combination should be set to try to reduce the flow of frames through that frame handler. The frame handler has some choice as to which logical connections should be alerted to congestion. If congestion is becoming quite serious, all logical connections through a frame handler might be notified. In the early stages of congestion, the frame handler might just notify users for those connections that are generating the most traffic.

In one of the frame relay specifications, an algorithm for monitoring queue lengths is suggested; this is shown in Figure V.7. A cycle begins when the outgoing circuit goes from idle (queue empty) to busy (nonzero queue size, including the current frame). If a threshold value is exceeded, then the circuit is in a state of incipient congestion, and the congestion avoidance bits should be set on some or all logical connections that use that circuit. Describe the algorithm in words and explain its advantages.

CELLULAR WIRELESS NETWORKS

After the fire of 1805, Judge Woodward was the central figure involved in reestablishing the town. Influenced by Major Pierre L'Enfant's plans for Washington, DC, Judge Woodward envisioned a modern series of hexagons with major diagonal avenues centered on circular parks, or circuses, in the center of the hexagons. Frederick Law Olmstead said, "nearly all of the most serious mistakes of Detroit's past have arisen from a disregard of the spirit of Woodward's plan."

— *Endangered Detroit*, Friends of the Book-Cadillac Hotel

KEY POINTS

◆ The essence of a cellular network is the use of multiple low-power transmitters. The area to be covered is divided into cells in a hexagonal tile pattern that provide full coverage of the area.

◆ A major technical problem for cellular networks is fading, which refers to the time variation of received signal power caused by changes in the transmission medium or path(s).

◆ First-generation cellular networks were analog, making use of frequency division multiplexing.

◆ Second-generation cellular networks are digital. One technique in widespread use is based on code division multiple access (CDMA).

◆ The objective of the third-generation (3G) of wireless communication is to provide fairly high-speed wireless communications to support multimedia, data, and video in addition to voice.

Of all the tremendous advances in data communications and telecommunications, perhaps the most revolutionary is the development of cellular networks. Cellular technology is the foundation of mobile wireless communications and supports users in locations that are not easily served by wired networks. Cellular technology is the underlying technology for mobile telephones, personal communications systems, wireless Internet and wireless Web applications, and much more.

We begin this chapter with a look at the basic principles used in all cellular networks. Then we look at specific cellular technologies and standards, which are conveniently grouped into three generations. The first generation is analog based and, while still widely used, is passing from the scene. The dominant technology today is the digital second-generation systems. Finally, third-generation high-speed digital systems have begun to emerge.

14.1 PRINCIPLES OF CELLULAR NETWORKS

Cellular radio is a technique that was developed to increase the capacity available for mobile radio telephone service. Prior to the introduction of cellular radio, mobile radio telephone service was only provided by a high-power transmitter/receiver.

A typical system would support about 25 channels with an effective radius of about 80 km. The way to increase the capacity of the system is to use lower-power systems with shorter radius and to use numerous transmitters/receivers. We begin this section with a look at the organization of cellular systems and then examine some of the details of their implementation.

Cellular Network Organization

The essence of a cellular network is the use of multiple low-power transmitters, on the order of 100 W or less. Because the range of such a transmitter is small, an area can be divided into cells, each one served by its own antenna. Each cell is allocated a band of frequencies and is served by a **base station**, consisting of transmitter, receiver, and control unit. Adjacent cells are assigned different frequencies to avoid interference or crosstalk. However, cells sufficiently distant from each other can use the same frequency band.

The first design decision to make is the shape of cells to cover an area. A matrix of square cells would be the simplest layout to define (Figure 14.1a). However, this geometry is not ideal. If the width of a square cell is d, then a cell has four neighbors at a distance d and four neighbors at a distance $\sqrt{2}d$. As a mobile user within a cell moves toward the cell's boundaries, it is best if all of the adjacent antennas are equidistant. This simplifies the task of determining when to switch the user to an adjacent antenna and which antenna to choose. A hexagonal pattern provides for equidistant antennas (Figure 14.1b). The radius of a hexagon is defined to be the radius of the circle that circumscribes it (equivalently, the distance from the center to each vertex; also equal to the length of a side of a hexagon). For a cell radius R, the distance between the cell center and each adjacent cell center is $d = \sqrt{3}R$.

In practice, a precise hexagonal pattern is not used. Variations from the ideal are due to topographical limitations, local signal propagation conditions, and practical limitation on siting antennas.

A wireless cellular system limits the opportunity to use the same frequency for different communications because the signals, not being constrained, can interfere

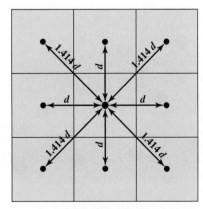
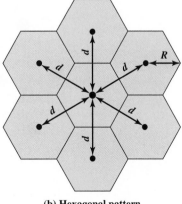

(a) Square pattern   **(b) Hexagonal pattern**

Figure 14.1   Cellular Geometries

with one another even if geographically separated. Systems supporting a large number of communications simultaneously need mechanisms to conserve spectrum.

FREQUENCY REUSE In a cellular system, each cell has a base transceiver. The transmission power is carefully controlled (to the extent that it is possible in the highly variable mobile communication environment) to allow communication within the cell using a given frequency, while limiting the power at that frequency that escapes the cell into adjacent ones. The objective is to use the same frequency in other nearby (but not adjacent) cells, thus allowing the frequency to be used for multiple simultaneous conversations. Generally, 10 to 50 frequencies are assigned to each cell, depending on the traffic expected.

The essential issue is to determine how many cells must intervene between two cells using the same frequency so that the two cells do not interfere with each other. Various patterns of frequency reuse are possible. Figure 14.2 shows some examples. If the pattern consists of N cells and each cell is assigned the same number of frequencies, each cell can have K/N frequencies, where K is the total number of frequencies allotted to the system. For AMPS (Section 14.2), $K = 395$ and $N = 7$ is the smallest pattern that can provide sufficient isolation between two uses of the same frequency. This implies that there can be at most 57 frequencies per cell on average.

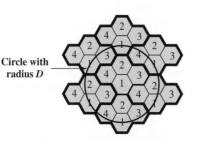

Circle with radius D

(a) Frequency reuse pattern for $N = 4$

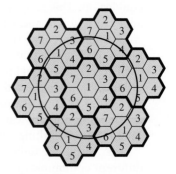

(b) Frequency reuse pattern for $N = 7$

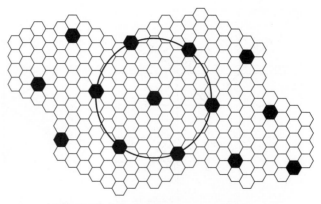

(c) Black cells indicate a frequency reuse for $N = 19$

Figure 14.2 Frequency Reuse Patterns

In characterizing frequency reuse, the following parameters are commonly used:

D = minimum distance between centers of cells that use the same band of frequencies (called cochannels)

R = radius of a cell

d = distance between centers of adjacent cells ($d = \sqrt{3}R$)

N = number of cells in a repetitious pattern (each cell in the pattern uses a unique band of frequencies), termed the **reuse factor**

In a hexagonal cell pattern, only the following values of N are possible:

$$N = I^2 + J^2 + (I \times J) \quad I, J = 0, 1, 2, 3, \ldots$$

Hence, possible values of N are 1, 3, 4, 7, 9, 12, 13, 16, 19, 21, and so on. The following relationship holds:

$$\frac{D}{R} = \sqrt{3N}$$

This can also be expressed as $D/d = \sqrt{N}$.

INCREASING CAPACITY In time, as more customers use the system, traffic may build up so that there are not enough frequencies assigned to a cell to handle its calls. A number of approaches have been used to cope with this situation, including the following:

- **Adding new channels:** Typically, when a system is set up in a region, not all of the channels are used, and growth and expansion can be managed in an orderly fashion by adding new channels.

- **Frequency borrowing:** In the simplest case, frequencies are taken from adjacent cells by congested cells. The frequencies can also be assigned to cells dynamically.

- **Cell splitting:** In practice, the distribution of traffic and topographic features is not uniform, and this presents opportunities for capacity increase. Cells in areas of high usage can be split into smaller cells. Generally, the original cells are about 6.5 to 13 km in size. The smaller cells can themselves be split; however, 1.5-km cells are close to the practical minimum size as a general solution (but see the subsequent discussion of microcells). To use a smaller cell, the power level used must be reduced to keep the signal within the cell. Also, as the mobile units move, they pass from cell to cell, which requires transferring of the call from one base transceiver to another. This process is called a *handoff*. As the cells get smaller, these handoffs become much more frequent. Figure 14.3 indicates schematically how cells can be divided to provide more capacity. A radius reduction by a factor of F reduces the coverage area and increases the required number of base stations by a factor of F^2.

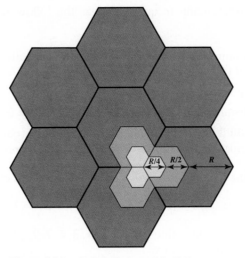

Figure 14.3 Cell Splitting with Cell
Reduction Factor of $F = 2$

- **Cell sectoring:** With cell sectoring, a cell is divided into a number of wedge-shaped sectors, each with its own set of channels, typically three or six sectors per cell. Each sector is assigned a separate subset of the cell's channels, and directional antennas at the base station are used to focus on each sector.

- **Microcells:** As cells become smaller, antennas move from the tops of tall buildings or hills, to the tops of small buildings or the sides of large buildings, and finally to lamp posts, where they form microcells. Each decrease in cell size is accompanied by a reduction in the radiated power levels from the base stations and the mobile units. Microcells are useful in city streets in congested areas, along highways, and inside large public buildings.

Table 14.1 suggests typical parameters for traditional cells, called macrocells, and microcells with current technology. The average delay spread refers to multipath delay spread (i.e., the same signal follows different paths and there is a time delay between the earliest and latest arrival of the signal at the receiver). As indicated, the use of smaller cells enables the use of lower power and provides superior propagation conditions.

Table 14.1 Typical Parameters for Macrocells and Microcells [ANDE95]

	Macrocell	**Microcell**
Cell Radius	1–20 km	0.1–1 km
Transmission Power	1–10 W	0.1–1 W
Average Delay Spread	0.1–10 μs	10–100 ns
Maximum Bit Rate	0.3 Mbps	1 Mbps

EXAMPLE 14.1 Assume a system of 32 cells with a cell radius of 1.6 km, a total of 32 cells, a total frequency bandwidth that supports 336 traffic channels, and a reuse factor of $N = 7$. If there are 32 total cells, what geographic area is covered, how many channels are there per cell, and what is the total number of concurrent calls that can be handled? Repeat for a cell radius of 0.8 km and 128 cells.

Figure 14.4a shows an approximately square pattern. The area of a hexagon of radius R is $1.5R^2\sqrt{3}$. A hexagon of radius 1.6 km has an area of 6.65 km^2, and the total area covered is $6.65 \times 32 = 213$ km^2. For $N = 7$, the number of channels per cell is $336/7 = 48$, for a total channel capacity of $48 \times 32 = 1536$ channels. For the layout of Figure 14.4b, the area covered is $1.66 \times 128 = 213$ km^2. The number of channels per cell is $336/7 = 48$, for a total channel capacity of $48 \times 128 = 6144$ channels.

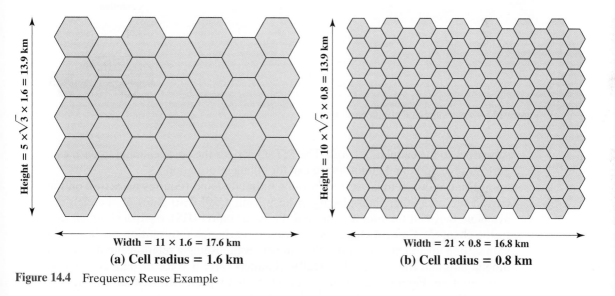

(a) Cell radius = 1.6 km   (b) Cell radius = 0.8 km

Figure 14.4   Frequency Reuse Example

Operation of Cellular Systems

Figure 14.5 shows the principal elements of a cellular system. In the approximate center of each cell is a base station (BS). The BS includes one or more antennas, a controller, and a number of transceivers, for communicating on the channels assigned to that cell. The controller is used to handle the call process between the mobile unit and the rest of the network. At any time, a number of mobile user units may be active and moving about within a cell, communicating with the BS. Each BS is connected to a mobile telecommunications switching office (MTSO), with one MTSO serving multiple BSs. Typically, the link between an MTSO and a BS is by a wire line, although a wireless link is also possible. The MTSO connects calls between mobile units. The MTSO is also connected to the public telephone or telecommunications network and can make a connection between a fixed subscriber to the public network and a mobile

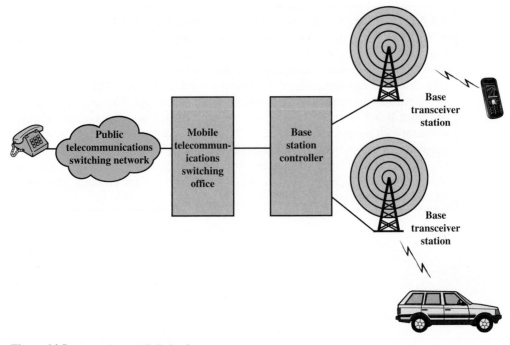

Figure 14.5   Overview of Cellular System

subscriber to the cellular network. The MTSO assigns the voice channel to each call, performs handoffs, and monitors the call for billing information.

The use of a cellular system is fully automated and requires no action on the part of the user other than placing or answering a call. Two types of channels are available between the mobile unit and the base station (BS): control channels and traffic channels. **Control channels** are used to exchange information having to do with setting up and maintaining calls and with establishing a relationship between a mobile unit and the nearest BS. **Traffic channels** carry a voice or data connection between users. Figure 14.6 illustrates the steps in a typical call between two mobile users within an area controlled by a single MTSO:

- **Mobile unit initialization:** When the mobile unit is turned on, it scans and selects the strongest setup control channel used for this system (Figure 14.6a). Cells with different frequency bands repetitively broadcast on different setup channels. The receiver selects the strongest setup channel and monitors that channel. The effect of this procedure is that the mobile unit has automatically selected the BS antenna of the cell within which it will operate.[1] Then a handshake takes place between the mobile unit and the MTSO controlling this cell, through the BS in this cell. The handshake is used to identify the user and register its location. As long as the mobile unit is on, this scanning procedure is repeated

---

[1]Usually, but not always, the antenna and therefore the base station selected is the closest one to the mobile unit. However, because of propagation anomalies, this is not always the case.

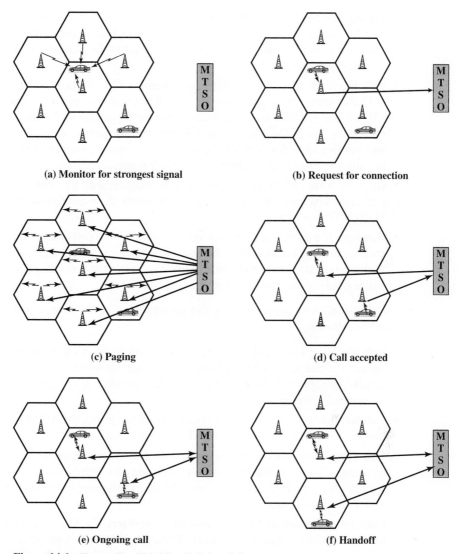

(a) Monitor for strongest signal

(b) Request for connection

(c) Paging

(d) Call accepted

(e) Ongoing call

(f) Handoff

Figure 14.6   Example of Mobile Cellular Cell

periodically to account for the motion of the unit. If the unit enters a new cell, then a new BS is selected. In addition, the mobile unit is monitoring for pages, discussed subsequently.

- **Mobile-originated call:** A mobile unit originates a call by sending the number of the called unit on the preselected setup channel (Figure 14.6b). The receiver at the mobile unit first checks that the setup channel is idle by examining information in the forward (from the BS) channel. When an idle condition is detected, the mobile may transmit on the corresponding reverse (to BS) channel. The BS sends the request to the MTSO.

- **Paging:** The MTSO then attempts to complete the connection to the called unit. The MTSO sends a paging message to certain BSs depending on the called mobile number (Figure 14.6c). Each BS transmits the paging signal on its own assigned setup channel.

- **Call accepted:** The called mobile unit recognizes its number on the setup channel being monitored and responds to that BS, which sends the response to the MTSO. The MTSO sets up a circuit between the calling and called BSs. At the same time, the MTSO selects an available traffic channel within each BS's cell and notifies each BS, which in turn notifies its mobile unit (Figure 14.6d). The two mobile units tune to their respective assigned channels.

- **Ongoing call:** While the connection is maintained, the two mobile units exchange voice or data signals, going through their respective BSs and the MTSO (Figure 14.6e).

- **Handoff:** If a mobile unit moves out of range of one cell and into the range of another during a connection, the traffic channel has to change to one assigned to the BS in the new cell (Figure 14.6f). The system makes this change without either interrupting the call or alerting the user.

Other functions performed by the system but not illustrated in Figure 14.6 include the following:

- **Call blocking:** During the mobile-initiated call stage, if all the traffic channels assigned to the nearest BS are busy, then the mobile unit makes a preconfigured number of repeated attempts. After a certain number of failed tries, a busy tone is returned to the user.

- **Call termination:** When one of the two users hangs up, the MTSO is informed and the traffic channels at the two BSs are released.

- **Call drop:** During a connection, because of interference or weak signal spots in certain areas, if the BS cannot maintain the minimum required signal strength for a certain period of time, the traffic channel to the user is dropped and the MTSO is informed.

- **Calls to/from fixed and remote mobile subscriber:** The MTSO connects to the public switched telephone network. Thus, the MTSO can set up a connection between a mobile user in its area and a fixed subscriber via the telephone network. Further, the MTSO can connect to a remote MTSO via the telephone network or via dedicated lines and set up a connection between a mobile user in its area and a remote mobile user.

Mobile Radio Propagation Effects

Mobile radio communication introduces complexities not found in wire communication or in fixed wireless communication. Two general areas of concern are signal strength and signal propagation effects.

- **Signal strength:** The strength of the signal between the base station and the mobile unit must be strong enough to maintain signal quality at the receiver but not so strong as to create too much cochannel interference with channels in another cell using the same frequency band. Several complicating factors exist. Human-made noise varies considerably, resulting in a variable noise level. For example, automobile ignition noise in the cellular frequency range is greater in the city than in a suburban area. Other signal sources vary from place to place. The signal strength varies as a function of distance from the BS to a point within its cell. Moreover, the signal strength varies dynamically as the mobile unit moves.

- **Fading:** Even if signal strength is within an effective range, signal propagation effects may disrupt the signal and cause errors. Fading is discussed subsequently in this section.

In designing a cellular layout, the communications engineer must take account of these various propagation effects, the desired maximum transmit power level at the base station and the mobile units, the typical height of the mobile unit antenna, and the available height of the BS antenna. These factors will determine the size of the individual cell. Unfortunately, as just described, the propagation effects are dynamic and difficult to predict. The best that can be done is to come up with a model based on empirical data and to apply that model to a given environment to develop guidelines for cell size. One of the most widely used models was developed by Okumura et al. [OKUM68] and subsequently refined by Hata [HATA80]. The original was a detailed analysis of the Tokyo area and produced path loss information for an urban environment. Hata's model is an empirical formulation that takes into account a variety of environments and conditions. For an urban environment, predicted path loss is

$$L_{dB} = 69.55 + 26.16 \log f_c - 13.82 \log h_t - A(h_r) + (44.9 - 6.55 \log h_t) \log d \quad \textbf{(14.1)}$$

where

f_c = carrier frequency in MHz from 150 to 1500 MHz
h_t = height of transmitting antenna (base station) in m, from 30 to 300 m
h_r = height of receiving antenna (mobile station) in m, from 1 to 10 m
d = propagation distance between antennas in km, from 1 to 20 km
$A(h_r)$ = correction factor for mobile antenna height

For a small- or medium-sized city, the correction factor is given by

$$A(h_r) = (1.1 \log f_c - 0.7) h_r - (1.56 \log f_c - 0.8) \text{ dB}$$

And for a large city it is given by

$$A(h_r) = 8.29 [\log(1.54 h_r)]^2 - 1.1 \text{ dB} \qquad \text{for } f_c \leq 300 \text{ MHz}$$
$$A(h_r) = 3.2 [\log(11.75 h_r)]^2 - 4.97 \text{ dB} \qquad \text{for } f_c \geq 300 \text{ MHz}$$

To estimate the path loss in a suburban area, the formula for urban path loss in Equation (14.1) is modified as:

$$L_{dB}(\text{suburban}) = L_{dB}(\text{urban}) - 2[\log (f_c/28)]^2 - 5.4$$

And for the path loss in open areas, the formula is modified as

$$L_{dB}(\text{open}) = L_{dB}(\text{urban}) - 4.78\,(\log f_c)^2 - 18.733\,(\log f_c) - 40.98$$

The Okumura/Hata model is considered to be among the best in terms of accuracy in path loss prediction and provides a practical means of estimating path loss in a wide variety of situations [FREE07].

EXAMPLE 14.2 Let $f_c = 900$ MHz, $h_t = 40$ m, $h_r = 5$ m, and $d = 10$ km. Estimate the path loss for a medium-size city.

$$A(h_r) = (1.1 \log 900 - 0.7)\,5 - (1.56 \log 900 - 0.8) \text{ dB}$$
$$= 12.75 - 3.8 = 8.95 \text{ dB}$$
$$L_{dB} = 69.55 + 26.16 \log 900 - 13.82 \log 40 - 8.95 + (44.9 - 6.55 \log 40) \log 10$$
$$= 69.55 + 77.28 - 22.14 - 8.95 + 34.4 = 150.14 \text{ dB}$$

Fading in the Mobile Environment

Perhaps the most challenging technical problem facing communications systems engineers is fading in a mobile environment. The term *fading* refers to the time variation of received signal power caused by changes in the transmission medium or path(s). In a fixed environment, fading is affected by changes in atmospheric conditions, such as rainfall. But in a mobile environment, where one of the two antennas is moving relative to the other, the relative location of various obstacles changes over time, creating complex transmission effects.

MULTIPATH PROPAGATION Three propagation mechanisms, illustrated in Figure 14.7, play a role. **Reflection** occurs when an electromagnetic signal encounters a surface that is large relative to the wavelength of the signal. For example, suppose a ground-reflected wave near the mobile unit is received. Because the ground-reflected wave has a 180° phase shift after reflection, the ground wave and the line-of-sight (LOS) wave may tend to cancel, resulting in high signal loss.[2] Further, because the mobile antenna is lower than most human-made structures in the area, multipath interference occurs. These reflected waves may interfere constructively or destructively at the receiver.

Diffraction occurs at the edge of an impenetrable body that is large compared to the wavelength of the radio wave. When a radio wave encounters such an edge, waves propagate in different directions with the edge as the source. Thus, signals can be received even when there is no unobstructed LOS from the transmitter.

If the size of an obstacle is on the order of the wavelength of the signal or less, **scattering** occurs. An incoming signal is scattered into several weaker outgoing

---

[2]On the other hand, the reflected signal has a longer path, which creates a phase shift due to delay relative to the unreflected signal. When this delay is equivalent to half a wavelength, the two signals are back in phase.

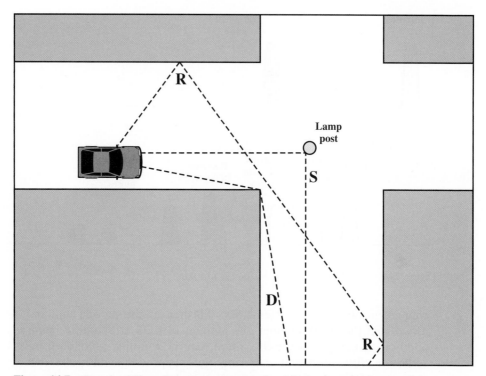

Figure 14.7   Sketch of Three Important Propagation Mechanisms: Reflection (R), Scattering (S), Diffraction (D) [ANDE95]

signals. At typical cellular microwave frequencies, there are numerous objects, such as lamp posts and traffic signs, that can cause scattering. Thus, scattering effects are difficult to predict.

These three propagation effects influence system performance in various ways depending on local conditions and as the mobile unit moves within a cell. If a mobile unit has a clear LOS to the transmitter, then diffraction and scattering are generally minor effects, although reflection may have a significant impact. If there is no clear LOS, such as in an urban area at street level, then diffraction and scattering are the primary means of signal reception.

THE EFFECTS OF MULTIPATH PROPAGATION As just noted, one unwanted effect of multipath propagation is that multiple copies of a signal may arrive at different phases. If these phases add destructively, the signal level relative to noise declines, making signal detection at the receiver more difficult.

A second phenomenon, of particular importance for digital transmission, is intersymbol interference (ISI). Consider that we are sending a narrow pulse at a given frequency across a link between a fixed antenna and a mobile unit. Figure 14.8 shows what the channel may deliver to the receiver if the impulse is sent at two different times. The upper line shows two pulses at the time of transmission. The lower line shows the resulting pulses at the receiver. In each case the first received pulse is the desired LOS signal. The magnitude of that pulse may change because of

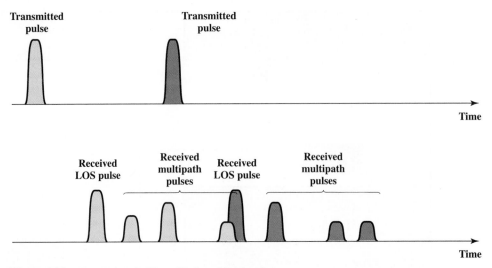

Figure 14.8 Two Pulses in Time-Variant Multipath

changes in atmospheric attenuation. Further, as the mobile unit moves farther away from the fixed antenna, the amount of LOS attenuation increases. But in addition to this primary pulse, there may be multiple secondary pulses due to reflection, diffraction, and scattering. Now suppose that this pulse encodes one or more bits of data. In that case, one or more delayed copies of a pulse may arrive at the same time as the primary pulse for a subsequent bit. These delayed pulses act as a form of noise to the subsequent primary pulse, making recovery of the bit information more difficult.

As the mobile antenna moves, the location of various obstacles changes; hence the number, magnitude, and timing of the secondary pulses change. This makes it difficult to design signal-processing techniques that will filter out multipath effects so that the intended signal is recovered with fidelity.

TYPES OF FADING Fading effects in a mobile environment can be classified as either fast or slow. Referring to Figure 14.7, as the mobile unit moves down a street in an urban environment, rapid variations in signal strength occur over distances of about one-half a wavelength. At a frequency of 900 MHz, which is typical for mobile cellular applications, a wavelength is 0.33 m. Changes of amplitude can be as much as 20 or 30 dB over a short distance. This type of rapidly changing fading phenomenon, known as **fast fading**, affects not only mobile phones in automobiles, but even a mobile phone user walking down an urban street.

As the mobile user covers distances well in excess of a wavelength, the urban environment changes, as the user passes buildings of different heights, vacant lots, intersections, and so forth. Over these longer distances, there is a change in the average received power level about which the rapid fluctuations occur. This is referred to as **slow fading**.

Fading effects can also be classified as flat or selective. **Flat fading**, or nonselective fading, is that type of fading in which all frequency components of the received signal fluctuate in the same proportions simultaneously. **Selective fading** affects unequally the different spectral components of a radio signal. The term *selective fading* is usually significant only relative to the bandwidth of the overall communications channel. If attenuation occurs over a portion of the bandwidth of the signal, the fading is considered to be selective; nonselective fading implies that the signal bandwidth of interest is narrower than, and completely covered by, the spectrum affected by the fading.

ERROR COMPENSATION MECHANISMS The efforts to compensate for the errors and distortions introduced by multipath fading fall into three general categories: forward error correction, adaptive equalization, and diversity techniques. In the typical mobile wireless environment, techniques from all three categories are combined to combat the error rates encountered.

Forward error correction is applicable in digital transmission applications: those in which the transmitted signal carries digital data or digitized voice or video data. Typically in mobile wireless applications, the ratio of total bits sent to data bits sent is between 2 and 3. This may seem an extravagant amount of overhead, in that the capacity of the system is cut to one-half or one-third of its potential, but the mobile wireless environment is so difficult that such levels of redundancy are necessary. Chapter 6 discusses forward error correction.

Adaptive equalization can be applied to transmissions that carry analog information (e.g., analog voice or video) or digital information (e.g., digital data, digitized voice or video) and is used to combat intersymbol interference. The process of equalization involves some method of gathering the dispersed symbol energy back together into its original time interval. Equalization is a broad topic; techniques include the use of so-called lumped analog circuits as well as sophisticated digital signal processing algorithms.

Diversity is based on the fact that individual channels experience independent fading events. We can therefore compensate for error effects by providing multiple logical channels in some sense between transmitter and receiver and sending part of the signal over each channel. This technique does not eliminate errors but it does reduce the error rate, since we have spread the transmission out to avoid being subjected to the highest error rate that might occur. The other techniques (equalization, forward error correction) can then cope with the reduced error rate.

Some diversity techniques involve the physical transmission path and are referred to as **space diversity**. For example, multiple nearby antennas may be used to receive the message, with the signals combined in some fashion to reconstruct the most likely transmitted signal. Another example is the use of collocated multiple directional antennas, each oriented to a different reception angle with the incoming signals again combined to reconstitute the transmitted signal.

More commonly, the term *diversity* refers to frequency diversity or time diversity techniques. With **frequency diversity**, the signal is spread out over a larger- frequency bandwidth or carried on multiple frequency carriers. The most important example of this approach is spread spectrum, which is examined in Chapter 9.

14.2 FIRST-GENERATION ANALOG

The original cellular telephone networks provided analog traffic channels; these are now referred to as first-generation systems. Since the early 1980s the most common first-generation system in North America has been the **Advanced Mobile Phone Service (AMPS)** developed by AT&T. This approach is also common in South America, Australia, and China. Although gradually being replaced by second-generation systems, AMPS is still in common use. In this section, we provide an overview of AMPS.

Spectral Allocation

In North America, two 25-MHz bands are allocated to AMPS (Table 14.2), one for transmission from the base station to the mobile unit (869–894 MHz), the other for transmission from the mobile to the base station (824–849 MHz). Each of these bands is split in two to encourage competition (i.e., so that in each market two operators can be accommodated). An operator is allocated only 12.5 MHz in each direction for its system. The channels are spaced 30 kHz apart, which allows a total of 416 channels per operator. Twenty-one channels are allocated for control, leaving 395 to carry calls. The control channels are data channels operating at 10 kbps. The conversation channels carry the conversations in analog using frequency modulation. Control information is also sent on the conversation channels in bursts as data. This number of channels is inadequate for most major markets, so some way must be found either to use less bandwidth per conversation or to reuse frequencies. Both approaches have been taken in the various approaches to mobile telephony. For AMPS, frequency reuse is exploited.

Operation

Each AMPS-capable cellular telephone includes a *numeric assignment module* (NAM) in read-only memory. The NAM contains the telephone number of the

Table 14.2 AMPS Parameters

Base station transmission band	869–894 MHz
Mobile unit transmission band	824–849 MHz
Spacing between forward and reverse channels	45 MHz
Channel bandwidth	30 kHz
Number of full-duplex voice channels	790
Number of full-duplex control channels	42
Mobile unit maximum power	3 W
Cell size, radius	2 to 20 km
Modulation, voice channel	FM, 12-kHz peak deviation
Modulation, control channel	FSK, 8-kHz peak deviation
Data transmission rate	10 kbps
Error control coding	BCH (48, 36, 5) and (40, 28, 5)

phone, which is assigned by the service provider, and the serial number of the phone, which is assigned by the manufacturer. When the phone is turned on, it transmits its serial number and phone number to the MTSO (Figure 14.5); the MTSO maintains a database with information about mobile units that have been reported stolen and uses serial number to lock out stolen units. The MTSO uses the phone number for billing purposes. If the phone is used in a remote city, the service is still billed to the user's local service provider.

When a call is placed, the following sequence of events occurs [COUC07]:

1. The subscriber initiates a call by keying in the telephone number of the called party and presses the send key.
2. The MTSO verifies that the telephone number is valid and that the user is authorized to place the call; some service providers require the user to enter a PIN (personal identification number) as well as the called number to counter theft.
3. The MTSO issues a message to the user's cell phone indicating which traffic channels to use for sending and receiving.
4. The MTSO sends out a ringing signal to the called party. All of these operations (steps 2 through 4) occur within 10 s of initiating the call.
5. When the called party answers, the MTSO establishes a circuit between the two parties and initiates billing information.
6. When one party hangs up, the MTSO releases the circuit, frees the radio channels, and completes the billing information.

AMPS Control Channels

Each AMPS service includes 21 full-duplex 30-kHz control channels, consisting of 21 reverse control channels (RCCs) from subscriber to base station, and 21 forward channels from base station to subscriber. These channels transmit digital data using FSK. In both channels, data are transmitted in frames.

Control information can be transmitted over a voice channel during a conversation. The mobile unit or the base station can insert a burst of data by turning off the voice FM transmission for about 100 ms and replacing it with an FSK-encoded message. These messages are used to exchange urgent messages, such as change power level and handoff.

14.3 SECOND-GENERATION CDMA

This section begins with an overview and then looks in detail at one type of second-generation cellular system.

First- and Second-Generation Cellular Systems

First-generation cellular networks, such as AMPS, quickly became highly popular, threatening to swamp available capacity. Second-generation systems have been developed to provide higher-quality signals, higher data rates for support of digital services, and greater capacity. [BLAC99b] lists the following as the key differences between the two generations:

- **Digital traffic channels:** The most notable difference between the two generations is that first-generation systems are almost purely analog, whereas second-generation systems are digital. In particular, the first-generation systems are designed to support voice channels using FM; digital traffic is supported only by the use of a modem that converts the digital data into analog form. Second-generation systems provide digital traffic channels. These readily support digital data; voice traffic is first encoded in digital form before transmitting. Of course, for second-generation systems, the user traffic (data or digitized voice) must be converted to an analog signal for transmission between the mobile unit and the base station (e.g., see Figure 5.15).

- **Encryption:** Because all of the user traffic, as well as control traffic, is digitized in second-generation systems, it is a relatively simple matter to encrypt all of the traffic to prevent eavesdropping. All second-generation systems provide this capability, whereas first-generation systems send user traffic in the clear, providing no security.

- **Error detection and correction:** The digital traffic stream of second-generation systems also lends itself to the use of error detection and correction techniques, such as those discussed in Chapter 6. The result can be very clear voice reception.

- **Channel access:** In first-generation systems, each cell supports a number of channels. At any given time a channel is allocated to only one user. Second-generation systems also provide multiple channels per cell, but each channel is dynamically shared by a number of users using time division multiple access (TDMA) or code division multiple access (CDMA). We look at CDMA-based systems in this section.

Beginning around 1990, a number of different second-generation systems have been deployed. A good example is the IS-95 scheme using CDMA.

Code Division Multiple Access

CDMA for cellular systems can be described as follows. As with FDMA, each cell is allocated a frequency bandwidth, which is split into two parts, half for reverse (mobile unit to base station) and half for forward (base station to mobile unit). For full-duplex communication, a mobile unit uses both reverse and forward channels. Transmission is in the form of direct-sequence spread spectrum (DS-SS), which uses a chipping code to increase the data rate of the transmission, resulting in an increased signal bandwidth. Multiple access is provided by assigning orthogonal chipping codes (defined in Chapter 9) to multiple users, so that the receiver can recover the transmission of an individual unit from multiple transmissions.

CDMA has a number of advantages for a cellular network:

- **Frequency diversity:** Because the transmission is spread out over a larger bandwidth, frequency-dependent transmission impairments, such as noise bursts and selective fading, have less effect on the signal.

- **Multipath resistance:** In addition to the ability of DS-SS to overcome multipath fading by frequency diversity, the chipping codes used for CDMA not only exhibit low cross correlation but also low autocorrelation.[3] Therefore, a version of the signal that is delayed by more than one chip interval does not interfere with the dominant signal as much as in other multipath environments.

- **Privacy:** Because spread spectrum is obtained by the use of noiselike signals, where each user has a unique code, privacy is inherent.

- **Graceful degradation:** With FDMA or TDMA, a fixed number of users can access the system simultaneously. However, with CDMA, as more users access the system simultaneously, the noise level and hence the error rate increases; only gradually does the system degrade to the point of an unacceptable error rate.

Two drawbacks of CDMA cellular should also be mentioned:

- **Self-jamming:** Unless all of the mobile users are perfectly synchronized, the arriving transmissions from multiple users will not be perfectly aligned on chip boundaries. Thus, the spreading sequences of the different users are not orthogonal and there is some level of cross correlation. This is distinct from either TDMA or FDMA, in which for reasonable time or frequency guardbands, respectively, the received signals are orthogonal or nearly so.

- **Near–far problem:** Signals closer to the receiver are received with less attenuation than signals farther away. Given the lack of complete orthogonality, the transmissions from the more remote mobile units may be more difficult to recover.

Mobile Wireless CDMA Design Considerations

Before turning to the specific example of IS-95, it will be useful to consider some general design elements of a CDMA cellular system.

Rake Receiver In a multipath environment, which is common in cellular systems, if the multiple versions of a signal arrive more than one chip interval apart from each other, the receiver can recover the signal by correlating the chip sequence with the dominant incoming signal. The remaining signals are treated as noise. However, even better performance can be achieved if the receiver attempts to recover the

---

[3]See Appendix N for a discussion of correlation and orthogonality.

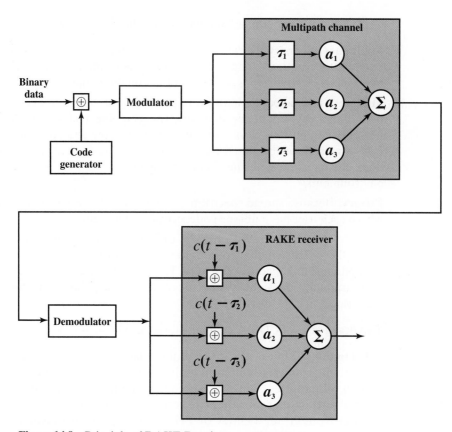

Figure 14.9 Principle of RAKE Receiver

signals from multiple paths and then combine them, with suitable delays. This principle is used in the RAKE receiver.

Figure 14.9 illustrates the principle of the RAKE receiver. The original binary signal to be transmitted is spread by the exclusive-OR (XOR) operation with the transmitter's chipping code. The spread sequence is then modulated for transmission over the wireless channel. Because of multipath effects, the channel generates multiple copies of the signal, each with a different amount of time delay (τ_1, τ_2, etc.), and each with a different attenuation factors (a_1, a_2, etc.). At the receiver, the combined signal is demodulated. The demodulated chip stream is then fed into multiple correlators, each delayed by a different amount. These signals are then combined using weighting factors estimated from the channel.

IS-95

The most widely used second-generation CDMA scheme is IS-95, which is primarily deployed in North America. Here we describe the transmission structure on the forward link; the reverse link is similar.

Table 14.3 IS-95 Forward Link Channel Parameters

Channel	Sync	Paging		Traffic Rate Set 1				Traffic Rate Set 2			
Data rate (bps)	1200	4800	9600	1200	2400	4800	9600	1800	3600	7200	14400
Code repetition	2	2	1	8	4	2	1	8	4	2	1
Modulation symbol rate (sps)	4800	19,200	19,200	19,200	19,200	19,200	19,200	19,200	19,200	19,200	19,200
PN chips/modulation symbol	256	64	64	64	64	64	64	64	64	64	64
PN chips/bit	1024	256	128	1024	512	256	128	682.67	341.33	170.67	85.33

Table 14.3 lists forward link channel parameters. The forward link consists of up to 64 logical CDMA channels each occupying the same 1228-kHz bandwidth (Figure 14.10a). The forward link supports four types of channels:

- **Pilot (channel 0):** A continuous signal on a single channel. This channel allows the mobile unit to acquire timing information, provides phase reference for the demodulation process, and provides a means for signal strength comparison for the purpose of handoff determination. The pilot channel consists of all zeros.
- **Synchronization (channel 32):** A 1200-bps channel used by the mobile station to obtain identification information about the cellular system (system time, long code state, protocol revision, etc.).

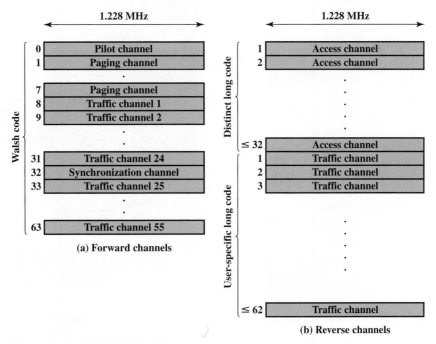

Figure 14.10 IS-95 Channel Structure

- **Paging (channels 1 to 7):** Contain messages for one or more mobile stations.
- **Traffic (channels 8 to 31 and 33 to 63):** The forward channel supports 55 traffic channels. The original specification supported data rates of up to 9600 bps. A subsequent revision added a second set of rates up to 14,400 bps.

Note that all of these channels use the same bandwidth. The chipping code is used to distinguish among the different channels. For the forward channel, the chipping codes are the 64 orthogonal 64-bit codes derived from a 64×64 matrix known as the Walsh matrix (discussed in [STAL05]).

Figure 14.11 shows the processing steps for transmission on a forward traffic channel using rate set 1. For voice traffic, the speech is encoded at a data rate of

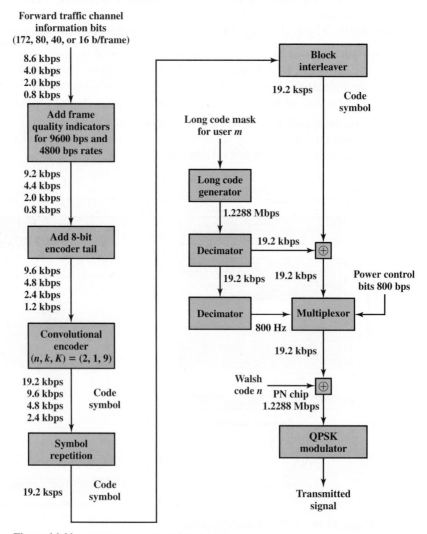

Figure 14.11 IS-95 Forward Link Transmission

8550 bps. After additional bits are added for error detection, the rate is 9600 bps. The full channel capacity is not used when the user is not speaking. During quiet periods the data rate is lowered to as low as 1200 bps. The 2400-bps rate is used to transmit transients in the background noise, and the 4800 bps rate is used to mix digitized speech and signaling data.

The data or digitized speech is transmitted in 20-ms blocks with forward error correction provided by a convolutional encoder with rate 1/2, thus doubling the effective data rate to a maximum of 19.2 kbps. For lower data rates, the encoder output bits (called code symbols) are replicated to yield the 19.2-kbps rate. The data are then interleaved in blocks to reduce the effects of errors by spreading them out.

Following the interleaver, the data bits are scrambled. The purpose of this is to serve as a privacy mask and to prevent the sending of repetitive patterns, which in turn reduces the probability of users sending at peak power at the same time. The scrambling is accomplished by means of a long code that is generated as a pseudo-random number from a 42-bit-long shift register. The shift register is initialized with the user's electronic serial number. The output of the long code generator is at a rate of 1.2288 Mbps, which is 64 times the rate of 19.2 kbps, so only one bit in 64 is selected (by the decimator function). The resulting stream is XORed with the output of the block interleaver.

The next step in the processing inserts power control information in the traffic channel, to control the power output of the antenna. The power control function of the base station robs the traffic channel of bits at a rate of 800 bps. These are inserted by stealing code bits. The 800-bps channel carries information directing the mobile unit to increment, decrement, or keep stable its current output level. This power control stream is multiplexed into the 19.2 kbps by replacing some of the code bits, using the long code generator to encode the bits.

The next step in the process is the DS-SS function, which spreads the 19.2 kbps to a rate of 1.2288 Mbps using one row of the 64×64 Walsh matrix. One row of the matrix is assigned to a mobile station during call setup. If a 0 bit is presented to the XOR function, then the 64 bits of the assigned row are sent. If a 1 is presented, then the bitwise XOR of the row is sent. Thus, the final bit rate is 1.2288 Mbps. This digital bit stream is then modulated onto the carrier using a QPSK modulation scheme. Recall from Chapter 5 that QPSK involves creating 2two-bit streams that are separately modulated (see Figure 5.11). In the IS-95 scheme, the data are split into I and Q (in-phase and quadrature) channels and the data in each channel are XORed with a unique short code. The short codes are generated as pseudorandom numbers from a 15-bit-long shift register.

14.4 THIRD-GENERATION SYSTEMS

The objective of the third generation (3G) of wireless communication is to provide fairly high-speed wireless communications to support multimedia, data, and video in addition to voice. The ITU's International Mobile Telecommunications for the year

2000 (IMT-2000) initiative has defined the ITU's view of third-generation capabilities as follows:

- Voice quality comparable to the public switched telephone network
- 144 kbps data rate available to users in high-speed motor vehicles over large areas
- 384 kbps available to pedestrians standing or moving slowly over small areas
- Support (to be phased in) for 2.048 Mbps for office use
- Symmetrical and asymmetrical data transmission rates
- Support for both packet-switched and circuit-switched data services
- An adaptive interface to the Internet to reflect efficiently the common asymmetry between inbound and outbound traffic
- More efficient use of the available spectrum in general
- Support for a wide variety of mobile equipment
- Flexibility to allow the introduction of new services and technologies

More generally, one of the driving forces of modern communication technology is the trend toward universal personal telecommunications and universal communications access. The first concept refers to the ability of a person to identify himself or herself easily and use conveniently any communication system in an entire country, over a continent, or even globally, in terms of a single account. The second refers to the capability of using one's terminal in a wide variety of environments to connect to information services (e.g., to have a portable terminal that will work in the office, on the street, and on airplanes equally well). This revolution in personal computing will obviously involve wireless communication in a fundamental way.

Third-generation services are intended to keep up with demand as more people use their mobile devices to check Facebook and watch videos online. Table 14.4 provides estimates of how much capacity is used per person for various activities on different mobile devices [FARZ10].

Alternative Interfaces

Figure 14.12 shows the alternative schemes that have been adopted as part of IMT-2000. The specification covers a set of radio interfaces for optimized performance in different radio environments. A major reason for the inclusion of five alternatives was to enable a smooth evolution from existing first- and second-generation systems.

The five alternatives reflect the evolution from the second generation. Two of the specifications grow out of the work at the European Telecommunications Standards Institute (ETSI) to develop a UMTS (universal mobile telecommunications system) as Europe's 3G wireless standard. UMTS includes two standards. One of these is known as wideband CDMA, or W-CDMA. This scheme fully exploits CDMA technology to provide high data rates with efficient use of bandwidth. Table 14.5 shows some of the key parameters of W-CDMA. The other European effort under UMTS is known as IMT-TC, or TD-CDMA. This approach is a combination of W-CDMA and TDMA technology. IMT-TC is intended to provide an upgrade path for the TDMA-based GSM systems.

Table 14.4 Typical Mobile Device Capacity Demands

Device	Applications	Usage during Online Session	Average Monthly Capacity Requirement
Feature phone	Phones such as the Motorola Razr are used primarily to make calls and texts. They have limited Web activity with a stripped-down Web browser.	Voice calls: 4 MB/hr Web browsing: 4–5 MB/hr	100 MB
Smartphone	Smartphones such as Blackberry are used for phone calls, email, and light Web browsing.	Voice calls: 4 MB/hr Web browsing: 4–5 MB/hr	185 MB
Superphone	Advanced devices, such as iPhone, make it easy to surf the Web and watch online videos	Voice calls: 4 MB/hr Web browsing: 4–5 MB/hr Net radio: 60 MB/hr YouTube videos: 200 MB/hr	560 MB
Tablet computer	Devices such as iPad greatly increase capacity demand.	Web browsing: 50–60 MB/hr Net radio: 60 MB/hr YouTube videos: 300–400 MB/hr	800–1000 MB

Another CDMA-based system, known as cdma2000, has a North American origin. This scheme is similar to, but incompatible with, W-CDMA, in part because the standards use different chip rates. Also, cdma2000 uses a technique known as multicarrier, not used with W-CDMA.

Two other interface specifications are shown in Figure 14.12. IMT-SC is primarily designed for TDMA-only networks. IMT-FT can be used by both TDMA and FDMA carriers to provide some 3G services; it is an outgrowth of the Digital European Cordless Telecommunications (DECT) standard.

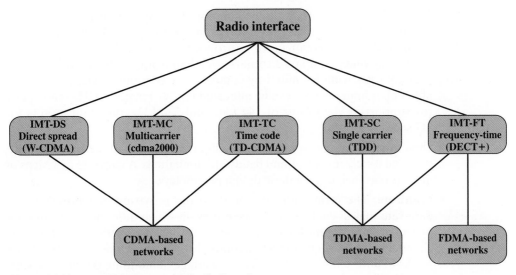

Figure 14.12   IMT-2000 Terrestrial Radio Interfaces

Table 14.5 W-CDMA Parameters

Channel bandwidth	5 MHz
Forward RF channel structure	Direct spread
Chip rate	3.84 Mcps
Frame length	10 ms
Number of slots/frame	15
Spreading modulation	Balanced QPSK (forward) Dual channel QPSK (reverse) Complex spreading circuit
Data modulation	QPSK (forward) BPSK (reverse)
Coherent detection	Pilot symbols
Reverse channel multiplexing	Control and pilot channel time multiplexed. I and Q multiplexing for data and control channels
Multirate	Various spreading and multicode
Spreading factors	4–256
Power control	Open and fast closed loop (1.6 kHz)
Spreading (forward)	Variable length orthogonal sequences for channel separation. Gold sequences 2^{18} for cell and user separation.
Spreading (reverse)	Same as forward, different time shifts in I and Q channels.

CDMA Design Considerations

The dominant technology for 3G systems is CDMA. Although three different CDMA schemes have been adopted, they share some common design issues. [OJAN98] lists the following:

- **Bandwidth:** An important design goal for all 3G systems is to limit channel usage to 5 MHz. There are several reasons for this goal. On the one hand, a bandwidth of 5 MHz or more improves the receiver's ability to resolve multipath when compared to narrower bandwidths. On the other hand, available spectrum is limited by competing needs, and 5 MHz is a reasonable upper limit on what can be allocated for 3G. Finally, 5 MHz is adequate for supporting data rates of 144 kHz and 384 kHz, the main targets for 3G services.

- **Chip rate:** Given the bandwidth, the chip rate depends on desired data rate, the need for error control, and bandwidth limitations. A chip rate of 3 Mcps or more is reasonable given these design parameters.

- **Multirate:** The term *multirate* refers to the provision of multiple fixed-data-rate logical channels to a given user, in which different data rates are provided on different logical channels. Further, the traffic on each logical channel can be switched independently through the wireless and fixed networks to different destinations. The advantage of multirate is that the system can flexibly support multiple simultaneous applications from a given user

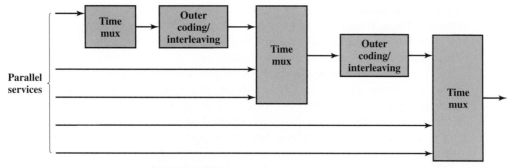

(a) Time multiplexing

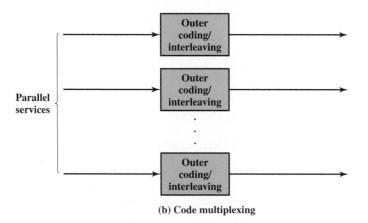

(b) Code multiplexing

Figure 14.13   Time and Code Multiplexing Principles [OJAN98]

and can efficiently use available capacity by only providing the capacity required for each service. Multirate can be achieved with a TDMA scheme within a single CDMA channel, in which a different number of slots per frame are assigned to achieve different data rates. All the subchannels at a given data rate would be protected by error correction and interleaving techniques (Figure 14.13a). An alternative is to use multiple CDMA codes, with separate coding and interleaving, and map them to separate CDMA channels (Figure 14.13b).

14.5 FOURTH-GENERATION SYSTEMS

Third-generation and enhanced 3G systems have gone a long way toward meeting the digital, high data rate requirements for which they were designed. However, current public wireless networks are experiencing a rapid increase in data traffic. As pointed out in [RISS09], this increased demand is linked to the recent availability of new types of terminals offering easy access to Internet services, a permanent connection to mail systems, and new rich multimedia entertainment services like video messaging and all forms of mobile commerce. There is also a need to support always-on capabilities, such as presence, instant messaging, and other real-time services. These requirements have led to the development of a fourth generation (4G) of mobile wireless technology that is designed to maximize bandwidth and throughput while maximizing spectral efficiency.

Two candidates have emerged for 4G standardization. One is known as Long-Term Evolution (LTE), which has been developed by the Third-Generation Partnership Project (3GPP), a consortium of Asian, European, and North American telecommunications standards organizations. The other effort is being made by the IEEE 802.16 committee, which has developed standards for high-speed fixed wireless operations known as WiMax. The committee has specified an enhancement of WiMax to meet 4G needs. The two efforts are similar both in terms of performance and technology. Both are based on the use of orthogonal frequency division multiple access (OFDMA) to support multiple access to network resources. WiMax uses a pure OFDMA approach of both uplink and downlink. LTE uses pure OFDMA on the downlink but a technique that is based on OFDMA but that offers enhanced power efficiency. It appears likely that LTE will become the universal standard for 4G wireless.

Table 14.6 summarizes key aspects of mobile wireless network generations. In the remainder of this section we examine the key 4G technology, OFDMA.

Orthogonal Frequency Division Multiplexing

OFDM, also called multicarrier modulation, uses multiple carrier signals at different frequencies, sending some of the bits on each channel. This is similar to FDM. However, in the case of OFDM, all of the subcarriers are dedicated to a single data source.

Figure 14.14 illustrates OFDM. Suppose we have a data stream operating at R bps and an available bandwidth of Nf_b, centered at f_0. The entire bandwidth could be used to send the data stream, in which case each bit duration would be $1/R$. The alternative is to split the data stream into N substreams, using a serial-to-parallel converter. Each substream has a data rate of R/N bps and is transmitted on a separate subcarrier, with a spacing between adjacent subcarriers of f_b. Now the bit duration is N/R.

Table 14.6 Wireless Network Generations

Technology	1G	2G	2.5G	3G	4G
Design began	1970	1980	1985	1990	2000
Implementation	1984	1991	1999	2002	2010
Services	Analog voice	Digital voice	Higher capacity packetized data	Higher capacity, broadband	Completely IP based
Data rate	1.9. kbps	14.4 kbps	384 kbps	2 Mbps	200 Mbps
Multiplexing	FDMA	TDMA, CDMA	TDMA, CDMA	CDMA	OFDMA
Core network	PSTN	PSTN	PSTN, packet network	Packet network	IP backbone

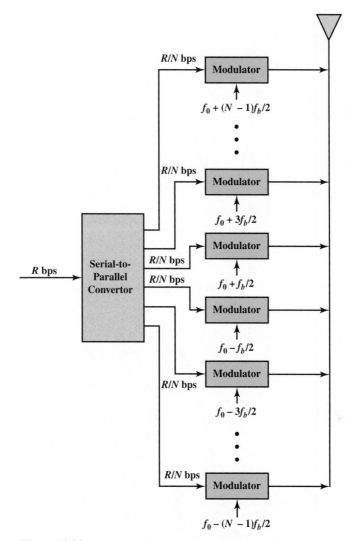

Figure 14.14   Orthogonal Frequency Division Multiplexing

To gain a clearer understanding of OFDM, let us consider the scheme in terms of its base frequency, f_b. This is the lowest-frequency subcarrier. All of the other subcarriers are integer multiples of the base frequency, namely $2f_b$, $3f_b$, and so on, as shown in Figure 14.15a. The OFDM scheme uses advanced digital signal-processing techniques to distribute the data over multiple carriers at precise frequencies. The precise relationship among the subcarriers is referred to as orthogonality. The result, as shown in Figure 14.15b, is that the peaks of the power spectral density of each subcarrier occur at a point at which the power of other subcarriers is zero. With OFDM, the subcarriers can be packed tightly together because there is minimal interference between adjacent subcarriers.

Note that Figure 14.14 depicts the set of OFDM subcarriers in a frequency band beginning with the base frequency. For transmission, the set of OFDM subcarriers

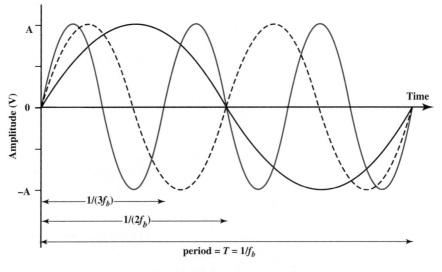

(a) Three subcarriers in time domain

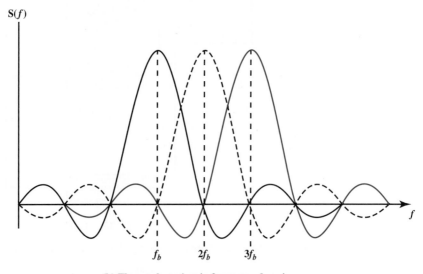

(b) Three subcarriers in frequency domain

Figure 14.15 Illustration of Orthogonality of OFDM

is further modulated to a higher-frequency band. For example, for the IEEE 802.11a LAN standard, discussed in Chapter 11, the OFDM scheme consists of a set of 52 subcarriers with a base frequency of 0.3125 MHz. This set of subcarriers is then translated to the 5-GHz range for transmission.

OFDM has several advantages. First, frequency selective fading only affects some subcarriers and not the whole signal. If the data stream is protected by a forward error-correcting code, this type of fading is easily handled. More important, OFDM overcomes intersymbol interference (ISI) in a multipath environment. As discussed in Chapter 3, ISI has a greater impact at higher bit rates, because the distance between bits, or symbols, is smaller. With OFDM, the data rate is reduced by a factor of N, which increases the symbol time by a factor of N. Thus, if the symbol period is T_s for the source stream, the period for the OFDM signals is NT_s. This dramatically reduces the effect of ISI. As a design criterion, N is chosen so that NT_s is significantly greater than the root-mean-square delay spread of the channel.

As a result of these considerations, with the use of OFDM, it may not be necessary to deploy equalizers, which are complex devices whose complexity increases with the number of symbols over which ISI is present.

A common modulation scheme used with OFDM is quadrature phase shift keying (QPSK). In this case, each transmitted symbol represents two bits. An example of an OFDM/QPSK scheme [CISC00] occupies 6 MHz made up of 512 individual carriers, with a carrier separation of a little under 12 kHz. To minimize ISI, data are transmitted in bursts, with each burst consisting of a cyclic prefix followed by data symbols. The cyclic prefix is used to absorb transients from previous bursts caused by multipath. For this system, 64 symbols constitute the cyclic prefix, followed by 512 QPSK symbols per burst. On each subcarrier, therefore, QPSK symbols are separated by a prefix of duration 64/512 symbol times. In general, by the time the prefix is over, the resulting waveform created by the combined multipath signals is not a function of any samples from the previous burst. Hence there is no ISI.

Orthogonal Frequency Division Multiple Access

Like OFDM, OFDMA employs multiple closely spaced subcarriers, but the subcarriers are divided into groups of subcarriers. Each group is named a subchannel. The subcarriers that form a subchannel need not be adjacent. In the downlink, a subchannel may be intended for different receivers. In the uplink, a transmitter may be assigned one or more subchannels. Figure 14.16 contrasts OFDM and OFDMA; in the OFDMA case the use of adjacent subcarriers to form a subchannel is illustrated.

Subchannelization defines subchannels that can be allocated to subscriber stations (SSs) depending on their channel conditions and data requirements. Using subchannelization, within the same time slot, a 4G base station can allocate more transmit power to user devices (SSs) with lower SNR (signal-to-noise ratio), and less power to user devices with higher SNR. Subchannelization also enables the BS to allocate higher power to subchannels assigned to indoor SSs resulting in better in-building coverage. Subchannels are further grouped into bursts, which can be allocated to wireless users. Each burst allocation can be changed from frame to frame as well as within the modulation order. This allows the base station to dynamically adjust the bandwidth usage according to the current system requirements.

Subchannelization in the uplink can save user-device transmit power because it can concentrate power only on certain subchannel(s) allocated to it. This power-saving feature is particularly useful for battery-powered user devices, the likely case in mobile 4G.

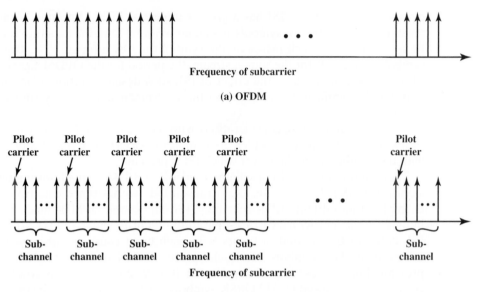

(a) OFDM

(b) OFDMA (adjacent subcarriers)

Figure 14.16 OFDM and OFDMA

14.6 RECOMMENDED READING AND WEB SITES

[BERT94] and [ANDE95] are instructive surveys of cellular wireless propagation effects. [BLAC99b] is one of the best technical treatments of second-generation cellular systems.

[TANT98] contains reprints of numerous important papers dealing with CDMA in cellular networks. [DINA98] provides an overview of both PN and orthogonal spreading codes for cellular CDMA networks.

[OJAN98] provides an overview of key technical design considerations for 3G systems. Another useful survey is [ZENG00]. [PRAS00] is a much more detailed analysis. [FRAT06] and [KHAN09] provide 4G overviews.

ANDE95 Anderson, J.; Rappaport, T.; and Yoshida, S. "Propagation Measurements and Models for Wireless Communications Channels." *IEEE Communications Magazine*, January 1995.

BERT94 Bertoni, H.; Honcharenko, W.; Maciel, L.; and Xia, H. "UHF Propagation Prediction for Wireless Personal Communications." *Proceedings of the IEEE*, September 1994.

BLAC99b Black, U. *Second-Generation Mobile and Wireless Networks.* Upper Saddle River, NJ: Prentice Hall, 1999.

DINA98 Dinan, E., and Jabbari, B. "Spreading Codes for Direct Sequence CDMA and Wideband CDMA Cellular Networks." *IEEE Communications Magazine*, September 1998.

FRAT06 Frattasi, S., et al. "Defining 4G Technology from the User's Perspective." *IEEE Network*, January/February 2006.

KHAN09   Khan, A., et al. "4G as a Next Generation Wireless Network." *Proceedings, 2009 International Conference on Future Computer and Communications,* 2009.

OJAN98   Ojanpera, T., and Prasad, G. "An Overview of Air Interface Multiple Access for IMT-2000/UMTS." *IEEE Communications Magazine,* September 1998.

PRAS00   Prasad, R.; Mohr, W.; and Konhauser, W., eds. *Third-Generation Mobile Communication Systems.* Boston: Artech House, 2000.

TANT98   Tantaratana, S., and Ahmed, K., eds. *Wireless Applications of Spread Spectrum Systems: Selected Readings.* Piscataway, NJ: IEEE Press, 1998.

ZENG00   Zeng, M.; Annamalai, A.; and Bhargava, V. "Harmonization of Global Third-generation Mobile Systems." *IEEE Communications Magazine,* December 2000.

Recommended Web sites:

- **Wireless World Research Forum:** Useful collection of white papers and briefings on mobile wireless networks.
- **Cellular telecommunications and Internet Association:** An industry consortium that provides information on successful applications of wireless technology.
- **CDMA development group:** Information and links for IS-95 and CDMA generally.
- **3G Americas:** A trade group of Western Hemisphere companies supporting a variety of second- and third-generation schemes. Includes industry news, white papers, and other technical information.

14.7 KEY TERMS, REVIEW QUESTIONS, AND PROBLEMS

Key Terms

adaptive equalization	fast fading	reflection
Advanced Mobile Phone Service (AMPS)	flat fading	reuse factor
	first-generation (1G) network	reverse channel
base station	forward channel	scattering
cellular network	forward error correction	second-generation (2G) network
code division multiple access (CDMA)	frequency diversity	
	frequency reuse	selective fading
diffraction	handoff	slow fading
diversity	mobile radio	space diversity
fading	power control	third-generation (3G) network

Review Questions

14.1   What geometric shape is used in cellular system design?

14.2   What is the principle of frequency reuse in the context of a cellular network?

14.3   List five ways of increasing the capacity of a cellular system.

14.4 Explain the paging function of a cellular system.

14.5 What is fading?

14.6 What is the difference between diffraction and scattering?

14.7 What is the difference between fast and slow fading?

14.8 What is the difference between flat and selective fading?

14.9 What are the key differences between first- and second-generation cellular systems?

14.10 What are the advantages of using CDMA for a cellular network?

14.11 What are the disadvantages of using CDMA for a cellular network?

14.12 What are some key characteristics that distinguish third-generation cellular systems from second-generation cellular systems?

Problems

14.1 Consider four different cellular systems that share the following characteristics. The frequency bands are 825 to 845 MHz for mobile unit transmission and 870 to 890 MHz for base station transmission. A duplex circuit consists of one 30-kHz channel in each direction. The systems are distinguished by the reuse factor, which is 4, 7, 12, and 19, respectively.
  a. Suppose that in each of the systems, the cluster of cells (4, 7, 12, 19) is duplicated 16 times. Find the number of simultaneous communications that can be supported by each system.
  b. Find the number of simultaneous communications that can be supported by a single cell in each system.
  c. What is the area covered, in cells, by each system?
  d. Suppose the cell size is the same in all four systems and a fixed area of 100 cells is covered by each system. Find the number of simultaneous communications that can be supported by each system.

14.2 Describe a sequence of events similar to that of Figure 14.6 for
  a. a call from a mobile unit to a fixed subscriber
  b. a call from a fixed subscriber to a mobile unit

14.3 An analog cellular system has a total of 33 MHz of bandwidth and uses two 25-kHz simplex (one-way) channels to provide full-duplex voice and control channels.
  a. What is the number of channels available per cell for a frequency reuse factor of (1) 4 cells, (2) 7 cells, and (3) 12 cells?
  b. Assume that 1 MHz is dedicated to control channels but that only one control channel is needed per cell. Determine a reasonable distribution of control channels and voice channels in each cell for the three frequency reuse factors of part (a).

14.4 A cellular system uses FDMA with a spectrum allocation of 12.5 MHz in each direction, a guard band at the edge of the allocated spectrum of 10 kHz, and a channel bandwidth of 30 kHz. What is the number of available channels?

14.5 For a cellular system, FDMA spectral efficiency is defined as $\eta_a = \dfrac{B_c N_T}{B_w}$ where

B_c = channel bandwidth

B_w = total bandwidth in one direction

N_T = total number of voice channels in the covered area

What is an upper bound on η_a?

14.6 Walsh codes are the most common orthogonal codes used in CDMA applications. A set of Walsh codes of length n consists of the n rows of an $n \times n$ Walsh matrix.

That is, there are n codes, each of length n. The matrix is defined recursively as follows:

$$\mathbf{W}_1 = (0) \qquad \mathbf{W}_{2n} = \begin{pmatrix} \mathbf{W}_n & \mathbf{W}_n \\ \mathbf{W}_n & \overline{\mathbf{W}_n} \end{pmatrix}$$

where n is the dimension of the matrix and the overscore denotes the logical NOT of the bits in the matrix. The Walsh matrix has the property that every row is orthogonal to every other row and to the logical NOT of every other row. Show the Walsh matrices of dimensions 2, 4, and 8.

14.7 Demonstrate that the codes in an 8×8 Walsh matrix are orthogonal to each other by showing that multiplying any code by any other code produces a result of zero.

14.8 Consider a CDMA system in which users A and B have the Walsh codes $(-1\,1\,-1\,1\,-1\,1\,-1\,1)$ and $(-1\,-1\,1\,1\,-1\,-1\,1\,1)$, respectively.

   a. Show the output at the receiver if A transmits a data bit 1 and B does not transmit.

   b. Show the output at the receiver if A transmits a data bit 0 and B does not transmit.

   c. Show the output at the receiver if A transmits a data bit 1 and B transmits a data bit 1. Assume the received power from both A and B is the same.

   d. Show the output at the receiver if A transmits a data bit 0 and B transmits a data bit 1. Assume the received power from both A and B is the same.

   e. Show the output at the receiver if A transmits a data bit 1 and B transmits a data bit 0. Assume the received power from both A and B is the same.

   f. Show the output at the receiver if A transmits a data bit 0 and B transmits a data bit 0. Assume the received power from both A and B is the same.

   g. Show the output at the receiver if A transmits a data bit 1 and B transmits a data bit 1. Assume the received power from B is twice the received power from A. This can be represented by showing the received signal component from A as consisting of elements of magnitude $1(+1, -1)$ and the received signal component from B as consisting of elements of magnitude $2(+2, -2)$.

   h. Show the output at the receiver if A transmits a data bit 0 and B transmits a data bit 1. Assume the received power from B is twice the received power from A.

LOCAL AREA NETWORK OVERVIEW

The whole of this operation is described in minute detail in the official British Naval History, and should be studied with its excellent charts by those who are interested in its technical aspect. So complicated is the full story that the lay reader cannot see the wood for the trees. I have endeavored to render intelligible the broad effects.

— The World Crisis, Winston Churchill

KEY POINTS

◆ A LAN consists of a shared transmission medium and a set of hardware and software for interfacing devices to the medium and regulating the orderly access to the medium.

◆ The topologies that have been used for LANs are ring, bus, tree, and star. A ring LAN consists of a closed loop of repeaters that allow data to circulate around the ring. A repeater may also function as a device attachment point. Transmission is generally in the form of frames. The bus and tree topologies are passive sections of cable to which stations are attached. A transmission of a frame by any one station can be heard by any other station. A star LAN includes a central node to which stations are attached.

◆ A set of standards has been defined for LANs that specifies a range of data rates and encompasses a variety of topologies and transmission media.

◆ In most cases, an organization will have multiple LANs that need to be interconnected. The simplest approach to meeting this requirement is the bridge.

◆ Hubs and switches form the basic building blocks of most LANs.

We turn now to a discussion of **local area networks (LANs)**. Whereas wide area networks may be public or private, LANs usually are owned by the organization that is using the network to interconnect equipment. LANs have much greater capacity than wide area networks to carry what is generally a greater internal communications load.

In this chapter we look at the underlying technology and protocol architecture of LANs. Chapters 16 and 17 are devoted to a discussion of specific LAN systems.

15.1 TOPOLOGIES AND TRANSMISSION MEDIA

The key elements of a LAN are these:

• Topology
• Transmission medium
• Wiring layout
• Medium access control

Together, these elements determine not only the cost and capacity of the LAN but also the type of data that may be transmitted, the speed and efficiency of communications, and even the kinds of applications that can be supported.

This section provides a survey of the major technologies in the first two of these categories. It will be seen that there is interdependence among the choices in different categories. Accordingly, a discussion of pros and cons relative to specific applications is best done by looking at preferred combinations. This, in turn, is best done in the context of standards, which is a subject of a later section.

Topologies

In the context of a communication network, the term *topology* refers to the way in which the end points, or stations, attached to the network are interconnected. Historically common topologies for LANs are bus, tree, ring, and star (Figure 15.1). The bus is a special case of the tree, with only one trunk and no branches. In contemporary LANs, the star topology dominates. However, it is useful to look at the operation of the different topologies, especially since the Ethernet LAN, discussed in the next chapter, developed initially as a bus topology.

BUS AND TREE TOPOLOGIES Both bus and tree topologies are characterized by the use of a multipoint medium. For the **bus**, all stations attach, through appropriate hardware interfacing known as a tap, directly to a linear transmission medium, or

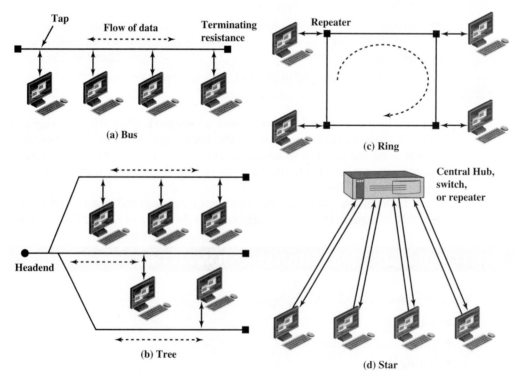

Figure 15.1 LAN Topologies

bus. Full-duplex operation between the station and the tap allows data to be transmitted onto the bus and received from the bus. A transmission from any station propagates the length of the medium in both directions and can be received by all other stations. At each end of the bus is a terminator, which absorbs any signal, removing it from the bus.

The **tree topology** is a generalization of the bus topology. The transmission medium is a branching cable with no closed loops. The tree layout begins at a point known as the *headend*. One or more cables start at the headend, and each of these may have branches. The branches in turn may have additional branches to allow quite complex layouts. Again, a transmission from any station propagates throughout the medium and can be received by all other stations.

Two problems present themselves in this arrangement. First, because a transmission from any one station can be received by all other stations, there needs to be some way of indicating for whom the transmission is intended. Second, a mechanism is needed to regulate transmission. To see the reason for this, consider that if two stations on the bus attempt to transmit at the same time, their signals will overlap and become garbled. Or consider that if one station decides to transmit continuously for a long period of time, other stations will be blocked from transmitting.

To solve these problems, stations transmit data in small blocks, known as frames. Each frame consists of a portion of the data that a station wishes to transmit, plus a frame header that contains control information. Each station on the bus is assigned a unique address, or identifier, and the destination address for a frame is included in its header.

EXAMPLE 15.1 Figure 15.2 illustrates the bus scheme. In this example, station C wishes to transmit a frame of data to A. The frame header includes A's address. As the frame propagates along the bus, it passes B. B observes the address and ignores the frame. A, on the other hand, sees that the frame is addressed to itself and therefore copies the data from the frame as it goes by.

So the frame structure solves the first problem mentioned previously: It provides a mechanism for indicating the intended recipient of data. It also provides the basic tool for solving the second problem, the regulation of access. In particular, the stations take turns sending frames in some cooperative fashion. This involves putting additional control information into the frame header, as discussed later.

With the bus or tree, no special action needs to be taken to remove frames from the medium. When a signal reaches the end of the medium, it is absorbed by the terminator.

RING TOPOLOGY In the **ring topology**, the network consists of a set of *repeaters* joined by point-to-point links in a closed loop. The repeater is a comparatively simple device, capable of receiving data on one link and transmitting them, bit by bit, on the other link as fast as they are received. The links are unidirectional; that is, data are transmitted in one direction only, so that data circulate around the ring in one direction (clockwise or counterclockwise).

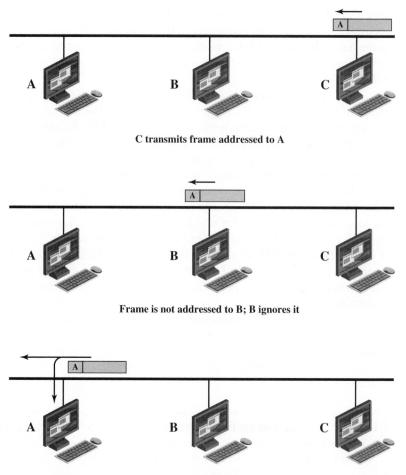

Figure 15.2 Frame Transmission on a Bus LAN

Each station attaches to the network at a repeater and can transmit data onto the network through the repeater. As with the bus and tree, data are transmitted in frames. As a frame circulates past all the other stations, the destination station recognizes its address and copies the frame into a local buffer as it goes by. The frame continues to circulate until it returns to the source station, where it is removed. Because multiple stations share the ring, medium access control is needed to determine at what time each station may insert frames.

EXAMPLE 15.2 Figure 15.3 illustrates the ring scheme. In this example, station C wishes to transmit a frame of data to A. The frame header includes A's address. As the frame circulates around the ring, it passes B. B observes the address and ignores the frame. A, on the other hand, sees that the frame is addressed to itself and therefore copies the data from the frame as it goes by.

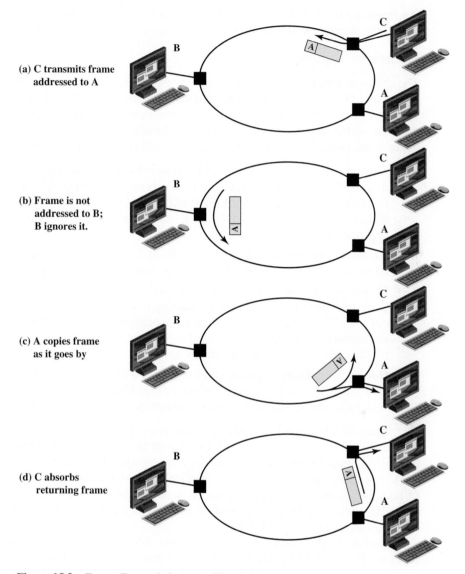

(a) C transmits frame addressed to A

(b) Frame is not addressed to B; B ignores it.

(c) A copies frame as it goes by

(d) C absorbs returning frame

Figure 15.3 Frame Transmission on a Ring LAN

STAR TOPOLOGY In the **star** LAN topology, each station is directly connected to a common central node. Typically, each station attaches to a central node via two point-to-point links, one for transmission and one for reception.

In general, there are two alternatives for the operation of the central node. One approach is for the central node to operate in a broadcast fashion. A transmission of a frame from one station to the node is retransmitted on all of the outgoing links. In this case, although the arrangement is physically a star, it is logically a bus: A transmission from any station is received by all other stations, and only one station at a time may successfully transmit. In this case, the central element is referred to as a **hub**. Another approach is for the central node to act as a frame-switching device.

An incoming frame is buffered in the node and then retransmitted on an outgoing link to the destination station. These approaches are explored in Section 15.4.

Choice of Topology

The choice of topology depends on a variety of factors, including reliability, expandability, and performance. This choice is part of the overall task of designing a LAN and thus cannot be made in isolation, independent of the choice of transmission medium, wiring layout, and access control technique. A few general remarks can be made at this point. There are four alternative media that can be used for a bus LAN:

- **Twisted pair:** In the early days of LAN development, voice-grade twisted pair was used to provide an inexpensive, easily installed bus LAN. A number of systems operating at 1 Mbps were implemented. Scaling twisted pair up to higher data rates in a shared-medium bus configuration is not practical, so this approach was dropped long ago.
- **Baseband coaxial cable:** A baseband coaxial cable is one that makes use of digital signaling. The original Ethernet scheme makes use of baseband coaxial cable.
- **Broadband coaxial cable:** Broadband coaxial cable is the type of cable used in cable television systems. Analog signaling is used at radio and television frequencies. This type of system is more expensive and more difficult to install and maintain than baseband coaxial cable. This approach never achieved popularity and such LANs are no longer made.
- **Optical fiber:** There has been considerable research relating to this alternative over the years, but the expense of the optical fiber taps and the availability of better alternatives have resulted in the demise of this option as well.

Thus, for a bus topology, only baseband coaxial cable has achieved widespread use, primarily for Ethernet systems. Compared to a star-topology twisted pair or optical fiber installation, the bus topology using baseband coaxial cable is difficult to work with. Even simple changes may require access to the coaxial cable, movement of taps, and rerouting of cable segments. Accordingly, few if any new installations are being attempted. Despite its limitations, there is a considerable installed base of baseband coaxial cable bus LANs.

Very-high-speed links over considerable distances can be used for the ring topology. Hence, the ring has the potential of providing the best throughput of any topology. One disadvantage of the ring is that a single link or repeater failure could disable the entire network.

The star topology takes advantage of the natural layout of wiring in a building. It is generally best for short distances and can support a small number of devices at high data rates.

Choice of Transmission Medium

The choice of transmission medium is determined by a number of factors. It is, we shall see, constrained by the topology of the LAN. Other factors come into play, including

- **Capacity:** To support the expected network traffic
- **Reliability:** To meet requirements for availability

- **Types of data supported:** Tailored to the application
- **Environmental scope:** To provide service over the range of environments required

The choice is part of the overall task of designing a local network, which is addressed in Chapter 16. Here we can make a few general observations.

Voice-grade unshielded twisted pair (UTP) is an inexpensive, well-understood medium; this is the Category 3 UTP referred to in Chapter 4. Typically, office buildings are wired to meet the anticipated telephone system demand plus a healthy margin; thus, there are no cable installation costs in the use of Category 3 UTP. However, the data rate that can be supported is generally quite limited, with the exception of very small LAN. Category 3 UTP is likely to be the most cost-effective for a single-building, low-traffic LAN installation.

Shielded twisted pair and baseband coaxial cable are more expensive than Category 3 UTP but provide greater capacity. Broadband cable is even more expensive but provides even greater capacity. However, in recent years, the trend has been toward the use of high-performance twisted pair, especially Category 6, Category 6A, and Category 7, as discussed in Chapter 4. These high-performance twisted-pair alternatives are well suited for use with the star topology.

Optical fiber has a number of attractive features, such as electromagnetic isolation, high capacity, and small size, which have attracted a great deal of interest. Market penetration of fiber LANs has increased rapidly in recent years, as the cost of fiber components has dropped and the availability of skilled personnel to install and maintain fiber systems has increased.

15.2 LAN PROTOCOL ARCHITECTURE

The architecture of a LAN is best described in terms of a layering of protocols that organize the basic functions of a LAN. This section opens with a description of the standardized protocol architecture for LANs, which encompasses physical, medium access control (MAC), and logical link control (LLC) layers. The physical layer encompasses topology and transmission medium, and is covered in Section 15.1. This section provides an overview of the MAC and LLC layers.

IEEE 802 Reference Model

Protocols defined specifically for LAN and metropolitan area networks (MAN) transmission address issues relating to the transmission of blocks of data over the network. In OSI terms, higher layer protocols (layer 3 or 4 and above) are independent of network architecture and are applicable to LANs, MANs, and WANs. Thus, a discussion of LAN protocols is concerned principally with lower layers of the OSI model.

Figure 15.4 relates the LAN protocols to the OSI architecture. This architecture was developed by the IEEE 802 LAN standards committee[1] and has been adopted by all organizations working on the specification of LAN standards. It is generally referred to as the IEEE 802 reference model.

---

[1] This committee has developed standards for a wide range of LANs. See Appendix C for details.

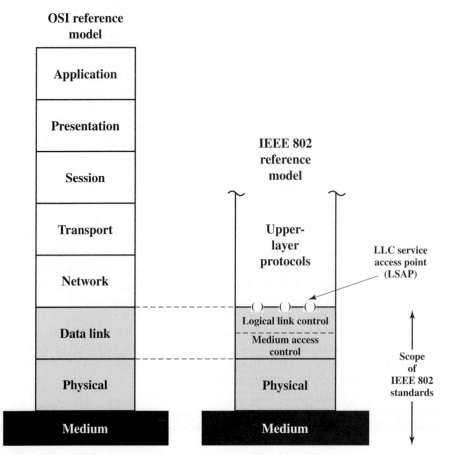

Figure 15.4 IEEE 802 Protocol Layers Compared to OSI Model

Working from the bottom up, the lowest layer of the IEEE 802 reference model corresponds to the **physical layer** of the OSI model and includes such functions as

- Encoding/decoding of signals
- Preamble generation/removal (for synchronization)
- Bit transmission/reception

In addition, the physical layer of the 802 model includes a specification of the transmission medium and the topology. Generally, this is considered "below" the lowest layer of the OSI model. However, the choice of transmission medium and topology is critical in LAN design, and so a specification of the medium is included.

Above the physical layer are the functions associated with providing service to LAN users. These include the following:

- On transmission, assemble data into a frame with address and error-detection fields.
- On reception, disassemble frame and perform address recognition and error detection.

- Govern access to the LAN transmission medium.
- Provide an interface to higher layers and perform flow and error control.

These are functions typically associated with OSI layer 2. The set of functions in the last bullet item are grouped into a **logical link control (LLC)** layer. The functions in the first three bullet items are treated as a separate layer, called **medium access control (MAC)**. The separation is done for the following reasons:

- The logic required to manage access to a shared-access medium is not found in traditional layer 2 data link control.
- For the same LLC, several MAC options may be provided.

Figure 15.5 illustrates the relationship between the levels of the architecture (compare Figure 2.5). Higher-level data are passed down to LLC, which appends control information as a header, creating an *LLC protocol data unit* (*PDU*). This control information is used in the operation of the LLC protocol. The entire LLC PDU is then passed down to the MAC layer, which appends control information at the front and back of the packet, forming a *MAC frame*. Again, the control information in the frame is needed for the operation of the MAC protocol. For context, the figure also shows the use of TCP/IP and an application layer above the LAN protocols.

Logical Link Control

The LLC layer for LANs is similar in many respects to other link layers in common use. Like all link layers, LLC is concerned with the transmission of a link-level PDU between two stations, without the necessity of an intermediate switching node. LLC has two characteristics not shared by most other link control protocols:

1. It must support the multiaccess, shared-medium nature of the link (this differs from a multidrop line in that there is no primary node).
2. It is relieved of some details of link access by the MAC layer.

Addressing in LLC involves specifying the source and destination LLC users. Typically, a user is a higher-layer protocol or a network management function in the station. These LLC user addresses are referred to as service access points (SAPs), in keeping with OSI terminology for the user of a protocol layer.

We look first at the services that LLC provides to a higher-level user, and then at the LLC protocol.

LLC Services LLC specifies the mechanisms for addressing stations across the medium and for controlling the exchange of data between two users. The operation and format of this standard is based on HDLC. Three services are provided as alternatives for attached devices using LLC:

- **Unacknowledged connectionless service:** This service is a datagram-style service. It is a very simple service that does not involve any of the flow- and error-control mechanisms. Thus, the delivery of data is not guaranteed. However, in most devices, there will be some higher layer of software that deals with reliability issues.

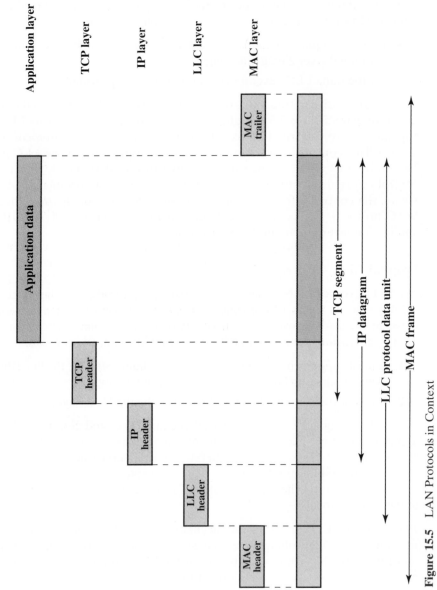

Figure 15.5 LAN Protocols in Context

- **Connection-mode service:** This service is similar to that offered by HDLC. A logical connection is set up between two users exchanging data, and flow control and error control are provided.

- **Acknowledged connectionless service:** This is a cross between the previous two services. It provides that datagrams are to be acknowledged, but no prior logical connection is set up.

Typically, a vendor will provide these services as options that the customer can select when purchasing the equipment. Alternatively, the customer can purchase equipment that provides two or all three services and select a specific service based on application.

The **unacknowledged connectionless service** requires minimum logic and is useful in two contexts. First, it will often be the case that higher layers of software will provide the necessary reliability and flow-control mechanism, and it is efficient to avoid duplicating them. For example, TCP could provide the mechanisms needed to ensure that data is delivered reliably. Second, there are instances in which the overhead of connection establishment and maintenance is unjustified or even counterproductive (e.g., data collection activities that involve the periodic sampling of data sources, such as sensors and automatic self-test reports from security equipment or network components). In a monitoring application, the loss of an occasional data unit would not cause distress, as the next report should arrive shortly. Thus, in most cases, the unacknowledged connectionless service is the preferred option.

The **connection-mode service** could be used in very simple devices, such as terminal controllers, that have little software operating above this level. In these cases, it would provide the flow control and reliability mechanisms normally implemented at higher layers of the communications software.

The **acknowledged connectionless service** is useful in several contexts. With the connection-mode service, the logical link control software must maintain some sort of table for each active connection, to keep track of the status of that connection. If the user needs guaranteed delivery but there are a large number of destinations for data, then the connection-mode service may be impractical because of the large number of tables required. An example is a process control or automated factory environment where a central site may need to communicate with a large number of processors and programmable controllers. Another use of this is the handling of important and time-critical alarm or emergency control signals in a factory. Because of their importance, an acknowledgment is needed so that the sender can be assured that the signal got through. Because of the urgency of the signal, the user might not want to take the time first to establish a logical connection and then send the data.

LLC PROTOCOL The basic LLC protocol is modeled after HDLC and has similar functions and formats. The differences between the two protocols can be summarized as follows:

- LLC makes use of the asynchronous balanced mode of operation of HDLC, to support connection-mode LLC service; this is referred to as type 2 operation. The other HDLC modes are not employed.

- LLC supports an unacknowledged connectionless service using the unnumbered information PDU; this is known as type 1 operation.

- LLC supports an acknowledged connectionless service by using two new unnumbered PDUs; this is known as type 3 operation.
- LLC permits multiplexing by the use of LLC service access points (LSAPs).

All three LLC protocols employ the same PDU format (Figure 15.6), which consists of four fields. The DSAP (Destination Service Access Point) and SSAP (Source Service Access Point) fields each contain a 7-bit address, which specify the destination and source users of LLC. One bit of the DSAP indicates whether the DSAP is an individual or group address. One bit of the SSAP indicates whether the PDU is a command or response PDU. The format of the LLC control field is identical to that of HDLC (Figure 7.7), using extended (7-bit) sequence numbers.

For **type 1 operation**, which supports the unacknowledged connectionless service, the unnumbered information (UI) PDU is used to transfer user data. There is no acknowledgment, flow control, or error control. However, there is error detection and discard at the MAC level.

Two other PDUs are used to support management functions associated with all three types of operation. Both PDUs are used in the following fashion. An LLC entity may issue a command (C/R bit = 0) XID or TEST. The receiving LLC entity issues a corresponding XID or TEST in response. The XID PDU is used to exchange two types of information: types of operation supported and window size. The TEST PDU is used to conduct a loopback test of the transmission path between two LLC entities. Upon receipt of a TEST command PDU, the addressed LLC entity issues a TEST response PDU as soon as possible.

With **type 2 operation**, a data link connection is established between two LLC SAPs prior to data exchange. Connection establishment is attempted by the type 2 protocol in response to a request from a user. The LLC entity issues a SABME

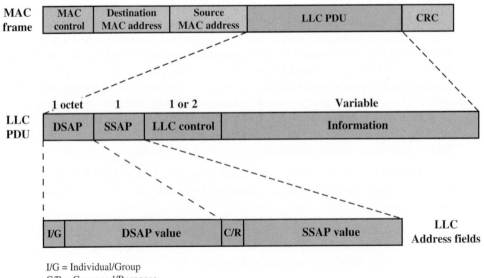

I/G = Individual/Group
C/R = Command/Response

Figure 15.6   LLC PDU in a Generic MAC Frame Format

PDU[2] to request a logical connection with the other LLC entity. If the connection is accepted by the LLC user designated by the DSAP, then the destination LLC entity returns an unnumbered acknowledgment (UA) PDU. The connection is henceforth uniquely identified by the pair of user SAPs. If the destination LLC user rejects the connection request, its LLC entity returns a disconnected mode (DM) PDU.

Once the connection is established, data are exchanged using information PDUs, as in HDLC. The information PDUs include send and receive sequence numbers, for sequencing and flow control. The supervisory PDUs are used, as in HDLC, for flow control and error control. Either LLC entity can terminate a logical LLC connection by issuing a disconnect (DISC) PDU.

With **type 3 operation**, each transmitted PDU is acknowledged. A new (not found in HDLC) unnumbered PDU, the Acknowledged Connectionless (AC) Information PDU, is defined. User data are sent in AC command PDUs and must be acknowledged using an AC response PDU. To guard against lost PDUs, a 1-bit sequence number is used. The sender alternates the use of 0 and 1 in its AC command PDU, and the receiver responds with an AC PDU with the opposite number of the corresponding command. Only one PDU in each direction may be outstanding at any time.

Medium Access Control

All LANs and MANs consist of collections of devices that must share the network's transmission capacity. Some means of controlling access to the transmission medium is needed to provide for an orderly and efficient use of that capacity. This is the function of a medium access control (MAC) protocol.

The key parameters in any medium access control technique are where and how. *Where* refers to whether control is exercised in a centralized or distributed fashion. In a centralized scheme, a controller is designated that has the authority to grant access to the network. A station wishing to transmit must wait until it receives permission from the controller. In a decentralized network, the stations collectively perform a medium access control function to determine dynamically the order in which stations transmit. A centralized scheme has certain advantages, including the following:

- It may afford greater control over access for providing such things as priorities, overrides, and guaranteed capacity.
- It enables the use of relatively simple access logic at each station.
- It avoids problems of distributed coordination among peer entities

The principal disadvantages of centralized schemes are as follows:

- It creates a single point of failure; that is, there is a point in the network that, if it fails, causes the entire network to fail.
- It may act as a bottleneck, reducing performance.

The pros and cons of distributed schemes are mirror images of the points just made.

---

[2]This stands for Set Asynchronous Balanced Mode Extended. It is used in HDLC to choose ABM and to select extended sequence numbers of seven bits. Both ABM and 7-bit sequence numbers are mandatory in type 2 operation.

The second parameter, *how*, is constrained by the topology and is a trade-off among competing factors, including cost, performance, and complexity. In general, we can categorize access control techniques as being either synchronous or asynchronous. With synchronous techniques, a specific capacity is dedicated to a connection. This is the same approach used in circuit switching, frequency division multiplexing (FDM), and synchronous time division multiplexing (TDM). Such techniques are generally not optimal in LANs and MANs because the needs of the stations are unpredictable. It is preferable to be able to allocate capacity in an asynchronous (dynamic) fashion, more or less in response to immediate demand. The asynchronous approach can be further subdivided into three categories: round robin, reservation, and contention.

ROUND ROBIN With round robin, each station in turn is given the opportunity to transmit. During that opportunity, the station may decline to transmit or may transmit subject to a specified upper bound, usually expressed as a maximum amount of data transmitted or time for this opportunity. In any case, the station, when it is finished, relinquishes its turn, and the right to transmit passes to the next station in logical sequence. Control of sequence may be centralized or distributed. Polling is an example of a centralized technique.

When many stations have data to transmit over an extended period of time, round-robin techniques can be very efficient. If only a few stations have data to transmit over an extended period of time, then there is a considerable overhead in passing the turn from station to station, because most of the stations will not transmit but simply pass their turns. Under such circumstances other techniques may be preferable, largely depending on whether the data traffic has a stream or bursty characteristic. Stream traffic is characterized by lengthy and fairly continuous transmissions; examples are voice communication, telemetry, and bulk file transfer. Bursty traffic is characterized by short, sporadic transmissions; interactive terminal-host traffic fits this description.

RESERVATION For stream traffic, reservation techniques are well suited. In general, for these techniques, time on the medium is divided into slots, much as with synchronous TDM. A station wishing to transmit reserves future slots for an extended or even an indefinite period. Again, reservations may be made in a centralized or distributed fashion.

CONTENTION For bursty traffic, contention techniques are usually appropriate. With these techniques, no control is exercised to determine whose turn it is; all stations contend for time in a way that can be, as we shall see, rather rough and tumble. These techniques are of necessity distributed in nature. Their principal advantage is that they are simple to implement and, under light-to-moderate load, efficient. For some of these techniques, however, performance tends to collapse under heavy load.

Although both centralized and distributed reservation techniques have been implemented in some LAN products, round-robin and contention techniques are the most common.

MAC FRAME FORMAT The MAC layer receives a block of data from the LLC layer and is responsible for performing functions related to medium access and for transmitting the data. As with other protocol layers, MAC implements these functions making use of a protocol data unit at its layer. In this case, the PDU is referred to as a MAC frame.

The exact format of the MAC frame differs somewhat for the various MAC protocols in use. In general, all of the MAC frames have a format similar to that of Figure 15.6. The fields of this frame are as follows:

- **MAC Control:** This field contains any protocol control information needed for the functioning of the MAC protocol. For example, a priority level could be indicated here.

- **Destination MAC Address:** The destination physical attachment point on the LAN for this frame.

- **Source MAC Address:** The source physical attachment point on the LAN for this frame.

- **LLC:** The LLC data from the next higher layer.

- **CRC:** The Cyclic Redundancy Check field (also known as the frame check sequence, FCS, field). This is an error-detecting code, as we have seen in HDLC and other data link control protocols (Chapter 7).

In most data link control protocols, the data link protocol entity is responsible not only for detecting errors using the CRC, but for recovering from those errors by retransmitting damaged frames. In the LAN protocol architecture, these two functions are split between the MAC and LLC layers. The MAC layer is responsible for detecting errors and discarding any frames that are in error. The LLC layer optionally keeps track of which frames have been successfully received and retransmits unsuccessful frames.

15.3 BRIDGES

In virtually all cases, there is a need to expand beyond the confines of a single LAN, to provide interconnection to other LANs and to wide area networks. Two general approaches are used for this purpose: bridges and routers. The bridge is the simpler of the two devices and provides a means of interconnecting similar LANs. The router is a more general-purpose device, capable of interconnecting a variety of LANs and WANs. We explore bridges in this section and look at routers in Part Five.

The bridge is designed for use between local area networks (LANs) that use identical protocols for the physical and link layers (e.g., all conforming to IEEE 802.3). Because the devices all use the same protocols, the amount of processing required at the bridge is minimal. More sophisticated bridges are capable of mapping from one MAC format to another (e.g., to interconnect an Ethernet and a token ring LAN).

Because the bridge is used in a situation in which all the LANs have the same characteristics, the reader may ask, why not simply have one large LAN? Depending on circumstance, there are several reasons for the use of multiple LANs connected by bridges:

- **Reliability:** The danger in connecting all data processing devices in an organization to one network is that a fault on the network may disable communication for all devices. By using bridges, the network can be partitioned into self-contained units.

- **Performance:** In general, performance on a LAN declines with an increase in the number of devices or the length of the wire. A number of smaller LANs will often give improved performance if devices can be clustered so that intranetwork traffic significantly exceeds internetwork traffic.

- **Security:** The establishment of multiple LANs may improve security of communications. It is desirable to keep different types of traffic (e.g., accounting, personnel, strategic planning) that have different security needs on physically separate media. At the same time, the different types of users with different levels of security need to communicate through controlled and monitored mechanisms.

- **Geography:** Clearly, two separate LANs are needed to support devices clustered in two geographically distant locations. Even in the case of two buildings separated by a highway, it may be far easier to use a microwave bridge link than to attempt to string coaxial cable between the two buildings.

Functions of a Bridge

EXAMPLE 15.3 Figure 15.7 illustrates the action of a bridge connecting two LANs, A and B, using the same MAC protocol. In this example, a single bridge attaches to both LANs; frequently, the bridge function is performed by two "half-bridges," one on each LAN. The functions of the bridge are few and simple:

- Read all frames transmitted on A and accept those addressed to any station on B.

- Using the medium access control protocol for B, retransmit each frame on B.

- Do the same for B-to-A traffic.

Several design aspects of a bridge are worth highlighting:

- The bridge makes no modification to the content or format of the frames it receives, nor does it encapsulate them with an additional header. Each frame to be transferred is simply copied from one LAN and repeated with exactly the same bit pattern on the other LAN. Because the two LANs use the same LAN protocols, it is permissible to do this.

- The bridge should contain enough buffer space to meet peak demands. Over a short period of time, frames may arrive faster than they can be retransmitted.

- The bridge must contain addressing and routing intelligence. At a minimum, the bridge must know which addresses are on each network to know which frames to pass. Further, there may be more than two LANs interconnected by a number of bridges. In that case, a frame may have to be routed through several bridges in its journey from source to destination.

- A bridge may connect more than two LANs.

In summary, the bridge provides an extension to the LAN that requires no modification to the communications software in the stations attached to the LANs.

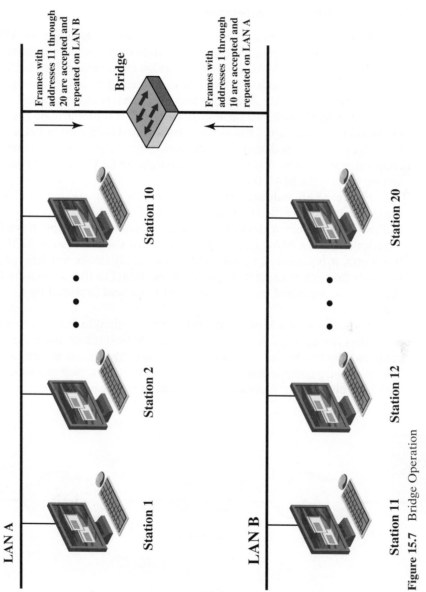

Figure 15.7 Bridge Operation

It appears to all stations on the two (or more) LANs that there is a single LAN on which each station has a unique address. The station uses that unique address and need not explicitly discriminate between stations on the same LAN and stations on other LANs; the bridge takes care of that.

Bridge Protocol Architecture

The IEEE 802.1D specification defines the protocol architecture for MAC bridges. Within the 802 architecture, the endpoint or station address is designated at the MAC level. Thus, it is at the MAC level that a bridge can function. Figure 15.8 shows the simplest case, which consists of two LANs connected by a single bridge. The LANs employ the same MAC and LLC protocols. The bridge operates as previously described. A MAC frame whose destination is not on the immediate LAN is captured by the bridge, buffered briefly, and then transmitted on the other LAN. As far as the LLC layer is concerned, there is a dialogue between peer LLC entities in the two endpoint stations. The bridge need not contain an LLC layer because it is merely serving to relay the MAC frames.

Figure 15.8b indicates the way in which data are encapsulated using a bridge. Data are provided by some user to LLC. The LLC entity appends a header and passes the resulting data unit to the MAC entity, which appends a header and a trailer to form a MAC frame. On the basis of the destination MAC address in the frame, it is captured by the bridge. The bridge does not strip off the MAC fields; its function is to relay the MAC frame intact to the destination LAN. Thus, the frame is deposited on the destination LAN and captured by the destination station.

The concept of a MAC relay bridge is not limited to the use of a single bridge to connect two nearby LANs. If the LANs are some distance apart, then they can be connected by two bridges that are in turn connected by a communications facility. The intervening communications facility can be a network, such as a wide area packet-switching network, or a point-to-point link. In such cases, when a bridge captures

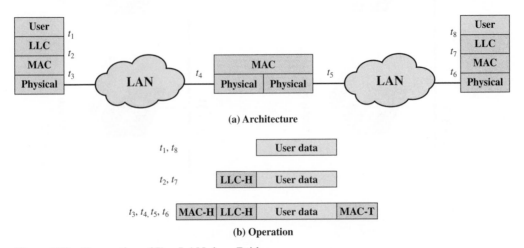

(a) Architecture

(b) Operation

Figure 15.8   Connection of Two LANs by a Bridge

a MAC frame, it must encapsulate the frame in the appropriate packaging and transmit it over the communications facility to a target bridge. The target bridge strips off these extra fields and transmits the original, unmodified MAC frame to the destination station.

Fixed Routing

There is a trend within many organizations to an increasing number of LANs interconnected by bridges. As the number of LANs grows, it becomes important to provide alternate paths between LANs via bridges for load balancing and reconfiguration in response to failure. Thus, many organizations will find that static, preconfigured routing tables are inadequate and that some sort of dynamic routing is needed.

EXAMPLE 15.4 Consider the configuration of Figure 15.9. Suppose that station 1 transmits a frame on LAN A intended for station 6. The frame will be read by bridges 101, 102, and 107. For each bridge, the addressed station is not on a LAN to which the bridge is attached. Therefore, each bridge must make a decision whether or not to retransmit the frame on its other LAN, in order to move it closer to its intended destination. In this case, bridge 102 should repeat the frame on LAN C, whereas bridges 101 and 107 should refrain from retransmitting the frame. Once the frame has been transmitted on LAN C, it will be picked up by both bridges 105 and 106. Again, each must decide whether or not to forward the frame. In this case, bridge 105 should retransmit the frame on LAN F, where it will be received by the destination, station 6.

Thus we see that, in the general case, the bridge must be equipped with a routing capability. When a bridge receives a frame, it must decide whether or not to forward it. If the bridge is attached to two or more networks, then it must decide whether or not to forward the frame and, if so, on which LAN the frame should be transmitted.

The routing decision may not always be a simple one. Figure 15.9 also shows that there are two routes between LAN A and LAN E. Such redundancy provides for higher overall Internet availability and creates the possibility for load balancing. In this case, if station 1 transmits a frame on LAN A intended for station 5 on LAN E, then either bridge 101 or bridge 107 could forward the frame. It would appear preferable for bridge 107 to forward the frame, since it will involve only one hop, whereas if the frame travels through bridge 101, it must suffer two hops. Another consideration is that there may be changes in the configuration. For example, bridge 107 may fail, in which case subsequent frames from station 1 to station 5 should go through bridge 101. So we can say that the routing capability must take into account the topology of the internet configuration and may need to be dynamically altered.

A variety of routing strategies have been proposed and implemented in recent years. The simplest and most common strategy is **fixed routing**. This strategy is suitable for small internets and for internets that are relatively stable. In addition, two groups within the IEEE 802 committee have developed specifications for routing strategies. The IEEE 802.1 group has issued a standard for routing based on the use of a **spanning tree** algorithm. The token ring committee, IEEE 802.5, has issued its

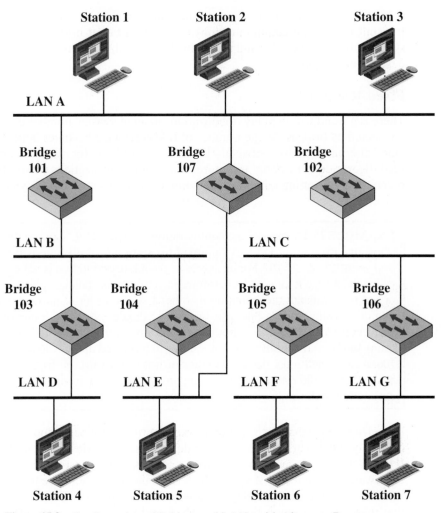

Figure 15.9 Configuration of Bridges and LANs, with Alternate Routes

own specification, referred to as **source routing**. In the remainder of this section, we look at fixed routing and the spanning tree algorithm, which is the most commonly used bridge routing algorithm.

For fixed routing, a route is selected for each source-destination pair of LANs in the configuration. If alternate routes are available between two LANs, then typically the route with the least number of hops is selected. The routes are fixed, or at least only change when there is a change in the topology of the internet.

The strategy for developing a fixed routing configuration for bridges is similar to that employed in a packet-switching network (Figure 12.2). A central routing matrix is created, to be stored perhaps at a network control center. The matrix shows, for each source-destination pair of LANs, the identity of the first bridge on the route.

EXAMPLE 15.5 The route from LAN E to LAN F begins by going through bridge 107 to LAN A. Again consulting the matrix, the route from LAN A to LAN F goes through bridge 102 to LAN C. Finally, the route from LAN C to LAN F is directly through bridge 105. Thus, the complete route from LAN E to LAN F is bridge 107, LAN A, bridge 102, and LAN C, bridge 105.

From this overall matrix, routing tables can be developed and stored at each bridge. Each bridge needs one table for each LAN to which it attaches. The information for each table is derived from a single row of the matrix. Thus, bridge 105 has two tables, one for frames arriving from LAN C and one for frames arriving from LAN F. The table shows, for each possible destination MAC address, the identity of the LAN to which the bridge should forward the frame.

Once the directories have been established, routing is a simple matter. A bridge copies each incoming frame on each of its LANs. If the destination MAC address corresponds to an entry in its routing table, the frame is retransmitted on the appropriate LAN.

The fixed routing strategy is widely used in commercially available products. It requires that a network manager manually load the data into the routing tables. It has the advantage of simplicity and minimal processing requirements. However, in a complex internet, in which bridges may be dynamically added and in which failures must be allowed for, this strategy is too limited.

The Spanning Tree Approach

The spanning tree approach is a mechanism in which bridges automatically develop a routing table and update that table in response to changing topology. The algorithm consists of three mechanisms: frame forwarding, address learning, and loop resolution.

FRAME FORWARDING In this scheme, a bridge maintains a **forwarding database** for each port attached to a LAN. The database indicates the station addresses for which frames should be forwarded through that port. We can interpret this in the following fashion. For each port, a list of stations is maintained. A station is on the list if it is on the "same side" of the bridge as the port. For example, for bridge 102 of Figure 15.9, stations on LANs C, F, and G are on the same side of the bridge as the LAN C port, and stations on LANs A, B, D, and E are on the same side of the bridge as the LAN A port. When a frame is received on any port, the bridge must decide whether that frame is to be forwarded through the bridge and out through one of the bridge's other ports. Suppose that a bridge receives a MAC frame on port x. The following rules are applied:

1. Search the forwarding database to determine if the MAC address is listed for any port except port x.

2. If the destination MAC address is not found, forward frame out all ports except the one from which is was received. This is part of the learning process described subsequently.

3. If the destination address is in the forwarding database for some port y, then determine whether port y is in a blocking or forwarding state. For reasons explained later, a port may sometimes be blocked, which prevents it from receiving or transmitting frames.

4. If port y is not blocked, transmit the frame through port y onto the LAN to which that port attaches.

ADDRESS LEARNING The preceding scheme assumes that the bridge is already equipped with a forwarding database that indicates the direction, from the bridge, of each destination station. This information can be preloaded into the bridge, as in fixed routing. However, an effective automatic mechanism for learning the direction of each station is desirable. A simple scheme for acquiring this information is based on the use of the source address field in each MAC frame.

The strategy is this. When a frame arrives on a particular port, it clearly has come from the direction of the incoming LAN. The source address field of the frame indicates the source station. Thus, a bridge can update its forwarding database for that port on the basis of the source address field of each incoming frame. To allow for changes in topology, each element in the database is equipped with a timer. When a new element is added to the database, its timer is set. If the timer expires, then the element is eliminated from the database, since the corresponding direction information may no longer be valid. Each time a frame is received, its source address is checked against the database. If the element is already in the database, the entry is updated (the direction may have changed) and the timer is reset. If the element is not in the database, a new entry is created, with its own timer.

SPANNING TREE ALGORITHM The address learning mechanism described previously is effective if the topology of the internet is a tree, that is, if there are no alternate routes in the network. The existence of alternate routes means that there is a closed loop. For example in Figure 15.9, the following is a closed loop: LAN A, bridge 101, LAN B, bridge 104, LAN E, bridge 107, LAN A.

To see the problem created by a closed loop, consider Figure 15.10. At time t_0, station A transmits a frame addressed to station B. The frame is captured by both bridges. Each bridge updates its database to indicate that station A is in the direction of LAN X, and retransmits the frame on LAN Y. Say that bridge α retransmits at time t_1 and bridge β a short time later t_2. Thus B will receive two copies of the frame. Furthermore, each bridge will receive the other's transmission on LAN Y. Note that each transmission is a frame with a source address of A and a destination address of B. Thus each bridge will update its database to indicate that station A is in the direction of LAN Y. Neither bridge is now capable of forwarding a frame addressed to station A.

To overcome this problem, a simple result from graph theory is used: For any connected graph, consisting of nodes and edges connecting pairs of nodes, there is a spanning tree of edges that maintains the connectivity of the graph but contains no closed loops. In terms of internets, each LAN corresponds to a graph node, and each bridge corresponds to a graph edge. Thus, in Figure 15.9, the removal of one (and only one) of bridges 107, 101, and 104 results in a spanning tree. What is desired is to develop a simple algorithm by which the bridges of the internet can exchange sufficient information to automatically (without user intervention) derive a spanning tree. The

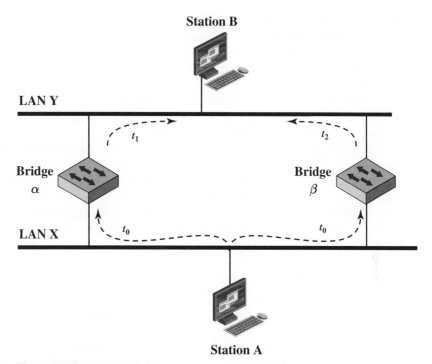

Figure 15.10   Loop of Bridges

algorithm must be dynamic. That is, when a topology change occurs, the bridges must be able to discover this fact and automatically derive a new spanning tree.

The spanning tree algorithm developed by IEEE 802.1, as the name suggests, is able to develop such a spanning tree. All that is required is that each bridge be assigned a unique identifier and that costs be assigned to each bridge port. In the absence of any special considerations, all costs could be set equal; this produces a minimum-hop tree. The algorithm involves a brief exchange of messages among all of the bridges to discover the minimum-cost spanning tree. Whenever there is a change in topology, the bridges automatically recalculate the spanning tree.

For more information on the spanning tree algorithm, see Appendix K.

15.4 HUBS AND SWITCHES

In recent years, there has been a proliferation of types of devices for interconnecting LANs that goes beyond the bridges discussed in Section 15.4 and the routers discussed in Part Five. These devices can conveniently be grouped into the categories of hubs and switches.

Hubs

Earlier, we used the term *hub* in reference to a star-topology LAN. The hub is the active central element of the star layout. Each station is connected to the hub by two lines (transmit and receive). The hub acts as a repeater: When a single station transmits, the hub repeats the signal on the outgoing line to each station. Ordinarily, the line consists of two unshielded twisted pairs. Because of the high data rate and the poor transmission qualities of unshielded twisted pair, the length of a line is limited to about 100 m. As an alternative, an optical fiber link may be used. In this case, the maximum length is about 500 m.

Note that although this scheme is physically a star, it is logically a bus: A transmission from any one station is received by all other stations, and if two stations transmit at the same time there will be a collision.

Multiple levels of hubs can be cascaded in a hierarchical configuration. Figure 15.11 illustrates a two-level configuration. There is one **header hub (HHUB)** and one or more **intermediate hubs (IHUB)**. Each hub may have a mixture of stations and other hubs attached to it from below. This layout fits well with building wiring practices. Typically, there is a wiring closet on each floor of an office building, and a hub can be placed in each one. Each hub could service the stations on its floor.

Layer 2 Switches

In recent years, a new device, the layer 2 switch, has replaced the hub in popularity, particularly for high-speed LANs. The layer 2 switch is also sometimes referred to as a switching hub.

To clarify the distinction between hubs and switches, Figure 15.12a shows a typical bus layout of a traditional 10-Mbps LAN. A bus is installed that is laid out so that all the devices to be attached are in reasonable proximity to a point on the bus. In the figure, station B is transmitting. This transmission goes from B, across the lead

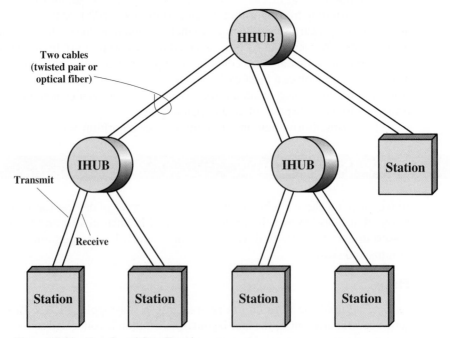

Figure 15.11 Two-Level Star Topology

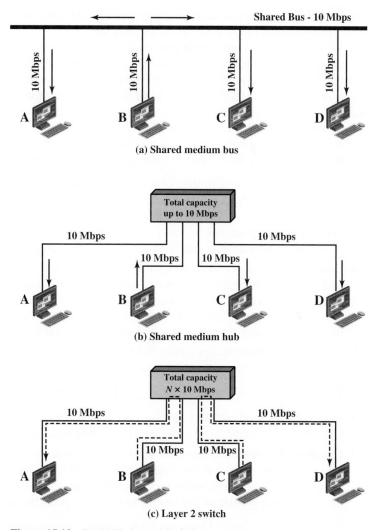

Figure 15.12   LAN Hubs and Switches

from B to the bus, along the bus in both directions, and along the access lines of each of the other attached stations. In this configuration, all the stations must share the total capacity of the bus, which is 10 Mbps.

A hub, often in a building wiring closet, uses a star wiring arrangement to attach stations to the hub. In this arrangement, a transmission from any one station is received by the hub and retransmitted on all of the outgoing lines. Therefore, to avoid collision, only one station can transmit at a time. Again, the total capacity of the LAN is 10 Mbps. The hub has several advantages over the simple bus arrangement. It exploits standard building wiring practices in the layout of cable. In addition, the hub can be configured to recognize a malfunctioning station that is jamming the network and to cut that station out of the network. Figure 15.12b illustrates the operation of a hub. Here again, station B is transmitting. This transmission goes from B, across the transmit line from B to the hub, and from the hub along the receive lines of each of the other attached stations.

We can achieve greater performance with a layer 2 switch. In this case, the central hub acts as a switch, much as a packet switch or circuit switch. With a layer 2 switch, an incoming frame from a particular station is switched to the appropriate output line to be delivered to the intended destination. At the same time, other unused lines can be used for switching other traffic. Figure 15.12c shows an example in which B is transmitting a frame to A and at the same time C is transmitting a frame to D. So, in this example, the current throughput on the LAN is 20 Mbps, although each individual device is limited to 10 Mbps. The layer 2 switch has several attractive features:

1. No change is required to the software or hardware of the attached devices to convert a bus LAN or a hub LAN to a switched LAN. In the case of an Ethernet LAN, each attached device continues to use the Ethernet medium access control protocol to access the LAN. From the point of view of the attached devices, nothing has changed in the access logic.

2. Each attached device has a dedicated capacity equal to that of the entire original LAN, assuming that the layer 2 switch has sufficient capacity to keep up with all attached devices. For example, in Figure 15.12c, if the layer 2 switch can sustain a throughput of 20 Mbps, each attached device appears to have a dedicated capacity for either input or output of 10 Mbps.

3. The layer 2 switch scales easily. Additional devices can be attached to the layer 2 switch by increasing the capacity of the layer 2 switch correspondingly.

Two types of layer 2 switches are available as commercial products:

- **Store-and-forward switch:** The layer 2 switch accepts a frame on an input line, buffers it briefly, and then routes it to the appropriate output line.

- **Cut-through switch:** The layer 2 switch takes advantage of the fact that the destination address appears at the beginning of the MAC (medium access control) frame. The layer 2 switch begins repeating the incoming frame onto the appropriate output line as soon as the layer 2 switch recognizes the destination address.

The cut-through switch yields the highest possible throughput but at some risk of propagating bad frames, because the switch is not able to check the CRC prior to retransmission. The store-and-forward switch involves a delay between sender and receiver but boosts the overall integrity of the network.

A layer 2 switch can be viewed as a full-duplex version of the hub. It can also incorporate logic that allows it to function as a multiport bridge. The following are differences between layer 2 switches and bridges:

- Bridge frame handling is done in software. A layer 2 switch performs the address recognition and frame forwarding functions in hardware.

- A bridge can typically only analyze and forward one frame at a time, whereas a layer 2 switch has multiple parallel data paths and can handle multiple frames at a time.

- A bridge uses store-and-forward operation. With a layer 2 switch, it is possible to have cut-through instead of store-and-forward operation.

Because a layer 2 switch has higher performance and can incorporate the functions of a bridge, the bridge has suffered commercially. New installations typically include layer 2 switches with bridge functionality rather than bridges.

15.5 VIRTUAL LANS

Figure 15.13 shows a relatively common type of hierarchical LAN configuration. In this example, the devices on the LAN are organized into four groups, each served by a LAN switch. The three lower groups might correspond to different departments,

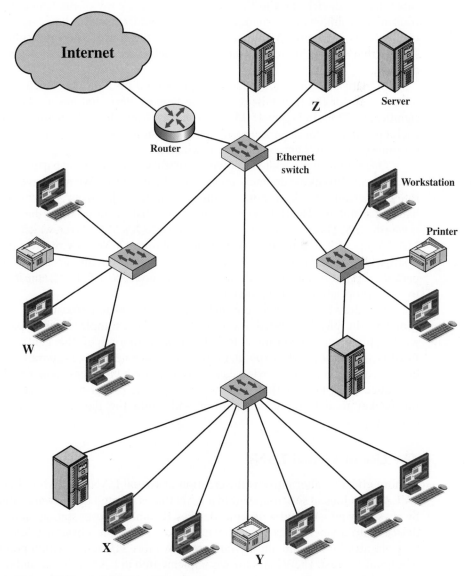

Figure 15.13 A LAN Configuration

which are physically separated, and the upper group could correspond to a centralized server farm that is used by all the departments.

Let us consider the transmission of a single MAC frame from workstation X. Suppose the destination MAC address in the frame (see Figure 15.6) is workstation Y. This frame is transmitted from X to the local switch, which then directs the frame along the link to Y. If X transmits a frame addressed to Z or W, then its local switch routes the MAC frame through the appropriate switches to the intended destination. All these are examples of **unicast addressing**, in which the destination address in the MAC frame designates a unique destination. A MAC frame may also contain a **broadcast address**, in which case the destination MAC address indicates that all devices on the LAN should receive a copy of the frame. Thus, if X transmits a frame with a broadcast destination address, all of the devices on all of the switches in Figure 15.13 receive a copy of the frame. The total collection of devices that receive broadcast frames from each other is referred to as a **broadcast domain**.

In many situations, a broadcast frame is used for a purpose, such as network management or the transmission of some type of alert, that has a relatively local significance. Thus, in Figure 15.13, if a broadcast frame has information that is only useful to a particular department, then transmission capacity is wasted on the other portions of the LAN and on the other switches.

One simple approach to improving efficiency is to physically partition the LAN into separate broadcast domains, as shown in Figure 15.14. We now have four separate LANs connected by a router. In this case, an IP packet from X intended for Z is handled as follows. The IP layer at X determines that the next hop to the destination is via router V. This information is handed down to X's MAC layer, which prepares a MAC frame with a destination MAC address of router V. When V receives the frame, it strips off the MAC header, determines the destination, and encapsulates the IP packet in a MAC frame with a destination MAC address of Z. This frame is then sent to the appropriate Ethernet switch for delivery.

The drawback to this approach is that the traffic pattern may not correspond to the physical distribution of devices. For example, some departmental workstations may generate a lot of traffic with one of the central servers. Further, as the networks expand, more routers are needed to separate users into broadcast domains and provide connectivity among broadcast domains. Routers introduce more latency than switches because the router must process more of the packet to determine destinations and route the data to the appropriate end node.

The Use of Virtual LANs

A more effective alternative is the creation of virtual LANs (VLANs). In essence, a VLAN is a logical subgroup within a LAN that is created by software rather than by physically moving and separating devices. It combines user stations and network devices into a single broadcast domain regardless of the physical LAN segment they are attached to and allows traffic to flow more efficiently within populations of mutual interest. The VLAN logic is implemented in LAN switches and functions at the MAC layer. Because the objective is to isolate traffic within the VLAN, in

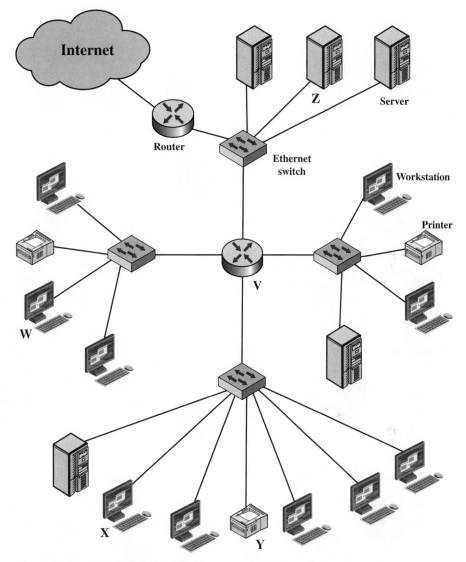

Figure 15.14   A Partitioned LAN

order to link from one VLAN to another, a router is required. Routers can be implemented as separate devices, so that traffic from one VLAN to another is directed to a router, or the router logic can be implemented as part of the LAN switch, as shown in Figure 15.15.

VLANs provide the ability for any organization to be physically dispersed throughout the company while maintaining its group identity. For example, accounting personnel can be located on the shop floor, in the research and development center, in the cash disbursement office, and in the corporate offices, while at the same time all members reside on the same virtual network, sharing traffic only with each other.

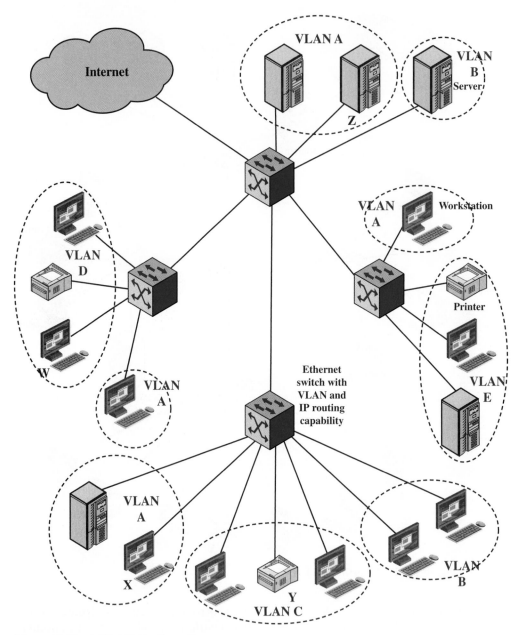

Figure 15.15 A VLAN Configuration

In Figure 15.15, five VLANs are defined. A transmission from workstation X to server Z is within the same VLAN, so it is efficiently switched at the MAC level. A broadcast MAC frame from X is transmitted to all devices in all portions of the same VLAN. But a transmission from X to printer Y goes from one VLAN to another. Accordingly, router logic at the IP level is required to move the IP packet from X to Y. In Figure 15.15, that logic is integrated into the switch, so that the switch determines whether or not the incoming MAC frame is destined for another device on the same VLAN. If not, the switch routes the enclosed IP packet at the IP level.

Defining VLANs

A VLAN is a broadcast domain consisting of a group of end stations, perhaps on multiple physical LAN segments, that are not constrained by their physical location and can communicate as if they were on a common LAN. Some means is therefore needed for defining VLAN membership. A number of different approaches have been used for defining membership, including the following:

- **Membership by port group:** Each switch in the LAN configuration contains two types of ports: a trunk port, which connects two switches, and an end port, which connects the switch to an end system. A VLAN can be defined by assigning each end port to a specific VLAN. This approach has the advantage that it is relatively easy to configure. The principle disadvantage is that the network manager must reconfigure VLAN membership when an end system moves from one port to another.

- **Membership by MAC address:** Since MAC-layer addresses are hardwired into the workstation's network interface card (NIC), VLANs based on MAC addresses enable network managers to move a workstation to a different physical location on the network and have that workstation automatically retain its VLAN membership. The main problem with this method is that VLAN membership must be assigned initially. In networks with thousands of users, this is no easy task. Also, in environments where notebook PCs are used, the MAC address is associated with the docking station and not with the notebook PC. Consequently, when a notebook PC is moved to a different docking station, its VLAN membership must be reconfigured.

- **Membership based on protocol information:** VLAN membership can be assigned based on IP address, transport protocol information, or even higher-layer protocol information. This is a quite flexible approach, but it does require switches to examine portions of the MAC frame above the MAC layer, which may have a performance impact.

Communicating VLAN Membership

Switches must have a way of understanding VLAN membership (i.e., which stations belong to which VLAN) when network traffic arrives from other switches; otherwise, VLANs would be limited to a single switch. One possibility is to configure the information manually or with some type of network management signaling protocol, so that switches can associate incoming frames with the appropriate VLAN.

A more common approach is frame tagging, in which a header is typically inserted into each frame on interswitch trunks to uniquely identify to which VLAN a particular MAC-layer frame belongs. The IEEE 802 committee has developed a standard for frame tagging, IEEE 802.1Q, which we examine in the next chapter.

15.6 RECOMMENDED READING AND WEB SITE

[HIER10] provides an overview of all of the IEEE 802.11 standards efforts. [RAJA97] is a good summary of VLAN principles.

HIER10 Hiertz, G., et al. "The IEEE 802.11 Universe." *IEEE Communications Magazine*, January 2010.

RAJA97 Rajaravivarma, V. "Virtual Local Area Network Technology and Applications." *Proceedings, 29th Southeastern Symposium on System Theory*, 1997.

Recommended Web site:

- **IEEE 802 LAN/MAN Standards Committee:** Status and documents for all of the working groups

15.7 KEY TERMS, REVIEW QUESTIONS, AND PROBLEMS

Key Terms

Acknowledged	hub	source routing
connectionless	fixed routing	spanning tree
bridge	forwarding database	star topology
broadcast address	intermediate hubs	switch
broadcast domain	(IHUB)layer 2 switch	tree topology
bus topology	local area network (LAN)	type 1 operation
connectionless service	logical link control (LLC)	type 2 operation
connection-mode service	medium access control (MAC)	type 3 operation
fixed routing	physical layer	unicast addressing
forwarding database	ring topology	virtual LAN (VLAN)
header hub (HHUB)	service	unacknowledged

Review Questions

15.1 What is network topology?

15.2 List four common LAN topologies and briefly describe their methods of operation.

15.3 What is the purpose of the IEEE 802 committee?

15.4 Why are there multiple LAN standards?

15.5 List and briefly define the services provided by LLC.

15.6 List and briefly define the types of operation provided by the LLC protocol.

15.7 List some basic functions performed at the MAC layer.

15.8   What functions are performed by a bridge?

15.9   What is a spanning tree?

15.10   What is the difference between a hub and a layer 2 switch?

15.11   What is the difference between a store-and-forward switch and a cut-through switch?

Problems

15.1   Instead of LLC, could HDLC be used as a data link control protocol for a LAN? If not, what is lacking?

15.2   An asynchronous device, such as a teletype, transmits characters one at a time with unpredictable delays between characters. What problems, if any, do you foresee if such a device is connected to a LAN and allowed to transmit at will (subject to gaining access to the medium)? How might such problems be resolved?

15.3   Consider the transfer of a file containing one million 8-bit characters from one station to another. What is the total elapsed time and effective throughput for the following cases:

   a.   A circuit-switched, star-topology local network. Call setup time is negligible and the data rate on the medium is 64 kbps.

   b.   A bus topology local network with two stations a distance D apart, a data rate of B bps, and a frame size of P with 80 bits of overhead per frame. Each frame is acknowledged with an 88-bit frame before the next is sent. The propagation speed on the bus is 200 m/μs. Solve for:

      1. $D = 1$ km, $B = 1$ Mbps, $P = 256$ bits

      2. $D = 1$ km, $B = 10$ Mbps, $P = 256$ bits

      3. $D = 10$ km, $B = 1$ Mbps, $P = 256$ bits

      4. $D = 1$ km, $B = 50$ Mbps, $P = 10,000$ bits

   c.   A ring topology local network with a total circular length of $2D$, with the two stations a distance D apart. Acknowledgment is achieved by allowing a frame to circulate past the destination station, back to the source station, with an acknowledgment bit set by the destination. There are N repeaters on the ring, each of which introduces a delay of one bit time. Repeat the calculation for each of b1 through b4 for $N = 10; 100; 1000$.

15.4   Consider a baseband bus with a number of equally spaced stations with a data rate of 10 Mbps and a bus length of 1 km.

   a.   What is the mean time to send a frame of 1000 bits to another station, measured from the beginning of transmission to the end of reception? Assume a propagation speed of 200 m/μs.

   b.   If two stations begin to transmit at exactly the same time, their packets will interfere with each other. If each transmitting station monitors the bus during transmission, how long before it notices an interference, in seconds? In bit times?

15.5   Repeat Problem 15.4 for a data rate of 100 Mbps.

15.6   At a propagation speed of 200 m/μs, what is the effective length added to a ring by a bit delay at each repeater?

   a.   At 1 Mbps

   b.   At 40 Mbps

15.7   A tree topology is to be provided that spans two buildings. If permission can be obtained to string cable between the two buildings, one continuous tree layout will be used. Otherwise, each building will have an independent tree topology network and a point-to-point link will connect a special communications station on one network with a communications station on the other network. What functions must the communications stations perform? Repeat for ring and star.

15.8 System A consists of a single ring with 300 stations, one per repeater. System B consists of three 100-station rings linked by a bridge. If the probability of a link failure is P^1, a repeater failure is P_r, and a bridge failure is P_b, derive an expression for parts (a) through (d):

  a. Probability of failure of system A

  b. Probability of complete failure of system B

  c. Probability that a particular station will find the network unavailable, for systems A and B

  d. Probability that any two stations, selected at random, will be unable to communicate, for systems A and B

  e. Compute values for parts (a) through (d) for $P_1 = P_b = P_r = 10^{-2}$.

15.9 Draw figures similar to Figure 15.8 for a configuration in which

  a. Two LANs are connected via two bridges that are connected by a point-to-point link.

  b. Two LANs are connected via two bridges that are connected by an ATM packet-switching network.

15.10 For the configuration of Figure 15.9, show the central routing matrix and the routing tables at each bridge.

ETHERNET

Congratulations. I knew the record would stand until it was broken.

— Yogi Berra

KEY POINTS

♦ The IEEE 802.3 standard, known as Ethernet, now encompasses data rates of 10 Mbps, 100 Mbps, 1 Gbps, and 10 Gbps. For the lower data rates, the CSMA/CD MAC protocol is used. For the 1-Gbps and 10-Gbps options, a switched technique is used.

♦ A variety of signal-encoding techniques are used in the various LAN standards to achieve efficiency and to make the high data rates practical.

Recent years have seen rapid changes in the technology, design, and commercial applications for local area networks (LANs). A major feature of this evolution is the introduction of a variety of new schemes for high-speed local area networking. To keep pace with the changing local networking needs of business, a number of approaches to high-speed LAN design have become commercial products. The most important of these are as follows:

- **Fast Ethernet and Gigabit Ethernet:** The extension of 10-Mbps CSMA/CD (carrier sense multiple access with collision detection) to higher speeds is a logical strategy, because it tends to preserve the investment in existing systems.

- **Fibre Channel:** This standard provides a low-cost, easily scalable approach to achieving very high data rates in local areas.

- **High-speed wireless LANs:** Wireless LAN technology and standards have at last come of age, and high-speed standards and products are being introduced.

Table 16.1 lists some of the characteristics of these approaches. The remainder of this is devoted to Ethernet. Chapter 17 covers wireless LANs. Appendix M covers Fibre Channel.

Table 16.1 Characteristics of Some High-Speed LANs

	Fast Ethernet	**Gigabit Ethernet**	**Fibre Channel**	**Wireless LAN**
Data Rate	100 Mbps	1 Gbps, 10 Gbps, 100 Gbps	100 Mbps–3.2 Gbps	1 Mbps–54 Mbps
Transmission Media	UTP, STP, optical fiber	UTP, shielded cable, optical fiber	Optical fiber, coaxial cable, STP	2.4-GHz, 5-GHz microwave
Access Method	CSMA/CD	Switched	Switched	CSMA/Polling
Supporting Standard	IEEE 802.3	IEEE 802.3	Fibre Channel Association	IEEE 802.11

16.1 TRADITIONAL ETHERNET

The most widely used high-speed LANs today are based on Ethernet and were developed by the IEEE 802.3 standards committee. As with other LAN standards, there is both a medium access control layer and a physical layer, which are discussed in turn in what follows.

IEEE 802.3 Medium Access Control

It is easier to understand the operation of CSMA/CD if we look first at some earlier schemes from which CSMA/CD evolved.

PRECURSORS CSMA/CD and its precursors can be termed *random access*, or *contention*, techniques. They are random access in the sense that there is no predictable or scheduled time for any station to transmit; station transmissions are ordered randomly. They exhibit contention in the sense that stations contend for time on the shared medium.

The earliest of these techniques, known as ALOHA, was developed for packet radio networks. However, it is applicable to any shared transmission medium. ALOHA, or pure ALOHA as it is sometimes called, specifies that a station may transmit a frame at any time. The station then listens for an amount of time equal to the maximum possible round-trip propagation delay on the network (twice the time it takes to send a frame between the two most widely separated stations) plus a small fixed time increment. If the station hears an acknowledgment during that time, fine; otherwise, it resends the frame. If the station fails to receive an acknowledgment after repeated transmissions, it gives up. A receiving station determines the correctness of an incoming frame by examining a frame-check sequence field, as in HDLC. If the frame is valid and if the destination address in the frame header matches the receiver's address, the station immediately sends an acknowledgment. The frame may be invalid due to noise on the channel or because another station transmitted a frame at about the same time. In the latter case, the two frames may interfere with each other at the receiver so that neither gets through; this is known as a **collision**. If a received frame is determined to be invalid, the receiving station simply ignores the frame.

ALOHA is as simple as can be, and pays a penalty for it. Because the number of collisions rises rapidly with increased load, the maximum utilization of the channel is only about 18%.

To improve efficiency, a modification of ALOHA, known as slotted ALOHA, was developed. In this scheme, time on the channel is organized into uniform slots whose size equals the frame transmission time. Some central clock or other technique is needed to synchronize all stations. Transmission is permitted to begin only at a slot boundary. Thus, frames that do overlap will do so totally. This increases the maximum utilization of the system to about 37%.

Both ALOHA and slotted ALOHA exhibit poor utilization. Both fail to take advantage of one of the key properties of both packet radio networks and LANs, which is that propagation delay between stations may be very small compared to frame transmission time. Consider the following observations. If the station-to-station propagation time is large compared to the frame transmission time, then, after a station launches a frame, it will be a long time before other stations know about it. During that time, one of the other stations may transmit a frame; the two frames may interfere with each other and neither gets through. Indeed, if the distances are great enough, many stations may begin transmitting, one after the other, and none of their frames get through unscathed. Suppose, however, that the propagation time is small compared to frame transmission time. In that case, when a station launches a frame, all the other stations know it almost immediately. So, if they had any sense, they would not try transmitting until the first station was done. Collisions would be rare because they would occur only when two stations began to transmit almost simultaneously. Another way to look at it is that a short propagation delay provides the stations with better feedback about the state of the network; this information can be used to improve efficiency.

The foregoing observations led to the development of carrier sense multiple access (CSMA). With CSMA, a station wishing to transmit first listens to the medium to determine if another transmission is in progress (carrier sense). If the medium is in use, the station must wait. If the medium is idle, the station may transmit. It may happen that two or more stations attempt to transmit at about the same time. If this happens, there will be a collision; the data from both transmissions will be garbled and not received successfully. To account for this, a station waits a reasonable amount of time after transmitting for an acknowledgment, taking into account the maximum round-trip propagation delay and the fact that the acknowledging station must also contend for the channel to respond. If there is no acknowledgment, the station assumes that a collision has occurred and retransmits.

One can see how this strategy would be effective for networks in which the average frame transmission time is much longer than the propagation time. Collisions can occur only when more than one user begins transmitting within a short time interval (the period of the propagation delay). If a station begins to transmit a frame, and there are no collisions during the time it takes for the leading edge of the packet to propagate to the farthest station, then there will be no collision for this frame because all other stations are now aware of the transmission.

The maximum utilization achievable using CSMA can far exceed that of ALOHA or slotted ALOHA. The maximum utilization depends on the length of the frame and on the propagation time; the longer the frames or the shorter the propagation time, the higher the utilization.

With CSMA, an algorithm is needed to specify what a station should do if the medium is found busy. Three approaches are depicted in Figure 16.1. One algorithm is **nonpersistent CSMA**. A station wishing to transmit listens to the medium and obeys the following rules:

1. If the medium is idle, transmit; otherwise, go to step 2.

2. If the medium is busy, wait an amount of time drawn from a probability distribution (the retransmission delay) and repeat step 1.

The use of random delays reduces the probability of collisions. To see this, consider that two stations become ready to transmit at about the same time while another transmission is in progress; if both stations delay the same amount of time

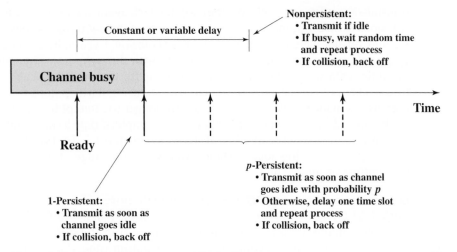

Figure 16.1 CSMA Persistence and Backoff

before trying again, they will both attempt to transmit at about the same time. A problem with nonpersistent CSMA is that capacity is wasted because the medium will generally remain idle following the end of a transmission even if there are one or more stations waiting to transmit.

To avoid idle channel time, the **1-persistent protocol** can be used. A station wishing to transmit listens to the medium and obeys the following rules:

1. If the medium is idle, transmit; otherwise, go to step 2.
2. If the medium is busy, continue to listen until the channel is sensed idle; then transmit immediately.

Whereas nonpersistent stations are deferential, 1-persistent stations are self-ish. If two or more stations are waiting to transmit, a collision is guaranteed. Things get sorted out only after the collision.

A compromise that attempts to reduce collisions, like nonpersistent, and reduce idle time, like 1-persistent, is **p-persistent**. The rules are given:

1. If the medium is idle, transmit with probability p, and delay one time unit with probability $(1 - p)$. The time unit is typically equal to the maximum propagation delay.
2. If the medium is busy, continue to listen until the channel is idle and repeat step 1.
3. If transmission is delayed one time unit, repeat step 1.

The question arises as to what is an effective value of p. The main problem to avoid is one of instability under heavy load. Consider the case in which n stations have frames to send while a transmission is taking place. At the end of the transmission, the expected number of stations that will attempt to transmit is equal to the number of stations ready to transmit times the probability of transmitting, or np. If np is greater than 1, on average multiple stations will attempt to transmit and there will be a collision. What is more, as soon as all these stations realize that their transmission suffered a collision, they will be back again, almost guaranteeing more collisions. Worse yet, these retries will compete with new transmissions from other stations, further increasing the probability of collision. Eventually, all stations will be trying to send, causing continuous collisions, with throughput dropping to zero. To avoid this catastrophe, np must be less than one for the expected peaks of n; therefore, if a heavy load is expected to occur with some regularity, p must be small. However, as p is made smaller, stations must wait longer to attempt transmission. At low loads, this can result in very long delays. For example, if only a single station desires to transmit, the expected number of iterations of step 1 is $1/p$ (see Problem 16.2). Thus, if $p = 0.1$, at low load, a station will wait an average of 9 time units before transmitting on an idle line.

DESCRIPTION OF CSMA/CD CSMA, although more efficient than ALOHA or slotted ALOHA, still has one glaring inefficiency. When two frames collide, the medium remains unusable for the duration of transmission of both damaged frames. For long frames, compared to propagation time, the amount of wasted capacity can be considerable. This waste can be reduced if a station continues to listen to the medium while transmitting. This leads to the following rules for CSMA/CD:

1. If the medium is idle, transmit; otherwise, go to step 2.
2. If the medium is busy, continue to listen until the channel is idle, then transmit immediately.
3. If a collision is detected during transmission, transmit a brief jamming signal to assure that all stations know that there has been a collision and then cease transmission.
4. After transmitting the jamming signal, wait a random amount of time, referred to as the **backoff**, then attempt to transmit again (repeat from step 1).

Figure 16.2 illustrates the technique for a baseband bus. The upper part of the figure shows a bus LAN layout. At time t_0, station A begins transmitting a packet addressed to D. At t_1, both B and C are ready to transmit. B senses a transmission and so defers. C, however, is still unaware of A's transmission (because the leading edge of A's transmission has not yet arrived at C) and begins its own transmission. When A's transmission reaches C, at t_2, C detects the collision and ceases transmission. The effect of the collision propagates back to A, where it is detected by A some time later, t_3, at which time A ceases transmission.

With CSMA/CD, the amount of wasted capacity is reduced to the time it takes to detect a collision. Question: How long does that take? Let us consider the case of a baseband bus and consider two stations as far apart as possible. For example, in Figure 16.2, suppose that station A begins a transmission and that just before that transmission reaches D, D is ready to transmit. Because D is not yet aware of A's transmission, it begins to transmit. A collision occurs almost immediately and is recognized by D. However, the collision must propagate all the way back to A before A is aware of the collision. By this line of reasoning, we conclude that the amount of time that it takes to detect a collision is no greater than twice the end-to-end propagation delay.

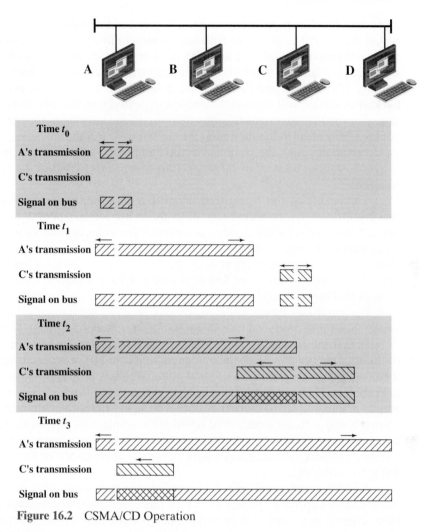

Figure 16.2 CSMA/CD Operation

An important rule followed in most CSMA/CD systems, including the IEEE standard, is that frames should be long enough to allow collision detection prior to the end of transmission. If shorter frames are used, then collision detection does not occur, and CSMA/CD exhibits the same performance as the less efficient CSMA protocol.

For a CSMA/CD LAN, the question arises as to which persistence algorithm to use. You may be surprised to learn that the algorithm used in the IEEE 802.3 standard is 1-persistent. Recall that both nonpersistent and p-persistent have performance problems. In the nonpersistent case, capacity is wasted because the medium will generally remain idle following the end of a transmission even if there are stations waiting to send. In the p-persistent case, p must be set low enough to avoid instability, with the result of sometimes atrocious delays under light load. The 1-persistent algorithm, which means, after all, that $p = 1$, would seem to be even more unstable than *p*-persistent due to the greed of the stations. What saves the day is that the wasted time due to collisions is mercifully short (if the frames are long relative to propagation delay), and with random backoff, the two stations involved in a collision are unlikely to collide on their next tries. To ensure that backoff maintains stability, IEEE 802.3 and Ethernet use a technique known as **binary exponential backoff**. A station will attempt to transmit repeatedly in the face of repeated collisions. For the first 10 retransmission attempts, the mean value of the random delay is doubled. This mean value then remains the same for 6 additional attempts. After 16 unsuccessful attempts, the station gives up and reports an error. Thus, as congestion increases, stations back off by larger and larger amounts to reduce the probability of collision.

The beauty of the 1-persistent algorithm with binary exponential backoff is that it is efficient over a wide range of loads. At low loads, 1-persistence guarantees that a station can seize the channel as soon as it goes idle, in contrast to the non- and *p*-persistent schemes. At high loads, it is at least as stable as the other techniques. However, one unfortunate effect of the backoff algorithm is that it has a last-in first-out effect; stations with no or few collisions will have a chance to transmit before stations that have waited longer.

For baseband bus, a collision should produce substantially higher voltage swings than those produced by a single transmitter. Accordingly, the IEEE standard dictates that the transmitter will detect a collision if the signal on the cable at the transmitter tap point exceeds the maximum that could be produced by the transmitter alone. Because a transmitted signal attenuates as it propagates, there is a potential problem: If two stations far apart are transmitting, each station will receive a greatly attenuated signal from the other. The signal strength could be so small that when it is added to the transmitted signal at the transmitter tap point, the combined signal does not exceed the CD threshold. For this reason, among others, the IEEE standard restricts the maximum length of coaxial cable to 500 m for 10BASE5 and 200 m for 10BASE2.

A much simpler collision detection scheme is possible with the twisted-pair star-topology approach (Figure 15.11). In this case, collision detection is based on logic rather than sensing voltage magnitudes. For any hub, if there is activity (signal) on more than one input, a collision is assumed. A special signal called the collision presence signal is generated. This signal is generated and sent out as long as activity is sensed on any of the input lines. This signal is interpreted by every node as an occurrence of a collision.

For a discussion of LAN performance, see Appendix L.

MAC FRAME IEEE 802.3 defines three types of MAC frames. The **basic frame** is the original frame format. In addition, to support data link layer protocol encapsulation within the data portion of the frame, two additional frame types have been added. A **Q-tagged frame** supports 802.1Q VLAN capability, as described in Section 16.3. An **envelope frame** is intended to allow inclusion of additional prefixes and suffixes to the data field required by higher-layer encapsulation protocols such as those defined by the IEEE 802.1 working group (such as Provider Bridges and MAC Security), ITU-T, or IETF (such as MPLS).

Figure 16.3 depicts the frame format for all three types of frames; the differences are contained in the MAC Client Data field. Several additional fields encapsulate the frame to form an 802.3 packet. The fields are as follows:

- **Preamble:** A 7-octet pattern of alternating 0s and 1s used by the receiver to establish bit synchronization.

- **Start Frame Delimiter (SFD):** The sequence 10101011, which that delimits the actual start of the frame and enables the receiver to locate the first bit the frame.

- **Destination Address (DA):** Specifies the station(s) for which the frame is intended. It may be a unique physical address, a multicast address, or a broadcast address.

- **Source Address (SA):** Specifies the station that sent the frame.

- **Length/Type:** Takes on one of two meanings, depending on its numeric value. If the value of this field is less than or equal to 1500 decimal, then the Length/Type field indicates the number of MAC Client Data octets contained in the subsequent MAC Client Data field of the basic frame (length interpretation). If the

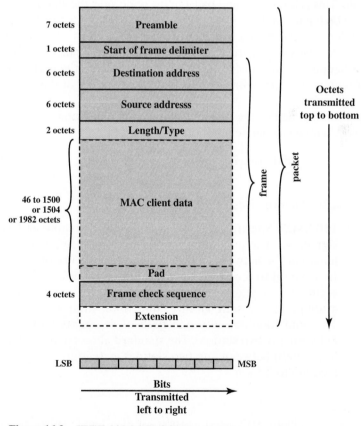

Figure 16.3   IEEE 802.3 MAC Frame Format

value of this field is greater than or equal to 1536 decimal then the Length/Type field indicates the nature of the MAC client protocol (Type interpretation). The Length and Type interpretations of this field are mutually exclusive.

- **MAC Client Data:** Data unit supplied by LLC. The maximum size of this field is 1500 octets for a basic frame, 1504 octets for a Q-tagged frame, and 1982 octets for an envelope frame.
- **Pad:** Octets added to ensure that the frame is long enough for proper CD operation.
- **Frame Check Sequence (FCS):** A 32-bit cyclic redundancy check, based on all fields except preamble, SFD, and FCS.
- **Extension:** This field is added, if required for 1-Gbps half-duplex operation. The extension field is necessary to enforce the minimum carrier event duration on the medium in half-duplex mode at an operating speed of 1 Gbps.

IEEE 802.3 10-Mbps Specifications (Ethernet)

The IEEE 802.3 committee has defined a number of alternative physical configurations. This is both good and bad. On the good side, the standard has been responsive to evolving technology. On the bad side, the customer, not to mention the potential vendor, is faced with a bewildering array of options. However, the committee has been at pains to ensure that the various options can be easily integrated into a configuration that satisfies a variety of needs. Thus, the user that has a complex set of requirements may find the flexibility and variety of the 802.3 standard to be an asset.

To distinguish the various implementations that are available, the committee has developed a concise notation:

<data rate in Mbps> <signaling method><maximum segment length in hundreds of meters>

The defined alternatives for 10-Mbps are[1]:

- **10BASE5:** Specifies the use of 50-Ω coaxial cable and Manchester digital signaling.[2] The maximum length of a cable segment is set at 500 m. The length of the network can be extended by the use of repeaters. A repeater is transparent to the MAC level; as it does no buffering, it does not isolate one segment from another. So, for example, if two stations on different segments attempt to transmit at the same time, their transmissions will collide. To avoid looping, only one path of segments and repeaters is allowed between any two stations. The standard allows a maximum of four repeaters in the path between any two stations, extending the effective length of the medium to 2.5 km.

---

[1]There is also a 10BROAD36 option, specifying a 10-Mbps broadband bus; this option is rarely used.
[2]See Section 5.1.

Table 16.2 IEEE 802.3 10-Mbps Physical Layer Medium Alternatives

	10BASE5	**10BASE2**	**10BASE-T**	**10BASE-FP**
Transmission Medium	Coaxial cable (50 Ω)	Coaxial cable (50 Ω)	Unshielded twisted pair	850-nm optical fiber pair
Signaling Technique	Baseband (Manchester)	Baseband (Manchester)	Baseband (Manchester)	Manchester/on-off
Topology	Bus	Bus	Star	Star
Maximum Segment Length (m)	500	185	100	500
Nodes per Segment	100	30	—	33
Cable Diameter (mm)	10	5	0.4–0.6	62.5/125 μm

- **10BASE2:** Similar to 10BASE5 but uses a thinner cable, which supports fewer taps over a shorter distance than the 10BASE5 cable. This is a lower-cost alternative to 10BASE5.

- **10BASE-T:** Uses unshielded twisted pair in a star-shaped topology. Because of the high data rate and the poor transmission qualities of unshielded twisted pair, the length of a link is limited to 100 m. As an alternative, an optical fiber link may be used. In this case, the maximum length is 500 m.

- **10BASE-F:** Contains three specifications: a passive-star topology for interconnecting stations and repeaters with up to 1 km per segment, a point-to-point link that can be used to connect stations or repeaters at up to 2 km, and a point-to-point link that can be used to connect repeaters at up to 2 km.

Note that 10BASE-T and 10-BASE-F do not quite follow the notation: "T" stands for twisted pair and "F" stands for optical fiber. Table 16.2 summarizes the remaining options. All of the alternatives listed in the table specify a data rate of 10 Mbps.

16.2 HIGH-SPEED ETHERNET

IEEE 802.3 100–Mbps Specifications (Fast Ethernet)

Fast Ethernet refers to a set of specifications developed by the IEEE 802.3 committee to provide a low-cost, Ethernet-compatible LAN operating at 100 Mbps. The blanket designation for these standards is 100BASE-T. The committee defined a number of alternatives to be used with different transmission media.

Table 16.3 summarizes key characteristics of the 100BASE-T options. All of the 100BASE-T options use the IEEE 802.3 MAC protocol and frame format. 100BASE-X refers to a set of options that use two physical links between nodes: one for transmission and one for reception. 100BASE-TX makes use of shielded twisted pair (STP) or high-quality (Category 5) unshielded twisted pair (UTP). 100BASE-FX uses optical fiber.

Table 16.3 IEEE 802.3 100BASE-T Physical Layer Medium Alternatives

	100BASE-TX		**100BASE-FX**	**100BASE-T4**
Transmission Medium	2 pair, STP	2 pair, Category 5 UTP	2 optical fibers	4 pair, Category 3, 4, or 5 UTP
Signaling Technique	MLT-3	MLT-3	4B5B, NRZI	8B6T, NRZ
Data Rate	100 Mbps	100 Mbps	100 Mbps	100 Mbps
Maximum Segment Length	100 m	100 m	100 m	100 m
Network Span	200 m	200 m	400 m	200 m

In many buildings, any of the 100BASE-X options requires the installation of new cable. For such cases, 100BASE-T4 defines a lower-cost alternative that can use Category 3, voice-grade UTP in addition to the higher-quality Category 5 UTP.[3] To achieve the 100-Mbps data rate over lower-quality cable, 100BASE-T4 dictates the use of four twisted-pair lines between nodes, with the data transmission making use of three pairs in one direction at a time.

For all of the 100BASE-T options, the topology is similar to that of 10BASE-T, namely a star-wire topology.

100BASE-X For all of the transmission media specified under 100BASE-X, a unidirectional data rate of 100 Mbps is achieved transmitting over a single link (single twisted pair, single optical fiber). For all of these media, an efficient and effective signal-encoding scheme is required. The one chosen is referred to as 4B/5B-NRZI. This scheme is further modified for each option. See Appendix 16A for a description.

The 100BASE-X designation includes two physical medium specifications: one for twisted pair, known as 100BASE-TX, and one for optical fiber, known as 100-BASE-FX.

100BASE-TX makes use of two pairs of twisted-pair cable, one pair used for transmission and one for reception. Both STP and Category 5 UTP are allowed. The MTL-3 signaling scheme is used (described in Appendix 16A).

100BASE-FX makes use of two optical fiber cables: one for transmission and one for reception. With 100BASE-FX, a means is needed to convert the 4B/5B-NRZI code group stream into optical signals. The technique used is known as intensity modulation. A binary 1 is represented by a burst or pulse of light; a binary 0 is represented by either the absence of a light pulse or a light pulse at very low intensity.

100BASE-T4 100BASE-T4 is designed to produce a 100-Mbps data rate over lower-quality Category 3 cable, thus taking advantage of the large installed base of Category 3 cable in office buildings. The specification also indicates that the use of Category 5 cable is optional. 100BASE-T4 does not transmit a continuous signal between packets, which makes it useful in battery-powered applications.

---

[3]See Chapter 4 for a discussion of Category 3 and Category 5 cable.

For 100BASE-T4 using voice-grade Category 3 cable, it is not reasonable to expect to achieve 100 Mbps on a single twisted pair. Instead, 100BASE-T4 specifies that the data stream to be transmitted is split up into three separate data streams, each with an effective data rate of $33\frac{1}{3}$ Mbps. Four twisted pairs are used. Data are transmitted using three pairs and received using three pairs. Thus, two of the pairs must be configured for bidirectional transmission.

As with 100BASE-X, a simple NRZ encoding scheme is not used for 100BASE-T4. This would require a signaling rate of 33 Mbps on each twisted pair and does not provide synchronization. Instead, a ternary signaling scheme known as 8B6T is used (described in Appendix 16A).

FULL-DUPLEX OPERATION A traditional Ethernet is half duplex: A station can either transmit or receive a frame, but it cannot do both simultaneously. With full-duplex operation, a station can transmit and receive simultaneously. If a 100-Mbps Ethernet ran in full-duplex mode, the theoretical transfer rate becomes 200 Mbps.

Several changes are needed to operate in full-duplex mode. The attached stations must have full-duplex rather than half-duplex adapter cards. The central point in the star wire cannot be a simple multiport repeater but rather must be a switching hub. In this case each station constitutes a separate collision domain. In fact, there are no collisions and the CSMA/CD algorithm is no longer needed. However, the same 802.3 MAC frame format is used and the attached stations can continue to execute the CSMA/CD algorithm, even though no collisions can ever be detected.

MIXED CONFIGURATION One of the strengths of the Fast Ethernet approach is that it readily supports a mixture of existing 10-Mbps LANs and newer 100-Mbps LANs. For example, the 100-Mbps technology can be used as a backbone LAN to support a number of 10-Mbps hubs. Many of the stations attach to 10-Mbps hubs using the 10BASE-T standard. These hubs are in turn connected to switching hubs that conform to 100BASE-T and that can support both 10-Mbps and 100-Mbps links. Additional high-capacity workstations and servers attach directly to these 10/100 switches. These mixed-capacity switches are in turn connected to 100-Mbps hubs using 100-Mbps links. The 100-Mbps hubs provide a building backbone and are also connected to a router that provides connection to an outside WAN.

Gigabit Ethernet

In late 1995, the IEEE 802.3 committee formed a High-Speed Study Group to investigate means for conveying packets in Ethernet format at speeds in the gigabits per second range. The strategy for Gigabit Ethernet is the same as that for Fast Ethernet. While defining a new medium and transmission specification, Gigabit Ethernet retains the CSMA/CD protocol and Ethernet format of its 10-Mbps and 100-Mbps predecessors. It is compatible with 100BASE-T and 10BASE-T, preserving a smooth migration path. As more organizations move to 100BASE-T, putting huge traffic loads on backbone networks, demand for Gigabit Ethernet has intensified.

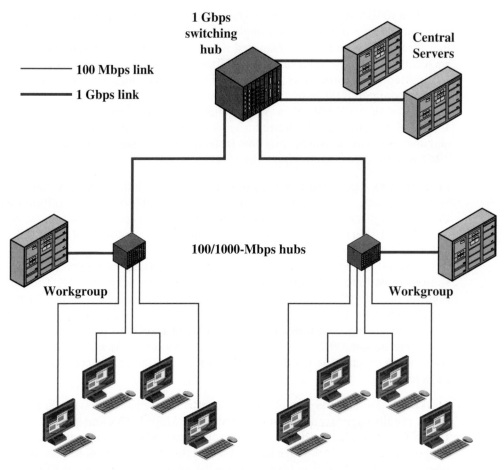

Figure 16.4 Example Gigabit Ethernet Configuration

Figure 16.4 shows a typical application of Gigabit Ethernet. A 1-Gbps switching hub provides backbone connectivity for central servers and high-speed workgroup hubs. Each workgroup LAN switch supports both 1-Gbps links, to connect to the backbone LAN switch and to support high-performance workgroup servers, and 100-Mbps links, to support high-performance workstations, servers, and 100-Mbps LAN switches.

MEDIA ACCESS LAYER The 1000-Mbps specification calls for the same CSMA/CD frame format and MAC protocol as used in the 10-Mbps and 100-Mbps version of IEEE 802.3. For shared-medium hub operation (Figure 15.12b), there are two enhancements to the basic CSMA/CD scheme:

- **Carrier extension:** Carrier extension appends a set of special symbols to the end of short MAC frames so that the resulting block is at least 4096 bit-times in duration, up from the minimum 512 bit-times imposed at 10 and 100 Mbps. This is so that the frame length of a transmission is longer than the propagation time at 1 Gbps.

- **Frame bursting:** This feature allows for multiple short frames to be transmitted consecutively, up to a limit, without relinquishing control for CSMA/CD between frames. Frame bursting avoids the overhead of carrier extension when a single station has a number of small frames ready to send.

With a switching hub (Figure 15.12c), which provides dedicated access to the medium, the carrier extension and frame bursting features are not needed. This is because data transmission and reception at a station can occur simultaneously without interference and with no contention for a shared medium.

Physical Layer The current 1-Gbps specification for IEEE 802.3 includes the following physical layer alternatives (Figure 16.5):

- **1000BASE-SX:** This short-wavelength option supports duplex links of up to 275 m using 62.5-μm multimode or up to 550 m using 50-μm multimode fiber. Wavelengths are in the range of 770 to 860 nm.
- **1000BASE-LX:** This long-wavelength option supports duplex links of up to 550 m of 62.5-μm or 50-μm multimode fiber or 5 km of 10-μm single-mode fiber. Wavelengths are in the range of 1270 to 1355 nm.
- **1000BASE-CX:** This option supports 1-Gbps links among devices located within a single room or equipment rack, using copper jumpers (specialized shielded twisted-pair cable that spans no more than 25 m). Each link is composed of a separate shielded twisted pair running in each direction.
- **1000BASE-T:** This option makes use of four pairs of Category 5 unshielded twisted pair to support devices over a range of up to 100 m, transmitting and receiving on all four pairs at the same time, with echo cancellation circuitry.

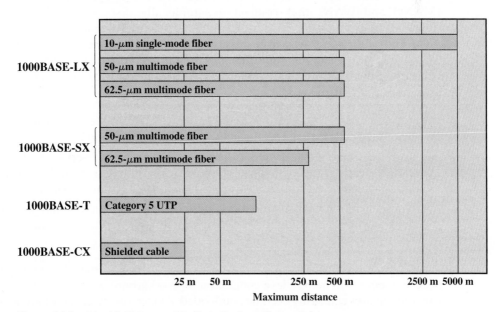

Figure 16.5 Gigabit Ethernet Medium Options (log scale)

The signal-encoding scheme used for the first three Gigabit Ethernet options just listed is 8B/10B, which is described in Appendix 16A. The signal-encoding scheme used for 1000BASE-T is 4D-PAM5, a complex scheme whose description is beyond our scope.

10-Gbps Ethernet

With gigabit products still fairly new, attention has turned in the past several years to a 10-Gbps Ethernet capability. The principle driving requirement for 10-Gigabit Ethernet is the increase in Internet and intranet traffic. A number of factors contribute to the explosive growth in both Internet and intranet traffic:

- An increase in the number of network connections
- An increase in the connection speed of each end-station (e.g., 10 Mbps users moving to 100 Mbps, analog 56-kbps users moving to DSL and cable modems)
- An increase in the deployment of bandwidth-intensive applications such as high-quality video
- An increase in Web hosting and application hosting traffic

Initially network managers will use 10-Gbps Ethernet to provide high-speed, local backbone interconnection between large-capacity switches. As the demand for bandwidth increases, 10-Gbps Ethernet will be deployed throughout the entire network and will include server farm, backbone, and campuswide connectivity. This technology enables Internet service providers (ISPs) and network service providers (NSPs) to create very high-speed links at a low cost, between co-located, carrier-class switches and routers.

The technology also allows the construction of metropolitan area networks (MANs) and WANs that connect geographically dispersed LANs between campuses or points of presence (PoPs). Thus, Ethernet begins to compete with ATM and other wide area transmission and networking technologies. In most cases where the customer requirement is data and TCP/IP transport, 10-Gbps Ethernet provides substantial value over ATM transport for both network end users and service providers:

- No expensive, bandwidth-consuming conversion between Ethernet packets and ATM cells is required; the network is Ethernet, end to end.
- The combination of IP and Ethernet offers quality of service and traffic-policing capabilities that approach those provided by ATM, so that advanced traffic-engineering technologies are available to users and providers.
- A wide variety of standard optical interfaces (wavelengths and link distances) have been specified for 10-Gbps Ethernet, optimizing its operation and cost for LAN, MAN, or WAN applications.

Figure 16.6 illustrates potential uses of 10-Gbps Ethernet. Higher-capacity backbone pipes will help relieve congestion for workgroup switches, where Gigabit Ethernet uplinks can easily become overloaded, and for server farms, where 1-Gbps network interface cards are already in widespread use.

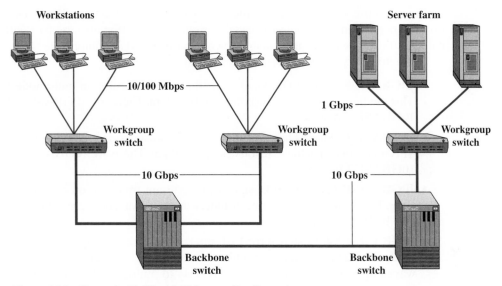

Figure 16.6   Example 10 Gigabit Ethernet Configuration

The goal for maximum link distances covers a range of applications: from 300 m to 40 km. The links operate in full-duplex mode only, using a variety of optical fiber physical media.

Four physical layer options are defined for 10-Gbps Ethernet (Figure 16.7). The first three of these have two suboptions: an "R" suboption and a "W" suboption. The R designation refers to a family of physical layer implementations that use a signal-encoding technique known as 64B/66B, described in Appendix 16A. The R implementations are designed for use over *dark fiber*, meaning a fiber optic cable

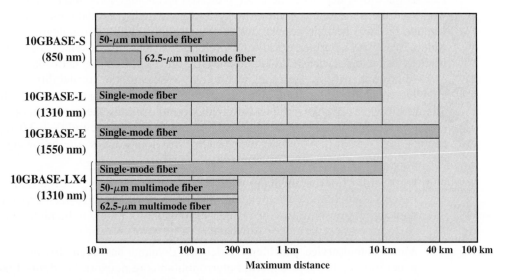

Figure 16.7   10-Gbps Ethernet Distance Options (log scale)

that is not in use and that is not connected to any other equipment. The W designation refers to a family of physical layer implementations that also use 64B/66B signaling but that are then encapsulated to connect to SONET equipment.

The four physical layer options are as follows:

- **10GBASE-S (short):** Designed for 850-nm transmission on multimode fiber. This medium can achieve distances up to 300 m. There are 10GBASE-SR and 10GBASE-SW versions.

- **10GBASE-L (long):** Designed for 1310-nm transmission on single-mode fiber. This medium can achieve distances up to 10 km. There are 10GBASE-LR and 10GBASE-LW versions.

- **10GBASE-E (extended):** Designed for 1550-nm transmission on single-mode fiber. This medium can achieve distances up to 40 km. There are 10GBASE-ER and 10GBASE-EW versions.

- **10GBASE-LX4:** Designed for 1310-nm transmission on single-mode or multimode fiber. This medium can achieve distances up to 10 km. This medium uses wavelength-division multiplexing (WDM) to multiplex the bit stream across four light waves.

The success of Fast Ethernet, Gigabit Ethernet, and 10-Gbps Ethernet highlights the importance of network management concerns in choosing a network technology. Both ATM and Fibre Channel may be technically superior choices for a high-speed backbone, because of their flexibility and scalability. However, the Ethernet alternatives offer compatibility with existing installed LANs, network management software, and applications. This compatibility has accounted for the survival of a nearly 30-year-old technology (CSMA/CD) in today's fast-evolving network environment.

100–Gbps Ethernet

Ethernet is widely deployed and is the preferred technology for wired local area networking. Ethernet dominates enterprise LANs, broadband access, data center networking, and has also become popular for communication across metropolitan and even wide area networks. Further, it is now the preferred carrier wire line vehicle for bridging wireless technologies, such as Wi-Fi and WiMAX, into local Ethernet networks.

This popularity of Ethernet technology is due to the availability of cost-effective, reliable, and interoperable networking products from a variety of vendors. The development of converged and unified communications, the evolution of massive server farms, and the continuing expansion of VoIP, TVoIP, and Web 2.0 applications have driven the need for ever faster Ethernet switches. The following are market drivers for 100-Gbps Ethernet:

- **Data center/Internet media providers:** To support the growth of Internet multimedia content and Web applications, content providers have been expanding data centers, pushing 10-Gbps Ethernet to its limits. Likely to be high-volume early adopters of 100-Gbps Ethernet.

- **Metro-video/service providers:** Video on demand has been driving a new generation of 10-Gbps Ethernet metropolitan/core network buildouts. Likely to be high-volume adopters in the medium term.

- **Enterprise LANs:** Continuing growth in convergence of voice/video/data and in unified communications is driving up network switch demands. However, most enterprises still rely on 1-Gbps or a mix of 1-Gbps and 10-Gbps Ethernet, and adoption of 100-Gbps Ethernet is likely to be slow.

- **Internet exchanges/ISP core routing:** With the massive amount of traffic flowing through these nodes, these installations are likely to be early adopters of 100-Gbps Ethernet.

In 2007, the IEEE 802.3 working group authorized the *IEEE P802.3ba 40Gb/s and 100Gb/s Ethernet Task Force*. The 802.3ba project authorization request provided the following as the rationale for the two different speeds:

> The project is necessary to provide a solution for applications that have been demonstrated to need bandwidth beyond the existing capabilities. These include data center, internet exchanges, high performance computing and video-on-demand delivery. Network aggregation and end-station bandwidth requirements are increasing at different rates, and is recognized by the definition of two distinct speeds to serve the appropriate applications.

The first products in this category appeared in 2009, and the IEEE 802.3ba standard was finalized in 2010.

An example of the application of 100-Gbps Ethernet is shown in Figure 16.8, taken from [NOWE07]. The trend at large data centers, with substantial banks of blade servers,[4] is the deployment of 10-Gbps ports on individual servers to handle the massive multimedia traffic provided by these servers. Such arrangements are stressing the on-site switches needed to interconnect large numbers of servers. A 100GbE rate was proposed to provide the bandwidth required to handle the increased traffic load. It is expected that 100GbE will be deployed in switch uplinks inside the data center as well as providing interbuilding, intercampus, MAN, and WAN connections for enterprise networks.

The success of Fast Ethernet, Gigabit Ethernet, and 10-Gbps Ethernet highlights the importance of network management concerns in choosing a network technology. The 40-Gbps and 100-Gbps Ethernet specifications offer compatibility with existing installed LANs, network management software, and applications. This compatibility has accounted for the survival of 30-year-old technology in today's fast-evolving network environment.

MULTILANE DISTRIBUTION The 802.3ba standard uses a technique known as multilane distribution to achieve the required data rates. There are two separate concepts we need to address: multilane distribution and virtual lanes.

The general idea of **multilane distribution** is that, in order to accommodate the very high data rates of 40 and 100 Gbps, the physical link between an end station and an Ethernet switch or the physical link between two switches may be implemented as

---

[4]A blade server is a server architecture that houses multiple server modules ("blades") in a single chassis. It is widely used in data centers to save space and improve system management. Either self-standing or rack mounted, the chassis provides the power supply, and each blade has its own CPU, memory, and hard disk (definition from pcmag.com encyclopedia).

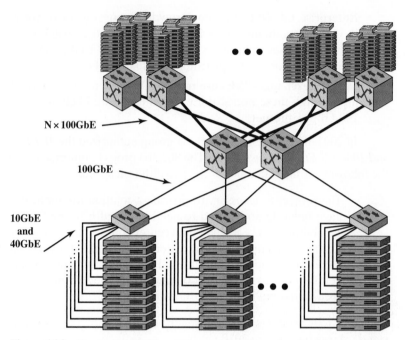

Figure 16.8 Example 100-Gbps Ethernet Configuration for Massive Blade
Server Site

multiple parallel channels. These parallel channels could be separate physical wires,
such as the use of four parallel twisted-pair links between nodes. Alternatively, the
parallel channels could be separate frequency channels, such as provided by wavelength division multiplexing over a single optical fiber link.

For simplicity and manufacturing ease, we would like to specify a specific multiple-
lane structure in the electrical physical sublayer of the device, known as the physical
medium attachment (PMA) sublayer. The lanes produced are referred to as **virtual
lanes**. If a different number of lanes are actually in use in the electrical or optical link,
then the virtual lanes are distributed into the appropriate number of physical lanes in
the physical medium dependent (PMD) sublayer. This is a form of inverse multiplexing.

Figure 16.9a shows the virtual lane scheme at the transmitter. The user data
stream is encoded using the 64B/66B, which is also used in 10-Gbps Ethernet. Data is
distributed to the virtual lanes one 66-bit word at a time using a simple round robin
scheme (first word to first lane, second word to second lane, etc.). A unique 66-bit alignment block is added to each virtual lane periodically. The alignment blocks are used to
identify and reorder the virtual lanes and thus reconstruct the aggregate data stream.

The virtual lanes are then transmitted over physical lanes. If the number of
physical lanes is smaller than the number of virtual lanes, then bit-level multiplexing
is used to transmit the virtual lane traffic. The number of virtual lanes must be an
integer multiple (1 or more) of the number of physical lanes.

Figure 16.9b shows the format of the alignment block. The block consists of
8 single-byte fields preceded by the two-bit synchronization field, which has the
value 10. The Frm fields contain a fixed framing pattern common to all virtual lanes

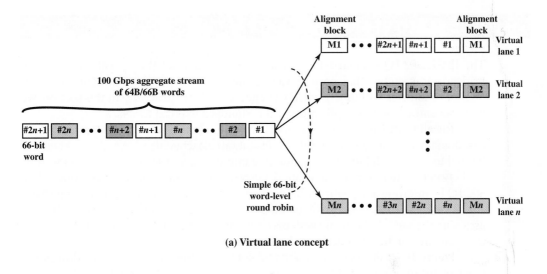

(a) Virtual lane concept

1	0	Frm1	Frm2	reserved	reserved	reserved	reserved	~VL#	VL#

(b) Alignment block

Figure 16.9   Multilane Distribution for 100-Gbps Ethernet

and used by the receiver to locate the alignment blocks. The VL# fields contain a pattern unique to the virtual lane: one of the fields is the binary inverse of the other.

MEDIA OPTIONS IEEE 802.3ba specifies three types of transmission media (Table 16.4): copper backplane, twin axial (a type of cable similar to coaxial cable), and optical fiber. For copper media, four separate physical lanes are specified. For optical fiber, either 4 or 10 wavelength lanes are specified, depending on data rate and distance.

Table 16.4   Media Options for 40-Gbps and 100-Gbps Ethernet

	40 Gbps	**100 Gbps**
1m backplane	40GBASE-KR4	
10 m copper	40GBASE-CR4	1000GBASE-CR10
100 m multimode fiber	40GBASE-SR4	1000GBASE-SR10
10 km single mode fiber	40GBASE-LR4	1000GBASE-LR4
40 km single mode fiber		1000GBASE-ER4

Naming nomenclature:
  Copper: K = backplane; C = cable assembly
  Optical: S = short reach (100 m); L = long reach (10 km); E = extended long
    reach (40 km)
  Coding scheme: R = 64B/66B block coding
  Final number: number of lanes (copper wires or fiber wavelengths)

16.3 IEEE 802.1Q VLAN STANDARD

The IEEE 802.1Q standard, last updated in 2005, defines the operation of VLAN bridges and switches that permits the definition, operation, and administration of VLAN topologies within a bridged/switched LAN infrastructure. In this section, we will concentrate on the application of this standard to 802.3 LANs.

Recall from Chapter 15 that a VLAN is an administratively configured broadcast domain, consisting of a subset of end stations attached to a LAN. A VLAN is not limited to one switch but can span multiple interconnected switches. In that case, traffic between switches must indicate VLAN membership. This is accomplished in 802.1Q by inserting a tag with a VLAN identifier (VID) with a value in the range from 1 to 4094. Each VLAN in a LAN configuration is assigned a globally unique VID. By assigning the same VID to end systems on many switches, one or more VLAN broadcast domains can be extended across a large network.

Figure 16.10 shows the position and content of the 802.1 tag, referred to as Tag Control Information (TCI). The presence of the 2-octet TCI field is indicated by setting the Length/Type field in the 802.3 MAC frame to a value of 8100 hex. The TCI consists of three subfields:

- **User priority (3 bits):** The priority level for this frame.

- **Canonical format indicator (1 bit):** Is always set to zero for Ethernet switches. CFI is used for compatibility between Ethernet type networks and token ring type networks. If a frame received at an Ethernet port has a CFI set to 1, then that frame should not be forwarded as it is to an untagged port.

- **VLAN identifier (12 bits):** The identification of the VLAN. Of the 4096 possible VIDs, a VID of 0 is used to identify that the TCI contains only a priority value, and 4095 (FFF) is reserved, so the maximum possible number of VLAN configurations is 4094.

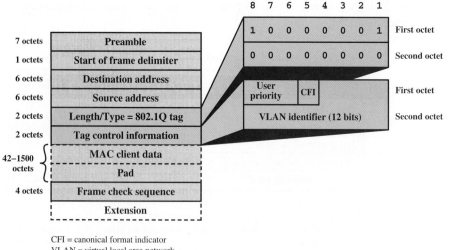

CFI = canonical format indicator
VLAN = virtual local area network

Figure 16.10 Tagged IEEE 802.3 MAC Frame Format

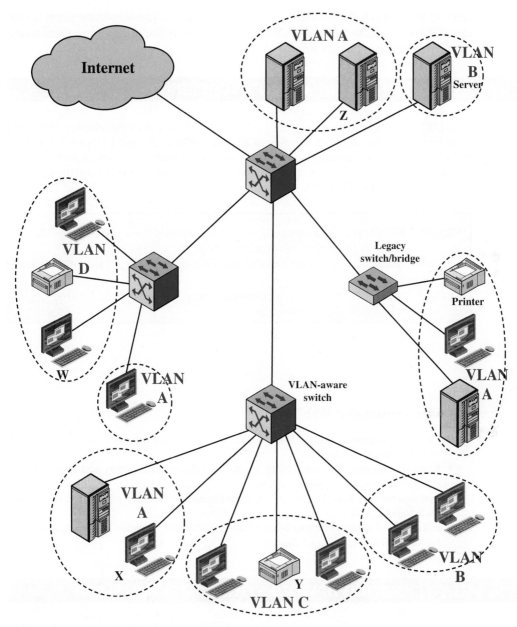

Figure 16.11   A VLAN Configuration

Figure 16.11 illustrates a LAN configuration that includes three switches that implement 802.1Q and one "legacy" switch or bridge that does not. In this case, all of the end systems of the legacy device must belong to the same VLAN. The MAC frames that traverse trunks between VLAN-aware switches include the 802.1Q TCI tag. This tag is stripped off before a frame is routed to a legacy switch. For end systems connected to a VLAN-aware switch, the MAC frame may or may not include the TCI tag, depending on the implementation. The important point is that the TCI tag is used between VLAN-aware switches so that appropriate routing and frame handling can be performed.

16.4 RECOMMENDED READING AND WEB SITES

[STAL00] covers in greater detail the LAN systems discussed in this chapter. [SPUR00] provides a concise but thorough overview of all of the 10-Mbps through 1-Gbps 802.3 systems, including configuration guidelines for a single segment of each media type, as well as guidelines for building multisegment Ethernets using a variety of media types. A good survey article on Gigabit Ethernet is [FRAZ99].

FRAZ99   Frazier, H., and Johnson, H. "Gigabit Ethernet: From 100 to 1,000 Mbps." *IEEE Internet Computing*, January/February 1999.

SPUR00   Spurgeon, C. *Ethernet: The Definitive Guide*. Cambridge, MA: O'Reilly and Associates, 2000.

STAL00   Stallings, W. *Local and Metropolitan Area Networks*, Sixth Edition. Upper Saddle River, NJ: Prentice Hall, 2000.

Recommended Web sites:

- **Charles Spurgeon's Ethernet Web site:** Provides extensive information about Ethernet, including links and documents
- **Ethernet Alliance:** This consortium promotes Ethernet technology and products. This site includes numerous white papers.
- **Interoperability Lab:** University of New Hampshire site for equipment testing for high-speed LANs
- **IEEE 802.3 Ethernet Working Group:** Latest documents, including task force documents for 40-Gbps and 100-Gbps Ethernet.

16.5 KEY TERMS, REVIEW QUESTIONS, AND PROBLEMS

Key Terms

1-persistent CSMA	carrier sense multiple access	nonpersistent CSMA
ALOHA	with collision detection	*p*-persistent CSMA
binary exponential	(CSMA/CD)	repeater
backoff	Collision	scrambling
carrier sense multiple access	Ethernet	slotted ALOHA
(CSMA)	full-duplex operation	

Review Questions

16.1   What is a server farm?

16.2   Explain the three persistence protocols that can be used with CSMA.

16.3   What is CSMA/CD?

16.4   Explain binary exponential backoff.

16.5   What are the transmission medium options for Fast Ethernet?

16.6   How does Fast Ethernet differ from 10BASE-T, other than the data rate?

16.7   In the context of Ethernet, what is full-duplex operation?

16.8   List the levels of Fibre Channel and the functions of each level (see Appendix M).

16.9   What are the topology options for Fibre Channel?

Problems

16.1   A disadvantage of the contention approach for LANs, such as CSMA/CD, is the capacity wasted due to multiple stations attempting to access the channel at the same time. Suppose that time is divided into discrete slots, with each of N stations attempting to transmit with probability p during each slot. What fraction of slots are wasted due to multiple simultaneous transmission attempts?

16.2   For p-persistent CSMA, consider the following situation. A station is ready to transmit and is listening to the current transmission. No other station is ready to transmit, and there will be no other transmission for an indefinite period. If the time unit used in the protocol is T, show that the average number of iterations of step 1 of the protocol is $1/p$ and that therefore the expected time that the station will have to wait after the current transmission is $T\left(\dfrac{1}{P} - 1\right)$. *Hint:* use the equality $\displaystyle\sum_{i=1}^{\infty} iX^{i-1} = \dfrac{1}{(1 - X)^2}$.

16.3   The binary exponential backoff algorithm is defined by IEEE 802 as follows:

> The delay is an integral multiple of slot time. The number of slot times to delay before the nth retransmission attempt is chosen as a uniformly distributed random integer r in the range $0 \le r < 2^K$, where $K = \min(n,10)$.

Slot time is, roughly, twice the round-trip propagation delay. Assume that two stations always have a frame to send. After a collision, what is the mean number of retransmission attempts before one station successfully retransmits? What is the answer if three stations always have frames to send?

16.4   Describe the signal pattern produced on the medium by the Manchester-encoded preamble of the IEEE 802.3 MAC frame.

16.5   Analyze the advantages of having the FCS field of IEEE 802.3 frames in the trailer of the frame rather than in the header of the frame.

16.6   The most widely used MAC approach for a ring topology is token ring, defined in IEEE 802.5. The token ring technique is based on the use of a small frame, called a token, that circulates when all stations are idle. A station wishing to transmit must wait until it detects a token passing by. It then seizes the token by changing 1one bit in the token, which transforms it from a token to a start-of-frame sequence for a data frame. The station then appends and transmits the remainder of the fields needed to construct a data frame.

> When a station seizes a token and begins to transmit a data frame, there is no token on the ring, so other stations wishing to transmit must wait. The frame on the ring will make a round trip and be absorbed by the transmitting station. The transmitting station will insert a new token on the ring when both of the following conditions have been met: (1) The station has completed transmission of its frame. (2) The leading edge of the transmitted frame has returned (after a complete circulation of the ring) to the station.

    a. An option in IEEE 802.5, known as early token release, eliminates the second condition just listed. Under what conditions will early token release result in improved utilization?

    b. Are there any potential disadvantages to early token release? Explain.

16.7 For a token ring LAN, suppose that the destination station removes the data frame and immediately sends a short acknowledgment frame to the sender rather than letting the original frame return to sender. How will this affect performance?

16.8 Another medium access control technique for rings is the slotted ring. A number of fixed-length slots circulate continuously on the ring. Each slot contains a leading bit to designate the slot as empty or full. A station wishing to transmit waits until an empty slot arrives, marks the slot full, and inserts a frame of data as the slot goes by. The full slot makes a complete round trip, to be marked empty again by the station that marked it full. In what sense are the slotted ring and token ring protocols the complement (dual) of each other?

16.9 Consider a slotted ring of length 10 km with a data rate of 10 Mbps and 500 repeaters, each of which introduces a 1-bit delay. Each slot contains room for one source address byte, one destination address byte, two data bytes, and five control bits for a total length of 37 bits. How many slots are on the ring?

16.10 With 8B6T coding, the effective data rate on a single channel is 33 Mbps with a signaling rate of 25 Mbaud. If a pure ternary scheme were used, what is the effective data rate for a signaling rate of 25 Mbaud?

16.11 With 8B6T coding, the DC algorithm sometimes negates all of the ternary symbols in a code group. How does the receiver recognize this condition? How does the receiver discriminate between a negated code group and one that has not been negated? For example, the code group for data byte 00 is $+ - 0\,0 + -$ and the code group for data byte 38 is the negation of that, namely, $- + 0\,0 - +$.

16.12 Draw the MLT decoder state diagram that corresponds to the encoder state diagram of Figure 16.12.

16.13 For the bit stream 0101110, sketch the waveforms for NRZ-L, NRZI, Manchester, and differential Manchester, and MLT-3.

16.14 Consider a token ring system with N stations in which a station that has just transmitted a frame releases a new token only after the station has completed transmission of its frame and the leading edge of the transmitted frame has returned (after a complete circulation of the ring) to the station.

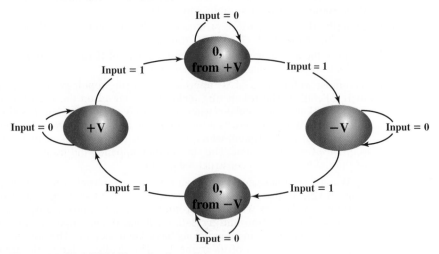

Figure 16.12 MLT-3 Encoder State Diagram

        a. Show that utilization can be approximated by $1/(1 + a/N)$ for $a < 1$ and by $1/(a + a/N)$ for $a > 1$.

        b. What is the asymptotic value of utilization as N increases?

16.15 **a.** Verify that the division illustrated in Figure 16.18a corresponds to the implementation of Figure 16.17a by calculating the result step by step using Equation (16.1).

        b. Verify that the multiplication illustrated in Figure 16.18b corresponds to the implementation of Figure 16.17b by calculating the result step by step using Equation (16.2).

16.16 Draw a figure similar to Figure 16.16 for the MLT-3 scrambler and descrambler.

APPENDIX 16A DIGITAL SIGNAL ENCODING FOR LANS

In Chapter 5, we looked at some of the common techniques for encoding digital data for transmission, including Manchester and differential Manchester, which are used in some of the LAN standards. In this appendix, we examine some additional encoding schemes referred to in this chapter.

4B/5B-NRZI

This scheme, which is actually a combination of two encoding algorithms, is used for 100BASE-X. To understand the significance of this choice, first consider the simple alternative of a NRZ (nonreturn to zero) coding scheme. With NRZ, one signal state represents binary one and one signal state represents binary zero. The disadvantage of this approach is its lack of synchronization. Because transitions on the medium are unpredictable, there is no way for the receiver to synchronize its clock to the transmitter. A solution to this problem is to encode the binary data to guarantee the presence of transitions. For example, the data could first be encoded using Manchester encoding. The disadvantage of this approach is that the efficiency is only 50%. That is, because there can be as many as two transitions per bit time, a signaling rate of 200 million signal elements per second (200 Mbaud) is needed to achieve a data rate of 100 Mbps. This represents an unnecessary cost and technical burden.

Greater efficiency can be achieved using the 4B/5B code. In this scheme, encoding is done 4 bits at a time; each 4 bits of data are encoded into a symbol with five *code bits*, such that each code bit contains a single signal element; the block of five code bits is called a *code group*. In effect, each set of 4 bits is encoded as 5 bits. The efficiency is thus raised to 80%: 100 Mbps is achieved with 125 Mbaud.

To ensure synchronization, there is a second stage of encoding: Each code bit of the 4B/5B stream is treated as a binary value and encoded using nonreturn to zero inverted (NRZI) (see Figure 5.2). In this code, a binary 1 is represented with a transition at the beginning of the bit interval and a binary 0 is represented with no transition at the beginning of the bit interval; there are no other transitions. The advantage of NRZI is that it employs differential encoding. Recall from Chapter 5 that in differential encoding, the signal is decoded by comparing the polarity of adjacent signal elements rather than the absolute value of a signal element. A benefit of this scheme is that it is generally more reliable to detect a transition in the presence of noise and distortion than to compare a value to a threshold.

Now we are in a position to describe the 4B/5B code and to understand the selections that were made. Table 16.5 shows the symbol encoding. Each 5-bit code group pattern is shown, together with its NRZI realization. Because we are encoding 4 bits with a 5-bit pattern, only 16 of the 32 possible patterns are needed for data encoding. The codes selected to represent the 16 4-bit data blocks are such that a transition is present at least twice for each 5-code group code. No more than three zeros in a row are allowed across one or more code groups

Table 16.5   4B/5B Code Groups

Data Input (4 bits)	Code Group (5 bits)	NRZI Pattern	Interpretation
0000	11110		Data 0
0001	01001		Data 1
0010	10100		Data 2
0011	10101		Data 3
0100	01010		Data 4
0101	01011		Data 5
0110	01110		Data 6
0111	01111		Data 7
1000	10010		Data 8
1001	10011		Data 9
1010	10110		Data A
1011	10111		Data B
1100	11010		Data C
1101	11011		Data D
1110	11100		Data E
1111	11101		Data F
	11111		Idle
	11000		Start of stream delimiter, part 1
	10001		Start of stream delimiter, part 2
	01101		End of stream delimiter, part 1
	00111		End of stream delimiter, part 2
	00100		Transmit error
	other		Invalid codes

The encoding scheme can be summarized as follows:

1. A simple NRZ encoding is rejected because it does not provide synchronization; a string of 1s or 0s will have no transitions.

2. The data to be transmitted must first be encoded to assure transitions. The 4B/5B code is chosen over Manchester because it is more efficient.

3. The 4B/5B code is further encoded using NRZI so that the resulting differential signal will improve reception reliability.

4. The specific 5-bit patterns for the encoding of the 16 4-bit data patterns are chosen to guarantee no more than three zeros in a row to provide for adequate synchronization.

Those code groups not used to represent data are either declared invalid or assigned special meaning as control symbols. These assignments are listed in Table 16.5. The nondata symbols fall into the following categories:

- **Idle:** The idle code group is transmitted between data transmission sequences. It consists of a constant flow of binary ones, which in NRZI comes out as a continuous alternation between the two signal levels. This continuous fill pattern establishes and maintains synchronization and is used in the CSMA/CD protocol to indicate that the shared medium is idle.

- **Start of stream delimiter:** Used to delineate the starting boundary of a data transmission sequence; consists of two different code groups.

- **End of stream delimiter:** Used to terminate normal data transmission sequences; consists of two different code groups.

- **Transmit error:** This code group is interpreted as a signaling error. The normal use of this indicator is for repeaters to propagate received errors.

MLT-3

Although 4B/5B-NRZI is effective over optical fiber, it is not suitable as is for use over twisted pair. The reason is that the signal energy is concentrated in such a way as to produce undesirable radiated emissions from the wire. MLT-3, which is used on 100BASE-TX, is designed to overcome this problem.

The following steps are involved:

1. **NRZI to NRZ conversion.** The 4B/5B NRZI signal of the basic 100BASE-X is converted back to NRZ.
2. **Scrambling.** The bit stream is scrambled to produce a more uniform spectrum distribution for the next stage.
3. **Encoder.** The scrambled bit stream is encoded using a scheme known as MLT-3.
4. **Driver.** The resulting encoding is transmitted.

The effect of the MLT-3 scheme is to concentrate most of the energy in the transmitted signal below 30 MHz, which reduces radiated emissions. This in turn reduces problems due to interference.

The MLT-3 encoding produces an output that has a transition for every binary one and that uses three levels: a positive voltage ($+V$), a negative voltage ($-V$), and no voltage (0). The encoding rules are best explained with reference to the encoder state diagram shown in Figure 16.12:

1. If the next input bit is zero, then the next output value is the same as the preceding value.
2. If the next input bit is one, then the next output value involves a transition:
   - **a.** If the preceding output value was either $+V$ or $-V$, then the next output value is 0.
   - **b.** If the preceding output value was 0, then the next output value is nonzero, and that output is of the opposite sign to the last nonzero output.

Figure 16.13 provides an example. Every time there is an input of 1, there is a transition. The occurrences of $+V$ and $-V$ alternate.

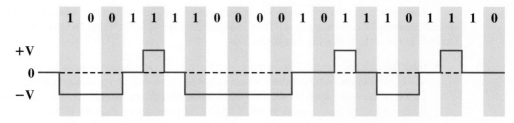

Figure 16.13 Example of MLT-3 Encoding

8B6T

The 8B6T encoding algorithm uses ternary signaling. With ternary signaling, each signal element can take on one of three values (positive voltage, negative voltage, zero voltage). A pure ternary code is one in which the full information-carrying capacity of the ternary signal is exploited. However, pure ternary is not attractive for the same reasons that a pure binary (NRZ) code is rejected: the lack of synchronization. However, there are schemes referred to as *block-coding methods* that approach the efficiency of ternary and overcome this disadvantage. A new block-coding scheme known as 8B6T is used for 100BASE-T4.

With 8B6T the data to be transmitted are handled in 8-bit blocks. Each block of 8 bits is mapped into a code group of 6 ternary symbols. The stream of code groups is then transmitted in round-robin fashion across the three output channels (Figure 16.14). Thus the ternary transmission rate on each output channel is

$$\frac{6}{8} \times 33\frac{1}{3} = 25 \text{ Mbaud}$$

Table 16.6 shows a portion of the 8B6T code table; the full table maps all possible 8-bit patterns into a unique code group of 6 ternary symbols. The mapping was chosen with two requirements in mind: synchronization and DC balance. For synchronization, the codes were chosen to maximize the average number of transitions per code group. The second requirement is to maintain DC balance, so that the average voltage on the line is zero. For this purpose all of the selected code groups either have an equal number of positive and negative symbols or an excess of one positive symbol. To maintain balance, a DC balancing algorithm is used. In essence, this algorithm monitors the cumulative weight of all code groups transmitted on a single twisted pair. Each code group has a weight of 0 or 1. To maintain balance, the algorithm may negate a transmitted code group (change all + symbols to − symbols and all − symbols to + symbols), so that the cumulative weight at the conclusion of each code group is always either 0 or 1.

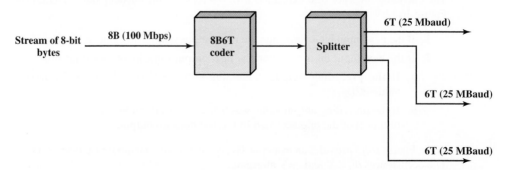

Figure 16.14 8B6T Transmission Scheme

Table 16.6 Portion of 8B6T Code Table

Data Octet	6T Code Group	Data Octet	6T Code Group	Data Octet	6T Code Group	Data Octet	6T Code Group
00	+ − 0 0 + −	10	+ 0 + − − 0	20	0 0 − + + −	30	+ − 0 0 − +
01	0 + − + − 0	11	+ + 0 − 0 −	21	− − + 0 0 +	31	0 + − − + 0
02	+ − 0 + − 0	12	+ 0 + − 0 −	22	+ + − 0 + −	32	+ − 0 − + 0
03	− 0 + + − 0	13	0 + + − 0 −	23	+ + − 0 − +	33	− 0 + − + 0
04	− 0 + 0 + −	14	0 + + − − 0	24	0 0 + 0 − +	34	− 0 + 0 − +
05	0 + − − 0 +	15	+ + 0 0 − −	25	0 0 + 0 + −	35	0 + − + 0 −
06	+ − 0 − 0 +	16	+ 0 + 0 − −	26	0 0 − 0 0 +	36	+ − 0 + 0 −
07	− 0 + − 0 +	17	0 + + 0 − −	27	− − + + + −	37	− 0 + + 0 −
08	− + 0 0 + −	18	0 + − 0 + −	28	− 0 − + + 0	38	− + 0 0 − +
09	0 − + + − 0	19	0 + − 0 − +	29	− − 0 + 0 +	39	0 − + − + 0
0A	− + 0 + − 0	1A	0 + − + + −	2A	− 0 − + 0 +	3A	− + 0 − + 0
0B	+ 0 − + − 0	1B	0 + − 0 0 +	2B	0 − − + 0 +	3B	+ 0 − − + 0
0C	+ 0 − 0 + −	1C	0 − + 0 0 +	2C	0 − − + + 0	3C	+ 0 − 0 − +
0D	0 − + − 0 +	1D	0 − + + + −	2D	− − 0 0 + +	3D	0 − + + 0 −
0E	− + 0 − 0 +	1E	0 − + 0 − +	2E	− 0 − 0 + +	3E	− + 0 + 0 −
0F	+ 0 − − 0 +	1F	0 − + 0 + −	2F	0 − − 0 + +	3F	+ 0 − + 0 −

8B/10B

The encoding scheme used for Fibre Channel and Gigabit Ethernet is 8B/10B, in which each 8 bits of data is converted into 10 bits for transmission. This scheme has a similar philosophy to the 4B/5B scheme discussed earlier. The 8B/10B scheme, developed and patented by IBM for use in its 200-megabaud ESCON interconnect system [WIDM83], is more powerful than 4B/5B in terms of transmission characteristics and error detection capability.

The developers of this code list the following advantages:

- It can be implemented with relatively simple and reliable transceivers at low cost.
- It is well balanced, with minimal deviation from the occurrence of an equal number of 1 and 0 bits across any sequence.
- It provides good transition density for easier clock recovery.
- It provides useful error detection capability.

The 8B/10B code is an example of the more general mBnB code, in which m binary source bits are mapped into n binary bits for transmission. Redundancy is built into the code to provide the desired transmission features by making $n > m$.

The 8B/10B code actually combines two other codes, a 5B/6B code and a 3B/4B code. The use of these two codes is simply an artifact that simplifies the definition of the mapping and the implementation; the mapping could have been defined directly as an 8B/10B code. In any case, a mapping is defined that maps each of the possible 8-bit source blocks into a 10-bit code block. There is also a function called *disparity control*. In essence, this function keeps track of the excess of zeros over ones or ones over zeros. An excess in either direction is referred to as a disparity. If there is a disparity, and if the current code block would add to that disparity, then the disparity control block complements the 10-bit code block. This has the effect of either eliminating the disparity or at least moving it in the opposite direction of the current disparity.

64B/66B

The 8B/10B code results in an overhead of 25%. To achieve greater efficiency at a higher data rate, the 64B/66B code maps a block of 64 bits into an output block of 66 bits, for an overhead of just 3%. This code is used in 10-Gbps and 100-Gbps Ethernet. The entire Ethernet frame, including control fields, is considered "data" for this process. In addition, there are nondata symbols, called "control," and which include those defined for the 4B/5B code discussed previously plus a few other symbols.

The first step in the process is to encode an input block into a 64-bit block, to which is preopended a 2-bit synchronization field, as show in Figure 16.15. If the input block consists

Input data	sync	Data-only field bits							
DDDD DDDD	01	D0	D1	D2	D3	D4	D5	D6	D7

Input data		Type	Data/control field bits							
CCCC CCCC	10	0x1E	C0	C1	C2	C3	C4	C5	C6	C7
CCCC ODDD	10	0x2D	C0	C1	C2	C3	O	D5	D6	D7
CCCC SDDD	10	0x33	C0	C1	C2	C3		D5	D6	D7
ODDD SDDD	10	0x66	D1	D2	D3	O		D5	D6	D7
ODDD ODDD	10	0x55	D1	D2	D3	O	O	D5	D6	D7
SDDD DDDD	10	0x78	D1	D2	D3	D4		D5	D6	D7
ODDD CCCC	10	0x4B	D1	D2	D3	O	C4	C5	C6	C7
TCCC CCCC	10	0x87		C1	C2	C3	C4	C5	C6	C7
DTCC CCCC	10	0x99	D0		C2	C3	C4	C5	C6	C7
DDTC CCCC	10	0xAA	D0	D1		C3	C4	C5	C6	C7
DDDT DDDT	10	0xB4	D0	D1	D2		C4	C5	C6	C7
DDDD TCCC	10	0xCC	D0	D1	D2	D3		C5	C6	C7
DDDD DTCC	10	0xD2	D0	D1	D2	D3	D4		C6	C7
DDDD DDTC	10	0xE1	D0	D1	D2	D3	D4	D5		C7
DDDD DDDT	10	0xFF	D0	D1	D2	D3	D4	D5	D6	

D = data octet
C = input control octet
Ci = 7-bit output control field
S = start of packet field
T = terminate = end of packet field
O = ordered set control character

Figure 16.15 64B/66B Block Formats

entirely of data octets, then the encoded block consists of the sync field value 10 followed by the 8 data octets unchanged. Otherwise, the input block consists of 8 control octets or a mixture of control octets and data octets. In this case the sync value is 01. This is followed by an 8-bit control type field, which defines the format of the remaining 56-bits of the block. To understand how the 56-bit block is formed, we need to indicate the types of control octets that might be included in the input block, which include the following:

- **Start of packet (S):** Indicates the start of a stream that includes an entire 802.3 MAC packet plus some 64B/66B control characters. This octet is encoded as either 4 bits or 0 bits.

- **End of packet (T):** Marks the termination of the packet. It is encoded using from 0 through 7 bits

- **Ordered set (0):** Used to adapt clock rates. It is encoded in 4 bits.

- **Other control octets:** Includes idle and error control characters. These octets are encoded in 7 bits.

It is necessary to reduce the number of bits in the input control characters so that the 64-bit input block can be accommodated in 56 bits. Figure 16.15 indicates how this is done. In the input block, the start of packet character is always aligned to be the first or fifth octet. If it occurs as the first octet in the input block, then the remaining seven octets are always data octets. To accommodate all seven data octets, the S field is implied by the block type field but takes up no bits in the encoded block. If the S character is the fifth input octet, then it occupies 4 bits of the encoded block. Similarly, the position and size of the T field is specified by the block type field and varies from 0 bits to 7 bits depending on the mixture of control and data octets in the input block.

Figure 16.16 shows the overall scheme for 64B/66B transmission. First, the input block is encoded and the 2-bit sync field is added. Then, scrambling is performed on the encoded

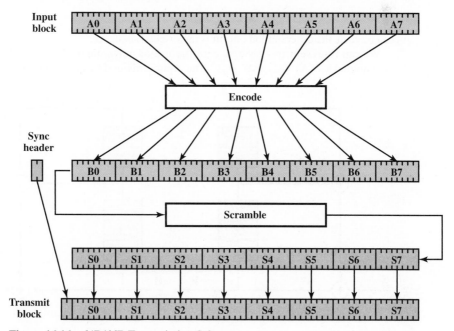

Figure 16.16   64B/66B Transmission Scheme

64-bit block using the polynomial $1 + X^{39} + X^{58}$. See Appendix 16B for a discussion of scrambling. The unscrambled 2-bit synchronization field is then prepended to the scrambled block. The sync field provides block alignment and a means of synchronizing when long streams of bits are sent.

Note that for this scheme, no specific coding technique is used to achieve the desired synchronization and frequency of transitions. Rather the scrambling algorithm provides the required characteristics.

APPENDIX 16B SCRAMBLING

For some digital data encoding techniques, a long string of binary zeros or ones in a transmission can degrade system performance. Also, other transmission properties, such as spectral properties, are enhanced if the data are more nearly of a random nature rather than constant or repetitive. A technique commonly used to improve signal quality is scrambling and descrambling. The scrambling process tends to make the data appear more random.

The scrambling process consists of a feedback shift register, and the matching descrambler consists of a feedforward shift register. An example is shown in Figure 16.17. In this example, the scrambled data sequence may be expressed as follows:

$$B_m = A_m \oplus B_{m-3} \oplus B_{m-5} \qquad (16.1)$$

where $\oplus$ indicates the exclusive-or operation. The shift register is initialized to contain all zeros. The descrambled sequence is

$$
\begin{aligned}
C_m &= B_m \oplus B_{m-3} \oplus B_{m-5} \\
&= (A_m \oplus B_{m-3} \oplus B_{m-5}) \oplus B_{m-3} \oplus B_{m-5} \\
&= A_m (\oplus B_{m-3} \oplus B_{m-3} \oplus) B_{m-5} \oplus B_{m-5} \\
&= A_m \qquad (16.2)
\end{aligned}
$$

As can be seen, the descrambled output is the original sequence.

We can represent this process with the use of polynomials. Thus, for this example, the polynomial is $P(X) = 1 + X^3 + X^5$. The input is divided by this polynomial to produce

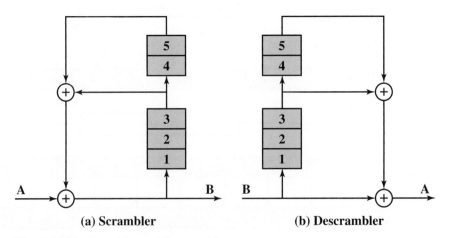

(a) Scrambler   **(b) Descrambler**

Figure 16.17 Scrambler and Descrambler

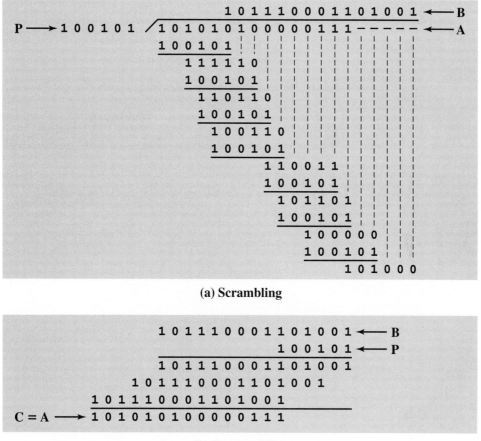

(a) Scrambling

(b) Descrambling

Figure 16.18 Example of Scrambling with $P(X) = 1 + X^{-3} + X^{-5}$

the scrambled sequence. At the receiver the received scrambled signal is multiplied by the same polynomial to reproduce the original input. Figure 16.18 is an example using the polynomial $P(X)$ and an input of 101010100000111.[5] The scrambled transmission, produced by dividing by $P(X)$ (100101), is 101110001101001. When this number is multiplied by $P(X)$, we get the original input. Note that the input sequence contains the periodic sequence 10101010 as well as a long string of zeros. The scrambler effectively removes both patterns.

For the MLT-3 scheme, which is used for 100BASE-TX, the scrambling equation is:

$$B_m = A_m \oplus X_9 \oplus X_{11}$$

In this case the shift register consists of nine elements, used in the same manner as the 5-element register in Figure 16.17. However, in the case of MLT-3, the shift register is not fed

---

[5]We use the convention that the leftmost bit is the first bit presented to the scrambler; thus the bits can be labeled $A_0A_1A_2$.... Similarly, the polynomial is converted to a bit string from left to right. The polynomial $B_0 + B_1X + B_2X^2 + \ldots$ is represented as $B_0B_1B_2\ldots$

by the output . Instead, after each bit transmission, the register is shifted one unit up, and the result of the previous XOR is fed into the first unit. This can be expressed as:

$$X_i(t) = X_{i-1}(t-1); \quad 2 \leq i \leq 9$$
$$X_i(t) = X_9(t-1) \oplus X_{11}(t-1)$$

If the shift register contains all zeros, no scrambling occurs (we just have $B_m = A_m$) and the above equations produce no change in the shift register. Accordingly, the standard calls for initializing the shift register with all ones and reinitializing the register to all ones when it takes on a value of all zeros.

For the 4D-PAM5 scheme, two scrambling equations are used, one in each direction:

$$B_m = A_m \oplus B_{m-13} \oplus B_{m-33}$$
$$B_m = A_m \oplus B_{m-20} \oplus B_{m-33}$$

WIRELESS LANS

Investigators have published numerous reports of birds taking turns vocalizing; the bird spoken to gave its full attention to the speaker and never vocalized at the same time, as if the two were holding a conversation. Researchers and scholars who have studied the data on avian communication carefully write the (a) the communication code of birds such as crows has not been broken by any means; (b) probably all birds have wider vocabularies than anyone realizes; and (c) greater complexity and depth are recognized in avian communication as research progresses.

—The Human Nature of Birds, Theodore Barber

KEY POINTS

◆ The principal technologies used for wireless LANs are infrared, spread spectrum, and narrowband microwave.

◆ The IEEE 802.11 standard defines a set of services and physical-layer options for wireless LANs.

◆ The IEEE 802.11 services include managing associations, delivering data, and security.

◆ The IEEE 802.11 physical layer includes infrared and spread spectrum and covers a range of data rates.

In recent years, wireless LANs have come to occupy a significant niche in the local area network market. Increasingly, organizations are finding that wireless LANs are an indispensable adjunct to traditional wired LANs, to satisfy requirements for mobility, relocation, ad hoc networking, and coverage of locations difficult to wire.

This chapter provides a survey of wireless LANs. We begin with an overview that looks at the motivations for using wireless LANs and summarize the various approaches in current use. The next section examines the three principal types of wireless LANs, classified according to transmission technology: infrared, spread spectrum, and narrowband microwave.

The most prominent specification for wireless LANs was developed by the IEEE 802.11 working group. This chapter focuses on this standard.

17.1 OVERVIEW

As the name suggests, a wireless LAN is one that makes use of a wireless transmission medium. Until relatively recently, wireless LANs were little used. The reasons for this included high prices, low data rates, occupational safety concerns, and licensing requirements. As these problems have been addressed, the popularity of wireless LANs has grown rapidly.

In this section, we survey the key wireless LAN application areas and then look at the requirements for and advantages of wireless LANs.

Wireless LAN Applications

[PAHL95] lists four application areas for wireless LANs: LAN extension, cross-building interconnect, nomadic access, and ad hoc networks. Let us consider each of these in turn.

LAN EXTENSION Early wireless LAN products, introduced in the late 1980s, were marketed as substitutes for traditional wired LANs. A wireless LAN saves the cost of the installation of LAN cabling and eases the task of relocation and other modifications to network structure. However, this motivation for using wireless LANs was overtaken by events. First, as awareness of the need for LANs became greater, architects designed new buildings to include extensive prewiring for data applications. Second, with advances in data transmission technology, there is an increasing reliance on twisted pair cabling for LANs. Most buildings are now wired with an abundance of data-grade cable, and many newer buildings are prewired with Category 5 cable. Thus, the use of a wireless LAN to replace wired LANs has not happened to any great extent.

However, in a number of environments, there is a role for the wireless LAN as an alternative to a wired LAN. Examples include buildings with large open areas, such as manufacturing plants, stock exchange trading floors, and warehouses; historical buildings with insufficient twisted pair and where drilling holes for new wiring is prohibited; and small offices where installation and maintenance of wired LANs is not economical. In all of these cases, a wireless LAN provides an effective and more attractive alternative. In most of these cases, an organization will also have a wired LAN to support servers and some stationary workstations. For example, a manufacturing facility typically has an office area that is separate from the factory floor but that must be linked to it for networking purposes. Therefore, typically, a wireless LAN will be linked into a wired LAN on the same premises. Thus, this application area is referred to as LAN extension.

Figure 17.1 indicates a simple wireless LAN configuration that is typical of many environments. There is a backbone wired LAN, such as Ethernet, that supports servers, workstations, and one or more bridges or routers to link with other networks. In addition, there is a control module (CM) that acts as an interface to a wireless LAN. The control module includes either bridge or router functionality to link the wireless LAN to the backbone. It includes some sort of access control logic, such as a polling or token-passing scheme, to regulate the access from the end systems. Note that some of the end systems are stand-alone devices, such as a workstation or a server. Hubs or other user modules (UMs) that control a number of stations off a wired LAN may also be part of the wireless LAN configuration.

The configuration of Figure 17.1 can be referred to as a single-cell wireless LAN; all of the wireless end systems are within range of a single control module. Another common configuration, suggested by Figure 17.2, is a multiple-cell wireless LAN. In this case, there are multiple control modules interconnected by a wired LAN. Each control module supports a number of wireless end systems within its transmission range. For example, with an infrared LAN, transmission is limited to a single room; therefore, one cell is needed for each room in an office building that requires wireless support.

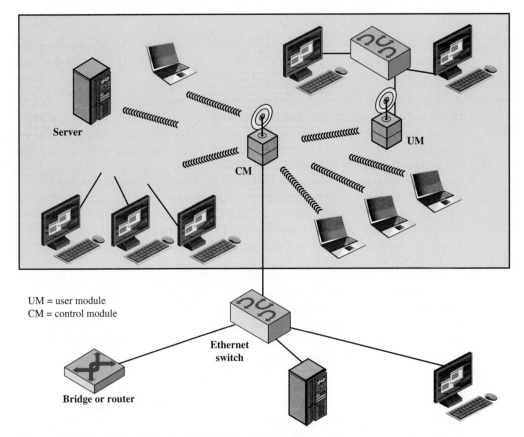

UM = user module
CM = control module

Figure 17.1 Example of Single-Cell Wireless LAN Configuration

CROSS-BUILDING INTERCONNECT Another use of wireless LAN technology is to connect LANs in nearby buildings, be they wired or wireless LANs. In this case, a point-to-point wireless link is used between two buildings. For example, two microwave or infrared transmitter/receiver units can be placed on the rooftops of two buildings within the line of sight of each other. The devices so connected are typically bridges or routers. This single point-to-point link is not a LAN per se, but it is usual to include this application under the heading of wireless LAN.

NOMADIC ACCESS Nomadic access provides a wireless link between a LAN hub and a mobile data terminal equipped with an antenna, such as a laptop computer or notepad computer. One example of the utility of such a connection is to enable an employee returning from a trip to transfer data from a personal portable computer to a server in the office. Nomadic access is also useful in an extended environment such as a campus or a business operating out of a cluster of buildings. In both of these cases, users may move around with their portable computers and may wish access to the servers on a wired LAN from various locations.

AD HOC NETWORKING An ad hoc network is a peer-to-peer network (no centralized server) set up temporarily to meet some immediate need. For example, a group of

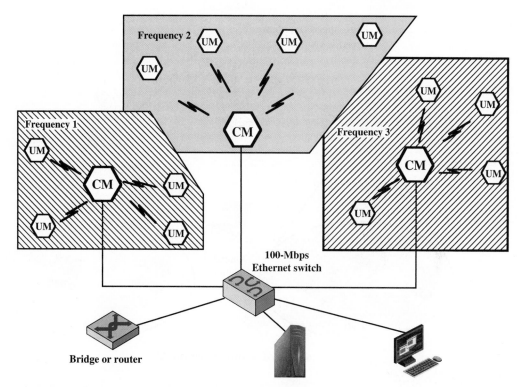

Figure 17.2 Example of Multiple-Cell Wireless LAN Configuration

employees, each with a laptop or palmtop computer, may convene in a conference room for a business or classroom meeting. The employees link their computers in a temporary network just for the duration of the meeting.

Figure 17.3 suggests the differences between a wireless LAN that supports LAN extension and nomadic access requirements and an ad hoc wireless LAN. In the former case, the wireless LAN forms a stationary infrastructure consisting of one or more cells with a control module for each cell. Within a cell, there may be a number of stationary end systems. Nomadic stations can move from one cell to another. In contrast, there is no infrastructure for an ad hoc network. Rather, a peer collection of stations within range of each other may dynamically configure themselves into a temporary network.

Wireless LAN Requirements

A wireless LAN must meet the same sort of requirements typical of any LAN, including high capacity, ability to cover short distances, full connectivity among attached stations, and broadcast capability. In addition, there are a number of requirements specific to the wireless LAN environment. The following are among the most important requirements for wireless LANs:

- **Throughput:** The medium access control (MAC) protocol should make as efficient use as possible of the wireless medium to maximize capacity.

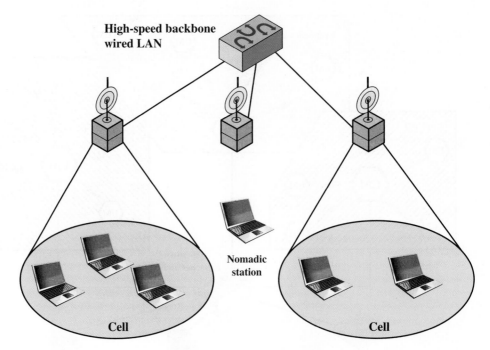

(a) Infrastructure wireless LAN

(b) Ad hoc LAN

Figure 17.3 Wireless LAN Configurations

- **Number of nodes:** Wireless LANs may need to support hundreds of nodes across multiple cells.

- **Connection to backbone LAN:** In most cases, interconnection with stations on a wired backbone LAN is required. For infrastructure wireless LANs, this is easily accomplished through the use of control modules that connect to both types of LANs. There may also need to be accommodation for mobile users and ad hoc wireless networks.

- **Service area:** A typical coverage area for a wireless LAN has a diameter of 100 to 300 m.

- **Battery power consumption:** Mobile workers use battery-powered workstations that need to have a long battery life when used with wireless adapters. This suggests that a MAC protocol that requires mobile nodes to monitor access points constantly or engage in frequent handshakes with a base station is inappropriate. Typical wireless LAN implementations have features to reduce power consumption while not using the network, such as a sleep mode.

- **Transmission robustness and security:** Unless properly designed, a wireless LAN may be especially vulnerable to interference and network eavesdropping. The design of a wireless LAN must permit reliable transmission even in a noisy environment and should provide some level of security from eavesdropping.

- **Collocated network operation:** As wireless LANs become more popular, it is quite likely for two or more wireless LANs to operate in the same area or in some area where interference between the LANs is possible. Such interference may thwart the normal operation of a MAC algorithm and may allow unauthorized access to a particular LAN.

- **License-free operation:** Users would prefer to buy and operate wireless LAN products without having to secure a license for the frequency band used by the LAN.

- **Handoff/roaming:** The MAC protocol used in the wireless LAN should enable mobile stations to move from one cell to another.

- **Dynamic configuration:** The MAC addressing and network management aspects of the wireless LAN should permit dynamic and automated addition, deletion, and relocation of end systems without disruption to other users.

17.2 WIRELESS LAN TECHNOLOGY

Wireless LANs are generally categorized according to the transmission technique that is used. All current wireless LAN products fall into one of the following categories:

- **Spread spectrum LANs:** This type of LAN makes use of spread spectrum transmission technology. In most cases, these LANs operate in the ISM (industrial, scientific, and medical) 2.4-GHz microwave bands so that no Federal Communications Commission (FCC) licensing is required for their use in the United States.

- **OFDM LANs:** For higher speeds, a technology known as orthogonal frequency division multiplexing (OFDM) is superior to spread spectrum, and products with this technology are now common. These LANs typically operate in either the 2.4-GHz band or the 5-GHz band.

- **Infrared (IR) LANs:** An individual cell of an IR LAN is limited to a single room, because infrared light does not penetrate opaque walls. This type of LAN is little used.

The remainder of this section provides a brief overview of some aspects of spread spectrum and OFDM LANs.

Configuration

Except for quite small offices, a wireless LAN makes use of a multiple-cell arrangement, as was illustrated in Figure 17.2. Adjacent cells make use of different center frequencies within the same band to avoid interference.

Within a given cell, the topology can be either hub or peer to peer. In a hub topology, indicated in Figure 17.2, the hub is typically mounted on the ceiling and connected to a backbone wired LAN to provide connectivity to stations attached to the wired LAN and to stations that are part of wireless LANs in other cells. The hub may also control access, as in the IEEE 802.11 point coordination function, described subsequently. The hub may also control access by acting as a multiport repeater with similar functionality to Ethernet multiport repeaters. In this case, all stations in the cell transmit only to the hub and receive only from the hub. Alternatively, and regardless of access control mechanism, each station may broadcast using an omnidirectional antenna so that all other stations in the cell may receive; this corresponds to a logical bus configuration.

One other potential function of a hub is automatic handoff of mobile stations. At any time, a number of stations are dynamically assigned to a given hub based on proximity. When the hub senses a weakening signal, it can automatically hand off to the nearest adjacent hub.

A peer-to-peer topology is one in which there is no hub. A MAC algorithm such as carrier sense multiple access (CSMA) is used to control access. This topology is appropriate for ad hoc LANs.

Transmission Issues

A desirable, though not necessary, characteristic of a wireless LAN is that it be usable without having to go through a licensing procedure. The licensing regulations differ from one country to another, which complicates this objective. Within the United States, the FCC has authorized two unlicensed applications within the ISM band: spread spectrum systems, which can operate at up to 1 W, and very low power systems, which can operate at up to 0.5 W. Since the FCC opened up this band, its use for spread spectrum wireless LANs has become popular.

In the United States, three microwave bands have been set aside for unlicensed spread spectrum use: 902–928 MHz (915-MHz band), 2.4–2.4835 GHz (2.4-GHz band), and 5.725–5.825 GHz (5.8-GHz band). Of these, the 2.4 GHz is also used in this manner in Europe and Japan. The higher the frequency, the higher the potential bandwidth, so the three bands are of increasing order of attractiveness from a capacity point of view. In addition, the potential for interference must be considered. There are a number of devices that operate at around 900 MHz, including cordless telephones, wireless microphones, and amateur radio. There are fewer devices operating at 2.4 GHz; one notable example is the microwave oven, which tends to have greater leakage of radiation with increasing age. At present there is little competition at the 5.8-GHz band; however, the higher the frequency band, in general the more expensive the equipment.

17.3 IEEE 802.11 ARCHITECTURE AND SERVICES

In 1990, the IEEE 802 Committee formed a new working group, IEEE 802.11, specifically devoted to wireless LANs, with a charter to develop a MAC protocol and physical medium specification. Since that time, the demand for WLANs, at different frequencies and data rates, has exploded. Keeping pace with this demand, the IEEE 802.11 working group has issued an ever-expanding list of standards (Table 17.1). Table 17.2 briefly defines key terms used in the IEEE 802.11 standard.

Table 17.1 IEEE 802.11 Standards

Standard	Scope
IEEE 802.11	Medium access control (MAC): One common MAC for WLAN applications
	Physical layer: Infrared at 1 Mbps and 2 Mbps
	Physical layer: 2.4-GHz FHSS at 1 Mbps and 2 Mbps
	Physical layer: 2.4-GHz DSSS at 1 Mbps and 2 Mbps
IEEE 802.11a	Physical layer: 5-GHz OFDM at rates from 6 to 54 Mbps
IEEE 802.11b	Physical layer: 2.4-GHz DSSS at 5.5 Mbps and 11 Mbps
IEEE 802.11c	Bridge operation at 802.11 MAC layer
IEEE 802.11d	Physical layer: Extend operation of 802.11 WLANs to new regulatory domains (countries)
IEEE 802.11e	MAC: Enhance to improve quality of service and enhance security mechanisms
IEEE 802.11f	Recommended practices for multivendor access point interoperability
IEEE 802.11g	Physical layer: Extend 802.11b to data rates >20 Mbps
IEEE 802.11h	Physical/MAC: Enhance IEEE 802.11a to add indoor and outdoor channel selection and to improve spectrum and transmit power management
IEEE 802.11i	MAC: Enhance security and authentication mechanisms
IEEE 802.11j	Physical layer: Enhance IEEE 802.11a to conform to Japanese requirements
IEEE 802.11k	Radio resource measurement enhancements to provide interface to higher layers for radio and network measurements
IEEE 802.11m	Maintenance of IEEE 802.11-1999 standard with technical and editorial corrections
IEEE 802.11n	Physical/MAC: Enhancements to enable higher throughput
IEEE 802.11p	Physical/MAC: Wireless access in vehicular environments
IEEE 802.11r	Physical/MAC: Fast roaming (fast BSS transition)
IEEE 802.11s	Physical/MAC: ESS mesh networking
IEEE 802.11T	Recommended practice for the evaluation of 802.11 wireless performance
IEEE 802.11u	Physical/MAC: Interworking with external networks

(Continued)

Table 17.1 IEEE 802.11 Standards (Continued)

Standard	Scope
IEEE 802.11w	MAC: data integrity, data origin authenticity, replay protection, and data confidentiality for MAC management frames
IEEE 802.11y	Physical layer: Extend 802.11a to include 3650–3700 MHz band
IEEE 802.11z	MAC: Amendment to define a new direct link setup (DLS) mechanism to allow operation with non-DLS capable access points
IEEE 802.11aa	MAC: Enhancements for robust audio video streaming
IEEE 802.11ad	Operation in the 60-GHz band
IEEE 802.11ae	Mechanisms for prioritizing IEEE 802.11 management frames
IEEE 802.11af	Modifications to allow 802.11 wireless networks to be used in the TV white space

Table 17.2 IEEE 802.11 Terminology

Access point (AP)	Any entity that has station functionality and provides access to the distribution system via the wireless medium for associated stations
Basic service set (BSS)	A set of stations controlled by a single coordination function
Coordination function	The logical function that determines when a station operating within a BSS is permitted to transmit and may be able to receive Protocol data units (PDUs)
Distribution system (DS)	A system used to interconnect a set of BSSs and integrated LANs to create an extended service set (ESS)
Extended service set	A set of one or more interconnected BSSs and integrated LANs that appear as a single BSS to the logical link control (LLC) layer at any station associated with one of these BSSs
MAC protocol data unit (MPDU)	The unit of data exchanged between two peer MAC entities using the services of the physical layer
MAC service data unit (MSDU)	Information that is delivered as a unit between MAC users
Station	Any device that contains an IEEE 802.11 conformant MAC and physical layer

The Wi-Fi Alliance

The first 802.11 standard to gain broad industry acceptance was 802.11b. Although 802.11b products are all based on the same standard, there is always a concern whether products from different vendors will successfully interoperate. To meet this concern, the Wireless Ethernet Compatibility Alliance (WECA), an industry consortium, was formed in 1999. This organization, subsequently renamed the Wi-Fi (Wireless Fidelity) Alliance, created a test suite to certify interoperability for 802.11b products. The term used for certified 802.11b products is *Wi-Fi*. Wi-Fi certification has been extended to 802.11g products. The Wi-Fi Alliance has also developed a certification process for 802.11a products, called *Wi-Fi5*. The Wi-Fi Alliance is concerned with a range of market areas for WLANs, including enterprise, home, and hot spots.

IEEE 802.11 Architecture

Figure 17.4 illustrates the model developed by the 802.11 working group. The smallest building block of a wireless LAN is a **basic service set (BSS)**, which consists of some number of stations executing the same MAC protocol and competing for access to the same shared wireless medium. A BSS may be isolated or it may connect to a backbone **distribution system (DS)** through an **access point (AP)**. The AP functions as a bridge and a relay point. In a BSS, client stations do not communicate directly with one another. Rather, if one station in the BSS wants to communicate with another station in the same BSS, the MAC frame is first sent from the originating station to the AP, and then from the AP to the destination station. Similarly, a MAC frame from a station in the BSS to a remote station is sent from the local station to the AP and then relayed by the AP over the DS on its way to the destination station. The BSS generally corresponds to what is referred to as a cell in the literature. The DS can be a switch, a wired network, or a wireless network.

When all the stations in the BSS are mobile stations, with no connection to other BSSs, the BSS is called an **independent BSS (IBSS)**. An IBSS is typically an ad hoc network. In an IBSS, the stations all communicate directly, and no AP is involved.

A simple configuration is shown in Figure 17.4, in which each station belongs to a single BSS; that is, each station is within wireless range only of other stations within the same BSS. It is also possible for two BSSs to overlap geographically, so that a single station could participate in more than one BSS. Further, the association between a station and a BSS is dynamic. Stations may turn off, come within range, and go out of range.

An **extended service set (ESS)** consists of two or more BSSs interconnected by a distribution system. Typically, the distribution system is a wired backbone LAN

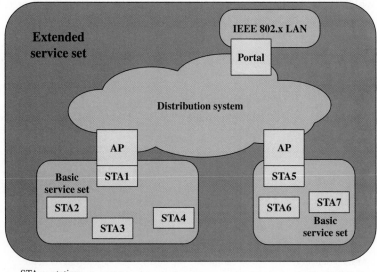

STA = station
AP = access point

Figure 17.4   IEEE 802.11 Architecture

but can be any communications network. The ESS appears as a single logical LAN to the logical link control (LLC) level.

Figure 17.4 indicates that an AP is implemented as part of a station; the AP is the logic within a station that provides access to the DS by providing DS services in addition to acting as a station. To integrate the IEEE 802.11 architecture with a traditional wired LAN, a **portal** is used. The portal logic is implemented in a device, such as a bridge or router, that is part of the wired LAN and that is attached to the DS.

IEEE 802.11 Services

IEEE 802.11 defines nine services that need to be provided by the wireless LAN to provide functionality equivalent to that which is inherent to wired LANs. Table 17.3 lists the services and indicates two ways of categorizing them.

1. The service provider can be either the station or the DS. Station services are implemented in every 802.11 station, including AP stations. Distribution services are provided between BSSs; these services may be implemented in an AP or in another special-purpose device attached to the distribution system.

2. Three of the services are used to control IEEE 802.11 LAN access and confidentiality. Six of the services are used to support delivery of MAC service data units (MSDUs) between stations. The MSDU is a block of data passed down from the MAC user to the MAC layer; typically this is a LLC PDU. If the MSDU is too large to be transmitted in a single MAC frame, it may be fragmented and transmitted in a series of MAC frames. Fragmentation is discussed in Section 17.4.

Following the IEEE 802.11 document, we next discuss the services in an order designed to clarify the operation of an IEEE 802.11 ESS network. **MSDU delivery**, which is the basic service, has already been mentioned. Services related to security are discussed in Section 17.6.

DISTRIBUTION OF MESSAGES WITHIN A DS The two services involved with the distribution of messages within a DS are distribution and integration. **Distribution** is

Table 17.3   IEEE 802.11 Services

Service	Provider	Used to Support
Association	Distribution system	MSDU delivery
Authentication	Station	LAN access and security
Deauthentication	Station	LAN access and security
Disassociation	Distribution system	MSDU delivery
Distribution	Distribution system	MSDU delivery
Integration	Distribution system	MSDU delivery
MSDU delivery	Station	MSDU delivery
Privacy	Station	LAN access and security
Reassociation	Distribution system	MSDU delivery

the primary service used by stations to exchange MAC frames when the frame must traverse the DS to get from a station in one BSS to a station in another BSS. For example, suppose a frame is to be sent from station 2 (STA2) to STA7 in Figure 17.4. The frame is sent from STA2 to STA1, which is the AP for this BSS. The AP gives the frame to the DS, which has the job of directing the frame to the AP associated with STA5 in the target BSS. STA5 receives the frame and forwards it to STA7. How the message is transported through the DS is beyond the scope of the IEEE 802.11 standard.

If the two stations that are communicating are within the same BSS, then the distribution service logically goes through the single AP of that BSS.

The **integration** service enables transfer of data between a station on an IEEE 802.11 LAN and a station on an integrated IEEE 802.x LAN. The term *integrated* refers to a wired LAN that is physically connected to the DS and whose stations may be logically connected to an IEEE 802.11 LAN via the integration service. The integration service takes care of any address translation and media conversion logic required for the exchange of data.

ASSOCIATION-RELATED SERVICES The primary purpose of the MAC layer is to transfer MSDUs between MAC entities; this purpose is fulfilled by the distribution service. For that service to function, it requires information about stations within the ESS that is provided by the association-related services. Before the distribution service can deliver data to or accept data from a station, that station must be *associated*. Before looking at the concept of association, we need to describe the concept of mobility. The standard defines three transition types, based on mobility:

- **No transition:** A station of this type is either stationary or moves only within the direct communication range of the communicating stations of a single BSS.
- **BSS transition:** This is defined as a station movement from one BSS to another BSS within the same ESS. In this case, delivery of data to the station requires that the addressing capability be able to recognize the new location of the station.
- **ESS transition:** This is defined as a station movement from a BSS in one ESS to a BSS within another ESS. This case is supported only in the sense that the station can move. Maintenance of upper-layer connections supported by 802.11 cannot be guaranteed. In fact, disruption of service is likely to occur.

To deliver a message within a DS, the distribution service needs to know where the destination station is located. Specifically, the DS needs to know the identity of the AP to which the message should be delivered in order for that message to reach the destination station. To meet this requirement, a station must maintain an association with the AP within its current BSS. Three services relate to this requirement:

- **Association:** Establishes an initial association between a station and an AP. Before a station can transmit or receive frames on a wireless LAN, its identity and address must be known. For this purpose, a station must establish an association with an AP within a particular BSS. The AP can then communicate this information to other APs within the ESS to facilitate routing and delivery of addressed frames.

- **Reassociation:** Enables an established association to be transferred from one AP to another, allowing a mobile station to move from one BSS to another.

- **Disassociation:** A notification from either a station or an AP that an existing association is terminated. A station should give this notification before leaving an ESS or shutting down. However, the MAC management facility protects itself against stations that disappear without notification.

17.4 IEEE 802.11 MEDIUM ACCESS CONTROL

The IEEE 802.11 MAC layer covers three functional areas: reliable data delivery, access control, and security. This section covers the first two topics.

Reliable Data Delivery

As with any wireless network, a wireless LAN using the IEEE 802.11 physical and MAC layers is subject to considerable unreliability. Noise, interference, and other propagation effects result in the loss of a significant number of frames. Even with error correction codes, a number of MAC frames may not successfully be received. This situation can be dealt with by reliability mechanisms at a higher layer, such as TCP. However, timers used for retransmission at higher layers are typically on the order of seconds. It is therefore more efficient to deal with errors at the MAC level. For this purpose, IEEE 802.11 includes a frame exchange protocol. When a station receives a data frame from another station, it returns an acknowledgment (ACK) frame to the source station. This exchange is treated as an atomic unit, not to be interrupted by a transmission from any other station. If the source does not receive an ACK within a short period of time, either because its data frame was damaged or because the returning ACK was damaged, the source retransmits the frame.

Thus, the basic data transfer mechanism in IEEE 802.11 involves an exchange of two frames. To further enhance reliability, a four-frame exchange may be used. In this scheme, a source first issues a Request to Send (RTS) frame to the destination. The destination then responds with a Clear to Send (CTS). After receiving the CTS, the source transmits the data frame, and the destination responds with an ACK. The RTS alerts all stations that are within reception range of the source that an exchange is under way; these stations refrain from transmission in order to avoid a collision between two frames transmitted at the same time. Similarly, the CTS alerts all stations that are within reception range of the destination that an exchange is under way. The RTS/CTS portion of the exchange is a required function of the MAC but may be disabled.

Medium Access Control

The 802.11 working group considered two types of proposals for a MAC algorithm: distributed access protocols, which, like Ethernet, distribute the decision to transmit over all the nodes using a carrier sense mechanism; and centralized access protocols, which involve regulation of transmission by a centralized decision maker. A distributed access protocol makes sense for an ad hoc network of peer workstations (typically an IBSS) and may also be attractive in other wireless LAN configurations that consist primarily of bursty traffic. A centralized access protocol is natural for configurations in which a number of wireless stations are interconnected with each other and some sort of base station that attaches to a backbone wired LAN; it is especially useful if some of the data is time sensitive or high priority.

The end result for 802.11 is a MAC algorithm called DFWMAC (distributed foundation wireless MAC) that provides a distributed access control mechanism with an optional centralized control built on top of that. Figure 17.5 illustrates the architecture. The lower sublayer of the MAC layer is the distributed coordination function (DCF). DCF uses a contention algorithm to provide access to all traffic. Ordinary asynchronous traffic directly uses DCF. The point coordination function (PCF) is a centralized MAC algorithm used to provide contention-free service. PCF is built on top of DCF and exploits features of DCF to assure access for its users. Let us consider these two sublayers in turn.

DISTRIBUTED COORDINATION FUNCTION The DCF sublayer makes use of a simple CSMA (carrier sense multiple access) algorithm. If a station has a MAC frame to transmit, it listens to the medium. If the medium is idle, the station may transmit; otherwise the station must wait until the current transmission is complete before transmitting. The DCF does not include a collision detection function (i.e., CSMA/CD) because collision detection is not practical on a wireless network. The dynamic range of the signals on the medium is very large, so that a transmitting

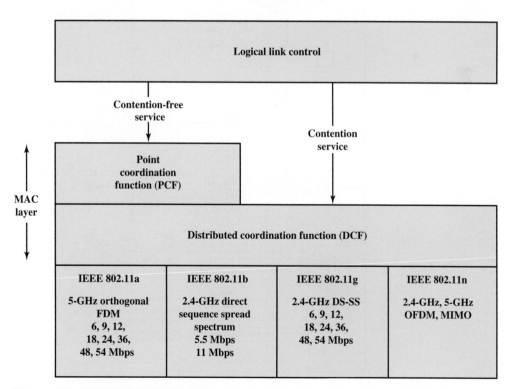

Figure 17.5   IEEE 802.11 Protocol Architecture

station cannot effectively distinguish incoming weak signals from noise and the effects of its own transmission.

To ensure the smooth and fair functioning of this algorithm, DCF includes a set of delays that amounts to a priority scheme. Let us start by considering a single delay known as an interframe space (IFS). In fact, there are three different IFS values, but the algorithm is best explained by initially ignoring this detail. Using an IFS, the rules for CSMA access are as follows (Figure 17.6):

1. A station with a frame to transmit senses the medium. If the medium is idle, it waits to see if the medium remains idle for a time equal to IFS. If so, the station may transmit immediately.

2. If the medium is busy (either because the station initially finds the medium busy or because the medium becomes busy during the IFS idle time), the station defers transmission and continues to monitor the medium until the current transmission is over.

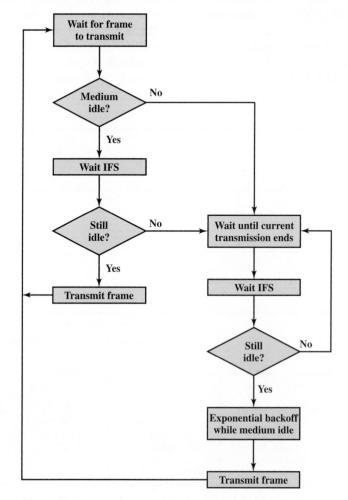

Figure 17.6   IEEE 802.11 Medium Access Control Logic

3. Once the current transmission is over, the station delays another IFS. If the medium remains idle for this period, then the station backs off a random amount of time and again senses the medium. If the medium is still idle, the station may transmit. During the backoff time, if the medium becomes busy, the backoff timer is halted and resumes when the medium becomes idle.

4. If the transmission is unsuccessful, which is determined by the absence of an acknowledgement, then it is assumed that a collision has occurred.

To ensure that backoff maintains stability, binary exponential backoff, described in Chapter 16, is used. Binary exponential backoff provides a means of handling a heavy load. Repeated failed attempts to transmit result in longer and longer backoff times, which helps to smooth out the load. Without such a backoff, the following situation could occur: Two or more stations attempt to transmit at the same time, causing a collision. These stations then immediately attempt to retransmit, causing a new collision.

The preceding scheme is refined for DCF to provide priority-based access by the simple expedient of using three values for IFS:

- **SIFS (short IFS):** The shortest IFS, used for all immediate response actions, as explained in the following discussion
- **PIFS (point coordination function IFS):** A midlength IFS, used by the centralized controller in the PCF scheme when issuing polls
- **DIFS (distributed coordination function IFS):** The longest IFS, used as a minimum delay for asynchronous frames contending for access

Figure 17.7a illustrates the use of these time values. Consider first the SIFS. Any station using SIFS to determine transmission opportunity has, in effect, the highest priority, because it will always gain access in preference to a station waiting an amount of time equal to PIFS or DIFS. The SIFS is used in the following circumstances:

- **Acknowledgment (ACK):** When a station receives a frame addressed only to itself (not multicast or broadcast), it responds with an ACK frame after waiting only for an SIFS gap. This has two desirable effects. First, because collision detection is not used, the likelihood of collisions is greater than with CSMA/CD, and the MAC-level ACK provides for efficient collision recovery. Second, the SIFS can be used to provide efficient delivery of an LLC protocol data unit (PDU) that requires multiple MAC frames. In this case, the following scenario occurs. A station with a multiframe LLC PDU to transmit sends out the MAC frames one at a time. Each frame is acknowledged by the recipient after SIFS. When the source receives an ACK, it immediately (after SIFS) sends the next frame in the sequence. The result is that once a station has contended for the channel, it will maintain control of the channel until it has sent all of the fragments of an LLC PDU.
- **Clear to Send (CTS):** A station can ensure that its data frame will get through by first issuing a small RTS frame. The station to which this frame is addressed should immediately respond with a CTS frame if it is ready to receive. All other stations receive the RTS and defer using the medium.
- **Poll response:** This is explained in the following discussion of PCF.

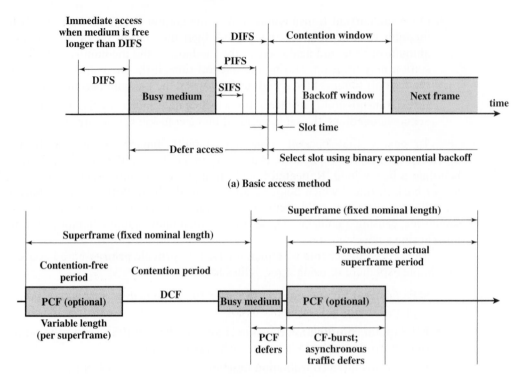

Figure 17.7   IEEE 802.11 MAC Timing

The next longest IFS interval is the PIFS. This is used by the centralized controller in issuing polls and takes precedence over normal contention traffic. However, those frames transmitted using SIFS have precedence over a PCF poll.

Finally, the DIFS interval is used for all ordinary asynchronous traffic.

POINT COORDINATION FUNCTION   PCF is an alternative access method implemented on top of the DCF. The operation consists of polling by the centralized polling master (point coordinator). The point coordinator makes use of PIFS when issuing polls. Because PIFS is smaller than DIFS, the point coordinator can seize the medium and lock out all asynchronous traffic while it issues polls and receives responses.

As an extreme, consider the following possible scenario. A wireless network is configured so that a number of stations with time-sensitive traffic are controlled by the point coordinator while remaining traffic contends for access using CSMA. The point coordinator could issue polls in a round-robin fashion to all stations configured for polling. When a poll is issued, the polled station may respond using SIFS. If the point coordinator receives a response, it issues another poll using PIFS. If no response is received during the expected turnaround time, the coordinator issues a poll.

If the discipline of the preceding paragraph were implemented, the point coordinator would lock out all asynchronous traffic by repeatedly issuing polls. To prevent this, an interval known as the superframe is defined. During the first part of this interval, the point coordinator issues polls in a round-robin fashion to all stations configured for polling. The point coordinator then idles for the remainder of the superframe, allowing a contention period for asynchronous access.

Figure 17.7b illustrates the use of the superframe. At the beginning of a super-frame, the point coordinator may optionally seize control and issue polls for a given period of time. This interval varies because of the variable frame size issued by responding stations. The remainder of the superframe is available for contention-based access. At the end of the superframe interval, the point coordinator contends for access to the medium using PIFS. If the medium is idle, the point coordinator gains immediate access and a full superframe period follows. However, the medium may be busy at the end of a superframe. In this case, the point coordinator must wait until the medium is idle to gain access; this results in a foreshortened superframe period for the next cycle.

MAC Frame

Figure 17.8 shows the IEEE 802.11 frame format. This general format is used for all data and control frames, but not all fields are used in all contexts. The fields are as follows:

- **Frame Control:** Indicates the type of frame (control, management, or data) and provides control information. Control information includes whether the frame is to or from a DS, fragmentation information, and privacy information.

- **Duration/Connection ID:** If used as a duration field, indicates the time (in microseconds) the channel will be allocated for successful transmission of a MAC frame. In some control frames, this field contains an association, or connection, identifier.

- **Addresses:** The number and meaning of the 48-bit address fields depend on context. The **transmitter address** and **receiver address** are the MAC addresses of stations joined to the BSS that are transmitting and receiving frames over the wireless LAN. The **service set ID (SSID)** identifies the wireless LAN over which a frame is transmitted. For an IBSS, the SSID is a random number generated at the time the network is formed. For a wireless LAN that is part of a larger con-figuration, the SSID identifies the BSS over which the frame is transmitted; specifically, the SSID is the MAC-level address of the AP for this BSS (Figure 17.4). Finally the **source address** and **destination address** are the MAC addresses of stations, wireless or otherwise, that are the ultimate source and des-tination of this frame. The source address may be identical to the transmitter address and the destination address may be identical to the receiver address.

- **Sequence Control:** Contains a 4-bit fragment number subfield, used for fragmentation and reassembly, and a 12-bit sequence number used to number frames sent between a given transmitter and receiver.

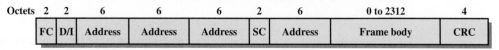

FC = frame control
D/I = duration/connection ID
SC = sequence control

Figure 17.8   IEEE 802.11 MAC Frame Format

- **Frame Body:** Contains an MSDU or a fragment of an MSDU. The MSDU is a LLC PDU or MAC control information.
- **Frame Check Sequence:** A 32-bit cyclic redundancy check.

We now look at the three MAC frame types.

CONTROL FRAMES Control frames assist in the reliable delivery of data frames. There are six control frame subtypes:

- **Power Save-Poll (PS-Poll):** This frame is sent by any station to the station that includes the AP (access point). Its purpose is to request that the AP transmit a frame that has been buffered for this station while the station was in power-saving mode.
- **Request to Send (RTS):** This is the first frame in the four-way frame exchange discussed under the subsection on reliable data delivery at the beginning of Section 17.3. The station sending this message is alerting a potential destination, and all other stations within reception range, that it intends to send a data frame to that destination.
- **Clear to Send (CTS):** This is the second frame in the four-way exchange. It is sent by the destination station to the source station to grant permission to send a data frame.
- **Acknowledgment:** Provides an acknowledgment from the destination to the source that the immediately preceding data, management, or PS-Poll frame was received correctly.
- **Contention-Free (CF)-end:** Announces the end of a contention-free period that is part of the point coordination function.
- **CF-End + CF-Ack:** Acknowledges the CF-end. This frame ends the contention-free period and releases stations from the restrictions associated with that period.

DATA FRAMES There are eight data frame subtypes, organized into two groups. The first four subtypes define frames that carry upper-level data from the source station to the destination station. The four data-carrying frames are as follows:

- **Data:** This is the simplest data frame. It may be used in both a contention period and a contention-free period.
- **Data + CF-Ack:** May only be sent during a contention-free period. In addition to carrying data, this frame acknowledges previously received data.
- **Data + CF-Poll:** Used by a point coordinator to deliver data to a mobile station and also to request that the mobile station send a data frame that it may have buffered.
- **Data + CF-Ack + CF-Poll:** Combines the functions of the Data + CF-Ack and Data + CF-Poll into a single frame.

The remaining four subtypes of data frames do not in fact carry any user data. The Null Function data frame carries no data, polls, or acknowledgments. It is used only to carry the power management bit in the frame control field to the AP, to indicate that the station is changing to a low-power operating state. The remaining three frames (CF-Ack, CF-Poll, CF-Ack + CF-Poll + have the same functionality as the corresponding data frame subtypes in the preceding list (Data + CF-Ack, Data + CF-Poll, Data + CF-Ack + CF-Poll) but without the data.

MANAGEMENT FRAMES Management frames are used to manage communications between stations and APs. Functions covered include management of associations (request, response, reassociation, dissociation, and authentication).

17.5 IEEE 802.11 PHYSICAL LAYER

The physical layer for IEEE 802.11 has been issued in five stages. The first part, simply called **IEEE 802.11**, includes the MAC layer and three physical-layer specifications, two in the 2.4-GHz band (ISM) and one in the infrared, all operating at 1 and 2 Mbps. **IEEE 802.11a** operates in the 5-GHz band at data rates up to 54 Mbps. **IEEE 802.11b** operates in the 2.4-GHz band at 5.5 and 11 Mbps. **IEEE 802.11g** also operates in the 2.4-GHz band, at data rates up to 54 Mbps. Finally, **IEEE 802.11n** operates in either the 2.4-GHz band or the 5-GHz band with data rates in the hundreds of Gbps. Table 17.4 provides some details. We look at each of these in turn.

Original IEEE 802.11 Physical Layer

Three physical media are defined in the original 802.11 standard:

- **Direct sequence spread spectrum (DSSS)** operating in the 2.4-GHz ISM band, at data rates of 1 Mbps and 2 Mbps. In the United States, the FCC (Federal Communications Commission) requires no licensing for the use of this band. The number of channels available depends on the bandwidth allocated by the various national regulatory agencies. This ranges from 13 in most European countries to just one available channel in Japan.

Table 17.4   IEEE 802.11 Physical Layer Standards

	802.11a	802.11b	802.11g	802.11n
Peak Data Throughput*	23 Mbps	6 Mbps	23 Mbps	60 Mbps (20-MHz channel)
				90 Mbps (40-MHz channel)
Peak Signaling Rate	54 Mbps	11 Mbps	54 Mbps	124 Mbps (20-MHz channel)
				248 Mbps (40-MHz channel)
RF Band	5 GHz	2.4 GHz	2.4 GHz	2.4 GHz or 5 GHz
Channel Width	20 MHz	20 MHz	20 Mhz	20 MHz or 40 MHz
Number of Spatial Streams	1	1	1	1, 2, 3, or 4

* This is the actual data throughput you get with real equipment under ideal conditions. Real world performance is lower than this due to noise. This is also shared capacity among wireless clients. When two devices use the same access point, the capacity is typically divided in two, though it's possible some clients will use more of the capacity than others. Source: [OU07].

- **Frequency-hopping spread spectrum (FHSS)** operating in the 2.4-GHz ISM band, at data rates of 1 Mbps and 2 Mbps. The number of channels available ranges from 23 in Japan to 70 in the United States.
- **Infrared** at 1 Mbps and 2 Mbps operating at a wavelength between 850 and 950 nm

DIRECT SEQUENCE SPREAD SPECTRUM Up to three nonoverlapping channels, each with a data rate of 1 Mbps or 2 Mbps, can be used in the DSSS scheme. Each channel has a bandwidth of 5 MHz. The encoding scheme that is used is DBPSK (differential binary phase shift keying) for the 1-Mbps rate and DQPSK (differential quadrature phase shift keying) for the 2-Mbps rate.

Recall from Chapter 9 that a DSSS system makes use of a chipping code, or pseudonoise sequence, to spread the data rate and hence the bandwidth of the signal. For IEEE 802.11, a Barker sequence is used.

A **Barker sequence** is a binary $\{-1, +1\}$ sequence $\{s(t)\}$ of length n with the property that its autocorrelation values $R(\tau)$ satisfy $|R(\tau)| \leq 1$ for all $|\tau| \leq (n-1)$.

Autocorrelation is defined by the following formula: $R(\tau) = \dfrac{1}{N}\sum_{k=1}^{N} B_k B_{k-\tau}$, where the B_k are the bits of the sequence.[1]

Further, the Barker property is preserved under the following transformations:

$$s(t) \rightarrow -s(t) \qquad s(t) \rightarrow (-1)^t s(t) \quad and) \quad s(t) \rightarrow -s(n-1-t)$$

as well as under compositions of these transformations. Only the following Barker sequences are known:

$n = 2$	+ +
$n = 3$	+ + −
$n = 4$	+ + + −
$n = 5$	+ + + − +
$n = 7$	+ + + − − + −
$n = 11$	+ − + + − + + + − − −
$n = 13$	+ + + + + − − + + − + − +

IEEE 802.11 DSSS uses the 11-chip Barker sequence. Each data binary 1 is mapped into the sequence { + − + + − + + + − − − }, and each binary 0 is mapped into the sequence { − + − − + − − − + + + }.

Important characteristics of Barker sequences are their robustness against interference and their insensitivity to multipath propagation.

FREQUENCY-HOPPING SPREAD SPECTRUM Recall from Chapter 9 that a FHSS system makes use of a multiple channels, with the signal hopping from one channel to

---

[1]See Appendix N for a discussion of correlation and orthogonality.

another based on a pseudonoise sequence. In the case of the IEEE 802.11 scheme, 1-MHz channels are used.

The details of the hopping scheme are adjustable. For example, the minimum hop rate for the United States is 2.5 hops per second. The minimum hop distance in frequency is 6 MHz in North America and most of Europe and 5 MHz in Japan.

For modulation, the FHSS scheme uses two-level Gaussian FSK for the 1-Mbps system. The bits zero and one are encoded as deviations from the current carrier frequency. For 2 Mbps, a four-level GFSK scheme is used, in which four different deviations from the center frequency define the four 2-bit combinations.

INFRARED The IEEE 802.11 infrared scheme is omnidirectional rather than point to point. A range of up to 20 m is possible. The modulation scheme for the 1-Mbps data rate is known as 16-PPM (pulse position modulation). In PPM, the input value determines the position of a narrow pulse relative to the clocking time. The advantage of PPM is that it reduces the output power required of the infrared source. For 16-PPM, each group of 4 data bits is mapped into one of the 16-PPM symbols; each symbol is a string of 16 pulse positions. Each 16-pulse string consists of fifteen pulse positions with no pulse and one pulse. For the 2-Mbps data rate, each group of 2 data bits is mapped into one of four 4-pulse-position sequences. Each sequence consists of three 0s and one binary 1. The actual transmission uses an intensity modulation scheme, in which the presence of a signal corresponds to a binary 1 and the absence of a signal corresponds to binary 0.

IEEE 802.11b

IEEE 802.11b is an extension of the IEEE 802.11 DSSS scheme, providing data rates of 5.5 and 11 Mbps in the ISM band. The chipping rate is 11 MHz, which is the same as the original DSSS scheme, thus providing the same occupied bandwidth. To achieve a higher data rate in the same bandwidth at the same chipping rate, a modulation scheme known as complementary code keying (CCK) is used.

The CCK modulation scheme is quite complex and is not examined in detail here. Figure 17.9 provides an overview of the scheme for the 11-Mbps rate. Input data are treated in blocks of 8 bits at a rate of 1.375 MHz (8bits/symbol $\times$ 1.375MHz = 11Mbps). Six of these bits are mapped into one of 64 codes sequences derived from a 64×64 matrix known as the Walsh matrix

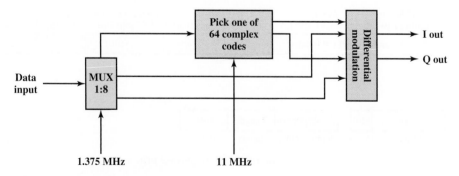

Figure 17.9 11-Mbps CCK Modulation Scheme

(discussed in [STAL05]). The output of the mapping, plus the two additional bits, forms the input to a QPSK modulator.

An optional alternative to CCK is known as packet binary convolutional coding (PBCC). PBCC provides for potentially more efficient transmission at the cost of increased computation at the receiver. PBCC was incorporated into 802.11b in anticipation of its need for higher data rates for future enhancements to the standard.

PHYSICAL-LAYER FRAME STRUCTURE IEEE 802.11b defines two physical-layer frame formats, which differ only in the length of the preamble. The long preamble of 144 bits is the same as used in the original 802.11 DSSS scheme and allows interoperability with other legacy systems. The short preamble of 72 bits provides improved throughput efficiency. Figure 17.10b illustrates the physical-layer frame format with the short preamble. The **PLCP (physical layer conversion protocol) Preamble** field enables the receiver to acquire an incoming signal and synchronize the demodulator. It consists of two subfields: a 56-bit **Sync** field for synchronization and a 16-bit start-of-frame delimiter (**SFD**). The preamble is transmitted at 1 Mbps using differential BPSK and Barker code spreading.

Following the preamble is the **PLCP Header**, which is transmitted at 2 Mbps using DQPSK. It consists of the following subfields:

- **Signal:** Specifies the data rate at which the MPDU portion of the frame is transmitted.

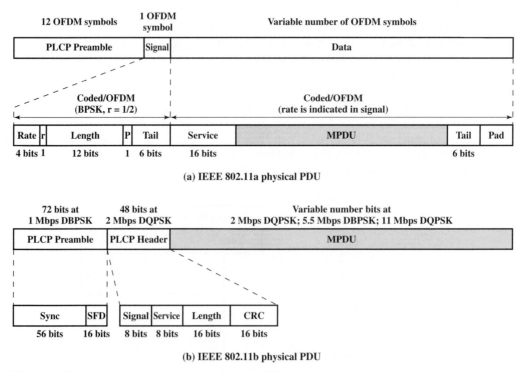

(a) IEEE 802.11a physical PDU

(b) IEEE 802.11b physical PDU

Figure 17.10   IEEE 802.11 Physical-Level Protocol Data Units

- **Service:** Only 3 bits of this 8-bit field are used in 802.11b. One bit indicates whether the transmit frequency and symbol clocks use the same local oscillator. Another bit indicates whether CCK or PBCC encoding is used. A third bit acts as an extension to the Length subfield.

- **Length:** Indicates the length of the MPDU field by specifying the number of microseconds necessary to transmit the MPDU. Given the data rate, the length of the MPDU in octets can be calculated. For any data rate over 8 Mbps, the length extension bit from the Service field is needed to resolve a rounding ambiguity.

- **CRC:** A 16-bit error-detection code used to protect the Signal, Service, and Length fields.

The **MPDU** field consists of a variable number of bits transmitted at the data rate specified in the Signal subfield. Prior to transmission, all of the bits of the physical-layer PDU are scrambled (see Appendix 16B for a discussion of scrambling).

IEEE 802.11a

Although 802.11b achieved a certain level of success, its limited data rate results in limited appeal. To meet the needs for a truly high-speed wireless LAN, **IEEE 802.11a** was developed.

CHANNEL STRUCTURE IEEE 802.11a makes use of the frequency band called the Universal Networking Information Infrastructure (UNNI), which is divided into three parts. The UNNI-1 band (5.15–5.25 GHz) is intended for indoor use; the UNNI-2 band (5.25–5.35 GHz) can be used either indoor or outdoor; and the UNNI-3 band (5.725–5.825 GHz) is for outdoor use.

IEEE 802.11a has several advantages over IEEE 802.11b/g:

- IEEE 802.11a utilizes more available bandwidth than 802.11b/g. Each UNNI band provides four nonoverlapping channels for a total of 12 across the allocated spectrum.

- IEEE 802.11a provides much higher data rates than 802.11b and the same maximum data rate as 802.11g.

- IEEE 802.11a uses a different, relatively uncluttered frequency spectrum (5 GHz).

CODING AND MODULATION Unlike the 2.4-GHz specifications, IEEE 802.11a does not use a spread spectrum scheme but rather uses OFDM (orthogonal frequency division multiplexing). Recall from Section 14.5 that OFDM, also called multicarrier modulation, uses multiple carrier signals at different frequencies, sending some of the bits on each channel. This is similar to FDM. However, in the case of OFDM, all of the subchannels are dedicated to a single data source.

To complement OFDM, the specification supports the use of a variety of modulation and coding alternatives. The system uses up to 48 subcarriers that are modulated using BPSK, QPSK, 16-QAM, or 64-QAM. Subcarrier frequency spacing is 0.3125 MHz, and each subcarrier transmits at a rate of 250 kbaud. A convolutional code at a rate of 1/2, 2/3, or 3/4 provides forward error correction. The combination of modulation technique and coding rate determines the data rate.

PHYSICAL-LAYER FRAME STRUCTURE The primary purpose of the physical layer is to transmit MAC protocol data units (MPDUs) as directed by the 802.11 MAC layer. The PLCP sublayer provides the framing and signaling bits needed for the OFDM transmission and the PMD sublayer performs the actual encoding and transmission operation.

Figure 17.10a illustrates the physical-layer frame format. The **PLCP Preamble** field enables the receiver to acquire an incoming OFDM signal and synchronize the demodulator. Next is the **Signal** field, which consists of 24 bits encoded as a single OFDM symbol. The Preamble and Signal fields are transmitted at 6 Mbps using BPSK. The signal field consists of the following subfields:

- **Rate:** Specifies the data rate at which the data field portion of the frame is transmitted
- **r:** reserved for future use
- **Length:** Number of octets in the MAC PDU
- **P:** An even parity bit for the 17 bits in the Rate, r, and Length subfields
- **Tail:** Consists of 6 zero bits appended to the symbol to bring the convolutional encoder to zero state

The **Data** field consists of a variable number of OFDM symbols transmitted at the data rate specified in the Rate subfield. Prior to transmission, all of the bits of the Data field are scrambled (see Appendix 16B for a discussion of scrambling). The Data field consists of four subfields:

- **Service:** Consists of 16 bits, with the first 7 bits set to zeros to synchronize the descrambler in the receiver and the remaining 9 bits (all zeros) reserved for future use.
- **MAC PDU:** Handed down from the MAC layer. The format is shown in Figure 17.8.
- **Tail:** Produced by replacing the six scrambled bits following the MPDU end with 6 bits of all zeros; used to reinitialize the convolutional encoder.
- **Pad:** The number of bits required to make the Data field a multiple of the number of bits in an OFDM symbol (48, 96, 192, or 288).

IEEE 802.11g

IEEE 802.11g extends 802.11b to data rates above 20 Mbps, up to 54 Mbps. Like 802.11b, 802.11g operates in the 2.4-GHz range and thus the two are compatible. The standard is designed so that 802.11b devices will work when connected to an 802.11g AP, and 802.11g devices will work when connected to an 802.11b AP, in both cases using the lower 802.11b data rate.

IEEE 802.11g offers a wide array of data rate and modulation scheme options. IEEE 802.11g provides compatibility with 802.11 and 802.11b by specifying the same modulation and framing schemes as these standards for 1, 2, 5.5, and 11 Mbps. At data rates of 6, 9, 12, 18, 24, 36, 48, and 54 Mbps, 802.11g adopts the 802.11a OFDM scheme, adapted for the 2.4-GHz rate; this is referred to as ERP-OFDM, with ERP standing for extended rate physical layer. In addition, an ERP-PBCC scheme is used to provide data rates of 22 and 33 Mbps.

The IEEE 802.11 standards do not include a specification of speed versus distance objectives. Different vendors will give different values, depending on environment. Table 17.5, based on [LAYL04], gives estimated values for a typical office environment.

IEEE 802.11n

With increasing demands being placed on wireless LANs, the 802.11 committee looked for ways to increase the data throughput and overall capacity of 802.11 networks. The goal of this effort is to not just increase the bit rate of the transmitting antennas but to increase the effective throughput of the network. Increasing effective throughput involves looking not only at the signal encoding scheme, but also at the antenna architecture and the MAC frame structure. The result of these efforts is a package of improvements and enhancements embodied in IEEE 802.11n. This standard is defined to operate in both the 2.4-GHz and the 5-GHz bands and can therefore be made upwardly compatible with either 802.11a or 802.11b/g.

IEEE 802.11n embodies changes in three general areas: use of MIMO, enhancements in radio transmission, and MAC enhancements. We briefly examine each of these.

Multiple-input-multiple-output (MIMO) antenna architecture is the most important of the enhancements provided by 802.11n. A discussion of MIMO is beyond our scope, so we content ourselves with a brief overview (see Figure 17.11). In a MIMO scheme, the transmitter employs multiple antennas. The source data stream is divided into n substreams, one for each of the n transmitting antennas. The individual substreams are the input to the transmitting antennas (multiple input). At the receiving end, m antennas receive the transmissions from the n source antennas via a combination of line-of-sight transmission and multipath. The outputs from the m receiving antennas (multiple output) are combined with the signals from the other receive radios. With a lot of complex math, the result is a much better receive signal than can be achieved with either a single antenna or multiple frequency channels. 802.11n defines a number of different combinations for the number of

Table 17.5 Estimated Distance (m) Versus Data Rate

Data Rate (Mbps)	802.11b	802.11a	802.11g
1	90+	—	90+
2	75	—	75
5.5(b)/6(a/g)	60	60+	65
9	—	50	55
11(b)/12(a/g)	50	45	50
18	—	40	50
24	—	30	45
36	—	25	35
48	—	15	25
54	—	10	20

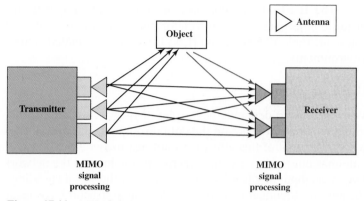

Figure 17.11 MIMO Scheme

transmitters and the number of receivers, from 2×1 to 4×4. Each additional transmitter or receiver in the system increases the SNR (signal-to-noise ratio). However, the incremental gains from each additional transmitter or receiver diminish rapidly. The gain in SNR is large for each step from 2×1 to 2×2 and to 3×2, but the improvement with 3×3 and beyond is relatively small [CISC07].

In addition to MIMO, 802.11n makes a number of changes in the **radio transmission scheme** to increase capacity. The most significant of these techniques, known as channel bonding, combines two 20-MHz channels to create a 40-MHz channel. Using OFDM, this allows for twice as many subchannels, doubling the transmission rate.

Finally, 802.11n provides some **MAC enhancements**. The most significant change is to aggregate multiple MAC frames into a single block for transmission. Once a station acquires the medium for transmission, it can transmit long packets without significant delays between transmissions. The receiver sends a single block acknowledgement. Frame aggregation can result in significantly improved efficiency in the use of the transmission capacity.

Figure 17.12 gives an indication of the effectiveness of 802.11n compared to 802.11g [DEBE07]. The chart shows the average throughput per user on a shared

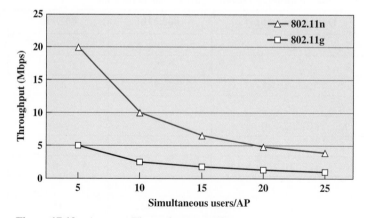

Figure 17.12 Average Throughput per User

system. As expected, the more active users competing for the wireless capacity, the smaller the average throughput per user. IEEE 802.11n provides a significant improvement, especially for networks in which a small number of users are actively competing for transmission time.

17.6 IEEE 802.11 SECURITY CONSIDERATIONS

There are two characteristics of a wired LAN that are not inherent in a wireless LAN.

1. In order to transmit over a wired LAN, a station must be physically connected to the LAN. On the other hand, with a wireless LAN, any station within radio range of the other devices on the LAN can transmit. In a sense, there is a form of authentication with a wired LAN, in that it requires some positive and presumably observable action to connect a station to a wired LAN.

2. Similarly, in order to receive a transmission from a station that is part of a wired LAN, the receiving station must also be attached to the wired LAN. On the other hand, with a wireless LAN, any station within radio range can receive. Thus, a wired LAN provides a degree of privacy, limiting reception of data to stations connected to the LAN.

Access and Privacy Services

IEEE 802.11 defines three services that provide a wireless LAN with these two features:

- **Authentication:** Used to establish the identity of stations to each other. In a wired LAN, it is generally assumed that access to a physical connection conveys authority to connect to the LAN. This is not a valid assumption for a wireless LAN, in which connectivity is achieved simply by having an attached antenna that is properly tuned. The authentication service is used by stations to establish their identity with stations they wish to communicate with. IEEE 802.11 supports several authentication schemes and allows for expansion of the functionality of these schemes. The standard does not mandate any particular authentication scheme, which could range from relatively unsecure handshaking to public-key encryption schemes. However, IEEE 802.11 requires mutually acceptable, successful authentication before a station can establish an association with an AP.

- **Deauthentication:** This service is invoked whenever an existing authentication is to be terminated.

- **Privacy:** Used to prevent the contents of messages from being read by other than the intended recipient. The standard provides for the optional use of encryption to assure privacy.

Wireless LAN Security Standards

The original 802.11 specification included a set of security features for privacy and authentication that, unfortunately, were quite weak. For **privacy**, 802.11 defined the Wired Equivalent Privacy (WEP) algorithm. The privacy portion of the 802.11

standard contained major weaknesses. Subsequent to the development of WEP, the 802.11i task group has developed a set of capabilities to address the WLAN security issues. In order to accelerate the introduction of strong security into WLANs, the Wi-Fi Alliance promulgated **Wi-Fi Protected Access (WPA)** as a Wi-Fi standard. WPA is a set of security mechanisms that eliminates most 802.11 security issues and was based on the current state of the 802.11i standard. As 802.11i evolves, WPA will evolve to maintain compatibility.

WPA is examined in Chapter 24.

17.7 RECOMMENDED READING AND WEB SITES

A brief but useful survey of 802.11 is [MCFA03]. [GEIE01] has a good discussion of IEEE 802.11a. [PETR00] summarizes IEEE 802.11b. [SHOE02] provides an overview of IEEE 802.11g. [XIAO04] discusses 802.11e. [CISC07] is a detailed treatment of IEEE 802.11n. [SKOR08] is a thorough examination of the 802.11n MAC frame aggregation scheme. [HALP10] examines the 802.11n MIMO scheme.

CISC07 Cisco Systems, Inc. "802.11n: The Next Generation of Wireless Performance." Cisco White Paper, 2007, cisco.com

GEIE01 Geier, J. "Enabling Fast Wireless Networks with OFDM." *Communications System Design*, www.csdmag.com, February 2001.

HALP10 Halperin, D., et al. "802.11 with Multiple Antennas for Dummies." *Computer Communication Review*, January 2010.

MCFA03 McFarland, B., and Wong, M. "The Family Dynamics of 802.11." *ACM Queue*, May 2003.

PETR00 Petrick, A. "IEEE 802.11b—Wireless Ethernet." *Communications System Design*, June 2000, www.commsdesign.com

SHOE02 Shoemake, M. "IEEE 802.11g Jells as Applications Mount." *Communications System Design*, April 2002, www.commsdesign.com.

SKOR08 Skordoulis, D., et al. "IEEE 802.11n MAC Frame Aggregation Mechanisms for Next-Generation High-Throughput WLANs." *IEEE Wireless Communications*, February 2008.

XIAO04 Xiao, Y. "IEEE 802.11e: QoS Provisioning at the MAC Layer." *IEEE Communications Magazine*, June 2004.

Recommended Web sites:

- **The IEEE 802.11 Wireless LAN working group:** Contains working-group documents plus discussion archives.
- **Wi-Fi Alliance:** An industry group promoting the interoperability of 802.11 products with each other and with Ethernet.

17.8 KEY TERMS, REVIEW QUESTIONS, AND PROBLEMS

Key Terms

access point (AP) ad hoc networking Barker sequence basic service set (BSS) complementary code keying (CCK) coordination function	distributed coordination function (DCF) distribution system (DS) extended service set (ESS) infrared LAN LAN extension	narrowband microwave LAN nomadic access point coordination function (PCF) spread spectrum LAN wireless LAN

Review Questions

17.1 List and briefly define four application areas for wireless LANs.

17.2 List and briefly define key requirements for wireless LANs.

17.3 What is the difference between a single-cell and a multiple-cell wireless LAN?

17.4 What is the difference between an access point and a portal?

17.5 Is a distribution system a wireless network?

17.6 List and briefly define IEEE 802.11 services.

17.7 How is the concept of an association related to that of mobility?

Problems

17.1 Consider the sequence of actions within a BSS depicted in Figure 17.13. Draw a time-line, beginning with a period during which the medium is busy and ending with a period in which the CF-End is broadcast from the AP. Show the transmission periods and the gaps.

17.2 Find the autocorrelation for the 11-bit Barker sequence as a function of τ.

17.3 **a.** For the 16-PPM scheme used for the 1-Mbps IEEE 802.11 infrared standard,

      a1. What is the period of transmission (time between bits)?
            For the corresponding infrared pulse transmission,
      a2. What is the average time between pulses (1 values) and the corresponding average rate of pulse transmission?
      a3. What is the minimum time between adjacent pulses?
      a4. What is the maximum time between pulses?

    b. Repeat (a) for the 4-PPM scheme used for the 2-Mbps infrared standard.

17.4 For IEEE 802.11a, show how the modulation technique and coding rate determine the data rate.

17.5 The 802.11a and 802.11b physical layers make use of data scrambling (see Appendix 16B). For 802.11, the scrambling equation is

$$P(X) = 1 + X^4 + X^7$$

In this case the shift register consists of seven elements, used in the same manner as the five-element register in Figure 16.17. For the 802.11 scrambler and descrambler,

    a. Show the expression with exclusive-or operators that corresponds to the polynomial definition.

    b. Draw a figure similar to Figure 16.17.

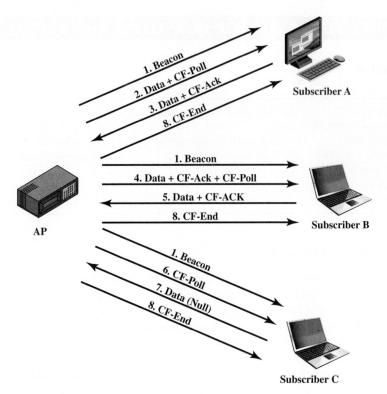

Figure 17.13 Configuration for Problem 17.1

17.6 Answer the following questions about your wireless network:
  a. What is the SSID?
  b. Who is the equipment vendor?
  c. What standard are you using?
  d. What is the size of the network?

17.7 Using what you know about wired and wireless networks, draw the topology of your network.

17.8 There are many free tools and applications available for helping decipher wireless networks. One of the most popular is Netstumbler. Obtain the software at www.netstumbler.com and follow the links for downloads. The site has a list of supported wireless cards. Using the Netstumbler software, determine the following:
  a. How many access points in your network have the same SSID?
  b. What is your signal strength to your access point?
  c. How many other wireless networks and access points can you find?

17.9 Most wireless cards come with a small set of applications that can perform tasks similar to Netstumbler. Using your own client software, determine the same items you did with Netstumbler. Do they agree?

17.10 Try this experiment: How far can you go and still be connected to your network? This will depend to a large extent on your physical environment.

17.11 Compare and contrast wired and wireless LANs. What unique concerns must be addressed by the designer of a wireless LAN network?

17.12 Two documents related to safety concerns associated with wireless media are the FCC OET-65 Bulletin and the ANSI/IEEE C95.1-1999. Briefly describe the purpose of these documents and briefly outline the safety concerns associated with wireless LAN technology.

INTERNET PROTOCOLS

She occupied herself with studying a map on the opposite wall because she knew she would have to change trains at some point. Tottenham Court Road must be that point, an interchange from the black line to the red. This train would take her there, was bearing her there rapidly now, and at the station she would follow the signs, for signs there must be, to the Central Line going westward.

—*King Solomon's Carpet,* Barbara Vine (Ruth Rendell)

KEY POINTS

◆ An internet consists of multiple separate networks that are interconnected by routers. Data are transmitted in packets from a source system to a destination across a path involving multiple networks and routers. Typically, a connectionless or datagram operation is used. A router accepts datagrams and relays them on toward their destination and is responsible for determining the route, much the same way as packet-switching nodes operate.

◆ The most widely used protocol for internetworking is the **Internet Protocol (IP)**. IP attaches a header to upper-layer (e.g., TCP) data to form an IP datagram.

◆ A next-generation IP, known as IPv6, has been defined. IPv6 provides longer address fields and more functionality than the current IP.

The purpose of this chapter is to examine the Internet Protocol, which is the foundation on which all of the internet-based protocols and internetworking are based. First, it will be useful to provide a general discussion of internetworking. Next, the chapter focuses on the two standard internet protocols: IPv4 and IPv6. Finally, the topic of IP security is introduced.

Refer to Figure 2.8 to see the position within the TCP/IP suite of the protocols discussed in this chapter.

18.1 PRINCIPLES OF INTERNETWORKING

Packet-switching and packet-broadcasting networks grew out of a need to allow the computer user to have access to resources beyond that available in a single system. In a similar fashion, the resources of a single network are often inadequate to meet users' needs. Because the networks that might be of interest exhibit so many differences, it is impractical to consider merging them into a single network. Rather, what is needed is the ability to interconnect various networks so that any two stations on any of the constituent networks can communicate.

Table 18.1 lists some commonly used terms relating to the interconnection of networks, or internetworking. An interconnected set of networks, from a user's point of view, may appear simply as a larger network. However, if each of the

Table 18.1 Internetworking Terms

Communication Network
A facility that provides a data transfer service among devices attached to the network.

Internet
A collection of communication networks interconnected by bridges and/or routers.

Intranet
An internet used by a single organization that provides the key Internet applications, especially the World Wide Web. An intranet operates within the organization for internal purposes and can exist as an isolated, self-contained internet, or may have links to the Internet.

Subnetwork
Refers to a constituent network of an internet. This avoids ambiguity because the entire internet, from a user's point of view, is a single network.

End System (ES)
A device attached to one of the networks of an internet that is used to support end-user applications or services.

Intermediate System (IS)
A device used to connect two networks and permit communication between end systems attached to different networks.

Bridge
An IS used to connect two LANs that use similar LAN protocols. The bridge acts as an address filter, picking up packets from one LAN that are intended for a destination on another LAN and passing those packets on. The bridge does not modify the contents of the packets and does not add anything to the packet. The bridge operates at layer 2 of the OSI model.

Router
An IS used to connect two networks that may or may not be similar. The router employs an internet protocol present in each router and each end system of the network. The router operates at layer 3 of the OSI model.

constituent networks retains its identity and special mechanisms are needed for communicating across multiple networks, then the entire configuration is often referred to as an **internet**.

Each constituent network in an internet supports communication among the devices attached to that network; these devices are referred to as **end systems (ESs)**. In addition, networks are connected by devices referred to in the ISO documents as **intermediate systems (ISs)**. Intermediate systems provide a communications path and perform the necessary relaying and routing functions so that data can be exchanged between devices attached to different networks in the internet.

Two types of ISs of particular interest are bridges and routers. The differences between them have to do with the types of protocols used for the internetworking logic. In essence, a **bridge** operates at layer 2 of the open systems interconnection (OSI) seven-layer architecture and acts as a relay of frames between similar networks; bridges are discussed in Chapter 15. A **router** operates at layer 3 of the OSI architecture and routes packets between potentially different networks. Both the bridge and the router assume that the same upper-layer protocols are in use.

We begin our examination of internetworking with a discussion of the basic principles of internetworking. We then examine the most important architectural approach to internetworking: the connectionless router.

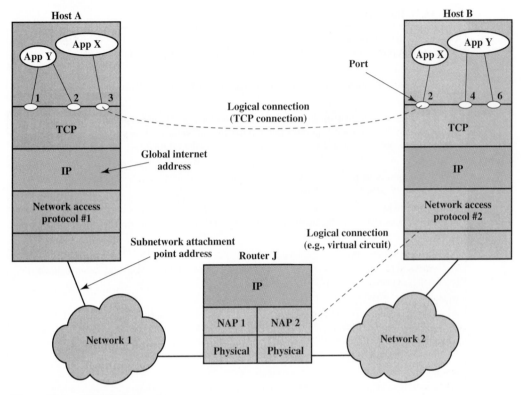

Figure 18.1   TCP/IP Concepts

Requirements

The overall requirements for an internetworking facility are as follows (we refer to Figure 18.1, which repeats Figure 2.4, as an example throughout):

1. **Provide a link between networks.** At minimum, a physical and link control connection is needed. (Router J has physical links to N1 and N2, and on each link there is a data link protocol.)

2. **Provide for the routing and delivery of data between processes on different networks.** (Application X on host A exchanges data with application X on host B.)

3. **Provide an accounting service** that keeps track of the use of the various networks and routers and maintains status information.

4. **Provide the services just listed in such a way** as not to require modifications to the networking architecture of any of the constituent networks. This means that the internetworking facility must accommodate a number of differences among networks. These include:

   - **Different addressing schemes:** The networks may use different endpoint names and addresses and directory maintenance schemes. Some form of global network addressing must be provided, as well as a directory service. (Hosts A and B and router J have globally unique IP addresses.)

- **Different maximum packet size:** Packets from one network may have to be broken up into smaller pieces for another. This process is referred to as fragmentation. (N1 and N2 may set different upper limits on packet sizes.)
- **Different network access mechanisms:** The network access mechanism between station and network may be different for stations on different networks. (e.g., N1 may be a frame relay network and N2 an Ethernet network.)
- **Different timeouts:** Typically, a connection-oriented transport service will await an acknowledgment until a timeout expires, at which time it will retransmit its block of data. In general, longer times are required for successful delivery across multiple networks. Internetwork timing procedures must allow successful transmission that avoids unnecessary retransmissions.
- **Error recovery:** Network procedures may provide anything from no error recovery up to reliable end-to-end (within the network) service. The internetwork service should not depend on nor be interfered with by the nature of the individual network's error recovery capability.
- **Status reporting:** Different networks report status and performance differently. Yet it must be possible for the internetworking facility to provide such information on internetworking activity to interested and authorized processes.
- **Routing techniques:** Intranetwork routing may depend on fault detection and congestion control techniques peculiar to each network. The internetworking facility must be able to coordinate these to route data adaptively between stations on different networks.
- **User access control:** Each network will have its own user access control technique (authorization for use of the network). These must be invoked by the internetwork facility as needed. Further, a separate internetwork access control technique may be required.
- **Connection, connectionless:** Individual networks may provide connection-oriented (e.g., virtual circuit) or connectionless (datagram) service. It may be desirable for the internetwork service not to depend on the nature of the connection service of the individual networks.

The Internet Protocol meets some of these requirements. Others require additional control and application software, as we shall see in this chapter and the next.

Connectionless Operation

In virtually all implementation, internetworking involves connectionless operation at the level of the Internet Protocol. Whereas connection-oriented operation corresponds to the virtual circuit mechanism of a packet-switching network (Figure 10.10), connectionless-mode operation corresponds to the datagram mechanism of a packet-switching network (Figure 10.9). Each network protocol data unit is treated independently and routed from source ES to destination ES through a series of routers and networks. For each data unit transmitted by A, A makes a decision as to which router should receive the data unit. The data unit hops across the internet from one router to the next until it reaches the destination network. At each router, a routing decision is made (independently for each data unit) concerning the next hop. Thus, different data units may travel different routes between source and destination ES.

All ESs and routers share a common network-layer protocol known generically as the Internet Protocol. An Internet Protocol was initially developed for the DARPA internet project and published as RFC 791 and has become an Internet Standard. Below this Internet Protocol, a protocol is needed to access a particular network. Thus, there are typically two protocols operating in each ES and router at the network layer: an upper sublayer that provides the internetworking function and a lower sublayer that provides network access. Figure 18.2 shows an example. We discuss this example in detail in the next section.

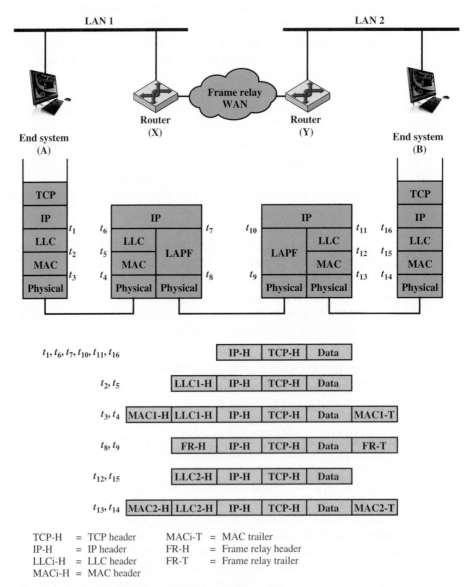

TCP-H   = TCP header   MACi-T = MAC trailer
IP-H   = IP header   FR-H   = Frame relay header
LLCi-H = LLC header   FR-T   = Frame relay trailer
MACi-H = MAC header

Figure 18.2 Example of Internet Protocol Operation

18.2 INTERNET PROTOCOL OPERATION

In this section, we examine the essential functions of an internetwork protocol. For convenience, we refer specifically to the Internet Standard IPv4, but the narrative in this section applies to any connectionless Internet Protocol, such as IPv6.

Operation of a Connectionless Internetworking Scheme

IP provides a connectionless, or datagram, service between end systems. There are a number of advantages to this approach:

- A connectionless internet facility is flexible. It can deal with a variety of networks, some of which are themselves connectionless. In essence, IP requires very little from the constituent networks.

- A connectionless internet service can be made highly robust. This is basically the same argument made for a datagram network service versus a virtual circuit service. For a further discussion, see Section 10.5.

- A connectionless internet service is best for connectionless transport protocols, because it does not impose unnecessary overhead.

Figure 18.2 depicts a typical example using IP, in which two LANs are interconnected by a frame relay WAN. The figure depicts the operation of the Internet Protocol for data exchange between host A on one LAN (network 1) and host B on another LAN (network 2) through the WAN. The figure shows the protocol architecture and format of the data unit at each stage. The end systems and routers must all share a common Internet Protocol. In addition, the end systems must share the same protocols above IP. The intermediate routers need only implement up through IP.

The IP at A receives blocks of data to be sent to B from a higher layer of software in A (e.g., TCP or UDP). IP attaches a header (at time t_1) specifying, among other things, the global internet address of B. That address is logically in two parts: network identifier and end system identifier. The combination of IP header and upper-level data is called an Internet Protocol data unit (PDU), or simply a datagram. The datagram is then encapsulated with the LAN protocol (LLC header at t_2; MAC header and trailer at t_3) and sent to the router, which strips off the LAN fields to read the IP header (t_6). The router modifies the IP header if necessary (t_7) and then encapsulates the datagram with the frame relay protocol fields (t_8) and transmits it across the WAN to another router. This router strips off the frame relay fields and recovers the datagram, which it then wraps in LAN fields appropriate to LAN 2 and sends it to B.

Let us now look at this example in more detail. End system A has a datagram to transmit to end system B; the datagram includes the internet address of B. The IP module in A recognizes that the destination (B) is on another network. So the first step is to send the data to a router, in this case router X. To do this, IP passes the datagram down to the next lower layer (in this case LLC) with instructions to send it to router X. LLC in turn passes this information down to the MAC layer, which inserts the MAC-level address of router X into the MAC header. Thus, the block of data transmitted onto LAN 1 includes data from a layer or layers above TCP, plus a TCP header, an IP header, an LLC header, and a MAC header and trailer (time t_3 in Figure 18.2).

Next, the packet travels through network 1 to router X. The router removes MAC and LLC fields and analyzes the IP header to determine the ultimate destination of the data, in this case B. The router must now make a routing decision. There are three possibilities:

1. The destination B is connected directly to one of the networks to which the router is attached. If so, the router sends the datagram directly to the destination.

2. To reach the destination, one or more additional routers must be traversed. If so, a routing decision must be made: To which router should the datagram be sent?

3. The router does not know the destination address. In this case, the router returns an error message to the source of the datagram.

In both cases 1 and 2, the IP module in the router sends the datagram down to the next lower layer with the destination network address. Please note that we are speaking here of a lower-layer address that refers to this network.

In this example, the data must pass through router Y before reaching the destination. So router X constructs a new frame by appending a frame relay (LAPF) header and trailer to the IP datagram. The frame relay header indicates a logical connection to router Y. When this frame arrives at router Y, the frame header and trailer are stripped off. The router determines that this IP data unit is destined for B, which is connected directly to a network to which this router is attached. The router therefore creates a frame with a layer-2 destination address of B and sends it out onto LAN 2. The data finally arrive at B, where the LAN and IP headers can be stripped off.

At each router, before the data can be forwarded, the router may need to fragment the datagram to accommodate a smaller maximum packet size limitation on the outgoing network. If so, the data unit is split into two or more fragments, each of which becomes an independent IP datagram. Each new data unit is wrapped in a lower-layer packet and queued for transmission. The router may also limit the length of its queue for each network to which it attaches so as to avoid having a slow network penalize a faster one. Once the queue limit is reached, additional data units are simply dropped.

The process just described continues through as many routers as it takes for the data unit to reach its destination. As with a router, the destination end system recovers the IP datagram from its network wrapping. If fragmentation has occurred, the IP module in the destination end system buffers the incoming data until the entire original data field can be reassembled. This block of data is then passed to a higher layer in the end system.[1]

This service offered by IP is an unreliable one. That is, IP does not guarantee that all data will be delivered or that the data that are delivered will arrive in the proper order. It is the responsibility of the next higher layer (e.g., TCP) to recover from any errors that occur. This approach provides for a great deal of flexibility.

With the Internet Protocol approach, each unit of data is passed from router to router in an attempt to get from source to destination. Because delivery is not guaranteed, there is no particular reliability requirement on any of the networks. Thus, the protocol will work with any combination of network types. Because the sequence of delivery is not guaranteed, successive data units can follow different

---

[1]Appendix O provides a more detailed example, showing the involvement of all protocol layers.

paths through the internet. This allows the protocol to react to both congestion and failure in the internet by changing routes.

Design Issues

With that brief sketch of the operation of an IP-controlled internet, we now examine some design issues in greater detail:

- Routing
- Datagram lifetime
- Fragmentation and reassembly
- Error control
- Flow control

As we proceed with this discussion, note the many similarities with design issues and techniques relevant to packet-switching networks. To see the reason for this, consider Figure 18.3, which compares an internet architecture with a

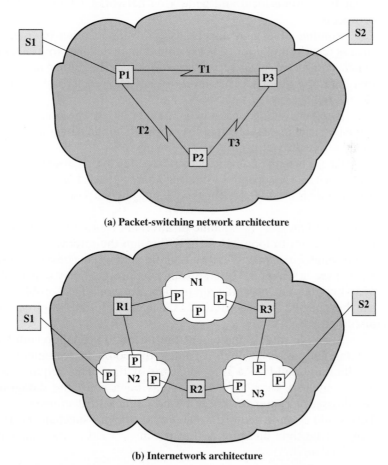

(a) Packet-switching network architecture

(b) Internetwork architecture

Figure 18.3   The Internet as a Network (based on [HIND83])

packet-switching network architecture. The routers (R1, R2, R3) in the internet correspond to the packet-switching nodes (P1, P2, P3) in the network, and the networks (N1, N2, N3) in the internet correspond to the transmission links (T1, T2, T3) in the networks. The routers perform essentially the same functions as packet-switching nodes and use the intervening networks in a manner analogous to transmission links.

ROUTING For the purpose of routing, each end system and router maintains a routing table that lists, for each possible destination network, the next router to which the internet datagram should be sent.

The routing table may be static or dynamic. A static table, however, could contain alternate routes if a particular router is unavailable. A dynamic table is more flexible in responding to both error and congestion conditions. In the Internet, for example, when a router goes down, all of its neighbors will send out a status report, allowing other routers and stations to update their routing tables. A similar scheme can be used to control congestion. Congestion control is particularly important because of the mismatch in capacity between local and wide area networks. Chapter 19 discusses routing protocols.

Routing tables may also be used to support other internetworking services, such as security and priority. For example, individual networks might be classified to handle data up to a given security classification. The routing mechanism must assure that data of a given security level are not allowed to pass through networks not cleared to handle such data.

Another routing technique is source routing. The source station specifies the route by including a sequential list of routers in the datagram. This, again, could be useful for security or priority requirements.

Finally, we mention a service related to routing: route recording. To record a route, each router appends its internet address to a list of addresses in the datagram. This feature is useful for testing and debugging purposes.

DATAGRAM LIFETIME If dynamic or alternate routing is used, the potential exists for a datagram to loop indefinitely through the internet. This is undesirable for two reasons. First, an endlessly circulating datagram consumes resources. Second, we will see in Chapter 22 that a transport protocol may depend on the existence of an upper bound on datagram lifetime. To avoid these problems, each datagram can be marked with a lifetime. Once the lifetime expires, the datagram is discarded.

A simple way to implement lifetime is to use a hop count. Each time that a datagram passes through a router, the count is decremented. Alternatively, the lifetime could be a true measure of time. This requires that the routers must somehow know how long it has been since the datagram or fragment last crossed a router, to know by how much to decrement the lifetime field. This would seem to require some global clocking mechanism. The advantage of using a true time measure is that it can be used in the reassembly algorithm, described next.

Fragmentation and Reassembly The Internet Protocol accepts a block of data from a higher-layer protocol, such as TCP or UDP, and may divide this block into multiple blocks of some smaller bounded size to form multiple IP packets. This process is called **fragmentation**.[2]

There are a number of motivations for fragmentation, depending on the context. Among the typical reasons for fragmentation are the following:

- The communications network may only accept blocks of data up to a certain size. For example, an ATM network is limited to blocks of 53 octets; Ethernet imposes a maximum size of 1526 octets.

- Error control may be more efficient with a smaller PDU size. With smaller PDUs, fewer bits need to be retransmitted when a PDU suffers an error.

- More equitable access to shared transmission facilities, with shorter delay, can be provided. For example, without a maximum block size, one station could monopolize a multipoint medium.

- A smaller PDU size may mean that receiving entities can allocate smaller buffers.

- An entity may require that data transfer comes to some sort of "closure" from time to time, for checkpoint and restart/recovery operations.

There are several disadvantages to fragmentation that argue for making PDUs as large as possible:

- Because each PDU contains a certain amount of control information, smaller blocks have a greater percentage of overhead.

- PDU arrival may generate an interrupt that must be serviced. Smaller blocks result in more interrupts.

- More time is spent processing smaller, more numerous PDUs.

If datagrams can be fragmented (perhaps more than once) in the course of their travels, the question arises as to where they should be reassembled. The easiest solution is to have reassembly performed at the destination only. The principal disadvantage of this approach is that fragments can only get smaller as data move through the internet. This may impair the efficiency of some networks. However, if intermediate router reassembly is allowed, the following disadvantages result:

1. Large buffers are required at routers, and there is the risk that all of the buffer space will be used up storing partial datagrams.

2. All fragments of a datagram must pass through the same router. This inhibits the use of dynamic routing.

---

[2]The term *segmentation* is used in OSI-related documents, but in protocol specifications related to the TCP/IP suite, the term *fragmentation* is used. The meaning is the same.

In IP, datagram fragments are reassembled at the destination end system. The IP fragmentation technique uses the following information in the IP header:

- Data Unit Identifier (ID)
- Data Length[3]
- Offset
- More Flag

The *ID* is a means of uniquely identifying an end-system-originated datagram. In IP, it consists of the source and destination addresses, a number that corresponds to the protocol layer that generated the data (e.g., TCP), and an identification supplied by that protocol layer. The *Data Length* is the length of the user data field in octets, and the *Offset* is the position of a fragment of user data in the data field of the original datagram, in multiples of 64 bits.

The source end system creates a datagram with a *Data Length* equal to the entire length of the data field, with *Offset* = 0 and a *More Flag* set to 0 (false). To fragment a long datagram into two pieces, an IP module in a router performs the following tasks:

1. Create two new datagrams and copy the header fields of the incoming datagram into both.

2. Divide the incoming user data field into two portions along a 64-bit boundary (counting from the beginning), placing one portion in each new datagram. The first portion must be a multiple of 64 bits (8 octets).

3. Set the *Data Length* of the first new datagram to the length of the inserted data, and set *More Flag* to 1 (true). The *Offset* field is unchanged.

4. Set the *Data Length* of the second new datagram to the length of the inserted data, and add the length of the first data portion divided by 8 to the *Offset* field. The *More Flag* remains the same.

EXAMPLE 18.1 Figure 18.4 gives an example in which two fragments are created from an original IP datagram. The procedure is easily generalized to an *n*-way split. In this example, the payload of the original IP datagram is a TCP segment, consisting of a TCP header and application data. The IP header from the original datagram is used in both fragments, with the appropriate changes to the fragmentation-related fields. Note that the first fragment contains the TCP header; this header is not replicated in the second fragment, because all of the IP payload, including the TCP header is transparent to IP. That is, IP is not concerned with the contents of the payload of the datagram.

---

[3]In the IPv6 header, there is a Payload Length field that corresponds to Data Length in this discussion. In the IPv4 header, there is Total Length field whose value is the length of the header plus data; the data length must be calculated by subtracting the header length.

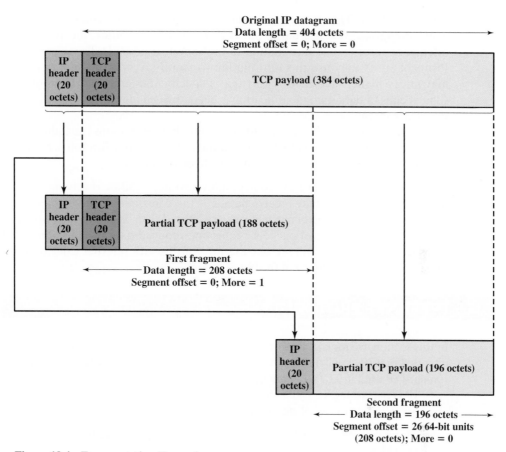

Figure 18.4 Fragmentation Example

To reassemble a datagram, there must be sufficient buffer space at the reassembly point. As fragments with the same ID arrive, their data fields are inserted in the proper position in the buffer until the entire data field is reassembled, which is achieved when a contiguous set of data exists starting with an *Offset* of zero and ending with data from a fragment with a false *More Flag*.

One eventuality that must be dealt with is that one or more of the fragments may not get through; the IP service does not guarantee delivery. Some method is needed to decide when to abandon a reassembly effort to free up buffer space. Two approaches are commonly used. First, assign a reassembly lifetime to the first fragment to arrive. This is a local, real-time clock assigned by the reassembly function and decremented while the fragments of the original datagram are being buffered. If the time expires prior to complete reassembly, the received fragments are discarded. A second approach is to make use of the datagram lifetime, which is part of the header of each incoming fragment. The lifetime field continues to be decremented by the reassembly function; as with the first approach, if the lifetime expires prior to complete reassembly, the received fragments are discarded.

ERROR CONTROL The internetwork facility does not guarantee successful delivery of every datagram. When a datagram is discarded by a router, the router should attempt to return some information to the source, if possible. The source Internet Protocol entity may use this information to modify its transmission strategy and may notify higher layers. To report that a specific datagram has been discarded, some means of datagram identification is needed. Such identification is discussed in the next section.

Datagrams may be discarded for a number of reasons, including lifetime expiration, congestion, and FCS error. In the latter case, notification is not possible because the source address field may have been damaged.

FLOW CONTROL Internet flow control allows routers and/or receiving stations to limit the rate at which they receive data. For the connectionless type of service we are describing, flow control mechanisms are limited. The best approach would seem to be to send flow control packets, requesting reduced data flow, to other routers and source stations. We will see one example of this with Internet Control Message Protocol (ICMP), discussed in the next section.

18.3 INTERNET PROTOCOL

In this section, we look at version 4 of IP, officially defined in RFC 791. Although it is intended that IPv4 will ultimately be replaced by IPv6, IPv4 is currently the dominant standard IP used in TCP/IP networks.

IP is part of the TCP/IP suite and is the most widely used internetworking protocol. As with any protocol standard, IP is specified in two parts (see Figure 2.10):

- The interface with a higher layer (e.g., TCP), specifying the services that IP provides
- The actual protocol format and mechanisms

In this section, we examine first IP services and then the protocol. This is followed by a discussion of IP address formats. Finally, the ICMP, which is an integral part of IP, is described.

IP Services

The services to be provided across adjacent protocol layers (e.g., between IP and TCP) are expressed in terms of primitives and parameters. A primitive specifies the function to be performed, and the parameters are used to pass data and control information. The actual form of a primitive is implementation dependent. An example is a procedure call.

IP provides two service primitives at the interface to the next higher layer. The Send primitive is used to request transmission of a data unit. The Deliver primitive is used by IP to notify a user of the arrival of a data unit. The parameters associated with the two primitives are as follows:

- **Source address:** Internetwork address of sending IP entity.
- **Destination address:** Internetwork address of destination IP entity.

- **Protocol:** Recipient protocol entity (an IP user, such as TCP).
- **Type-of-service indicators:** Used to specify the treatment of the data unit in its transmission through component networks.
- **Identification:** Used in combination with the source and destination addresses and user protocol to identify the data unit uniquely. This parameter is needed for reassembly and error reporting.
- **Don't fragment identifier:** Indicates whether IP can fragment data to accomplish delivery.
- **Time to live (TTL):** Measured in seconds.
- **Data length:** Length of data being transmitted.
- **Option data:** Options requested by the IP user.
- **Data:** User data to be transmitted.

The *identification*, *don't fragment identifier*, and *time to live* parameters are present in the Send primitive but not in the Deliver primitive. These three parameters provide instructions to IP that are not of concern to the recipient IP user.

The options parameter allows for future extensibility and for inclusion of parameters that are usually not invoked. The currently defined options are the following:

- **Security:** Allows a security label to be attached to a datagram.
- **Source routing:** A sequenced list of router addresses that specifies the route to be followed. Routing may be strict (only identified routers may be visited) or loose (other intermediate routers may be visited).
- **Route recording:** A field is allocated to record the sequence of routers visited by the datagram.
- **Stream identification:** Names reserved resources used for stream service. This service provides special handling for volatile periodic traffic (e.g., voice).
- **Timestamping:** The source IP entity and some or all intermediate routers add a timestamp (precision to milliseconds) to the data unit as it goes by.

Internet Protocol

The protocol between IP entities is best described with reference to the IP datagram format, shown in Figure 18.5. The fields are as follows:

- **Version (4 bits):** Indicates version number, to allow evolution of the protocol; the value is 4.
- **Internet Header Length (IHL) (4 bits):** Length of header in 32-bit words. The minimum value is 5, for a minimum header length of 20 octets.
- **DS (8 bits):** This field supports the Differentiated Service function, described in Chapter 20.
- **ECN (2 bits):** The Explicit Congestion Notification field, defined in RFC 3168, enables routers to indicate to end nodes packets that are experiencing congestion, without the necessity of immediately dropping such packets. A value of

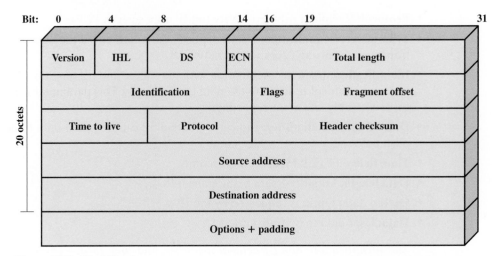

Figure 18.5 IPv4 Header

00 indicates a packet that is not using ECN. A value of 01 or 10 is set by the data sender to indicate that the end-points of the transport protocol are ECN-capable. A value of 11 is set by a router to indicate congestion has been encountered.

- **Total Length (16 bits):** Total datagram length, including header plus data, in octets.

- **Identification (16 bits):** A sequence number that, together with the source address, destination address, and user protocol, is intended to identify a datagram uniquely. Thus, this number should be unique for the datagram's source address, destination address, and user protocol for the time during which the datagram will remain in the internet.

- **Flags (3 bits):** Only two of the bits are currently defined. The More bit is used for fragmentation and reassembly, as previously explained. The Don't Fragment bit prohibits fragmentation when set. This bit may be useful if it is known that the destination does not have the capability to reassemble fragments. However, if this bit is set, the datagram will be discarded if it exceeds the maximum size of an en route network. Therefore, if the bit is set, it may be advisable to use source routing to avoid networks with small maximum packet size.

- **Fragment Offset (13 bits):** Indicates where in the original datagram this fragment belongs, measured in 64-bit units. This implies that fragments other than the last fragment must contain a data field that is a multiple of 64 bits in length.

- **Time to Live (8 bits):** Specifies how long, in seconds, a datagram is allowed to remain in the internet. Every router that processes a datagram must decrease the TTL by at least one, so the TTL is similar to a hop count.

- **Protocol (8 bits):** Indicates the next higher level protocol that is to receive the data field at the destination; thus, this field identifies the type of the next header in the packet after the IP header. Example values are TCP = 6; UDP = 17.

A complete list is maintained at http://www.iana.org/assignments/protocol-numbers.

- **Header Checksum (16 bits):** An error-detecting code applied to the header only. Because some header fields may change during transit (e.g., Time to Live, fragmentation-related fields), this is reverified and recomputed at each router. The checksum is formed by taking the ones complement of the 16-bit ones complement addition of all 16-bit words in the header. For purposes of computation, the checksum field is itself initialized to a value of zero.[4]
- **Source Address (32 bits):** Coded to allow a variable allocation of bits to specify the network and the end system attached to the specified network, as discussed subsequently.
- **Destination Address (32 bits):** Same characteristics as source address.
- **Options (variable):** Encodes the options requested by the sending user.
- **Padding (variable):** Used to ensure that the datagram header is a multiple of 32 bits in length.
- **Data (variable):** The data field must be an integer multiple of 8 bits in length. The maximum length of the datagram (data field plus header) is 65,535 octets.

It should be clear how the IP services specified in the Send and Deliver primitives map into the fields of the IP datagram.

IP Addresses

The source and destination address fields in the IP header each contain a 32-bit global internet address, generally consisting of a network identifier and a host identifier.

NETWORK CLASSES The address is coded to allow a variable allocation of bits to specify network and host, as depicted in Figure 18.6. This encoding provides flexibility in assigning addresses to hosts and allows a mix of network sizes on an internet. The three principal network classes are best suited to the following conditions:

- **Class A:** Few networks, each with many hosts
- **Class B:** Medium number of networks, each with a medium number of hosts
- **Class C:** Many networks, each with a few hosts

In a particular environment, it may be best to use addresses all from one class. For example, a corporate internetwork that consist of a large number of departmental local area networks may need to use Class C addresses exclusively. However, the format of the addresses is such that it is possible to mix all three classes of addresses on the same internetwork; this is what is done in the case of the Internet itself. A mixture of classes is appropriate for an internetwork consisting of a few large networks, many small networks, plus some medium-sized networks.

IP addresses are usually written in **dotted decimal notation**, with a decimal number representing each of the octets of the 32-bit address. For example, the IP address 11000000 11100100 00010001 00111001 is written as 192.228.17.57.

---

[4]A discussion of this checksum is contained in Appendix P.

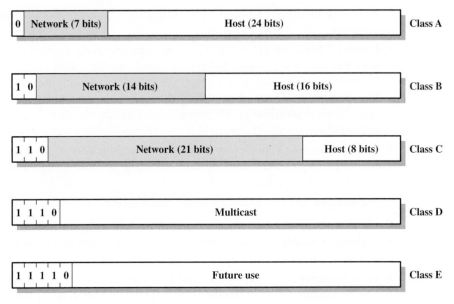

Figure 18.6 IPv4 Address Formats

Note that all Class A network addresses begin with a binary 0. Network addresses with a first octet of 0 (binary 00000000) and 127 (binary 01111111) are reserved, so there are 126 potential Class A network numbers, which have a first dotted decimal number in the range 1 to 126. Class B network addresses begin with a binary 10, so that the range of the first decimal number in a Class B address is 128 to 191(binary 10000000 to 10111111). The second octet is also part of the Class B address, so that there are 2^{14} = 16,384 Class B addresses. For Class C addresses, the first decimal number ranges from 192 to 223 (11000000 to 11011111). The total number of Class C addresses is 2^{21} = 2,097,152.

SUBNETS AND SUBNET MASKS The concept of subnet was introduced to address the following requirement. Consider an internet that includes one or more WANs and a number of sites, each of which has a number of LANs. We would like to allow arbitrary complexity of interconnected LAN structures within an organization while insulating the overall internet against explosive growth in network numbers and routing complexity. One approach to this problem is to assign a single network number to all of the LANs at a site. From the point of view of the rest of the internet, there is a single network at that site, which simplifies addressing and routing. To allow the routers within the site to function properly, each LAN is assigned a subnet number. The *host* portion of the internet address is partitioned into a subnet number and a host number to accommodate this new level of addressing.

Within the subnetted network, the local routers must route on the basis of an extended network number consisting of the *network* portion of the IP address and the subnet number. The address mask indicates the bit positions containing this extended network number. The use of the address mask allows the host to determine whether an outgoing datagram is destined for a host on the same LAN (send directly) or another LAN (send datagram to router). It is assumed that some other means (e.g., manual configuration) are used to create address masks and make them known to the local routers.

Table 18.2a shows the calculations involved in the use of a subnet mask. Note that the effect of the subnet mask is to erase the portion of the host field that refers to an actual host on a subnet. What remains is the network number and the subnet number.

EXAMPLE 18.2 Figure 18.7 shows an example of the use of subnetting. The figure shows a local complex consisting of three LANs and two routers. To the rest of the internet, this complex is a single network with a Class C address of the form 192.228.17.x, where the leftmost three octets are the network number and the rightmost octet contains a host number x. Both routers R1 and R2 are configured with a subnet mask with the value 255.255.255.224 (see Table 18.2a). For example, if a datagram with the destination address 192.228.17.57 arrives at R1 from either the rest of the internet or from LAN Y, R1 applies the subnet mask to determine that this address refers to subnet 1, which is LAN X, and so forwards the datagram to LAN X. Similarly, if a datagram with that destination address arrives at R2 from LAN Z, R2 applies the mask and then determines from its forwarding database that datagrams destined for subnet 1 should be forwarded to R1. Hosts must also employ a subnet mask to make routing decisions.

Table 18.2   IP Addresses and Subnet Masks

(a) Dotted decimal and binary representations of IP address and subnet masks

	Binary Representation	Dotted Decimal
IP address	11000000.11100100.00010001.00111001	192.228.17.57
Subnet mask	11111111.11111111.11111111.11100000	255.255.255.224
Bitwise AND of address and mask (resultant network/subnet number)	11000000.11100100.00010001.00100000	192.228.17.32
Subnet number	11000000.11100100.00010001.001	1
Host number	00000000.00000000.00000000.00011001	25

(b) Default subnet masks

	Binary Representation	Dotted Decimal
Class A default mask	11111111.00000000.00000000.00000000	255.0.0.0
Example Class A mask	11111111.11000000.00000000.00000000	255.192.0.0
Class B default mask	11111111.11111111.00000000.00000000	255.255.0.0
Example Class B mask	11111111.11111111.11111000.00000000	255.255.248.0
Class C default mask	11111111.11111111.11111111.00000000	255. 255. 255.0
Example Class C mask	11111111.11111111.11111111.11111100	255. 255. 255.252

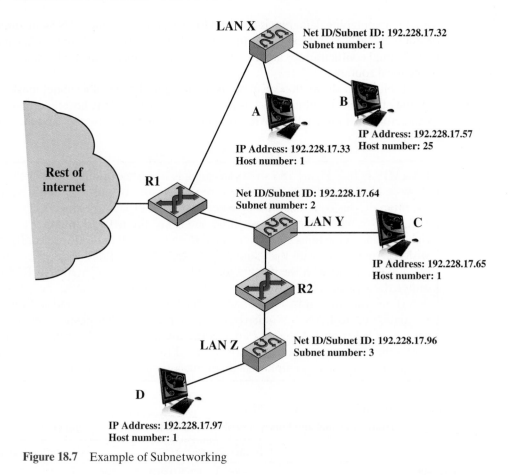

Figure 18.7 Example of Subnetworking

The default subnet mask for a given class of addresses is a null mask (Table 18.2b), which yields the same network and host number as the nonsubnetted address.

Internet Control Message Protocol (ICMP)

The IP standard specifies that a compliant implementation must also implement ICMP (RFC 792). ICMP provides a means for transferring messages from routers and other hosts to a host. In essence, ICMP provides feedback about problems in the communication environment. Examples of its use are when a datagram cannot reach its destination, when the router does not have the buffering capacity to forward a datagram, and when the router can direct the station to send traffic on a shorter route. In most cases, an ICMP message is sent in response to a datagram, either by a router along the datagram's path or by the intended destination host.

Although ICMP is, in effect, at the same level as IP in the TCP/IP architecture, it is a user of IP. An ICMP message is constructed and then passed down to IP, which encapsulates the message with an IP header and then transmits the resulting datagram in the usual fashion. Because ICMP messages are transmitted in IP datagrams, their delivery is not guaranteed and their use cannot be considered reliable.

Figure 18.8 shows the format of the various ICMP message types. An ICMP message starts with a 64-bit header consisting of the following:

- **Type (8 bits):** Specifies the type of ICMP message.
- **Code (8 bits):** Used to specify parameters of the message that can be encoded in one or a few bits.
- **Checksum (16 bits):** Checksum of the entire ICMP message. This is the same checksum algorithm used for IP.
- **Parameters (32 bits):** Used to specify more lengthy parameters.

These fields are generally followed by additional information fields that further specify the content of the message.

In those cases in which the ICMP message refers to a prior datagram, the information field includes the entire IP header plus the first 64 bits of the data field of the original datagram. This enables the source host to match the incoming ICMP message with the prior datagram. The reason for including the first 64 bits of the data field is that this will enable the IP module in the host to determine which upper-level protocol or protocols were involved. In particular, the first 64 bits would include a portion of the TCP header or other transport-level header.

The **destination unreachable** message covers a number of contingencies. A router may return this message if it does not know how to reach the destination network. In some networks, an attached router may be able to determine if a particular host is unreachable and returns the message. The destination host itself may return this

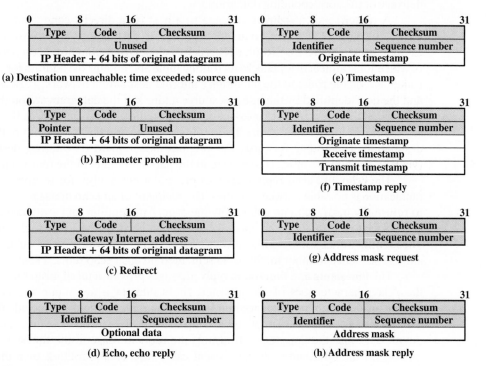

Figure 18.8   ICMP Message Formats

message if the user protocol or some higher-level service access point is unreachable. This could happen if the corresponding field in the IP header was set incorrectly. If the datagram specifies a source route that is unusable, a message is returned. Finally, if a router must fragment a datagram but the Don't Fragment flag is set, the datagram is discarded and a message is returned.

A router will return a **time exceeded** message if the lifetime of the datagram expires. A host will send this message if it cannot complete reassembly within a time limit.

A syntactic or semantic error in an IP header will cause a **parameter problem** message to be returned by a router or host. For example, an incorrect argument may be provided with an option. The Parameter field contains a pointer to the octet in the original header where the error was detected.

The **source quench** message provides a rudimentary form of flow control. Either a router or a destination host may send this message to a source host, requesting that it reduce the rate at which it is sending traffic to the internet destination. On receipt of a source quench message, the source host should cut back the rate at which it is sending traffic to the specified destination until it no longer receives source quench messages. The source quench message can be used by a router or host that must discard datagrams because of a full buffer. In that case, the router or host will issue a source quench message for every datagram that it discards. In addition, a system may anticipate congestion and issue source quench messages when its buffers approach capacity. In that case, the datagram referred to in the source quench message may well be delivered. Thus, receipt of a source quench message does not imply delivery or non-delivery of the corresponding datagram.

A router sends a **redirect** message to a host on a directly connected router to advise the host of a better route to a particular destination. The following is an example, using Figure 18.7. Router R1 receives a datagram from host C on network Y, to which R1 is attached. R1 checks its routing table and obtains the address for the next router, R2, on the route to the datagram's internet destination network, Z. Because R2 and the host identified by the internet source address of the datagram are on the same network, R1 sends a redirect message to C. The redirect message advises the host to send its traffic for network Z directly to router R2, because this is a shorter path to the destination. The router forwards the original datagram to its internet destination (via R2). The address of R2 is contained in the parameter field of the redirect message.

The **echo** and **echo reply** messages provide a mechanism for testing that communication is possible between entities. The recipient of an echo message is obligated to return the message in an echo reply message. An identifier and sequence number are associated with the echo message to be matched in the echo reply message. The identifier might be used like a service access point to identify a particular session, and the sequence number might be incremented on each echo request sent.

The **timestamp** and **timestamp reply** messages provide a mechanism for sampling the delay characteristics of the internet. The sender of a timestamp message may include an identifier and sequence number in the parameters field and include the time that the message is sent (originate timestamp). The receiver records the time it received the message and the time that it transmits the reply message in the timestamp reply message. If the timestamp message is sent using strict source routing, then the delay characteristics of a particular route can be measured.

The **address mask request** and **address mask reply** messages are useful in an environment that includes subnets. The address mask request and reply messages allow a host to learn the address mask for the LAN to which it connects. The host broadcasts an address mask request message on the LAN. The router on the LAN responds with an address mask reply message that contains the address mask.

Address Resolution Protocol (ARP)

Earlier in this chapter, we referred to the concepts of a global address (IP address) and an address that conforms to the addressing scheme of the network to which a host is attached (subnetwork address). For a local area network, the latter address is a MAC address, which provides a physical address for a host port attached to the LAN. Clearly, to deliver an IP datagram to a destination host, a mapping must be made from the IP address to the subnetwork address for that last hop. If a datagram traverses one or more routers between source and destination hosts, then the mapping must be done in the final router, which is attached to the same subnetwork as the destination host. If a datagram is sent from one host to another on the same subnetwork, then the source host must do the mapping. In the following discussion, we use the term *system* to refer to the entity that does the mapping.

For mapping from an IP address to a subnetwork address, a number of approaches are possible:

- Each system can maintain a local table of IP addresses and matching subnetwork addresses for possible correspondents. This approach does not accommodate easy and automatic additions of new hosts to the subnetwork.

- The subnetwork address can be a subset of the network portion of the IP address. However, the entire internet address is 32 bits long and for most subnetwork types (e.g., Ethernet) the host address field is longer than 32 bits.

- A centralized directory can be maintained on each subnetwork that contains the IP-subnet address mappings. This is a reasonable solution for many networks.

- An address resolution protocol can be used. This is a simpler approach than the use of a centralized directory and is well suited to LANs.

RFC 826 defines an Address Resolution Protocol, which allows dynamic distribution of the information needed to build tables to translate an IP address A into a 48-bit Ethernet address; the protocol can be used for any broadcast network. ARP exploits the broadcast property of a LAN; namely, that a transmission from any device on the network is received by all other devices on the network. ARP works as follows:

1. Each system on the LAN maintains a table of known IP-subnetwork address mappings.
2. When a subnetwork address is needed for an IP address, and the mapping is not found in the system's table, the system uses ARP directly on top of the LAN protocol (e.g., IEEE 802) to broadcast a request. The broadcast message contains the IP address for which a subnetwork address is needed.

3. Other hosts on the subnetwork listen for ARP messages and reply when a match occurs. The reply includes both the IP and subnetwork addresses of the replying host.

4. The original request includes the requesting host's IP address and subnetwork address. Any interested host can copy this information into its local table, avoiding the need for later ARP messages.

5. The ARP message can also be used simply to broadcast a host's IP address and subnetwork address, for the benefit of others on the subnetwork.

18.4 IPv6

IPv4 has been the foundation of the Internet and virtually all multivendor private internetworks. This protocol is reaching the end of its useful life and a new protocol, known as IPv6 (IP version 6), has been defined to ultimately replace IP.[5]

We first look at the motivation for developing a new version of IP and then examine some of its details.

IP Next Generation

The driving motivation for the adoption of a new version of IP was the limitation imposed by the 32-bit address field in IPv4. With a 32-bit address field, it is possible in principle to assign 232 different addresses, which is over 4 billion possible addresses. One might think that this number of addresses was more than adequate to meet addressing needs on the Internet. However, in the late 1980s it was perceived that there would be a problem, and this problem began to manifest itself in the early 1990s. Reasons for the inadequacy of 32-bit addresses include the following:

- The two-level structure of the IP address (network number, host number) is convenient but wasteful of the address space. Once a network number is assigned to a network, all of the host-number addresses for that network number are assigned to that network. The address space for that network may be sparsely used, but as far as the effective IP address space is concerned, if a network number is used, then all addresses within the network are used.

- The IP addressing model generally requires that a unique network number be assigned to each IP network whether or not it is actually connected to the Internet.

- Networks are proliferating rapidly. Most organizations boast multiple LANs, not just a single LAN system. Wireless networks have rapidly assumed a major role. The Internet itself has grown explosively for years.

- Growth of TCP/IP usage into new areas will result in a rapid growth in the demand for unique IP addresses. Examples include using TCP/IP to interconnect electronic point-of-sale terminals and for cable television receivers.

---

[5]The currently deployed version of IP is IP version 4; previous versions of IP (1 through 3) were successively defined and replaced to reach IPv4. Version 5 is the number assigned to the Stream Protocol, a connection-oriented internet-layer protocol. Hence the use of the label version 6.

- Typically, a single IP address is assigned to each host. A more flexible arrangement is to allow multiple IP addresses per host. This, of course, increases the demand for IP addresses.

So the need for an increased address space dictated that a new version of IP was needed. In addition, IP is a very old protocol, and new requirements in the areas of address configuration, routing flexibility, and traffic support had been defined.

In response to these needs, the Internet Engineering Task Force (IETF) issued a call for proposals for a next generation IP (IPng) in July of 1992. A number of proposals were received, and by 1994 the final design for IPng emerged. A major milestone was reached with the publication of RFC 1752, "The Recommendation for the IP Next Generation Protocol," issued in January 1995. RFC 1752 outlines the requirements for IPng, specifies the PDU formats, and highlights the IPng approach in the areas of addressing, routing, and security. A number of other Internet documents defined details of the protocol, now officially called IPv6; these include an overall specification of IPv6 (RFC 2460), an RFC dealing with addressing structure of IPv6 (RFC 4291), and numerous others.

IPv6 includes the following enhancements over IPv4:

- **Expanded address space:** IPv6 uses 128-bit addresses instead of the 32-bit addresses of IPv4. This is an increase of address space by a factor of 296. It has been pointed out [HIND95] that this allows on the order of 6×10^{23} unique addresses per square meter of the surface of the Earth. Even if addresses are very inefficiently allocated, this address space seems inexhaustible.

- **Improved option mechanism:** IPv6 options are placed in separate optional headers that are located between the IPv6 header and the transport-layer header. Most of these optional headers are not examined or processed by any router on the packet's path. This simplifies and speeds up router processing of IPv6 packets compared to IPv4 datagrams.[6] It also makes it easier to add additional options.

- **Address autoconfiguration:** This capability provides for dynamic assignment of IPv6 addresses.

- **Increased addressing flexibility:** IPv6 includes the concept of an anycast address, for which a packet is delivered to just one of a set of nodes. The scalability of multicast routing is improved by adding a scope field to multicast addresses.

- **Support for resource allocation:** IPv6 enables the labeling of packets belonging to a particular traffic flow for which the sender requests special handling. This aids in the support of specialized traffic such as real-time video.

All of these features are explored in the remainder of this section.

---

[6]The protocol data unit for IPv6 is referred to as a packet rather than a datagram, which is the term used for IPv4 PDUs.

IPv6 Structure

An IPv6 protocol data unit (known as a packet) has the following general form:

IPv6 header	Extension header	• • •	Extension header	Transport-level PDU

←— 40 octets —→   ←——————————— 0 or more ———————————→

The only header that is required is referred to simply as the IPv6 header. This is of fixed size with a length of 40 octets, compared to 20 octets for the mandatory portion of the IPv4 header (Figure 18.5). The following extension headers have been defined:

- **Hop-by-Hop Options header:** Defines special options that require hop-by-hop processing
- **Routing header:** Provides extended routing, similar to IPv4 source routing
- **Fragment header:** Contains fragmentation and reassembly information
- **Authentication header:** Provides packet integrity and authentication
- **Encapsulating Security Payload header:** Provides privacy
- **Destination Options header:** Contains optional information to be examined by the destination node

The IPv6 standard recommends that when multiple extension headers are used, the IPv6 headers appear in the following order:

1. IPv6 header: Mandatory, must always appear first
2. Hop-by-Hop Options header
3. Destination Options header: For options to be processed by the first destination that appears in the IPv6 Destination Address field plus subsequent destinations listed in the Routing header
4. Routing header
5. Fragment header
6. Authentication header
7. Encapsulating Security Payload header
8. Destination Options header: For options to be processed only by the final destination of the packet

Figure 18.9 shows an example of an IPv6 packet that includes an instance of each header, except those related to security. Note that the IPv6 header and each extension header include a Next Header field. This field identifies the type of the immediately following header. If the next header is an extension header, then this field contains the type identifier of that header. Otherwise, this field contains the protocol identifier of the upper-layer protocol using IPv6 (typically a transport-level protocol), using the same values as the IPv4 Protocol field. In Figure 18.9, the upper-layer protocol is TCP; thus, the upper-layer data carried by the IPv6 packet consist of a TCP header followed by a block of application data.

We first look at the main IPv6 header and then examine each of the extensions in turn.

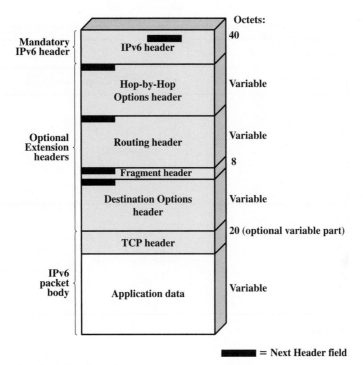

Octets:

Mandatory IPv6 header — IPv6 header — 40

Hop-by-Hop Options header — Variable

Optional Extension headers — Routing header — Variable

Fragment header — 8

Destination Options header — Variable

TCP header — 20 (optional variable part)

IPv6 packet body — Application data — Variable

▬▬▬▬ = Next Header field

Figure 18.9   IPv6 Packet with Extension Headers (containing a TCP Segment)

IPv6 Header

The IPv6 header has a fixed length of 40 octets, consisting of the following fields (Figure 18.10):

- **Version (4 bits):** Internet protocol version number; the value is 6.
- **DS/ECN (8 bits):** Available for use by originating nodes and/or forwarding routers for differentiated services and congestion functions, as described for the IPv4 DS/ECN field.
- **Flow Label (20 bits):** May be used by a host to label those packets for which it is requesting special handling by routers within a network, discussed subsequently.
- **Payload Length (16 bits):** Length of the remainder of the IPv6 packet following the header, in octets. In other words, this is the total length of all of the extension headers plus the transport-level PDU.
- **Next Header (8 bits):** Identifies the type of header immediately following the IPv6 header; this will either be an IPv6 extension header or a higher-layer header, such as TCP or UDP.
- **Hop Limit (8 bits):** The remaining number of allowable hops for this packet. The hop limit is set to some desired maximum value by the source and decremented by 1 by each node that forwards the packet. The packet is discarded if Hop Limit is decremented to zero. This is a simplification over the processing required for

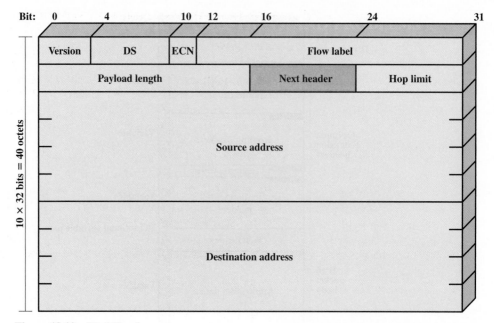

Figure 18.10   IPv6 Header

the Time to Live field of IPv4. The consensus was that the extra effort in accounting for time intervals in IPv4 added no significant value to the protocol. In fact, IPv4 routers, as a general rule, treat the Time to Live field as a hop limit field.

- **Source Address (128 bits):** The address of the originator of the packet.
- **Destination Address (128 bits):** The address of the intended recipient of the packet. This may not in fact be the intended ultimate destination if a Routing header is present, as explained subsequently.

Although the IPv6 header is longer than the mandatory portion of the IPv4 header (40 octets versus 20 octets), it contains fewer fields (8 versus 12). Thus, routers have less processing to do per header, which should speed up routing.

FLOW LABEL RFC 3697 defines a flow as a sequence of packets sent from a particular source to a particular (unicast, anycast, or multicast) destination for which the source desires special handling by the intervening routers. A flow is uniquely identified by the combination of a source address, destination address, and a nonzero 20-bit flow label. Thus, all packets that are to be part of the same flow are assigned the same flow label by the source.

From the source's point of view, a flow typically will be a sequence of packets that are generated from a single application instance at the source and that have the same transfer service requirements. A flow may comprise a single TCP connection or even multiple TCP connections; an example of the latter is a file transfer application, which could have one control connection and multiple data connections. A single application may generate a single flow or multiple flows. An example of the latter is multimedia conferencing, which might have one flow for audio and one for graphic windows, each with different transfer requirements in terms of data rate, delay, and delay variation.

From the router's point of view, a flow is a sequence of packets that share attributes that affect how these packets are handled by the router. These include path, resource allocation, discard requirements, accounting, and security attributes. The router may treat packets from different flows differently in a number of ways, including allocating different buffer sizes, giving different precedence in terms of forwarding, and requesting different quality of service from networks.

There is no special significance to any particular flow label. Instead the special handling to be provided for a packet flow must be declared in some other way. For example, a source might negotiate or request special handling ahead of time from routers by means of a control protocol, or at transmission time by information in one of the extension headers in the packet, such as the Hop-by-Hop Options header. Examples of special handling that might be requested include some sort of nondefault quality of service and some form of real-time service.

In principle, all of a user's requirements for a particular flow could be defined in an extension header and included with each packet. If we wish to leave the concept of flow open to include a wide variety of requirements, this design approach could result in very large packet headers. The alternative, adopted for IPv6, is the flow label, in which the flow requirements are defined prior to flow commencement and a unique flow label is assigned to the flow. In this case, the router must save flow requirement information about each flow.

The following rules apply to the flow label:

1. Hosts or routers that do not support the Flow Label field must set the field to zero when originating a packet, pass the field unchanged when forwarding a packet, and ignore the field when receiving a packet.

2. All packets originating from a given source with the same nonzero Flow Label must have the same Destination Address, Source Address, Hop-by-Hop Options header contents (if this header is present), and Routing header contents (if this header is present). The intent is that a router can decide how to route and process the packet by simply looking up the flow label in a table and without examining the rest of the header.

3. The source assigns a flow label to a flow. New flow labels must be chosen (pseudo-) randomly and uniformly in the range 1 to $2^{20} - 1$, subject to the restriction that a source must not reuse a flow label for a new flow within the lifetime of the existing flow. The zero flow label is reserved to indicate that no flow label is being used.

This last point requires some elaboration. The router must maintain information about the characteristics of each active flow that may pass through it, presumably in some sort of table. To forward packets efficiently and rapidly, table lookup must be efficient. One alternative is to have a table with 2^{20} (about 1 million) entries, one for each possible flow label; this imposes an unnecessary memory burden on the router. Another alternative is to have one entry in the table per active flow, include the flow label with each entry, and require the router to search the entire table each time a packet is encountered. This imposes an unnecessary processing burden on the router. Instead, most router designs are likely to use some sort of hash table approach. With this approach a moderate-sized table is used, and each flow entry is mapped into the table using a hashing function on the flow label. The hashing function might simply be the low-order few bits (say 8 or 10) of the flow label or some simple calculation on the 20 bits of the flow label. In any case, the efficiency of the hash approach typically depends on the flow labels being uniformly distributed over their possible range. Hence requirement number 3 in the preceding list.

IPv6 Addresses

IPv6 addresses are 128 bits in length. Addresses are assigned to individual interfaces on nodes, not to the nodes themselves.[7] A single interface may have multiple unique unicast addresses. Any of the unicast addresses associated with a node's interface may be used to uniquely identify that node.

The combination of long addresses and multiple addresses per interface enables improved routing efficiency over IPv4. In IPv4, addresses generally do not have a structure that assists routing, and therefore a router may need to maintain huge table of routing paths. Longer internet addresses allow for aggregating addresses by hierarchies of network, access provider, geography, corporation, and so on. Such aggregation should make for smaller routing tables and faster table lookups. The allowance for multiple addresses per interface would allow a subscriber that uses multiple access providers across the same interface to have separate addresses aggregated under each provider's address space.

IPv6 allows three types of addresses:

- **Unicast:** An identifier for a single interface. A packet sent to a unicast address is delivered to the interface identified by that address.
- **Anycast:** An identifier for a set of interfaces (typically belonging to different nodes). A packet sent to an anycast address is delivered to one of the interfaces identified by that address (the "nearest" one, according to the routing protocols' measure of distance).
- **Multicast:** An identifier for a set of interfaces (typically belonging to different nodes). A packet sent to a multicast address is delivered to all interfaces identified by that address.

Hop-by-Hop Options Header

The Hop-by-Hop Options header carries optional information that, if present, must be examined by every router along the path. This header consists of (Figure 18.11a):

- **Next Header (8 bits):** Identifies the type of header immediately following this header.
- **Header Extension Length (8 bits):** Length of this header in 64-bit units, not including the first 64 bits.
- **Options:** A variable-length field consisting of one or more option definitions. Each definition is in the form of three subfields: Option Type (8 bits), which identifies the option; Length (8 bits), which specifies the length of the Option Data field in octets; and Option Data, which is a variable-length specification of the option.

---

[7]In IPv6, a *node* is any device that implements IPv6; this includes hosts and routers.

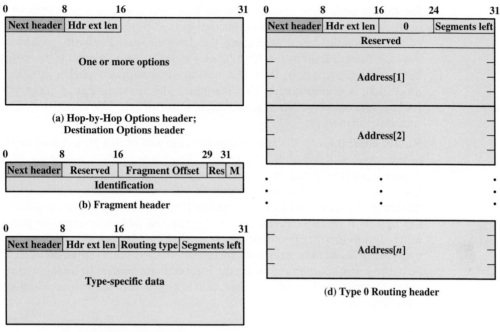

(a) Hop-by-Hop Options header;
Destination Options header

(b) Fragment header

(c) Generic Routing header

(d) Type 0 Routing header

Figure 18.11 IPv6 Extension Header

It is actually the lowest-order five bits of the Option Type field that are used to specify a particular option. The high-order two bits indicate the action to be taken by a node that does not recognize this option type, as follows:

- 00—Skip over this option and continue processing the header.
- 01—Discard the packet.
- 10—Discard the packet and send an ICMP Parameter Problem message to the packet's Source Address, pointing to the unrecognized Option Type.
- 11—Discard the packet and, only if the packet's Destination Address is not a multicast address, send an ICMP Parameter Problem message to the packet's Source Address, pointing to the unrecognized Option Type

The third highest-order bit specifies whether the Option Data field does not change (0) or may change (1) en route from source to destination. Data that may change must be excluded from authentication calculations, as discussed in Chapter 24.

These conventions for the Option Type field also apply to the Destination Options header.

Four hop-by-hop options have been specified so far:

- **Pad1:** Used to insert one byte of padding into the Options area of the header.
- **PadN:** Used to insert N bytes ($N \geq 2$) of padding into the Options area of the header. The two padding options ensure that the header is a multiple of 8 bytes in length.

- **Jumbo payload:** Used to send IPv6 packets with payloads longer than 65,535 octets. The Option Data field of this option is 32 bits long and gives the length of the packet in octets, excluding the IPv6 header. For such packets, the Payload Length field in the IPv6 header must be set to zero, and there must be no Fragment header. With this option, IPv6 supports packet sizes up to more than 4 billion octets. This facilitates the transmission of large video packets and enables IPv6 to make the best use of available capacity over any transmission medium.

- **Router alert:** Informs the router that the contents of this packet is of interest to the router and to handle any control data accordingly. The absence of this option in an IPv6 datagram informs the router that the packet does not contain information needed by the router and hence can be safely routed without further packet parsing. Hosts originating IPv6 packets are required to include this option in certain circumstances. The purpose of this option is to provide efficient support for protocols such as RSVP (Chapter 20) that generate packets that need to be examined by intermediate routers for purposes of traffic control. Rather than requiring the intermediate routers to look in detail at the extension headers of a packet, this option alerts the router when such attention is required.

Fragment Header

In IPv6, fragmentation may only be performed by source nodes, not by routers along a packet's delivery path. To take full advantage of the internetworking environment, a node must perform a path discovery algorithm that enables it to learn the smallest maximum transmission unit (MTU) supported by any network on the path. With this knowledge, the source node will fragment, as required, for each given destination address. Otherwise the source must limit all packets to 1280 octets, which is the minimum MTU that must be supported by each network.

The fragment header consists of the following (Figure 18.11b):

- **Next Header (8 bits):** Identifies the type of header immediately following this header.

- **Reserved (8 bits):** For future use.

- **Fragment Offset (13 bits):** Indicates where in the original packet the payload of this fragment belongs, measured in 64-bit units. This implies that fragments (other than the last fragment) must contain a data field that is a multiple of 64 bits long.

- **Res (2 bits):** Reserved for future use.

- **M Flag (1 bit):** 1 = more fragments; 0 = last fragment.

- **Identification (32 bits):** Intended to uniquely identify the original packet. The identifier must be unique for the packet's source address and destination address for the time during which the packet will remain in the internet. All fragments with the same identifier, source address, and destination address are reassembled to form the original packet.

The fragmentation algorithm is the same as that described in Section 18.2.

Routing Header

The Routing header contains a list of one or more intermediate nodes to be visited on the way to a packet's destination. All routing headers start with a 32-bit block consisting of four 8-bit fields, followed by routing data specific to a given routing type (Figure 18.11c). The four 8-bit fields are as follows:

- **Next Header:** Identifies the type of header immediately following this header.
- **Header Extension Length:** Length of this header in 64-bit units, not including the first 64 bits.
- **Routing Type:** Identifies a particular Routing header variant. If a router does not recognize the Routing Type value, it must discard the packet.
- **Segments Left:** Number of route segments remaining; that is, the number of explicitly listed intermediate nodes still to be visited before reaching the final destination.

The only specific routing header format defined in RFC 2460 is the Type 0 Routing header (Figure 18.11d). When using the Type 0 Routing header, the source node does not place the ultimate destination address in the IPv6 header. Instead, that address is the last address listed in the Routing header (Address[n] in Figure 18.11d), and the IPv6 header contains the destination address of the first desired router on the path. The Routing header will not be examined until the packet reaches the node identified in the IPv6 header. At that point, the IPv6 and Routing header contents are updated and the packet is forwarded. The update consists of placing the next address to be visited in the IPv6 header and decrementing the Segments Left field in the Routing header.

Destination Options Header

The Destination Options header carries optional information that, if present, is examined only by the packet's destination node. The format of this header is the same as that of the Hop-by-Hop Options header (Figure 18.11a).

18.5 VIRTUAL PRIVATE NETWORKS AND IP SECURITY

In today's distributed computing environment, the **virtual private network (VPN)** offers an attractive solution to network managers. In essence, a VPN consists of a set of computers that interconnect by means of a relatively unsecure network and that make use of encryption and special protocols to provide security. At each corporate site, workstations, servers, and databases are linked by one or more LANs. The LANs are under the control of the network manager and can be configured and tuned for cost-effective performance. The Internet or some other public network can be used to interconnect sites, providing a cost savings over the use of a private network and offloading the wide area network management task to the public network provider. That same public network provides an access path for telecommuters and other mobile employees to log on to corporate systems from remote sites.

But the manager faces a fundamental requirement: security. Use of a public network exposes corporate traffic to eavesdropping and provides an entry point for unauthorized users. To counter this problem, the manager may choose from a variety of encryption and authentication packages and products. Proprietary solutions raise a number of problems. First, how secure is the solution? If proprietary encryption or authentication schemes are used, there may be little reassurance in the technical literature as to the level of security provided. Second is the question of compatibility. No manager wants to be limited in the choice of workstations, servers, routers, firewalls, and so on by a need for compatibility with the security facility. This is the motivation for the IP Security (IPsec) set of Internet standards.

IPsec

In 1994, the Internet Architecture Board (IAB) issued a report titled "Security in the Internet Architecture" (RFC 1636). The report stated the general consensus that the Internet needs more and better security and identified key areas for security mechanisms. Among these were the need to secure the network infrastructure from unauthorized monitoring and control of network traffic and the need to secure end-user-to-end-user traffic using authentication and encryption mechanisms.

To provide security, the IAB included authentication and encryption as necessary security features in the next-generation IP, which has been issued as IPv6. Fortunately, these security capabilities were designed to be usable both with the current IPv4 and the future IPv6. This means that vendors can begin offering these features now, and many vendors do now have some IPsec capability in their products. The IPsec specification now exists as a set of Internet standards.

Applications of IPsec

IPsec provides the capability to secure communications across a LAN, across private and public WANs, and across the Internet. Examples of its use include the following:

- **Secure branch office connectivity over the Internet:** A company can build a secure virtual private network over the Internet or over a public WAN. This enables a business to rely heavily on the Internet and reduce its need for private networks, saving costs and network management overhead.
- **Secure remote access over the Internet:** An end user whose system is equipped with IP security protocols can make a local call to an Internet service provider (ISP) and gain secure access to a company network. This reduces the cost of toll charges for traveling employees and telecommuters.
- **Establishing extranet and intranet connectivity with partners:** IPsec can be used to secure communication with other organizations, ensuring authentication and confidentiality and providing a key exchange mechanism.
- **Enhancing electronic commerce security:** Even though some Web and electronic commerce applications have built-in security protocols, the use of IPsec enhances that security. IPsec guarantees that all traffic designated by the network administrator is both encrypted and authenticated, adding an additional layer of security to whatever is provided at the application layer.

The principal feature of IPsec that enables it to support these varied applications is that it can encrypt and/or authenticate *all* traffic at the IP level. Thus, all distributed applications, including remote logon, client/server, e-mail, file transfer, Web access, and so on, can be secured.

Figure 18.12 is a typical scenario of IPsec usage. An organization maintains LANs at dispersed locations. Nonsecure IP traffic is conducted on each LAN. For traffic offsite, through some sort of private or public WAN, IPsec protocols are used. These protocols operate in networking devices, such as a router or firewall, that connect each LAN to the outside world. The IPsec networking device will typically encrypt and compress all traffic going into the WAN, and decrypt and decompress traffic coming from the WAN; these operations are transparent to workstations and servers on the LAN. Secure transmission is also possible with individual users who dial into the WAN. Such user workstations must implement the IPsec protocols to provide security.

Benefits of IPsec

Some of the benefits of IPsec are as follows:

- When IPsec is implemented in a firewall or router, it provides strong security that can be applied to all traffic crossing the perimeter. Traffic within a company or workgroup does not incur the overhead of security-related processing.

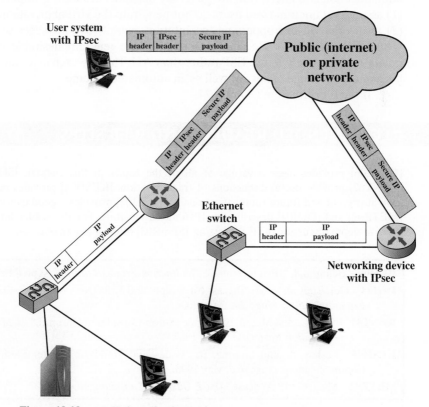

Figure 18.12   An IP Security Scenario

- IPsec in a firewall is resistant to bypass if all traffic from the outside must use IP and the firewall is the only means of entrance from the Internet into the organization.
- IPsec is below the transport layer (TCP, UDP) and so is transparent to applications. There is no need to change software on a user or server system when IPsec is implemented in the firewall or router. Even if IPsec is implemented in end systems, upper-layer software, including applications, is not affected.
- IPsec can be transparent to end users. There is no need to train users on security mechanisms, issue keying material on a per-user basis, or revoke keying material when users leave the organization.
- IPsec can provide security for individual users if needed. This is useful for offsite workers and for setting up a secure virtual subnetwork within an organization for sensitive applications.

IPsec Functions

IPsec provides three main facilities: an authentication-only function referred to as Authentication Header (AH), a combined authentication/encryption function called Encapsulating Security Payload (ESP), and a key exchange function. For VPNs, both authentication and encryption are generally desired, because it is important both to (1) assure that unauthorized users do not penetrate the virtual private network and (2) assure that eavesdroppers on the Internet cannot read messages sent over the virtual private network. Because both features are generally desirable, most implementations are likely to use ESP rather than AH. The key exchange function allows for manual exchange of keys as well as an automated scheme.

IPsec is explored in Chapter 24.

18.6 RECOMMENDED READING AND WEB SITES

[PARZ06] provides clear coverage of all of the topics in this chapter. [SHAN02] and [KENT87] provide useful discussions of fragmentation. [KESH98] provides an instructive look at present and future router functionality. [BEIJ06] provides a good overview of IPv6. [METZ02] and [DOI04] describe the IPv6 anycast feature. For the reader interested in a more in-depth discussion of IP addressing, [SPOR03] offers a wealth of detail.

BEIJ06 Beijnum, I. "IPv6 Internals." *The Internet Protocol Journal*, September 2006.

DOI04 Doi, S., et al. "IPv6 Anycast for Simple and Effective Communications." *IEEE Communications Magazine*, May 2004.

KENT87 Kent, C., and Mogul, J. "Fragmentation Considered Harmful." *ACM Computer Communication Review*, October 1987.

KESH98 Keshav, S., and Sharma, R. "Issues and Trends in Router Design." *IEEE Communications Magazine*, May 1998.

METZ02 Metz, C. "IP Anycast." *IEEE Internet Computing*, March 2002.

PARZ06   Parziale, L., et al. *TCP/IP Tutorial and Technical Overview*. IBM Redbook
GG24-3376-07, 2006. http://www.redbooks.ibm.com/abstracts/gg243376.html

SHAN02   Shannon, C.; Moore, D.; and Claffy, K. "Beyond Folklore: Observations
on Fragmented Traffic." *IEEE/ACM Transactions on Networking*, December
2002.

SPOR03   Sportack, M. *IP Addressing Fundamentals*. Indianapolis, IN: Cisco Press, 2003.

Recommended Web sites:

- **IPv6:** Information about IPv6 and related topics.
- **IPv6 Forum:** An industry consortium that promotes IPv6-related products. Includes a number of white papers and articles.

18.7 KEY TERMS, REVIEW QUESTIONS, AND PROBLEMS

Key Terms

broadcast	Internet Protocol (IP)	router
datagram lifetime	internetworking	segmentation
end system	intranet	subnet
fragmentation	IPv4	subnet mask
intermediate system (IS)	IPv6	subnetwork
Internet Control Message	multicast	traffic class
Protocol (ICMP)	reassembly	unicast

Review Questions

18.1   List the requirements for an internetworking facility.

18.2   Give some reasons for using fragmentation and reassembly.

18.3   What are the pros and cons of limiting reassembly to the endpoint as compared to allowing en route reassembly?

18.4   Explain the function of the three flags in the IPv4 header.

18.5   How is the IPv4 header checksum calculated?

18.6   What is the difference between the traffic class and flow label fields in the IPv6 header?

18.7   Briefly explain the three types of IPv6 addresses.

18.8   What is the purpose of each of the IPv6 header types?

Problems

18.1 Although not explicitly stated, the Internet Protocol (IP) specification, RFC 791, defines the minimum packet size a network technology must support to allow IP to run over it.

    a. Read Section 3.2 of RFC 791 to find out that value. What is it?

    b. Discuss the reasons for adopting that specific value.

18.2 In the discussion of IP, it was mentioned that the *identifier*, *don't fragment identifier*, and *time to live* parameters are present in the Send primitive but not in the Deliver primitive because they are only of concern to IP. For each of these parameters indicate whether it is of concern to the IP entity in the source, the IP entities in any intermediate routers, and the IP entity in the destination end systems. Justify your answer.

18.3 What is the header overhead in the IP protocol?

18.4 Describe some circumstances where it might be desirable to use source routing rather than let the routers make the routing decision.

18.5 Because of fragmentation, an IP datagram can arrive in several pieces, not necessarily in the correct order. The IP entity at the receiving end system must accumulate these fragments until the original datagram is reconstituted.

    a. Consider that the IP entity creates a buffer for assembling the data field in the original datagram. As assembly proceeds, the buffer will contain blocks of data and "holes" between the data blocks. Describe an algorithm for reassembly based on this concept.

    b. For the algorithm in part (a), it is necessary to keep track of the holes. Describe a simple mechanism for doing this.

18.6 A 4480-octet datagram is to be transmitted and needs to be fragmented because it will pass through an Ethernet with a maximum payload of 1500 octets. Show the Total Length, More Flag, and Fragment Offset values in each of the resulting fragments.

18.7 Consider a header that consists of 10 octets, with the checksum in the last two octets (this does not correspond to any actual header format) with the following content (in hexadecimal): 01 00 F6 F7 F4 F5 F2 03 00 00

    a. Calculate the checksum. Show your calculations.

    b. Show the resulting packet.

    c. Verify the checksum.

18.8 The IP checksum needs to be recalculated at routers because of changes to the IP header, such as the lifetime field. It is possible to recalculate the checksum from scratch. Suggest a procedure that involves less calculation. *Hint:* Suppose that the value in 16-bit word k is changed by $Z = \text{new–value} - \text{old–value}$; consider the effect of this change on the checksum.

18.9 An IP datagram is to be fragmented. Which options in the option field need to be copied into the header of each fragment, and which need only be retained in the first fragment? Justify the handling of each option.

18.10 A transport layer message consisting of 1500 bits of data and 160 bits of header is sent to an internet layer, which appends another 160 bits of header. This is then transmitted through two networks, each of which uses a 24-bit packet header. The destination network has a maximum packet size of 800 bits. How many bits, including headers, are delivered to the network-layer protocol at the destination?

18.11 The architecture suggested by Figure 18.1 is to be used. What functions could be added to the routers to alleviate some of the problems caused by the mismatched local and long-haul networks?

18.12 Should internetworking be concerned with a network's internal routing? Why or why not?

18.13 Provide the following parameter values for each of the network classes A, B, and C. Be sure to consider any special or reserved addresses in your calculations.
  a. Number of bits in network portion of address
  b. Number of bits in host portion of address
  c. Number of distinct networks allowed
  d. Number of distinct hosts per network allowed
  e. Integer range of first octet

18.14 What percentage of the total IP address space does each of the network classes represent?

18.15 What is the difference between the subnet mask for a Class A address with 16 bits for the subnet ID and a Class B address with 8 bits for the subnet ID?

18.16 Is the subnet mask 255.255.0.255 valid for a Class A address?

18.17 Given a network address of 192.168.100.0 and a subnet mask of 255.255.255.192,
  a. How many subnets are created?
  b. How many hosts are there per subnet?

18.18 Given a company with six individual departments and each department having ten computers or networked devices, what mask could be applied to the company network to provide the subnetting necessary to divide up the network equally?

18.19 In contemporary routing and addressing, the notation commonly used is called classless interdomain routing or CIDR. With CIDR, the number of bits in the mask is indicated in the following fashion: 192.168.100.0/24. This corresponds to a mask of 255.255.255.0. If this example would provide for 256 host addresses on the network, how many addresses are provided with the following?
  a. 192.168.100.0/23
  b. 192.168.100.0/25

18.20 Find out about your network. Using the command "ipconfig", "ifconfig", or "winipcfg", we can learn not only our IP address but other network parameters as well. Can you determine your mask, gateway, and the number of addresses available on your network?

18.21 Using your IP address and your mask, what is your network address? This is determined by converting the IP address and the mask to binary and then proceeding with a bitwise logical AND operation. For example, given the address 172.16.45.0 and the mask 255.255.224.0, we would discover that the network address would be 172.16.32.0.

18.22 Compare the individual fields of the IPv4 header with the IPv6 header. Account for the functionality provided by each IPv4 field by showing how the same functionality is provided in IPv6.

18.23 Justify the recommended order in which IPv6 extension headers appear (i.e., why is the Hop-by-Hop Options header first, why is the Routing header before the Fragment header, and so on).

18.24 The IPv6 standard states that if a packet with a nonzero flow label arrives at a router and the router has no information for that flow label, the router should ignore the flow label and forward the packet.
  a. What are the disadvantages of treating this event as an error, discarding the packet, and sending an ICMP message?
  b. Are there situations in which routing the packet as if its flow label were zero will cause the wrong result? Explain.

18.25 The IPv6 flow mechanism assumes that the state associated with a given flow label is stored in routers, so they know how to handle packets that carry that flow label. A design requirement is to flush flow labels that are no longer being used (stale flow label) from routers.
  a. Assume that a source always send a control message to all affected routers deleting a flow label when the source finishes with that flow. In that case, how could a stale flow label persist?

    b. Suggest router and source mechanisms to overcome the problem of stale flow labels.

18.26 The question arises as to which packets generated by a source should carry nonzero IPv6 flow labels. For some applications, the answer is obvious. Small exchanges of data should have a zero flow label because it is not worth creating a flow for a few packets. Real-time flows should have a flow label; such flows are a primary reason flow labels were created. A more difficult issue is what to do with peers sending large amounts of best-effort traffic (e.g., TCP connections). Make a case for assigning a unique flow label to each long-term TCP connection. Make a case for not doing this.

18.27 The original IPv6 specifications combined the Traffic Class and Flow Label fields into a single 28-bit Flow Label field. This allowed flows to redefine the interpretation of different values of priority. Suggest reasons why the final specification includes the Priority field as a distinct field.

18.28 For Type 0 IPv6 routing, specify the algorithm for updating the IPv6 and Routing headers by intermediate nodes.

INTERNETWORK OPERATION

Prior to the recent explosion of sophisticated research, scientists believed that birds required no special awareness or intelligence to perform their migrations and their navigational and homing feats. Accumulated research shows that in addition to performing the difficult tasks of correcting for displacement (by storms, winds, mountains, and other hindrances), birds integrate an astonishing variety of celestial, atmospheric, and geological information to travel between their winter and summer homes. In brief, avian navigation is characterized by the ability to gather a variety of informational cues and to interpret and coordinate them so as to move closer toward a goal.

—The Human Nature of Birds, Theodore Barber

KEY POINTS

◆ The act of sending a packet from a source to multiple destinations is referred to as multicasting. Multicasting raises design issues in the areas of addressing and routing.

◆ Routing protocols in an internet function in a similar fashion to those used in packet-switching networks. An internet routing protocol is used to exchange information about reachability and traffic delays, allowing each router to construct a next-hop routing table for paths through the internet. Typically, relatively simple routing protocols are used between autonomous systems within a larger internet and more complex routing protocols are used within each autonomous system.

◆ Mobile IP defines extensions to IP for accommodating mobile and nomadic hosts.

This chapter begins with a discussion of multicasting. Next, we explore the issue of internetwork routing algorithms. The chapter then introduces the topic of Mobile IP. Refer to Figure 2.5 to see the position within the TCP/IP suite of the protocols discussed in this chapter.

19.1 MULTICASTING

Typically, an IP address refers to an individual host on a particular network. IP also accommodates addresses that refer to a group of hosts on one or more networks. Such addresses are referred to as **multicast addresses**, and the act of sending a packet from a source to the members of a multicast group is referred to as **multicasting**.

Multicasting has a number of practical applications. For example,

• **Multimedia:** A number of users "tune in" to a video or audio transmission from a multimedia source station.

• **Teleconferencing:** A group of workstations form a multicast group such that a transmission from any member is received by all other group members.

- **Database:** All copies of a replicated file or database are updated at the same time.
- **Distributed computation:** Intermediate results are sent to all participants.
- **Real-time workgroup:** Files, graphics, and messages are exchanged among active group members in real time.

Multicasting done within the scope of a single LAN segment is straightforward. IEEE 802 and other LAN protocols include provision for MAC-level multicast addresses. A packet with a multicast address is transmitted on a LAN segment. Those stations that are members of the corresponding multicast group recognize the multicast address and accept the packet. In this case, only a single copy of the packet is ever transmitted. This technique works because of the broadcast nature of a LAN: a transmission from any one station is received by all other stations on the LAN.

In an internet environment, multicasting is a far more difficult undertaking. To see this, consider the configuration of Figure 19.1; a number of LANs are interconnected by routers. Routers connect to each other either over high-speed links or

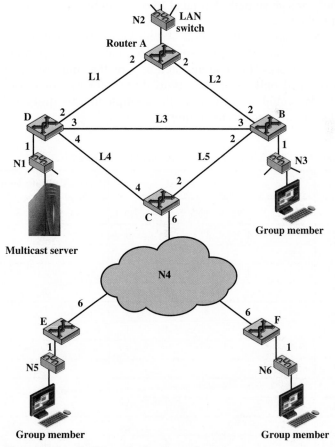

Figure 19.1   An Example Configuration

across a wide area network (network N4). A cost is associated with each link or network in each direction, indicated by the value shown leaving the router for that link or network. Suppose that the multicast server on network N1 is transmitting packets to a multicast address that represents the workstations indicated on networks N3, N5, and N6. Suppose that the server does not know the location of the members of the multicast group. Then one way to assure that the packet is received by all members of the group is to **broadcast** a copy of each packet to each network in the configuration, over the least-cost route for each network. For example, one packet would be addressed to N3 and would traverse N1, link L3, and N3. Router B is responsible for translating the IP-level multicast address to a MAC-level multicast address before transmitting the MAC frame onto N3. Table 19.1 summarizes the number of packets generated on the various links and networks in order to transmit one packet to a multicast group by this method. In this table, the source is the multicast server on network N1 in Figure 19.1; the multicast address includes the group members on N3, N5, and N6. Each column in the table refers to the path taken from the source host to a destination router attached to a particular destination network. Each row of the table refers to a network or link in the configuration of Figure 19.1. Each entry in the table gives the number of packets that traverse a given network or link for a given path. A total of 13 copies of the packet are required for the broadcast technique.

Now suppose the source system knows the location of each member of the multicast group. That is, the source has a table that maps a multicast address into a list of networks that contain members of that multicast group. In that case, the source need only send packets to those networks that contain members of the group. We could refer to this as the **multiple unicast** strategy. Table 19.1 shows that in this case, 11 packets are required.

Table 19.1 Traffic Generated by Various Multicasting Strategies

	Broadcast					**Multiple Unicast**				**Multicast**
	S→N2	S→N3	S→N5	S→N6	Total	S→N3	S→N5	S→N6	Total	
N1	1	1	1	1	4	1	1	1	3	1
N2										
N3		1			1	1			1	1
N4			1	1	2		1	1	2	2
N5			1		1		1		1	1
N6				1	1			1	1	1
L1	1				1					
L2										
L3		1			1	1			1	1
L4			1	1	2		1	1	2	1
L5										
Total	2	3	4	4	13	3	4	4	11	8

Both the broadcast and multiple unicast strategies are inefficient because they generate unnecessary copies of the source packet. In a true **multicast** strategy, the following method is used:

1. The least-cost path from the source to each network that includes members of the multicast group is determined. This results in a spanning tree[1] of the configuration. Note that this is not a full spanning tree of the configuration. Rather, it is a spanning tree that includes only those networks containing group members.

2. The source transmits a single packet along the spanning tree.

3. The packet is replicated by routers only at branch points of the spanning tree.

Figure 19.2a shows the spanning tree for transmissions from the source to the multicast group, and Figure 19.2b shows this method in action. The source transmits a single packet over N1 to router D. D makes two copies of the packet, to transmit over links L3 and L4. B receives the packet from L3 and transmits it on N3, where it is read by members of the multicast group on the network. Meanwhile, C receives the packet sent on L4. It must now deliver that packet to both E and F. If network N4 were a broadcast network (e.g., an IEEE 802 LAN), then C would only need to transmit one instance of the packet for both routers to read. If N4 is a packet-switching WAN, then C must make two copies of the packet and address one to E

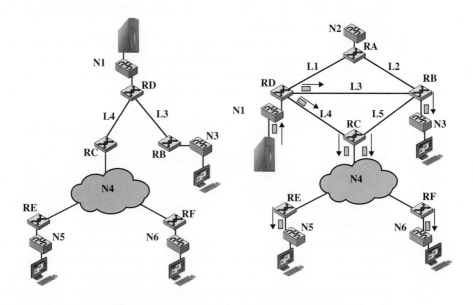

(a) Spanning tree from source to multicast group   (b) Packets generated for multicast transmission

Figure 19.2   Multicast Transmission Example

---

[1]The concept of spanning tree was introduced in our discussion of bridges in Chapter 15. A spanning tree of a graph consists of all the nodes of the graph plus a subset of the links (edges) of the graph that provides connectivity (a path exists between any two nodes) with no closed loops (there is only one path between any two nodes).

and one to F. Each of these routers, in turn, retransmits the received packet on N5 and N6, respectively. As Table 19.1 shows, the multicast technique requires only eight copies of the packet.

Requirements for Multicasting

In ordinary unicast transmission over an internet, in which each datagram has a unique destination network, the task of each router is to forward the datagram along the shortest path from that router to the destination network. With multicast transmission, the router may be required to forward two or more copies of an incoming datagram. In our example, routers D and C both must forward two copies of a single incoming datagram.

Thus, we might expect that the overall functionality of multicast routing is more complex than unicast routing. The following is a list of required functions:

1. A convention is needed for identifying a multicast address. In IPv4, Class D addresses are reserved for this purpose. These are 32-bit addresses with 1110 as their high-order 4 bits, followed by a 28-bit group identifier. In IPv6, a 128-bit multicast address consists of an 8-bit prefix of all ones, a 4-bit flags field, a 4-bit scope field, and a 112-bit group identifier. The flags field, currently, only indicates whether this address is permanently assigned or not. The scope field indicates the scope of applicability of the address, ranging from a single network to global.

2. Each node (router or source node participating in the routing algorithm) must translate between an IP multicast address and a list of networks that contain members of this group. This information allows the node to construct a shortest-path spanning tree to all of the networks containing group members.

3. A router must translate between an IP multicast address and a network multicast address in order to deliver a multicast IP datagram on the destination network. For example, in IEEE 802 networks, a MAC-level address is 48 bits long; if the highest-order bit is 1, then it is a multicast address. Thus, for multicast delivery, a router attached to an IEEE 802 network must translate a 32-bit IPv4 or a 128-bit IPv6 multicast address into a 48-bit IEEE 802 MAC-level multicast address.

4. Although some multicast addresses may be assigned permanently, the more usual case is that multicast addresses are generated dynamically and that individual hosts may join and leave multicast groups dynamically. Thus, a mechanism is needed by which an individual host informs routers attached to the same network as itself of its inclusion in and exclusion from a multicast group. Internet Group Management Protocol (IGMP), described subsequently, provides this mechanism.

5. Routers must exchange two sorts of information. First, routers need to know which networks include members of a given multicast group. Second, routers need sufficient information to calculate the shortest path to each network

containing group members. These requirements imply the need for a multicast routing protocol. A discussion of such protocols is beyond the scope of this book.

6. A routing algorithm is needed to calculate shortest paths to all group members.

7. Each router must determine multicast routing paths on the basis of both source and destination addresses.

The last point is a subtle consequence of the use of multicast addresses. To illustrate the point, consider again Figure 19.1. If the multicast server transmits a unicast packet addressed to a host on network N5, the packet is forwarded by router D to C, which then forwards the packet to E. Similarly, a packet addressed to a host on network N3 is forwarded by D to B. But now suppose that the server transmits a packet with a multicast address that includes hosts on N3, N5, and N6. As we have discussed, D makes two copies of the packet and sends one to B and one to C. What will C do when it receives a packet with such a multicast address? C knows that this packet is intended for networks N3, N5, and N6. A simple-minded approach would be for C to calculate the shortest path to each of these three networks. This produces the shortest-path spanning tree shown in Figure 19.3. As a result, C sends two copies of the packet out over N4, one intended for N5 and one intended for N6. But it also sends a copy of the packet to B for delivery on N3. Thus B will receive two copies of the packet, one from D and one from C. This is clearly not what was intended by the host on N1 when it launched the packet.

To avoid unnecessary duplication of packets, each router must route packets on the basis of both source and multicast destination. When C receives a packet intended for the multicast group from a source on N1, it must calculate the spanning tree with N1 as the root (shown in Figure 19.2a) and route on the basis of that spanning tree.

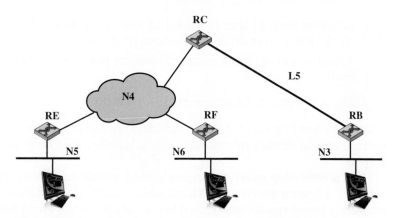

Figure 19.3　Spanning Tree from Router C to Multicast Group

Internet Group Management Protocol (IGMP)

IGMP, defined in RFC 3376, is used by hosts and routers to exchange multicast group membership information over a LAN. IGMP takes advantage of the broadcast nature of a LAN to provide an efficient technique for the exchange of information among multiple hosts and routers. In general, IGMP supports two principal operations:

1. Hosts send messages to routers to subscribe to and unsubscribe from a multicast group defined by a given multicast address.
2. Routers periodically check which multicast groups are of interest to which hosts.

IGMP is currently at version 3. In IGMPv1, hosts could join a multicast group and routers used a timer to unsubscribe group members. IGMPv2 enabled a host to request to be unsubscribed from a group. The first two versions used essentially the following operational model:

- Receivers have to subscribe to multicast groups.
- Sources do not have to subscribe to multicast groups.
- Any host can send traffic to any multicast group.

This paradigm is very general, but it also has some weaknesses:

1. Spamming of multicast groups is easy. Even if there are application level filters to drop unwanted packets, still these packets consume valuable resources in the network and in the receiver that has to process them.
2. Establishment of the multicast distribution trees is problematic. This is mainly because the location of sources is not known.
3. Finding globally unique multicast addresses is difficult. It is always possible that another multicast group uses the same multicast address.

IGMPv3 addresses these weaknesses by

1. Allowing hosts to specify the list of hosts from which they want to receive traffic. Traffic from other hosts is blocked at routers.
2. Allowing hosts to block packets that come from sources that send unwanted traffic.

The remainder of this section discusses IGMPv3.

IGMP MESSAGE FORMAT All IGMP messages are transmitted in IP datagrams. The current version defines two message types: Membership Query and Membership Report.

A **membership query** message is sent by a multicast router. There are three subtypes: a **general query**, used to learn which groups have members on an attached network; a **group-specific query**, used to learn if a particular group has any members on an attached network; and a **group-and-source specific query**, used to learn if any attached device desires reception of packets sent to a specified multicast address, from any of a specified list of sources. Figure 19.4a shows the message format, which consists of the following fields:

- **Type:** Defines this message type.
- **Max Response Code:** Indicates the maximum allowed time before sending a responding report in units of 0.1 s.
- **Checksum:** An error-detecting code, calculated as the 16-bit ones complement addition of all the 16-bit words in the message. For purposes of computation, the Checksum field is itself initialized to a value of zero. This is the same checksum algorithm used in IPv4.
- **Group Address:** Zero for a general query message; a valid IP multicast group address when sending a group-specific query or group-and-source-specific query.
- **S Flag:** When set to one, indicates to any receiving multicast routers that they are to suppress the normal timer updates they perform upon hearing a query.
- **QRV (querier's robustness variable):** If nonzero, the QRV field contains the RV value used by the querier (i.e., the sender of the query). Routers adopt the RV value from the most recently received query as their own RV value, unless that most recently received RV was zero, in which case the receivers use the default value or a statically configured value. The RV dictates how many times a host will retransmit a report to assure that it is not missed by any attached multicast routers.
- **QQIC (querier's querier interval code):** Specifies the QI value used by the querier, which is a timer for sending multiple queries. Multicast routers that are not the current querier adopt the QI value from the most recently received query as their own QI value, unless that most recently received QI was zero, in which case the receiving routers use the default QI value.
- **Number of Sources:** Specifies how many source addresses are present in this query. This value is nonzero only for a group-and-source specific query.
- **Source Addresses:** If the number of sources is N, then there are N 32-bit unicast addresses appended to the message.

A **membership report** message consists of the following fields:

- **Type:** Defines this message type.
- **Checksum:** An error-detecting code, calculated as the 16-bit ones complement addition of all the 16-bit words in the message.
- **Number of Group Records:** Specifies how many group records are present in this report.
- **Group Records:** If the number of group records is M, then there are M 32-bit unicast group records appended to the message.

A group record includes the following fields:

- **Record Type:** Defines this record type, as described subsequently.
- **Aux Data Length:** Length of the auxiliary data field, in 32-bit words.

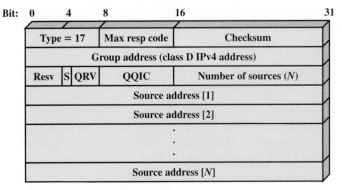

(a) Membership query message

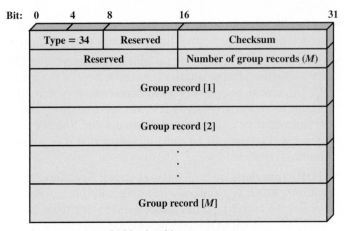

(b) Membership report message

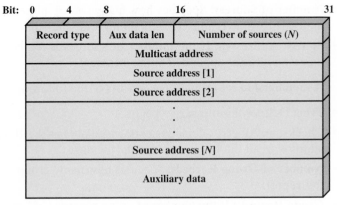

(c) Group record

Figure 19.4 IGMPv3 Message Formats

- **Number of Sources:** Specifies how many source addresses are present in this record.
- **Multicast Address:** The IP multicast address to which this record pertains.
- **Source Addresses:** If the number of sources is N, then there are N 32-bit unicast addresses appended to the message.
- **Auxiliary Data:** Additional information pertaining to this record. Currently, no auxiliary data values are defined.

IGMP OPERATION The objective of each host in using IGMP is to make itself known as a member of a group with a given multicast address to other hosts on the LAN and to all routers on the LAN. IGMPv3 introduces the ability for hosts to signal group membership with filtering capabilities with respect to sources. A host can either signal that it wants to receive traffic from all sources sending to a group except for some specific sources (called EXCLUDE mode) or that it wants to receive traffic only from some specific sources sending to the group (called INCLUDE mode). To join a group, a host sends an IGMP membership report message, in which the multicast address field is the multicast address of the group. This message is sent in an IP datagram with the same multicast destination address. In other words, the Multicast Address field of the IGMP message and the Destination Address field of the encapsulating IP header are the same. All hosts that are currently members of this multicast group will receive the message and learn of the new group member. Each router attached to the LAN must listen to all IP multicast addresses in order to hear all reports.

To maintain a valid current list of active group addresses, a multicast router periodically issues an IGMP general query message, sent in an IP datagram with an *all-hosts* multicast address. Each host that still wishes to remain a member of one or more multicast groups must read datagrams with the all-hosts address. When such a host receives the query, it must respond with a report message for each group to which it claims membership.

Note that the multicast router does not need to know the identity of every host in a group. Rather, it needs to know that there is at least one group member still active. Therefore, each host in a group that receives a query sets a timer with a random delay. Any host that hears another host claim membership in the group will cancel its own report. If no other report is heard and the timer expires, a host sends a report. With this scheme, only one member of each group should provide a report to the multicast router.

When a host leaves a group, it sends a leave group message to the all-routers static multicast address. This is accomplished by sending a membership report message with the INCLUDE option and a null list of source addresses; that is, no sources are to be included, effectively leaving the group. When a router receives such a message for a group that has group members on the reception interface, it needs to determine if there are any remaining group members. For this purpose, the router uses the group-specific query message.

GROUP MEMBERSHIP WITH IPv6 IGMP was defined for operation with IPv4 and makes use of 32-bit addresses. IPv6 internets need this same functionality. Rather than defining a separate version of IGMP for IPv6, its functions have been incorporated into the new version of the Internet Control Message Protocol (ICMPv6). ICMPv6 includes all of the functionality of ICMPv4 and IGMP. For multicast support, ICMPv6 includes both a group-membership query and a group-membership report message, which are used in the same fashion as in IGMP.

19.2 ROUTING PROTOCOLS

The routers in an internet are responsible for receiving and forwarding packets through the interconnected set of networks. Each router makes routing decision based on knowledge of the topology and traffic/delay conditions of the internet. In a simple internet, a fixed routing scheme is possible. In more complex internets, a degree of dynamic cooperation is needed among the routers. In particular, the router must avoid portions of the network that have failed and should avoid portions of the network that are congested. To make such dynamic routing decisions, routers exchange routing information using a special routing protocol for that purpose. Information is needed about the status of the internet, in terms of which networks can be reached by which routes, and the delay characteristics of various routes.

In considering the routing function, it is important to distinguish two concepts:

- **Routing information:** Information about the topology and delays of the internet
- **Routing algorithm:** The algorithm used to make a routing decision for a particular datagram, based on current routing information

Autonomous Systems

To proceed with our discussion of routing protocols, we need to introduce the concept of an **autonomous system (AS)**. An AS exhibits the following characteristics:

1. An AS is a set of routers and networks managed by a single organization.
2. An AS consists of a group of routers exchanging information via a common routing protocol.
3. Except in times of failure, an AS is connected (in a graph-theoretic sense); that is, there is a path between any pair of nodes.

A shared routing protocol, which we shall refer to as an **interior router protocol (IRP)**, passes routing information between routers within an AS. The protocol used within the AS does not need to be implemented outside of the system. This flexibility allows IRPs to be custom tailored to specific applications and requirements.

It may happen, however, that an internet will be constructed of more than one AS. For example, all of the LANs at a site, such as an office complex or campus, could be linked by routers to form an AS. This system might be linked through a wide area network to other ASs. The situation is illustrated in Figure 19.5. In this case, the routing algorithms and information in routing tables used by routers in different ASs may differ. Nevertheless, the routers in one AS need at least a minimal level of information concerning networks outside the system that can be reached.

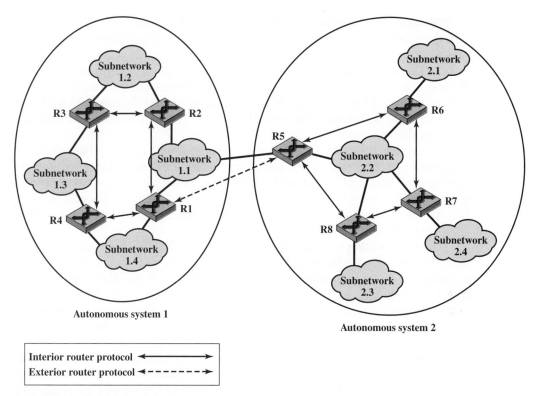

Figure 19.5   Application of Exterior and Interior Routing Protocols

We refer to the protocol used to pass routing information between routers in different ASs as an **exterior router protocol (ERP)**.[2]

We can expect that an ERP will need to pass less information than an IRP for the following reason. If a datagram is to be transferred from a host in one AS to a host in another AS, a router in the first system need only determine the target AS and devise a route to get into that target system. Once the datagram enters the target AS, the routers within that system can cooperate to deliver the datagram; the ERP is not concerned with, and does not know about, the details of the route followed within the target AS.

In the remainder of this section, we look at what are perhaps the most important examples of these two types of routing protocols: Broader Gateway Protocol (BGP) and Open Shortest Path First (OSPF) Protocol. But first, it is useful to look at a different way of characterizing routing protocols.

Approaches to Routing

Internet routing protocols employ one of three approaches to gathering and using routing information: distance-vector routing, link-state routing, and path-vector routing.

---

[2]In the literature, the terms *interior gateway protocol* (IGP) and *exterior gateway protocol* (EGP) are often used for what are referred to here as IRP and ERP. However, because the terms *IGP* and *EGP* also refer to specific protocols, we avoid their use when referring to general concepts.

Distance-vector routing requires that each node (router or host that implements the routing protocol) exchange information with its neighboring nodes. Two nodes are said to be neighbors if they are both directly connected to the same network. This approach is that used in the first-generation routing algorithm for ARPANET, as described in Section 12.2. For this purpose, each node maintains a vector of link costs for each directly attached network and distance and next-hop vectors for each destination. The relatively simple Routing Information Protocol (RIP) uses this approach.

Distance-vector routing requires the transmission of a considerable amount of information by each router. Each router must send a distance vector to all of its neighbors, and that vector contains the estimated path cost to all networks in the configuration. Furthermore, when there is a significant change in a link cost or when a link is unavailable, it may take a considerable amount of time for this information to propagate through the internet.

Link-state routing is designed to overcome the drawbacks of distance-vector routing. When a router is initialized, it determines the link cost on each of its network interfaces. The router then advertises this set of link costs to all other routers in the internet topology, not just neighboring routers. From then on, the router monitors its link costs. Whenever there is a significant change (e.g., a link cost increases or decreases substantially, a new link is created, or an existing link becomes unavailable), the router again advertises its set of link costs to all other routers in the configuration.

Because each router receives the link costs of all routers in the configuration, each router can construct the topology of the entire configuration and then calculate the shortest path to each destination network. Having done this, the router can construct its routing table, listing the first hop to each destination. Because the router has a representation of the entire network, it does not use a distributed version of a routing algorithm, as is done in distance-vector routing. Rather, the router can use any routing algorithm to determine the shortest paths. In practice, Dijkstra's algorithm is used. The OSPF protocol is an example of a routing protocol that uses link-state routing. The second-generation routing algorithm for ARPANET also uses this approach.

Both link-state and distance-vector approaches have been used for interior router protocols. Neither approach is effective for an exterior router protocol.

In a distance-vector routing protocol, each router advertises to its neighbors a vector listing each network it can reach, together with a distance metric associated with the path to that network. Each router builds up a routing database on the basis of these neighbor updates but does not know the identity of intermediate routers and networks on any particular path. There are two problems with this approach for an exterior router protocol:

1. This distance-vector protocol assumes that all routers share a common distance metric with which to judge router preferences. This may not be the case among different ASs. If different routers attach different meanings to a given metric, it may not be possible to create stable, loop-free routes.

2. A given AS may have different priorities from other ASs and may have restrictions that prohibit the use of certain other AS. A distance-vector algorithm gives no information about the ASs that will be visited along a route.

In a link-state routing protocol, each router advertises its link metrics to all other routers. Each router builds up a picture of the complete topology of the configuration and then performs a routing calculation. This approach also has problems if used in an exterior router protocol:

1. Different ASs may use different metrics and have different restrictions. Although the link-state protocol does allow a router to build up a picture of the entire topology, the metrics used may vary from one AS to another, making it impossible to perform a consistent routing algorithm.

2. The flooding of link- state information to all routers implementing an exterior router protocol across multiple ASs may be unmanageable.

An alternative, known as **path-vector routing**, is to dispense with routing metrics and simply provide information about which networks can be reached by a given router and the ASs that must be crossed to get there. The approach differs from a distance-vector algorithm in two respects: First, the path-vector approach does not include a distance or cost estimate. Second, each block of routing information lists all of the ASs visited in order to reach the destination network by this route.

Because a path vector lists the ASs that a datagram must traverse if it follows this route, the path information enables a router to perform policy routing. That is, a router may decide to avoid a particular path in order to avoid transiting a particular AS. For example, information that is confidential may be limited to certain kinds of ASs. Or a router may have information about the performance or quality of the portion of the internet that is included in an AS that leads the router to avoid that AS. Examples of performance or quality metrics include link speed, capacity, tendency to become congested, and overall quality of operation. Another criterion that could be used is minimizing the number of transit ASs.

Border Gateway Protocol

BGP was developed for use in conjunction with internets that employ the TCP/IP suite, although the concepts are applicable to any internet. BGP has become the preferred exterior router protocol for the Internet.

FUNCTIONS BGP was designed to allow routers, called gateways in the standard, in different autonomous systems (ASs) to cooperate in the exchange of routing information. The protocol operates in terms of messages, which are sent over TCP connections. The repertoire of messages is summarized in Table 19.2. The current version of BGP is known as BGP-4 (RFC 4271).

Three functional procedures are involved in BGP:

- Neighbor acquisition
- Neighbor reachability
- Network reachability

Two routers are considered to be neighbors if they are attached to the same network. If the two routers are in different autonomous systems, they may wish to exchange routing information. For this purpose, it is necessary first to perform **neighbor acquisition**. In essence, neighbor acquisition occurs when two neighboring routers in

Table 19.2 BGP-4 Messages

Open	Used to open a neighbor relationship with another router.
Update	Used to (1) transmit information about a single route and/or (2) list multiple routes to be withdrawn.
Keepalive	Used to (1) acknowledge an Open message and (2) periodically confirm the neighbor relationship.
Notification	Send when an error condition is detected.

different autonomous systems agree to exchange routing information regularly. A formal acquisition procedure is needed because one of the routers may not wish to participate. For example, the router may be overburdened and does not want to be responsible for traffic coming in from outside the system. In the neighbor acquisition process, one router sends a request message to the other, which may either accept or refuse the offer. The protocol does not address the issue of how one router knows the address or even the existence of another router nor how it decides that it needs to exchange routing information with that particular router. These issues must be dealt with at configuration time or by active intervention of a network manager.

To perform neighbor acquisition, two routers send Open messages to each other after a TCP connection is established. If each router accepts the request, it returns a Keepalive message in response.

Once a neighbor relationship is established, the **neighbor reachability** procedure is used to maintain the relationship. Each partner needs to be assured that the other partner still exists and is still engaged in the neighbor relationship. For this purpose, the two routers periodically issue Keepalive messages to each other.

The final procedure specified by BGP is **network reachability**. Each router maintains a database of the networks that it can reach and the preferred route for reaching each network. When a change is made to this database, the router issues an Update message that is broadcast to all other routers implementing BGP. Because the Update message is broadcast, all BGP routers can build up and maintain their routing information.

BGP Messages Figure 19.6 illustrates the formats of all of the BGP messages. Each message begins with a 19-octet header containing three fields, as indicated by the shaded portion of each message in the figure:

- **Marker:** Reserved for authentication. The sender may insert a value in this field that would be used as part of an authentication mechanism to enable the recipient to verify the identity of the sender.
- **Length:** Length of message in octets.
- **Type:** Type of message: Open, Update, Notification, Keepalive.

To acquire a neighbor, a router first opens a TCP connection to the neighbor router of interest. It then sends an Open message. This message identifies the AS to which the sender belongs and provides the IP address of the router. It also includes a Hold Time parameter, which indicates the number of seconds that the sender proposes for the value of the Hold Timer. If the recipient is prepared to open a neighbor relationship, it calculates a value of Hold Timer that is the minimum of its Hold Time and the Hold Time in the Open message. This calculated value is the

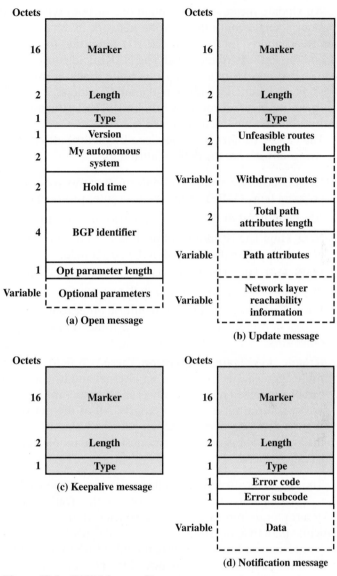

Figure 19.6 BGP Message Formats

maximum number of seconds that may elapse between the receipt of successive Keepalive and/or Update messages by the sender.

The Keepalive message consists simply of the header. Each router issues these messages to each of its peers often enough to prevent the Hold Timer from expiring.

The Update message communicates two types of information:

- Information about a single route through the internet. This information is available to be added to the database of any recipient router.
- A list of routes previously advertised by this router that are being withdrawn.

An Update message may contain one or both types of information. Information about a single route through the network involves three fields: the Network Layer Reachability Information (NLRI) field, the Total Path Attributes Length field, and the Path Attributes field. The NLRI field consists of a list of identifiers of networks that can be reached by this route. Each network is identified by its IP address, which is actually a portion of a full IP address. Recall that an IP address is a 32-bit quantity of the form {network, host}. The left-hand or prefix portion of this quantity identifies a particular network.

The Path Attributes field contains a list of attributes that apply to this particular route. The following are the defined attributes:

- **Origin:** Indicates whether this information was generated by an interior router protocol (e.g., OSPF) or an exterior router protocol (in particular, BGP).
- **AS_Path:** A list of the ASs that are traversed for this route.
- **Next_Hop:** The IP address of the border router that should be used as the next hop to the destinations listed in the NLRI field.
- **Multi_Exit_Disc:** Used to communicate some information about routes internal to an AS. This is described later in this section.
- **Local_Pref:** Used by a router to inform other routers within the same AS of its degree of preference for a particular route. It has no significance to routers in other ASs.
- **Atomic_Aggregate, Aggregator:** These two fields implement the concept of route aggregation. In essence, an internet and its corresponding address space can be organized hierarchically (i.e., as a tree). In this case, network addresses are structured in two or more parts. All of the networks of a given subtree share a common partial internet address. Using this common partial address, the amount of information that must be communicated in NLRI can be significantly reduced.

The AS_Path attribute actually serves two purposes. Because it lists the ASs that a datagram must traverse if it follows this route, the AS_Path information enables a router to implement routing policies. That is, a router may decide to avoid a particular path to avoid transiting a particular AS. For example, information that is confidential may be limited to certain kinds of ASs. Or a router may have information about the performance or quality of the portion of the internet that is included in an AS that leads the router to avoid that AS. Examples of performance or quality metrics include link speed, capacity, tendency to become congested, and overall quality of operation. Another criterion that could be used is minimizing the number of transit ASs.

The reader may wonder about the purpose of the Next_Hop attribute. The requesting router will necessarily want to know which networks are reachable via the responding router, but why provide information about other routers? This is best explained with reference to Figure 19.5. In this example, router R1 in autonomous system 1 and router R5 in autonomous system 2 implement BGP and acquire a neighbor relationship. R1 issues Update messages to R5, indicating which networks it can reach and the distances (network hops) involved. R1 also provides the same information on behalf of R2. That is, R1 tells R5 what networks are reachable via R2. In this example, R2 does not implement BGP. Typically, most of the routers in an autonomous system will not implement BGP. Only a few routers will be assigned responsibility for communicating with routers in other autonomous systems. A final point: R1 is in possession of the necessary information about R2, because R1 and R2 share an interior router protocol.

The second type of update information is the withdrawal of one or more routes. In this case, the route is identified by the IP address of the destination network.

Finally, the Notification message is sent when an error condition is detected. The following errors may be reported:

- **Message header error:** Includes authentication and syntax errors.
- **Open message error:** Includes syntax errors and options not recognized in an Open message. This message can also be used to indicate that a proposed Hold Time in an Open message is unacceptable.
- **Update message error:** Includes syntax and validity errors in an Update message.
- **Hold timer expired:** If the sending router has not received successive Keepalive and/or Update and/or Notification messages within the Hold Time period, then this error is communicated and the connection is closed.
- **Finite state machine error:** Includes any procedural error.
- **Cease:** Used by a router to close a connection with another router in the absence of any other error.

BGP Routing Information Exchange The essence of BGP is the exchange of routing information among participating routers in multiple ASs. This process can be quite complex. In what follows, we provide a simplified overview.

Let us consider router R1 in autonomous system 1 (AS1), in Figure 19.5. To begin, a router that implements BGP will also implement an internal routing protocol such as OSPF. Using OSPF, R1 can exchange routing information with other routers within AS1 and build up a picture of the topology of the networks and routers in AS1 and construct a routing table. Next, R1 can issue an Update message to R5 in AS2. The Update message could include the following:

- **AS_Path:** The identity of AS1
- **Next_Hop:** The IP address of R1
- **NLRI:** A list of all of the networks in AS1

This message informs R5 that all of the networks listed in NLRI are reachable via R1 and that the only autonomous system traversed is AS1.

Suppose now that R5 also has a neighbor relationship with another router in another autonomous system, say R9 in AS3. R5 will forward the information just received from R1 to R9 in a new Update message. This message includes the following:

- **AS_Path:** The list of identifiers {AS2, AS1}
- **Next_Hop:** The IP address of R5
- **NLRI:** A list of all of the networks in AS1

This message informs R9 that all of the networks listed in NLRI are reachable via R5 and that the autonomous systems traversed are AS2 and AS1. R9 must now decide if this is its preferred route to the networks listed. It may have knowledge of an alternate route to some or all of these networks that it prefers for reasons of performance or some other policy metric. If R9 decides that the route provided in R5's update message is preferable, then R9 incorporates that routing information into its routing database and forwards this new routing information to other neighbors. This new message will include an AS_Path field of {AS3, AS2, AS1}.

In this fashion, routing update information is propagated through the larger internet, consisting of a number of interconnected autonomous systems. The AS_Path field is used to assure that such messages do not circulate indefinitely: if an Update message is received by a router in an AS that is included in the AS_Path field, that router will not forward the update information to other routers.

Routers within the same AS, called internal neighbors, may exchange BGP information. In this case, the sending router does not add the identifier of the common AS to the AS_Path field. When a router has selected a preferred route to an external destination, it transmits this route to all of its internal neighbors. Each of these routers then decides if the new route is preferred, in which case the new route is added to its database and a new Update message goes out.

When there are multiple entry points into an AS that are available to a border router in another AS, the Multi_Exit_Disc attribute may be used to choose among them. This attribute contains a number that reflects some internal metric for reaching destinations within an AS. For example, suppose in Figure 19.5 that both R1 and R2 implement BGP and both have a neighbor relationship with R5. Each provides an Update message to R5 for network 1.3 that includes a routing metric used internal to AS1, such as a routing metric associated with the OSPF internal router protocol. R5 could then use these two metrics as the basis for choosing between the two routes.

Open Shortest Path First (OSPF) Protocol

The OSPF protocol (RFC 2328) is now widely used as the interior router protocol in TCP/IP networks. OSPF computes a route through the internet that incurs the least cost based on a user-configurable metric of cost. The user can configure the cost to express a function of delay, data rate, dollar cost, or other factors. OSPF is able to equalize loads over multiple equal-cost paths.

Each router maintains a database that reflects the known topology of the autonomous system of which it is a part. The topology is expressed as a directed graph. The graph consists of the following:

- Vertices, or nodes, of two types:
  1. router
  2. network, which is in turn of two types
     a. transit, if it can carry data that neither originate nor terminate on an end system attached to this network
     b. stub, if it is not a transit network

- Edges of two types:
  1. graph edges that connect two router vertices when the corresponding routers are connected to each other by a direct point-to-point link
  2. graph edges that connect a router vertex to a network vertex when the router is directly connected to the network

Figure 19.7, based on one in RFC 2328, shows an example of an autonomous system, and Figure 19.8 is the resulting directed graph. The mapping is straightforward:

- Two routers joined by a point-to-point link are represented in the graph as being directly connected by a pair of edges, one in each direction (e.g., routers 6 and 10).
- When multiple routers are attached to a network (such as a LAN or packet-switching network), the directed graph shows all routers bidirectionally

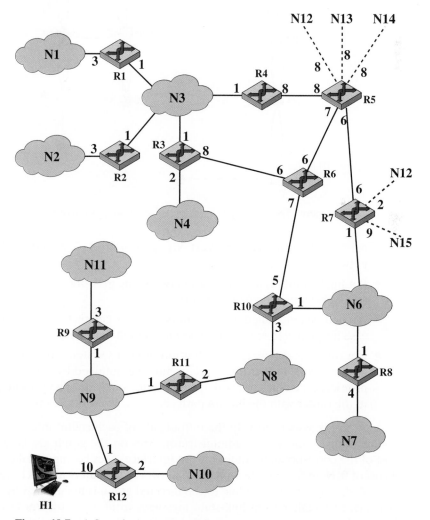

Figure 19.7 A Sample Autonomous System

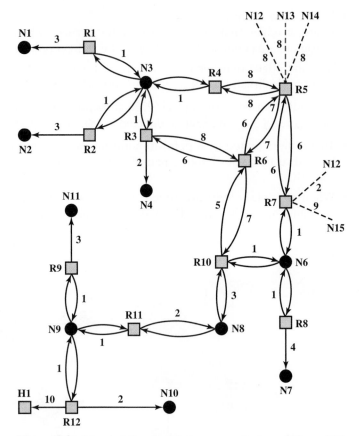

Figure 19.8 Directed Graph of Autonomous System of Figure 19.7

connected to the network vertex (e.g., routers 1, 2, 3, and 4 all connect to network 3).

- If a single router is attached to a network, the network will appear in the graph as a stub connection (e.g., network 7).
- An end system, called a host, can be directly connected to a router, in which case it is depicted in the corresponding graph (e.g., host 1).
- If a router is connected to other autonomous systems, then the path cost to each network in the other system must be obtained by some exterior router protocol. Each such network is represented on the graph by a stub and an edge to the router with the known path cost (e.g., networks 12 through 15).

A cost is associated with the output side of each router interface. This cost is configurable by the system administrator. Arcs on the graph are labeled with the cost of the corresponding router output interface. Arcs having no labeled cost have a cost of 0. Note that arcs leading from networks to routers always have a cost of 0.

A database corresponding to the directed graph is maintained by each router. It is pieced together from link-state messages from other routers in the internet. Using Dijkstra's algorithm (see Section 12.3), a router calculates the least-cost path

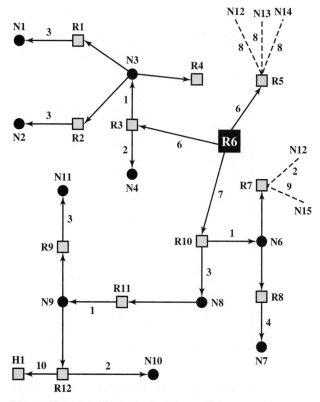

Figure 19.9   The SPF Tree for Router R6

to all destination networks. The result for router 6 of Figure 19.7 is shown as a tree in Figure 19.9, with R6 as the root of the tree. The tree gives the entire route to any destination network or host. However, only the next hop to the destination is used in the forwarding process. The resulting routing table for router 6 is shown in Table 19.3. The table includes entries for routers advertising external routes (routers 5 and 7). For external networks whose identity is known, entries are also provided.

19.3 MOBILE IP

In response to the increasing popularity of palmtop and other mobile computers, Mobile IP was developed to enable computers to maintain Internet connectivity while moving from one Internet attachment point to another. Although Mobile IP can work with wired connections, in which a computer is unplugged from one physical attachment point and plugged into another, it is particularly suited to wireless connections.

The term *mobile* in this context implies that a user is connected to one or more applications across the Internet, that the user's point of attachment changes dynamically, and that all connections are automatically maintained despite the change. This is in contrast to a user, such as a business traveler, with a portable computer of some sort who arrives at a destination and uses the computer's notebook to dial into an

Table 19.3 Routing Table for R6

Destination	Next Hop	Distance
N1	R3	10
N2	R3	10
N3	R3	7
N4	R3	8
N6	R10	8
N7	R10	12
N8	R10	10
N9	R10	11
N10	R10	13
N11	R10	14
H1	R10	21
R5	R5	6
R7	R10	8
N12	R10	10
N13	R5	14
N14	R5	14
N15	R10	17

Internet service provider (ISP). In this latter case, the user's Internet connection is terminated each time the user moves and a new connection is initiated when the user dials back in. Each time an Internet connection is established, software in the point of attachment (typically an ISP) is used to obtain a new, temporarily assigned IP address. This temporary IP address is used by the user's correspondent for each application-level connection (e.g., FTP, Web connection). A better term for this kind of use is *nomadic*.

We begin with a general overview of Mobile IP and then look at some of the details.

Operation of Mobile IP

As was described earlier in this chapter, routers make use of the IP address in an IP datagram to perform routing. In particular, the **network portion** of an IP address (Figure 18.6) is used by routers to move a datagram from the source computer to the network to which the target computer is attached. Then the final router on the path, which is attached to the same network as the target computer, uses the **host portion** of the IP address to deliver the IP datagram to the destination. Further, this IP address is known to the next higher layer in the protocol architecture (Figure 18.1). In particular, most applications over the Internet are supported by TCP connections. When a TCP connection is set up, the TCP entity on each side of the connection knows the IP address of the correspondent host. When a TCP segment is handed down to the IP layer for delivery, TCP provides the IP address, and IP creates an IP datagram with that IP address in the IP header and sends the datagram out for routing and delivery. However, with a mobile host, the IP address may change while one or more TCP connections are active.

Figure 19.10 shows in general terms how Mobile IP deals with the problem of dynamic IP addresses. A mobile node is assigned to a particular network, known as its **home network**. Its IP address on that network, known as its **home address**, is static. When the mobile node moves its attachment point to another network, that network is considered a **foreign network** for this host. Once the mobile node is reattached, it makes its presence known by registering with a network node, typically a router, on the foreign network known as a **foreign agent**. The mobile node then communicates with a similar agent on the user's home network, known as a **home agent**, giving the home agent the **care-of address** of the mobile node; the care-of address identifies the foreign agent's location. Typically, one or more routers on a network will implement the roles of both home and foreign agents.

When IP datagrams are exchanged over a connection between the mobile node and another host (a server in Figure 18.10), the following operations occur:

1. Server X transmits an IP datagram destined for mobile node A, with A's home address in the IP header. The IP datagram is routed to A's home network.

2. At the home network, the incoming IP datagram is intercepted by the home agent. The home agent encapsulates the entire datagram inside a new IP datagram that has the A's care-of address in the header, and retransmits the

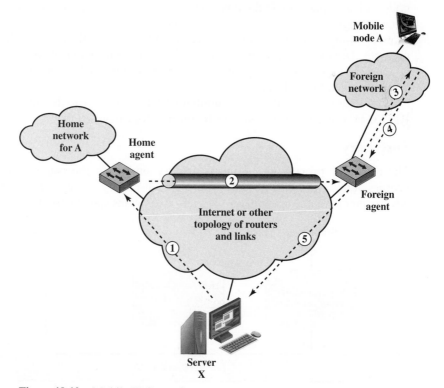

Figure 19.10 Mobile IP Scenario

datagram. The use of an outer IP datagram with a different destination IP address is known as **tunneling**. This IP datagram is routed to the foreign agent.

3. The foreign agent strips off the outer IP header, encapsulates the original IP datagram in a network-level PDU (e.g., a LAN LLC frame), and delivers the original datagram to A across the foreign network.

4. When A sends IP traffic to X, it uses X's IP address. In our example, this is a fixed address; that is, X is not a mobile node. Each IP datagram is sent by A to a router on the foreign network for routing to X. Typically, this router is also the foreign agent.

5. The IP datagram from A to X travels directly across the Internet to X, using X's IP address.

To support the operations illustrated in Figure 19.10, Mobile IP includes three basic capabilities:

- **Discovery:** A mobile node uses a discovery procedure to identify prospective home agents and foreign agents.
- **Registration:** A mobile node uses an authenticated registration procedure to inform its home agent of its care-of address.
- **Tunneling:** Tunneling is used to forward IP datagrams from a home address to a care-of address.

Figure 19.11 indicates the underlying protocol support for the Mobile IP capability. The registration protocol communicates between an application on the mobile node and an application in the home agent and hence uses a transport-level protocol. Because registration is a simple request-response transaction, the overhead of the connection-oriented TCP is not required, and therefore UDP is used as the transport protocol. Discovery makes use of the existing Internet Control Message Protocol (ICMP) by adding the appropriate extensions to the ICMP header. Finally, tunneling is performed at the IP level.

Mobile IP is specified in a number of RFCs. The basic defining document is RFC 3344. Table 19.4 lists some useful terminology from RFC 3344.

Discovery

The discovery process in Mobile IP is very similar to the router advertisement process defined in ICMP. Accordingly, agent discovery makes use of ICMP router advertisement messages, with one or more extensions specific to Mobile IP.

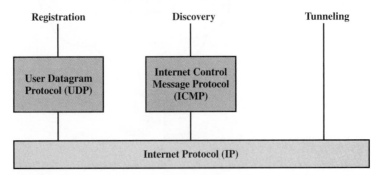

Figure 19.11 Protocol Support for Mobile IP

Table 19.4 Mobile IP Terminology (RFC 3334)

Mobile node	A host or router that changes its point of attachment from one network or subnetwork to another. A mobile node may change its location without changing its IP address; it may continue to communicate with other Internet nodes at any location using its (constant) IP address, assuming link-layer connectivity to a point of attachment is available.
Home address	An IP address that is assigned for an extended period of time to a mobile node. It remains unchanged regardless of where the node is attached to the Internet.
Home agent	A router on a mobile node's home network which tunnels datagrams for delivery to the mobile node when it is away from home, and maintains current location information for the mobile node.
Home network	A network, possibly virtual, having a network prefix matching that of a mobile node's home address. Note that standard IP routing mechanisms will deliver datagrams destined to a mobile node's Home Address to the mobile node's Home Network.
Foreign agent	A router on a mobile node's visited network which provides routing services to the mobile node while registered. The foreign agent detunnels and delivers datagrams to the mobile node that were tunneled by the mobile node's home agent. For datagrams sent by a mobile node, the foreign agent may serve as a default router for registered mobile nodes.
Foreign network	Any network other than the mobile node's Home Network.
Care-of address	The termination point of a tunnel toward a mobile node, for datagrams forwarded to the mobile node while it is away from home. The protocol can use two different types of care-of address: a "foreign agent care-of address" is an address of a foreign agent with which the mobile node is registered, and a "co-located care-of address" is an externally obtained local address which the mobile node has associated with one of its own network interfaces.
Correspondent node	A peer with which a mobile node is communicating. A correspondent node may be either mobile or stationary.
Link	A facility or medium over which nodes can communicate at the link layer. A link underlies the network layer.
Node	A host or a router.
Tunnel	The path followed by a datagram while it is encapsulated. The model is that, while it is encapsulated, a datagram is routed to a knowledgeable decapsulating agent, which decapsulates the datagram and then correctly delivers it to its ultimate destination.

The mobile node is responsible for an ongoing discovery process. It must determine if it is attached to its home network, in which case IP datagrams may be received without forwarding, or if it is attached to a foreign network. Because hand-off from one network to another occurs at the physical layer, a transition from the home network to a foreign network can occur at any time without notification to the network layer (i.e., the IP layer). Thus, discovery for a mobile node is a continuous process.

For the purpose of discovery, a router or other network node that can act as an agent periodically issues a router advertisement ICMP message (Figure 18.8d) with an advertisement extension. The router advertisement portion of the message includes the IP address of the router. The advertisement extension includes additional information about the router's role as an agent, as discussed subsequently. A mobile node listens for these **agent advertisement messages**. Because a foreign agent could be on the mobile node's home network (set up to serve visiting mobile nodes), the arrival of an agent advertisement does not necessarily tell the mobile node that it is on a foreign network. The mobile node must compare the network portion of the router's IP address with the network portion of its own home address. If these network portions do not match, then the mobile node is on a foreign network.

The **agent advertisement extension** follows the ICMP router advertisement fields. The extension includes the following 1-bit flags:

- **R:** Registration with this foreign agent is required (or another foreign agent on this network). Even those mobile nodes that have already acquired a care-of address from this foreign agent must re-register.
- **B:** Busy. The foreign agent will not accept registrations from additional mobile nodes.
- **H:** This agent offers services as a home agent on this network.
- **F:** This agent offers services as a foreign agent on this network.
- **M:** This agent can receive tunneled IP datagrams that use minimal encapsulation, explained subsequently.
- **G:** This agent can receive tunneled IP datagrams that use generic routing encapsulation (GRE), explained subsequently.
- **r:** Reserved.
- **T:** Foreign agent supports reverse tunneling.

In addition, the extension includes zero or more **care-of addresses** supported by this agent on this network. There must be at least one such address if the F bit is set. There may be multiple addresses.

AGENT SOLICITATION Foreign agents are expected to issue agent advertisement messages periodically. If a mobile node needs agent information immediately, it can issue an ICMP router solicitation message (Figure 18.8e). Any agent receiving this message will then issue an agent advertisement.

MOVE DETECTION As was mentioned, a mobile node may move from one network to another due to some handoff mechanism, without the IP level being aware of it. The agent discovery process is intended to enable the agent to detect such a move. The agent may use one of two algorithms for this purpose:

- **Use of lifetime field:** When a mobile node receives an agent advertisement from a foreign agent that it is currently using or that it is now going to register with, it records the lifetime field as a timer. If the timer expires before the mobile node receives another agent advertisement from the agent, then the node assumes that it has lost contact with that agent. If, in the meantime, the mobile node has received an agent advertisement from another agent and that advertisement has not yet expired, the mobile node can register with this new agent. Otherwise, the mobile node should use agent solicitation to find an agent.
- **Use of network prefix:** The mobile node checks whether any newly received agent advertisement is on the same network as the node's current care-of address. If it is not, the mobile node assumes that it has moved and may register with the agent whose advertisement the mobile node has just received.

CO-LOCATED ADDRESSES The discussion so far has involved the use of a care-of address associated with a foreign agent; that is, the care-of address is an IP address for the foreign agent. This foreign agent will receive datagrams at this care-of address, intended for the mobile node, and then forward them across the foreign network to the mobile node. However, in some cases a mobile node may move to a network that has no foreign agents or on which all foreign agents are busy. As an alternative, the mobile node may act as its own foreign agent by using a co-located care-of address. A co-located care-of address is an IP address obtained by the mobile node that is associated with the mobile node's current interface to a network.

The means by which a mobile node acquires a co-located address is beyond the scope of Mobile IP. One means is to dynamically acquire a temporary IP address through an Internet service such as Dynamic Host Configuration Protocol (DHCP). Another alternative is that the co-located address may be owned by the mobile node as a long-term address for use only while visiting a given foreign network.

Registration

Once a mobile node has recognized that it is on a foreign network and has acquired a care-of address, it needs to alert a home agent on its home network and request that the home agent forward its IP traffic. The registration process involves four steps:

1. The mobile node requests the forwarding service by sending a registration request to the foreign agent that the mobile node wants to use.
2. The foreign agent relays this request to the mobile node's home agent.
3. The home agent either accepts or denies the request and sends a registration reply to the foreign agent.
4. The foreign agent relays this reply to the mobile node.

If the mobile node is using a co-located care-of address, then it registers directly with its home agent, rather than going through a foreign agent.

The registration operation uses two types of messages carried in UDP segments. The **registration request message** includes the following 1-bit flags:

- **S:** Simultaneous bindings. The mobile node is requesting that the home agent retain its prior mobility bindings. When simultaneous bindings are in effect, the home agent will forward multiple copies of the IP datagram, one to each care-of address currently registered for this mobile node. Multiple simultaneous bindings can be useful in wireless handoff situations to improve reliability.

- **B:** Broadcast datagrams. Indicates that the mobile node would like to receive copies of broadcast datagrams that it would have received if it were attached to its home network.

- **D:** Decapsulation by mobile node. The mobile node is using a co-located care-of address and will decapsulate its own tunneled IP datagrams.

- **M:** Indicates that the home agent should use minimal encapsulation, explained subsequently.

- **G:** Indicates that the home agent should use GRE, explained subsequently.
- **T:** Reverse tunneling requested.

In addition, the message includes the following fields:

- **Home Address:** The home IP address of the mobile node. The home agent can expect to receive IP datagrams with this as a destination address, and must forward those to the care-of address.
- **Home Agent:** The IP address of the mobile node's home agent. This informs the foreign agent of the address to which this request should be relayed.
- **Care-of Address:** The IP address at this end of the tunnel. The home agent should forward IP datagrams that it receives with mobile node's home address to this destination address.
- **Identification:** A 64-bit number generated by the mobile node, used for matching registration requests to registration replies and for security purposes, explained subsequently.
- **Extensions:** The only extension so far defined is the authentication extension, explained subsequently.

The **registration reply message** includes a code that indicates whether the request is accepted and, if not, the reason for denial.

SECURING THE REGISTRATION PROCEDURE A key concern with the registration procedure is security. Mobile IP is designed to resist two types of attacks:

1. A node may pretend to be a foreign agent and send a registration request to a home agent so as to divert traffic intended for a mobile node to itself.
2. A malicious agent may replay old registration messages, effectively cutting the mobile node from the network.

The technique that is used to protect against such attacks involves the use of message authentication and the proper use of the identification field of the registration request and reply messages.

For purposes of message authentication, each registration request and reply contains an **authentication extension**, which includes the following fields:

- **Security Parameter Index (SPI):** An index that identifies a security context between a pair of nodes. This security context is configured so that the two nodes share a secret key and parameters relevant to this association (e.g., authentication algorithm).
- **Authenticator:** A code used to authenticate the message. The sender inserts this code into the message using a shared secret key. The receiver uses the code to ensure that the message has not been altered or delayed. The authenticator protects the entire registration request or reply message, any extensions prior to this extension, and the type and length fields of this extension.

The default authentication algorithm is HMAC-MD5, defined in RFC 2104, which produces a 128-bit message digest. HMAC-MD4 is an example of what is known as a keyed hash code. Appendix Q describes such codes. The digest is computed over a shared secret key, and the protected fields from the registration message.

Three types of authentication extensions are defined:

- **Mobile-home:** This extension must be present and provides for authentication of the registration messages between the mobile node and the home agent.
- **Mobile-foreign:** The extension may be present when a security association exists between the mobile node and the foreign agent. The foreign agent will strip this extension off before relaying a request message to the home agent and add this extension to a reply message coming from a home agent.
- **Foreign-home:** The extension may be present when a security association exists between the foreign agent and the home agent.

Note that the authenticator protects the identification field in the request and reply messages. As a result, the identification value can be used to thwart replay types of attacks. As was mentioned, the identification value enables the mobile node to match a reply to a request. Further, if the mobile node and the home agent maintain synchronization, so that the home agent can distinguish a reasonable identification value from a suspicious one, then the home agent can reject suspicious messages. One way to do this is to use a timestamp value. As long as the mobile node and home agent have reasonably synchronized values of time, the timestamp will serve the purpose. Alternatively, the mobile node could generate values using a pseudorandom number generator. If the home agent knows the algorithm, then it knows what identification value to expect next.

Tunneling

Once a mobile node is registered with a home agent, the home agent must be able to intercept IP datagrams sent to the mobile node's home address so that these datagrams can be forwarded via tunneling. The standard does not mandate a specific technique for this purpose but references the Address Resolution Protocol (ARP) as a possible mechanism. The home agent needs to inform other nodes on the same network (the home network) that IP datagrams with a destination address of the mobile node in question should be delivered (at the link level) to this agent. In effect, the home agent steals the identity of the mobile node in order to capture packets destined for that node that are transmitted across the home network.

For example, suppose that R3 in Figure 19.12 is acting as the home agent for a mobile node that is attached to a foreign network elsewhere on the Internet. That is, there is a host H whose home network is LAN Z that is now attached to some foreign network. If host D has traffic for H, it will generate an IP datagram with H's home address in the IP destination address field. The IP module in D recognizes that this destination address is on LAN Z and so passes the datagram down to the link layer with instructions to deliver it to a particular MAC-level address on Z. Prior to this time, R3 has informed the IP layer at D that datagrams destined for that particular address should be sent to R3. Thus, D inserts the MAC address of R3 in the destination MAC address field of the outgoing MAC frame. Similarly, if an IP datagram with the mobile node's home address arrives at router R2, it recognizes that the destination address is on LAN Z and will attempt to deliver the datagram

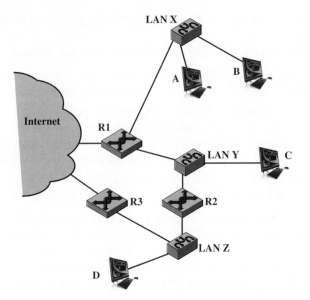

Figure 19.12 A Simple Internetworking Example

to a MAC-level address on Z. Again, R2 has previously been informed that the MAC-level address it needs corresponds to R3.

For traffic that is routed across the Internet and arrives at R3 from the Internet, R3 must simply recognize that for this destination address, the datagram is to be captured and forwarded.

To forward an IP datagram to a care-of address, the home agent puts the entire IP datagram into an outer IP datagram. This is a form of encapsulation, just as placing an IP header in front of a TCP segment encapsulates the TCP segment in an IP datagram. Three options for encapsulation are allowed for Mobile IP:

- **IP-within-IP encapsulation:** This is the simplest approach, defined in RFC 2003.

- **Minimal encapsulation:** This approach involves fewer fields, defined in RFC 2004.

- **Generic routing encapsulation (GRE):** This is a generic encapsulation procedure that was developed prior to the development of Mobile IP, defined in RFC 1701.

We review the first two of these methods.

IP-WITHIN-IP ENCAPSULATION With this approach, the entire IP datagram becomes the payload in a new IP datagram (Figure 19.13a). The inner, original IP header is unchanged except to decrement Time to Live (TTL) by 1. The outer header is a full IP header. Two fields (indicated as unshaded in the figure) are copied from the inner header: The version number is 4, which is the protocol identifier for IPv4, and the type of service requested for the outer IP datagram is the same as that requested for the inner IP datagram.

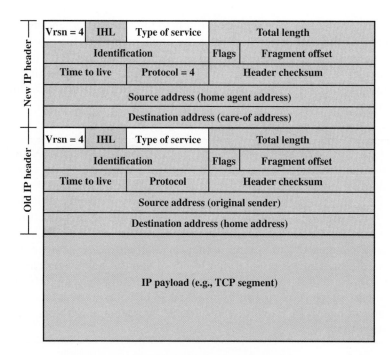

Unshaded fields are copied
from the inner IP header to
the outer IP header.

(a) IP-within-IP encapsulation

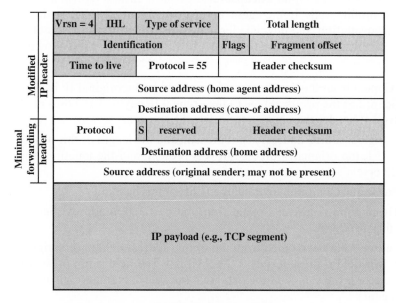

Unshaded fields in the inner
IP header are copied from the
original IP header. Unshaded
fields in the outer IP header
are modified from the original
IP header.

(b) Minimal encapsulation

Figure 19.13   Mobile IP Encapsulation

In the inner IP header, the source address refers to the host that is sending the original datagram, and the destination address is the home address of the intended recipient. In the outer IP header, the source and destination addresses refer to the entry and exit points of the tunnel. Thus, the source address typically is the IP address of the home agent, and the destination address is the care-of address for the intended destination.

EXAMPLE 19.1 Consider an IP datagram that originates at server X in Figure 19.10 and that is intended for mobile node A. The original IP datagram has a source address equal to the IP address of X and a destination address equal to the IP home address of A. The network portion of A's home address refers to A's home network, and so the datagram is routed through the Internet to A's home network, where it is intercepted by the home agent. The home agent encapsulates the incoming datagram with an outer IP header, which includes a source address equal to the IP address of the home agent and a destination address equal to the IP address of the foreign agent on the foreign network to which A is currently attached. When this new datagram reaches the foreign agent, it strips off the outer IP header and delivers the original datagram to A.

MINIMAL ENCAPSULATION Minimal encapsulation results in less overhead and can be used if the mobile node, home agent, and foreign agent all agree to do so. With minimal encapsulation, the new header is inserted between the original IP header and the original IP payload (Figure 19.13b). It includes the following fields:

- **Protocol:** Copied from the destination address field in the original IP header. This field identifies the protocol type of the original IP payload and thus identifies the type of header than begins the original IP payload.
- **S:** If 0, the original source address is not present, and the length of this header is 8 octets. If 1, the original source address is present, and the length of this header is 12 octets.
- **Header Checksum:** Computed over all the fields of this header.
- **Original Destination Address:** Copied from the destination address field in the original IP header.
- **Original Source Address:** Copied from the source address field in the original IP header. This field is present only if the S bit is 1. The field is not present if the encapsulator is the source of the datagram (i.e., the datagram originates at the home agent).

The following fields in the original IP header are modified to form the new outer IP header:

- **Total Length:** Incremented by the size of the minimal forwarding header (8 or 12).
- **Protocol:** 55; this is the protocol number assigned to minimal IP encapsulation.

- **Header Checksum:** Computed over all the fields of this header; because some of the fields have been modified, this value must be recomputed.
- **Source Address:** The IP address of the encapsulator, typically the home agent.
- **Destination Address:** The IP address of the exit point of the tunnel. This is the care-of address and may either be the IP address of the foreign agent or the IP address of the mobile node (in the case of a co-located care-of address).

The processing for minimal encapsulation is as follows. The encapsulator (home agent) prepares the encapsulated datagram with the format of Figure 19.13b. This datagram is now suitable for tunneling and is delivered across the Internet to the care-of address. At the care-of address, the fields in the minimal forwarding header are restored to the original IP header and the forwarding header is removed from the datagram. The total length field in the IP header is decremented by the size of the minimal forwarding header (8 or 12) and the header checksum field is recomputed.

19.4 RECOMMENDED READING AND WEB SITES

A number of worthwhile books provide detailed coverage of various routing algorithms: [HUIT00], [BLAC00], and [PERL00]. [MOY98] provides a thorough treatment of OSPF.

[LI05] provides an overview of Mobile IP. A more detailed discussion is found in [VENK05].

BLAC00 Black, U. *IP Routing Protocols: RIP, OSPF, BGP, PNNI & Cisco Routing Protocols.* Upper Saddle River, NJ: Prentice Hall, 2000.

HUIT00 Huitema, C. *Routing in the Internet.* Upper Saddle River, NJ: Prentice Hall, 2000.

LI05 Li, J., and Chen, H. "Mobility Support for IP-Based Networks." *IEEE Communications Magazine*, October 2005.

MOY98 Moy, J. *OSPF: Anatomy of an Internet Routing Protocol.* Reading, MA: Addison-Wesley, 1998.

PERL00 Perlman, R. *Interconnections: Bridges, Routers, Switches, and Internetworking Protocols.* Reading, MA: Addison-Wesley, 2000.

VENK05 Venkataraman, N. "Inside Mobile IP." *Dr. Dobb's Journal*, September 2005.

Recommended Web sites:

- **Inter-Domain Routing working group:** Chartered by IETF to revise BGP and related standards. The Web site includes all relevant RFCs and Internet drafts.
- **OSPF working group:** Chartered by IETF to develop OSPF and related standards. The Web site includes all relevant RFCs and Internet drafts.

19.5 KEY TERMS, REVIEW QUESTIONS, AND PROBLEMS

Key Terms

autonomous system (AS)	Internet Group Management	neighbor reachability
Border Gateway Protocol	Protocol (IGMP)	network reachability
(BGP)	link-state routing	Open Shortest Path First
broadcast address	Mobile IP	(OSPF)
distance-vector routing	multicast address	path-vector routing
exterior router protocol (ERP)	multicasting	unicast address
interior router protocol (IRP)	neighbor acquisition	

Review Questions

19.1 List some practical applications of multicasting.

19.2 Summarize the differences among unicast, multicast, and broadcast addresses.

19.3 List and briefly explain the functions that are required for multicasting.

19.4 What operations are performed by IGMP?

19.5 What is an autonomous system?

19.6 What is the difference between an interior router protocol and an exterior router protocol?

19.7 Compare the three main approaches to routing.

19.8 List and briefly explain the three main functions of BGP.

19.9 List and briefly define the capabilities provided by Mobile IP.

19.10 What is the relationship between Mobile IP discovery and ICMP?

19.11 What are the two different types of destination addresses that can be assigned to a mobile node while it is attached to a foreign network?

19.12 Under what circumstances would a mobile node choose to use each of the types of address referred to in Question 12.5?

Problems

19.1 Most operating systems include a tool named "traceroute" (or "tracert") that can be used to determine the path packets follow to reach a specified host from the system the tool is being run on. A number of sites provide web access to the "traceroute" tool, for example:

http://www.supporttechnique.net/traceroute.ihtml

http://www.t1shopper.com/tools/traceroute

Use the "traceroute" tool to determine the path packets follow to reach the host williamstallings.com.

19.2 A connected graph may have more than one spanning tree. Find all spanning trees of this graph:

19.3 In the discussion of Figure 19.1, three alternatives for transmitting a packet to a multicast address were discussed: broadcast, multiple unicast, and true multicast. Yet another alternative is flooding. The source transmits one packet to each neighboring router. Each router, when it receives a packet, retransmits the packet on all outgoing interfaces except the one on which the packet is received. Each packet is labeled with a unique identifier so that a router does not flood the same packet more than once. Fill out a matrix similar to those of Table 19.1 and comment on the results.

19.4 In a manner similar to Figure 19.3, show the spanning tree from router B to the multicast group.

19.5 IGMP specifies that query messages are sent in IP datagrams that have the Time to Live field set to 1. Why?

19.6 In IGMPv1 and IGMPv2, a host will cancel sending a pending membership report if it hears another host claiming membership in that group, in order to control the generation of IGMP traffic. However, IGMPv3 removes this suppression of host membership reports. Analyze the reasons behind this design decision.

19.7 IGMP membership queries include a "Max Resp Code" field that specifies the maximum time allowed before sending a responding report. The actual time allowed, called the Max Resp Time, is represented in units of 0.1 s and is derived from the Max Resp Code as follows:

If MaxRespCode $<$ 128, MaxRespTime = Max Resp Code

If MaxRespCode $\geq$ 128, MaxRespTime is a floating-point value as follows:

0	1	2	3	4	5	6	7
1		exp			mant		

MaxRespTime = (mant|0 $\times$ 10) $\ll$ (exp + 3) in C notation

MaxRespTime = (mant OR 16) $\times$ $2^{(exp+3)}$

Explain the motivation for the smaller values and the larger values.

19.8 Multicast applications call an API function on their sockets in order to ask the IP layer to enable or disable reception of packets sent from some specific IP address(es) to a specific multicast address.

For each of these sockets, the system records the desired multicast reception state. In addition to these per-socket multicast reception states, the system must maintain a multicast reception state for each of its interfaces, which is derived from the per-socket reception states.

Suppose four multicast applications run on the same host, and participate in the same multicast group, M1. The first application uses an EXCLUDE{A1, A2, A3} filter. The second one uses an EXCLUDE{A1, A3, A4} filter. The third one uses an INCLUDE{A3, A4} filter. And the fourth one uses an INCLUDE{A3} filter. What's the resulting multicast state (multicast-address, filter-mode, source-list) for the network interface?

19.9 Multicast applications commonly use UDP or RTP (Real-Time Transport Protocol) as their transport protocol. Multicast applications do not use TCP as its transport protocol. What's the problem with TCP?

19.10 With multicasting, packets are delivered to multiple destinations. Thus, in case of errors (such as routing failures), one IP packet might trigger multiple ICMP error packets, leading to a packet storm. How is this potential problem avoided? *Hint:* consult RFC 1122.

19.11 BGP's AS_PATH attribute identifies the autonomous systems through which routing information has passed. How can the AS_PATH attribute be used to detect routing information loops?

19.12   BGP provides a list of autonomous systems on the path to the destination. However, this information cannot be considered a distance metric. Why?

19.13   This problem refers to Figure 19.12. Suppose that LAN Z is the home network for host E and that D sends a block of data to E via IP.

    a.   Show the PDU structure, including the fields of the IP header and the lower-level headers (MAC, LLC) with the contents of address fields indicated for the case in which E is on its home network.

    b.   Repeat part (a) for the case in which E is on a foreign network reachable via the Internet through R3. Show formats for the MAC frame leaving D and the IP datagram leaving R3. Assume that IP-to-IP encapsulation is used.

    c.   Repeat part (b) for the IP datagram leaving R3, but now assume that minimal encapsulation is used.

19.14   Again referring to Figure 19.12, assume that A is a mobile node and that LAN X is a foreign network for A. Assume that an IP datagram arrives at R1 from the Internet to be delivered to A. Show the format of the IP datagram arriving at R1 and the MAC frame leaving R1 (include the IP header or headers) for the following cases:

    a.   IP-to-IP encapsulation is used and R1 is the care-of address.

    b.   Minimal encapsulation is used and R1 is the care-of address.

    c.   IP-to-IP encapsulation is used and A is the care-of address.

    d.   Minimal encapsulation is used and A is the care-of address.

19.15   In a typical Mobile IP implementation in a home agent, the agent maintains a mobility binding table to map a mobile node's home address to its care-of address for packet forwarding. What entries are essential for each row of the table?

19.16   In a typical Mobile IP implementation in a foreign agent, the agent maintains a visitor table that contains information about the mobile nodes currently visiting this network. What entries are essential for each row of the table?

INTERNETWORK QUALITY OF SERVICE

At St. Paul's a great throng crammed the platform. She saw a sea of faces, each stamped with a kind of purposeful, hungry urgency, a determination to get into this train. As before, when she was on the Northern Line, she thought there must be some rule, some operating law, that would stop more than a limited, controlled number getting in. Authority would appear and stop it.

—*King Solomon's Carpet,* Barbara Vine (Ruth Rendell)

KEY POINTS

♦ The integrated services architecture is a response to the growing variety and volume of traffic experienced in the Internet and intranets. It provides a framework for the development of protocols such as RSVP to handle multimedia/multicast traffic and provides guidance to router vendors on the development of efficient techniques for handling a varied load.

♦ The differentiated services architecture is designed to provide a simple, easy-to-implement, low-overhead tool to support a range of network services that are differentiated on the basis of performance. Differentiated services are provided on the basis of a 6-bit label in the IP header, which classifies traffic in terms of the type of service to be given by routers for that traffic.

The traffic that the Internet and other internetworks must carry continues to grow and change. The demand generated by traditional data-based applications, such as electronic mail, Usenet news, file transfer, and remote logon, is sufficient to challenge these systems. But the driving factors are the heavy use of the World Wide Web, which demands real-time response, and the increasing use of audio, image, and video over internetwork architectures.

These internetwork schemes are essentially datagram packet-switching technology with routers functioning as the switches. This technology was not designed to handle voice and video and is straining to meet the demands placed on it.

To cope with these demands, it is not enough to increase Internet capacity. Sensible and effective methods for managing the traffic and controlling congestion are needed. Historically, IP-based internets have been able to provide a simple best-effort delivery service to all applications using an internet. But the needs of users have changed. A company may have spent millions of dollars installing an IP-based internet designed to transport data among LANs but now finds that new real-time, multimedia, and multicasting applications are not well supported by such a configuration.

Thus, there is a strong need to be able to support a variety of traffic with a variety of quality-of-service (QoS) requirements, within the TCP/IP architecture. This chapter looks at the internetwork functions and services designed to meet this need.

Next, we look at the Integrated Services Architecture (ISA), which provides a framework for current and future internet services. We then look at a key protocol related to ISA called RSVP. Then, we examine differentiated services. Finally, we introduce the topics of service level agreements and IP performance metrics.

20.1 INTEGRATED SERVICES ARCHITECTURE

To meet the requirement for QoS-based service, the IETF is developing a suite of standards under the general umbrella of the Integrated Services Architecture (ISA). ISA, intended to provide QoS transport over IP-based internets, is defined in overall terms in RFC 1633, while a number of other documents fill in the details. Already, a number of vendors have implemented portions of the ISA in routers and end-system software.

This section provides an overview of ISA.

Internet Traffic

Traffic on a network or internet can be divided into two broad categories: elastic and inelastic. A consideration of their differing requirements clarifies the need for an enhanced internet architecture.

ELASTIC TRAFFIC Elastic traffic is that which can adjust, over wide ranges, to changes in delay and throughput across an internet and still meet the needs of its applications. This is the traditional type of traffic supported on TCP/IP-based internets and is the type of traffic for which internets were designed. Applications that generate such traffic typically use TCP or UDP as a transport protocol. In the case of UDP, the application will use as much capacity as is available up to the rate that the application generates data. In the case of TCP, the application will use as much capacity as is available up to the maximum rate that the end-to-end receiver can accept data. Also with TCP, traffic on individual connections adjusts to congestion by reducing the rate at which data are presented to the network; this is described in Chapter 22.

Applications that can be classified as elastic include the common applications that operate over TCP or UDP, including file transfer (FTP), electronic mail (SMTP), remote login (TELNET), network management (SNMP), and Web access (HTTP). However, there are differences among the requirements of these applications. For example,

- E-mail is generally insensitive to changes in delay.
- When file transfer is done interactively, as it frequently is, the user expects the delay to be proportional to the file size and so is sensitive to changes in throughput.
- With network management, delay is generally not a serious concern. However, if failures in an internet are the cause of congestion, then the need for SNMP messages to get through with minimum delay increases with increased congestion.
- Interactive applications, such as remote logon and Web access, are sensitive to delay.

It is important to realize that it is not per-packet delay that is the quantity of interest. As noted in [CLAR95], observation of real delays across the Internet suggest that wide variations in delay do not occur. Because of the congestion control mechanisms in TCP, when congestion develops, delays only increase modestly before the arrival rate from the various TCP connections slow down. Instead, the QoS perceived by the user relates to the total elapsed time to transfer an element of the current application. For an interactive TELNET-based application, the element may be a single keystroke or single line. For a Web access, the element is a Web page, which could be as little as a few kilobytes or could be substantially larger for an image-rich page. For a scientific application, the element could be many megabytes of data.

For very small elements, the total elapsed time is dominated by the delay time across the internet. However, for larger elements, the total elapsed time is dictated by the sliding-window performance of TCP and is therefore dominated by the throughput achieved over the TCP connection. Thus, for large transfers, the transfer time is proportional to the size of the file and the degree to which the source slows due to congestion.

It should be clear that even if we confine our attention to elastic traffic, a QoS-based internet service could be of benefit. Without such a service, routers are dealing evenhandedly with arriving IP packets, with no concern for the type of application and whether a particular packet is part of a large transfer element or a small one. Under such circumstances, and if congestion develops, it is unlikely that resources will be allocated in such a way as to meet the needs of all applications fairly. When inelastic traffic is added to the mix, the results are even more unsatisfactory.

INELASTIC TRAFFIC Inelastic traffic does not easily adapt, if at all, to changes in delay and throughput across an internet. The prime example is real-time traffic. The requirements for inelastic traffic may include the following:

- **Throughput:** A minimum throughput value may be required. Unlike most elastic traffic, which can continue to deliver data with perhaps degraded service, many inelastic applications absolutely require a given minimum throughput.

- **Delay:** An example of a delay-sensitive application is stock trading; someone who consistently receives later service will consistently act later, and with greater disadvantage.

- **Jitter:** The magnitude of delay variation, called jitter, is a critical factor in real-time applications. Because of the variable delay imposed by the Internet, the interarrival times between packets are not maintained at a fixed interval at the destination. To compensate for this, the incoming packets are buffered, delayed sufficiently to compensate for the jitter, and then released at a constant rate to the software that is expecting a steady real-time stream. The larger the allowable delay variation, the longer the real delay in delivering the data and the greater the size of the delay buffer required at receivers. Real-time interactive applications, such as teleconferencing, may require a reasonable upper bound on jitter.

- **Packet loss:** Real-time applications vary in the amount of packet loss, if any, that they can sustain.

These requirements are difficult to meet in an environment with variable queuing delays and congestion losses. Accordingly, inelastic traffic introduces two new requirements into the internet architecture. First, some means is needed to give preferential treatment to applications with more demanding requirements. Applications need to be able to state their requirements, either ahead of time in some sort of service request function, or on the fly, by means of fields in the IP packet header. The former approach provides more flexibility in stating requirements, and it enables the network to anticipate demands and deny new requests if the required resources are unavailable. This approach implies the use of some sort of resource reservation protocol.

An additional requirement in supporting inelastic traffic in an internet architecture is that elastic traffic must still be supported. Inelastic applications typically do not back off and reduce demand in the face of congestion, in contrast to TCP-based applications. Therefore, in times of congestion, inelastic traffic will continue to supply a high load, and elastic traffic will be crowded off the internet. A reservation protocol can help control this situation by denying service requests that would leave too few resources available to handle current elastic traffic.

ISA Approach

The purpose of ISA is to enable the provision of QoS support over IP-based internets. The central design issue for ISA is how to share the available capacity in times of congestion.

For an IP-based internet that provides only a best-effort service, the tools for controlling congestion and providing service are limited. In essence, routers have two mechanisms to work with:

- **Routing algorithm:** Most routing protocols in use in internets allow routes to be selected to minimize delay. Routers exchange information to get a picture of the delays throughout the internet. Minimum-delay routing helps to balance loads, thus decreasing local congestion, and helps to reduce delays seen by individual TCP connections.

- **Packet discard:** When a router's buffer overflows, it discards packets. Typically, the most recent packet is discarded. The effect of lost packets on a TCP connection is that the sending TCP entity backs off and reduces its load, thus helping to alleviate internet congestion.

These tools have worked reasonably well. However, as the discussion in the preceding subsection shows, such techniques are inadequate for the variety of traffic now coming to internets.

ISA is an overall architecture within which a number of enhancements to the traditional best-effort mechanisms are being developed. In ISA, each IP packet can be associated with a flow. RFC 1633 defines a flow as a distinguishable stream of related IP packets that results from a single user activity and requires the same QoS. For example, a flow might consist of one transport connection or one video stream distinguishable by the ISA. A flow differs from a TCP connection in two respects: A flow is unidirectional, and there can be more than one recipient of a flow (multicast). Typically, an IP packet is identified as a member of a flow on the basis of source and destination IP addresses and port numbers, and protocol type. The flow identifier in the IPv6 header is not necessarily equivalent to an ISA flow, but in future the IPv6 flow identifier could be used in ISA.

ISA makes use of the following functions to manage congestion and provide QoS transport:

- **Admission control:** For QoS transport (other than default best-effort transport), ISA requires that a reservation be made for a new flow. If the routers collectively determine that there are insufficient resources to guarantee the requested QoS, then the flow is not admitted. The protocol RSVP is used to make reservations.

- **Routing algorithm:** The routing decision may be based on a variety of QoS parameters, not just minimum delay. For example, the routing protocol OSPF, discussed in Section 19.2, can select routes based on QoS.

- **Queuing discipline:** A vital element of the ISA is an effective queuing policy that takes into account the differing requirements of different flows.

- **Discard policy:** A discard policy determines which packets to drop when a buffer is full and new packets arrive. A discard policy can be an important element in managing congestion and meeting QoS guarantees.

ISA Components

Figure 20.1 is a general depiction of the implementation architecture for ISA within a router. Below the thick horizontal line are the forwarding functions of the router; these are executed for each packet and therefore must be highly optimized. The remaining functions, above the line, are background functions that create data structures used by the forwarding functions.

The principal background functions are as follows:

- **Reservation protocol:** This protocol is to reserve resources for a new flow at a given level of QoS. It is used among routers and between routers and end systems. The reservation protocol is responsible for maintaining flow-specific state information at the end systems and at the routers along the path of the flow. RSVP is used for this purpose. The reservation protocol updates the traffic control database used by the packet scheduler to determine the service provided for packets of each flow.

- **Admission control:** When a new flow is requested, the reservation protocol invokes the admission control function. This function determines if sufficient resources are available for this flow at the requested QoS. This determination is based on the current level of commitment to other reservations and/or on the current load on the network.

- **Management agent:** A network management agent is able to modify the traffic control database and to direct the admission control module in order to set admission control policies.

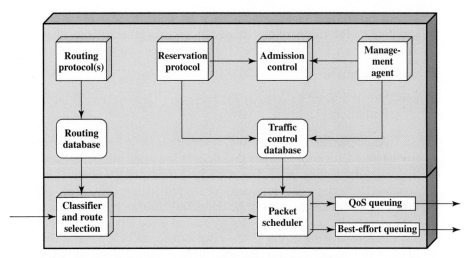

Figure 20.1   Integrated Services Architecture Implemented in Router

- **Routing protocol:** The routing protocol is responsible for maintaining a routing database that gives the next hop to be taken for each destination address and each flow.

These background functions support the main task of the router, which is the forwarding of packets. The two principal functional areas that accomplish forwarding are the following:

- **Classifier and route selection:** For the purposes of forwarding and traffic control, incoming packets must be mapped into classes. A class may correspond to a single flow or to a set of flows with the same QoS requirements. For example, the packets of all video flows or the packets of all flows attributable to a particular organization may be treated identically for purposes of resource allocation and queuing discipline. The selection of class is based on fields in the IP header. Based on the packet's class and its destination IP address, this function determines the next-hop address for this packet.

- **Packet scheduler:** This function manages one or more queues for each output port. It determines the order in which queued packets are transmitted and the selection of packets for discard, if necessary. Decisions are made based on a packet's class, the contents of the traffic control database, and current and past activity on this outgoing port. Part of the packet scheduler's task is that of policing, which is the function of determining whether the packet traffic in a given flow exceeds the requested capacity and, if so, deciding how to treat the excess packets.

ISA Services

ISA service for a flow of packets is defined on two levels. First, a number of general categories of service are provided, each of which provides a certain general type of service guarantees. Second, within each category, the service for a particular flow is specified by the values of certain parameters; together, these values are referred to as a traffic specification (TSpec). Currently, three categories of service are defined:

- Guaranteed
- Controlled load
- Best effort

An application can request a reservation for a flow for a guaranteed or controlled load QoS, with a TSpec that defines the exact amount of service required. If the reservation is accepted, then the TSpec is part of the contract between the data flow and the service. The service agrees to provide the requested QoS as long as the flow's data traffic continues to be described accurately by the TSpec. Packets that are not part of a reserved flow are by default given a best-effort delivery service.

Before looking at the ISA service categories, one general concept should be defined: the token bucket traffic specification. This is a way of characterizing traffic that has three advantages in the context of ISA:

1. Many traffic sources can be defined easily and accurately by a token bucket scheme.
2. The token bucket scheme provides a concise description of the load to be imposed by a flow, enabling the service to determine easily the resource requirement.
3. The token bucket scheme provides the input parameters to a policing function.

A token bucket traffic specification consists of two parameters: a token replenishment rate R and a bucket size B. The token rate R specifies the continually sustainable data rate; that is, over a relatively long period of time, the average data rate to be supported for this flow is R. The bucket size B specifies the amount by which the data rate can exceed R for short periods of time. The exact condition is as follows: during any time period T, the amount of data sent cannot exceed $RT + B$.

Figure 20.2 illustrates this scheme and explains the use of the term *bucket*. The bucket represents a counter that indicates the allowable number of octets of IP data that can be sent at any time. The bucket fills with *octet tokens* at the rate of R (i.e., the counter is incremented R times per second), up to the bucket capacity (up to the maximum counter value). IP packets arrive and are queued for processing. An IP packet may be processed if there are sufficient octet tokens to match the IP data size. If so, the packet is processed and the bucket is drained of the corresponding number of tokens. If a packet arrives and there are insufficient tokens available, then the packet exceeds the TSpec for this flow. The treatment for such packets is not specified in the ISA documents; common actions are relegating the packet to best-effort service, discarding the packet, or marking the packet in such a way that it may be discarded in future.

Over the long run, the rate of IP data allowed by the token bucket is R. However, if there is an idle or relatively slow period, the bucket capacity builds up, so that at most an additional B octets above the stated rate can be accepted. Thus, B is a measure of the degree of burstiness of the data flow that is allowed.

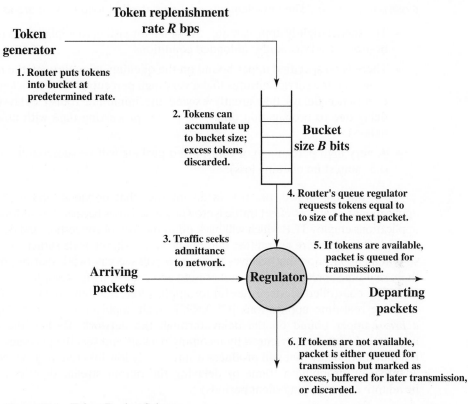

Token generator

Token replenishment rate _R_ bps

1. Router puts tokens into bucket at predetermined rate.

2. Tokens can accumulate up to bucket size; excess tokens discarded.

Bucket size _B_ bits

4. Router's queue regulator requests tokens equal to to size of the next packet.

3. Traffic seeks admittance to network.

5. If tokens are available, packet is queued for transmission.

Arriving packets

Regulator

Departing packets

6. If tokens are not available, packet is either queued for transmission but marked as excess, buffered for later transmission, or discarded.

Figure 20.2   Token Bucket Scheme

GUARANTEED SERVICE The key elements of the guaranteed service are as follows:

- The service provides assured capacity, or data rate.
- There is a specified upper bound on the queuing delay through the network. This must be added to the propagation delay, or latency, to arrive at the bound on total delay through the network.
- There are no queuing losses. That is, no packets are lost due to buffer overflow; packets may be lost due to failures in the network or changes in routing paths.

With this service, an application provides a characterization of its expected traffic profile, and the service determines the end-to-end delay that it can guarantee.

One category of applications for this service is those that need an upper bound on delay so that a delay buffer can be used for real-time playback of incoming data, and that do not tolerate packet losses because of the degradation in the quality of the output. Another example is applications with hard real-time deadlines.

The guaranteed service is the most demanding service provided by ISA. Because the delay bound is firm, the delay has to be set at a large value to cover rare cases of long queuing delays.

CONTROLLED LOAD The key elements of the controlled load service are as follows:

- The service tightly approximates the behavior visible to applications receiving best-effort service under unloaded conditions.
- There is no specified upper bound on the queuing delay through the network. However, the service ensures that a very high percentage of the packets do not experience delays that greatly exceed the minimum transit delay (i.e., the delay due to propagation time plus router processing time with no queuing delays).
- A very high percentage of transmitted packets will be successfully delivered (i.e., almost no queuing loss).

As was mentioned, the risk in an internet that provides QoS for real-time applications is that best-effort traffic is crowded out. This is because best-effort types of applications employ TCP, which will back off in the face of congestion and delays. The controlled load service guarantees that the network will set aside sufficient resources so that an application that receives this service will see a network that responds as if these real-time applications were not present and competing for resources.

The controlled service is useful for applications that have been referred to as adaptive real-time applications [CLAR92]. Such applications do not require an *a priori* upper bound on the delay through the network. Rather, the receiver measures the jitter experienced by incoming packets and sets the playback point to the minimum delay that still produces a sufficiently low loss rate (e.g., video can be adaptive by dropping a frame or delaying the output stream slightly; voice can be adaptive by adjusting silent periods).

Queuing Discipline

An important component of an ISA implementation is the queuing discipline used at the routers. Routers traditionally have used a first-in-first-out (FIFO) queuing discipline at each output port. A single queue is maintained at each output port. When a new packet arrives and is routed to an output port, it is placed at the end of the queue. As long as the queue is not empty, the router transmits packets from the queue, taking the oldest remaining packet next.

There are several drawbacks to the FIFO queuing discipline:

- No special treatment is given to packets from flows that are of higher priority or are more delay sensitive. If a number of packets from different flows are ready to be forwarded, they are handled strictly in FIFO order.
- If a number of smaller packets are queued behind a long packet, then FIFO queuing results in a larger average delay per packet than if the shorter packets were transmitted before the longer packet. In general, flows of larger packets get better service.
- A greedy TCP connection can crowd out more altruistic connections. If congestion occurs and one TCP connection fails to back off, other connections along the same path segment must back off more than they would otherwise have to do.

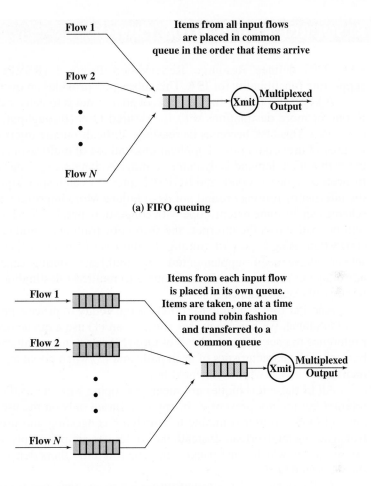

(a) FIFO queuing

(b) Fair queuing

Figure 20.3 FIFO and Fair Queuing

To overcome the drawbacks of FIFO queuing, some sort of fair queuing scheme is used, in which a router maintains multiple queues at each output port (Figure 20.3). With simple fair queuing, each incoming packet is placed in the queue for its flow. The queues are serviced in round-robin fashion, taking one packet from each non-empty queue in turn. Empty queues are skipped over. This scheme is fair in that each busy flow gets to send exactly one packet per cycle. Further, this is a form of load balancing among the various flows. There is no advantage in being greedy. A greedy flow finds that its queues become long, increasing its delays, whereas other flows are unaffected by this behavior.

A number of vendors have implemented a refinement of fair queuing known as weighted fair queuing (WFQ). In essence, WFQ takes into account the amount of traffic through each queue and gives busier queues more capacity without completely shutting out less busy queues. In addition WFQ can take into account the amount of service requested by each traffic flow and adjust the queuing discipline accordingly.

20.2 RESOURCE RESERVATION PROTOCOL

RFC 2205 defines Resource ReSerVation Protocol (RSVP), which provides supporting functionality for ISA. This subsection provides an overview.

A key task, perhaps the key task, of an internet is to deliver data from a source to one or more destinations with the desired QoS (throughput, delay, delay variance, etc.). This task becomes increasingly difficult on any internet with increasing number of users, data rate of applications, and use of multicasting. One tool for coping with a high demand is dynamic routing. A dynamic routing scheme, supported by protocols such as OSPF and BGP (Chapter 19), can respond quickly to failures in the internet by routing around points of failure. More important, a dynamic routing scheme can, to some extent, cope with congestion, first by load balancing to smooth out the load across the internet, and second by routing around areas of developing congestion using least-cost routing. In the case of multicasting, dynamic routing schemes have been supplemented with multicast routing capabilities that take advantage of shared paths from a source to multicast destinations to minimize the number of packet duplications.

Another tool available to routers is the ability to process packets on the basis of a QoS label. We have seen that routers can (1) use a queue discipline that gives preference to packets on the basis of QoS; (2) select among alternate routes on the basis of QoS characteristics of each path; and (3) when possible, invoke QoS treatment in the subnetwork of the next hop.

All of these techniques are means of coping with the traffic presented to the internet but are not preventive in any way. Based only on the use of dynamic routing and QoS, a router is unable to anticipate congestion and prevent applications from causing an overload. Instead, the router can simply supply a best-effort delivery service, in which some packets may be lost and others delivered with less than the requested QoS.

As the demands on internets grow, it appears that prevention as well as reaction to congestion is needed. As this section shows, a means to implement a prevention strategy is resource reservation.

Preventive measures can be useful in both unicast and multicast transmission. For **unicast**, two applications agree on a specific QoS for a session and expect the internet to support that QoS. If the internet is heavily loaded, it may not provide the desired QoS and instead deliver packets at a reduced QoS. In that case, the applications may have preferred to wait before initiating the session or at least to have been alerted to the potential for reduced QoS. A way of dealing with this situation is to have the unicast applications reserve resources in order to meet a given QoS. Routers along an intended path could then preallocate resources (queue space, outgoing capacity) to assure the desired QoS. If a router could not meet the resource reservation because of prior outstanding reservations, then the applications could be informed. The applications may then decide to try again at a reduced QoS reservation or may decide to try later.

Multicast transmission also present a compelling case for implementing resource reservation. A multicast transmission can generate a tremendous amount of internet traffic if either the application is high volume (e.g., video) or the group of multicast destinations is large and scattered, or both. What makes the case for multicast resource reservation is that much of the potential load generated by a multicast source may easily be prevented. This is so for two reasons:

1. Some members of an existing multicast group may not require delivery from a particular source over some given period of time. For example, there may be two "channels" (two multicast sources) broadcasting to a particular multicast group at the same time. A multicast destination may wish to "tune in" to only one channel at a time.

2. Some members of a group may only be able to handle a portion of the source transmission. For example, a video source may transmit a video stream that consists of two components: a basic component that provides a reduced picture quality, and an enhanced component. Some receivers may not have the processing power to handle the enhanced component, or may be connected to the internet through a subnetwork or link that does not have the capacity for the full signal.

Thus, the use of resource reservation can enable routers to decide ahead of time if they can meet the requirement to deliver a multicast transmission to all designated multicast receivers and to reserve the appropriate resources if possible.

Internet resource reservation differs from the type of resource reservation that may be implemented in a connection-oriented network, such as ATM or frame relay. An internet resource reservation scheme must interact with a dynamic routing strategy that allows the route followed by packets of a given transmission to change. When the route changes, the resource reservations must be changed. To deal with this dynamic situation, the concept of *soft state* is used. A soft state is simply a set of state information at a router that expires unless regularly refreshed from the entity that requested the state. If a route for a given transmission changes, then some soft states will expire and new resource reservations will invoke the appropriate soft states on the new routers along the route. Thus, the end systems requesting resources must periodically renew their requests during the course of an application transmission.

We now turn to the protocol that has been developed for performing resource reservation in an internet environment: RSVP, defined in RFC 2205.

RSVP Goals and Characteristics

Based on these preceding considerations, RFC 2205 lists the following characteristics of RSVP:

- **Unicast and multicast:** RSVP makes reservations for both unicast and multicast transmissions, adapting dynamically to changing group membership as well as to changing routes, and reserving resources based on the individual requirements of multicast members.

- **Simplex:** RSVP makes reservations for unidirectional data flow. Data exchanges between two end systems require separate reservations in the two directions.

- **Receiver-initiated reservation:** The receiver of a data flow initiates and maintains the resource reservation for that flow.

- **Maintaining soft state in the internet:** RSVP maintains a soft state at intermediate routers and leaves the responsibility for maintaining these reservation states to end users.

- **Providing different reservation styles:** These allow RSVP users to specify how reservations for the same multicast group should be aggregated at the intermediate switches. This feature enables a more efficient use of internet resources.

- **Transparent operation through non-RSVP routers:** Because reservations and RSVP are independent of routing protocol, there is no fundamental conflict in a mixed environment in which some routers do not employ RSVP. These routers will simply use a best-effort delivery technique.

It is worth elaborating on two of these design characteristics: receiver-initiated reservations, and soft state.

RECEIVER-INITIATED RESERVATION In previous attempts at resource reservation, including the approach taken in frame relay and ATM networks, the source of a data flow requests a given set of resources. In a strictly unicast environment, this approach is reasonable. A transmitting application is able to transmit data at a certain rate and has a given QoS designed into the transmission scheme. However, this approach is inadequate for multicasting. As was mentioned, different members of the same multicast group may have different resource requirements. If the source transmission flow can be divided into component subflows, then some multicast members may only require a single subflow. If there are multiple sources transmitting to a multicast group, then a particular multicast receiver may want to select only one or a subset of all sources to receive. Finally, the QoS requirements of different receivers may differ depending on the output equipment, processing power, and link speed of the receiver.

It therefore makes sense for receivers rather than senders to make resource reservations. A sender needs to provide the routers with the traffic characteristics of the transmission (data rate, variability), but it is the receivers that must specify the desired QoS. Routers can then aggregate multicast resource reservations to take advantage of shared path segments along the distribution tree.

SOFT STATE RSVP makes use of the concept of a soft state. This concept was first introduced by David Clark in [CLAR88], and it is worth quoting his description[1]:

> While the datagram has served very well in solving the most important goals of the Internet, the goals of resource management and accountability have proved difficult to achieve. Most datagrams are part of some sequence of packets from source to destination, rather than isolated units at the application level. However, the gateway cannot directly see the existence of this sequence, because it is forced to deal with each packet in isolation. Therefore, resource management decisions or accounting must be done on each packet separately.

---

[1]*Gateway* is the term used for *router* in most of the earlier RFCs and TCP/IP literature; it is still occasionally used today (e.g., Border Gateway Protocol).

This suggests that there may be a better building block than the datagram for the next generation of architecture. The general characteristic of this building block is that it would identify a sequence of packets traveling from source to destination. I have used the term *flow* to characterize this building block. It would be necessary for the gateways to have flow state in order to remember the nature of the flows which are passing through them, but the state information would not be critical in maintaining the described type of service associated with the flow. Instead, that type of service would be enforced by the end points, which would periodically send messages to ensure that the proper type of service was being associated with the flow. In this way, the state information associated with the flow could be lost in a crash without permanent disruption of the service features being used. I call this concept *soft state*.

In essence, a connection-oriented scheme takes a hard-state approach, in which the nature of the connection along a fixed route is defined by the state information in the intermediate switching nodes. RSVP takes a soft-state, or connectionless, approach, in which the reservation state is cached information in the routers that is installed and periodically refreshed by end systems. If a state is not refreshed within a required time limit, the router discards the state. If a new route becomes preferred for a given flow, the end systems provide the reservation to the new routers on the route.

Data Flows

Three concepts relating to data flows form the basis of RSVP operation: session, flow specification, and filter specification.

A session is a data flow identified by its destination. The reason for using the term *session* rather than simply *destination* is that it reflects the soft-state nature of RSVP operation. Once a reservation is made at a router by a particular destination, the router considers this as a session and allocates resources for the life of that session. In particular, a session is defined by:

Session:	Destination IP address
	IP protocol identifier
	Destination port

The destination IP address may be unicast or multicast. The protocol identifier indicates the user of IP (e.g., TCP or UDP), and the destination port is the TCP or UDP port for the user of this transport-layer protocol. If the address is multicast, the destination port may not be necessary, because there is typically a different multicast address for different applications.

A reservation request issued by a destination end system is called a *flow descriptor* and consists of a *flowspec* and a *filter spec*. The flowspec specifies a desired QoS and is used to set parameters in a node's packet scheduler. That is, the router will transmit packets with a given set of preferences based on the current flowspecs. The filter spec defines the set of packets for which a reservation is requested. Thus, the filter spec together with the session define the set of packets, or flow, that are to receive the desired QoS. Any other packets addressed to the same destination are handled as best-effort traffic.

The content of the flowspec is beyond the scope of RSVP, which is merely a carrier of the request. In general, a flowspec contains the following elements:

Flowspec:	Service class
	RSpec
	TSpec

The service class is an identifier of a type of service being requested; it includes information used by the router to merge requests. The other two parameters are sets of numeric values. The RSpec (R for reserve) parameter defines the desired QoS, and the TSpec (T for traffic) parameter describes the data flow. The contents of Rspec and TSpec are opaque to RSVP.

In principle, the filter spec may designate an arbitrary subset of the packets of one session (i.e., the packets arriving with the destination specified by this session). For example, a filter spec could specify only specific sources, or specific source protocols, or in general only packets that have a match on certain fields in any of the protocol headers in the packet. The current RSVP version uses a restricted filter spec consisting of the following elements:

Filter spec:	Source address
	UDP/TCP source port

Figure 20.4 indicates the relationship among session, flowspec, and filter spec. Each incoming packet is part of at most one session and is treated according to the logical flow indicated in the figure for that session. If a packet belongs to no session, it is given a best-effort delivery service.

RSVP Operation

Much of the complexity of RSVP has to do with dealing with multicast transmission. Unicast transmission is treated as a special case. In what follows, we examine the general operation of RSVP for multicast resource reservation. The internet configuration shown in Figure 20.5a is used in the discussion. This configuration consists of four routers connected as shown. The link between two routers, indicated by a line, could be a point-to-point link or a subnetwork. Three hosts, G1, G2, and G3, are members of a multicast group and can receive datagrams with the corresponding destination multicast address. Two hosts, S1 and S2, transmit data to this multicast address. The thick black lines indicate the routing tree for source S1 and this multicast group, and

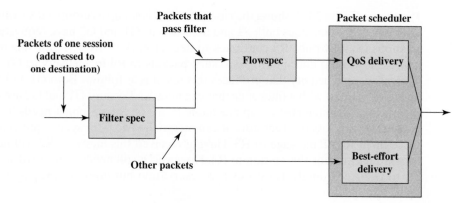

Figure 20.4 Treatment of Packets of One Session at One Router

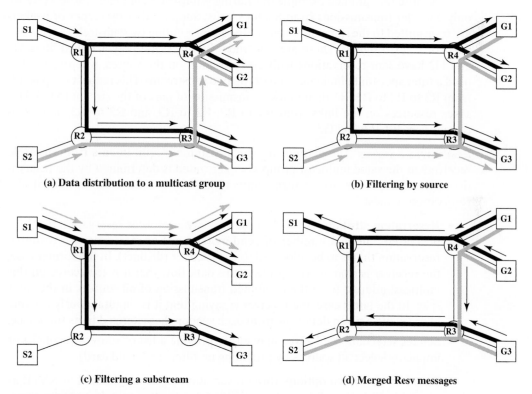

(a) Data distribution to a multicast group

(b) Filtering by source

(c) Filtering a substream

(d) Merged Resv messages

Figure 20.5 RSVP Operation

the thick shaded lines indicate the routing tree for source S2 and this multicast group. The arrowed lines indicate packet transmission from S1 (black) and S2 (gray).

We can see that all four routers need to be aware of the resource reservations of each multicast destination. Thus, resource requests from the destinations must propagate backward through the routing trees toward each potential host.

FILTERING Figure 20.5b shows the case that G3 has set up a resource reservation with a filter spec that includes both S1 and S2, whereas G1 and G2 have requested transmissions from S1 only. R3 continues to deliver packets from S2 for this multicast address to G3 but does not forward such packets to R4 for delivery to G1 and G2. The reservation activity that produces this result is as follows. Both G1 and G2 send an RSVP request with a filter spec that excludes S2. Because G1 and G2 are the only members of the multicast group reachable from R4, R4 no longer needs to forward packets for this session. Therefore, it can merge the two filter spec requests and send these in an RSVP message to R3. Having received this message, R3 will no longer forward packets for this session to R4. However, it still needs to forward such packets to G3. Accordingly, R3 stores this reservation but does not propagate it back up to R2.

Data packets that are addressed to a particular session but do not match any of the filter specs are treated as best-effort traffic.

A more fine-grained example of filtering is illustrated in Figure 20.5c. Here we only consider transmissions from S1, for clarity. Suppose that two types of packets are transmitted to the same multicast address representing two substreams (e.g., two parts of a video signal). These are illustrated by black and gray arrowed lines. G1 and G2 have sent reservations with no restriction on the source, whereas G3 has used a filter spec that eliminates one of the two substreams. This request propagates from R3 to R2 to R1. R1 then blocks transmission of part of the stream to G3. This saves resources on the links from R1 to R2, R2 to R3, and R3 to G3, as well as resources in R2, R3, and G3.

RESERVATION STYLES The manner in which resource requirements from multiple receivers in the same multicast group are aggregated is determined by the reservation style. These styles are, in turn, characterized by two different options in the reservation request:

- **Reservation attribute:** A receiver may specify a resource reservation that is to be shared among a number of senders (shared) or may specify a resource reservation that is to be allocated to each sender (distinct). In the former case, the receiver is characterizing the entire data flow that it is to receive on this multicast address from the combined transmission of all sources in the filter spec. In the latter case, the receiver is saying that it is simultaneously capable of receiving a given data flow from each sender characterized in its filter spec.
- **Sender selection:** A receiver may either provide a list of sources (explicit) or implicitly select all sources by providing no filter spec (wild card).

Based on these two options, three reservation styles are defined in RSVP, as shown in Table 20.1. The **wildcard-filter (WF) style** specifies a single resource reservation to be shared by all senders to this address. If all of the receivers use this style, then we can think of this style as a shared pipe whose capacity (or quality) is the largest of the resource requests from all receivers downstream from any point on the distribution tree. The size is independent of the number of senders using it. This type of reservation is propagated upstream to all senders. Symbolically, this style is represented in the form WF(*{Q}), where the asterisk represents wildcard sender selection and Q is the flowspec.

Table 20.1   Reservation Attributes and Styles

Sender Selection	Reservation Attribute	
	Distinct	**Shared**
Explicit	Fixed-filter (FF) style	Shared-explicit (SE) style
Wildcard	—	Wildcard-filter (WF) style

To see the effects of the WF style, we use the router configuration of Figure Figure 20.6 taken from the RSVP specification. This is a router along the distribution tree that forwards packets on port y for receiver R1 and on port z for receivers R2 and R3. Transmissions for this group arrive on port w from S1 and on port x from S2 and S3. Transmissions from all sources are forwarded to all destinations through this router.

Figure 20.6b shows the way in which the router handles WF requests. For simplicity, the flowspec is a one-dimensional quantity in multiples of some unit resource B. The *Receive* column shows the requests that arrive from the receivers. The *Reserve* column shows the resulting reservation state for each outgoing port. The *Send* column indicates the requests that are sent upstream to the previous-hop nodes. Note that the router must reserve a pipe of capacity 4B for port y and of capacity 3B for port z. In the latter case, the router has merged the requests from R2 and R3 to support the maximum requirement for that port. However, in passing requests upstream the router must merge all outgoing requests and send a request for 4B upstream on both ports w and x.

Now suppose that the distribution tree is such that this router forwards packets from S1 on both ports y and z but forwards packets from S2 and S3 only on port z, because the internet topology provides a shorter path from S2 and S3 to R1. Figure 20.6c indicates the way in which resource requests are merged in this case. The only change is that the request sent upstream on port x is for 3B. This is because packets arriving from this port are only to be forwarded on port z, which has a maximum flowspec request of 3B.

A good example of the use of the WF style is for an audio teleconference with multiple sites. Typically, only one person at a time speaks, so a shared capacity can be used by all senders.

The **fixed-filter (FF) style** specifies a distinct reservation for each sender and provides an explicit list of senders. Symbolically, this style is represented in the form FF($S1\{Q1\}$, $S2\{Q2\}$, ...), where Si is a requested sender and Qi is the resource request for that sender. The total reservation on a link for a given session is the sum of the Qi for all requested senders.

Figure 20.6d illustrates the operation of the FF style. In the *Reserve* column, each box represents one reserved pipe on the outgoing link. All of the incoming requests for S1 are merged to send a request for 4B out on port w. The flow descriptors for senders S2 and S3 are packed (not merged) into the request sent of port x; for this request, the maximum requested flowspec amount for each source is used.

A good example of the use of the FF style is for video distribution. To receive video signals simultaneously from different sources requires a separate pipe for

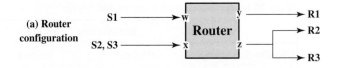

(a) Router configuration

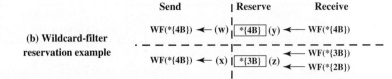

(b) Wildcard-filter reservation example

(c) Wildcard-filter reservation example: partial routing

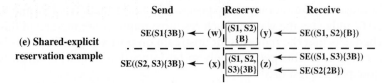

(d) Fixed-filter reservation example

(e) Shared-explicit reservation example

Figure 20.6 Examples of Reservation Styles

each of the streams. The merging and packing operations at the routers assure that adequate resources are available. For example, in Figure 20.5a, R3 must reserve resources for two distinct video streams going to G3, but it needs only a single pipe on the stream going to R4 even though that stream is feeding two destinations (G1 and G2). Thus, with FF style, it may be possible to share resources among multiple receivers but it is never possible to share resources among multiple senders.

The **shared-explicit (SE) style** specifies a single resource reservation to be shared among an explicit list of senders. Symbolically, this style is represented in the form SE(S1, S2, … {Q}). Figure 20.6e illustrates the operation of this style. When SE-style reservations are merged, the resulting filter spec is the union of the original filter specs, and the resulting flowspec is the largest flowspec.

As with the WF style, the SE style is appropriate for multicast applications in which there are multiple data sources but they are unlikely to transmit simultaneously.

RSVP Protocol Mechanisms

RSVP uses two basic message types: Resv and Path. Resv messages originate at multicast group receivers and propagate upstream through the distribution tree, being merged and packed when appropriate at each node along the way. These messages create soft states within the routers of the distribution tree that define the resources reserved for this session (this multicast address). Ultimately, the merged Resv messages reach the sending hosts, enabling the hosts to set up appropriate traffic control parameters for the first hop. Figure 20.5d indicates the flow of Resv messages. Note that messages are merged so that only a single message flows upstream along any branch of the combined distribution trees. However, these messages must be repeated periodically to maintain the soft states.

The Path message is used to provide upstream routing information. In all of the multicast routing protocols currently in use, only a downstream route, in the form of a distribution tree, is maintained. However, the Resv messages must propagate upstream through all intermediate routers and to all sending hosts. In the absence of reverse routing information from the routing protocol, RSVP provides this with the Path message. Each host that wishes to participate as a sender in a multicast group issues a Path message that is transmitted throughout the distribution tree to all multicast destinations. Along the way, each router and each destination host creates a path state that indicates the reverse hop to be used for this source. Figure 20.5a indicates the paths taken by these messages, which is the same as the paths taken by data packets.

Figure 20.7 illustrates the operation of the protocol, with events numbered from the perspective of each host. The following events occur:

a. A receiver joins a multicast group by sending an IGMP (Internet Group Message Protocol) join message to a neighboring router.

b. A potential sender issues a Path message to the multicast group address.

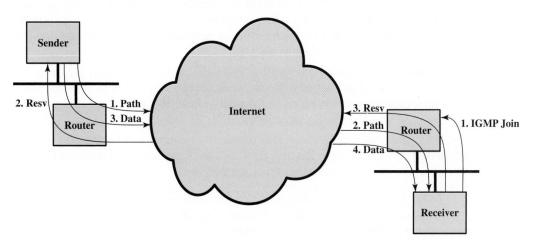

Figure 20.7 RSVP Host Model

    c. A receiver receives a Path message identifying a sender.

    d. Now that the receiver has reverse path information, it may begin sending Resv messages, specifying the desired flow descriptors.

    e. The Resv message propagates through the internet and is delivered to the sender.

    f. The sender starts sending data packets.

    g. The receiver starts receiving data packets.

Events a and b may happen in either order.

20.3 DIFFERENTIATED SERVICES

ISA and RSVP are intended to support QoS capability in the Internet and in private internets. Although ISA in general and RSVP in particular are useful tools in this regard, these features are relatively complex to deploy. Further, they may not scale well to handle large volumes of traffic because of the amount of control signaling required to coordinate integrated QoS offerings and because of the maintenance of state information required at routers.

As the burden on the Internet grows, and as the variety of applications grow, there is an immediate need to provide differing levels of QoS to different traffic flows. The differentiated services (DS) architecture (RFC 2475) is designed to provide a simple, easy-to-implement, low-overhead tool to support a range of network services that are differentiated on the basis of performance.

Several key characteristics of DS contribute to its efficiency and ease of deployment:

- IP packets are labeled for differing QoS treatment using the existing IPv4 (Figure 18.5) or IPv6 (Figure 18.10) DS field. Thus, no change is required to IP.

- A service level agreement (SLA) is established between the service provider (Internet domain) and the customer prior to the use of DS. This avoids the need to incorporate DS mechanisms in applications. Thus, existing applications need not be modified to use DS.

- DS provides a built-in aggregation mechanism. All traffic with the same DS octet is treated the same by the network service. For example, multiple voice connections are not handled individually but in the aggregate. This provides for good scaling to larger networks and traffic loads.

- DS is implemented in individual routers by queuing and forwarding packets based on the DS octet. Routers deal with each packet individually and do not have to save state information on packet flows.

Today, DS is the most widely accepted QoS mechanism in enterprise networks.

Although DS is intended to provide a simple service based on relatively simple mechanisms, the set of RFCs related to DS is relatively complex. Table 20.2 summarizes some of the key terms from these specifications.

Table 20.2 Terminology for Differentiated Services

Behavior Aggregate	A set of packets with the same DS codepoint crossing a link in a particular direction.
Classifier	Selects packets based on the DS field (BA classifier) or on multiple fields within the packet header (MF classifier).
DS Boundary Node	A DS node that connects one DS domain to a node in another domain
DS Codepoint	A specified value of the 6-bit DSCP portion of the 8-bit DS field in the IP header.
DS Domain	A contiguous (connected) set of nodes, capable of implementing differentiated services, that operate with a common set of service provisioning policies and per-hop behavior definitions.
DS Interior Node	A DS node that is not a DS boundary node.
DS Node	A node that supports differentiated services. Typically, a DS node is a router. A host system that provides differentiated services for applications in the host is also a DS node.
Dropping	The process of discarding packets based on specified rules; also called **policing**.
Marking	The process of setting the DS codepoint in a packet. Packets may be marked on initiation and may be re-marked by an en route DS node.
Metering	The process of measuring the temporal properties (e.g., rate) of a packet stream selected by a classifier. The instantaneous state of that process may affect marking, shaping, and dropping functions.
Per-Hop Behavior (PHB)	The externally observable forwarding behavior applied at a node to a behavior aggregate.
Service Level Agreement (SLA)	A service contract between a customer and a service provider that specifies the forwarding service a customer should receive.
Shaping	The process of delaying packets within a packet stream to cause it to conform to some defined traffic profile.
Traffic Conditioning	Control functions performed to enforce rules specified in a TCA, including metering, marking, shaping, and dropping.
Traffic Conditioning Agreement (TCA)	An agreement specifying classifying rules and traffic conditioning rules that are to apply to packets selected by the classifier.

Services

The DS type of service is provided within a DS domain, which is defined as a contiguous portion of the Internet over which a consistent set of DS policies are administered. Typically, a DS domain would be under the control of one administrative entity. The services provided across a DS domain are defined in an SLA, which is a service contract between a customer and the service provider that specifies the forwarding service that the customer should receive for various classes of packets. A customer may be a user organization or another DS domain. Once the SLA is established, the customer submits packets with the DS octet marked to indicate the packet class. The service provider must assure that the customer gets at least the agreed QoS for each packet class. To provide that QoS, the service provider must configure the appropriate forwarding policies at each router (based on DS octet value) and must measure the performance being provided for each class on an ongoing basis.

If a customer submits packets intended for destinations within the DS domain, then the DS domain is expected to provide the agreed service. If the destination is beyond the customer's DS domain, then the DS domain will attempt to forward the packets through other domains, requesting the most appropriate service to match the requested service.

A draft DS framework document lists the following detailed performance parameters that might be included in an SLA:

- Detailed service performance parameters such as expected throughput, drop probability, latency
- Constraints on the ingress and egress points at which the service is provided, indicating the scope of the service
- Traffic profiles that must be adhered to for the requested service to be provided, such as token bucket parameters
- Disposition of traffic submitted in excess of the specified profile

The framework document also gives some examples of services that might be provided:

1. Traffic offered at service level A will be delivered with low latency.
2. Traffic offered at service level B will be delivered with low loss.
3. Ninety percent of in-profile traffic delivered at service level C will experience no more than 50 ms latency.
4. Ninety-five percent of in-profile traffic delivered at service level D will be delivered.
5. Traffic offered at service level E will be allotted twice the bandwidth of traffic delivered at service level F.
6. Traffic with drop precedence X has a higher probability of delivery than traffic with drop precedence Y.

The first two examples are qualitative and are valid only in comparison to other traffic, such as default traffic that gets a best-effort service. The next two examples are quantitative and provide a specific guarantee that can be verified by measurement on the actual service without comparison to any other services offered at the same time. The final two examples are a mixture of quantitative and qualitative.

DS Field

Packets are labeled for service handling by means of the 6-bit DS field in the IPv4 header or the IPv6 header. The value of the DS field, referred to as the **DS code-point**, is the label used to classify packets for differentiated services. Figure 20.8a shows the DS field.

With a 6-bit codepoint, there are in principle 64 different classes of traffic that could be defined. These 64 codepoints are allocated across three pools of code-points, as follows:

- Codepoints of the form xxxxx0, where x is either 0 or 1, are reserved for assignment as standards.

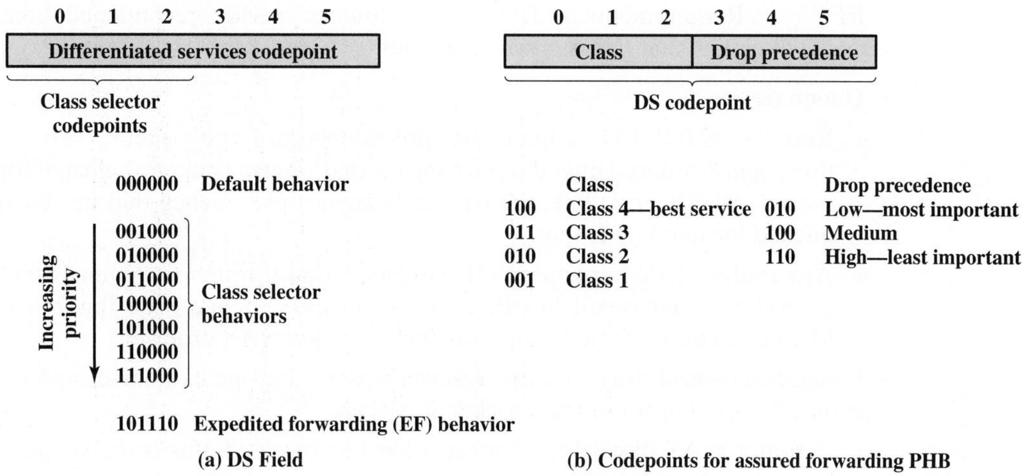

	0	1	2	3	4	5
Differentiated services codepoint						

Class selector
codepoints

	0	1	2	3	4	5
Class			Drop precedence			

DS codepoint

000000	Default behavior	
001000		
010000		
011000		
100000	Class selector	
101000	behaviors	
110000		
111000		

Increasing priority

Class		
100	Class 4—best service	010
011	Class 3	100
010	Class 2	110
001	Class 1	

Drop precedence	
Low—most important	
Medium	
High—least important	

101110 Expedited forwarding (EF) behavior

(a) DS Field

(b) Codepoints for assured forwarding PHB

Figure 20.8   DS Field

- Codepoints of the form xxxx11 are reserved for experimental or local use.
- Codepoints of the form xxxx01 are also reserved for experimental or local use but may be allocated for future standards action as needed.

Within the first pool, several assignments are made in RFC 2474. The codepoint 000000 is the default packet class. The default class is the best-effort forwarding behavior in existing routers. Such packets are forwarded in the order that they are received as soon as link capacity becomes available. If other higher-priority packets in other DS classes are available for transmission, these are given preference over best-effort default packets.

Codepoints of the form xxx000 are reserved to provide backward compatibility with the IPv4 precedence service. To explain this requirement, we need to digress to an explanation of the IPv4 precedence service. The IPv4 type of service (TOS) field includes two subfields: a 3-bit precedence subfield and a 4-bit TOS subfield. These subfields serve complementary functions. The TOS subfield provides guidance to the IP entity (in the source or router) on selecting the next hop for this datagram, and the precedence subfield provides guidance about the relative allocation of router resources for this datagram.

The precedence field is set to indicate the degree of urgency or priority to be associated with a datagram. If a router supports the precedence subfield, there are three approaches to responding:

- **Route selection:** A particular route may be selected if the router has a smaller queue for that route or if the next hop on that route supports network precedence or priority (e.g., a token ring network supports priority).
- **Network service:** If the network on the next hop supports precedence, then that service is invoked.
- **Queuing discipline:** A router may use precedence to affect how queues are handled. For example, a router may give preferential treatment in queues to datagrams with higher precedence.

RFC 1812, Requirements for IP Version 4 Routers, provides recommendations for queuing discipline that fall into two categories:

- **Queue service**

  a. Routers SHOULD implement precedence-ordered queue service. Precedence-ordered queue service means that when a packet is selected for output on a (logical) link, the packet of highest precedence that has been queued for that link is sent.

  b. Any router MAY implement other policy-based throughput management procedures that result in other than strict precedence ordering, but it MUST be configurable to suppress them (i.e., use strict ordering).

- **Congestion control**. When a router receives a packet beyond its storage capacity, it must discard it or some other packet or packets.

  a. A router MAY discard the packet it has just received; this is the simplest but not the best policy.

  b. Ideally, the router should select a packet from one of the sessions most heavily abusing the link, given that the applicable QoS policy permits this. A recommended policy in datagram environments using FIFO queues is to discard a packet randomly selected from the queue. An equivalent algorithm in routers using fair queues is to discard from the longest queue. A router MAY use these algorithms to determine which packet to discard.

  c. If precedence-ordered queue service is implemented and enabled, the router MUST NOT discard a packet whose IP precedence is higher than that of a packet that is not discarded.

  d. A router MAY protect packets whose IP headers request the maximize reliability TOS, except where doing so would be in violation of the previous rule.

  e. A router MAY protect fragmented IP packets, on the theory that dropping a fragment of a datagram may increase congestion by causing all fragments of the datagram to be retransmitted by the source.

  f. To help prevent routing perturbations or disruption of management functions, the router MAY protect packets used for routing control, link control, or network management from being discarded. Dedicated routers (i.e., routers that are not also general purpose hosts, terminal servers, etc.) can achieve an approximation of this rule by protecting packets whose source or destination is the router itself.

The DS codepoints of the form xxx000 should provide a service that at minimum is equivalent to that of the IPv4 precedence functionality.

DS Configuration and Operation

Figure 20.9 illustrates the type of configuration envisioned in the DS documents. A DS domain consists of a set of contiguous routers; that is, it is possible to get from any router in the domain to any other router in the domain by a path that does not include routers outside the domain. Within a domain, the interpretation of DS codepoints is uniform, so that a uniform, consistent service is provided.

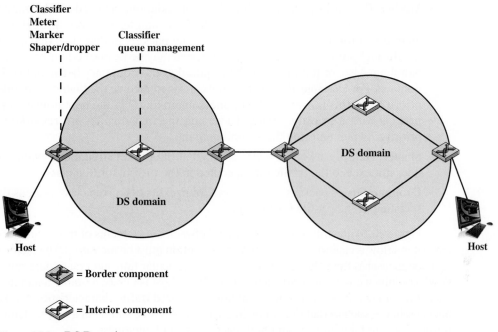

Figure 20.9 DS Domains

Routers in a DS domain are either boundary nodes or interior nodes. Typically, the interior nodes implement simple mechanisms for handling packets based on their DS codepoint values. This includes queuing discipline to give preferential treatment depending on codepoint value, and packet-dropping rules to dictate which packets should be dropped first in the event of buffer saturation. The DS specifications refer to the forwarding treatment provided at a router as per-hop behavior (PHB). This PHB must be available at all routers, and typically PHB is the only part of DS implemented in interior routers.

The boundary nodes include PHB mechanisms but more sophisticated traffic conditioning mechanisms are also required to provide the desired service. Thus, interior routers have minimal functionality and minimal overhead in providing the DS service, while most of the complexity is in the boundary nodes. The boundary node function can also be provided by a host system attached to the domain, on behalf of the applications at that host system.

The traffic conditioning function consists of five elements:

- **Classifier:** Separates submitted packets into different classes. This is the foundation of providing differentiated services. A classifier may separate traffic only on the basis of the DS codepoint (behavior aggregate classifier) or based on multiple fields within the packet header or even the packet payload (multifield classifier).

- **Meter:** Measures submitted traffic for conformance to a profile. The meter determines whether a given packet stream class is within or exceeds the service level guaranteed for that class.

- **Marker:** Re-marks packets with a different codepoint as needed. This may be done for packets that exceed the profile; for example, if a given throughput is guaranteed for a particular service class, any packets in that class that exceed the throughput in some defined time interval may be re-marked for best-effort handling. Also, re-marking may be required at the boundary between two DS domains. For example, if a given traffic class is to receive the highest supported priority, and this is a value of 3 in one domain and 7 in the next domain, then packets with a priority 3 value traversing the first domain are remarked as priority 7 when entering the second domain.

- **Shaper:** Delays packets as necessary so that the packet stream in a given class does not exceed the traffic rate specified in the profile for that class.

- **Dropper:** Drops packets when the rate of packets of a given class exceeds that specified in the profile for that class.

Figure 20.10 illustrates the relationship between the elements of traffic conditioning. After a flow is classified, its resource consumption must be measured. The metering function measures the volume of packets over a particular time interval to determine a flow's compliance with the traffic agreement. If the host is bursty, a simple data rate or packet rate may not be sufficient to capture the desired traffic characteristics. A token bucket scheme, such as that illustrated in Figure 20.2, is an example of a way to define a traffic profile to take into account both packet rate and burstiness.

If a traffic flow exceeds some profile, several approaches can be taken. Individual packets in excess of the profile may be re-marked for lower-quality handling and allowed to pass into the DS domain. A traffic shaper may absorb a burst of packets in a buffer and pace the packets over a longer period. A dropper may drop packets if the buffer used for pacing becomes saturated.

Per–Hop Behavior

As part of the DS standardization effort, specific types of PHB need to be defined, which can be associated with specific differentiated services. Currently, two standards-track PHBs have been issued: expedited forwarding PHB (RFCs 3246 and 3247) and assured forwarding PHB (RFC 2597).

EXPEDITED FORWARDING PHB RFC 3246 defines the expedited forwarding (EF) PHB as a building block for low-loss, low-delay, and low-jitter end-to-end services

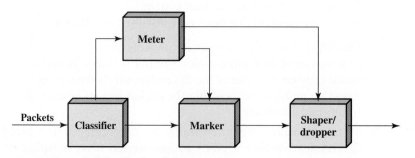

Figure 20.10 DS Traffic Conditioner

through DS domains. In essence, such a service should appear to the endpoints as providing close to the performance of a point-to-point connection or leased line.

In an internet or packet-switching network, a low-loss, low-delay, and low-jitter service is difficult to achieve. By its nature, an internet involves queues at each node, or router, where packets are buffered waiting to use a shared output link. It is the queuing behavior at each node that results in loss, delays, and jitter. Thus, unless the internet is grossly oversized to eliminate all queuing effects, care must be taken in handling traffic for EF PHB to assure that queuing effects do not result in loss, delay, or jitter above a given threshold. RFC 3246 declares that the intent of the EF PHB is to provide a PHB in which suitably marked packets usually encounter short or empty queues. The relative absence of queues minimizes delay and jitter. Furthermore, if queues remain short relative to the buffer space available, packet loss is also kept to a minimum.

The EF PHB is designed to configuring nodes so that the traffic aggregate[2] has a well-defined minimum departure rate. (*Well-defined* means "independent of the dynamic state of the node." In particular, independent of the intensity of other traffic at the node.) The general concept outlined in RFC 3246 is this: The border nodes control the traffic aggregate to limit its characteristics (rate, burstiness) to some predefined level. Interior nodes must treat the incoming traffic in such a way that queuing effects do not appear. In general terms, the requirement on interior nodes is that the aggregate's maximum arrival rate must be less than the aggregate's minimum departure rate.

RFC 3246 does not mandate a specific queuing policy at the interior nodes to achieve the EF PHB. The RFC notes that a simple priority scheme could achieve the desired effect, with the EF traffic given absolute priority over other traffic. So long as the EF traffic itself did not overwhelm an interior node, this scheme would result in acceptable queuing delays for the EF PHB. However, the risk of a simple priority scheme is that packet flows for other PHB traffic would be disrupted. Thus, some more sophisticated queuing policy might be warranted.

ASSURED FORWARDING PHB The assured forwarding (AF) PHB is designed to provide a service superior to best effort but one that does not require the reservation of resources within an internet and does not require the use of detailed discrimination among flows from different users. The concept behind the AF PHB was first introduced in [CLAR98] and is referred to as explicit allocation. The AF PHB is more complex than explicit allocation, but it is useful to first highlight the key elements of the explicit allocation scheme:

1. Users are offered the choice of a number of classes of service for their traffic. Each class describes a different traffic profile in terms of an aggregate data rate and burstiness.

2. Traffic from a user within a given class is monitored at a boundary node. Each packet in a traffic flow is marked *out* or *in* based on whether it does or does not exceed the traffic profile.

---

[2]The term *traffic aggregate* refers to the flow of packets associated with a particular service for a particular user.

3. Inside the network, there is no separation of traffic from different users or even traffic from different classes. Instead, all traffic is treated as a single pool of packets, with the only distinction being whether each packet has been marked *in* or *out*.

4. When congestion occurs, the interior nodes implement a dropping scheme in which *out* packets are dropped before *in* packets.

5. Different users will see different levels of service because they will have different quantities of *in* packets in the service queues.

The advantage of this approach is its simplicity. Very little work is required by the internal nodes. Marking of the traffic at the boundary nodes based on traffic profiles provides different levels of service to different classes.

The AF PHB defined in RFC 2597 expands on the preceding approach in the following ways:

1. Four AF classes are defined, allowing the definition of four distinct traffic profiles. A user may select one or more of these classes to satisfy requirements.

2. Within each class, packets are marked by the customer or by the service provider with one of three drop precedence values. In case of congestion, the drop precedence of a packet determines the relative importance of the packet within the AF class. A congested DS node tries to protect packets with a lower drop precedence value from being lost by preferably discarding packets with a higher drop precedence value.

This approach is still simpler to implement than any sort of resource reservation scheme but provides considerable flexibility. Within an interior DS node, traffic from the four classes can be treated separately, with different amounts of resources (buffer space, data rate) assigned to the four classes. Within each class, packets are handled based on drop precedence. Thus, as RFC 2597 points out, the level of forwarding assurance of an IP packet depends on the following:

- How much forwarding resources has been allocated to the AF class to which the packet belongs
- The current load of the AF class, and, in case of congestion, within the class
- The drop precedence of the packet

RFC 2597 does not mandate any mechanisms at the interior nodes to manage the AF traffic. It does reference the RED algorithm as a possible way of managing congestion.

Figure 20.8b shows the recommended codepoints for AF PHB in the DS field.

20.4 SERVICE LEVEL AGREEMENTS

A service level agreement (SLA) is a contract between a network provider and a customer that defines specific aspects of the service that is to be provided. The definition is formal and typically defines quantitative thresholds that must be met. An SLA typically includes the following information:

- **A description of the nature of service to be provided:** A basic service would be IP-based network connectivity of enterprise locations plus access to the Internet. The service may include additional functions such as Web hosting, maintenance of domain name servers, and operation and maintenance tasks.

- **The expected performance level of the service:** The SLA defines a number of metrics, such as delay, reliability, and availability, with numerical thresholds.

- **The process for monitoring and reporting the service level:** This describes how performance levels are measured and reported.

The types of service parameters included in an SLA for an IP network are similar to those provided for frame relay and ATM networks. A key difference is that, because of the unreliable datagram nature of an IP network, it is more difficult to realize tightly defined constraints on performance, compared to the connection-oriented frame relay and ATM networks.

Figure 20.11 shows a typical configuration that lends itself to an SLA. In this case, a network service provider maintains an IP-based network. A customer has a number of private networks (e.g., LANs) at various sites. Customer networks are connected to the provider via access routers at the access points. The SLA dictates service and performance levels for traffic between access routers across the provider network. In addition, the provider network links to the Internet and thus

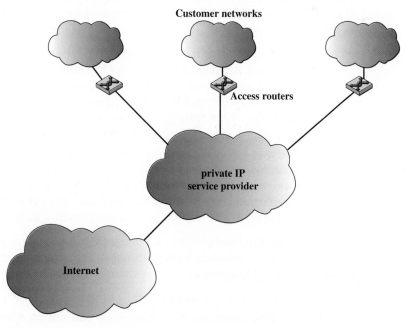

Figure 20.11 Typical Framework for Service Level Agreement

provides Internet access for the enterprise. For example, for the Internet Dedicated Service provided by MCI, the SLA includes the following items:

- **Availability:** 100% availability.
- **Latency (delay):** Average round-trip transmissions of ≤ 45 ms between access routers in the contiguous U.S. Average round-trip transmissions of ≤ 90 ms between an access router in the New York metropolitan area and an access router in the London metropolitan area. Latency is calculated by averaging sample measurements taken during a calendar month between routers.
- **Network packet delivery (reliability):** Successful packet delivery rate of ≥ 99.5%.
- **Denial of service (DoS):** Responds to DoS attacks reported by customer within 15 minutes of customer opening a complete trouble ticket. MCI defines a DoS attack as more than 95% bandwidth utilization.
- **Network jitter:** Jitter is defined as the variation or difference in the end-to-end delay between received packets of an IP or packet stream. Jitter performance will not exceed 1 ms between access routers.

An SLA can be defined for the overall network service. In addition, SLAs can be defined for specific end-to-end services available across the carrier's network, such as a virtual private network, or differentiated services.

20.5 IP PERFORMANCE METRICS

The IPPM Performance Metrics Working Group (IPPM) is chartered by IETF to develop standard metrics that relate to the quality, performance, and reliability of Internet data delivery. Two trends dictate the need for such a standardized measurement scheme:

1. The Internet has grown and continues to grow at a dramatic rate. Its topology is increasingly complex. As its capacity has grown, the load on the Internet has grown at an even faster rate. Similarly, private internets, such as corporate intranets and extranets, have exhibited similar growth in complexity, capacity, and load. The sheer scale of these networks makes it difficult to determine quality, performance, and reliability characteristics.
2. The Internet serves a large and growing number of commercial and personal users across an expanding spectrum of applications. Similarly, private networks are growing in terms of user base and range of applications. Some of these applications are sensitive to particular QoS parameters, leading users to require accurate and understandable performance metrics.

A standardized and effective set of metrics enables users and service providers to have an accurate common understanding of the performance of the Internet and private internets. Measurement data is useful for a variety of purposes, including

- Supporting capacity planning and troubleshooting of large complex internets
- Encouraging competition by providing uniform comparison metrics across service providers

- Supporting Internet research in such areas as protocol design, congestion control, and quality of service
- Verification of service level agreements

Table 20.3 lists the metrics that have been defined in RFCs at the time of this writing. Table 20.3a lists those metrics which result in a value estimated based on a sampling technique. The metrics are defined in three stages:

- **Singleton metric:** The most elementary, or atomic, quantity that can be measured for a given performance metric. For example, for a delay metric, a singleton metric is the delay experienced by a single packet.
- **Sample metric:** A collection of singleton measurements taken during a given time period. For example, for a delay metric, a sample metric is the set of delay values for all of the measurements taken during a one-hour period.
- **Statistical metric:** A value derived from a given sample metric by computing some statistic of the values defined by the singleton metric on the sample. For example, the mean of all the one-way delay values on a sample might be defined as a statistical metric

The measurement technique can be either active or passive. **Active techniques** require injecting packets into the network for the sole purpose of measurement. There are several drawbacks to this approach. The load on the network is increased. This in turn can affect the desired result. For example, on a heavily loaded network, the injection of measurement packets can increase network delay, so that the measured delay is greater than it would be without the measurement traffic. In addition, an active measurement policy can be abused for denial-of-service attacks disguised as legitimate measurement activity. **Passive techniques** observe and extract metrics from existing traffic. This approach can expose the contents of Internet traffic to unintended recipients, creating security and privacy concerns. So far, the metrics defined by the IPPM working group are all active.

For the sample metrics, the simplest technique is to take measurements at fixed time intervals, known as periodic sampling. There are several problems with this approach. First, if the traffic on the network exhibits periodic behavior, with a period that is an integer multiple of the sampling period (or vice versa), correlation effects may result in inaccurate values.

Also, the act of measurement can perturb what is being measured (e.g., injecting measurement traffic into a network alters the congestion level of the network), and repeated periodic perturbations can drive a network into a state of synchronization (e.g., [FLOY94]), greatly magnifying what might individually be minor effects. Accordingly, RFC 2330 (*Framework for IP Performance Metrics*) recommends Poisson sampling. This method uses a Poisson distribution to generate random time intervals with the desired mean value.

Most of the statistical metrics listed in Table 20.3a are self-explanatory. The percentile metric is defined as follows: The xth percentile is a value y such that $x\%$ of measurements $\geq y$. The inverse percentile of x for a set of measurements is the percentage of all values $\leq x$.

Table 20.3 IP Performance Metrics

(a) Sampled metrics

Metric Name	Singleton Definition	Statistical Definitions
One-Way Delay	Delay = dT, where Src transmits first bit of packet at T and Dst received last bit of packet at $T + dT$	Percentile, median, minimum, inverse percentile
Round-Trip Delay	Delay = dT, where Src transmits first bit of packet at T and Src received last bit of packet immediately returned by Dst at $T + dT$	Percentile, median, minimum, inverse percentile
One-Way Loss	Packet loss = 0 (signifying successful transmission and reception of packet); = 1 (signifying packet loss)	Average
One-Way Loss Pattern	Loss distance: Pattern showing the distance between successive packet losses in terms of the sequence of packets	Number or rate of loss distances below a defined threshold, number of loss periods, pattern of period lengths, pattern of inter-loss period lengths.
	Loss period: Pattern showing the number of bursty losses (losses involving consecutive packets)	
Packet Delay Variation	Packet delay variation (pdv) for a pair of packets with a stream of packets = difference between the one-way-delay of the selected packets	Percentile, inverse percentile, jitter, peak-to-peak pdv

Src = IP address of a host

Dst = IP address of a host

(b) Other metrics

Metric Name	General Definition	Metrics
Connectivity	Ability to deliver a packet over a transport connection.	One-way instantaneous connectivity, Two-way instantaneous connectivity, one-way interval connectivity, two-way interval connectivity, two-sway temporal connectivity
Bulk Transfer Capacity	Long-term average data rate (bps) over a single congestion-aware transport connection.	BTC = (data sent)/(elapsed time)

Figure 20.12 illustrates the packet delay variation metric. This metric is used to measure jitter, or variability, in the delay of packets traversing the network. The singleton metric is defined by selecting two packet measurements and measuring the difference in the two delays. The statistical measures make use of the absolute values of the delays.

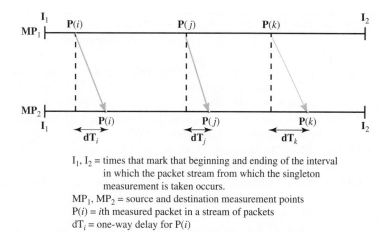

I_1, I_2 = times that mark that beginning and ending of the interval
in which the packet stream from which the singleton
measurement is taken occurs.
MP_1, MP_2 = source and destination measurement points
$P(i)$ = ith measured packet in a stream of packets
dT_i = one-way delay for $P(i)$

Figure 20.12   Model for Defining Packet Delay Variation

Table 20.3b lists two metrics that are not defined statistically. Connectivity deals with the issue of whether a transport-level connection is maintained by the network. The current specification (RFC 2678) does not detail specific sample and statistical metrics but provides a framework within which such metrics could be defined. Connectivity is determined by the ability to deliver a packet across a connection within a specified time limit. The other metric, bulk transfer capacity, is similarly specified (RFC 3148) without sample and statistical metrics but begins to address the issue of measuring the transfer capacity of a network service with the implementation of various congestion control mechanisms.

20.6 RECOMMENDED READING AND WEB SITES

[XIAO99] provides an overview and overall framework for Internet QoS as well as integrated and differentiated services. [MEDD10] is a more recent survey. [CLAR92] and [CLAR95] provide valuable surveys of the issues involved in internet service allocation for real-time and elastic applications, respectively. [SHEN95] is a masterful analysis of the rationale for a QoS-based internet architecture. [ZHAN95] is a broad survey of queuing disciplines that can be used in an ISA, including an analysis of FQ and WFQ.

[ZHAN93] is a good overview of the philosophy and functionality of RSVP, written by its developers. [WHIT97] is a broad survey of both ISA and RSVP.

[CARP02] and [WEIS98] are instructive surveys of differentiated services, while [KUMA98] looks at differentiated services and supporting router mechanisms that go beyond the current RFCs.

Two papers that compare IS and DS in terms of services and performance are [BERN00] and [HARJ00].

[VERM04] is an excellent survey of service level agreements for IP networks. [BOUI02] covers the more general case of data networks. [MART02] examines limitations of IP network SLAs compared to data networks such as frame relay.

[CHEN02] is a useful survey of Internet performance measurement issues. [PAXS96] provides an overview of the framework of the IPPM effort.

BERN00 Bernet, Y. "The Complementary Roles of RSVP and Differentiated Services in the Full-Service QoS Network." *IEEE Communications Magazine*, February 2000.

BOUI02 Bouillet, E.; Mitra, D.; and Ramakrishnan, K. "The Structure and Management of Service Level Agreements in Networks." *IEEE Journal on Selected Areas in Communications*, May 2002.

CARP02 Carpenter, B., and Nichols, K. "Differentiated Services in the Internet." *Proceedings of the IEEE*, September 2002.

CHEN02 Chen, T. "Internet Performance Monitoring." *Proceedings of the IEEE*, September 2002.

CLAR92 Clark, D.; Shenker, S.; and Zhang, L. "Supporting Real-Time Applications in an Integrated Services Packet Network: Architecture and Mechanism." *Proceedings, SIGCOMM '92*, August 1992.

CLAR95 Clark, D. *Adding Service Discrimination to the Internet*. MIT Laboratory for Computer Science Technical Report, September 1995, http://ana-www.lcs.mit.edu/anaWeb/papers.html

HARJ00 Harju, J., and Kivimaki, P. "Cooperation and Comparison of DiffServ and IntServ: Performance Measurements." *Proceedings, 23rd Annual IEEE Conference on Local Computer Networks*, November 2000.

KUMA98 Kumar, V.; Lakshman, T.; and Stiliadis, D. "Beyond Best Effort: Router Architectures for the Differentiated Services of Tomorrow's Internet." *IEEE Communications Magazine*, May 1998.

MART02 Martin, J., and Nilsson, A. "On Service Level Agreements for IP Networks." *Proceedings, IEEE INFOCOMM'02*, 2002.

MEDD10 Meddeb, A. "Internet QoS: Pieces of the Puzzle." *IEEE Communications Magazine*, January 2010.

PAXS96 Paxson, V. "Toward a Framework for Defining Internet Performance Metrics." *Proceedings, INET '96*, 1996, http://www-nrg.ee.lbl.gov

SHEN95 Shenker, S. "Fundamental Design Issues for the Future Internet." *IEEE Journal on Selected Areas in Communications*, September 1995.

VERM04 Verma, D. "Service Level Agreements on IP Networks." *Proceedings of the IEEE*, September 2004.

WEIS98 Weiss, W. "QoS with Differentiated Services." *Bell Labs Technical Journal*, October–December 1998.

WHIT97 White, P., and Crowcroft, J. "The Integrated Services in the Internet: State of the Art." *Proceedings of the IEEE*, December 1997.

XIAO99 Xiao, X., and Ni, L. "Internet QoS: A Big Picture." *IEEE Network*, March/April 1999.

ZHAN93 Zhang, L.; Deering, S.; Estrin, D.; Shenker, S.; and Zappala, D. "RSVP: A New Resource ReSerVation Protocol." *IEEE Network*, September 1993.

ZHAN95 Zhang, H. "Service Disciplines for Guaranteed Performance Service in Packet-Switching Networks." *Proceedings of the IEEE*, October 1995.

Recommended Web sites:

- **RSVP Project:** Home page for RSVP development.
- **IP Performance Metrics Working Group:** Chartered by IETF to develop a set of standard metrics that can be applied to the quality, performance, and reliability of Internet data delivery services. The Web site includes all relevant RFCs and Internet drafts.

20.7 KEY TERMS, REVIEW QUESTIONS, AND PROBLEMS

Key Terms

classifier	Integrated Services	quality of service (QoS)
differentiated	Architecture (ISA)	queuing discipline
services (DS)	jitter	Resource ReSerVation
dropper	marker	Protocol (RSVP)
elastic traffic	meter	shaper
inelastic traffic	per-hop behavior (PHB)	

Review Questions

20.1 What is the Integrated Services Architecture?

20.2 What is the difference between elastic and inelastic traffic?

20.3 What are the major functions that are part of an ISA?

20.4 List and briefly describe the three categories of service offered by ISA.

20.5 What is the difference between FIFO queuing and WFQ queuing?

20.6 What is the purpose of a DS codepoint?

20.7 List and briefly explain the five main functions of DS traffic conditioning.

20.8 What is meant by per-hop behavior?

Problems

20.1 When multiple equal-cost routes to a destination exist, OSPF may distribute traffic equally among the routes. This is called *load balancing*. What effect does such load balancing have on a transport layer protocol, such as TCP?

20.2 It is clear that if a router gives preferential treatment to one flow or one class of flows, then that flow or class of flows will receive improved service. It is not as clear that the overall service provided by the internet is improved. This question is intended to illustrate an overall improvement. Consider a network with a single link modeled by an exponential server of rate $T_s = 1$, and consider two classes of flows with Poisson arrival rates of $\lambda1 = \lambda2 = 0.25$ that have utility functions $U_1 = 4 - 2\,T_{q1}$ and $U_2 = 4 - T_{q2}$, where T_{qi} represents the average queuing delay to class i. Thus, class 1 traffic is more sensitive to delay than class 2. Define the total utility of the network as $V = U_1 + U_2$.

   a. Assume that the two classes are treated alike and that FIFO queuing is used. What is V?

   b. Now assume a strict priority service so that packets from class 1 are always transmitted before packets in class 2. What is V? Comment.

20.3 Provide three examples (each) of elastic and inelastic Internet traffic. Justify each example's inclusion in their respective category.

20.4 In RSVP, because the UDP/TCP port numbers are used for packet classification, each router must be able to examine these fields. This requirement raises problems in the following areas:

   a. IPv6 header processing

   b. IP-level security

Indicate the nature of the problem in each area, and suggest a solution.

20.5 Why does a differentiated services (DS) domain consist of a set of contiguous routers? How are the boundary node routers different from the interior node routers in a DS domain?

20.6 The token bucket scheme places a limit on the length of time at which traffic can depart at the maximum data rate. Let the token bucket be defined by a bucket size B octets and a token arrival rate of R octets/second, and let the maximum output data rate be M octets/s.

   a. Derive a formula for S, which is the length of the maximum-rate burst. That is, for how long can a flow transmit at the maximum output rate when governed by a token bucket?

   b. What is the value of S for $B = 250$ KB, $R = 2$ MB/s, and $M = 25$ MB/s?

Hint: The formula for S is not so simple as it might appear, because more tokens arrive while the burst is being output.

20.7 RFC 2330 (*Framework for IP Performance Metrics*) defines percentile in the following way. Given a collection of measurements, define the function $F(x)$, which for any x gives the percentage of the total measurements that were $\leq x$. If x is less than the minimum value observed, then $F(x) = 0\%$. If it is greater or equal to the maximum value observed, then $F(x) = 100\%$. The yth percentile refer to the smallest value of x for which $F(x) \geq y$. Consider that we have the following measurements: $-2, 7, 7, 4, 18, -5$. Determine the following percentiles: 0, 25, 50, 100.

20.8 For the one-way and two-way delay metrics, if a packet fails to arrive within a reasonable period of time, the delay is taken to be undefined (informally, infinite). The threshold of reasonable is a parameter of the methodology. Suppose we take a sample of one-way delays and get the following results: 100 ms, 110 ms, undefined, 90 ms, 500 ms. What is the 50th percentile?

20.9 RFC 2330 defines the median of a set of measurements to be equal to the 50th percentile if the number of measurements is odd. For an even number of measurements, sort the measurements in ascending order; the median is then the mean of the two central values. What is the median value for the measurements in the preceding two problems?

20.10 RFC 2679 defines the inverse percentile of x for a set of measurements to be the percentage of all values $\leq x$. What is the inverse percentile of 103 ms for the measurements in Problem 20.14?

MULTIPROTOCOL LABEL SWITCHING

No ticket! Dear me, Watson, this is really very singular. According to my experience it is not possible to reach the platform of a Metropolitan train without exhibiting one's ticket.

— *The Adventure of the Bruce-Partington Plans,* Sir Arthur Conan Doyle

KEY POINTS

◆ Multiprotocol Label Switching (MPLS) is a set of protocols, designed to address a number of issues, including traffic engineering, QoS, virtual private networks, and IP/ATM integration.

◆ An MPLS network or internet consists of a set of nodes, called label switching routers (LSRs), capable of switching and routing packets on the basis of which a label has been appended to each packet.

◆ A key component of an MPLS network is the use of traffic engineering to optimize and manage the load.

◆ MPLS is well suited to implementing virtual private networks.

In Chapter 19, we examined a number of IP-based mechanisms designed to improve the performance of IP-based networks and to provide different levels of quality of service (QoS) to different service users. Although the routing protocols discussed in Chapter 19 have as their fundamental purpose dynamically finding a route through an internet between any source and any destination, they also provide support for performance goals in two ways:

1. Because these protocols are distributed and dynamic, they can react to congestion by altering routes to avoid pockets of heavy traffic. This tends to smooth out and balance the load on the Internet, improving overall performance.
2. Routes can be based on various metrics, such as hop count and delay. Thus a routing algorithm develops information that can be used in determining how to handle packets with different service needs.

More directly, some of the mechanisms discussed in Chapter 20 (IS, DS) provide enhancements to an IP-based internet that explicitly provide support for QoS. However, none of the mechanisms or protocols discussed in Chapter 20 directly addresses the performance issue: How to improve the overall throughput and delay characteristics of an internet. MPLS is intended to provide connection-oriented QoS with features similar to those found in differentiated services, and support traffic management to improve network throughput and retain the flexibility of an IP-based networking approach.

Multiprotocol Label Switching (MPLS) is a set of Internet Engineering Task Force (IETF) specifications for including routing and traffic engineering information in packets. Thus, MPLS comprises a number of interrelated protocols, which can be referred to as the MPLS protocol suite. It can be used in IP networks but also in other types of packet-switching networks. MPLS is used to ensure that all packets in a particular flow take the same route over a backbone. Deployed by many telecommunication companies and service providers, MPLS delivers the quality of service required to support real-time voice and video as well as service level agreements (SLAs) that guarantee bandwidth.

We begin this chapter with an overview of the current status of MPLS as a networking technology.

Although the basic principles of MPLS are straightforward, the set of protocols and procedures that have been built up around MPLS is formidable. As of this writing, the IETF MPLS working group has issued 70 RFCs and has 29 active Internet Drafts. In addition, there are five other IETF working groups developing RFCs on topics related to MPLS. Thus, even a book-length treatment fails to capture the full extent of MPLS. Accordingly, the goal of this chapter is to present the fundamental concepts and an overview of the breadth of MPLS.

21.1 THE ROLE OF MPLS

In essence, MPLS is an efficient technique for forwarding and routing packets. MPLS was designed with IP networks in mind, but the technology can be used without IP to construct a network with any link-level protocol, including ATM and frame relay. In an ordinary packet-switching network, packet switches must examine various fields within the packet header to determine destination, route, quality of service, and any traffic management functions (such as discard or delay) that may be supported. Similarly, in an IP-based network, routers examine a number of fields in the IP header to determine these functions. In an MPLS network, a fixed-length label encapsulates an IP packet or a data link frame. The MPLS label contains all the information needed by an MPLS-enabled router to perform routing, delivery, QoS, and traffic management functions. Unlike IP, MPLS is connection oriented.

The IETF MPLS working group is the lead organization in developing MPLS-related specifications and standards. A number of other working groups deal with MPLS-related issues. Briefly, the objectives of these groups are as follows:

- **MPLS:** Responsible for standardizing a base technology for using label switching and for the implementation of label switched paths over various packet-based link-level technologies, such as Packet-over-SONET, Frame Relay, ATM, and LAN technologies (e.g., all forms of Ethernet, Token Ring, etc.). This includes procedures and protocols for the distribution of labels between routers and encapsulation.

- **Common control and measurement plane (CCAMP):** Responsible for defining a common control plane and a separate common measurement plane for physical path and core tunneling technologies of Internet and telecom service providers (ISPs and SPs), for example, O-O and O-E-O optical switches, TDM switches, Ethernet switches, ATM and frame relay switches, IP encapsulation tunneling technologies, and MPLS.

- **Layer 2 Virtual Private Networks (l2VPN):** Responsible for defining and specifying a limited number of solutions for supporting provider-provisioned Layer- 2

Virtual Private Networks (l2VPNs). The objective is to support link layer interfaces, such as ATM and Ethernet, for providing VPNs for an MPLS-enabled IP
packet- switched network.

- **Layer 3 Virtual Private Networks (l3VPN):** Responsible for defining and specifying a limited number of solutions for supporting provider-provisioned Layer- 3
  (routed) Virtual Private Networks (L3VPNs). Standardization includes supporting VPNs for end systems that have an IP interface over an MPLS-enabled
  IP packet -switched network.

- **Pseudowire Emulation Edge to Edge (pwe3):** Responsible for specifying protocols for pseudowire emulation over an MPLS network. A pseudowire emulates
  a point-to-point or point-to-multipoint link, and provides a single service that is
  perceived by its user as an unshared link or circuit of the chosen service.

- **Path Computation Element (PCE):** Focuses on the architecture and techniques
  for constraint-based path computation.

The magnitude of this effort suggests the importance, indeed the coming
dominance, of MPLS. A 2009 survey found that 84% of companies are now using
MPLS for their wide area networks [REED09]. MPLS is deployed in almost every
major IP network. [MARS09] lists the following reasons for the dramatic growth in
MPLS acceptance.

1. MPLS embraced IP. In the early 1990s, the telecom industry was pinning their
   hopes on ATM as the network backbone technology of the future, and made
   substantial investment. But as Internet usage exploded, carriers needed to
   refocus their efforts. At the same time, IETF was looking for ways to make
   circuit-oriented ATM technology run over IP. The result was the MPLS effort,
   which was quickly adopted by ATM proponents.

2. MPLS has built-in flexibility in several ways. MPLS separates out a control
   component, which enables various applications to directly manipulate label
   bindings, and a forwarding component, which uses a simple label-swapping
   paradigm. Also, MPLS allows labels to be stacked, enabling multiple control
   planes to act on a packet.

3. MPLS is protocol neutral. MPLS is designed to work in a multiple protocol
   environment. This enables MPLS to work with ATM, frame relay, SONET, or
   Ethernet at the core.

4. MPLS is pragmatic. The architecture created only two new protocols: Label
   Distribution Protocol and Link Management Protocol. Everything else incorporates or adapts existing protocols.

5. MPLS is adaptable. MPLS has evolved over time to support new applications
   and services, including layer 2 and layer 3 virtual private networks, Ethernet
   services, and traffic engineering.

6. MPLS supports metrics. MPLS allows carriers to collect a wide variety of
   statistics that can be used for network traffic trend analysis and planning. With
   MPLS, it is possible to measure traffic volume, latency, and delay between two
   routers. Carriers also can measure traffic between hubs, metropolitan areas,
   and regions.

7. MPLS scales. For example, Verizon uses MPLS for several global networks including its public and private IP networks. Verizon's Public IP network spans 410 points of presence on six continents and spans more than 150 countries.

It is clear that MPLS will permeate virtually all areas of networking. Hence the need for students to gain a basic understanding of its technology and protocols.

21.2 BACKGROUND

The roots of MPLS go back to a number of efforts in the mid-1990s to provide a comprehensive set of QoS and traffic engineering capabilities in IP-based networks. The first such effort to reach the marketplace was IP switching, developed by Ipsilon. To compete with this offering, numerous other companies announced their own products, notably Cisco Systems (tag switching), IBM (aggregate route-based IP switching), and Cascade (IP navigator). The goal of all these products was to improve the throughput and delay performance of IP, and all took the same basic approach: Use a standard routing protocol such as OSPF to define paths between endpoints and assign packets to these paths as they enter the network.

In response to these proprietary initiatives, the IETF set up the MPLS working group in 1997 to develop a common, standardized approach. The working group issued its first set of Proposed Standards in 2001. The key specification is RFC 3031. MPLS reduces the amount of per-packet processing required at each router in an IP-based network, enhancing router performance even more. More significantly, MPLS provides significant new capabilities in four areas that have ensured its popularity: QoS support, traffic engineering, virtual private networks, and multiprotocol support. Before turning to the details of MPLS, we briefly examine each of these.

Connection–Oriented QoS Support

Network managers and users require increasingly sophisticated QoS support for a number of reasons. [SIKE00] lists the following key requirements:

- Guarantee a fixed amount of capacity for specific applications, such as audio/video conference.
- Control latency and jitter and ensure capacity for voice.
- Provide very specific, guaranteed, and quantifiable service level agreements, or traffic contracts.
- Configure varying degrees of QoS for multiple network customers.

A connectionless network, such as in IP-based internet, cannot provide truly firm QoS commitments. A differentiated service (DS) framework works in only a general way and upon aggregates of traffic from a number of sources. An integrated services (IS) framework, using RSVP, has some of the flavor of a connection-oriented approach but is nevertheless limited in terms of its flexibility and scalability. For services such as voice and video that require a network with high predictability, the DS and IS approaches, by themselves, may prove inadequate on a heavily loaded network. By contrast, a connection-oriented network, as we have seen with ATM, has powerful traffic management and QoS capabilities. MPLS imposes a connection-oriented framework on an IP-based internet and thus provides the foundation for sophisticated and reliable QoS traffic contracts.

Traffic Engineering

MPLS makes it easy to commit network resources in such a way as to balance the load in the face of a given demand and to commit to differential levels of support to meet various user traffic requirements. The ability to define routes dynamically, plan resource commitments on the basis of known demand, and optimize network utilization is referred to as **traffic engineering**. Prior to the advent of MPLS, the one networking technology that provided strong traffic engineering capabilities was ATM.

   With the basic IP mechanism, there is a primitive form of automated traffic engineering. Specifically, routing protocols such as OSPF enable routers to dynamically change the route to a given destination on a packet-by-packet basis to try to balance load. But such dynamic routing reacts in a very simple manner to congestion and does not provide a way to support QoS. All traffic between two endpoints follows the same route, which may be changed when congestion occurs. MPLS, on the other hand, is aware of not just individual packets but flows of packets in which each flow has certain QoS requirements and a predictable traffic demand. With MPLS, it is possible to set up routes on the basis of these individual flows, with two different flows between the same endpoints perhaps following different routers. Further, when congestion threatens, MPLS paths can be rerouted intelligently. That is, instead of simply changing the route on a packet-by-packet basis, with MPLS, the routes are changed on a flow-by-flow basis, taking advantage of the known traffic demands of each flow. Effective use of traffic engineering can substantially increase usable network capacity.

Virtual Private Network (VPN) Support

MPLS provides an efficient mechanism for supporting VPNs. With a VPN, the traffic of a given enterprise or group passes transparently through an internet in a way that effectively segregates that traffic from other packets on the internet, proving performance guarantees and security.

Multiprotocol Support

MPLS can be used on a number of networking technologies. Our focus in this chapter is on IP-based internets, and this is likely to be the principal area of use. MPLS is an enhancement to the way a connectionless IP-based internet is operated, requiring an upgrade to IP routers to support the MPLS features. MPLS-enabled routers can coexist with ordinary IP routers, facilitating the evolution to MPLS schemes. MPLS is also designed to work in ATM and frame relay networks. Again, MPLS-enabled ATM switches and MPLS-enabled frame relay switches can be configured to coexist with ordinary switches. Furthermore, MPLS can be used in a pure IP-based

Table 21.1   MPLS Terminology

Forwarding equivalence class (FEC) A group of IP packets that are forwarded in the same manner (e.g., over the same path, with the same forwarding treatment).	**Label stack** An ordered set of labels.
	Merge point A node at which label merging is done.
Frame merge Label merging, when it is applied to operation over frame based media, so that the potential problem of cell interleave is not an issue.	**MPLS domain** A contiguous set of nodes that operate MPLS routing and forwarding and that are also in one Routing or Administrative Domain.
Label merging The replacement of multiple incoming labels for a particular FEC with a single outgoing label.	**MPLS edge node** An MPLS node that connects an MPLS domain with a node that is outside of the domain, either because it does not run MPLS, and/or because it is in a different domain. Note that if an LSR has a neighboring host that is not running MPLS, then that LSR is an MPLS edge node.
Label swap The basic forwarding operation consisting of looking up an incoming label to determine the outgoing label, encapsulation, port, and other data handling information.	
	MPLS egress node An MPLS edge node in its role in handling traffic as it leaves an MPLS domain.
Label swapping A forwarding paradigm allowing streamlined forwarding of data by using labels to identify classes of data packets that are treated indistinguishably when forwarding.	**MPLS ingress node** An MPLS edge node in its role in handling traffic as it enters an MPLS domain.
	MPLS label A short, fixed-length physically contiguous identifier that is used to identify a FEC, usually of local significance. A label is carried in a packet header.
Label switched hop The hop between two MPLS nodes, on which forwarding is done using labels.	
Label switched path The path through one or more LSRs at one level of the hierarchy followed by a packets in a particular FEC.	**MPLS node** A node that is running MPLS. An MPLS node will be aware of MPLS control protocols, will operate one or more L3 routing protocols, and will be capable of forwarding packets based on labels. An MPLS node may optionally be also capable of forwarding native L3 packets.
Label switching router (LSR) An MPLS node that is capable of forwarding native L3 packets.	

internet, a pure ATM network, a pure frame relay network, or an internet that includes two or even all three technologies. This universal nature of MPLS should appeal to users who currently have mixed network technologies and seek ways to optimize resources and expand QoS support.

For the remainder of this discussion, we focus on the use of MPLS in IP-based internets, with brief comments about formatting issues for ATM and frame relay networks. Table 21.1 defines key MPLS terms used in our discussion.

21.3 MPLS OPERATION

An MPLS network or internet[1] consists of a set of nodes, called **label switching routers (LSRs)**, capable of switching and routing packets on the basis of a label appended to each packet. Labels define a flow of packets between two

---

[1]For simplicity, we will use the term *network* for the remainder of this section. In the case of an IP-based internet, we are referring to the Internet or a private internet, where the IP routers function as MPLS nodes.

endpoints or, in the case of multicast, between a source endpoint and a multicast group of destination endpoints. For each distinct flow, called a **forwarding equivalence class (FEC)**, a specific path through the network of LSRs is defined, called a **label switched path (LSP)**. In essence, an FEC represents a group of packets that share the same transport requirements. All packets in an FEC receive the same treatment en route to the destination. These packets follow the same path and receive the same QoS treatment at each hop. In contrast to forwarding in ordinary IP networks, the assignment of a particular packet to a particular FEC is done just once, when the packet enters the network of MPLS routers.

Thus, MPLS is a connection-oriented technology. Associated with each FEC is a traffic characterization that defines the QoS requirements for that flow. The LSRs need not examine or process the IP header but rather simply forward each packet based on its label value. Each LSR builds a table, called a **label information base (LIB)**, to specify how a packet must be treated and forwarded. Thus, the forwarding process is simpler than with an IP router.

Label assignment decisions (i.e., the assignment of a packet to a give FEC and hence a given LSP) may be based on the following criteria:

- **Destination unicast routing:** In the absence of other criteria, packets flowing from one source to one destination may be assigned to the same FEC.
- **Traffic engineering:** Packet flows may be split up or aggregated to accommodate traffic engineering requirements.
- **Multicast:** Multicast routes through the network may be defined.
- **Virtual private network (VPN):** Traffic among end systems for a particular customer may be segregated from other traffic on a public MPLS network by means of a dedicated set of LSPs.
- **QoS:** Traffic may be assigned different FECs for different QoS requirements.

Figure 21.1 depicts the operation of MPLS within a domain of MPLS-enabled routers. The following are key elements of the operation:

1. Prior to the routing and delivery of packets in a given FEC, a path through the network, known as a **label switched path (LSP)**, must be defined and the QoS parameters along that path must be established. The QoS parameters determine (1) how much resources to commit to the path, and (2) what queuing and discarding policy to establish at each LSR for packets in this FEC. To accomplish these tasks, two protocols are used to exchange the necessary information among routers:

   a. An interior routing protocol, such as OSPF, is used to exchange reachability and routing information.

   b. Labels must be assigned to the packets for a particular FEC. Because the use of globally unique labels would impose a management burden and limit the number of usable labels, labels have local significance only, as discussed subsequently. A network operator can specify explicit routes manually and assign the appropriate label values. Alternatively,

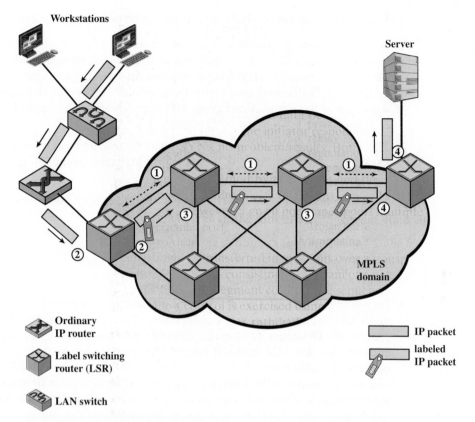

Figure 21.1 MPLS Operation

a protocol is used to determine the route and establish label values between adjacent LSRs. Either of two protocols can be used for this purpose: the Label Distribution Protocol (LDP) or an enhanced version of RSVP. LDP is now considered the standard technique.

2. A packet enters an MPLS domain through an ingress edge LSR, where it is processed to determine which network-layer services it requires, defining its QoS. The LSR assigns this packet to a particular FEC, and therefore a particular LSP; appends the appropriate label to the packet; and forwards the packet. If no LSP yet exists for this FEC, the edge LSR must cooperate with the other LSRs in defining a new LSP.

3. Within the MPLS domain, as each LSR receives a labeled packet, it

   a. removes the incoming label and attaches the appropriate outgoing label to the packet

   b. forwards the packet to the next LSR along the LSP

4. The egress edge LSR strips the label, reads the IP packet header, and forwards the packet to its final destination.

Several key features of MLSP operation can be noted at this point:

1. An MPLS domain consists of a contiguous, or connected, set of MPLS-enabled routers. Traffic can enter or exit the domain from an endpoint on a directly connected network, as shown in the upper-right corner of Figure 21.1. Traffic may also arrive from an ordinary router that connects to a portion of the internet not using MPLS, as shown in the upper-left corner of Figure 21.1.

2. The FEC for a packet can be determined by one or more of a number of parameters, as specified by the network manager. Some of the possible parameters are the following:

   - Source and/or destination IP addresses or IP network addresses
   - Source and/or destination port numbers
   - IP protocol ID
   - Differentiated services codepoint
   - IPv6 flow label

3. Forwarding is achieved by doing a simple lookup in a predefined table that maps label values to next hop addresses. There is no need to examine or process the IP header or to make a routing decision based on destination IP address. This not only makes it possible to separate types of traffic, such as best-effort traffic from mission-critical traffic, it also renders an MPLS solution highly scalable. MPLS decouples packet forwarding from IP header information because it uses different mechanisms to assign labels. Labels have local significance only; therefore, it is nearly impossible to run out of labels. This characteristic is essential to implementing advanced IP services such as QoS, VPNs, and traffic engineering.

4. A particular per-hop behavior (PHB) can be defined at an LSR for a given FEC. The PHB defines the queuing priority of the packets for this FEC and the discard policy.

5. Packets sent between the same endpoints may belong to different FECs. Thus, they will be labeled differently, will experience different PHB at each LSR, and may follow different paths through the network.

Figure 21.2 shows the label-handling and forwarding operation in more detail. Each LSR maintains a forwarding table for each LSP passing through the LSR. When a labeled packet arrives, the LSR indexes the forwarding table to determine the next hop. For scalability, as was mentioned, labels have local significance only. Thus, the LSR removes the incoming label from the packet and attaches the matching outgoing label before forwarding the packet. The ingress edge LSR determines the FEC for each incoming unlabeled packet and, on the basis of the FEC, assigns the packet to a particular LSP, attaches the corresponding label, and forwards the packet. In this example, the first packet arrives at the edge LSR, which reads the IP header for the destination address prefix, 128.89. The LSR then looks up the destination address in the switching table, inserts a label with a 20-bit label

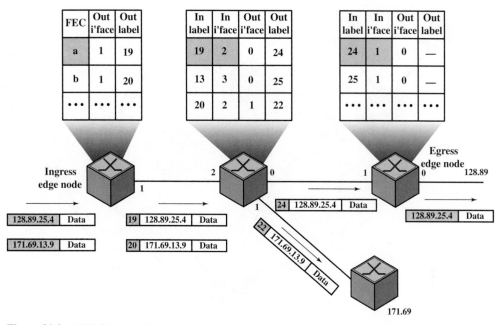

FEC	Out i'face	Out label
a	1	19
b	1	20
...	...	...

In label	In i'face	Out i'face	Out label
19	2	0	24
13	3	0	25
20	2	1	22

In label	In i'face	Out i'face	Out label
24	1	0	—
25	1	0	—
...	...	...	...

Figure 21.2 MPLS Packet Forwarding

value of 19, and forwards the labeled packet out interface 1. This interface is attached via a link to a core LSR, which receives the packet on its interface 2. The LSR in the core reads the label and looks up its match in its switching table, replaces label 19 with label 24, and forwards it out interface 0. The egress LSR reads and looks up label 4 in its table, which says to strip the label and forward the packet out interface 0.

Let us now look at an example that illustrates the various stages of operation of MPLS, using Figure 21.3. We examine the path of a packet as it travels from a source workstation to a destination server. Across the MPLS network, the packet enters at egress node LSR 1. Assume that this is the first occurrence of a packet on a new flow of packets, so that LSR 1 does not have a label for the packet. LSR 1 consults the IP header to find the destination address and then determine the next hop. Assume in this case that the next hop is LSR 3. Then, LSR 1 initiates a label request toward LSR 3. This request propagates through the network as indicated by the dashed green line.

Each intermediate router receives a label from its downstream router starting from LSR 7 and going upstream until LSR 1, setting up an LSP. The LSP setup is indicated by the dashed gray line. The setup can be performed using LDP and may or may not involve traffic engineering considerations.

LSR 1 is now able to insert the appropriate label and forward the packet to LSR 3. Each subsequent LSR (LSR 5, LSR 6, LSR 7) examines the label in the received packet, replaces it with the outgoing label, and forwards it. When the packet reaches LSR 7, the LSR removes the label because the packet is departing the MPLS domain and delivers the packet to the destination.

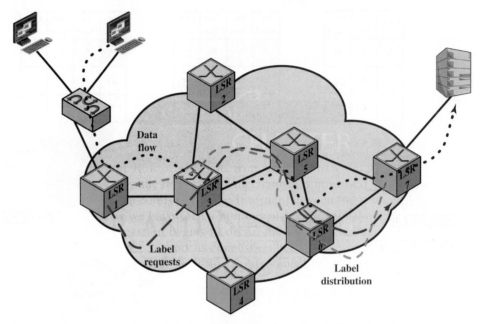

Figure 21.3 LSP Creation and Packet Forwarding through an MPLS Domain

21.4 LABELS

Label Stacking

One of the most powerful features of MPLS is label stacking. A labeled packet may carry a number of labels, organized as a last-in-first-out stack. Processing is always based on the top label. At any LSR, a label may be added to the stack (push operation) or removed from the stack (pop operation). Label stacking allows the aggregation of LSPs into a single LSP for a portion of the route through a network, creating a tunnel. The term *tunnel* refers to the fact that traffic routing is determined by labels, and is exercised below normal IP routing and filtering mechanisms. At the beginning of the tunnel, an LSR assigns the same label to packets from a number of LSPs by pushing the label onto each packet's stack. At the end of the tunnel, another LSR pops the top element from the label stack, revealing the inner label. This is similar to ATM, which has one level of stacking (virtual channels inside virtual paths) but MPLS supports unlimited stacking.

Label stacking provides considerable flexibility. An enterprise could establish MPLS-enabled networks at various sites and a number of LSPs at each site. The enterprise could then use label stacking to aggregate multiple flows of its own traffic before handing it to an access provider. The access provider could aggregate traffic from multiple enterprises before handing it to a larger service provider. Service providers could aggregate many LSPs into a relatively small number of tunnels between points of presence. Fewer tunnels mean smaller tables, making it easier for a provider to scale the network core.

Label Format

An MPLS label is a 32-bit field consisting of the following elements (Figure 21.4), defined in RFC 3032:

- **Label value:** Locally significant 20-bit label. Values 0 through 15 are reserved.
- **Traffic class (TC):** 3 bits used to carry traffic class information.
- **S:** Set to one for the oldest entry in the stack, and zero for all other entries. Thus, this bit marks the bottom of the stack.
- **Time to live (TTL):** 8 bits used to encode a hop count, or time to live, value.

TRAFFIC CLASS RFCs 3270 and 5129 discuss the use of the TC field to convey information to support differentiated services and explicit congestion notification (ECN), respectively. With respect to DS, one approach is to assign a unique label value to each DS per-hop-behavior scheduling class, in which case, the TC field is not necessarily needed. The other approach is to map the drop precedence or some other DS information into the TC field. With respect to ECN, the three possible ECN values (not ECN capable, ECN capable, congestion marked) are mapped into the TC field. RFC 5129 discusses strategies in which both DS and ECN might be supported in the TC field. At present, no unique definition of the TC bits has been standardized.

TIME TO LIVE PROCESSING A key field in the IP packet header is the TTL field (IPv4, Figure 2.7a), or hop limit (IPv6, Figure 2.7b). In an ordinary IP-based internet, this field is decremented at each router and the packet is dropped if the count falls to zero. This is done to avoid looping or having the packet remain too long in the Internet due to faulty routing. Because an LSR does not examine the IP header, the TTL field is included in the label so that the TTL function is still supported. The rules for processing the TTL field in the label are as follows:

1. When an IP packet arrives at an ingress edge LSR of an MPLS domain, a single label stack entry is added to the packet. The TTL value of this label stack entry is set to the value of the IP TTL value. If the IP TTL field needs to be decremented, as part of the IP processing, it is assumed that this has already been done.

2. When an MPLS packet arrives at an internal LSR of an MPLS domain, the TTL value in the top label stack entry is decremented. Then

   a. If this value is zero, the MPLS packet is not forwarded. Depending on the label value in the label stack entry, the packet may be simply discarded, or it may be passed to the appropriate "ordinary" network layer for error processing (e.g., for the generation of an ICMP error message).

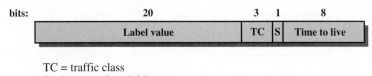

bits:	20	3	1	8
	Label value	TC	S	Time to live

TC = traffic class
S = bottom of stack bit

Figure 21.4 MPLS Label Format

  b. If this value is positive, it is placed in the TTL field of the top label stack entry for the outgoing MPLS packet, and the packet is forwarded. The outgoing TTL value is a function solely of the incoming TTL value and is independent of whether any labels are pushed or popped before forwarding. There is no significance to the value of the TTL field in any label stack entry that is not at the top of the stack.

 3. When an MPLS packet arrives at an egress edge LSR of an MPLS domain, the TTL value in the single label stack entry is decremented and the label is popped, resulting in an empty label stack. Then

  a. If this value is zero, the IP packet is not forwarded. Depending on the label value in the label stack entry, the packet may be simply discarded, or it may be passed to the appropriate "ordinary" network layer for error processing.

  b. If this value is positive, it is placed in the TTL field of the IP header, and the IP packet is forwarded using ordinary IP routing. Note that the IP header checksum must be modified prior to forwarding

Label Placement

The label stack entries appear after the data link layer headers, but before any network layer headers. The top of the label stack appears earliest in the packet (closest to the data link header), and the bottom appears latest (closest to the network layer header), as shown in Figure 21.5. The network layer packet immediately follows the label stack entry that has the S bit set. In data link frame, such as for PPP (point-to-point protocol), the label stack appears between the IP header and the data link header (Figure 21.6a). For an IEEE 802 frame, the label stack appears between the IP header and the LLC (logical link control) header (Figure 21.6b).

  If MPLS is used over a connection-oriented network service, a slightly different approach may be taken, as shown in Figures 21.6c and d. For ATM cells, the label value in the topmost label is placed in the VPI/VCI field in the ATM cell header. The entire top label remains at the top of the label stack, which is inserted between the cell header and the IP header. Placing the label value in the ATM cell

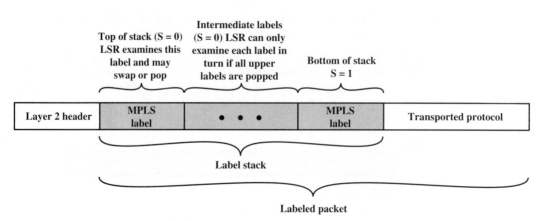

Figure 21.5 Encapsulation for Labeled Packet

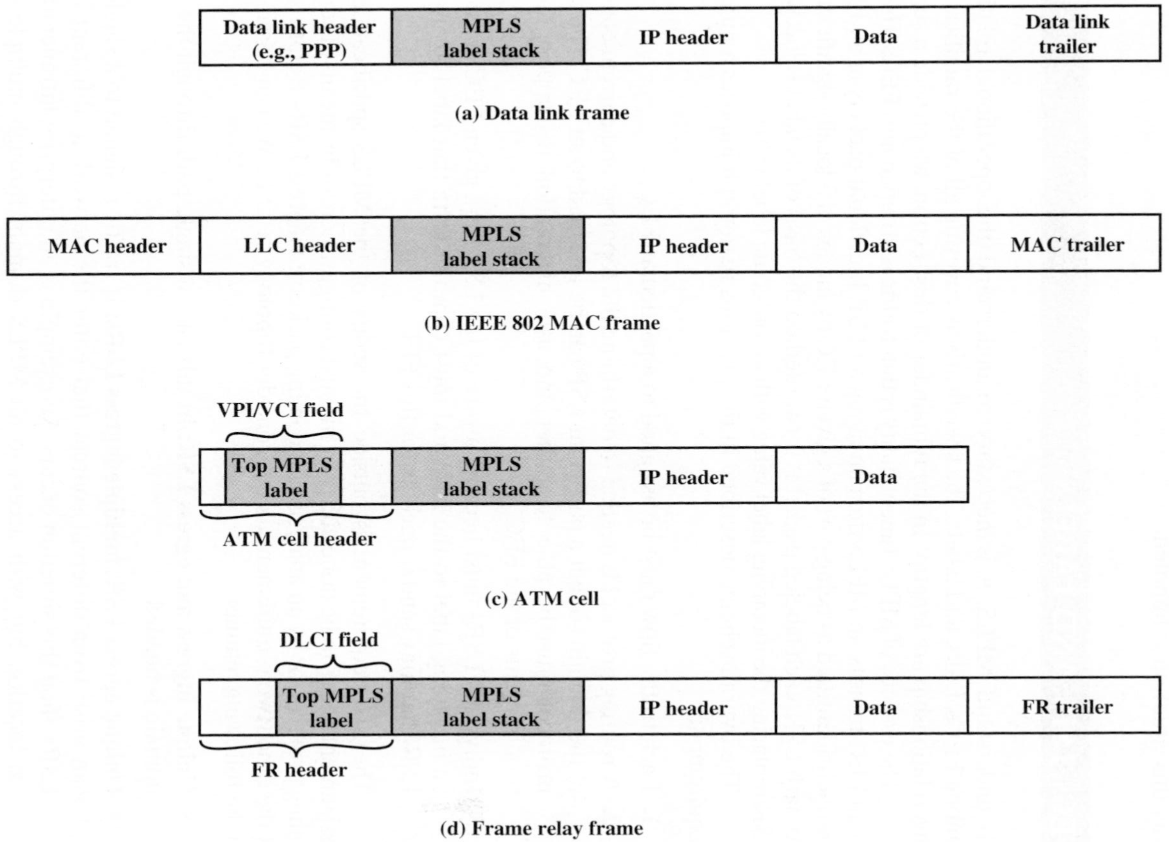

Figure 21.6 Position of MPLS Label Stack

(a) Data link frame

(b) IEEE 802 MAC frame

(c) ATM cell

(d) Frame relay frame

| Data link header (e.g., PPP) | MPLS label stack | IP header | Data | Data link trailer |

| MAC header | LLC header | MPLS label stack | IP header | Data | MAC trailer |

VPI/VCI field — Top MPLS label
ATM cell header

| Top MPLS label | MPLS label stack | IP header | Data |

DLCI field — Top MPLS label
FR header

| Top MPLS label | MPLS label stack | IP header | Data | FR trailer |

header facilitates switching by an ATM switch, which would, as usual, only need to look at the cell header. Similarly, the topmost label value can be placed in the DLCI (data link connection identifier) field of a frame relay header. Note that in both these cases, the time to live field is not visible to the switch and so is not decremented. The reader should consult the MPLS specifications for the details of the way this situation is handled.

21.5 FECs, LSPs, AND LABELS

To understand MPLS, it is necessary to understand the operational relationship among FECs, LSPs, and labels. The specifications covering all of the ramifications of this relationship are lengthy. In the remainder of this section, we provide a summary.

The essence of MPLS functionality is that traffic is grouped into FECs. The traffic in an FEC transits an MPLS domain along an LSP. Individual packets in an FEC are uniquely identified as being part of a given FEC by means of a locally significant label. At each LSR, each labeled packet is forwarded on the basis of its label value, with the LSR replacing the incoming label value with an outgoing label value.

The overall scheme described in the previous paragraph imposes a number of requirements:

1. Each traffic flow must be assigned to a particular FEC.
2. A routing protocol is needed to determine the topology and current conditions in the domain so that a particular LSP can be assigned to an FEC. The routing protocol must be able to gather and use information to support the QoS requirements of the FEC.
3. Individual LSRs must become aware of the LSP for a given FEC, must assign an incoming label to the LSP, and must communicate that label to any other LSR that may send it packets for this FEC.

The first requirement is outside the scope of the MPLS specifications. The assignment needs to be done either by manual configuration, or by means of some signaling protocol, or by an analysis of incoming packets at ingress LSRs. Before looking at the other two requirements, let us consider topology of LSPs. We can classify these in the following manner:

- **Unique ingress and egress LSR:** In this case a single path through the MPLS domain is needed.
- **Unique egress LSR, multiple ingress LSRs:** If traffic assigned to a single FEC can arise from different sources that enter the network at different ingress LSRs, then this situation occurs. An example is an enterprise intranet at a single location but with access to an MPLS domain through multiple MPLS ingress LSRs. This situation would call for multiple paths through the MPLS domain, probably sharing a final few hops.
- **Multiple egress LSRs for unicast traffic:** RFC 3031 states that, most commonly, a packet is assigned to an FEC based (completely or partially) on its network layer destination address. If not, then it is possible that the FEC would require

paths to multiple distinct egress LSRs. However, more likely, there would be a cluster of destination networks all of which are reached via the same MPLS egress LSR.

- **Multicast:** RFC 5332 defines techniques for handling multicast packets.

Route Selection

Route selection refers to the selection of an LSP for a particular FEC. The MPLS architecture supports two options: hop-by-hop routing and explicit routing.

With **hop-by-hop routing**, each LSR independently chooses the next hop for each FEC. RFC 3031 implies that this option makes use of an ordinary routing protocol, such as OSPF. This option provides some of the advantages of MPLS, including rapid switching by labels, the ability to use label stacking, and differential treatment of packets from different FECs following the same route. However, because of the limited use of performance metrics in typical routing protocols, hop-by-hop routing does not readily support traffic engineering or policy routing (defining routes based on some policy related to QoS, security, or some other consideration).

With **explicit routing**, a single LSR, usually the ingress or egress LSR, specifies some or all of the LSRs in the LSP for a given FEC. For strict explicit routing, an LSR specifies all of the LSRs on an LSP. For loose explicit routing, only some of the LSRs are specified. Explicit routing provides all of the benefits of MPLS, including the ability to do traffic engineering and policy routing.

Explicit routes can be selected by configuration, that is, set up ahead of time, or dynamically. Dynamic explicit routing would provide the best scope for traffic engineering. For dynamic explicit routing, the LSR setting up the LSP would need information about the topology of the MPLS domain as well as QoS-related information about that domain. An MPLS traffic engineering specification (RFC 2702) suggests that the QoS-related information falls into two categories:

- A set of attributes associated with an FEC or a collection of similar FECs that collectively specify their behavioral characteristics
- A set of attributes associated with resources (nodes, links) that constrain the placement of LSPs through them

A routing algorithm that takes into account the traffic requirements of various flows and that takes into account the resources available along various hops and through various nodes is referred to as a **constraint-based routing algorithm**. In essence, a network that uses a constraint-based routing algorithm is aware of current utilization, existing capacity, and committed services at all times. Traditional routing algorithms, such as OSPF and BGP, do not employ a sufficient array of cost metrics in their algorithms to qualify as constraint based. Furthermore, for any given route calculation, only a single-cost metric (e.g., number of hops, delay) can be used. For MPLS, it is necessary either to augment an existing routing protocol or to deploy a new one. For example, an enhanced version of OSPF has been defined (RFC 2676) that provides at least some of the support required for MPLS. Examples of metrics that would be useful to constraint-based routing are as follows:

- Maximum link data rate
- Current capacity reservation
- Packet loss ratio
- Link propagation delay

21.6 LABEL DISTRIBUTION

Requirements for Label Distribution

Route selection consists of defining an LSP for an FEC. A separate function is the actual setting up of the LSP. For this purpose, each LSR on the LSP must do the following:

1. Assign a label to the LSP to be used to recognize incoming packets that belong to the corresponding FEC.
2. Inform all potential upstream nodes (nodes that will send packets for this FEC to this LSR) of the label assigned by this LSR to this FEC, so that these nodes can properly label packets to be sent to this LSR.
3. Learn the next hop for this LSP and learn the label that the downstream node (LSR that is the next hop) has assigned to this FEC. This will enable this LSR to map an incoming label to an outgoing label.

The first item in the preceding list is a local function. Items 2 and 3 must either be done by manual configuration or require the use of some sort of label distribution protocol. Thus, the essence of a label distribution protocol is that it enables one LSR to inform others of the label/FEC bindings it has made. In addition, a label distribution protocol enables two LSRs to learn each other's MPLS capabilities. The MPLS architecture does not assume a single label distribution protocol but allows for multiple such protocols. Specifically, RFC 3031 refers to a new label distribution protocol and to enhancements to existing protocols, such as RSVP and BGP, to serve the purpose.

The relationship between label distribution and route selection is complex. It is best to look at in the context of the two types of route selection.

With hop-by-hop route selection, no specific attention is paid to traffic engineering or policy routing concerns, as we have seen. In such a case, an ordinary routing protocol such as OSPF is used to determine the next hop by each LSR. A relatively straightforward label distribution protocol can operate using the routing protocol to design routes.

With explicit route selection, a more sophisticated routing algorithm must be implemented, one that does not employ a single metric to design a route. In this case, a label distribution protocol could make use of a separate route selection protocol, such as an enhanced OSPF, or incorporate a routing algorithm into a more complex label distribution protocol.

Label Distribution Protocol

Protocols that communicate which label goes with which FEC are called label distribution protocols. A number of label distribution protocols exist, most commonly Label Distribution Protocol (LDP; RFC 5036), Resource Reservation Protocol-Traffic Engineering (RSVP-TE; RFC 3209), and multiprotocol BGP as extended for Layer 3 VPNs (L3VPNs; RFC 4364). LDP has emerged as the preferred solution and we provide a brief introduction here.

LDP has a simple objective: It is a protocol defined for distributing labels. It is the set of procedures and messages by which label switching routers (LSRs) establish label switched paths (LSPs) through a network by mapping network-layer routing information directly to data-link layer switched paths. These LSPs may have an endpoint at a directly attached neighbor (comparable to IP hop-by-hop forwarding), or may have an endpoint at a network egress node, enabling switching via all intermediary nodes. LDP associates a forwarding equivalence class (FEC) with each LSP it creates. The FEC associated with an LSP specifies which packets are mapped to that LSP. LSPs are extended through a network as each LSR splices incoming labels for a FEC to the outgoing label assigned to the next hop for the given FEC.

Two LSRs that use LDP to exchange FEC label binding information are known as LDP peers. In order to exchange information, two LDP peers first establish a session over a TCP connection. LDP includes a mechanism by which an LSR can discover potential LDP peers. The discovery mechanism makes it unnecessary for operators to explicitly configure each LSR with its LDP peers. When an LSR discovers another LSR it follows the LDP session setup procedure to establish an LDP session. By means of this procedure the LSRs establish a session TCP connection and use it to negotiate parameters for the session, such as the label distribution method to be used. After the LSRs agree on the parameters, the session is operational and the LSRs use the TCP connection for label distribution.

LDP supports two different methods for label distribution. An LSR using Downstream Unsolicited distribution advertises FEC-label bindings to its peers when it is ready to forward packets in the FEC by means of MPLS. An LSR using Downstream on Demand distribution provides FEC-label bindings to a peer in response to specific requests from the peer for a label for the FEC.

LDP depends on a routing protocol, such as OSPF, to initially establish reachability between two LSRs. The routing protocol can also be used to define the route for the LSP. Alternatively, traffic engineering considerations can determine the exact route of the LSP, as discussed in Section 21.7. Once a route is established for an LSP, LDP is used to establish the LSP and assign labels. Figure 21.7 suggests the operation of LDP. Each LSP is unidirectional, and label assignment propagate back from the end point of the LSP to the originating point.

LDP Messages

LDP operates by the exchange of messages over a TCP connection between LDP peers. There are four categories of messages, reflecting the four major functions of LDP:

- **Discovery:** Each LSR announces and maintains its presence in a network. LSRs indicate their presence in a network by sending Hello messages periodically.

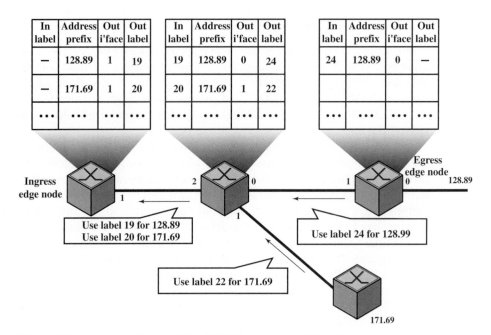

Figure 21.7 Assigning Labels Using LDP Downstream Allocation

Hello messages are transmitted as UDP packets to the LDP port at the group multicast address for all routers on the subnet.

- **Session establishment and maintenance:** If two LSRs have discovered each other by means of the LDP Hellos, they can then establish, maintain, and terminate sessions as LDP peers. When a router establishes a session with another router learned through the Hello message, it uses the LDP initialization procedure over TCP transport. When the initialization procedure is completed successfully, the two routers are LDP peers and can exchange advertisement messages.

- **Advertisement:** Advertising label mappings or label bindings is the main purpose of LDP. Advertisement messages are used to create, change, and delete label mappings for FECs. Requesting a label or advertising a label mapping to a peer is a decision made by the local router. In general, the router requests a label mapping from a neighboring router when it needs one and advertises a label mapping to a neighboring router when it wants the neighbor to use a label.

- **Notification messages:** Used to provide advisory information and to signal error information. LDP sends notification messages to report errors and other events of interest. There are two kinds of LDP notification messages:

    Error notifications, which signal fatal errors. If a router receives an error notification from a peer for an LDP session, it terminates the LDP session by closing the TCP transport connection for the session and discarding all label mappings learned through the session.

    Advisory notifications, which pass information to a router about the LDP session or the status of some previous message received from the peer.

LDP Message Format

Figure 21.8 illustrates the format of LDP messages. Each LDP protocol data unit (PDU) consists of an LDP header followed by one or more LDP messages. The header contains three fields:

- **Version:** Version number for this protocol. The current version is 1.
- **PDU length:** Length of this PDU in octets.
- **LDP identifier:** Identifies the LSR uniquely.

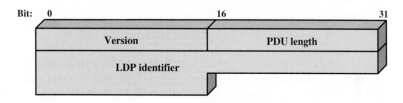

(a) Header format

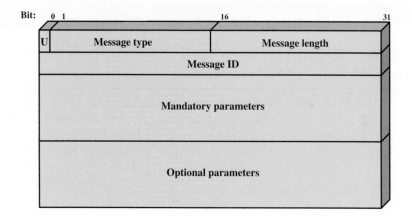

(b) Message format

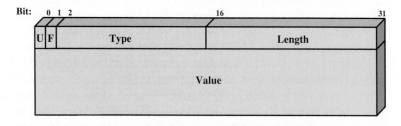

(c) Type-length-value (TLV) parameter encoding

Figure 21.8 LDP PDU Formats

Each message consists of the following fields:

- **U bit:** Indicates how to handle a message of an unknown type (forward or discard). This facilitates backward compatibility.
- **Message type:** Identifies the specific type of message (e.g., Hello).
- **Message length:** Length of this message in octets.
- **Message ID:** Identifies this specific message with a sequence number. This is used to facilitate identifying subsequent notification messages that may apply to this message.
- **Mandatory parameters:** Variable length set of required message parameters. Some messages have no required parameters.
- **Optional parameters:** Variable length set of optional message parameters. Many messages have no optional parameters.

Each parameter has a type-length-value (TLV) format. An LDP TLV is encoded as a 2-octet field that uses 14 bits to specify a Type and 2 bits to specify behavior when an LSR doesn't recognize the Type, followed by a 2-octet Length field, followed by a variable length Value field.

21.7 TRAFFIC ENGINEERING

RFC 2702 (Requirements for Traffic Engineering Over MPLS) describes traffic engineering as follows:

> **TRAFFIC ENGINEERING.** Traffic Engineering (TE) is concerned with performance optimization of operational networks. In general, it encompasses the application of technology and scientific principles to the measurement, modeling, characterization, and control of Internet traffic, and the application of such knowledge and techniques to achieve specific performance objectives. The aspects of traffic engineering that are of interest concerning MPLS are measurement and control.

The goal of MPLS traffic engineering is twofold. First, traffic engineering seeks to allocate traffic to the network to maximize utilization of the network capacity. And second, traffic engineering seeks to ensure the most desirable route through the network for packet traffic, taking into account the QoS requirements of the various packet flows. In performing traffic engineering, MPLS may override the shortest path or least-cost route selected by the interior routing protocol for a given source-destination flow.

Figure 21.9 provides a simple example of traffic engineering. Both R1 and R8 have a flow of packets to send to R5. Using OSPF or some other routing protocol, the shortest path is calculated as R2-R3-R4. However, if we assume that R8 has a steady-state traffic flow of 20 Mbps and R1 has a flow of 40 Mbps, then the aggregate flow over this route will be 60 Mbps, which will exceed the capacity of the R3-R4 link. As an alternative, a traffic engineering approach is to determine a route from source to destination ahead of time and reserve the required resources along the way by setting up an LSP and associating resource requirements with that LSP. In this case, the traffic

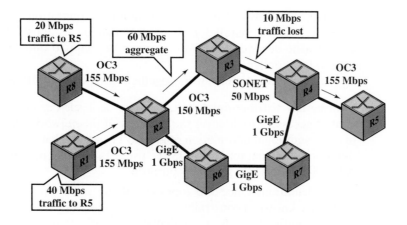

(a) A shortest-path solution

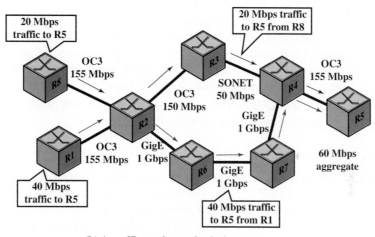

(b) A traffic-engineered solution

Figure 21.9   Traffic Engineering Example

from R8 to R5 follows the shortest route, but the traffic from R1 to R5 follows a longer route that avoids overloading the network.

Elements of MPLS Traffic Engineering

MPLS TE works by learning about the topology and resources available in a network. It then maps the traffic flows to a particular path based on the resources that the traffic flow requires and the available resources. MPLS TE builds unidirectional LSPs from a source to the destination, which are then used for forwarding traffic. The point where the LSP begins is called LSP headend or LSP source, and the node where the LSP ends is called LSP tailend or LSP tunnel destination.

LSP tunnels allow the implementation of a variety of policies related to network performance optimization. For example, LSP tunnels can be automatically or manually routed away from network failures, congestion, and bottlenecks. Furthermore, multiple parallel LSP tunnels can be established between two nodes, and traffic between the two nodes can be mapped onto the LSP tunnels according to local policy.

The following components work together to implement MPLS TE:

- **Information distribution:** A link state protocol, such as Open Shortest-Path First, is necessary to discover the topology of the network. OSPF is enhanced to carry additional information related to TE, such as bandwidth available and other related parameters. OSPF uses Type 10 (opaque) Link State Advertisements (LSAs) for this purpose.

- **Path calculation:** Once the topology of the network and the alternative routes are known, a constraint-based routing scheme is used for finding the shortest path through a particular network that meets the resource requirements of the traffic flow. The constrained shortest-path first algorithm (discussed subsequently), which operates on the LSP headend is used for this functionality.

- **Path setup:** A signaling protocol to reserve the resources for a traffic flow and to establish the LSP for a traffic flow. IETF has defined two alternative protocols for this purpose. RSVP has been enhanced with TE extensions for carrying labels and building the LSP. The other approach is an enhancement to LDP known as Constraint-based Routing Label Distribution Protocol (CR-LDP).

- **Traffic forwarding:** This is accomplished with MPLS, using the LSP set up by the traffic engineering components just described.

Constrained Shortest-Path First Algorithm

The CSPF algorithm is an enhanced version of the shortest-path first (SPF) algorithm used in OSPF. CSPF computes paths taking into account multiple constraints. When computing paths for LSPs, CSPF considers the topology of the network, the attributes of the individual links between LSRs, and the attributes of existing LSPs. CSPF attempts to satisfy the requirements for a new LSP while minimizing congestion by balancing the network load.

Figure 21.10 suggests the context in which CSPF is used. In setting up a new LSP, CSPF operates on the basis of three inputs:

- **Unicast link attributes:** These include the capacity of the link and the administrative groups that are allowed to use this link. For example, some links may be reserved for the exclusive use of one or several groups or, alternatively, some groups may be specifically excluded from using this link. The term *color* is used to refer to a unique administrative group.

- **User-specified LSP constraints:** When an application requests an LSP to a given unicast destination, the application specifies the required attributes of the path, including data rate, hop limitations, link color requirements, priority, and explicit route requirements.

- **Traffic engineering database:** The TE database maintains current topology information, current reservable capacity of links, and link colors.

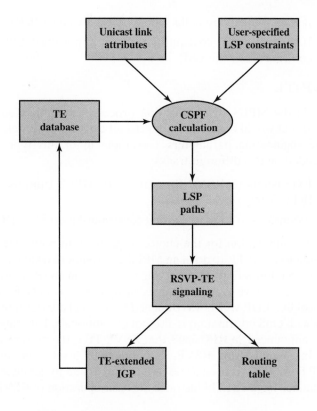

RSVP-TE = Resource Reservation Protocol - Traffic Engineering
CSPF = constrained shortest-path first
IGP = interior gateway protocol (interior routing protocol; e.g., OSPF)
LSP = label switching path
TE = traffic engineering

Figure 21.10   CSPF Flowchart

Based on these three inputs, the CSPF algorithm selects a route for the requested LSP. This information is used by RSVP-TE to set up the path and to provide information to the routing algorithm, which in turn updates the TE database. In general terms, the CSPF path selection procedure involves the following steps:

1. If multiple LSPs are to be determined, calculate LSPs one at a time, beginning with the highest priority LSP. Among LSPs of equal priority, CSPF starts with those that have the highest capacity requirement.

2. Prune the TE database of all the links that do not have sufficient reservable capacity. If the LSP configuration includes the include statement, prune all links that do not share any included colors. If the LSP configuration includes the exclude statement, prune all links that contain excluded colors and do not contain a color.

3. Find the shortest path toward the LSP's egress router, taking into account explicit-path constraints. For example, if the path must pass through Router A, two separate SPFs are computed, one from the ingress router to Router A, the other from Router A to the egress router.

4. If several equal-cost paths remain, select the one with the fewest number of hops.

5. If several equal-cost paths remain, apply the CSPF load-balancing rule configured on the LSP.

RSVP-TE

Early in the MPLS standardization process, it became clear that a protocol was needed that would enable providers to set up LSPs that took into account QoS and traffic engineering parameters. Development of this type of signaling protocol proceeded on two different tracks:

- Extensions to RSVP for setting up MPLS tunnels, known as RSVP-TE [RFC 3209]
- Extensions to LDP for setting constraint-based LSPs [RFC 3212]

The motivation for the choice of protocol in both cases was straightforward. Extending RSVP-TE to do in an MPLS environment what it already was doing (handling QoS information and reserving resources) in an IP environment is comprehensible; you only have to add the label distribution capability. Extending a native MPLS protocol like LDP, which was designed to do label distribution, to handle some extra TLVs with QoS information is also not revolutionary. Ultimately, the MPLS working group announced, in RFC 3468, that RSVP-TE is the preferred solution.

In general terms, RSVP-TE operates by associating an MPLS label with an RSVP flow. RSVP is used to reserve resources and to define an explicit router for an LSP tunnel. Figure 21.11 illustrates the basic operation of RSVP-TE. An ingress node

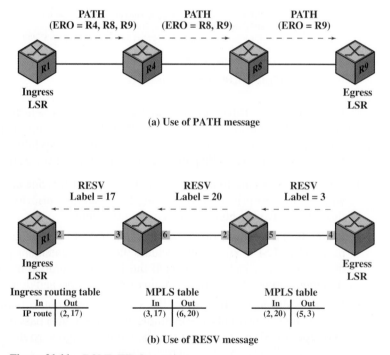

(b) Use of RESV message

Figure 21.11 RSVP-TE Operation

uses the RSVP PATH message to request an LSP to be defined along an explicit route. The PATH message includes a label request object and an explicit route object (ERO). The ERO defines the explicit route to be followed by the LSP.

The destination node of a label switched path responds to a LABEL_ REQUEST by including a LABEL object in its response RSVP Resv message. The LABEL object is inserted in the filter spec list immediately following the filter spec to which it pertains. The Resv message is sent back upstream toward the sender, following the path state created by the Path message, in reverse order.

21.8 VIRTUAL PRIVATE NETWORKS

A virtual private network is a private network that is configured within a public network (a carrier's network or the Internet) in order to take advantage of the economies of scale and management facilities of large networks. VPNs are widely used by enterprises to create wide area networks that span large geographic areas, to provide site-to-site connections to branch offices, and to allow mobile users to dial up their company LANs. From the point of view of the provider, the pubic network facility is shared by many customers, with the traffic of each customer segregated from other traffic. Traffic designated as VPN traffic can only go from a VPN source to a destination in the same VPN. It is often the case that encryption and authentication facilities are provided for the VPN.

The subject of VPNs, even when limited to MPLS-enabled VPNs, is extraordinarily complex. In this section, we provide a brief overview of two of the most common approaches to VPN implementation using MPLS: the layer 2 VPNs (L2VPN) and the layer 3 VPN (L3VPN).

Table 21.2, based on RFC 4026 (*Provider Provisioned Virtual Private Network Terminology*), defines key VPN terms used in our discussion.

Layer 2 Virtual Private Network

With a layer 2 VPN, there is mutual transparency between the customer network and the provider network. In effect, the customer requests a mesh of unicast LSPs among customer switches that attach to the provider network. Each LSP is viewed as a layer 2 circuit by the customer. In an L2VPN, the provider's equipment forwards customer data based on information in the Layer 2 headers, such as an Ethernet MAC address, an ATM virtual channel identifier, or a frame relay data link connection identifier.

Figure 21.12 depicts key elements in an L2VPN. Customers connect to the provider by means of a layer 2 device, such as an Ethernet switch, or a frame relay or ATM node; the customer device that connects to the MPLS network is generally referred to as a customer edge (CE) device. The MPLS edge router is referred to as a provider edge (PE) device. The link between the CE and the PE operates at the link layer (e.g., Ethernet), and is referred to as an attachment circuit. The MPLS network then sets up an LSP that acts as a tunnel between two edge routers (i.e., two PEs) that attach to two networks of the same enterprise. This tunnel can carry multiple virtual channels (VCs) using label stacking.

Table 21.2 VPN Terminology

Attachment circuit (AC) In a Layer 2 VPN the CE is attached to PE via an AC. The AC may be a physical or logical link.	packets from one PE to another. Separation of one customer's traffic from another customer's traffic is done based on tunnel multiplexers.
Customer edge (CE) A device or set of devices on the customer premises that attaches to a provider provisioned VPN.	**Tunnel multiplexer** An entity that is sent with the packets traversing the tunnel to make it possible to decide which instance of a service a packet belongs to and from which sender it was received. In an MPLS network, the tunnel multiplexor is formatted as an MPLS label.
Layer 2 VPN (L2VPN) An L2VPN interconnects sets of hosts and routers based on Layer 2 addresses.	
Layer 3 VPN (L3VPN) An L3VPN interconnects sets of hosts and routers based on Layer 3 addresses.	**Virtual channel (VC)** A VC is transported within a tunnel and identified by its tunnel multiplexer. In an MPLS-enabled IP network, a VC label is an MPLS label used to identify traffic within a tunnel that belongs to a particular VPN; i.e., the VC label is the tunnel multiplexer in networks that use MPLS labels.
Packet switched network (PSN) A network through which the tunnels supporting the VPN services are set up.	
Provider edge (PE) A device or set of devices at the edge of the provider network with the functionality that is needed to interface with the customer.	**Virtual private network (VPN)** A generic term that covers the use of public or private networks to create groups of users that are separated from other network users and that may communicate among them as if they were on a private network.
Tunnel Connectivity through a PSN that is used to send traffic across the network from one PE to another. The tunnel provides a means to transport	

When a link-layer frame arrives at the PE from the CE, the PE creates an MPLS packet. The PE pushes a label that corresponds to the VC assigned to this frame. Then the PE pushes a second label onto the label stack for this packet that corresponds to the tunnel between the source and destination PE for this VC. The packet is then routed across the LSP associated with this tunnel, using the top label for label switched routing. At the destination edge, the destination PE pops the tunnel label and examines the VC label. This tells the PE how to construct a link layer frame to deliver the payload across to the destination CE.

If the payload of the MPLS packet is, for example, an ATM AAL5 PDU, the VC label will generally correspond to a particular ATM VC at PE2. That is, PE2 needs to be able to infer from the VC label the outgoing interface and the VPI/VCI (virtual path identifier/virtual circuit identifier) value for the AAL5 PDU. If the payload is a frame relay PDU, then PE2 needs to be able to infer from the VC label the outgoing interface and the DLCI (data link connection identifier) value. If the payload is an Ethernet frame, then PE2 needs to be able to infer from the VC label the outgoing interface, and perhaps the VLAN identifier. This process is unidirectional, and will be repeated independently for bidirectional operation.

The virtual circuits in the tunnel can all belong to a single enterprise, or it is possible for a single tunnel to manage virtual circuits from multiple enterprises. In any case, from the point of view of the customer, a virtual circuit is a dedicated link-layer point-to-point channel. If multiple VCs connect a PE to a CE this is logically the multiplexing of multiple link-layer channels between the customer and the provider.

Layer 3 Virtual Private Network

Whereas L2VPNs are constructed based on link level addresses (e.g., MAC addresses), L3VPNs are based on VPN routes between CEs based on IP addresses. As

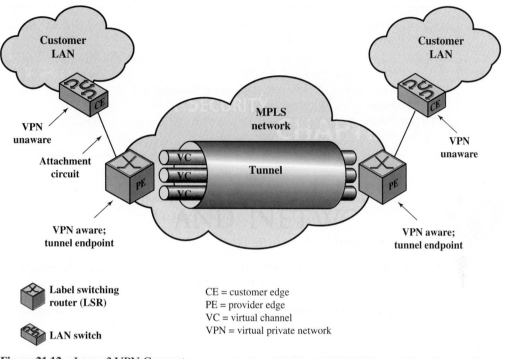

Figure 21.12 Layer 2 VPN Concepts

with an L2VPN, an MPLS-based L3VPN typically uses a stack of two labels. The inner label identifies a specific VPN instance; the outer label identifies a tunnel or route through the MPLS provider network. The tunnel label is associated with an LSP and is used for label swapping and forwarding. At the egress PE, the tunnel label is stripped off and the VPN label is used to direct the packet to the proper CE and to the proper logical flow at that CE.

For an L3VPN, the CE implements IP and is thus a router, such as is illustrated in Figure 21.1. The CE routers advertise their networks to the provider. The provider network can then use an enhanced version of BGP to establish VPNs between CEs. Inside the provider network, MPLS tools, such as CR-LDP, are used to establish routes between edge PEs supporting a VPN. Thus, the provider's routers participate in the customer's L3 routing function.

21.9 RECOMMENDED READING AND WEB SITES

[HARN02] provides a thorough treatment of MPLS. [WANG01] covers not only MPLS but IS and DS; it also has an excellent chapter on MPLS traffic engineering. [VISW98] includes a concise overview of the MPLS architecture and describes the various proprietary efforts that preceded MPLS. [LAWR01] looks at the design of MPLS switches.

HARN02 Harnedy, S. *The MPLS Primer: An Introduction to Multiprotocol Label Switching.* Upper Saddle River, NJ: Prentice Hall, 2002.

LAWR01 Lawrence, J. "Designing Multiprotocol Label Switching Networks." *IEEE Communications Magazine*, July 2001.

VISW98 Viswanathan, A., et al. "Evolution of Multiprotocol Label Switching." *IEEE Communications Magazine*, May 1998.

WANG01 Wang, Z. *Internet QoS: Architectures and Mechanisms for Quality of Service.* San Francisco, CA: Morgan Kaufmann, 2001.

Recommended Web sites:

- **MPLS Working Group:** Chartered by IETF to develop standards related to MPLS. The Web site includes all relevant RFCs and Internet drafts.
- **Broadband Forum:** Forum to promote MPLS interoperability and standards.
- **MPLS Resource Center:** Provides a clearinghouse for information on MPLS; includes a useful FAQ.

21.10 KEY TERMS, REVIEW QUESTIONS, AND PROBLEMS

Key Terms

constrained shortest-path first algorithm	label stacking	Multiprotocol Label Switching (MPLS)
constraint-based routing algorithm	label switched path (LSP)	pseudowire
forwarding equivalence class (FEC)	label switching router (LSR)	Resource Reservation Protocol-Traffic
label distribution	Layer 2 Virtual Private Network (L2VPN)	Engineering (RSVP-TE)
Label Distribution Protocol (LDP)	Layer 3 Virtual Private Network (L3VPN)	traffic engineering
	LSP tunnel	

Review Questions

21.1 What is traffic engineering?

21.2 What is an MPLS forwarding equivalence class?

21.3 What is an MPLS label switched path?

21.4 Explain label stacking.

21.5 What is meant by a constraint-based routing algorithm?

Problems

21.1 The MPLS specification allows an LSR to use a technique known as *penultimate hop popping*. With this technique, the next-to-last LSR in an LSP is allowed to remove the label from a packet and send it without the label to the last LSR in that LSP.

    a. Explain why this action is possible, that is, why it results in correct behavior.

    b. What is the advantage of penultimate hop popping?

21.2 In the TCP/IP protocol suite, it is standard practice for the header corresponding to a given protocol layer to contain information that identifies the protocol used in the next higher layer. This information is needed so that the recipient of the PDU, when stripping off a given header, knows how to interpret the remaining bits so as to identify and process the header portion. For example, the IPv4 and IPv6 headers have a Protocol and Next Header field, respectively (Figure 2.12); TCP and UDP both have a Port field (Figure 2.12), which can be used to identify the protocol on top of TCP or UDP. However, each MPLS node processes a packet whose top element is the MPLS label field, which contains no explicit information about the protocol that is encapsulated. Typically, that protocol is IPv4, but it could be some other network-layer protocol.

    a. Along an LSP, which MPLS nodes would need to identify the packet's network layer protocol?

    b. What conditions must we impose on the MPLS label in order for proper processing to occur?

    c. Are such restrictions needed on all of the labels in an MPLS label stack or, if not, which ones?

21.3 Figure 21.5 indicates that the topmost label in a label stack is adjacent to the encapsulating layer 2 header and the label at the bottom of the stack is adjacent to the header of the transported protocol (e.g., IP header). Explain why this is the proper order, rather than the reverse.

21.4 In an MPLS-enabled IP network, isn't it the case that the IP layer at each router still has to examine the IP header to make a routing decision? Explain.

21.5 Consider that we have two applications using MPLS with traffic engineering. One application is delay sensitive (DS), such as a real-time voice or video application. The other application is throughput sensitive (TS), such as a file transfer application or a high-volume remote sensor feed. Now consider the following settings defined by the user for the ingress node of a requested LSP:

	PDR	PBS	CDR	CBS	EBS	Frequency
1	S	S	=PDR	=PBS	0	Frequent
2	S	S	S	S	0	Unspecified

Where the S values are user specified and may differ for each entry.

    a. Which row is more appropriate for DS and which for TS?

    b. Consider the following two policies: (1) drop packet if PDR is exceeded. (2) drop packet if PDR or PBS is exceeded; mark packet as potentially to be dropped, if needed, if CDR or CBS is exceeded. Which policy is more appropriate for DS and which for TS?

TRANSPORT PROTOCOLS

692

The foregoing observations should make us reconsider the widely held view that birds live only in the present. In fact, birds are aware of more than immediately present stimuli; they remember the past and anticipate the future.

— *The Minds of Birds,* Alexander Skutch

KEY POINTS

♦ The transport protocol provides an end-to-end data transfer service that shields upper-layer protocols from the details of the intervening network or networks. A transport protocol can be either connection oriented, such as TCP, or connectionless, such as UDP.

♦ If the underlying network or internetwork service is unreliable, such as with the use of IP, then a reliable connection-oriented transport protocol becomes quite complex. The basic cause of this complexity is the need to deal with the relatively large and variable delays experienced between end systems. These large, variable delays complicate the flow control and error control techniques.

♦ TCP uses a credit-based flow control technique that is somewhat different from the sliding-window flow control found in X.25 and HDLC. In essence, TCP separates acknowledgments from the management of the size of the sliding window.

♦ Although the TCP credit-based mechanism was designed for end-to-end flow control, it is also used to assist in internetwork congestion control. When a TCP entity detects the presence of congestion in the Internet, it reduces the flow of data onto the Internet until it detects an easing in congestion.

In a protocol architecture, the transport protocol sits above a network or internetwork layer, which provides network-related services, and just below application and other upper-layer protocols. The transport protocol provides services to transport service (TS) users, such as FTP, SMTP, and TELNET. The local transport entity communicates with some remote transport entity, using the services of some lower layer, such as the Internet Protocol. The general service provided by a transport protocol is the end-to-end transport of data in a way that shields the TS user from the details of the underlying communications systems.

We begin this chapter by examining the protocol mechanisms required to provide these services. We find that most of the complexity relates to reliable connection-oriented services. As might be expected, the less the network service provides, the more the transport protocol must do. The remainder of the chapter looks at two widely used transport protocols: Transmission Control Protocol (TCP) and User Datagram Protocol (UDP).

Refer to Figure 2.8 to see the position within the TCP/IP suite of the protocols discussed in this chapter.

22.1 CONNECTION-ORIENTED TRANSPORT PROTOCOL MECHANISMS

Two basic types of transport service are possible: connection oriented and connectionless or datagram service. A connection-oriented service provides for the establishment, maintenance, and termination of a logical connection between TS users. This has, so far, been the most common type of protocol service available and has a wide variety of applications. The connection-oriented service generally implies that the service is reliable. This section looks at the transport protocol mechanisms needed to support the connection-oriented service.

A full-feature connection-oriented transport protocol, such as TCP, is very complex. For purposes of clarity, we present the transport protocol mechanisms in an evolutionary fashion. We begin with a network service that makes life easy for the transport protocol by guaranteeing the delivery of all transport data units in order and defining the required mechanisms. Then we will look at the transport protocol mechanisms required to cope with an unreliable network service. All of this discussion applies in general to transport-level protocols. In Section 22.2, we apply the concepts developed in this section to describe TCP.

Reliable Sequencing Network Service

Let us assume that the network service accepts messages of arbitrary length and, with virtually 100 percent reliability, delivers them in sequence to the destination. Examples of such networks include the following:

- A highly reliable packet-switching network with an X.25 interface
- A frame relay network using the LAPF control protocol
- An IEEE 802.3 LAN using the connection-oriented LLC service

In all of these cases, the transport protocol is used as an end-to-end protocol between two systems attached to the same network, rather than across an internet.

The assumption of a reliable sequencing networking service allows the use of a quite simple transport protocol. Four issues need to be addressed:

- Addressing
- Multiplexing
- Flow control
- Connection establishment/termination

ADDRESSING The issue concerned with addressing is simply this: A user of a given transport entity wishes either to establish a connection with or make a data transfer to a user of some other transport entity using the same transport protocol. The target user needs to be specified by all of the following:

- User identification
- Transport entity identification

- Host address
- Network number

The transport protocol must be able to derive the information listed above from the TS user address. Typically, the user address is specified as (Host, Port). The **Port** variable represents a particular TS user at the specified host. Generally, there will be a single transport entity at each host, so a transport entity identification is not needed. If more than one transport entity is present, there is usually only one of each type. In this latter case, the address should include a designation of the type of transport protocol (e.g., TCP, UDP). In the case of a single network, **Host** identifies an attached network device. In the case of an internet, *Host* is a global internet address. In TCP, the combination of port and host is referred to as a **socket**.

Because routing is not a concern of the transport layer, it simply passes the *Host* portion of the address down to the network service. *Port* is included in a transport header, to be used at the destination by the destination transport protocol entity.

One question remains to be addressed: How does the initiating TS user know the address of the destination TS user? Two static and two dynamic strategies suggest themselves:

1. The TS user knows the address it wishes to use ahead of time. This is basically a system configuration function. For example, a process may be running that is only of concern to a limited number of TS users, such as a process that collects statistics on performance. From time to time, a central network management routine connects to the process to obtain the statistics. These processes generally are not, and should not be, well known and accessible to all.

2. Some commonly used services are assigned "well-known addresses." Examples include the server side of FTP, SMTP, and some other standard protocols.

3. A name server is provided. The TS user requests a service by some generic or global name. The request is sent to the name server, which does a directory lookup and returns an address. The transport entity then proceeds with the connection. This service is useful for commonly used applications that change location from time to time. For example, a data entry process may be moved from one host to another on a local network to balance load.

4. In some cases, the target user is to be a process that is spawned at request time. The initiating user can send a process request to a well-known address. The user at that address is a privileged system process that will spawn the new process and return an address. For example, a programmer has developed a private application (e.g., a simulation program) that will execute on a remote server but be invoked from a local workstation. A request can be issued to a remote job-management process that spawns the simulation process.

MULTIPLEXING With respect to the interface between the transport protocol and higher-level protocols, the transport protocol performs a multiplexing/demultiplexing function. That is, multiple users employ the same transport protocol and are distinguished by port numbers or service access points.

The transport entity may also perform a multiplexing function with respect to the network services that it uses. We define upward multiplexing as the multiplexing of multiple connections on a single lower-level connection, and downward multiplexing as the splitting of a single connection among multiple lower-level connections.

Consider, for example, a transport entity making use of an X.25 service. Why should the transport entity employ upward multiplexing? There are, after all, 4095 virtual circuits available. In the typical case, this is more than enough to handle all active TS users. However, most X.25 networks base part of their charge on virtual circuit connect time, because each virtual circuit consumes some node buffer resources. Thus, if a single virtual circuit provides sufficient throughput for multiple TS users, upward multiplexing is indicated.

On the other hand, downward multiplexing or splitting might be used to improve throughput. For example, each X.25 virtual circuit is restricted to a 3-bit or 7-bit sequence number. A larger sequence space might be needed for high-speed, high-delay networks. Of course, throughput can only be increased so far. If there is a single host-node link over which all virtual circuits are multiplexed, the throughput of a transport connection cannot exceed the data rate of that link.

FLOW CONTROL   Whereas flow control is a relatively simple mechanism at the link layer, it is a rather complex mechanism at the transport layer, for two main reasons:

- The transmission delay between transport entities is generally long compared to actual transmission time. This means that there is a considerable delay in the communication of flow control information.

- Because the transport layer operates over a network or internet, the amount of the transmission delay may be highly variable. This makes it difficult to effectively use a timeout mechanism for retransmission of lost data.

In general, there are two reasons why one transport entity would want to restrain the rate of segment[1] transmission over a connection from another transport entity:

- The user of the receiving transport entity cannot keep up with the flow of data.
- The receiving transport entity itself cannot keep up with the flow of segments.

How do such problems manifest themselves? Presumably a transport entity has a certain amount of buffer space. Incoming segments are added to the buffer. Each buffered segment is processed (i.e., the transport header is examined) and the data are sent to the TS user. Either of the two problems just mentioned will cause the buffer to fill up. Thus, the transport entity needs to take steps to stop or slow the flow of segments to prevent buffer overflow. This requirement is difficult to fulfill because of the annoying time gap between sender and receiver. We return to this

---

[1]Recall from Chapter 2 that the blocks of data (protocol data units) exchanged by TCP entities are referred to as TCP segments.

point subsequently. First, we present four ways of coping with the flow control requirement. The receiving transport entity can

1. Do nothing.
2. Refuse to accept further segments from the network service.
3. Use a fixed sliding-window protocol.
4. Use a credit scheme.

Alternative 1 means that the segments that overflow the buffer are discarded. The sending transport entity, failing to get an acknowledgment, will retransmit. This is a shame, because the advantage of a reliable network is that one never has to retransmit. Furthermore, the effect of this maneuver is to exacerbate the problem. The sender has increased its output to include new segments plus retransmitted old segments.

The second alternative is a backpressure mechanism that relies on the network service to do the work. When a buffer of a transport entity is full, it refuses additional data from the network service. This triggers flow control procedures within the network that throttle the network service at the sending end. This service, in turn, refuses additional segments from its transport entity. It should be clear that this mechanism is clumsy and coarse grained. For example, if multiple transport connections are multiplexed on a single network connection (virtual circuit), flow control is exercised only on the aggregate of all transport connections.

The third alternative is already familiar to you from our discussions of link-layer protocols in Chapter 7. The key ingredients, recall, are

- The use of sequence numbers on data units
- The use of a window of fixed size
- The use of acknowledgments to advance the window

With a reliable network service, the sliding-window technique would work quite well. For example, consider a protocol with a window size of 7. When the sender receives an acknowledgment to a particular segment, it is automatically authorized to send the succeeding seven segments (of course, some may already have been sent). When the receiver's buffer capacity gets down to seven segments, it can withhold acknowledgment of incoming segments to avoid overflow. The sending transport entity can send at most seven additional segments and then must stop. Because the underlying network service is reliable, the sender will not time out and retransmit. Thus, at some point, a sending transport entity may have a number of segments outstanding for which no acknowledgment has been received. Because we are dealing with a reliable network, the sending transport entity can assume that the segments will get through and that the lack of acknowledgment is a flow control tactic. This tactic would not work well in an unreliable network, because the sending transport entity would not know whether the lack of acknowledgment is due to flow control or a lost segment.

The fourth alternative, a credit scheme, provides the receiver with a greater degree of control over data flow. Although it is not strictly necessary with a reliable network service, a credit scheme should result in a smoother traffic flow. Further, it is a more effective scheme with an unreliable network service, as we shall see.

The credit scheme decouples acknowledgment from flow control. In fixed sliding-window protocols, such as X.25 and High-Level Data Link Control (HDLC), the two are synonymous. In a credit scheme, a segment may be acknowledged without granting new credit, and vice versa. For the credit scheme, each individual octet of data that is transmitted is considered to have a unique sequence number. In addition to data, each transmitted segment includes in its header three fields related to flow control: **sequence number (SN)**, **acknowledgment number (AN)**, and **window (W)**. When a transport entity sends a segment, it includes the sequence number of the first octet in the segment data field. Implicitly, the remaining data octets are numbered sequentially following the first data octet. A transport entity acknowledges an incoming segment with a return segment that includes $(AN = i, W = j)$, with the following interpretation:

- All octets through sequence number $SN = i - 1$ are acknowledged; the next expected octet has sequence number i.
- Permission is granted to send an additional window of $W = j$ octets of data; that is, the j octets corresponding to sequence numbers i through $i + j - 1$.

Figure 22.1 illustrates the mechanism (compare Figure 7.4). For simplicity, we show data flow in one direction only and assume that 200 octets of data are sent in each segment. Initially, through the connection establishment process, the sending and receiving sequence numbers are synchronized and A is granted an initial credit allocation of 1400 octets, beginning with octet number 1001. The first segment transmitted by A contains data octets numbered 1001 through 1200. After sending

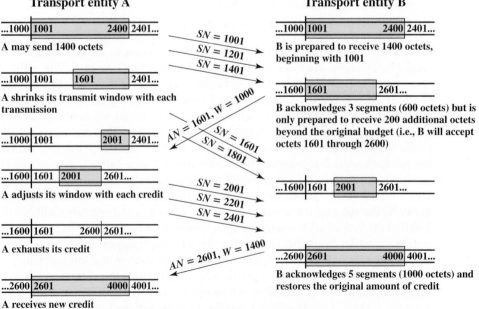

Figure 22.1 Example of TCP Credit Allocation Mechanism

600 octets in three segments, A has shrunk its window to a size of 800 octets (numbers 1601 through 2400). After B receives these three segments, 600 octets out of its original 1400 octets of credit are accounted for, and 800 octets of credit are outstanding. Now suppose that, at this point, B is capable of absorbing 1000 octets of incoming data on this connection. Accordingly, B acknowledges receipt of all octets through 1600 and issues a credit of 1000 octets. This means that A can send octets 1601 through 2600 (5 segments). However, by the time that B's message has arrived at A, A has already sent two segments, containing octets 1601 through 2000 (which was permissible under the initial allocation). Thus, A's remaining credit upon receipt of B's credit allocation is only 600 octets (3 segments). As the exchange proceeds, A advances the trailing edge of its window each time that it transmits and advances the leading edge only when it is granted credit.

Figure 22.2 shows the view of this mechanism from the sending and receiving sides (compare Figure 7.3). Typically, both sides take both views because data may be exchanged in both directions. Note that the receiver is not required to immediately acknowledge incoming segments but may wait and issue a cumulative acknowledgment for a number of segments.

The receiver needs to adopt some policy concerning the amount of data it permits the sender to transmit. The conservative approach is to only allow new segments up to the limit of available buffer space. If this policy were in effect in

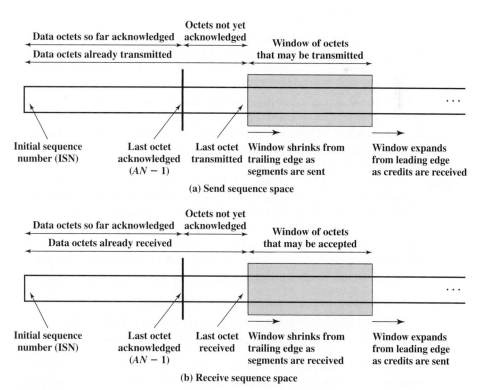

(a) Send sequence space

(b) Receive sequence space

Figure 22.2   Sending and Receiving Flow Control Perspectives

Figure 22.1, the first credit message implies that B has 1000 available octets in its buffer, and the second message that B has 1400 available octets.

A conservative flow control scheme may limit the throughput of the transport connection in long-delay situations. The receiver could potentially increase throughput by optimistically granting credit for space it does not have. For example, if a receiver's buffer is full but it anticipates that it can release space for 1000 octets within a round-trip propagation time, it could immediately send a credit of 1000. If the receiver can keep up with the sender, this scheme may increase throughput and can do no harm. If the sender is faster than the receiver, however, some segments may be discarded, necessitating a retransmission. Because retransmissions are not otherwise necessary with a reliable network service (in the absence of internet congestion), an optimistic flow control scheme will complicate the protocol.

CONNECTION ESTABLISHMENT AND TERMINATION Even with a reliable network service, there is a need for connection establishment and termination procedures to support connection-oriented service. Connection establishment serves three main purposes:

- It allows each end to assure that the other exists.
- It allows exchange or negotiation of optional parameters (e.g., maximum segment size, maximum window size, quality of service).
- It triggers allocation of transport entity resources (e.g., buffer space, entry in connection table).

Connection establishment is by mutual agreement and can be accomplished by a simple set of user commands and control segments, as shown in the state diagram of Figure 22.3. To begin, a TS user is in a CLOSED state (i.e., it has no open transport connection). The TS user can signal to the local TCP entity that it will passively wait for a request with a Passive Open command. A server program, such as time-sharing or a file transfer application, might do this. The TS user may change its mind by sending a Close command. After the Passive Open command is issued, the transport entity creates a connection object of some sort (i.e., a table entry) that is in the LISTEN state.

From the CLOSED state, a TS user may open a connection by issuing an Active Open command, which instructs the transport entity to attempt connection establishment with a designated remote TS user, which triggers the transport entity to send a SYN (for synchronize) segment. This segment is carried to the receiving transport entity and interpreted as a request for connection to a particular port. If the destination transport entity is in the LISTEN state for that port, then a connection is established by the following actions by the receiving transport entity:

- Signal the local TS user that a connection is open.
- Send a SYN as confirmation to the remote transport entity.
- Put the connection object in an ESTAB (established) state.

When the responding SYN is received by the initiating transport entity, it too can move the connection to an ESTAB state. The connection is prematurely aborted if either TS user issues a Close command.

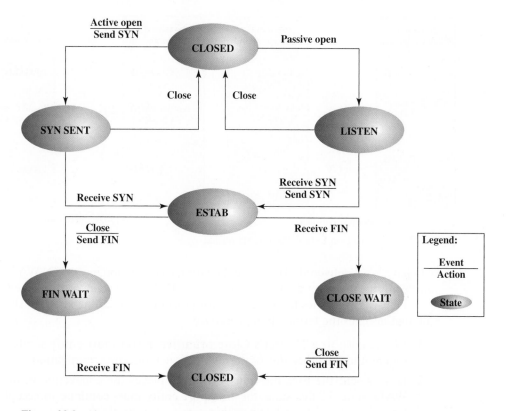

Figure 22.3 Simple Connection State Diagram

Figure 22.4 shows the robustness of this protocol. Either side can initiate a connection. Further, if both sides initiate the connection at about the same time, it is established without confusion. This is because the SYN segment functions both as a connection request and a connection acknowledgment.

The reader may ask what happens if a SYN comes in while the requested TS user is idle (not listening). Three courses may be followed:

- The transport entity can reject the request by sending a RST (reset) segment back to the other transport entity.
- The request can be queued until the local TS user issues a matching Open.
- The transport entity can interrupt or otherwise signal the local TS user to notify it of a pending request.

Note that if the third mechanism is used, a Passive Open command is not strictly necessary but may be replaced by an Accept command, which is a signal from the user to the transport entity that it accepts the request for connection.

Connection termination is handled similarly. Either side, or both sides, may initiate a close. The connection is closed by mutual agreement. This strategy allows for either abrupt or graceful termination. With abrupt termination, data in transit may be lost; a graceful termination prevents either side from closing the connection until all

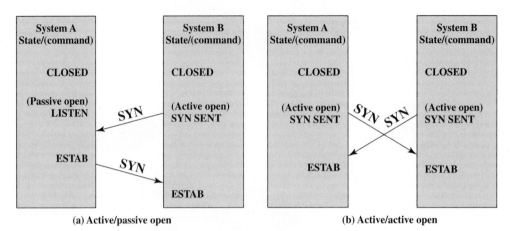

Figure 22.4 Connection Establishment Scenarios

data have been delivered. To achieve the latter, a connection in the FIN WAIT state must continue to accept data segments until a FIN (finish) segment is received.

Figure 22.3 defines the procedure for graceful termination. First, consider the side that initiates the termination procedure:

1. In response to a TS user's Close primitive, a transport entity sends a FIN segment to the other side of the connection, requesting termination.

2. Having sent the FIN, the transport entity places the connection in the FIN WAIT state. In this state, the transport entity must continue to accept data from the other side and deliver that data to its user.

3. When a FIN is received in response, the transport entity informs its user and closes the connection.

From the point of view of the side that does not initiate a termination,

1. When a FIN segment is received, the transport entity informs its user of the termination request and places the connection in the CLOSE WAIT state. In this state, the transport entity must continue to accept data from its user and transmit it in data segments to the other side.

2. When the user issues a Close primitive, the transport entity sends a responding FIN segment to the other side and closes the connection.

This procedure ensures that both sides have received all outstanding data and that both sides agree to connection termination before actual termination.

Unreliable Network Service

A more difficult case for a transport protocol is that of an unreliable network service. Examples of such networks include the following:

- An internetwork using IP
- A frame relay network using only the LAPF core protocol
- An IEEE 802.3 LAN using the unacknowledged connectionless LLC service

The problem is not just that segments are occasionally lost, but that segments may arrive out of sequence due to variable transit delays. As we shall see, elaborate machinery is required to cope with these two interrelated network deficiencies. We shall also see that a discouraging pattern emerges. The combination of unreliability and nonsequencing creates problems with every mechanism we have discussed so far. Generally, the solution to each problem raises new problems. Although there are problems to be overcome for protocols at all levels, it seems that there are more difficulties with a reliable connection-oriented transport protocol than any other sort of protocol.

In the remainder of this section, unless otherwise noted, the mechanisms discussed are those used by TCP. Seven issues need to be addressed:

- Ordered delivery
- Retransmission strategy
- Duplicate detection
- Flow control
- Connection establishment
- Connection termination
- Failure recovery

ORDERED DELIVERY With an unreliable network service, it is possible that segments, even if they are all delivered, may arrive out of order. The required solution to this problem is to number segments sequentially. We have seen that for data link control protocols, such as HDLC, and for X.25, each data unit (frame, packet) is numbered sequentially with each successive sequence number being one more than the previous sequence number. This scheme is used in some transport protocols, such as the ISO transport protocols. However, TCP uses a somewhat different scheme in which each data octet that is transmitted is implicitly numbered. Thus, the first segment may have a sequence number of 1. If that segment has 200 octets of data, then the second segment would have the sequence number 201, and so on. For simplicity in the discussions of this section, we will continue to assume that each successive segment's sequence number is 200 more than that of the previous segment; that is, each segment contains exactly 200 octets of data.

RETRANSMISSION STRATEGY Two events necessitate the retransmission of a segment. First, a segment may be damaged in transit but nevertheless arrive at its destination. If a checksum is included with the segment, the receiving transport entity can detect the error and discard the segment. The second contingency is that a segment fails to arrive. In either case, the sending transport entity does not know that the segment transmission was unsuccessful. To cover this contingency, a positive acknowledgment scheme is used: The receiver must acknowledge each successfully received segment by returning a segment containing an acknowledgment number. For efficiency, we do not require one acknowledgment per segment. Rather, a cumulative acknowledgment can be used, as we have seen many times in this book. Thus, the receiver may receive segments numbered 1, 201, and 401, but only send $AN = 601$ back. The sender must interpret $AN = 601$ to mean that the segment with $SN = 401$ and all previous segments have been successfully received.

If a segment does not arrive successfully, no acknowledgment will be issued and a retransmission is in order. To cope with this situation, there must be a timer associated with each segment as it is sent. If the timer expires before the segment is acknowledged, the sender must retransmit.

So the addition of a timer solves that problem. Next problem: At what value should the timer be set? Two strategies suggest themselves. A fixed timer value could be used, based on an understanding of the network's typical behavior. This suffers from an inability to respond to changing network conditions. If the value is too small, there will be many unnecessary retransmissions, wasting network capacity. If the value is too large, the protocol will be sluggish in responding to a lost segment. The timer should be set at a value a bit longer than the round-trip time (send segment, receive ACK). Of course, this delay is variable even under constant network load. Worse, the statistics of the delay will vary with changing network conditions.

An adaptive scheme has its own problems. Suppose that the transport entity keeps track of the time taken to acknowledge data segments and sets its **retransmission timer** based on the average of the observed delays. This value cannot be trusted for three reasons:

- The peer transport entity may not acknowledge a segment immediately. Recall that we gave it the privilege of cumulative acknowledgments.
- If a segment has been retransmitted, the sender cannot know whether the received acknowledgment is a response to the initial transmission or the retransmission.
- Network conditions may change suddenly.

Each of these problems is a cause for some further tweaking of the transport algorithm, but the problem admits of no complete solution. There will always be some uncertainty concerning the best value for the retransmission timer. We return to this issue in Section 22.3.

Incidentally, the retransmission timer is only one of a number of timers needed for proper functioning of a transport protocol. These are listed in Table 22.1, together with a brief explanation.

DUPLICATE DETECTION If a segment is lost and then retransmitted, no confusion will result. If, however, one or more segments in sequence are successfully delivered, but the corresponding ACK is lost, then the sending transport entity will time out and

Table 22.1 Transport Protocol Timers

Retransmission timer	Retransmit an unacknowledged segment
MSL (maximum segment lifetime) timer	Minimum time between closing one connection and opening another with the same destination address
Persist timer	Maximum time between ACK/CREDIT segments
Retransmit-SYN timer	Time between attempts to open a connection
Keepalive timer	Abort connection when no segments are received

one or more segments will be retransmitted. If these retransmitted segments arrive successfully, they will be duplicates of previously received segments. Thus, the receiver must be able to recognize duplicates. The fact that each segment carries a sequence number helps, but, nevertheless, duplicate detection and handling is not simple. There are two cases:

- A duplicate is received prior to the close of the connection.
- A duplicate is received after the close of the connection.

The second case is discussed in the subsection on connection establishment. We deal with the first case here.

Notice that we say "a" duplicate rather than "the" duplicate. From the sender's point of view, the retransmitted segment is the duplicate. However, the retransmitted segment may arrive before the original segment, in which case the receiver views the original segment as the duplicate. In any case, two tactics are needed to cope with a duplicate received prior to the close of a connection:

- The receiver must assume that its acknowledgment was lost and therefore must acknowledge the duplicate. Consequently, the sender must not get confused if it receives multiple acknowledgments to the same segment.
- The sequence number space must be long enough so as not to "cycle" in less than the maximum possible segment lifetime (time it takes segment to transit network).

Figure 22.5 illustrates the reason for the latter requirement. In this example, the sequence space is of length 1600; that is, after $SN = 1600$, the sequence numbers cycle back and begin with $SN = 1$. For simplicity, we assume the receiving transport entity maintains a credit window size of 600. Suppose that A has transmitted data segments with $SN = 1, 201$, and 401. B has received the two segments with $SN = 201$ and $SN = 401$, but the segment with $SN = 1$ is delayed in transit. Thus, B does not send any acknowledgments. Eventually, A times out and retransmits segment $SN = 1$. When the duplicate segment $SN = 1$ arrives, B acknowledges 1, 201, and 401 with $AN = 601$. Meanwhile, A has timed out again and retransmits $SN = 201$, which B acknowledges with another $AN = 601$. Things now seem to have sorted themselves out and data transfer continues. When the sequence space is exhausted, A cycles back to $SN = 1$ and continues. Alas, the old segment $SN = 1$ makes a belated appearance and is accepted by B before the new segment $SN = 1$ arrives. When the new segment $SN = 1$ does arrive, it is treated as a duplicate and discarded.

It should be clear that the untimely emergence of the old segment would have caused no difficulty if the sequence numbers had not yet wrapped around. The larger the sequence number space (number of bits used to represent the sequence number), the longer the wraparound is avoided. How big must the sequence space be? This depends on, among other things, whether the network enforces a maximum packet lifetime, and the rate at which segments are being transmitted. Fortunately, each addition of a single bit to the sequence number field doubles the sequence space, so it is rather easy to select a safe size.

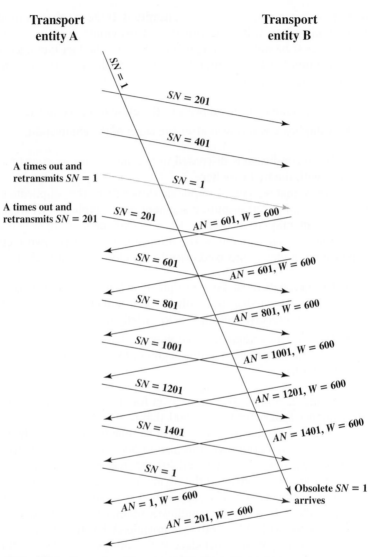

Figure 22.5 Example of Incorrect Duplicate Detection

FLOW CONTROL The credit allocation flow control mechanism described earlier is quite robust in the face of an unreliable network service and requires little enhancement. As was mentioned, a segment containing $(AN = i, W = j)$ acknowledges all octets through number $i - 1$ and grants credit for an additional j octets beginning with octet i. The credit allocation mechanism is quite flexible. For example, suppose that the last octet of data received by B was octet number $i - 1$ and that the last segment issued by B was $(AN = i, W = jk)$. Then

- To increase credit to an amount $k(k > j)$ when no additional data have arrived, B issues $(AN = i, W = k)$.

- To acknowledge an incoming segment containing m octets of data ($m < j$) without granting additional credit, B issues ($AN = i + m, W = j - m$).

If an ACK/CREDIT segment is lost, little harm is done. Future acknowledgments will resynchronize the protocol. Further, if no new acknowledgments are forthcoming, the sender times out and retransmits a data segment, which triggers a new acknowledgment. However, it is still possible for deadlock to occur. Consider a situation in which B sends ($AN = i, W = 0$), temporarily closing the window. Subsequently, B sends ($AN = i, W = j$), but this segment is lost. A is awaiting the opportunity to send data and B thinks that it has granted that opportunity. To overcome this problem, a **persist timer** can be used. This timer is reset with each outgoing segment (all segments contain the AN and W fields). If the timer ever expires, the protocol entity is required to send a segment, even if it duplicates a previous one. This breaks the deadlock and also assures the other end that the protocol entity is still alive.

CONNECTION ESTABLISHMENT As with other protocol mechanisms, connection establishment must take into account the unreliability of a network service. Recall that a connection establishment calls for the exchange of SYNs, a procedure sometimes referred to as a two-way handshake. Suppose that A issues a SYN to B. It expects to get a SYN back, confirming the connection. Two things can go wrong: A's SYN can be lost or B's answering SYN can be lost. Both cases can be handled by use of a **retransmit-SYN timer** (Table 22.1). After A issues a SYN, it will reissue the SYN when the timer expires.

This gives rise, potentially, to duplicate SYNs. If A's initial SYN was lost, there are no duplicates. If B's response was lost, then B may receive two SYNs from A. Further, if B's response was not lost, but simply delayed, A may get two responding SYNs. All of this means that A and B must simply ignore duplicate SYNs once a connection is established.

There are other problems to contend with. Just as a delayed SYN or lost response can give rise to a duplicate SYN, a delayed data segment or lost acknowledgment can give rise to duplicate data segments, as we have seen in Figure 22.5. Such a delayed or duplicated data segment can interfere with data transfer, as illustrated in Figure 22.6. Assume that with each new connection, each transport protocol entity begins numbering its data segments with sequence number 1. In the figure, a duplicate copy of segment $SN = 401$ from an old connection arrives during the lifetime of a new connection and is delivered to B before delivery of the legitimate data segment $SN = 401$. One way of attacking this problem is to start each new connection with a different sequence number that is far removed from the last sequence number of the most recent connection. For this purpose, the connection request is of the form SYN $i + 1$, where i is the sequence number of the first data segment that will be sent on this connection.

Now consider that a duplicate SYN i may survive past the termination of the connection. Figure 22.7 depicts the problem that may arise. An old SYN i arrives at B after the connection is terminated. B assumes that this is a fresh request and responds with SYN j, meaning that B accepts the connection request and will begin transmitting with $SN = j + 1$. Meanwhile, A has decided to open a new connection with B and sends SYN k. B discards this as a duplicate. Now

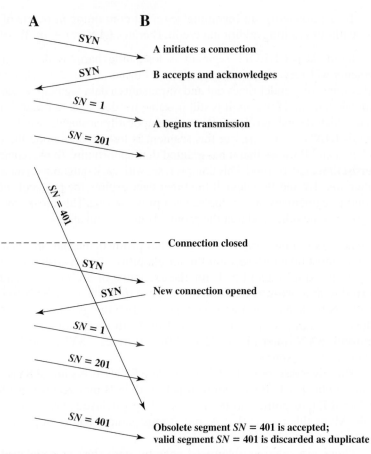

A

B

SYN — A initiates a connection

SYN — B accepts and acknowledges

$SN = 1$ — A begins transmission

$SN = 201$

$SN = 401$

- Connection closed

SYN

SYN — New connection opened

$SN = 1$

$SN = 201$

$SN = 401$ — Obsolete segment $SN = 401$ is accepted;
valid segment $SN = 401$ is discarded as duplicate

Figure 22.6 The Two-Way Handshake: Problem with Obsolete Data Segment

both sides have transmitted and subsequently received a SYN segment, and therefore think that a valid connection exists. However, when A initiates data transfer with a segment numbered $k + 1$, B rejects the segment as being out of sequence.

The way out of this problem is for each side to acknowledge explicitly the other's SYN and sequence number. The procedure is known as a **three-way handshake**. The revised connection state diagram, which is the one employed by TCP, is shown in the upper part of Figure 22.8. A new state (SYN RECEIVED) is added. In this state, the transport entity hesitates during connection opening to assure that the SYN segments sent by the two sides have both been acknowledged before the connection is declared established. In addition to the new state, there is a control segment (RST) to reset the other side when a duplicate SYN is detected.

Figure 22.9 illustrates typical three-way handshake operations. In Figure 22.9a, transport entity A initiates the connection, with a SYN including the sending sequence number, i. The value i is referred to as the initial sequence number (ISN)

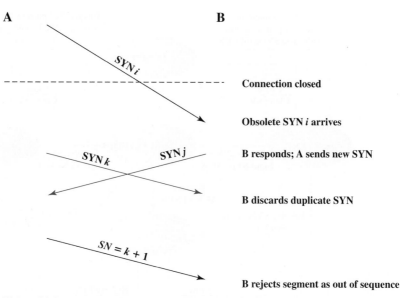

Figure 22.7 Two-Way Handshake: Problem with Obsolete SYN Segments

and is associated with the SYN; the first data octet to be transmitted will have sequence number $i + 1$. The responding SYN acknowledges the ISN with $(AN = i + 1)$ and includes its ISN. A acknowledges B's SYN/ACK in its first data segment, which begins with sequence number $i + 1$. Figure 22.9b shows a situation in which an old SYN i arrives at B after the close of the relevant connection. B assumes that this is a fresh request and responds with SYN j, $AN = i + 1$. When A receives this message, it realizes that it has not requested a connection and therefore sends an RST, $AN = j$. Note that the $AN = j$ portion of the RST message is essential so that an old duplicate RST does not abort a legitimate connection establishment. Figure 22.9c shows a case in which an old SYN/ACK arrives in the middle of a new connection establishment. Because of the use of sequence numbers in the acknowledgments, this event causes no mischief.

For simplicity, the upper part of Figure 22.8 does not include transitions in which RST is sent. The basic rule is as follows: Send an RST if the connection state is not yet OPEN and an invalid ACK (one that does not reference something that was sent) is received. The reader should try various combinations of events to see that this connection establishment procedure works in spite of any combination of old and lost segments.

CONNECTION TERMINATION The state diagram of Figure 22.3 defines the use of a simple two-way handshake for connection establishment, which was found to be unsatisfactory in the face of an unreliable network service. Similarly, the two-way handshake defined in that diagram for connection termination is inadequate for an unreliable network service. Misordering of segments could cause the following scenario. A transport entity in the CLOSE WAIT state sends its last data segment, followed by a FIN segment, but the FIN segment arrives at the other side before the

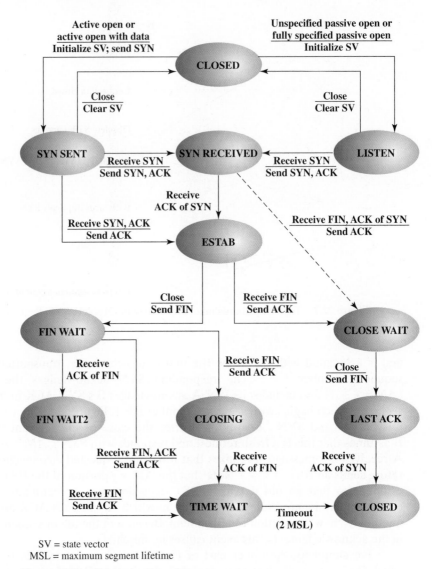

SV = state vector
MSL = maximum segment lifetime

Figure 22.8 TCP Entity State Diagram

last data segment. The receiving transport entity will accept that FIN, close the connection, and lose the last segment of data. To avoid this problem, a sequence number can be associated with the FIN, which can be assigned the next sequence number after the last octet of transmitted data. With this refinement, the receiving transport entity, upon receiving a FIN, will wait if necessary for the late-arriving data before closing the connection.

A more serious problem is the potential loss of segments and the potential presence of obsolete segments. Figure 22.8 shows that the termination procedure

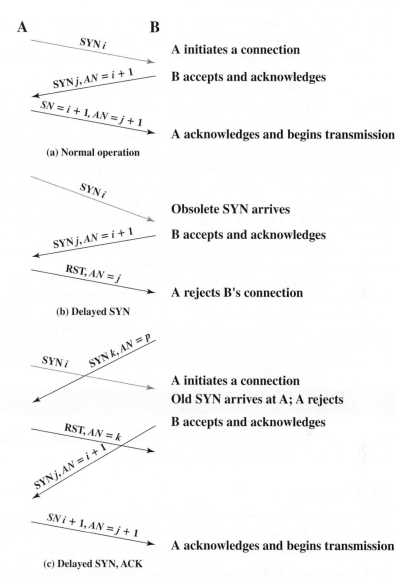

Figure 22.9 Examples of Three-Way Handshake

adopts a similar solution to that used for connection establishment. Each side must explicitly acknowledge the FIN of the other, using an ACK with the sequence number of the FIN to be acknowledged. For a graceful close, a transport entity requires the following:

- It must send a FIN i and receive $AN = i + 1$.
- It must receive a FIN j and send $AN = j + 1$.
- It must wait an interval equal to twice the maximum expected segment lifetime.

FAILURE RECOVERY When the system upon which a transport entity is running fails and subsequently restarts, the state information of all active connections is lost. The affected connections become *half open* because the side that did not fail does not yet realize the problem.

The still active side of a half-open connection can close the connection using a **keepalive timer**. This timer measures the time the transport machine will continue to await an acknowledgment (or other appropriate reply) of a transmitted segment after the segment has been retransmitted the maximum number of times. When the timer expires, the transport entity assumes that the other transport entity or the intervening network has failed, closes the connection, and signals an abnormal close to the TS user.

In the event that a transport entity fails and quickly restarts, half-open connections can be terminated more quickly by the use of the RST segment. The failed side returns an RST *i* to every segment *i* that it receives. When the RST *i* reaches the other side, it must be checked for validity based on the sequence number *i*, because the RST could be in response to an old segment. If the reset is valid, the transport entity performs an abnormal termination.

These measures clean up the situation at the transport level. The decision as to whether to reopen the connection is up to the TS users. The problem is one of synchronization. At the time of failure, there may have been one or more outstanding segments in either direction. The TS user on the side that did not fail knows how much data it has received, but the other user may not, if state information were lost. Thus, there is the danger that some user data will be lost or duplicated.

22.2 TCP

In this section, we look at TCP (RFC 793), first at the service it provides to the TS user and then at the internal protocol details.

TCP Services

TCP is designed to provide reliable communication between pairs of processes (TCP users) across a variety of reliable and unreliable networks and internets. TCP provides two useful facilities for labeling data: push and urgent.

- **Data stream push**: Ordinarily, TCP decides when sufficient data have accumulated to form a segment for transmission. The TCP user can require TCP to transmit all outstanding data up to and including that labeled with a push flag. On the receiving end, TCP will deliver these data to the user in the same manner. A user might request this if it has come to a logical break in the data.

- **Urgent data signaling**: This provides a means of informing the destination TCP user that significant or "urgent" data is in the upcoming data stream. It is up to the destination user to determine appropriate action.

As with IP, the services provided by TCP are defined in terms of primitives and parameters. The services provided by TCP are considerably richer than those provided by IP, and hence the set of primitives and parameters is more complex. Table 22.2 lists TCP service request primitives, which are issued by a TCP user to

Table 22.2   TCP Service Request Primitives

Primitive	Parameters	Description
Unspecified Passive Open	source-port, [timeout], [timeout-action], [precedence], [security-range]	Listen for connection attempt at specified security and precedence from any remote destination.
Fully Specified Passive Open	source-port, destination-port, destination-address, [timeout], [timeout-action], [precedence], [security-range]	Listen for connection attempt at specified security and precedence from specified destination.
Active Open	source-port, destination-port, destination-address, [timeout], [timeout-action], [precedence], [security]	Request connection at a particular security and precedence to a specified destination.
Active Open with Data	source-port, destination-port, destination-address, [timeout], [timeout-action], [precedence], [security], data, data-length, PUSH-flag, URGENT-flag	Request connection at a particular security and precedence to a specified destination and transmit data with the request.
Send	local-connection-name, data, data-length, PUSH-flag, URGENT-flag, [timeout], [timeout-action]	Transfer data across named connection.
Allocate	local-connection-name, data-length	Issue incremental allocation for receive data to TCP.
Close	local-connection-name	Close connection gracefully.
Abort	local-connection-name	Close connection abruptly.
Status	local-connection-name	Query connection status.

Note: Square brackets indicate optional parameters.

TCP, and Table 22.3 lists TCP service response primitives, which are issued by TCP to a local TCP user. Table 22.4 provides a brief definition of the parameters involved. The two passive open commands signal the TCP user's willingness to accept a connection request. The active open with data allows the user to begin transmitting data with the opening of the connection.

TCP Header Format

TCP uses only a single type of protocol data unit, called a TCP segment. The header is shown in Figure 22.10. Because one header must serve to perform all protocol mechanisms, it is rather large, with a minimum length of 20 octets. The fields are as follows:

- **Source Port (16 bits):** Source TCP user. Example values are Telnet = 23; TFTP = 69; HTTP = 80. A complete list is maintained at http://www.iana.org/assignments/port-numbers.

- **Destination Port (16 bits):** Destination TCP user.

- **Sequence Number (32 bits):** Sequence number of the first data octet in this segment except when the SYN flag is set. If SYN is set, this field contains the initial sequence number (ISN) and the first data octet in this segment has sequence number ISN + 1.

Table 22.3 TCP Service Response Primitives

Primitive	Parameters	Description
Open ID	local-connection-name, source-port, destination-port*, destination-address*,	Informs TCP user of connection name assigned to pending connection requested in an Open primitive
Open Failure	local-connection-name	Reports failure of an Active Open request
Open Success	local-connection-name	Reports completion of pending Open request
Deliver	local-connection-name, data, data-length, URGENT-flag	Reports arrival of data
Closing	local-connection-name	Reports that remote TCP user has issued a Close and that all data sent by remote user has been delivered
Terminate	local-connection-name, description	Reports that the connection has been terminated; a description of the reason for termination is provided
Status Response	local-connection-name, source-port, source-address, destination-port, destination-address, connection-state, receive-window, send-window, amount-awaiting-ACK, amount-awaiting-receipt, urgent-state, precedence, security, timeout	Reports current status of connection
Error	local-connection-name, description	Reports service-request or internal error

* = Not used for Unspecified Passive Open.

- **Acknowledgment Number (32 bits):** Contains the sequence number of the next data octet that the TCP entity expects to receive.
- **Data Offset (4 bits):** Number of 32-bit words in the header.
- **Reserved (4 bits):** Reserved for future use.
- **Flags (8 bits):** For each flag, if set to 1, the meaning is
  CWR: congestion window reduced.

  ECE: ECN-Echo; the CWR and ECE bits, defined in RFC 3168, are used for the explicit congestion notification function; a discussion of this function is beyond our scope.

  URG: urgent pointer field significant.

  ACK: acknowledgment field significant.

  PSH: push function.

  RST: reset the connection.

  SYN: synchronize the sequence numbers.

  FIN: no more data from sender.
- **Window (16 bits):** Flow control credit allocation, in octets. Contains the number of data octets, beginning with the sequence number indicated in the acknowledgment field that the sender is willing to accept.

Table 22.4 TCP Service Parameters

Source Port	Local TCP user
Timeout	Longest delay allowed for data delivery before automatic connection termination or error report; user specified
Timeout-action	Indicates whether the connection is terminated or an error is reported to the TCP user in the event of a timeout
Precedence	Precedence level for a connection. Takes on values zero (lowest) through seven (highest); same parameter as defined for IP
Security-range	Allowed ranges in compartment, handling restrictions, transmission control codes, and security levels
Destination Port	Remote TCP user
Destination Address	Internet address of remote host
Security	Security information for a connection, including security level, compartment, handling restrictions, and transmission control code.; same parameter as defined for IP
Data	Block of data sent by TCP user or delivered to a TCP user
Data Length	Length of block of data sent or delivered
PUSH flag	If set, indicates that the associated data are to be provided with the data stream push service
URGENT flag	If set, indicates that the associated data are to be provided with the urgent data signaling service
Local Connection Name	Identifier of a connection defined by a (local socket, remote socket) pair; provided by TCP
Description	Supplementary information in a Terminate or Error primitive
Source Address	Internet address of the local host
Connection State	State of referenced connection (CLOSED, ACTIVE OPEN, PASSIVE OPEN, ESTABLISHED, CLOSING)
Receive Window	Amount of data in octets the local TCP entity is willing to receive
Send Window	Amount of data in octets permitted to be sent to remote TCP entity
Amount Awaiting ACK	Amount of previously transmitted data awaiting acknowledgment
Amount Awaiting Receipt	Amount of data in octets buffered at local TCP entity pending receipt by local TCP user
Urgent State	Indicates to the receiving TCP user whether there are urgent data available or whether all urgent data, if any, have been delivered to the user

- **Checksum (16 bits):** The ones complement of the ones complement sum of all the 16-bit words in the segment plus a pseudoheader, described subsequently.[2]
- **Urgent Pointer (16 bits):** This value, when added to the segment sequence number, contains the sequence number of the last octet in a sequence of

---

[2]A discussion of this checksum is contained in Appendix P.

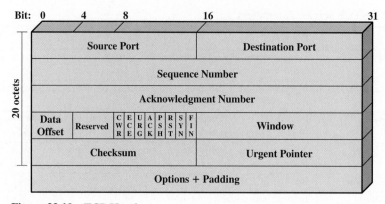

Figure 22.10   TCP Header

urgent data. This allows the receiver to know how much urgent data is coming.

- **Options (Variable):** An example is the option that specifies the maximum segment size that will be accepted.

The **Sequence Number** and **Acknowledgment Number** are bound to octets rather than to entire segments. For example, if a segment contains sequence number 1001 and includes 600 octets of data, the sequence number refers to the first octet in the data field; the next segment in logical order will have sequence number 1601. Thus, TCP is logically stream oriented: It accepts a stream of octets from the user, groups them into segments as it sees fit, and numbers each octet in the stream.

The **Checksum** field applies to the entire segment plus a pseudoheader prefixed to the header at the time of calculation (at both transmission and reception). The pseudoheader includes the following fields from the IP header: source and destination internet address and protocol, plus a segment length field. By including the pseudoheader, TCP protects itself from misdelivery by IP. That is, if IP delivers a packet to the wrong host, even if the packet contains no bit errors, the receiving TCP entity will detect the delivery error.

By comparing the TCP header to the TCP user interface defined in Tables 22.2 and 22.3, the reader may feel that some items are missing from the TCP header—that is indeed the case. TCP is intended to work with IP. Hence, some TCP user parameters are passed down by TCP to IP for inclusion in the IP header. The precedence parameter can be mapped into the Differentiated Services (DS) field, and the security parameter into the Optional Security field in the IP header.

It is worth observing that this TCP/IP linkage means that the required minimum overhead for every data unit is 40 octets.

TCP Mechanisms

We can group TCP mechanisms into the categories of connection establishment, data transfer, and connection termination.

CONNECTION ESTABLISHMENT Connection establishment in TCP always uses a three-way handshake. When the SYN flag is set, the segment is essentially a request for connection and functions as explained in Section 22.1. To initiate a connection, an entity sends a SYN, $SN = X$, where X is the initial sequence number. The receiver responds with SYN, $SN = Y, AN = X + 1$ by setting both the SYN and ACK flags. Note that the acknowledgment indicates that the receiver is now expecting to receive a segment beginning with data octet $X + 1$, acknowledging the SYN, which occupies $SN = X$. Finally, the initiator responds with $AN = Y + 1$. If the two sides issue crossing SYNs, no problem results: Both sides respond with SYN/ACKs (Figure 22.4).

A connection is uniquely determined by the source and destination sockets (host, port). Thus, at any one time, there can only be a single TCP connection between a unique pair of ports. However, a given port can support multiple connections, each with a different partner port.

DATA TRANSFER Although data are transferred in segments over a transport connection, data transfer is viewed logically as consisting of a stream of octets. Hence every octet is numbered, modulo 232. Each segment contains the sequence number of the first octet in the data field. Flow control is exercised using a credit allocation scheme in which the credit is a number of octets rather than a number of segments, as explained in Section 22.1.

Data are buffered by the transport entity on both transmission and reception. TCP normally exercises its own discretion as to when to construct a segment for transmission and when to release received data to the user. The PUSH flag is used to force the data so far accumulated to be sent by the transmitter and passed on by the receiver. This serves an end-of-block function.

The user may specify a block of data as urgent. TCP will designate the end of that block with an urgent pointer and send it out in the ordinary data stream. The receiving user is alerted that urgent data are being received.

If, during data exchange, a segment arrives that is apparently not meant for the current connection, the RST flag is set on an outgoing segment. Examples of this situation are delayed duplicate SYNs and an acknowledgment of data not yet sent.

CONNECTION TERMINATION The normal means of terminating a connection is a graceful close. Each TCP user must issue a CLOSE primitive. The transport entity sets the FIN bit on the last segment that it sends out, which also contains the last of the data to be sent on this connection.

An abrupt termination occurs if the user issues an ABORT primitive. In this case, the entity abandons all attempts to send or receive data and discards data in its transmission and reception buffers. An RST segment is sent to the other side.

TCP Implementation Policy Options

The TCP standard provides a precise specification of the protocol to be used between TCP entities. However, certain aspects of the protocol admit several possible implementation options. Although two implementations that choose alternative options will be interoperable, there may be performance implications. The design areas for which options are specified are the following:

- Send policy
- Deliver policy
- Accept policy
- Retransmit policy
- Acknowledge policy

SEND POLICY In the absence of both pushed data and a closed transmission window (see Figure 22.2a), a sending TCP entity is free to transmit data at its own convenience, within its current credit allocation. As data are issued by the user, they are buffered in the transmit buffer. TCP may construct a segment for each batch of data provided by its user or it may wait until a certain amount of data accumulates before constructing and sending a segment. The actual policy will depend on performance considerations. If transmissions are infrequent and large, there is low overhead in terms of segment generation and processing. On the other hand, if transmissions are frequent and small, the system is providing quick response.

DELIVER POLICY In the absence of a Push, a receiving TCP entity is free to deliver data to the user at its own convenience. It may deliver data as each in-order segment is received, or it may buffer data from a number of segments in the receive buffer before delivery. The actual policy will depend on performance considerations. If deliveries are infrequent and large, the user is not receiving data as promptly as may be desirable. On the other hand, if deliveries are frequent and small, there may be unnecessary processing both in TCP and in the user software, as well as an unnecessary number of operating system interrupts.

ACCEPT POLICY When all data segments arrive in order over a TCP connection, TCP places the data in a receive buffer for delivery to the user. It is possible, however, for segments to arrive out of order. In this case, the receiving TCP entity has two options:

- **In-order:** Accept only segments that arrive in order; any segment that arrives out of order is discarded.
- **In-window:** Accept all segments that are within the receive window (see Figure 22.2b).

The in-order policy makes for a simple implementation but places a burden on the networking facility, as the sending TCP must time out and retransmit segments that were successfully received but discarded because of misordering. Furthermore, if a single segment is lost in transit, then all subsequent segments must be retransmitted once the sending TCP times out on the lost segment.

The in-window policy may reduce transmissions but requires a more complex acceptance test and a more sophisticated data storage scheme to buffer and keep track of data accepted out of order.

RETRANSMIT POLICY TCP maintains a queue of segments that have been sent but not yet acknowledged. The TCP specification states that TCP will retransmit a segment if it fails to receive an acknowledgment within a given time. A TCP implementation may employ one of three retransmission strategies:

- **First-only:** Maintain one retransmission timer for the entire queue. If an acknowledgment is received, remove the appropriate segment or segments from the queue and reset the timer. If the timer expires, retransmit the segment at the front of the queue and reset the timer.
- **Batch:** Maintain one retransmission timer for the entire queue. if an acknowledgment is received, remove the appropriate segment or segments from the queue and reset the timer. If the timer expires, retransmit all segments in the queue and reset the timer.
- **Individual:** Maintain one timer for each segment in the queue. If an acknowledgment is received, remove the appropriate segment or segments from the queue and destroy the corresponding timer or timers. If any timer expires, retransmit the corresponding segment individually and reset its timer.

The first-only policy is efficient in terms of traffic generated, because only lost segments (or segments whose ACK was lost) are retransmitted. Because the timer for the second segment in the queue is not set until the first segment is acknowledged, however, there can be considerable delays. The individual policy solves this problem at the expense of a more complex implementation. The batch policy also reduces the likelihood of long delays but may result in unnecessary retransmissions.

The actual effectiveness of the retransmit policy depends in part on the accept policy of the receiver. If the receiver is using an in-order accept policy, then it will discard segments received after a lost segment. This fits best with batch retransmission. If the receiver is using an in-window accept policy, then a first-only or individual retransmission policy is best. Of course, in a mixed network of computers, both accept policies may be in use.

ACKNOWLEDGE POLICY When a data segment arrives that is in sequence, the receiving TCP entity has two options concerning the timing of acknowledgment:

- **Immediate:** When data are accepted, immediately transmit an empty (no data) segment containing the appropriate acknowledgment number.
- **Cumulative:** When data are accepted, record the need for acknowledgment, but wait for an outbound segment with data on which to piggyback the acknowledgment. To avoid long delay, set a persist timer (Table 22.1); if the timer expires before an acknowledgment is sent, transmit an empty segment containing the appropriate acknowledgment number.

The immediate policy is simple and keeps the remote TCP entity fully informed, which limits unnecessary retransmissions. However, this policy results in extra segment transmissions, namely, empty segments used only to ACK. Furthermore, the policy can cause a further load on the network. Consider that a TCP entity receives a segment and immediately sends an ACK. Then the data in the segment are released to the application, which expands the receive window, triggering another empty TCP segment to provide additional credit to the sending TCP entity.

Because of the potential overhead of the immediate policy, the cumulative policy is typically used. Recognize, however, that the use of this policy requires more processing at the receiving end and complicates the task of estimating round-trip time (RTT) by the sending TCP entity.

22.3 TCP CONGESTION CONTROL

The credit-based flow control mechanism of TCP was designed to enable a destination to restrict the flow of segments from a source to avoid buffer overflow at the destination. This same flow control mechanism is now used in ingenious ways to provide congestion control over the Internet between the source and destination. Congestion, as we have seen a number of times in this book, has two main effects. First, as congestion begins to occur, the transit time across a network or internetwork increases. Second, as congestion becomes severe, network or internet nodes drop packets. The TCP flow control mechanism can be used to recognize the onset of congestion (by recognizing increased delay times and dropped segments) and to react by reducing the flow of data. If many of the TCP entities operating across a network exercise this sort of restraint, internet congestion is relieved.

Since the publication of RFC 793, a number of techniques have been implemented that are intended to improve TCP congestion control characteristics. Table 22.5 lists some of the most popular of these techniques. None of these techniques extends or violates the original TCP standard; rather the techniques represent implementation policies that are within the scope of the TCP specification. Many of these techniques are mandated for use with TCP in RFC 1122 (*Requirements for Internet Hosts*) while some of them are specified in RFC 5681. The labels Tahoe, Reno, and NewReno refer to implementation packages available on many operating systems that support TCP. The techniques fall roughly into two categories: retransmission timer management and window management. In this section, we look at some of the most important and most widely implemented of these techniques.

Table 22.5 Implementation of TCP Congestion Control Measures

Measure	RFC 1122	TCP Tahoe	TCP Reno	NewReno
RTT Variance Estimation	✓	✓	✓	✓
Exponential RTO Backoff	✓	✓	✓	✓
Karn's Algorithm	✓	✓	✓	✓
Slow Start	✓	✓	✓	✓
Dynamic Window Sizing on Congestion	✓	✓	✓	✓
Fast Retransmit		✓	✓	✓
Fast Recovery			✓	✓
Modified Fast Recovery				✓

Retransmission Timer Management

As network or internet conditions change, a static retransmission timer is likely to be either too long or too short. Accordingly, virtually all TCP implementations attempt to estimate the current round-trip time by observing the pattern of delay for recent segments, and then set the timer to a value somewhat greater than the estimated round-trip time.

SIMPLE AVERAGE   A simple approach is to take the average of observed round-trip times over a number of segments. If the average accurately predicts future round-trip times, then the resulting retransmission timer will yield good performance. The simple averaging method can be expressed as:

$$ARTT(K + 1) = \frac{1}{K + 1} \sum_{i=1}^{K+1} RTT(i) \qquad (22.1)$$

where $RTT(i)$ is the round-trip time observed for the ith transmitted segment, and $ARTT(K)$ is the average round-trip time for the first K segments.

This expression can be rewritten as

$$ARTT(K + 1) = \frac{K}{K + 1} ARTT(K) + \frac{1}{K + 1} RTT(K + 1) \qquad (22.2)$$

With this formulation, it is not necessary to recalculate the entire summation each time.

EXPONENTIAL AVERAGE   Note that each term in the summation is given equal weight; that is, each term is multiplied by the same constant $1/(K + 1)$. Typically, we would like to give greater weight to more recent instances because they are more likely to reflect future behavior. A common technique for predicting the next value on the basis of a time series of past values, and the one specified in RFC 793, is exponential averaging:

$$SRTT(K + 1) = \alpha \times SRTT(K) + (1 - \alpha) \times RTT(K + 1) \qquad (22.3)$$

where $SRTT(K)$ is called the smoothed round-trip time estimate, and we define $SRTT(0) = 0$. Compare this with Equation (22.2). By using a constant value of $\alpha (0 < \alpha < 1)$, independent of the number of past observations, we have a circumstance in which all past values are considered, but the more distant ones have less weight. To see this more clearly, consider the following expansion of Equation (22.3):

$$SRTT(K + 1) = (1 - \alpha)RTT(K + 1) + \alpha(1 - \alpha)RTT(K) +$$
$$\alpha^2(1 - \alpha)RRT(K - 1) + \dots + \alpha^K(1 - \alpha)RTT(1)$$

Because both α and $((1 - \alpha))$ are less than one, each successive term in the preceding equation is smaller. For example, for $\alpha = 0.8$, the expansion is

$$SRTT(K + 1) = (0.2)RTT(K + 1) + (0.16)RTT(K) +$$
$$(0.128)RTT(K - 1) + \dots$$

The older the observation, the less it is counted in the average.

The smaller the value of α, the greater the weight given to the more recent observations. For $\alpha = 0.5$, virtually all of the weight is given to the four or five most recent observations, whereas for $\alpha = 0.875$, the averaging is effectively spread out over the ten or so most recent observations. The advantage of using a small value of α is that the average will quickly reflect a rapid change in the observed quantity. The disadvantage is that if there is a brief surge in the value of the observed quantity and it then settles back to some relatively constant value, the use of a small value of α will result in jerky changes in the average.

Figure 22.11 compares simple averaging with exponential averaging (for two different values of α). In part (a) of the figure, the observed value begins at 1, grows

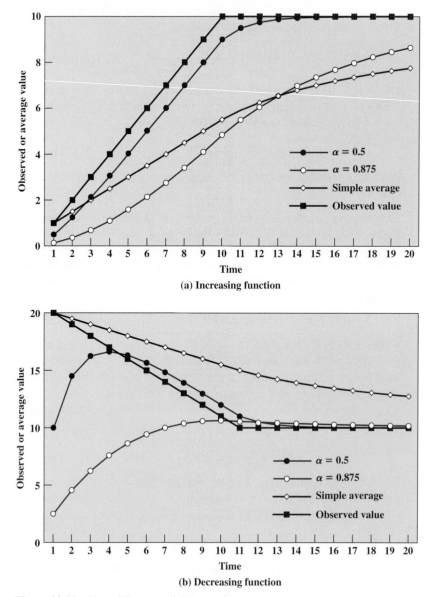

Figure 22.11   Use of Exponential Averaging

gradually to a value of 10, and then stays there. In part (b) of the figure, the observed value begins at 20, declines gradually to 10, and then stays there. Note that exponential averaging tracks changes in RTT faster than does simple averaging and that the smaller value of α results in a more rapid reaction to the change in the observed value.

Equation (22.3) is used in RFC 793 to estimate the current round-trip time. As was mentioned, the retransmission timer should be set at a value somewhat greater than the estimated round-trip time. One possibility is to use a constant value:

$$\text{RTO}(K + 1) = \text{SRTT}(K + 1) + \Delta$$

where RTO is the retransmission timer (also called the retransmission timeout) and Δ is a constant. The disadvantage of this is that Δ is not proportional to SRTT. For large values of SRTT, Δ is relatively small and fluctuations in the actual RTT will result in unnecessary retransmissions. For small values of SRTT, Δ is relatively large and causes unnecessary delays in retransmitting lost segments. Accordingly, RFC 793 specifies the use of a timer whose value is proportional to SRTT, within limits:

$$\text{RTO}(K + 1) = \text{MIN}(\text{UBOUND}, \text{MAX}(\text{LBOUND}, \beta \times \text{SRTT}(K + 1))) \quad \textbf{(22.4)}$$

where UBOUND and LBOUND are prechosen fixed upper and lower bounds on the timer value and β is a constant. RFC 793 does not recommend specific values but does list as "example values" the following: α between 0.8 and 0.9 and β between 1.3 and 2.0.

RTT VARIANCE ESTIMATION (JACOBSON'S ALGORITHM) The technique specified in the TCP standard, and described in Equations (22.3) and (22.4), enables a TCP entity to adapt to changes in round-trip time. However, it does not cope well with a situation in which the round-trip time exhibits a relatively high variance. [ZHAN86] points out three sources of high variance:

1. If the data rate on the TCP connection is relatively low, then the transmission delay will be relatively large compared to propagation time and the variance in delay due to variance in IP datagram size will be significant. Thus, the SRTT estimator is heavily influenced by characteristics that are a property of the data and not of the network.

2. Internet traffic load and conditions may change abruptly due to traffic from other sources, causing abrupt changes in RTT.

3. The peer TCP entity may not acknowledge each segment immediately because of its own processing delays and because it exercises its privilege to use cumulative acknowledgments.

The original TCP specification tries to account for this variability by multiplying the RTT estimator by a constant factor, as shown in Equation (22.4). In a stable environment, with low variance of RTT, this formulation results in an unnecessarily high value of RTO, and in an unstable environment a value of $\beta = 2$ may be inadequate to protect against unnecessary retransmissions.

A more effective approach is to estimate the variability in RTT values and to use that as input into the calculation of an RTO. A variability measure that is easy to estimate is the mean deviation, defined as

$$MDEV(X) = E[|X - E[X]|]$$

where $E[X]$ is the expected value of X.

As with the estimate of RTT, a simple average could be used to estimate MDEV:

$$AERR(K + 1) = RTT(K + 1) - ARTT(K)$$

$$ADEV(K + 1) = \frac{1}{K + 1} \sum_{i=1}^{K+1} |AERR(i)|$$

$$= \frac{1}{K + 1} ADEV(K) + \frac{1}{K + 1} |AERR(K + 1)|$$

where $ARTT(K)$ is the simple average defined in Equation (22.1) and $AERR(K)$ is the sample mean deviation measured at time K.

As with the definition of ARTT, each term in the summation of ADEV is given equal weight; that is, each term is multiplied by the same constant $1/(K + 1)$. Again, we would like to give greater weight to more recent instances because they are more likely to reflect future behavior. Jacobson, who proposed the use of a dynamic estimate of variability in estimating RTT [JACO88], suggests using the same exponential smoothing technique as is used for the calculation of SRTT. The complete algorithm proposed by Jacobson can be expressed as follows:

$$SRTT(K + 1) = (1 - g) \times SRTT(K) + g \times RTT(K + 1)$$
$$SERR(K + 1) = RTT(K + 1) - SRTT(K)$$
$$SDEV(K + 1) = (1 - h) \times SDEV(K + h) \times |SERR(K + 1)|$$
$$RTO(K + 1) = SRTT(K + 1) + f \times SDEV(K + 1) \qquad \textbf{(22.5)}$$

As in the RFC 793 definition [Equation (22.3)], SRTT is an exponentially smoothed estimate of RTT, with $(1 - g)$ equivalent to α. Now, however, instead of multiplying the estimate SRTT by a constant [Equation (22.4)], a multiple of the estimated mean deviation is added to SRTT to form the retransmission timer. Based on his timing experiments, Jacobson proposed the following values for the constants in his original paper [JACO88]:

$$g = 1/8 = 0.125$$

$$h = 1/4 = 0.25$$

$$f = 2$$

After further research [JACO90a], Jacobson recommended using $f = 4$, and this is the value used in current implementations.

Figure 22.12 illustrates the use of Equation (22.5) on the same data set used in Figure 22.11. Once the arrival times stabilize, the variation estimate SDEV declines. The values of RTO for both $f = 2$ and $f = 4$ are quite conservative as long as RTT is changing but then begin to converge to RTT when it stabilizes.

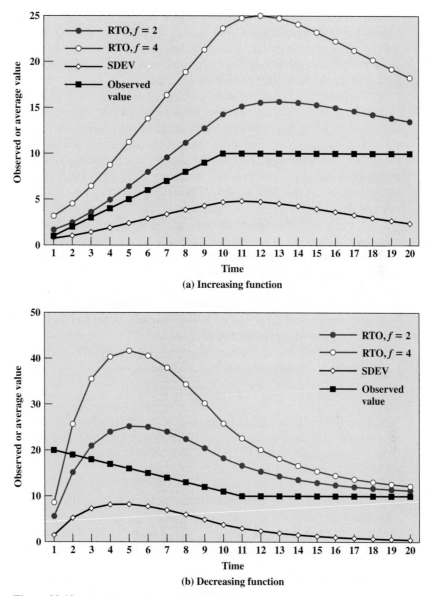

Figure 22.12   Jacobson's RTO Calculation

Experience has shown that Jacobson's algorithm can significantly improve TCP performance. However, it does not stand by itself. Two other factors must be considered:

1. What RTO value should be used on a retransmitted segment? The exponential RTO backoff algorithm is used for this purpose.
2. Which round-trip samples should be used as input to Jacobson's algorithm? Karn's algorithm determines which samples to use.

EXPONENTIAL RTO BACKOFF When a TCP sender times out on a segment, it must retransmit that segment. RFC 793 assumes that the same RTO value will be used for this retransmitted segment. However, because the timeout is probably due to network congestion, manifested as a dropped packet or a long delay in round-trip time, maintaining the same RTO value is ill advised.

Consider the following scenario. There are a number of active TCP connections from various sources sending traffic into an internet. A region of congestion develops such that segments on many of these connections are lost or delayed past the RTO time of the connections. Therefore, at roughly the same time, many segments will be retransmitted into the internet, maintaining or even increasing the congestion. All of the sources then wait a local (to each connection) RTO time and retransmit yet again. This pattern of behavior could cause a sustained condition of congestion.

A more sensible policy dictates that a sending TCP entity increase its RTO each time a segment is retransmitted; this is referred to as a *backoff* process. In the scenario of the preceding paragraph, after the first retransmission of a segment on each affected connection, the sending TCP entities will all wait a longer time before performing a second retransmission. This may give the internet time to clear the current congestion. If a second retransmission is required, each sending TCP entity will wait an even longer time before timing out for a third retransmission, giving the internet an even longer period to recover.

A simple technique for implementing RTO backoff is to multiply the RTO for a segment by a constant value for each retransmission:

$$RTO = q \times RTO \qquad \textbf{(22.6)}$$

Equation (22.6) causes RTO to grow exponentially with each retransmission. The most commonly used value of q is 2. With this value, the technique is referred to as *binary exponential backoff*. This is the same technique used in the Ethernet CSMA/CD protocol (Chapter 16).

KARN'S ALGORITHM If no segments are retransmitted, the sampling process for Jacobson's algorithm is straightforward. The RTT for each segment can be included in the calculation. Suppose, however, that a segment times out and must be retransmitted. If an acknowledgment is subsequently received, there are two possibilities:

1. This is the ACK to the first transmission of the segment. In this case, the RTT is simply longer than expected but is an accurate reflection of network conditions.
2. This is the ACK to the second transmission.

The sending TCP entity cannot distinguish between these two cases. If the second case is true and the TCP entity simply measures the RTT from the first transmission until receipt of the ACK, the measured time will be much too long. The measured RTT will be on the order of the actual RTT plus the RTO. Feeding this false RTT into Jacobson's algorithm will produce an unnecessarily high value of SRTT and therefore RTO. Furthermore, this effect propagates forward a number of iterations, since the SRTT value of one iteration is an input value in the next iteration.

An even worse approach would be to measure the RTT from the *second* transmission to the receipt of the ACK. If this is in fact the ACK to the first transmission, then the measured RTT will be much too small, producing a too low value of SRTT and RTO. This is likely to have a positive feedback effect, causing additional retransmissions and additional false measurements.

Karn's algorithm [KARN91] solves this problem with the following rules:

1. Do not use the measured RTT for a retransmitted segment to update SRTT and SDEV [Equation (22.5)].

2. Calculate the backoff RTO using Equation (22.6) when a retransmission occurs.

3. Use the backoff RTO value for succeeding segments until an acknowledgment arrives for a segment that has not been retransmitted.

When an acknowledgment is received to an unretransmitted segment, Jacobson's algorithm is again activated to compute future RTO values.

Window Management

In addition to techniques for improving the effectiveness of the retransmission timer, a number of approaches to managing the send window have been examined. The size of TCP's send window can have a critical effect on whether TCP can be used efficiently without causing congestion. We discuss two techniques found in virtually all modern implementations of TCP: slow start and dynamic window sizing on congestion.[3]

SLOW START The larger the send window used in TCP, the more segments that a sending TCP entity can send before it must wait for an acknowledgment. This can create a problem when a TCP connection is first established, because the TCP entity is free to dump the entire window of data onto the internet.

One strategy that could be followed is for the TCP sender to begin sending from some relatively large but not maximum window, hoping to approximate the window size that would ultimately be provided by the connection. This is risky because the sender might flood the internet with many segments before it realized from timeouts that the flow was excessive. Instead, some means is needed of gradually expanding the window until acknowledgments are received. This is the purpose of the slow-start mechanism.

With slow start, TCP transmission is constrained by the following relationship:

$$awnd = MIN[credit, cwnd] \qquad (22.7)$$

---

[3]These algorithms were developed by Jacobson [JACO88] and are also described in RFC 2581. Van Jacobson describes things in units of TCP segments, whereas RFC 2581 relies primarily on units of TCP data octets, with some reference to calculations in units of segments. We follow the development in [JACO88].

where

> *awnd* = allowed window, in segments. This is the number of segments that TCP is currently allowed to send without receiving further acknowledgments.
>
> *cwnd* = congestion window, in segments. A window used by TCP during start-up and to reduce flow during periods of congestion.
>
> *credit* = the amount of unused credit granted in the most recent acknowledgment, in segments. When an acknowledgment is received, this value is calculated as *window/segment_size*, where *window* is a field in the incoming TCP segment (the amount of data the peer TCP entity is willing to accept).

When a new connection is opened, the TCP entity initializes *cwnd* = 1. That is, TCP is only allowed to send 1 segment and then must wait for an acknowledgment before transmitting a second segment. Each time an acknowledgment to new data is received, the value of *cwnd* is increased by 1, up to some maximum value.

In effect, the slow-start mechanism probes the internet to make sure that the TCP entity is not sending too many segments into an already congested environment. As acknowledgments arrive, TCP is able to open up its window until the flow is controlled by the incoming ACKs rather than by *cwnd*.

The term *slow start* is a bit of a misnomer, because *cwnd* actually grows exponentially. When the first ACK arrives, TCP opens *cwnd* to 2 and can send two segments. When these two segments are acknowledged, TCP can slide the window 1 segment for each incoming ACK and can increase *cwnd* by 1 for each incoming ACK. Therefore, at this point TCP can send four segments. When these four are acknowledged, TCP will be able to send eight segments.

DYNAMIC WINDOW SIZING ON CONGESTION   The slow-start algorithm has been found to work effectively for initializing a connection. It enables the TCP sender to determine quickly a reasonable window size for the connection. Might not the same technique be useful when there is a surge in congestion? In particular, suppose a TCP entity initiates a connection and goes through the slow-start procedure. At some point, either before or after *cwnd* reaches the size of the credit allocated by the other side, a segment is lost (timeout). This is a signal that congestion is occurring. It is not clear how serious the congestion is. Therefore, a prudent procedure would be to reset *cwnd* = 1 and begin the slow-start process all over.

This seems like a reasonable, conservative procedure, but in fact it is not conservative enough. Jacobson [JACO88] points out that "it is easy to drive a network into saturation but hard for the net to recover." In other words, once congestion occurs, it may take a long time for the congestion to clear.[4] Thus, the exponential growth of *cwnd* under slow start may be too aggressive and may worsen the congestion. Instead, Jacobson proposed the use of slow start to begin with, followed by a linear growth in *cwnd*. The rules are as follows. When a timeout occurs,

---

[4]Kleinrock refers to this phenomenon as the long-tail effect during a rush-hour period. See Sections 2.7 and 2.10 of [KLEI76] for a detailed discussion.

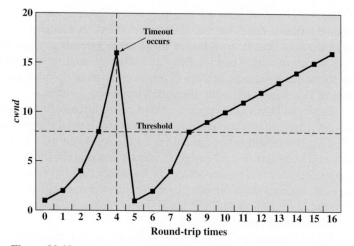

Figure 22.13 Illustration of Slow Start and Congestion Avoidance

1. Set a slow-start threshold equal to half the current congestion window; that is, set *ssthresh* = *cwnd*/2.

2. Set *cwnd* = 1 and perform the slow-start process until *cwnd* = *ssthresh*. In this phase, *cwnd* is increased by 1 for every ACK received.

3. For *cwnd* ≥ *ssthresh*, increase *cwnd* by 1 for each round-trip time.

Figure 22.13 illustrates this behavior. Note that it takes 11 round-trip times to recover to the *cwnd* level that initially took 4 round-trip times to achieve.

FAST RETRANSMIT The retransmission timer (RTO) that is used by a sending TCP entity to determine when to retransmit a segment will generally be noticeably longer than the actual round-trip time (RTT) that the ACK for that segment will take to reach the sender. Both the original RFC 793 algorithm and the Jacobson algorithm set the value of RTO at somewhat greater than the estimated round-trip time SRTT. Several factors make this margin desirable:

1. RTO is calculated on the basis of a prediction of the next RTT, estimated from past values of RTT. If delays in the network fluctuate, then the estimated RTT may be smaller than the actual RTT.

2. Similarly, if delays at the destination fluctuate, the estimated RTT becomes unreliable.

3. The destination system may not ACK each segment but cumulatively ACK multiple segments, while at the same time sending ACKs when it has any data to send. This behavior contributes to fluctuations in RTT.

A consequence of these factors is that if a segment is lost, TCP may be slow to retransmit. If the destination TCP is using an in-order accept policy (see Section 6.3), then many segments may be lost. Even in the more likely case that the destination TCP is using an in-window accept policy, a slow retransmission can cause problems. To see this, suppose that A transmits a sequence of segments, the first of which is lost.

So long as its send window is not empty and RTO does not expire, A can continue to transmit without receiving an acknowledgment. B receives all of these segments except the first. But B must buffer all of these incoming segments until the missing one is retransmitted; it cannot clear its buffer by sending the data to an application until the missing segment arrives. If retransmission of the missing segment is delayed too long, B will have to begin discarding incoming segments.

Jacobson [JACO90b] proposed two procedures, called fast retransmit and fast recovery, that under some circumstances improve on the performance provided by RTO. Fast retransmit takes advantage of the following rule in TCP. If a TCP entity receives a segment out of order, it must immediately issue an ACK for the last in-order segment that was received. TCP will continue to repeat this ACK with each incoming segment until the missing segment arrives to "plug the hole" in its buffer. When the hole is plugged, TCP sends a cumulative ACK for all of the in-order segments received so far.

When a source TCP receives a duplicate ACK, it means that either (1) the segment following the ACKed segment was delayed so that it ultimately arrived out of order or (2) that segment was lost. In case (1), the segment does ultimately arrive and therefore TCP should not retransmit. But in case (2), the arrival of a duplicate ACK can function as an early warning system to tell the source TCP that a segment has been lost and must be retransmitted. To make sure that we have case (2) rather than case (1), Jacobson recommends that a TCP sender wait until it receives three duplicate ACKs to the same segment (i.e., a total of four ACKs to the same segment). Under these circumstances, it is highly likely that the following segment has been lost and should be retransmitted immediately, rather than waiting for a timeout.

FAST RECOVERY When a TCP entity retransmits a segment using fast retransmit, it knows (or rather assumes) that a segment was lost, even though it has not yet timed out on that segment. Accordingly, the TCP entity should take congestion avoidance measures. One obvious strategy is the slow-start/congestion avoidance procedure used when a timeout occurs. That is, the entity could set *ssthresh* to *cwnd*/2, set*cwnd* = 1 and begin the exponential slow-start process until *cwnd* = *ssthresh*, and then increase *cwnd* linearly. Jacobson [JACO90b] argues that this approach is unnecessarily conservative. As was just pointed out, the very fact that multiple ACKs have returned indicates that data segments are getting through fairly regularly to the other side. So Jacobson proposes a fast recovery technique: retransmit the lost segment, cut *cwnd* in half, and then proceed with the linear increase of *cwnd*. This technique avoids the initial exponential slow-start process.

RFC 3782 (The NewReno Modification to TCP's Fast Recovery Mechanism) modifies the fast recovery algorithm to improve the response when two segments are lost within a single window. Using fast retransmit, a sender retransmits a segment before timeout because it infers that the segment was lost. If the sender subsequently receives an acknowledgement that does not cover all of the segments transmitted before fast retransmit was initiated, the sender may infer that two segments were lost from the current window and retransmit an additional segment. The details of both fast recovery and modified fast recovery are complex; the reader is referred to RFCs 5681 and 3782.

22.4 UDP

In addition to TCP, there is one other transport-level protocol that is in common use as part of the TCP/IP suite: the user datagram protocol (UDP), specified in RFC 768. UDP provides a connectionless service for application-level procedures. Thus, UDP is basically an unreliable service; delivery and duplicate protection are not guaranteed. However, this does reduce the overhead of the protocol and may be adequate in many cases. An example of the use of UDP is in the context of network management, as described in Chapter 25.

The strengths of the connection-oriented approach are clear. It allows connection-related features such as flow control, error control, and sequenced delivery. Connectionless service, however, is more appropriate in some contexts. At lower layers (internet, network), a connectionless service is more robust (e.g., see discussion in Section 10.5). In addition, it represents a "least common denominator" of service to be expected at higher layers. Further, even at transport and above there is justification for a connectionless service. There are instances in which the overhead of connection establishment and termination is unjustified or even counterproductive. Examples include the following:

- **Inward data collection:** Involves the periodic active or passive sampling of data sources, such as sensors, and automatic self-test reports from security equipment or network components. In a real-time monitoring situation, the loss of an occasional data unit would not cause distress, because the next report should arrive shortly.

- **Outward data dissemination:** Includes broadcast messages to network users, the announcement of a new node or the change of address of a service, and the distribution of real-time clock values.

- **Request-response:** Applications in which a transaction service is provided by a common server to a number of distributed TS users, and for which a single request-response sequence is typical. Use of the service is regulated at the application level, and lower-level connections are often unnecessary and cumbersome.

- **Real-time applications:** Such as voice and telemetry, involving a degree of redundancy and/or a real-time transmission requirement. These must not have connection-oriented functions such as retransmission.

Thus, there is a place at the transport level for both a connection-oriented and a connectionless type of service.

UDP sits on top of IP. Because it is connectionless, UDP has very little to do. Essentially, it adds a port addressing capability to IP. This is best seen by examining the UDP header, shown in Figure 22.14. The header includes a source port and destination port. The Length field contains the length of the entire UDP segment, including header and data. The checksum is the same algorithm used for TCP and IP. For UDP, the checksum applies to the entire UDP segment plus a pseudoheader prefixed to the UDP header at the time of calculation and which is the same pseudoheader used for TCP. If an error is detected, the segment is discarded and no further action is taken.

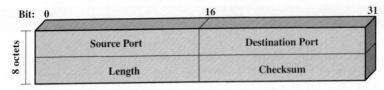

Figure 22.14 UDP Header

The checksum field in UDP is optional. If it is not used, it is set to zero. However, it should be pointed out that the IP checksum applies only to the IP header and not to the data field, which in this case consists of the UDP header and the user data. Thus, if no checksum calculation is performed by UDP, then no check is made on the user data at either the transport or internet protocol layers.

22.5 RECOMMENDED READING AND WEB SITES

[IREN99] is a comprehensive survey of transport protocol services and protocol mechanisms, with a brief discussion of a number of different transport protocols. Perhaps the best coverage of the various TCP strategies for flow and congestion control is to be found in [STEV94]. An essential paper for understanding the issues involved is the classic [JACO88].

IREN99 Iren, S.; Amer, P.; and Conrad, P. "The Transport Layer: Tutorial and Survey." *ACM Computing Surveys*, December 1999.

JACO88 Jacobson, V. "Congestion Avoidance and Control." *Proceedings, SIGCOMM '88, Computer Communication Review*, August 1988; reprinted in *Computer Communication Review*, January 1995; a slightly revised version is available at ftp.ee.lbl.gov/papers/congavoid.ps.Z

STEV94 Stevens, W. *TCP/IP Illustrated, Volume 1: The Protocols*. Reading, MA: Addison-Wesley, 1994.

Recommended Web sites:

- **Internet Congestion Control Research Group:** An Internet Research Task Force (IRTF) Research Group for the discussion and review of TCP congestion control mechanisms.
- **Center for Internet Research:** One of the most active groups in the areas covered in this chapter. The site contains many papers and useful pointers.
- **TCP Maintenance Working Group:** Chartered by IETF to make minor revisions to TCP and to update congestion strategies and protocols. The Web site includes all relevant RFCs and Internet drafts.
- **TCP-Friendly Web site:** Summarizes some of the recent work on adaptive congestion control algorithms for non-TCP-based applications, with a specific focus on schemes that share bandwidth fairly with TCP connections.

22.6 KEY TERMS, REVIEW QUESTIONS, AND PROBLEMS

Key Terms

checksum	port	Transmission Control Protocol
credit	retransmission strategy	(TCP)
data stream push	sequence number	transport protocol
duplicate detection	slow start	urgent data signaling
exponential average	socket	User Datagram Protocol
flow control	TCP congestion control	(UDP)
Karn's algorithm	TCP implementation policy	
Multiplexing	options	

Review Questions

22.1 What addressing elements are needed to specify a target transport service (TS) user?

22.2 Describe four strategies by which a sending TS user can learn the address of a receiving TS user.

22.3 Explain the use of multiplexing in the context of a transport protocol.

22.4 Briefly describe the credit scheme used by TCP for flow control.

22.5 What is the key difference between the TCP credit scheme and the sliding-window flow control scheme used by many other protocols, such as HDLC?

22.6 Explain the two-way and three-way handshake mechanisms.

22.7 What is the benefit of the three-way handshake mechanism?

22.8 Define the urgent and push features of TCP.

22.9 What is a TCP implementation policy option?

22.10 How can TCP be used to deal with network or internet congestion?

22.11 What does UDP provide that is not provided by IP?

Problems

22.1 It is common practice in most transport protocols (indeed, most protocols at all levels) for control and data to be multiplexed over the same logical channel on a per-user-connection basis. An alternative is to establish a single control transport connection between each pair of communicating transport entities. This connection would be used to carry control signals relating to all user-transport connections between the two entities. Discuss the implications of this strategy.

22.2 The discussion of flow control with a reliable network service referred to a backpressure mechanism utilizing a lower-level flow control protocol. Discuss the disadvantages of this strategy.

22.3 Two transport entities communicate across a reliable network. Let the normalized time to transmit a segment equal 1. Assume that the end-to-end propagation delay is 3, and that it takes a time 2 to deliver data from a received segment to the transport user. The sender is initially granted a credit of seven segments. The receiver uses a conservative flow control policy and updates its credit allocation at every opportunity. What is the maximum achievable throughput?

22.4 Someone posting to comp.protocols.tcp-ip complained about a throughput of 122 kbps on a 256 kbps link with a 128-ms round-trip delay between the United States and Japan, and a throughput of 33 kbps when the link was routed over a satellite.
  a. What is the utilization over the two links? Assume a 500-ms round-trip delay for the satellite link.
  b. What does the window size appear to be for the two cases?
  c. How big should the window size be for the satellite link?

22.5 Draw diagrams similar to Figure 22.4 for the following (assume a reliable sequenced network service):
  a. Connection termination: active/passive
  b. Connection termination: active/active
  c. Connection rejection
  d. Connection abortion: User issues an OPEN to a listening user, and then issues a CLOSE before any data are exchanged

22.6 With a reliable sequencing network service, are segment sequence numbers strictly necessary? What, if any, capability is lost without them?

22.7 Consider a connection-oriented network service that suffers a reset. How could this be dealt with by a transport protocol that assumes that the network service is reliable except for resets?

22.8 The discussion of retransmission strategy made reference to three problems associated with dynamic timer calculation. What modifications to the strategy would help to alleviate those problems?

22.9 Consider a transport protocol that uses a connection-oriented network service. Suppose that the transport protocol uses a credit allocation flow control scheme, and the network protocol uses a sliding-window scheme. What relationship, if any, should there be between the dynamic window of the transport protocol and the fixed window of the network protocol?

22.10 In a network that has a maximum packet size of 128 bytes, a maximum packet lifetime of 30 s, and an 8-bit packet sequence number, what is the maximum data rate per connection?

22.11 Is a deadlock possible using only a two-way handshake instead of a three-way handshake? Give an example or prove otherwise.

22.12 Listed are four strategies that can be used to provide a transport user with the address of the destination transport user. For each one, describe an analogy with the Postal Service user.
  a. Know the address ahead of time.
  b. Make use of a "well-known address."
  c. Use a name server.
  d. Addressee is spawned at request time.

22.13 In a credit flow control scheme such as that of TCP, what provision could be made for credit allocations that are lost or misordered in transit?

22.14 What happens in Figure 22.3 if a SYN comes in while the requested user is in CLOSED? Is there any way to get the attention of the user when it is not listening?

22.15 In discussing connection termination with reference to Figure 22.8, it was stated that in addition to receiving an acknowledgement of its FIN and sending an acknowledgement of the incoming FIN, a TCP entity must wait an interval equal to twice the maximum expected segment lifetime (the TIME WAIT state). Receiving an ACK to its FIN assures that all of the segments it sent have been received by the other side. Sending an ACK to the other side's FIN assures the other side that all its segments have been received. Give a reason why it is still necessary to wait before closing the connection.

22.16 Ordinarily, the Window field in the TCP header gives a credit allocation in octets. When the Window Scale option is in use, the value in the Window field is multiplied by a $2F$, where F is the value of the window scale option. The maximum value of F that TCP accepts is 14. Why is the option limited to 14?

22.17 Suppose the round-trip time (RTT) between two hosts is 100 ms, and that both hosts use a TCP window of 32 Kbytes. What is the maximum throughput that can be achieved by means of TCP in this scenario?

22.18 Suppose two hosts are connected with each other by means of a 100-Mbps link, and assume the round-trip time between them is 1 ms. What is the minimum TCP window size that would let TCP achieve the maximum possible throughput between these two hosts? (*Note:* Assume no overhead.)

22.19 A host is receiving data from a remote peer by means of TCP segments with a payload of 1460 bytes. If TCP acknowledges every other segment, what is the minimum uplink bandwidth needed to achieve a data throughput of 1 Mbytes per second, assuming there is no overhead below the network layer? (*Note:* Assume no options are used by TCP and IP.)

22.20 Analyze the advantages and disadvantages of performing congestion control at the transport layer, rather than at the network layer.

22.21 Jacobson's congestion control algorithm assumes most packet losses are caused by routers dropping packets due to network congestion. However, packets may be also dropped if they are corrupted in their path to destination. Analyze the performance of TCP in such a lossy environment, due to Jacobson's congestion control algorithm.

22.22 One difficulty with the original TCP SRTT estimator is the choice of an initial value. In the absence of any special knowledge of network conditions, the typical approach is to pick an arbitrary value, such as 3 s, and hope that this will converge quickly to an accurate value. If this estimate is too small, TCP will perform unnecessary retransmissions. If it is too large, TCP will wait a long time before retransmitting if the first segment is lost. Also, the convergence may be slow, as this problem indicates.
  a. Choose $\alpha = 0.85$ and $SRTT(0) = 3$ s, and assume all measured RTT values $= 1$ s and no packet loss. What is $SRTT(19)$? *Hint:* Equation (22.3) can be rewritten to simplify the calculation, using the expression $(1 - \alpha^n)/(1 - \alpha)$.
  b. Now let $SRTT(0) = 1$ s and assume measured RTT values $= 3$ s and no packet loss. What is $SRTT(19)$?

22.23 A poor implementation of TCP's sliding-window scheme can lead to extremely poor performance. There is a phenomenon known as the Silly Window Syndrome (SWS), which can easily cause degradation in performance by several factors of 10. As an example of SWS, consider an application that is engaged in a lengthy file transfer, and that TCP is transferring this file in 200-octet segments. The receiver initially provides a credit of 1000. The sender uses up this window with 5 segments of 200 octets. Now suppose that the receiver returns an acknowledgment to each segment and provides an additional credit of 200 octets for every received segment. From the receiver's point of view, this opens the window back up to 1000 octets. However, from the sender's point of view, if the first acknowledgment arrives after five segments have been sent, a window of only 200 octets becomes available. Assume that at some point, the sender calculates a window of 200 octets but has only 50 octets to send until it reaches a "push" point. It therefore sends 50 octets in one segment, followed by 150 octets in the next segment, and then resumes transmission of 200-octet segments. What might now happen to cause a performance problem? State the SWS in more general terms.

22.24 TCP mandates that both the receiver and the sender should incorporate mechanisms to cope with SWS.
  a. Suggest a strategy for the receiver. *Hint:* Let the receiver "lie" about how much buffer space is available under certain circumstances. State a reasonable rule of thumb for this.
  b. Suggest a strategy for the sender. *Hint:* Consider the relationship between the maximum possible send window and what is currently available to send.

22.25 Derive Equation (22.2) from Equation (22.1).

22.26 In Equation (22.5), rewrite the definition of $SRTT(K + 1)$ so that it is a function of $SERR(K + 1)$. Interpret the result.

22.27 A TCP entity opens a connection and uses slow start. Approximately how many round-trip times are required before TCP can send N segments.

22.28 Although slow start with congestion avoidance is an effective technique for coping with congestion, it can result in long recovery times in high-speed networks, as this problem demonstrates.

    a. Assume a round-trip time of 60 ms (about what might occur across a continent) and a link with an available bandwidth of 1 Gbps and a segment size of 576 octets. Determine the window size needed to keep the pipe full and the time it will take to reach that window size after a timeout using Jacobson's approach.

    b. Repeat (a) for a segment size of 16 Kbytes.

COMPUTER AND NETWORK SECURITY THREATS

The art of war teaches us to rely not on the likelihood of the enemy's not coming, but on our own readiness to receive him; not on the chance of his not attacking, but rather on the fact that we have made our position unassailable.

— *The Art of War,* Sun Tzu

KEY POINTS

◆ **Security attacks** are classified as either passive attacks, which include unauthorized reading of a message of file and traffic analysis, or active attacks, such as modification of messages or files, and denial of service.

◆ Unauthorized intrusion into a computer system or network is one of the most serious threats to computer security.

◆ Malicious software is a software that is intentionally included or inserted in a system for a harmful purpose.

◆ A virus is a piece of software that can "infect" other programs by modifying them; the modification includes a copy of the virus program, which can then go on to infect other programs.

◆ A worm is a program that can replicate itself and send copies from computer to computer across network connections. Upon arrival, the worm may be activated to replicate and propagate again. In addition to propagation, the worm usually performs some unwanted functions.

This chapter provides an overview of security threats. We begin with a discussion of what we mean by computer security. In essence, computer security deals with computer-related assets that are subject to a variety of threats and for which various measures are taken to protect those assets. The remainder of the chapter looks at the two broad categories of computer and network security threats: intruders and malicious software.

Cryptographic algorithms, such as encryption and hash functions, play a role both in computer security threats and computer security techniques. Appendix Q provides an overview of encryption.

23.1 COMPUTER SECURITY CONCEPTS

The NIST *Computer Security Handbook* [NIST95] defines the term *computer security* as follows:

> **Computer Security:** The protection afforded to an automated information system in order to attain the applicable objectives of preserving the integrity, availability, and confidentiality of information system resources (includes hardware, software, firmware, information/data, and telecommunications).

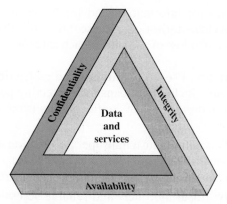

Figure 23.1 The Security Requirements Triad

This definition introduces three key objectives that are at the heart of computer security:

- **Confidentiality:** This term covers two related concepts:
  - **Data[1] confidentiality:** Assures that private or confidential information is not made available or disclosed to unauthorized individuals
  - **Privacy:** Assures that individuals control or influence what information related to them may be collected and stored and by whom and to whom that information may be disclosed
- **Integrity:** This term covers two related concepts:
  - **Data integrity:** Assures that information and programs are changed only in a specified and authorized manner
  - **System integrity:** Assures that a system performs its intended function in an unimpaired manner, free from deliberate or inadvertent unauthorized manipulation of the system
- **Availability:** Assures that systems work promptly and service is not denied to authorized users

These three concepts form what is often referred to as the **CIA triad** (Figure 23.1). The three concepts embody the fundamental security objectives for both data and for information and computing services. For example, the NIST standard FIPS 199 (*Standards for Security Categorization of Federal Information and Information Systems*) lists confidentiality, integrity, and availability as the three

---

[1]RFC 2828 (*Internet Security Glossary*) defines *information* as "facts and ideas, which can be represented (encoded) as various forms of data," and *data* as "information in a specific physical representation, usually a sequence of symbols that have meaning; especially a representation of information that can be processed or produced by a computer." Security literature typically does not make much of a distinction; nor does this chapter.

security objectives for information and for information systems. FIPS PUB 199 provides a useful characterization of these three objectives in terms of requirements and the definition of a loss of security in each category:

- **Confidentiality:** Preserving authorized restrictions on information access and disclosure, including means for protecting personal privacy and proprietary information. A loss of confidentiality is the unauthorized disclosure of information.

- **Integrity:** Guarding against improper information modification or destruction, including ensuring information nonrepudiation and authenticity. A loss of integrity is the unauthorized modification or destruction of information.

- **Availability:** Ensuring timely and reliable access to and use of information. A loss of availability is the disruption of access to or use of information or an information system.

Although the use of the CIA triad to define security objectives is well established, some in the security field feel that additional concepts are needed to present a complete picture. Two of the most commonly mentioned are as follows:

- **Authenticity:** The property of being genuine and being able to be verified and trusted; confidence in the validity of a transmission, a message, or message originator. This means verifying that users are who they say they are and that each input arriving at the system came from a trusted source.

- **Accountability:** The security goal that generates the requirement for actions of an entity to be traced uniquely to that entity. This supports nonrepudiation, deterrence, fault isolation, intrusion detection and prevention, and after-action recovery and legal action. Because truly secure systems aren't yet an achievable goal, we must be able to trace a security breach to a responsible party. Systems must keep records of their activities to permit later forensic analysis to trace security breaches or to aid in transaction disputes.

Note that FIPS PUB 199 includes authenticity under integrity.

23.2 THREATS, ATTACKS, AND ASSETS

We turn now to a look at threats, attacks, and assets as related to computer security.

Threats and Attacks

Table 23.1, based on RFC 2828, describes four kinds of threat consequences and lists the kinds of attacks that result in each consequence.

Unauthorized disclosure is a threat to confidentiality. The following types of attacks can result in this threat consequence:

- **Exposure:** This can be deliberate, as when an insider intentionally releases sensitive information, such as credit card numbers, to an outsider. It can also be the result of a human, hardware, or software error, which results in an entity

Table 23.1 Threat Consequences, and the Types of Threat Actions That Cause Each Consequence (based on RFC 2828)

Threat Consequence	Threat Action (attack)
Unauthorized Disclosure A circumstance or event whereby an entity gains access to data for which the entity is not authorized.	**Exposure:** Sensitive data are directly released to an unauthorized entity. **Interception:** An unauthorized entity directly accesses sensitive data traveling between authorized sources and destinations. **Inference:** A threat action whereby an unauthorized entity indirectly accesses sensitive data (but not necessarily the data contained in the communication) by reasoning from characteristics or byproducts of communications. **Intrusion:** An unauthorized entity gains access to sensitive data by circumventing a system's security protections.
Deception A circumstance or event that may result in an authorized entity receiving false data and believing it to be true.	**Masquerade:** An unauthorized entity gains access to a system or performs a malicious act by posing as an authorized entity. **Falsification:** False data deceive an authorized entity. **Repudiation:** An entity deceives another by falsely denying responsibility for an act.
Disruption A circumstance or event that interrupts or prevents the correct operation of system services and functions.	**Incapacitation:** Prevents or interrupts system operation by disabling a system component. **Corruption:** Undesirably alters system operation by adversely modifying system functions or data. **Obstruction:** A threat action that interrupts delivery of system services by hindering system operation.
Usurpation A circumstance or event that results in control of system services or functions by an unauthorized entity.	**Misappropriation:** An entity assumes unauthorized logical or physical control of a system resource. **Misuse:** Causes a system component to perform a function or service that is detrimental to system security.

gaining unauthorized knowledge of sensitive data. There have been numerous instances of this, such as universities accidentally posting student confidential information on the Web.

- **Interception:** Interception is a common attack in the context of communications. On a shared local area network (LAN), such as a wireless LAN or a broadcast Ethernet, any device attached to the LAN can receive a copy of packets intended for another device. On the Internet, a determined hacker can gain access to e-mail traffic and other data transfers. All of these situations create the potential for unauthorized access to data.

- **Inference:** An example of inference is traffic analysis, in which an adversary is able to gain information from observing the pattern of traffic on a network, such as the amount of traffic between particular pairs of hosts on the network. Another example is the inference of detailed information from a database by a user who has only limited access; this is accomplished by repeated queries whose combined results enable inference.

- **Intrusion:** An example of intrusion is an adversary gaining unauthorized access to sensitive data by overcoming the system's access control protections.

Deception is a threat to either system integrity or data integrity. The following types of attacks can result in this threat consequence:

- **Masquerade:** One example of masquerade is an attempt by an unauthorized user to gain access to a system by posing as an authorized user; this could happen if the unauthorized user has learned another user's logon ID and password. Another example is malicious logic, such as a Trojan horse, that appears to perform a useful or desirable function but actually gains unauthorized access to system resources or tricks a user into executing other malicious logic.
- **Falsification:** This refers to the altering or replacing of valid data or the introduction of false data into a file or database. For example, a student may alter his or her grades on a school database.
- **Repudiation:** In this case, a user either denies sending data or a user denies receiving or possessing the data.

Disruption is a threat to availability or system integrity. The following types of attacks can result in this threat consequence:

- **Incapacitation:** This is an attack on system availability. This could occur as a result of physical destruction of or damage to system hardware. More typically, malicious software, such as Trojan horses, viruses, or worms, could operate in such a way as to disable a system or some of its services.
- **Corruption:** This is an attack on system integrity. Malicious software in this context could operate in such a way that system resources or services function in an unintended manner. Or a user could gain unauthorized access to a system and modify some of its functions. An example of the latter is a user placing backdoor logic in the system to provide subsequent access to a system and its resources by other than the usual procedure.
- **Obstruction:** One way to obstruct system operation is to interfere with communications by disabling communication links or altering communication control information. Another way is to overload the system by placing excess burden on communication traffic or processing resources.

Usurpation is a threat to system integrity. The following types of attacks can result in this threat consequence:

- **Misappropriation:** This can include theft of service. An example is a distributed denial of service attack, when malicious software is installed on a number of hosts to be used as platforms to launch traffic at a target host. In this case, the malicious software makes unauthorized use of processor and operating system resources.
- **Misuse:** Misuse can occur either by means of malicious logic or a hacker that has gained unauthorized access to a system. In either case, security functions can be disabled or thwarted.

Threats and Assets

The assets of a computer system can be categorized as hardware, software, data, and communication lines and networks. In this subsection, we briefly describe these four categories and relate these to the concepts of integrity, confidentiality, and availability introduced in Section 23.1 (see Figure 23.2 and Table 23.2).

HARDWARE A major threat to computer system hardware is the threat to availability. Hardware is the most vulnerable to attack and the least susceptible to automated controls. Threats include accidental and deliberate damage to equipment as well as theft. The proliferation of personal computers and workstations and the widespread use of LANs increase the potential for losses in this area. Theft of CD-ROMs and DVDs can lead to loss of confidentiality. Physical and administrative security measures are needed to deal with these threats.

SOFTWARE Software includes the operating system, utilities, and application programs. A key threat to software is an attack on availability. Software, especially application software, is often easy to delete. Software can also be altered or damaged to render it useless. Careful software configuration management, which includes making backups of the most recent version of software, can maintain high availability. A more difficult problem to deal with is software modification that results in a program that still functions but that behaves differently than before, which is a threat to integrity and authenticity. Computer viruses and related attacks fall into this category. A final problem is protection against software piracy. Although certain countermeasures are available, by and large the problem of unauthorized copying of software has not been solved.

DATA Hardware and software security are typically concerns of computing center professionals or individual concerns of personal computer users. A much more widespread problem is data security, which involves files and other forms of data controlled by individuals, groups, and business organizations.

Security concerns with respect to data are broad, encompassing availability, secrecy, and integrity. In the case of availability, the concern is with the destruction of data files, which can occur either accidentally or maliciously.

The obvious concern with secrecy is the unauthorized reading of data files or databases, and this area has been the subject of perhaps more research and effort than any other area of computer security. A less obvious threat to secrecy involves the analysis of data and manifests itself in the use of so-called statistical databases, which provide summary or aggregate information. Presumably, the existence of aggregate information does not threaten the privacy of the individuals involved. However, as the use of statistical databases grows, there is an increasing potential for disclosure of personal information. In essence, characteristics of constituent individuals may be identified through careful analysis. For example, if one table records the aggregate of the incomes of respondents A, B, C, and D and another records the aggregate of the incomes of A, B, C, D, and E, the difference between the two aggregates would be the income of E. This problem is exacerbated by the increasing desire to combine data sets. In many cases, matching several sets of data for consistency at different levels of aggregation

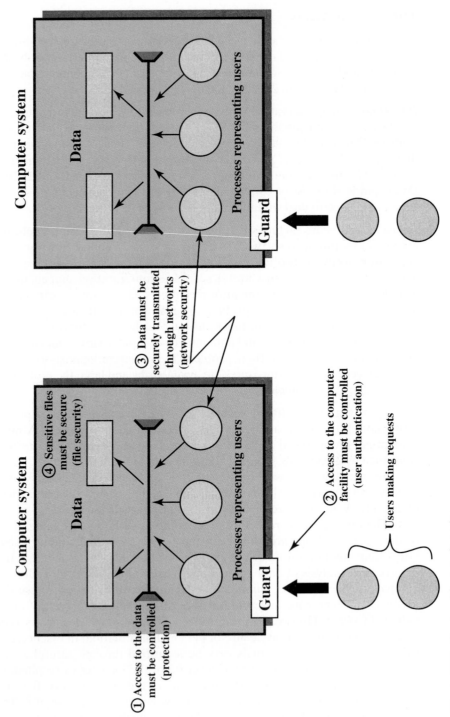

Figure 23.2 Scope of System Security

Table 23.2   Computer and Network Assets, with Examples of Threats

	Availability	Confidentiality	Integrity
Hardware	Equipment is stolen or disabled, thus denying service.		
Software	Programs are deleted, denying access to users.	An unauthorized copy of software is made.	A working program is modified, either to cause it to fail during execution or to cause it to do some unintended task.
Data	Files are deleted, denying access to users.	An unauthorized read of data is performed. An analysis of statistical data reveals underlying data.	Existing files are modified or new files are fabricated.
Communication Lines	Messages are destroyed or deleted. Communication lines or networks are rendered unavailable.	Messages are read. The traffic pattern of messages is observed.	Messages are modified, delayed, reordered, or duplicated. False messages are fabricated.

requires access to individual units. Thus, the individual units, which are the subject of privacy concerns, are available at various stages in the processing of data sets.

Finally, data integrity is a major concern in most installations. Modifications to data files can have consequences ranging from minor to disastrous.

COMMUNICATION LINES AND NETWORKS   Network security attacks can be classified as *passive attacks* and *active attacks*. A passive attack attempts to learn or make use of information from the system but does not affect system resources. An active attack attempts to alter system resources or affect their operation.

Passive attacks are in the nature of eavesdropping on, or monitoring of, transmissions. The goal of the attacker is to obtain information that is being transmitted. Two types of passive attacks are release of message contents and traffic analysis.

The **release of message contents** is easily understood. A telephone conversation, an electronic mail message, and a transferred file may contain sensitive or confidential information. We would like to prevent an opponent from learning the contents of these transmissions.

A second type of passive attack, **traffic analysis**, is subtler. Suppose that we had a way of masking the contents of messages or other information traffic so that opponents, even if they captured the message, could not extract the information from the message. The common technique for masking contents is encryption. If we had encryption protection in place, an opponent might still be able to observe the pattern of these messages. The opponent could determine the location and identity of communicating hosts and could observe the frequency and length of messages being exchanged. This information might be useful in guessing the nature of the communication that was taking place.

Passive attacks are very difficult to detect because they do not involve any alteration of the data. Typically, the message traffic is sent and received in an apparently normal fashion and neither the sender nor the receiver is aware that a third party has read the messages or observed the traffic pattern. However, it is feasible to prevent the success of these attacks, usually by means of encryption. Thus, the emphasis in dealing with passive attacks is on prevention rather than detection.

Active attacks involve some modification of the data stream or the creation of a false stream and can be subdivided into four categories: replay, masquerade, modification of messages, and denial of service.

Replay involves the passive capture of a data unit and its subsequent retransmission to produce an unauthorized effect.

A **masquerade** takes place when one entity pretends to be a different entity. A masquerade attack usually includes one of the other forms of active attack. For example, authentication sequences can be captured and replayed after a valid authentication sequence has taken place, thus enabling an authorized entity with few privileges to obtain extra privileges by impersonating an entity that has those privileges.

Modification of messages simply means that some portion of a legitimate message is altered, or that messages are delayed or reordered, to produce an unauthorized effect. For example, a message stating, "Allow John Smith to read confidential file accounts" is modified to say "Allow Fred Brown to read confidential file accounts."

The **denial of service** prevents or inhibits the normal use or management of communications facilities. This attack may have a specific target; for example, an entity may suppress all messages directed to a particular destination (e.g., the security audit service). Another form of service denial is the disruption of an entire network, either by disabling the network or by overloading it with messages so as to degrade performance.

Active attacks present the opposite characteristics of passive attacks. Whereas passive attacks are difficult to detect, measures are available to prevent their success. On the other hand, it is quite difficult to prevent active attacks absolutely, because to do so would require physical protection of all communications facilities and paths at all times. Instead, the goal is to detect them and to recover from any disruption or delays caused by them. Because the detection has a deterrent effect, it may also contribute to prevention.

23.3 INTRUDERS

One of the two most publicized threats to security is the intruder (the other is viruses), often referred to as a hacker or cracker. In an important early study of intrusion, Anderson [ANDE80] identified three classes of intruders:

- **Masquerader:** An individual who is not authorized to use the computer and who penetrates a system's access controls to exploit a legitimate user's account

- **Misfeasor:** A legitimate user who accesses data, programs, or resources for which such access is not authorized, or who is authorized for such access but misuses his or her privileges
- **Clandestine user:** An individual who seizes supervisory control of the system and uses this control to evade auditing and access controls or to suppress audit collection

The masquerader is likely to be an outsider; the misfeasor generally is an insider; and the clandestine user can be either an outsider or an insider.

Intruder attacks range from the benign to the serious. At the benign end of the scale, there are many people who simply wish to explore internets and see what is out there. At the serious end are individuals who are attempting to read privileged data, perform unauthorized modifications to data, or disrupt the system.

[GRAN04] lists the following examples of intrusion:

- Performing a remote root compromise of an e-mail server
- Defacing a Web server
- Guessing and cracking passwords
- Copying a database containing credit card numbers
- Viewing sensitive data, including payroll records and medical information, without authorization
- Running a packet sniffer on a workstation to capture usernames and passwords
- Using a permission error on an anonymous FTP server to distribute pirated software and music files
- Dialing into an unsecured modem and gaining internal network access
- Posing as an executive, calling the help desk, resetting the executive's e-mail password, and learning the new password
- Using an unattended, logged-in workstation without permission

Intruder Behavior Patterns

The techniques and behavior patterns of intruders are constantly shifting, to exploit newly discovered weaknesses and to evade detection and countermeasures. Even so, intruders typically follow one of a number of recognizable behavior patterns, and these patterns typically differ from those of ordinary users. In the following, we look at three broad examples of intruder behavior patterns to give the reader some feel for the challenge facing the security administrator. Table 23.3, based on [RADC04], summarizes the behavior.

HACKERS Traditionally, those who hack into computers do so for the thrill of it or for status. The hacking community is a strong meritocracy in which status is determined by level of competence. Thus, attackers often look for targets of opportunity and then share the information with others. A typical example is a break-in at a large financial institution reported in [RADC04]. The intruder took advantage of the fact that the corporate network was running unprotected services, some of which were not even needed. In this case, the key to the break-in was the

Table 23.3   Some Examples of Intruder Patterns of Behavior

(a) Hacker

1. Select the target using IP lookup tools such as NSLookup, Dig, and others.
2. Map network for accessible services using tools such as NMAP.
3. Identify potentially vulnerable services (in this case, pcAnywhere).
4. Brute force (guess) pcAnywhere password.
5. Install remote administration tool called DameWare.
6. Wait for administrator to log on and capture his password.
7. Use that password to access remainder of network.

(b) Criminal Enterprise

1. Act quickly and precisely to make their activities harder to detect.
2. Exploit perimeter through vulnerable ports.
3. Use Trojan horses (hidden software) to leave backdoors for reentry.
4. Use sniffers to capture passwords.
5. Do not stick around until noticed.
6. Make few or no mistakes.

(c) Internal Threat

1. Create network accounts for themselves and their friends.
2. Access accounts and applications they wouldn't normally use for their daily jobs.
3. E-mail former and prospective employers.
4. Conduct furtive instant-messaging chats.
5. Visit Web sites that cater to disgruntled employees, such as f'dcompany.com.
6. Perform large downloads and file copying.
7. Access the network during off hours.

pcAnywhere application. The manufacturer, Symantec, advertises this program as a remote control solution that enables secure connection to remote devices. But the attacker had an easy time gaining access to pcAnywhere; the administrator used the same three-letter username and password for the program. In this case, there was no intrusion detection system on the 700-node corporate network. The intruder was only discovered when a vice president walked into her office and saw the cursor moving files around on her Windows workstation.

Benign intruders might be tolerable, although they do consume resources and may slow performance for legitimate users. However, there is no way in advance to know whether an intruder will be benign or malign. Consequently, even for systems with no particularly sensitive resources, there is a motivation to control this problem.

Intrusion detection systems (IDSs) and intrusion prevention systems (IPSs), of the type described in Chapter 24, are designed to counter this type of hacker threat. In addition to using such systems, organizations can consider restricting remote logons to specific IP addresses and/or use virtual private network technology.

One of the results of the growing awareness of the intruder problem has been the establishment of a number of computer emergency response teams (CERTs).

These cooperative ventures collect information about system vulnerabilities and disseminate it to systems managers. Hackers also routinely read CERT reports. Thus, it is important for system administrators to quickly insert all software patches to discovered vulnerabilities. Unfortunately, given the complexity of many IT systems and the rate at which patches are released, this is increasingly difficult to achieve without automated updating. Even then, there are problems caused by incompatibilities resulting from the updated software (hence the need for multiple layers of defense in managing security threats to IT systems).

CRIMINALS Organized groups of hackers have become a widespread and common threat to Internet-based systems. These groups can be in the employ of a corporation or government but often are loosely affiliated gangs of hackers. Typically, these gangs are young, often Eastern European, Russian, or Southeast Asian hackers who do business on the Web [ANTE06]. They meet in underground forums with names like DarkMarket.org and theftservices.com to trade tips and data and coordinate attacks. A common target is a credit card file at an e-commerce server. Attackers attempt to gain root access. The card numbers are used by organized crime gangs to purchase expensive items and are then posted to carder sites, where others can access and use the account numbers; this obscures usage patterns and complicates investigation.

Whereas traditional hackers look for targets of opportunity, criminal hackers usually have specific targets, or at least classes of targets in mind. Once a site is penetrated, the attacker acts quickly, scooping up as much valuable information as possible and exiting.

IDSs and IPSs can also be used for these types of attackers but may be less effective because of the quick in-and-out nature of the attack. For e-commerce sites, database encryption should be used for sensitive customer information, especially credit cards. For hosted e-commerce sites (provided by an outsider service), the e-commerce organization should make use of a dedicated server (not used to support multiple customers) and closely monitor the provider's security services.

INSIDER ATTACKS Insider attacks are among the most difficult to detect and prevent. Employees already have access to and knowledge of the structure and content of corporate databases. Insider attacks can be motivated by revenge or simply a feeling of entitlement. An example of the former is the case of Kenneth Patterson, fired from his position as data communications manager for American Eagle Outfitters. Patterson disabled the company's ability to process credit card purchases during five days of the holiday season of 2002. As for a sense of entitlement, there have always been many employees who felt entitled to take extra office supplies for home use, but this now extends to corporate data. An example is that of a vice president of sales for a stock analysis firm who quit to go to a competitor. Before she left, she copied the customer database to take with her. The offender reported feeling no animus toward her former employee; she simply wanted the data because it would be useful to her.

Although IDS and IPS facilities can be useful in countering insider attacks, other more direct approaches are of higher priority. Examples include the following:

- Enforce least privilege, only allowing access to the resources employees need to do their job.
- Set logs to see what users access and what commands they are entering.

- Protect sensitive resources with strong authentication.
- Upon termination, delete employee's computer and network access.
- Upon termination, make a mirror image of employee's hard drive before reissuing it. That evidence might be needed if your company information turns up at a competitor.

Intrusion Techniques

The objective of the intruder is to gain access to a system or to increase the range of privileges accessible on a system. Most initial attacks use system or software vulnerabilities that allow a user to execute code that opens a back door into the system. Intruders can get access to a system by exploiting attacks such as buffer overflows on a program that runs with certain privileges.

Alternatively, the intruder attempts to acquire information that should have been protected. In some cases, this information is in the form of a user password. With knowledge of some other user's password, an intruder can log in to a system and exercise all the privileges accorded to the legitimate user.

23.4 MALICIOUS SOFTWARE OVERVIEW

Perhaps the most sophisticated types of threats to computer systems are presented by programs that exploit vulnerabilities in computing systems. Such threats are referred to as **malicious software**, or **malware**. In this context, we are concerned with application programs as well as utility programs, such as editors and compilers. Malware is software designed to cause damage to or use up the resources of a target computer. It is frequently concealed within or masquerades as legitimate software. In some cases, it spreads itself to other computers via e-mail or infected floppy disks.

The terminology in this area presents problems because of a lack of universal agreement on all of the terms and because some of the categories overlap. Table 23.4 is a useful guide.

Malicious software can be divided into two categories: those that need a host program and those that are independent. The former, referred to as **parasitic**, are essentially fragments of programs that cannot exist independently of some actual application program, utility, or system program. Viruses, logic bombs, and backdoors are examples. The latter are self-contained programs that can be scheduled and run by the operating system. Worms and bot programs are examples.

We can also differentiate between those software threats that do not replicate and those that do. The former are programs or fragments of programs that are activated by a trigger. Examples are logic bombs, backdoors, and bot programs. The latter consist of either a program fragment or an independent program that, when executed, may produce one or more copies of itself to be activated later on the same system or some other system. Viruses and worms are examples.

In the remainder of this section, we briefly survey some of the key categories of malicious software, deferring discussion on the key topics of viruses, worms, and bots until the following section.

Table 23.4 Terminology of Malicious Programs

Name	Description
Virus	Malware that, when executed, tries to replicate itself into other executable code; when it succeeds the code is said to be infected. When the infected code is executed, the virus also executes.
Worm	A computer program that can run independently and can propagate a complete working version of itself onto other hosts on a network.
Logic bomb	A program inserted into software by an intruder. A logic bomb lies dormant until a predefined condition is met; the program then triggers an unauthorized act.
Trojan horse	A computer program that appears to have a useful function, but also has a hidden and potentially malicious function that evades security mechanisms, sometimes by exploiting legitimate authorizations of a system entity that invokes the Trojan horse program.
Backdoor (trapdoor)	Any mechanism that bypasses a normal security check; it may allow unauthorized access to functionality.
Mobile code	Software (e.g., script, macro, or other portable instruction) that can be shipped unchanged to a heterogeneous collection of platforms and execute with identical semantics.
Exploits	Code specific to a single vulnerability or set of vulnerabilities.
Downloaders	Program that installs other items on a machine that is under attack. Usually, a downloader is sent in an e-mail.
Auto-rooter	Malicious hacker tools used to break into new machines remotely.
Kit (virus generator)	Set of tools for generating new viruses automatically.
Spammer programs	Used to send large volumes of unwanted e-mail.
Flooders	Used to attack networked computer systems with a large volume of traffic to carry out a denial-of-service (DoS) attack.
Keyloggers	Captures keystrokes on a compromised system.
Rootkit	Set of hacker tools used after attacker has broken into a computer system and gained root-level access.
Zombie, bot	Program activated on an infected machine that is activated to launch attacks on other machines.
Spyware	Software that collects information from a computer and transmits it to another system.
Adware	Advertising that is integrated into software. It can result in pop-up ads or redirection of a browser to a commercial site.

Backdoor

A **backdoor**, also known as a **trapdoor**, is a secret entry point into a program that allows someone who is aware of the backdoor to gain access without going through the usual security access procedures. Programmers have used backdoors legitimately for many years to debug and test programs; such a backdoor is called a **maintenance hook**. This is usually done when the programmer is developing an application that has an authentication procedure, or a long setup, requiring the user to enter many different values to run the application. To debug the program, the developer may wish to gain special privileges or to avoid all the necessary setup and authentication. The programmer may also want to ensure that there is a method of activating the program should something be wrong with the authentication procedure that is being built into the application. The backdoor is code that recognizes some special sequence of input or is triggered by being run from a certain user ID or by an unlikely sequence of events.

Backdoors become threats when unscrupulous programmers use them to gain unauthorized access. The backdoor was the basic idea for the vulnerability portrayed in the movie *War Games*. Another example is that during the development of Multics, penetration tests were conducted by an Air Force "tiger team" (simulating adversaries). One tactic employed was to send a bogus operating system update to a site running Multics. The update contained a Trojan horse (described later) that could be activated by a backdoor and that allowed the tiger team to gain access. The threat was so well implemented that the Multics developers could not find it, even after they were informed of its presence [ENGE80].

It is difficult to implement operating system controls for backdoors. Security measures must focus on the program development and software update activities.

Logic Bomb

One of the oldest types of program threat, predating viruses and worms, is the logic bomb. The logic bomb is code embedded in some legitimate program that is set to "explode" when certain conditions are met. Examples of conditions that can be used as triggers for a logic bomb are the presence or absence of certain files, a particular day of the week or date, or a particular user running the application. Once triggered, a bomb may alter or delete data or entire files, cause a machine halt, or do some other damage. A striking example of how logic bombs can be employed was the case of Tim Lloyd, who was convicted of setting a logic bomb that cost his employer, Omega Engineering, more than $10 million, derailed its corporate growth strategy, and eventually led to the layoff of 80 workers [GAUD00]. Ultimately, Lloyd was sentenced to 41 months in prison and ordered to pay $2 million in restitution.

Trojan Horse

A Trojan horse is a useful, or apparently useful, program or command procedure containing hidden code that, when invoked, performs some unwanted or harmful function.

Trojan horse programs can be used to accomplish functions indirectly that an unauthorized user could not accomplish directly. For example, to gain access to the files of another user on a shared system, a user could create a Trojan horse program that, when executed, changes the invoking user's file permissions so that the files are readable by any user. The author could then induce users to run the program by placing it in a common directory and naming it such that it appears to be a useful utility program or application. An example is a program that ostensibly produces a listing of the user's files in a desirable format. After another user has run the program, the author of the program can then access the information in the user's files. An example of a Trojan horse program that would be difficult to detect is a compiler that has been modified to insert additional code into certain programs as they are compiled, such as a system login program [THOM84]. The code creates a backdoor in the login program that permits the author to log on to the system using a special password. This Trojan horse can never be discovered by reading the source code of the login program.

Another common motivation for the Trojan horse is data destruction. The program appears to be performing a useful function (e.g., a calculator program), but it may also be quietly deleting the user's files. For example, a CBS executive was victimized by a Trojan horse that destroyed all information contained in his computer's memory [TIME90]. The Trojan horse was implanted in a graphics routine offered on an electronic bulletin board system.

Trojan horses fit into one of three models:

- Continuing to perform the function of the original program and additionally performing a separate malicious activity
- Continuing to perform the function of the original program but modifying the function to perform malicious activity (e.g., a Trojan horse version of a login program that collects passwords) or to disguise other malicious activity (e.g., a Trojan horse version of a process listing program that does not display certain processes that are malicious)
- Performing a malicious function that completely replaces the function of the original program

Mobile Code

Mobile code refers to programs (e.g., script, macro, or other portable instruction) that can be shipped unchanged to a heterogeneous collection of platforms and execute with identical semantics [JANS01]. The term also applies to situations involving a large homogeneous collection of platforms (e.g., Microsoft Windows).

Mobile code is transmitted from a remote system to a local system and then executed on the local system without the user's explicit instruction. Mobile code often acts as a mechanism for a virus, worm, or Trojan horse to be transmitted to the user's workstation. In other cases, mobile code takes advantage of vulnerabilities to perform its own exploits, such as unauthorized data access or root compromise. Popular vehicles for mobile code include Java applets, ActiveX, JavaScript, and VBScript. The most common ways of using mobile code for malicious operations on local system are cross-site scripting, interactive and dynamic Web sites, e-mail attachments, and downloads from untrusted sites or of untrusted software.

Multiple-Threat Malware

Viruses and other malware may operate in multiple ways. The terminology is far from uniform; this subsection gives a brief introduction to several related concepts that could be considered multiple-threat malware.

A **multipartite** virus infects in multiple ways. Typically, the multipartite virus is capable of infecting multiple types of files, so that virus eradication must deal with all of the possible sites of infection.

A **blended attack** uses multiple methods of infection or transmission, to maximize the speed of contagion and the severity of the attack. Some writers characterize a blended attack as a package that includes multiple types of malware. An example of a blended attack is the Nimda attack, erroneously referred to as simply a worm. Nimda uses four distribution methods:

- **E-mail:** A user on a vulnerable host opens an infected e-mail attachment; Nimda looks for e-mail addresses on the host and then sends copies of itself to those addresses.

- **Windows shares:** Nimda scans hosts for unsecured Windows file shares; it can then use NetBIOS86 as a transport mechanism to infect files on that host in the hopes that a user will run an infected file, which will activate Nimda on that host.

- **Web servers:** Nimda scans Web servers, looking for known vulnerabilities in Microsoft IIS. If it finds a vulnerable server, it attempts to transfer a copy of itself to the server and infect it and its files.

- **Web clients:** If a vulnerable Web client visits a Web server that has been infected by Nimda, the client's workstation will become infected.

Thus, Nimda has worm, virus, and mobile code characteristics. Blended attacks may also spread through other services, such as instant messaging and peer-to-peer file sharing.

23.5 VIRUSES, WORMS, AND BOTS

Viruses

A computer virus is a piece of software that can "infect" other programs by modifying them; the modification includes injecting the original program with a routine to make copies of the virus program, which can then go on to infect other programs.

Biological viruses are tiny scraps of genetic code—DNA or RNA—that can take over the machinery of a living cell and trick it into making thousands of flawless replicas of the original virus. Like its biological counterpart, a computer virus carries in its instructional code the recipe for making perfect copies of itself. The typical virus becomes embedded in a program on a computer. Then, whenever the infected computer comes into contact with an uninfected piece of software, a fresh copy of the virus passes into the new program. Thus, the infection can be spread from computer to computer by unsuspecting users who either swap disks or send programs to one another over a network. In a network environment, the ability to access applications and system services on other computers provides a perfect culture for the spread of a virus.

THE NATURE OF VIRUSES A virus can do anything that other programs do. The only difference is that it attaches itself to another program and executes secretly when the host program is run. Once a virus is executing, it can perform any function that is allowed by the privileges of the current user, such as erasing files and programs.

A computer virus has three parts [AYCO06]:

- **Infection mechanism:** The means by which a virus spreads, enabling it to replicate. The mechanism is also referred to as the **infection vector**.
- **Trigger:** The event or condition that determines when the payload is activated or delivered.
- **Payload:** What the virus does, besides spreading. The payload may involve damage or may involve benign but noticeable activity.

During its lifetime, a typical virus goes through the following four phases:

- **Dormant phase:** The virus is idle. The virus will eventually be activated by some event, such as a date, the presence of another program or file, or the capacity of the disk exceeding some limit. Not all viruses have this stage.
- **Propagation phase:** The virus places an identical copy of itself into other programs or into certain system areas on the disk. Each infected program will now contain a clone of the virus, which will itself enter a propagation phase.
- **Triggering phase:** The virus is activated to perform the function for which it was intended. As with the dormant phase, the triggering phase can be caused by a variety of system events, including a count of the number of times that this copy of the virus has made copies of itself.
- **Execution phase:** The function is performed. The function may be harmless, such as a message on the screen, or damaging, such as the destruction of programs and data files.

Most viruses carry out their work in a manner that is specific to a particular operating system and, in some cases, specific to a particular hardware platform. Thus, they are designed to take advantage of the details and weaknesses of particular systems.

VIRUS STRUCTURE A virus can be prepended or postpended to an executable program, or it can be embedded in some other fashion. The key to its operation is that the infected program, when invoked, will first execute the virus code and then execute the original code of the program.

A very general depiction of virus structure is shown in Figure 23.3 (based on [COHE94]). In this case, the virus code, V, is prepended to infected programs, and it is assumed that the entry point to the program, when invoked, is the first line of the program.

The infected program begins with the virus code and works as follows. The first line of code is a jump to the main virus program. The second line is a special marker that is used by the virus to determine whether or not a potential victim program has already been infected with this virus. When the program is invoked, control is immediately transferred to the main virus program. The virus program may first seek out uninfected executable files and infect them. Next, the virus may perform some action, usually detrimental to the system. This action could be performed every time

```
        program V :=

{goto main;
    1234567;

    subroutine infect-executable :=
        {loop:
        file := get-random-executable-file;
        if (first-line-of-file = 1234567)
            then goto loop
            else prepend V to file; }

    subroutine do-damage :=
        {whatever damage is to be done}

    subroutine trigger-pulled :=
        {return true if some condition holds}

main:  main-program :=
        {infrect-executable;
        if trigger-pulled then do-damage;
        goto next;}

next:

}
```

Figure 23.3   A Simple Virus

the program is invoked, or it could be a logic bomb that triggers only under certain conditions. Finally, the virus transfers control to the original program. If the infection phase of the program is reasonably rapid, a user is unlikely to notice any difference between the execution of an infected and an uninfected program.

A virus such as the one just described is easily detected because an infected version of a program is longer than the corresponding uninfected one. A way to thwart such a simple means of detecting a virus is to compress the executable file so that both the infected and uninfected versions are of identical length. Figure 23.4 [COHE94] shows in general terms the logic required. The important lines in this virus are numbered. We assume that program P_1 is infected with the virus CV. When this program is invoked, control passes to its virus, which performs the following steps:

1. For each uninfected file P_2 that is found, the virus first compresses that file to produce P'_2, which is shorter than the original program by the size of the virus.

2. A copy of the virus is prepended to the compressed program.

3. The compressed version of the original infected program, P'_1, is uncompressed.

4. The uncompressed original program is executed.

In this example, the virus does nothing other than propagate. As previously mentioned, the virus may include a logic bomb.

```
    program CV :=

{goto main;
    01234567;

    subroutine infect-executable :=
            {loop:
                file := get-random-executable-file;
            if (first-line-of-file = 1234567) then goto loop;
        (1)    compress file;
        (2)    prepend CV to file;
        }

main:   main-program :=
            {if ask-permission then infect-executable;
        (3)    uncompress rest-of-file;
        (4)    run uncompared file;
        }
```

Figure 23.4   Logic for a Compression Virus

INITIAL INFECTION Once a virus has gained entry to a system by infecting a single program, it is in a position to potentially infect some or all other executable files on that system when the infected program executes. Thus, viral infection can be completely prevented by preventing the virus from gaining entry in the first place. Unfortunately, prevention is extraordinarily difficult because a virus can be part of any program outside a system. Thus, unless one is content to take an absolutely bare piece of iron and write all one's own system and application programs, one is vulnerable. Many forms of infection can also be blocked by denying normal users the right to modify programs on the system.

The lack of access controls on early PCs is a key reason why traditional machine code based viruses spread rapidly on these systems. In contrast, while it is easy enough to write a machine code virus for UNIX systems, they were almost never seen in practice because the existence of access controls on these systems prevented effective propagation of the virus. Traditional machine code based viruses are now less prevalent, because modern PC operating systems have more effective access controls. However, virus creators have found other avenues, such as macro and e-mail viruses, as discussed subsequently.

VIRUSES CLASSIFICATION There has been a continuous arms race between virus writers and writers of antivirus software since viruses first appeared. As effective countermeasures are developed for existing types of viruses, newer types are developed. There is no simple or universally agreed upon classification scheme for viruses. In this section, we follow [AYCO06] and classify viruses along two orthogonal axes: the type of target the virus tries to infect and the method the virus uses to conceal itself from detection by users and antivirus software.

A virus **classification by target** includes the following categories:

- **Boot sector infector:** Infects a master boot record or boot record and spreads when a system is booted from the disk containing the virus
- **File infector:** Infects files that the operating system or shell consider to be executable
- **Macro virus:** Infects files with macro code that is interpreted by an application

A virus classification by concealment strategy includes the following categories:

- **Encrypted virus:** A typical approach is as follows: A portion of the virus creates a random encryption key and encrypts the remainder of the virus. The key is stored with the virus. When an infected program is invoked, the virus uses the stored random key to decrypt the virus. When the virus replicates, a different random key is selected. Because the bulk of the virus is encrypted with a different key for each instance, there is no constant bit pattern to observe.
- **Stealth virus:** A form of virus explicitly designed to hide itself from detection by antivirus software. Thus, the entire virus, not just a payload is hidden.
- **Polymorphic virus:** A virus that mutates with every infection, making detection by the "signature" of the virus impossible.
- **Metamorphic virus:** As with a polymorphic virus, a metamorphic virus mutates with every infection. The difference is that a metamorphic virus rewrites itself completely at each iteration, increasing the difficulty of detection. Metamorphic viruses may change their behavior as well as their appearance.

One example of a **stealth virus** was discussed earlier: a virus that uses compression so that the infected program is exactly the same length as an uninfected version. Far more sophisticated techniques are possible. For example, a virus can place intercept logic in disk I/O routines, so that when there is an attempt to read suspected portions of the disk using these routines, the virus will present back the original, uninfected program. Thus, *stealth* is not a term that applies to a virus as such but, rather, refers to a technique used by a virus to evade detection.

A **polymorphic virus** creates copies during replication that are functionally equivalent but have distinctly different bit patterns. As with a stealth virus, the purpose is to defeat programs that scan for viruses. In this case, the "signature" of the virus will vary with each copy. To achieve this variation, the virus may randomly insert superfluous instructions or interchange the order of independent instructions. A more effective approach is to use encryption. The strategy of the encryption virus is followed. The portion of the virus that is responsible for generating keys and performing encryption/decryption is referred to as the *mutation engine*. The mutation engine itself is altered with each use.

VIRUS KITS Another weapon in the virus writers' armory is the virus-creation toolkit. Such a toolkit enables a relative novice to quickly create a number of different viruses. Although viruses created with toolkits tend to be less sophisticated than viruses designed from scratch, the sheer number of new viruses that can be generated using a toolkit creates a problem for antivirus schemes.

MACRO VIRUSES In the mid-1990s, macro viruses became by far the most prevalent type of virus. Macro viruses are particularly threatening for a number of reasons:

1. A macro virus is platform independent. Many macro viruses infect Microsoft Word documents or other Microsoft Office documents. Any hardware platform and operating system that supports these applications can be infected.
2. Macro viruses infect documents, not executable portions of code. Most of the information introduced onto a computer system is in the form of a document rather than a program.
3. Macro viruses are easily spread. A very common method is by electronic mail.
4. Because macro viruses infect user documents rather than system programs, traditional file system access controls are of limited use in preventing their spread.

Macro viruses take advantage of a feature found in Word and other office applications such as Microsoft Excel—namely, the macro. In essence, a macro is an executable program embedded in a word processing document or other type of file. Typically, users employ macros to automate repetitive tasks and thereby save keystrokes. The macro language is usually some form of the Basic programming language. A user might define a sequence of keystrokes in a macro and set it up so that the macro is invoked when a function key or special short combination of keys is input.

Successive releases of MS Office products provide increased protection against macro viruses. For example, Microsoft offers an optional Macro Virus Protection tool that detects suspicious Word files and alerts the customer to the potential risk of opening a file with macros. Various antivirus product vendors have also developed tools to detect and correct macro viruses. As in other types of viruses, the arms race continues in the field of macro viruses, but they no longer are the predominant virus threat.

E-MAIL VIRUSES A more recent development in malicious software is the e-mail virus. The first rapidly spreading e-mail viruses, such as Melissa, made use of a Microsoft Word macro embedded in an attachment. If the recipient opens the e-mail attachment, the Word macro is activated. Then

1. The e-mail virus sends itself to everyone on the mailing list in the user's e-mail package.
2. The virus does local damage on the user's system.

In 1999, a more powerful version of the e-mail virus appeared. This newer version can be activated merely by opening an e-mail that contains the virus rather than opening an attachment. The virus uses the Visual Basic scripting language supported by the e-mail package.

Thus we see a new generation of malware that arrives via e-mail and uses e-mail software features to replicate itself across the Internet. The virus propagates itself as soon as it is activated (either by opening an e-mail attachment or by opening the e-mail) to all of the e-mail addresses known to the infected host. As a result, whereas viruses used to take months or years to propagate, they now do so in hours. This makes it very difficult for antivirus software to respond before much damage is done. Ultimately, a greater degree of security must be built into Internet utility and application software on PCs to counter the growing threat.

Worms

A worm is a program that can replicate itself and send copies from computer to computer across network connections. Upon arrival, the worm may be activated to replicate and propagate again. In addition to propagation, the worm usually performs some unwanted function. An e-mail virus has some of the characteristics of a worm because it propagates itself from system to system. However, we can still classify it as a virus because it uses a document modified to contain viral macro content and requires human action. A worm actively seeks out more machines to infect and each machine that is infected serves as an automated launching pad for attacks on other machines.

Network worm programs use network connections to spread from system to system. Once active within a system, a network worm can behave as a computer virus or bacteria, or it could implant Trojan horse programs or perform any number of disruptive or destructive actions.

To replicate itself, a network worm uses some sort of network vehicle. Examples include the following:

- **Electronic mail facility:** A worm mails a copy of itself to other systems, so that its code is run when the e-mail or an attachment is received or viewed.
- **Remote execution capability:** A worm executes a copy of itself on another system, either using an explicit remote execution facility or by exploiting a program flaw in a network service to subvert its operations.
- **Remote login capability:** A worm logs onto a remote system as a user and then uses commands to copy itself from one system to the other, where it then executes.

The new copy of the worm program is then run on the remote system, where, in addition to any functions that it performs at that system, it continues to spread in the same fashion.

A network worm exhibits the same characteristics as a computer virus: a dormant phase, a propagation phase, a triggering phase, and an execution phase. The propagation phase generally performs the following functions:

1. Search for other systems to infect by examining host tables or similar repositories of remote system addresses.
2. Establish a connection with a remote system.
3. Copy itself to the remote system and cause the copy to be run.

The network worm may also attempt to determine whether a system has previously been infected before copying itself to the system. In a multiprogramming system, it may also disguise its presence by naming itself as a system process or using some other name that may not be noticed by a system operator.

As with viruses, network worms are difficult to counter.

WORM PROPAGATION MODEL [ZOU05] describes a model for worm propagation based on an analysis of recent worm attacks. The speed of propagation and the total number of hosts infected depend on a number of factors, including the mode of propagation, the vulnerability or vulnerabilities exploited, and the degree of similarity to preceding attacks. For the latter factor, an attack that is a variation of a recent previous attack may be countered more effectively than a more novel attack. Figure 23.5 shows the dynamics for one typical set of parameters. Propagation proceeds through three phases. In the initial phase, the number of hosts increases exponentially. To see that this is so, consider a simplified case in which a worm is launched from a single host and infects two nearby hosts. Each of these hosts infects two more hosts, and so on. This results in exponential growth. After a time, infecting hosts waste some time attacking already infected hosts, which reduces the rate of infection. During this middle phase, growth is approximately linear, but the rate of infection is rapid. When most vulnerable computers have been infected, the attack enters a slow finish phase as the worm seeks out those remaining hosts that are difficult to identify.

Clearly, the objective in countering a worm is to catch the worm in its slow start phase, at a time when few hosts have been infected.

STATE OF WORM TECHNOLOGY The state of the art in worm technology includes the following:

- **Multiplatform:** Newer worms are not limited to Windows machines but can attack a variety of platforms, especially the popular varieties of UNIX.

- **Multi-exploit:** New worms penetrate systems in a variety of ways, using exploits against Web servers, browsers, e-mail, file sharing, and other network-based applications.

- **Ultrafast spreading:** One technique to accelerate the spread of a worm is to conduct a prior Internet scan to accumulate Internet addresses of vulnerable machines.

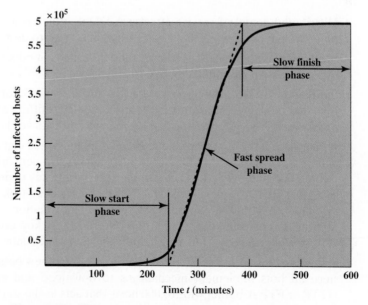

Figure 23.5 Worm Propagation Model

- **Polymorphic:** To evade detection, skip past filters, and foil real-time analysis, worms adopt the virus polymorphic technique. Each copy of the worm has new code generated on the fly using functionally equivalent instructions and encryption techniques.

- **Metamorphic:** In addition to changing their appearance, metamorphic worms have a repertoire of behavior patterns that are unleashed at different stages of propagation.

- **Transport vehicles:** Because worms can rapidly compromise a large number of systems, they are ideal for spreading other distributed attack tools, such as distributed denial-of-service bots.

- **Zero-day exploit:** To achieve maximum surprise and distribution, a worm should exploit an unknown vulnerability that is only discovered by the general network community when the worm is launched.

Bots

A bot (robot), also known as a zombie or drone, is a program that secretly takes over another Internet-attached computer and then uses that computer to launch attacks that are difficult to trace to the bot's creator. The bot is typically planted on hundreds or thousands of computers belonging to unsuspecting third parties. The collection of bots often is capable of acting in a coordinated manner; such a collection is referred to as a **botnet.**

A botnet exhibits three characteristics: the bot functionality, a remote control facility, and a spreading mechanism to propagate the bots and construct the botnet. We examine each of these characteristics in turn.

Uses of Bots [HONE05] lists the following uses of bots:

- **Distributed denial-of-service attacks:** A DDoS attack is an attack on a computer system or network that causes a loss of service to users.

- **Spamming:** With the help of a botnet and thousands of bots, an attacker is able to send massive amounts of bulk e-mail (spam).

- **Sniffing traffic:** Bots can also use a packet sniffer to watch for interesting cleartext data passing by a compromised machine. The sniffers are mostly used to retrieve sensitive information like usernames and passwords.

- **Keylogging:** If the compromised machine uses encrypted communication channels (e.g., HTTPS or POP3S), then just sniffing the network packets on the victim's computer is useless because the appropriate key to decrypt the packets is missing. But by using a keylogger, which captures keystrokes on the infected machine, an attacker can retrieve sensitive information. An implemented filtering mechanism (e.g., "I am only interested in key sequences near the keyword 'paypal.com' ") further helps in stealing secret data.

- **Spreading new malware:** Botnets are used to spread new bots. This is very easy since all bots implement mechanisms to download and execute a file via HTTP or FTP. A botnet with 10,000 hosts that acts as the start base for a worm or mail virus allows very fast spreading and thus causes more harm.

- **Installing advertisement add-ons and browser helper objects (BHOs):** Botnets can also be used to gain financial advantages. This works by setting up a fake Web site with some advertisements: The operator of this Web site negotiates a deal with some hosting companies that pay for clicks on ads. With the help of a botnet, these clicks can be "automated" so that instantly a few thousand bots click on the pop-ups. This process can be further enhanced if the bot hijacks the start page of a compromised machine so that the "clicks" are executed each time the victim uses the browser.

- **Attacking IRC chat networks:** Botnets are also used for attacks against Internet Relay Chat (IRC) networks. Popular among attackers is especially the so-called clone attack: In this kind of attack, the controller orders each bot to connect a large number of clones to the victim IRC network. The victim is flooded by service requests from thousands of bots or thousands of channel-joins by these cloned bots. In this way, the victim IRC network is brought down, similar to a DDoS attack.

- **Manipulating online polls/games:** Online polls/games are getting more and more attention, and it is rather easy to manipulate them with botnets. Since every bot has a distinct IP address, every vote will have the same credibility as a vote cast by a real person. Online games can be manipulated in a similar way.

REMOTE CONTROL FACILITY The remote control facility is what distinguishes a bot from a worm. A worm propagates itself and activates itself, whereas a bot is controlled from some central facility, at least initially.

A typical means of implementing the remote control facility is on an IRC server. All bots join a specific channel on this server and treat incoming messages as commands. More recent botnets tend to avoid IRC mechanisms and use covert communication channels via protocols such as HTTP. Distributed control mechanisms are also used, to avoid a single point of failure.

Once a communications path is established between a control module and the bots, the control module can activate the bots. In its simplest form, the control module simply issues command to the bot that causes the bot to execute routines that are already implemented in the bot. For greater flexibility, the control module can issue update commands that instruct the bots to download a file from some Internet location and execute it. The bot in this latter case becomes a more general-purpose tool that can be used for multiple attacks.

CONSTRUCTING THE ATTACK NETWORK The first step in a botnet attack is for the attacker to infect a number of machines with bot software that will ultimately be used to carry out the attack. The essential ingredients in this phase of the attack are the following:

1. Software that can carry out the attack. The software must be able to run on a large number of machines, must be able to conceal its existence, must be able to communicate with the attacker or have some sort of time-triggered mechanism, and must be able to launch the intended attack toward the target.

2. A vulnerability in a large number of systems. The attacker must become aware of a vulnerability that many system administrators and individual users have failed to patch and that enables the attacker to install the bot software.

3. A strategy for locating and identifying vulnerable machines, a process known as **scanning** or **fingerprinting**.

In the scanning process, the attacker first seeks out a number of vulnerable machines and infects them. Then, typically, the bot software that is installed in the infected machines repeats the same scanning process, until a large distributed network of infected machines is created. [MIRK04] lists the following types of scanning strategies:

- **Random:** Each compromised host probes random addresses in the IP address space, using a different random number generation seed. This technique produces a high volume of Internet traffic, which may cause generalized disruption even before the actual attack is launched.

- **Hit list:** The attacker first compiles a long list of potential vulnerable machines. This can be a slow process done over a long period to avoid detection that an attack is underway. Once the list is compiled, the attacker begins infecting machines on the list. Each infected machine is provided with a portion of the list to scan. This strategy results in a very short scanning period, which may make it difficult to detect that infection is taking place.

- **Topological:** This method uses information contained on an infected victim machine to find more hosts to scan.

- **Local subnet:** If a host can be infected behind a firewall, that host then looks for targets in its own local network. The host uses the subnet address structure to find other hosts that would otherwise be protected by the firewall.

23.6 RECOMMENDED READING AND WEB SITES

The topics in this chapter are covered in more detail in [STAL08].

STAL08   Stallings, W., and Brown L. *Computer Security: Principles and Practice*. Upper Saddle River, NJ: Prentice Hall, 2008.

Recommended Web sites:

- **Computer Security Resource Center:** Maintained by the National Institute on Standards and Technology (NIST). Contains a broad range of information on security threats, technology, and standards.
- **CERT Coordination Center:** The organization that grew from the computer emergency response team formed by the Defense Advanced Research Projects Agency. This site provides good information on Internet security threats, vulnerabilities, and attack statistics.
- **Vmyths:** Dedicated to exposing virus hoaxes and dispelling misconceptions about real viruses.

23.7 KEY TERMS, REVIEW QUESTIONS, AND PROBLEMS

Key Terms

accountability	exposure	passive attack
active attack	falsification	privacy
asset	hacker	replay
attack	insider attack	repudiation
authenticity	integrity	system integrity
availability	interception	threat
backdoor	intruder	traffic analysis
confidentiality	intrusion	trapdoor
data integrity	logic bomb	Trojan horse
deception	macro virus	usurpation
denial of service	malicious software	virus
disruption	malware	virus kit
e-mail virus	masquerade	worm

Review Questions

23.1 Define *computer security*.

23.2 What are the fundamental requirements addressed by computer security?

23.3 What is the difference between passive and active security threats?

23.4 List and briefly define three classes of intruders.

23.5 List and briefly define three intruder behavior patterns.

23.6 What is the role of compression in the operation of a virus?

23.7 What is the role of encryption in the operation of a virus?

23.8 What are typical phases of operation of a virus or worm?

23.9 In general terms, how does a worm propagate?

Problems

23.1 Consider an automated teller machine (ATM) in which users provide a personal identification number (PIN) and a card for account access. Give examples of confidentiality, integrity, and availability requirements associated with the system and, in each case, indicate the degree of importance of the requirement.

23.2 Repeat the preceding problem for a telephone switching system that routes calls through a switching network based on the telephone number requested by the caller.

23.3 Consider a desktop publishing system used to produce documents for various organizations.

  a. Give an example of a type of publication for which confidentiality of the stored data is the most important requirement.

  b. Give an example of a type of publication in which data integrity is the most important requirement.

  c. Give an example in which system availability is the most important requirement.

23.4 For each of the following assets, assign a low, moderate, or high impact level for the loss of confidentiality, availability, and integrity, respectively. Justify your answers.

   a. An organization managing public information on its Web server.

   b. A law enforcement organization managing extremely sensitive investigative information.

   c. A financial organization managing routine administrative information (not privacy-related information).

   d. An information system used for large acquisitions in a contracting organization contains both sensitive, presolicitation phase contract information and routine administrative information. Assess the impact for the two data sets separately and the information system as a whole.

   e. A power plant contains a SCADA (supervisory control and data acquisition) system controlling the distribution of electric power for a large military installation. The SCADA system contains both real-time sensor data and routine administrative information. Assess the impact for the two data sets separately and the information system as a whole.

23.5 Assume that passwords are selected from four-character combinations of 26 alphabetic characters. Assume that an adversary is able to attempt passwords at a rate of one per second.

   a. Assuming no feedback to the adversary until each attempt has been completed, what is the expected time to discover the correct password?

   b. Assuming feedback to the adversary flagging an error as each incorrect character is entered, what is the expected time to discover the correct password?

23.6 There is a flaw in the virus program of Figure 23.3. What is it?

23.7 The question arises as to whether it is possible to develop a program that can analyze a piece of software to determine if it is a virus. Consider that we have a program D that is supposed to be able to do that. That is, for any program P, if we run D(P), the result returned is TRUE (P is a virus) or FALSE (P is not a virus). Now consider the following program:

```
Program CV :=
    { ...
    main-program :=
        {if D(CV) then goto next:
            else infect-executable;
        }
    next:
    }
```

In the preceding program, infect-executable is a module that scans memory for executable programs and replicates itself in those programs. Determine if D can correctly decide whether CV is a virus.

23.8 The point of this problem is to demonstrate the type of puzzles that must be solved in the design of malicious code and, therefore, the type of mind-set that one wishing to counter such attacks must adopt.

   a. Consider the following C program:

```
begin
    print (*begin print (); end.*);
end
```

   What do you think the program was intended to do? Does it work?

   b. Answer the same questions for the following program:

```
char [] = {'0', ' ', '}', ';', 'm', 'a', 'i',
'n', '(', ')', '{',
and so on... 't', ')', '0'};
```

```
main ()
{
  int I;
  printf(*char t[] = (*);
  for (i=0; t[i]!=0; i=i+1)
      printf("%d, ", t[i]);
  printf("%s", t);
}
```

c. What is the specific relevance of this problem to this chapter?

23.9 Consider the following fragment:

```
legitimate code
if data is Friday the 13th;
   crash_computer();
legitimate code
```

What type of malicious software is this?

23.10 Consider the following fragment in an authentication program:

```
username = read_username();
password = read_password();
if username is "133t h4ck0r"
   return ALLOW_LOGIN;
if username and password are valid
   return ALLOW_LOGIN
else return DENY_LOGIN
```

What type of malicious software is this?

23.11 The following code fragments show a sequence of virus instructions and a polymorphic version of the virus. Describe the effect produced by the metamorphic code.

Original Code	Metamorphic Code
mov eax, 5 add eax, ebx call [eax]	mov eax, 5 push ecx pop ecx add eax, ebx swap eax, ebx swap ebx, eax call[eax] nop

COMPUTER AND NETWORK SECURITY TECHNIQUES

To guard against the baneful influence exerted by strangers is therefore an elementary dictate of savage prudence. Hence before strangers are allowed to enter a district, or at least before they are permitted to mingle freely with the inhabitants, certain ceremonies are often performed by the natives of the country for the purpose of disarming the strangers of their magical powers, or of disinfecting, so to speak, the tainted atmosphere by which they are supposed to be surrounded.

— The Golden Bough, Sir James George Frazer

KEY POINTS

◆ IPsec (Internet Protocol Security) provides authentication, encryption, and key exchange functions for IP-based networks, and can be used to construct virtual private networks (VPN).

◆ Secure Sockets Layer (SSL) and the follow-on Internet standard known as Transport Layer Security (TLS) provide a transport-level security service for Web access.

◆ Wi-Fi Protected Access (WPA) is a set of protocols that provides a variety of security services for IEEE 802.11 wireless LANs.

◆ An intrusion detection system (IDS) is a security service that monitors and analyzes system events for the purpose of finding, and providing real-time or near-real-time warning of, attempts to access system resources in an unauthorized manner.

◆ A firewall protects the system of network behind the firewall from Internet-based attacks.

◆ Malicious software is a software that is intentionally included or inserted in a system for a harmful purpose.

This chapter introduces common measures and protocols used to counter the security threats discussed in Chapter 23.

24.1 VIRTUAL PRIVATE NETWORKS AND IPSEC

Virtual private networks (VPNs) and IPsec (Internet Protocol Security) were introduced in Chapter 18, where we looked at the applications and benefits of IPsec. This section provides some of the technical details.

IPsec Functions

IPsec provides three main facilities: an authentication-only function referred to as Authentication Header (AH), a combined authentication/encryption function called Encapsulating Security Payload (ESP), and a key exchange function. For VPNs, both authentication and encryption are generally desired, because it is important both to

(1) assure that unauthorized users do not penetrate the virtual private network, and (2) assure that eavesdroppers on the Internet cannot read messages sent over the virtual private network. Because both features are generally desirable, most implementations are likely to use ESP rather than AH. The key exchange function allows for manual exchange of keys as well as an automated scheme.

The current specification requires that IPsec support the Data Encryption Standard (DES) for encryption, but a variety of other encryption algorithms may also be used. Because of concern about the strength of DES, it is likely that other algorithms, such as triple DES, will be widely used. For authentication, a relatively new scheme, known as HMAC, is required.

Transport and Tunnel Modes

ESP supports two modes of use: transport and tunnel mode.

Transport mode provides protection primarily for upper-layer protocols. That is, transport mode protection extends to the payload of an IP packet. Typically, transport mode is used for end-to-end communication between two hosts (e.g., a client and a server, or two workstations). ESP in transport mode encrypts and optionally authenticates the IP payload but not the IP header (Figure 24.1b). This configuration is useful for relatively small networks, in which each host and server is equipped with IPsec. However, for a full-blown VPN, tunnel mode is far more efficient.

Tunnel mode provides protection to the entire IP packet. To achieve this, after the ESP fields are added to the IP packet, the entire packet plus security fields is treated as the payload of new "outer" IP packet with a new outer IP header. The entire

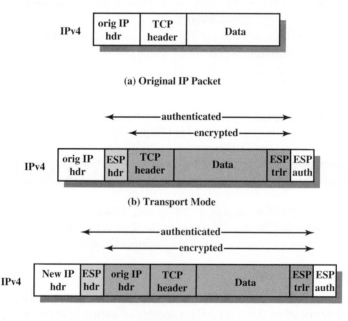

(a) Original IP Packet

(b) Transport Mode

(c) Tunnel Mode

Figure 24.1 Scope of Esp Encryption and Authentication

original, or inner, packet travels through a "tunnel" from one point of an IP network to another; no routers along the way are able to examine the inner IP header. Because the original packet is encapsulated, the new, larger packet may have totally different source and destination addresses, adding to the security. Tunnel mode is used when at least on of the two ends is a security gateway, such as a firewall or router that implements IPsec. With tunnel mode, a number of hosts on networks behind firewalls may engage in secure communications without implementing IPsec. The unprotected packets generated by such hosts are tunneled through external networks by using tunnel mode, set up by the IPsec software in the firewall or secure router at the boundary of the local network.

Here is an example of how tunnel-mode IPsec operates. Host A on a network generates an IP packet with the destination address of host B on another network. This packet is routed from the originating host to a firewall or secure router at the boundary of A's network. The firewall filters all outgoing packets to determine the need for IPsec processing. If this packet from A to B requires IPsec, the firewall performs IPsec processing and encapsulates the packet in an outer IP header. The source IP address of this outer IP packet is this firewall, and the destination address may be a firewall that forms the boundary to B's local network. This packet is now routed to B's firewall, with intermediate routers examining only the outer IP header. At B's firewall, the outer IP header is stripped off, and the inner packet is delivered to B.

ESP in tunnel mode encrypts and optionally authenticates the entire inner IP packet, including the inner IP header.

Key Management

The key management portion of IPsec involves the determination and distribution of secret keys. The IPsec Architecture document mandates support for two types of key management:

- **Manual:** A system administrator (SA) manually configures each system with its own keys and with the keys of other communicating systems. This is practical for small, relatively static environments.

- **Automated:** An automated system enables the on-demand creation of keys and facilitates the use of keys in a large distributed system with an evolving configuration. An automated system is the most flexible but requires more effort to configure and requires more software, so smaller installations are likely to opt for manual key management.

IPsec and VPNs

The driving force for the acceptance and deployment of secure IP is the need for business and government users to connect their private WAN/LAN infrastructure to the Internet for (1) access to Internet services, and (2) use of the Internet as a component of the WAN transport system. Users need to secure their networks and at the same time send and receive traffic over the Internet. The authentication and privacy mechanisms of secure IP provide the basis for a security strategy.

Because IP security mechanisms have been defined independent of their use with either the current IP or IPv6, deployment of these mechanisms does not depend on deployment of IPv6. Indeed, it is likely that we will see widespread use of secure IP features long before IPv6 becomes popular, because the need for IP-level security is greater than the need for the added functions that IPv6 provides compared to the current IP.

With the arrival of IPsec, managers have a standardized means of implementing security for VPNs. Further, all of the encryption and authentication algorithms, and security protocols, used in IPsec are well studied and have survived years of scrutiny. As a result, the user can be confident that the IPsec facility indeed provides strong security.

IPsec can be implemented in routers or firewalls owned and operated by the organization. This gives the network manager complete control over security aspects of the VPN, which is much to be desired. However, IPsec is a complex set of functions and modules and the management and configuration responsibility is formidable. The alternative is to seek a solution from a service provider. A service provider can simplify the job of planning, implementing, and maintaining Internet-based VPNs for secure access to network resources and secure communication between sites.

24.2 SSL AND TLS

One of the most widely used security services is the Secure Sockets Layer (SSL) and the follow-on Internet standard known as Transport Layer Security (TLS), the latter defined in RFC 2246. SSL is a general-purpose service implemented as a set of protocols that rely on TCP. At this level, there are two implementation choices. For full generality, SSL (or TLS) could be provided as part of the underlying protocol suite and therefore be transparent to applications. Alternatively, SSL can be embedded in specific packages. For example, Netscape and Microsoft Explorer browsers come equipped with SSL, and most Web servers have implemented the protocol.

SSL Architecture

SSL is designed to make use of TCP to provide a reliable end-to-end secure service. SSL is not a single protocol but rather two layers of protocols, as illustrated in Figure 24.2.

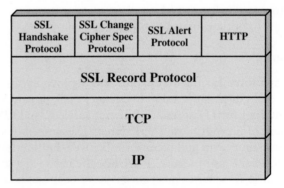

Figure 24.2 SSL Protocol Stack

The SSL Record Protocol provides basic security services to various higher-layer protocols. In particular, the Hypertext Transfer Protocol (HTTP), which provides the transfer service for Web client/server interaction, can operate on top of SSL. Three higher-layer protocols are defined as part of SSL: the Handshake Protocol, the Change Cipher Spec Protocol, and the Alert Protocol. These SSL-specific protocols are used in the management of SSL exchanges and are examined later in this section.

Two important SSL concepts are the SSL session and the SSL connection, which are defined in the specification as follows:

- **Connection:** A connection is a transport (in the OSI layering model definition) that provides a suitable type of service. For SSL, such connections are peer-to-peer relationships. The connections are transient. Every connection is associated with one session.

- **Session:** An SSL session is an association between a client and a server. Sessions are created by the Handshake Protocol. Sessions define a set of cryptographic security parameters, which can be shared among multiple connections. Sessions are used to avoid the expensive negotiation of new security parameters for each connection.

Between any pair of parties (applications such as HTTP on client and server), there may be multiple secure connections. In theory, there may also be multiple simultaneous sessions between parties, but this feature is not used in practice.

SSL Record Protocol

The SSL Record Protocol provides two services for SSL connections:

- **Confidentiality:** The Handshake Protocol defines a shared secret key that is used for symmetric encryption of SSL payloads.

- **Message integrity:** The Handshake Protocol also defines a shared secret key that is used to form a message authentication code (MAC).

Figure 24.3 indicates the overall operation of the SSL Record Protocol. The first step is **fragmentation**. Each upper-layer message is fragmented into blocks of 2^{14} bytes (16,384 bytes) or less. Next, **compression** is optionally applied. The next step in processing is to compute a **message authentication code** over the compressed data. Next, the compressed message plus the MAC are **encrypted** using symmetric encryption.[1]

The final step of SSL Record Protocol processing is to prepend a header, consisting of the following fields:

- **Content Type (8 bits):** The higher-layer protocol used to process the enclosed fragment.

- **Major Version (8 bits):** Indicates major version of SSL in use. For SSLv3, the value is 3.

---

[1]The cryptographic concepts referenced in this chapter are discussed in Appendix Q.

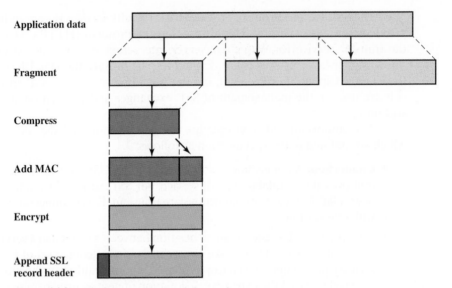

Figure 24.3 SSL Record Protocol Operation

- **Minor Version (8 bits):** Indicates minor version in use. For SSLv3, the value is 0.
- **Compressed Length (16 bits):** The length in bytes of the plaintext fragment (or compressed fragment if compression is used). The maximum value is $2^{14} + 2048$.

The content types that have been defined are change_cipher_spec, alert, handshake, and application_data. The first three are the SSL-specific protocols, discussed next. Note that no distinction is made among the various applications (e.g., HTTP) that might use SSL; the content of the data created by such applications is opaque to SSL.

The Record Protocol then transmits the resulting unit in a TCP segment. Received data are decrypted, verified, decompressed, and reassembled, and then delivered to higher-level users.

Change Cipher Spec Protocol

The Change Cipher Spec Protocol is one of the three SSL-specific protocols that use the SSL Record Protocol, and it is the simplest. This protocol consists of a single message, which consists of a single byte with the value 1. The sole purpose of this message is to cause the pending state to be copied into the current state, which updates the cipher suite to be used on this connection.

Alert Protocol

The Alert Protocol is used to convey SSL-related alerts to the peer entity. As with other applications that use SSL, alert messages are compressed and encrypted, as specified by the current state.

Each message in this protocol consists of two bytes. The first byte takes the value warning (1) or fatal (2) to convey the severity of the message. If the level is fatal, SSL immediately terminates the connection. Other connections on the same session may continue, but no new connections on this session may be established. The second byte contains a code that indicates the specific alert. An example of a fatal alert is an incorrect MAC. An example of a nonfatal alert is a close_notify message, which notifies the recipient that the sender will not send any more messages on this connection.

Handshake Protocol

The most complex part of SSL is the Handshake Protocol. This protocol allows the server and client to authenticate each other and to negotiate an encryption and MAC algorithm and cryptographic keys to be used to protect data sent in an SSL record. The Handshake Protocol is used before any application data are transmitted.

The Handshake Protocol consists of a series of messages exchanged by client and server. The exchange can be viewed as having four phases.

Phase 1 is used to initiate a logical connection and to establish the security capabilities that will be associated with it. The exchange is initiated by the client, which sends a client_hello message with the following parameters:

- **Version:** The highest SSL version understood by the client.

- **Random:** A client-generated random structure, consisting of a 32-bit timestamp and 28 bytes generated by a secure random number generator. These values are used during key exchange to prevent replay attacks.

- **Session ID:** A variable-length session identifier. A nonzero value indicates that the client wishes to update the parameters of an existing connection or create a new connection on this session. A zero value indicates that the client wishes to establish a new connection on a new session.

- **CipherSuite:** This is a list that contains the combinations of cryptographic algorithms supported by the client, in decreasing order of preference. Each element of the list (each cipher suite) defines both a key exchange algorithm and a CipherSpec.

- **Compression method:** This is a list of the compression methods the client supports.

After sending the client_hello message, the client waits for the server_hello message, which contains the same parameters as the client_hello message.

The details of **phase 2** depend on the underlying public-key encryption scheme that is used. In some cases, the server passes a certificate to the client, possibly additional key information, and a request for a certificate from the client.

The final message in phase 2, and one that is always required, is the server_done message, which is sent by the server to indicate the end of the server hello and associated messages. After sending this message, the server will wait for a client response.

In **phase 3**, upon receipt of the server_done message, the client should verify that the server provided a valid certificate if required and check that the server_hello parameters are acceptable. If all is satisfactory, the client sends one or more messages back to the server, depending on the underlying public-key scheme.

Phase 4 completes the setting up of a secure connection. The client sends a change_cipher_spec message and copies the pending CipherSpec into the current CipherSpec. Note that this message is not considered part of the Handshake Protocol but is sent using the Change Cipher Spec Protocol. The client then immediately sends the finished message under the new algorithms, keys, and secrets. The finished message verifies that the key exchange and authentication processes were successful.

In response to these two messages, the server sends its own change_cipher_spec message, transfers the pending to the current CipherSpec, and sends its finished message. At this point the handshake is complete and the client and server may begin to exchange application layer data.

24.3 WI-FI PROTECTED ACCESS

As discussed in Chapter 17, the 802.11i task group has developed a set of capabilities to address the WLAN security issues. In order to accelerate the introduction of strong security into WLANs, the Wi-Fi Alliance promulgated **Wi-Fi Protected Access (WPA)** as a Wi-Fi standard. WPA is a set of security mechanisms that eliminates most 802.11 security issues and was based on the current state of the 802.11i standard. As 802.11i evolves, WPA will evolve to maintain compatibility.

IEEE 802.11i addresses three main security areas: authentication, key management, and data transfer privacy. To improve authentication, 802.11i requires the use of an authentication server (AS) and defines a more robust authentication protocol. The AS also plays a role in key distribution. For privacy, 802.11i provides three different encryption schemes. The scheme that provides a long-term solution makes use of the Advanced Encryption Standard (AES) with 128-bit keys. However, because the use of AES would require expensive upgrades to existing equipment, alternative schemes based on 104-bit RC4 are also defined.

Figure 24.4 gives a general overview of 802.11i operation. First, an exchange between a station and an AP enables the two to agree on a set of security capabilities to be used. Then, an exchange involving the AS and the station provides for

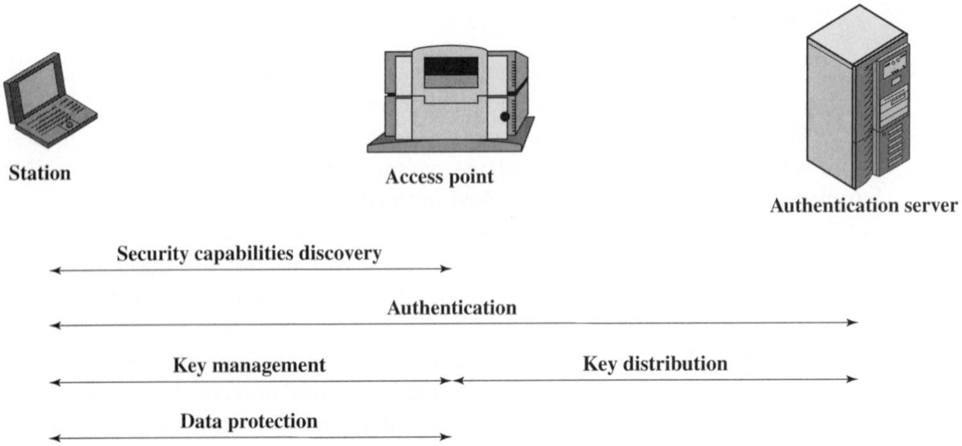

Station   Access point   Authentication server

Security capabilities discovery

Authentication

Key management   Key distribution

Data protection

Figure 24.4   802.11i Operational Phases

secure authentication. The AS is responsible for key distribution to the AP, which in turn manages and distributes keys to stations. Finally, strong encryption is used to protect data transfer between the station and the AP.

The 802.11i architecture consists of three main ingredients:

- **Authentication:** A protocol is used to define an exchange between a user and an AS that provides mutual authentication and generates temporary keys to be used between the client and the AP over the wireless link.

- **Access control:** This function enforces the use of the authentication function, routes the messages properly, and facilitates key exchange. It can work with a variety of authentication protocols.

- **Privacy with message integrity:** MAC-level data (e.g., an LLC PDU) are encrypted, along with a message integrity code that ensures that the data have not been altered.

Authentication operates at a level above the LLC and MAC protocols and is considered beyond the scope of 802.11. There are a number of popular authentication protocols in use, including the Extensible Authentication Protocol (EAP) and the Remote Authentication Dial-In User Service (RADIUS). These are not covered in this book. The remainder of this section examines access control and privacy with message integrity.

Access Control

IEEE 802.11i makes use of another standard that was designed to provide access control functions for LANs. The standard is IEEE 802.1X, Port-Based Network Access Control. IEEE 802.1X uses the terms *supplicant, authenticator*, and *authentication server* (AS). In the context of an 802.11 WLAN, the first two terms correspond to the wireless station and the AP. The AS is typically a separate device on the wired side of the network (i.e., accessible over the DS) but could also reside directly on the authenticator.

Before a supplicant is authenticated by the AS, using an authentication protocol, the authenticator only passes control or authentication messages between the supplicant and the AS; the 802.1X control channel is unblocked but the 802.11 data channel is blocked. Once a supplicant is authenticated and keys are provided, the authenticator can forward data from the supplicant, subject to predefined access control limitations for the supplicant to the network. Under these circumstances, the data channel is unblocked.

As indicated in Figure 24.5, 802.1X uses the concepts of controlled and uncontrolled ports. Ports are logical entities defined within the authenticator and refer to physical network connections. For a WLAN, the authenticator (the AP) may have only two physical ports, one connecting to the DS and one for wireless communication within its BSS. Each logical port is mapped to one of these two physical ports. An uncontrolled port allows the exchange of PDUs between the supplicant and other the AS regardless of the authentication state of the supplicant. A controlled port allows the exchange of PDUs between a supplicant and other systems on the LAN only if the current state of the supplicant authorizes such an exchange.

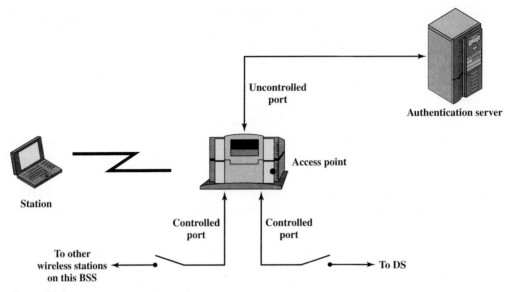

Figure 24.5   802.11i Access Control

The 802.1X framework, with an upper-layer authentication protocol, fits nicely with a BSS architecture that includes a number of wireless stations and an AP. However, for an IBSS, there is no AP. For an IBSS, 802.11i provides a more complex solution that, in essence, involves pairwise authentication between stations on the IBSS.

Privacy with Message Integrity

IEEE 802.11i defines two schemes for protecting data transmitted in 802.11 MAC PDUs. The first scheme is known as the Temporal Key Integrity Protocol (TKIP) or WPA-1. TKIP is designed to require only software changes to devices that are implemented with an older wireless LAN security approach called Wired Equivalent Privacy (WEP); it uses the same RC4 stream encryption algorithm as WEP. The second scheme is known as Counter Mode-CBC MAC Protocol (CCMP) or WPA-2. CCMP makes use of the Advanced Encryption Standard (AES) encryption protocol.[2]

Both TKIP and WPA-2 add a message integrity code (MIC) to the 802.11 MAC frame after the data field. The MIC is generated by an algorithm, called Michael, that computes a 64-bit value calculated using the source and destination MAC address values and the data field. This value is then encrypted using a separate key from that used for encrypting the data fields. Thus, both the data and MIC fields are encrypted. The use of a more complex algorithm, a separate encryption key, and a 64-bit length, all make the MIC a substantially stronger message authentication feature than the ICV. The MIC serves the purpose of message authentication.

---

[2]The AES algorithm is described in detail in [STAL11].

24.4 INTRUSION DETECTION

The following definitions from RFC 2828 (Internet Security Glossary) are relevant to our discussion:

> **Security Intrusion:** A security event, or a combination of multiple security events, that constitutes a security incident in which an intruder gains, or attempts to gain, access to a system (or system resource) without having authorization to do so.
>
> **Intrusion Detection:** A security service that monitors and analyzes system events for the purpose of finding, and providing real-time or near-real-time warning of, attempts to access system resources in an unauthorized manner.

Intrusion detection systems (IDSs) can be classified as follows:

- **Host-based IDS:** Monitors the characteristics of a single host and the events occurring within that host for suspicious activity
- **Network-based IDS:** Monitors network traffic for particular network segments or devices and analyzes network, transport, and application protocols to identify suspicious activity

An IDS comprises three logical components:

- **Sensors:** Sensors are responsible for collecting data. The input for a sensor may be any part of a system that could contain evidence of an intrusion. Types of input to a sensor include network packets, log files, and system call traces. Sensors collect and forward this information to the analyzer.
- **Analyzers:** Analyzers receive input from one or more sensors or from other analyzers. The analyzer is responsible for determining if an intrusion has occurred. The output of this component is an indication that an intrusion has occurred. The output may include evidence supporting the conclusion that an intrusion occurred. The analyzer may provide guidance about what actions to take as a result of the intrusion.
- **User interface:** The user interface to an IDS enables a user to view output from the system or control the behavior of the system. In some systems, the user interface may equate to a manager, director, or console component.

Basic Principles

Authentication facilities, access control facilities, and firewalls all play a role in countering intrusions. Another line of defense is intrusion detection, and this has been the focus of much research in recent years. This interest is motivated by a number of considerations, including the following:

1. If an intrusion is detected quickly enough, the intruder can be identified and ejected from the system before any damage is done or any data are compromised. Even if the detection is not sufficiently timely to preempt the intruder,

the sooner that the intrusion is detected, the less the amount of damage and the more quickly that recovery can be achieved.

2. An effective IDS can serve as a deterrent, thus acting to prevent intrusions.

3. Intrusion detection enables the collection of information about intrusion techniques that can be used to strengthen intrusion prevention measures.

Intrusion detection is based on the assumption that the behavior of the intruder differs from that of a legitimate user in ways that can be quantified. Of course, we cannot expect that there will be a crisp, exact distinction between an attack by an intruder and the normal use of resources by an authorized user. Rather, we must expect that there will be some overlap.

Figure 24.6 suggests, in abstract terms, the nature of the task confronting the designer of an IDS. Although the typical behavior of an intruder differs from the typical behavior of an authorized user, there is an overlap in these behaviors. Thus, a loose interpretation of intruder behavior, which will catch more intruders, will also lead to a number of **false positives**, or authorized users identified as intruders. On the other hand, an attempt to limit false positives by a tight interpretation of intruder behavior will lead to an increase in **false negatives**, or intruders not identified as intruders. Thus, there is an element of compromise and art in the practice of intrusion detection.

In Anderson's study [ANDE80], it was postulated that one could, with reasonable confidence, distinguish between a masquerader and a legitimate user. Patterns of

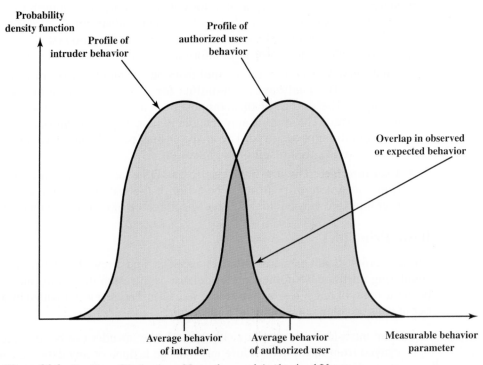

Figure 24.6 Profiles of Behavior of Intruders and Authorized Users

legitimate user behavior can be established by observing past history, and significant deviation from such patterns can be detected. Anderson suggests that the task of detecting a misfeasor (legitimate user performing in an unauthorized fashion) is more difficult, in that the distinction between abnormal and normal behavior may be small. Anderson concluded that such violations would be undetectable solely through the search for anomalous behavior. However, misfeasor behavior might nevertheless be detectable by intelligent definition of the class of conditions that suggest unauthorized use. Finally, the detection of the clandestine user was felt to be beyond the scope of purely automated techniques. These observations, which were made in 1980, remain true today.

For the remainder of this section, we concentrate on host-based intrusion detection.

Host–Based Intrusion Detection Techniques

Host-based IDSs add a specialized layer of security software to vulnerable or sensitive systems; examples include database servers and administrative systems. The host-based IDS monitors activity on the system in a variety of ways to detect suspicious behavior. In some cases, an IDS can halt an attack before any damage is done, but its primary purpose is to detect intrusions, log suspicious events, and send alerts.

The primary benefit of a host-based IDS is that it can detect both external and internal intrusions, something that is not possible either with network-based IDSs or firewalls.

Host-based IDSs follow one of two general approaches to intrusion detection:

1. **Anomaly detection:** Involves the collection of data relating to the behavior of legitimate users over a period of time. Then statistical tests are applied to observed behavior to determine with a high level of confidence whether that behavior is not legitimate user behavior. The following are two approaches to statistical anomaly detection:

2. **a.** *Threshold detection:* This approach involves defining thresholds, independent of user, for the frequency of occurrence of various events.

   b. *Profile based:* A profile of the activity of each user is developed and used to detect changes in the behavior of individual accounts.

3. **Signature detection:** Involves an attempt to define a set of rules or attack patterns that can be used to decide that a given behavior is that of an intruder.

In essence, anomaly approaches attempt to define normal, or expected, behavior, whereas signature-based approaches attempt to define proper behavior.

In terms of the types of attackers listed earlier, anomaly detection is effective against masqueraders, who are unlikely to mimic the behavior patterns of the accounts they appropriate. On the other hand, such techniques may be unable to deal with misfeasors. For such attacks, signature-based approaches may be able to recognize events and sequences that, in context, reveal penetration. In practice, a system may employ a combination of both approaches to be effective against a broad range of attacks.

24.5 FIREWALLS

The firewall is an important complement to host-based security services such as intrusion detection systems. Typically, a firewall is inserted between the premises network and the Internet to establish a controlled link and to erect an outer security wall or perimeter. The aim of this perimeter is to protect the premises network from Internet-based attacks and to provide a single choke point where security and auditing can be imposed.

The firewall provides an additional layer of defense, insulating the internal systems from external networks. This follows the classic military doctrine of "defense in depth," which is just as applicable to IT security.

Firewall Characteristics

[BELL94] lists the following design goals for a firewall:

1. All traffic from inside to outside, and vice versa, must pass through the firewall. This is achieved by physically blocking all access to the local network except via the firewall. Various configurations are possible, as explained later in this chapter.

2. Only authorized traffic, as defined by the local security policy, will be allowed to pass. Various types of firewalls are used, which implement various types of security policies, as explained later in this chapter.

3. The firewall itself is immune to penetration. This implies the use of a hardened system with a secured operating system. Trusted computer systems are suitable for hosting a firewall and often required in government applications.

[SMIT97] lists four general techniques that firewalls use to control access and enforce the site's security policy. Originally, firewalls focused primarily on service control, but they have since evolved to provide all four:

- **Service control:** Determines the types of Internet services that can be accessed, inbound or outbound. The firewall may filter traffic on the basis of IP address, protocol, or port number; may provide proxy software that receives and interprets each service request before passing it on; or may host the server software itself, such as a Web or mail service.

- **Direction control:** Determines the direction in which particular service requests may be initiated and allowed to flow through the firewall.

- **User control:** Controls access to a service according to which user is attempting to access it. This feature is typically applied to users inside the firewall perimeter (local users). It may also be applied to incoming traffic from external users; the latter requires some form of secure authentication technology, such as is provided in IPsec.

- **Behavior control:** Controls how particular services are used. For example, the firewall may filter e-mail to eliminate spam, or it may enable external access to only a portion of the information on a local Web server.

Before proceeding to the details of firewall types and configurations, it is best to summarize what one can expect from a firewall. The following capabilities are within the scope of a firewall:

1. A firewall defines a single choke point that keeps unauthorized users out of the protected network, prohibits potentially vulnerable services from entering or leaving the network, and provides protection from various kinds of IP spoofing and routing attacks. The use of a single choke point simplifies security management because security capabilities are consolidated on a single system or set of systems.

2. A firewall provides a location for monitoring security-related events. Audits and alarms can be implemented on the firewall system.

3. A firewall is a convenient platform for several Internet functions that are not security related. These include a network address translator, which maps local addresses to Internet addresses, and a network management function that audits or logs Internet usage.

4. A firewall can serve as the platform for IPsec. Using the tunnel mode capability described in Section 24.1, the firewall can be used to implement virtual private networks.

Firewalls have their limitations, including the following:

1. The firewall cannot protect against attacks that bypass the firewall. Internal systems may have dial-out capability to connect to an ISP. An internal LAN may support a modem pool that provides dial-in capability for traveling employees and telecommuters.

2. The firewall may not protect fully against internal threats, such as a disgruntled employee or an employee who unwittingly cooperates with an external attacker.

3. An improperly secured wireless LAN may be accessed from outside the organization. An internal firewall that separates portions of an enterprise network cannot guard against wireless communications between local systems on different sides of the internal firewall.

4. A laptop, PDA, or portable storage device may be used and infected outside the corporate network, and then attached and used internally.

Types of Firewalls

A firewall may act as a packet filter. It can operate as a positive filter, allowing to pass only packets that meet specific criteria, or as a negative filter, rejecting any packet that meets certain criteria. Depending on the type of firewall, it may examine one or more protocol headers in each packet, the payload of each packet, or the pattern generated by a sequence of packets. In this section, we look at the principal types of firewalls.

PACKET FILTERING FIREWALL A packet filtering firewall applies a set of rules to each incoming and outgoing IP packet and then forwards or discards the packet (Figure 24.7b). The firewall is typically configured to filter packets going in both

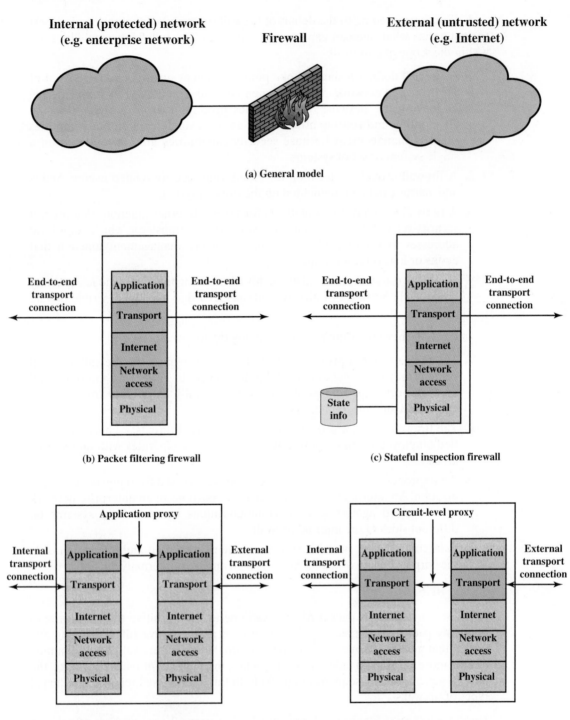

Figure 24.7 Types of Firewalls

directions (from and to the internal network). Filtering rules are based on information contained in a network packet:

- **Source IP address:** The IP address of the system that originated the IP packet (e.g., 192.178.1.1)
- **Destination IP address:** The IP address of the system the IP packet is trying to reach (e.g., 192.168.1.2)
- **Source and destination transport-level address:** The transport-level (e.g., TCP or UDP) port number, which defines applications such as SNMP or TELNET
- **IP protocol field:** Defines the transport protocol
- **Interface:** For a firewall with three or more ports, which interface of the firewall the packet came from or which interface of the firewall the packet is destined for

The packet filter is typically set up as a list of rules based on matches to fields in the IP or TCP header. If there is a match to one of the rules, that rule is invoked to determine whether to forward or discard the packet. If there is no match to any rule, then a default action is taken. Two default policies are possible:

- **Default = discard:** That which is not expressly permitted is prohibited.
- **Default = forward:** That which is not expressly prohibited is permitted.

The default = discard policy is more conservative. Initially, everything is blocked, and services must be added on a case-by-case basis. This policy is more visible to users, who are more likely to see the firewall as a hindrance. However, this is the policy likely to be preferred by businesses and government organizations. Further, visibility to users diminishes as rules are created. The default = forward policy increases ease of use for end users but provides reduced security; the security administrator must, in essence, react to each new security threat as it becomes known. This policy may be used by generally more open organizations, such as universities.

Table 24.1, from [BELL94], gives some examples of packet filtering rule sets. In each set, the rules are applied top to bottom. The "*" in a field is a wildcard designator that matches everything. We assume that the default = discard policy is in force.

A. Inbound mail is allowed (port 25 is for SMTP incoming), but only to a gateway host. However, packets from a particular external host, SPIGOT, are blocked because that host has a history of sending massive files in e-mail messages.

B. This is an explicit statement of the default policy. All rule sets include this rule implicitly as the last rule.

C. This rule set is intended to specify that any inside host can send mail to the outside. A TCP packet with a destination port of 25 is routed to the SMTP server on the destination machine. The problem with this rule is that the use of port 25 for SMTP receipt is only a default; an outside machine could be configured to have some other application linked to port 25. As this rule is written, an attacker could gain access to internal machines by sending packets with a TCP source port number of 25.

Table 24.1   Packet Filtering Examples

Rule Set A

action	ourhost	port	theirhost	port	comment
block	*	*	SPIGOT	*	we don't trust these people
allow	OUR-GW	25	*	*	connection to our SMTP port

Rule Set B

action	ourhost	port	theirhost	port	comment
block	*	*	*	*	default

Rule Set C

action	ourhost	port	theirhost	port	comment
allow	*	*	*	25	connection to their SMTP port

Rule Set D

action	src	port	dest	port	flags	comment
allow	{our hosts}	*	*	25		our packets to their SMTP port
allow	*	25	*	*	ACK	their replies

Rule Set E

action	src	port	dest	port	flags	comment
allow	{our hosts}	*	*	*		our outgoing calls
allow	*	*	*	*	ACK	replies to our calls
allow	*	*	*	>1024		traffic to nonservers

D. This rule set achieves the intended result that was not achieved in C. The rules take advantage of a feature of TCP connections. Once a connection is set up, the ACK flag of a TCP segment is set to acknowledge segments sent from the other side. Thus, this rule set states that it allows IP packets where the source IP address is one of a list of designated internal hosts and the destination TCP port number is 25. It also allows incoming packets with a source port number of 25 that include the ACK flag in the TCP segment. Note that we explicitly designate source and destination systems to define these rules explicitly.

E. This rule set is one approach to handling FTP connections. With FTP, two TCP connections are used: a control connection to set up the file transfer and a data connection for the actual file transfer. The data connection uses a different port number that is dynamically assigned for the transfer. Most servers, and hence most attack targets, use low-numbered ports; most outgoing calls tend to use a higher-numbered port, typically above 1023. Thus, this rule set allows

— Packets that originate internally

— Reply packets to a connection initiated by an internal machine

— Packets destined for a high-numbered port on an internal machine

This scheme requires that the systems be configured so that only the appropriate port numbers are in use.

Rule set E points out the difficulty in dealing with applications at the packet filtering level. Another way to deal with FTP and similar applications is either stateful packet filters or an application-level gateway, both described subsequently in this section.

One advantage of a packet filtering firewall is its simplicity. Also, packet filters typically are transparent to users and are very fast. [WACK02] lists the following weaknesses of packet filter firewalls:

- Because packet filter firewalls do not examine upper-layer data, they cannot prevent attacks that employ application-specific vulnerabilities or functions. For example, a packet filter firewall cannot block specific application commands; if a packet filter firewall allows a given application, all functions available within that application will be permitted.

- Because of the limited information available to the firewall, the logging functionality present in packet filter firewalls is limited. Packet filter logs normally contain the same information used to make access control decisions (source address, destination address, and traffic type).

- Most packet filter firewalls do not support advanced user authentication schemes. Once again, this limitation is mostly due to the lack of upper-layer functionality by the firewall.

- Packet filter firewalls are generally vulnerable to attacks and exploits that take advantage of problems within the TCP/IP specification and protocol stack, such as *network layer address spoofing*. Many packet filter firewalls cannot detect a network packet in which the OSI Layer 3 addressing information has been altered. Spoofing attacks are generally employed by intruders to bypass the security controls implemented in a firewall platform.

- Finally, due to the small number of variables used in access control decisions, packet filter firewalls are susceptible to security breaches caused by improper configurations. In other words, it is easy to accidentally configure a packet filter firewall to allow traffic types, sources, and destinations that should be denied based on an organization's information security policy.

Some of the attacks that can be made on packet filtering firewalls and the appropriate countermeasures are the following:

- **IP address spoofing:** The intruder transmits packets from the outside with a source IP address field containing an address of an internal host. The attacker hopes that the use of a spoofed address will allow penetration of systems that employ simple source address security, in which packets from specific trusted internal hosts are accepted. The countermeasure is to discard packets with an inside source address if the packet arrives on an external interface. In fact, this countermeasure is often implemented at the router external to the firewall.

- **Source routing attacks:** The source station specifies the route that a packet should take as it crosses the Internet, in the hopes that this will bypass security measures that do not analyze the source routing information. The countermeasure is to discard all packets that use this option.

- **Tiny fragment attacks:** The intruder uses the IP fragmentation option to create extremely small fragments and force the TCP header information into a separate packet fragment. This attack is designed to circumvent filtering rules that depend on TCP header information. Typically, a packet filter will make a filtering decision on the first fragment of a packet. All subsequent fragments of that packet are filtered out solely on the basis that they are part of the packet whose first fragment was rejected. The attacker hopes that the filtering firewall examines only the first fragment and that the remaining fragments are passed through. A tiny fragment attack can be defeated by enforcing a rule that the first fragment of a packet must contain a predefined minimum amount of the transport header. If the first fragment is rejected, the filter can remember the packet and discard all subsequent fragments.

STATEFUL INSPECTION FIREWALLS A traditional packet filter makes filtering decisions on an individual packet basis and does not take into consideration any higher-layer context. To understand what is meant by *context* and why a traditional packet filter is limited with regard to context, a little background is needed. Most standardized applications that run on top of TCP follow a client/server model. For example, for the Simple Mail Transfer Protocol (SMTP), e-mail is transmitted from a client system to a server system. The client system generates new e-mail messages, typically from user input. The server system accepts incoming e-mail messages and places them in the appropriate user mailboxes. SMTP operates by setting up a TCP connection between client and server, in which the TCP server port number, which identifies the SMTP server application, is 25. The TCP port number for the SMTP client is a number between 1024 and 65535 that is generated by the SMTP client.

In general, when an application that uses TCP creates a session with a remote host, it creates a TCP connection in which the TCP port number for the remote (server) application is a number less than 1024 and the TCP port number for the local (client) application is a number between 1024 and 65535. The numbers less than 1024 are the "well-known" port numbers and are assigned permanently to particular applications (e.g., 25 for server SMTP). The numbers between 1024 and 65535 are generated dynamically and have temporary significance only for the lifetime of a TCP connection.

A simple packet filtering firewall must permit inbound network traffic on all these high-numbered ports for TCP-based traffic to occur. This creates a vulnerability that can be exploited by unauthorized users.

A stateful inspection packet firewall tightens up the rules for TCP traffic by creating a directory of outbound TCP connections, as shown in Table 24.2. There is an entry for each currently established connection. The packet filter will now allow incoming traffic to high-numbered ports only for those packets that fit the profile of one of the entries in this directory.

Table 24.2 Example Stateful Firewall Connection State Tables

Source Address	Source Port	Destination Address	Destination Port	Connection State
192.168.1.100	1030	210.9.88.29	80	Established
192.168.1.102	1031	216.32.42.123	80	Established
192.168.1.101	1033	173.66.32.122	25	Established
192.168.1.106	1035	177.231.32.12	79	Established
223.43.21.231	1990	192.168.1.6	80	Established
219.22.123.32	2112	192.168.1.6	80	Established
210.99.212.18	3321	192.168.1.6	80	Established
24.102.32.23	1025	192.168.1.6	80	Established
223.21.22.12	1046	192.168.1.6	80	Established

A stateful packet inspection firewall reviews the same packet information as a packet filtering firewall, but also records information about TCP connections (Figure 24.7c). Some stateful firewalls also keep track of TCP sequence numbers to prevent attacks that depend on the sequence number, such as session hijacking. Some even inspect limited amounts of application data for some well-known protocols like FTP, IM, and SIPS commands, in order to identify and track related connections.

APPLICATION-LEVEL GATEWAY An application-level gateway, also called an **application proxy**, acts as a relay of application-level traffic (Figure 24.7d). The user contacts the gateway using a TCP/IP application, such as Telnet or FTP, and the gateway asks the user for the name of the remote host to be accessed. When the user responds and provides a valid user ID and authentication information, the gateway contacts the application on the remote host and relays TCP segments containing the application data between the two endpoints. If the gateway does not implement the proxy code for a specific application, the service is not supported and cannot be forwarded across the firewall. Further, the gateway can be configured to support only specific features of an application that the network administrator considers acceptable while denying all other features.

Application-level gateways tend to be more secure than packet filters. Rather than trying to deal with the numerous possible combinations that are to be allowed and forbidden at the TCP and IP level, the application-level gateway need only scrutinize a few allowable applications. In addition, it is easy to log and audit all incoming traffic at the application level.

A prime disadvantage of this type of gateway is the additional processing overhead on each connection. In effect, there are two spliced connections between the end users, with the gateway at the splice point, and the gateway must examine and forward all traffic in both directions.

CIRCUIT-LEVEL GATEWAY A fourth type of firewall is the circuit-level gateway or **circuit-level proxy** (Figure 24.7e). This can be a stand-alone system or it can be a specialized function performed by an application-level gateway for certain applications. As with an application gateway, a circuit-level gateway does not permit an end-to-end

TCP connection; rather, the gateway sets up two TCP connections, one between itself and a TCP user on an inner host and one between itself and a TCP user on an outside host. Once the two connections are established, the gateway typically relays TCP segments from one connection to the other without examining the contents. The security function consists of determining which connections will be allowed.

A typical use of circuit-level gateways is a situation in which the system administrator trusts the internal users. The gateway can be configured to support application-level or proxy service on inbound connections and circuit-level functions for outbound connections. In this configuration, the gateway can incur the processing overhead of examining incoming application data for forbidden functions but does not incur that overhead on outgoing data.

24.6 MALWARE DEFENSE

Antivirus Approaches

The ideal solution to the threat of viruses is prevention: Do not allow a virus to get into the system in the first place. This goal is, in general, impossible to achieve, although prevention can reduce the number of successful viral attacks. The next best approach is to be able to do the following:

- **Detection:** Once the infection has occurred, determine that it has occurred and locate the virus.
- **Identification:** Once detection has been achieved, identify the specific virus that has infected a program.
- **Removal:** Once the specific virus has been identified, remove all traces of the virus from the infected program and restore it to its original state. Remove the virus from all infected systems so that the disease cannot spread further.

If detection succeeds but either identification or removal is not possible, then the alternative is to discard the infected program and reload a clean backup version.

Advances in virus and antivirus technology go hand in hand. Early viruses were relatively simple code fragments and could be identified and purged with relatively simple antivirus software packages. As the virus arms race has evolved, both viruses and, necessarily, antivirus software have grown more complex and sophisticated. Increasingly sophisticated antivirus approaches and products continue to appear. In this subsection, we highlight two of the most important.

GENERIC DECRYPTION Generic decryption (GD) technology enables the antivirus program to easily detect even the most complex polymorphic viruses while maintaining fast scanning speeds [NACH97]. Recall that when a file containing a polymorphic virus is executed, the virus must decrypt itself to activate. In order to detect such a structure, executable files are run through a GD scanner, which contains the following elements:

- **CPU emulator:** A software-based virtual computer. Instructions in an executable file are interpreted by the emulator rather than executed on the underlying processor. The emulator includes software versions of all registers and other processor hardware, so that the underlying processor is unaffected by programs interpreted on the emulator.

- **Virus signature scanner:** A module that scans the target code looking for known virus signatures.
- **Emulation control module:** Controls the execution of the target code.

At the start of each simulation, the emulator begins interpreting instructions in the target code, one at a time. Thus, if the code includes a decryption routine that decrypts and hence exposes the virus, that code is interpreted. In effect, the virus does the work for the antivirus program by exposing the virus. Periodically, the control module interrupts interpretation to scan the target code for virus signatures.

During interpretation, the target code can cause no damage to the actual personal computer environment, because it is being interpreted in a completely controlled environment.

The most difficult design issue with a GD scanner is to determine how long to run each interpretation. Typically, virus elements are activated soon after a program begins executing, but this need not be the case. The longer the scanner emulates a particular program, the more likely it is to catch any hidden viruses. However, the antivirus program can take up only a limited amount of time and resources before users complain of degraded system performance.

DIGITAL IMMUNE SYSTEM The digital immune system is a comprehensive approach to virus protection developed by IBM [KEPH97a, KEPH97b, WHIT99] and subsequently refined by Symantec [SYMA01]. The motivation for this development has been the rising threat of Internet-based virus propagation. We first say a few words about this threat and then summarize IBM's approach.

Traditionally, the virus threat was characterized by the relatively slow spread of new viruses and new mutations. Antivirus software was typically updated on a monthly basis, and this was sufficient to control the problem. Also traditionally, the Internet played a comparatively small role in the spread of viruses. But as [CHES97] points out, two major trends in Internet technology have had an increasing impact on the rate of virus propagation in recent years:

- **Integrated mail systems:** Systems such as Lotus Notes and Microsoft Outlook make it very simple to send anything to anyone and to work with objects that are received.
- **Mobile-program systems:** Capabilities such as Java and ActiveX allow programs to move on their own from one system to another.

In response to the threat posed by these Internet-based capabilities, IBM has developed a prototype digital immune system. This system expands on the use of program emulation discussed in the preceding subsection and provides a general-purpose emulation and virus-detection system. The objective of this system is to provide rapid response time so that viruses can be stamped out almost as soon as they are introduced. When a new virus enters an organization, the immune system automatically captures it, analyzes it, adds detection and shielding for it, removes it, and passes information about that virus to systems running IBM AntiVirus so that it can be detected before it is allowed to run elsewhere.

Figure 24.8 illustrates the typical steps in digital immune system operation:

1. A monitoring program on each PC uses a variety of heuristics based on system behavior, suspicious changes to programs, or family signature to infer that a virus may be present. The monitoring program forwards a copy of any program thought to be infected to an administrative machine within the organization.
2. The administrative machine encrypts the sample and sends it to a central virus analysis machine.
3. This machine creates an environment in which the infected program can be safely run for analysis. Techniques used for this purpose include emulation, or the creation of a protected environment within which the suspect program can be executed and monitored. The virus analysis machine then produces a prescription for identifying and removing the virus.
4. The resulting prescription is sent back to the administrative machine.
5. The administrative machine forwards the prescription to the infected client.
6. The prescription is also forwarded to other clients in the organization.
7. Subscribers around the world receive regular antivirus updates that protect them from the new virus.

The success of the digital immune system depends on the ability of the virus analysis machine to detect new and innovative virus strains. By constantly analyzing

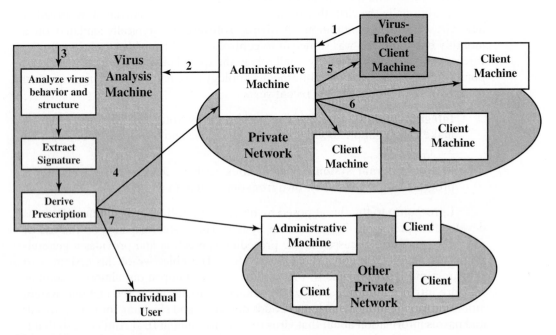

Figure 24.8 Digital Immune System

and monitoring the viruses found in the wild, it should be possible to continually update the digital immune software to keep up with the threat.

BEHAVIOR-BLOCKING SOFTWARE Unlike heuristics or fingerprint-based scanners, behavior-blocking software integrates with the operating system of a host computer and monitors program behavior in real time for malicious actions [CONR02, NACH02]. The behavior-blocking software then blocks potentially malicious actions before they have a chance to affect the system. Monitored behaviors can include the following:

- Attempts to open, view, delete, and/or modify files;
- Attempts to format disk drives and other unrecoverable disk operations;
- Modifications to the logic of executable files or macros;
- Modification of critical system settings, such as start-up settings;
- Scripting of e-mail and instant messaging clients to send executable content; and
- Initiation of network communications.

Figure 24.9 illustrates the operation of a behavior blocker. Behavior-blocking software runs on server and desktop computers and is instructed through policies set by the network administrator to let benign actions take place but to intercede when unauthorized or suspicious actions occur. The module blocks any suspicious software from executing. A blocker isolates the code in a sandbox, which restricts

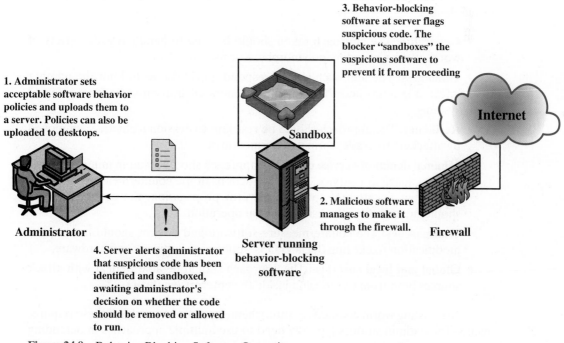

Figure 24.9 Behavior-Blocking Software Operation

the code's access to various OS resources and applications. The blocker then sends an alert.

Because a behavior blocker can block suspicious software in real time, it has an advantage over such established antivirus detection techniques as fingerprinting or heuristics. While there are literally trillions of different ways to obfuscate and rearrange the instructions of a virus or worm, many of which will evade detection by a fingerprint scanner or heuristic, eventually malicious code must make a well-defined request to the operating system. Given that the behavior blocker can intercept all such requests, it can identify and block malicious actions regardless of how obfuscated the program logic appears to be.

Behavior blocking alone has limitations. Because the malicious code must run on the target machine before all its behaviors can be identified, it can cause harm before it has been detected and blocked. For example, a new virus might shuffle a number of seemingly unimportant files around the hard drive before infecting a single file and being blocked. Even though the actual infection was blocked, the user may be unable to locate his or her files, causing a loss to productivity or possibly worse.

Worm Countermeasures

There is considerable overlap in techniques for dealing with viruses and worms. Once a worm is resident on a machine, antivirus software can be used to detect it. In addition, because worm propagation generates considerable network activity, network activity and usage monitoring can form the basis of a worm defense.

To begin, let us consider the requirements for an effective worm countermeasure scheme:

- **Generality:** The approach taken should be able to handle a wide variety of worm attacks, including polymorphic worms.
- **Timeliness:** The approach should respond quickly so as to limit the number infected systems and the number of generated transmissions from infected systems.
- **Resiliency:** The approach should be resistant to evasion techniques employed by attackers to evade worm countermeasures.
- **Minimal denial-of-service costs:** The approach should result in minimal reduction in capacity or service due to the actions of the countermeasure software. That is, in an attempt to contain worm propagation, the countermeasure should not significantly disrupt normal operation.
- **Transparency:** The countermeasure software and devices should not require modification to existing (legacy) OSs, application software, and hardware.
- **Global and local coverage:** The approach should be able to deal with attack sources both from outside and inside the enterprise network.

No existing worm countermeasure scheme appears to satisfy all these requirements. Thus, administrators typically need to use multiple approaches in defending against worm attacks.

Following [JHI07], we list six classes of worm defense:

A. Signature-based worm scan filtering: This type of approach generates a worm signature, which is then used to prevent worm scans from entering/leaving a network/host. Typically, this approach involves identifying suspicious flows and generating a worm signature. This approach is vulnerable to the use of polymorphic worms: Either the detection software misses the worm or, if it is sufficiently sophisticated to deal with polymorphic worms, the scheme may take a long time to react.

B. Filter-based worm containment: This approach is similar to class A but focuses on worm content rather than a scan signature. The filter checks a message to determine if it contains worm code. This approach can be quite effective but requires efficient detection algorithms and rapid alert dissemination.

C. Payload-classification-based worm containment: These network-based techniques examine packets to see if they contain a worm. Various anomaly detection techniques can be used, but care is needed to avoid high levels of false positives or negatives. This approach does not generate signatures based on byte patterns but rather looks for control and data flow structures that suggest an exploit.

D. Threshold random walk (TRW) scan detection: TRW exploits randomness in picking destinations to connect to as a way of detecting if a scanner is in operation. TRW is suitable for deployment in high-speed, low-cost network devices. It is effective against the common behavior seen in worm scans.

E. Rate limiting: This class limits the rate of scanlike traffic from an infected host. Various strategies can be used, including limiting the number of new machines a host can connect to in a window of time, detecting a high connection failure rate, and limiting the number of unique IP addresses a host can scan in a window of time. This class of countermeasures may introduce longer delays for normal traffic. This class is also not suited for slow, stealthy worms that spread slowly to avoid detection based on activity level.

F. Rate halting: This approach immediately blocks outgoing traffic when a threshold is exceeded either in outgoing connection rate or diversity of connection attempts [JHI07]. The approach must include measures to quickly unblock mistakenly blocked hosts in a transparent way. Rate halting can integrate with a signature- or filter-based approach so that once a signature or filter is generated, every blocked host can be unblocked. Rate halting appears to offer a very effective countermeasure. As with rate limiting, rate halting techniques are not suitable for slow, stealthy worms.

Bot Countermeasures

A number of the countermeasures discussed in this chapter make sense against bots, including IDSs and digital immune systems. Once bots are activated and an attack is underway, these countermeasures can be used to detect the attack. But the primary objective is to try to detect and disable the botnet during its construction phase.

24.7 RECOMMENDED READING AND WEB SITES

The topics in this chapter are covered in greater detail in [STAL11].

> **STAL11** Stallings, W. *Cryptography and Network Security: Principles and Practice, Fourth Edition*. Upper Saddle River, NJ: Prentice Hall, 2011.

Recommended Web sites:

- **AntiVirus online:** IBM's site on virus information
- **VirusList:** Site maintained by commercial antivirus software provider. Good collection of useful information

24.8 KEY TERMS, REVIEW QUESTIONS, AND PROBLEMS

Key Terms

antivirus	intrusion detection	stateful inspection firewall
Bot	intrusion detections system	Transport Layer Security
digital immune system	(IDS)	(TLS)
firewall	malware	Wi-Fi Protected Access
host-based IDS	packet filtering firewall	(WPA)
IP security (IPsec)	Secure Sockets Layer (SSL)	Worm

Review Questions

24.1 What services are provided by IPsec?

24.2 What protocols comprise SSL?

24.3 What is the difference between an SSL connection and an SSL session?

24.4 What services are provided by the SSL Record Protocol?

24.5 What security areas are addressed by IEEE 802.11i?

24.6 Explain the difference between anomaly intrusion detection and signature intrusion detection.

24.7 List three design goals for a firewall.

24.8 List four techniques used by firewalls to control access and enforce a security policy.

24.9 What information is used by a typical packet filtering router?

24.10 What are some weaknesses of a packet filtering router?

24.11 What is the difference between a packet filtering router and a stateful inspection firewall?

24.12 What is a digital immune system?

24.13 How does behavior-blocking software work?

24.14 Describe some worm countermeasures.

Problems

24.1 The authentication header (AH) in IPsec includes a message authentication code (MAC), which is calculated over all of the fields of the IPsec packet except IP header fields that either do not change in transit (immutable) or that are predictable in value upon arrival at the endpoint for the AH SA. Fields that may change in transit and whose value on arrival are unpredictable are set to zero for purposes of calculation at both source and destination.

    a. For each of the fields in the IPv4 header, indicate whether the field is immutable, mutable but predictable, or mutable.

    b. Do the same for the IPv6 header.

    In each case, justify your decision for each field.

24.2 In SSL and TLS, why is there a separate Change Cipher Spec Protocol rather than including a change_cipher_spec message in the Handshake Protocol?

24.3 In the context of an IDS, we define a false positive to be an alarm generated by an IDS in which the IDS alerts to a condition that is actually benign. A false negative occurs when an IDS fails to generate an alarm when an alert-worthy condition is in effect. Using the following diagram, depict two curves that roughly indicate false positives and false negatives, respectively.

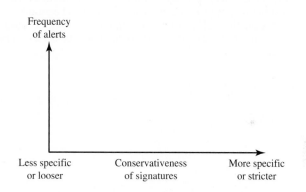

24.4 The overlapping area of the two probability density functions of Figure 24.6 represents the region in which there is the potential for false positives and false negatives. Further, Figure 24.6 is an idealized and not necessarily representative depiction of the relative shapes of the two density functions. Suppose there is 1 actual intrusion for every 1000 authorized users, and the overlapping area covers 1% of the authorized users and 50% of the intruders.

    a. Sketch such a set of density functions and argue that this is not an unreasonable depiction.

    b. What is the probability that an event that occurs in this region is that of an authorized user? Keep in mind that 50% of all intrusions fall in this region.

24.5 An example of a host-based intrusion detection tool is the tripwire program. This is a file integrity checking tool that scans files and directories on the system on a regular basis and notifies the administrator of any changes. It uses a protected database of cryptographic checksums for each file checked and compares this value with that recomputed on each file as it is scanned. It must be configured with a list of files and directories to check, and what changes, if any, are permissible to each. It can allow, for example, log files to have new entries appended, but not for existing entries to be changed. What are the advantages and disadvantages of using such a tool? Consider the problem of determining which files should only change rarely, which files may change more often and how, and which change frequently and hence cannot be checked. Consider the amount of work in both the configuration of the program and on the system administrator monitoring the responses generated.

24.6 Test the vulnerability of a machine at the following site: http://grc.com/default.htm. Follow the ShieldsUP! link for a series of free tests listed midway down the page.

24.7 As was mentioned in Section 24.5, one approach to defeating the tiny fragment attack is to enforce a minimum length of the transport header that must be contained in the first fragment of an IP packet. If the first fragment is rejected, all subsequent fragments can be rejected. However, the nature of IP is such that fragments may arrive out of order. Thus, an intermediate fragment may pass through the filter before the initial fragment is rejected. How can this situation be handled?

24.8 In an IPv4 packet, the size of the payload in the first fragment, in octets, is equal to Total Length – $(4 \times \text{IHL})$. If this value is less than the required minimum (8 octets for TCP), then this fragment and the entire packet are rejected. Suggest an alternative method of achieving the same result using only the Fragment Offset field.

24.9 RFC 791, the IPv4 protocol specification, describes a reassembly algorithm that results in new fragments overwriting any overlapped portions of previously received fragments. Given such a reassembly implementation, an attacker could construct a series of packets in which the lowest (zero-offset) fragment would contain innocuous data (and thereby be passed by administrative packet filters), and in which some subsequent packet having a non-zero offset would overlap TCP header information (destination port, for instance) and cause it to be modified. The second packet would be passed through most filter implementations because it does not have a zero fragment offset. Suggest a method that could be used by a packet filter to counter this attack.

FOURIER ANALYSIS

"I cannot conceal from myself, in spite of your distinguished politeness, that I am becoming intolerably tiresome with my commonplace talk."

"On the contrary," replied Kai Lung, "while listening to your voice I seemed to hear the beating of many gongs of the finest and most polished brass."

— *The Wallet of Kai Lung,* Ernest Bramah

In this appendix, we provide an overview of key concepts in Fourier analysis.

A.1 FOURIER SERIES REPRESENTATION OF PERIODIC SIGNALS

With the aid of a good table of integrals, it is a remarkably simple task to determine the frequency domain nature of many signals. We begin with periodic signals. Any periodic signal can be represented as a sum of sinusoids, known as a Fourier series:[1]

$$x(t) = \frac{A_0}{2} + \sum_{n=1}^{\infty} [A_n \cos (2\pi n f_0 t) + B_n \sin (2\pi n f_0 t)]$$

where f_0 is the reciprocal of the period of the signal ($f_0 = 1/T$). The frequency f_0 is referred to as the **fundamental frequency** or **fundamental harmonic**; integer multiples of f_0 are referred to as **harmonics**. Thus a periodic signal with period T consists of the fundamental frequency $f_0 = 1/T$ plus integer multiples of that frequency. If $A_0 \neq 0$, then $x(t)$ has a **dc component**.

The values of the coefficients are calculated as follows:

$$A_0 = \frac{2}{T} \int_0^T x(t) \, dt$$

$$A_n = \frac{2}{T} \int_0^T x(t) \cos(2\pi n f_0 t) \, dt$$

$$B_n = \frac{2}{T} \int_0^T x(t) \sin (2\pi n f_0 t) dt$$

This form of representation, known as the sine-cosine representation, is the easiest form to compute but suffers from the fact that there are two components at each frequency. A more meaningful representation, the amplitude-phase representation, takes the form

$$x(t) = \frac{C_0}{2} + \sum_{n=1}^{\infty} C_n \cos (2\pi n f_0 t + \theta_n)$$

---

[1]Mathematicians typically write Fourier series and transform expressions using the variable w_0, which has a dimension of radians per second and where $w_0 = 2\pi f_0$. For physics and engineering, the f_0 formulation is preferred; it makes for simpler expressions, and it is intuitively more satisfying to have frequency expressed in Hz rather than radians per second.

This relates to the earlier representation as follows:

$$C_0 = A_0$$
$$C_n = \sqrt{A_n^2 + B_n^2}$$

$$\theta_n = \tan^{-1}\left(2\,\frac{-B_n}{A_n}\right)$$

Examples of the Fourier series for periodic signals are shown in Figure A.1.

A.2 FOURIER TRANSFORM REPRESENTATION OF APERIODIC SIGNALS

For a periodic signal, we have seen that its spectrum consists of discrete frequency components, at the fundamental frequency and its harmonics. For an aperiodic signal, the spectrum consists of a continuum of frequencies. This spectrum can be defined by the Fourier transform. For a signal $x(t)$ with a spectrum $X(f)$, the following relationships hold:

$$x(t) = \int_{-\infty}^{\infty} X(f)e^{j2\pi ft}df$$

$$X(f) = \int_{-\infty}^{\infty} X(t)e^{-j2\pi ft}dt$$

where $j = \sqrt{-1}$. The presence of an imaginary number in the equations is a matter of convenience. The imaginary component has a physical interpretation having to do with the phase of a waveform, and a discussion of this topic is beyond the scope of this book.

Figure A.2 presents some examples of Fourier transform pairs.

Power Spectral Density and Bandwidth

The absolute bandwidth of any time-limited signal is infinite. In practical terms, however, most of the power in a signal is concentrated in some finite band, and the effective bandwidth consists of that portion of the spectrum that contains most of the power. To make this concept precise, we need to define the power spectral density (PSD). In essence, the PSD describes the power content of a signal as a function of frequency, so that it shows how much power is present over various frequency bands.

First, we observe the power in the time domain. A function $x(t)$ usually specifies a signal in terms of either voltage or current. In either case, the instantaneous power in the signal is proportional to $|x(t)|^2$. We define the average power of a time-limited signal as

$$P = \frac{1}{t_1 - t_2}\int_{t_1}^{t_2} |x(t)|^2\, dt$$

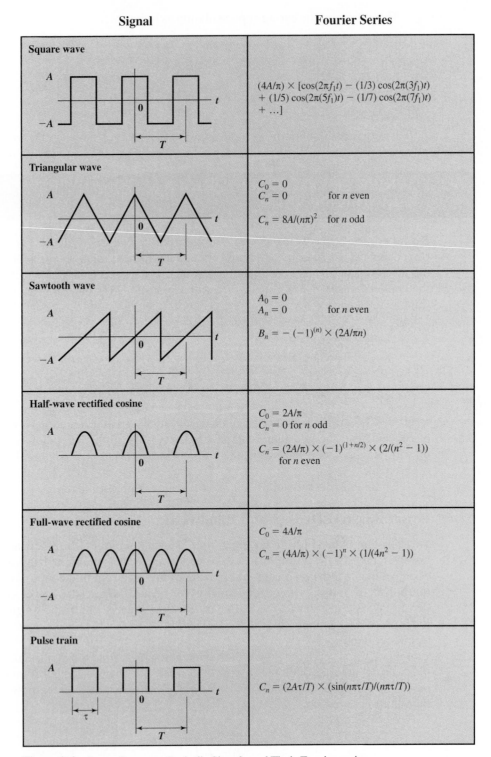

Figure A.1 Some Common Periodic Signals and Their Fourier series

Signal $x(t)$	**Fourier Transform $X(f)$**

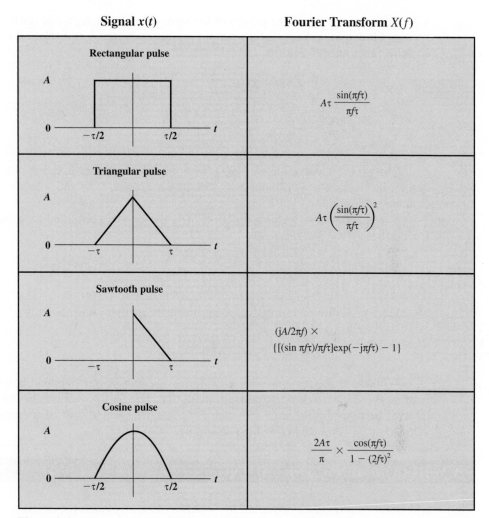

Figure A.2   Some Common Aperiodic Signals and Their Fourier Transforms

For a periodic signal the average power in one period is

$$P = \frac{1}{T} \int_0^T |x(t)|^2 \, dt$$

We would like to know the distribution of power as a function of frequency. For periodic signals, this is easily expressed in terms of the coefficients of the Fourier series. The power spectral density $S(f)$ obeys

$$S(f) = \sum_{n=-\infty}^{\infty} |C_n|^2 \delta(f - nf_0)$$

where f_0 is the inverse of the period of the signal ($f_0 = 1/T$), C_n is the coefficient in the amplitude-phase representation of a Fourier series, and $\delta(t)$ is the unit impulse, or delta, function, defined as:

$$\delta(t) = \begin{cases} 0 & \text{if } t \neq 0 \\ \infty & \text{if } t = 0 \end{cases}$$

$$\int_{-\infty}^{\infty} \delta(t)dt = 1$$

The power spectral density $S(f)$ for aperiodic functions is more difficult to define. In essence, it is obtained by defining a "period" T_0 and allowing T_0 to increase without limit.

For a continuous valued function $S(f)$, the power contained in a band of frequencies, $f_1 < f < f_2$, is

$$P = 2 \int_{f_1}^{f_2} S(f) \, df$$

For a periodic waveform, the power through the first j harmonics is

$$P = \frac{1}{4} C_0^2 + \frac{1}{2} \sum_{n=1}^{j} C_n^2$$

With these concepts, we can now define the half-power bandwidth, which is perhaps the most common bandwidth definition. The half-power bandwidth is the interval between frequencies at which $S(f)$ has dropped to half of its maximum value of power, or 3 dB below the peak value.

A.3 RECOMMENDED READING

A very accessible treatment of Fourier series and Fourier transforms is [JAME03]. For a thorough understanding of Fourier series and transforms, the book to read is [KAMM00]. [BHAT05] is a useful short introduction to Fourier series.

BHAT05 Bhatia, R. *Fourier Series.* Washington, DC: Mathematical Association of America, 2005.

JAME03 James, J. *A Student's Guide to Fourier Transforms.* Cambridge, England: Cambridge University Press, 2003.

KAMM00 Kammler, D. *A First Course in Fourier Analysis.* Upper Saddle River, NJ: Prentice Hall, 2000.

PROJECTS AND OTHER STUDENT EXERCISES FOR TEACHING DATA AND COMPUTER COMMUNICATIONS

Analysis and observation, theory and experience must never disdain or exclude each other; on the contrary, they support each other.

— *On War*, Carl Von Clausewitz

Many instructors believe that research or implementation projects are crucial to the clear understanding of the concepts of data and computer communications. Without projects, it may be difficult for students to grasp some of the basic concepts and interactions among components. Projects reinforce the concepts introduced in the book, give the student a greater appreciation of how protocols and transmission schemes work, and can motivate students and give them confidence that they have mastered the material.

In this text, I have tried to present the concepts as clearly as possible and have provided nearly 400 homework problems to reinforce those concepts. Many instructors will wish to supplement this material with projects. This appendix provides some guidance in that regard and describes support material available in the **Instructor's Resource Center (IRC)** for this book accessible from Prentice Hall for instructors. The support material covers nine types of projects and other student exercises:

- Animations
- Practical exercises
- Sockets programming projects
- Wireshark projects
- Simulation projects
- Performance modeling projects
- Research projects
- Reading/report assignments
- Writing assignments
- Discussion topics

B.1 ANIMATIONS AND ANIMATION PROJECTS

Animations provide a powerful tool for understanding the complex mechanisms of network protocols. A number of Web-based animations are used to illustrate protocol behavior. Each animation allows the users to step through the operation of the protocol by selecting the next step at each point in the protocol exchange. The animations will be made available to professors at the IRC for this book in such a way as to enable online access by students.

The animations can be used in two ways. In a **passive mode**, the student can click more or less randomly on the next step at each point in the animation and watch as the given concept or principle is illustrated. The **active mode** can be used for two types of assignments. First, the student can be given a specific set of steps to invoke and watch the animation, and then be asked to analyze and comment on the results. Second, the student can be given a specific end point and required to devise a sequence of steps that achieve the desired result. The IRC includes a set of assignments for each of the animations, plus suggested solutions so that instructors can assess the student's work.

These animations were developed at the University of Stirling in Scotland by Iain Robin and Ken Turner, with contributions from Paul Johnson and Kenneth Whyte. Larry Tan of the University of Stirling developed the animation assignments.

B.2 PRACTICAL EXERCISES

The IRC includes Web pages that provide a set of practical exercises for an introduction to the use of IP over a LAN. The exercises naturally follow one another and build on the experience of the previous exercises. They do not, however, need to be attempted one after another. The four exercises may more easily be done on four separate occasions. The practical exercises are designed to help the student understand the operation of an Ethernet LAN and an IP network. The exercises involve using simple network commands available on most computers. About an hour is needed to perform all four exercises. The exercises cover the following topics: your own network connection, computers on your LAN, computers on remote networks, and the Internet.

B.3 SOCKETS PROJECTS

The concept of sockets and sockets programming was developed in the 1980s in the UNIX environment as the Berkeley Sockets Interface. In essence, a socket enables communications between a client and server process and may be either connection oriented or connectionless. A socket can be considered an endpoint in a communication. A client socket in one computer uses an address to call a server socket on another computer. Once the appropriate sockets are engaged, the two computers can exchange data.

Typically, computers with server sockets keep a TCP or UDP port open, ready for unscheduled incoming calls. The client typically determines the socket identification of the desired server by finding it in a Domain Name System (DNS) database. Once a connection is made, the server switches the dialog to a different port number to free up the main port number for additional incoming calls.

Internet applications, such as TELNET and remote login (rlogin), make use of sockets, with the details hidden from the user. However, sockets can be constructed from within a program (in a language such as C or Java), enabling the programmer to easily support networking functions and applications. The sockets programming mechanism includes sufficient semantics to permit unrelated processes on different hosts to communicate.

The Berkeley Sockets Interface is the de facto standard application programming interface (API) for developing networking applications, spanning a wide range of operating systems. The sockets API provides generic access to interprocess communications services. Thus, the sockets capability is ideally suited for students to learn the principles of protocols and distributed applications by hands-on program development.

Appendix T provides an overview of sockets programming prepared especially for this book plus links to sites with more information on the subject. In addition, the IRC includes a set of programming projects.

B.4 WIRESHARK PROJECTS

Wireshark, formerly known as Ethereal, is used by network professionals around the world for troubleshooting, analysis, software and protocol development, and education. It has all of the standard features you would expect in a protocol analyzer and several features not seen in any other product. Its open source license allows talented experts in the networking community to add enhancements. It runs on all popular computing platforms, including UNIX, Linux, Windows, and Mac OS X.

Wireshark is ideal for allowing students to study the behavior of protocols not only because of its many features and multiplatform capability but also because students may subsequently use Wireshark in their professional life.

The IRC includes a Student User's Manual and a set of project assignments for Wireshark created specifically for use with the book. In addition, there is a very useful video tutorial that introduces the student to the use of Wireshark.

Michael Harris of Indiana University initially developed the Ethereal exercises and user's guide. Dave Bremer of Otago Polytechnic in New Zealand updated the material for the most recent Wireshark release; he also developed the online video tutorial.

B.5 SIMULATION AND MODELING PROJECTS

An excellent way to obtain a grasp of the operation of communication protocols and network configurations, and to study and appreciate some of the design trade-offs and performance implications, is by simulating key elements. A tool that is useful for this purpose is *cnet*.

Compared to actual hardware/software implementation, simulation provides two advantages for both research and educational use:

- With simulation, it is easy to modify various elements of a network configuration or various features of a protocol, to vary the performance characteristics of various components and then to analyze the effects of such modifications.

- Simulation provides for detailed performance statistics collection, which can be used to understand performance trade-offs.

The *cnet* network simulator [MCDO91] enables experimentation with various data link layer, network layer, routing and transport layer protocols, and with various network configurations. It has been specifically designed for undergraduate computer networking courses and used worldwide by thousands of students since 1991.

The *cnet* simulator was developed by Professor Chris McDonald at the University of Western Australia. Professor McDonald has developed a Student User's Manual and a set of project assignments specifically for use with *Data and Computer Communications* and available to professors on request.

The *cnet* simulator runs under a variety of UNIX and Linux platforms. The software can be downloaded from the *cnet* Web site. It is available at no cost for noncommercial use.

B.6 PERFORMANCE MODELING

An alternative to simulation for assessing the performance of a communications system or networking protocol is analytic modeling. As used here, analytic modeling refers to tools for doing queuing analysis, as well as tools for doing simple statistical tests on network traffic data and tools for generating time series for analysis.

A powerful and easy-to-use set of tools has been developed by Professor Kenneth Christensen at the University of South Florida. His *tools page* contains downloadable tools primarily related to performance evaluation of computer networks and to TCP/IP sockets programming. Each tool is written in ANSI C. The format for each tool is the same, with the program header describing tool purpose, general notes, sample input, sample output, build instructions, execution instructions, and author/contact information. The code is documented with extensive inline comments and header blocks for all functions. The goal for each tool is that it can serve as a teaching tool for the concept implemented by the tool (and as a model for good programming practices). Thus, the emphasis is on simplicity and clarity. It is assumed that the student will have access to a C compiler and have at least moderate experience in C programming.

Professor Christensen has developed a Student User's Manual and a set of project assignments specifically for use with *Data and Computer Communications* and available to professors on request. The software can be downloaded from the *tools* Web site. It is available at no cost for noncommercial use.

In addition, OPNET, a professional modeling tool for networking configurations, can be used. An academic version is available and a student lab manual prepared for this book is available from Prentice Hall.

B.7 RESEARCH PROJECTS

An effective way of reinforcing basic concepts from the course and for teaching students research skills is to assign a research project. Such a project could involve a literature search as well as a Web search of vendor products, research lab activities, and standardization efforts. Projects could be assigned to teams or, for smaller projects, to individuals. In any case, it is best to require some sort of project proposal early in the term, giving the instructor time to evaluate the proposal for appropriate topic and appropriate level of effort. Student handouts for research projects should include the following:

- A format for the proposal
- A format for the final report
- A schedule with intermediate and final deadlines
- A list of possible project topics

The students can select one of the listed topics or devise their own comparable project. The IRC includes a suggested format for the proposal and final report plus a list of possible research topics.

B.8 READING/REPORT ASSIGNMENTS

Another excellent way to reinforce concepts from the course and to give students research experience is to assign papers from the literature to be read and analyzed. The IRC includes a suggested list of papers, one or two per chapter, to be assigned. The IRC provides a PDF copy of each of the papers. The IRC also includes a suggested assignment wording.

B.9 WRITING ASSIGNMENTS

Writing assignments can have a powerful multiplier effect in the learning process in a technical discipline such as cryptography and network security. Adherents of the Writing Across the Curriculum (WAC) movement (http://wac.colostate.edu/) report substantial benefits of writing assignments in facilitating learning. Writing assignments lead to more detailed and complete thinking about a particular topic. In addition, writing assignments help to overcome the tendency of students to pursue a subject with a minimum of personal engagement, just learning facts and problem-solving techniques without obtaining a deep understanding of the subject matter.

The IRC contains a number of suggested writing assignments, organized by chapter. Instructors may ultimately find that this is an important part of their approach to teaching the material. I would greatly appreciate any feedback on this area and any suggestions for additional writing assignments.

B.10 DISCUSSION TOPICS

One way to provide a collaborative experience is discussion topics, a number of which are included in the IRC. Each topic relates to material in the book. The instructor can set it up so that students can discuss a topic either in a class setting, an online chat room, or a message board. Again, I would greatly appreciate any feedback on this area and any suggestions for additional discussion topics.

REFERENCES

In matters of this kind everyone feels he is justified in writing and publishing the first thing that comes into his head when he picks up a pen, and thinks his own idea as axiomatic as the fact that two and two make four. If critics would go to the trouble of thinking about the subject for years on end and testing each conclusion against the actual history of war, as I have done, they would undoubtedly be more careful of what they wrote.

On War, Carl von Clausewitz

ABBREVIATIONS

ACM   Association for Computing Machinery
IEEE   Institute of Electrical and Electronics Engineers
NIST   National Institute of Standards and Technology

ADAM91   Adamek, J. *Foundations of Coding.* New York: Wiley, 1991.

ANDE80   Anderson, J. *Computer Security Threat Monitoring and Surveillance.* Fort Washington, PA: James P. Anderson Co., April 1980.

ANDE95   Anderson, J.; Rappaport, T.; and Yoshida, S. "Propagation Measurements and Models for Wireless Communications Channels." *IEEE Communications Magazine*, January 1995.

ANDR99   Andrikopoulos, I.; Liakopoulous, A.; Pavlou, G.; and Sun, Z. "Providing Rate Guarantees for Internet Application Traffic Across ATM Networks." *IEEE Communications Surveys*, Third Quarter 1999, http://www.comsoc.org/pubs/surveys.

ANTE06   Ante, S., and Grow, B. "Meet the Hackers." *Business Week*, May 29, 2006.

ARAS94   Aras, C.; Kurose, J.; Reeves, D.; and Schulzrinne, H. "Real-Time Communication in Packet-Switched Networks." *Proceedings of the IEEE*, January 1994.

ARMI93   Armitage, G., and Adams, K. "Packet Reassembly During Cell Loss." *IEEE Network*, September 1993.

ASH90   Ash, R. *Information Theory.* New York: Dover, 1990.

AYCO06   Aycock, J. *Computer Viruses and Malware.* New York: Springer, 2006.

BALL89   Ballart, R., and Ching, Y. "SONET: Now It's the Standard Optical Network." *IEEE Communications Magazine*, March 1989.

BARA02   Baran, P. "The Beginnings of Packet Switching: Some Underlying Concepts." *IEEE Communications Magazine*, July 2002.

BEIJ06   Beijnum, I. "IPv6 Internals." *The Internet Protocol Journal*, September 2006.

BELL94   Bellovin, S., and Cheswick, W. "Network Firewalls." *IEEE Communications Magazine*, September 1994.

BELL00   Bellamy, J. *Digital Telephony.* New York: Wiley, 2000.

BENE64   Benice, R. "An Analysis of Retransmission Systems." *IEEE Transactions on Communication Technology*, December 1964.

BERG96   Bergmans, J. *Digital Baseband Transmission and Recording.* Boston: Kluwer, 1996.

BERL87   Berlekamp, E.; Peile, R.; and Pope, S. "The Application of Error Control to Communications." *IEEE Communications Magazine*, April 1987.

BERN00   Bernet, Y. "The Complementary Roles of RSVP and Differentiated Services in the Full-Service QoS Network." *IEEE Communications Magazine*, February 2000.

BERT92   Bertsekas, D., and Gallager, R. *Data Networks.* Englewood Cliffs, NJ: Prentice Hall, 1992.

BERT94   Bertoni, H.; Honcharenko, W.; Maciel, L.; and Xia, H. "UHF Propagation Prediction for Wireless Personal Communications." *Proceedings of the IEEE*, September 1994.

BHAR83   Bhargava, V. "Forward Error Correction Schemes for Digital Communications." *IEEE Communications Magazine*, January 1983.

BHAT05   Bhatia, R. *Fourier Series.* Washington, DC: Mathematical Association of America, 2005.

BLAC99a Black, U. *ATM Volume I: Foundation for Broadband Networks.* Upper Saddle River, NJ: Prentice Hall, 1999.

BLAC99b Black, U. *Second-Generation Mobile and Wireless Networks.* Upper Saddle River, NJ: Prentice Hall, 1999.

BLAC00   Black, U. *IP Routing Protocols: RIP, OSPF, BGP, PNNI & Cisco Routing Protocols.* Upper Saddle River, NJ: Prentice Hall, 2000.

BOEH90   Boehm, R. "Progress in Standardization of SONET." *IEEE LCS*, May 1990.

BONA01   Bonaventure, O., and Nelissen, J. "Guaranteed Frame Rate: A Better Service for TCP/IP in ATM Networks." *IEEE Network*, January/February 2001.

BORE97   Borella, M., et al. "Optical Components for WDM Lightwave Networks." *Proceedings of the IEEE*, August 1997.

BOUI02   Bouillet, E.; Mitra, D.; and Ramakrishnan, K. "The Structure and Management of Service Level Agreements in Networks." *IEEE Journal on Selected Areas in Communications*, May 2002.

BURG91   Burg, J., and Dorman, D. "Broadband ISDN Resource Management: The Role of Virtual Paths." *IEEE Communications Magazine*, September 1991.

BUX80   Bux, W.; Kummerle, K.; and Truong, H. "Balanced HDLC Procedures: A Performance Analysis." *IEEE Transactions on Communications*, November 1980.

CARN99   Carne, E. *Telecommunications Primer: Data, Voice, and Video Communications.* Upper Saddle River, NJ: Prentice Hall, 1999.

CARP02   Carpenter, B., and Nichols, K. "Differentiated Services in the Internet." *Proceedings of the IEEE*, September 2002.

CERF74   Cerf, V., and Kahn, R. "A Protocol for Packet Network Interconnection." *IEEE Transactions on Communications*, May 1974.

CHEN02   Chen, T. "Internet Performance Monitoring." *Proceedings of the IEEE*, September 2002.

CHES97   Chess, D. "The Future of Viruses on the Internet." *Proceedings, Virus Bulletin International Conference*, October 1997.

CICI01   Ciciora, W. "The Cable Modem Traffic Jam." *IEEE Spectrum*, June 2001.

CISC00   Cisco Systems, Inc. *Overcoming Multipath in Non-Line-of-Sight High-Speed Microwave Communication Links.* White Paper, 2000, www.cisco.com.

CISC07   Cisco Systems, Inc. "802.11n: The Next Generation of Wireless Performance." Cisco White Paper, 2007, cisco.com.

CLAR88   Clark, D. "The Design Philosophy of the DARPA Internet Protocols." *ACM SIGCOMM Computer Communications Review*, August 1988.

CLAR90   Clark, D., and Tennenhouse, D. "Architectural Considerations for a New Generation of Protocols." *Proceedings, SIGCOMM '90, Computer Communication Review*, September 1990.

CLAR92   Clark, D.; Shenker, S.; and Zhang, L. "Supporting Real-Time Applications in an Integrated Services Packet Network: Architecture and Mechanism" *Proceedings, SIGCOMM '92*, August 1992.

CLAR95   Clark, D. *Adding Service Discrimination to the Internet.* MIT Laboratory for Computer Science Technical Report, September 1995, http://ana-www.lcs.mit.edu/anaWeb/papers.html.

CLAR98   Clark, D., and Fang, W. "Explicit Allocation of Best-Effort Packet Delivery Service." *IEEE/ACM Transactions on Networking*, August 1998.

COHE94   Cohen, F. *A Short Course on Computer Viruses.* New York: Wiley, 1994.

COME99   Comer, D., and Stevens, D. *Internetworking with TCP/IP, Volume II: Design Implementation, and Internals.* Upper Saddle River, NJ: Prentice Hall, 1999.

COME01   Comer, D., and Stevens, D. *Internetworking with TCP/IP, Volume III: Client-Server Programming and Applications.* Upper Saddle River, NJ: Prentice Hall, 2001.

COME06   Comer, D. *Internetworking with TCP/IP, Volume I: Principles, Protocols, and Architecture.* Upper Saddle River, NJ: Prentice Hall, 2006.

CONR02   Conry-Murray, A. "Behavior-Blocking Stops Unknown Malicious Code." *Network Magazine*, June 2002.

CORM09   Cormen, T., et al. *Introduction to Algorithms.* Cambridge, MA: MIT Press, 2009.

COUC07   Couch, L. *Digital and Analog Communication Systems.* Upper Saddle River, NJ: Prentice Hall, 2007.

CROW92   Crowcroft, J.; Wakeman, I.; Wang, Z.; and Sirovica, D. "Is Layering Harmful?" *IEEE Network Magazine*, January 1992.

DEBE07   Debeasi, P. "802.11n: Beyond the Hype." *Burton Group White Paper*, July 2007, www.burtongroup.com.

DIAN02   Dianda, J.; Gurbani, V.; and Jones, M. "Session Initiation Protocol Services Architecture." *Bell Labs Technical Journal*, Volume 7, Number 1, 2002.

DIJK59   Dijkstra, E. "A Note on Two Problems in Connection with Graphs." *Numerical Mathematics*, October 1959.

ELSA02   El-Sayed, M., and Jaffe, J. "A View of Telecommunications Network Evolution." *IEEE Communications Magazine*, December 2002.

DINA98   Dinan, E., and Jabbari, B. "Spreading Codes for Direct Sequence CDMA and Wideband CDMA Cellular Networks." *IEEE Communications Magazine*, September 1998.

DOI04   Doi, S., et al. "IPv6 Anycast for Simple and Effective Communications." *IEEE Communications Magazine*, May 2004.

ENGE80   Enger, N., and Howerton, P. *Computer Security.* New York: Amacom, 1980.

FARZ10   Farzad, R. "AT&T's iMess." *Business Week*, February 15, 2010.

FELL01   Fellows, D., and Jones, D. "DOCSIS Cable Modem Technology." *IEEE Communications Magazine*, March 2001.

FIOR95   Fiorini, D.; Chiani, M.; Tralli, V.; and Salati, C. "Can We Trust HDLC?" *ACM Computer Communications Review*, October 1995.

FLOY94   Floyd, S., and Jacobson, V. "The Synchronization of Periodic Routing Messages," *IEEE/ACM Transactions on Networking*, April 1994.

FORD62   Ford, L., and Fulkerson, D. *Flows in Networks.* Princeton, NJ: Princeton University Press, 1962.

FRAT06   Frattasi, S., et al. "Defining 4G Technology from the User's Perspective." *IEEE Network*, January/February 2006.

FRAZ99   Frazier, H., and Johnson, H. "Gigabit Ethernet: From 100 to 1,000 Mbps." *IEEE Internet Computing*, January/February 1999.

FREE98a   Freeman, R. "Bits, Symbols, Baud, and Bandwidth." *IEEE Communications Magazine*, April 1998.

FREE98b   Freeman, R. *Telecommunication Transmission Handbook.* New York: Wiley, 1998.

FREE02   Freeman, R. *Fiber-Optic Systems for Telecommunications.* New York: Wiley, 2002.

FREE04   Freeman, R. *Telecommunication System Engineering.* New York: Wiley, 2004.

FREE05   Freeman, R. *Fundamentals of Telecommunications.* New York: Wiley, 2005.

FREE07   Freeman, R. *Radio System Design for Telecommunications.* New York: Wiley, 2007.

FURH94   Furht, B. "Multimedia Systems: An Overview." *IEEE Multimedia*, Spring 1994.

GARR96   Garrett, M. "A Service Architecture for ATM: From Applications to Scheduling." *IEEE Network*, May/June 1996.

GAUD00   Gaudin, S. "The Omega Files." *Network World*, June 26, 2000.

GEIE01   Geier, J. "Enabling Fast Wireless Networks with OFDM." *Communications System Design*, February 2001, www.csdmag.com.

GERL80   Gerla, M., and Kleinrock, L. "Flow Control: A Comparative Survey." *IEEE Transactions on Communications*, April 1980.

GERS91   Gersht, A., and Lee, K. "A Congestion Control Framework for ATM Networks." *IEEE Journal on Selected Areas in Communications*, September 1991.

GIBS93   Gibson, J. *Principles of Digital and Analog Communications.* New York: Macmillan, 1993.

GIRO99   Giroux, N., and Ganti, S. *Quality of Service in ATM Networks.* Upper Saddle River, NJ: Prentice Hall, 1999.

GONZ00   Gonzalez, R. "Disciplining Multimedia." *IEEE Multimedia*, July–September 2000.

GOOD02   Goode, B. "Voice Over Internet Protocol (VoIP)." *Proceedings of the IEEE*, September 2002.

GOYA98   Goyal, R., et al. "Providing Rate Guarantees to TCP over the ATM GFR Service." *Proceedings of the Local Computer Networks Conference*, October 1998.

GOUR02   Gourley, D., et al. *HTTP: The Definitive Guide.* Sebastopol, CA: O'Reilly, 2002.

GRAN04   Grance, T.; Kent, K.; and Kim, B. *Computer Security Incident Handling Guide.* NIST Special Publication SP 800-61, January 2004.

GREE80   Green, P. "An Introduction to Network Architecture and Protocols." *IEEE Transactions on Communications*, April 1980.

GRIM91   Grimes, J., and Potel, M. "What is Multimedia?" *IEEE Computer Graphics and Applications*, January 1991.

HALP10   Halperin, D., et al. "802.11 with Multiple Antennas for Dummies." *Computer Communication Review*, January 2010.

HARJ00   Harju, J., and Kivimaki, P. "Cooperation and Comparison of DiffServ and IntServ: Performance Measurements." *Proceedings, 23rd Annual IEEE Conference on Local Computer Networks*, November 2000.

HARN02   Harnedy, S. *The MPLS Primer: An Introduction to Multiprotocol Label Switching.* Upper Saddle River, NJ: Prentice Hall, 2002.

HATA80   Hata, M. "Empirical Formula for Propagation Loss in Land Mobile Radio Services." *IEEE Transactions on Vehicular Technology*, March 1980.

HAWL97   Hawley, G. "Systems Considerations for the Use of xDSL Technology for Data Access." *IEEE Communications Magazine*, March 1997.

HAYK09   Haykin, S. *Communication Systems*. New York: Wiley, 2009.

HEGG84   Heggestad, H. "An Overview of Packet Switching Communications." *IEEE Communications Magazine*, April 1984.

HELL01   Heller, R., et al. "Using a Theoretical Multimedia Taxonomy Framework." *ACM Journal of Educational Resources in Computing*, Spring 2001.

HIER10   Hiertz, G., et al. "The IEEE 802.11 Universe." IEEE Communications Magazine, January 2010.

HIND95   Hinden, R. "IP Next Generation Overview." *Connexions*, March 1995.

HONE05   Honeynet Project. *Knowing Your Enemy: Tracking Botnets*. Honeynet White Paper, March 2005, http://honeynet.org/papers/bots.

HUIT00   Huitema, C. *Routing in the Internet*. Upper Saddle River, NJ: Prentice Hall, 2000.

HUMP97   Humphrey, M., and Freeman, J. "How xDSL Supports Broadband Services to the Home." *IEEE Network*, January/March 1997.

IBM95   IBM International Technical Support Organization. *Asynchronous Transfer Mode (ATM) Technical Overview*. IBM Redbook SG24-4625-00, 1995, www.redbooks.ibm.com.

IPAT05   Ipatov, V. *Spread Spectrum and CDMA: Principles and Applications*. New York: Wiley, 2005.

IREN99   Iren, S.; Amer, P.; and Conrad, P. "The Transport Layer: Tutorial and Survey." *ACM Computing Surveys*, December 1999.

JACO88   Jacobson, V. "Congestion Avoidance and Control." *Proceedings, SIGCOMM '88, Computer Communication Review*, August 1988; reprinted in *Computer Communication Review*, January 1995; a slightly revised version is available at ftp.ee.lbl.gov/papers/congavoid.ps.Z.

JACO90a   Jacobson, V. "Berkeley TCP Evolution from 4.3 Tahoe to 4.3-Reno." *Proceedings of the Eighteenth Internet Engineering Task Force*, September 1990.

JACO90b   Jacobson, V. "Modified TCP Congestion Avoidance Algorithm." *end2end-interest mailing list*, April 20, 1990, ftp://ftp.ee.lbl.gov/email/vanj.90apr30.txt.

JAIN90   Jain, R. "Congestion Control in Computer Networks: Issues and Trends." *IEEE Network Magazine*, May 1990.

JAIN92   Jain, R. "Myths About Congestion Management in High-Speed Networks." *Internetworking: Research and Experience*, Volume 3, 1992.

JAIN94   Jain, R. "What Is Multimedia, Anyway?" *IEEE Multimedia*, Fall 1994.

JAME03   James, J. *A Student's Guide to Fourier Transforms.* Cambridge, England: Cambridge University Press, 2003.

JANS01   Jansen, W. *Guidelines on Active Content and Mobile Code.* NIST Special Publication SP 800-28, October 2001.

JHI07   Jhi, Y., et al. "Proactive Containment of Fast Scanning Worms through White Detection." *Proceedings of 3rd International Conference on Security and Privacy in Communication Networks*, September 2007.

KAMM00   Kammler, D. *A First Course in Fourier Analysis.* Upper Saddle River, NJ: Prentice Hall, 2000.

KARN91   Karn, P., and Partridge, C. "Improving Round-Trip Estimates in Reliable Transport Protocols." *ACM Transactions on Computer Systems*, November 1991.

KENT87   Kent, C., and Mogul, J. "Fragmentation Considered Harmful." *ACM Computer Communication Review*, October 1987.

KEPH97a   Kephart, J.; Sorkin, G.; Chess, D.; and White, S. "Fighting Computer Viruses." *Scientific American*, November 1997.

KEPH97b   Kephart, J.; Sorkin, G.; Swimmer, B.; and White, S. "Blueprint for a Computer Immune System." *Proceedings, Virus Bulletin International Conference*, October 1997.

KESH98   Keshav, S., and Sharma, R. "Issues and Trends in Router Design." *IEEE Communications Magazine*, May 1998.

KHAN89   Khanna, A. and Zinky, J. "The Revised ARPANET Routing Metric." *Proceedings, SIGCOMM '89 Symposium*, 1989.

KHAN09   Khan, A., et al. "4G as a Next Generation Wireless Network." *Proceedings, 2009 International Conference on Future Computer and Communications*, 2009.

KHAR98   Khare, R. "The Spec's in the Mail." *IEEE Internet Computing*, September/October 1998.

KLEI92   Kleinrock, L. "The Latency/Bandwidth Tradeoff in Gigabit Networks." *IEEE Communications Magazine*, April 1992.

KLEI93   Kleinrock, L. "On the Modeling and Analysis of Computer Networks." *Proceedings of the IEEE*, August 1993.

KNUT98   Knuth, D. *The Art of Computer Programming, Volume 2: Seminumerical Algorithms.* Reading, MA: Addison-Wesley, 1998.

KONH80   Konheim, A. "A Queuing Analysis of Two ARQ Protocols." *IEEE Transactions on Communications*, July 1980.

KRIS01   Krishnamurthy, B., and Rexford, J. *Web Protocols and Practice: HTTP/1.1, Networking Protocols, Caching, and Traffic Measurement.* Upper Saddle River, NJ: Prentice Hall, 2001.

KUMA98   Kumar, V.; Lakshman, T.; and Stiliadis, D. "Beyond Best Effort: Router Architectures for the Differentiated Services of Tomorrow's Internet." *IEEE Communications Magazine*, May 1998.

LAWR01   Lawrence, J. "Designing Multiprotocol Label Switching Networks." *IEEE Communications Magazine*, July 2001.

LAYL04   Layland, R. "Understanding Wi-Fi Performance." *Business Communications Review*, March 2004.

LEBO98   Lebow, I. *Understanding Digital Transmission and Recording.* New York: IEEE Press, 1998.

LEIN85   Leiner, B.; Cole, R.; Postel, J.; and Mills, D. "The DARPA Internet Protocol Suite." *IEEE Communications Magazine*, March 1985.

LI05   Li, J., and Chen, H. "Mobility Support for IP-Based Networks." *IEEE Communications Magazine*, October 2005.

LIN84   Lin, S.; Costello, D.; and Miller, M. "Automatic-Repeat-Request Error-Control Schemes." *IEEE Communications Magazine*, December 1984.

LIN04   Lin, S., and Costello, D. *Error Control Coding.* Upper Saddle River, NJ: Prentice Hall, 2004.

LUIN97   Luinen, S.; Budrikis, Z.; and Cantoni, A. "The Controlled Cell Transfer Capability." *Computer Communications Review*, January 1997.

MARS09   Marsan, C. "7 Reasons MPLS Has Been Wildly Successful." *Network World*, March 27, 2009.

MART02   Martin, J., and Nilsson, A. "On Service Level Agreements for IP Networks." *Proceedings, IEEE INFOCOMM '02*, 2002.

MAXE90   Maxemchuk, N., and Zarki, M. "Routing and Flow Control in High-Speed Wide-Area Networks." *Proceedings of the IEEE*, January 1990,

MAXW96   Maxwell, K. "Asymmetric Digital Subscriber Line: Interim Technology for the Next Forty Years." *IEEE Communications Magazine*, October 1996.

MEDD10   Meddeb, A. "Internet QoS: Pieces of the Puzzle." *IEEE Communications Magazine*, January 2010.

METZ02   Metz C. "IP Anycast." *IEEE Internet Computing*, March 2002.

MCDO91   McDonald, C. "A Network Specification Language and Execution Environment for Undergraduate Teaching." *Proceedings of the ACM Computer Science Educational Technical Symposium*, March 1991.

MCFA03   McFarland, B., and Wong, M. "The Family Dynamics of 802.11." *ACM Queue*, May 2003.

MCDY99   McDysan, D., and Spohn, D. *ATM: Theory and Application.* New York: McGraw-Hill, 1999.

MCQU80   McQuillan, J.; Richer, I.; and Rosen, E. "The New Routing Algorithm for the ARPANET." *IEEE Transactions on Communications*, May 1980.

MELL07   Melle, S., et al. "Market Drivers and Implementation Options for 100-BgE Transport Over the WAN." *IEEE Applications and Practice*, November 2007.

MILL05   Miller, H.; Levine, H.; and Bates, S. "Welcome to Convergence." *IT Pro*, May/June 2005.

MIRK04   Mirkovic, J., and Relher, P. "A Taxonomy of DDoS Attack and DDoS Defense Mechanisms." *ACM SIGCOMM Computer Communications Review*, April 2004.

MOCK88   Mockapetris, P., and Dunlap, K. "Development of the Domain Name System." *ACM Computer Communications Review*, August 1988.

MOGU02   Mogul, J. "Clarifying the Fundamentals of HTTP." *Proceedings of the Eleventh International Conference on World Wide Web*, 2002.

MOY98   Moy, J. *OSPF: Anatomy of an Internet Routing Protocol.* Reading, MA: Addison-Wesley, 1998.

MUKH00   Mukherjee, B. "WDM Optical Communication Networks: Progress and Challenges." *IEEE Journal on Selected Areas in Communications*, October 2000.

NACH97   Nachenberg, C. "Computer Virus-Antivirus Coevolution." *Communications of the ACM*, January 1997.

NACH02   Nachenberg, C. "Behavior Blocking: The Next Step in Anti-Virus Protection." *White Paper*, March 2002, SecurityFocus.com.

NIST95   National Institute of Standards and Technology. *An Introduction to Computer Security: The NIST Handbook.* Special Publication 800-12, October 1995.

NOWE07   Nowell, M.; Vusirikala, V.; and Hays, R. "Overview of Requirements and Applications for 40 Gigabit and 100 Gigabit Ethernet." *Ethernet Alliance White Paper*, August 2007.

OJAN98   Ojanpera, T., and Prasad, G. "An Overview of Air Interface Multiple Access for IMT-2000/UMTS." *IEEE Communications Magazine*, September 1998.

OKUM68   Okumura, T., et al., "Field Strength and Its Variability in VHF and UHF Land-Mobile Radio Service." *Rev. Elec. Communication Lab*, 1968.

OLIV09   Oliviero, A., and Woodward, B. *Cabling: The Complete Guide to Copper and Fiber-Optic Networking.* Indianapolis: Sybex, 2009.

PACK99   Packer, R. "Just What Is Multimedia, Anyway?" *IEEE Multimedia*, January–March 1999.

PAHL95   Pahlavan, K.; Probert, T.; and Chase, M. "Trends in Local Wireless Networks." *IEEE Communications Magazine*, March 1995.

PARE88   Parekh, S., and Sohraby, K. "Some Performance Trade-Offs Associated with ATM Fixed-Length vs. Variable-Length Cell Formats." *Proceedings, GlobeCom*, November 1988.

PARK88   Park, S., and Miller, K. "Random Number Generators: Good Ones are Hard to Find." *Communications of the ACM*, October 1988.

PARZ06   Parziale, L., et al. *TCP/IP Tutorial and Technical Overview.* IBM Redbook GG24-3376-07, 2006, http://www.redbooks.ibm.com/abstracts/gg243376.html.

PAXS96   Paxson, V. "Toward a Framework for Defining Internet Performance Metrics." *Proceedings, INET '96*, 1996, http://www-nrg.ee.lbl.gov.

PERL00   Perlman, R. *Interconnections: Bridges, Routers, Switches, and Internetworking Protocols.* Reading, MA: Addison-Wesley, 2000.

PETE61   Peterson, W., and Brown, D. "Cyclic Codes for Error Detection." *Proceedings of the IEEE*, January 1961.

PETR00   Petrick, A. "IEEE 802.11b—Wireless Ethernet." *Communications System Design*, June 2000, www.commsdesign.com

PICK82   Pickholtz, R.; Schilling, D.; and Milstein, L. "Theory of Spread Spectrum Communications—A Tutorial." *IEEE Transactions on Communications*, May 1982. Reprinted in [TANT98].

POL07   Pol, C., and Russo, P. "Convergence: Worth the Journey." *Business Trends Quarterly*, Q1 2007.

PRAS00   Prasad, R.; Mohr, W.; and Konhauser, W., eds. *Third-Generation Mobile Communication Systems.* Boston: Artech House, 2000.

PROA05   Proakis, J. *Fundamentals of Communication Systems.* Upper Saddle River, NJ: Prentice Hall, 2005.

PURC98   Purchase, H. "Defining Multimedia." *IEEE Multimedia*, January–March 1998.

RADC04   Radcliff, D. "What Are They Thinking?" *Network World*, March 1, 2004.

RAJA97   Rajaravivarma, V. "Virtual Local Area Network Technology and Applications." *Proceedings, 29th Southeastern Symposium on System Theory*, 1997.

RAMA88   Ramabadran, T., and Gaitonde, S. "A Tutorial on CRC Computations." *IEEE Micro*, August 1988.

RAMA06   Ramaswami, R. "Optical Network Technologies: What Worked and What Didn't." *IEEE Communications Magazine*, September 2006.

RAPP02   Rappaport, T. *Wireless Communications.* Upper Saddle River, NJ: Prentice Hall, 2002.

REED09   Reed, B. "What's Next for MPLS?" *Network World*, December 21, 2009.

REEV95   Reeve, W. *Subscriber Loop Signaling and Transmission Handbook.* Piscataway, NJ: IEEE Press, 1995.

RISS09   Risson, J., and Soni, R. "The Evolution of 4G Systems." *Bell Labs Technical Journal*, Winter 2009.

ROBE78   Roberts, L. "The Evolution of Packet Switching." *Proceedings of the IEEE*, November 1978.

SATO90   Sato, K.; Ohta, S.; and Tokizawa, I. "Broad-band ATM Network Architecture Based on Virtual Paths." *IEEE Transactions on Communications*, August 1990.

SATO91   Sato, K.; Ueda, H.; and Yoshikai, M. "The Role of Virtual Path Crossconnection." *IEEE LTS*, August 1991.

SCHU98   Schulzrinne, H., and Rosenberg, J. "The Session Initiation Protocol: Providing Advanced Telephony Access Across the Internet." *Bell Labs Technical Journal*, October–December 1998.

SCHU99   Schulzrinne, H., and Rosenberg, J. "The IETF Internet Telephony Architecture and Protocols." *IEEE Network*, May/June 1999.

SCHW80   Schwartz, M., and Stern, T. "Routing Techniques Used in Computer Communication Networks." *IEEE Transactions on Communications*, April 1980.

SCHW96   Schwartz, M. *Broadband Integrated Networks.* Upper Saddle River, NJ: Prentice Hall PTR, 1996.

SHAN02   Shannon, C.; Moore, D.; and Claffy, K. "Beyond Folklore: Observations on Fragmented Traffic." *IEEE/ACM Transactions on Networking*, December 2002.

SHEN95   Shenker, S. "Fundamental Design Issues for the Future Internet." *IEEE Journal on Selected Areas in Communications*, September 1995.

SHER04   Sherburne, P., and Fitzgerald, C. "You Don't Know Jack About VoIP." *ACM Queue*, September 2004.

SHOE02   Shoemake, M. "IEEE 802.11g Jells as Applications Mount." *Communications System Design*, April 2002, www.commsdesign.com.

SIKE00   Siket, J., and Proch, D. "MPLS—Bring IP Networks and Connection-Oriented Networks Together." *Business Communications Review*, April 2000.

SKLA93   Sklar, B. "Defining, Designing, and Evaluating Digital Communication Systems." *IEEE Communications Magazine*, November 1993.

SKLA01   Sklar, B. *Digital Communications: Fundamentals and Applications.* Englewood Cliffs, NJ: Prentice Hall, 2001.

SKOR08   Skordoulis, D., et al. "IEEE 802.11n MAC Frame Aggregation Mechanisms for Next-Generation High-Throughput WLANs." *IEEE Wireless Communications*, February 2008.

SMIT97   Smith, R. *Internet Cryptography.* Reading, MA: Addison-Wesley, 1997.

SPAR07   Sparks, R., and Systems, E. "SIP—Basics and Beyond." *ACM Queue*, March 2007.

SPOR03   Sportack, M. *IP Addressing Fundamentals.* Indianapolis, IN: Cisco Press, 2003.

SPRA91   Spragins, J.; Hammond, J.; and Pawlikowski, K. *Telecommunications Protocols and Design.* Reading, MA: Addison-Wesley, 1991.

SPUR00   Spurgeon, C. *Ethernet: The Definitive Guide.* Cambridge, MA: O'Reilly and Associates, 2000.

STAL99   Stallings, W. *ISDN and Broadband ISDN, with Frame Relay and ATM.* Upper Saddle River, NJ: Prentice Hall, 1999.

STAL00   Stallings, W. *Local and Metropolitan Area Networks*, Sixth Edition. Upper Saddle River, NJ: Prentice Hall, 2000.

STAL05   Stallings, W. *Wireless Communications and Networks*, Second Edition. Upper Saddle River, NJ: Prentice Hall, 2005.

STAL08   Stallings, W., and Brown L. *Computer Security: Principles and Practice.* Upper Saddle River, NJ: Prentice Hall, 2008.

STAL11   Stallings, W. *Cryptography and Network Security: Principles and Practice, Fourth Edition.* Upper Saddle River, NJ: Prentice Hall, 2011.

STEV94   Stevens, W. *TCP/IP Illustrated, Volume 1: The Protocols.* Reading, MA: Addison-Wesley, 1994.

STEV96   Stevens, W. *TCP/IP Illustrated, Volume 3: TCP for Transactions, HTTP, NNTP, and the UNIX(R) Domain Protocol.* Reading, MA: Addison-Wesley, 1996.

SYMA01   Symantec Corp. *The Digital Immune System.* Symantec Technical Brief, 2001.

SUZU94   Suzuki, T. "ATM Adaptation Layer Protocol." *IEEE Communications Magazine*, April 1994.

TANE03   Tanenbaum, A. *Computer Networks.* Upper Saddle River, NJ: Prentice Hall, 2003.

TANT98   Tantaratana, S., and Ahmed, K., eds. *Wireless Applications of Spread Spectrum Systems: Selected Readings.* Piscataway, NJ: IEEE Press, 1998.

TEKT01   Tektronix. *SONET Telecommunications Standard Primer.* Tektronix White Paper, 2001, www.tektronix.com/optical.

THOM84   Thompson, K. "Reflections on Trusting Trust (Deliberate Software Bugs)." *Communications of the ACM*, August 1984.

TIME90   Time, Inc. *Computer Security, Understanding Computers Series.* Alexandria, VA: Time-Life Books, 1990.

TORR05   Torrieri, D. *Principles of Spread-Spectrum Communication Systems.* New York: Springer, 2005.

VENK05   Venkataraman, N. "Inside Mobile IP." *Dr. Dobb's Journal*, September 2005.

VERM04   Verma, D. "Service Level Agreements on IP Networks." *Proceedings of the IEEE*, September 2004.

VIN98   Vin, H. "Supporting Next-Generation Distributed Applications." *IEEE Multimedia*, July–September 1998.

VISW98   Viswanathan, A., et al. "Evolution of Multiprotocol Label Switching." *IEEE Communications Magazine*, May 1998.

VOGE95   Vogel, A., et al. "Distributed Multimedia and QoS: A Survey." *IEEE Multimedia*, Summer 1995.

WACK02   Wack, J.; Cutler, K.; and Pole, J. *Guidelines on Firewalls and Firewall Policy.* NIST Special Publication SP 800-41, January 2002.

WANG01   Wang, Z. *Internet QoS: Architectures and Mechanisms for Quality of Service.* San Francisco, CA: Morgan Kaufmann, 2001.

WHIT97   White, P., and Crowcroft, J. "The Integrated Services in the Internet: State of the Art." *Proceedings of the IEEE*, December 1997.

WHIT99   White, S. *Anatomy of a Commercial-Grade Immune System.* IBM Research White Paper, 1999.

WIDM83   Widmer, A., and Franaszek, P. "A DC-Balanced, Partitioned, 8B/10B Transmission Code." *IBM Journal of Research and Development,* September 1983.

WILL97   Willner, A. "Mining the Optical Bandwidth for a Terabit per Second." *IEEE Spectrum*, April 1997.

WRIG95   Wright, G., and Stevens, W. *TCP/IP Illustrated, Volume 2: The Implementation.* Reading, MA: Addison-Wesley, 1995.

XIAO99   Xiao, X., and Ni, L. "Internet QoS: A Big Picture." *IEEE Network*, March/April 1999.

XIAO04   Xiao, Y. "IEEE 802.11e: QoS Provisioning at the MAC Layer." *IEEE Communications Magazine*, June 2004.

XION00   Xiong, F. *Digital Modulation Techniques.* Boston: Artech House, 2000.

YANG95   Yang, C., and Reddy, A. "A Taxonomy for Congestion Control Algorithms in Packet Switching Networks." *IEEE Network*, July/August 1995.

ZENG00   Zeng, M.; Annamalai, A.; and Bhargava, V. "Harmonization of Global Third-generation Mobile Systems. *IEEE Communications Magazine,* December 2000.

ZHAN93   Zhang, L.; Deering, S.; Estrin, D.; Shenker, S.; and Zappala, D. "RSVP: A New Resource ReSerVation Protocol." *IEEE Network*, September 1993.

ZHAN86   Zhang, L. "Why TCP Timers Don't Work Well." *Proceedings, SIGCOMM '86 Symposium*, August 1986.

ZHAN95   Zhang, H. "Service Disciplines for Guaranteed Performance Service in Packet-Switching Networks." *Proceedings of the IEEE*, October 1995.

ZORZ96   Zorzi, M., and Rao, R. "On the Use of Renewal Theory in the Analysis of ARQ Protocols." *IEEE Transactions on Communications*, September 1996.

ZOU05   Zou, C., et al. "The Monitoring and Early Detection of Internet Worms." *IEEE/ACM Transactions on Networking*, October 2005.

INDEX

ACRONYMS

AAL	ATM Adaptation Layer	IDN	Integrated Digital Network
ADSL	Asymmetric Digital Subscriber Line	IEEE	Institute of Electrical and Electronics Engineers
AES	Advanced Encryption Standard	IETF	Internet Engineering Task Force
AM	Amplitude Modulation	IGMP	Internet Group Management
AMI	Alternate Mark Inversion		Protocol
ANS	American National Standard	IP	Internet Protocol
ANSI	American National Standard Institute	IPng	Internet Protocol-Next Generation
ARP	Address Resolution Protocol	IRA	International Reference Alphabet
ARQ	Automatic Repeat Request	ISA	Integrated Services Architecture
ASCII	American Standard Code for Information Interchange	ISDN	Integrated Services Digital Network
ASK	Amplitude-Shift Keying	ISO	International Organization for Standardization
ATM	Asynchronous Transfer Mode	ITU	International Telecommunication
BER	Bit Error Rate		Union
B-ISDN	Broadband ISDN	ITU-T	ITU Telecommunication
BGP	Border Gateway Protocol		Standardization Sector
BOC	Bell Operating Company	LAN	Local Area Network
CBR	Constant Bit Rate	LAPB	Link Access Procedure-Balanced
CCITT	International Consultative Committee on Telegraphy and Telephony	LAPD	Link Access Procedure on the D Channel
		LAPF	Link Access Procedure for Frame Mode Bearer Services
CIR	Committed Information Rate	LLC	Logical Link Control
CMI	Coded Mark Inversion	MAC	Medium Access Control
CRC	Cyclic Redundancy Check	MAN	Metropolitan Area Network
CSMA/CD	Carrier Sense Multiple Access with Collision Detection	MIME	Multi-Purpose Internet Mail Extension
DCE	Data Circuit-Terminating Equipment	MPLS	Multiprotocol Label Switching
DEA	Data Encryption Algorithm	NRZI	Nonreturn to Zero, Inverted
DES	Data Encryption Standard	NRZL	Nonreturn to Zero, Level
DS	Differentiated Services	NT	Network Termination
DTE	Data Terminal Equipment	OSI	Open Systems Interconnection
FCC	Federal Communications Commission	OSPF	Open Shortest Path First
		PBX	Private Branch Exchange
FCS	Frame Check Sequence	PCM	Pulse-Code Modulation
FDM	Frequency-Division Multiplexing	PDU	Protocol Data Unit
FSK	Frequency-Shift Keying	PSK	Phase-Shift Keying
FTP	File Transfer Protocol	PTT	Postal, Telegraph, and Telephone
FM	Frequency Modulation	PM	Phase Modulation
GFR	Guaranteed Frame Rate	QAM	Quadrature Amplitude Modulation
GPS	Global Positioning System		
HDLC	High-Level Data Link Control	QoS	Quality of Service
HTML	Hypertext Markup Language	QPSK	Quadrature Phase Shift Keying
HTTP	Hypertext Transfer Protocol	RBOC	Regional Bell Operating Company
IAB	Internet Architecture Board		
ICMP	Internet Control Message Protocol	RF	Radio Frequency